The Oxford Dictionary of

Foreign Words and Phrases

The Oxford Dictionary of

Foreign Words and Phrases

EDITED BY

Jennifer Speake

Oxford   New York

OXFORD UNIVERSITY PRESS

1997

Oxford University Press, Great Clarendon Street, Oxford OX2 6DP

Oxford New York
Athens Auckland Bangkok Bogota Bombay Buenos Aires
Calcutta Cape Town Dar es Salaam Delhi Florence Hong Kong Istanbul
Karachi Kuala Lumpur Madras Madrid Melbourne Mexico City
Nairobi Paris Singapore Taipei Tokyo Toronto Warsaw

and associated companies in
Berlin Ibadan

Oxford is a trade mark of Oxford University Press

Published in the United States
by Oxford University Press Inc., New York

© *Oxford University Press 1997*
First published 1997

British Library Cataloguing in Publication Data
Data available

Library of Congress Cataloging in Publication Data
Oxford Dictionary of Foreign Words and Phrases / edited by Jennifer Speake
p.   cm.
1. English language—Foreign words and phrases—Dictionaries.
I. Speake, Jennifer.
PE1582.A3094   1997   96-49006
422'.4'03—dc21   CIP

ISBN 0-19-863159-6

10 9 8 7 6 5 4 3 2 1

Data-capture by Jayvee, Trivandrum, India
Designed by Jane Stevenson
Typeset in Swift and Arial by ISL, Gloucester

Printed in the United States of America
on acid free paper

Contents

Preface

....

The Oxford Dictionary of Foreign Words and Phrases records the influx of words from a variety of other languages into both American and British English, concentrating especially on those introduced during the course of the twentieth century. Older dictionaries in this field tend to have a preponderance of French and Latin expressions; many of these are indeed still current and are represented in the present work by 1990s citations, but the English language is now open to new words on a worldwide basis. Many recent introductions reflect an unprecedented cultural eclecticism, particularly in what might be called 'lifestyle' words—those dealing with areas such as fashion, cuisine, ethnic music, and recreation.

There is nothing new about sources for foreign words being indicative of historical or cultural events. The influx of French military terms in the early eighteenth century, for instance, can be linked to the Continental campaigns of the Duke of Marlborough. More recently, the British Raj in India spawned a large number of Anglo-Indian terms for the various functionaries and institutions necessary to keep the wheels of empire turning. However, neither of these two categories is heavily represented in late twentieth-century speech, *nouvelle cuisine* being more fashionable than fortification and *karma* having a higher profile than imperial administration.

The criteria for currency that have been applied in the selection of entries mean that there is a bias in favour of words first introduced during this century. An exception to this is the large category of words, particularly from the classical languages, that are recent introductions or revivals with exclusively scientific senses; these are excluded on the grounds that they do not fulfil the other criterion of currency, namely that the word may be encountered in non-specialist literature. However, many other words have both technical and more general senses, and in such cases the technical senses are generally included or mentioned in the entry, as the evolution of the various senses once they have entered the language is often interesting in itself. For instance, *flèche*, which occurs in Middle English with its basic French meaning of 'arrow', soon became obsolete after its first introduction (most probably because it duplicated an already established word); reintroduced from Modern French with a variety of special applications, it has fared better. Terms that have been introduced purely as terms of art in particular sports or other fields of activity and have remained so (or have not had time to move beyond their restricted area) have been excluded; admitting terms for bullfighting passes or judo throws would have considerably increased the proportion of, respectively, Spanish and Japanese entries.

Introduced expressions have met with varying fortunes in English, but certain patterns can be seen. On the whole, phrases tend to be more resistant to naturalization than single words. At one end of the scale of naturalization, many words, especially those from Old French and Latin, have become totally assimilated in spelling, pronunciation, and plural form, and are thus no longer thought of as foreign in any sense other than the purely etymological. Others (such as *restaurant*) are nearing the end of this process of assimilation, with only some slight variation in standard pronunciation as a gesture towards an alien origin. Others, particularly Latin and French phrases, have remained obstinately 'foreign' over several centuries.

Italicization is a helpful but not infallible clue to the extent of assimilation, the rule of thumb being that the more 'foreign' a word is felt to be the more likely it is to be distinguished in this way. However, italics are generally retained in practice even for well-established words where there might be any possibility of confusion with an English word, as between *pace* (Latin ablative singular of *pax* used as a preposition) and 'pace' English noun and verb. Practice regarding italics however varies between British and American English and between publisher and publisher. For this reason, and to avoid the appearance of prescription, no attempt has been made to distinguish between italic and non-italic in the headwords in this dictionary.

Retention of accents is another indicator of awareness of the foreign origin of a word, since the native English writer has a strong tendency to drop them. In this respect the spelling *detour*, to take a common example, is well down the route to total assimilation, but the pronunciation still has a faint echo of the original *détour*.

How far spelling can move away from the original before a word can be said to be wholly Anglicized is not only a matter of the dropping or retention of accents. Various words from the Romance languages have doubled or single consonants in the original and the opposite in the usual English spelling: examples are *concessionnaire* in French, but 'concessionaire' in English, *improvvisatore* in Italian, but 'improvisatore' in English; on the other hand it is 'commando' in English but *comando* in Portuguese. Some variation in unstressed vowels also appears (*imprimitura* in Italian, but predominantly 'imprimatura' in English). However, in none of these cases does the fluctuation in spelling seriously affect the perception of the word as 'foreign'.

More latitude has been allowed in the case of words transcribed from non-Roman alphabets, and significant variants have been noted. For instance, Greek *kappa*, formerly often transcribed as *c*, is now more frequently rendered *k*, particularly in specialist contexts. Variation between *s* and *sh* and between *c* and *ch* occurs in transliterations from various languages of the Indian subcontinent. Attempts by users to make transliterations conform to English spelling norms have not disqualified words, since they generally do not disguise the alien origin of the word itself.

To keep the dictionary within reasonable bounds, several whole categories of words have been excluded, unless there is some strong reason to make an exception for a particular member of the class. If a word has a transferred meaning in English or is sufficiently at home to be used figuratively, it is generally included; thus, made-up words, even those with impeccable classical Greek or Latin elements such as *homophobia*, *megalomania*, are usually not admitted, but *utopia* is included. A very few other words such as *braggadocio* that are not genuine foreign words at all have been allowed in on the basis of their being so easily mistaken for a genuine borrowing. Also in are Latin phrases such as *infra dig.* that are seldom or never given their full form in English usage. Currencies, obsolete coins, weights and measures, and scientific units are excluded, but exceptions are made for *shekel* and *sou* on account of their metaphorical uses. Plant and animal names do not have entries unless they are also the names of a commodity that is widely traded or used; thus *jojoba* and *vicuña* are both in.

Evidence for use in the latter part of the twentieth century almost always guarantees inclusion, although some items which duplicate good English expressions and which are therefore unlikely to move beyond an entirely literary ambience have been omitted (e.g. *dialogue des sourds* smacks of affectation as an alternative to 'dialogue of the deaf'). Sometimes a foreign expression fulfils a valid function as a euphemism: *faux marbre* sounds considerably more up-market than *fake* (or *false*) *marble*. Words that are current but used only in the context of the country of origin have been looked at individually on the basis of likelihood of applications outside the particular national context; for example, *ragazza* as a word for 'girl' is most unlikely to be encountered anywhere except in a text specifically about or set in Italy, while *wagon-lit* on the other hand is much less country-specific. Greetings and polite forms of address have generally been excluded on similar grounds, *gnädige Frau* and such expressions belonging more properly in a foreign-language phrase book.

The tables given in the Appendix break down the headwords in the *Dictionary* by country of origin and century of introduction. They are intended as a snapshot of the foreign expressions for which there is evidence in twentieth-century texts and are in no sense a statistical exercise. Dates are given in abbreviated form, following the scheme used for the *New Shorter Oxford English Dictionary* (see below).

OE	Old English	pre-1149
ME	Middle English	1150–1349
LME	late Middle English	1350–1469
L15	late fifteenth century	1470–1499
E16	early sixteenth century	1500–1529
M16	mid sixteenth century	1530–1569
L16	late sixteenth century	1570–1599
E17	early seventeenth century	1600–1629
M17	mid seventeenth century	1630–1669
L17	late seventeenth century	1670–1699
E18	early eighteenth century	1700–1729
M18	mid eighteenth century	1730–1769
L18	late eighteenth century	1770–1799
E19	early nineteenth century	1800–1829
M19	mid nineteenth century	1830–1869
L19	late nineteenth century	1870–1899
E20	early twentieth century	1900–1929
M20	mid twentieth century	1930–1969
L20	late twentieth century	1970–

Pronunciation Guide

Guidance on pronunciation follows the International Phonetic Alphabet system (IPA), and is based on the pronunciation associated especially with southern England (sometimes referred to as 'Received Pronunciation'). Many foreign words and phrases, however, have widely varying pronunciations, ranging from the wholly naturalized to a conscious attempt to reproduce what the speaker believes to be the 'foreign' pronunciation, and it is neither feasible nor particularly helpful to include every possibility.

Stress

' indicates primary stress on the following syllable
, indicates secondary stress on the following syllable

Consonants and Semivowels

b, d, f, h, k, l, m, n, p, r, s, t, v, w, and z all have their usual English values. Other sounds are represented by the following symbols:

g	get	x	loch	ð	this	j	yes
tʃ	chip	ŋ	ring	ʃ	she	dʒ	jar
θ	thin	ʒ	decision	ç	(German) echt		
ɲ	(French) seigneur			ɥ	(French) nuit		

(r) indicates an r that is sometimes sounded when a vowel follows, as in *cha-chaing*.

Vowels

The following symbols represent vowel sounds that appear in English and foreign languages:

short vowels		long vowels (: indicates length)		diphthongs	
a	cat	ɑː	arm	ʌɪ	my
ɛ	bed	ɛː	hair	aʊ	how
ə	ago	əː	her	eɪ	day
ɪ	sit	iː	see	əʊ	no
i	cosy	ɔː	saw	ɪə	near
ɒ	hot	uː	too	ɔɪ	boy
ʌ	run			ʊə	poor
ʊ	put			ʌɪə	fire
				aʊə	sour

(ə) signifies the indeterminate sound as in the final syllables of *garden*, *carnal*, and *rhythm*.

The following symbols are used for vowel sounds that do not occur in English:

short vowels	*long vowels* (: *indicates length*)
ɑ (French) pas*s*é	
e (French) démod*é* (Italian) dol*c*e	e: (German) We*h*rmacht (Italian) comm*e*dia
o (French) *au*berge (German) Bildungsroman (Italian) amorett*o*	o: (German) verb*o*ten (Italian) cass*o*ne
ɔ (French) borné (German) Doppelgänger (Italian) donna	
œ (French) bo*eu*f	œ: (French) accouch*eu*r
ø (French) bl*eu*	ø: (French) berc*eu*se (German) Gasthöfe
u (French) bij*ou* (Italian) fig*u*rante	
y (French) cr*u*	y: (German) gemütlich

The following symbols are used for other sounds that do not occur in English:

nasalized vowels (˜ *indicates nasality*)	*diphthongs*
õ (French) cord*on* bleu	aɪ (German) Gl*ei*chschaltung
ã (French) *en*	
ɛ̃ (French) disti*n*gué	ɔy (German) Haken*kreu*z
ɔ̃ (French) co*n*gé	

A

aa /'ɑːɑː/ noun M19 Hawaiian ('a-'a). *Geology* Rough, clinkery, scoriaceous lava. Cf. PAHOEHOE.

aba /'abə/ noun (also **abba**) E19 Arabic ('abā'). A sleeveless outer garment of various forms, worn by Arabs. Cf. ABAYA.

abacus /'abəkəs/ noun plural **abaci** /'abəsʌɪ/, **abacuses** M16 Latin (from Greek *abakos*, *abax* slab, originally drawing-board covered with dust, from Semitic: cf. Hebrew *'ābāq* dust). **1** M16 *Architecture* The upper member of a capital, supporting the architrave. **2** L17 A calculating frame, *especially* one with balls sliding on wires. **3** L18 *Classical Antiquities* A sideboard.

■ The word was first introduced (LME) in its antique sense of 'a board strewn with sand, for drawing figures, etc.' but this sense is not found after the medieval period.

à bas /a bɑ/ interjection M19 French. Down with ... !

■ Always followed by the name of a person or thing.

abatis /'abətɪs/ noun (also **abattis** /ə'batɪs/) plural **abat(t)is**, **abatises** M18 French (from Old French *abatre*, ultimately from Latin *batt(u)ere* to beat). *Military* A defence formed by placing felled trees lengthwise one over the other with their branches towards the enemy line. Also, a barricade of barbed wire.

abattoir /'abətwɑː/ noun E19 French (from *abattre* to fell). A slaughterhouse.

abaya /ə'beɪjə/ noun M19 Arabic. An ABA.

Abba /'abə/ noun LME ecclesiastical Latin (from New Testament Greek, from Aramaic *'abbā* father). *Christian Church* **1** LME Abba, father: an invocation to God as Father (Mark 14:36 etc.). **2** M17 A title given to bishops and patriarchs in the Syrian Orthodox and Coptic Churches.

abba see ABA.

abbé /'abeɪ/, *foreign* /abe/ (plural same) noun M16 French (from ecclesiastical Latin *abbat-* abbot). In France: an abbot, a secular priest, or *loosely* anyone, with or without official duties, who is entitled to wear ecclesiastical dress.

ab extra /ab 'ɛkstrə/ adverb phrase M17 Late Latin. From outside.

ab initio /ab ɪ'nɪʃɪəʊ/ adverb phrase E17 Latin. From the beginning.

1996 *Spectator* An unthinking agnosticism is taken for granted everywhere, so atheists are seldom called on to put their case *ab initio*.

ab intra /ab 'ɪntrə/ adverb phrase L17 Modern Latin. From inside.

Abitur /abi'tuːr/ noun (also **abitur**) M20 German (abbreviation of *Abiturientenexamen* leavers' examination). In Germany: a set of examinations taken in the final year of secondary school (success in which formerly ensured a university place).

Abiturient /ˌabituri'ɛnt/ noun (also **abiturient**) plural **Abiturienten** M19 German (from Modern Latin *abiturire* to wish to leave). A candidate for the ABITUR.

ablaut /'ablaʊt/ noun M19 German (from *ab* off + *Laut* sound). *Philology* Vowel change in related words, *especially* that in Indo-European, which survives in English in, e.g., *sing, sang, sung, song*.

abonné /abɔne/ noun plural pronounced same L19 French (past participle of *abonner* to subscribe). A subscriber; a season-ticket holder.

abonnement /abɔnmɑ̃/ noun plural pronounced same L19 French (from *abonner* to subscribe). A subscription, as for a newspaper etc.; a season ticket.

ab origine /ab ə'rɪdʒmi/ adverb phrase M16 Latin (from *ab* from + *origine* ablative of *origo* beginning, source). From the beginning; from the creation of the world.

abortus /ə'bɔːtəs/ noun plural **aborti** /ə'bɔːtʌɪ/, **abortuses** M19 Latin (= miscarriage). *Medicine* **1** M19 Abortion. **2** E20 An aborted foetus.

ab ovo /ab 'əʊvəʊ/ adverb phrase L16 Latin (= from the egg). From the (very) beginning.

abrazo /a'braθo/, /a'braso/, /ə'brɑːzəʊ/ noun plural **abrazos** /a'braθos/,

/a'brasos/, /ə'brɑːzəʊz/ E20 **Spanish.** An embrace, a hug, especially as a salutation.

abri /ə'briː/ *noun* E19 **French.** A shelter; *specifically* in *Archaeology*, an overhanging rock affording shelter.

abscissa /ab'sɪsə/ *noun* plural **abscissae** /ab'sɪsiː/, **abscissas** L17 **Modern Latin** (*abscissa* use as noun (sc. *linea* line) of feminine past participle of *abscindere* to cut asunder). **1** L17 *Mathematics* Originally, the portion of a line between a fixed point on it and the point of intersection with an ordinate. Now, the distance of a point from the *y*-axis measured parallel to the *x*-axis. **2** L19 *Botany absciss layer*, a distinctive layer of cells at which separation occurs on leaf-fall.

abseil /'abzʌɪl/, /'abseɪl/ *noun & intransitive verb* M20 **German** (*abseilen*, from *ab* down + *Seil* rope). **1** M20 *Mountaineering* (Make) a descent of a steep rock-face by means of a doubled rope fixed at a higher point. **2** L20 (Make) a similar descent from a helicopter.

absinth /'absɪnθ/ *noun* (also (in sense 2 usually) **absinthe**) LME **French** (*absinthe* from Latin *absinthium* from Greek *apsinthion* wormwood). **1** LME Wormwood, the plant *Artemisia absinthium* or its essence; *figuratively* bitterness, sorrow. **2** M19 A green liqueur made (at least originally) from wine and wormwood. **b** L19 A green colour resembling that of the liqueur.

absit omen /'absɪt ˌəʊmən/ *interjection* L16 **Latin** (= may this (ill) omen be absent). May this evil foreboding not become fact.

absurdum /əb'səːdəm/ *noun* plural **absurda** /əb'səːdə/ M19 **Latin** (neuter singular of *absurdus* absurd, used as noun). An absurd or illogical conclusion or condition. See also REDUCTIO AD ABSURDUM.

ab urbe condita /ab ˌəːbeɪ kɒn'dɪtə/ *adverbial phrase* E17 **Latin** (= since the foundation of the city). (In the Roman annual dating system) since the founding of Rome.

■ The traditional date of the founding of Rome was 753 BC, which was the point of departure for the computation of dates. A variant form of the phrase is *anno urbis conditae* in the year of the founding of the city. Both version are abbreviated AUC.

AC abbreviation of APPELLATION CONTRÔLÉE.

academia /akə'diːmɪə/ *noun* M20 **Latin** (from Greek *akadem(e)ia*, adjective from *Akademos*). The world of higher learning; the university environment or community.

■ Akademos was the man or demigod who gave his name to the garden just outside ancient Athens where Plato conducted his philosophical school.

acanthus /ə'kanθəs/ *noun* M16 **Latin** (from Greek *akanthos*, from *akantha* thorn, perhaps from *akē* sharp point). **1** M16 Any of several erect herbaceous plants belonging to the genus *Acanthus* (family Acanthaceae), having decorative spiny leaves; especially *Acanthus spinosus*, native to the Mediterranean region. **2** M18 *Architecture* A conventionalized form of the leaf of *Acanthus spinosus*, used to decorate Corinthian and Composite capitals; hence, a similar decorative motif used on furniture and fabrics.

a cappella /a kə'pɛlə/, /ɑː/ *adjective & adverb phrase* L19 **Italian** (= in chapel style). Of choral music or choirs: unaccompanied. Cf. ALLA CAPELLA.

■ Used both as a premodifier and postpositively (see quotations).
1995 *Times* No doubt the uninviting weather had something to do with it [the smallness of the audience], although admittedly it is difficult to imagine a programme of 20th-century German and Dutch *a cappella* music ever causing a traffic jam in Smith Square.
1996 *Times* He [sc. Bruce Springsteen] remained at the Ivy the other night until all other diners had left, then regaled staff with a short concert *a cappella*.

accelerando /əkˌsɛlə'randəʊ/, /əˌtʃɛlə'randəʊ/ *adverb, adjective, & noun* E19 **Italian.** *Music* E19 **A** *adverb & adjective* (A direction:) with gradual increase of speed. **B** *noun* L19 plural **accelerandos, accelerandi.** A gradual increase of speed; a passage (to be) played with a gradual increase of speed; also *figurative*.

B **1996** *Bookseller* There are fewer and fewer prerequisites to studying the humanities, but ... the entrance exams in mathematics and physics for the first-year student, were what, less than 15 years ago, would have been post-doctoral research. That is your accelerando.

acciaccatura /əˌtʃakə'tʊərə/, *foreign* /atˌtʃakka'tuːra/ *noun* plural **acciaccaturas, acciaccature** /atˌtʃakka'tuːre/ E19 **Italian** (from *acciaccare* to crush). *Music* A grace-note performed quickly before an essential note of a melody.

accidie /'aksɪdi/ *noun* ME **Anglo-Norman** (= Old French *accide* from medieval Latin

accouchement | adage

accidia, alteration of late Latin ACEDIA). Sloth, torpor, apathy. Now also, despair.
■ Became obsolete (E16), but subsequently revived (L19).

accouchement /əˈkuːʃmɒ̃/, *foreign* /akuʃmɑ̃/ *noun* L18 French (from *accoucher* to give birth). Childbirth.

accoucheur /akuːˈʃəː/, *foreign* /akuʃœr/ (*plural same*) *noun* M18 French (from *accoucher* to give birth). A man (formerly also a woman) who acts as midwife.

accra /ˈakrə/, /əˈkrɑː/ *noun* (also **akkra**, **akara** /əˈkarə/, and other variants) L19 Yoruba (*àkàrà* bean cake). A West African and West Indian fritter made with black-eyed peas or a similar pulse. Also, a West Indian fritter made with mashed fish.

acedia /əˈsiːdɪə/ *noun* E17 Late Latin (*acedia* from Greek *akēdia*, from *a-* not + *kēdos* care, concern). ACCIDIE.

Aceldama /əˈkɛldəmə/, /əˈsɛldəmə/ *noun* M17 Greek (*Akeldama* from Aramaic *ḥăqel děmā* field of blood). A scene of bloodshed; a place of slaughter.

achar /əˈtʃɑː/ *noun* L16 Hindustani (ultimately from Persian *āchār*). Pickles, as prepared in the Indian subcontinent.

acharnement /aʃarnəmɑ̃/, /əˈʃɑːnmɒ̃/ *noun* M18 French (from *acharner* to give a taste of flesh (to dogs etc.)). Bloodthirsty fury; ferocity, gusto.

acharya /ɑːˈtʃɑːrjə/ *noun* E19 Sanskrit (*ācārya* master, teacher). In the Indian subcontinent: (a title given to) a spiritual teacher or leader; *transferred* an influential mentor.

à cheval /a ʃəval/, /ɑː ʃəˈval/ *adverb phrase* M19 French (= on horseback). With one foot on each side; in command of two lines of communication; with a stake risked equally on two chances.

achkan /ˈatʃk(ə)n/ *noun* E20 Hindustani (*ackan*). A knee-length coat, buttoned in front, worn by men in the Indian subcontinent.

acme /ˈakmi/ *noun* L16 Greek (*akmē* highest point). The highest point; the point or period of perfection.
■ Long after its introduction into English it was consciously used as a Greek word and written in Greek letters. It was formerly also used in the specific senses of 'the period of full growth; the flower or full bloom of life' (L16–M19) and 'the crisis of an illness' (M17–M19).

à contrecœur /a kɔ̃trəkœr/ *adverb phrase* E19 French (literally, 'against the heart'). Against one's will, reluctantly.
1996 *Spectator* A pragmatist, he accepted, *contre coeur*, the liberalisation of the economy as the only alternative to bankruptcy . . .

acropolis /əˈkrɒpəlɪs/ *noun* E17 Greek (*akropolis*, from as *akros* tip, peak + *polis* city). The citadel or elevated fortified part of a Greek city, especially of Athens.

acroterion /akrəˈtɪərɪən/ *noun* plural **acroteria** /akrəˈtɪərɪə/ (also **acroter** /ˈakrətə/, plural **acroters**; **acroterium** /akrəˈtɪərɪəm/, **acroteria** /akrəˈtɪərɪə/; **akroterion** /akrəˈtɪərɪən/, **akroteria** /akrə ˈtɪərɪə/) M17 Greek (*akrōtērion* extremity. Variants from French *acrotère* and (its source) Latin *acroterium* from Greek). *Architecture* **1** collectively singular and (usually) in *plural* Ornaments in ranges on roofs of classical buildings. **2** E18 A pedestal for a statue or the like on the centre or side of a pediment.

acte gratuit /akt ɡratɥi/ *noun phrase* plural **actes gratuits** (pronounced same) M20 French. A gratuitous, random, or inconsequent action performed on impulse.
■ The concept of the *acte gratuit* was given currency by the works of the French novelist and essayist André Gide (1869–1951) and explored in such works as *Les Caves du Vatican* (1914).
1933 'Rebecca West' *St Augustine* It was simply a demonstration against order . . . ; in fact, it was an *acte gratuit* of the sort that fills M. André Gide with such ecstasy.

actio in distans /ˌaktɪəʊ ɪn ˈdɪstanz/ M19 Latin (= action on something apart). Action at a distance, the exertion of force by one body upon another separated from it by space; *figurative* the exertion of influence from afar.

acumen /ˈakjʊmən/, /əˈkjuːmən/ *noun* L16 Latin (= point, acuteness, from *acuere* to sharpen, from *acus* needle). **1** L16 Sharpness of wit; penetration of perception; keenness of discrimination. **2** L18 *Botany* A tapering point.
■ Of the two pronunciations, /əˈkjuːmən/ is the older and more etymological.

AD abbreviation of ANNO DOMINI.

adage /ˈadɪdʒ/ *noun* 1 M16 French (from Latin *adagium*, from *ad* to + an early form of *aio* I say). A saying expressing common experience, a folk maxim.

adage /adɑʒ/ *noun* 2 plural pronounced same M20 French (from Italian, as next). ADAGIO *noun* 2.

> **1996** *Spectator* . . . the standard sequence of the various parts of the pas de deux, namely *adage*, variations and coda . . .

adagio /əˈdɑː(d)ʒɪəʊ/ *adverb, adjective, & noun* L17 Italian (from *ad agio* at ease). *Music* **A** *adverb & adjective* L17 In slow time, leisurely. **B** *noun* plural **adagios**. **1** M18 A musical piece or movement in slow time. **2** M18 A dance or ballet movement in slow time.

adat /ˈadat/ *noun* L18 Malay (from Arabic '*āda*). Custom, or customary law, in the Islamic regions of South-East Asia, especially in contrast to Islamic religious law.

■ Also in the phrase *adat law.*

ADC abbreviation of AIDE-DE-CAMP.

ad captandum vulgus /ad kapˌtandəm ˈvʌlgəs/ *adverb & adjective phrase* M18 Latin (= for alluring the crowd). (Designed) to appeal to the emotions (of the rabble).

■ Also used in the abbreviated form *ad captandum.*

addendum /əˈdɛndəm/ *noun* plural **addenda** /əˈdɛndə/ L17 Latin (neuter gerundive of *addere* to add). A thing to be added, especially because of omission; an appendix, an addition; *singular* and (especially) in *plural* (occasionally treated as *singular*), additional matter at the end of a book.

addio /adˈdiːo/ *interjection* L18 Italian (from *a* to + *Dio* god: cf. ADIEU, ADIOS). Goodbye.

■ Formerly in general use in the subscription of letters etc.

ad eundem /ad ɪˈʌndəm/ *adverb phrase* E18 Latin (= to the same (degree)). (Admitted) to the same degree or rank at another university or institution.

à deux /a dø/ *adverb & adjective phrase* L19 French. Of, for, or between, two. Cf. FOLIE À DEUX, MÉNAGE.

ad hoc /ad ˈhɒk/ *adverb & adjective phrase* M17 Latin (literally, 'to this'). For this particular purpose; special(ly).

> **1996** *Spectator* [In] 1899, government ministries were relatively small affairs, but the ad hoc jumble of Georgian buildings that housed them in Whitehall was deemed neither to be efficient, nor to reflect the dignity of the largest empire the world had ever seen.

ad hominem /ad ˈhɒmmɛm/ *adverb & adjective phrase* L16 Latin (= to the person). Of an argument etc.: directed to the individual, personal; appealing to an opponent's known personal views rather than reason.

■ Such an argument, which plays upon an opponent's own premisses, seeking to draw from them a conclusion that is rejected by that same opponent, is a legitimate debating tactic, unlike the kind of ARGUMENTUM AD HOMINEM which is really no more than a personal attack.

ad idem /ad ˈɪdɛm/ *adverb phrase* L16 Latin (= to the same thing). On the same point, in agreement.

adieu /əˈdjuː/ *interjection & noun* LME French (Anglo-Norman *adeu*, Old French *adieu*, from *à* to + *Dieu* god: cf. ADDIO, ADIOS). **A** *interjection* LME Goodbye. *Archaic*. **B** *noun* LME plural **adieus, adieux** /əˈdjuːz/. A leave-taking; a parting word; a farewell.

ad infinitum /ad ˌɪnfɪˈnʌɪtəm/ *adverb & adjective phrase* E17 Latin (literally, 'to infinity'). Without limit, for ever.

ad interim /ad ˈɪntərɪm/ *adverb & adjective phrase* L18 Latin (*ad* to + *interim* adverb 'meanwhile' used as noun). For the meantime.

adios /adɪˈəʊs/, /adɪˈɒs/ *interjection* M19 Spanish (*adiós*, from *a* to + *Dios* god: cf. ADIEU, ADDIO). Goodbye.

> **1996** *Times* . . . Señor Nuñez has decided that since he had neither cups nor courtesy from the coach, it is time to say *adios* to Mr Cruyff.

ad lib /ad ˈlɪb/ *adverb, adjective, verb & noun* (also **ad-lib**, when used as attributive adjective or verb) E19 Latin (abbreviation of next). **A** *adverb* E19 AD LIBITUM. **B** *adjective* E20 Extemporized; spontaneous. **C** *transitive & intransitive verb* E20 To speak extempore, to improvise. **D** *noun* M20 Something extemporized; an ad-lib remark.

ad libitum /ad ˈlɪbɪtəm/ *adverb & adjective phrase* E17 Latin. According to pleasure; to any desired extent.

■ Often used in the abbreviated form AD LIB.

> *adjective phrase* **1995** *New Scientist* The joke—though it wasn't a funny joke—in our lab is that the most deadly thing we've tested has been a perfectly healthy diet given in ad libitum amounts. We literally kill them [sc. the rats] with kindness.

ad litem /ad ˈlʌɪtɛm/ *adverb & adjective phrase* M18 Latin (= for the lawsuit). *Law* Of a guardian, etc.: appointed to act, in a lawsuit, on behalf of a child or other incapable person.

ad nauseam /ad 'nɔ:zɪam/, /ad 'nɔ:sɪam/ *adverb phrase* M17 Latin (literally, 'to sickness'). To a disgusting or tiresome extent.

■ The phrase was earlier (E17) introduced in the form *ad nauseam usque* (right up to sickness), and also occurs as *usque ad nauseam*, but these have been superseded by the shorter form.
1996 *Times* As we argued ad nauseam at the time, the Government should have consulted the people when the Maastricht treaty was drummed through Parliament . . .

adobe /ə'dəʊb(ɪ)/ *noun* M18 Spanish (from *adobar* to plaster, from Arabic *aṭ-ṭūb*, from *al* the + *ṭūb* bricks). **1** M18 An unburnt brick dried in the sun. **b** E19 A house built of such bricks. *United States*. **2** L18 Clay or earth prepared for making into such bricks or suitable for this purpose.

ad personam /ad pə:'səʊnam/ *adverb & adjective phrase* M20 Latin (literally, 'to the person'). Personal(ly); on an individual basis.

ad referendum /ad rɛfə'rɛndəm/ *adverb phrase* L18 Modern Latin (literally, 'for reference'). Subject to the assent of a higher authority.

ad rem /ad 'rɛm/ *adverb & adjective phrase* L16 Latin (literally, 'to the matter'). To the point; to the purpose.

adsuki variant of ADZUKI.

adsum /'adsʌm/ *interjection* L16 Latin (1st singular present indicative of *adesse* to be present). I am present.
■ As an answer to a roll-call etc.

ad usum Delphini /ad ˌju:səm dɛl'fmɪ/ *adjective phrase* L18 Latin (= for the use of the Dauphin). Originally, designating or pertaining to an edition of the classics prepared for the use of the son of Louis XIV of France; hence, expurgated.

ad valorem /ad və'lɔ:rɛm/ *adverb & adjective phrase* L17 Latin (= according to the value). Of taxes: in proportion to the estimated value of goods.

adversaria /advə'sɛ:rɪə/ *noun plural* E18 Latin (use as noun of neuter plural (sc. *scripta* writings) of *adversarius* facing one). Miscellaneous remarks and observations; *collectively singular* a commonplace-book.

ad vivum /ad 'vi:vəm/ *adverb & adjective phrase* M17 Latin (= according to the living (model)). (Painted) from life.

1996 *Country Life* . . . this ad vivum rendering captures perhaps better than any other, the physical presence and psychology of the future King.

advocatus diaboli /advə,ka:təs di:'abəli:/, /advə,keɪtəs dʌɪ'abəlʌɪ/ *noun phrase* E19 Modern Latin (literally, 'devil's advocate'). *Roman Catholic Church* The official whose function is to put the case against a person's beatification or canonization; *transferred* a person who provokes argument or debate by supporting the opposing side or by pointing out the weaknesses in his or her own case.
■ The phrase, particularly in its transferred sense, is now much more familiar in its English form: 'devil's advocate'.
1933 *Music and Letters* It is a pleasant thing to play advocatus diaboli with the knowledge that one is going to allow oneself to cross over to the angels' bench later.

adytum /'adɪtəm/ *noun* plural **adyta** /'adɪtə/ E17 Latin (from Greek *aduton* use as noun of neuter singular of *adutos* impenetrable). The innermost part of a temple; a private chamber, a sanctum.

adzuki /əd'zu:ki/ *noun* (also **adsuki**, **azuki**) E18 Japanese (*azuki*). A bushy leguminous plant, *Vigna angularis*, cultivated in China and Japan; the edible bean of this plant.
■ Also in the phrase *adzuki bean*.

aegis /'i:dʒɪs/ *noun* (also **egis** (chiefly United States)) E17 Greek (from Greek *aigis* shield of Zeus). **1** E17 A shield, defensive armour, *especially* that of Jupiter or Minerva. **2** L18 *figurative* Protection; an impregnable defence.
■ Most frequently in the phrase *under the aegis of* 'under the protection of' (see quotation).
1996 *Country Life* Here under the aegis of Jan Brueghel, Roelandt Savery and Bosschaert we can see the format evolving.

aegrotat /ʌɪ'grəʊtat/, /'i:grəʊtat/, /i:'grəʊtat/ *noun* L18 Latin (*aegrotat* 3rd singular present indicative of *aegrotare* to be ill, from *aeger* sick, ill). In universities, a certificate that a student is too ill to attend an examination etc.; an examination pass or (*North America*) a credit awarded to a student having such a certificate.

aetatis /ʌɪ'ta:tɪs/, /i:'teɪtɪs/ *adjective* (usually abbreviated as **aet.**) /ʌɪt/, /i:t/ or **aetat** /'ʌɪtat/, /'i:tat/ E19 Latin. Of or at the age of.
■ The formula *aetatis, aetatis suae*, or one of the abbreviations, plus a figure, is found

much earlier, in England and elsewhere, inscribed on portraits to give the age of the sitter. The full formula *anno aetatis suae* is also occasionally found.

affaire /afɛr/ *noun* plural pronounced same E19 **French**. A temporary sexual relationship outside marriage; a love affair. Also *generally* a sensational event, case, or scandal.

■ Originally more usual in its full form *affaire de* (or *du*) *cœur* /daʃ/, /dy/, /kœr/ (literally, 'affair of the heart'). In its more general sense, used with the definite article (either French or English), followed by the name of the person(s) involved (see quotation 1995).
1958 A. Wilson *Middle Age of Mrs. Eliot* It would be so awful to have one of those office affaires that they have in the women's mags.
1995 *Times* Robbed of its most lurid aspect—money—*l'affaire* O.J. [sc. Simpson] may now serve a more contemplative purpose.

affairé /afere/ *adjective* E20 **French**. Busy; involved.

affaire de (or **du**) **cœur** see AFFAIRE.

affiche /afiʃ/ (*plural same*); /əˈfiːʃ/ *noun* E19 **French**. A notice affixed to a wall etc.; a poster.

affidavit /afɪˈdeɪvɪt/ *noun* M16 **Medieval Latin** (= he/she has affirmed, 3rd person singular perfect indicative of *affidare* to declare on oath). *Law* A written statement, confirmed by oath, to be used as evidence.

■ In legal phraseology a deponent *swears* an affidavit, the judge *takes* it; in popular use, however, the deponent *takes* or *makes* it.
1996 *Oldie* For my part, once I am sure that everyone knows who I am talking about, I shall sign an affidavit that all the characters are fictitious, and publish the book anonymously.

afflatus /əˈfleɪtəs/ *noun* M17 **Latin** (from *afflat-* past participial stem of *afflare*, from *ad* on + *flare* to blow). The communication of supernatural knowledge; divine impulse; (especially poetic) inspiration.

aficionado /afɪsjəˈnɑːdəʊ/, *foreign* /aˌfiθjo ˈnado/, *noun* plural **aficionados** /aˌfɪsjə ˈnɑːdəʊz/, *foreign* /aˌfiθjoˈnados/ M19 **Spanish** (= amateur, use as noun of past participle of *aficionar* to become fond of, from *afición* from Latin *affectio* favourable disposition). **1** M19 A devotee of bullfighting. **2** L19 An ardent follower of any activity or interest.

1 **1996** *Spectator* For those of us who are *aficionados*, it is satisfying to report that the bullfight is flourishing today as never before.

2 **1996** *Times* Dennis Potter *aficionados* may care to take notice of Keeley Hawes . . . who will be making something of a splash as the female star of *Karaoke*.

à fond /a fɔ̃/ *adverb phrase* E19 **French** (literally, 'to bottom'). Thoroughly, fully.

a fortiori /eɪ fɔːtɪˈɔːrʌɪ/, /fɔːtɪˈɔːriː/ *adverb phrase* E17 **Latin**. With yet stronger reason; more conclusively; even more so.
1961 *New Scientist* Anyone who . . . loses his sight after leaving school—or *a fortiori* in mid-career—cannot easily escape feelings of deep dismay.

afreet /ˈafriːt/ *noun* (also **afrit**, **efreet** /ˈɛfriːt/) L18 **Arabic** ('ifrīt, colloquial 'afrīt). A powerful jinnee in Arabian stories and Muslim mythology.

aga /ˈɑːɡə/ *noun* (also **agha**) M16 **Turkish** (ağa master, lord from Mongolian aqa). An Ottoman title, now abolished, for (originally) a military commander and (later) officials of various ranks. Now, a title of respect for landowners among Turkish village people.

agal /aˈɡɑːl/ *noun* M19 **Arabic** (representing Bedouin pronunciation of Arabic 'iḳāl bond, rope for hobbling a camel). A fillet worn around the head by Bedouin Arabs to keep the KEFFIYEH in position.

agape /ˈaɡəpi/ *noun* plural **agapae** /ˈaɡəpiː/, **agapes** E17 **Greek** (agapē brotherly love). **1** E17 A love-feast held by early Christians in connection with the Eucharist; *transferred* a parochial feast at a festival time. **2** M19 Christian love, charity.

agapemone /aɡəˈpiːməni/, /aɡəˈpɛməni/ *noun* M19 **Greek** (irregular formation from agapē love + monē abode). An abode of love; an establishment where free love is practised.

■ Originally with capital initial, the name of a community founded in Somerset, England, *c.*1850 by H. J. Prince.

agar-agar /ˌeɪɡɑːˈeɪɡɑː/ *noun* (in sense 2 usually simply **agar**) E19 **Malay**. **1** E19 Any of certain South-East Asian seaweeds from which a gelatinous substance is extracted. **2** M19 The substance itself, used especially to make soups and to form biological culture media.

agenda /əˈdʒɛndə/ *noun* plural, also used as *singular* (less commonly in singular **agendum** /əˈdʒɛndəm/) E17 **Latin** (plural of agendum, use as noun of gerundive of agere to do). **1** E17 *plural* Things to be done; matters of practice. **2** M18 *collective singular* A memorandum book. *archaic.*

3 L19 As *plural*, items of business to be considered at a meeting or to be otherwise attended to. As *singular*, a list of such items.

agent provocateur /aʒã prɔvɔkatœr/ *noun phrase* plural **agents provocateurs** (pronounced same) L19 French (= provocative agent). An agent employed to tempt suspected persons into committing an incriminating act.

1996 *Times* Either try persuading people that cycling is a realistic mode of transport in London. Or—forgive me for sounding like an *agent provocateur*—start shooting motorists.

aggiornamento /adˌdʒɔrnaˈmento/, /əˌdʒɔːnəˈmɛntəʊ/ *noun* M20 Italian. Bringing up to date, especially of Roman Catholic Church policy by and after the Second Vatican Council (1962–5).

agio /ˈadʒɪəʊ/ *noun* plural **agios** L17 Italian (*ag(g)io*). **1** L17 The percentage charged for changing paper money into cash, or an inferior for a more valuable currency; the excess value of one currency over another. **2** E19 *loosely.* Money-changing.

agiotage /ˈadʒɪətɪdʒ/ *noun* L18 French (from *agioter* to speculate, from Italian *ag(g)io* from as preceding). Money-changing business; speculation in stocks; stock-jobbing.

agitato /adʒɪˈtɑːtəʊ/ *adverb, adjective, & noun* E19 Italian. *Music* **A** *adverb & adjective* E19 (A direction:) in an agitated manner. **B** *noun* E19 plural **agitati** /adʒɪˈtɑːti/, **agitatos**. A passage (to be) played or sung in an agitated manner. *rare.*

agitprop /ˈadʒɪtprɒp/, /ˈagɪtprɒp/ *noun* (also **Agitprop**) E20 Russian (from *agit(atsiya)* agitation + *prop(aganda)* propaganda). *History* Soviet Communist propaganda; the system or activity of disseminating this.

agloo, aglu see IGLOO.

agnolotti /ˌanjəˈlɒti/ *noun* plural L20 Italian. Pasta made into cases with meat or other stuffing. Cf. RAVIOLI.

agnomen /agˈnəʊmɛn/ *noun* M17 Latin (*agnomen*, from *ad* to + (g)*nomen* name). A name given or acquired during the course of one's life, a nickname; *Roman History* a fourth name occasionally given as an honour.

Agnus Dei /ˌagnʊs ˈdeɪiː/, *in sense 1 also* /ˌanjʊs/; /ˌagnəs ˈdiːʌɪ/ *noun phrase* LME Latin (= Lamb of God). *Christian Church* **1** LME Part of the Mass beginning with the words *Agnus Dei*; a musical setting of this. **2** LME A figure of a lamb bearing a cross or flag, as an emblem of Christ. **b** L16 A cake of wax stamped with such a figure and blessed by the Pope.

■ In sense 2 the Agnus Dei is the emblem of St John the Baptist in art, who is very often depicted with it and holding a scroll with the words ECCE AGNUS DEI 'Behold the Lamb of God'.

a gogo /ə ˈɡəʊɡəʊ/ *adverb & postpositive adjective phrase* M20 French (*à gogo*). In abundance, galore. *colloquial.*

agon /ˈaɡɒn/ *noun* plural **agones** /əˈɡəʊniːz/ E17 Greek (*agōn* contest). *Greek History* **1** E17 A public celebration comprising athletic games; a contest for the prize at such games or *transferred* elsewhere. **2** L19 A verbal contest between two characters in a play.

agonistes /aɡəˈnɪstiːz/ *postpositive adjective* L17 Greek (= contestant). Who is an agonist.

■ First used in the title of John Milton's *Samson Agonistes* (1671) and imitated by later authors.

agora /ˈaɡɒrə/ *noun* plural **agorae** /ˈaɡɒriː/, **agorai** /ˈaɡɒrʌɪ/, **agoras** L16 Greek. *Greek History* An assembly; a place of assembly, *especially* a market-place.

1996 *Times* If there was ever an opportunity to create a new European *agora*, the Net's unsupervised electronic anarchy is surely the place.

agoraphobia /ˌaɡ(ə)rəˈfəʊbɪə/ *noun* L19 pseudo-Greek (from AGORA + -PHOBIA). Irrational terror of open spaces.

■ Coined by the German psychologist Carl Westphal in 1871.

agraphon /ˈaɡrəfɒn/ *noun* plural **agrapha** /ˈaɡrəfə/ L19 Greek (neuter of *agraphos* unwritten). A saying attributed to Jesus but not in the canonical Gospels. Usually in *plural.*

agrément /aɡremã/ *noun* plural **agréments, agrémens** (pronounced same) E18 French. **1** E18 In *plural* Agreeable qualities, circumstances, etc. **2** L18 *Music* In *plural* Grace-notes; embellishments. **3** E20 Official approval given to a diplomatic representative of another country.

1 1996 *Spectator* The continentals like to have their *agréments*, the comfortable pleasures of civilisation without its pomp.

aguardiente /ˌaɡwardiˈente/, /əˌɡwɑːdɪˈɛnti/ *noun* E19 Spanish (from *agua* water + *ardiente* fiery). Coarse Spanish brandy; in

Spanish-speaking areas of America, a similar distilled liquor, *especially* one made from sugar cane.

AH see under HEGIRA.

ahimsa /əˈhɪmsɑː/ *noun* L19 Sanskrit (from *a* non- + *himsā* violence). The doctrine in Hindu, Buddhist, and Jain philosophy that there should be no violence or killing of any living creature, however humble.

à huis clos /a yi klɔ/ *adverb phrase* E17 French. In secret, IN CAMERA.

aide-de-camp /eɪddəˈkɒ̃/, *foreign* /ɛddəkɑ̃/ *noun* (also **aid-de-camp, aide de camp**) plural **aides-de-camp, aids-de-camp** (*chiefly United States*), /eɪdzdəˈkɒ̃/, *foreign* /ɛddəkɑ̃/ L17 French (= camp adjutant). *Military* An officer acting as a confidential assistant to a senior officer, or assisting on a ceremonial occasion; *transferred* anyone acting in a similar capacity to a more senior person.

■ Often abbreviated in military use to ADC.

1996 *Times* The culprits were John Redwood, MP for Wokingham, and his ebullient *aide de camp*, Hywel Williams.

aide-mémoire /ˌeɪdmɛmˈwɑː/; *foreign* /ɛdmemwar/ (*plural same*) *noun* M19 French. (A book or document serving as) an aid to the memory; (in diplomats' use) a memorandum.

1995 *Spectator* Then I had a bright idea and dug out of a trunk all my account books going back to the 1950s. They are a wonderful *aide-mémoire*.

aigre-doux /ɛgrədu/, /ɛgrəˈdu:/ *adjective* (also **aigre-douce** /ɛgrədus/, /ɛgrəˈdu:s/) LME French. Compounded of sweet and sour; bitter-sweet.

aigrette /ˈeɪgrɛt/, /eɪˈgrɛt/ *noun* M18 French. An egret's plume; a tuft of feathers or hair; a spray of gems etc. worn on the head.

aiguille /ˈeɪgwiːl/ *noun* M18 French (= needle). A sharply pointed peak of rock, especially in the Alps.

aikido /ʌɪˈkiːdəʊ/ *noun* M20 Japanese (*aikidō*, from *ai* together, unify + *ki* spirit + *dō* way). A Japanese form of self-defence and martial art, developed from ju-jitsu and involving holds and throws.

aileron /ˈeɪlərɒn/ *noun* E20 French (diminutive of *aile* wing). A movable aerofoil used to control the balance of an aircraft in flight, usually a hinged flap in the trailing edge of a wing.

aïoli /ʌɪˈjəʊli/, *foreign* /ajɔli/ *noun* E20 French (from Provençal *ai* garlic + *oli* oil). Mayonnaise seasoned with garlic.

akara, akkra variants of ACCRA.

akroterion variant of ACROTERION.

akvavit variant of AQUAVIT.

à la /ɑː lɑː/, *foreign* /a la/ *preposition phrase* L16 French (abbreviation of À LA MODE). In the manner, method, or style of.

■ Followed by a French noun in standard phrases (see following entries), but also often with an English noun (see quotation).

1995 *Spectator* And how long can the Labour leader go on talking about newness *à la* Newt before someone notices that, unlike with Mr Gingrich, there is no real radicalism behind the rhetoric?

à la bonne femme see BONNE FEMME.

à la broche /ɑː lɑː ˈbrɒʃ/, *foreign* /a la brɔʃ/*adverb & adjective phrase* E20 French. (Cooked) on a spit; spit-roasted. Cf. À LA BROCHETTE.

à la brochette /ɑː lɑː brɒˈʃɛt/, *foreign* /a la brɔʃɛt/ *adverb & adjective phrase* M19 French. (Cooked) on a skewer. Cf. À LA BROCHE.

à la carte /ɑː lɑː ˈkɑːt/, *foreign* /a la kart/ *adverb & adjective phrase* E19 French. By the bill of fare; ordered as a separately priced item or as separately priced items from a menu, not as part of a table d'hôte meal.

à la daube /ɑː lɑː dəʊb/, *foreign* /a la dob/ *adverb & adjective phrase* E18 French. (Of poultry, meat, or game) stewed, braised.

à la Florentine /ɑː lɑː ˈflɒr(ə)ntiːn/, *foreign* /a la flɔrɑ̃tin/ *adverb & adjective phrase* E20 French (= in the Florentine manner). (Of eggs, fish, etc.) served on a bed of spinach or with a spinach sauce.

■ Now generally just 'Florentine'.

à la fourchette /ɑː lɑː fʊəˈʃɛt/, *foreign* /a la furʃɛt/ *adverb & adjective phrase* E19 French. (Of a meal) requiring the use (only) of a fork.

à la lanterne /ɑː lɑː lɑ̃tɛrn(ə)/ *interjection* L18 French (= to the lantern). Away with (them)!

■ The phrase is a quotation from the refrain of the French Revolutionary song 'Ça ira'. It records the Revolutionary mobs' practice of hanging their victims from the street lamps.

1995 *Country Life* Did they hear the trundle of the tumbrels on Blenheim's drive and distant cries of 'A la lanterne' from the streets of Woodstock?

alameda /alə'meɪdə/ *noun* L18 Spanish. In Spain and Spanish-speaking areas: a public walk, shaded with trees; an ALLÉE.

à la mode /ɑː lɑː 'məʊd/, *foreign* /a la mɔd/ *adverb & adjective phrase* L16 French (= in the fashion). **1** L16 In or according to the fashion; fashionable. **2** *Cookery* **a** M17 Of beef: braised or made into a rich stew, usually with wine. **b** E20 Of food: served with ice cream. Chiefly *United States*.

■ Also in use (M–L17) as a noun (phrase), usually as one word, meaning 'a fashion, a temporary mood' or (M17) 'a thin glossy usually black silk'.

1 1996 *Spectator* He ends with a chapter describing what the book might have been, if it had been longer . . . All very much *à la mode*, but why not save the space and cut the price to the public?

à la page /a la paʒ/, /ɑː lɑː 'pɑːʒ/ *adverb & adjective phrase* M20 French (literally, 'at the page'). Up to date, up to the minute.

à la russe /ɑː lɑː 'ruːs/, *foreign* /a la rys/ *adverb & adjective phrase* (also **à la Russe**) E19 French. In the Russian manner.

■ In the mid nineteenth century *à la russe* often alluded to the then new-fangled custom in smart society of serving meals on a table dressed with flowers and dessert, with the individual courses brought in from another room or served from side-tables.

alba /'albə/ *noun* E19 Provençal (ultimately from Latin *albus* white). A medieval Provençal song at dawn. Cf. AUBADE.

albarello /albə'rɛləʊ/ *noun* plural **albarelli** /albə'rɛli/ L19 Italian (*alberello* pot, phial). A majolica jar used especially as a container for drugs.

1995 *Country Life* The form of the *albarello* came from Persia in the 15th century, and was popular with northern European potteries as well as the makers of maiolica.

albedo /al'biːdəʊ/ *noun* plural **albedos** M19 ecclesiastical Latin (= whiteness, from Latin *albus* white). The proportion of incident radiation reflected by a surface, especially of a planet or moon.

albergo /al'bɛrgo/, /al'bəːgəʊ/ *noun* plural **alberghi** /al'bɛrgi/, /al'bəːgiː/ E17 Italian. An Italian inn. Cf. AUBERGE.

albino /al'biːnəʊ/ *noun & adjective* E18 Spanish **and** Portuguese (from *albo* white). **A** *noun* plural **albinos** **1** E18 A human being having a congenital defi-ciency of pigmentation in the skin and hair, which are white, and the eyes, which are usually pink. **2** E19 An abnormally white animal or plant. **B** *adjective* E19 Congenitally lacking in pigmentation; abnormally white.

■ Originally applied by the Portuguese to albinos among African Blacks.

album /'albəm/ *noun* E17 Latin (= blank tablet, use as noun of neuter of *albus* white). **I** A blank book for the insertion of collected items. **1** E17 A blank book in which people other than the owner insert autographs, memorial verses, etc. **2** M19 A blank book for the insertion of stamps, photographs, etc. **II 3** E20 A holder for a set of discs or tape recordings; an integral set of discs or tapes; a disc or tape comprising several pieces of music etc.

■ First taken into English from the German use of the Latin phrase *album amicorum* album of friends, i.e. an autograph book.

albumen /'albjʊmm/ *noun* (also **albumin** in sense 3) L16 Latin (from *albus* white). **1** L16 The white of an egg. **2** L17 *Botany* The nutritive material surrounding the embryo in some plant seeds; the endosperm. **3** E19 Soluble protein, such as that in egg-white.

alcade variant of ALCALDE.

alcaide /al'kʌɪdi/, *foreign* /al'kaide/ *noun* (also **alcaid, alcayde**) E16 Spanish (from Arabic *al-ḳāʾid* the leader, the commander). The governor of a Spanish, Portuguese, Moorish, etc., fortress; a jailer.

alcalde /al'kaldi/, *foreign* /al'kalde/ *noun* (also **alcade** /al'kɑːd/, *foreign* /al'kad/) M16 Spanish (*alcalde* (French *alcade*) from Arabic *al-ḳāḍī* the judge). A mayor, magistrate, or similar administrative officer in Spain, Portugal, and parts of South America and the south-western United States.

alcayde variant of ALCAIDE.

alcazar /alkə'zɑː/, *foreign* /al'kaθar/, /al'kasar/ *noun* plural **alcazars** /alkə'zɑːz/, **alcazares** /al'kaθares/, /al'kasares/ E17 Spanish (*alcázar* from Arabic *al-ḳaṣr* the castle). A Spanish palace or fortress.

alcheringa /altʃə'rɪŋgə/ *noun* L19 Aranda (= in the dream-time). A golden age in the mythology of some Australian Aborigine groups.

aldea /al'deɪə/, *foreign* /al'dea/ *noun* E17 Portuguese (*aldeia*, Spanish *aldea* from Arabic *al-ḍay'a*, from *al* the + *ḍay'a* agricultural village, farm). A small village or a farm in Portugal, Spain, or one of their former territories.

al dente /al 'dɛnti/, *foreign* /al 'dɛnte/ *adverb & adjective phrase* M20 Italian (literally, 'to the tooth'). Of pasta, vegetables, etc.: (cooked) so as to be still slightly firm when bitten.

> **1995** *Spectator* [The] pasta, although it had swollen wonderfully with the pale coral juices of the seafood, was just a bit too *al dente*.

aleatico /alɪˈatɪkəʊ/ *noun* (also **Aleatico**) E19 Italian. A sweet Italian red wine.

aleph /'ɑːlɛf/ *noun* ME Hebrew ('ālep, literally, 'ox'; cf. ALPHA). **1** ME The first letter of the Hebrew, Phoenician, and other Semitic alphabets. **2** E20 *Mathematics* A transfinite cardinal numeral.

alfa /'alfə/ *noun* (also **halfa** /'halfə/) M19 Arabic (*ḥalfā'*, colloquial *ḥalfa*). Esparto grass.

alfalfa /ˌalˈfalfə/ *noun* M19 Spanish (from Arabic *al-fasfaṣa* a green fodder). A leguminous plant, *Medicago sativa*, cultivated for green fodder; lucerne.

alfilaria /ˌalfɪləˈriːə/ *noun* M19 Mexican Spanish (from Spanish *alfiler* pin, with reference to the long-beaked carpels). In the United States: the common stork's-bill, *Erodium cicutarium*, grown as fodder; pin clover.

alforja /alˈfɔːhə/, *foreign* /alˈfɔrxa/ *noun* Also formerly written **alforge** E17 Spanish (*alforja*, Portuguese *alforge* from Arabic *al-ḳurj* the saddle-bag). In Spain, Portugal, Latin America, and other areas of Spanish influence (as the south-western United States): a wallet, a saddle-bag.

alfresco /alˈfrɛskəʊ/ *adverb & adjective* (also **al fresco**) M18 Italian (*al fresco*). **A** *adverb* **1** M18 In the open air. **2** M18 *Art* In fresco. **B** *adjective* E19 Open-air.

> **B 1996** *Times: Weekend* This situation, naturally, has many possibilities, especially when complicated by extra-mural, even *al fresco*, couplings, one of which leads to a sacking.

alga /'algə/ *noun* plural **algae** /'aldʒiː/, /'algiː/ M16 Latin (= seaweed). Originally, seaweed; now, any of a large group of non-vascular mainly aquatic cryptogams capable of photosynthesis, including seaweeds and many unicellular and filamentous organisms. Also *collectively*, the mass formed by such organisms.

alguacil /algwəˈsɪl/, *foreign* /algwaˈθil/, /algwaˈsil/ *noun* plural **alguacils** /algwəˈsɪlz/, *foreign* **alguaciles** /algwaˈθiles/, /algwaˈsiles/ (also **alguazil** /algwəˈzɪl/ plural **alguazils** /algwəˈzɪlz/, **alguaziles** /algwəˈziːləz/) E16 Spanish ((earlier *alguazil*) from Arabic *al-wazīr*, from *al* the + *wazīr* vizier). **1** E16 In Spain: an officer of justice, a warrant-officer, a sergeant. In Latin America or other areas of Spanish influence: a sheriff, a constable. **2** *Bullfighting* E20 A mounted official at a bullfight.

alhaji /alˈhadʒi/ *noun* (also as a title **Alhaji**) M20 Hausa (from Arabic *al* the + *ḥajj* pilgrimage). In West Africa: a Muslim who has been to Mecca as a pilgrim.

alias /'eɪlɪəs/ *adverb & noun* LME Latin (= at another time, otherwise). **A** *adverb* LME Otherwise called or named; called at other times. **B** *noun* E17 A name by which a person is or has been called on other occasions; an assumed name.

> **B 1996** *Times: Magazine* So, for whom is Grace an alias?

alibi /'alɪbʌɪ/ *adverb, noun, & verb* L17 Latin (= elsewhere). **A** *noun* L18 A plea by the person accused of an act that he or she was elsewhere when it took place; evidence to support such a plea; *colloquially* an excuse of any kind. **B** *transitive & intransitive verb* E20 Provide an alibi, offer an excuse, (for).

> ■ *Alibi* was originally used in English as an adverb, following the Latin, but during the late eighteenth century this usage became obsolete and was superseded by the modern nominal usage.

aliquot /'alɪkwɒt/ *adjective & noun* L16 French (*aliquote* from Latin *aliquot* some, several, from *alius* one of two + *quot* how many). Originally *Mathematics*. **A** *adjective* L16 That is contained in the whole an integral number of times. Chiefly in *aliquot part*. **B** *noun* E17 An aliquot part, integral factor; *loosely* any fraction of a whole, a sample.

alla breve /alə 'breɪvi/ *adverb, adjective, & noun phrase* M18 Italian (= according to the breve). *Music* With increased speed, at two minim beats in a bar instead of four crotchets; such a tempo or time signature.

alla cappella /alǝ kǝ'pɛlǝ/ *adverb & adjective phrase* M18 Italian. Of choral music or choirs: unaccompanied.
■ Introduced earlier than A CAPPELLA.

alla marcia /ˌalǝ 'mɑːtʃǝ/ *adverb, adjective, & noun phrase* L19 Italian. *Music* (A piece, movement, etc.) in the style of a march.

allargando /alɑː'gandǝʊ/ *adverb, adjective, & noun* L19 Italian (= broadening). *Music* **A** *adverb & adjective* L19 (A direction:) getting slower and slower and often also fuller in tone. **B** *noun* M20 *plural* **allargandi** /alɑː'gandi/, **allargandos**. A passage (to be) so played.

allée /ale/ *noun plural pronounced same* M18 French. A walk or passage in a garden, park, etc., usually flanked and shaded by trees or shrubs; an alley.
  1996 *Country Life: Garden Year* The grotto is approached through an ominously dark *allée* of tall yews extending south of the house.

allegretto /alɪ'grɛtǝʊ/ *adverb, adjective, & noun* M18 Italian (diminutive of ALLEGRO). *Music* **A** *adverb & adjective* M18 (A direction:) in fairly quick time, but not as quick(ly) as allegro. **B** *noun* L19 *plural* **allegrettos, allegretti** /alɪ'grɛti/. A movement or piece in fairly quick time. Also, a short movement or piece in quick time.

allegro /ǝ'leɪgrǝʊ/, /ǝ'lɛgrǝʊ/ *adverb, adjective, & noun* L17 Italian (= lively, gay). *Music* **A** *adverb & adjective* L17 (A direction:) in quick time; *transferred* (of forms of words and phrases) used in speech and shortened (e.g. *we'll* for *we will*). **B** *noun* M18 *plural* **allegros, allegri** /ǝ'leɪgri/. A movement or piece in quick time.

allemande /'almɑːnd/, /almɑ̃d/ (*plural same*) *noun* L17 French (= German (feminine)). **1** L17 A piece of music for a German dance or in its rhythm, *especially* one which forms a movement of a suite. **2** E18 Any of various German dances. **b** E19 A figure in square dancing in which adjacent dancers link arms or join hands and make a full or partial turn. Also used as a call to dancers to execute this figure turning in the specified direction. **3** *Cookery* E19 A rich velouté sauce thickened with egg yolks.
■ The earliest sense (M17) in which *Allemande* was used in English was 'a German woman', but this is not attested outside this period.

allumette /alu:'mɛt/, *foreign* /alymɛt/ (*plural same*) *noun* E17 French (from *allumer* to set light to). A match for lighting or setting things alight.

■ Rare before the nineteenth century.

alluvium /ǝ'l(j)uːvɪǝm/ *noun plural* (*now rare*) **alluvia** /ǝ'l(j)uːvɪǝ/, **alluviums** M17 Latin, (neuter of *alluvius* washed against, from *ad* to + *luere* to wash). A deposit of clay, silt, sand, etc., left by flowing water, as in a river valley or delta.

Alma Mater /ˌalmǝ 'mɑːtǝ/, /'meɪtǝ/ *noun phrase* (also **alma mater**) *plural* **Alma Maters**, (*rare*) **Almae Matres** /ˌalmʌɪ 'mɑːtrɛz/, /ˌalmi: 'meɪtriːz/ M17 Latin (= bounteous mother, a title given to various Roman goddesses, especially Ceres and Cybele). **1** M17 Someone or something providing nourishment and care. **2** L17 *especially* A university or school as regarded by its past and present members.
  2 1996 *Spectator* After representing the Emperor and Empress ... at King George VI's coronation, and visiting his *alma mater* at Oxford, he [sc. the Crown Prince] returned to Japan ...

aloe vera /ˌalǝʊ 'vɛːrǝ/ *noun phrase* L20 Latin (= true aloe). A plant resembling a cactus from which an extract used in skin care and other health products is obtained.
  1989 A. Tan *Joy Luck Club* A cutting of aloe vera that Lena gave me did not belong anywhere because we had no other succulents.

aloha /ǝ'lǝʊhǝ/ *interjection & noun* E19 Hawaiian. Used in Hawaii especially as greeting or parting: love, affection; an utterance of this.

à l'outrance *variant of* À OUTRANCE.

alpaca /al'pakǝ/ *noun* L18 Spanish (from Aymara *allpaca*). A domesticated Peruvian animal, *Lama pacos*, resembling the llama, with long fine woolly hair and usually brown and white colouring; the wool of the alpaca; fabric or a garment made from this.

alpargata /alpɑː'gɑːtǝ/ *noun* E19 Spanish. An ESPADRILLE.

alpenhorn /'alpǝnhɔːn/ *noun* L19 German (= Alp-horn). A long wooden horn used by Alpine herdsmen.

alpenstock /'alpǝnstɒk/ *noun* E19 German (= Alp-stick). A long iron-tipped staff used in mountain-climbing.

alpha /'alfǝ/ *noun* ME Latin (from Greek). **1** ME The first letter (A, a) of the Greek alphabet; the beginning of anything. **2** E17 Denoting the first in a numerical or other sequence. **3** *attributive Science* M18 First, most important; as in *Astronomy* (preceding the genitive of the Latin name of the constellation) designating the chief star in a constellation; thus *Alpha Centauri* is the brightest star in the constellation Centaurus. **4** E20 (A person gaining) a first-class mark in an examination etc.

■ In sense 1 *alpha* often appears in the phrase *the alpha and* (*the*) *omega*, which originally referred to God (see Revelation 1:8), but now is also used in the transferred sense of 'the beginning and the end' (see quotation 1996). In scientific terminology *alpha* has specialist applications in Chemistry, Medicine, and Computing, as well as Astronomy.

1 1996 *Times* The 100 metres is the alpha and omega of sport.
3 1995 *New Scientist* If the female deigns to mate, the honour goes to the senior partner, or alpha male. The junior, or beta male reaps his reward years later: when the alpha dies, the beta inherits his mentor's alpha status, and recruits his own apprentice.

al segno /al 'sɛnjəʊ/ *adverb phrase* L18 Italian (= to the sign). *Music* (A direction:) go back (= DAL SEGNO) or continue to the point indicated by the sign.

alter ego /ˌaltər 'ɛgəʊ/, /ˌɒltər/, /ˈiːgəʊ/ *noun phrase* plural **alter egos** M16 Latin (= other self). A person's second self; an intimate friend; a representative of another person.

1996 *Times* If . . . Anne is ever-faithful Auden to Kallman's rake, then the poet could not have asked for a more sympathetic alter ego.
1996 *Oldie* 'Simply put, one of the greatest writers ever.' This is Scott Turow's considered judgment on Ruth Rendall and her alter ego Barbara Vine.

althorn /ˈalthɔːn/ *noun* M19 German (*alt* alto + *horn* horn). *Music* A wind instrument of the saxhorn family.

altiplano /altɪˈplɑːnəʊ/, *foreign* /altiˈplano/ *noun* E20 Spanish. The high tableland of central South America.

alto /ˈaltəʊ/ *noun & adjective* L16 Italian (= high (sc. song) from Latin *altus* high). *Music* **A** *noun* plural **altos 1a** L16 The highest adult male voice, with range above the tenor, the counter-tenor voice; a part written for such a voice. **b** E19 A female voice of similar range, a contralto voice; a part written for such a voice. **2** L18 A person who has a counter-tenor or contralto voice. **3** L19 An alto wind instrument (see **B**). **B** *adjective* E18 Designating, pertaining to, or intended for a counter-tenor or contralto voice. Also, designating that member of a group of

similar instruments with a range or relative pitch comparable to an alto voice (among wind instruments usually the second or third highest member of the family).

alto-relievo /ˌaltəʊrɪˈliːvəʊ/ *noun* (also **alto-rilievo** /ˌaltəʊrɪˈljeɪvəʊ/) plural **alto-relievos** M17 Italian (*alto-rilievo*). (A sculpture, moulding, carving, etc., in) high relief.

alumna /əˈlʌmnə/ *noun* plural **alumnae** /əˈlʌmniː/ L19 Latin (feminine of next). A female graduate or former student of a school, college, university, or other educational institution.

alumnus /əˈlʌmnəs/ *noun* plural **alumni** /əˈlʌmnʌɪ/, /əˈlʌmniː/ M17 Latin (= nursling, pupil, from *alere* to nourish). Formerly, a pupil. Now *specifically*, a (male) graduate or former student of a school, college, university, or other educational institution.

a.m. abbreviation of ANTE MERIDIEM.

ama /ˈamə/ *noun* plural same M20 Japanese. A Japanese woman who dives for shellfish and edible seaweed.

amah /ˈɑːmə/ *noun* M19 Portuguese (*ama* nurse). In parts of the Indian subcontinent and the Far East: a wet-nurse, a children's nurse, a house-servant.

amanuensis /əˌmanjʊˈɛnsɪs/ *noun* plural **amanuenses** /əˌmanjʊˈɛnsiːz/ E17 Latin (from *a manu* in *servus a manu* slave at hand + -*ensis* belonging to). A person who writes from dictation or copies manuscript; a literary assistant.

■ The Latin phrase *servus a manu* was used by Suetonius (Life of Julius Caesar: 74) and by the Latin legal writers to denote a slave who acted as a secretary.

amateur /ˈamətə/, /ˈamətjʊə/ *noun & adjective* L18 French (from Italian *amatore* from Latin *amator* lover). **A** *noun* **1** L18 A person who is fond *of* something; a person who has a taste for something. **2** L18 A person who practises something, especially an art or game, only as a pastime; an unpaid player, performer, etc. (opposed *professional*); also (*depreciative*), a dabbler. **B** E19 *attributive* or as *adjective* Done by amateurs, not professional; also (*depreciative*), unskilful.

ambiance /ãbjãs/ *noun* M20 French (from *ambiant* from Latin *ambire* to go round). Environment, ambience; also *specifically*, the combination of the accessory elements of a painting to support the main effect of a piece.

■ The Anglicized *ambience* tends to be used in general contexts, with *ambiance* suggesting a more contrived or specially created atmosphere, as in the *ambiance* of a club or restaurant (see quotation).
1996 *Times* Now there are theme restaurants: hang the food, feel the ambiance is the premise on which they operate.

ambiente /ambi'ente/, /ambr'ɛnti/ *noun* E20 **Italian and Spanish**. Surroundings, ambience.

ambo /'ambəʊ/ *noun* plural **ambos** also written in Latin form **ambones** /am 'bəʊni:z/ M17 **Medieval Latin** (from Greek *ambōn* rim, edge of a cup). The pulpit or reading-desk in early Christian churches; an oblong enclosure with steps at both ends.

ambrosia /am'brəʊzjə/ *noun* M16 **Latin** (from Greek = immortality, elixir of life, from *ambrotos* immortal; in Dioscurides and Pliny applied to one or more herbs). **I 1** M16 *Classical Mythology* The food, drink, or unguent of the gods. **2** E17 (Honey and) pollen used as food by bees, beebread. **3** M17 Something divinely sweet to taste or smell. **4** L17 Water, oil, and fruits mixed as a libation; also, a perfumed or flavoured drink. **5** L19 A fungal product which forms the food of the pinhole borer. **II 6** M16 Wood-sage and certain other plants. Now only as Modern Latin name of a genus of plants of the Compositae family.

ameba variant of AMOEBA.

âme damnée /am dɑne/ *noun phrase* plural **âmes damnées** (pronounced same) E19 **French** (= damned soul). A devoted adherent; a stooge.

ameer mainly US variant of AMIR.

amende honorable /amɑ̃d ɔnɔrabl/ *noun phrase* plural **amendes honorables** (pronounced same) E17 **French** (= honourable reparation). Public or open apology and reparation; an instance of this.

a mensa et thoro /eɪ ˌmɛnsə ɛt 'tɔːrəʊ/ *adverb & adjective phrase* E17 **Latin** (= from table and bed). *Law.* Formerly (before 1857) of a divorce: decreed by an ecclesiastical court on grounds sanctioned by law (having the effect of a modern judicial separation).

à merveille /a mɛrvɛj/ *adverb phrase* M18 **French** (= to a marvel). Admirably, wonderfully.

âmes damnées plural of ÂME DAMNÉE.

amicus curiae /aˌmʌɪkəs 'kjʊəriːi/ *noun phrase* plural **amici curiae** /aˌmiːsiː 'kjʊəriːi/ E17 **Modern Latin** (= friend of the court). *Law* A disinterested adviser who assists the court by drawing attention to points that might otherwise fail to be mentioned.
1996 *Times* At the High Court's Chancery Division, the Government will argue that the traitor [sc. George Blake] has no right to royalties ... Lord Lester of Herne Hill has been appointed amicus curiae to ensure Blake gets a fair hearing.

amigo /ə'miːgəʊ/ *noun* plural **amigos** M19 **Spanish**. A friend, a comrade.

■ Frequently used as a colloquial form of address, mainly in the United States.
1996 *Times* Herro thought the 'amigos' who had been with the brothers since time began ... would never walk away from their fat-cat accoutrements, pensions, chauffeured cars, and so on. But they did.

amir /ə'miːə/ *noun* (also **ameer**) L16 **Persian and Urdu** (from Arabic *'amīr* commander, governor, prince, from *amara* to command; cf. EMIR). A title of various Muslim rulers.

amnesia /am'niːzjə/ *noun* L18 **Greek** (*amnēsia* forgetfulness). Loss of memory.

amoeba /ə'miːbə/ *noun* (also **ameba**) plural **amoebas**, **amoebae** /ə'miːbiː/ M19 **Modern Latin** (from Greek *amoibē* change, alternation). A single-celled aquatic protozoan, characterized by a constantly changing shape.

amok /ə'mɒk/ *adjective, noun, & adverb* (also **amuck** /ə'mʌk/, (earliest) **am(o)uco**) E16 **Portuguese** (*am(o)uco* from Malay *amuk* fighting furiously, in a homicidal frenzy). **A** *adjective* E16 In a homicidal frenzy. *rare.* Only in E16. **B** *noun* **1** M17 A Malay in a homicidal frenzy. **2** M19 A homicidal frenzy; an act of running amok. **C** *adverb* L17 **run amok**, run about in a frenzied thirst for blood; go on a destructive rampage; rush wildly and heedlessly.

amole /ə'məʊli/ *noun* M19 **Mexican Spanish**. The root of any of several plants of Mexico and the southern United States, used as a detergent; any of these plants.

amontillado /əˌmɒntɪ'lɑːdəʊ/, /əˌmɒntɪl-'jɑːdəʊ/ *noun* (also **Amontillado**) plural **amontillados** E19 **Spanish** (from *Montilla* a town in southern Spain). Formerly, a wine of the sherry type produced in Montilla. Now, a medium sherry of a matured type. Also, a drink or glass of either of these wines.

amoretto /aməˈrɛtəʊ/, *foreign* /amoˈretto/ *noun* plural **amoretti** /amoˈrɛtti/, **amoretto(e)s** /aməˈrɛtəʊz/ L16 Italian (diminutive of *amore* love). **1** L16–E18 A sweetheart; a love poem. **2** E17 A cupid.

amorino /aməˈriːnəʊ/, *foreign* /amoˈriːno/ *noun* plural **amorini** /aməˈriːni/, **amorinos** M19 Italian (diminutive of *amore* love). A cupid.

> **1996** *Times* Last month the auction house predicted a sale of £1 million plus for the *amorino*, discovered in a garden in Wales.

amoroso /aməˈrəʊsəʊ/ *noun, adverb, & adjective* E17 Spanish and Italian (from medieval Latin *amorosus* amorous). **A** *noun* plural **amorosi** /aməˈrəʊsi/, **amorosos** **1** E17–E19 A lover; a gallant. **2** L19 A type of sweetened oloroso sherry. **B** *adverb & adjective* L18 *Music* (A direction:) tender(ly).

amour /əˈmʊə/, *foreign* /amur/ *noun* ME Old and Modern French (from Latin *amor*). **1** ME Love; affection. Now *rare* except in AMOUR COURTOIS, AMOUR PROPRE. **2** LME–E18 In *plural*. Sexual or romantic love. **3** L16 A love affair, especially a secret one.

> **3 1996** *Times* The final swapping of amours [in *Twelfth Night*] does not seem a tricky matter.

amour courtois /amur kurtwa/ *noun phrase* L19 French (= courtly love). A highly conventionalized medieval code of love and etiquette first developed by the troubadours among the chivalric aristocracy of southern France.

amourette /amʊəˈrɛt/, *foreign* /amurɛt/ (*plural same*) *noun* E19 French. **1** E19 A brief or unimportant love affair. **2** M19 A cupid, an amoretto.

amour propre /ˌamʊə ˈprɒpr(ə)/, *foreign* /amur prɔpr/ *noun phrase* (also **amour-propre**) L18 French. Self-esteem; vanity.

> **1996** *Times* [N]ot only is hurling yourself about the court and going for every shot healthier both for body and for *amour-propre*, it is the best excuse there is for losing to those younger than you.
> **1996** *Spectator* Although it would be a blow to the *amour propre* of Mr Preston and friends to sell the Sunday paper after only three years, they may have to do so.

amphisbaena /ˌamfɪsˈbiːnə/ *noun* LME Latin (from Greek *amphisbaina*, from *amphis* both ways + *bainein* to go, walk). **1** LME A fabled serpent with a head at each end and able to move in either direction. **2** M19 A wormlike burrowing lizard of the genus *Amphisbaena*.

> ■ Pliny describes the mythical serpent in the eighth book of his *Natural History*, and Lucan (*Pharsalia* ix.719) lists it amongst the poisonous monsters of Libya that sprang from the dripping blood of the gorgon Medusa's severed head.

amphora /ˈamf(ə)rə/ *noun* plural **amphorae** /ˈamf(ə)riː/, **amphoras** /ˈamf(ə)rɪz/ ME Latin (from Greek *amphoreus*, or French *amphore*). **1** ME A Greek or Roman two-handled vessel. **2** LME A Greek or Roman liquid measure of varying capacity.

ampoule /ˈampuːl/ *noun* M17 Modern French. **1** M17 An AMPULLA 2. *rare*. **2** E20 A small sealed glass vessel for holding sterilized materials for injection, poisons, air-sensitive chemicals, etc.

ampulla /amˈpʊlə/ *noun* plural **ampullae** /amˈpʊliː/ LME Latin (diminutive of *ampora* variant of AMPHORA). **1** LME *Roman Antiquities* A small two-handled globular flask or bottle. **2** L16 A vessel for holding consecrated oil or for other sacred uses. **3** M19 *Anatomy* A vessel or cavity shaped like the ancient ampulla.

amuck variant of AMOK.

amuse-gueule /amyzɡœl/ *noun* L20 French (literally, 'amusement for the mouth'). A snack, an appetizer.

> **1996** *Spectator* Before our starters came an amuse-gueule.

anabasis /aˈnabəsɪs/ *noun literary* plural **anabases** /aˈnabəsiːz/ E18 Greek (= going up, from *ana-* up + *basis* going. A military advance, an up-country march.

> ■ The original *anabasis* was that of ten thousand Greek auxiliaries under the Persian Cyrus the Younger into Asia in 401 BC. The Athenian writer Xenophon narrated the story of the ill-fated expedition, which turned into a *katabasis* or retreat in which he played a conspicuous role, in his *Anabasis*.

anacoluthon /ˌanəkəˈluːθɒn/, /ˌanəkəˈluːθ(ə)n/ *noun* plural **anacolutha** /ˌanəkəˈluːθə/ E18 Late Latin (from Greek *anakolouthon* neuter singular of adjective = lacking sequence, from as *an-* not + *akolouthos* following). A sentence or construction lacking grammatical sequence.

anacrusis /anəˈkruːsɪs/ *noun* plural **anacruses** /anəˈkruːsiːz/ M19 Modern Latin (from Greek *anakrousis* prelude, from *anakrouein*, from as *ana-* not + *krouein* to strike). **1** M19 *Prosody* An unstressed syllable at the beginning of a verse. **2** E20 *Music* An unstressed note or unstressed notes before the first strong beat of a phrase.

anaesthesia /anɪs'θiːzjə/ *noun* (also **anesthesia**) E18 Modern Latin (from Greek *anaisthēsia*, from as *an-* not + *aisthēsis* sensation). Absence of sensation; *especially* artificially induced inability to feel pain.

anagnorisis /anəg'nɒrɪsɪs/ *noun* plural **anagnorises** /anəg'nɒrɪsiːz/ L18 Greek (*anagnōrisis*). Recognition; the dénouement in a drama.

analemma /anə'lɛmə/ *noun* plural **analemmae**, /anə'lɛmiː/, **analemmas** M17 Latin ((Vitruvius) = sundial, from Greek *analēmma* support, (base of a) sundial). **1** M17 (An astronomical instrument incorporating) an orthographic projection of the sphere on the plane of the meridian. **2** M19 A figure representing the sun's daily declination and the difference between the right ascension of the mean sun and that of the true sun, drawn especially on terrestrial globes.

analgesia /an(ə)l'dʒiːzjə/ *noun* E18 Greek (*analgēsia* painlessness, ultimately from *an-* not + *algein* to feel pain). *Medicine* Absence or reduction of ability to feel pain; relief of pain, especially by drugs.

anamnesis /anəm'niːsɪs/ *noun* plural **anamneses** /anəm'niːsiːz/ L16 Greek (*anamnēsis* remembrance). **1** L16 The recalling of things past; reminiscence. **2** L19 *Christian Church* That part of the Eucharistic canon in which the sacrifice of Christ is recalled. **3** L19 A patient's account of his or her medical history.

anamorphosis /anə'mɔːfəsɪs/ *noun* plural **anamorphoses** /anə'mɔːfəsiːz/ E18 Greek (*anamorphōsis* transformation). **1** E18 A distorted projection or drawing of anything, which appears normal when viewed from a particular point or by means of a suitable mirror. **2** M19 *Botany* and *Zoology* Progression to a higher type. Now *specifically* development of the adult form through a series of small changes.

anaphora /ə'naf(ə)rə/ *noun* L16 Latin and Greek (branch I, Latin from Greek = repetition, from as *ana-* back, again + *pherein* carry; branch II Late Greek). **I 1** L16 *Rhetoric* The repetition of the same word or phrase in several successive clauses. **2** M20 *Linguistics* The use of an expression which refers to or stands for an earlier word or group of words. **II 3** M18 *Christian*

Church The part of the Eucharist at which the oblation is made.

anastrophe /ə'nastrəfi/ *noun* M16 Greek (*anastrophē* turning back, from as *ana-* back + *strephein* to turn). *Rhetoric* Inversion or unusual order of words or clauses.

anathema /ə'naθəmə/ *noun* plural **anathemas**, in sense 3 also **anathemata** /anə'θiːmətə/ E16 ecclesiastical Latin ((as senses 1 and 2) from Greek originally 'a thing devoted' (sense 3), later 'an accursed thing', originally variant of *anathēma* votive offering, from *anatithenai* to set up). **1** E16 Something or someone accursed or assigned to damnation; something or someone detested. **2** L16 The formal act or formula of consigning to damnation; the curse of God; the curse of the Church, excommunicating a person or denouncing a doctrine etc.; a denunciation of alleged impiety, heresy, etc.; an imprecation. **3** L16 Something devoted or consecrated to divine use. Now *rare*.

anchoveta /antʃə'vɛtə/ *noun* M20 Spanish (diminutive of *anchova*). A Pacific anchovy, *Cetengraulis mysticetus*, used as bait or to make fish-meal.

ancien régime /ɑ̃sjɛ̃ reʒim/ *noun phrase* L18 French (= former regime). The system of government in France before the Revolution of 1789. Also *transferred*, the old system or style of things.

> **1995** *Spectator* Sponsored by the Home Office under the auspices of the Centre of Criminological Research at the University of Oxford, it [sc. the researchers' visitation] set the fear of God into Grendon's *ancien régime*.

ancona /an'koːna/, /an'kəʊnə/ *noun* plural **ancone** /an'koːne/, /an'kəʊni/ L19 Italian (from medieval Latin, of uncertain origin: perhaps alteration of Greek *eikona* accusative of *eikōn* icon). An altarpiece, *especially* one consisting of a group of paintings connected by architectural structure.

andante /an'danti/ *adverb, adjective, & noun* E18 Italian (present participle of *andare* to go). *Music* **A** *adverb & adjective* E18 (A direction:) (originally) distinct(ly); (now) moderately slow(ly). **B** *noun* L18 A moderately slow movement or piece.

andantino /ˌandan'tiːnəʊ/ *adverb, adjective, & noun* E19 Italian (diminutive of preceding). *Music* **A** *adverb & adjective* E19 (A direction:) (originally) rather slower than andante; (now usually) with less of andante, i.e. rather quicker than andante.

B *noun* M19 plural **andantinos**. A movement or piece rather quicker (originally slower) than an andante.

andouille /ˈāduj/ *noun* plural pronounced same E17 Old and Modern French (of unknown origin). A kind of pork sausage, usually served as an hors d'oeuvre.

andouillette /ˈādujɛt/ *noun* plural pronounced same (also **andouillet**) E17 French (diminutive of preceding). A sausage made from a paste of minced veal, bacon, and other ingredients.

angekok /ˈaŋgɪkɒk/ *noun* M18 Eskimo ((Greenlandic) *angakkoq*). An Eskimo sorcerer or medicine man.

angelus /ˈandʒ(ə)ləs/ *noun* M17 Latin (from the opening words *Angelus domini* the angel of the Lord). **1** M17 A devotional exercise commemorating the Incarnation, said by Roman Catholics at morning, noon, and sunset. **2** M19 The bell rung at the times for the angelus. More fully *angelus bell*.

angina pectoris /anˌdʒʌmə ˈpɛktərɪs/ *noun* M18 Latin (*angina* quinsy (from Greek *agkhonē* strangling, assimilated to Latin *angere* to squeeze) + *pectoris* of the chest). *Medicine* Severe pain in the chest, and often also the arms and neck, due to inadequate blood supply to the heart muscles.

■ *Angina* alone was earlier (M16) used of any condition marked by a suffocating, oppressive pain or discomfort, especially quinsy. It is now rare in this sense and is current only as a shortened form of *angina pectoris*.

anglice /ˈaŋglɪsi/ *adverb* (also **Anglice**) E17 Medieval Latin (from Latin *Anglus* English). In (plain) English.

angst /aŋst/ *noun* E20 German. Anxiety, neurotic fear; guilt, remorse.

1995 *Times* 'Oh, I'm seriously rich,' hoots Rhys Jones, not altogether seriously. 'I am covered in angst because I am so rich.'

an-hua /anˈhwɑː/ *noun & adjective* E20 Chinese (*ànhuā*, from *àn* obscure + *huā* flower). (Of) a type of decoration of Chinese porcelain or fabrics that is visible only by transmitted light.

anima /ˈanɪmə/ *noun* E20 Latin (= (i) air, breath, life; (ii) mind, soul). *Psychoanalysis* The inner self (opposed to PERSONA). Also, the source of the feminine component of a personality. Cf. ANIMUS.

anima mundi /ˌanɪmə ˈmʌndʌɪ/, /ˈmʊndi:/ *noun phrase* L16 Medieval Latin (= soul of the world; apparently formed to render Greek *psukhē tou kosmou*). A power supposed to organize the whole universe and to coordinate its parts.

■ The concept is first found in the writings of the French philosopher and theologian Peter Abelard (1079–1142), who was accused in 1140 by his detractors of identifying it with the Holy Spirit. The phrase was introduced into English philosophical discourse in the seventeenth century by the alchemist Thomas Vaughan in *Anima Magica Abscondita* (1650), who defined it as 'the universal spirit of Nature', and given wider currency by the Cambridge Platonist Ralph Cudworth (1617–88) in *The True Intellectual System of the Universe* (1678) and by the writings of John Locke.

animus /ˈanɪməs/ *noun* E19 Latin (= spirit, mind). **1** E19 Actuating feeling, animating spirit, usually hostile; animosity shown in speech or action. **2** E20 *Psychoanalysis* The source of the masculine component of a personality. Cf. ANIMA.

1 1995 *Spectator* The greatest animus felt by British, Australian and New Zealand troops alike was against the politicians.

anis /ani(s)/ *noun* L19 French. A liqueur or aperitif flavoured with aniseed; occasionally, aniseed.

ankh /aŋk/ *noun* L19 Egyptian (= life, soul). An object resembling a cross, but with a loop in place of the upper limb, used in ancient Egyptian art as a symbol of life.

■ Also called CRUX ANSATA.

ankus /ˈaŋkəs/ *noun* L19 Hindustani (*ā̃kus*, *aṅkas* from Sanskrit *aṅkuśa*). In the Indian subcontinent: an elephant-goad.

anlaut /ˈanlaʊt/ *noun* L19 German (from *an* on + *Laut* sound). *Philology* The initial sound of a word.

anno aetatis suae see under AETATIS.

Anno Domini /ˌanəʊ ˈdɒmmʌɪ/, /ˈdɒmmi/ *adverb & noun phrase* M16 Latin (= in the year of the Lord). **A** *adverb* M16 Of the Christian era. Usually written AD. **B** *noun* **1** L17 A particular year. **2** L19 Advanced or advancing age. *colloquial*.

B.2 1906 E. V. Lucas *Fireside and Sunshine* When the time came for A. to take the bat he was unable to do so. *Anno Domini* asserted itself.

annulus /ˈanjʊləs/ *noun* plural **annuli** /ˈanjʊlʌɪ/, /ˈanjʊli/ M16 Latin (late form of *anulus* diminutive of *anus* ring). Chiefly

Mathematics and *Botany* A ring, a circle that is not filled in; *specifically* a partial veil forming a collar round the stalk in some agarics.

annus horribilis /ˌanəs hɒˈrɪbɪlɪs/ *noun phrase* L20 Modern Latin (= horrible year; formed after ANNUS MIRABILIS). A dreadful or miserable year.

■ The phrase leapt into circulation after H.M. the Queen used it with reference to 1992, a year of much-publicized matrimonial troubles within the British royal family and a serious fire at Windsor Castle.
1995 *Times* Against this background, the EU has let itself in for an *annus horribilis* in 1998.

annus mirabilis /ˌanəs mɪˈrɑːbɪlɪs/ *noun phrase* M17 Modern Latin (= wonderful year). A remarkable or auspicious year.

■ The origin of the phrase is the title of Dryden's poem *Annus Mirabilis: The Year of Wonders* (1667), which chronicled events in 1666, including British naval battles against the Dutch and the Great Fire of London. Dryden's use of *mirabilis* as 're-markable in both good and bad senses' has tended to be superseded by the more positive sense of 'marvellous' (see quotation), a tendency reinforced by the currency of ANNUS HORRIBILIS in the 1990s.
1995 *Spectator* All peoples have their *annus mirabilis*, the crucial period of their history which defines them . . . : great political or constitutional acts, like 1776 to the Americans or 1789 to the French, or great military events like 1812 in Russia . . . or 1813 in Prussia.

anomie /ˈanəmi/ *noun* (also **anomy**) M20 French (from Greek *anomia*, from *anomos* lawless). Lack of the usual social standards in a group or person.

■ The term was resurrected in its current sense by the French sociologist Emile Durkheim in *Suicide* (1897). It occurs in English in technical sociological contexts, but also more generally (see quotation).
1995 *Spectator* Today, . . . travelling to work by car is guaranteed to whip up anger, alienation and *anomie*.

anonym /ˈanənɪm/ *noun* (also **anonyme**) E19 French (*anonyme* from Greek *anōnumos* anonymous). **1** E19 An anonymous person or publication. **2** M19 A pseudonym.

anorak /ˈanərak/ *noun* E20 Eskimo (Greenlandic *annoraaq*). **1** A hooded jacket made of skin or cloth and worn by Eskimos and so by others in polar regions; a similar weatherproof garment worn elsewhere. **2** A person who wears an anorak; an obsessive hobbyist. *derogatory*.

2 1995 *Times* Should they pick up a point or three at Barnsley on Saturday, it will be a sad day for expectant anoraks everywhere.

anorexia /anəˈrɛksɪə/ *noun* M17 Late Latin (from Greek *an-* no + *orexis* appetite). *Medicine* Absence of appetite.

■ First introduced in 1598 in the French form *anorexie*, which, like the Anglicized form *anorexy*, is now obsolete. *Anorexia* now very often refers to the specific complaint of ANOREXIA NERVOSA.

anorexia nervosa /anəˌrɛksɪə nəːˈvəʊsə/ *noun phrase* L19 Late Latin (= nervous anorexia) Chronic anorexia induced by emotional disturbance.

Anschauung /ˈanʃaʊʊŋ/ *noun* plural **Anschauungen** /ˈanʃaʊʊŋən/ M19 German (= looking at). **1** M19 *Philosophy* (especially *Kantian*) A sense-perception, an intuition, an immediate apprehension by sense. **2** E20 An outlook, an attitude, a point of view. Cf. WELTANSCHAUUNG.

Anschluss /ˈanʃlʊs/ *noun* E20 German (from *anschliessen* to join, annex). Union, annexation; *specifically* the annexation of Austria by Germany in 1938.
1958 *Economist* Ability to opt to join the Commonwealth might give certain states a valuable policy counter, when other forms of Anschluss seem to be in the offing.

an sich /an zɪç/ *adjective & adverb phrase* M19 German. In itself; in the abstract; not in relation to anything else. See also DING AN SICH.

anta /ˈantə/ *noun* plural **antae** /ˈantiː/, **antas** L16 Latin. *Architecture* A square pilaster at either side of a door or at the corner of a building. Cf. ANTES, IN ANTIS.

ante /ˈanti/ *noun* E19 Latin (= before). **1** E19 In poker and similar games: a stake put up by a player before drawing cards. **2** L19 *transferred* An advance payment; a sum of money for a payment.

■ Chiefly North American. Often in the phrase *upping* (or *to up*) *the ante*, that is, 'raising the stakes'.
2 1996 *Times* That would have balanced the market and raised the negotiating ante.

ante-bellum /antɪˈbɛləm/ *adjective* (also **antebellum**) M19 Latin (*ante bellum* before the war). Occurring or existing before a particular war, especially (*United States*) the American Civil War. Opposed to POST-BELLUM.
1996 *Times* Kenneth Greenberg's aim is to enlarge our understanding of a dead world . . . The world? The antebellum slave South.

antefix /'antɪfɪks/ *noun* (also in Latin form **antefixum** /'antɪfɪksəm/, plural **antefixa** /'antɪfɪksə/) M19 Latin (*antefixum*, from as *ante-* before + use as noun of *fixus* fixed). *Classical Architecture* An ornament on an eave or cornice to conceal the ends of tiles; also, as ornamental head etc. making a spout from a gutter. Usually in *plural*.

ante meridiem /ˌantɪ məˈrɪdɪəm/ *adjective & adverb phrase* M16 Latin. Before midday; between midnight and the following noon.

■ Abbreviated to *a.m.*

ante-mortem /antɪˈmɔːtəm/ *adjective* L19 Latin (*ante mortem* before death). Made before death. Cf. POST-MORTEM.

antenna /anˈtɛnə/ *noun* plural **antennae** /anˈtɛniː/ (especially sense 4) **antennas** M17 Latin (alteration of *antemna* sailyard, used in plural as translation of Aristotle's *keraioi* 'horns' of insects). **1** M17 *Zoology* Either of a pair of sensory appendages on the heads of insects, crustaceans, and some other arthropods; a feeler. **2** M19 *figurative* In plural. Receptive senses, means of exploration. **3** M19 *Botany* Either of a pair of projections on the male flowers of certain orchids. **4** E20 A metal wire, rod, or other structure used to transmit or receive radio or other electromagnetic waves; an aerial. Chiefly *United States* and in *technical use*.

2 1996 *Spectator* He had developed sensitive antennae over the years as to when a man was on the way out and who was to succeed him . . .

4 1995 *New Scientist* Instead [of fuel tanks], slung beneath its [sc. the airship's] belly is a giant, square receiving antenna designed to convert microwaves into electric power.

antependium /antɪˈpɛndɪəm/ *noun* L16 Medieval Latin (from as *ante-* before + Latin *pendere* to hang). A veil or hanging for the front of an altar.

antepenultima /ˌantɪpɪˈnʌltɪmə/ *noun* plural **antepenultimae** /ˌantɪpɪˈnʌltɪmiː/, **antepenultimas** L16 Late Latin ((*syllaba*) *antepaenultima*, from as *ante-* before + *penultima* feminine of *paenultimus* last but one). *Prosody* The last syllable but two of a word or verse.

ante rem /'antɪ rɛm/ *adjective & adverb phrase* L19 Medieval Latin (= before the thing). *Philosophy* Prior to the existence of something else; *specifically* (of a universal) prior to the particular; of or pertaining to the theory that the universal is logically prior to the particular. Cf. IN RE 2, POST REM.

■ The phrase occurs in the writings of the thirteenth-century scholastic philosopher Albertus Magnus.

antes /'antɪz/ *noun plural* L16 French (representing Latin *antae* plural of ANTA). *Architecture* Square pilasters.

anthemion /anˈθiːmɪən/ *noun* plural **anthemia** /anˈθiːmɪə/ M19 Greek (= flower). A figure or ornament resembling a stylized honeysuckle.

anthrax /'anθraks/ *noun* L19 Latin (= carbuncle, from Greek *anthrax, anthrak-* coal, carbuncle). *Medicine* Infection with the bacterium *Bacillus anthracis*, which in animals usually takes the form of a fatal acute septicaemia, and in humans usually affects the skin, causing development of a pustule, or the lungs, causing a form of pneumonia.

■ Originally (LME) with its Latin sense, but this is now rare or obsolete.

anthropophagi /anθrəˈpɒfəgʌɪ/, /anθrə ˈpɒfədʒʌɪ/ *noun plural* M16 Latin (*anthropophagus* from Greek *anthrōpophagos* man-eating). Cannibals.

■ The singular *anthropophagus* is rare.

anti /'anti/ *noun & adjective* L18 Greek (*anti-* = opposite, against). **A** *noun* L18 Someone who is opposed to someone or something; *especially United States* an anti-Federalist. **B** *adjective* M19 Against or antagonistic to someone or something.

■ The use of *anti-* as a prefix in words adopted (ultimately) from Greek, and in English words modelled on these, long predates the use of *anti* as an independent word, and as a prefix *anti-* has been freely used with nouns and adjectives in the twentieth century with the sense 'opposite, against, preventing'.

A 1996 *Spectator* In those days, the antis were marginal figures, more numerous than the League of Empire loyalists but with hardly greater purchase on the future.

antipasto /antɪˈpastəʊ/ *noun* plural **antipasti**, /antɪˈpasti/, **antipastos** E17 Italian. An appetizer, an hors d'oeuvre.

■ Rare before the mid twentieth century. Also used figuratively (see quotation).

1996 *Times* An artistic *antipasto* can stimulate the appetite for more substantial fare.

antipodes /anˈtɪpədiːz/ *noun plural* (sense 3 also treated as *singular*) (also **Antipodes**) LME French (or late Latin from Greek plural of *antipous* having the feet opposite, from as *anti-* opposite + *pous, pod-* foot).

1 LME-M19 Those who live on the opposite side of the earth to each other or to one-self.   **2** M16 Places on the surface of the earth directly or diametrically opposite to each other; a place diametrically oppo-site to another, *especially* Australasia as the region on the opposite side of the earth to Europe.   **3** E17 Exact opposites. Also as *singular.* (Followed by *of, to.*)

▪ Formerly pronounced as a trisyllable /'antɪpəʊdz/; present pronunciation fol-lows Greek and Latin.

antistrophe /anˈtɪstrəfi/ *noun* M16 Late Latin (from Greek *antistrophē*, from *anti-strephein* to turn against).   **1** M16 *Rhetoric* The repetition of words in inverse order.   **2** E17 The returning movement, from left to right, in Greek choruses and dances, answering to the strophe; the lines of choral song recited during this move-ment; *transferred* any choral response.   **3** E17 An inverse correspondence.

antithesis /anˈtɪθəsɪs/ *noun* plural **antith-eses** /anˈtɪθəsiːz/ LME Late Latin (from Greek, from *antitithenai*, from as *anti-* against + *tithenai* to set, place: cf. THESIS).   **1** *Grammar* **a** The substitution of one case for another. Only in LME.   **b** L16-M17 The substitution of one sound for an-other.   **2** E16 *Rhetoric* (An) opposition or contrast of ideas, expressed by parallel-ism of words which are the opposites of, or strongly contrasted with, each other. Also, repetition of the same word at the end of successive clauses.   **3** M16 The sec-ond of two opposed clauses or sentences; a counter-thesis.   **4** E17 Direct or striking opposition of character or function (*of, be-tween* two things).   **5** M17 The direct oppo-site, a complete contrast, (*of, to*).   **6** L19 In Hegelian philosophy: the negation of the THESIS as the second stage in the process of dialectical reasoning. Cf. SYNTHESIS 2.

antonomasia /ˌantənəˈmeɪzɪə/ *noun* M16 Latin (from Greek, from *antonomazein* to name instead, from as *anti-* instead + *onoma* name). The substitution of an epi-thet etc. or the name of an office or dig-nity, for a proper name (e.g. *the Iron Lady* for Margaret Thatcher). Also, conversely, use of a proper name to express a general idea (e.g. *Jezebel* for 'a wicked woman').

AOC see under APPELLATION CONTRÔLÉE.

à outrance /a utrãs/ *adverb phrase* Also **à l'outrance** /a lutrãs/, **à toute outrance** /a tut utrãs/ E17 French (= to beyond bounds). To the death; to the bitter end.

1996 *Spectator* . . . he [sc. President Clinton] may find it difficult to shift the blame onto the opposition as he did so brilliantly when Newt Gingrich unwisely engaged him in war *à outrance* over the budget.

Apache *in senses* A.1, B.1 /əˈpatʃi/; *in senses* A.2, B.2 /əˈpaʃ/, *foreign* /apaʃ/ (*plural of noun same*) *noun & adjective* (senses A.2, B.2 also written **apache**) M18 Mexican Spanish (probably from Zuñi *Ápachu*, literally, 'enemy'; senses A.2, B.2 through French). **A** *noun* plural **Apaches**, same.   **1** M18 A member of an Athapaskan Indian people of New Mexico and Arizona; the language of this people.   **2** E20 A violent street ruf-fian, originally in Paris.   **B** *attributive* or as *adjective*   **1** M19 Of or pertaining to the Apache or their language.   **2** E20 Desig-nating a vigorous dance for two associ-ated with street ruffians or apaches.

aparejo /apəˈreɪhəʊ/ *noun* plural **apare-jos** M19 Spanish (= preparation, harness, tackle). A pack-saddle.

▪ Only in United States.

apartheid /əˈpɑːtheɪt/ *noun* M20 Afri-kaans (literally, 'separateness', from Dutch *apart* apart + *-heid* -hood). The for-mer South African (policy of) racial segre-gation of the White inhabitants from the remainder. Also *transferred* and *figurative*, any other form of segregation.

1996 *Times* Men became more involved in parenting and women entered the workplace. But the end of sexual apartheid brought its own problems.

aperçu /apɛrsy/ (*plural same*), /apɛːˈsjuː/ *noun* E19 French. A summary, a conspec-tus; an insight, a revealing glimpse.

1995 *Spectator* Nowhere, though, have I seen mentioned one of Amis's best *aperçus* . . . that the surest harbinger of boredom and *longueurs* is the question, perfunctory and ominous—'Red or white, sir?'

aperitif /əˈpɛrɪtiːf/, /əpɛrɪˈtiːf/ *noun* (also **apéritif** /aperitif/ (*plural same*)) L19 French (*apéritif* (noun and adjective) from medi-eval Latin *aperitivus* (adjective) variant of late Latin *aperitivus*, from *apertus* open). An alcoholic drink taken as an appetizer. Also *figurative*.

apex /ˈeɪpɛks/ *noun* plural **apexes, apices** /ˈeɪpɪsiːz/ E17 Latin.   **1** The tip, top, peak, or pointed end of anything; the vertex of a triangle, cone, etc.; *Botany* the growing point of a shoot etc.   **2** L18 *Astronomy* The point on the celestial sphere towards which the sun is moving. Also *solar apex.*

apfelstrudel /ˈapf(ə)lˌʃtruːd(ə)l/ *noun* M20 German (from *Apfel* apple + STRUDEL). A flaky pastry with a spicy apple filling.
■ Also very frequently in partially Anglicized form *apple strudel*.

aphasia /əˈfeɪzɪə/ *noun* M19 Greek (from *aphatos* speechless, from *a-* without + *phanai* to speak). Loss or impairment of the faculty of speech or of understanding of language (or both), due to cerebral disease or damage.

aplomb /əˈplɒm/ *noun* L18 French (from *à plomb* according to the plummet). **1** L18 Perpendicularity; steadiness. Now *rare* or *obsolete*. **2** E19 Self-possession, coolness; assurance.

2 1996 *Spectator* Some ministers stamp their personality on their department with such aplomb that, ever after, they become archetypes.

apocatastasis variant of APOKATASTASIS.

Apocrypha /əˈpɒkrɪfə/ *noun* (usually treated as *singular*; rarely as *plural*, with *singular* **Apocryphon** /əˈpɒkrɪfɒn/) (also **apocrypha**) LME ecclesiastical Latin (neuter plural (sc. *scripta* writings) of *apocryphus* from Greek *apokruphos* hidden, from *apokruptein* to hide). A writing or statement of doubtful authorship or authenticity; *specifically* **a** those Old Testament books included in the Septuagint and Vulgate which are not included in the Hebrew Scriptures, and which were excluded from the Protestant canon at the Reformation; **b** *New Testament Apocrypha*, various early Christian writings parallel to but excluded from the New Testament canon.

apodyterium /ˌapədɪˈtɪərɪəm/ *noun* plural **apodyteria** /ˌapədɪˈtɪərɪə/ E17 Latin (from Greek *apodutērion*, from *apoduein* to strip). *Classical History* A room adjacent to a bath or palaestra where clothes were deposited.

à point /a pwɛ̃/ *adverb phrase* E20 French (= to the point). Especially *Cookery*. At or to exactly the right point; just enough, without overcooking or undercooking.

apokatastasis /ˌapə(ʊ)kəˈtastəsɪs/ *noun* (also **apocatastasis**) L17 Greek (= re-establishment). Restoration, renewal; *specifically* in *Theology* the ultimate salvation of all moral beings.

apo koinou /ˌapəʊ ˈkɔɪnuː/, /ˈkɔɪnaʊ/ *adjective & adverb phrase* L19 Greek (literally, 'in common'). *Grammar* Designating a construction comprising two clauses having an unrepeated word or phrase in common; so as to form such a construction.

apologia /apəˈləʊdʒɪə/ *noun* L18 Latin. A written defence of one's own (or someone else's) opinions or conduct.

■ The currency of *apologia* is largely due to the impact of John Henry Newman's *Apologia pro Vita Sua* (1864), charting his intellectual and spiritual progress from Anglicanism to Roman Catholicism. The complete phrase is sometimes used of an autobiography, especially one by a controversial figure.

1996 *Times* . . . we are told that there is respect for human rights in China. To prove it (and this gets very macabre), the Chinese Government has published a weird kind of apologia.

aporia /əˈpɔːrɪə/, /əˈpɒrɪə/ *noun* M16 Late Latin (from Greek, from *aporos* impassable). **1** M16 *Rhetoric* The expression of doubt. **2** L19 A doubtful matter, a perplexing difficulty.

a posteriori /eɪ/, /ɑː/, /pɒˌstɛrɪˈɔːrʌɪ/, /pɒˌstɪərɪɔːrʌɪ/ *adverb & adjective phrase* E17 Latin (= from what comes after). **1** E17 Of reasoning: (by) proceeding from effects to causes; inductive(ly), empirical(ly). Opposed (to) A PRIORI. **2** M18 From behind; on the buttocks. *facetious*.

1 1991 W. Charlton *The Analytic Ambition* This general belief is dispositional. It could be applied in action or prediction but here it is applied in a posteriori inference.

apotheosis /əˌpɒθɪˈəʊsɪs/ *noun* plural **apotheoses** /əˌpɒθɪˈəʊsiːz/ L16 ecclesiastical Latin (from Greek *apotheōsis*, from *apotheoun* to deify, from *apo-* + *theos* god). **1** L16 (Elevation to) divine status. **2** E17 Glorification or exaltation of a person, principle, or practice; canonization; idealization. **3** M17 Ascension to glory, resurrection, triumph; highest development, culmination.

apparat /apəˈrɑːt/ *noun* M20 Russian (through German from Latin *apparatus* from *apparare* to make ready). The Communist Party machine in the former USSR and other countries.

apparatchik /apəˈratʃɪk/ *noun* plural **apparatchiki** /apəˈratʃɪki/, **apparatchiks** M20 Russian (from preceding). **1** M20 A member of the APPARAT; a Communist agent. **2** L20 *transferred* An implementer of party or official policy; an executive officer.

21

apparatus criticus | apsara

2 1996 *Spectator* What usually happens now is that the prime minister assembles a committee of favoured ministers, placemen and apparatchiks to decide the date.

apparatus criticus /apəˌreɪtəs ˈkrɪtɪkəs/ *noun phrase* plural **apparatus critici** /apə ˌreɪtəs ˈkrɪtɪsʌɪ/ M19 **Modern Latin**. A collection of material, as variant readings and other palaeographical and critical matter, for the textual study of a document.

1996 *Spectator* On what grounds is this a *Selected* and not a *Collected*? How much surviving comic verse [of A. E. Housman's] do we in fact have? We are not going to find out from the present *apparatus criticus*, so to dignify it.

appellation contrôlée /apɛlasjɔ̃ kɔ̃trole/ *noun phrase* M20 **French** (= controlled appellation). (A guarantee of) the description of a bottle of French wine (or other item of food) in conformity with statutory regulations as to its origin.

■ Abbreviated to AC. Also *appellation d'origine contrôlée* /apɛlasjɔ̃ dɔriʒin kɔ̃trole/, abbreviated to AOC.

1996 *Times* Without any form of *appellation contrôlée*, the quality of what we are served in the name quickly deteriorates.

appliqué /əˈpliːkeɪ/ *noun & verb* M18 **French** (use as noun of past participle of *appliquer* from Latin *applicare* to apply (to)). Chiefly *Needlework*. **A** *noun* M18 (A piece of) ornamental work cut out from one material and affixed to the surface of another; the technique of ornamenting in this way. **B** *transitive verb* L19 Decorate in this way. Chiefly as *appliquéd* participial adjective.

appoggiatura /əˌpɒdʒəˈtʊərə/ *noun* plural **appoggiature**/əˌpɒdʒəˈtʊəreɪ/ M18 **Italian** (from *appoggiare* to lean upon, rest). *Music* A grace-note just above or below a primary note, which it precedes and delays; the use of such notes.

après /ˈapreɪ/, *foreign* /ɑprɛ/ *preposition* M20 **French**. After.

■ Combined with English words in (jocular) imitation of APRÈS-SKI, as *après-bath*, *après-sex*, etc.

après coup /ˈapreɪ kuː/ *adverb phrase* M19 **French** (literally, 'after stroke'). After the event; as an afterthought.

après nous le déluge /apre nu lə delyʒ/ *adverb phrase* M19 **French** (literally, 'after us the flood'). (Used to express the feeling that) the present state of affairs or order of things will not long survive us.

■ Attributed in the *Mémoires* of Mme de Hausset (1824) to Mme de Pompadour (1721–64), mistress of King Louis XV of France, who had premonitions of catastrophe after the French defeat by the Prussians at Rossbach in 1757. It is very often quoted by English speakers in the version *après moi le déluge*.

1995 *Times* Evidently, the only way we can truly face our own demise is by hoping that, so to speak, *après moi, le déluge*. If we have to go, then we want everyone to go with us.

après-ski /ˌapreɪˈskiː/ *noun & adjective* M20 **French**. (Worn, done, etc., at) the time when skiing is over for the day at a resort.

a priori /eɪ prʌɪˈɔːrʌɪ, /ɑː prɪˈɔːri/ *adverb & adjective phrase* L16 **Latin** (*a priori* from what is before). **1** L16 Of reasoning: (by) proceeding from causes to effects; deductive(ly). Opposed to A POSTERIORI. **2** E19 loosely Presumptive(ly); without previous investigation; as far as one knows. **3** M19 *Philosophy* Of knowledge or concepts: not derived from sensory experience; innate(ly).

2 1995 *Spectator* What would be limited is the phenomenon by which European law could be said to apply *a priori*, regardless of national legislatures.

3 1996 *Times* His *a priori* melancholic disposition becomes whipped into a religious fever.

apropos /aprəˈpəʊ/, /ˈaprəpəʊ/ *adverb, adjective, & preposition* (also **à propos** /a prɔpo/) M17 **French** (à *propos*, from à to + *propos* purpose). **A** *adverb* **1** M17 To the point; fitly, opportunely. **2** M18 In respect or as a relevant association of (now less commonly, to). **b** M18 *absolutely* Incidentally, by the way. **B** *adjective* M17 Pertinent, appropriate, opportune. (Followed by of, to.) **C** *preposition* M20 Concerning, with regard to. *colloquial*.

C 1996 *Times* A propos the medicinal habits of Florence Nightingale . . . , there is convincing evidence in biographical literature that she took laudanum . . .

à propos de bottes /aprəˈpəʊ də bɔt/ *adverb phrase* M18 **French** (= with regard to boots, i.e. to something quite irrelevant). Without rhyme or reason, motiveless.

apsara /ˈʌpsərɑː/ *noun* (also **upsara**) M19 **Hindi** (*apsarā* from Sanskrit *apsarās*). *Hindu Mythology* Any of a class of celestial nymphs, frequently regarded as the wives of the gandharvas or heavenly musicians.

aqua fortis /ˌakwə ˈfɔːtɪs/ *noun phrase* (also **aquafortis**) L15 Latin (= strong water). Nitric acid; originally, any powerful solvent. Now *archaic*.

aqua regia /ˌakwə ˈriːʤə/ *noun phrase* (also formerly **aqua regis**) E17 Latin (= royal water). *Chemistry* A concentrated mixture of nitric and hydrochloric acids, able to dissolve gold, platinum, etc.

aquarelle /akwəˈrɛl/ *noun* M19 French (from Italian *acquarella* watercolour, from *acqua* from Latin *aqua* water). A style of painting in thin, usually transparent, watercolours; a painting in this style.

aquarium /əˈkwɛːrɪəm/ *noun* plural **aquaria** /əˈkwɛːrɪə/, **aquariums** M19 Modern Latin (use as noun of neuter singular of *aquarius* pertaining to water, after VIVARIUM). An artificial pond or tank (usually with transparent sides) for keeping live aquatic plants and animals; a place containing such tanks.

aquavit /akwəˈviːt/ *noun* (also **akvavit** /akvəˈviːt/) L19 Norwegian, Swedish, Danish (*akvavit* AQUA VITAE). An alcoholic spirit distilled from potatoes or other starch-containing plants.

aqua vitae /ˌakwə ˈvʌɪtiː/, /ˈviːtʌɪ/, /ˈviːtiː/ *noun phrase* (also **aqua-vitae**) LME Latin (= water of life: cf. French *eau de vie*). Alcoholic spirits, especially of the first distillation.

arabesque /arəˈbɛsk/ *noun & adjective* M17 French (from Italian *arabesco*, from *arabo* Arabic). **A** *noun* **1** M17 Decorative work of a kind which originated in Arabic or Moorish art, consisting of flowing lines of branches, leaves, scrollwork, etc., fancifully intertwined; an ornamental design of this kind. **2** M19 *Ballet* A posture in which the body is bent forwards and supported on one leg with the other leg extended horizontally backwards, with the arms extended one forwards and one backwards. **3** M19 *Music* A passage or composition with fanciful ornamentation of the melody. **B** *adjective* L18 Of ornamental design: decorated with arabesques (sense 1).

arak /ˈarək/ *noun* (also **arrack**) E17 Arabic (*'araḳ* sweat, especially in *'araḳ at-tamr* fermented and distilled juice of dates). In Eastern countries: an alcoholic spirit of local manufacture, especially distilled

from the sap of the coco palm or from rice.

arbiter elegantiae /ˌɑːbɪtə ɛlɪˈgantɪʌɪ/ E19 Latin (= judge of elegance). An authority on matters of taste or etiquette.

■ First introduced in the form *arbiter elegantiarum* 'judge in matters of taste', which was current in English in the nineteenth century, but the singular form of the genitive, *elegantiae*, is now usual. It has classical sanction in being applied by Tacitus (*Annales* xvi.18) to Titus Petronius, *elegantiae arbiter* at the court of Nero.

arboretum /ɑːbəˈriːtəm/ *noun* plural **arboreta** /ɑːbəˈriːtə/, (chiefly *North American*) **arboretums** E19 Latin (= place with trees, from *arbor* tree). A place devoted to the cultivation and exhibition of rare trees; a botanical tree-garden.

arbor vitae /ˌɑːbə ˈvʌɪtiː/, /ˈviːtʌɪ/ *noun phrase* (also (especially in sense 1) **arbor-vitae** plural same) E17 Latin (= tree of life). E17 Any of a number of North American or Far Eastern evergreen conifers, belonging chiefly to the genus *Thuja*.

Arcades ambo /ˌɑːkədiːz ˈambəʊ/ *noun phrase* E19 Latin (= both Arcadians, i.e. both pastoral poet-musicians). Two people of the same (often literary or aesthetic) tastes, profession, or character.

■ The phrase is a quotation from Virgil (*Eclogues* vii. 4) and, following Byron (see quotation), is frequently used derogatorily with overtones of 'idle layabouts' or worse.
1821 *Don Juan* With Raucocanti lucklessly was chain'd The tenor . . . 'Arcades ambo,' *id est*—blackguards both.

arcanum /ɑːˈkeməm/ *noun* plural **arcana** /ɑːˈkemə/ L16 Latin (use as noun of neuter singular of *arcanus* concealed). Usually in plural. **1** L16 A hidden thing; a mystery, a profound secret. **2** E17 *specifically* Any of the supposed secrets of nature sought by alchemists; a marvellous remedy, an elixir. *archaic*.

1 1996 *Spectator* One has always heard it bruited that such [obscene] compositions survive, shrouded away on the duskier, dustier shelves of the British and Cambridge Libraries . . . surely the age has now come when the arcana may finally be opened?

archi plural of ARCO.

archon /ˈɑːkən/ *noun* plural **archons**, **archontes** /ɑːˈkɒntiːz/ L16 Greek (*arkhōn*, *arkhont-* ruler, use as noun of present participle of *arkhein* to rule). **1** L16 The chief magistrate, or, after the time of Solon, each of the nine chief magistrates, of ancient Athens. **2** M18 A ruler, a president. **3** M18 A power subordinate to God, held by some of the Gnostics to have created the world.

arco /'arko/, /'ɑːkəʊ/ *noun, adverb & adjective* M18 Italian. *Music* **A** *noun* M18 plural **archi** /'arki/, **arcos** /'ɑːkəʊz/. A bow for a stringed instrument. **B** *adverb & adjective* E19 (A direction:) resuming use of the bow after a pizzicato passage.

à rebours /a rəbur/ *adverb phrase* E20 Old French (*à* from + *rebors* (modern *rebours*) rough, perverse, the wrong side, etc., from popular Latin *rebursum*, Latin *reburrum* rough-haired, bristly). In the wrong way, against the grain; through perversity.

■ *Rebours* was formerly naturalized in the Scottish phrase *at rebours*. The adoption of the phrase in its modern form may be on account of its having been the title of an influential book (1884) by the French novelist Joris-Karl Huysmans.

areg plural of ERG.

arête /əˈrɛt/, /əˈreɪt/ *noun* E19 French (from Latin *arista* ear of corn, fish-bone or -spine). A sharp mountain ridge with steep sides.

argot /'ɑːgəʊ/ *noun* M19 French (of unknown origin). The jargon, slang, or peculiar phraseology of a social class or group; originally, rogues' and thieves' cant.

1996 *Times* European football has always had its own argot too . . .

argumentum ad hominem /ɑːgjʊ ˌmɛntəm ad 'hɒmmɛm/ *noun phrase* M17 Latin. An argument, usually vilificatory, attacking the personal circumstances or character of an opponent rather than employing sound reasoning to make the point. Cf. AD HOMINEM.

■ In attributive use often shortened to *ad hominem*; see quotation.

1995 *Times* Ad hominem attacks smack of an insolence intolerable to most leaders . . .

argumentum e silentio /ɑːgjʊˌmɛntəm eɪ sɪˈlɛntɪəʊ/, /sɪˈlɛnʃɪəʊ/ *noun phrase* (also **argumentum ex silentio** /ɑːgjʊˌmɛntəm ɛks sɪˈlɛntɪəʊ/, /sɪˈlɛnʃɪəʊ/) M20 Latin (= argument from silence). A conclusion based on silence, i.e. on lack of contrary evidence.

■ The more (classically) correct *argumentum ex silentio* is also found.

1962 *Listener* Doesn't Dr Needham . . . give the Chinese the benefit of a doubt, sometimes, with an *argumentum e silentio*?

Arhat /'ɑːhat/ *noun* (also **Arahat** /'arəhat/, **arahat**) L19 Sanskrit (*arhat*, Pali *arahat* meritorious). *Buddhism* and *Jainism* A saint of one of the highest ranks.

aria /'ɑːrɪə/ *noun* E18 Italian (from Latin *aera* accusative of *aer* from Greek *aēr* air). *Music* A long song for one voice usually with accompaniment; *especially* such a song in an opera, oratorio, etc.

arietta /arɪˈɛtə/ *noun* E18 Italian (diminutive of ARIA). *Music* A short tune or song.

arioso /arɪˈəʊsəʊ/ *adjective, adverb, & noun* E18 Italian (from ARIA). *Music* **A** *adjective* E18 Melodious, songlike, cantabile; having something of the quality of an aria. Also as *adverb* as a direction. **B** *noun* L19 plural **ariosos**. A piece of vocal or instrumental music of this kind.

armada /ɑːˈmɑːdə/ *noun* (also **armado** and in sense 1b **Armada**) M16 Spanish (from Proto-Romance *armata* army). **1** M16 A fleet of warships. **b** L16 *specifically* The Spanish Armada, the fleet sent by Philip II of Spain to attack England in 1588. **2** L16–M17 A single warship. **3** E18 *transferred* and *figurative* A large army or airborne force; a large fleet of vessels of any kind.

■ Formerly pronounced /ɑːˈmeɪdə/.

armamentarium /ˌɑːməmɛnˈtɛːrɪəm/ *noun* plural **armamentaria** /ˌɑːməmɛn ˈtɛːrɪə/ L19 Latin (= arsenal, armoury). The medicines, equipment, and techniques available to a medical practitioner.

arme blanche /arm blɑ̃ʃ/ *noun phrase* plural **armes blanches** (pronounced same) L19 French (literally, 'white arm'). A cavalry sword or lance; the cavalry.

armiger /'ɑːmɪdʒə/ *noun* M16 Latin (= bearing arms, from *arma* arms). An esquire: originally, a person who attended a knight to bear his shield; now, a person entitled to heraldic arms.

armilla /ɑːˈmɪlə/ *noun* plural **armillae** /ɑːˈmɪliː/, **armillas** M17 Latin (diminutive of *armus* shoulder). **1** M17 An ancient astronomical instrument consisting of a graduated ring or hoop fixed in the plane of the equator (*equinoctial armilla*), sometimes crossed by another in the plane of the meridian (*solstitial armilla*). **2** L17 A coronation stole; an armil. **3** E18 Chiefly *Archaeology*. A bracelet, an armlet.

armoire /ɑːˈmwɑː/ *noun* L16 French. A cupboard, a wardrobe; *especially* one that is ornate or antique.

arpeggio /ɑːˈpɛdʒɪəʊ/ *noun* plural **arpeggios** E18 Italian (from *arpeggiare* to play on the harp, from *arpa* harp). *Music* The sounding of the notes of a chord in (usually rapid upward) succession, not simultaneously; a chord so sounded.

1996 *Country Life* ... the playfulness of Opus 110 dissolved into a moment of perfect stillness before the joyous arpeggios came bubbling back.

arrack variant of ARAK.

arrêt /arɛ/ (plural same), /əˈrɛt/ *noun* M17 French. An authoritative sentence or decision, specifically of the monarch (historical) or parliament of France.

arrière-pensée /arjɛrpɑ̃se/ *noun* plural pronounced same E19 French (literally, 'behind-thought'). A concealed thought or intention; an ulterior motive; a mental reservation.

arrivisme /arrivism/ *noun* (also in Anglicized form **arrivism**) M20 French (from Old French *ariver* to arrive, ultimately from Latin *ad* to + *ripa* shore). The behaviour or character of an ARRIVISTE.

arriviste /arivist/ *noun* plural pronounced same (also in Anglicized form **arrivist**) E20 French (from as preceding). An ambitious or self-seeking person.

1995 *Spectator* The shameless effrontery with which these two power-greedy arrivistes bought and sold office for votes quite takes one's breath away.

arrondissement /arɔ̃dismɑ̃/ *noun* plural pronounced same E19 French (from *arrondiss-* lengthened stem of *arrondir* make round). In France: an administrative subdivision of a city or department.

arroyo /əˈrɔɪəʊ/ *noun* plural **arroyos** M19 Spanish. A steep gully, a watercourse. *North American.*

arsis /ˈɑːsɪs/ *noun* plural **arses** /ˈɑːsiːz/ LME Late Latin (from Greek = lifting, raising, from *airein* to raise). The syllable or part of a metrical foot that is stressed (originally, *Classical Prosody*, by raised pitch or volume); the unstressed beat in barred music. Opposed to THESIS I sense 1.

art brut /ar bryt/ *noun phrase* M20 French (literally, 'raw art'). Primitive or pseudo-primitive art.

■ *L'Art brut* was the title of an exhibition of paintings in Paris in 1949, which included works by children and psychiatric patients.

1996 *Economist Art brut*—raw art—is the term that the French artist and collector Jean Dubuffet coined to describe works by intuitive artists outside the common run.

artel /ɑːˈtɛl/ *noun* L19 Russian (*artel'*). A Russian or Soviet collective enterprise of craftsmen or skilled workers.

artiste /ɑːˈtiːst/ *noun* E19 French. A performing artist; a professional singer, dancer, actor, etc.

art nouveau /ɑː nuːˈvəʊ/, *foreign* /ar nuvo/ *noun phrase* E20 French (literally, 'new art'). A decorative style in French and English art of the late nineteenth century characterized by ornamented and flowing lines. Cf. JUGENDSTIL.

1996 *Spectator* Bakst's original setting for the 1906 exhibition in Paris ... gives a lift to some overripe Russian art nouveau sculpture.

aryballos /arɪˈbaləs/ *noun* M19 Greek (*aruballos* bag, purse, oil-flask). *Greek Antiquities* A globular flask with a narrow neck used to hold oil or unguent.

ascesis /əˈsiːsɪs/ *noun* (also **askesis** /əˈskiːsɪs/) L19 Greek (*askēsis* exercise, training, from *askein* to exercise). The practice of self-discipline.

ashram /ˈaʃrəm/ *noun* E20 Sanskrit (*āśrama* hermitage). **1** E20 In the Indian subcontinent: a hermitage, a place of religious retreat. **2** M20 *transferred* Any group with shared spiritual or social aims living together.

askari /əˈskɑːri/ *noun* plural **askaris**, same L19 Arabic (*'askarī* soldier). An East African soldier or police officer.

askesis variant of ASCESIS.

asphyxia /əsˈfɪksɪə/ *noun* M19 Modern Latin (from Greek *asphuxia*, from *a-* without + *sphuxis* pulsation). *Medicine* The condition of defective aeration of the blood caused by failure of the oxygen supply; suffocation.

■ Earlier (E18) in the sense of 'stoppage of the pulse', but there is no apparent evidence of this outside dictionaries.

assai /aˈsʌɪ/ *adverb* E18 Italian. *Music* (In directions:) very.

assegai /ˈasəgʌɪ/ *noun* (also **assagai**) E17 French (*azagaie* (now *zagaie, sagaie*)) or Portuguese (*azagaia*, Spanish *azagaya* from colloquial Arabic *az-zaġāya from al* the + Berber *zaġāya* spear). An iron-bladed spear with a hardwood shaft used for stabbing or as a missile by South African indigenous peoples.

assemblé /asɑble/ *noun* plural pronounced same L18 French (past participle of *assembler* to bring together). *Ballet* A leap in which the feet are brought together before landing.

assemblée /asãble/ *noun* plural pronounced same E18 French. An assembly; *especially* a gathering of polite society for recreational purposes.

assiette /asjɛt/ (*plural same*), /asɪˈɛt/ *noun* M18 French (= plate, course of a meal; seat, site; bed, foundation). A prepared dish of food.

■ Usually with qualifying word or phrase, as in *assiette anglaise* 'a platter of assorted cold meats'.

ataman /ˈatəman/ *noun* M19 Russian. A Cossack leader. Cf. HETMAN.

ataraxia /atəˈraksɪə/ *noun* M19 Greek (= impassiveness, from *a-* not + *tarassein* to disturb). Imperturbability; ataraxy.

atelier /əˈtɛlɪeɪ/ *noun* L17 French. A workshop or studio, especially of an artist or couturier.

1995 *Times* Gone are the days when . . . the *ateliers* of craftspeople were busy, not just with clothes and hats for a wedding, but with custom-made jewels.

a tempo /ɑːˈtɛmpəʊ/ *adverb phrase* M18 Italian (= in time). *Music* (A direction:) in the tempo indicated previously, before the direction to deviate from it.

à terre /a tɛr/ *adverb & adjective phrase* E20 French. Chiefly *Ballet*. On the ground.

atlantes /atˈlantiːz/ *noun plural* E17 Greek (*Atlas, Atlant-*, the Titan supposed to hold up the pillars of the universe, and a mountain range in western North Africa also regarded mythically as supporting the heavens). *Architecture* Male figures used as pillars to support an entablature.

■ The singular form of the word, meaning 'a person who supports a great burden' was introduced via Latin (L16) and soon afterwards (M17) became the name for 'a collection of maps or charts bound in a volume'. In this sense, and in other senses derived from it, *atlas* has long been entirely naturalized. The connection between the world-supporting Titan and the book of maps was first made in the mid sixteenth century, when Antonio Lafreri, a French publisher working in Rome, put together collections of maps to his customers' specifications and bound them with a standard titlepage depicting Atlas carrying the world on his shoulders. The use of 'Atlas' as a title for a book of maps originated with the Flemish geographers Gerhard and Rumold Merca-

tor, whose complete 107-map *Atlas* was published in 1595. The Mercator *Atlas* in various versions and editions so dominated European cartography in the first half of the seventeenth century (it appeared in English in 1636) that the name became used generically for all such books.

atman /ˈɑːtmən/ *noun* L18 Sanskrit (*ātman*). *Hindu Philosophy* The self as the subject of individual consciousness, the soul; the supreme personal principle of life in the universe.

atole /əˈtəʊli/ *noun* M17 American Spanish (from Nahuatl *atolli*). Gruel or porridge made of maize or other meal.

■ Chiefly United States.

à tort et à travers /a tɔr e a travɛr/ *adverb phrase* M18 French (= wrongly and across). At random, haphazardly.

à toute outrance variant of λ OUTRANCE.

atrium /ˈeɪtrɪəm/ *noun* plural **atria** /ˈeɪtrɪə/, **atriums** L16 Latin. **1** L16 *Architecture* A central court, originally that of an ancient-Roman house; a covered court or portico; (a building with) a large lightwell; a central hall or glassed-in court in a building. **2** L19 *Anatomy* and *Zoology* Any of various chambers into which one or more passages open; *specifically* (**a**) either of the two upper chambers of the heart into which the veins conduct blood; (**b**) the tympanic chamber of the ear.

1 1995 *Times* Office accommodation for tenants has a separate entrance with escalators leading up to a glass and cream-coloured marble atrium.

à trois /a trwa/ *adjective & adverb phrase* L19 French. Shared by, or in a group of, three people. Cf. MÉNAGE À TROIS.

1996 *Spectator* In 1956 Gottfried, Budge and I went to dine *à trois* wearing black tie.

attaché /əˈtaʃeɪ/ *noun* E19 French (past participle of *attacher* to attach). A junior official attached to the staff of an ambassador etc.; a representative of his or her government in a foreign country.

■ Frequently in the combination *attaché case* a small rectangular case, usually with a handle, for carrying documents.

attar /ˈatə/ *noun* (also (earlier) **otto** /ˈɒtəʊ/) M17 Persian ('*itr*, Arabic '*itr*, colloquial Arabic '*atar* perfume, essence). A fragrant volatile essence, *especially* (more fully *attar of roses*) that obtained from rose-petals.

attentat in sense 1 foreign /atɑ̃ta/; (*plural same*); in sense 2 /əˈtɛntət/ *noun* (also (now only in sense 2) **attentate** /əˈtɛnteɪt/ E17 Old and Modern French (or medieval Latin *attentatum*, from *attentatum* past participial stem of *attentare* variant of Latin *attemptare* to attempt). **1** E17 An attack; an attempted assassination. **2** E18 *Law* Something wrongfully done by a judge in a proceeding, pending an appeal.

attentisme /atãtism/ *noun* M20 French (from *attente* wait, waiting). The policy of waiting to see what happens.

attrait /atrɛ/ *noun* E20 French (from *attraire* to attract). *Theology* Vocation; inclination.

aubade /əʊˈbɑːd/, *foreign* /obad/ (*plural same*) *noun* L17 French (from Spanish *albada*, from *alba* (= French *aube*) dawn). A piece of music or a poem written to be heard at or appropriate to dawn.

auberge /əʊˈbɛːʒ/; *foreign* /obɛrʒ/ (*plural same*) *noun* L16 French (from Provençal *alberga* lodging). An inn, *especially* one in France.

aubergine /ˈəʊbəʒiːn/ *noun & adjective* L18 French (from Catalan *alberginia*, from Arabic *al-bādinjān*, from *al-* the + Persian *bādingān*, *bādinjān* from Sanskrit *vātiṃgaṇa*). **A** *noun* **1** L18 The fruit of the eggplant, *Solanum melongena*, eaten as a vegetable; the plant itself. Cf. BRINJAL. **2** L19 A dark purple colour typical of the skin of the fruit. **B** *adjective* L19 Of the colour aubergine, dark purple.

aubusson /obysɔ̃/ *noun* (also more correctly **Aubusson**) plural pronounced same E20 French (Aubusson = a town in central France). Tapestry or (especially) a tapestry carpet woven at Aubusson.

AUC abbreviation of AB URBE CONDITA.

au contraire /o kɔ̃trɛr/, /əʊ kɒnˈtrɛː/ *adverb phrase* M18 French. On the contrary.
 1995 D. Lodge *Therapy* Don't get the idea that I'm an enthusiast for British Rail's Inter-City service to London. *Au contraire*, as Amy would say.

au courant /o kurã/ *adverb & adjective phrase* M18 French. In an informed position; aware of current developments.
 ■ Usually followed by *with*, *of*, but can also be used absolutely.
 1996 *Times* . . . to find out what the in-your-face young are wearing, or were ten minutes ago when in-your-face was still an *au courant* fashion statement . . .

auditorium /ɔːdɪˈtɔːrɪəm/ *noun* plural **auditoriums**, **auditoria** /ɔːdɪˈtɔːrɪə/ E17 Latin. **1** E17 *general* A place for hearing.

rare. **2** M19 *specifically* The part of a theatre, lecture-hall, or other public building occupied by the audience; (*North America*) such a building as a whole.

au fait /əʊ feɪ/, *foreign* /o fɛ/ *adverb & predicative adjective phrase* M18 French (literally, 'to the fact', 'to the point'). Thoroughly conversant (*with*), well instructed (*in*), expert or skilful (*at*).
 1996 *Times: Weekend* The Tuscans are not entirely au fait with the idea of walking for pleasure.

Aufklärung /ˈaʊfklɛːrʊŋ/ *noun* E19 German (literally, 'clearing up'). The intellectual and philosophical movement in eighteenth-century Europe that promoted reason and individualism against traditional religion and ancient authority; the Enlightenment.

au fond /o fɔ̃/ *adverb phrase* L18 French. At bottom, basically.
 1996 *Spectator* . . . Mrs Lancaster was *au fond* nostalgic, a sentiment she vehemently denies possessing . . .

au grand sérieux /o grã serjø/ *adverb phrase* M19 French. In all seriousness. Cf. AU SÉRIEUX.

au gratin /o gratɛ̃/ *adverb & predicative adjective phrase* E19 French (from *au* with the + GRATIN). *Cookery* Sprinkled with breadcrumbs and/or grated cheese and browned.

auguste /ˈɔːɡuːst/; *foreign* /oɡyst/ (*plural same*) *noun* E20 French (from German *August*, male forename, (*slang*) clown, fool). A circus clown wearing ill-fitting or dishevelled clothes.

au mieux /o mjø/ *adverb phrase* M19 French (= at the best). On the best of, or on very intimate, terms *with* (someone).

aumônière /omonjɛr/ *noun* plural pronounced same E19 French (feminine of *aumônier* almoner). A purse carried at the waist.

au naturel /o natyrɛl/ *adverb phrase* E19 French. In the natural state; cooked plainly; uncooked.
 1996 *New Scientist* Now the company is paying people to look for weedy pastures around the state [sc. Nebraska] and pick the [milkweed] pods *au naturel*.

au pair /əʊ pɛː/ *adjective & noun phrase* L19 French (= on equal terms). **A** *adjective phrase* L19 Of arrangements between two parties: paid for (entirely or largely) by mutual services. Of a person: party to such an arrangement; *specifically* (of a (usually foreign) girl) undertaking domestic duties in return for room and board. **B** *noun* M20 An au pair girl.

au pied de la lettre /o pje də la lɛtr/ *adverb phrase* L18 French (= to the foot of the letter). Down to the last detail; literally.

aura /'ɔːrə/ *noun plural* **auras,** *(rare)* **aurae** /'ɔːriː/ LME Latin (from Greek = breath, breeze). **1** LME A gentle breeze, a zephyr. *archaic* and *poetic*. **2** M18 A subtle emanation or exhalation; a surrounding glow; *figurative* an atmosphere diffused by or attending a person, place, etc.; a distinctive impression of character or aspect. **3** L18 A premonitory sensation experienced before an epileptic fit.

> **2 1996** *Oldie* Esther, who is also a medium, says she can tell whether an animal is sick by its aura.

aureola /ɔːˈriːələ/ *noun plural* **aureolae,** /ɔːˈriːəli/, **aureolas** L15 Latin (feminine (sc. *corona* crown) of *aureolus* adjective, diminutive of *aureus* golden, from *aurum* gold). A celestial crown; a halo; an aureole.

au reste /o rɛst/ *adverb phrase* E17 French. As for the rest.

au revoir /o rəvwar/, /əu rəˈvwɑː/ *interjection & noun phrase* L17 French (literally, 'to the seeing again'). (Goodbye) until we meet again; a farewell for the present.

aurora /ɔːˈrɔːrə/ *noun* (also **Aurora**) plural **aurorae** /ɔːˈrɔːriː/, **auroras** LME Latin (*Aurora* the Roman goddess of the dawn). **1** LME The rising light of the morning; the dawn. **b** *figurative* M19 The beginning, the early period. **2** M17 A rich orange colour, as of the sky at sunrise. **3** E18 A luminous phenomenon, often taking the form of variable streamers or resembling drapery, seen in the upper atmosphere of high northern (*borealis*) and southern (*australis*) latitudes.

aurora australis /ɔːˌrɔːrə ɔːˈstreɪlɪs/ M18 Latin (= southern dawn). The aurora of the southern polar regions, the southern lights.

■ Coined after AURORA BOREALIS.

aurora borealis /ɔːˌrɔːrə bɔːrɪˈeɪlɪs/ E18 Latin (= northern dawn). The aurora of the northern polar regions, the northern lights.

■ The phrase was coined to describe the phenomenon in 1621 by the French physicist and philosopher Pierre Gassendi (1592–1655).

au sérieux /o serjø/ *adverb phrase* M19 French. Seriously. Cf. AU GRAND SÉRIEUX.

Auslese /'ausleːzə/ *noun* (also **auslese**) plural **Auslesen** /'ausleːzən/, **Ausleses** M19 German (from *aus* out + *lese* picking, vintage). A white wine made (especially in Germany) from selected bunches of grapes picked later than the general harvest.

auteur /otœr/ *noun plural* pronounced same M20 French (= author). *Cinema* A director who so greatly influences the films directed as to be able to rank as their author.

> **1995** *Spectator* But then why would anyone go hire a writer when everyone keeps telling him that he's an *auteur*?

auto /'auto/ *noun plural* **autos** /'autos/ M16 Spanish and Portuguese (from Latin *actus* act). **1** M16 An AUTO-DA-FÉ. **2** L18 A play (by a Spanish or Portuguese author).

autobahn /'ɔːtəbɑːn/, *foreign* /'autobɑːn/ *noun plural* **autobahns, autobahnen** /'autobɑːnən/ M20 German (from *Auto* automobile + *Bahn* road). In Germany, Switzerland, or Austria: a motorway.

> **1996** *Independent* Germany gave us prototypical motorways in Hitler's *Autobahn*.

auto-da-fé /ˌautadaˈfe/, /ˌɔːtəudaːˈfeɪ/, /ˌautəudaˈfeɪ/ *noun plural* **autos-da-fé** /ˌautosdaˈfe/, /ɔːtəuzdaːˈfeɪ/, /ˌautəuzdɑːˈfeɪ/, **auto-da-fés** E18 Portuguese (= act of the faith (Spanish *auto de fe*)). (The execution of) a judicial sentence of the Inquisition; *especially* the public burning of a heretic; *transferred* a public burning.

> **1997** G. Kepel *Allah in West* . . . television viewers saw the scenes [of the burning of Rushdie's *Satanic Verses*] differently: they recalled engravings of Inquisition bonfires or black-and-white images of Nazis burning books . . . whilst commentators in the Western press used these images to wax indignant about the *auto-da-fé* . . .

autogiro /ɔːtəuˈdʒaɪrəu/ *noun* (also **autogyro**) plural **autogiros** E20 Spanish (from as *auto-* self + *giro* gyration). A type of aircraft having a propeller and freely rotating horizontal vanes.

automat /'ɔːtəmat/ *noun* L17 German (from French *automate* from Latin AUTOMATON). **1** L17 An *automaton* **2** E20 A cafeteria in which food is obtained from a slot-machine; a slot-machine.

■ Sense 2 is chiefly a United States usage.

automaton /ɔːˈtɒmət(ə)n/ *noun plural* **automatons, automata** /ɔːˈtɒmətə/ E17 Latin ((also *automatum*) from Greek, use as noun of neuter of *automatos* acting of itself). **1** E17 Something having the power of spontaneous motion; *especially* a living being viewed as a machine. **2** M17 A piece of mechanism with concealed motive power, *especially* one simulating a living being; a robot. **3** L17 A living being whose actions are purely involuntary or mechanical; a person behaving without active intelligence or mechanically in a set pattern or routine. **4** M20 *Computing* A machine whose responses to all possible inputs are specified in advance.

autopista /ɔːtəˈpiːstə/, *foreign* /autoˈpista/ *noun* M20 **Spanish** (from *auto* automobile + *pista* track, PISTE). In Spain and Spanish-speaking countries: a motorway.

autoroute /ˈɔːtəruːt/, *foreign* /otorut/ (*plural same*) *noun* M20 **French** (from *auto* automobile + *route* road). In France: a motorway.

autostrada /ɔːtəˈstrɑːdə/, *foreign* /auto ˈstrɑːda/ *noun* plural **autostradas, autostrade** /autoˈstrɑːde/ E20 **Italian** (from *auto* automobile + *strada* road from Latin STRA-TUM). In Italy: a motorway.

avalanche /ˈavəlɑːnʃ/ *noun* & *verb* L18 **French** (from Romansh, alteration of Alpine French dialect *lavanche* (of unknown origin), by blending with *avaler* descend: cf. Provençal *lavanca*, Italian *valanga*). **A** *noun* **1** L18 A large mass of snow, rocks, and ice, moving swiftly down a mountainside. **2** *transferred* and *figurative* M19 A sudden onrush or descent; a rapidly descending mass. **b** *Physics* M20 A process of cumulative ionization in which each electron and ion generates further charged particles. Also more fully *Townsend avalanche*. Frequently *attributive*. **B** *intransitive verb* L19 Descend in or like an avalanche.

avant-garde /ˌavɒ̃ˈɡɑːd/ *noun* & *adjective* LME **French** (from *avant* forward, before + *garde* guard). **A** *noun* **1** LME The vanguard of an army. Now *archaic* or *historical*. **2** E20 The pioneering or innovative writers, artists, etc., in a particular period. **B** *adjective* E20 Of or pertaining to the artistic avant-garde; progressive, ultramodern.

A.2 1996 *Times* The punk singer, who wowed the avant-garde of Madrid in the frenzied years after Franco's death, has mellowed into a chubby 45-year-old in jeans and a stripey jumper.

B 1996 *Country Life* [Stockhausen's] *Gruppen* has always been considered an avant-garde landmark.

avant la lettre /avɒ̃ la lɛtr/ *adverb phrase* M20 **French** (literally, 'before the letter'). Before the word, definition, etc., was invented.

1995 *Spectator* He was a Eurosceptic avant la lettre.

avatar /ˈavətɑː/ *noun* L18 **Sanskrit** (*avatāra* descent, from *ava* off, away, down + *tar-* to pass over). **1** L18 *Hindu Mythology* The descent of a god to earth in incarnate form. **2** E19 An incarnation or embodiment (of another person, an idea, etc.). **3** E19 A manifestation to the world as a ruling power or as an object of worship; *generally* a manifestation, a phase.

2 1995 *Times* Most are interpreted as avatars of anti-imperialism, which requires some dedicated pummelling into shape.

3 1995 *New Scientist* For example, members of the online communities . . . can create avatars for themselves, complete with the body and head of their choice—which is more flexibility than you get offline in real life.

ave /ˈɑːvi/, /ˈɑːveɪ/ *noun* & *interjection* (also *Ave* in sense A.1) ME **Latin** (as imperative singular of *avere* to be or fare well, used as an expression of greeting or farewell). **A** *noun* **1** ME An AVE MARIA. **b** ME A bead on a rosary (as used for counting the number of aves recited). **2** E17 A shout of welcome or farewell. **B** *interjection* LME Hail! Farewell!

■ The earliest use of the noun was short for AVE MARIA.

ave atque vale /ˌɑːveɪ atkwi ˈvɑːleɪ/ *interjection* M19 **Latin** (= hail and farewell). Hello and goodbye, hail and farewell.

■ The concluding words of Catullus's graveside address to his dead brother (*Carmina* ci.10), the exclamation is now sometimes used jocularly as a greeting to someone whom one has seen or will see for only a short time.

Ave Maria /ˌɑːvi məˈriːə/, /ˌɑːveɪ məˈriːə/ *interjection* & *noun phrase* (also **Ave Mary** /ˈmɛːri/) ME **Latin** (= hail, Mary!). **1** ME The angel's greeting to the Virgin Mary combined with that of Elizabeth (cf. Luke 1:28, 42), used as a devotional recitation; the prayer to the Virgin as Mother of God beginning with these words; a recitation of this devotional phrase or prayer (often shortened to AVE). **2** L16 (The time of) the ave-bell.

avoirdupois /ˌavədəˈpɔɪz/, /ˌavwɑːdjʊ ˈpwɑː/ *noun* ME **Old French** (*aveir de peis* goods of weight, from *ave(i)r* (modern *avoir*) use as noun of *avoir* to have (from Latin *habere*) + *de* of + *peis, pois* (modern *poids*) weight. **1** ME-L17 Merchandise sold by weight. **2** L15 A system of weights based on a pound (the *avoirdupois pound*) of 16 ounces or 7,000 grains. More fully *avoirdupois weight*. **3** L16 Weight, heaviness; *colloquially* excess bodily weight.

■ The substitution of *du* for the earlier *de* was established in the seventeenth century.

3 1995 *Times* It may be wish-fulfilment or simply *avoirdupois*, but Paula Yates's famously tiny waist seems to have expanded.

avoué /avwe/ *noun* plural pronounced same E19 French. **1** E19 A person who holds the advowson of an ecclesiastical house or benefice; an advowee. **2** E19 A French solicitor.

awabi /əˈwɑːbi/ *noun* E18 Japanese. The Japanese abalone, *Haliotis gigantea*.

axiomata media /aksɪˌɒmətə ˈmiːdɪə/ *noun phrase plural* M19 Modern Latin (= middle principles). *Philosophy* Principles above simple empirical laws but below the highest generalizations or fundamental laws.

■ The phrase is Francis Bacon's in his *Novum Organum* (I.xix), published in Latin in 1620. It was introduced into English philosophical discourse by J. S. Mill in the mid nineteenth century.

ayah /ˈʌɪə/ *noun* L18 Portuguese (*aia* feminine of *aio* tutor). A nurse or maidservant, especially of Europeans in India, Southeast Asia, etc.

1996 *Times: Weekend* Olive, like many children born in colonies and brought up by an *ayah*, has divided loyalties.

ayahuasca /ˌajaˈwaska/ *noun* L20 South American Spanish (From Quechua *aya-*

wáskha from *aya* corpse + *waskha* rope). A hallucinogenic drug made from the bark of a tropical vine found in the Amazon basin; the vine itself. Also called *yagé*.

1991 M. Talbot *Holographic Universe* He had to take a shamanic sacred drink made from a hallucinogenic plant known as *ayahuasca*, the 'soul vine'.

ayatollah /ʌɪəˈtɒlə/ *noun* (also (as a title) **Ayatollah**) M20 Persian (from Arabic *'āyatu-llāh* miraculous sign of God). A Shiite religious leader in Iran; *figurative* a dogmatic leader, an influential or powerful person.

ayurveda /ɑːjəˈveɪdə/ *noun* (also **Ayurveda**) E20 Sanskrit (*āyur-veda* science of life, medicine). An ancient Indian health system.

1995 *Guardian: Weekend* Ayurveda recommends that red meat in particular is to be avoided as it is extremely hard to digest.

azan /əˈzɑːn/ *noun* M19 Arabic ('*aḏān* announcement). The Muslim call to ritual prayer, often made by a muezzin or broadcast through loudspeakers from the minaret of a mosque.

azotea /aθoˈtea/, /azoˈtea/ *noun* E19 Spanish. In Spain and Spanish-speaking countries: the flat roof of a house used as a terrace.

azuki variant of ADZUKI.

azulejo /aθuˈlexo/, /asuˈlexo/, /azjʊˈleɪhəʊ/ *noun* plural **azulejos** /aθuˈlexos/, /asuˈlexos/, /azjʊˈleɪhəʊz/ M19 Spanish (from *azul* blue). A kind of coloured glazed tile used in Spanish buildings.

B

baas /bɑːs/ *noun* L18 Dutch. In South Africa: a (usually White) employer, master, overseer, etc.

■ The word was first used in English in 1625 (*Purchas his Pilgrimes* I. ii. 117) for a sea-captain: 'Our Baase (for so a Dutch capitaine is called)'. It travelled to South Africa with the Dutch settlers of that country and became, in both Afrikaans and South African English, the normal form of address used by Black or Coloured South Africans for those in authority (hence BAASSKAP),

baasskap /ˈbɑːskap/ *noun* M20 Afrikaans (from Dutch *baasschap*, from BAAS + -*schap* -ship). Domination, especially of non-Whites by Whites.

baba /ˈbɑːbɑː/ *noun* E19 French (from Polish, literally, 'married (peasant) woman'). A rich sponge cake; *specifically* one served in a rum syrup. More fully *rum baba* or *baba au rhum*.

babiche /bəˈbiːʃ/ *noun* E19 Canadian French (from Micmac *aːpapiːč*). In North America: thongs or thread made of rawhide, sinew, etc.

babu /ˈbɑːbuː/ *noun* (also **baboo** or (as title) **Babu**) L18 Hindustani (*bābū*). **1** L18–E19 Originally, a Hindu title of respect. Later, a Hindu gentleman. **2** M19 *History* An Indian clerk or official who could write English; *derogatory* an Indian, especially in Bengal, who had had a superficial English education; *attributive* the ornate and often unidiomatic English written by such a person.

2 *attributive* **1936** C. S. Lewis *Allegory of Love* The fantastical 'babu' ornaments of the style [of the *De Nuptiis*] were admired.

babushka /bəˈbʊʃkə/ *noun* M20 Russian (= grandmother). **1** M20 In Russia: a grandmother, an old woman. **2** M20 A headscarf folded diagonally and tied under the chin. Chiefly *North American*.

bac abbreviation of BACCALAUREATE or BACCARAT.

bacalao /bakaˈlao/ *noun* (also **bacalhau** /bakaˈʎau/) M16 Spanish (*bacal(l)ao*, Portuguese *bacalhau*). Codfish, especially dried or salted.

baccalaureate /bakəˈlɔːrɪət/ *noun* M17 French (*baccalauréat* or medieval Latin *baccalaureatus*, from *baccalaureus*, originally with reference to *bacca lauri* laurel berry). **1** M17 The university degree of bachelor. **2** L20 (A qualification awarded for satisfactory performance in) a set of examinations intended to qualify successful candidates for higher education in any of several countries; hence also known as the *International Baccalaureate*.

■ *Bac* or *bachot*, the colloquial French abbreviations of *baccalauréat*, are also found.

baccarat /ˈbakərɑː/ *noun* (also **baccara**) M19 French (*baccara*, of unknown origin). A gambling card-game, played between a banker and one punter, or several punters in turn, in which the best one- or two-card hand is that yielding the highest remainder when its total face value is divided by 10.

bach /bɑːx/ *noun* L19 Welsh ((dialect) literally, 'little'). Dear, beloved; little one; friend.

■ Chiefly vocative and often placed appositionally after personal names.

bachot abbreviation of BACCALAUREATE.

bacillus /bəˈsɪləs/ *noun* plural **bacilli** /bəˈsɪlʌɪ/, /bəˈsɪliː/ L19 Late Latin (= little rod, diminutive of *baculus* rod, stick). Any rod-shaped bacterium; *loosely* any pathogenic bacterium.

backfisch /ˈbakfɪʃ/ *noun* plural **backfische** /ˈbakfɪʃə/ L19 German (literally, 'fish for frying'). A girl in late adolescence, a teenage girl.

1966 *Observer* Marlene Dietrich . . . conjures up the little Berlin *backfisch* . . . who auditioned for 'The Blue Angel'.

backsheesh variant of BAKSHEESH.

bacterium /bakˈtɪərɪəm/ *noun* plural **bacteria** /bakˈtɪərɪə/ M19 Modern Latin (from Greek *baktērion* diminutive of *baktēria* staff, cane). Any of the very widely distributed group *Bacteria* of microscopic prokaryotic mainly single-celled organisms, many of which are symbiotic or pathogenic in animals and plants.

badigeon /bəˈdɪdʒ(ə)n/ *noun* M18 French (of unknown origin). A composition used to fill up gaps in stone or wood.

■ Now United States.

badinage /ˌbadɪ'nɑːʒ/ *noun & verb* M17 French (from *badiner* to joke, from *badin* fool from Provençal, from *badar* to gape, from Proto-Romance). **A** *noun* M17 Humorous banter or ridicule. **B** *verb* E19 Banter playfully.
1996 *Spectator* The jokes and the badinage now were for real; and so were the author's anxieties.

badmash /'bʌdmɑːʃ/ *noun* M19. Urdu (from Persian, from *bad* evil + Arabic *ma'āš* means of livelihood). In the Indian subcontinent: a rascal, a hooligan.

bagarre /bagar/ *noun* plural pronounced same L19 French. A tumult; a scuffle, a brawl.

bagasse /bə'gas/ *noun* E19 French (from Spanish *bagazo*). The residue left after the extraction of juice from sugar cane or sugar beet.

bagatelle /bagə'tɛl/ *noun* M17 French (from Italian *bagatella* perhaps diminutive of Latin *baca* berry, or from Italian *baga* baggage). **1** M17 A trifle, a thing of no value or importance; a negligible amount. **2** M18 A piece of verse or music in a light style. **3** E19 A game in which small balls are struck (usually by a mechanical striker operated by the player) towards numbered holes on a board with a semicircular end.
1 **1996** *Spectator* What if I had confused a treaty? Phooey, a mere bagatelle.

bagel /'beɪg(ə)l/ *noun* (also **beigel** /'bʌɪg(ə)l/) E20 Yiddish (*beygel*). A usually hard ring-shaped roll of bread.

bagnio /'bɑːnjəʊ/ *noun* plural **bagnios** L16 Italian (*bagno* from Latin *balneum* bath). **1** L16 An oriental prison; a slave-house. Now only *historical*. **2** E17–E19 A bath, a bathing-house. **3** E17 A brothel.

baguette /ba'gɛt/ *noun* E18 French (from Italian *bacchetta* diminutive of *bacchio* from Latin *baculum* staff). **1** E18 *Architecture* A small moulding of semicircular section, like an astragal. **2** E20 A gem, usually a diamond, cut in a long rectangular shape. **3** M20 A long narrow French loaf.

bahada variant of BAJADA.

bahut /bay/ *noun* plural pronounced same M19 French. An ornamental chest or cabinet.

baignoire /bɛɲwar/ *noun* plural pronounced same M19 French (= bath-tub). A box at a theatre on the same level as the stalls.

bain-marie /ˌbanmə'riː/, *foreign* /bɛmari/ *noun* plural **bains-marie** (pronounced same) E18 French (translation of medieval Latin *balneum Mariae* translation of medieval Greek *kaminos Marias* furnace of Maria, a supposed Jewish alchemist). A vessel of hot water in which cooking-pans and their contents are slowly heated; a double saucepan. Also, a dish prepared in this.

bajada /bə'hɑːdə/ *noun* (also **bahada**) M19 Spanish (= descent, slope). A broad slope of alluvial material at the foot of an escarpment.
■ Originally south-western United States but subsequently more general (see quotation).
1960 B. W. Sparks *Geomorphology* The whole slope from the range to the infilled playa lake is usually termed a piedmont. The upper part is often, but not always, a rock-cut surface, normally termed a pediment, while the lower part is an aggradation feature formed of detritus from the ranges and termed a bahada.

baklava /'bɑːkləvə/ *noun* M17 Turkish. An originally eastern Mediterranean dessert made of thin pieces of flaky pastry, honey or syrup, and nuts.

baksheesh /bak'ʃiːʃ/ *noun* (also **backsheesh**) M18 Persian (ultimately from *bakšiš* from *bakšīdan* to give). In Eastern countries: a gratuity, a tip.

balafon /'balafɒn/ *noun* L20 African. A West African musical instrument similar to a xylophone.
1991 P. Matthiessen *African Silences* The group included . . . three players of the balafon, a kind of xylophone with hardwood strips.

balalaika /balə'lʌɪkə/ *noun* L18 Russian (of Tartar origin). A musical instrument of the guitar kind, with a triangular body and from two to four strings, popular in Slavonic countries.

balancé /balɑ̃se/ *noun* plural pronounced same L18 French (= balanced (sc. *pas* step)). *Dancing* A swaying step from one foot to the other.

bal costumé /bal kɔstyme/ *noun phrase* plural **bals costumés** (pronounced same) E19 French. A fancy-dress ball.

baldachin /'baldəkɪn/, /'bɔːldəkɪn/ *noun* (also **baldaquin**) M17 Italian (*baldacchino*, ultimately from *Baldacco* Italian form of *Baghdad*). A canopy supported on columns or fixed to a roof or wall, and placed over an altar, throne, or doorway.

■ When first introduced into English (L16), *baldacchino* denoted rich brocade of a type that had originally been made in Baghdad. It was later (M17) transferred to describe a canopy made out of this material, and in current usage the canopy can be of any material.

ballabile /baˈlɑːbile/ *noun* plural **ballabili** /baˈlɑːbili/ M19 Italian (from *ballare* to dance). A dance by the *corps de ballet* or by the chorus in an opera; a piece of music for this; any piece of instrumental music suggestive of a dance.

ballade /baˈlɑːd/ *noun* LME French (from Provençal *balada* dance, song, or poem to dance to, from *balar* to dance). **A** *noun* **1** LME A poem (originally for singing with accompaniment) of one or more triplets of stanzas having 7, 8, or 10 lines, each usually ending with the same refrain line, and an envoy; more *generally*, a poem divided into stanzas of equal length, usually of 7 or 8 lines. Also *collectively*, poetry of this form. **2** M19 *Music* An extended, usually dramatic, piece usually for the piano.

ballerina /baləˈriːnə/ *noun* plural **ballerinas** L18 Italian (feminine of *ballerino* dancing-master, from *ballare* to dance). *Ballet* A female dancer, *especially* one who undertakes a leading role in classical ballet.

ballet /ˈbaleɪ/, /ˈbali/ *noun* M17 French (from Italian *balletto* diminutive of *ballo* ball). (A theatrical performance of) dancing and mime to music; a company performing this.

ballet blanc /ˈbaleɪ blɑ̃/ *noun phrase* M20 French (= white ballet). A ballet in which the female dancers wear long white tutus.
1996 *Spectator* La Sylphide is conventionally regarded as the work that introduced Romantic elements on stage such as the long white tutus—hence the term *ballet blanc* or 'white ballet' used to describe that particular genre . . .

ballista /bəˈlɪstə/ *noun* plural **ballistae** /bəˈlɪstiː/, **ballistas** E16 Latin (ultimately from Greek *ballein* to throw). A large military engine used in antiquity for hurling stones and other missiles.

ballon /balɔ̃/ *noun* plural pronounced same M19 French. **1** M19 Elasticity and buoyancy in dancing; smooth passage from step to step. **2** M20 A spherical glass for brandy, a brandy balloon.
1 1995 *Times* Tetsuya Kumakawa as the Blue Boy turns and jumps with the flashy *ballon* and clarity that has made him such a hit . . .

ballon d'essai /balɔ̃ desɛ/ *noun phrase* plural **ballons d'essai** (pronounced same) L19 French (= trial balloon). An experiment to see how a new policy or project will be received; a tentative proposal.
1942 *Mind* A good deal of Hume's theory of belief is rather a *ballon d'essai* than meant altogether seriously.

ballonné /balɔne/ *noun* plural pronounced same L18 French (past participle of *ballonner* to swell or puff out, distend). A bouncing step in dancing.

bal masqué /bal maske/ *noun phrase* plural **bals masqués** (pronounced same) M18 French. A masked ball.

bal musette /bal myzɛt/ *noun phrase* plural **bals musettes** (pronounced same) E20 French. In France: a popular dancehall (with an accordion band).

balsa /ˈbɒlsə/ *noun* E17 Spanish (= raft). **1** E17 A raft or fishing boat, used chiefly on the Pacific coasts of South America. **2** M19 A tropical American tree, *Ochroma pyramidale* (more fully *balsa tree*); its strong, very light wood, used for rafts, floats, etc. (more fully *balsa-wood*).

balti /ˈbɔːlti/, /ˈbalti/ *noun* L20 Urdu (*bāltī* bucket). A type of Indian cuisine apparently originating in Northern Pakistan and served in metal pans.
1994 *Guardian* Among the 8,000 restaurants now doing business, previous vogues have been superseded by balti (bucket) cuisine. 'Balti is the current fashion and it hasn't peaked yet,' he said.

bambino /bamˈbiːno/, /bamˈbiːnəʊ/ *noun* plural **bambini** /bamˈbiːni/, **bambinos** E18 Italian (diminutive of *bambo* silly). In Italy: a young child or baby; *specifically* an image of the infant Jesus in swaddling-clothes.

banco /ˈbaŋkəʊ/ *interjection* L18 French (from Italian). In baccarat etc.: expressing a player's willingness to meet single-handed the banker's whole stake. Cf. VA BANQUE.

bandar-log /ˈbʌndələʊg/ L19 Hindustani (*bādar*, from Sanskrit *vānara* rhesus monkey + *log* people, from Sanskrit *loka*). The monkeys collectively; *figurative* a group of irresponsible chatterers.

bandeau /'bandəʊ/, *foreign* /bɑ̃do/ *noun* plural **bandeaux** /'bandəʊz/, *foreign* /bɑ̃do/ E18 French (from Old French *bandel* diminutive of *bande*). A band or strip of material, *especially* one used for binding a woman's hair.

banderilla /bandeˈriʎa/, /bandəˈrɪljə/ *noun* plural **banderillas** /bandeˈriʎas/, /bandəˈrɪljəz/ L18 Spanish (diminutive of *bandera* banner). *Bullfighting* A decorated dart thrust into a bull's neck or shoulders during a bullfight.

banderillero /banderiˈʎero/, /bandərɪˈljɛːrəʊ/ *noun* plural **banderilleros** /banderiˈʎeros/, /bandərɪˈljɛːrəʊz/ L18 Spanish (from BANDERILLA). *Bullfighting* A bullfighter who uses banderillas. Also called PEON.

banderole /'bandərəʊl/ *noun* (also **banderol**; /'bandərəʊl/, /'bandər(ə)l/; (especially in sense 2, earlier form) **bannerol** /'banərəʊl/, /'banər(ə)l/) M16 French (*ban-(n)erole*, later *banderole*, from Italian *banderuola* diminutive of *bandiera* banner). **1** M16 A long narrow flag with a cleft end, flown from the masthead of a ship. **2** M16 A rectangular banner borne at the funerals of public figures and placed over the tomb. **3** L16 An ornamental streamer of the kind attached to a knight's lance. **4** E17 A ribbon-like scroll bearing a device or inscription.

bandobast variant of BUNDOBUST.

bandolero /bandəˈlɛːrəʊ/ *noun* plural **bandoleros** M17 Spanish. A Spanish bandit.

bania /'bʌnɪə/ *noun* L18 Hindustani (*baniyā* from Sanskrit *vāṇija*). A Hindu trader or merchant.

banian variant of BANYAN.

bannerol variant of BANDEROLE.

banquette /baŋˈkɛt/ *noun* E17 French (from Italian *banchetta* diminutive of *banca* bench, shelf). **1** E17 A raised step or way running along the inside of a rampart, at the bottom of a trench, etc., on which soldiers stand to fire at the enemy. **2** M19 A long upholstered seat along a wall.

banyan /'banɪən/, /'banjən/ *noun* (also **banian**) L16 Portuguese (from Gujarati *vāṇiyo* man of the trading caste, from Sanskrit *vāṇija* merchant). **1** L16 A BANIA. **2** M17 An Indian broker or steward attached to a firm or individual. **3** E18 In full *banyan shirt* etc. A loose flannel shirt or jacket. **4** M17 In full *banyan tree*. An Indian fig tree, *Ficus benghalensis*, the branches of which root themselves over a wide area.

■ *Banyan* has tended this century to supersede the generally preferred earlier spelling *banian*. In sense 4 the word was originally applied by Europeans to a particular tree of the species growing in a port on the Persian Gulf, under which Hindu merchants had set up a shrine; in 1634 Sir Thomas Herbert wrote of 'A tree . . . named by us the Bannyan Tree, from their adorning and adoring it with ribbons and streamers of varicoloured Taffata' (*Travels* II (1638)). The tree is not known by this name in any Indian language.

banzai /banˈzʌɪ/ *interjection & adjective* L19 Japanese (= ten thousand years (of life to you)). **A** L19 *interjection* A form of acclamation used by the Japanese especially to their Emperor, a cheer used in battle etc. **B** E20 *attributive* or as *adjective* (As if) shouting 'banzai'; uproarious; (of an attack by Japanese) reckless. *slang*.

banzuke /banˈzuːki/ *noun* L20 Japanese. The ranking list of sumo wrestlers.

baragouin /baragwɛ̃/, /barəˈgwɪn/ *noun* E17 French. Gibberish; unintelligible jargon.

baraza /bəˈrɑːzə/ *noun* L19 Kiswahili. In East Africa: a place of public audience or reception; a meeting, a reception.

barbette /bɑːˈbɛt/ *noun* L18 French (from *barbe* beard + diminutive *-ette*). A platform in a fort or ship from which guns fire over a parapet etc. and not through an embrasure.

barbotine /'bɑːbətiːn/, /'bɑːbətiːn/ *noun* M19 French. (Pottery ornamented with) a slip of kaolin clay.

barcarole /'bɑːkərəʊl/, /bɑːkəˈrəʊl/ *noun* (also **barcarolle** /'bɑːkərɒl/) L18 French (*barcarolle* from Venetian Italian *barcarola* related to *barcarolo* gondolier, from *barca* boat). A song sung by Venetian gondoliers; a piece of music in imitation of such songs or suggestive of the rocking motion of a boat.

barchan /'bɑːk(ə)n/ *noun* (also **barchane**, **barkhan**, **barkan**) L19 Turkic (*barkhan*). A shifting crescent-shaped sand-dune, concave on the leeward side.

barège /barɛʒ/ *noun & adjective* E19 French (from *Barèges* a village in south-west France). **A** *noun* E19 plural pronounced same. (A garment made of) a gauzelike fabric of silk and wool. **B** *adjective* M19 Made of barège.

barkan, barkhan variants of BARCHAN.

bar mitzvah /bɑː 'mɪtsvə/ *noun phrase* (also **Bar mitzvah**) M19 Hebrew (*bar miṣwāh* son of commandment). (A religious initiation ceremony for) a Jewish boy aged thirteen, regarded as liable to observe the religious precepts and eligible to take part in public worship. Cf. BAT MITZVAH.

barouche /bəˈruːʃ/ *noun* E19 German (dialect *Barutsche* from Italian *baroccio* (Spanish *barrocho*) two-wheeled, ultimately from Latin *birotus*, from *bi-* two + *rota* wheel). A four-wheeled horse-drawn carriage with a collapsible half-hood, a seat in front for the driver, and seats facing each other for passengers. Chiefly *historical*.

barre /bɑː/ *noun* E20 French. **1** E20 *Music* (A finger used as) a CAPOTASTO. **2** M20 A waist-level horizontal bar to help dancers keep their balance during some exercises.

barré /bare/ *adjective & noun* plural of noun pronounced same L19 French (past participle of *barrer* to bar). *Music* (A chord) played with strings stopped by a CAPOTASTO or finger.

barrera /baˈrrera/ *noun* E20 Spanish (= barrier). *Bullfighting* (The row of seats nearest to) the barrier encircling a bullring.

barrette /baˈrɛt/ *noun* E20 French (diminutive of BARRE). A bar-shaped clip or ornament for a woman's or girl's hair.

> **1996** *Times* Jil Sander and Prada favoured twisted buns sometimes held in place with a slim barrette.

barrio /ˈbarɪəʊ/ *noun* plural **barrios** M19 Spanish (perhaps from Arabic). A ward or quarter of a town or city in Spain and Spanish-speaking countries; a Spanish-speaking quarter of a United States town or city.

bas bleu /bɑ blə/ *noun phrase* plural **bas bleus** (pronounced same) L18 French (translation from English). A bluestocking; a serious-minded and learned woman.

bascule /ˈbaskjuːl/ *noun* L17 French ((earlier *bacule*) = see-saw, from stem of *battre* to beat + *cul* buttocks). A lever apparatus of which one end is raised when the other is lowered.

basha, bashaw variants of PASHA.

basho /ˈbaʃəʊ/ *noun* plural same, **bashos** L20 Japanese. A sumo wrestling tournament.

basilica /bəˈsɪlɪkə/, /bəˈzɪlɪkə/ *noun* M16 Latin (branch I, literally, 'royal palace' from Greek *basilikē* use as noun of feminine of *basilikos* royal, from *basileus* king; branch II from Greek *basilika* neuter plural of *basilikos*). **I** *singular* (pl. **basilicas**, (*rare*) **basilicae** /bəˈsɪlɪkiː/) **1** M16 *History* A large oblong hall or building, with double colonnades and a semicircular apse, used for courts of law and public assemblies. **2** M16 A building of this form used as a Christian church. Also, used as the title of certain churches granted privileges by the Pope. **II** *plural* **3** M17 *History* (**Basilica**) The 9th-century Byzantine legal code initiated by the emperor Basil I.

basmati /basˈmɑːti/, /bɑːzˈmɑːti/ *noun* M19 Hindustani (*bāsmatī* literally, 'fragrant'). A kind of rice with very long thin grains and a delicate fragrance. More fully *basmati rice*.

basse-taille /bastaj/ *noun* L19 French (from *basse* feminine of *bas* low + *taille* cut). A technique of applying translucent enamels to metal reliefs so that the shade of the enamel is darkest where the relief is most deeply cut.

bassetto /bəˈsɛtəʊ/ *noun* plural **bassettos** E18 Italian (diminutive of BASSO). A violoncello.

bassinet /basɪˈnɛt/ *noun* (also **bassinette**) M19 French (diminutive of *bassin* basin). A wicker cradle or pram with a curved hood.

> ■ A buttercup is called a bassinet in Normandy, and *bacinetz* occurs in a 1509 French list of vernacular flower names. In English too, *bassinet* was for a long time (L16-E18) used solely in a botanical context, with Lyte's 1578 herbal referring to the marsh marigold as the 'Brave Bassinet'; later herbalists recorded it as a dialect name for a geranium or various species of ranunculus.

basso /ˈbasəʊ/ *noun & adjective* plural **bassos, bassi** /ˈbasi/ E18 Italian (= low, from Latin *bassus*). *Music* Bass.

basso buffo /ˌbasəʊ ˈbʊfəʊ/ plural **bassi buffi** /ˌbasi ˈbʊfi/, **bassos buffos** E20 Italian (BASSO + *buffo* buffoon). *Music* A bass singer who takes comic parts in opera.

basso cantante /ˌbasəʊ kanˈtanteɪ/ plural **bassi cantanti** /ˌbasi kanˈtanti/ L19

Italian (BASSO + *cantante*, literally, 'singing'). *Music* (A singer with) a voice in the upper register of the bass range.

basso continuo /ˌbasəʊ kənˈtɪnjʊəʊ/ plural **basso continuos** E18 Italian (BASSO + CONTINUO). *Music* A figured bass, a thorough bass.

basso ostinato /ˌbasəʊ ɒstɪˈnɑːtəʊ/ plural **basso ostinatos** L19 Italian (BASSO + OSTINATO). *Music* A short passage usually in the bass, constantly repeated with varying melody and harmony, a ground bass.

basso profundo /ˌbasəʊ prəˈfʌndəʊ/ (occasionally **profondo** /prəˈfɒndəʊ/) plural **bassi profundi** /ˌbasi prəˈfʌndi/, **bassos profundos** M19 Italian (BASSO + *profundo*, literally, 'deep'). *Music* (A singer with) a very deep and rich voice.

basso-relievo /ˌbasəʊrɪˈliːvəʊ/ *noun* (also **basso-rilievo** /ˌbasəʊrɪˈljervəʊ/) plural **basso-relievos** M17 Italian (*basso-rilievo*). (A sculpture, carving, etc. in) low relief; bas-relief.

basta /ˈbasta/ *interjection* L16 Italian. Enough! No matter!

bastide /baˈstiːd/ *noun* E16 Old French (Provençal *bastida* (medieval Latin *bastida*) use as noun of feminine past participle of *bastir* to build). **1** E16 *History* A fortified village or town. **2** E18 A country house in southern France.

> **2 1996** *Times Magazine* . . . centuries-old village houses, abandoned *mas* or farmhouses, grand *bastides*, dressed up for today's tastes but retaining their nobility.

basuco /bəˈzuːkəʊ/, /bəˈsuːkəʊ/ *noun* (also **basuko**, **bazuco**, **bazuko**) L20 Colombian Spanish (perhaps connected with Spanish *basura* waste; or with Spanish *bazucar* to shake violently). A cheap form of impure cocaine made from adulterated coca paste and highly addictive when smoked as a drug.

> ■ The explosive effect of *basuco* has led to an alternative suggestion for the etymology, linking it with the English word *bazooka*, adopted in Spanish and applied figuratively to the drug and then borrowed back into English in a slightly altered form. Other names for the drug, which first appeared in the English-speaking world in the mid 1980s, are *little devil* and *Suzuki*.
> **1985** C. Nicholl *The Fruit Palace* There's a big internal market; a lot of coke and basuko used by the street boys.

batardeau /batardo/ *noun* plural **batardeaux** /batardo/ M18 French (earlier *bastardeau* diminutive of Old French *bastard* of unknown origin). A coffer-dam. Also, a wall built across the moat or ditch surrounding a fortification.

batata /bəˈtɑːtə/ *noun* M16 Spanish (from Taino). Sweet potato.

bateau /ˈbatəʊ/, *foreign* /bato/ *noun* plural **bateaux** /ˈbatəʊz/, *foreign* /bato/ E18 French (= boat). A light riverboat, especially of a flat-bottomed kind used in Canada. Cf. BATEAU-MOUCHE.

> ■ *Bateau* is also used attributively as an alternative to 'boat' in *bateau neck*, *bateau-necked*, etc., used of a garment with shallow curved neckline running from shoulder to shoulder.

bateau-mouche /batomuʃ/ plural **bateaux-mouches** (pronounced same) E20 French. A riverboat which takes sightseers on the Seine in Paris.

bathos /ˈbeɪθɒs/ *noun* E18 Greek (= depth). **1** E18 *Rhetoric* Ludicrous descent from the elevated to the commonplace; anticlimax. **2** E19 A comedown; a performance absurdly unequal to the occasion.

> ■ First introduced (M17) with its original Greek meaning of 'depth, lowest phase, bottom', *bathos* is now rare or obsolete in this sense, which has been superseded by the two senses above. Alexander Pope was primarily responsible for sense 1 in *Peri Bathous: or the Art of Sinking in Poetry* (1727), a parody of the work by the ancient Greek rhetorician Longinus *On the Sublime*.
> **2 1996** *Country Life* The series attempted to marry the bathos of the quiz show to the nitpicking of scholarship.

batik /ˈbatɪk/, /bəˈtiːk/ *noun & adjective* L19 Javanese (literally, 'painted'). **A** L19 *noun* A method (originally used in Java) of making coloured designs on textiles by waxing the parts not to be dyed; (a garment made of) a fabric dyed by this method. **B** E20 *attributive* or as *adjective* Executed or ornamented by this method.

batiste /bəˈtiːst/ *noun & adjective* E19 French ((earlier *batiche*) perhaps from base of *battre* to beat). (Of) a fine light cotton or linen fabric like cambric.

bat mitzvah /bɑːt ˈmɪtsvə/ *noun phrase* (also **Bat mitzvah**) M20 Hebrew (*baṭ miṣwāh* daughter of commandment, after BAR MITZVAH). (A religious initiation ceremony for) a Jewish girl aged twelve years and one day, regarded as the age of religious maturity.

baton /'bat(ə)n/, *in senses 4 and 6 also foreign* /batɔ̃/ *noun* E16 French (bâton (earlier baston) = Provençal, Spanish baston Italian bastone from Proto-Romance, from late Latin bastum stick). **1** E16 A stick or staff used as a weapon. **b** L19 A police officer's cudgel, *especially* a relatively long one. **2** L16 A staff carried as symbol of office, *especially* that of a field marshal. **3** *Heraldry* M18 A narrow truncated bend. **4** *Music* L18 A conductor's wand; a drum-major's stick. **5** M19 A long loaf or stick of bread. **6** E20 A short stick carried in a relay race and passed from one participant to the next.

■ Although *baton* or *batton* was used by Scots writers in the sixteenth century, the commoner spelling in England until the nineteenth century was *batoon*. *Baton* in the general sense 1 is now much less common than in its various specialized senses.

battement /batmã/ *plural same*, /'batmɔ̃/ *noun* M19 French (= beating). *Dancing* Any of a number of beating leg movements. Cf. GRAND BATTEMENT, PETIT BATTEMENT.

batterie /batri/ *noun plural pronounced same* E18 French. **1** *Dancing* E18 A movement in which the feet or calves are beaten together during a leap. **2** L18 Abbreviation of BATTERIE DE CUISINE. **3** *Music* M20 Percussion instruments in an orchestra or band.

■ French *batterie* in its commoner senses (electrical or military) has been fully assimilated in English as *battery*, but it is retained in more specialist meanings, such as 'drum-kit' (see sense 3).

batterie de cuisine /batri də kɥizin/ *noun phrase* L18 French (= articles for cookery). Apparatus or utensils for preparing or serving a meal.

battue /bə't(j)uː/; *foreign* /baty/ (*plural same*) *noun* E19 French (use as noun of feminine past participle of *battre* to beat). **1** E19 A driving of game towards the guns by beaters; a shooting-party on this plan. **2** *transferred* **a** M19 A thorough search. **b** M19 A wholesale slaughter.

batture /bə'tjʊə/ *noun* E19 French. **1** E19 A stretch of river shore, usually formed by deposition, between the natural embankment and the low-water mark. **2** E19 A sand bar in a river.

■ Both senses North American; sense 2 Canadian.

battuta /bə'tuːtə/ *noun* E18 Italian (from *battere* to beat). *Music* The beating of time; a strong beat; the regular beat.

Bauhaus /'baʊhaʊs/ *noun* E20 German (*Bau* building + *Haus* house). (The principles of) a German school of architecture and design founded in 1919 by Walter Gropius and closed in 1933.

bavaroise /bavə'waːz/, *foreign* /bavarwaz/ *noun* (also **bavarois** /bavə'waː/, *foreign* /bavarwa/) M19 French (use as noun of feminine adjective *bavaroise* Bavarian). A dessert containing gelatin and whipped cream, served cold.

bayadère /beɪjə'dɛː/, /beɪjə'dɪə/ *noun* L16 French (from Portuguese *bailadeira*, from *bailar* to dance, related to medieval Latin *ballare* to dance). **1** L16 A Hindu dancing-girl (especially at a southern Indian temple). **2** M19 A striped textile fabric.

bayou /'baɪuː/ *noun* M18 American French (from Choctaw *bayuk*). In the southern United States: a marshy offshoot of a river, lake, etc.

bazaar /bə'zɑː/ *noun* L16 Italian (*bazarro* from Turkish from Persian *bāzār* market). **1** L16 An oriental market. **2** E19 A large shop, or arcade of shops, selling fancy goods, bric-à-brac, etc. **3** E19 A sale of miscellaneous new or second-hand goods in aid of charity.

bazuco, bazuko variants of BASUCO.

béarnaise /beɪə'neɪz/, *foreign* /bearnɛz/ *adjective* (also **Béarnaise**) L19 French (feminine of *béarnais* of Béarn, a region of south-west France). A rich white sauce flavoured with tarragon. In full, *béarnaise sauce* (also *sauce béarnaise*).

beau /bəʊ/ *noun plural* **beaux** /bəʊz/, **beaus** L17 French (use as noun of adjective, ultimately from Latin *bellus* fine, beautiful). **1** L17 A fashionable man, a ladies' man; a fop, a dandy. **2** E18 A lady's male companion, a suitor; a boyfriend, a lover. Now chiefly *North America*.

beau geste /bəʊ ʒɛst/ *noun phrase plural* **beaux gestes** (pronounced same) E20 French (= splendid gesture). A display of magnanimity; a generous act.

beau ideal /bəʊ ʌɪ'dɪəl/ *noun phrase* E19 French (*beau idéal* = ideal beauty). One's highest or ideal type of excellence or beauty; the perfect model.

■ Now often misunderstood to mean 'beautiful ideal'.

Beaujolais nouveau /ˌbəʊʒəleɪ nuːˈvəʊ/, *foreign* /boʒɔlɛ nuvo/ L20 **French** (= new Beaujolais). A light, usually red, burgundy wine of the latest vintage produced in the Beaujolais district of France.

beau monde /bəʊ ˈmɒnd/, *foreign* /bo mɔ̃d/ *noun phrase* L17 **French** (= fine world). (The world of) fashionable society.

1995 *Times* Teresa Lady Rothschild was never deeply interested in the glittering *beau monde* which circled around the international banking dynasty into which she married.

beau rôle /bo rol/ *noun phrase* plural **beaux rôles** (pronounced same) L19 **French** (= fine role). A fine acting part; the leading part.

beau sabreur /bo sabrœr/ *noun phrase* plural **beaux sabreurs** (pronounced same) M19 **French** (= fine (or handsome) swordsman). A gallant warrior, a handsome or dashing adventurer.

■ Originally a sobriquet of Joachim Murat (1767–1815), French cavalry officer and brother-in-law of Napoleon.

beauté du diable /bote dy djabl/ *noun phrase* M19 **French** (= devil's beauty). Superficial attractiveness; captivating charm.

beaux arts /boz ɑr/ *noun & adjective phrase* (also **beaux-arts**) E19 **French** (*beaux-arts*). **A** *noun phrase* plural E19 Fine arts. Also *elliptical*, the *École des Beaux-Arts* in Paris. **B** *adjective phrase* E20 Of or pertaining to the classical decorative style maintained by the *École des Beaux-Arts* especially in the nienteenth century.

beaux esprits plural of BEL ESPRIT.

beaux gestes plural of BEAU GESTE.

beaux yeux /boz jø/ *noun phrase* E19 **French**. Beautiful eyes; admiring glances; favourable regard.

bebung /ˈbeːbʊŋ/ *noun* L19 **German** (= trembling). *Music* A pulsating or trembling effect given to a sustained note; *specifically* such an effect produced on the clavichord by rocking the fingertip.

beccafico /bɛkəˈfiːkəʊ/ *noun* plural **beccaficos** E17 **Italian** (from *beccare* to peck + *fico* fig). Any of a number of small birds (warblers, etc.) esteemed as a delicacy in the Mediterranean region.

béchamel /ˈbeɪʃəmɛl/, *foreign* /beʃamɛl/ *noun* M18 **French**. *Cookery* A fine savoury white sauce, frequently made with added cream or milk. More fully *béchamel sauce*.

■ Called after the Marquis de *Béchamel*, steward of Louis XIV.

bêche-de-mer /bɛʃdəˈmɛː/ *noun* plural same, **bêches-de-mer** /bɛʃdəˈmɛː/ L18 **pseudo-French** (from Portuguese *bicho do mar*, literally, 'worm of the sea'). **1** L18 A sea cucumber eaten as a Chinese delicacy. **2** L19 An English-based pidgin used formerly as a trade language and contact vernacular in the southwest Pacific. Also *bêche-de-mer English* or *beach-la-mar*.

Bedouin /ˈbɛdʊɪn/ *noun & adjective* (also **Beduin, beduin**) LME **Old French** (*beduin* (modern *bédouin*) ultimately (through medieval Latin *beduini* plural) from Arabic *badawī*, plural *badawīn* (from *badw* desert) nomadic desert tribes). **A** *noun* **1** LME An Arab of the desert. **2** M19 A person living a nomadic life. **B** *adjective* M19 Of the desert or Bedouins; nomadic, wandering.

Bedu /ˈbɛdu/ *noun & adjective* plural of noun same E20 **Arabic** (*badw*). (Of) a Bedouin; *collective* (of) Bedouins.

beebee variant of BIBI.

Beerenauslese /ˈbeːrənˌaʊsleːzə/ *noun* (also **beerenauslese**) plural **Beerenauslesen**, /ˈbeːrənˌaʊsleːzən/, **Beerenausleses** E20 **German** (from *Beeren* berries, grapes + AUSLESE). A white wine made (especially in Germany) from selected individual grapes picked later than the general harvest.

béguin /begɛ̃/ *noun* plural pronounced same E20 **French**. An infatuation, a fancy.

■ *Avoir le béguin de* (or *pour*) is 'to have a crush on' in colloquial French.

beguine /beɪˈɡiːn/ *noun* 1 (also **béguine**) LME **Old and Modern French** (*béguine* (Middle Dutch, Middle High German *begīne*), medieval Latin *Beguina*, perhaps ultimately from Middle Dutch verb meaning 'to mutter (prayers)'). A member of a lay sisterhood in the Low Countries, formed in the twelfth century and not bound by vows.

beguine /bɪˈɡiːn/ *noun* 2 E20 **American French** (from French BÉGUIN). (The distinctive rhythm of) a dance of West Indian origin.

begum /ˈbeɪɡəm/ *noun* (also (as title) **Begum**) M17 **Urdu** (*begam* from Early Turkic *begim*, from *beg* bey + 1st person singular possessive suffix -*im*). In the Indian subcontinent: a Muslim noblewoman or lady of high rank. Also (**Begum**), a title given to a married Muslim woman (= Mrs).

beignet /'bɛnjeɪ/, /bɛn'jɛ/, *foreign* /bɛɲɛ/ (*plural same*) *noun* M19 French. A fritter; *specifically* (*United States*) a square of fried dough sprinkled with icing sugar and eaten hot. Usually in *plural*.

> **1995** *Observer* The French beignets, golden balls of molten cheese, must rank high in the world of the fritter fancier . . .

bel canto /bɛl 'kantəʊ/ *noun phrase* L19 Italian (= fine song). (A style of) singing characterized by full rich broad tone, legato phrasing, and accomplished technique.

> **1996** *Spectator* Not only is his voice beautiful, but he always sings beautifully—'bel canto', in other words . . .

bel esprit /bɛl ɛspri/ *noun phrase* plural **beaux esprits** /boz ɛspri/ M17 French (= fine mind). A brilliant or witty person.

belle /bɛl/ *noun* E17 French (feminine of *bel*, BEAU, from Latin *bella* feminine of *bellus* beautiful). A beautiful woman, *especially* the outstanding beauty of a place, time, etc.

belle époque /bɛl eɪ'pɒk/ *noun phrase* (also **belle epoque, Belle Epoque**) plural **belles époques** /bɛlz eɪ'pɒk/ M20 French (= fine period). A period of settled comfort and prosperity.

> ■ Originally and specifically used of the period in France from the late nineteenth century to the war of 1914–18; see quotation at DOUCEUR DE VIVRE.

belle laide /bɛl lɛd/ *noun phrase* (also **belle-laide**) plural **belles laides** (pronounced same) E20 French (from feminine adjectives *belle* beautiful + *laide* ugly). An attractive though ugly woman. Cf. JOLIE LAIDE.

> *transferred* **1956** L. E. Jones *Edwardian Youth* Like that of an ugly woman with many lovers, Balliol's uncomeliness only serves to underline the greatness and ardour of her soul . . . and her lovers at Eton . . . were long past the stage of minding . . . the physical failings of that fascinating *belle-laide*.

belles-lettres /bɛllɛtr/ *noun plural* (occasionally treated as *singular*) M17 French (literally, 'fine letters'). Studies or writings of a purely literary character, *especially* essays, criticism, etc. Originally more widely, literature generally, the humanities.

belote /bə'lɒt/ *noun* (also **belotte**) M20 French. A card-game like pinochle, played with a 32-card pack, popular in France;

the combination of king and queen of trumps in this game.

> ■ Perhaps from F. Belot, a Frenchman said to have developed the game.

bema /'biːmə/ *noun* plural **bemas, bemata** /biːmətə/ L17 Greek (*bēma* a step, a raised place to speak from). **1** L17 *Christian Church* The altar part or sanctuary in ancient and Orthodox churches; the chancel. **2** E19 *Greek Antiquities* The platform from which Athenian orators spoke.

benedicite /bɛnɪ'dʌɪsɪti/ *interjection & noun* ME Latin (2nd person plural imperative of *benedicere* to wish well to, bless, from *bene* well + *dicere* to say). **A** *interjection* **1** ME Expressing a wish: God bless you! **2** ME Expression of astonishment: Good gracious! **B** *noun* **1** ME An invocation of a blessing; *especially* a grace at table. **2** M17 *Christian Church* the Benedicite, the canticle beginning *Benedicite, omnia opera* 'O all ye works [of the Lord], bless ye [the Lord]', known also as 'The Song of the Three Children', which is an alternative to the *Te Deum* at matins in the *Book of Common Prayer*.

bene esse /'bɛnɪ ɛsi/ *noun phrase* E17 Modern Latin. Well-being, welfare, especially opposed to ESSE.

benthos /'bɛnθɒs/ *noun* L19 Greek (= depth of the sea). The flora and fauna of the bottom of the sea (or of a lake).

ben trovato /ben trɒ'vɑːtɒ/ *adjective phrase* L19 Italian (literally, 'well found'). Of a story etc.: happily invented; appropriate though untrue.

> ■ *Se non è vero, è molto ben trovato* 'if it is not true, it is a happy invention' was apparently a well-known saying in sixteenth-century Italy, being found for example in the writings of Giordano Bruno. Smollett used the phrase in 1771 in the form *ben trovata*.
>
> **1952** R. M. Hare *Language of Morals* We might say that to tell a story about someone, which every one knows is *ben trovato*, is not lying.
>
> **1996** *Spectator* Beaverbrook, who was a fund of good stories (*ben trovato* anyhow), was the source for the famous story of an old friend visiting Bottomley in prison finding him mending mailbags, as was usual then.

berceau /bɛrso/ *noun* plural **berceaux** (pronounced same) L17 French (literally, 'cradle'). An arbour; a shaded or leafy walk.

berceuse /bɛrsøz/, /bɛː'səːz/ *noun* plural pronounced same L19 French (from *bercer* to rock + feminine agent-suffix *-euse*). *Music* A lullaby; an instrumental piece with a gently rocking rhythm.

beret /'bɛreɪ/, /'bɛri/ *noun* E19 French (*béret* from south-west French dialect and Old Provençal *berret*). A round felt or cloth cap that lies flat on the head, covering it closely (as traditionally worn by Basque peasantry); such a cap forming part of military uniform.

beretta variant of BIRETTA.

berg /bə:g/, *foreign* /berx/ *noun* E19 Afrikaans (from Dutch (= Old English *beorg* barrow, hill)). A mountain; a mountain range.

bergère /bɛrʒɛr/ *noun* plural pronounced same M18 French (= shepherdess). A long-seated upholstered armchair fashionable in the eighteenth century. Also, a chair with canework seat, back, and sides.

> **1995** *Country Life* There are at least two types of *bergère*. One is a rectangular seat with high arms sweeping up to the back, which may be caned or covered in leather . . . .The second type is the 'curricle', which is a rounded, and usually slightly smaller, version of the same thing.

bergerette /bə:ʒə'rɛt/ *noun* LME French (from *berger* shepherd). A pastoral or rustic song about shepherds, for dancing to.

bergschrund /'bə:gʃrʊnd/ *noun* M19 German (from *Berg* mountain + *schrund* cleft). A crevasse or gap at the junction of a glacier or snowfield with a steep upper slope.

bersaglieri /ˌbɛrsaʎˈʎeːri/, /ˌbɛːsɑːlrˈɛːri/ *noun plural* M19 Italian (from *bersaglio* target). Highly trained Italian infantry, originally riflemen or sharpshooters.

bertillonage /bɛrtijɔnaʒ/ *noun* L19 French (*bertillonnage*). The system of identification of criminals by anthropometric measurements, etc.

■ The system is named after its inventor, the French criminologist Alphonse Bertillon (1853–1914), who introduced it in 1882. It was soon supplemented, and in the early years of the twentieth century superseded, by fingerprinting.

beta /'biːtə/ *noun* ME Latin (from Greek). **1** ME The second letter (B, β) of the Greek alphabet. **2** L17 Denoting the second in a numerical sequence. **3** *attributive Science* L19 (Frequently written β); as in *Astronomy* (preceding the genitive of the Latin name of the constellation) designating the second brightest star in a constellation. **4** E20 A second-class mark in an examination etc.

■ Like *alpha*, *beta* has a number of specialist applications in scientific terminology and often appears in the same context to designate the entity secondary to the *alpha* one; see quotation at ALPHA.

betel /'biːt(ə)l/ *noun* M16 Portuguese (from Malayalam *veṟṟila*). The leaf of a climbing evergreen shrub, *Piper betle*, which is chewed in the East with acreca-nut parings and a little lime. Also (more fully *betel pepper*), the plant itself.

bête noire /bert 'nwɑː/, *foreign* /bɛt nwar/ *noun phrase* plural **bêtes noires** (pronounced same) M19 French (literally, 'black beast'). The bane of someone's life; an insufferable person or thing; an object of strong or obsessive aversion.

> **1995** *Spectator* [F. R. Leavis's] *bête noire*, David Cecil at Oxford, taught literature as something to be enjoyed without benefit of Leavisite scrutiny.

bethel /'bɛθ(ə)l/ *noun* E17 Hebrew (*bēṯ, ēl* from *bēṯ* house of + *'ēl* god). **1** E17 A place where God is worshipped. **2** E19 *transferred* A Nonconformist chapel; a seamen's church.

bêtise /bɛtiz/, /ber'tiːz/ *noun* (also **betise**) plural pronounced same E19 French (= stupidity, from *bête* foolish, from Old French *beste* beast). An ill-judged or ill-timed remark or action; a piece of folly.

> **1996** *Spectator* They . . . at once went to Zimbabwe where their *betises* included, in an attempt to portray the sundowner life, a room full of ancient people served by a black man in a fancy uniform, in the kind of grand house that scarcely existed then. Wrong on every count.

beur /bœr/ *noun* L20 French. In France: a child of immigrant parents, born in France.

beurre manié /bœr manje/, /bə: man'jeɪ/ *noun phrase* M20 French (= handled butter). *Cookery* A mixture of flour and butter used for thickening sauces or soups.

beurre noir /bœr nwar/, /bə: 'nwɑː/ *noun phrase* M19 French (= butter). *Cookery* A sauce made by heating butter until it is brown, usually mixing it with vinegar.

bévue /bevy/ *noun* plural pronounced same. L17 French. A blunder.

bey /beɪ/ *noun* (also (as title) **Bey**) L16 Turkish (modern form of *beg* governor). The governor of a district or province in the Ottoman Empire. Also (**Bey** following name) formerly used in Turkey and Egypt as a courtesy title.

bezesteen /ˈbɛzɪstiːn/ *noun* M17 Turkish ((perhaps through French or Italian, from Turkish) *bezesten* (now *bedesten*) covered market for fine cloth and valuables, from Persian *bazistān*, from *baz* (Turkish *bez*) from Arabic *bazz* cloth + suffix of place *-istān*). An exchange, bazaar, or marketplace in the Middle East.

bhajan /ˈbʌdʒ(ə)n/ *noun* E20 Sanskrit (*bhajana*). Hinduism A devotional song.

bhaji /ˈbɑːdʒi/ *noun* L20 Hindi (*bhájī* fried vegetables from Sanskrit *bhrajj* to fry). In Indian cooking, a fritter, generally made with onions, but also with other vegetables.

bhakta /ˈbʌktə/ *noun* E19 Sanskrit. Hinduism A religious devotee.

bhakti /ˈbʌkti/ *noun* M19 Sanskrit. Hinduism Religious devotion or piety as a means of salvation.

bhang /bɑːŋ/ *noun* (also **bang**) L16 Persian and Urdu (*bang* (through Portuguese *bangue*), later assimilated to Hindustani *bhāṅ* from Sanskrit *bhaṅg*). A preparation of the cannabis or Indian hemp plant (*Cannabis sativa*) used as an intoxicating or hallucinogenic drug or for medicinal purposes.

bhangra /ˈbɑːŋgrə/ *noun* M20 Panjabi (*bhāṅgrā*). **1** M20 A type of Punjabi folkdance for men associated with the harvest. **2** L20 A style of popular (especially dance) music combining Punjabi folk music with rock and roll or disco music.

■ In Britain *bhangra* (also known as *bhangra beat*), originated in the Asian communities in the 1980s, but by the end of the decade had won a wider following.

2 1987 *Independent* An up and coming group . . . set the seemingly incompatible rhythmic stridency of funk and Bhangra dance to a compulsive harmony.

bhikkhu /ˈbɪkuː/ *noun* (also **bhikku**) M19 Pali (*bhikkhu* from as BHIKSHU). A Buddhist mendicant or religious devotee.

bhikshu /ˈbɪkʃuː/ *noun* plural **bhikshus**, same E19 Sanskrit (*bhikṣu* beggar, from *bhikṣ* beg). A brahminical or Buddhist mendicant or religious devotee. Cf. BHIKKHU.

bianco sopra bianco /ˌbjaŋko ˌsopra ˈbjaŋko/ *noun phrase* L19 Italian (literally, 'white upon white'). A form of white decoration upon white porcelain.

■ Earlier in English (M19) in the elliptical form *sopra bianco*.

bibelot /ˈbɪbələʊ/, *foreign* /biblo/ (*plural same*) *noun* L19 French (from reduplication of *bel* beautiful). A small curio or artistic trinket.

1996 *Times* Nor can he tell us who is the famous actress and beauty who slid bibelots into her handbag at Sir Harold Acton's villa outside Florence . . .

biberon /bibrɔ̃/ *noun* plural pronounced same M19 French. A drinking-vessel with elongated spout, formerly used by travellers, invalids, and children.

bibi /ˈbiːbiː/ *noun* (also **beebee**) E19 Urdu (*bībī* from Persian). In the Indian subcontinent: a mistress of a household; a non-European female consort.

bibliotheca /ˌbɪbliəˈθiːkə/ *noun* E18 Latin (from Greek *bibliothēkē* library, from *biblion* book + *thēkē* repository). A collection of books or treatises; a library; a bibliographer's catalogue.

■ Following St Jerome, *bibliotheca* was used in both medieval Latin and Old English to mean 'the Bible'. In Anglo-Latin it occurs interchangeably with *biblia* in an eleventh-century catalogue of the library of Lindisfarne, but by time of the compilation of the thirteenth-century Durham catalogue only *biblia* appears. By the end of that century the Middle English *bibul* and its many variants, from which Modern English *bible* derives, had replaced *bibliotheca* in the vernacular. The modern reintroduction into English of *bibliotheca* in a bibliographical sense is thus entirely separate from the earlier biblical sense and relies on learned Latin usage. *Bibliotheca annua* (1700–4), an annual catalogue of English and Latin books published in England, was an early example. Since the nineteenth century *bibliotheca* has been used in titles of series (e.g. *Bryophytorum bibliotheca*; *Bibliotheca Americana Vetustissima*) or individual bibliographies (e.g. *Bibliotheca arcana* (1885), a catalogue of banned erotica; *Bibliotheca chemica* (1906), a catalogue of alchemical works).

bibliothèque /bibljɔtɛk/ *noun* plural pronounced same M16 French (from as BIBLIOTHECA). A library.

■ Formerly naturalized, but now treated as French.

bidet /'bi:deɪ/ *noun* M17 French (from earlier sense 'pony', from *bider* to trot, of unknown origin). **1** M17 A small horse. *archaic.* **2** L18 A shallow oval basin on a low stand used for washing especially the genital and anal regions.

■ The evolution of sense 2 from sense 1 is explained in Grose's definition of *bidet* in his *Dictionary of the Vulgar Tongue* (1785): 'commonly pronounced biddy, a kind of tub, contrived for ladies to wash themselves, for which purpose they bestride it like a little French poney, ... called in France bidets.

bidon /bidɔ̃/ *noun* plural pronounced same M19 French. A container for liquids; a petrol tin, oil can, etc.

    1964 E. Ambler *Kind of Anger* Get the car filled up. Adèle left me two *bidons* for emergencies.

bidonville /'bi:d(ə)nvɪl/; *foreign* /bidɔ̃vil/ (*plural same*) *noun* M20 French (from BIDON + *ville* town). A shanty-town built of oil drums etc., *especially* a slum on the outskirts of a French or North African city.

bien entendu /bjɛ̃ ɑ̃tɑ̃dy/ *adverb phrase* M19 French (from *bien* well + *entendu* past participle of *entendre* to hear, understand). Of course; that goes without saying.

bien-être /bjɛ̃nɛtr/ *noun* M19 French (from *bien* well + *être* to be). A state of well-being.

biennale /bi:ɛ'nɑ:li/ *noun* M20 Italian (from Latin *biennis* of two years). A large art exhibition or music festival, especially one held every two years.

■ Originally a specific festival, the Biennale, held biennially in Venice, Italy.

biennium /bʌɪ'ɛnɪəm/ *noun* plural **bienniums, biennia** /bʌɪ'ɛnɪə/ E20 Latin (from as *bi-* two + *annus* year). A period of two years.

bien pensant /bjɛ̃ pɑ̃sɑ̃/ *adjective & noun phrase* Also **bien-pensant** (plural pronounced same) E20 French (*bien* well, *pensant* present participle of *penser* to think). (A person who is) right-thinking.

■ Often with a derogatory implication of timorous or mindless compliance with current intellectual or moral fashion (see quotations).

    noun phrase **1995** *Times* In this form of journo-speak, a Tory 'right winger' is someone who believes in: hanging, low taxes, large armies, standards in schools, . . . and a ragbag of other items which offend the *bien pensants*.

adjective phrase **1996** *Spectator* I ask him if Ms Roddick's liberal embrace of every *bien-pensant* cause does not lead to jumping on every passing bandwagon.

bienséance /bjɛ̃seɑ̃s/ *noun* L17 French (from *bien* well + *séant*, from *seoir* to befit). Decorum.

bierhaus /'bi:rhaʊs/ *noun* plural **bierhäuser** /'bi:rhɔyzər/ M20 German (from *Bier* beer + *Haus* house). In a German-speaking country: a public house or alehouse.

Bierstube /'bi:rʃtu:bə/, *noun* plural **Bierstuben** /'bi:rʃtu:bən/, **Bierstubes** E20 German (from *Bier* beer + *Stube* room). A German tavern, taproom, or bar. Cf. WEINSTUBE.

bigarade /bɪgə'rɑ:d/ *foreign* /bigarad/ (*plural same*) *noun* E18 French (from Provençal *bigarrado*). The Spanish bitter orange.

bigarreau /'bɪgərəʊ/ *noun* plural **bigarreaus, bigareaux** (pronounced same) E17 French (from *bigarré* variegated). A variety of sweet cherry, usually heart-shaped and with firm flesh. In full *bigarreau cherry*.

bijou /'bi:ʒu:/, *foreign* /biʒu/ *noun & adjective* M17 French (from Breton *bizoù* fingerring, from *biz* finger). **A** *noun* M17 plural **bijoux** /'bi:ʒu:(z)/, *foreign* /biʒu/. A jewel, a trinket. **B** *adjective* M19 Small and elegant.

    B 1996 *Bookseller* Shops dealing exclusively in English language books in the south of France tend to be bijou in size.

bijouterie /biʒutri/ *noun* E19 French. Jewellery, trinkets, etc.

Bildungsroman /'bɪldʊŋzro͵mɑ:n/ *noun* plural **Bildungsromane** /'bɪldʊŋzro͵mɑ:nə/ E20 German (from *Bildung* education + *Roman* novel). A novel dealing with one person's formative years or spiritual education.

    1995 *Times* His long, indulgent autobiography, *What's It All About?*, is a kind of *bildungsroman* about how Maurice Joseph Micklewhite, Jr. became Michael Caine.

billabong /'bɪləbɒŋ/ *noun* M19 Aboriginal (*Billibang* Bell River, from *billa* water + *bang* channel dry except after rain). In Australia: a branch of a river, forming a blind channel, backwater, or stagnant pool.

billet-doux /bɪlɪ'du:/ *noun* plural **billets-doux** /bɪlɪ'du:z/ L17 French (literally, 'sweet note'). A love-letter.

■ Now chiefly jocular.

biltong /ˈbɪltɒŋ/ *noun* E19 Afrikaans (from Dutch *bil* buttock + *tong* tongue). In South Africa: lean meat cut into strips and dried.

bimbo /ˈbɪmbəʊ/ *noun* plural **bimbos, bimboes** E20 Italian (= small child, baby). **1** E20 A chap, *especially* a young and foolish one. **2** E20 A young woman, *especially* one that is sexually attractive but empty-headed.

■ Now used in a slang and almost always derogatory sense, *bimbo* was originally a direct borrowing from Italian. P. G. Wodehouse used it in sense 1 (see quotation 1947), but it was already current in the 1920s with the sense of a pretty but brainless tart. *Bimbo* was revived in the 1980s media to designate a young woman who has an affair with a rich or famous man and then sells the 'revelations' to the popular press. The word has also spawned a number of derivatives: *bimbette* (a teenage bimbo), *bimboy* (a male bimbo), *bimboland*, etc.

1 1947 P. G. Wodehouse *Full Moon* ... bimbos who went about the place making passes at innocent girls after discarding their wives.

2 1988 *Independent* In the strict sense the bimbo exists on the fringes of pornography, and some cynics might say she has the mental capacity of a minor kitchen appliance.

binghi /ˈbɪŋʌɪ/ *noun* M19 Aboriginal. An Aborigine.

■ Originally a neutral word (R. Dawson in *Present State of Australia* (1831) mentions having been greeted by Aborigines as 'bingeye, or brother'), *binghi* has become an Australian slang term and usually derogatory.

bint /bɪnt/ *noun* M19 Arabic (= daughter, girl). A girl, a woman; (formerly) a girl friend.

■ Mainly servicemen's slang, used by personnel stationed in Egypt and elsewhere in the Middle East during the two world wars; usually derogatory.

1958 K. Amis *I Like It Here* As the R.A.F. friend would have put it, you could never tell with these foreign bints.

biretta /bɪˈrɛtə/ *noun* (also **beretta, birretta**) L16 Italian (*berretta* or Spanish *birreta*, feminine diminutives corresponding to Old Provençal *berret* beret, based on late Latin *birrus, birettum* hooded cape or cloak, perhaps of Celtic origin). A square cap worn by Roman Catholic ecclesiastics (black by priests, purple by bishops, red by cardinals) or by other clergymen.

biriani variant of BIRYANI.

birretta variant of BIRETTA.

biryani /brˈrjɑːni/, /bɪrɪˈɑːni/ *noun* (also **biriani** and other variants) M20 Urdu (from Persian *biryānī*, from *biriyān* fried, grilled). A dish of the Indian subcontinent consisting of spiced meat or vegetables and cooked rice.

bis /bis/ *adverb* E17 French and Italian (from Latin *bis* twice). Encore; again; twice; *specifically* as a direction in a musical score indicating that a passage is to be repeated.

bismillah /bɪsˈmɪlə/ *interjection & noun* L18 Arabic (*bi-smi-llāh(i)*, the first word of the Koran). (The exclamation) in the name of God: used by Muslims at the beginning of any undertaking.

bisque /bɪsk/ *noun* 1 M17 French (of unknown origin). In various games, especially tennis, croquet, and golf, (the allowing of) a point or stroke to be scored or taken when desired as a handicapping advantage.

bisque /bɪsk/ *noun* 2 M17 French (from Old French *bescuit, besquit*, ultimately from Latin *bis* twice + *coctus* past participle of *coquere* to cook). A variety of unglazed white porcelain used for statuettes etc. Also porcelain that has undergone firing but no other treatment; biscuit.

bisque /bɪsk/, /biːsk/ *noun* 3 (also **bisk** /bɪsk/) M17 French (= crayfish soup). A rich soup usually made from shellfish but also from birds etc.

bistre /ˈbɪstə/ *noun* (also **bister**) E18 French (of unknown origin). (The colour of) a brown pigment prepared from soot.

bistro /ˈbiːstrəʊ/, /ˈbɪstrəʊ/ *noun* (also **bistrot**) plural **bistros** E20 French. A small wine-bar or restaurant.

bivouac /ˈbɪvʊak/, /ˈbɪvwak/ *noun & verb* E18 French (probably from Swiss German *Biwacht*, literally, 'extra watch'). **A** *noun* E18 Originally, a night-watch by a whole army. Later, a temporary encampment, usually for the night, without tents; the place of such an encampment. **B** *intransitive & intransitive verb* E19 in pass. Inflected **bivouack**. Remain in the open air (especially during the night) without tents etc.

■ The Swiss word is said to have been used in Aargau and Zürich to denote a patrol of citizens to assist the ordinary town watch.

bizarre /brˈzɑː/ *adjective & noun* M17 French (from Italian *bizzarro* angry, of unknown origin. Cf. Spanish and Portuguese *bizarro* handsome, brave). **A** *adjective* **1** M17 Eccentric, fantastic, grotesque. **2** M18 Designating variegated forms of garden flowers, as carnations, tulips, etc. **B** *noun* **1** L18 A bizarre carnation, tulip, etc. **2** M19 *absolutely* The bizarre quality of things; bizarre things.

blague /blag/ *noun* M19 French. Humbug, claptrap.

blagueur /blagœr/ *noun* plural pronounced same L19 French (from BLAGUE). A pretentious talker; a joker, a teller of tall stories.

blanc /blɑ̃/ *noun* plural pronounced same M18 French (= white). **1** M18 White paint, especially for the face. Now *archaic* or *historical*. **2** M19 A type of light-coloured stock or gravy.

blancbec /blɑ̃bɛk/ *noun* plural pronounced same M19 French (literally, 'white beak'). A raw youngster, a greenhorn.

blanc de blanc /blɑ̃ də blɑ̃/ *noun phrase* M20 French. A (usually sparkling) white wine made from white grapes only.

blanc de chine /blɑ̃ də ʃin/ *noun phrase* L19 French. A white glazed Chinese porcelain, especially of the Ming period. Also called Dehua after its place of origin.

blanc de perle /blɑ̃ də pɛrl/ *adjective phrase* L19 French. Pearl-white.

blanc fixe /blɑ̃ fiks/ *noun phrase* M19 French. Barium sulphate, especially as used in paints.

blancmange /bləˈmɒnʒ/, /bləˈmɑːnʒ/ *noun* (also (earlier) **blancmanger**) LME Old French (*blanc mangier* (modern *blancmanger*), from *blanc* white + *mang(i)er* food, use as noun of *mang(i)er* to eat.). **1** LME–L15 A dish of white meat or fish in a cream sauce. **2** M16 An opaque jelly made with isinglass or gelatin and milk or (now usually) cornflour and milk, often flavoured and sweetened.

■ The terminal 'r' was dropped in the eighteenth century.

blanquette /blɑ̃kɛt/ *noun* plural pronounced same M18 French (from Old French *blanchet* from *blanc*, *blanche* white). A dish of light meat, especially veal, cooked in a white sauce.

blasé /ˈblɑːzeɪ/ *adjective* E19 French. Cloyed with or tired of pleasure; bored or unimpressed by things from having seen or experienced them too often.

1996 *Oldie* We have also survived scares about yoghurt . . . , microwave cookers, television sets, computers, salami (contains nitrate), etc, and have now got blasé about it all.

bled /blɛd/ *noun* M20 French (from colloquial (Algerian) Arabic, corresponding to classical Arabic *balad* vast stretch of country, *bilād* land, country). In north-west Africa: uncultivated land behind a fertile populated area.

bleu-du-roi /blødyrwa/ *noun & adjective* (also **bleu-de-roi** /blødərwa/) M19 French (= king's blue). (Of) the ultramarine blue of Sèvres porcelain.

blin /blm/ *noun* plural **blini, bliny** /ˈblmi/, **blinis** /ˈblmɪz/ L19 Russian. A kind of pancake, frequently stuffed. Cf. BLINTZE.

blintze /blm(t)s/ *noun* E20 Yiddish (*blintse* from Russian *blinets* diminutive of *blin*). A BLIN.

blitzkrieg /ˈblɪtskriːg/ *noun* (also **Blitzkrieg**) M20 German (from *Blitz* lightning + *Krieg* war). A violent campaign intended to bring about speedy victory.

■ Used specifically of the German military campaigns in World War Two, *Blitzkrieg* is usually found in the abbreviated form *Blitz* with reference to the Luftwaffe's bombardment of British cities. Both *blitzkrieg* and *blitz* are in general metaphorical use (see quotation).

1996 *New Scientist* The Japanese blitzkrieg on Western markets was in full swing in the early 1980s.

bloc /blɒk/ *noun* E20 French (= block, from Middle Dutch *blok*, Middle and Modern Low German *block*, of unknown origin). A combination of nation-states, parties, groups, or people, formed to promote a particular interest.

blond /blɒnd/ *adjective & noun* (also **blonde**) L15 Old and Modern French (from medieval Latin *blundus*, *blondus* yellow, perhaps of Germanic origin). **A** *adjective* L15 (Especially of the hair) of a light golden-brown colour, flaxen, fair; (of the complexion) light-coloured with fair hair. **B** *noun* M18 A person (especially a woman) with blond hair and complexion.

■ The feminine form of the adjective *blonde* was introduced from French in the seventeenth century, but the masculine/feminine distinction is often not observed in English usage, with *blonde* being used of both men and women.

blouson /'blu:zɒn/, *foreign* /bluzɔ̃/ (*plural same*) *noun* E20 French. A short jacket fitting loosely on the body like a blouse.

blutwurst /'blʌtwɜːst/ *foreign* /'blʊtvʊrst/ *noun* M19 German (from *Blut* blood + *Wurst* sausage). (A) black pudding.

bocage /bə'kɑːʒ/, *foreign* /bɔkaʒ/ (*plural same*) *noun* L16 French. **1** L16 Wooded country interspersed with pasture (in France); a thicket, a wood. **2** *Ceramics* E20 (A, the) representation of silvan scenery (especially a leafy tree stump or flowery arbour) as a decorative element but also as a support for a figure during firing. Frequently *attributive*.

boccaro /'bɒkərəʊ/ *noun* (also **bucaro, buccaro** /'bʌkərəʊ/) plural **boccaros** L19 Spanish (*búcaro* from Portuguese *púcaro* clay cup, ultimately from Latin *poculum* cup). A scented red unglazed earthenware of a type originally made in Mexico and imitated in Spain and Portugal.

bodega /bə'diːgə/, *foreign* /bo'dega/ *noun* M19 Spanish (from Latin *apotheca* from Greek *apothēkē* storehouse; *cf.* BOUTIQUE). (Originally in Spain) a shop selling wine.

bodegón /bode'gon/ *noun* plural **bodegones** /bode'gones/ M19 Spanish (from BODEGA, as originally representing a bodega scene). A Spanish picture representing still life or a genre subject.

Boer /bɔː/, /'bəʊə/, /bʊə/ *noun & adjective* (also **boer**) M19 Dutch (*boer* farmer). **A** *noun* M19 A South African of Dutch descent, an Afrikaner; *History* an early Dutch inhabitant of the Cape. **B** *attributive* or as *adjective* Of, made by, or typical of Boers.

boerewors /'bɔːrəvɔːs/ *noun* M20 Afrikaans (from *boer* farmer + *wors* sausage). (A) coarse sausage made with beef and pork.

1950 L. G. Green *Land of Afternoon* Boerewors is another farm product which some still make in the old way; a sausage in which the meat has been pounded with a wooden stamper rather than minced.

bœuf /bœf/ *noun* E20 French (= beef). *Cookery* Used in the names of various beef dishes.

bœuf bourguignon /bœf burgiɲɔ̃/ *noun phrase* E20 French (= beef of Burgundy). *Cookery* A casserole of beef cooked slowly in red wine.

bois brûlé /bwa bryle/ *noun phrase* plural **bois brûlés** (pronounced same) E19 French (= burnt wood). In North America: a half-breed, especially one of French and American Indian descent.

boiserie /bwazri/ *noun* M19 French. Wainscoting, wooden panelling.

boîte /bwat/ *noun* plural (pronounced same) E20 French (= box). A small (French) restaurant or nightclub.

bolas /'bəʊləs/ *noun singular* (with plural **bolases**) or *plural* (also *singular* **bola** /'bəʊlə/) E19 Spanish and Portuguese (plural of *bola* ball). A missile (chiefly South American) consisting of balls connected by a strong cord, which is thrown to entangle the legs of a quarry.

bolero /bə'lɛːrəʊ/, in sense 2 also /'bɒlərəʊ/ *noun* plural **boleros** L18 Spanish. **1** L18 A lively Spanish dance; a piece of music for this dance. **2** L19 A short jacket just reaching the waist, worn by men in Spain; a woman's short open jacket, with or without sleeves.

boletus /bə'liːtəs/ *noun* (also Anglicized as **bolet** /bə'lɛt/, **bolete** /bə'liːt/) E16 Latin (*boletus* from Greek *bōlitēs*, perhaps from *bōlos* lump). A mushroom or toadstool of the large genus *Boletus*, having the undersurface of the cap full of pores.

Bolshevik /'bɒlʃɪvɪk/ *noun & adjective* (also **bolshevik**) E20 Russian (*bol'shevik* = member of the majority, from *bol'she* greater, from *bol'shoi* big). **A** *noun* **1** E20 *History* A member of the majority faction of the Russian Social-Democratic Party, which in 1903 favoured extreme measures; an advocate of proletarian dictatorship in Russia by soviets; a Russian Communist. **2** E20 *general* A socialist revolutionary. **B** *adjective* E20 Of or pertaining to Bolsheviks or Bolshevism.

bolson /'bəʊls(ə)n/ *noun* M19 Spanish (*bolsón* augmentative of *bolsa* purse). A basin-shaped depression surrounded by mountains, especially in the southern United States and Mexico.

■ Originally United States; *cf.* Bolsón de Mapimí, the name of a high desert in Mexico.

bolus /'bəʊləs/ *noun* M16 Late Latin (from Greek *bōlos* clod, lump of earth). **1** M16 A large pill of medicine. Often *contemptuous* or *archaic* except in *Veterinary Medicine*. **2** L18 A small rounded mass of anything, especially of masticated food at the moment of swallowing. **3** M20 *Medicine* A single dose of a pharmaceutical preparation given intravenously.

boma /ˈbəʊmə/ *noun* L19 Kiswahili. In East Africa: a defensible enclosure, especially for animals; hence, a police or military post; a magistrate's office.

bombachas /bɒmˈbatʃəz/ *noun plural* M20 South American Spanish (from *bombacho* loose-fitting, wide). Baggy trousers worn in some South American countries.

bombe /bɒmb/, *foreign* /bɔ̃b/ (*plural same*) *noun* L19 French (= bomb). A conical or cup-shaped confection, frequently frozen.

bombé /bɔ̃be/ *adjective* E20 French (past participle of *bomber* to swell out). Especially of furniture: rounded, convex.

bombilla /bɒmˈbɪljə/ *noun* M19 American Spanish (diminutive of Spanish *bomba* strainer). A tube with a strainer at the end, from which maté is drunk in South America.

bombora /bɒmˈbɔːrə/ *noun* M20 Aboriginal. In Australia and New Zealand: a dangerous stretch of water where waves break over a submerged reef.

bon /bɔ̃/ *adjective* L16 French (= good (masculine; cf. BONNE)). Good.
■ In various phrases used in English (see entries below).

bona fide /ˌbəʊnə ˈfʌɪdi/ *adverb & adjective phrase* M16 Latin (= with good faith (ablative of next)). (Acting or done) in good faith; sincere(ly), genuine(ly).
1996 *Times* We hear echoes of it in Top 40 songs, but we seldom, if ever, see a bona fide gospel singer in the chart shows.

bona fides /ˌbəʊnə ˈfʌɪdiːz/ *noun phrase* L18 Latin (= good faith). **1** L18 Good faith, freedom from intent to deceive. **2** M20 (erroneously treated as plural) Guarantees of good faith, credentials.

bonanza /bəˈnanzə/ *noun & adjective* E19 Spanish (= fair weather, prosperity, from Latin *bonus* good). **A** *noun* E19 A run of good luck, an unexpected success; prosperity; a source of great wealth or good fortune. **B** *adjective* L19 Greatly prospering or productive.
■ Originally used among miners in the United States for 'a rich find' or 'lucky strike'.
1996 *Country Life* Daffodil growers . . . , who missed their usual £10 million bonanza on Mothering Sunday because cold weather delayed flowering, are setting their sights on Easter.

bon appétit /bɔn apeti/, /bɒn apəˈtiː/ *interjection* M19 French. Good appetite!
■ Used as a salutation to people about to eat.

bon-bon /ˈbɒnbɒn/ *noun* L18 French (literally, 'good-good'). A piece of confectionery, a sweet.

bonbonnière /bɔ̃bɔnjɛr/ *noun plural* pronounced same E19 French. A fancy box for holding sweets.
1996 *Country Life* As an amusement, I would far rather have had a bonbonnière by an unidentified 18th-century German factory. It was of a crouching and concentrating cat . . .

bond /bɒnt/ *noun* (also **Bond**) L19 Afrikaans (from Dutch (= German *Bund*), from *binden* bind). In South Africa: an Afrikaner league or association, especially the extreme nationalist *Broederbond*.

bondieuserie /bɔ̃djøzri/ *noun plural* pronounced same M20 French (from *bon* good + *Dieu* God). A church ornament or devotional object, *especially* one of little artistic merit; such objects collectively.
■ The French journalist and novelist Jules Vallès (1832–85) is credited with the invention of the term.

bon enfant /bɔn ɑ̃fɑ̃/ *noun phrase* M19 French (literally, 'good child'). An agreeable companion.

bongo /ˈbɒŋgəʊ/ *noun plural* **bongo(e)s** E20 American Spanish (*bongó*). Either of a pair of small drums, usually held between the knees and played with the fingers. Also *bongo-drum(s)*.

bon gré mal gré /bɔ̃ gre mal gre/ *adverb phrase* E19 French (literally, 'good will, bad will'). (Whether) willingly or unwillingly.

bonheur du jour /bɔnœr dy ʒur/ *noun phrase plural* **bonheurs du jour** (pronounced same) L19 French (literally, 'happiness of the day'). A small writing-table, usually fitted to hold toilet accessories, popular in eighteenth-century France.

bonhomie /ˈbɒnəmi/ *noun* (also formerly written **bonhommie**) L18 French (from *bonhomme* good man, from medieval Latin *bonus homo* + suffix *-ie*). Good-natured friendliness, geniality.
1992 A. Lambert *A Rather English Marriage* Reginald was bluff and cheery, spreading enough bonhomie to fuel a party.

bonito /bəˈniːtəʊ/ *noun plural* **bonitos** (also **boneta** /bəˈniːtə/) L16 Spanish. Any of various striped tuna, especially *Sarda sarda* of the Atlantic and Mediterranean.

bonjour /'bɔʒur/ *interjection* L16 French. Good day! Hallo!

■ Used as a general greeting.

bon mot /bɔ̃ mo/ *noun phrase* plural **bons mots** (pronounced same) M18 French (literally, 'good word'). A witty remark, a clever saying.

1995 *Spectator* When King Louis-Philippe was told that Talleyrand had died he was heard to mutter: 'Died, has he? I wonder what he meant by that.' It seems a shame to deprive Louis-Philippe of some of his few recorded *bons mots* and ascribe it to Talleyrand, who has plenty to his credit.

bonne /bɔn/ *adjective & noun* E16 French (feminine of BON). **A** *adjective* E16 Good. **B** *noun* L18 A (French) nursemaid or personal servant.

■ Use as an adjective has long been restricted to certain phrases adopted from French (see below) and the nominal use too is now rare.

bonne bouche /bɔn buʃ/ *noun phrase* (also **bonne-bouche**) plural **bonnes bouches** (pronounced same) M18 French (literally, 'good mouth'). A dainty morsel, a titbit, especially one at the end of a meal; also *figurative*.

■ In French the sense is 'a pleasing taste in the mouth', which has been understood in English as the delicacy that gives this.

1996 *Times* Let us begin with a *bonne-bouche* before we tuck in.

bonne femme /bɔn fam/ *adjective phrase* E19 French (literally, 'in the manner of a good housewife'). *Cookery* (Of a dish of food) prepared in a particular way.

■ Also in the fuller form *à la bonne femme*, both used postpositively, as in 'sole *bonne femme*'.

bonne fortune /bɔn fɔrtyn/ *noun phrase* plural **bonnes fortunes** (pronounced same) E19 French (literally, 'good fortune'). A lady's favours, seen as a cause for self-congratulation on the part of their receipient.

bonsai /'bɒnsʌɪ/ *noun* plural same E20 Japanese (from *bon* tray + *sai* planting). The (Japanese) practice of cultivating artificially dwarfed potted plants or small trees; a plant or tree cultivated by this method.

bon ton /bɔn tɔ̃/ *noun phrase* M18 French (literally, 'good tone') . The fashionable world.

bon vivant /bɔ̃ vivã/ *noun phrase* plural **bons vivants** (pronounced same) L17 French (literally, '(a person) who lives well'). A gourmand, an epicure.

■ In contemporary usage *bon vivant* and BON VIVEUR appear interchangeably in a general sense of someone with a self-indulgent lifestyle (see quotation).

1996 *Times* Nor does it mean that the *bon vivant* has renounced his ways. 'Don't worry, . . . [the] fun and sex are not over yet.'

bon viveur /bɔ̃ vivœr/ *noun phrase* plural **bons viveurs** (pronounced same) M19 pseudo-French (formed after BON VIVANT). A person who indulges a taste for the good things of life.

1995 *Spectator* Roy Hattersley, politician, man of letters, *bon viveur*, is one of public life's polymaths.

bon voyage /bɒn vwa'jɑ:ʒ/ *interjection* L17 French (literally, 'good journey'). Pleasant journey!

■ Used as a farewell to a person about to travel.

bonze /bɒnz/ *noun* L16 French (*bonze* or Portuguese *bonzo* probably from Japanese *bonzō, bonsō* priest). A Japanese or Chinese Buddhist religious teacher.

boomerang /'bu:məraŋ/ *noun & verb* L18 Aboriginal (perhaps modified: cf. Kamilaroi *būmarin*). **A** *noun* **1** L18 A thin curved hardwood missile (of a kind) used by Australian Aborigines as a hunting weapon, *especially* one that can be thrown so as to return to the thrower. **2** M19 *figurative* A scheme etc. that recoils on its originator. **B** *intransitive verb* L19 Act as a boomerang; *figurative* recoil on the originator.

boondock /'bu:ndɒk/ *noun* M20 Tagalog (*bundok* mountain). Rough or isolated country; remote parts.

■ North American slang, originally used by service personnel. It appears infrequently in the singular, more usually in the plural, and often in the phrase (*out*) *in the boondocks*.

bordello /bɔː'dɛləʊ/ *noun* plural **bordellos** L16 Italian (from medieval Latin *bordellum*). A brothel.

1996 *Times* The management skills involved in running a chain of hotels, discotheques, pubs or theme restaurants are no different from those needed for bordellos.

bordereau /bɔːdə'rəʊ/, *foreign* /bɔrdəro/ *noun* plural **bordereaux** /bɔːdə'rəʊz/, *foreign* /bɔrdəro/ L19 French (diminutive of *bord* board). A memorandum of contents, a schedule, a docket.

borné /bɔrne/ *adjective* L18 French (past participle of *borner* to limit). Limited in scope, intellect, outlook, etc.

bortsch /bɔːtʃ/ *noun* (also **borsch** /bɔːʃ/, **borstch** /bɔːstʃ/) E19 Russian (*borshch*). A Russian or Polish soup of various ingredients including beetroot and cabbage.

bosquet /'bɒskɪt/ *noun* (also **bosket**) M18 French (from Italian *boschetto* diminutive of *bosco* wood; cf. BOUQUET). A plantation of small trees in a garden, park, etc.; a thicket.

bossage /'bɒsɪdʒ/ *noun* E18 French (from *bosse* boss). *Architecture* Projecting stonework, bosses; *especially* a type of rustic work.

bossa nova /ˌbɒsə 'nəʊvə/ *noun phrase* M20 Portuguese (*bossa* tendency, *nova* feminine singular of *novo* new). A style of Brazilian music related to the samba; a dance to this music.

> **1995** *Spectator* A 'bossa' is a hump on an ox's back, and thus idiomatically 'bossa nova' means something like 'new commotion' or 'new wrinkle'.

botargo /bə'tɑːgəʊ/ *noun* plural **botargo(e)s** L16 Italian (from (medieval) Greek *arghotarakho*, perhaps through Pontic dialect *ovotarakho*). A relish made of the roe of the mullet or tuna.

boucan /'buːk(ə)n/ *noun* (also **buccan** /'bʌk(ə)n/) E17 French (from Tupi *mukem*, *mocaém*). **1** E17 In South America: a wooden frame for cooking, smoking, or drying meat over an open fire. **2** M19 Meat cooked or cured on such a frame. **3** M19 An open floor on which coffee beans etc. may be spread out to dry.

bouchée /buʃe/ *noun* plural pronounced same M19 French (= mouthful, from *bouche* mouth). A small baked confection.
> ■ Usually in plural.

bouclé /'buːkleɪ/ *adjective & noun* L19 French (= buckled, curled). (Fabric) woven with a knotted and curled appearance; (yarn) of looped or curled ply.

boudin /'buːdɪn/, *foreign* /budɛ̃/ (*plural* same) *noun* E20 French. *Geology* Any of a number of roughly parallel elongated sections resulting from the fracturing of a rock stratum during folding.
> ■ Although recorded earlier (M19) with its current French meaning of 'a black pudding', *boudin* has never been entirely naturalized in this sense.

boudoir /'buːdwɑː/ *noun* L18 French (literally, 'place to sulk in', from *bouder* to pout, sulk). A (woman's) small private room.

bouffant /'buːfɑ̃/ *noun & adjective* E19 French (present participle of *bouffer* to swell). **A** *noun* E19 A puffed-out part of a dress etc.; a puffed-out hairstyle. **B** *adjective* L19 Of a dress, hairstyle, etc.: puffed out.
> **A 1996** *Times* Hoddle has come a long way since the days when he sported first a Keeganesque bouffant and then hair straggling sweatily down his neck.

bougie /'buːʒi/ *noun* M18 French (from *Bougie* (Arabic *Bijāya*) a town in Algeria which carried on a trade in wax). **1** M18 A wax candle. **2** M18 *Medicine* A rod or tube for exploring or dilating the passages of the body.

bouillabaisse /buːjə'beɪs/, *foreign* /bujabɛs/ *noun* M19 French (from Modern Provençal *bouiabaisso*). A Provençal dish of fish stewed in water or white wine. Also *figurative*.
> **1996** *Times* Emerging from this bouillabaisse of complaints, however, is one certainty.

bouilli /'buːji/, *foreign* /buji/ *noun* E17 French (use as noun of past participle of *bouillir* to boil). Boiled or stewed meat, especially beef.
> ■ Since the mid eighteenth century often Anglicized as *bully*, especially when referring to beef in the form used for army rations.

bouillon /'buːjɔ̃/, *foreign* /bujɔ̃/ *noun* M17 French (from *bouillir* to boil). Broth, thin soup. See also COURT BOUILLON.

boule /'buːli/ *noun* 1 M19 Greek (*boulē* senate). A legislative body of ancient or modern Greece.

boule /buːl/, *foreign* /bul/ *noun* 2 plural **boules** in sense 2 /buːl/, in sense 3 /buːlz/, *foreign* /bul/ E20 French (= bowl). **1** E20 A form of roulette. **2** E20 (*singular* and in *plural*) A French form of bowls played on rough ground, usually with metal bowls. **3** M20 A small pear-shaped mass of synthetic sapphire, ruby, etc., made by fusing suitably tinted alumina.

boul(l)e variant of BUHL.

boulevard /'buːləvɑː(r)d/, *foreign* /bulvar/ (*plural* same) *noun* M18 French ((originally) = rampart, (later) a promenade on the site of this). A broad street (especially in France) with rows of trees planted along it; *United States* a broad main urban road.

boulevardier /bulvardje/ *noun* plural pronounced same L19 French (from *boulevard* + *-ier*). A person who frequents (French) boulevards.

bouleversé /bulvɛrse/ *adjective* M19 French (past participle of *bouleverser* to turn as a ball, from as BOULE (*noun* 2) + *verser* to turn). Amazed, upset, completely taken aback.

1995 *Times* The rest of the world was *bouleversé* by this week's letter from Pope John Paul lauding feminism and apologising to women for centuries of hardship and exclusion.

bouleversement /bulvɛrsəmɑ̃/ *noun* plural pronounced same L18 French (from as preceding). An inversion, *especially* a violent one; an upset, an upheaval.

bouquet /bʊ'keɪ/, /bəʊ'keɪ/, /'bʊkeɪ/ *noun* E18 French ((earlier = clump of trees), from dialectal variant of Old French *bos*, *bois* wood). **1** E18 A bunch of flowers, *especially* a large attractive one for use at a ceremony. **b** E20 *figurative* A compliment. **2** M19 The perfume of wine etc. **3** M19 A BOUQUET GARNI. **4** L19 A number of rockets etc. fired together.

bouquet garni /bʊkeɪ 'gɑːni/ *noun phrase* M19 French (literally, 'garnished bouquet'). *Cookery* A bunch of assorted herbs for flavouring.

bouquetier /bʊkə'tɪə/, *foreign* /buktje/ *noun* L18 French. A small holder for a posy of flowers, especially one to be carried in the hand.

bourdon /'bʊəd(ə)n/ *noun* (also **burdoun**) ME Old and Modern French (= drone, from Proto-Romance, of imitative origin). **1** ME The bass or undersong of a melody. **2** M19 A low-pitched stop in an organ or harmonium; the drone pipe of a bagpipe. **3** E20 The lowest-pitched in a peal of bells.

■ *Bourdon* in sense 1 soon merged with the same sense of *burden* and is now rare or obsolete with its original meaning; sense 2 is a reintroduction.

bourg /bʊəg/ *noun* LME Old and Modern French (from medieval Latin *burgus* borough). A town or village under the shadow of a castle (*historical*); an ancient town in continental Europe.

bourgade /burgad/ *noun* plural pronounced same E17 French (from as preceding + *-ade*). A large village or straggling unwalled town in Europe.

bourgeois /'bʊəʒwɑː/, *foreign* /burʒwa/ *adjective* & *noun* M16 French. **A** *adjective* **1** M16 Of, pertaining to, characteristic of, or resembling, the bourgeois (see sense B below); middle-class; conventionally respectable and unimaginative, humdrum; selfishly materialistic; capitalistic, reactionary. **2** E20 Of French wine: next in quality to wines classified as the best. **B** *noun* plural same. **1** L17 Originally, a (French) citizen or freeman of a city or burgh, as distinct from a peasant or a gentleman. Now, any member of the middle class. **2** L19 In Communist or socialist writing: a capitalist, an exploiter of the proletariat. *derogatory*. **3** M20 A socially or aesthetically conventional person, a philistine. *derogatory*.

bourgeoise /'bʊəʒwɑːz/, *foreign* /burʒwaz/ *noun* & *adjective* plural of noun pronounced same L18 French (feminine of preceding). **A** *noun* L18 A female bourgeois. **B** *adjective* M20 Of a female: bourgeois.

bourgeoisie /ˌbʊəʒwɑː'ziː/, *foreign* /burʒwazi/ *noun* E18 French (from BOURGEOIS). The bourgeois collectively; the middle class.

bourrée /'bʊəreɪ/, *foreign* /bure/ (*plural* same) *noun* L17 French. A lively dance of French origin, resembling the gavotte; a piece of music for this dance or in its rhythm, *especially* one which forms a movement of a suite.

■ In a *bourrée* step the dancer moves sideways, with one foot crossing behind or in front of the other.

bourse /bʊəs/ *noun* L16 French. A money market; *especially* (the Bourse) the Paris stock exchange; *transferred* an exchange.

1996 *Times* For diplomats used to trading sovereignty for influence in the Brussels *bourse*, the thought that sovereignty might be retrieved, and independence asserted, is deeply uncongenial.

boustrophedon /baʊstrə'fiːd(ə)n/, /buːstrə'fiːd(ə)n/ *adverb* & *adjective* E17 Greek (= as the ox turns in ploughing, from *bous* ox + *strophos* twist + adverbial suffix *-don*). (Written) from right to left and from left to right in alternate lines.

boutade /buː'tɑːd/ *noun* E17 French (from *bouter* to thrust). A sudden outburst or outbreak.

boutique /buːˈtiːk/ *noun* M18 French (from Old Provençal *botica* (Italian *bottega*) from Latin *apotheca* from Greek *apothēkē* storehouse: cf. BODEGA). A small shop. Now usually a shop, or a department in a large store, selling (especially fashionable) clothes or accessories.

bouton /ˈbuːtɒn/ *noun* M19 French (= button). **1** M19 A round pearl with a flat back. In full *bouton pearl*. **2** M20 Anatomy An enlarged part of a nerve fibre or cell, especially an axon, where it forms a synapse.

boutonnière /ˌbuːtɒnˈjɛː/, *foreign* /butɔnjɛr/ (*plural same*) *noun* L19 French. A flower or posy worn in a lapel buttonhole.

> **1996** *Times: Weekend* Reno is noted for being a wedding factory town, where one enterprising local chapel offers an all-inclusive nuptial special for $129 . . . in addition to a free *boutonnière* for the groom . . .

bouts rimés /buː riːˈmeɪ/ *noun phrase plural* E18 French (= rhymed endings). Rhyming words upon which verses are (to be) composed.

bouzouki /buˈzuːki/ *noun* M20 Modern Greek (*mpouzouki*: cf. Turkish *bozuk* spoilt, i.e. roughly made (instruments)). In Greece: a form of long-necked lute much used in traditional folk music.

boyar /bəʊˈjɑː/ *noun* L16 Russian (*boyarin* grandee). History A member of an order of Russian aristocracy (abolished by Peter the Great), next in rank to a prince.

braai /ˈbrɑːɪ/ *noun & verb* M20 Afrikaans (abbreviation of next). **A** *noun* M20 In South Africa: a barbecue, a BRAAIVLEIS. **B** *transitive & intransitive verb* M20 Grill (meat) over an open fire.

braaivleis /ˈbrɑːɪfleɪs/ *noun* M20 Afrikaans (= grilled meat, from *braai* to grill + *vleis* meat). In South Africa: meat grilled over an open fire; a picnic, barbecue, etc., at which meat is cooked in this way.

braggadocio /bragəˈdəʊtʃɪəʊ/ *noun plural* **braggadocios** L16 pseudo-Italian (fictional name formed from *brag* or *braggart* + Italian augmentative suffix *-occio*). **1** L16 A loud-mouthed braggart, an idle boaster. **2** M18 Empty boasting, bluster.

> ■ *Braggadocchio* is the name of a cowardly braggart in Spenser's *Faerie Queene*, the first part of which was published in 1590: 'Proud *Braggadocchio*, that in vaunting vaine / His glory did repose, and credit did maintaine' (III.viii.11).

> **1996** *Spectator* He drank unwisely and not too well, went in for a deal of Celtic fist-flaying and had a bully's *braggadocio* . . .

brahmacharya /brɑːməˈtʃɑːrɪə/ *noun* E20 Sanskrit (*brahmacarya*, from *bráhman* prayer, worship + *carya* conduct). Purity of life, especially regarding sexual matters.

> ■ Frequently used with reference to the life and teachings of M. K. Gandhi, through whose writings the word entered English.

brahman /ˈbrɑːmən/ *noun* (also **brahma** /ˈbrɑːmə/, **brahm**, **Brahman**) L18 Sanskrit (*bráhman* sacred utterance). In Hindu philosophy: the ultimate reality underlying all phenomena.

brandade /brɑ̃dad/ *noun* E19 French (from Modern Provençal *brandado*, literally, 'thing which has been moved or shaken'). A Provençal dish made from salt cod.

brasserie /ˈbrasəri/ *noun* M19 French ((originally = brewery), from *brasser* to brew). A (French) saloon selling beer and usually food; *generally* an informal restaurant.

brassière /ˈbrasɪə/, /ˈbrazɪə/ *noun* (also **brassiere**) E20 French (= child's reins, camisole, etc.). A woman's shaped undergarment worn to support the breasts.

> ■ The abbreviation *bra* is almost universal in informal contexts.

bratwurst /ˈbratwəːst/, /ˈbratvəːst/ E20 German (from *Brat* a spit (*braten* roast etc.) + *Wurst* sausage). (A) mild-flavoured German pork sausage.

brava /ˈbrɑːvə/ *noun & interjection* E19 Italian (feminine of *bravo*). (A cry addressed to a woman or girl meaning) excellent, well done!

bravo /ˈbrɑːvəʊ/ *noun* 1 plural **bravo(e)s** L16 Italian. A hired ruffian; a desperado.

bravo /brɑːˈvəʊ/, /ˈbrɑːvəʊ/ *interjection & noun* 2 M18 French (from as preceding: cf. BRAVA). **A** *interjection* M18 Excellent, well done! **B** *noun* plural **bravos** M19 A cry of 'bravo!', a cheer.

> **B 1996** *Country Life* There was silence at the close, broken finally by bravos.

bravura /brəˈv(j)ʊərə/ *noun & adjective* M18 Italian (from *bravo* brave). **1** Music M18 (A passage or style, especially of singing) requiring exceptional powers of execution. **2** E19 (A performance that is) brilliant or ambitious; (a display that is) daring, dash(ing).

2 1996 *Spectator* But behind all the bravura lies a new novelist of prodigious talent; one whose voice, only audible when his own comedy has subsided, is a moving, melancholic one.

breccia /'brɛtʃə/, /'brɛtʃɪə/ *noun* L18 Italian (= gravel, rubble, cognate with French *brèche*, German *brechen* from Germanic base of break). *Geology* Rock consisting of angular fragments cemented together e.g. by lime.

brei /brʌɪ/ *noun* M20 German (= pulp, mush, jelly). *Biology* A homogenized pulp of organic tissue prepared for experimental work.

breitschwanz /'brʌɪtʃvɑːnts/ *noun* E20 German (= broad tail). The lustrous pelt of a young karakul lamb.

breloque /brə'ləʊk/ *noun* M19 French. A small ornament fastened to a watch-chain; a trinket.

bretelle /brə'tɛl/ *noun* M19 French (= strap, sling, (in plural) trouser-braces). Each of a pair of ornamental straps extending over the shoulders from the belt on the front of a dress to the belt on the back. Usually in *plural*.

bric-à-brac /'brɪkəbrak/ *noun* (also **bric-a-brac, bricabrac**) M19 French (from *à bric et à brac* at random). Miscellaneous old ornaments, trinkets, small pieces of furniture, etc; antiquarian knick-knacks.
1996 *Spectator* For many years the great auction houses of London sold only fine art in all its forms. If you wanted to dispose of the bric-à-brac of life you had to look for others to sell it for you.

bricolage /brɪkə'lɑːʒ/, *foreign* /brɪkɔlaʒ/ (*plural same*) *noun* M20 French (from *bricoler* to do odd jobs, repair, from as next). Construction or creation from whatever is immediately available for use; something constructed or created in this way, an assemblage of haphazard or incongruous elements.

bricole /'brɪk(ə)l/, /brɪ'kəʊl/ *noun* E16 Old and Modern French (from Provençal *bricola* or Italian *briccola*, of unknown origin). **1** E16 An engine or catapult for discharging stones or bolts. *obsolete* except *historical*. **2** L16 A rebound of the ball from a side-wall or cushion in real tennis, billiards, etc.

bricoleur /brɪkə'ləː/; *foreign* /brikɔlœr/ (*plural same*) *noun* M20 French (= handyman, from *bricoler* to do odd jobs). A person who engages in BRICOLAGE; a constructor or creator of bricolages.

brillante /brɪ'lanteɪ/ *adverb & adjective* M18 Italian. *Music* (A direction:) in a showy or sparkling style.

brinjal /'brɪndʒaːl/ *noun* E17 Anglo-Indian (ultimately from Portuguese *berinjela*, from as AUBERGINE). Especially in the Indian subcontinent: an aubergine.

brio /'briːəʊ/ *noun* M18 Italian. Vivacity, liveliness, verve.
1996 *Country Life* At a time when the RSC has been looking a bit wobbly, it restores some much-needed brio and confidence to Stratford Shakespeare.

brioche /briː'ɒʃ/, /'briːɒʃ/ *noun* E19 French. A small usually round sweet cake made with light yeast dough.

briquette /brɪ'kɛt/ *noun & verb* (also **briquet**) L19 French (diminutive of *brique* brick). **A** *noun* L19 A small block or slab, especially of compressed coal-dust or other inflammable material for use as fuel. **B** *transitive verb* L19 Form into briquettes.

brisé /brize/ *noun* plural pronounced same L18 French (past participle of *briser* to break). *Ballet* A movement in which the feet or legs are lightly beaten together in the air.

brise-soleil /brizsɔlej/, /ˌbriːzsɒ'leɪ/ *noun* plural pronounced same M20 French (literally, 'sun-breaker'). A device (such as a perforated screen, louvre, etc.) for shutting out direct or excessive sunlight.

brocard /'brəʊkəd/, *foreign* /brɔkar/ (*plural same*) *noun* M16 French (or medieval Latin *brocardus*, appellative use of the Latinized form of the proper name *Burchart*). **1** M16 A cutting speech, a gibe. *rare*. **2** E17 An elementary legal principle or maxim.
■ Burchart was an eleventh-century bishop of Worms and the compiler of volumes of ecclesiastical rules and regulations.

broché /'brəʊʃeɪ/, *foreign* /brɔʃe/ *adjective & noun* L19 French (past participle of *brocher* to stitch). (A material, especially silk) woven with a pattern on the surface.

brochette /brɒ'ʃɛt/ *noun* L15 French (diminutive of *broche* spit). **1** L15 A small skewer or spit; *specifically* a skewer on which chunks of meat are cooked (cf. À LA BROCHETTE). **2** M19 A pin or bar used to fasten medals, orders, etc., to clothing; a set of decorations worn in this way.

brochure /'brəʊʃə/, /brɒ'ʃʊə/ *noun* M18 French (literally, 'stitching, stitched work', from *brocher* to stitch + *-ure*). A booklet or pamphlet, especially giving information about the amenities of a place etc.

■ The literal French meaning refers to the fact that, before the days of staplers, such a pamphlet would have been made by stitching a few sheets of paper together.

broderie anglaise /ˌbrəʊd(ə)rɪ ɒŋ'ɡleɪz/ *noun phrase* M19 French (= English embroidery). Open embroidery on linen, cambric, etc.; fabric so embroidered.

brogan /'brəʊg(ə)n/ *noun* M19 Irish (*brógán*, Gaelic *brógán* diminutive of *bróg* brogue). A coarse stout leather shoe reaching to the ankle.

bronco /'brɒŋkəʊ/ *noun & adjective* (also **broncho**) M19 Spanish (= rough, rude). **A** *noun* M19 plural **broncos**. A wild or half-tamed horse, especially of the western United States. **B** *adjective* M19. Wild, uncontrollable, rough. *United States, colloquial.*

brouhaha /'bruːhɑːhɑː/ *noun* L19 French. A commotion, a sensation; uproar, hubbub.

brouillon /brujɔ̃/ *noun* plural pronounced same L17 French. A rough draft.

bruit /bruːt/, *in sense 4 foreign* /brɥi/ (*plural same*) *noun* LME Old and Modern French (use as noun of past participle of *bruire* to roar, from Proto-Romance alteration of Latin *rugire* to roar, by association with Proto-Romance source of 'bray'). **1** LME Noise, clamour. **2** LME Rumour, report. **3** L15–E17 Fame, reputation. **4** M19 Medicine Any sound (especially an abnormal one) heard in auscultation.

brunet /bruː'nɛt/, /bru'nɛt/ *noun & adjective* (also (feminine) **brunette**) M16 French (*brunet* masculine, *brunette* feminine, diminutive of *brun* brown). (A White person) with a dark complexion or (now usually) brown hair. Of the complexion: dark.

■ The form *brunette*, especially a woman or girl, is far more frequent than the masculine form.

brusque /brʊsk/, /bruːsk/ *adjective* (also **brusk**) M17 French (= lively, fierce, harsh, from Italian *brusco* sour, tart, use as adjective of noun = Spanish, Portuguese *brusco* butcher's broom (a spiny bush) from Proto-Romance). Rough or rude in manner or speech; blunt, off-hand, abrupt.

■ Earliest (only in E17) in the sense of 'tart'.

brut /bruːt/, *foreign* /bryt/ *adjective* L19 French. Of wine: unsweetened, very dry.

brutum fulmen /ˌbruːtəm 'fʌlmen/ *noun phrase* plural **bruta fulmina** /ˌbruːtə 'fʌlmmə/ E17 Latin (literally, 'unfeeling thunderbolt'). A mere noise; an ineffective act, an empty threat.

■ The phrase *bruta fulmina et vana* 'insensate and ineffectual thunderbolts' occurs in Pliny's *Natural History* II.xliii.

bubo /'bjuːbəʊ/ *noun* plural **buboes** LME Latin (from Greek *boubōn* groin, swelling in the groin). A swollen inflamed lymph node especially in the groin or armpit.

bucaro, buccaro variants of BOCCARO.

buccan variant of BOUCAN.

buccra variant of BUCKRA.

bucellas /bjuː'sɛləs/ *noun* E19 Portuguese (name of a village near Lisbon). A Portuguese white wine; a drink of this.

buckaroo see VAQUERO.

buckling /'bʌklɪŋ/ *noun* E20 German (*Bückling* bloater). A smoked herring.

buckra /'bʌkrə/ *noun* (also **buccra** and other variants) M18 Ibibio and Efik ((m)*bakara* European, master). (A Blacks' name for) a White man, a master.

■ Used in the West Indies and southern United States and frequently derogatory.

buffet /'bʊfeɪ/, *in sense 1 also* /'bʌfɪt/ *noun* E18 French (from Old French *buf(f)et*, of unknown origin). **1** E18 A sideboard or recessed cupboard for china, plate, etc. **2** L18 (A place offering) a service of food from a sideboard or counter where guests or customers can help themselves.

buffo /'bʊfəʊ/ *noun & adjective* M18 Italian (= puff of wind, buffoon, from *buffare* to puff, from Proto-Romance verb of imitative origin). **A** *noun* M18 plural **buffos**. A comic actor, a singer in OPERA BUFFA. **B** *adjective* L18 Comic, burlesque.

bugaku /'bʊgakuː/ *noun* L19 Japanese (from *bu* dancing + *gaku* music). A Japanese classical dance in which pure dance form and symmetry are emphasized, and masks are used.

buhl /buːl/ *noun & adjective* (also **boul(l)e**, **Buhl**) E19 German (*buhl*, French *boule*, from André Charles *Boulle* (1642–1732), French cabinet-maker). (Of) brass, tortoise-shell, etc., worked into ornamental patterns for inlaying; (work) inlaid thus.

bulgur /'bʌlgə/ *noun* (also **bulghur**) M20 Turkish (= Persian *bulgūr* bruised grain). Cracked wheat, BURGHUL.

bund /bʊnd/, *foreign* /bʊnt/ *noun* (also **Bund**) plural **bunds, bunde** /'bʊndə/ M19 German. A German league, confederacy, or association. Cf. BOND.

bundobust /'bʌndəbʌst/ *noun* (also **bandobast**) L18 Urdu (from Persian *band-o-bast* tying and binding). In the Indian subcontinent: arrangements, organization.

Bunraku /'bʊnrakuː/, *foreign* /'bunraku/ *noun & adjective* E20 Japanese. (Of, pertaining to, or characteristic of) Japanese puppet drama, *specifically* as practised by the Bunraku-za company.

bunyip /'bʌnjɪp/ *noun* M19 **Aboriginal**. In Australia: a fabulous monster of swamps and lagoons.

bureau /'bjʊərəʊ/ *noun* plural **bureaux** /'bjʊərəʊz/, **bureaus** L17 French (Old French *burel*, originally = woollen stuff, baize (used for covering writing-desks), probably from *bure*, variant of *buire* dark brown, from Proto-Romance alteration of Latin *burrus* fiery red, from Greek *purros* red). **1** L17 A writing-desk with drawers for papers etc. **b** E19 A chest of drawers. *North America*. **2** L17 An office, especially for the transaction of public business; a department of public administration. **b** E20 An office or business with a specified function; an agency for the coordination of related activities, the distribution of information, etc.

burette /bjʊ'rɛt/ *noun* (also **buret**) M19 French. A graduated glass tube with tap, used for measuring small quantities of liquid in chemical analysis.

burghul /bə'guːl/ *noun* (also **burgul**) E20 Arabic (*burgul* from Persian *burġūl* variant of *bulġūr*). Wholewheat partially boiled and then dried; a dish made from this.

burin /'bjʊərɪn/ *noun* M17 French (related to Italian *burino* (*bulino*), perhaps connected with Old High German *bora* boring-tool). A tool for engraving on copper or wood.

burka /'bʊəkə/ *noun* M19 Urdu (Persian *burka'* from Arabic *burḳu'*). A Muslim woman's long enveloping garment worn in public. Also, a yashmak.

burlesque /bə:'lɛsk/ *adjective, noun, and verb* M17 French (from Italian *burlesco*, from *burla* ridicule, joke, fun, of unknown origin). **A** *adjective* **1** M17–M19 Jocular, odd, grotesque. **2** M17 Derisively or amusingly imitative; mock-heroic or mock-pathetic; bombastic. (Now chiefly of literary composition or dramatic representation.) **B** *noun* **1** M17 Derisively or amusingly imitative literary or dramatic composition, bombast; mock-seriousness; an instance or example of this; (a) parody; (a) caricature. **2a** M19 *History* The concluding portion of a blackface minstrel entertainment, containing dialogue and sketches. *United States*. **b** L19 A variety show, frequently featuring striptease. Originally and chiefly *United States*. **C** *transitive verb* L17 Imitate to deride or amuse; parody; caricature.

burnous /bə:'nuːs/ *noun* (also **burnoose** and other variants) L16 French (from Arabic *burnus, burnūs*). An Arab or Moorish hooded cloak; a fashion garment resembling this.

burra /'bʌrə/ *adjective* E19 **Hindustani** (*baṛā, barā* great, greatest). In the Indian subcontinent: high-ranking, great.

■ Occurs only in phrases such as *burra sahib* and *burra memsahib*, used to refer to important people.

burrito /bʊ'riːtəʊ/ *noun* plural **burritos** M20 **American Spanish** (diminutive of BURRO). A tortilla rolled round a filling of spiced beef and other ingredients.

burro /'bʊrəʊ/ *noun* plural **burros** E19 Spanish. A small donkey used as a pack-animal. Chiefly *North American*.

bushido /'buːʃɪdəʊ/, /buˈʃiːdəʊ/ *noun* L19 Japanese (= military knight's way). The code of honour and morals evolved by the samurai.

bustier /'bʌstɪeɪ/, /'bʊstɪeɪ/, *foreign* /bystje/ (*plural same*) *noun* L20 French (from *buste* bust). A close-fitting usually strapless bodice or top worn by women.

■ The revival of the *bustier* as a fashion item in the 1980s was closely associated with the rock star Madonna, who frequently wore one for her public appearances.

1987 *London Evening News* ... bustiers in scarlet and black sat atop wafts of brightly coloured chiffon skirts for evening.

butoh /'buto/ *noun* L20 **Japanese** ('dark art'). A Japanese dance style influenced by Western dance.

1996 *Spectator* Dramatic tension and the exploration of man's dark inner depths should also be the ingredients of *butoh*, the Japanese theatre art halfway between dance and drama.

butte /bju:t/ *noun* M19 **French.** *Physical Geography* In North America: an isolated hill with steep sides and a flat top, similar to but narrower than a MESA.

bwana /'bwɑːnə/ *noun* L19 **Kiswahili.** In East Africa: master, sir.

■ Frequently used, particularly in colonial times, as a term of respectful address by a Black person to a White man.

C

c., ca. abbreviations of CIRCA.

caba /kə'bɑ:/ *noun* (also **cabas** /kə'bɑ:s/) M19 French (*cabas* basket, pannier). A small satchel or handbag. Chiefly *United States*.

cabaia variant of KEBAYA.

cabala variant of CABBALA.

caballada /kabə'ljɑːdə/ *noun* M19 Spanish (from *caballo* horse). A drove of horses or mules.
■ United States; earlier in the form CAVA-YARD.

caballero /kabə'ljɛːrəʊ/ *noun* plural **caballeros** M19 Spanish (= French *chevalier*, Italian *cavaliere*). A Spanish gentleman.

cabana /kə'bɑːnə/ *noun* (also **cabaña** /kə'bɑːnjə/) L19 Spanish (*cabaña* from late Latin *capanna*, *cavana* cabin). A cabin; *specifically* a shelter at a beach or swimming pool. Chiefly *United States*.
1957 F. Richards *Practise to Deceive* He asked why Lane had gone into the bath-house cabaña.

cabane /kə'bɑːn/ *noun* M19 French. **1** M19 A hut, a cabin. *French Canadian.* **2** E20 A pyramidal structure supporting the wings of an aircraft.

cabaret /'kabəreɪ/; *in sense 1 also foreign* /kabəre/ (*plural same*) *noun* M17 Old and Modern French (originally Walloon and Picard, from Middle Dutch variant of *camaret*, *cambret* from Old Picard *camberet* little room). **1** M17 A public house in France etc. **2** E20 An entertainment provided in a restaurant etc. while customers are at table; a restaurant, nightclub, etc., providing such entertainment.

cabas variant of CABA.

cabbala /kə'bɑːlə/, /'kabələ/ *noun* (also **cabala**, **kabbala**, and (in sense 1) with initial capital) E16 Medieval Latin (*cab(b)ala* from rabbinical Hebrew *qabbālāh* tradition, from *qibbēl* to receive, accept). **1** E16 The esoteric and mystical Jewish tradition, first transmitted orally, of which the Zohar (thirteenth century) is the basic text. **2** *generally* **a** M-L17 (An) oral tradition. **b** M17 (An) esoteric doctrine; (a) mystic interpretation; occult lore.

cabildo /ka'bildo/, /kə'bɪldəʊ/ *noun* plural **cabildos** /ka'bildos/, /kə'bɪldəʊz/ E19 Spanish (from late Latin *capitulum* chapter-house). In Spain and Spanish-speaking countries: a town hall or town council.

cabob variant of KEBAB.

cabochon /'kabəʃɒn/ *adjective & noun* M16 Old and Modern French (diminutive of *caboche*, Picard variant of Old French *caboce* head, of unknown origin). (A gem) polished but not faceted.
■ Also in the phrase EN CABOCHON.

cabotage /'kabəta:ʒ/, /'kabətɪdʒ/ *noun* M19 French (from *caboter* to coast along (a shore), perhaps ultimately from Spanish *cabo* cape, promontory). **1** M19 Coastal trade. **2** M20 The reservation to a country of (especially air) traffic operation within its territory.

cabotin /kabɔtɛ̃/ *noun* (feminine **cabotine** /kabɔtin/) plural pronounced same E20 French (= strolling player, perhaps from as preceding from resemblance to vessels travelling from port to port). A third-rate or low-class actor.

cabriole /'kabrɪəʊl/, *foreign* /kabrijɔl/ (*plural same*) *noun* L18 French (from *cabrioler*, earlier *caprioler*, from Italian *capriolare* to leap; cf. CAPRIOLE). **1** L18 A springing dance step in which one leg is extended and the other brought up to it. **2** L18 *History* More fully *cabriole chair*. A kind of small armchair. **3** L18 A CABRIOLET sense 1. Chiefly *historical*. **4** L19 A kind of curved leg characteristic of Chippendale and Queen Anne furniture.

cabriolet /'kabrɪəleɪ/ *noun* M18 French (from as preceding). **1** M18 A light two-wheeled hooded one-horse chaise. Chiefly *historical*. **2** L18 A bonnet or hat shaped like a cabriolet. **3** E20 A motor car with a folding top.

cache /kaʃ/ *noun & verb* L18 French (from *cacher* to hide). **A** *noun* **1** L18 A hiding place for goods, provisions, ammunition, treasure, etc. **2** M19 A hidden store of provisions etc. **3** M20 An auxiliary computer memory from which high-speed retrieval is possible. Also *cache memory*. **B** *transitive verb* E19 Place or store in a cache.

B 1986 *Personal Computer World* Window images are normally cached in a form to allow fast screen redraw.

cache-peigne /kaʃpɛɲ/ *noun* plural pronounced same L19 French (from *cacher* to hide + *peigne* comb). A bow or other trimming for a hat, usually worn at the back.

cache-pot /kaʃpo/ (*plural same*), /ˈkaʃpɒt/ *noun* L19 French (from *cacher* to hide + *pot* pot). An ornamental holder for a flowerpot.

cache-sexe /kaʃsɛks/ (*plural same*), /ˈkaʃsɛks/ *noun* E20 French (from *cacher* to hide + *sexe* sex). A covering for the genitals.

cachet /ˈkaʃeɪ/ *noun* E17 French (from *cacher* (in sense 'press', represented now in *écacher* to crush) from Proto-Romance alteration of Latin *coactare* to constrain). **1** E17 A seal for letters, documents, etc. Now *rare* or *obsolete*. **2** M19 A characteristic or distinguishing mark; a characteristic feature or quality conferring prestige or distinction; high status. **3** L19 A small digestible case enclosing a dose of medicine.

2 1995 *Times* Suddenly perfume is losing its luxury cachet and becoming an everyday purchase—and buyers are no longer showing brand loyalty.

cachou /ˈkaʃuː/, /kəˈʃuː/ *noun* L16 French (from Portuguese *cachu* from Malay *kacu*). **1** L16 Catechu, any of various astringent tannin-rich vegetable extracts used especially in tanning. **2** E18 A lozenge taken to sweeten the breath.

cacique /kəˈsiːk/ *noun* M16 Spanish or French (from Taino). **1** M16 A West Indian or South American Indian native chief. **2** L19 In Spain or Latin America: a political boss.

cacodemon /kakəˈdiːmən/ *noun* (also **cacodaemon**) L16 Greek (*kakodaimōn* from as *kako-* evil + *daimōn* genius). **1** L16 An evil spirit. **2** E18 A malignant or deprecated person.

cacoethes /kakəʊˈiːθiːz/ *noun* M16 Latin (from Greek *kakoēthes* use as noun of adjective *kakoēthes* ill-disposed, from as *kako-* evil + ETHOS). An evil habit; a passion or 'itch' for doing something inadvisable.

■ Although also formerly used of a malignant tendency in a medical sense, *cacoethes* mainly occurs in English with reference to the Latin poet Juvenal (*Satire* vii): *tenet insanabile multos / scribendi cacoethes* 'the incurable itch to write grips many'.

cadastre /kəˈdastə/ *noun* L18 French (from Modern Provençal *cadastro* from Italian *catast(r)o* earlier *catastico* from late Greek *katastikhon* list, register, from *kata stikhon* line by line). A register of property showing the extent, value, and ownership, of land for taxation.

cadeau /kado/ *noun* plural **cadeaux** plural pronounced same L18 French. A gift.

cadenza /kəˈdɛnzə/ *noun* M18 Italian. *Music* A (sometimes improvised) flourish or passage for a solo instrument or voice, usually near the close or between the divisions of a movement; *specifically* such a passage in a concerto in which the main themes of the movement (usually the first or last) are developed.

cadet /kəˈdɛt/ *noun* E17 French (earlier *capdet* from Gascon dialect (= Provençal *capdel*) from Proto-Romance diminutive of Latin *caput* head). **1** E17 A younger son or brother; also occasionally (a member of) a younger branch of a family. **b** M17 *The* youngest son or brother. **2** M17 *History* A gentleman who entered the army without a commission, to learn the profession. **3** L18 A student in a naval, military, or air force college. **4** M19 A young man learning sheep-farming. *New Zealand*. **5** L19 A member of a corps receiving elementary military or police training.

cadi /ˈkɑːdi/, /ˈkeɪdi/ *noun* (also **kadi, qadi**) L16 Arabic ((*al-*)*ḳāḍī*). A civil judge in a Muslim country.

cadre /ˈkɑːdə/, /ˈkɑːdr(ə)/, /ˈkadri/ *noun* M19 French (from Italian *quadro* from Latin *quadrus* square). **1** M19 A frame, a framework; a plan. *rare*. **2** M19 *Military* **a** A permanent establishment of trained personnel forming a nucleus for expansion at need. **b** M19 (A list of) the complement of the officers of a regiment etc. **3** M20 (A member of) a group of workers acting to promote the aims and interests of the Communist Party. **b** M20 In the People's Republic of China: an officeholder in a Party, governmental, or military organization.

caduceus /kəˈdjuːsɪəs/ *noun* plural **caducei** /kəˈdjuːsɪʌɪ/ L16 Latin (*caduceus, caduceum* from Doric Greek *karuk(e)ion* = Attic *kērukeion* neuter adjective used as noun, from *kērux* herald). *Classical History* A Greek or Roman herald's wand; *specifically* the wand carried by the messenger-god Hermes or Mercury, usually represented with two serpents twined round it.

caesura /sɪ'zjʊərə/ *noun* M16 Latin (*caesura*, from *caes-* past participial stem of *caedere* to cut). **1** M16 *Prosody* A break or pause between words within a metrical foot in classical prosody or near the middle of a line in English etc. *prosody*. **2** L16 *generally* A break, a stop, an interruption.

cafard /ka'fɑ:/, *foreign* /kafar/ *noun* M16 French (= cockroach, hypocrite, probably from late Latin *caphardum*). **1** M16–M17 A hypocrite. **2** E20 Melancholia.

café /'kafeɪ/, /'kafi/; *also jocular or slang* /kaf/, /keɪf/ *noun* (also **cafe** and (reflecting slang pronunciation) **caf(f)**) E19 French (= coffee (house)). A coffee-house; a teashop; an informal restaurant; a bar (*United States*).

■ Both the 'coffee' and the 'coffee-house' senses of the French occur in various phrases used in English (see entries below).

café au lait /kafe o lɛ/ *noun & adjective phrase* M18 French (= coffee with milk). **A** *noun phrase* M18 Coffee with milk, white coffee. **B** *adjective phrase* E20 Of the light brown colour of this.

café chantant /kafe ʃɑ̃tɑ̃/ *noun phrase* plural **cafés chantants** (pronounced same) M19 French (literally, 'singing café'). A café with live musical entertainment.

café complet /kafe kɔ̃plɛ/ *noun phrase* plural **cafés complets** (pronounced same) M20 French (literally, 'complete coffee'). A light breakfast including coffee and usually croissants. Cf. THÉ COMPLET.

café noir /kafe nwar/ *noun phrase* M19 French (= black coffee). Coffee without milk, black coffee.

cafeteria /kafɪ'tɪərɪə/ *noun* M19 American Spanish (*cafetería*, from *café* coffee). A coffee-house; a restaurant; now *especially* a self-service restaurant as part of the facilities in a workplace, institution or public building.

■ Originally United States, but apparently spread to Europe in the 1920s, when the *Glasgow Herald* (30 July 1925) observed that 'Cafeterias, although a commonplace in America, are just beginning to have a hold in Paris.'

cafetière /kaftjɛr/ *noun* plural pronounced same M19 French (from *café* coffee). A coffee-pot; a coffee-making machine; a coffee-percolator.

1996 *Times Magazine* Every household member believes that he or she is the only person who ever . . . deals with coffee-grounds in the cafetière . . . .

cafila /'kɑ:fɪlə/ *noun* L16 Arabic (*ḳāfila*). A company of travellers in the Middle East, a caravan.

■ *Coffle*, an eighteenth-century derivation from *ḳāfila*, refers specifically to a line of slaves or animals fastened together.

caftan /'kaftan/, /kaf'tɑ:n/ *noun* (also **kaftan**) L16 Turkish (*kaftan* from Persian *ḳaftān*, partly through French *cafetan*). **1** L16 An Eastern man's long tunic with a waist girdle. **2** M20 A long loose dress; a loose-fitting shirt.

2 1996 *Times* Quant simply was not a kaftan sort of person, nor was she a glitzy shoulder-padded woman either.

cagnotte /kaɲɔt/ *noun* L19 French. Money reserved from the stakes for the bank at certain gambling games.

cagoule /kə'gu:l/ *noun* (also **kagoule**) M20 French (literally, 'cowl'). A hooded thin waterproof garment pulled on over the head.

caique /kʌɪ'i:k/, /keɪ'i:k/ *noun* E17 French (*caïque* from Italian *caicco* from Turkish *kayik*). **1** E17 A light rowing boat or skiff used on the Bosporus. **2** M17 An eastern Mediterranean sailing vessel.

caisson /'keɪs(ə)n/, /kə'su:n/ *noun* L17 French (= large chest, from Italian *cassone* with assimilation to *caisse* case). **1** L17 A large watertight chamber open at the bottom, from which the water is kept out by air pressure, used in laying foundations under water. **b** M19 A floating vessel used as a dock gate. **2** E18 An ammunition chest; an ammunition wagon.

calabrese /'kaləbri:s/, *noun* M20 Italian (= Calabrian). A variety of usually green sprouting broccoli.

calamari /kalə'mɑ:ri/ *noun plural* L20 Italian (plural of *calamaro* squid). Squid, especially as used in cooking.

calando /kə'landəʊ/, *foreign* /ka'lando/ *adverb* E19 Italian (= slackening). *Music* Gradually decreasing in speed and volume.

caldarium /kal'dɛːrɪʊm/ *noun* plural **caldaria** /kal'dɛːrɪə/ M18 Latin. *History* A (Roman) hot bath or bathroom.

caldera /kal'dɛːrə/, /kal'dɪərə/ *noun* L17 Spanish (from late Latin *caldaria* pot for boiling). A volcanic crater of great size;

specifically one whose breadth greatly exceeds that of the vent(s) within it.

calembour /kalăbur/ *noun* (also **calembourg** /kalăbur/ plural pronounced same E19 French. A pun.

calinda /kə'lɪmdə/ *noun* M18 American Spanish. A Black American dance found in Latin America and the southern United States.

calliope /kə'lʌɪəpi/ *noun* M19 Greek (*Kalliopē* (literally, 'beautiful-voiced') the Muse of epic poetry). A set of steam-whistles producing musical notes, played by a keyboard like that of an organ. Also *steam calliope. North American.*

callus /'kaləs/ *noun & verb* M16 Latin (more commonly *callum*). **A** *noun* **1** M16 A thickened and hardened part of the skin or soft tissue, a callosity. **2** L17 *Medicine* The bony healing tissue which forms around the ends of broken bone. **3** L19 *Botany* A hard formation of tissue; new tissue formed over a wound. **B** *verb intransitive* Form a callus (*over*).

calotte /kə'lɒt/ *noun* M17 French (perhaps related to *cale* caul). **1** M17 A skullcap, especially as worn by Roman Catholic priests. **2** L19 A snowcap, an ice-cap.

caloyer /'kalɔɪə/, *foreign* /kalɔje/ (*plural same noun* L16 French (from Italian *caloiero* from ecclesiastical Greek *kalogēros*, from *kalos* beautiful + *gērōs* old age). A Greek Orthodox monk.

calque /kalk/ *noun & verb* M20 French (= copy, tracing, from *calquer* to trace, from Italian *calcare* from Latin *calcare* to tread). **A** *noun* M20 A loan-translation (*of, on*). **B** *transitive verb* M20 Form as a calque. Usually in *passive* (followed by *on*).

■ A modern example of a calque is 'that goes without saying', which is calqued on French *cela va sans dire*.
1957 G. V. Smithers *Kyng Alisaunder Fecche mood . . .* is evidently a calque on OF. *porter ire*, as in *Chanson de Roland.*

calumet /'kaljʊmɛt/ *noun* L17 French (dialectal variant of *chalumeau* from late Latin *calamellus* diminutive of *calamus* reed). An American Indian tobacco-pipe with a clay bowl and reed stem, smoked especially as a sign of peace; *transferred* and *figurative* a symbol of peace.

calvados /'kalvədɒs/ *noun* E20 French (*Calvados*, a department in Normandy, France). Apple brandy, traditionally made in the Calvados region; a drink of this.

calyx /'kalɪks/, /'kelɪks/ *noun* plural **calyces** /'kalɪsiːz/, **calyxes** L17 Latin (*calyx, -yc-* from Greek *kalux* shell, husk, pod, from base of *kaluptein* to hide). *Botany* A whorl of leaves (sepals), forming the outer case of a bud or the envelope of a flower.

calzone /kal'tsəʊni/ *noun* L20 Italian (literally, 'trousers'). In Italian cookery, pizza dough with a stuffing of savoury ingredients.

camaieu /kamajø/ *noun* plural pronounced same L16 French. **1** L16–L18 A cameo. **2** E18 A method of monochrome painting.

camaraderie /kamə'rɑːd(ə)ri/, /kamə'rɑːd(ə)riː/ *noun* M19 French (from *camarade* comrade). The mutual trust and sociability of comrades.
1995 *Spectator* Banter goes on across tables. The camaraderie is palpable and so is the air. Everybody smokes.

camarilla /kamə'rɪlə/, /kamə'rɪljə/ *noun* M19 Spanish (diminutive of *camara* chamber). A cabal, a clique.

camaron /kamə'rəʊn/, /'kamər(ə)n/ *noun* L19 Spanish (*camarón* shrimp). A freshwater shrimp or prawn resembling a crayfish.

cambré /kɑ̃bre/ *adjective* E20 French (past participle of *cambrer* to camber, from Old French *cambre* from dialect variant of *chambre* arched, from Latin *camur* curved inwards). Curved, arched; *Ballet* (of the body) bent from the waist sideways or backwards.

cameo /'kamɪəʊ/ *noun* plural **cameos** LME Old French (*came(h)u, camahieu* (modern CAMAIEU): cf. medieval Latin *camahutus* etc. Later influenced by Italian *cam(m)eo*, corresponding to medieval Latin *cammaeus*). **1** LME A small piece of relief-carving in onyx, agate, etc., usually with colour-layers, the lower of which serves as ground; a relief design of similar form. **2** M19 A short literary sketch or acted scene; (more fully *cameo part*) a small character part in a play, film, etc.
2 1950 E. Crispin *Frequent Hearses* A cameo part . . . the film equivalent of a bit part on the stage.

camera lucida /,kam(ə)rə 'luːsɪdə/ *noun phrase* plural **camera lucidas** M18 Latin (= bright chamber). An instrument by which the rays of light from an object are reflected by a prism and produce an image on paper placed beneath the instrument, traceable with a pencil.

camera obscura | canard

camera obscura /ˌkam(ə)rə ɒbsˈkjʊərə/
noun phrase plural **camera obscuras** E18
Latin (= dark chamber). A darkened box
or enclosure with an aperture for projecting an image of external objects on a
screen placed at the focus of the lens; a
building containing such a box or enclosure.

camisole /ˈkamɪsəʊl/ *noun* E19 French
(from Italian *camiciola* or Spanish *cami-
sola*, diminutive of (respectively) *camicia*,
camisa from late Latin *camisia*). **1** E19 *History* A type of sleeved short jacket worn by
men. **2** M19 *History* A short loose jacket
worn by women when dressed in négligé.
3 M19 A woman's underbodice, usually
straight with shoulder-straps and embroidered or otherwise ornamentally
trimmed.

Camorra /kəˈmɔːrə/, /kəˈmɒrə/ *noun* (also
camorra) M19 Italian (perhaps from Spanish *camorra* dispute, quarrel). A secret society akin to the Mafia operating in the
Neapolitan district; *generally* any organized body engaged in extortion or other
dishonest activities.

camouflage /ˈkaməflɑːʒ/ *noun and verb*
E20 French (from *camoufler* (thieves' slang)
to cover up, from Italian *camuffare* disguise, deceive, perhaps associated with
French *camouflet* whiff of smoke in the
face). **A** *noun* E20 The disguising or con-
cealment of guns, ships, aircraft, etc., by
obscuring with splashes of various colours, foliage, netting, smokescreens, etc.;
the disguise so used; *generally* any means
of disguise or evasion. **B** *verb transitive*
E20 Conceal by camouflage.

campagna /kamˈpɑːnjə/, *foreign* /kam
ˈpaɲɲa/ *noun* (also **campa(g)nia**) L16 Italian (from late Latin *campania*). Open
country.
■ Now rare except with reference to the
Campagna di Roma. In the mid seventeenth century the word was also briefly
used with the sense of 'military campaign'.
1996 *Country Life* Its long, curving terrace
looks over the once heavily wooded
Warwickshire plain . . . , as if it were an English
version of the Roman *campagna*.

campana /kamˈpɑːnə/ *noun* E17 Late Latin
(*campana* bell). **1** E17 A bell; a bell-shaped
flower. Now *rare* or *obsolete*. **2** E19 A bell-
shaped vase.

campanile /kampəˈniːli/ *noun* M17 Italian
(from *campana* bell + *-ile*). A (usually lofty
and detached) bell-tower, especially in
Italy.

campesino /kampeˈsino/, /kampəˈsiːnəʊ/
noun plural **campesinos** /kampeˈsinos/,
/kampəˈsiːnəʊz/ M20 Spanish. In Spain
and Spanish-speaking countries: a peasant farmer.

campo /ˈkampəʊ/ *noun* plural **campos**
M19 American Spanish or Portuguese (=
field, open country, from Latin *campus*).
In South America (especially Brazil): a
grass plain with occasional stunted trees;
a savannah.
■ Frequently in plural.

campus /ˈkampəs/ *noun* L18 Latin. The
grounds and buildings of a college, university, etc., especially where forming a
distinct area; a separate part of a university; university or college life.
■ Originally used of the grounds of Prince-
ton University, New Jersey, then of similar
open spaces in other United States universities, and now worldwide.

canaille /kanaj/ *noun* L16 French (from
Italian *canaglia*, literally, 'pack of dogs',
from *cane* dog). The rabble, the populace.

canapé /ˈkanəpeɪ/, /ˈkanəpi/ *noun* L19
French. **1** L19 A piece of bread, toast, etc.,
with a small savoury on top. **2** L19 A sofa,
a settee.
■ In sense 2 the history of the Romance
word *canapé* is closely linked to that of English *canopy*, both of them deriving from medieval Latin *canopeum* baldachin, a variant
of classical Latin *conopeum* bed with net
curtains, from Greek *kōnōpeion* Egyptian
bed with mosquito curtains, from *kōnōps*
mosquito. In English the sense of *canopy*
has adhered to the 'curtain' sense of the
Latin, while *canapé* in the Romance languages (Spanish and Portuguese as well as
French) has retained the primary sense of
'couch, sofa'. By the late eighteenth century sense 1, now by far the more familiar
in English, had evolved in French.

canard /kəˈnɑːd/, /kanad/ *noun* M19
French (literally, 'duck'). **1** M19 A false report, a hoax. **2** E20 An extra surface attached to an aircraft, hydrofoil, etc., for
stability or control. Also, an aircraft fitted
with this.
1 1995 *New Scientist* This is a common
misunderstanding and is a canard on a par
with the belief that long ago insurance
companies which provided fire engines would
not put out fires unless the building displayed
their company's mark.

canasta /kə'nastə/ *noun* M20 Spanish (= basket, ultimately from Latin *canistrum* bread (or flower) basket). A two-pack card-game of the rummy family and of Uruguayan origin, usually played by four in two partnerships; a meld of seven or more cards in this game.

cancan /'kankan/ *noun* M19 French (reduplication of *canard* duck). A lively dance of French origin, originally a form of quadrille, now performed by a woman and involving high kicks, usually while holding up the front of the skirts.

cancellandum /kansə'landəm/ *noun* plural **cancellanda** /kansə'landə/ E20 Latin (neuter gerundive of *cancellare* to cancel). *Printing* A leaf for which another is substituted. In full *cancellandum leaf*. Cf. next.

cancellans /'kanselanz/ *noun & adjective* E20 Latin (present participle of *cancellare* to cancel). *Printing* **A** *noun* E20 A leaf which replaces another. Cf. preceding. **B** *adjective* M20 Designating a leaf, sheet, fold, etc., which replaces another, or a slip which cancels text.

cancrizans /'kaŋkrɪzanz/ *adjective, adverb, & noun* L18 Medieval Latin (present participle of *cancrizare* to walk backwards, from Latin *cancer* crab). *Music* (Designating, pertaining to, in the manner of) a canon in which the theme or subject is repeated backwards in the second part.

candelabrum /kandɪ'lɑːbrəm/, /kandɪ'leɪbrəm/ *noun* plural **candelabra** /kandɪ'lɑːbrə/, **candelabrums** (also **candelabra**, plural same, **candelabras**) E19 Latin (from *candela* candle). A large usually branched ornamental candlestick or lamp-holder carrying several lights.

candida /'kandɪdə/ *noun* (also *Candida*) M20 Modern Latin (feminine of Latin *candidus* white). **1** M20 A yeastlike fungus of the genus *Candida*, especially *C. albicans*. **2** L20 *Medicine* and *Veterinary Medicine* Infection with candida, especially one causing vaginal or oral thrush; candidiasis.

1990 *News of the World* Certain food's OK for the Candida, but bad for the liver.

canephora /kə'nɛf(ə)rə/, /kə'niːf(ə)rə/ *noun* plural **canephorae** /kə'nɛf(ə)riː/ E17 Latin (*canephora* feminine, from Greek *kanēphoros*, from *kaneon* basket + *-phoros* carrying). In ancient Greece, each of the maidens who carried on their heads baskets bearing sacred things used at certain feasts; in *Architecture*, a caryatid representing or resembling such a maiden.

cannelloni /kanə'ləʊni/ *noun plural* M20 Italian (augmentative plural of *cannello* stalk). Rolls of pasta filled with meat or cheese and seasonings; an Italian dish consisting largely of this and usually a sauce.

cannelure /'kan(ə)ljʊə/ *noun* M18 French (from *canneler* to groove, flute, from *canne* reed). A groove or fluting, especially around a bullet etc.

cañon variant of CANYON.

cantabile /kan'tɑːbɪli/ *adverb, adjective, & noun* E18 Italian (= that can be sung). *Music* **A** *adverb & adjective* E18 In a smooth flowing style, as if singing. **B** *noun* M18 Cantabile style; a piece or movement in this style.

cantaloup /'kantəluːp/ *noun* (also **cantaloupe**) L18 French. A small round ribbed variety of melon, with orange flesh. Also called *rock melon*.

■ The French name is taken from *Cantaluppi*, the name of the place near Rome, where, on its introduction from Armenia, the melon was first grown in Europe.

cantata /kan'tɑːtə/ *noun* E18 Italian ((sc. *aria* air), feminine past participle of *cantare* to sing). *Music* An extended composition for one or more voices with instrumental accompaniment; original, a narrative recitative or sequence of recitatives and ariettas, for solo voice; later, a choral work resembling a short oratorio.

cantatrice /'kantətriːs/ *noun* E19 French and Italian (from Latin *cantatrix*). A female professional singer.

cante hondo /ˌkante 'xondo/, /ˌkanteɪ 'hɒndəʊ/ *noun phrase* (also **cante jondo**) M20 Spanish (= deep song). Flamenco singing, songs, of a predominantly mournful or tragic character.

canti fermi plural of CANTO FERMO.

cantilena /kantɪ'leɪnə/, /kantɪ'liːnə/ *noun* M18 Italian (or Latin *cantilena*). *Music* A simple or sustained vocal melody, or an instrumental passage performed in a smooth lyrical style. Also, the (highest) melodic part in a composition.

cantina /kan'tiːnə/ *noun* L19 Spanish and Italian. In Spain, Spanish-speaking countries, and the south-western United States: a bar-room, a saloon; in Italy: a wine-shop.

canto /'kantəʊ/ *noun* plural **cantos** L16 Italian (literally, 'song', from Latin CANTUS). **1** L16 Each of the divisions of a long poem. **2** E17–E18 A song, a ballad. **3** E18 *Music* The upper part or melody in a composition.

canto fermo /ˌkantəʊ ˈfəːməʊ/ *noun phrase* plural **canti fermi** /ˌkanti ˈfəːmi/ L16 Italian (translating medieval Latin CANTUS FIRMUS). *Music* Originally, an unadorned melody, plainsong; later *specifically* a melody used as a basis for counterpoint. Now also, an existing melody, taken as a basis for a new polyphonic composition.

canton /ˈkantən/, *in sense 1 also* /kanˈtɒn/ *noun* E16 Old and Modern French (from Provençal from oblique case of Proto-Romance variant of Latin *cant(h)us*). A subdivision of a country; a small district; *specifically* one of the several States which form the Swiss confederation.

cantor /ˈkantɔː/, /ˈkantə/ *noun* M16 Latin (= singer, from *canere* to chant). **1** M16 A precentor in a church. **2** L19 An official who sings liturgical music and leads prayer in a synagogue, a HAZZAN.

cantoris /kanˈtɔːrɪs/ *adjective* M17 Latin (genitive of CANTOR). Of or pertaining to the north side of the choir of a church where the precentor usually sits; *Music* to be sung by the cantorial side in antiphonal singing (cf. DECANI).

cantus /ˈkantəs/ *noun* plural **cantus** /ˈkantuːs/, /ˈkantəs/ L16 Latin (= song). *Early Music* A song, a melody, especially in church music. Also, the highest voice in a polyphonic song.

cantus firmus /ˌkantəs ˈfəːməs/ *noun phrase* plural **cantus firmi** /ˈfəːmʌɪ/ M19 Medieval Latin (= firm song). *Music* CANTO FERMO.

canyon /ˈkanjən/ *noun* (also **cañon**) M19 Spanish (*cañón* tube, pipe, gun barrel, etc. augmentative of *caña* from Latin *canna* reed). A deep gorge (especially in the United States or Mexico), frequently with a stream at its bottom.

canzona /kanˈtsəʊnə/ *noun* L19 Italian (from next). (A musical setting of the words of) a canzone; an instrumental piece resembling a madrigal in character.

canzone /kanˈtsəʊni/ *noun* plural **canzoni** /kanˈtsəʊni/ L16 Italian (= song (corresponding to Old and Modern French *chanson*) from Latin *cantio(n)* singing, from *cant-* past participle of *canere* to sing). An Italian or Provençal song or bal

lad; a style of lyric resembling a madrigal.

caoine /ˈkiːnə/ *noun* E18 Irish (from *caoinim* I wail). An Irish funeral song accompanied by wailing in lamentation of the dead.

caoutchouc /ˈkaʊtʃʊk/ *noun & adjective* L18 French (from obsolete Spanish *cauchuc* from Quechua *kauchuk*). (Of) unvulcanized natural rubber.

capable de tout /kapabl də tu/ *adjective phrase* L19 French. Capable of anything; without scruple or restraint.

cap-à-pie /kapəˈpiː/ *adverb* E16 Old French (*cap a pie* (Modern French *de pied en cap*)). From head to foot, fully (armed, ready, etc.). Now *archaic*.

capataz /kapaˈtaθ/, /kapaˈtas/ *noun* plural **capataces** /kapaˈtaθes/, /kapaˈtases/ E19 Spanish (irregular from Latin *caput* head). In Spain or Spanish-speaking America: an overseer, a superintendent, a boss.

capeador /ˌkapɪəˈdɔː/ *noun* E20 Spanish (from *capear* to trick a bull with a cape, from *capa* cloak). *Bullfighting* A person who aids a bullfighter by distracting the bull with his cloak.

capitonné /kapɪtɔne/ *adjective* L19 French (past participle of *capitonner* to upholster, quilt). Designating or characterized by a style of upholstery or embroidery in which the material is drawn in at intervals to present a quilted appearance.

capo /ˈkapəʊ/ *noun* plural **capos** M20 Italian (from Latin *caput* head). The head of a crime syndicate or one of its branches. Chiefly *United States*.

capo abbreviated form of CAPOTASTO.

capot /kəˈpɒt/ *noun & verb* M17 French (perhaps from *capoter* dialectal variant of *chapoter* to castrate). *Piquet* **A** *noun* M17 The winning of all the tricks by one player; a score awarded for this. **B** *transitive verb* M17 Win all the tricks from.

■ Formerly stressed on the first syllable. *Capot* is the source of the German *kaputt*, from which the dated English slang KAPUT is taken.

capot /ˈkapəʊ/, /kəˈpɒt/; *foreign* /kapo/ (*plural same*) *noun* L17 French (masculine form of CAPOTE). A long hooded cloak worn by soldiers, travellers, etc.

capotasto /kapəʊˈtastəʊ/ *noun* plural **capotastos** (also **capo tasto**) L19 Italian (literally, 'head stop': cf. TASTO). *Music* A

movable bar attached to the finger-board of a stringed instrument to make possible the simultaneous adjustment of the pitch of all the strings.
■ Generally known as a *capo*.

capote /kə'pəʊt/ *noun* E19 French (diminutive of *cape* cape, cloak). **1 a** E19 A long hooded cloak worn by soldiers, travellers, etc. **b** M19 A long mantle worn by women. **2** E19 A bonnet with a soft crown and stiff projecting brim.

capouch variant of CAPUCHE.

cappuccino /kapʊ'tʃi:nəʊ/ *noun* plural **cappuccinos** M20 Italian. (A cup of) coffee with milk, especially made with espresso coffee and topped with white foam.

capriccio /kə'prɪtʃɪəʊ/ *noun* plural **capriccios** E17 Italian. **1** E17–E19 A CAPRICE, a whim. **2** M17–M19 A sudden movement; a trick, a prank, a caper. **3** L17 A thing or work of lively fancy in art etc.; *especially* a lively usually short musical composition, more or less free in form.

capriccioso /kəprɪtʃɪ'əʊsəʊ/ *adverb* M18 Italian. *Music* (A direction:) in a free and impulsive style.

caprice /kə'pri:s/ *noun* M17 French (from Italian *capriccio*, literally, 'head with the hair standing on end', (hence) horror; later (by association with *capra* goat) sudden start, from *capo* head + *riccio* hedgehog, ultimately from Latin *(h)ericius* urchin). **1** M17 An unaccountable change of mind or conduct; a whim; a freakish fancy. **b** M17 Inclination or disposition to such changes etc.; capriciousness. **2** E18 A CAPRICCIO.

capriole /'kaprɪəʊl/ *noun & verb* L16 French ((now *cabriole*), from Italian *capriola*, from *capriolare* to leap, from *capriolo* roebuck, from Latin *capreolus* diminutive of *caper* goat). **A** *noun* **1** L16 A leap or caper, especially as made in dancing (cf. CABRIOLE 1). **2** *Equestrianism* L16 A trained horse's horizontal leap with the hind legs kicking vigorously. **B** *intransitive verb* L16 Perform a capriole; skip, leap, caper.

capuche /kə'pu:ʃ/ *noun* (also **capouch**) L16 French ((now *capuce*) from Italian *cappuccio*). The hood of a cloak, *especially* that of a Capuchin.

caput mortuum /,kapət 'mɔ:tu:əm/ *noun phrase* M17 Latin (= dead head). **1** A death's head, a skull. Only in M17. **2** M17

Alchemy The residue remaining after distillation or sublimation. **3** E18 Worthless residue.

carabinero /,karabi'nero/, /,karəbɪ'nε:rəʊ/ *noun* plural **carabineros** /,karabi'neros/, /,karabɪ'nε:rəʊz/ M19 Spanish (literally, 'carabineer'). A (Spanish) customs or revenue officer; a (Spanish) frontier guard.

carabiniere /,karabi'njere/, /,karəbɪ'njε:ri/ *noun* plural **carabinieri** /,karabɪ'njeri/ M19 Italian (literally, 'carabineer'). An Italian soldier in a corps serving as a police force.
> **1995** *Times* Away from skiing, Tomba is facing possible expulsion from the Italian *carabinieri* after a photographer, who had sold nude photographs of him to a magazine, alleged that the Italian had thrown a heavy glass trophy at him after a World Cup race on Sunday.

caracole /'karəkəʊl/ *noun* (also **caracol** /'karəkɒl/) E17 French (*caracol(e)* snail's shell, spiral). *Equestrianism* E17 A half-turn or wheel to the right or left by a horse or rider. Formerly also, a series of such turns alternately to right and left.
■ The word was also formerly used in English for short periods in senses deriving directly from its basic French meanings: 'a spiral shell' (only E17) and in architectural contexts 'a helical staircase' (E18).

caracul variant of KARAKUL.

carafe /kə'raf/, /kə'rɑ:f/ *noun* L18 French (from Italian *caraffa*, of unknown origin). A glass bottle for water or wine at a table, in a bedroom, etc.

caramba /kə'rambə/, *foreign* /ka'ramba/ *interjection* M19 Spanish. Expressive of surprise or dismay.

carambole /'kar(ə)mbəʊl/ *noun & intransitive verb* L18 Spanish (*carambola* whence French *carambole* red ball in billiards), apparently from *bola* ball). (Make) a cannon in billiards.

cara sposa /,kɑ:ra 'spo:za/ *noun phrase* plural **care spose** /,kɑ:re 'spo:ze/ L18 Italian. (One's) dear wife; a devoted wife. Cf. CARO SPOSO.

caravanserai /karə'vansərʌɪ/, /karə'vansəri/ *noun* (also **caravansary**, **caravansery**, and other variants) L16 Persian (kārwānsarāy, from kārvān (desert) caravan + SERAI). An Eastern inn with a large inner court where caravans rest.

carcinoma /kɑ:sɪ'nəʊmə/ *noun* plural **carcinomas**, **carcinomata** /kɑ:sɪ-

'nəʊmətə/ E18 **Latin** (from Greek *karki-nōma* from *karkinos* crab + suffix *-oma*). *Medicine* A cancer; now *specifically* a malignant tumour of epithelial origin.

care spose plural of CARA SPOSA.

caret /'karət/ *noun* L17 **Latin** (3rd person singular present indicative of *carere* to be without, lack). A mark (strictly ^) placed below a line of writing or printing, in a margin, etc., to show the place of an omission.

carezza variant of KAREZZA.

cargador /kɑːgə'dɔː/ *noun* plural **carga-dores** /kɑːgə'dɔːrɪz/ E19 **Spanish** (from *cargo* cargo). In Spanish-speaking parts of America: a porter.

caries /'kɛːriːz/ *noun* plural same L16 **Latin**. Decay of a tooth or bone.

carillon /'karıljən/, /'karılɒn/, /kə'rıljən/ *noun* L18 **French** (alteration of Old French *car(e)ignon, quarregnon,* from Proto-Romance = peal of four bells). **1** L18 A set of bells sounded either from a keyboard or mechanically. **2** L18 A tune played on such bells. **3** E19 A musical instrument or part of an organ designed to imitate a peal of bells.

carioca /karɪ'əʊkə/ *noun* M19 **Portuguese**. **1** M19 A native of Rio de Janeiro, Brazil. **2** M20 A Brazilian dance resembling a samba; a piece of music for this dance.

cariole variant of CARRIOLE.

cari sposi plural of CARO SPOSO.

carissima /ka'rissima/ *adjective* M19 **Italian** (superlative of *cara* dear). A term of endearment to a woman: dearest, darling.

carmagnole /karmaɲɔl/ *noun* plural pronounced same L18 **French**. **1** L18 A popular song and round dance of the French Revolutionary period. **2** L18 A French revolutionary soldier; *transferred* an author of mischief.

■ In French, originally a style of jacket popular during the French Revolution, the name ultimately deriving from Carmagnola, a town in Piedmont.

carnet /'kɑːneɪ/, *foreign* /karnɛ/ *(plural same) noun* E19 **French**. **1** E19 A notebook *rare.* **2** E20 A permit; *specifically* **(a)** one allowing a motorist to drive across a frontier; **(b)** one allowing use of some campsites.

caro sposo /'kɑːro 'spoːzo/ *noun phrase* plural **cari sposi** /ˌkɑːri 'spoːzi/ L18 **Ital-**

ian. (One's) dear husband; a devoted husband. Cf. CARA SPOSA.

carousel /karə'sɛl/, /karə'zɛl/ *noun* (also **carrousel**) M17 **French** (*carrousel* from Italian *carosello, garosello*). **1** M17 *History* A kind of tournament in which variously dressed companies of knights engaged in plays, chariot races, exercises, etc. **2** L17 A merry-go-round; a roundabout. Chiefly *North American.* **3** M20 A rotating delivery or conveyor system, *especially* one in an airport for the delivery of passengers' luggage.

carriole /'karɪəʊl/ *noun* (also **cariole**) M18 **French** (from Italian *carriuola,* diminutive of *carro* car). **1** M18 A small open carriage for one; a covered light cart. Chiefly *historical.* **2** E19 A kind of sledge used in Canada.

carrousel variant of CAROUSEL.

carte /kɑːt/ *noun* LME **French** (from Latin *c(h)arta* papyrus leaf, paper). **1** LME–M18 A charter, a document; an exposition; a chart, a diagram. **2** L15 A playing-card; in *plural,* a game of cards. *Scottish.* **3** E19 A bill of fare. Cf. À LA CARTE. **4** M19 A CARTE-DE-VISITE.

carte blanche /kɑːt 'blɑːnʃ/, *foreign* /kart blɑ̃ʃ/ *noun phrase* plural **cartes blanches** /kɑːts 'blɑːnʃ/, *foreign* /kart blɑ̃ʃ/ L17 **French** (= blank paper). **1** L17 A blank sheet of paper to be filled in as a person wishes; *figurative* full discretionary power granted. **2** E19 *Cards* In piquet and bezique, a hand containing no court-cards as dealt, and attracting a compensatory score.

■ The figurative use of sense 1 is now the one usually encountered (see quotation 1996).

1996 *Times* That is greatly to the credit of the company, which gave *carte blanche* to . . . an experienced American business academic who spent 60 days coming up with a more down-to-earth 'audit' than sceptics might have expected.

carte-de-visite /ˌkɑːtdəvɪ'ziːt/ *noun* plural **cartes-de-visite** (pronounced same) M19 **French** (= visiting-card). A small photographic portrait mounted on a card. Now *archaic* or *historical.*

carte d'identité /kart didãtite/ *noun phrase* plural **cartes d'identité** (pronounced same) E20 **French**. An identity card.

carte du pays /kart dy pei/ *noun phrase* plural **cartes du pays** (pronounced same) M18 French (literally, 'map of the country'). (A statement of) the state of affairs.

cartel branch I /ˈkɑːt(ə)l/, branch II /kɑːˈtɛl/ noun (branch I also **chartel**) M16 French (branch I from Italian *cartello* placard, challenge, diminutive of *carta* from Latin *c(h)arta*; branch II from German *Kartell* from French). **I 1** M16 A written challenge. In full *cartel of defiance*. Now *archaic* or *historical*. **2** L17 *History* A written agreement relating to the exchange or ransom of prisoners; an exchange or ransom of prisoners; (in full *cartel ship*) a ship commissioned for the exchange of prisoners. **3** L17 *generally* A paper or card bearing writing or printing. **II 4** L19 A combination between political parties to promote a mutual interest. **5** E20 A manufacturers' agreement or association formed to control marketing arrangements, regulate prices, etc.

cartes blanches, cartes-de-visite, etc. plural of CARTE BLANCHE, CARTE-DE-VISITE, etc.

cartonnage /ˈkɑːt(ə)nɪdʒ/ noun (also **cartonage**) M19 French (from *carton* cardboard (from Italian *cartone* augmentative of *carta*, from Latin *c(h)arta* paper) + -*age*). *Egyptology* A mummy-case made of tightly fitting layers of linen or papyrus glued together.

carton-pierre /kartɔ̃pjɛr/ noun M19 French (literally, 'cardboard (of) stone'). Papier mâché made to resemble stone or bronze.

cartouche /kɑːˈtuːʃ/ noun E17 French (from Italian *cartoccio* from *carta* paper). **I 1a** E17 A case for containing propellent explosive, a cartridge. *obsolete* except *historical*. **b** E17–M18 A case of wood, pasteboard, etc., for cannon-balls. **II 2a** E17 *Architecture* A scroll-shaped ornament; a tablet representing a scroll with rolled-up ends or edges, with or without an inscription. **b** L18 A painting or drawing of a scroll with rolled-up ends, with or without a text; an ornate frame in the shape of such a scroll. **3** M19 *Egyptology* An elongated oval with a straight bar at the end containing the hieroglyphic names and titles of rulers.

casbah variant of KASBAH.

cascara sagrada /kaˈskɑːrə səˌgrɑːdə/ noun phrase L19 Spanish (*cáscara sagrada*, literally, 'sacred bark'). The bark of a Cali-

fornian buckthorn, *Rhamnus purshiana*; an extract of this, used as a purgative.
■ Often shortened to *cascara*.

casha variant of KASHA.

casino /kəˈsiːnəʊ/ noun plural **casinos** M18 Italian (diminutive of *casa* house, from Latin *casa* cottage). **1** M18 Originally, a public room used for social meetings; *especially* a public room for music or dancing saloon. Now, a building for gambling, often with other amenities. **2** M18 A summer-house (*specifically* in Italy).
■ See also CASSINO, originally a variant of *casino*.

2 1996 *Spectator* [Sir William Hamilton] took a *casino* on the beach at Posillipo for sea-bathing . . .

casque /kɑːsk/ noun L17 French (from Spanish *casco*). **1** L17 A piece of armour to cover the head; a helmet. Now *historical* or *poetical*. **2** L18 *Zoology* A helmet-like structure, as in the cassowaries and hornbills.

cassareep /ˈkasəriːp/ noun M19 Caribbean. A thick brown syrup prepared by boiling down the juice of the cassava with sugar, spices, etc.

cassata /kəˈsɑːtə/ noun E20 Italian. A Neapolitan ice-cream containing fruit and nuts.

casse /kas/ noun L19 French (from *casser* to break). Souring of certain wines, accompanied by the loss of colour and the throwing of a sediment.

casserole /ˈkasərəʊl/ noun & verb E18 French (extension of *cassole* diminutive of *casse* from Provençal *casa*, from late Latin *cattia* ladle, pan, from Greek *kuathion*, *kuatheion* diminutive of *kuathos* cup). **A** noun A covered heatproof vessel in which food is cooked and served (now also *casserole dish*, *pan*, etc.); (a dish of) food cooked in this. **B** *transitive verb* M20 Cook in a casserole.

cassette /kəˈsɛt/ noun L18 French (diminutive of *casse*, *caisse* case). **1** L18 A casket. Now *rare*. **2** L19 A container for transporting photographic plates; a frame or holder for an X-ray plate or film. **3** M20 A container for a spool of magnetic tape, photographic film, etc., fashioned so as to be immediately usable on insertion into equipment designed for it; (now usually) such a container together with its tape, film, etc.; a video or audio magnetic recording on such a tape etc. **4** L20 *Genetics* A block of genetic material which can be inserted or moved as a unit, *especially* one which is expressed only at one location.

cassino /kə'si:nəʊ/ *noun* L18 Italian (variant of CASINO). A two-handed card-game in which players match or combine cards exposed on the table with cards from their hands. Also, either of two high-scoring cards in this game, (a) *big cassino*, (now *rare*) *great cassino*, the ten of diamonds, (b) *little cassino*, the two of spades.

cassis /ka'si:s/, /'kasɪs/ *noun* L19 French (= blackcurrant, apparently from Latin *cassia*). A (frequently alcoholic) syrup made from blackcurrants and used to flavour drinks etc.

cassolette /kasə'lɛt/ *noun* (also **cassolet**) M17 French (from Provençal *casoleta* diminutive of *casola*, from *casa*; cf. CASSEROLE). **1** M17 A vessel in which perfumes are burned. **2** E19 A box with a perforated cover for diffusing the odour of perfume in it. **3** E19 A small casserole dish; (a dish of) food cooked in this.

cassone /ka'səʊni/, *foreign* /kas'so:ne/ *noun* plural **cassones** /ka'səʊniz/, **cassoni** /kas'so:ni/ L19 Italian (augmentative of *cassa* chest). A large Italian coffer, especially to hold a bride's trousseau.

cassoulet /'kasʊleɪ/ *noun* M20 French (diminutive of dialect *cassolo* stew-pan, tureen). A ragout of meat and beans.

castrato /ka'strɑ:təʊ/ *noun* plural **castrati** /ka'strɑ:ti/ M18 Italian (use as noun of past participle of *castrare* to castrate). *History* An adult male singer castrated in boyhood so as to retain a soprano or alto voice.

castrum /'kastrəm/ *noun* plural **castra** /'kastrə/ M19 Latin. A Roman encampment or fortress.

casus belli /ˌkɑ:sʊs 'bɛli:/, /ˌkeɪsəs 'bɛlʌɪ/ *noun phrase* M19 Latin (from *casus* case + *belli* genitive of *bellum* war). An act or situation justifying or precipitating war.
> **1996** *Spectator* There must be clear provocation, a satisfactory *casus belli*.

casus foederis /ˌkɑ:sʊs 'fɔɪdərɪs/, /ˌkeɪsəs 'fi:dərɪs/ *noun phrase* L18 Latin (from *casus* case + *foederis* genitive of *foedus* treaty). An event which, under the terms of a treaty of alliance, entitles one of the allies to help from the other(s).

catafalque /'katəfalk/ *noun* (also (now *rare*) **catafalco** /katə'falkəʊ/, plural **catafalco(e)s** M17 French (from Italian *cata-*

falco, of unknown origin). **1** M17 A decorated structure fashioned so as to carry the coffin or effigy of a distinguished person during a funeral service or for a lying in state. **2** M19 A structure on which a coffin is drawn in procession.

catalogue raisonné /katalɔg rezɔne/ *noun phrase* plural **catalogues raisonnés** (pronounced same) L18 French (= reasoned catalogue). A descriptive catalogue with explanations or comments; *figurative* an exhaustive account.
> **1996** *Country Life* Paul McCarron has produced a *catalogue raisonné* of the prints of Martin Lewis . . . *figurative*
> **1995** *Spectator* That is the import of *The Sleaze File* by Judith Cook, a new *catalogue raisonné* of British scandal and microscandal over the last two or three years.

catalysis /kə'talɪsɪs/ *noun* plural **catalyses** /kə'talɪsi:z/ M17 Modern Latin (from Greek *katalusis*, from *kataluein* to dissolve). **1** M-L17 Dissolution, destruction. **2** M19 *Chemistry* The action or effect of a substance in increasing the rate of a reaction without itself being consumed; an instance of this.

catamaran /ˌkatəmə'ran/, /'katəmərən/ *noun* E17 Tamil (*kaṭṭumaram*, literally, 'tied wood'). **1** E17 A raft or float of logs tied side by side with the longest in the middle; a raft of two boats fastened side by side; a sailing boat with two hulls side by side. **2** E19 *History* A naval weapon consisting of a floating chest packed with gunpowder. **3** M19 A quarrelsome woman. *colloquial*.

catastasis /kə'tastəsɪs/ *noun* plural **catastases** /kə'tastəsi:z/ M16 Greek (*katastasis* settling, appointment, from as *cata-* + *stasis*). The third part of the ancient drama, in which the action is heightened for the catastrophe.

catechesis /katɪ'ki:sɪs/ *noun* plural **catecheses** /katɪ'ki:si:z/ M18 ecclesiastical Latin (from Greek *katēkhēsis* instruction by word of mouth, from *katēkhein*). **1** M18 Oral instruction given to catechumens; catechizing. **2** M18 A book for the instruction of catechumens.

catechumen /katɪ'kju:mɛn/ *noun* LME Old and Modern French (*catéchumène* or ecclesiastical Latin *catechumenus* from Greek *katēkhoumenos* being instructed, present participle passive of *katēkhein*). A Christian convert under instruction before baptism. Also, a young Christian preparing for confirmation.

catharsis /kəˈθɑːsɪs/ *noun* (in sense 2 also **katharsis**) plural **catharses** /kəˈθɑːsiːz/ E19 Modern Latin (from Greek *katharsis*, from *kathairein* to cleanse, from *katharos* pure). **1** E19 *Medicine* Purgation. **2** M19 (A) purification of the emotions by vicarious experience, especially through drama, or, in psychotherapy, by abreaction.

■ In sense 2 from Aristotle's *Poetics*.

cathedra /kəˈθiːdrə/ *noun* LME Latin (from Greek *kathedra* chair). A seat; *specifically* the chair of a bishop in his church; the episcopal see.

■ Most commonly in the phrase EX CATHEDRA.

catheter /ˈkaθɪtə/ *noun* (also **katheter**) E17 Late Latin (*catheter* from Greek *kathetēr*, from *kathienai* to send or let down). *Medicine* A tube which can be passed into the bladder or other body cavity or canal to allow the draining of fluid.

cathexis /kəˈθɛksɪs/ *noun* E20 Greek (*kathexis* holding, retention). *Psychoanalysis* The concentration or accumulation of libidinal energy on a particular object.

■ A rendering of Freud's German term (*Libido*)*besetzung*.

caudillo /kaʊˈdiːljəʊ/ *noun* plural **caudillos** M19 Spanish (from late Latin *capitellum* diminutive of *caput* head). In Spain and Spanish-speaking countries: a head of State, a military or political leader.

cause célèbre /koz selɛbr/ *noun phrase* plural **causes célèbres** (pronounced same) M18 French. A notorious legal case; *generally* a controversy or scandal that attracts much attention.

1996 *Times* The rape of Artemisia Gentileschi is a cause célèbre in art history.

causerie /kozri/ *noun* plural pronounced same E19 French (from *causer* to talk). Informal (especially literary) talk; a chatty article in a magazine or journal.

causes célèbres plural of CAUSE CÉLÈBRE.

causeuse /kozøz/ *noun* plural pronounced same M19 French (from *causer* to talk). A small sofa for two people.

cavaliere servente /kavaˈljeːre ser ˈvɛnte/ *noun phrase* M18 Italian (literally, 'gentleman-in-waiting'). The lover or solicitous admirer of a (married) woman.

cavallard variant of CAVAYARD.

cavatina /kavəˈtiːnə/ *noun* E19 Italian. *Music* A short simple song; a songlike piece of instrumental music, usually slow and emotional.

cavayard /ˈkavrjɑːd/ *noun* (also **cavallard** /ˈkav(ə)ljɑːd/, **cavy-yard**, and other variants) E19 Spanish (alteration of CABALLADA). A drove of horses or mules. *United States*.

cave /ˈkeɪvi/ *noun & interjection* LME Latin (imperative singular of *cavere* to beware). **A** *noun* **1** LME–L15 A warning; an injunction. **2** E20 *keep cave*, act as a lookout. *school slang*. **B** M19 *interjection* As a warning cry: look out! *school slang*.

cavea /ˈkeɪvɪə/ *noun* plural **caveae** /ˈkeɪviː/ E17 Latin (= a hollow). *Roman Antiquities* The (concave) auditorium of a theatre; a theatre.

caveat /ˈkavɪat/, /ˈkeɪvɪat/ *noun* M16 Latin (3rd person singular present subjunctive of *cavere* to beware). **1** M16 A warning, a proviso; *specifically* in *Law* a process or notice suspending or delaying proceedings. **2** L16–L17 A precaution.

■ Also formerly as a transitive verb (M17) in legal terminology or an intransitive verb (M17) in fencers' jargon meaning 'disengage'. Current verbal use is confined to the phrase CAVEAT EMPTOR.

1 **1996** *Times* I started to offer Wiesenthal Lord Shawcross's objections, but he stopped me with a caveat about using the euphemism 'war criminals'.

caveat emptor /ˌkavɪat ˈɛmptɔː/ *interjection* E16 Latin. (A maxim:) let the buyer beware!

■ A robust antique principle that the purchaser, rather than the seller, is responsible for making sure that the quality of the goods purchased is satisfactory. Frequently invoked in the context of horse-dealing—the earliest recorded use in English is in J. Fitzherbert's *A newe tracte . . . for all husbande men* (1523)—it fails to find much favour under modern consumer protection legislation.

1950 T. H. Marshall *Citizenship and Social Class* The principle of caveat emptor is at least plausible when you are buying a horse.

cavy-yard variant of CAVAYARD.

cedilla /sɪˈdɪlə/ *noun* (formerly (L16–M19) also **cerilla** L16 Spanish ((now *zedilla*), diminutive of *zeda* letter Z). The diacritic mark , written under *c* to show that it is sibilant /s/ or /ts/, as before *a*, *o*, *u* in French and Portuguese and (formerly)

Spanish; a similar mark under *c* and *s* indicating a manner of articulation in various other contexts, as distinguishing the voiceless from the voiced consonants in Turkish.

ceilidh /'keɪlɪ/ *noun* L19 Irish (*céilidhe* (now *céilí*), Gaelic *cèilidh*, from Old Irish *céilide* visit, act of visiting, from *céile* companion). An informal gathering for (especially Scottish or Irish) folk music, dancing, song, etc.

ceinture /sɛ̃tyr/ *noun* plural pronounced same LME French (from Latin *cinctura*, from *cinctus* past participle of *cingere* to gird). A girdle, a cincture.
■ Fell into disuse after the Middle English period, but was reintroduced in the early nineteenth century as part of the enthusiasm for all things Gothic and medieval.

celadon /'sɛlədɒn/ *noun & adjective* M18 French (*céladon*). **A** *noun* **1** M18 A pale greyish shade of green. **2** M19 A glaze of this colour used on (especially Chinese) pottery or porcelain; ceramic ware thus glazed. **B** L19 *attributive* or as *adjective* Of this colour; covered with this glaze.
■ From the name of the shepherd-hero of D'Urfé's immensely popular pastoral romance *L'Astrée* (1607–27).

celebret /'sɛlɪbrɛt/ *noun* M19 Latin (= let him celebrate, 3rd person singular present subjunctive of *celebrare* to celebrate). *Roman Catholic Church* A document granting permission by a bishop to a priest to celebrate mass in a particular parish.

celesta /sɪ'lɛstə/ *noun* L19 pseudo-Latin (apparently based on French CÉLESTE). *Music* A small keyboard instrument in which hammers strike on steel plates, producing an ethereal bell-like sound.

celeste /sɪ'lɛst/ *noun* L19 French (*céleste* from Latin *caelestis* from *caelum* heaven). **1** L19 A stop on the organ and harmonium with a soft tremulous tone (French *voix céleste*). Also, a form of soft pedal on a piano. **2** M20 A CELESTA.

cella /'kɛlə/ *noun* plural **cellae** /'kɛli:/ L17 Latin. *Architecture* The internal section of a Greek or Roman temple housing the hidden cult image; a similar part of other ancient temples.

cembalo /'tʃɛmbələʊ/ *noun* plural **cembalos** M19 Italian (abbreviation of CLAVICEMBALO). A harpsichord.

cenacle /'sɛnək(ə)l/ *noun* LME Old and Modern French (*cénacle* from Latin *cenac-* *ulum*, from *cena* dinner). **1** LME A dining-room; *specifically* the room in which the Last Supper was held. **2** L19 A place where a discussion group, literary clique, etc., meets; the group itself.

cenobium variant of COENOBIUM.

cenote /se'note/ *noun* M19 Yucatan Spanish (from Maya *tzonot*). A natural underground reservoir of water, such as occurs in the limestone of Yucatan, Mexico.

census /'sɛnsəs/ *noun* E17 Latin (from *censere* to assess). **1** E17-M19 A tax, a tribute; *especially* a poll tax. **2** M17 *History* The registration of citizens and their property in ancient Rome, usually for taxation purposes. **3** M18 An official enumeration of the population of a country etc., or of a class of things, usually with statistics relating to them.

cento /'sɛntəʊ/ *noun* plural **centos** E17 Latin (literally, 'patchwork garment'). **1** E-M17 A piece of patchwork; a patchwork garment. **2** E17 A hotchpotch, a medley; *specifically* a composition made up of quotations from other authors.

centrifuge /'sɛntrɪfjuːdʒ/ *adjective, noun, & verb* E18 French (from Modern Latin *centrifugus* centrifugal). **A** *adjective* E18-E19 Moving or tending to move away from the centre, centrifugal. **B** *noun* L19 A centrifugal machine; *especially* a device for effecting separation, usually of one liquid from another or of a solid from a liquid, by rapid rotation. **C** E20 *transitive verb* Subject to centrifugal motion; separate by means of a centrifuge.

centum see PER CENTUM.

cep /sɛp/ *noun* (also **cèpe** /sɛp/ (*plural* same)) M19 French (*cèpe* from Gascon *cep* tree-trunk, mushroom, from Latin *cippus* stake). An edible boletus.

cerebellum /sɛrɪ'bɛləm/ *noun* M16 Latin (diminutive of CEREBRUM). *Anatomy* The larger part of the hindbrain, responsible for the control of muscle tone and balance.
1996 *Oldie* We are all so dull, without discernment . . . But flabby cerebellums, arise! Address yourselves to a new noise.

cerebrum /'sɛrɪbrəm/ *noun* E17 Latin (= brain). *Anatomy* The larger, anterior part of the brain, responsible for voluntary activity and mental processes.

cerilla obsolete variant of CEDILLA.

cerise /sɛ'riːz/, /sɛ'riːs/ *adjective & noun* M19 French (= cherry). (Of) a light clear red.

ceroon variant of SERON.

cervelat /'sə:vəlɑ:/ *noun* E17 French ((now *cervelas*) from Italian *cervellata* Milanese sausage). A kind of smoked pork sausage.

cervix /'sə:vɪks/ *noun* plural **cervices** /'sə:vɪsiːz/ M18 Latin. *Anatomy* The neck; a part of an organ resembling or forming a neck; *specifically* the narrow passage forming the lower end of the womb adjacent to the vagina.

c'est la guerre /ˌseɪ la 'gɛː/ *interjection* F20 French (= that's war). (An expression of resignation:) that's the kind of thing that happens!

c'est la vie /ˌseɪ la 'viː/ *interjection* E20 French. (An expression of resignation:) that's life!

> **1995** *Country Life* Thanks to my inattention, and a low-flying helicopter . . . , I was bucked off this morning. *C'est la vie.*

cestui /'sɛti/ *noun* M16 Anglo-Norman and Old French (from Proto-Romance, from Latin *ecce* lo! + *iste* that (one), with element *-ui* as in *cui* dative of *quis* who). *Law* The person (who), he (who).

> ■ Only in the following legal phrases: *cestui que trust*, *cestui que use* the person for whose benefit something is given in trust to another; *cestui que vie* a person for whose lifetime an estate or interest in property is held by another.

cestus /'sɛstəs/ *noun* 1 plural **cesti** /'sɛstʌɪ/ M16 Latin (from Greek *kestos* use as noun of participial adjective = stitched). A (bridal) belt or girdle for the waist, *especially* that of Aphrodite or Venus.

cestus /'sɛstəs/ *noun* 2 plural same L17 Latin (*caestus*, from *caedere* to strike). *History* A covering for the hand made of thongs of bull-hide loaded with metallic strips, used by boxers in ancient Rome.

ceteris paribus /ˌkeɪtərɪs 'parɪbəs/, /ˌsetərɪs 'parɪbəs/, /ˌsiːtərɪs 'parɪbəs/ *adverb phrase* E17 Modern Latin. Other things being equal or unchanged.

> **1995** *Spectator* The new Rowntree Trust report merely gives the latest gloss on the problem. Thousands of years from now, Rowntree-type people will be producing, *ceteris paribus*, similar gloomy reports.

ceviche variant of SEVICHE.

cha-cha /'ʧɑːʧɑː/ *noun & verb* (also **cha-cha-cha** /ˈʧɑːʧɑːˈʧɑː/ M20 American Spanish. **A** *noun* M20 A type of ballroom dance to a Latin American rhythm; a piece of music for this dance. **B** *transitive verb* M20 Perform this dance.

> **1996** *Times* Ballroom dancing is divided into Latin (cha-cha, jive, rumba, samba, paso doblé) and Modern . . .

chacham variant of HAHAM.

chaconne /ʃə'kɒn/ *noun* L17 French (from Spanish *chacona*). A moderately slow musical composition on a ground bass, usually in triple time; a dance to this music.

> **1996** *Country Life* . . . a theme by Bach is worked into a *chaconne* which is one of the wonders of 19th-century music.

chacun à son goût /ʃakœ̃ a sɔ̃ gu/ *interjection* L19 French. Everyone to his or her taste.

> ■ Also occasionally in the form usual in French: *à chacun son goût*.
> **1996** *Country Life* People must think I'm totally halfwitted. There are some who would give their eye-teeth to fish this beautiful stretch of river. But *chacun à son goût*.

chadar /'ʧɑːdə/ *noun* (also **chaddar**, **chador**, **chuddar** /'ʧʌdə/, and other variants) E17 Urdu (*chādar*, *chaddar* from Persian *čādar* sheet, veil). A large piece of material worn as a long shawl or cloak especially by Muslim women in the Indian subcontinent and Iran.

chaebol /keɪ'bɒl/ *noun* L20 Korean. In South Korea: a large business conglomerate comparable to the Japanese ZAIBATSU.

chagrin /'ʃagrɪn/ *noun & verb* M17 French (literally, 'rough skin', of unknown origin). **A** *noun* **1** M17-M19 Anxiety; melancholy. **2** E18 Vexation arising from disappointment or failure; acute annoyance. **B** also /ʃə'griːn/ *transitive verb* M17 Affect with chagrin. Usually in *passive*.

> ■ The spelling *shagreen* of the noun is an obsolete (L17-M19) variant that is now used solely in senses that retain the literal French meaning, being applied to a kind of untanned leather with a rough granular surface (often dyed green) or to the rough scaly skin of sharks or rays especially as used for polishing.

chaîné /ʃɛne/ *noun* M20 French (= linked). *Ballet* A quick step or turn from one foot to the other, or a series of these, performed in a line.

chaise /ʃeɪz/ noun plural pronounced same M17 French (variant of *chaire* chair). **1** M17 A pleasure or travelling carriage, especially a light open one for one or two people. Chiefly *historical*. **2** M20 A CHAISE LONGUE.

chaise longue /ʃeɪz 'lɒŋg/, foreign /ʃɛz lɔ̃g/ noun phrase plural **chaise longues** /ʃeɪz 'lɒŋgz/, **chaises longues** /ʃeɪz 'lɒŋg(z)/, foreign /ʃɛz lɔ̃g/ E19 French (= long chair). A kind of sofa with a backrest at only one end.

chaise percée /ʃɛz pɛrse/ noun phrase plural **chaises percées** (pronounced same) M20 French (= pierced chair). A chair incorporating a chamber-pot.

chaitya /'tʃʌɪtjə/ noun L19 Sanskrit (*caitya* (resembling) a funeral pile, mound, etc., from *citā* funeral mound). A Buddhist place or object of reverence.

chakra /'tʃʌkrə/ noun L18 Sanskrit (*cakra*; cf. Greek *kuklos* cycle). **1** L18 A thin knife-edged disc of steel formerly used as a weapon by Sikhs. **2** L19 A discus or mystic circle depicted in the hands of Hindu deities. **3** L19 *Yoga* Each of the centres of spiritual power in the human body. **4** M20 The circular emblem on the flag of the Indian Union.

chal /tʃal/ noun M19 Romany (= person, fellow). A male Gypsy. Also *Romany chal*.

chalet /'ʃaleɪ/ noun L18 Swiss French (diminutive of Old French *chasel* farmstead from Proto-Romance derivative of Latin *casa* hut, cottage). A Swiss mountain cowherd's hut; a Swiss peasant's wooden cottage; a house with a widely overhanging roof; a small villa; a small house in a holiday camp etc.

chalifa variant of KHALIFA.

challah /'hɑːlə/, foreign /'xɑːlɑː/ noun L20 Hebrew. Jewish ceremonial bread for the Sabbath.

chalumeau /ʃalymo/ noun plural **chalumeaux** /ʃalymo/ E18 French (from late Latin *calamellus* diminutive of *calamus* reed). A musical pipe of reed or straw; an instrument having a reed mouthpiece, *especially* the forerunner of the clarinet. Also (in full *chalumeau register*), the lowest register of the clarinet.

chalutzim variant of HALUTZIM.

cham /kam/ noun LME French (*cham, chan* from Turkic *kăn* KHAN). A khan. Now only *transferred* and *figurative*, an autocrat, a dominant critic, etc.

■ The transferred use alludes to an expression of the Scottish author Tobias Smollett, who, in a letter to John Wilkes in 1759, referred to Samuel Johnson as the 'great Cham of literature'.

chambranle /ʃɑ̃brɑ̃l/ noun plural pronounced same E18 French. *Architecture* An ornamental bordering around a door, window, or fireplace.

chambré /ʃɒmbreɪ/, foreign /ʃɑ̃bre/ adjective M20 French (past participle of *chambrer* to bring to room temperature, from Old French *chambre* from Latin *camera* room). Of wine: at room temperature. Usually *predicative*.

1952 B. Pym *Excellent Women* My only fear is that it will scarcely be chambré by the time I shall want to drink it.

chametz variant of HAMETZ.

chamois /'ʃamwɑː/; in senses A2 and B2, usually /ʃami/ noun & adjective (senses A2 and B2 also **shammy** /'ʃami/) plural of noun same /'ʃamwɑːz/, /'ʃamɪz/ M16 Old and Modern French (probably ultimately from Swiss Proto-Romance; cf. Gallo-Latin *camox*). **A** noun **1** M16 A goatlike antelope, *Rupicapra rupicapra*, found in the mountains of Europe and Asia Minor. **2** L16 Soft pliable leather from the chamois or (now more usually) from sheep, goats, deer, etc.; a piece of this for polishing etc. More fully *chamois leather*. **B** *attributive* or as *adjective*. **1** E17 Made of chamois leather. **2** M17 Of the colour of chamois leather; yellowish brown.

champignon /tʃam'pmjən/, /'ʃampmjɒ̃/; foreign /ʃɑ̃piɲɔ̃/ (plural same) noun L16 French ((earlier *champaignon*), diminutive of *champagne*). A mushroom; a toadstool. Now specifically (a) the edible field mushroom *Agaricus campestris*; (b) an agaric, *Marismius oreades*, which often forms fairy-rings.

champlevé /'ʃampləveɪ/, foreign /ʃɑ̃ləve/ adjective & noun M19 French (from *champ* field + *levé* raised). (Designating) enamel-work in which the colours in the pattern are set into hollows made in the surface of the metal base. Cf. CLOISONNÉ.

1996 Country Life An example . . . is a Limoges engraved copper, gilt and champlevé enamel statue of the Virgin and Child.

chancre /'tʃaŋkə/ noun L16 French (from Latin *cancer* crab). *Medicine* A painless ulcer, *especially* one occurring on the genitals and resulting from syphilis.

chandelier /ʃandəˈlɪə/ *noun* M17 French (from *chandelle* candle, from Latin *candela*). **1** M17 *Military* A wooden frame filled with fascines to form a traverse in sapping. **2** M18 A branched hanging support for several lights, originally candles.

changement /ʃãʒmã/ *noun* plural pronounced same M19 French (from *changer* to change). *Ballet* A jump during which the dancer changes the position of the feet. In full *changement de pieds* /ʃãʒmãdə pje/ (literally, 'changing of feet').

chanson /ʃãsɔ̃/ *noun* plural pronounced same L15 Old and Modern French (from Latin *cantio* song). A French song.

chanson de geste /ʃãsɔ̃ də ʒɛst/ *noun phrase* plural **chansons de geste** (pronounced same) M19 French (= song of heroic deeds). Any of a group of medieval French epic poems dealing with chivalric and heroic subjects.

■ The earliest was the *Chanson de Roland*, written about 1100.

chansonette /ʃãsɔnɛt/ *noun* plural pronounced same E19 French. A short song.

chansonnier /[ʃãsɔnje/ *noun* plural pronounced same L19 French. In France: a writer or performer of songs, especially of satirical songs in a cabaret; a collection of (French) songs.

chantage /ʃãtaʒ/, /ˈtʃɑːntɪdʒ/ *noun* L19 French. Extortion of money by blackmail.

chanterelle /ˈtʃɑːntərɛl/, /ˈtʃɑːntəˈrɛl/ *noun* **1** E17 French (from *chanter* from Latin *cantare* frequentative of *canere* to sing). **1** A decoy-bird. Only in E17. **2** L18 The highest-pitched string of a plucked or bowed musical instrument.

chanterelle /ˈtʃɑːntəˈrɛl/ *noun* **2** (also **chantarelle**) L18 French (from Modern Latin *cantharellus* diminutive of *cantharus* from Greek *kantharos* drinking-vessel). A yellow funnel-shaped edible fungus, *Cantharellus cibarius*.

chanteuse /ʃãtøz/ *noun* plural pronounced same M19 French. A female singer of popular songs, originally in France.

1996 *Times Magazine* Stylistically, the work is a throwback to the golden age of confessional chanteuse à la Joni Mitchell . . .

chaparejos /ʃapəˈreɪhəʊs/, /ˈtʃapə ˈreɪhəʊs/ *noun* plural (also **chaparreras** /ʃapəˈrɛːrəs/, /ˈtʃapəˈrɛːrəs/) M19 Mexican Spanish (*chaparreras*, from *chaparra*, *chaparro* dwarf evergreen oak). Tough leather over-trousers worn by cowboys for protection against spiny vegetation.

■ *Chaparejos* is a later form than *chaparreras* and is probably influenced by Spanish *aparejo* 'equipment'. In the United States the abbreviation *chaps* has been commonly used from the late nineteenth century onwards.

chaparral /ʃapəˈral/, /ˈtʃapəˈral/ *noun* M19 Spanish (from as above). In United States: a thicket of dwarf evergreen oaks; dense tangled brushwood.

chaparreras variant of CHAPAREJOS.

chapatti /tʃəˈpɑːti/, /ˈtʃəˈpati/ *noun* (also **chapati**, **chupatti**, and other variants) E19 Hindustani (*capātī*, from *capānā* to flatten, roll out, ultimately from Dravidian). In Indian cookery: a small flat thin cake of coarse unleavened bread.

chapeau-bras /ʃapobra/ *noun* plural **chapeaux-bras** (pronounced same) M18 French (from *chapeau* (Old French *c(h)apel*, from Latin *cappellum* diminutive of *cappa* cap) hat + *bras* arm). A three-cornered flat silk hat able to be carried under the arm.

chapelle ardente /ʃapɛl ardãt/ *noun phrase* plural **chapelles ardentes** (pronounced same) E19 French (= burning chapel). A chamber prepared for the lying-in-state of a distinguished person, and lit up with candles, torches, etc.

chaperon /ˈʃapərəʊn/ *noun & verb* (also **chaperone**) LME Old and Modern French (from *chape* cape, hood, ultimately from Latin *caput* head). **A** *noun* **1** LME A hood, a capital. *obsolete except historical.* **2** L17–L18 A small escutcheon placed especially on the forehead of a horse drawing a hearse. **3** E18 A person who ensures propriety, *especially* a married or older woman accompanying a young unmarried woman on social occasions. **B** L18 *transitive verb* Act as a chaperon to.

chappal /ˈtʃap(ə)l/ *noun* (also **chappli** /ˈtʃapli/) L19 Hindustani (*cappal*, *caplī*). In the Indian subcontinent: a sandal, especially of leather.

chaprassi /tʃəˈprasi/ *noun* plural **chaprassi(e)s** (also **chuprassy**) E19 Urdu (*chaprāsī*, from *chaprās* official badge, from Persian *čaprǎst*). In the Indian sub-continent: an attendant, a messenger, a household official.

charabanc /'ʃarəbaŋ/ *noun* (also **char-à-banc**) E19 French (*char-à-bancs* literally, 'carriage with seats'). A long and light vehicle with transverse seats looking forward; a motor coach. Now *archaic* or *jocular*.

charade /ʃə'rɑːd/ *noun* L18 French (from Modern Provençal *charrado* conversation, from *charra* chatter, perhaps of imitative origin). **1** L18 A written or (now usually) acted clue from which a syllable of a word or a complete word is to be guessed. **b** M19 (in *plural* usually treated as *singular*) A game of guessing words from such clues. **2** L19 *figurative* An absurd pretence.

charcuterie /ʃarkytri/ (*plural same*), /ʃɑː'kuːt(ə)riː/ *noun* M19 French (from *char* (modern *chair*) *cuite* cooked flesh). Cold cooked meats; a shop selling these; a (French) pork-butcher's shop.
> **1996** *Times* He is capable of appreciating the elaborate display of a *charcuterie* . . .

chargé /'ʃɑːʒeɪ/; *foreign* /ʃarʒe/ (*plural same*) *noun* M19 French. Abbreviation of CHARGÉ D'AFFAIRES.

chargé d'affaires /,ʃɑːʒeɪ da'fɛː/, *foreign* /ʃarʒe dafɛr/ *noun phrase plural* **chargés d'affaires** (pronounced same) (also **chargé des affaires**) M18 French (= (a person) in charge of affairs). **1** M18 A minister who transacts diplomatic business during the temporary absence of an ambassador; a State's representative at a minor foreign court or government. **2** L18 *generally* A person temporarily in charge.

charisma /kə'rɪzmə/ *noun plural* **charismata** /kə'rɪzmətə/ M17 ecclesiastical Latin (from Greek *kharisma, -mat-*, from *kharis* favour, grace). **1** M17 *Christian Theology* A divinely conferred power or talent. **2** M20 A capacity to inspire devotion and enthusiasm; aura.
> **2 1996** *Times* In the entertainment world, the Sagittarian's charisma is matched by a determination to be different, to stamp originality on the most mundane or unlikely material.

charivari /ʃɑːrɪ'vɑːriː/ *noun* M17 French (of unknown origin). A cacophonous mock serenade in derision of an unpopular person, marriage, etc.; a discordant medley of sounds, a hubbub.

■ The variant *shivaree* (M19) is mainly found in the United States.

charlotte /'ʃɑːlət/ *noun* L18 French (possibly the feminine name). A pudding made of stewed fruit with a casing or covering of bread, biscuits, sponge cake, or breadcrumbs.
■ Usually with defining word, as in *apple charlotte, rhubarb charlotte*, etc. Cf. CHARLOTTE RUSSE.

charlotte russe /'ʃɑːlət ,ruːs/ *noun phrase plural* **charlottes russes, charlotte russes** M19 French (= Russian CHARLOTTE). A pudding with flavoured custard or cream inside a moulded sponge cake or biscuit casing.

charmeuse /ʃɑː'məːz/, *foreign* /ʃarmøz/ *noun* E20 French (feminine of *charmeur* charmer, from Old French *charme* charm, from Latin *carmen* song, incantation). A soft smooth silky dress-fabric.

charoset(h) variants of HAROSETH.

charpoy /'tʃɑːpɔɪ/ *noun* M17 Urdu (*chārpāī* from Persian). In the Indian subcontinent: a light bedstead.

charqui /'tʃɑːki/ *noun* E17 American Spanish (*charqui, charque* from Quechua *cc'arki*). Meat, especially beef, cut into thin slices and dried in the wind and sun.
■ English travellers to the New World in the seventeenth century apparently adopted the word from the Spanish, corrupting it in the process; from these corruptions the word *jerky* emerged (M19) to become the term widely used in North America. The South African equivalent is BILTONG; cf. PEMMICAN.

charro /'tʃɑːrəʊ/ *noun plural* **charros** E20 Mexican Spanish (from Spanish = rustic). A Mexican cowboy, *especially* one elaborately dressed.

chartreuse /ʃɑː'trəːz/, *foreign* /ʃartrøz/ (*plural same*) *noun* E19 French (feminine of *Chartreux*). **1** E19 *Cookery* A dish turned out from a mould, of meat, vegetables, or (now more usually) of fruit enclosed in jelly etc. **2** M19 A green or yellow liqueur of brandy and aromatic herbs etc., originally made by the monks of La Grande Chartreuse, near Grenoble, France. **3** L19 An apple-green colour.

chasid variant of HASID.

chasse /ʃas/, /ʃɑːs/ *noun* **1** LME French (*châsse* reliquary). A case for the relics of a saint.

chasse /ʃas/, /ʃɑːs/ *noun* 2 plural **chasses** /ʃas/, /ˈʃɑːsɪz/ M18 French (abbreviation of *chasse-café*, literally, 'chase-coffee'). A liqueur taken after coffee, tobacco, etc.; a chaser.

■ The full form *chasse-café* (E19) is now rare.

chassé /ʃase/ (*plural same*), /ˈʃaseɪ/ *noun* E19 French (literally, 'chasing, chase'). A sliding step in which one foot displaces the other in dancing.

■ A mainly North American alteration is *sashay* (noun and verb), '(to perform) a *chassé* in square dancing'; as a verb *sashay* also has a general colloquial sense of 'to walk with an ostentatiously gliding or swinging step' (see quotation at DERRIÈRE).
1995 *Times* A group of couples appear, confident in their skaters' *chassé* steps, with only one of the men later falling over.

chassé croisé /ʃase krwaze/ *noun phrase* L19 French (literally, 'crossed chassé'). A dance movement comprising a double chassé causing partners to change position; *figurative* an elaborate reversal of position, especially a mix-up in which people trying to meet constantly miss one another.

chasseur /ʃaˈsəː/; *foreign* /ʃasœr/ (*plural same*) *noun* M18 French (from *chasser* to hunt). **1** M18 *History* A soldier (especially French) equipped and trained for rapid movement. **2** M18 An attendant dressed in military style. Now *rare* or *obsolete*. **b** L19 A hotel messenger, especially in France. **3** L18 A huntsman.

■ The French equivalent of the German JÄGER.

chassid variant of HASID.

chassis /ˈʃasi/, /ˈʃasiː/ *noun* plural same /ˈʃasɪz/, /ˈʃasiːz/ M17 French (*châssis* from Proto-Romance, from Latin *capsa* case). **1** M17–E18 A window frame, a sash. **2** M19 The sliding base-frame of a mounted gun. **3** E20 The base-frame of a motor vehicle etc. **4** M20 A frame carrying radio etc. equipment. **5** M20 The human or animal frame, the body. *slang*.

château /ˈʃatəʊ/, *foreign* /ʃato/ *noun* plural **châteaux** /ˈʃatəʊz/, *foreign* /ʃato/ M18 French. A large country house in France (formerly also elsewhere); *especially* one giving its name to wine made in its neighbourhood.

■ Sometimes also used jocularly with the owner's name of an ostentatious or pretentious house anywhere, e.g. Château Jones.

1996 *Times Magazine* Buying en primeur . . . is often the only chance that claret lovers will get to buy their favourite châteaux.

Chateaubriand /ʃatobrijã/ *noun* plural pronounced same L19 French. A thick fillet beefsteak, grilled and garnished with herbs etc.

■ Called after François René, Vicomte de *Chateaubriand* (1768–1848), French writer and statesman. Also *Chateaubriand steak* or *steak à la Chateaubriand*.

chatelaine /ˈʃatəlem/ *noun* M19 French (*châtelaine* feminine of *châtelain*). **1** M19 A female castellan (*historical*); the mistress of a castle or (country) house. **2** M19 *History* A set of short chains attached to a woman's belt for carrying keys, a watch, a pencil, etc.

1 1995 *Times* If the chatelaine had spent all day lying down zonked out with Valium, these were suppers that required a minimum of preparation.

chaton /ʃatõ/ *noun* plural pronounced same L16 French (from German *Kasten* case (Old and Middle High German *kasto*)). The part of a finger-ring in which a stone is set or on which a device is engraved.

chatoyant /ʃəˈtɔɪənt/, *foreign* /ʃatwajã/ *noun* & *adjective* L18 French (present participle of *chatoyer*) to shimmer. (Of) iridescent undulating lustre.

■ Now *rare*.

chaud-froid /ʃəʊˈfrwɑː/, *foreign* /ʃofrwa/ (*plural same*) *noun* L19 French (literally, 'hot-cold'). A dish of cold cooked meat or fish in a jelly or sauce.

chaukidar variant of CHOKIDAR.

chaussée /ʃose/ *noun* plural pronounced same E19 French. In France, Belgium, etc.: a causeway; a high road.

chaussure /ʃosyr/ *noun* LME French (Anglo-Norman *chaucer* = Old French *chaucier* (modern *chaussure*), Provençal *causier* shoe; cf. medieval Latin *calceatura*). Footwear.

■ Formerly naturalized with the spelling *chawcer* and variants, but reintroduced as a borrowing from Modern French in the nineteenth century.

chayote /ˈtʃeɪəʊti/, *noun* L19 Spanish (from Nahuatl *chayotli*). A tropical American vine, *Sechium edule*, cultivated elsewhere for its fruit; the succulent fruit of this vine. Also called *chocho*.

chaz(z)an variants of HAZZAN.

chechia /'ʃeɪʃɪə/ noun M19 French (*chéchia* from Maghribi pronunciation of Arabic *šāšiyya*, from Arabic *šāš* Tashkent in Uzbekistan). A red felt cap worn in North-west Africa.

cheder variant of HEDER.

cheechako /tʃiːˈtʃɑːkəʊ/ noun L19 Chinook Jargon (= newcomer). A recently arrived immigrant to the mining districts of North America; a greenhorn.
■ North American colloquial.

chee-chee variant of CHI-CHI.

chef /ʃɛf/ noun E19 French (= head). A person (usually a man) who is (usually the chief) cook in a hotel, restaurant, etc.
■ Also in combinations such as *sous-chef* 'under-chef', COMMIS *chef*, etc.

chef d'école /ʃɛf dekɔl/ noun phrase plural **chefs d'école** (pronounced same) M19 French (= head of school). The initiator or leader of a school or style of music, painting, literature, etc.
1995 *Spectator* He found himself an unwilling and unsuitable *chef d'école*—unsuitable because his search for a modern language in painting became increasingly idiosyncratic.

chef d'équipe /ʃɛf dekip/ noun phrase plural **chefs d'équipe** (pronounced same) L20 French (= head of team; cf. ÉQUIPE). The manager of a sports team responsible for practical arrangements especially when travelling.
1996 *Times* Long after she [sc. Pat Smythe] had been forced to give up showjumping she remained involved in the sport as an international selector, and sometimes, chef d'equipe of British teams abroad.

chef-d'œuvre /ʃɛdœvr/ noun plural **chefs-d'œuvre** (pronounced same) E17 French (= chief (piece) of work). The greatest work of an artist etc.; a masterpiece.

chef d'orchestre /ʃɛf dɔrkɛstr/ noun phrase plural **chefs d'orchestre** (pronounced same) M19 French (= head of orchestra). The leader or conductor of an orchestra.

chela /'tʃeɪlə/ noun M19 Hindustani (*celā*). A disciple, a pupil, *specifically* in Hinduism.

chemin de fer /ʃ(ə)mɛ̃ də fɛr/, /ʃə'mɑ̃ də fɛ:/ noun L19 French (= railway, literally, 'road of iron'). A form of baccarat.

chemise /ʃə'miːz/ noun ME Old and Modern French (from late Latin *camisia* shirt, nightgown). 1 ME A garment for the upper body; *especially* a woman's loose-fit-ting undergarment or dress hanging straight from the shoulders. 2 E18 *History* A wall with which a bastion etc. is lined as a fortification. 3 L19 *History* A loose covering for a book.

chemisette /ʃɛmiˈzɛt/ noun E19 French (diminutive of CHEMISE). 1 E19 A bodice, resembling the upper part of a chemise. 2 E19 A piece of muslin, lace, etc., used to fill in the open front of a woman's dress.

chenille /ʃə'niːl/ noun M18 French (literally, 'hairy caterpillar', from Latin *canicula* diminutive of *canis* dog). Velvety cord with pile all round, used in trimming and bordering dresses and furniture.

cheongsam /tʃɪɒŋ'sam/, /tʃɒŋ'sam/ noun M20 Chinese (Cantonese (= Mandarin *chángshān*)). A Chinese woman's garment with a high neck and slit skirt.

cherchez la femme /ʃɛrʃe la fam/ interjection L19 French (= look for the woman). The principle that there is certain to be a woman behind an untoward event.
■ A catchphrase of Alexandre Dumas *père* in *Les Mohicans de Paris* (1864).
1996 *Times* [Lady Hollis] was credited with influencing Alan Howarth's decision to cross the floor—a canard put out by credulous Tories playing *cherchez la femme*.

chère amie /ʃɛr ami/ noun phrase plural **chères amies** /ʃɛrz ami/ L18 French (literally, 'dear (woman) friend'). A female lover; a mistress.

cherem /'xerem/, /'herem/ noun (also **herem**) E19 Hebrew (*ḥērem* from *ḥāram* devote, put under a curse). Excommunication from the Synagogue and the Jewish community.

cherimoya /tʃɛrɪ'mɔɪə/ noun (also **chirimoya** /tʃɪr'mɔɪə/) M18 Spanish (from Quechua, from *chiri* cold, refreshing + *muya* circle). (The pulpy edible fruit of) a small tree, *Annona cherimola*, native to the Andes of Peru and Ecuador.

cher maître /ʃɛr mɛtr/ noun phrase plural **chers maîtres** (pronounced same) E20 French (literally, 'dear master'). (A flattering form of address to) a famous writer.
■ Often used ironically (see quotation).
1995 *Country Life* For me at least, *cher maître*, you do not always succeed.

chernozem /'tʃɜːnəzɛm/ noun (also **chernosem**) M19 Russian (from *chërnyĭ* black + Slavonic base *zem*- (cf. Russian *zemlya*) earth). A dark, humus-rich, fertile soil characteristic of temperate or cool grassland.

■ Originally used of the soil of the Russian steppes, now generally for soils of this type.

chétif /ʃetif/ *adjective* E20 **French**. Puny, sickly, thin; miserable, wretched.

chetnik /ˈtʃetnɪk/ *noun* E20 **Serbo-Croat** (*četnik*, from *četa* band, troop). A guerrilla fighter in the Balkans; (*historical*) one of a royalist force led by General Draža Mihajlović in occupied Yugoslavia, 1941–5.

chevachee variant of CHEVAUCHÉE.

cheval /ʃəval/, /ʃəˈval/ *noun* plural **chevaux** /ʃəvo/, /ʃəˈvəʊ/ L15 **French** (= horse, frame). Horse; frame.

■ Never independently naturalized in English, *cheval* occurs in the combination *cheval-glass* (a tall glass set on a pivot in an upright frame) and in various phrases; see À CHEVAL, CHEVAL DE BATAILLE, CHEVAUX DE FRISE.

cheval de bataille /ʃəval də bataj/ *noun phrase* plural **chevaux de bataille** /ʃəvo də bataj/ E19 **French** (literally, 'battle-horse'). An obsession, a pet subject; something made boring by repetition or overuse.

■ Native English equivalents are 'hobby-horse' or 'warhorse', depending on context; see quotation for 'warhorse' sense.

1942 E. Blom *Music in England* The chief *chevaux de bataille* for new sopranos [are] the heroines in 'La Sonnambula' and 'Lucia di Lammermoor'.

chevalet /ʃəvale/ *noun* plural pronounced same E19 **French** (diminutive of CHEVAL). **1** A trestle for a bridge. Only in E19. **2** L19 The bridge of a bowed musical instrument.

chevalier /ʃɛvəˈlɪə/, *foreign* /ʃəvalje/ (*plural same*) *noun* LME **Anglo-Norman** (*chevaler*, Old and Modern French *chevalier*, from medieval Latin *caballarius*, from Latin *caballus* horse). **1** LME *History* A horseman, *especially* a mounted knight. **2** M17 A chivalrous man, a gallant. **3** E18 A member of certain orders of knighthood, or of the French Legion of Honour, etc.

■ Sometimes in the phrase *chevalier sans peur et sans reproche* literally, 'a knight without fear or stain', a perfect gentleman; see also SANS PEUR.

chevauchée /ʃəvoʃe/ *noun* Also formerly written **chevachee** LME **French** (from Old

French *chevauchiee* expedition on horseback, past participial formation on *chevauchier* (modern *chevaucher*) from Late Latin *caballicare* to ride, from *caballus* horse). *History* A mounted raid.

1995 *Spectator* These *chevauchées* involved the English soldiery running amok, marauding, looting, raping and laying waste the countryside.

chevaux de frise /ʃəvo də friz/ *noun phrase* L17 **French** (literally, 'horses of Friesland'). Iron spikes closely set in timber, originally to repel cavalry; a similar device, often with the spikes rotating around a rod, now set along the tops of walls, fences, etc. to deter intruders.

■ The name is an ironical reference to the fact that the Frieslanders possessed no cavalry and relied upon such devices to beat off the cavalry of others. Although the phrase is plural in form it is often treated as singular.

chevelure /ʃəvlyr/ *noun* plural pronounced same LME **Old French** (*cheveleûre* (modern *chevelure*), from Latin *capillatura*, from *capillatus* haired, from *capillus* hair). **1** LME The hair of the head, a head of hair; (formerly) a wig. **2** L17 A halo around a star etc.; a comet's coma.

chevet /ʃəˈveɪ/, *foreign* /ʃəvɛ/ (*plural same*) *noun* E19 **French** (= pillow). The apsidal termination of the east end of a church.

cheville /ʃəvij/ *noun* plural pronounced same L19 **French** (= peg, pin, plug). **1** L19 A meaningless or redundant word or phrase inserted to round off a sentence or complete a verse. **2** L19 A peg in a stringed musical instrument.

chevra variant of HEBRA.

chèvre /ʃɛvr/ *noun* M20 **French** (= goat, especially she-goat). French goat's-milk cheese.

chevron /ˈʃɛvrən/ *noun* LME **Old and Modern French** (from Proto-Romance, from Latin *caper* goat; cf. Latin *capreoli* pair of rafters). **1** *Heraldry* LME A charge consisting of a bent bar of an inverted V shape. **b** E17 This shape used in decorative art etc. **2** L16 A beam or rafters, *especially* in *plural*, the rafters of a roof that meet at an angle at the ridge. **3** E19 A badge in a V shape (whether inverted or not) on a uniform to denote rank and length of service; a V-shaped stripe.

chez /ʃe/, *before a vowel* /ʃez/ *preposition* M18 **French** (from Old French *chiese* from

Latin *casa* cottage). At the house or home of.

1996 *Spectator* The predominant political leaning *chez* Hart suggested that a special musical selection was called for—perhaps a K-Tel collection of Top Tunes for Troubled Tories.

chiaroscuro /kɪˌɑːrəˈskʊərəʊ/ *noun & adjective* M17 Italian (from *chiaro* clear, bright + *oscuro* dark, obscure). **A** *noun* plural **chiaroscuros**. **1** M17 A style of painting in which only light and shade are represented; black and white. **2** L17 The treatment or disposition of the light and shade, or brighter and darker masses, in a picture; an effect or contrast of light and shade in a picture or in nature. **3** E19 *figurative* The use of contrast in literature etc. **B** M19 *attributively* or as *adjective* In chiaroscuro.

chiasmus /kʌɪˈazməs/, /kɪˈazməs/ *noun* plural **chiasmi** /kʌɪˈazmʌɪ/ M17 Modern Latin (from Greek *khiasmos* from *khiazein* mark with a chi, from *khi* chi. **1** M17 *generally* A diagonal or crosswise arrangement. *rare*. **2** L19 *Rhetoric* The inversion in a second phrase or clause of the order of words in the first.

chibouk /tʃɪˈbuːk/ *noun* (also **chibouque**) E19 French ((*chibouque* from) Turkish *çubuk*, (earlier) *çıbık* tube, pipe). A long Turkish tobacco-pipe.

chic /ʃiːk/ *noun & adjective* M19 French (probably from German *Schick* skill). **A** *noun* M19 Stylishness; elegance in dress; skill, effectiveness. **B** *adjective* M19 Stylish, elegant.

chicane /ʃɪˈkeɪn/ *noun* L17 French (from as next). **1** L17 Trickery or subterfuge in legal matters, chicanery. **2** L17–M18 An instance of chicanery; a subterfuge, a quibble. **3** L19 *Cards* A hand without trumps or without cards of one suit as dealt. **4** M20 An artificial barrier or obstacle, especially a sharp double bend, on a motor-racing track.

chicane /ʃɪˈkeɪn/ *verb* L17 French (*chicaner* to pursue at law, quibble, of unknown origin). **1** L17 *intransitive verb* Employ chicanery; quibble, cavil. **2** L18 *transitive verb* Quibble over; argue *away* by chicanery. *rare*. **3** M19 *transitive verb* Deceive by chicanery, cheat, (*into, out of,* etc.).

chicano /tʃɪˈkɑːnəʊ/, /ʃɪˈkɑːnəʊ/, /tʃɪˈkeɪnəʊ/, /ʃɪˈkeɪnəʊ/ *noun & adjective* (also **Chicano**) M20 Spanish (alteration of *mejicano* Mexican, from *Méjico* Mexico). **A** *noun* M20 plural **chicanos** (feminine

chicana /tʃɪˈkɑːnə/) A North American of Mexican origin. **B** *adjective* M20 Of or pertaining to chicanos; Mexican American.

chicha /ˈtʃiːtʃə/ *noun* E17 American Spanish (from Cuna). In South and Central America: a fermented liquor made from maize.

chicharron /tʃiːtʃəˈrɒn/, *foreign* /tʃitʃa ˈrron/ *noun* plural **chicharrones** /tʃiːtʃə ˈrəʊnɪz/, *foreign* /tʃitʃaˈrrones/ M19 American Spanish (*chicharrón*). A piece of crackling, served as a delicacy in Mexico, parts of the southern United States, etc.

chichi /ˈʃiːʃiː/ *noun & adjective* E20 French. **A** *noun* E20 Showiness, fussiness; affectation; a frilly or showy thing. **B** *adjective* M20 Showy, frilly, fussy; affected.

chi-chi /ˈtʃiːtʃiː/ *adjective* (also **chee-chee**) L18 Anglo-Indian (perhaps from Hindustani *chī-chī* fie!). (Especially of a girl or woman) half-caste, Eurasian; (of speech) characteristic of the English formerly spoken by some Eurasians in India.

■ Usually derogatory in application, *chi-chi* mimicks an affected expression supposed by the Europeans to be used by Eurasians.

chicken variant of CHIKAN.

chicle /ˈtʃɪk(ə)l/, /ˈtʃɪkli/ *noun* L19 American Spanish (from Nahuatl *tzictli*). The coagulated latex of the sapodilla, *Manilkara zapota*, and several related trees, which forms the basis of chewing-gum.

chiffon /ˈʃɪfɒn/ *noun & adjective* M18 French (from *chiffe* rag). **A** *noun* **1** M18 In *plural* Trimmings or other adornments of women's dress. *archaic* **2** L19 A light diaphanous plain-woven fabric of silk, nylon, etc. **B** E20 *attributively* or as *adjective* Made of chiffon; light in weight.

chiffonier /ʃɪfəˈnɪə/ *noun* (also **chiffon-(n)ière**) M18 French (*chiffonnier, chiffonière,* transferred use of CHIFFONNIER). A movable low cupboard with a sideboard top.

chiffonnade /ʃɪfəˈnɑːd/, *foreign* /ʃifɔnad/ (*plural same*) *noun* L19 French. A selection of shredded or finely cut vegetables, used especially as a garnish for soup.

chiffonnier /ʃifɔnje/ *noun* plural pronounced same M19 French. A collector of scraps, a rag-picker.

chignon /ˈʃiːnjɒ̃/ *noun* L18 French (originally = nape of the neck, from Proto-Romance variant of Latin *catena* chain). A coil or mass of hair worn by women at the back of the head.

chikan /'ʧɪk(ə)n/ *noun* (also **chicken**) L19 Urdu (*chikan* from Persian *čikin*). A type of hand-embroidery of the Indian subcontinent.

chilli /'ʧɪli/ *noun* (also **chile, chili**) plural **chil(l)ies, chiles** E17 Spanish (*chile* from Nahuatl *chilli*). The (dried) red pod of the pepper *Capsicum annuum* var. *longum*, used in sauces, relishes, etc., and made into a hot cayenne; cayenne made from these dried pods. Also *chilli pepper.*

chilli con carne /ˌʧɪli kɒn 'kɑːni/ *noun phrase* (also **chile con carne, chili con carne**) M19 Spanish (= chilli with meat). A Mexican dish of minced beef, beans, and chilli.

chilli relleno /ˌʧɪli rɛ'ljemaʊ/ *noun phrase* Spanish (= stuffed chilli). A stuffed green pepper.

■ Sometimes abbreviated to *relleno* plural *rellenos* (E20).

chimera /kʌɪ'mɪərə/, /kɪ'mɪərə/ *noun* (also **chimaera**) LME Latin (*chimaera* from Greek *khimaira* she-goat, monster, from *khimaros* he-goat). **1** LME *Greek Mythology* A fire-breathing monster, with a lion's head, a goat's body, and a serpent's tail. **2** LME A grotesque monster represented in painting etc. **3a** E16 A bogey, a horrible phantasm. **b** L16 A wild or fanciful conception. **c** M19 A thing of hybrid character. **4** E19 (Usually **chimaera**.) Any cartilaginous fish of the family Chimaeridae. **5** E20 *Biology* An organism whose cells are not all derived from the same zygote.

chin variant of TCHIN.

chinchilla /ʧɪn'ʧɪlə/ *noun* E17 Spanish (probably from Aymara or Quechua). **I 1** E17 A South American rodent of the genus Chinchilla, with very soft grey fur. **2** L19 A cat of a silver-grey breed. **3** E20 A rabbit of a variety bred for its grey fur. **II 4** E19 The fur of the South American chinchilla or of the chinchilla rabbit.

chiné /ʃiː'neɪ/ *noun & adjective* M19 French (past participle of *chiner*, from *Chine* China). (A fabric) given a mottled pattern of (supposedly) Chinese style by colouring the warp or weft threads, or both, before weaving.

chino /'ʧiː:nəʊ/ *noun & adjective* M20 American Spanish (= toasted). **A** M20 *noun* plural **chinos** A cotton twill cloth, usually khaki-coloured; in *plural*, trousers made of this. **B** M20 *adjective* Of this cloth.

■ Originally United States.

chinoiserie /ʃɪn'wɑːzəri/, *foreign* /ʃinwazri/ (*plural same*) *noun* L19 French (from *chinois* Chinese + *-erie*). A Chinese or imitation Chinese artistic object, piece of furniture, etc.; the imitation of Chinese motifs in furniture etc.

> **1996** *Country Life* ... although chinoiserie is often thought of as a minor and frivolous flourish to the European decorative arts, it affected almost every palace and great house from the Danish Rosenborg Slot in the 17th century to the Brighton Pavilion ...

chipolata /ʧɪpə'lɑːtə/ *noun* L19 French (from Italian *cipollata* dish of onions, from *cipolla* onion). In full *chipolata sausage*. A small (often spicy) sausage.

chipotle /tʃɪ'pɒtleɪ/ *noun* L20 Mexican Spanish. A kind of dried and smoked chilli used in Mexican cooking.

chi-rho /kʌɪ'rəʊ/ *noun* M19 Greek (twenty-second letter of the alphabet *chi* + seventeenth letter *rho*). A monogram representing the first two letters of Greek *Khristos* Christ.

■ The *chi-rho* was adopted in AD 312 by the Byzantine emperor Constantine the Great as a device for his military banners, following on a vision in which he was told 'By this sign you shall conquer'. During the following centuries the *chi-rho* became ubiquitous in Christian art.

chirimoya variant of cherimoya.

chitarrone /kɪtə'rəʊni/ *noun* plural **chitarroni** /kɪtə'rəʊni/ M18 Italian (augmentative of *chitarra* guitar). A double-necked lute of great length, a theorbo.

chiton /'kʌɪtɒn/, /'kʌɪt(ə)n/ *noun* E19 Greek (*khitōn*; in sense 1 through Modern Latin *Chiton* genus name). **1** E19 A mollusc of the class Polyplacophora, characterized by a broad oval foot and a symmetrical dorsal shell composed of a series of eight overlapping plates. **2** M19 A long woollen tunic worn in ancient Greece.

chocolatier /ʧɒkə'latɪə/, *foreign* /ʃɔkɔlatje/ (*plural same*) *noun* L19 French (from *chocolat* (or Spanish *chocolate* from Nahuatl *chocolatl* item of food made from caocao seeds)). A maker or seller of chocolate.

chokidar /'ʧəʊkɪdɑː/ *noun* (also **chauki-dar** /'ʧəʊkɪdɑː/) E17 Urdu (*chaukīdār*, from Hindustani *cauki* toll, police station + Urdu and Persian *-dār* keeper). In the Indian subcontinent; a watchman.

chola see CHOLO.

cholent /'tʃɒl(ə)nt/, /'ʃɒl(ə)nt/ *noun* M20 Yiddish (*tscholnt*; cf. SCHALET). A Jewish Sabbath dish of slowly baked meat and vegetables, prepared on a Friday and cooked overnight.

choli /'tʃəʊli/ *noun* E20 Hindustani (*coli*). An Indian woman's short-sleeved bodice of a type worn under a SARI.

cholo /'tʃəʊləʊ/ *noun* (also **Cholo**; feminine **chola** /'tʃəʊlə/) plural **cholos** M19 American Spanish (from *Cholollán*, now *Cholula*, a district of México). An Indian of Latin America; a mestizo; *United States* (frequently *derogatory*) a lower-class Mexican.

chometz variant of HAMETZ.

chopsuey /tʃɒp'suːɪ/ *noun* L19 Chinese ((Cantonese) *tsaâp suì* mixed bits). A Chinese dish of pieces of meat or chicken fried with rice, onions, etc., often made with leftover food.

choragus /kɒ'reɪgəs/ *noun* (also **choregus**) plural **choragi** /kɒ'reɪgʌɪ/, /kɒ'reɪgiː/ E17 Latin (from Greek *khoragos*, *khorēgos*, from *khoros* chorus + *agein* to lead). Chiefly *Greek History* The leader of a chorus, or of any group; *specifically* at Athens, a person who defrayed the cost of bringing out a chorus.

chorea /kɒ'rɪə/ *noun* L17 Latin (from Greek *khoreia* dance). *Medicine* Jerky involuntary movements; a disease with symptoms of this kind.

chorizo /tʃə'riːzəʊ/ *noun* plural **chorizos** M19 Spanish. A Spanish sausage of which the chief ingredient is pork.

chose jugée /ʃoz ʒyʒe/ *noun phrase* plural **choses jugées** (pronounced same) L19 French. A settled or decided matter; something it is idle to discuss.

chota /'tʃəʊtə/ *adjective* E19 Anglo-Indian (Hindustani *choṭā*). Small, little; younger, junior.

■ Occurs often in such phrases as *chota hazri* (a light early breakfast) and *chota peg* (a small drink of whisky).

chott variant of SHOTT.

chou /ʃuː/, *foreign* /ʃu/ *noun* (also **choux** (pronounced same)) plural **choux** E18 French (= cabbage, from Latin *caulis*). **1** E18 A small ball of pastry filled with cream etc. **2** L19 A rosette or ornamental knot of ribbon, chiffon, etc., on a woman's hat or dress.

choucroute /ʃukrut/ *noun* M19 French (from German dialect *Surkrut* SAUERKRAUT, assimilated to French CHOU). A kind of pickled cabbage.

chouette /ʃuːˈɛt/ *noun* L19 French (literally, 'barn owl'). A player in a two-handed game (e.g. backgammon, piquet) who plays against a number of others successively or in combination, especially as a means of enabling three players to compete with one another.

chou moellier /ˌʃu: 'mɒlɪə/ *noun phrase* E20 French (= marrow-filled cabbage). A kind of kale grown as fodder, marrowstem. *Australia and New Zealand.*

choux see CHOU.

chow mein /tʃaʊ 'meɪn/ *noun phrase* L19 Chinese (*chǎo miàn* fried noodles). A Chinese dish of fried noodles usually in a sauce with shredded meat and vegetables.

chroma /'krəʊmə/ *noun* L19 Greek (*khrōma* colour). Purity or intensity as a colour quality, especially in colour television etc.

chronique scandaleuse /krɔnik skãdaløz/ *noun phrase* plural **chroniques scandaleuses** (pronounced same) M19 French. A compilation or body of gossip, scandal, etc.

chuddar variant of CHADAR.

chulo /'tʃulo/, /'tʃuːləʊ/ *noun* plural **chulos** /'tʃulos/, /'tʃuːləʊz/ L18 Spanish. *Bullfighting* A bullfighter's assistant.

chuño /'tʃuɲo/, /'tʃuːnjəʊ/ *noun* E17 American Spanish (from Quechua *ch'uñu*). (Flour prepared from) dried potatoes, as eaten by Andean Indians.

chupatti variant of CHAPATTI.

chuppah /'xʊpə/ *noun* (also **chuppaha**) L19 Hebrew (*huppāh* cover, canopy). A canopy beneath which Jewish marriage ceremonies are performed.

chuprassy variant of CHAPRASSI.

churinga variant of TJURUNGA.

churrasco /tʃʊ'rasko/, /tʃʊ'raskəʊ/ *noun* L20 South American Spanish (probably from dialect *churrascar* to burn; cf. Spanish *soccarar* to scorch). A grilled dish, usually of meat.

chutzpah /'xʊtspə/, /'hʊtspə/ *noun* L19 Yiddish (from Aramaic *huspā*). Shameless audacity, gall. *slang.*

1995 *Times* Celtic oratory—brooding, bombastic, and with a touch of Hergé's Captain Haddock . . . —meets a metropolitan Londoner's smoothness, zest and chutzpah.

chypre /ʃipr/ *noun* L19 French (= Cyprus, where perhaps originally made). A heavy perfume made from sandalwood.

ciabatta /tʃəˈbɑːtə/, *foreign* /tʃaˈbatta/ *noun* plural **ciabattas, ciabatte** /tʃaˈbaːtte/ L20 Italian ((dialect) literally, 'slipper' (from the shape of the loaf)). A type of moist aerated Italian bread made with olive oil; a loaf of this.

ciao /tʃaʊ/ *interjection* E20 Italian (dialectal alteration of *schiavo* (I am your) slave, from medieval Latin *sclavus* slave). Hello; goodbye.

■ A colloquial expression widespread in continental Europe, now also used as a casual greeting between Anglophones.

cibol variant of CIBOULE.

ciborium /sɪˈbɔːrɪəm/ *noun* plural **ciboria** /sɪˈbɔːrɪə/ M16 Medieval Latin (from Greek *kibōrion* cup-shaped seed-vessel of the Egyptian water lily, a drinking-cup made from this; sense 1 probably influenced by Latin *cibus* food). **1** M16 *Christian Church* A receptacle for the reservation of the Eucharist, shaped like a shrine, or a cup with an arched cover. **2** M18 *Architecture* A canopy; a canopied shrine.

ciboule /ˈsɪb(ə)l/ *noun* (also **cibol**) M17 French. The Welsh onion, *Allium fistulosum*, which resembles a spring onion.

cicada /sɪˈkɑːdə/ *noun* LME Latin (*cicada, cicala*). Any of the family Cicadidae of large-winged homopteran insects, the males of which make shrill chirping sounds.

■ The Old Provençal name *cigala* (cf. French *cigale*) was the usual form in English during the seventeenth and eighteenth centuries.

cicatrice /ˈsɪkətrɪs/ *noun* (also (especially *Medicine and Botany*) **cicatrix** /ˈsɪkətrɪks/) plural **cicatrices** /ˈsɪkətrɪsɪz/, *especially Medicine and Botany* /sɪkəˈtraɪsiːz/ LME Old and Modern French (or Latin *cicatrix, cicatric-*). **1** LME The scar of a healed wound, burn, etc.; a scar on the bark of a tree. **b** E19 *Botany* A scar. **2** L16 A mark or impression resembling a scar.

cicerone /tʃɪtʃəˈrəʊni/, /sɪsəˈrəʊni/ *noun & verb* plural **ciceroni** /tʃɪtʃəˈrəʊni/, /sɪsəˈrəʊni/ **cicerones** E18 Italian (from Latin name *Cicero, -onis*). **A** *noun* E18 A guide who understands and explains an-

tiquities etc.; any learned guide. **B** *transitive verb* L18 Act as a cicerone to.

■ Marcus Tullius Cicero (106–43 BC) was renowned for his learning, and it is surmised that English Grand Tourists dubbed the local Italian antiquaries who showed them round the sites *cicerones*, that is 'Ciceros'. The actual historical origin of the word is uncertain, as the earliest English use of *cicerone* (Addison was apparently the first, in 1726) antedates its appearance in Italian dictionaries.

1996 *Country Life* He made a good profit on the . . . 'Portland' vase bought from the Roman cicerone James Byres for £1,000 . . .

cicisbeo /tʃɪtʃɪzˈbeɪəʊ/ *noun* plural **cicisbei** /tʃɪtʃɪzˈbeiː/, **cicisbeos** E18 Italian (of unknown origin). A married (originally Italian) woman's male companion or lover.

ci-devant /sidvɑ̃/ *adjective & adverb* E18 French. Former(ly).

■ Used with the person's earlier name or status.

cigala see under CICADA.

cilantro /θiˈlantro/, /siˈlantro/ *noun* L20 Spanish. Coriander. *North American*.

cilium /ˈsɪlɪəm/ *noun* plural **cilia** /ˈsɪlɪə/ E18 Latin. **1** E18 An eyelash; (the edge of) an eyelid. **2** L18 A delicate hair like an eyelash, e.g. on the margin of a leaf, or the wing of an insect. **3** M19 A hairlike appendage, usually motile, which is found in numbers on the surfaces of some cells, and in many organisms is used in locomotion.

cimbalom /ˈsɪmb(ə)l(ə)m/ *noun* (also **zimbalom** /ˈzɪmb(ə)l(ə)m/) L19 Hungarian (from Italian CYMBALO). A dulcimer.

cinéaste /ˈsɪneɪast/, *foreign* /sineast/ (*plural same*) *noun* (also **cineast(e)** /ˈsɪniast/) E20 French (from *ciné* cine + *-aste* as in *enthousiaste* enthusiast). An enthusiast for or devotee of the cinema.

1995 *Spectator* It is outwardly the unfilmable script, far more imaginary than real, of a would-be English cinéaste, one Richard Arthur Thornby (RAT), currently lecturing in Texas on the cinema.

cinematheque /sɪnɪməˈtɛk/ *noun* (also **cinémathèque** /sinematɛk/ (*plural same*)) M20 French (*cinémathèque*, from *cinéma* cinema, after *bibliothèque* library). A library of cinema films; a (national) repository of old films. Also, a small cinema showing artistic films.

cinéma-vérité /sinemɑverite/, /ˌsɪnɪmɑ
'verɪteɪ/ *noun* M20 French. (The making of)
films which avoid artificiality and have
the appearance of real life.

ciné-vérité /sineverite/, /sɪnɪ'verɪteɪ/
noun M20 French. CINÉMA-VÉRITÉ.

cinq-à-sept /sĕk a set/ *noun* (also **cinq à
sept**) L20 French (literally, 'five to seven').
A visit to a mistress or a brothel, traditionally made between five and seven
p.m.
1996 *Spectator* The English like to stand
around a pool table and guffaw rather loudly.
Continental men prefer *le cinq à sept.*

cinquecento /ˌtʃɪŋkwɪ'tʃentəʊ/ *noun* M18
Italian (= five hundred). The sixteenth
century in Italy; the Italian style of art of
this period, with reversion to classical
forms.

cipolin /'sɪpəlɪn/ *noun* (also **cipollino**
/ˌtʃɪpə'liːnəʊ/, plural **cipolinos**) L18 French
((*cipolin* from) Italian *cipollino*, from *cipolla*
onion (Latin *cepa*); so called from the resemblance of its foliated structure to the
coats of an onion). An Italian marble in-
terfoliated with veins of talc, mica,
quartz, etc., showing alternations of (especially white and green) colourings.

cippus /'sɪpəs/ *noun* plural **cippi** /'sɪpʌɪ/
E18 Latin (= post, stake). *Architecture* A low
column, usually bearing an inscription,
used by the ancients as a landmark, funerary monument, etc.
■ Earlier (E17) in the sense of 'the stocks',
but this sense does not seem to have survived into the eighteenth century.

circa /'sə:kə/ *preposition* M19 Latin. About,
approximately in or at (with dates etc.).
■ Frequently in abbreviated form before a
date: *c.* or *ca.*

circiter /'sə:sɪtə/ *preposition* L19 Latin.
About, CIRCA.
■ Used with dates.

circulus vitiosus /ˌsə:kjʊləs vɪʃɪ'əʊsəs/,
/vɪtɪ'əʊsəs/ *noun phrase* plural **circuli vi-
tiosi** /ˌsə:kjʊlʌɪ vɪʃɪ'əʊsʌɪ/, /vɪtɪ'əʊsʌɪ/ E20
Latin. A vicious circle.

ciré /'si:reɪ/ *adjective & noun* E20 French (=
waxed). (Fabric) with a smooth polished
surface, obtained especially by heating
and waxing.

cire perdue /sir perdy/ *noun phrase* L19
French (= lost wax). A method of casting
bronze by pouring molten metal over a
wax-surfaced core within a mould, to

form a model in the space created by the
melting and running out of wax.

cirque /sə:k/ *noun* E17 French (from Latin
circus circle, circus, corresponding to
Greek *kirkos* ring, circle). **1** E17 Circus.
2 L17 A circle, a ring, a circlet. *literary.*
3 M19 *Physical Geography* A large bowl-
shaped hollow of glacial origin at the
head of a valley or on a mountainside.

cirrus /'sɪrəs/ *noun* (also **cirrhus**) plural
cirri /'sɪrʌɪ/ E18 Latin (= curl, fringe).
1 E18 A curl or tuft of hair. *rare.* **2** E18
Botany A tendril. **3** M18 *Zoology* A slender,
filamentary appendage, e.g. the limb of a
cirripede, a barbel of certain fishes. **4** E19
Meteorology A cloud-type occurring at high
altitude and having the appearance of
wispy filamentary tufts.

cithara /'sɪθ(ə)rə/, /'kɪθ(ə)rə/ *noun* (also **kithara** /'kɪθ(ə)rə/) L18 Latin (from Greek *kithara*). An ancient Greek and Roman
stringed musical instrument akin to the
lyre, having two arms rising vertically
from the soundbox.

civet /sivɛ/ *noun* plural pronounced same
E18 French (earlier *civé*, from *cive* chive). A
highly seasoned stew of hare, venison, or
other game.

clachan /'klax(ə)n/ *noun* LME Gaelic and
Irish (*clachán*). In Scotland and Northern
Ireland: a small village, a hamlet.

clair-de-lune /klerdəlyn/, /klɛ:də'lu:n/
noun L19 French (literally, 'moonlight'). A
soft white or pale blue-grey colour; a Chinese porcelain glaze of this colour.

clairschach /'klɑ:ʃax/ *noun* (also **clarschach**) L15 Irish (*cláirseach*, Gaelic *clàr-
sach*). The traditional Celtic harp strung
with wire.

clairvoyance /klɛ:'vɔɪəns/ *noun* M19
French (from as next). **1** M19 The supposed faculty of perceiving, as if by seeing, what is happening or exists out of
sight. **2** M19 Keenness of mental perception: exceptional insight.

clairvoyant /klɛ:'vɔɪənt/ *adjective & noun*
(occasionally feminine **clairvoyante**) L17
French (from *clair* clear + *voyant* present
participial adjective of *voir* to see). **A** *adjective* **1** L17 Clear-sighted, perceptive.
rare. **2** M19 Having or exercising the faculty of clairvoyance; pertaining to clairvoyance. **B** *noun* **1** L18 A clear-sighted
person. *rare.* **2** M19 A person having the
faculty of clairvoyance.

claque /klak/, /klɑːk/; *foreign* /klak/ (*plural same*) *noun* M19 French (from *claquer* to clap). A hired body of applauders; *transferred* a body of devoted or sycophantic followers.

> **1995** *Times* [The organizers] of events decreed that before every open race there would be competitions for juveniles and juniors. This encourages the young to participate, feeds talent into the sport and provides an enthusiastic claque to cheer on the stars.

claqueur /klɑːˈkə:/, *foreign* /klakœr/ (*plural same*) *noun* M19 French (from *claquer* to clap). A member of a claque.

claro /ˈklɑːrəʊ/ *noun* plural **claros** L19 Spanish (= light, clear). A light-coloured cigar.

clarschach variant of CLAIRSCHACH.

classico /ˈklasɪkəʊ/ *adjective* L20 Italian. Of an Italian wine: superior, in an established style of excellence.

■ Used after the name of a wine, as in *Bardolino classico.*

clave /kleɪv/, /klɑːv/ *noun* E20 American Spanish (from Spanish *clave* keystone, from Latin *clavis* key). *Music* Either of a pair of hardwood sticks used to make a hollow sound.

■ Usually in plural.

clavecin /ˈklavɪsɪn/ *noun* E19 French (from medieval Latin *clavicymbalum* from *clavis* key + *cymbalum* cymbal). A harpsichord, especially in or from France.

clavicembalo /klavɪˈtʃɛmbələʊ/ *noun* plural **clavicembalos** M18 Italian (from as CLAVECIN). A harpsichord, especially in or from Italy.

clementine /ˈklɛm(ə)ntʌɪn/, /ˈklɛm(ə)nti:n/ *noun* E20 French (*clémentine*). A variety of tangerine grown especially in North Africa.

clepsydra /ˈklɛpsɪdrə/ *noun* plural **clepsydras**, **clepsydrae** /ˈklɛpsɪdriː/ LME Latin (from Greek *klepsudra*, from *kleps-* combining form of *kleptein* to steal + *hudōr* water). An instrument used in antiquity to measure time by the flow of water; a water-clock.

cliché /ˈkliːʃeɪ/ *noun* M19 French (use as noun of past participle of *clicher* to stereotype, perhaps of imitative origin). **1** M19 *History* A metal stereotype or electrotype block. **2** L19 *figurative* A stereotyped expression, a hackneyed phrase or opinion; a stereotyped character, style, etc.

> **2 1996** *Spectator* [The] novel . . . simultaneously underlines and overturns whole layers of class clichés.

clientele /ˌkliːɒnˈtɛl/, *foreign* /kliɑ̃tɛl/ *noun* (also **clientèle**) M16 Latin and French (either, directly from Latin *clientela*, from *cliens*, *-ntis* (earlier *cluens*) client, use as noun of present participle of *cluere* to hear, obey; or, later, from French *clientèle* from Latin). **1** M16–L19 Clientship; patronage. **2** L16 A body of clients, a following; the customers (of a shop); the patrons (of a theatre etc.); persons seeking the professional advice of a lawyer, architect, etc.

clique /kliːk/ *noun* E18 Old and Modern French (from *cliquer* to make a noise, from Middle Dutch *klikken* to click). A small exclusive group; a coterie.

■ Possibly related to CLAQUE.

cloaca /kləʊˈeɪkə/ *noun* plural **cloacae** /kləʊˈeɪkiː/, **cloacas** L16 Latin (*cloaca*, *cluaca* related to *cluere* to cleanse). **1** L16 An underground conduit for drainage, a sewer. Also, a water-closet. **2** M19 *Zoology* A common cavity for the release of digestive and urogenital products in birds, reptiles, amphibians, most fish, and monotremes.

clobiosh variant of KLABERJASS.

clochard /klɔʃar/ *noun* plural pronounced same M20 French (from *clocher* to limp). In France: a beggar, a vagrant.

> **1996** *Times* When, after the war, he went back to France, he lived for years—legend has it—more or less as a clochard, looked after, for a time, by the French Communist Party.

cloche /klɒʃ/, /kləʊʃ/ *noun* L19 French (= bell). **1** L19 A bell-glass; a small translucent (especially glass) cover for forcing or protecting outdoor plants. **2** E20 A woman's close-fitting bell-shaped hat. In full *cloche hat.*

cloisonné /klwazɔne/ *adjective & noun* M19 French (past participle of *cloisonner* to partition, from *cloison* division). More fully *cloisonné enamel.* (Designating) enamelwork or -ware in which the colours in the pattern are separated by thin strips of metal attached to the base. Cf. CHAMPLEVÉ.

cloqué /ˈkləʊkeɪ/ *noun* (also Anglicized as **cloky** /ˈkləʊki/) E20 French (literally, 'blistered'). A fabric with an irregularly raised or embossed surface.

clou /klu/ *noun* L19 French (literally, 'nail, stud'). The chief attraction, the point of greatest interest, the central idea.

1959 *Observer* The *clou* of the ballet is to be found in these four female solos.

cocasse /kɔkas/ *adjective* M19 French. Droll; ridiculous.

coccyx /'kɒksɪks/ *noun* plural **coccyxes, coccyges** /'kɒksɪdʒi:z/ L16 Latin (from Greek *kokkux* (originally) cuckoo (from its resemblance (in humans) to a cuckoo's beak)). *Anatomy* The small triangular bone forming the lower end of the spinal column in humans and some apes; the analogous part in birds or other vertebrates.

coco-de-mer /ˌkəʊkəʊdə'mɛ:/ *noun* E19 French (= coco from the sea (as having been first known from the nuts found floating in the sea)). A tall palm tree *Lodoicea maldivica*, native to the Seychelles; its immense woody nut.

cocotte /kɒ'kɒt/ *noun* M19 French (sense 1 from a child's name for a hen; sense 2 from French *cocasse* from Latin *cucuma* cooking vessel). **1** M19 A fashionable prostitute. *archaic*. **2** E20 A small fireproof dish for cooking and serving an individual portion of food.

coda /'kəʊdə/ *noun* M18 Italian (from Latin *cauda* tail). **1** M18 *Music* An independent and often elaborate passage introduced after the end of the main part of a movement. **b** L19 *transferred* and *figurative* A concluding event, remark, literary passage, etc. **2** E20 *Ballet* The final section of a classical *pas de deux*; the concluding dance of a whole ballet.

codetta /kəʊ'dɛtə/ *noun* M19 Italian (diminutive of **CODA**). *Music* A short coda; a short passage connecting sections of a movement or fugue.

codex /'kəʊdɛks/ *noun* plural **codices** /'kəʊdɪsi:z/, /'kɒdɪsi:z/ L16 Latin (*codex, codic-* block of wood, block split into leaves or tablets). **1** L16–M18 A legal code; *generally* a set of rules on any subject. **2** L18 A manuscript volume, especially of ancient texts. **3** M19 A collection of pharmaceutical descriptions of drugs, preparations, etc.

coenobium /sɪ'nəʊbɪəm/ *noun* (also **cenobium** (mainly United States)) plural **coenobia** /sɪ'nəʊbɪə/ E19 ecclesiastical Latin (from Greek *koinobion* community life, convent, from *koinos* common + *bion* life). **1** E19 A monastic house, a coenoby. **2** L19 *Biology* A cluster of unicellular organisms,

e.g. green algae, that behaves as a colony.

cogida /ko'xiða/, /kə'hi:də/ *noun* E20 Spanish (literally, 'a gathering of the harvest', use as noun of feminine past participle of *coger* to seize, from Latin *colligare* to bind together). *Bullfighting* A tossing of a bullfighter by a bull.

cogito /'kɒdʒɪtəʊ/ *noun* M19 Latin (= I think, 1st person present of *cogitare* to cogitate). *Philosophy* The principle establishing the existence of the thinker from the fact of his or her thinking or awareness.

■ The principle derives from the formula *cogito, ergo sum* 'I think (or I am thinking), therefore I am' of the French philosopher René Descartes (1596–1650).

cognitum /'kɒgnɪtəm/ *noun* plural **cognita** /'kɒgnɪtə/ L19 Latin (neuter past participle of *cognoscere* to know). *Philosophy* An object of cognition.

cognomen /kɒg'nəʊmən/ *noun* plural **cognomens**, (earlier) **cognomina** E17 Latin (*cognomen* from as *co-* with + (g)*nomen* name). **1** E17 A surname; a nickname; *loosely* an appellation, a name. **2** L19 *Roman History* The third personal name of a Roman citizen (as Marcus Tullius *Cicero*); a fourth name or personal epithet (as Publius Cornelius Scipio *Africanus*).

cognoscente /kɒnjo'ʃɛnte/, /kɒnjə'ʃɛnti/ *noun* plural **cognoscenti** /kɒnjo'ʃɛnti/ M18 Italian ((now *conoscente*), literally, 'a person who knows', Latinized form of *conoscente* from Latin *cognoscent-* present participial stem of *cognoscere* to know). A connoisseur; a discerning expert.

1995 *Country Life* This steep, deep and funky resort [sc. Taos] is an extraordinary amalgam of Swiss, Pueblo Indian and Spanish cultures and attracts skiing *cognoscenti* from round the globe.

cohabitation /kəʊˌhabɪ'teɪʃ(ə)n/, *in sense* 3 *foreign* /kɔabitasjɔ̃/ *noun* LME French. **1** LME Living together; community of life. *archaic*. **2** M16 Living together as husband and wife, especially without legal marriage. **3** *Politics* L20 An alliance dictated by expediency between office-holders of differing political views (originally in France).

■ Fully naturalized in senses 1 and 2, the word in its general literal meaning, as used in Middle English, is now almost entirely superseded by the particular sense 2. As a recent introduction from the French political scene, sense 3 is often written in italics to differentiate it from sense 2 and is therefore accorded a version of the French pronunciation.

3 1995 *Times* That experience will be all the more important in dealings with the new Duma, where the election result will force *cohabitation à la russe.*

cohue /kɔy/ *noun* plural pronounced same M19 **French.** A mob, an unruly crowd.

coiffeur /kwɑːˈfəː/, /kwɒˈfəː/, *foreign* /kwafœr/ (*plural same*) *noun* M19 **French** (from *coiffer* to dress the hair). A hairdresser.

coiffure /kwɑːˈfjʊə/, /kwɒˈfjʊə/, *noun also foreign* /kwafyr/ (*plural same*) *noun & verb* M17 **French** (*coiffe* from Old French *coife* head-dress, from late Latin *cofia* helmet). **A** *noun* M17 The way the hair is arranged or (formerly) the head decorated or covered; a hairstyle, a head-dress. **B** *transitive verb* E20 Dress or arrange hair, coiff. Chiefly as *coiffured* participial adjective.

coitus /ˈkəʊɪtəs/ *noun* M19 **Latin.** Copulation.

cojones /koˈxones/, /kəˈhəʊneɪz/ *noun plural* M20 **Spanish** (plural of *cojón* testicle). Testicles; *figurative* courage, guts.

■ Colloquial, and in figurative use often euphemistic for 'balls' (see quotation 1996).

1932 E. Hemingway *Death in the Afternoon* It takes more cojones to be a sportsman where death is a closer game to the game.

1996 *Times Magazine* Corrigan is working his cojones off to give us kidneys, liver, sweetbreads, anything that has not been banned which might be banned.

col /kɒl/ *noun* M19 **French** (from Latin *collum* neck). **1** M19 A depression in the summit-line of a mountain chain; a saddle between two peaks. **2** L19 *Meteorology* An area of lower pressure between two anticyclones.

collage /kɒˈlɑːʒ/ *noun* E20 **French** (= gluing). An abstract form of art in which photographs, pieces of paper, string, matchsticks, etc., are placed in juxtaposition and glued to a surface; a work in this form; *figurative* a jumbled collection of impressions, events, styles, etc.

collectanea /kɒlɛkˈtɑːnɪə/, /kɒlɛkˈteɪnɪə/ *noun* M17 **Latin** (*collectanea* neuter plural (from *collect-*, past participial stem of *colligere* to assemble) as used as adjective in *Dicta collectanea* of Caesar, and as noun in

Collectanea of Solinus). As *plural*, passages, remarks, etc., collected from various sources. As *singular*, a miscellany.

collegium /kəˈliːdʒɪəm/ *noun* plural **collegia** /kəˈliːdʒɪə/ L19 **Latin.** **1** L19 A society of amateurs for performing music, now *especially* one attached to a German or American university. In full *collegium musicum* /ˈmjuːzɪkəm/, plural *collegia musica* /ˈmjuːzɪkə/. **2** E20 *History* (representing Russian *kollegiya*) An advisory or administrative board in Russia.

colloquium /kəˈləʊkwɪəm/ *noun* plural **colloquia** /kəˈləʊkwɪə/, **colloquiums** L16 **Latin** (from as *co(l)-* with + *loqui* to speak). **1** L16–M18 A conversation, a dialogue. **2** M19 A conference; *specifically* an academic conference or seminar.

colluvium /kəˈl(j)uːvɪəm/ *noun* M20 **Latin.** *Physical Geography* Material which accumulates at the foot of a steep slope.

colon /kɒˈlən/ *noun* E17 **French** (from Latin *colonus*). **1** E17 A husbandman. *rare.* **2** M20 *History* A colonial settler or farmer, especially in a French colony.

colophon /ˈkɒləf(ə)n/ *noun* E17 **Late Latin** (from Greek *kolophōn* summit, finishing touch). **1** E17 A crowning or finishing touch. *rare.* **2** L18 A statement, sometimes with a device, at the end of a manuscript or printed book, giving information about its authorship, production, etc. **b** M20 A publisher's or printer's imprint; *loosely* a publisher's device, especially on a title-page.

coloratura /kɒlərəˈtjʊərə/, /kɒlərəˈtʊərə/ *noun* M18 **Italian** (from late Latin *coloratura*, from *colorat-* past participial stem of *colorare* to colour). **1** M18 Florid passages in vocal music, with runs, trills, etc.; the singing of these. **2** M20 A singer of coloratura, especially a soprano.

1 1996 *Spectator* Thus Zerbinetta's display piece in *Ariadne auf Naxos* is every bit as riveting as the frustrated composer's outcry earlier on . . . its coloratura expresses the feelings of a free spirit . . .

colossus /kəˈlɒsəs/ *noun* plural **colossi** /kəˈlɒsʌɪ/ **colossuses** LME **Latin** (from Greek *kolossos* applied by Herodotus to the statues of Egyptian temples). **1** LME A statue of considerably more than life size. **2** E17 A gigantic or overawing person or thing; an empire etc. personified as standing astride over dominions.

■ The Colossus of Rhodes, a gigantic statue of the Hellenistic period that is said to have straddled the harbour entrance on the island of Rhodes, was one of the Seven Wonders of the World.

2 1996 *New Scientist* Freud was a colossus, a massive intellect, the keenest clinical observer of mental disorders in the past 200 years.

colostrum /kə'lɒstrəm/ *noun* (also (earlier) **colostra** L16 Latin. The first milk of a mammal after giving birth.

colportage /'kɒlpɔːtɪdʒ/ *noun* M19 French (from *colporter* to hawk, peddle (see next)). The work of a colporteur; the peddling of books, newspapers, bibles, etc.

colporteur /'kɒlpɔːtə/, /ˌkɒlpɔː'təː/ *noun* L18 French (from *colporter*, probably alteration of *comporter* from Latin *comportare* transport, from as *com-* with + *portare* to carry). A pedlar of books, newspapers, etc., *especially* one employed by a religious society to distribute bibles and other religious tracts.

columbarium /kɒl(ə)m'bɛːrɪəm/ *noun* plural **columbaria** /kɒl(ə)m'bɛːrɪə/, **columbariums** M18 Latin (*columbarium*, from *columba* dove + *-arium*). **1** M18 A vault or building with niches for the reception of cinerary urns; a niche in such a vault etc. **2** E19 A pigeon-hole; a columbary.

coma /'kəʊmə/ *noun* 1 plural **comae** /'kəʊmiː/ E17 Latin (from Greek *komē* hair of the head). **1** E17 Botany The top of a plant; *especially* a terminal tuft of bracts or leaves; a leafy crown of branches; a tuft of silky hairs at the end of some seeds. **2** M18 Astronomy The diffuse hazy region surrounding the nucleus of a comet. **3** M19 An optical aberration causing the image of an off-axis point to be flared, like a comet with a diverging tail; the flared image itself.

coma /'kəʊmə/ *noun* 2 M17 Modern Latin (from Greek *kōma*, *kōmat-*, related to *koitē* bed, *keisthai* to lie down). Medicine A prolonged state of unconsciousness from which the patient cannot be roused. Also *figurative*.

comble /kɔ̃bl/ *noun* plural pronounced same M19 French (from Latin *cumulus* heap). A culminating point, a crowning touch.

comédie humaine /kɔmedi ymɛn/ plural **comédie humaines** pronounced same L19 French (literally, 'human comedy'). The sum of human activities; a literary portrait of this.

■ The title given by Honoré de Balzac (1799–1850) to his series of novels on nineteenth-century French society.

comédie larmoyante /kɔmedi larmwajɑ̃t/ plural **comédie larmoyantes** pronounced same E19 French (literally, 'weeping comedy'). A sentimental, moralizing comedy.

■ Applied originally to the plays of P. C. Nivelle de La Chaussée (1692–1754), which were very fashionable in eighteenth-century France.

comedienne /kəˌmiːdɪ'ɛn/, /kəˌmɛdɪ'ɛn/ *noun* (also **comédienne** /kəˌmeɪdɪ'ɛn/) M19 French (feminine of *comédien* comedian). A female comedian.

comédie noire /kɔmedi nwar/ plural **comédie noires** pronounced same M20 French (literally, 'black comedy'). A macabre or farcical rendering of a violent or tragic theme.

■ Now more common in English translation, 'black comedy', but cf. NOIR.

comes /'kəʊmiːz/ *noun* plural **comites** /'kəʊmɪtiːz/ M18 Latin (= companion, from *com-* with + *ire* to go). Music An answering or imitating voice in a canon or fugue; the answer itself. Opposed to DUX sense 1.

commando /kə'mɑːndəʊ/ *noun* plural **commandos** L18 Portuguese ((now *comando*), from *commandar* to command). **1** L18 A party, originally of Boers or burghers in South Africa, called out for military purposes, a militia; a unit of the Boer army made up of the militia of an electoral district; a raiding-party, a raid; participation in such a raid. **2** M20 (A member of) a unit of British amphibious shock troops; (a member of) a similar unit elsewhere.

comme ci, comme ça /kɔm si kɔm sa/ *adverb & adjective phrase* M20 French (literally, 'like this like that'). So-so, middling(ly).

commedia dell'arte /kɔmˌmeːdia dɛll 'arte/, /kɒˌmɛdɪə dɛl'ɑːteɪ/ *noun phrase* L19 Italian (= comedy of art). The improvised popular comedy in Italian theatres between the sixteenth and eighteenth centuries with stock characters.

comme il faut /kɔm il fo/, /kɒm iːl fəʊ/ *adverb & predicative adjective phrase* M18 French (literally, 'as it is necessary'). Proper(ly), correct(ly), as it should be (especially of behaviour).

1984 A. Brookner *Hotel du Lac* It was implied that prolonged drinking, whether for purposes of business or as a personal indulgence, was not *comme il faut* . . .

commendatore /ˌkɒmɛndəˈtɔːri/ *noun* L19 Italian. A knight of an Italian order of chivalry.

commère /kɔmɛr/, /ˈkɒmɛː/ *noun plural* pronounced /kɔmɛr/, /ˈkɒmɛːz/ E20 French. A female COMPÈRE.

commis /ˈkɒmi/ *noun plural* same (pronounced same, /ˈkɒmiːz/) L16 French (use as noun of past participle of *commettre* to entrust). **1** L16–E19 A deputy, a clerk. **2** M20 A junior waiter or chef.

commissar /kɒmɪˈsɑː/ *noun* LME French (*commissaire* from medieval Latin *commissarius* commissary; in sense 2 from Russian *komissar* from French). **1** LME–M18 A deputy, a delegate, a commissary. Chiefly *Scottish*. **2** E20 *History* The head of a government department in the former USSR; also *transferred*, a powerful official.

> **2 1996** *Spectator* She assumed that because she was a commissar, she could exercise rights which she wished to deny to her constituents.

commissionaire /kəˌmɪʃəˈnɛː/ *noun* (also **commissionnaire** M17 French (*commissionnaire* from Latin *commissio(n-)* from *commiss-* past participial stem of *committere* to commit. **1** M17 A person entrusted with small commissions; a messenger. Now *rare*. **2** M19 A uniformed door-attendant at a theatre, hotel, office, etc.

■ The Corps of Commissionaires was founded in London in 1859 as an organization through which pensioned (originally wounded) soldiers could find light employment as messengers, porters, etc.

> **2 1996** *Times* The commissionaire, mistaking him for a bum, refused him access.

communard /ˈkɒmjʊnɑːd/ *noun* L19 French. A member of a commune; *especially* (**Communard**) an adherent of the Paris Commune (the socialist government March–May 1871); a communalist.

communautaire /ˌkɒmjʊnəʊˈtɛː/ *adjective* L20 French. Attentive to or serving the best interests of the wider community (often with reference to the European Community).

> **1995** *Spectator* [A united Ireland] simply isn't going to come about in any foreseeable future unless the Protestants are physically expelled from Ulster, and that would be a little tricky for the Irish to carry out in their new enlightened and *communautaire* pose.

communiqué /kəˈmjuːnɪkeɪ/ *noun* M19 French (use as noun of past participle of *communiquer* to communicate). An official communication; *especially* an official statement reporting on a meeting, conference, etc.

compactum /kəmˈpaktəm/ *noun* E20 Latin (use as noun of neuter of *compactus* past participle of *compingere* to put together). A structure or device intended to hold a number of articles; a container; *specifically* a wardrobe.

compadre /kɒmˈpɑːdri/ *noun* M19 Spanish (= godfather, (hence) benefactor, friend). Companion, friend.

■ Chiefly United States, often used as a form of address. The extension of meaning from 'godfather' to 'friend' is paralleled in the evolution of the native English word *gossip* from late Old English *godsibb* (from *god* God + *sib* kin) meaning a 'godparent' to mid-fourteenth-century *gossip* 'a familiar acquaintance'. (The usual modern sense of *gossip* follows from the restriction of the word to specifically *female friends*, and thence to mean the sort of talk enjoyed by women amongst themselves.)

compagnon de voyage /kɔ̃paɲɔ̃ də vwajaʒ/ *noun phrase* (also **compagnon du voyage** /kɔ̃paɲɔ̃ dy vwajaʒ/) *plural* **compagnons de voyage** (pronounced same) M18 French. A travelling companion, a fellow traveller.

compendium /kəmˈpɛndɪəm/ *noun plural* **compendiums**, **compendia** /kəmˈpɛndɪə/ L16 Latin (originally, 'profit, saving', from *compendere* to weigh together). **I 1** L16 A work presenting in brief the essential points of a subject; a digest, an epitome. **2** E17 *figurative* An embodiment in miniature. **3** M17–E19 Saving of labour, space, etc. **II 4** L19 An assortment, a varied collection. **5** L19 In full *compendium of games*. A box containing assorted table-games. **b** E20 A package of stationery for letter-writing.

compère /ˈkɒmpɛː/ *noun & verb* (also **compere**) M18 French (originally, 'godfather in relation to the actual parents', from medieval Latin *compater* from *com-* with + *pater* father). **A** *noun* **1** An elderly man who lavishes gifts on a younger woman. Only in M18. **2** E20 A person in a cabaret act, radio or television show, etc., who introduces the performers, comments on the turns, etc. **B** *transitive & intransitive verb* M20 Act as compère (to a show).

compluvium /kəmˈpluːvɪəm/ *noun* plural **compluvia** /kəmˈpluːvɪə/ M19 Latin (from *compluere* to flow together). *Roman Antiquities* A square opening in the roof of the atrium, through which fell the rainwater collected from the roof.

compos mentis /ˌkɒmpɒs ˈmɛntɪs/ *adjective phrase* E17 **Latin**. In one's right mind, having control of one's mind, not mad. Cf. NON COMPOS MENTIS.

■ Usually used predicatively and sometimes shortened to *compos* (E19).

1996 *Spectator* . . . even drunks have their sober and *compos mentis* lulls . . .

compote /ˈkɒmpəʊt/, /ˈkɒmpɒt/ *noun* (also **compôte**) L17 French (Old French *composte* from Latin *compos(i)ta, compos(i)tum* use as noun of feminine and neuter past participle of *componere* to place together, compound). **1** L17 (A dish of) fruit preserved or cooked in a syrup; a fruit salad, stewed fruit, especially with or in a syrup. **2** M18 A dish of stewed pigeon. **3** L19 A COMPOTIER.

compotier /kɔ̃pɔtje/ *noun* plural pronounced same M18 French (from as preceding). A bowl-shaped dessert dish with a stem; a dish for stewed fruit etc.

compte rendu /kɔ̃t rɑ̃dy/ *noun phrase* plural **comptes rendus** (pronounced same) E19 French (= account rendered). A report, a review, a statement.

comptoir /kɔ̃twar/ *noun* plural pronounced same E18 French. A commercial agency or factory in a foreign country.

comte /kɔ̃t/ (*plural same*), /kɒnt/, /kɒmt/ *noun* E17 French. A French nobleman corresponding in rank to an English earl.

comtesse /kɔ̃tes/ (*plural same*), /kɔ̃ˈtɛs/, /ˈkɒmtes/ *noun* E20 French (from as preceding + feminine suffix *-esse*). A French noblewoman corresponding in rank to an English countess.

con abbreviation of CONTRA.

con amore /kɒn əˈmɔːreɪ/, *foreign* /kɔn a ˈmoːre/ *adverb phrase* M18 Italian (= with love). With devotion or zeal; *Music* (a direction:) with tenderness.

con brio /kɒn ˈbriːəʊ/, *foreign* /kɔn ˈbrio/ *adverb phrase* E19 Italian. *Music* (A direction:) with vigour. Also *figurative*.

1996 *Times* He also signed autographs by the dozen—it is, incidentally, a signature that is bold, sweeping and exuberant, written *con brio*.

conceptus /kənˈsɛptəs/ *noun* M18 Latin (= conception, embryo, from *concept-* past participial stem of *concipere* to conceive). The product of conception in the womb, especially in the early stages of pregnancy.

concertante /kɒntʃəˈtanti/ *adjective & noun* plural of noun **concertanti** /kɒntʃə ˈtanti/ E18 Italian (participial adjective of *concertare* to bring into agreement or harmony). *Music* Formerly, (designating) those instrumental parts present throughout a piece of music. Now, (a piece of music) containing one or more solo parts (usually of less prominence or weight than in a concerto) playing with an orchestra; also, designating such a part.

concerti plural of CONCERTO.

concerti grossi plural of CONCERTO GROSSO.

concertino /kɒntʃəˈtiːnəʊ/ *noun* plural **concertinos** L18 Italian (diminutive of CONCERTO). *Music* **1** L18 A small or short concert. *rare.* **2** E19 The solo instrument(s) in a concerto. **3** L19 A simple or short concerto.

concerto /kənˈtʃəːtəʊ/, /kənˈtʃɛːtəʊ/ *noun* plural **concertos, concerti** /kənˈtʃəːti/ E18 Italian (from *concertare* to bring into agreement or harmony). *Music* Originally, a composition for various combinations of instruments. Now, a composition (in the classical form usually in three movements) for one, or sometimes more, solo instruments accompanied by orchestra.

concerto grosso /kənˌtʃəːtəʊ ˈɡrɒsəʊ/ *noun phrase* plural **concerti grossi** /kənˌtʃəːti ˈɡrɒsiː/ E18 Italian (= big concerto). *Music* A baroque concerto characterized by the use of a small group of solo instruments alternately with the full orchestra; a modern imitation of this.

concessionaire /kənˌsɛʃəˈnɛː/ *noun* (also **concessionnaire**) M19 French (*concessionnaire*, from Latin *concessio(n)-* (from *concess-* past participial stem of *concedere* to concede) + *-aire*). The holder of a concession or grant, especially of the use of land or trading rights.

concierge /ˈkɒnsɪɛːʒ/; *foreign* /kɔ̃sjɛrʒ/ (*plural same*) *noun* M16 French (from Old French *cumcerges* etc. = medieval Latin *consergius*, probably ultimately from Latin *conservus* fellow slave). **1** M16 The warden of a house, castle, or prison; (the title of) a high official in France and other European states, having custody of a royal palace etc. *obsolete except historical.* **2** L17 A doorkeeper, porter, etc., for a block of flats or other building, especially in France.

2 1996 *Times Magazine* Sympathetic Karen at concierge's desk calls doctor.

concordat /kən'kɔːdat/ *noun* E17 **French** or **Latin** (*concordatum* use as noun of neuter past participle of *concordare* to agree on). An agreement, a compact; *especially* one between the Vatican and a secular government relating to matters of mutual interest.

1996 *New Scientist* The lot of contract researchers was improved last week when universities and major research sponsors signed a concordat to give them some of the benefits enjoyed by permanent staff . . .

concours d'élégance /kɔ̃kur delegɑ̃s/ *noun phrase* plural same M20 **French** (= contest of elegance). A parade of motor vehicles in which prizes are awarded for the most elegant-looking.

■ Sometimes shortened to *concours*, especially when used attributively (see quotation).

1996 *Times* . . . Rolls-Royce would complete the work to *concours* condition and deliver the car 'in perfect working order, free of charge' in return for the right to use it for publicity.

conde /'kɔnde/ *noun* (also **Conde**) M17 **Spanish** (from Latin *comes, comitis* companion). A Spanish count.

condominium /kɒndə'mɪnɪəm/ *noun* E18 **Modern Latin** (from as *con-* with (others) + *dominium* rule). **1** E18 Joint control of a State's affairs vested in two or more other States. **2** M20 A set of flats, group of cottages, etc., rented or bought by a group of people; a unit of property so held. *North American.*

condor /'kɒndɔː/ *noun* E17 **Spanish** (*cóndor* from Quechua *kuntur*). Either of two very large vultures, *Vultur gryphus*, native to the Andes of South America (more fully *Andean condor*), and *Gymnogyps californianus*, of the mountains of California (more fully *Californian condor*).

condottiere /kɒndot'tjere/ *noun* plural **condottieri** /kɒndot'tjeri/ (also **condottiero**) L18 **Italian** (from *condotta* a contract, from feminine past participle of *condurre* to conduct, from as next). *History* A leader or member of a troop of mercenaries (originally and especially in Italy).

conférencier /kɔ̃ferɑ̃sje/ *noun* plural pronounced same L19 **French**. A lecturer, a public speaker; a (leading) member of a conference; a compère.

confetti /kən'feti/ *noun* E19 **Italian** (plural of *confetto* comfit, bonbon). Coloured paper shapes showered on the bride and bridegroom by the guests at a wedding. In Italy (the earlier sense), real or imitation bonbons thrown during carnival etc.

■ Originally plural but now usually treated as singular.

confiture /'kɒnfɪtjʊə/; (*foreign*) /kɔ̃fityr/ (*plural same*) *noun* M16 **French** (Old French *confit*). A preparation of fruit preserved in sugar; a confection.

■ The word was a rare import from Old French in the Middle English period with the meaning of 'a preparation of drugs'. In its present sense the forms *confiture* and *comfiture* were both used until the form in *-n-* was readopted (E19) from Modern French.

confrater /kən'freɪtə/ *noun* L16 **Medieval Latin**. A member of a brotherhood, especially of monks.

confrère /'kɒnfrɛː/ *noun* LME **French** (Old French from medieval Latin CONFRATER). **1** LME–L17 A fellow member of a fraternity. **2** M18 A fellow member of a profession, scientific body, etc.

2 1996 *Bookseller* His is a surprisingly Thatcherite credo, given how many of his confrères are running for cover in the face of the impending Tory bloodbath.

confrérie /kɔ̃freri/ *noun* plural pronounced same E19 **French** (from as preceding). A religious brotherhood; an association or group of people having similar interests, jobs, etc.

conga /'kɒŋgə/ *noun & verb* M20 **American Spanish** (from Spanish feminine of *congo* of or pertaining to the Congo). **A** *noun* **1** M20 A Latin American dance usually performed by people in single file who take three steps forward and then kick. **2** M20 In full *conga drum*. A tall, narrow, low-toned drum that is beaten with the hands. **B** *intransitive verb* L20 (past tense and participle **conga'd, congaed**). Perform the conga.

congé /kɔ̃ʒe/ (*plural same*), /'kɔ̃ʒeɪ/, /'kɒnʒeɪ/ *noun* (also (now *rare*) **congee** /'kɒndʒiː/) LME **Old French** (*congié* (modern *congé*) from Latin *commeatus* passage, leave to pass, furlough, from *commeare* to go and come). **1** LME Permission (for any act). **2** LME Ceremonious leave-taking. **3** L15–L18 Formal permission to depart. **4** L16 A bow. *archaic.* **5** M19 (from Modern

French) Unceremonious dismissal. Chiefly *jocular*.

1 1996 *Oldie* The primary articulation of the building gives congé to the decorative colour on the straight and curved planes, simple though they may be.
2 1996 *Spectator* What came to mind was not the anger of a statesman, but rather Tinkerbell in a huff. I made my *congés*.

con moto /kɒn ˈməʊtəʊ/, *foreign* /kɔn ˈmoto/ *adverb phrase* E19 Italian (= with movement). *Music* (A direction:) with spirited movement.

connoisseur /kɒnəˈsəː/ *noun* E18 French ((now *connaisseur*), from Old French *conoiss-* present participial stem of *conoistre* (modern *connaître*) to know). A person with a thorough knowledge and critical judgement of a subject, especially one of the fine arts; an expert in any matter of taste, e.g. wines, foods.

■ Often followed by *of*, *in*.

1996 *Country Life* Happily, this exhibition now re-unites more than 200 objects associated with Hamilton, attesting to the excellence of the connoisseur's taste . . .

conoscente /konoʃˈʃɛnte/ *noun* plural **conoscenti** /konoʃˈʃɛnti/ M18 Italian. CO-GNOSCENTE.

conquistador /kɒŋˈkwɪstədɔː/ *noun* plural **conquistadors**, **conquistadores** /kɒŋˌkwɪstəˈdɔːrɪz/ M19 Spanish. A conqueror; *specifically* any of the Spanish conquerors of Mexico and Peru in the sixteenth century.

1995 *New Scientist* Pauling's style was that of a conquistador in the realm of science, much as Freud had claimed to be.

consensus /kənˈsɛnsəs/ *noun* M17 Latin (= agreement, from *consens-* past participial stem of *consentire* to assent). Agreement or unity of or *of* opinion, testimony, etc.; the majority view, a collective opinion; (an agreement by different parties *to*) a shared body of views.

1996 *Country Life* Life is moving faster than the consensus of how to behave.

conservatoire /kənˈsəːvətwɑː/, *foreign* /kɔ̃sɛrvatwar/ (*plural same*) *noun* L18 French (from Italian CONSERVATORIO). An academy of music or other performing arts, especially in France or elsewhere in continental Europe.

■ Such an academy may also be called a CONSERVATORIO and CONSERVATORIUM in other parts of Europe (see below), while *conservatory* in this sense is chiefly North American.

conservatoria plural of CONSERVATOR-IUM.

conservatorio /kənˌsəːvəˈtɔːrɪəʊ/ *noun* plural **conservatorios** L18 Italian (from late Latin *conservatorium* use as noun of neuter of adjective *conservatorius* from *conservat-* past participial stem of *conservare* to conserve). An (Italian or Spanish) academy of music or other performing arts. Cf. CONSERVATOIRE, CONSERVATORIUM.

conservatorium /kənˌsəːvəˈtɔːrɪəm/ *noun* plural **conservatoriums**, **conservatoria** /kənˌsəːvəˈtɔːrɪə/ M19 German and Modern Latin (from as CONSERVATORIO *noun*). An academy of music or other performing arts, especially in Germany, Austria, or Australia. Cf. CONSERVATOIRE, CONSER-VATORIO.

consigne /kɔ̃siɲ/ *noun* plural pronounced same M19 French (from *consigner* to give instructions to a sentinel). **1** M19 An order given to a sentinel; a password. *rare*. **2** L19 A left-luggage office in France.

consolatio /kɒnsəˈleɪʃɪəʊ/, /ˌkɒnsəˈlɑːtɪəʊ/ *noun* plural **consolationes** /kɒnsəˌleɪʃɪˈəʊniːz/, /kɒnsəˌleɪtɪˈəʊniːz/ M20 Latin. A book, poem, etc. written to expound philosophical or religious themes as comfort for the misfortunes of life.

■ The much-translated *De Consolatione Philosophiae* of the Roman statesman Boethius (died AD 524) was the model for the *consolatio* genre in later European literature.

console /ˈkɒnsəʊl/ *noun* M17 French (perhaps from *consolider* to consolidate). **1** M17 *Architecture* An ornamental flat-sided bracket or corbel, usually incorporating a volute at each end. **2** E19 A table supported by consoles, and either fixed to a wall or free-standing. In full *console table*. **3** L19 A cabinet containing the keyboards, stops, and pedals of an organ. **4** E20 A cabinet for audio equipment, a television set, etc. **5** M20 A cabinet or panel where switches, meters, and controls are grouped together.

consommé /kənˈsɒmeɪ/ *noun* E19 French (use as noun of past participle of *consommer* from Latin *consummare* to finish up). A clear soup, originally made by boiling meat slowly for a long time.

con sordino /kɒn sɔːˈdiːnəʊ/ *adverb & adjective phrase* E19 Italian. *Music* (Played) with a mute or (*con sordini* /kɒn sɔːˈdiːniː/) mutes.

consortium /kənˈsɔːtɪəm/ *noun* plural **consortia** /kənˈsɔːtɪə/, **consortiums** E19 Latin (from *consors, consort-* having an equal share with). **1** E19 Partnership, association. *rare.* **2** M19 *Law.* The companionship, affection, and assistance which each spouse in a marriage is entitled to receive from the other. **3** L19 An association of organizations or States formed for commercial or financial purposes. **4** M20 A group; an assortment.

3 1996 *New Scientist* The main vehicle for this 'collaboration' between government and industry was the research and development consortium.

conspectus /kənˈspɛktəs/ *noun* M19 Latin (from *conspectus* past participial stem of *conspicere* to view). **1** M19 A comprehensive mental survey. **2** M19 A summary, a synopsis.

consul /ˈkɒns(ə)l/ *noun* LME Latin (related to *consulere* to take counsel). **1** LME *History* **a** A magistrate in ancient Rome. **b** E19 Each of the three chief magistrates of the French Republic, from 1799 to 1804, the first of whom was head of State. **2** L15 *History* A medieval earl or count. **3** E16–M18 A member of a council. **4** E16–L18 A foreign official or magistrate; *specifically* a representative head of the merchants of a particular nation resident in a foreign town. **5** M16 An agent appointed by a State to reside in a foreign town to protect the interests of the State's subjects and assist its commerce.

contadina /kɒntaˈdiːna/, /kɒntəˈdiːnə/ *noun* plural **contadine** /kɒntaˈdiːne/, /kɒntəˈdiːni/, **contadinas** E19 Italian (feminine of next). An Italian peasant girl or peasant woman.

contadino /kɒntaˈdiːno/, /kɒntəˈdiːnəʊ/ *noun* plural **contadini** /kɒntaˈdiːni/, **contadinos** M17 Italian (from *contado* county, (peasant population of) agricultural area round a city). An Italian peasant or countryman.

conte /kɔt/ *noun* plural pronounced same L19 French. A short story; as a form of literary composition, *specifically* a medieval narrative tale.

1996 *Bookseller* [Authors' agents] were always ready with scurrilous gossip or a mucky conte.

contessa /kɒnˈtɛsə/ *noun* (also (especially in titles) **Contessa**) E19 Italian (from medieval Latin *comitissa*). An Italian countess.

conteur /kɔtœr/ *noun* plural pronounced same M19 French (from CONTE). A composer of *contes*; a narrator.

continua plural of CONTINUUM.

continuo /kənˈtɪnjʊəʊ/ *noun* plural **continuos** E18 Italian (= continuous). A figured bass, a thorough bass, (= BASSO CONTINUO; an accompaniment, usually for keyboard, improvised from this. Also, the instrument(s) playing this part.

continuum /kənˈtɪnjʊəm/ *noun* plural **continua** /kənˈtɪnjʊə/ M17 Latin (use as noun of neuter singular of Latin *continuus* continuous, unbroken). A continuous thing, quantity, or substance; a continuous series of elements passing into each other; *Mathematics* the set of real numbers.

contra /ˈkɒntrə/ *adverb, preposition, & noun* LME Latin (= against (adverb and preposition), ablative feminine of a comparative from *com, cum* with). **A** *adverb* LME On or to the contrary; contrariwise. Chiefly in *pro and con(tra)* 'for and against'. **B** *preposition* LME Against. **C** *noun* **1** LME The opposing or opposite (side); an opposing factor or argument. **2** (Also *Contra.*) L20 A counter-revolutionary in Nicaragua, *especially* one opposing the government.

■ Often in abbreviated form in the noun phrase *pros and cons* (the points for and against (something)). See also quotation under PRO.

contrabasso /kɒntrəˈbasəʊ/ *noun* plural **contrabassos, contrabassi** /kɒntrəˈbasi/ E19 Italian. **1** E19 A double-bass, a contrabass. **2** M19 (A part within) the octave below the normal (bass) range, a contrabass.

contrafactum /kɒntrəˈfaktəm/ *noun* plural **contrafacta** /kɒntrəˈfaktə/ M20 Modern Latin (use as noun of neuter past participle of medieval Latin *contrafacere* to counterfeit). *Early Music* A rearrangement of a vocal composition whereby the music is retained and the words altered.

contrafagotto /ˌkɒntrəfəˈɡɒtəʊ/ *noun* plural **contrafagotti** /ˌkɒntrəfəˈɡɒti/ L19 Italian (now *controfagotto*). Double bassoon.

contralto /kənˈtraltəʊ/ *noun & adjective* M18 Italian (from as *contra-* + ALTO). *Music* **A** *noun* (plural **contraltos**) M18 The lowest female voice or (formerly) highest adult male voice; a singer having such a voice;

a part written for such a voice. **B** *adjective* M18 Possessing, belonging to, or written for a contralto voice.

1996 *Times* Heroines were supposed to be fragile blondes with light voices. Rawlings had raven hair, striking but not pretty looks and a mellow contralto voice.

contra mundum /ˌkɒntrə ˈmʌndəm/ *adverb phrase* M18 Latin. Against the world; defying or opposing everyone.

1995 *Country Life* Perhaps journalists and country people should gang up together. Us *contra mundum.*

contrapposto /kontrapˈposto/ *noun* plural **contrapposti** /kontrapˈposti/ E20 Italian (past participle of *contrapporre* from Latin *contraponere* to contrapose). In the visual arts, an arrangement of a figure in which the action of the arms and shoulders contrasts as strongly as possible with that of the hips and legs; a twisting of a figure on its own axis.

contra proferentem /ˌkɒntrə prɒfəˈrɛntɛm/ *adverb phrase* E20 Latin. *Law* Against the party which proposes or adduces a contract or a condition in a contract.

contrayerva /ˌkɒntrəˈjəːvə/ *noun* M17 Spanish (literally, 'counter-herb', i.e. one used as an antidote, from *contra-* against + *yerva* (now *hierba*) herb). (The root of) any of several tropical American plants used medicinally (formerly against snakebites).

contre cœur variant of À CONTRECŒUR.

contrecoup /ˈkɔːtrəkuː/ *noun* M18 French (from *contre* against + *coup* blow). **1** M18 A repercussion, an adverse consequence. *rare.* **2** M19 *Medicine* An injury of a part (especially one side of the brain) resulting from a blow on the opposite side.

contredanse /ˈkɒntrədɑːns/, *foreign* /kɔ̃trədɑ̃s/ (*plural same*) *noun* (also **contradance**) E19 French (alteration of *country dance* by association with *contre* against, opposite). A country dance, *especially* a social dance of which quadrille is a variant; a piece of music for such a dance.

contre-jour /ˈkɔː̃trəʒʊə/ *noun* E20 French (from *contre* against + *jour* daylight). *Photography* Back-lighting.

■ Usually attributive.

contretemps /ˈkɔ̃ːtrətɔ̃ː/, /ˈkɒntrətɔ̃ː/ *noun* plural pronounced same L17 French (originally 'motion out of time', from *contre* against + *temps* time). **1** L17 *Fencing* Originally, a thrust made at an inoppor-

tune moment or at the same time as one's opponent makes one. Now, a feint made with the intention of inducing a counter-thrust. **2** E18 An unexpected or untoward occurrence, especially of an embarrassing kind; a hitch, a mishap. **b** M20 A disagreement, an argument, a dispute. *colloquial.* **3** E18 *Dancing* A (ballet) step danced on the offbeat. Also, an academic ballet step involving a partial crossing of the feet and a small jump from a knees-bent position.

convenance /kɔ̃vnɑ̃s/ *noun* plural pronounced same L15 French (from *convenir* from Latin *convenire* to agree with). **1** L15–L17 Agreement, concurrence. *rare.* **2** M19 Conventional propriety or usage; in *plural*, the proprieties.

conversazione /ˌkɒnvəsatsɪˈəʊni/ *noun* plural **conversaziones, conversazioni** /ˌkɒnvəsatsɪˈəʊni/ M18 Italian (= conversation). **1** M18 In Italy: an evening gathering for conversation and recreation. **2** L18–L19 An at-home. **3** L18 A social gathering for discussion of the arts, literature, etc.; an educational soirée.

3 1995 *New Scientist* It [sc. the Royal Albert Hall] was to host science *conversaziones* and agricultural, industrial and scientific exhibitions.

conversus /kənˈvəːsəs/ *noun* plural **conversi** /kənˈvəːsʌɪ/ L18 Latin. *History* A lay member of a monastery or convent, *especially* one entering monastic life as a mature person.

cooee /ˈkuːɪ/, /ˈkuːiː/ *noun, interjection, & verb* (also **cooey**) L18 Aboriginal. **A** *noun & interjection* L18 (A call or cry) used as a signal to draw attention to the caller. **B** *intransitive verb* E19 Utter this call.

■ Chiefly Australia and New Zealand, imitative of a signal used by Aborigines and copied by settlers.

coon-can /ˈkuːnkan/ *noun* L19 Spanish (perhaps from *con quién?* with whom?). A card-game of Mexican origin, for two players and ancestral to (gin) rummy. Formerly also, a form of this played with two packs each with two jokers.

coontie /ˈkuːnti/ *noun* (also **coontah** /ˈkuːntə/) L18 Seminole (*kunti*). In the United States: any of several low-growing palmlike cycads of the genus *Zamia*, native to tropical and subtropical America; the arrowroot yielded by these plants.

copaiba /kəʊˈpʌɪbə/ *noun* (also **copaiva** /kəʊˈpʌɪvə/) E17 Portuguese (*copaíba* (whence Spanish *copaiba*) from Tupi *copaíba*, Guaraní *cupaíba*). A balsam of aromatic odour and acrid taste obtained from South American leguminous trees of the genus *Copaifera* and used in medicine and the arts. Formerly also, a tree yielding this.

copal /ˈkəʊp(ə)l/ *noun* L16 Spanish (from Nahuatl *copalli* incense). A hard translucent odoriferous resin obtained from various tropical trees and used to make a fine transparent varnish. Also *gum copal*.

coperta /kəˈpəːtə/ *noun* L19 Italian (= covering, from *coprire* from Latin *coperire*, *cooperire* to cover). A transparent lead glaze given as a final glaze to some majolica.

copita /kəʊˈpiːtə/ *noun* M19 Spanish (diminutive of *copa* from popular Latin *cuppa* cup). A tulip-shaped sherry glass of a type traditionally used in Spain; a glass of sherry.

copra /ˈkɒprə/ *noun* L16 Portuguese and Spanish (from Malayalam *koppara*). Dried coconut kernels, from which oil is obtained.

copula /ˈkɒpjʊlə/ *noun* E17 Latin (= connection, linking of words, from as *co-* + *apere* to fasten). **1** E17 *Logic* and *Grammar* That part of a proposition which connects the subject and the predicate. **2** M17 A connection, a link.

coq au vin /kɒk əʊ vɛ̃/ *noun phrase* M20 French (literally, 'cock in wine'). Chicken cooked in wine.

coque /kɒk/ *noun* 1 E19 French (= shell). A loop, a looped bow. Now *specifically* a small loop of ribbon in the trimming of a woman's hat.

coque /kəʊk/ *noun* 2 (also **coq** /kɒk/) E20 French (*coq* cock). A cock's feather used in the trimming of a hat etc. In full *coque feather*.

coquet /kɒˈkɛt/ *noun* & *adjective* L17 French (diminutive of *coq* cock; as adjective = forward, wanton, gallant). **A** *noun* L17 A man given to flirting or coquetry. **B** *adjective* L17 Coquettish.
■ The noun was formerly (L17–E19) both masculine and feminine; later the feminine became COQUETTE.

coquet /kɒˈkɛt/ *verb* (also **coquette**) L17 French (*coqueter*, from as preceding). **1** *intransitive & transitive verb* L17 with *it*. Of a woman, or (formerly) a man: flirt (*with*). **2** *transitive verb* Flirt with. Only in 18. **3** *intransitive verb* L18 Dally, trifle, or toy (*with* a matter etc.)

coquette /kɒˈkɛt/ *noun* & *adjective* M17 French (feminine of COQUET (noun)). **A** *noun* **1** M17 A woman who trifles with men's affections; a woman given to flirting or coquetry. **2** M19 A crested hummingbird of the genus *Lophornis*. **B** *adjective* M18 COQUET (adjective).
A.1 1996 *Spectator* . . . she can mock, tease, play the coquette . . .

coquillage /kɔkijaʒ/ *noun* M19 French (literally, 'shell-fish'; see next). Decoration in the form of shells or shellfish, *especially* on furniture.

coquille /kɔkij/ *noun* L19 French (from medieval Latin from medieval Greek *kokhulia* plural of *kokhulion* for Greek *kogkhulion*, from *kogkhē* conch). (Scallop) shell.
1995 D. Lodge *Therapy* The scallop shell, or coquille . . . is the traditional symbol of the pilgrimage to Santiago.

coquina /kəʊˈkiːnə/ *noun* M19 Spanish (= shellfish, cockle, from Old Spanish *coca* from medieval Latin by-form of Latin *concha* shell). A soft white limestone composed of broken marine shells cemented together and used for building in the West Indies and Florida. Also *coquina rock*, *coquina stone*.

coquito /kəʊˈkiːtəʊ/ *noun plural* **coquitos** M19 Spanish (diminutive of *coco* coconut). The Chilean wine palm, *Jubaea chilensis*, which yields palm honey and fibre. Also *coquito palm*.

coradgee variant of KORADJI.

corah /ˈkɔːrə/ *noun* & *adjective* E19 Hindi (*korā* new, unbleached). **A** *noun* E19 An Indian-pattern silk handkerchief. **B** *adjective* L19 Of silk: undyed.

coram /ˈkɔːrəm/ *preposition* M16 Latin. Before, in the presence of.
■ Occurs in various archaic legal phrases used in English, such as CORAM JUDICE, *coram nobis* 'in our presence', *coram populo* 'in the presence of the people' (i.e. in public).

coram judice /ˌkɔːrəm ˈjuːdɪsɪ/ *adverb phrase* E17 Latin (= in the presence of a judge). In a properly constituted or an appropriate court of law.

cor anglais /kɔːr ˈɑːŋgleɪ/, /kɔːr ˈɒŋgleɪ/ *noun phrase* L19 French (literally, 'English horn'). A musical instrument like an oboe but lower in pitch; a player of this. Also, an organ reed-stop of similar quality.

corbeau /'kɔːbəʊ/ noun & adjective E19 French (= crow, raven). In the drapery trade, (of) a dark green colour verging on black.

corbeille /kɔː'beɪ/ noun E19 French. An elegant basket of flowers or fruit.

cordelle /kɔː'dɛl/ noun & verb E16 French (diminutive of corde rope, from Latin chorda from Greek khordē gut, string (of musical instrument)). **A** noun **1** E16–E17 A rope, especially on a ship. Scottish. **2** E19 A ship's towing-line. North American **B** transitive & intransitive verb E19 Give a tow (to) with a cordelle. North American.

cordillera /kɔːdɪ'ljɛːrə/ noun E18 Spanish (from cordilla diminutive of cuerda from Latin chorda cord). Each of a series of parallel mountain ridges or chains, especially in the Andes; an extensive belt of mountains, valleys, etc., especially as a major continental feature.

cordon bleu /ˌkɔːdõ 'blə:/ noun & adjective phrase M18 French (cordon ribbon + bleu blue). **A** noun plural **cordons bleus** (pronounced same). M18 (A person having) a supreme distinction; specifically a first-class cook. **B** adjective M20 Of cooking: first-class.

■ In French history, a blue ribbon signified the highest order of chivalry under the Bourbon kings.

cordon sanitaire /ˌkɔːdõ sanɪ'tɛː/ noun phrase plural **cordons sanitaires** (pronounced same) M19 French (cordon ribbon, band + sanitaire sanitary). A guarded line placed between an area affected by disease and adjacent unaffected areas in order to prevent the infection from spreading. Also figurative.

■ Earlier (E19) simply cordon.

1996 Spectator Working in oils is a messy, smelly business which demands a cordon sanitaire from the rest of the household.

cordovan /'kɔːdəv(ə)n/ adjective & noun L16 Spanish (cordován (now cordobán) noun, cordovano adjective, from Córdova (now Cordoba) from Latin Corduba Córdoba). **A** adjective L16 Of or pertaining to the city of and province of Córdoba in Spain; made of cordovan. **B** noun L16 **1** A kind of pliable fine-grained leather used especially for shoes, made originally at Córdoba from goatskin and now from horsehide. **2** M17–E19 A skin of this leather.

cornada /kor'nada/, /kɔː'nɑːdə/ noun plural **cornadas** /kor'nadas/, /kɔː'nɑːdəz/ M20 Spanish (from cuerno from Latin cornu horn). Bullfighting The goring of a bull-fighter by a bull; a wound so caused.

corniche /'kɔːnɪʃ/, /kɔː'niːʃ/ noun M19 French. A road along the edge of a cliff; any coastal road with panoramic views. Also corniche road.

cornucopia /kɔːnjʊ'kəʊpɪə/ noun E16 Late Latin (cornucopia from Latin cornu copiae horn of plenty (a mythical horn able to provide whatever is desired)). **1** E16 A goat's horn depicted as a horn of plenty, overflowing with flowers, fruit, and corn; an ornamental vessel or other representation of this. **2** E17 figurative An overflowing stock; an abundant source.

corps /kɔː/, foreign /kɔr/ noun plural same /kɔz/, foreign /kɔr/ L16 French (from Latin CORPUS body). **1** L16 A tactical division of an army; an organized body of troops assigned to a special duty or a particular kind of work (medical, ordnance, intelligence, etc.). See also ESPRIT DE CORPS. **2** M18 A body of people engaged (collectively or as individuals) in a particular activity. **3** L19 A students' society in a German university.

■ The first appearance of corps in English was in the phrase CORPS DE GARDE. It was apparently first used as an independent word by Addison in 1711 in the Spectator in a letter peppered with up-to-the-minute military jargon, which was largely the product of the Duke of Marlborough's campaigns in Europe. It was probably at first pronounced as the English word corpse, and Johnson's Dictionary (1755) gives corps and corpse as alternative spellings. The desirability of distinguishing between the two sorts of 'body' has ensured that the French pronunciation and spelling have been retained for the 'group of people' sense.

corps à corps /kɔr a kɔr/ adverb phrase L19 French (= body to body). In close, especially bodily, contact; Fencing the position of two fencers so close that their bodies are in contact.

corps de ballet /kɔr də balɛ/, /ˌkɔːr də 'baleɪ/ noun phrase plural same E19 French. Dance The company of supporting dancers in a ballet.

transferred **1995** Spectator Those tough veterans had to sit down each year to be confronted by a corps de ballet of golden nymphs prancing down the table and saluting them with trumpets, laurel wreaths and skeins of silk.

corps de garde /kɔr də gard/, /ˌkɔːr də 'gɑːd/ noun phrase plural same L16 French.

A small body of soldiers set as a guard; the post they occupy, a guard-house.

corps d'élite /kɔr delit/, /kɔː deɾliːt/ *noun phrase* plural same L19 French. A body of specially picked men; a select group.

corps de logis /kɔr də lɔʒi/ *noun phrase* plural same M17 French (literally, 'body of dwelling'). *Architecture* The main (part of a) building; the central block of a house.

corps diplomatique /kɔr diplɔmatik/, /ˌkɔː dɪpləmaˈtiːk/ *noun phrase* plural **corps diplomatiques** (*pronounced same*) L18 French. The body of ambassadors and their staff attached to a particular seat of government; the diplomatic corps.

corpus /ˈkɔːpəs/ *noun* plural **corpora** /ˈkɔːp(ə)rə/, **corpuses** LME Latin (= body). **1** LME The body of a person or animal. Now *jocular*. **2** L17 *Anatomy* Any of various masses of tissue in the body that have a distinct structure or function. (Chiefly in technical terms such as *corpus callosum* etc.) **3** E18 A body or collection of writing, knowledge, etc.; the whole body of a particular category of literature etc. **b** M20 *specifically* A body of spoken or written material on which a linguistic analysis is based. **4** M19 Principal or capital, as opposed to interest or income. *archaic*. **5** M20 *Botany* The inner layers of cells in an apical meristem.

   3 1996 *Oldie* Some exercise of this sort . . . needs to be applied to the corpus of architectural criticism.

corral /kəˈrɑːl/ *noun & verb* L16 Spanish and Old Portuguese (*corral*, Portuguese *curral*: cf. KRAAL). **A** *noun* **1** L16 An enclosure for horses, cattle, etc. Chiefly *North American*. **2** M19 An enclosure in which to trap and capture wild animals. **3** M19 A defensive enclosure formed of wagons in an encampment. **B** *verb* inflected -ll-. **1** *transitive & intransitive verb* M19 Form (wagons) into a corral. **2** *transitive verb* M19 Shut up (as) in a corral, confine. **3** *transitive verb* M19 Obtain, get hold of. *North American colloquial*.

corrida /kɔˈriːdə/, *foreign* /koˈrrida/ *noun* L19 Spanish (literally, 'course (of bulls)'). A bullfight; bullfighting. In full *corrida de toros* /də ˈtɔːrəʊz/, *foreign* /ðe ˈtoros/.

corrigendum /kɒrɪˈdʒɛndəm/ *noun* plural **corrigenda** /kɒrɪˈdʒɛndə/ E19 Latin (neuter gerundive of *corrigere* to correct). Something requiring correction, *specifically* in a book. In plural *especially* errors listed with the corrections alongside.

corroboree /kəˈrɒbəri/ *noun* L18 Aboriginal. **A** *noun* **1** L18 A night-time dance of Australian Aborigines, which may be either festive or warlike; a song or chant for this. **2** L19 A noisy gathering; a disturbance.

corsetière /ˈkɔːsɪtjɛ/ *noun* M19 French (feminine of *corsetier*, from as Old French *cors* (modern *corps*) body + *-ière*). A woman who makes or fits corsets.

Corso /ˈkɔːsəʊ/ *noun* (also **corso**) plural **Corsos** L17 Italian (= course, main street from Latin *cursus* course). In Italy and some other Mediterranean countries: a procession of carriages; a social promenade; a street given over to this, or where races etc. were formerly held.

cortège /kɔːˈteɪʒ/ *noun* M17 French (from Italian *corteggio*, from *corteggiare* to attend court, from *corte* court). A train of attendants; a procession of people, especially mourners.

cortex /ˈkɔːtɛks/ *noun* plural **cortices** /ˈkɔːtɪsiːz/ LME Latin (= bark). **1** LME An outer layer of a part in an animal or plant; *specifically* (*Anatomy*) the outer layer of the cerebrum, composed of folded grey matter and playing an important role in consciousness; *Botany* a layer of plant tissue between the epidermis and the central vascular tissue. **2** M17-M18 *figurative* An outer shell or husk. **3** L17 The bark of a tree, or the peel or rind of a plant, as used medicinally; *specifically* cinchona bark.

cortile /korˈtiːle/, /kɔːˈtiːli/ *noun* E18 Italian (derivative of *corte* court). An enclosed usually roofless and arcaded area within or attached to an Italian building.

   1984 A. G. Lehmann *European Heritage* . . . for all the classical exhibition in the *cortile*, when it comes to furnishing their private apartments, the Medici lean rather towards the tastes of a European market, not a classical revival at all.

corvée /ˈkɔːveɪ/ *noun* ME Old and Modern French (= Provençal *corroada* from Proto-Romance use as noun (sc. *opera* work) of Latin *corrogata* neuter plural past participle of *corrogare* to summon). A day's unpaid work required of a vassal by a feudal lord; forced labour exacted as a tax, *specifically* that on public roads in France before 1776; *figurative* an unpleasant duty, an onerous task.

corvette /kɔːˈvɛt/ *noun* M17 French (ultimately diminutive of Middle and Modern Dutch *korf* basket, kind of ship). *History*

1 M17 Originally, a kind of small French vessel using both oars and sail. Later, a warship with a flush deck and one tier of guns. Now *historical*. **2** M20 An escort vessel smaller than a frigate used especially for protecting convoys against submarines in the war of 1939–45.

coryphaeus /kɒrɪˈfiːəs/ *noun* plural **coryphaei** /kɒrɪˈfiːʌɪ/ E17 Latin (from Greek *koruphaios* chief, chorus-leader, from *koruphē* head, top). **1** E17 The leader of a chorus. **2** E17 The leader of a party, sect, school of thought, etc.

coryphée /ˈkɒrɪfeɪ/ *noun* E19 French (from as preceding). A leading dancer of a CORPS DE BALLET.

coryza /kəˈrʌɪzə/ *noun* E16 Latin (from Greek *koruza* nasal mucus, catarrh). Acute catarrhal inflammation of the nose; *especially* the common cold.

Cosa Nostra /ˌkəʊzə ˈnɒstrə/ *noun phrase* M20 Italian (= our thing). The American branch of the Mafia.

cosmos /ˈkɒzmɒs/ *noun* ME Greek (*kosmos* order, ornament, world). **1** ME The universe as an ordered whole. **2** M19 Harmony, order. **3** L19 An ordered system of ideas etc.

costa /ˈkɒstə/ *noun* (also **Costa**) M20 Spanish (= coast). A coast, *especially* one developed as a holiday resort.
■ On the pattern of genuine place-names such as *Costa Brava* or *Costa del Sol*, jocular usage creates pseudo-Spanish names such as *Costa Geriatrica* (a sea-side resort or area mainly populated by elderly people) or *Costa del Crime* (an area favoured by criminals for enjoying their ill-gotten gains in luxury while remaining beyond the reach of extradition laws).
1995 *Times: Weekend* Goa is a long way yet from becoming another Spanish costa but the beach will be more crowded and there will no longer be any sense of solitude.

costumier /kɒˈstjuːmɪə/ *noun* M19 French (from *costumer* to costume). A person who makes or deals in costumes; *especially* a person who sells or hires out theatrical costumes and properties.

coteau /kɒˈtəʊ/, *foreign* /kɔto/ *noun* plural **coteaus, coteaux** /kɒˈtəʊz/ M19 French (= slope, hillside from Old French *costel*, from *coste* (modern *côte* rib, from Latin *costa*). Any of various kinds of elevated geographical features, as a plateau, a divide between valleys, etc. *North American*.

coterie /ˈkəʊt(ə)ri/ *noun* E18 French ((in Old French = tenants holding land together), ultimately from Middle Low German *kote* cote, cottage). **1** E18 A small exclusive group with common interests; *especially* a select social group. **2** E19 A meeting of such a group.

cotillion /kəˈtɪljən/ *noun* (in sense 1 also **cotillon** /kəˈtɪljən/, *foreign* /kɔtijɔ̃/ (*plural same*)) E18 French (*cotillon* petticoat, dance, diminutive of *cotte* coat). **1** E18 Any of several dances with elaborate steps and figures. **2** L19 A formal ball, *especially* one at which débutantes are presented. *United States*.

cotta /ˈkɒtə/ *noun* M19 Italian (from Proto-Romance, from Frankish, of unknown origin). *Christian Church* A short surplice.
1996 *Oldie* I . . . feel deeply uncomfortable with its atmosphere of unguents, incense, bells, mortifications and prayers directed at a world infected with cassocks and cottas . . .

cottage orné see under ORNÉ.

couac /kʊˈak/ *noun* L19 French (imitative). *Music* A quacking sound made by bad blowing on the clarinet, oboe, or bassoon.

couchant /ˈkaʊtʃ(ə)nt/ *adjective* LME Old and Modern French (present participle of *coucher* to couch, lie down). **1** LME Especially of an animal: lying down. **2** E16 *Heraldry* Of an animal: lying on its belly with its head up, lodged. Usually *postpositive*, as in *lion couchant*.

couchee /ˈkuːʃeɪ/, *foreign* /kuʃe/ (*plural same*) *noun* L17 French (*couché* variant of *coucher* lying down, going to bed, use as noun of *coucher* to couch). An evening reception.
■ The opposite of a LEVEE *noun* 1.

couchette /kuːˈʃɛt/, *foreign* /kuʃɛt/ (*plural same*) *noun* E20 French (literally, 'little bed', diminutive of *couche*). A railway carriage in which the seats convert into sleeping-berths; such a berth.

coudé /kuːˈdeɪ/ *adjective & noun* L19 French (past participle of *couder* to bend at right angles, from *coude* elbow from Latin *cubitum* cubit). (Of, pertaining to, or designating) a telescope in which the rays are bent to focus at a fixed point off the axis.

coulée /kuːˈleɪ/, /ˈkuːli/ *noun* (also **coulee**, (sense 1) **coulie** /ˈkuːli/) E19 French (= (lava) flow, from Latin *colare* to filter, strain, (in Proto-Romance) flow, from *cōlum* strainer). **1** E19 (The bed of) an intermittent stream; a dry valley; a gulch or valley with steep sides. *North American dialect.* **2** M19 *Geology* A stream of molten or solidified lava.

couleur de rose /kulœr də roz/ *noun & adjective phrase* LME French (= rose colour). **A** *noun phrase* LME Rose-colour, pink; *figurative* optimism, cheerfulness. **B** *adjective phrase* L18 Rose-coloured, pink; *figurative* optimistic, cheerful.

coulis /'ku:li/ *noun* L20 French (see next). A thin, flowing sauce.

> **1996** *Spectator* . . . a cassata . . . was very good, though I was less keen on the strawberry coulis draped around it.

coulisse /ku:'li:s/ *noun* E19 French (use as noun of feminine of *coulis* sliding (from *coulisser* to slide); cf. *portcullis* literally, 'sliding door'). **1** E19 *Theatre* Each of the side scenes of a stage; *singular* and (usually) in *plural*, the space between them, the wings. **2** M19 A groove in which a sluice-gate or other movable partition slides up and down. **3** L19 The body of outside dealers on the Paris Bourse; similar dealers in other stock exchanges; the place where they deal. **4** E20 A corridor; *figurative* a place of informal discussion or negotiation.

> **4 1968** D. Torr *Treason Line* The real business of the conference would begin . . . in the *coulisses.*

couloir /'ku:lwɑ:/, *foreign* /kulwar/ (*plural same*) *noun* E19 French (= channel, from *couler* to pour, from Latin *colare* to filter). A steep gully on a mountainside.

coup /ku:/, *foreign* /ku/ (*plural same*) *noun* LME Old and Modern French (from medieval Latin *colpus* from Latin *colaphus* from Greek *kolaphos* blow with the fist; in branch II reintroduced from French in figurative sense and also in a number of phrases (see below)). **I 1** LME-M16 A blow given or received in combat. **II 2** L18 A stroke or move that one makes; *especially* a notable or strikingly successful move. **b** M19 A COUP D'ÉTAT. **c** M19 *History* Among North American Indians: the act of touching an enemy, as a deed of bravery; the act of first touching an item of the enemy's in order to claim it. **3** L18 *Billiards* The direct pocketing of the cueball, which is a foul stroke.

coup de fors /ku də fɔrs/ *noun phrase* plural **coups de fors** (*pronounced same*) M19 French (literally, 'stroke of force'). A sudden violent action.

coup de foudre /ku də fudr/ *noun phrase* plural **coups de foudre** (*pronounced same*) L18 French (literally, 'stroke of lightning'). A sudden unforeseen event; a revelation; love at first sight.

coup de grâce /,ku: də 'grɑ:s/ *noun phrase* plural **coups de grâce** (*pronounced same*) L17 French (literally, 'stroke of grace'). A blow by which someone or something that has been mortally hurt is mercifully killed; *figurative* a decisive finishing stroke.

> **1996** *Times* It was de Villiers who administered the *coup de grâce*, dismissing Cork, Martin and Gough in successive overs . . .

coup de main /ku də mɛ̃/ *noun phrase* plural **coups de main** (*pronounced same*) M18 French (literally, 'stroke of hand'). Chiefly *Military* A sudden onslaught; a surprise attack.

coup d'état /ku: der'tɑ:/, *foreign* /ku deta/ *noun phrase* plural **coups d'état** /ku:z der 'tɑ:/, *foreign* /ku deta/, **coup d'états** /ku: der'tɑ:z/ M17 French (literally, 'blow of State'). A violent or illegal change in government. Formerly also, any sudden and decisive stroke of State policy.

> ■ Now often abbreviated to *coup* in all but the most formal contexts.
>
> **1996** *Spectator* Andreotti was once asked whether there could be a coup d'état in Italy. 'No,' he replied. 'There is no état.'

coup de théâtre /ku də teatr/ *noun phrase* plural **coups de théâtre** (*pronounced same*) M18 French (literally, 'stroke of theatre'). **1** A theatrical hit. **2** A sudden dramatic turn of events or action, *originally* in a play, now also *figurative* (see quotations).

> **2 1995** *Spectator* . . . the finale of the scene—where the Prince's girlfriend is shot dead—looks rather forced, instead of being a *coup de théâtre.*
>
> **2** *figurative* **1995** *Times* Tony Blair's most unexpected *coup de théâtre* this week was his announcement of a deal with British Telecom . . .

coup d'œil /ku dœj/ *noun phrase* M18 French (literally, 'stroke of eye'). A comprehensive glance; a general view; *Military* the faculty or action of rapidly assessing a position and sizing up its advantages etc.

> **1996** *Country Life* Also, they [sc. the rooms] are seen at the correct angles in the first views, with the chimneypieces being part of the first *coup d'œils* in all of them.

coupe /ku:p/ *noun* 1 L19 French (= goblet from medieval Latin *cuppa*). **1** L19 A shallow dish; a short-stemmed glass. **2** E20 A dessert of ice-cream, fruit, etc., served in a glass coupe.

coupe /kuːp/ *noun 2* E20 French (= felling, from *couper* to cut, slash). A periodic felling of trees; an area so cleared.

coupé /ˈkuːpeɪ/ *noun* (in sense 3b also **coupe** /kuːp/) E18 French (past participle of *couper* to cut; in branch II abbreviation of *carrosse coupé*, literally, 'cut carriage'). **I 1** E18 *Dancing* Formerly, coupee, a kind of bowing step. Now, a step in ballet in which one foot displaces another and weight is transferred to it. **2** L19 *Fencing* A movement of the sword similar to a disengage, but effected by drawing the sword along and over the point of the opponent's. **II 3a** M19 A four-wheeled carriage with a seat for two inside and an outside seat for the driver. Chiefly *historical*. **b** E20 An enclosed two-door motor car with two or four seats and (now) usually a sloping rear.

courante /kʊˈrɒ̃(n)t/, /kʊˈrɑːnt/ *noun* (also **courant** /kʊˈrant/) L16 French (use as noun of feminine present participle of *courir* to run). **1** L16 A court dance of the sixteenth and seventeenth centuries characterized by glides and light hops, a coranto. **2** L16 *Music* A piece of music for this dance; a piece of music in triple time, *especially* one which forms a movement of a suite.

courbette /kʊəˈbɛt/ *noun* M17 French (from Italian *corvetta*). *Equestrianism* A leap in *haute école* in which a trained horse rears up and jumps forward on the hind legs without the forelegs' touching the ground.

coureur /kuːrœr/ *noun* plural pronounced same E18 French (= (wood-)runner). *History* A woodsman, trader, etc., of French origin in Canada and the northern United States. In full *coureur de bois* /də bwaː/.

courge /kʊəʒ/ *noun* M19 French (= gourd from Old French *cohourde* from Latin *cucurbita*). A basket for holding live bait, towed behind a fishing boat.

courgette /kʊəˈʒɛt/ *noun* M20 French (from as preceding). A small variety of vegetable marrow. Also called ZUCCHINI.

course libre /kurs librʲ/ *noun phrase* plural **courses libres** (pronounced same) M20 French (= free course). A bullfight, as in France, in which the bull is baited but not killed.

court bouillon /kur bujɔ̃/ *noun phrase* M17 French (from *court* short + BOUILLON). A stock made from wine, vegetables, etc., in which fish is boiled.

couscous /ˈkuːskuːs/ *noun* (also **kouskous**, **couscoussou** /ˈkuːskuːsuː/) E17 French (from Arabic *kuskus*, *kuskusū* millet grain, probably of Berber origin). A spicy North African dish of crushed wheat or coarse flour steamed over broth, frequently with meat or fruit added; the granules of flour from which this dish is made.

couture /kuːˈtjʊə/ *noun* E20 French (from Old French *couture* sewing from late Latin *consutura*, from Latin *consutus* past participle of *consuere* to sew together). **1** Dressmaking; (the design and making of) fashionable garments, especially French ones. **2** Abbreviation of HAUTE COUTURE.

2 *attributive* **1995** *Times* How many women have the money to buy a couture dress?

couvade /kuːˈvaːd/ *noun* M19 French (from *couver* to hatch from Latin *cubare* to lie). A custom in some cultures by which a man takes to his bed and goes through certain rituals when his wife bears a child.

■ Adopted in French in this sense (M19) owing to a misunderstanding of the expression *faire le couvade* 'to sit doing nothing' in earlier writers.

couverture /ˈkuːvətjʊə/ *noun* M20 French (= covering). (A layer of) chocolate for coating sweets and cakes.

couvre-pied /kuvrəpje/ (*plural same*) *noun* (also **couvre-pieds** /kuvrəpje/) E19 French (literally, 'cover foot', from *couvrir* to cover). A rug to cover the feet.

coyote /ˈkɔɪəʊt/, /kɔɪˈəʊti/ *noun & verb* plural same, **coyotes** M18 Mexican Spanish (from Nahuatl *coyotl*). **A** *noun* M18 A small nocturnal wolflike animal, *Canis latrans*, of western North America, noted for its mournful howling. Also called *prairie-wolf*. **B** *intransitive verb* M19 *Mining* Make a small lateral tunnel from a shaft etc. *United States slang*.

■ The sense of the verb refers to the small tunnels dug out by the coyote; in California the phrase *coyote diggings* described such lateral shafts.

cracovienne /krakəʊvɪˈɛn/ *noun* M19 French (feminine adjective from *Cracovie* Kraków (Cracow), a city in southern Poland). A lively Polish dance; a ballet dance in a Polish style. Also called *krakowiak*.

cranium /ˈkreɪnɪəm/ *noun* plural **crania** /ˈkreɪnɪə/, **craniums** LME Medieval Latin (from Greek *kranion* skull). **1** LME The bones enclosing the brain; the bones of the whole head, the skull. **2** M17 The head. *jocular*.

2 1996 *Times Magazine* Never having had a book to promote before, *Like a Virgin* is chorusing through my cranium . . .

crannog /ˈkranəg/ *noun* E17 Irish (*crannóg*, Gaelic *crannag* timber structure, from *crann* tree, beam). In Scotland and Ireland: an ancient fortified settlement constructed in a lake or marsh on an artificial island made from timber.

craquelure /ˈkrakljʊə/, *foreign* /kraklyr/ *noun* E20 French. A network of small cracks in the pigment or varnish on the surface of a painting.

crèche /krɛʃ/, /kreɪʃ/ *noun* L18 French (from Old French *creche* wooden feeding rack for animals, from Proto-Romance from Germanic base related to *crib*). **1** L18 A model of the infant Jesus in the manger with attending figures, often displayed at Christmas. **2** M19 A day nursery for infants and young children.

■ *Crib* is now the more usual word for sense 1.

credenza /krɪˈdɛnzə/ *noun* L19 Italian (from medieval Latin *credentia* from Latin *credent-* present participial stem of *credere* to believe; see quotation 1996). A sideboard, a cupboard, a buffet.

1996 *Country Life* . . . although I knew what a credenza was—a sideboard or display cabinet with a blind door flanked by shelves or glazed cupboards—I was unsure of the derivation. A 'credence' in English furniture terminology began as a church table . . . but now means something more like a card-table. Although the Italian *credenza* shares the same origin, it developed into a sideboard, and the name was anglicized when such cabinets became popular in the 19th century.

credo /ˈkriːdəʊ/, /ˈkreɪdəʊ/ *noun* plural **credos** ME Latin (*credo* I believe). **1** ME The Apostles' Creed, the Nicene Creed, (from their first word). Now *especially* a musical setting of the Nicene Creed. **2** L16 *generally* A creed, a set of opinions or principles.

2 1996 *Bookseller* To any critic they can always call on their shabby mass-market credo, 'If that's what people want, who am I to patronise them by offering what someone else might think is better?'

creese variant of KRIS.

crémaillère /kremajɛr/ *noun* plural pronounced same E19 French (formerly *cramaillère*, from *cramail* pot-hanger, chimney-hook). *Fortification* A zig-zag or indented inside line of a parapet.

crème /krɛm/ (*plural same*), /kreɪm/ *noun* (also **crême**) E19 French (= cream). **1** E19 Cream; a cream, a custard. Used especially in names of desserts and liqueurs (see following entries). **2** M19 The CRÈME DE LA CRÈME.

crème brûlée /krɛm bryle/, /kreɪm ˈbruːleɪ/ *noun phrase* L19 French (literally, 'burnt cream'). A cream or custard dessert topped with caramelized sugar.

crème caramel /krɛm karamɛl/, /kreɪm ˈkarəmɛl/ *noun phrase* E20 French. A custard dessert topped with caramel. Cf. CRÈME RENVERSÉE.

■ Earlier (M19) as *crème au caramel*.

crème Chantilly /krɛm ʃɑ̃tiji/, /kreɪm ʃanˈtɪli/ *noun phrase* (also *crème chantilly*) E20 French. Whipped cream flavoured with vanilla and sweetened.

■ Earlier (L19) as *crème à la Chantilly*. Chantilly is the name of a town in France, not far from Paris.

crème de cacao /krɛm də kakao/, /ˌkreɪm də ˈkəˈkaʊ/ *noun phrase* M20 French. A chocolate-flavoured liqueur.

crème de la crème /krɛm də la krɛm/, /kreɪm də lɑː kreɪm/ *noun phrase* M19 French (literally, 'cream of the cream'). The pick of society; the élite in any field.

1996 *Spectator* In 1988, they played Liverpool, then seen as the *crème de la crème* of Europe, in the FA Cup Final.

crème de menthe /krɛm də mɑ̃t/, /kreɪm də ˈmɑːnt/, /kreɪm də ˈmɒnθ/ *noun phrase* E20 French. A peppermint-flavoured liqueur.

crème de noyau /krɛm də nwajo/, /kreɪm də ˈnwʌɪəʊ/ *noun phrase* L19 French. An almond-flavoured liqueur.

crème fraîche /krɛm frɛʃ/ *noun phrase* (also **creme fraiche**) L20 French. *Cookery* Soured cream.

1996 *Country Life* . . . one of my favourites is tartare of salmon with a *crème fraîche*, horseradish and dill sauce . . .

crème renversée /krɛm rɑ̃vɛrse/, /kreɪm ˈrɛnvəːseɪ/ *noun phrase* E20 French (literally, 'inverted cream'). A custard made in a mould and then turned out, often with a caramel topping (*crème caramel renversée*).

cremona variant of CROMORNE.

creole /'kriːəʊl/ *noun & adjective* (also (especially in strict use of sense A. 1 and corresponding uses of the adjective) **Creole**) E17 French (*créole*, earlier *criole* from Spanish *criollo* probably from Portuguese *crioulo* Black born in Brazil, home-born slave, from *criar* to nurse, breed, from Latin *creare* to create). **A** *noun* **1** E17 A descendant of European settlers or (occasionally) of Black slaves, in the West Indies or Central or South America; a descendant of French settlers in the southern United States, especially Louisiana. Also *loosely*, a person of mixed European and Black descent. **2** L19 A former pidgin language that has developed into the sole or native language of a community. **B** *adjective* **1** M18 That is a creole; of, pertaining to, or characteristic of a creole or creoles. **2** M18 Of a plant or animal: bred or grown in the West Indies but not of indigenous origin.

crêpe /kreɪp/ *noun & adjective* (also **crepe**) L18 French (earlier *crespe*, use as noun of Old French *crespe* curled, frizzed, from Latin *crispus* curled). **A** *noun* **1** L18 A fine cotton or gauzelike fabric with a crinkled surface. **2** E20 A type of raw rubber rolled into thin sheets with a wrinkled surface, used for shoe-soles etc. More fully *crêpe rubber*. **3** E20 A very thin pancake. **B** *attributive* or as *adjective* Made of crêpe; resembling crêpe.

■ The Anglicized spelling *crape* was current in the seventeenth century in sense A.1, but later came to be restricted to a specific kind of black silk cloth used especially for mourning dresses and funereal drapes.

crêpe de Chine /kreɪp də ʃiːn/ *noun phrase* L19 French. A fine crêpe of silk or similar fabric. Also called *China crêpe*.

crêpeline /'kreɪpəliːn/ *noun* (also **crêpoline**) L19 French (diminutive of CRÊPE). A thin light dress-material made of silk or silk and wool.

crêpe Suzette /kreɪp suːˈzɛt/ *noun phrase* plural **crêpes Suzette** (*pronounced same*) E20 French. A thin dessert pancake served hot in a sauce that usually contains spirit or liqueur.

crépinette /kreɪpɪˈnɛt/ *noun* L19 French (diminutive of *crépine* caul). A kind of flat sausage consisting of minced meat and savoury stuffing wrapped in pieces of pork caul.

crêpoline variant of CRÊPELINE.

crépon /'kreɪpən/ *noun & adjective* L19 French (from as CRÊPE *noun & adjective*). (Made of) a fabric resembling crêpe, but heavier.

crepusculum /krɪˈpʌskjʊləm/, /krɛˈpʌskjʊləm/ *noun* (also Anglicized as **crepuscle** /'krɛpəs(ə)l/, **crepuscule** /'krɛpəskjuːl/) LME Latin (related to *creper* dusky, dark). The period of half-dark at the beginning or end of the day; twilight, dusk.

crescendo /krɪˈʃɛndəʊ/ *adverb, adjective, noun, & verb* L18 Italian (present participle of *crescere* to increase from Latin *crescere* to grow). **A** *adverb & adjective* Music L18 (A direction:) with a gradual increase in loudness. **B** *noun* plural **crescendos**, **crescendi**. **1** *Music* L18 A gradual increase in loudness; a passage (to be) played or sung with such an increase. **2** L18 A progressive increase in force or effect. **3** E20 A climax. **C** *intransitive verb* Increase gradually in loudness or intensity.

> **A** 1995 *Spectator* . . . the composer Percy Grainger used the word 'louden', where less Australian musicians are content with 'crescendo' . . .

cresson /krɛsɔ̃/ *noun* M17 French (= cress). **1** In *plural* Cress. *rare* (only M17). **2** L19 A shade of green resembling that of watercress.

cretin /'krɛtɪn/ *noun* L18 French (*crétin* from Swiss French *creitin*, *crestin* from Latin *Christianus*). **1** L18 *Medicine* A person afflicted with cretinism. **2** L19 A fool; a person who behaves stupidly.

cretonne /krɛˈtɒn/, /'krɛtɒn/ *noun* L19 French (of unknown origin). A strong unglazed fabric printed on one or both sides with a (usually large floral) pattern, used for chair covers, curtains, etc.

crevasse /krɪˈvas/ *noun* E19 French (Old French *crevace*). **1** E19 A (usually deep) fissure or chasm in the ice of a glacier; *transferred* a deep crack or chasm. **2** E19 A breach in the bank or levee of a river, canal, etc. *United States*.

criard /kriar/ *adjective* (also (French feminine) **criarde** /kriard/) M19 French. Shrill; garish.

criblé /krible/ *noun & adjective* L19 French (from Old French *crible* from popular

Latin variant of Latin *cribrum* sieve). (Designating) a type of engraving with small punctures or depressions on a wood or metal ground. Cf. MANIÈRE CRIBLÉE.

■ The technique of using metalworkers' punches to create stippled areas on a printing plate was one of the earliest used in Renaissance metal engraving. The effect was to have patterns of white dots (likened to the holes of a sieve) against the black ground of the print.

cri de cœur /kri də kœr/ *noun phrase* plural **cris de cœur** (pronounced same) E20 French (= cry of or from the heart). An appeal in distress.

1996 *Times* Newcastle's social sides are not going down without a final *cri de cœur* for the essential amateurism which they . . . believe can co-exist with professional rugby.

crime passionnel /krim pasjɔnɛl/ *noun phrase* plural **crimes passionnels** (pronounced same) E20 French. A crime, especially murder, due to sexual jealousy.

criollo /krɪˈɒləʊ/ *noun & adjective* (also **Criollo**) plural of noun **criollos** L19 Spanish (= native to the locality). **1** L19 (Designating or pertaining to) a native of Spanish South or Central America, especially one of pure Spanish descent. **2** E20 (Designating) a cacao tree of a variety producing thin-shelled beans of high quality. **3** M20 (Designating) any of various South or Central American breeds of domestic animal, *especially* a small horse bred from native South American and Arab stock, or cattle of Spanish ancestry.

crise /kriz/ *noun* plural pronounced same LME French. Crisis.

■ Formerly fully naturalized, it now occurs only in the following phrases or as an abbreviation of them.

crise de conscience /kriz də kɔ̃sjɑ̃s/ *noun phrase* M20 French. A crisis of conscience.

crise de nerfs /kriz də nɛr/ *noun phrase* (also **crise des nerfs**) E20 French (= crisis of nerves). An attack of nerves; a fit of hysterics.

1970 *New Yorker* She has been a splendid advertisement for the benefits of a happy marriage—conspicuously more relaxed, far less subject to those old *crises des nerfs*.

critique /krɪˈtiːk/ *noun* Originally **critic** M17 French (ultimately from Greek *kritikē* (sc. *tekhnē*) the critical art, criticism). **1** M17 Criticism; *especially* the art of criticism. **2** M17 A criticism; *especially* a critical analysis, article, or essay.

crochet /ˈkrəʊʃeɪ/, /ˈkrəʊʃi/ *noun & verb* M19 French (diminutive of *croc* with *-ch-* from *crochié, crochu* hooked). **A** *noun* M19 A kind of knitting done using a single hooked needle to form intertwined loops; knitted material made in this way. **B** *verb* **1** *transitive verb* L19 Make in crochet. **2** *intransitive verb* L19 Do crochet work.

croisette /krwaˈzɛt/ *noun* L17 French (diminutive of *croix* cross). A small cross.

croissant /ˈkrwasɒ̃/ *noun* L16 French. L19 A flaky pastry roll in the shape of a crescent.

■ Earlier (L16–L17) found as an occasional variant of *crescent*, especially with reference to the crescent moon, *croissant* is now solely used for the pastry roll.

cromlech /ˈkrɒmlɛk/ *noun* L17 Welsh (from *crom* feminine of *crwm* bowed, arched + *llech* (flat) stone). A dolmen; any megalithic chamber-tomb.

cromorne /krəʊˈmɔːn/ *noun* (also **cremona**) E18 French (from German KRUMM-HORN). An organ reed stop, usually of 8-ft pitch, suggestive of a krummhorn or (later) a clarinet in sound.

croque-monsieur /ˈkrɔk məˌsjə/ *noun* M20 French. A toasted ham-and-cheese sandwich.

croquette /krɒˈkɛt/ *noun* E18 French (from *croquer* to crunch). A small ball or roll of vegetable, minced meat, or fish (to be) fried in breadcrumbs.

croquis /krɔki/, /krəʊˈkiː/ *noun* plural same /krɔki/, /krəʊˈkiːz/ E19 French (from *croquer* to sketch). A rough draft; a sketch.

crostini /krɒsˈtiːnɪ/ *noun plural* L20 Italian. Snacks consisting of bread, usually toasted or fried, with a savoury topping.

crotale /ˈkrəʊt(ə)l/ *noun* M20 French (from Latin CROTALUM). A small tuned cymbal; a kind of castanet or clapper; a crotalum.

crotalum /ˈkrɒt(ə)l(ə)m/, /ˈkrəʊt(ə)l(ə)m/ *noun* plural **crotala** /ˈkrɒt(ə)lə/, /ˈkrəʊt(ə)lə/ L18 Latin (from Greek *krotalon*). An ancient clapper or castanet the two halves of which were struck together with the finger and thumb.

croupade /krʊˈpeɪd/ *noun* M17 French (from Italian *groppata* (with assimilation to French *croupe* croup). *Equestrianism* In *haute école* a single leap with the horse's hind legs brought up under the belly.

Also, a high kick with the hind legs while the forelegs remain on the ground.

croupier /ˈkruːpɪə/, /ˈkruːpɪeɪ/ *noun* E18 French ((originally a person who rides behind on a horse's croup), from *croupe* from Proto-Romance from Germanic base related to *crop*). **1** A person who stands behind a gambler to give support and advice. Only in E18. **2** M18 A person who rakes in and pays out the money or tokens at a gaming-table. **3** L18 An assistant chairman sitting at the lower end of the table at a public dinner.

croustade /kruˈstɑːd/ *noun* M19 French (from Old French *crouste* (modern CROÛTE) or Italian *crostata* tart (from *crosta* crust)). A crisp piece of bread or pastry hollowed to receive a savoury filling.

croûte /kruːt/ *noun* plural pronounced same E20 French. A crisp piece of toasted or fried bread; a croûton. See also EN CROÛTE.

croûton /ˈkruːtɒn/, /kruːtɔ̃/ (*plural same*) *noun* (also **crouton**) E19 French (from CROÛTE). A small piece of toasted or fried bread served with soup or as a garnish.

cru /kry/ (*plural same*), /kruː/ *noun & adjective* (also **crû**) E19 French (from *crû* past participle of *croître* grow). *Wine* (The grade or quality of wine produced in) a French vineyard or wine-producing region; (designating) French wine of a specified quality.
▪ Often in phrases (see quotation); see also CRU CLASSÉ, GRAND CRU, PREMIER CRU.
1966 P. V. Price *France, Food & Wine Guide* Just below the classed growths come the *crus bourgeois* . . . then the *crus artisans*.

cru classé /kry klase/, /kruː ˈklaseɪ/ *noun phrase* plural **crus classés** (pronounced same) M20 French (= classed growth). *Wine* A Bordeaux wine belonging to one of the highest official categories.

crudités /krydite/, /ˈkruːdɪteɪ/ *noun plural* M20 French. *Cookery* Assorted raw vegetables as an hors d'oeuvre.

crumhorn variant of KRUMMHORN.

crux /krʌks/ *noun* plural **cruxes** /ˈkrʌksɪz/, **cruces** /ˈkruːsiːz/ M17 Latin (= cross). **1** M17 (A representation of) a cross. Chiefly in CRUX ANSATA. **2** E18 A difficult matter, a puzzle; the decisive point at issue; the central point. **3** M19 (Usually **Crux**) (The name of) the constellation of the Southern Cross.

crux ansata /krʌks anˈseɪtə/ *noun phrase* plural **cruces ansatae** /ˈkruːsiːz anˈseɪtiː/ M19 Latin (= cross with a handle). An ANKH.

crwth /kruːθ/ *noun* M19 Welsh (cf. Gaelic *cruit* harp, violin, Irish *cruit* small harp, Old Irish *crot* harp, cithara). An old Celtic musical instrument with three, or later six, strings which was held against the chest and played by bowing and plucking.
▪ Adopted earlier (ME) as *crowd*.

csardas /ˈtʃɑːdɑːʃ/, /ˈzɑːdəs/ *noun* (also **czardas**) plural same M19 Hungarian (*csárdás*, from *csárda* inn). A Hungarian dance usually having a slow start and a rapid wild finish, with many turns and leaps; a piece of music for this dance.

cuadrilla /kwadˈriʎa/, /kwɒdˈriːljə/ *noun* plural **cuadrillas** /kwadˈriʎas/, /kwɒd ˈriːljəz/ M19 Spanish. A company of people; *especially Bullfighting* A matador's team.

cuartel /kwarˈtel/, /kwɔːˈtɛl/ *noun* M19 Spanish (from *cuarta* quarter, from *cuarto* fourth, from Latin *quartus*). In Spain and Spanish-speaking countries: a military barracks.

cuesta /ˈkwɛstə/ *noun* E19 Spanish (= slope, from Latin *costa*). Originally (*United States dialect*), a steep slope that terminates a gently sloping plain; a plain in this configuration. Now (*Geography*), a ridge with a gentle slope on one side and a steep one on the other, a scarp and dip.

cui bono /kwiː ˈbɒnəʊ/, /kuːɪ ˈbɒnəʊ/, /kuːɪ ˈbəʊnəʊ/ *interjection* (interrogative), *adjective & noun phrase* E17 Latin (= to whom (is it) a benefit?). **A** *interjection* (interrogative) E17 What is the purpose (of)? Who stands to gain (and so might be responsible)? **B** *adjective phrase* M18 Of or pertaining to the question *cui bono?* **C** *noun phrase* M19 The question *cui bono?*
A 1996 *Spectator* Then, from the 1960s to the 1980s, yet more scholars . . . put the attribution back to Raphael and authenticated the Dürer inscription, to the general satisfaction. *Cui bono?* Well, it gave large numbers of dons and students . . . something to do.

cuir-ciselé /kwiːrˈsiːzleɪ/, *foreign* /kyirsizle/ *adjective* M20 French (= engraved leather). (Of a design on a leather binding) cut in relief with a pointed tool; having such a design.

cuisine /kwɪˈziːn/ *noun* L18 French (= kitchen, from Latin *coquina, cocina*, from *coquere* to cook). A culinary establishment; cookery as an art, especially as characteristic of a particular country or establishment. Cf. HAUTE CUISINE, NOUVELLE CUISINE.

cuivré /ˈkiːvreɪ/, *foreign* /kyivre/ *adverb & noun* M20 French (past participle of *cuivrer* to play with a brassy tone, from *cuivre* copper, from late Latin *cuprum*). *Music* (With) a harsh strident tone (in a brass instrument).

cul-de-sac /ˈkʌldəsak/, /kʊldəˈsak/ *noun* plural **culs-de-sac** (pronounced same), **cul-de-sacs** M18 French (= sack-bottom). **1** M18 *Anatomy* A vessel, tube, sac, etc., open only at one end; the closed end of such a vessel. **2** L18 A street, passage, etc., closed at one end; a blind alley; *Military* a position in which an army is hemmed in on all sides except behind.

> **2** *figurative* **1995** *New Scientist* Lock up the DNA libraries and information will simply not be available to other researchers. Life-saving research could then become stuck in a cul-de-sac.

culet /ˈkjuːlɪt/ *noun* (also (earlier) **collet** /ˈkɒlɪt/) L17 French (diminutive of *cul* bottom). **1** L17 The horizontal base of a diamond, formed by the blunting of a point, when the stone is cut as a brilliant. **2** M19 A piece of armour for protecting the hinder part of the body below the waist.

culmen /ˈkʌlmɛn/ *noun* M17 Latin (contraction of *columen* top, summit, etc). **1** M17 The top, the summit; *figurative* the acme, the culminating point. **2** M19 The upper ridge of a bird's bill.

culotte /kjuːˈlɒt/, *foreign* /kylɔt/ *noun* plural pronounced same M19 French (= knee-breeches; cf. SANSCULOTTE). **1** M19 Knee-breeches. *rare*. **2** E20 *singular* and (usually) in *plural*. A woman's garment that hangs like a skirt but has separate legs, as in trousers; a divided skirt. **3** E20 A fringe of soft hair on the back of the forelegs of some dogs.

culpa /ˈkʌlpə/ *noun* M19 Latin. *Law*. Neglect resulting in damage, negligence.

■ See also FELIX CULPA.

cultus /ˈkʌltəs/ *noun* M17 Latin (from past participial stem of *colere* to honour with worship). **1** Worship. *rare*. Only in M17.

2 M19 A system of religious worship or ritual; a cult.

cum /kʌm/ *preposition* LME Latin (= with). **1** LME Combined with. Used in names of combined parishes (e.g. Horton-cum-Studley). **2** With. Chiefly in Latin phrases and English ones imitating them (e.g. cum dividend). **3** And also. Denoting a combined role or nature (see quotation).

> **3** **1996** *New Scientist* ... she [sc. Sylvia Earle] co-founded Deep Ocean Technology and Deep Ocean Engineering, ... apparently running them as director-cum-secretary from her kitchen table.

cum laude /kʌm ˈlɔːdi/, /kʌm ˈlaʊdeɪ/ *adverb & adjective phrase* L19 Latin (= with praise). (Of a degree, diploma, etc.) with honours, with distinction.

■ Chiefly North American; cf. MAGNA CUM LAUDE, SUMMA CUM LAUDE.

cumulus /ˈkjuːmjʊləs/ *noun* plural **cumuli** /ˈkjuːmjʊlʌɪ/, /ˈkjuːmjʊliː/ M17 Latin. **1** M17 A heap, a pile; an accumulation; the conical top of a heap. **2** E19 *Meteorology* (A cloud-type consisting of) rounded masses of cloud heaped on each other and having a horizontal base at usually a low altitude. Also *cumulus cloud*.

cunnilingus /kʌnɪˈlɪŋgəs/ *noun* L19 Latin (= a person who licks the vulva, from *cunnus* female external genitals + *lingere* to lick). Stimulation of a woman's genitals with the tongue.

cupidon /ˈkjuːpɪdɒn/, *foreign* /kypidɔ̃/ (*plural same*) *noun* (also **Cupidon**) E19 French (from Latin *Cupido* Cupid, the personification of desire, the god of love). A beautiful youth; a cupid, an Adonis.

■ *Cupid* or *cupid* has been the normal form since Late Middle English, and *cupidon* is chiefly poetical.

cupola /ˈkjuːpələ/ *noun* M16 Italian (from late Latin *cupula* little cask, small burying-vault, diminutive of *cupa* cask). **1** M16 A rounded vault or dome forming the roof of (part of) a building; *specifically* a small rounded dome forming or adorning a roof; the ceiling of a dome. **b** M17 Something likened to such a dome. **2** E18 A tall usually cylindrical furnace, open at the top and tapped at the bottom, for melting metal that is to be cast. Also *cupola furnace*. **3** E19 *Anatomy* The small dome-shaped end of the cochlear duct. **4** M19 A revolving dome for protecting mounted guns on a warship etc. **5** E20 *Geology* A small dome-shaped projection on the top of a larger igneous intrusion.

curandero /kuran'dero/ *noun* plural **curanderos** /kuran'deros/ (feminine **curandera** /kuran'dera/) M20 Spanish (from *curar* to cure, from Latin *curare*). In Spain and Latin America: a healer who uses folk remedies.

curare /kjʊ'rɑːri/ *noun* L18 Spanish and Portuguese (from Carib word represented also by *wourali*). A resinous bitter substance obtained from the bark and stems of various tropical and subtropical South American plants of the genus *Strychnos*, which paralyses the motor nerves and was formerly used as an arrow poison by South American Indians and now in surgery etc. to relax the muscles.

curé /kyre/ *noun* plural pronounced same M17 French (from medieval Latin *curatus* a person who has a cure or charge (of a parish)). In France and French-speaking countries: a parish priest.

curettage /kjʊə'retɪʤ/, /kjʊərɪ'tɑːʒ/ *noun* L19 French (from as next). *Surgery* The scraping or cleaning of an internal surface of an organ or body cavity with a curette.
■ Often in the phrase *dilatation and curettage* (colloquially abbreviated *d&c*), a common operation on the womb which consists of this.

curette /kjʊə'ret/ *noun* & *verb* M18 French (from *curer* to take care of, clean, from Latin *curare* to heal). *Surgery* **A** *noun* M18 A small instrument resembling a scoop used to remove material by a scraping action, especially from the womb. **B** L19 *transitive & intransitive verb* Scrape or clean with a curette.

curia /'kjʊərɪə/ *noun* (also in sense 3 **Curia**) plural **curiae** /'kjʊəriː/, **curias** E17 Latin. **1** E17 *History* Each of the ten divisions into which each of the three tribes of ancient Rome was divided; the senate of an ancient Italian town, as distinguished from that of Rome. **2** E18 A court of justice, counsel, or administration, especially of the Roman Catholic Church or (*historical*) under the feudal system. **3** M19 *The Curia* Vatican tribunals, congregations, and other institutions through which the Pope directs the work of the Roman Catholic Church; the government departments of the Vatican.

curiosa /kjʊərɪ'əʊsə/ *noun* plural L19 Latin (*curiosa* neuter plural of *curiosus*). Curiosities, oddities; *specifically* erotic or pornographic books.

1996 *Independent on Sunday* It has beautiful women: . . . an absent-minded, gloriously disorganised, plump and pretty *assistante* sprung to life from the pages of some piece of Victorian *curiosa*.

curiosa felicitas /kjʊərɪˌəʊsə fə'lɪsɪtɑːs/ *noun phrase* M18 Latin (literally, 'careful felicity'). A studied appropriateness of expression.
■ The phrase is a quotation from Petronius (*Satyricon* cxviii).

currach /'kʌrə(x)/ *noun* (also **curragh**, **corrack**) LME Irish (Gaelic *curach* small boat, coracle). In Ireland and Scotland: a small boat made of slats or laths covered with watertight material (formerly hide, now usually tarred canvas).

curragh /'kʌrə(x)/ *noun* M17 Irish (*currach* marsh, Manx *curragh* moor, bog, fen). In Ireland and the Isle of Man: marshy waste ground.

currente calamo /kəˌrɛnteɪ 'kaləməʊ/ *adverb phrase* L18 Modern Latin (literally, 'with the pen running on'). Extempore; without deliberation or hesitation.

curriculum /kʌ'rɪkjʊləm/ *noun* plural **curricula** /kʌ'rɪkjʊlə/ E19 Latin (= running, course, race-chariot, from *currere* to run). A course of study at a school, university, etc.; the subjects making up such a course.

curriculum vitae /kʌˌrɪkjʊləm 'viːtʌɪ/, /'vʌɪtiː/ *noun phrase* plural **curricula vitae** /kʌ'rɪkjʊlə/ E20 Latin (from as preceding + Latin *vitae* of life). A brief account of one's life or career, especially as required in an application for employment.
■ In job advertisements and colloquial contexts usually abbreviated to *c.v.*
1996 *Times* None of the usual 'seeking other business opportunities', no attempt to deny a rift or gild the *curriculum vitae* for the benefit of future employers.

cursillo /kur'siʎo/; /kʊə'siːjəʊ/, /kur'siːljəʊ/ *noun* plural **cursillos** /kur'siʎos/, /kur'sijəʊz/, /kur'siːljəʊz/ M20 Spanish (literally, 'little course'). A short course of study etc., *specifically* of intensive religious studies and exercises, originally for Roman Catholics in Spain.

cursor /'kəːsə/ *noun* ME Latin (= runner, from *currere* to run). **1** ME–M17 A runner, a running messenger. **2** L16 A part of a mathematical or surveying instrument which can be slid back and forwards; *specifically* the transparent slide with a fine line with which the readings on a slide-rule are taken. **3** M20 A movable visual marker forming part of a VDU display, showing where the next character to be keyed will appear.

cursus /'kə:səs/ *noun* plural same, **cursuses** M18 Latin (= course, from *currere* to run). **1** M18 *Archaeology* A neolithic structure consisting of a long straight avenue, usually closed at the ends, formed by two earthen banks with a ditch on the outer side of each. **2** M19 A stated order of daily prayer or worship. **3** E20 One of the cadences which mark the ends of sentences and phrases, especially in Greek and Latin prose. **4** E20 Abbreviation of CURSUS HONORUM.

cursus honorum /ˌkə:səs ɒ'nɔ:rəm/ *noun phrase* plural same E20 Latin (= course of honours). An established hierarchy of positions through which a person may be promoted.

> **1995** *Spectator* His [sc. Isaiah Berlin's] *cursus honorum* (Fellow of All Souls, headship of an Oxford College . . . President of the British Academy and O.M.), might seem to make him a paid-up member of the establishment.

cuspidor /'kʌspɪdɔ:/ *noun* M18 **Portuguese** (= spitter, from *cuspir* to spit, from Latin *conspuere*). A spittoon. Chiefly *North American*.

custos /'kʌstɒs/ *noun* plural **custodes** /kʌ'stəʊdi:z/, (originally) **custoses** /kʌ'stəʊsi:z/ LME Latin. A keeper, a guardian, a custodian.

■ Now chiefly in titles from Modern Latin, as in *custos rotulorum* (literally, 'keeper of the rolls'), a title given to the chief Justice of the Peace in an English county, who has nominal responsibility for the records of the commission of the peace in that county.

cutcha variant of KUTCHA.

cuvée /kju:'veɪ/, *foreign* /kyve/ (*plural same*) *noun* M19 **French** (= vatful, from *cuve* from Latin *cupa* cask, vat). The contents of a vat of wine; a particular blend or batch of wine.

cuvette /kju:'vɛt/ *noun* L17 **French** (diminutive of *cuve* vat). **1** L17 *Fortification* A

trench along the middle of a dry ditch. **2** E18 A shallow vessel for holding liquid; a transparent vessel with flat sides for holding a spectrophotometric sample etc. **3** M19 A large clay basin or crucible used in making plate glass. **4** E20 *Geology* A basin in which sedimentation is occurring or has occurred.

cwm /kʊm/ *noun* M19 **Welsh** (= coomb). A bowl-shaped valley or hollow in (Welsh) mountains; *Physical Geography* A CIRQUE.

cyanosis /sʌɪə'nəʊsɪs/ *noun* plural **cyanoses** /sʌɪə'nəʊsi:z/ M19 **Modern Latin** (from Greek *kuanōsis* blueness). *Medicine* A blue discolouration of the skin due to deficient oxygenation of the blood.

cyma /'sʌɪmə/ *noun* M16 **Modern Latin** (from Greek *kuma* billow, wave, wavy moulding, from *kuein* to become pregnant). **1** M16 *Architecture* An ogee moulding of a cornice. **2** E18 *Botany* A CYME.

cymatium /sɪ'matɪəm/, /sɪ'meɪʃəm/ *noun* plural **cymatia** /sɪ'matɪə/, /sɪ'meɪʃə/ M16 Latin (*cymatium* ogee, Ionic volute from Greek *kumation* diminutive of *kuma* CYMA). *Architecture* A CYMA.

cymbalo /'sɪmbələʊ/ *noun* plural **cymbalos** L19 **Italian** (*cembalo, cimbalo* from Latin *cymbalum* cymbal; cf. CIMBALOM). A dulcimer.

cyme /sʌɪm/ *noun* (in sense 1 also written **cime**) E18 **French** (*cyme, cime* summit, top, from popular form of Latin CYMA). **1** The unopened head of a plant. rare. Only in E18. **2** L18 *Botany* An inflorescence (frequently forming a more or less flat head) in which the primary axis bears a single flower which develops first, flowers of secondary and higher order axes developing successively later.

czar variant of TSAR.

czardas variant of CSARDAS.

czarevich, czarevna, etc. variants of TSAREVICH, TSAREVNA, etc.

D

da capo /dɑː ˈkɑːpəʊ/ *adverb phrase* E18 Italian (= from the beginning). *Music* (A direction:) repeat from the beginning.

dacha /ˈdatʃə/ *noun* (also **datcha**) M19 Russian (= grant of land). In Russia: a small country house or villa.

1996 *Oldie* The Russians, who did not enjoy their time in Yemen, built *dachas* and Black Sea style hotels.

dacoit /dəˈkɔɪt/ *noun* L18 Hindustani (*ḍakait*, from *ḍākā* gang-robbery). A member of an Indian or Myanmar (Burmese) band of armed robbers.

dado /ˈdeɪdəʊ/ *noun* plural **dados** M17 Italian (= die, cube, from Latin *datum*). *Architecture* **1** M17 The plain portion of a pedestal between the base and the cornice. **2** L18 The lower part of an interior wall when faced or coloured differently from the upper part.

daemon /ˈdiːmən/, /ˈdʌɪməʊn/ *noun* (also formerly **demon**) M16 Latin (medieval Latin *demon*, Latin *daemon* from Greek *daimōn* divinity, genius). **1** *Greek Mythology* M16 A being of a nature between that of the gods and men, a spirit; the soul of a deceased person regarded as a minor divinity. **2** E17 An attendant or indwelling spirit; a DAIMON.

■ *Demon*, meaning specifically 'an evil spirit' or 'devil', was naturalized in Middle English, and this spelling was also occasionally used in Early Modern English in the senses above. However, the usefulness of being able to differentiate between an evil spirit and other morally neutral entities taken over from pagan classical religion ensured that the spelling *daemon* has survived in the latter senses. A similar consideration lay behind the later (M19) introduction of DAIMON.

dagesh /ˈdɑːɡɛʃ/ *noun* M16 Hebrew (*dāḡēš*). *Hebrew Grammar* A point or dot placed within a Hebrew letter, denoting either that it is doubled or that it is not aspirated.

dagga /ˈdaɡə/ *noun* L17 Afrikaans (from Nama *daχa*). In South Africa: Indian hemp used as a narcotic; any indigenous plant of the genus *Leonotis* which is similarly used.

dagoba /ˈdɑːɡəʊbə/ *noun* E19 Sinhalese (*dāḡaba* from Pali *dhātu-gabbha* receptacle for relics). A stupa or dome-shaped structure containing Buddhist relics.

daimon /ˈdʌɪməʊn/ *noun* M19 Greek (*daimōn*). An attendant or indwelling spirit, one's genius.

■ The direct transliteration of the Greek is intended to evoke the pagan classical concept of the personal spirit, unencumbered by the nuances of the earlier usages of d(a)emon; see also DAEMON.

daimyo /ˈdʌɪmɪəʊ/, /ˈdʌɪmjəʊ/ *noun* (also **daimio**) plural **daimyos** E18 Japanese (from *dai* great + *myō* name). *History* In feudal Japan: any of the chief land-owning nobles, vassals of the shogun.

dak /dɑːk/, /dɔːk/ *noun* (also **dawk**) E18 Hindustani (*ḍāk*). In the Indian subcontinent: originally, post or transport by relays; now, postal service, delivery of letters, mail.

dal variant of DHAL.

dalles /dalz/ *noun* plural L18 French (plural of *dalle* conduit, tube, etc.). In the western United States: rapids where a river is compressed into long narrow troughlike channels.

dal segno /dal ˈsɛmjəʊ/ *adverb phrase* L19 Italian (= from the sign). *Music* (A direction:) go back to the point indicated by the sign (not the beginning). Cf. AL SEGNO.

dame de compagnie /dam də kɔ̃paɲi/ *noun phrase* plural **dames de compagnie** (pronounced same) L18 French (literally, 'lady of company'). A paid female companion.

dame d'honneur /dam dɔnœr/ *noun phrase* plural **dames d'honneur** (pronounced same) E19 French (literally, 'lady of honour'). A maid of honour, a lady-in-waiting.

damna plural of DAMNUM.

damnatio memoriae /damˌnɑːtɪəʊ məˈmɔːrɪiː/ *noun phrase* M20 Latin (= condemnation of the memory). The attempt to obliterate the memory of a dead person by erasing inscriptions mentioning him or her, destroying statues and memorials, etc.

1985 H. Schutz *Romans in Central Europe* Nero's name had been erased after his death when the Roman Senate condemned his memory, the *damnatio memoriae*.

damnosa hereditas /dam͵nəʊsə hɪ ˈrɛdɪtas/ *noun phrase* M19 Latin (= inheritance that causes loss). An inheritance, tradition, etc., bringing more burden than profit.

1955 *Times* The rule that an executor was not compelled to accept a *damnosa hereditas* did not provide a reliable guide.

damnum /ˈdamnəm/ *noun plural* **damna** /ˈdamnə/ E19 Latin (= hurt, harm, damage). *Law* A loss, a wrong.

dan /dan/ *noun* M20 Japanese. Each of the (numbered) grades in the advanced level of proficiency in judo, karate, etc. (also *dan grade*; a person who has reached (a specified grade of) this level. Cf. KYU.

danse du ventre /dãs dy vãtr/ *noun phrase plural* **danses du ventre** (pronounced same) L19 French. A belly-dance.

danse macabre /dãs makabr/*noun phrase plural* **danses macabres** (pronounced same) L19 French. The dance of death; a musical piece or passage representing or suggestive of this.

■ Earlier (LME) Anglicized as *dance (of) macabre* (cf. MACABRE). As an allegory, the Dance of Death (called TOTENTANZ in German-speaking areas) was very popular in the late Middle Ages. Medieval and Renaissance representations of it show Death in the form of a skeleton approaching young and old, rich and poor, powerful and obscure, and leading them all away in a dance to the grave; the most famous of these images is the series of 50 woodcuts by Hans Holbein the Younger designed in the early 1520s and published in Lyons in 1538.

figurative **1996** *Spectator* . . . less like all-out war, more like a stately minuet between the command structure of the British state and that of the IRA, a *danse macabre* whose ritual bows to certain unwritten understandings about the rules of engagement.

danseur /dãsœr/ *noun plural pronounced same* E19 French (from *danser* to dance). *Ballet* A male dancer.

danseur noble /dãsœr nɔbl/ *noun phrase plural* **danseurs nobles** (*pronounced same*) M20 French (from as *danseur* + *noble* noble). *Ballet* A male dancer as partner of a ballerina.

1996 *Spectator* Wildor is now a complete ballerina . . . . Similarly, Trevitt is a true *danseur noble* who coped brilliantly with the complexities of the part . . .

danseuse /dãsøz/ *noun plural pronounced same* E19 French. A female dancer; a ballerina.

dariole /ˈdarɪəʊl/ *noun* LME Old and Modern French. **1** LME An individual sweet or savoury dish of various kinds; now *specifically* one made in a dariole mould. **2** M19 A small metal mould shaped like a flower-pot and used for making such a dish. In full *dariole mould*.

darshan /ˈdɑːʃən/ *noun* E20 Hindi (pronunciation of Sanskrit *darśana* sight, seeing, from *dr̥ś-* to see). In the Indian subcontinent etc.: the opportunity or occasion of seeing a holy person or the image of a deity.

Dasein /ˈdɑːzeɪn/ *noun* M19 German (from *dasein* to exist, from *da* there + *sein* to be). *Philosophy* In Hegelian terms, existence, determinate being; in existentialism, human existence, the being of a person in the world.

dashiki /ˈdɑːʃɪki/ *noun* M20 West African (probably Yoruba from Hausa: cf. Krio *da(n)shiki*). A loose brightly coloured West African shirt, also worn by Blacks in America etc.

data /ˈdeɪtə/ *noun* M17 Latin (plural of DATUM). *plural and collective singular* **1** M17 Things given or granted; things known or assumed as facts, and made the basis of reasoning or calculation. **2** L19 Facts, especially numerical facts, collected together for reference or information. **3** M20 The quantities, characters, or symbols on which operations are performed by computers and other automatic equipment, and which may be stored and transmitted in the form of electrical signals, records on magnetic, optical, or mechanical recording media, etc.

2 1996 *New Scientist* Much of the modern craze for collecting data is to avoid having to admit that we are just using our judgment.

datcha variant of DACHA.

datum /ˈdeɪtəm/ *noun singular plural* **data** /ˈdeɪtə/ M18 Latin (neuter past participle of *dare* to give). A thing given or granted; a thing known or assumed as a fact, and made the basis of reasoning or calculation; a fixed starting-point for a series of measurements etc.

■ Now much more frequent in the plural DATA.

daube /dəʊb/, *foreign* /dob/ (*plural same*) *noun* E18 French. A braised meat (usually beef) stew with wine, spices, etc.

dauphin /'dɔ:fm/, /'dəʊfã/ *noun* (also **Dauphin**) LME French ((Old French *daulphin*), family name of the lords of Viennois or Dauphiné). **1** LME *History* (The title of) the eldest son of the King of France, from 1349 to 1830. **2** A dolphin. *rare*. Only in L16.

■ See also AD USUM DELPHINI.

dazibao /'da:dzəbaʊ/ *noun* plural same M20 Chinese (*dàzìbào*, from *dà* big + *zì* character + *bào* newspaper, poster). In the People's Republic of China: a wall-poster written in large characters expressing an (especially political) opinion.

débâcle /deɪ'ba:k(ə)l/, /dɪ'ba:k(ə)l/ *noun* (also **debacle**) E19 French (from *débâcler* to unbar, from *dé-* + *bâcler* to bar). **1** E19 A breaking-up of ice in a river; a sudden flood or rush of water carrying along debris. **2** M19 A sudden and ignominious collapse or defeat; a humiliating and embarrassing situation.

2 1996 *Times Magazine* Fred Vermorel emerges from this débâcle as a sad individual trading on the reflected glory of his association with people from a bygone time.

débat /deba/ *noun* plural pronounced same L19 French (= debate). A poetic discussion between persons, personifications, or abstractions, on a question of morality, politics, or love, common in medieval European literature.

debitage /dɛbɪ'ta:ʒ/ *noun* M20 French (*débitage* cutting of stone). *Archaeology* Waste material produced in the making of prehistoric stone implements.

débouché /debuʃe/ *noun* plural pronounced same M18 French (from *déboucher* from *dé-* de- + *bouche* mouth (after synonymous Italian *sboccare*)). An opening where troops etc. (may) emerge; *generally* an outlet.

debris /'dɛbri:/, /'deɪbri:/ *noun* (also **débris**) E18 French (*débris*, from *débriser* to break down, break up, from *dé-* + *briser* to break). The remains of anything broken down or destroyed (originally *in figurative use*, of institutions, States, etc.); fragments, wreckage, ruins; accumulated waste matter; *Geology* fragmentary material accumulated from the breakdown of rocks etc.

début /'deɪb(j)u:/, /'dɛb(j)u:/; /deɪ'bju:/, /dɛ'bju:/ *noun* (also **debut**) M18 French (from *débuter* to lead off). Entry into society; the first appearance in public of a performer etc.

débutant /'dɛbjʊtõ/, /'deɪbjʊtõ/ *noun* (also **debutant**) E19 French (present participle of *débuter* to lead off). A male person making his début.

débutante /'dɛbjʊtɑ:nt/, /'deɪbjʊtɑ:nt/ *noun* (also **debutante**) E19 French (feminine of *débutant*: see preceding). **1** E19 A female performer etc. making her début. **2** E19 A young woman making her social début; *loosely* a young woman in fashionable society.

decalage /'di:kəlɑ:ʒ/ *noun* E20 French (*décalage* displacement, from *décaler* to displace). *Aeronautics* The difference in the angle of incidence between two aerofoils on an aeroplane.

decani /dɪ'keɪnʌɪ/ *adjective* M18 Latin (genitive of *decanus* dean). Of or pertaining to the south side of the choir of a church where the dean usually sits; *Music* to be sung by the decanal side in antiphonal singing (cf. CANTORIS).

decemvir /dɪ'sɛmvə/ *noun* LME Latin (singular of *decemviri*, originally *decem viri* ten men). **1** LME In *plural* A council or ruling body of ten. Originally and *especially* (*Roman History*) either of two bodies of magistrates appointed in 451 and 450 BC respectively. **2** E18 A member of such a body.

decennium /dɪ'sɛnɪəm/ *noun* plural **decennia** /dɪ'sɛnɪə/, **decenniums** L17 Latin (from *decennis*, from *decem* ten + *annus* year). A period of ten years, a decade.

déclassé /deklase/ (*plural same*), /deɪ'klaseɪ/ *adjective & noun* (feminine **déclassée**) L19 French (past participle of *déclasser* to (re)move from a class). (A person who is) reduced or degraded in social class or status.

1995 *Spectator* Forte (having for so long been accused of being too déclassé to own the Savoy) could point out the incongruity of a company whose most famous hostelry is the Rover's Return in Coronation Street becoming the landlord of the Grosvenor House in Park Lane.

décolletage /dekɔlta:ʒ/, /deɪkɒl'ta:ʒ/ *noun* L19 French (from *décolleter* to expose the neck). **1** L19 The low-cut neckline of a woman's garment. **2** L19 Exposure of the neck and shoulders by such a neckline.

2 1995 *Times Pride and Prejudice* convinced a nation of bra burners that a heaving décolletage was the only way to attract a Mr Darcy in time for Christmas.

décolleté /dekɔlte/, /deɪˈkɒl(ə)teɪ/ *adjective* (also **décolletée**) M19 French ((feminine *décolletée*), from *décolleter* to expose the neck, from *dé-* + *collet* collar of a dress etc). Of a (woman's) garment: having a low-cut neckline. Of a woman: wearing a low-necked garment. Also *figurative*, daring, slightly improper.

décor /ˈdeɪkɔː/ *noun* (also **decor**) L19 French (from *décorer* to decorate). **1** L19 The scenery and furnishings of a theatre stage; the set. **2** E20 (The overall effect of) the decoration and furnishings of a room, building, etc.

decorum /dɪˈkɔːrəm/ *noun* M16 Latin (use as noun of neuter singular of *decorus* seemly). **1** M16 Suitability of artistic or literary style to the subject; congruity, unity. **2** L16 Suitability to the dignity or circumstances of a person or occasion. *archaic*. **3** L16 Propriety of behaviour or demeanour; seemliness; etiquette.

3 1996 *Times* Correct posture, dress and decorum was all.

découpage /dekupaʒ/ *noun* plural pronounced same M20 French (from *découper* to cut up, cut out). **1** M20 The decoration of a surface with cut-out paper patterns or illustrations; an object so decorated. **2** M20 *Cinematography* The cutting or editing of a film.

1 1977 A. Jeffs *Creative Crafts* As découpage traveled through Europe in the 18th century, it was enthusiastically adopted by the women of the courts who amused themselves by imitating the then fashionable Chinese lacquerwork.

decrescendo /diːkrɪˈʃendəʊ/ *adverb, adjective, noun & intransitive verb* plural of noun **decrescendos** E19 Italian (present participle of *decrescere* to decrease). DIMINUENDO.

decretum /dɪˈkriːtəm/ *noun* plural **decreta** /dɪˈkriːtə/ E17 Latin. A decree.

de facto /deɪ ˈfaktəʊ/, /diː/ *adverb & adjective phrase* E17 Latin (= of fact). (Existing, held, etc.) in fact, in reality; in actual existence, force, or possession, whether by right or not.

■ Often used as the opposite to DE JURE.
1996 *Times* Old Compton Street on a Saturday night has become a *de facto* pedestrian precinct. It is thronged with people and almost impossible to drive down.

defluvium /dɪˈfluːvɪəm/ *noun* E19 Latin (*defluvium* loss by flowing or falling away). *Medicine* A complete shedding of hair, fingernails, etc., as a result of disease.

dégagé /degaʒe/, /deɪˈɡɑːʒeɪ/ *adjective* (feminine **dégagée**) L17 French (past participial adjective of *dégager* to set free). Unconstrained, relaxed; detached, unconcerned.

degras /ˈdɛɡrəs/ *noun* (also **dégras** /ˈdeɪɡrɑs/) L19 French (*dégras*, from *dégraisser* to remove grease from). **1** L19 A dark wax or grease obtained when fish-oils are rubbed into hides and recovered, used in the dressing of leather; a preparation containing this or synthesized in imitation of it; moellon. **2** L19 Wool-grease, wool-fat; a crude mixture of wax and fats obtained by scouring wool or treating it with organic solvents. *United States*.

dégringolade /degrɛ̃ɡɔlad/ *noun* plural pronounced same L19 French (from *dégringoler* to descend rapidly). A rapid descent or deterioration; decadence.

1996 *Spectator* After the happy Venetian years before the last war and the hardly less happy postwar ones . . . , there followed the ghastly and grotesque *dégringolade* of the final years.

de haut en bas /də o ã bɑ/ *adverb and adjective phrase* L17 French (= from above to below). Condescending(ly) or patronizing(ly).

1995 *Spectator* Maynard Keynes . . . had a very *de haut en bas* view that he knew best what forms of culture should be supported (opera and ballet) . . .

dehors /dəɔr/, /dəˈhɔː/ *preposition* E18 French (in Old French used as a preposition (Modern French as adverb and noun)). *Law* Outside of; not within the scope of.

Dei gratia /deɪ ˈɡrɑːtɪə/, /diːʌɪ ˈɡreɪʃə/ *adverb phrase* E17 Latin. By the grace of God.

déjà entendu /deʒa ɑ̃tɑ̃dy/, /ˌdeɪʒɑː ɒ̃tɒ̃ˈduː/ *noun phrase* (also **déjà-entendu**) M20 French (= already heard, after DÉJÀ VU). A feeling (correct or illusory) that one has already heard or understood the words, music, etc., currently under attention.

1995 *Spectator* From the moment Tony Blair uttered the fatal words, 'We will be opening discussions . . . about how we meet the goal of ensuring that every child has access to a laptop computer', the sense of *déjà-entendu* became almost too much to bear.

déjà lu /deʒa ly/, /ˌdeɪʒɑː ˈluː/ *noun phrase* M20 French (= already read, after next). A feeling that one may have read the present passage, or one very like it, before.

déjà vu /deʒa vy/, /ˌdeɪʒɑː ˈvuː/ *noun phrase* E20 French (= already seen). **1** E20 *Psychology* The illusory feeling of having already experienced the present moment or situation. **2** M20 The (correct) impression that something similar has been previously experienced; tedious familiarity.

2 1995 *Spectator* Huddled in the international departure lounge at Waterloo underneath a Eurostar board proudly exhibiting its cancelled trains, I felt a sudden nostalgic twinge of *déjà-vu* [sic].

déjeuner /deʒœne/ (*plural same*), /ˈdeɪʒə-neɪ/ *noun* L18 French (use as noun of infinitive = to break one's fast). **1** L18 A morning meal (early or late) in France or elsewhere; breakfast or (usually) lunch. **2** L18 A set of cups, saucers, plates, etc., for serving breakfast, breakfast service.

■ *Petit déjeuner* is commonly used for 'breakfast'.

de jure /diː ˈdʒʊəri/, /deɪ ˈjʊəreɪ/ *adverb & adjective phrase* M16 Latin (= of law). (Existing, held, etc.) rightfully, according to law.

■ Frequently used in contexts where it is the opposite to DE FACTO.

dekko /ˈdɛkəʊ/ *noun* plural **dekkos** L19 Hindustani (*dekho* polite imperative of *dekhnā* to look). A look.

■ Originally army slang. Although the word also existed (L19) as a transitive and intransitive verb, the verbal sense is usually expressed by *have* (or *take*) *a dekko*.

délassement /delɑsmã/ *noun* plural pronounced same E19 French (from *délasser* to relax, from *dé-* + *las* weary). Relaxation.

del credere /dɛl ˈkreɪdəri/, /dɛl ˈkrɛdəri/ *adjective, adverb, & noun phrase* L18 Italian (= of belief, of trust). *Commerce* (Subject or relating to) a selling agent's guarantee, for which a commission is charged, that the buyer is solvent.

délicatesse /delikatɛs/ *noun* L17 French (from *délicat* delicate). Delicacy.

delicatessen /ˌdɛlɪkəˈtɛs(ə)n/ *noun* L19 German (*Delikatessen* plural or Dutch *delicatessen* plural, from as preceding). **1** L19 Cooked meats, cheeses, and unusual or foreign prepared foods. **2** M20 A shop, or shop counter or department, selling delicatessen.

■ Originally in the United States. Sense 2 is often abbreviated colloquially to *deli*, which in Australia has undergone an extension of meaning to 'a small shop open long hours and selling perishable goods, newspapers, etc.'

delirium /dɪˈlɪrɪəm/ *noun* plural **deliriums**, **deliria** /dɪˈlɪrɪə/ M16 Latin (from *delirare* to deviate, be deranged, from *de-* + *lira* ridge between furrows). **1** M16 A disordered state of the mind resulting from disease, intoxication, etc., characterized by incoherent speech, hallucinations, restlessness, and often extreme excitement. **2** M17 Great excitement; ecstasy, rapturous frenzy.

delirium tremens /dɪˌlɪrɪəm ˈtriːmənz/, /dɪˌlɪrɪəm ˈtrɛmənz/ *noun phrase* E19 Modern Latin (= trembling delirium, from as DELIRIUM + *tremens* present participial adjective of *tremere* to shake). Delirium accompanied by tremors and terrifying illusions, usually as a symptom of withdrawal in cases of chronic alcoholism.

■ A term invented by a Dr T. Sutton in 1813 for a type of delirium that was worsened by bleeding but alleviated by opium; later medical writers established its modern sense.

delta /ˈdɛltə/ *noun* ME Latin (from Greek). **1** ME The fourth letter (Δ, δ) of the Greek alphabet. **2** M16 A tract of alluvial land, often more or less triangular in shape, enclosed or traversed by the diverging mouths of a river; originally (*the Delta*) specifically that of the River Nile. **3** M17 A triangle; a triangular area or formation. Usually *attributive*, as in *delta connection* (*Electricity*) and *delta wing* (*Aeronautics*). **4** L18 Denoting the fourth in a numerical sequence: *attributive Science* (frequently written δ) as *Astronomy* (preceding the genitive of the Latin name of the constellation): the fourth brightest star in a constellation; (**b**) *delta rays*, rays of low penetrative power consisting of slow electrons released from atoms by other particles; (**c**) *delta rhythm*, *delta waves*, slow electrical activity of the unconscious brain. **5** E20 A fourth-class or poor mark in an examination etc.

de luxe /dɪ ˈlʌks/, /ˈlʊks/, /də/ *adjective phrase* E19 French (= of luxury). Luxurious, sumptuous; of a superior kind.

■ Used either postpositively (see quotation 1996) or as a premodifier (see quotation 1970). Cf. POULE DE LUXE.
1970 K. Chesney *Victorian Underworld* These places were often little businesses engaged in

a de luxe trade, glovers, bonnet makers, perfumers and so on. **1996** *Spectator* Margaret Cooper, at the age of about 500 and as pretty as springtime, is a catalyst *de luxe.*

démarche /demarʃ/ (*plural same*), /deɪ ˈmaːʃ/ *noun* M17 French (from *démarcher* to take steps, from *dé-* + *marcher* to march). A step, a proceeding; *especially* a diplomatic action or initiative.
1996 *Spectator* John Lloyd . . . and Barry Cox . . . urged Mr Blair to stand against John Smith . . . . Mr Blair was right to disregard their advice . . . But the Cox/Lloyd *démarche* is interesting . . .

déménagement /demenaʒmɑ̃/ *noun* L19 French. The removal of household possessions from one place to another; moving house.

démenti /demɑ̃ti/ *noun* plural pronounced same L16 French (from *démentir* to contradict, from *dé-* from + *mentir* to lie). A contradiction, a denial; now *especially* an official denial of a published statement.

dementia /dɪˈmɛnʃə/ *noun* L18 Latin (from *demens* insane, from *de-* + *mens* mind). **1** L18 *Psychiatry* Chronic mental and emotional deterioration caused by organic brain disease. **2** L19 Madness, folly.

demi-caractère /ˌdɛmɪkarəkˈtɛː/, *foreign* /dəmikaraktɛr/ (*plural same*) *noun & adjective* L18 French (literally, 'half character'). *Ballet* **A** *noun* L18 A dance retaining the form of the character dance but executed with steps based on the classical technique. Also, a dancer of demi-caractères. **B** *adjective* E19 Of, pertaining to, or designating dancing of this kind.

demi-glace /ˈdɛmɪglas/ *noun* E20 French (literally, 'half-glaze'). *Cookery* A meat-stock from which the liquid has been partially evaporated. In full *demi-glace sauce.*

demilune /ˈdɛmɪluːn/ *noun & adjective* E18 French (literally, 'half-moon'). **A** *noun* **1** E18 *Fortification* An outwork resembling a bastion, with a crescent-shaped gorge. **2** M18 A half-moon, a crescent; a crescent-shaped body. **B** *adjective* L19 Crescent-shaped, semilunar.

demi-mondaine /dəmimɔ̃den/ (*plural same*), /ˌdɛmmmɒnˈdeɪn/ *noun* L19 French (from as next). A woman of the DEMI-MONDE.

1996 *Spectator* Most of my romantic entanglements have been less *demi-mondaine* than mundane.

demi-monde /dəmimɔ̃d/, /dɛmɪˈmɒnd/, /ˈdɛmmmɒnd/ *noun* M19 French (literally, 'half world'). The class of women of doubtful reputation and social standing; the class of kept women or *loosely* of prostitutes; *transferred* any social group regarded as behaving with doubtful propriety or legality.
■ *Le Demi-monde* was the title of a novel (1855) by the younger Alexandre Dumas.
1988 K. Adler *Unknown Impressionists* La Grenouillère was well known as a favourite place for Parisian bourgeois men to meet women of the demi-monde . . . .

de minimis /deɪ ˈmɪnɪmiːs/ *adverb and adjective phrase* E17 Latin (= about the smallest things (*de* about + use as noun of ablative plural of *minimus* least, smallest)). About petty details.
■ An elliptical use of the Latin legal tag *de minimis non curat lex* 'the law does not concern itself with petty matters', which is used as an injunction not to become over-concerned about trivia.
1996 *Times* At that level we must be getting very close to a *de minimis* argument.

demi-pension /dəmipɑ̃sjɔ̃/ *noun* M20 French. Originally in France and French-speaking countries: (the price of) bed, breakfast, and one meal at a hotel etc.; half-board.
attributive **1995** D. Lodge *Therapy* We were on *demi-pension* terms at the hotel.

demi-saison /dəmisɛzɔ̃/ *adjective* M18 French (literally, 'half season'). Of a style or fashion intermediate between that of the past and that of the coming season.

demi-sec /dɛmɪˈsɛk/, *foreign* /dəmisɛk/ *adjective* M20 French (literally, 'half-dry'). *Wine* Medium dry.

demitasse /ˈdɛmɪtas/, *foreign* /dəmitas/ (*plural same*) *noun* M19 French (literally, 'half-cup'). (The contents of) a small coffee-cup.

demi-vierge /dəmivjɛrʒ/ *noun* plural pronounced same E20 French (literally 'half-virgin'). A woman who behaves licentiously while remaining a virgin.
■ From the title of the novel *Les demi-vierges* (1874) by M. Prévost.

démodé /demɔde/, /deɪˈməʊdeɪ/ *adjective* L19 French (past participle of *démoder* to send, go out of fashion, from *dé-* from +

mode fashion). Out of fashion, unfashionable.

demoiselle /dɛmwɑːˈzɛl/ *noun* E16 French. **1** E16 A young lady, a girl. *archaic.* **2** L17 A Eurasian and North African crane, *Anthropoides virgo*, with elongated black breast-feathers and white neck-plumes. Now usually more fully *demoiselle crane*. **3** M19 A dragonfly or (*especially*) a damselfly. **4** L19 A damselfish.

de mortuis /deɪ ˈmɔːtuːiːs/ *noun phrase* Latin (= about the dead). (An injunction not to speak ill) of the dead.

■ An elliptical form of the Latin saying *de mortuis nil nisi bonum* '(say) nothing but good of the dead'. The saying is traditionally ascribed to Chilon of Sparta, one of the sages of ancient Greece.
1995 *Times* It is a real moment of casting-off for Jane who, ever a lady, is afflicted by *de mortuis*.

demos /ˈdiːmɒs/ *noun* plural **demi** /ˈdiːmaɪ/ L18 Greek (*dēmos*). **1** L18 A district of ancient Attica, Greece; a deme. *rare.* **2** M19 (**Demos**) The common people of an ancient Greek State; (a personification of) the populace, especially in a democracy.

dengue /ˈdɛŋgi/ *noun* (also **denga** /ˈdɛŋgə/) E19 West Indian Spanish (from Kiswahili *denga, dinga* (in full *kidinga-popo*), identified with Spanish *dengue* fastidiousness, prudery, with reference to the stiffness of the neck and shoulders caused by the disease). A debilitating tropical viral disease. Also *dengue-fever*.

dénigrement /denigrəmã/ *noun* L19 French. Blackening of character, denigration.

de nos jours /də no ʒur/ *postpositive adjective phrase* E20 French (= of our days). Of the present time; contemporary.
1995 *Times* Much was made in the late Eighties about comics being the rock stars *de nos jours* and so forth.

denouement /deɪˈnuːmõ/, /deɪˈnuːmɒŋ/ *noun* (also **dénouement**) M18 French (from *dénouer* (earlier *desnouement* to untie, from *des-, dé-* + *nouer* to knot). The unravelling of the complications of a plot, or of a confused situation or mystery; the final resolution of a play, novel, or other narrative.
1996 *Times* The denouement [of *An Ideal Husband*] depends on the accidental discovery of a brooch the villainess has stolen, by the very man who years before bought it.

de nouveau /də nuvo/ *adverb phrase* L18 French (= from new). Afresh, starting again from the beginning. Cf. next.

de novo /deɪ ˈnəʊvəʊ/, /diː/ *adverb phrase* E17 Latin (= from new). Starting again from the beginning.
1995 *Country Life* A splendid example of a private Jacobean chapel built *de novo* for Anglican worship is that at Hatfield House, Hertfordshire, created for Robert Cecil, 1st Earl of Salisbury, in 1607–12.

deoch an doris /dɒx (ə)n ˈdɒrɪs/, /dɒx/ *noun phrase* (also **doch an doris**) M17 Gaelic (*deoch an doruis* (Irish *deoch an dorais*) a drink at the door). In Scotland and Ireland: a drink taken at parting, a stirrup-cup.

Deo gratias /deɪəʊ ˈɡrɑːtɪəs/, /ˈɡrɑːʃɪəs/ *interjection* L16 Latin (= (we give) thanks to God). Thanks be to God.

Deo volente /ˌdeɪəʊ vɒˈlɛnteɪ/ *adverb phrase* M18 Latin. God willing; if nothing prevents it.

■ Abbreviated to *d.v.*.

dépaysé /depeize/ *adjective* (feminine **dépaysée**) E20 French (= (removed) from one's own country). Removed from one's habitual surroundings.

depot /ˈdɛpəʊ/ *noun* (also (now *rare*) **depôt**) L18 French (*dépôt*, Old French *depost* from Latin *depositum* use as noun of neuter past participle of *deponere* to place, put away). **1 a** L18–M19 The action or an act of depositing. *rare.* **b** M19 A deposit, a collection, a store. Now *specifically* (*transferred* from sense 4 below) a localized accumulation of a substance in the body. **2** L18 A military establishment at which stores are deposited, recruits or other troops assembled, etc.; *especially* a regimental headquarters. **3** L18 A place where goods etc. are deposited or stored, often for later dispatch; a warehouse, an emporium. **b** M19 A place where vehicles, locomotives, etc., are housed and maintained and from which they are dispatched for service; *North American* a railway or bus station. **4** E20 A site in the body at which a particular substance naturally concentrates or is deposited.

de profundis /deɪ prəˈfʊndiːs/ *noun & adverb phrase* LME Latin (= from the depths)). **A** *noun* LME A psalm of penitence; *specifically* Psalm 130 (129 in the Vulgate); *generally* a cry of appeal from the depths (of sorrow, humiliation, etc.). **B** *adverb phrase* LME Out of the depths (of sorrow etc.).

■ The initial words of Psalm 130 (129 in the Vulgate): 'Out of the deep have I called unto thee O Lord' (Book of Common Prayer). *De Profundis* was the title of Oscar Wilde's posthumously published apologia written after being sentenced to a term of imprisonment in Reading Gaol, and modern use of the phrase often contains an unspoken allusion to Wilde's work (see quotation).

A 1996 *Times* Johnson has given us an excellent Profession of Faith: his *De Profundis* has yet to come.

déraciné /derasine/ (*plural same*), /deɪ'rɑːsmeɪ/ *adjective & noun* (feminine **déracinée**) E20 French (= uprooted, past participial adjective of *déraciner*). **A** *adjective* E20 Uprooted from one's environment; displaced geographically or socially. **B** *noun* E20 A *déraciné* person.

derailleur /dɪ'reɪlə/, /dɪ'reɪljə/ *noun* M20 French (*dérailleur*, from *dérailler* to cause (a train) to run off the rails). A bicycle gear in which the ratio is changed by switching the line of the chain (while pedalling) so that it jumps to a different sprocket.

de rigueur /də rigœr/, /də rɪ'gə:/ *predicative adjective phrase* M19 French (literally, 'of strictness'). Required by custom or etiquette.

1995 *Spectator* It was *de rigueur* to dream on the eve of a battle, before giving birth to a hero, or before one's own assassination.

dernier /dɛrnje/, /'də:njeɪ/ *adjective* E17 French (from Old French *derrenier*, from *derrein* last). Last, ultimate, final.

■ Formerly fully naturalized, but now only in phrases (see below).

dernier cri /dɛrnje kri/, /ˌdə:njeɪ 'kri:/ *noun phrase* (also **le dernier cri**) L19 French (literally, '(the) last cry'). The very latest fashion.

1996 *Times* I loathed every minute of the staging, while recognising that it is probably the *dernier cri* (this week) of the producer's art.

dernier mot /dɛrnje mo/, /ˌdə:njeɪ 'məʊ/ *noun phrase* (also **le dernier mot**) M19 French. The last word.

dernier ressort /dɛrnje rəsɔr/, /ˌdə:njeɪ rə'sɔ:/ *noun phrase* (also **le dernier resort**) M17 French. A last refuge; *originally* the ultimate court of appeal.

derrière /dɛrjɛr/, /dɛrɪ'ɛ:/ (*plural same*) *noun* L18 French (= behind). The buttocks.

■ Usually only in jocular or colloquial use.

1995 *Times* At the autumn fashion collections, hourglass girls sashayed down the catwalk all décolletage and derrière with only a wasp waist to separate them.

dervish /'də:vɪʃ/ *noun* L16 Turkish (*derviş* from Persian *darvīš* poor, a religious mendicant). A Muslim (*specifically* Sufi) religious man who has taken vows of poverty and austerity; *specifically* (more fully *dancing, whirling, howling*, etc., *dervish*) one whose order includes the practice of dancing etc. as a spiritual exercise.

desaparecido /ˌdesapare'sido/ *noun* plural **desaparecidos** /ˌdesapare'sidos/ L20 Spanish (= (one who has) disappeared). In Argentina: a person who disappeared during the period of military rule between 1976 and 1983, presumed killed by members of the armed services or the police; a child removed from his or her arrested parents and placed with another family without consent.

■ By extension, the word is now also applied to any persons who have vanished or been separated from their real families under totalitarian regimes in South America.

1987 *New Yorker* People whose children or husbands or wives were *desaparecidos* —disappeared ones—would go to Cardinal Arns, and the Cardinal would stop whatever he was doing and drive to the prisons, the police, the Second Army headquarters.

désaxé /dezakse/ *adjective & adverb* E20 French. Of a motor-car crankshaft: (set) out of line with the centre of the cylinder.

descamisado /ˌdeskami'sado/, /ˌdɛsˌkamɪ'sɑːdəʊ/ *noun* plural **descamisados** /ˌdeskami'sados/, /ˌdɛsˌkami'sɑːdəʊz/ M19 Spanish (= shirtless). *History* An extreme liberal in the Spanish Revolutionary War of 1820–3; *transferred* an impoverished revolutionary.

■ A similar sartorial deficiency gave rise to the earlier French Revolutionary equivalent, SANSCULOTTE.

1979 J. M. Taylor *Evita Perón* His speech declared Eva the martyr of the descamisados, an example given by God to the Argentinian people of self-sacrifice and faith.

déshabillé /dezabije/ (*plural same*) *noun* (also **deshabille**, **déshabille** /deɪzə'biːl/, /deɪzə'biːjeɪ/, **dishabille** /dɪsə'biːl/) L17 French (*déshabillé* use as noun of past participle of *déshabiller* to undress). **1** L17 The state of being casually or only partially dressed. Chiefly in *in dishabille*, EN DÉSHABILLÉ. **2** L17 A garment or costume of a casual or informal style.

desideratum /dɪˌzɪdəˈrɑːtəm/, /dɪˌzɪdə ˈreɪtəm/, /dɪˌsɪdəˈrɑːtəm/ *noun* plural **desiderata** /dɪˌzɪdəˈrɑːtə/, /dɪˌzɪdəˈreɪtə/, /dɪ ˌsɪdəˈrɑːtə/ M17 Latin (use as noun of neuter singular of past participle of *desiderare* to feel the lack of, desire). A thing for which desire is felt; a thing lacked and wanted, a requirement.
1995 *Spectator* Stalin's demands changed remarkably little between 1939 and 1945; all that altered was his ability to obtain his desiderata.

détente /deɪˈtɑː(n)t/, /deɪˈtɑ̃(n)t/, /deɪ ˈtɑːnt/, /deɪˈtɒnt/ *noun* E20 French (= loosening, relaxation). The easing of strained relations, especially between States.

détenu /deɪtəˈnuː/; *foreign* /detəny/ (*plural same*) *noun* (also **detenu**) E19 French (use as noun of past participle of *détenir* to detain). A detainee, now especially in the Indian subcontinent.

detour /ˈdiːtʊə/ *noun & verb* (also **détour** /ˈdeɪtʊə/) M18 French (*détour* change of direction, from *détourner* to turn away). **A** *noun* M18 A deviation from one's route, a roundabout way; a digression. **B** *verb* **1** *intransitive* M19 Make a detour. **2** *transitive* E20 Send by a detour. **3** *transitive* M20 Bypass, make a detour round.

détraqué /detrake/ *adjective & noun* (feminine **détraquée**) E20 French (past participial adjective of *détraquer* to put out of order, derange). **A** *adjective* E20 Deranged; crazy; psychopathic. **B** *noun* E20 plural pronounced same. A deranged person, a psychopath.

detritus /dɪˈtrʌɪtəs/ *noun* L18 Latin (*detritus* rubbing away, from *deterere* to wear away; in sense 2 after French *détritus*). **1** L18–E19 Wearing away by rubbing; disintegration. **2** E19 Matter produced by detrition; *especially* material eroded or washed away, as gravel, sand, silt, etc. **3** M19 Debris of any kind.

de trop /də tro/, /də ˈtrəʊ/ *adjective phrase* M18 French (literally, 'excessive'). Not wanted, unwelcome, in the way.
1996 *Oldie* But now blackboards and chalk are rapidly becoming de trop, replaced by whiteboards and markers.

detur /ˈdɪːtə/ *noun* L18 Latin (= let there be given). Any of several prizes of books given annually at Harvard University.
■ Detur is the first word of the inscription accompanying these books.

deus absconditus /ˌdeɪəs abˈskɒndɪtəs/, /ˌdiːəs/ *noun phrase* M20 Latin (= hidden

god). *Theology* A divine being that is inaccessible to human perception.
■ Cf. Isaiah 45:15 'Verily thou art a God that hidest thyself, O God of Israel ... '

deus ex machina /ˌdeɪəs ɛks ˈmakɪnə/, /ˌdiːəs ɛks ˈmakɪnə/ *noun phrase* L17 Modern Latin (translation of Greek *theos ek mēkhanēs*, literally, 'god from the machinery'). A power, event, or person arriving in the nick of time to solve a difficulty; a providential (often rather contrived) interposition, especially in a novel or play.
■ The 'machine' was originally the device by which deities were suspended above the stage in the theatre in classical antiquity. The phrase is generally used in its entirety but also occurs abbreviated to *ex machina*, with another agent of providence substituted for *deus* (see quotation 1996(2)).
attributive **1996** *Spectator* The *deus ex machina* resolution of the drama may provide one of the most feeble dénouements in all opera ...
1996 *Times* In this ideal scenario, growth in Europe turns up and deficits come down without anyone on this side of the Atlantic having to do anything. EMU ex machina.

deva /ˈdeɪvə/ *noun* E19 Sanskrit (= a god, (originally) a shining one). Any of a class of deities in Vedic mythology; any of the lower-level gods in Hinduism and Buddhism.

devadasi /deɪvəˈdɑːsi/ *noun* E19 Sanskrit (*devadāsī*, literally, 'female servant of a god' (cf. preceding)). A hereditary female dancer in a Hindu temple.

développé /devlope/ *noun* plural pronounced same E20 French (use as noun of past participle of *développer* to develop). A ballet movement in which one leg is raised and then fully extended.

dévot /devo/ (*plural same*), /deɪˈvəʊ/ *noun* (feminine **dévote** /devɔt/ (*plural same*), /deɪˈvɒt/) E18 French (use as noun or adjective). A devotee; a devout person.

dey /deɪ/ *noun* (also (especially in titles) **Dey**) M17 French (from Turkish *dayl* maternal uncle, used also as a courtesy title). *History* (The title of) any of the supreme rulers of Algiers, 1710–1830. Also, (the title of) the local ruler of Tunis or Tripoli under nominal Ottoman suzerainty.

dhal /dɑːl/ *noun* (also **dal**) L17 Hindustani (*dāl*). Split pulses (especially the seed of the pigeon-pea, *Cajanus cajan*), a common ingredient in Indian cookery.

dhamma /'dɑːmə/, /'dʌmə/ *noun* E20 Pali (from as *dharma*). Especially among Theravada Buddhists, DHARMA.

dhania /'dɑːniə/ *noun* E20 Hindi (*dhaniyā*). In Indian cookery: coriander.

dharma /'dɑːmə/, /'dəːmə/ *noun* L18 Sanskrit (= something established, decree, custom; cf. DHAMMA). In *Hinduism*: social or caste custom, right behaviour, law; justice, virtue; natural or essential state or function, nature. In *Buddhism*: universal truth or law, especially as proclaimed by Buddha.

dharmsala /'dɑːmsɑːlə/, /'dəːmʃɑːlɑː/ *noun* (also **dharmasala** /'dɑːməsɑːlə/, /'dəːməʃɑːlɑː/) E19 Sanskrit (representing Hindustani pronunciation of Sanskrit *dharmaśālā*, from *dharma* + *śālā* house). In the Indian subcontinent: a building devoted to religious or charitable purposes, *especially* a rest-house for travellers.

dhobi /'dəʊbi/ *noun* (also **dhoby**, **dhobie**) M19 Hindustani (*dhobī*, from *dhob* washing). In the Indian subcontinent: a washerman or washerwoman.

dhoti /'dəʊti/ *noun* (also formerly **dhootie** /'duːti/ and other variants) E17 Hindustani (*dhotī*). A cloth worn by male Hindus, the ends being passed through the legs and tucked in at the waist.

dhow /daʊ/ *noun* (also **dow**) L18 Arabic (*dāwa*, probably related to Marathi *ḍāw*). A lateen-rigged sailing vessel of the Arabian Sea, with one or two masts. Formerly also *loosely*, an Arab slaver or other vessel.

diable /djɑbl/ *interjection* & *noun* L16 French (from ecclesiastical Latin *diabolus* devil). **A** *interjection* L16 Expressing impatience, amazement, dismay, etc. **B** *noun* M19 (*le diable*) DIABOLO. Now *rare* or *obsolete*.

diable au corps /djɑbl o kɔr/ *noun phrase* L19 French (literally, 'devil in the body'). Restless energy; a spirit of devilry.

diablerie /dɪˈrɑːbləri/ *noun* (also **diablery**) M18 French (from as DIABLE). **1** M18 Dealings with the Devil; sorcery, witchcraft. **b** M19 *figurative* Mischievous fun, devilment. **2** E19 The mythology or lore of devils; a description or representation of devils. **3** M19 The realm of devils.

1 1996 *Spectator* Fool! Ass! How had it happened? Was it some mysterious electric agency? Or was it *diablerie* playing tricks with my subconscious mind?

diabolo /dɪˈrɑːbələʊ/, /dʌɪˈabələʊ/ *noun* plural **diabolos** E20 Italian (from ecclesiastical Latin *diabolus* devil). A game in which a two-headed top is thrown up and caught on a string stretched between two sticks; the top used in this game.

diabolus in musica /dɪˈrɑːbələs in ˌmjuːzɪkə/ *noun phrase* M20 Latin (literally, 'the devil in music'). *Music* The interval of the diminished fifth.

■ So called because of its displeasing or unsettling effect.
attributive 1995 J. D. Barrow *Artful Universe* An acoustic form of this perceptual ambiguity exists with musical chord sequences displaying the *diabolus in musica* phenomenon.

diaeresis /dʌɪˈɪərɪsɪs/, /dʌɪˈɛrɪsɪs/ *noun* (also **dieresis**) plural **diaereses** /dʌɪˈɪərɪsiːz/ L16 Latin (from Greek *diairesis* noun of action from *diairein* to take apart, divide). **1** L16 The division of one syllable into two, especially by the resolution of a diphthong into two simple vowels. **2** E17 The sign placed over a vowel to indicate that it is pronounced separately, as in Brontë, naïve. **3** M19 *Prosody* A break in a line where the end of a foot coincides with the end of a word.

diamanté /dɪəˈmɒnteɪ/, *foreign* /djamɑ̃tɛ/ (*plural of noun same adjective* & *noun*) E20 French (past participle of *diamanter* to set with diamonds, from *diamant* diamond). (Material) given a sparkling effect by means of artificial gems, powdered crystal, etc.

Diaspora /dʌɪˈasp(ə)rə/ *noun* (also **diaspora**) L19 Greek (from *diaspeirein* to disperse, scatter). The dispersion of Jews among the Gentile nations; all those Jews who live outside the biblical land of Israel; (the situation of) any body of people living outside their traditional homeland.

dibbuk variant of DYBBUK.

dictum /'dɪktəm/ *noun* plural **dicta**, /'dɪktə/, **dictums** L16 Latin. **1** L16 A saying, an utterance; *especially* one that claims some authority, a pronouncement. **2** L18 *Law* An expression of opinion by a judge which is not essential to the decision and so has no binding authority as precedent. See also OBITER DICTUM. **3** E19 A common saying; a maxim.

1 1996 *Spectator* Conan Doyle's dictum—'When you have eliminated the impossible, whatever remains, *however improbable*, must be the truth'—simply doesn't apply.

didgeridoo /ˌdɪdʒ(ə)rɪˈduː/ *noun* (also **did-jeridoo, didgeridu**) E20 Aboriginal (of imitative origin). A long tubular wooden musical instrument of the Australian Aborigines which is blown to produce a resonant sound.

dieresis variant of DIAERESIS.

dies irae /ˌdiːeɪz ˈɪərʌɪ/, /ˌdiːeɪz ˈɪərəɪ/ *noun phrase* E19 Latin (= day of wrath). A thirteenth-century Latin hymn that was formerly an obligatory part of the requiem mass in the Roman Catholic Church; a musical setting of this part of the mass; *hence* the Day of Judgement or *transferred* any day of reckoning.

■ The text of which *Dies irae* is the opening phrase is attributed to Thomas of Celano (*c.*1250).

dies non /ˈdʌɪiːz ˌnɒn/ *noun phrase* plural same E19 Latin (literally, 'a non day'). A day that does not count because there has been no (specific) activity or because it cannot be used for a particular purpose.

■ Used in its original legal sense, it is an abbreviated form of the following, but it is also applied in other contexts.

dies non juridicus /ˌdʌɪiːz nɒn dʒʊəˈrɪdɪkəs/ *noun phrase* plural **dies non juridici** /ˌdʌɪiːz nɒn dʒʊəˈrɪdɪsʌɪ/ E17 Latin (literally, 'day not judicial'). *Law* A day on which no legal business is enacted.

differentia /dɪfəˈrɛnʃɪə/ *noun* plural **differentiae** /dɪfəˈrɛnʃiː/ L17 Latin. A distinguishing mark or characteristic, *especially* (*Logic*) that distinguishing a species from others of the same genus.

difficile /ˈdɪfɪsiːl/, *foreign* /difisil/ *adjective* LME French (from Latin *difficilis*, from *dif*- not + *facilis* easy). **1** LME–L17 Requiring physical or mental effort or skill. **2** L15–M17 Hard to understand; obscure. **3** M16 Of a person: not easy to get on with, stubborn, unaccommodating.

difficilior lectio /dɪfɪˌkɪlɪɔː ˈlɛktɪəʊ/ *noun phrase* plural **difficiliores lectiones** /dɪfɪkɪlɪˈɔːreɪz lɛktɪˈəʊneɪz/ E20 Latin (from the maxim *difficilior lectio potior* the harder reading is to be preferred). *Textual Criticism* The more difficult or unexpected of two variant readings and therefore the one that is less likely to be a copyist's error; (the principle of) giving preference to such a reading.

1996 *Spectator* A. E. H.[ousman], who would devote four pages of acerbic minutiae to the re-instatement of a *difficilior lectio* in Manilius, would have expired foaming on the spot.

digamma /dʌɪˈɡamə/ *noun* L17 Latin (from Greek, from *di*- twice + *gamma* (from the shape of the letter, a GAMMA with a doubled cross-stroke)). The sixth letter of the original Greek alphabet, probably equivalent to W, later disused.

digestif /diʒɛstif/ (*plural same*), /dʌɪˈdʒɛstɪf/ *noun* E20 French. Something which promotes good digestion, especially a drink taken after a meal.

diktat /ˈdɪktat/ *noun* M20 German (from Latin *dictatum* use as noun of neuter past participle of *dictare* to dictate). **1** M20 A severe settlement, especially one imposed by a victorious nation on a defeated one. **2** M20 A dictate; a categorical assertion.

2 1996 *Times* The essence of civilised behaviour is anyway to override the diktats of nature.

dilemma /dɪˈlɛmə/, /dʌɪˈlɛmə/ *noun* E16 Latin (from Greek *dilēmma*, from as *di*- twice + *lēmma* assumption, premiss). **1** E16 In *Rhetoric*, a form of argument involving an opponent in choice between two (or more) alternatives, both equally unfavourable. In *Logic*, a syllogism with two conditional major premisses and a disjunctive minor premiss. **2** L16 A choice between two (or several) alternatives which are equally unfavourable; a position of doubt or perplexity.

dilettante /dɪlɪˈtanti/ *noun & adjective* plural **dilettanti**, /dɪlɪˈtanti/, **dilettantes** M18 Italian (use as noun of verbal adjective from *dilettare* from Latin *delectare* to delight). **A** *noun* M18 A lover of the fine arts; a person who cultivates the arts as an amateur; a person who takes an interest in a subject merely as a pastime and without serious study, a dabbler. **B** *adjective* M18 Of, pertaining to, or characteristic of a dilettante; amateur.

■ The English use of the word is linked to the eighteenth-century British fashion for wealthy young aristocrats to travel to Italy on the so-called Grand Tour to study the remains of classical antiquity there and to purchase sculptures, coins, and other objects for their personal collections. In 1733–4 'some gentlemen who had travelled in Italy, desirous of encouraging, at home, a taste for those objects which had contributed so much to their entertainment abroad' founded the Society of Dilettanti. Despite Horace Walpole's unkind observation that the nominal qualification for membership of the Dilettanti was 'having been in Italy, and the real one, being drunk', the society subsequently financed some major expeditions and publications and generally played a key role in developing British knowledge of the ancient world.

A 1996 *Spectator* . . . the show is an oasis of antique elegance and calm—where would-be dilettanti can take wistful refuge from the mêlée of not-so-grand tourists in the Museum's entrance hall, and wish themselves transported to 18th-century Naples.

dilruba /dɪl'ruːbə/ *noun* E20 Hindustani (*dilrubā* = robber of the heart). An Indian musical instrument with a long neck, three or four strings played with a bow, and several sympathetic strings.

diminuendo /dɪˌmɪnjʊ'ɛndəʊ/ *noun, verb, adverb, & adjective* L18 Italian (= diminishing, present participle of *diminuire* from Latin *deminuere* to lessen). *Music* **A** *noun* L18 plural **diminuendos, diminuendi** /dɪ ˌmɪnjʊ'ɛndi/. A gradual decrease in loudness; a passage (to be) played or sung with such a decrease. **B** *intransitive verb* L18 Become quieter; grow less. **C** *adverb & adjective* E19 (A direction:) with a gradual decrease in loudness.

dim sum /dɪm 'sʌm/ *noun phrase* (also **dim sim** /dɪm 'sɪm/, and other variants) plural **dim sum(s)** etc. M20 Chinese (Cantonese) (*tím sam*, from *tím* dot + *sam* heart). A Chinese snack consisting of different hot savoury pastries.

dinanderie /dinãdri/ *noun* M19 French (from *Dinant* (formerly *Dinand*), a town near Liège, Belgium + -*erie*). Domestic and other utensils of brass (frequently embossed) made in late medieval times in and around Dinant; ornamental brassware from other parts, including India and the eastern Mediterranean region.

dinero /dɪ'nɛːrəʊ/ *noun* plural **dineros** L17 Spanish (= coin, money from Latin *denarius* a silver coin). **1** *History* L17 A monetary unit in Spain and Peru, now disused. **2** M19 Money. *United States slang.*

Ding an sich /dɪŋ an 'zɪç/ *noun phrase* M19 German (= thing in itself). *Philosophy* A thing as it really is, apart from human observation or experience of it. Cf. NOUMENON.

diorama /dʌɪə'rɑːmə/ *noun* E19 French (from as Greek *dia* through + *orama* view (after *panorama*). **1** E19 A scenic painting, viewed through a peephole, in which changes in lighting, colour, etc., are used to suggest different times of day, changes in weather, etc.; a building in which such paintings are exhibited. **2** E20 A small-scale tableau in which three-dimensional figures are shown against a painted background; a museum display of an animal etc. in its natural setting; a scale model of an architectural project in its surroundings. **3** M20 *Cinematography* A small-scale set used in place of a full-scale one for special effects, animation, etc.

diploma /dɪ'pləʊmə/ *noun & verb* M17 Latin (from Greek = folded paper, from *diploun* to make double, fold, from *diploos* double). **A** *noun* plural **diplomas**, (*rare*) **diplomata** /dɪ'pləʊmətə/. **1** M17 A State paper, an official document; a charter; in *plural*, historical or literary muniments. **2** M17 A document conferring some honour, privilege, or licence; a certificate of a university, college, or (*North American*) school degree or qualification; such a degree or qualification. **B** *transitive verb* M19 Award a diploma to. Chiefly as *diplomaed*, *diploma'd* participial adjective.

Directoire /dɪ'rɛktwɑː/, *foreign* /direktwar/ (*plural of noun same*) *noun & adjective* L18 French (from Late Latin *directorium* use as noun of neuter singular of *directorius* from *director* person who directs). **A** *noun* L18 *History* The French Directory (1795–9). **B** *adjective* L19 Also **directoire.** Of, pertaining to, or resembling an extravagant style of fashion, decorative art, etc., prevalent at the time of the Directory and characterized especially by an imitation of Greek and Roman modes.

■ The adjective is often found in the phrase *directoire knickers* (women's knee-length knickers elasticated at the knee and waist).

dirigisme /diriʒism/ *noun* (also **dirigism** /'dɪrɪdʒɪz(ə)m/) M20 French (from *diriger* from Latin *dirigere* to direct). The policy of State direction and control in economic and social matters.

1996 *Times* French dirigisme preserved their oyster. English *laisser faire* turned the oyster from poor man's food into an impossible luxury.

dirigiste /diriʒist/ *adjective & noun* M20 French (as preceding). (A proponent) of DIRIGISME.

adjective **1995** *New Scientist* But it is surely off-beam to suggest an outright ban is somehow less dirigiste than piecemeal regulation.

noun **1995** *Times* The European Community, which had been designed to make Europe more competitive, was already moving towards a bureaucratic model based on those old European *dirigistes* Bismarck and Colbert.

dirndl /'də:nd(ə)l/ *noun* M20 German (dialect, diminutive of *Dirne* girl). **1** M20 A dress in the style of Alpine peasant costume with a bodice and full skirt. **2** M20 A full skirt with a tight waistband. More fully *dirndl skirt*.

dis aliter visum /ˌdɪs alɪtə 'viːsəm/ *interjection* M20 Latin. The gods decided otherwise.

■ Quoted from Virgil *Aeneid* ii.428.
1948 R. Coupland *Zulu Battle Piece* The Zulu war, [Frere] had written, must begin and end with 'a sharp and decisive success'. *Dis aliter visum.*

discobolus /dɪ'skɒbələs/ *noun* plural **discoboli** /dɪ'skɒbələɪ/, /dɪ'skɒbəli:/ E18 Latin (from Greek *diskobolos*, from as *discus* + *-bolos* throwing, from *ballein* to throw). *Classical History* A discus-thrower; a statue representing one in action.

discothèque /'dɪskətɛk/ *noun* (also **discotheque**) M20 French (originally = record-library (after *bibliothèque*)). A place or event at which recorded pop music is played for dancing.
■ Now almost universally abbreviated to *disco*.

discus /'dɪskəs/ *noun* M17 Latin (from Greek *diskos*). **1** M17 A heavy thick-centred disc or plate thrown in ancient and modern athletic sports; the sporting event in which it is thrown. **2** L17–E18 Any disc or disc-shaped body.

diseuse /diː'zəːz/, *foreign* /dizøz/ *noun* plural pronounced same L19 French (= talker, feminine of *diseur*, from *dire* to say). A female artiste who specializes in monologue.

dishabille variant of DÉSHABILLÉ.

disinvoltura /ˌdisinvɔl'tuːra/ *noun* M19 Italian (from *disinvolto* unembarrassed, from *disinvolgere* to unwind). Self-assurance; lack of constraint.

disjecta membra /dɪsˌjɛktə 'mɛmbrə/ *noun phrase* plural (also **disiecta membra**) E18 Latin. Scattered remains.
■ Alteration of Latin *disjecti membra poetae* 'limbs of a dismembered poet' (Horace *Satires* I.iv.62). The word order *membra disjecta* is apparently a later (M20) variant.

dissensus /dɪ'sɛnsəs/ *noun* M20 Latin (= disagreement; or from *dis-* + *(con)sensus*). Widespread dissent; the reverse of consensus.

distingué /dɪ'staŋgeɪ/, *foreign* /distɛ̃ge/ *adjective* (feminine **distinguée**) E19 French. Having an air of distinction; having a distinguished appearance or manner.

distinguo /dɪ'stɪŋgwəʊ/ *noun* plural **distinguos** L19 Latin (= I distinguish). A distinction in thought or reasoning.

distrait /dɪ'streɪ/, /'dɪstreɪ/, *foreign* /distrɛ/ *adjective* (feminine **distraite** /dɪ'streɪt/, /'dɪstreɪt/, *foreign* /distrɛt/) LME French (from Old French *destrait* past participle of *destraire* from Latin *distrahere* to distract). **1** Only in LME. Distracted in mind. **2** LME–L16 Divided, separated. **3** M18 Absent-minded; not paying attention.
■ Sense 3 represents a re-borrowing from French after *distrait* had become obsolete in English in its two earlier senses.
3 1996 *Spectator* On my visit, . . . the place was crowded, though emptying, and the young, slightly inept staff *distrait*.

dithyramb /'dɪθɪram(b)/ *noun* (also in Latin form **dithyrambus** /ˌdɪθɪ'rambəs/, plural **dithyrambi** /ˌdɪθɪ'rambaɪ/) E17 Latin (*dithyrambus* from Greek *dithurambos*). **1** E17 An ancient Greek choric hymn, vehement and wild in character; a Bacchanalian song. **2** M17 A passionate or inflated poem, speech, or writing.

ditto /'dɪtəʊ/ *adjective, adverb, & noun* plural of noun **dittos** E17 Italian (dialect (Tuscan) variant of *detto* said, from Latin *dictus* past participle of *dicere* to say). **1** In or of the month already named; the aforesaid month. Only in 17. **2** L17 In the same way, similar(ly); the same; (the) aforesaid; (the same as, another of) what was mentioned above or previously. *colloquial* except in lists etc. (where usually represented by dots or commas under the matter repeated). **b** *noun* L19 A symbol representing the word 'ditto'. Also *ditto mark*. **3** *noun* M18 Cloth of the same material. Chiefly in *suit of dittos*, a suit of clothes of the same material and colour throughout. *archaic*. **4** *noun* L18 Something identical or similar; an exact resemblance; a repetition. **5** E20 (also **Ditto**) (Proprietary name for) a duplicator, a small offset press for copying.
2 1996 *Times* Anyway, neither Carman, QC, nor Gray, ditto, is going to beg his bread in the gutter . . .

diva /'diːvə/ *noun* L19 Italian (from Latin *diva* goddess). A distinguished female (especially operatic) singer; a prima donna.
1995 *Times* In person, she [sc. Dawn Upshaw] has few diva tendencies. The morning after her Berlin recital, she came to her interview minutes after stepping from the shower—hair still wet, face scrubbed.

divan /dɪ'van/, /dʌɪ'van/, /'dʌɪvan/ *noun*
L16 French (or Italian *divano*, from Turkish *dīvān* from Persian *dīvān* brochure, anthology, register, court, bench; cf.
DOUANE). **1** L16 An oriental council of
State; *specifically* (*historical*) the privy council of the Ottoman Empire. **b** E17 Any
council. *archaic.* **2** L16 The hall where the
Ottoman divan was held; an oriental
court of justice or council-chamber. **3** L17
In oriental countries: a room entirely
open at one side towards a court, garden,
river, etc. **4** E18 (Now the usual sense.) A
couch or bed without a head- or foot-
board. Originally, a low bench or a raised
part of a floor forming a long seat against
the wall of a room. **5** E19 (A smoking-
room attached to) a cigar-shop. *archaic.*
6 E19 An anthology of poems in Persian or
other oriental language; *specifically* a series of poems by one author, with rhymes
usually running through the alphabet.

divertimento /dɪˌvəːtɪ'mɛntəʊ/, /dɪˌvɛːtɪ
'mɛntəʊ/ *noun plural* **divertimenti** /dɪˌvəːtɪ
'mɛnti/, **divertimentos** M18 Italian (= di-
version). **1** M18 An amusement. Long
rare. **2** E19 *Music* A composition primarily
for entertainment, *especially* a suite for a
small group of instruments or a single instrument; a light orchestral piece.

divertissement /ˌdiːvɛː'tiːsmɔ̃/, *foreign*
/divɛrtismɑ̃/ (*plural pronounced same*) *noun*
E18 French (from *divertiss-* stem of *divertir*
to divert). **1** A short ballet or other entertainment between acts or longer pieces.
b L19 A DIVERTIMENTO sense 2. **2** E19 An
entertainment.

> **1.a** 1996 *Spectator* . . . the ballroom scene is
> constructed as a conventional 19th-century
> *divertissement*, where the well-regulated choral
> dancing frames virtuoso duets . . .

divisi /di'viːsi/ *adverb, adjective, & noun* M18
Italian (= divided, plural past participial
adjective of *dividere* to divide). *Music* **A** *adverb & adjective* M18 (A direction:) with a
section of players divided into two or
more groups each playing a different
part. **B** *noun* M20 (The use of) *divisi* playing or scoring.

divorcee /dɪvɔː'siː/ *noun* (also (earlier) **di-
vorcé**, feminine **divorcée**, /dɪvɔː'seɪ/ (*plural same*)), /dɪvɔː'seɪ/ E19 French (partly
from *divorcé(e)* use as noun of past participial adjective of *divorcer* to divorce,
partly from *divorce* + *-ee* after the French).
A divorced person.

dix-huitième /dizɥitjɛm/ *adjective & noun*
E20 French (= eighteenth). (Of or pertaining to) the eighteenth century.

dixit /'dɪksɪt/ *noun* L16 Latin (= he has said).
An utterance or statement (quoted as) already made.

djellaba(h) variant of JELLABA.

djibba(h) variant of *jibba*; see JUBBA.

djinn see JINNEE.

Dobos Torte /'dɒbɒʃ ˌtɔːtə/ *noun phrase*
(also **Dobos Torta, dobos torte**) plural
Dobos Torten /'tɔːt(ə)n/ E20 German (*Do-
bostorte*, from J. C. Dobós (1847–1924), Hungarian pastry-cook + *Torte* tart, pastry,
cake; cf. Hungarian *dobostorta*). A rich
cake made of alternate layers of sponge
and chocolate or mocha cream, with a
crisp caramel topping.

docent /'dəʊs(ə)nt/ *foreign* /do'tsɛnt/ *noun*
L19 German (*Docent, Dozent*, from Latin *do-
cent-* present participial stem of *docere* to
teach). **1** L19 Originally, a *Privatdozent*
(formerly in German universities, a
teacher paid by the students taught).
Now, in certain United States universities
and colleges, a member of the teaching
staff below professorial rank. **2** E20 A
(usually voluntary) guide in a museum,
art gallery, or zoo. Chiefly *United States.*

doch an doris variant of DEOCH AN
DORIS.

doctorand /'dɒktərand/ *noun* (also in
Latin form **doctorandus** /dɒktə'randəs/,
plural **doctorandi** /dɒktə'randʌɪ/) E20
German (from medieval Latin *doctorandus*). A candidate for a doctor's degree.

doctrinaire /ˌdɒktrɪ'nɛː/ *noun & adjective*
E19 French (from *doctrine* + *-aire*). **A** *noun*
1 E19 *History* In early nineteenth-century
France, a member of a political movement which supported constitutional
government and the reconciliation of the
principles of authority and liberty. **2** M19
A person who tries to apply principle
without allowance for circumstance; a
pedantic theorist. **B** *adjective* M19 Pertaining to or of the character of a doctrinaire;
determined to apply or promote a doctrine in all circumstances; theoretical
and unpractical.

> **B** 1996 *Country Life* [It] would be easy to
> imagine this tear-jerking technique being used
> for propaganda purposes. A clever, doctrinaire
> film-maker could have a wonderful time with fox
> cubs.

doek /dʊk/ *noun* L18 Afrikaans (= cloth). In
South Africa: a cloth, *especially* a headscarf.

dogana /dəʊˈgɑːnə/ *noun* M17 **Italian**. In Italy (and Spain): a custom-house; the customs.

dogaressa /dəʊgəˈrɛsə/ *noun* E19 **Italian** (irregular feminine of DOGE). *History* The wife of a doge.

doge /dəʊ(d)ʒ/ *noun* M16 **French** ((monosyllabic) from Italian (disyllabic) from Venetian Italian *doze* ultimately from Latin *dux, duc-* leader). *History* The chief magistrate in the former republics of Venice and Genoa.

dogma /ˈdɒgmə/ *noun* plural **dogmas, dogmata** /ˈdɒgmətə/ M16 **Late Latin** (from Greek *dogma, dogmat-* opinion, decree, from *dokein* to seem good, think). **1** M16 An opinion, a belief; *specifically* a tenet or doctrine authoritatively laid down, especially by a Church or sect; an arrogant declaration of opinion. **2** L18 A whole body of doctrines or opinions, especially on religious matters, laid down authoritatively or assertively.
> **2 1996** *Times* Treasury dogma opposes all tax allowances.

dojo /ˈdəʊdʒəʊ/ *noun* plural **dojos** M20 **Japanese** (from *dō* way, pursuit + *-jō* a place). A room or hall in which judo or other martial arts are practised; an area of padded mats for the same purpose.

dolce far niente /ˌdɒltʃe far niˈɛnte/ *noun phrase* E19 **Italian** (= sweet doing nothing). Delightful idleness.
> ■ Also in the shortened form FAR NIENTE.

dolce vita /ˌdɒltʃe ˈviːta/, /ˌdəʊltʃeɪ ˈviːtə/ *noun phrase* M20 **Italian** (= sweet life). A life of luxury, pleasure, and self-indulgence.
> ■ Frequently preceded by *the* or *la* /la/.
> **1996** *Country Life* . . . his talent and prospects were regularly undermined by his taste for *la dolce vita*.

doli capax /ˌdɒlɪ ˈkapaks/ *adjective phrase* L17 **Latin** (from *doli* genitive singular of *dolus* guile, fraud + *capax* capable). *Law* Capable of having the wrongful intention to commit a crime.

doli incapax /ˌdɒlɪ ɪnˈkapaks/ *adjective phrase* L17 **Latin** (from as DOLI CAPAX). *Law* Not *doli capax*, especially because under fourteen years old.
> *attributive* **1996** *Times* . . . the House of Lords shied away from changing the *doli incapax* rule concerning the criminal liability of children.

dolman /ˈdɒlmən/ *noun* (in sense 1 also written (earlier) **doliman** L16 **French** (in sense 1 from French *doliman*; in sense 2 from French *dolman* from German from Hungarian *dolmány*; both ultimately from Turkish *dolama(n)*). **1** L16 A long Turkish robe open in front and with narrow sleeves. **2** L19 A hussar's jacket worn with the sleeves hanging loose. **3** L19 A woman's mantle with dolman sleeves. **4** M20 A loose sleeve made in one piece with the body of a coat etc. In full *dolman sleeve*.

dolmas /ˈdɒlməs/ *noun* plural **dolmades** /dɒlˈmɑːdɛz/ (also **dolma**, plural **dolmas**) L17 **Modern Greek** (*ntolmas* from Turkish *dolma*, from *dolmak* to fill, be filled). In the cookery of Greece, Turkey, and other East European countries: a dish of seasoned chopped meat and rice enclosed in a vine leaf, cabbage, pepper, etc.

dolmen /ˈdɒlmɛn/ *noun* M19 **French** (perhaps from Cornish *tolmen* hole stone). A megalithic structure found especially in Britain and France, consisting of a large flat stone supported on stone slabs set vertically in the ground forming a burial chamber, probably originally covered by an earth mound.

dolmus /ˈdɒlmʊʃ/ *noun* M20 **Turkish** (*dolmuş* filled, (as noun) dolmus). In Turkey: a shared taxi.

dolus /ˈdɒləs/ *noun* E17 **Latin**. *Law* Deceit; intentional damage. Cf. DOLI CAPAX.

dom /dəʊm/ *noun* M19 **German** (from Latin *domus* house). In Germany, Austria, and other German-speaking areas: a cathedral church.

domaine /dəˈmeɪn/ *noun* M20 **French**. A vineyard.
> ■ Often in the phrase *domaine-bottled*, indicating that the wine has been bottled at the estate where the grapes of which it is made were grown.

domine /ˈduːmɪnɪ/, /ˈdʊəmmɪ/ *noun* (also (especially as a title) **Domine** M16 **Latin** (vocative of *dominus* lord, master; cf. DOMINEE, DOMINIE). **1** M16-L17 Lord, master; sir: used in respectful address to a clergyman or a member of one of the professions. **2** E17 DOMINIE sense 1. Now *rare* or *obsolete*. **3** M17 A member of the clergy, a pastor; *especially* a pastor of the Dutch Reformed Church. (Cf. DOMINEE, DOMINIE 2). *archaic*.

dominee /ˈduːmɪnɪ/, /ˈdʊəmmɪ/ *noun* (also (especially as a title) **Dominee**) M20 **Afrikaans** and **Dutch** (from Latin DOMINE). In South Africa: a pastor of the Dutch Reformed Church.

dominie *in sense 1* /'dɒmmi/; *in senses 2 and 3* /'dəʊmmi/, /'dɒmmi/ *noun* L17 Latin (alternative form of DOMINE). **1** L17 A schoolmaster. Now chiefly *Scottish*. **2** L17 A pastor of the Dutch Reformed Church; (*dialect*) any minister. *United States*. **3** E19 A variety of large apple. More fully *dominie apple*. *United States*.

dominium /də'mmɪəm/ *noun* M18 Latin. *Law* Lordship, ownership, dominion.

■ Chiefly in the phrases *dominium directum* 'direct ownership' and *dominium utile* 'ownership of use', differentiating the rights of the owner and those of the tenant who has the use only of something.

domino /'dɒmmaʊ/ *noun & interjection* L17 French (= hood worn by priests in winter (also in Spanish, = a masquerade garment), probably ultimately from Latin *dominus* lord, master, but unexplained). **A** *noun* plural **domino(e)s**. **1** L17 A garment worn to cover the head and shoulders; *specifically* a loose cloak with a mask for the upper part of the face, worn to conceal the identity at masquerades etc. **2** M18 A person wearing a domino. **3** L18 Each of a set of small oblong pieces, usually 28 in number and marked with 0 to 6 pips in each half, used in various matching and trick-taking games; in *plural* (treated as *singular*) or *singular*, the game played with such pieces. **4** M19 (From the interjection.) The end, the finish. Chiefly in *be all domino*, be all up (*with*). *slang*. **5** M19 Paper printed with a design from a woodblock and coloured, used as wallpaper etc. In full *domino paper*. **B** *interjection* M19 Notifying that one has matched up all one's dominoes; *transferred* notifying or registering the end of something.

■ The phrases *domino effect* and *domino theory*, much used in the mid twentieth century, allude to what happens when a row of dominoes (sense 3) is stood on end and the first one pushed over, resulting in the speedy collapse of the remainder; in political terms this is what Western governments feared would happen, particularly in South-east Asia but also in Africa, if one country became Communist-controlled.

don /dɒn/ *noun* E16 Spanish ((in sense 1c Italian) from Latin *dominus* lord, master). **1** E16 (**Don**) Used as a title of respect preceding the forename of a Spanish man (originally one of high rank) or (formerly, *jocular*) preceding the name or designation of any man. **b** E17 A Spanish lord or gentleman. **c** M20 A high-ranking or powerful member of the Mafia. *North Am-*

erican slang. **2** L16 A distinguished or skilled man; a man who is outstanding in some way. *archaic*. **3** M17 At British universities, especially Oxford and Cambridge: a head, fellow, or tutor of a college; a member of the teaching staff.

donatio mortis causa /də,neɪʃɪəʊ ,mɔːtɪs 'kɔːzə/ *noun phrase* plural **donationes mortis causa** /də,neɪʃɪ'əʊniːz/ M17 Latin (= gift by reason of death). *Law* A (revocable) gift of personal property made in expectation of the donor's imminent death and taking effect thereafter.

doner kebab /,dɒnə kɪ'bab/, /,dəʊnə/, /kə'bab/, /kə'bɑːb/ *noun phrase* M20 Turkish (*döner kebap*, from *döner* rotating + *kebap* KEBAB). A Turkish dish consisting of spiced lamb roasted on a vertical rotating spit and sliced thinly.

donga /'dɒŋgə/ *noun* L19 Nguni. **1** L19 A ravine or watercourse with steep sides. *South Africa*. **2** E20 A broad shallow depression in the ground. *Australia*. **3** E20 A makeshift shelter; a temporary dwelling. *Australia*.

donnée /dɒne/, /'dɒneɪ/ *noun* (also **donné**) L19 French (feminine past participial adjective of *donner* to give). **1** L19 A subject, theme, or motif of a literary work. **2** L19 A datum, a given fact; a basic assumption.

1 1995 *Spectator* In a preface, Vansittart reveals that he received the *donné* for his novel some 50 years before actually embarking on it.

dop /dɒp/ *noun* L19 Afrikaans (of uncertain origin). **1** L19 In South Africa: brandy, especially of a cheap or inferior kind. In full *dop brandy*. **2** M20 A tot of liquor, especially of wine as given to farm labourers in the Cape Province of South Africa.

doppelgänger /'dɒpəl,gɛŋər/, /'dɒp(ə)l,gɛŋə/, /'dɒp(ə)l,gaŋə/ *noun* (also **doppelganger**) M19 German (literally, 'double-goer'). A supposed spectral likeness or double of a living person.

1962 O. Sitwell *Tales My Father Taught Me* I was never able myself to discern the mysterious stranger, and my own feeling was that he must be . . . my father's Narcissus-like *doppelgänger*, a projection from and of his own personality . . .

doppione /dop'pjoːne/, /dɒprˈəʊni/ *noun* plural **doppioni** /dop'pjoːni/ M20 Italian (from *doppio* double). *Early Music* A double-bore woodwind instrument of the Italian Renaissance.

dormeuse /dɔrməz/ (plural same), /dɔːˈmɛːz/ noun M18 French (feminine of dormeur, literally, 'sleeper', from dormir to sleep). **1** A cap or hood worn in bed. Only in M18. **2** E19 A travelling-carriage adapted for sleeping in; obsolete except historical. **3** M19 A kind of couch or settee.

dos-à-dos /dozado/, /dəʊzəˈdəʊ/ adverb, noun, & adjective (also **do-se-do** /dəʊzɪˈdəʊ/, /dəʊsɪˈdəʊ/, **do-si-do**) M19 French (from dos back). **A** adverb M19 Back to back. **B** noun plural same. M19 A seat, carriage, etc., so constructed that the occupants sit back to back. archaic. **C** adjective M20 Designating binding or books in which two volumes are bound together facing in opposite directions and sharing a central board.

dot /dɒt/ noun M19 Old and Modern French (from Latin dos, dot-). A dowry only the income from which is at the husband's disposal.

dotaku /ˈdəʊtaku/ noun plural (also **dō-taku**) E20 Japanese. Prehistoric Japanese bronze objects, shaped like bells and usually decorated with geometric or figurative designs.

douane /duˈɑːn/ noun M17 French (from Italian do(g)ana from Arabic dīwān office, from Old Persian dīwān DIVAN). A customhouse in France or other Mediterranean country.

douanier /duːˈɑːnɪeɪ/ noun M18 French (from as preceding). A customs officer, especially one at a douane.

doublé /duble/ adjective M19 French (past participle of doubler to line). Covered or lined with; (of a book) having a doublure; plated with precious metal.

double entendre /ˌduːbˈ(ə)l ɒ̃ːˈtɒ̃ːdr(ə)/, foreign /dubl ɑ̃tɑ̃dr/ noun phrase plural **double entendres** (pronounced same) L17 French (now obsolete (modern double entente) = double understanding). A double meaning; an ambiguous expression; a phrase with two meanings, one usually indecent. Also, the use of such a meaning or phrase.

> **1996** Spectator It seemed as if only I was vulgar enough to be aware of the double entendre; one or two other ladies confessed that they were plonkers too.

double entente /dubl ɑ̃tɑ̃t/ noun phrase plural **doubles ententes** (pronounced same) L19 French. A DOUBLE ENTENDRE.

doublure /dəˈbluə/, /duˈbluə/, foreign /dublyr/ (plural same) noun L19 French (= lining, from doubler to line). An ornamental lining, usually of leather, on the inside of a book-cover.

douçaine /duːˈsem/ noun M20 French (from douce sweet). Early Music A soft-toned reed instrument.

douce /duːs/ adjective ME Old French (dous (modern doux), feminine douce from Latin dulcis sweet). **1** ME Pleasant, sweet. (Formerly a stock epithet of France.) Now Scottish and northern (dialect). **2** E18 Quiet, sober, sedate. Scottish and northern (dialect).

douceur /dusœr/, /duːˈsəː/ noun LME French (from Proto-Romance variant of Latin dulcor sweetness). **1** LME Originally, sweetness of manner, amiability, (of a person). Now, agreeableness, charm (chiefly in DOUCEUR DE VIVRE). **2** L17-E19 A complimentary speech or turn of phrase. **3** M18 A conciliatory present; a gratuity, a bribe. **4** L20 A tax benefit available to a person who sells a work of art by private treaty to a public collection rather than on the open market.

> **3 1996** Times: Magazine Journalists . . . take a stern, principled, even po-faced stance against bribery, corruption, inducements and douceurs.

douceur de vivre /dusœr də vivr/ noun phrase (also **douceur de (la) vie** /dusœr də (la) vi/) M20 French (literally, 'sweetness of living'). The pleasure or amenities of life.

> **1995** Spectator L'Heure de Gloire is also a panorama of the Belle Epoque and the years of douceur de vivre that were brought to an end by the first world war.

douche /duːʃ/ noun & verb M18 French (from Italian doccia conduit pipe, from docciare to pour by drops, from Proto-Romance from Latin ductus duct). **A** noun M18 (The application of) a jet of (especially cold) liquid or air to a part of the body, as a form of bathing or for medicinal purposes; specifically the flushing of the vagina, as a contraceptive measure. Also, a syringe or similar device for producing such a jet. **B** verb **1** transitive verb M19 Administer a douche to. **2** intransitive verb M19 Take a douche; specifically take a vaginal douche, especially as a contraceptive measure.

dow variant of DHOW.

doyen /ˈdɔɪən/, /ˈdwɑːjɑ̃/ noun L17 French (Old French d(e)ien from Late Latin decanus chief of a group of ten, from Latin decem ten, after primanus member of the first legion). The most senior or most prominent of a particular category or body of people.

■ Found as a rare borrowing from Old French in the Late Middle English period, with the sense of 'a leader or commander of ten', the word became obsolete after this period and was then reintroduced from Modern French in its modern sense. The English word *dean* (from Anglo-Norman *de(e)n*) is closely related.

1996 *Oldie* Any art critic who goes on the telly to talk about art runs the risk of being compared with the doyen of telly-savants, the late Lord Clark.

doyenne /'dɔɪɛn/, /dɔɪ'ɛn/, /dwɑ:'jɛn/ *noun* M19 **French** (feminine of DOYEN). The most senior or prominent woman in a particular group or category of people, a female doyen.

1996 *Times* Elma Browne, the wartime doyenne of London nightclubs, was impressed and offered her a two-week engagement at the Pigalle Club . . .

dragée /'drɑ:ʒeɪ/, *foreign* /draʒe/ (*plural same*) *noun* L17 **French** (Old French *dragie*, from medieval Latin *drageia*, *dragetum*, perhaps from Latin *tragemata* sweetmeats, from Greek). A sweet consisting of a centre covered with some coating, *especially* a sugared almond etc. or a chocolate; a small silver-coated sugar ball for use in cake decoration; a sweet used as a vehicle for a medicine or drug.

drageoir /draʒwar/ *noun* plural pronounced same M19 **French** (from as preceding). A box for holding sweets.

dramatis personae /,dramətɪs pə: 'səʊnʌɪ/, /,dramətɪs pə:'səʊni:/ *noun plural* (frequently treated as *singular*) M18 **Latin** (= persons of the drama). The (list of) characters in a play; *figurative* the participants in an event etc.

1996 *Spectator Rebecca* . . . is the only one of these films in which the terror seems to rise organically from character and psychology and situation—rather than just being imposed on the *dramatis personae* by the dictates of the formula.

figurative 1996 *Times* The *dramatis personae* are the usual cast of Catalan and Basque nationalists.

dramaturge /'dramətə:dʒ/ *noun* (also **dramaturg** /drama'tə:g/) M19 **French** (*dramaturge*, German *Dramaturg*, from Greek *dramatourgos*, from *dramat-* drama + *-ergos* worker). A dramatist; *specifically* a reader and literary editor etc. to a permanent theatrical company.

Drang /draŋ/ *noun* M19 **German**. Strong tendency, pressure; urge, strong desire.

■ Chiefly in phrases DRANG NACH OSTEN, STURM UND DRANG.

Drang nach Osten /,draŋ nax 'ɔstən/ *noun phrase* E20 **German** (literally, 'drive towards the east'). *History* The German imperialist policy of eastward expansion; *transferred* any political or economic drive eastwards.

dreidel /'dreɪd(ə)l/ *noun* (also **dreidl**) M20 **Yiddish** (*dreydl*, from Middle High German *dræ(je)n* (German *drehen*) to turn). A four-sided spinning-top with a Hebrew letter on each side; a game of put-and-take played with this, especially at Hanukkah. Chiefly *North American*.

dressage /'drɛsɑ:ʒ/, /'drɛsɑ:dʒ/ *noun* M20 **French** (literally, 'training', from *dresser* to train, drill). The training of a horse in obedience and deportment; the execution by a horse of precise movements in response to its rider.

droit /drɔɪt/, *foreign* /drwa/ *noun* LME **Old and Modern French** (from Proto-Romance use as noun of variant of Latin *directum* neuter of *directus* past participle of *dirigere* to direct, guide). **1** LME A right; a legal claim; something to which one has a legal claim; a due. **2** L15–M16 Law, right, justice; a law.

droit de seigneur /,drwa: də sɛn'jə:/, *foreign* /drwa də sɛɲœr/ *noun phrase* (also **droit du seigneur**) E19 **French** (literally, 'lord's right'). An alleged custom whereby a medieval feudal lord might have sexual intercourse with a vassal's bride on the latter's wedding-night.

1996 *Times Droit de seigneur* may be harder to trace in fact than in *The Marriage of Figaro*, but it represents the popular myth of lordly immorality.

dromos /'drɒmɒs/ *noun* plural **dromoi** /'drɒmɔɪ/ M19 **Greek**. *Greek Antiquities* An avenue or entrance-passage to an ancient temple, tomb, etc., often between rows of columns or statues.

droshky /'drɒʃki/ *noun* (also **drosky** /'drɒʃki/) E19 **Russian** (*drozhki* plural, diminutive of *drogi* wagon, hearse, plural of *droga* centre pole of a carriage). A low open horse-drawn carriage used especially in Russia; any horse-drawn passenger vehicle.

druzhina /'drʊʒi:nə/ *noun* plural **druzhinas**, **druzhiny** /'drʊʒi:ni/ L19 **Russian**

(from *drug* friend + group suffix *-ina*). *History* **1** L19 The retinue or bodyguards of a Russian prince. **2** M20 In the former USSR: a military or police unit; *specifically* a detachment of volunteers assuming police powers.

duce /'duːʧeɪ/ *noun* (also **Duce**) E20 Italian. A leader.

■ *Il* (Italian = the) *Duce* was the title assumed by Benito Mussolini (1883–1945), creator and leader of the Fascist State in Italy; hence *duce* in English usage generally has derogatory overtones (see quotation).
1996 *Times* Monday night saw Sir James Goldsmith, *duce* of the mono-policy Referendum Party, taking his message to the young ladies of the Kit Kat Club . . .

duchesse /duː'ʃɛs/, /'dʌʧɪs/, /'dʌʧɛs/, *foreign* /dyʃɛs/ (*plural same*) *noun* (also **Duchesse**) L18 French (from medieval Latin *ducissa* feminine from Latin *dux* leader). **1** L18 A chaise longue consisting of two facing armchairs connected by a detachable footstool. **2** M19 A dressing-table with a pivoting mirror. More fully *duchesse dressing-chest*, *(dressing)-table*. **3** L19 More fully *duchesse satin, satin duchesse*. A soft heavy kind of satin.

■ Also in several English phrases: e.g. *duchesse lace* (a kind of fine Brussels lace worked in large sprays); *duchesse potatoes* (mashed potatoes mixed with egg, moulded into small cakes and baked or fried); *duchesse set* (lace mats for a dressing-table); *duchesse sleeve* (a two-thirds-length sleeve with an elaborate trim).

duende /duː'ɛndeɪ/, *foreign* /'dwende/ *noun* E20 Spanish. **1** E20 A ghost, an evil spirit. **2** M20 Inspiration, magic.

duenna /djuː'ɛnə/ *noun* M17 Spanish (*dueña*, *duenna* from Latin *domina* lady, mistress). **1** M17 An older woman acting as governess and companion to one or more girls, especially within a Spanish family. **2** E18 A chaperon.

duettino /djuːɛ'tiːnəʊ/ *noun* plural **duettinos** M19 Italian (diminutive of next). A short duet.

duetto /djuː'ɛtəʊ/ *noun* plural **duettos** E18 Italian (from Latin *duo* = two). *Music* A duet.

dulciana /dʌlsɪ'ɑːnə/ *noun* L18 Medieval Latin (from Latin *dulcis* sweet). *Music* A small-scaled, soft, open metal diapason usually of 8-ft length and pitch.

dulia /djʊ'lʌɪə/ *noun* LME Medieval Latin (from Greek *douleia* servitude, from *doulos*

slave). *Roman Catholic Church* The veneration properly given to saints and angels.

■ Cf. HYPERDULIA and LATRIA. Similar distinctions in degrees of veneration obtain in the Orthodox Churches, *dulia* being the honour paid to icons as representative of the saints.

duma /'duːmə/, /'djuːmə/ *noun* L19 Russian. *History* A Russian elective municipal council; *specifically* the elective legislative council of state of 1905–17; the Russian parliament.

dum casta /dʌm 'kastə/ *noun* & *adjective phrase* L19 Latin (abbreviation of *dum sola et casta vixerit* as long as she shall live alone and chaste). *Law* (Designating) a clause conferring on a woman a benefit which is to cease should she (re)marry or cease to lead a chaste life.

dummkopf /'dʊmkɒpf/ *noun* (also **domcop**) E19 German (from *dumm* stupid + *Kopf* head; obsolete variant *domcop* from Dutch). A stupid person, a blockhead.

■ Slang, originating in the United States.

duo /'djuːəʊ/ *noun* plural **duos** L16 Italian ((whence also French) from Latin = two). **1** L16 *Music* A duet. **2** L19 Two people; a couple; *especially* a pair of entertainers.

duodecimo /ˌdjuːəʊ'dɛsɪməʊ/ *noun* & *adjective* M17 Latin ((*in*) *duodecimo* in a twelfth (sc. of a sheet), from Latin *duodecimus* twelfth). **A** *noun* plural **duodecimos** M17 A size of book or paper in which each leaf is one-twelfth of a standard printing-sheet. (Abbreviation *12mo*.) **B** L18 *attributive* or as *adjective* Of this size, in duodecimo; *figurative* diminutive.

duodenum /djuːə'diːnəm/ *noun* LME Medieval Latin (*duodenum* (so called from its length = twelve fingers' breadth), from Latin *duodeni* distributive of *duodecim* twelve). *Anatomy* The first portion of the small intestine immediately beyond the stomach.

duomo /'dwəʊməʊ/, *foreign* /'dwomo/ *noun* (also (earlier) **domo**) plural **duomos** /'dwəʊməʊz/, **duomi** /'dwomi/ M16 Italian. An Italian cathedral.

durbar /'dəːbɑː/ *noun* E17 Urdu (from Persian *darbār* court). **1** E17 A public levee held by an Indian ruler or by a British ruler in India. Also, the court of an Indian ruler. **2** E17 A hall or place of audience where durbars were held.

durchkomponiert /ˌdʊrçkɔmpo'niːrt/ *adjective* L19 German (from *durch* through

+ *komponiert* composed). *Music* (Of composition) having a formal design which does not rely on repeated sections; *especially* (of song) having different music for each stanza; through-composed.

du reste /dy rɛst/ *adverb phrase* E19 French (literally, 'of the rest'). Besides, moreover.

durgah /'də:gə/ *noun* L18 Persian (*dargāh* royal court). In the Indian subcontinent: the tomb and shrine of a Muslim holy man.

du tout /dy tu/ *adverb phrase* E19 French (abbreviation of PAS DU TOUT). Not at all; by no means.

duumvir /dju:'ʌmvə/ *noun* plural **duumvirs**, in Latin form **duumviri** /dju: 'ʌmvɪrʌɪ/ E17 Latin (singular from *duum virum* genitive plural of *duo viri* two men). In *Roman History*, either of a pair of co-equal magistrates or officials; *generally* either of two people with joint authority, a coalition of two people.

duvet /'dju:veɪ/, /'du:veɪ/ *noun* M18 French (= down) A thick soft quilt used instead of other bedclothes. Also called *continental quilt*, PLUMEAU.

dux /dʌks/ *noun* plural **duces** /'dju:si:z/, **duxes** M18 Latin (= leader). **1** M18 *Music* The subject of a fugue or canon; the leading voice or instrument in a fugue or canon. Opposed to COMES. **2** L18 The top pupil in a class or school. Chiefly in *Scotland*, *New Zealand*, and *South Africa*.

duxelles /'dʌks(ə)lz/, *foreign* /dyksɛl/ *noun* L19 French (Marquis *d'Uxelles*, seventeenth-century French nobleman). *Cookery* A mixture of finely chopped shallots, parsley, onions, and mushrooms, *especially* used to flavour a sauce.

d.v. abbreviation of DEO VOLENTE.

dybbuk /'dɪbʊk/ *noun* (also **dibbuk**) plural **dybbukim** /'dɪbʊkɪm/, **dybbuks** E20 Yiddish (*dibek* from Hebrew *dibbūq*, from *dāḇaq* to cling, cleave). In Jewish folklore, a malevolent wandering spirit that enters and possesses the body of a living person until exorcized.

dyspepsia /dɪs'pɛpsɪə/ *noun* E18 Latin (from Greek *duspepsia*, from *duspeptos* difficult of digestion, from *dus-* + *peptos* cooked, digested). Indigestion; abdominal pain or discomfort associated with taking food.

dysphoria /dɪs'fɔːrɪə/ *noun* M19 Greek (*dusphoria* malaise, discomfort, from *dusphoros* hard to bear, from *dus-* + *pherein* to bear). A state of unease or discomfort; *especially* an unpleasant state of mind marked by malaise, depression, or anxiety. Opposed to EUPHORIA.

dyspnoea /dɪsp'niːə/ *noun* (also **dyspnea**) M17 Latin (from Greek *duspnoia*, from *dus-* + *pnoē* breathing). *Medicine* Difficulty in breathing or shortness of breath, as a symptom of disease.

dystopia see UTOPIA.

E

eau /əʊ/, *foreign* /o/ *noun* plural **eaux** pronounced same E19 French. Water.

■ Occurs in English only in various phrases, mainly the names of liquids used in medicine or perfumery (see following, also JET D'EAU, SALLE D'EAU).

eau-de-Cologne /ˌəʊdəkə'ləʊn/ *noun* (also **eau de Cologne**) E19 French. A lightly scented perfume made mainly from alcohol and essential oils, originally produced at Cologne, Germany.

eau de Javel /ˌəʊ də ʒa'vɛl/ *noun phrase* (also **eau de Javelle**) E19 French. A solution of sodium or potassium hypochlorite, used as a bleach or disinfectant.

■ Also called *Javelle water*. Javel was a village just outside Paris, now a suburb, where this solution was first used.

eau-de-Nil /ˌəʊdə'niːl/, *foreign* /odnil/ *noun phrase* L19 French (literally, 'water of (the) Nile'). A pale greenish colour (purportedly resembling the waters of the River Nile).

eau de toilette /ˌəʊ də twa:'lɛt/, *foreign* /o də twalɛt/ *noun phrase* E20 French (= toilet water). A dilute form of perfume.

eau-de-vie /ˌəʊdə'vi:/, *foreign* /odvi/ *noun phrase* (also **eau de vie**) M18 French (literally, 'water of life'). Brandy.

eau sucrée /ˌəʊ 'su:kreɪ/, *foreign* /o sykre/ *noun phrase* E19 French (literally, 'sugared water'). Water with sugar dissolved in it.

ébauche / eboʃ/ *noun* plural pronounced same E18 French. **1** E18 A sketch; a rough-hewn sculpture; a first draft. **2** E20 A partly finished watch movement.

ébéniste /ebenist/ *noun* plural pronounced same E20 French (from *ébène* ebony). An ebonist; *specifically* a French cabinet-maker who veneers furniture (originally with ebony).

éboulement /ebulmɑ̃/ *noun* plural pronounced same E19 French (from *ébouler* to crumble). A crumbling and falling of rock etc.; a landslide.

écarté /eɪ'kɑːteɪ/, *foreign* /ekarte/ *noun* E19 French (past participle of *écarter* to discard, from *é-* + *carte* card). **1** E19 A card-game for two people in which cards may be exchanged for others and those from

the two to the six are excluded. **2** E20 *Ballet* A pose with one arm and one leg extended, the body being at an oblique angle to the audience.

ecce /'ɛki/, /'ɛtʃeɪ/, /'ɛksi/ *interjection* LME Latin. Lo!; behold.

■ Especially in the following phrases.

Ecce Homo /ˌɛki 'həʊməʊ/ *interjection & noun phrase* E17 Latin. **A** *interjection* Behold the Man! **B** *noun phrase* Art A portrayal of Jesus wearing the crown of thorns.

■ The source is the Latin text of the account of the presentation of Jesus to the crowd after his trial by Pontius Pilate: 'Then came Jesus forth, wearing the crown of thorns, and the purple robe. And Pilate saith unto them, Behold the man!' (John 19:5).

ecce signum /ˌɛki 'sɪɡnəm/ *interjection* L16 Latin. Behold the sign!

echelon /'ɛʃəlɒn/, /'eɪʃəlɒn/ *noun* (also **echellon**) L18 French (*échelon*, from *échelle* ladder, from Latin *scala*). **1** L18 An arrangement of troops or equipment in parallel lines such that the end of each line is stepped somewhat sideways from that in front; *generally* a formation of people or things arranged, individually or in groups, in a similar stepwise fashion. Also *echelon arrangement, echelon formation*, etc. Cf. EN ÉCHELON. **2** E19 Each of the divisions of an echelon formation. **b** E19 Each of the subdivisions of the main supply service for troops in warfare. **3** M20 (A group of people occupying) a particular level in any organization.

echinus /ɪ'kʌɪnəs/ *noun* plural **echini** /ɪ'kʌɪnʌɪ/ LME Latin (sense 1 from Greek *ekhinos* hedgehog, sea urchin; the origin of sense 2 (also in Latin and Greek) is unknown). **1** LME A sea urchin. Now *specifically* a member of the genus *E. chinus*, which includes the common edible sea urchin *E. esculentus*. **2** M16 *Architecture* An ovolo moulding next below the abacus of a capital.

echt /ɛçt/ *adjective & adverb* E20 German. Authentic(ally), genuine(ly), typical(ly).

1995 *Spectator* 'He [sc. Newt Gingrich] doesn't say he's a conservative, he says he's allied to the conservatives' is how Paul Weyrich, head of the *echt*-conservative Free Congress Foundation, explains the relationship.

éclair /eɪˈklɛː/, /ɪˈklɛː/ *noun* M19 French (literally, 'lightning'). A small finger-shaped cake of choux pastry, filled with cream and iced, especially with chocolate icing.

éclaircissement /eklɛrsismɑ̃/ *noun* plural pronounced same M17 French (from *éclairciss-* lengthened stem of *éclaircir* to clear up, from as *ex-*, *clair* clear *-ment*). A clarification of what is obscure or misunderstood; an explanation.

éclat /ɛˈklɑː/, /ˈeɪklɑː/, *foreign* /ekla/ *noun* L17 French (from *éclater* to burst out). 1 L17 Radiance, dazzling effect (now only *figurative*); brilliant display. 2 L17–L19 Ostentation, publicity; public exposure, scandal; a sensation. 3 M18 Social distinction; celebrity, renown. 4 M18 Conspicuous success; universal acclamation. Chiefly as *with* (great etc.) *éclat*.

> **1 1996** *Times* Puccini's La Rondine, staged with old-fashioned theatrical *éclat* by John Copley . . . , was almost as enjoyable.

écorché /ˈɛkɔːʃeɪ/, *foreign* /ekɔrʃe/ (*plural* same) *noun* M19 French (past participle of *écorcher* to flay). *Art* An anatomical subject treated so as to display the musculature.

écossaise /ɛkʊˈseɪz/, *foreign* /ekɔsɛz/ *noun* plural pronounced same M19 French (feminine of *écossais* Scottish). (A dance to) a lively tune in duple time.

écrevisse /ekrəvis/ *noun* plural pronounced same M18 French. A crayfish.

ecru /ˈeɪkruː/, /ɛˈkruː/ *adjective & noun* M19 French (*écru* raw, unbleached). (Of) the colour of unbleached linen; light fawn.

ecuelle /ɛˈkwɛl/ *noun* (also **écuelle**) M19 French (*écuelle* ultimately from Latin *scutella* small dish). 1 M19 A two-handled soup bowl. 2 L19 The process or apparatus by which oils are extracted from the peel of citrus fruit.

editio princeps /ɪˌdɪʃɪəʊ ˈprɪnsɛps/ *noun phrase* plural **editiones principes** /ɪˌdɪʃɪ ˌəʊniːz ˈprɪnsɪpiːz/ E19 Modern Latin (from Latin *editio* publication + *princeps* first). The first printed edition of a book.

effendi /ɛˈfɛndi/ *noun* E17 Turkish (*efendi* from Modern Greek *aphentē* vocative of *aphentēs* from Greek *authentēs* lord, master). A man of education or social standing in an eastern Mediterranean or Arab country. Frequently (usually *historical*) as

a title of respect or courtesy in Turkey or (former) Turkish territory.

effluvium /ɪˈfluːvɪəm/ *noun* plural **effluvia** /ɪˈfluːvɪə/, **effluviums** M17 Latin (from *effluere*, from *ef-* + *fluere* to flow). 1 M17–E18 A flowing out. 2 M17 Chiefly *History*. An outflow or stream of imperceptible particles, especially as supposedly transmitting electrical or magnetic influence etc. 3 M17 An (especially unpleasant) exhalation affecting the lungs or the sense of smell.

efreet variant of AFREET.

e.g. abbreviation of EXEMPLI GRATIA.

égalité /egalite/ *noun* L18 French (= equality, from *égal* from Latin *aequalis* equal). The condition of having equal rank, power, etc. with others.

> ■ Historically, as part of the rallying cry of the French Revolution: *Liberté, égalité, fraternité* 'Liberty, equality, brotherhood'.

églomisé /eglɔmize/ *adjective & noun* plural of noun pronounced same L19 French (from *Glomy*, eighteenth-century Parisian picture-framer). **A** *adjective* L19 Of glass: decorated on the back with engraved gold or silver leaf or paint. Frequently in VERRE ÉGLOMISÉ. **B** *noun* L19 (A panel of) verre églomisé.

ego /ˈiːgəʊ/, /ˈɛgəʊ/ *noun* plural **egos** E19 Latin (= I (pronoun)). 1 E19 *Metaphysics* Oneself, the conscious thinking subject. 2 L19 *Psychoanalysis* That part of the mind which has a sense of individuality and is most conscious of self. 3 L19 Self-esteem, self-importance.

> **3 1997** *Daily Telegraph* Mum can nurture her ego by fulfilling the career role set for her . . .

eheu fugaces /ˌeɪhjuː fuːˈgɑːsiːz/ *interjection* M19 Latin (= alas, the fleeting (years are hurrying by)). An expression of regret for the rapidity with which life passes.

> ■ The words are from the opening line of one of Horace's *Odes* (II.xiv).

eid /iːd/ *noun* (also **id**) L17 Arabic ('*īd* festival, from Aramaic). A Muslim feast-day; *specifically* that at the breaking of the fast at the end of Ramadan (cf. ID UL-FITR).

eidolon /ʌɪˈdəʊlɒn/ *noun* plural **eidola** /ʌɪˈdəʊlə/, **eidolons** M17 Greek (*eidōlon*). 1 An emanation considered by atomic philosophers to constitute the visible image of an object. *rare*. Only in M17.

2 E19 A spectre, a phantom. Also, an idealized image.

Einfühlung /'ʌmfy:lʊŋ/, /'ʌmfu:lən/ *noun* E20 German (from *ein-* into + *Fühlung* feeling, from *fühlen* to feel). Empathy.

eisteddfod /aɪ'stɛðvɒd/, /aɪ'stɛdvəd/ *noun* plural **eisteddfods**, **eisteddfodau** /aɪ'stɛðvɒdaɪ/ E19 Welsh (= session). A congress of Welsh bards; a gathering for competitions in Welsh poetry, music, etc.

Eiswein /'aɪsvaɪm/ *noun* M20 German (from *Eis* ice + *Wein* wine). Wine made from ripe grapes picked while covered with frost.

ejecta /ɪ'dʒɛktə/ *noun plural* (treated as *plural* or *singular*) L19 Latin (neuter plural of past participle of *e(j)icere* to eject). **1** L19 Matter that is thrown out of a volcano or a star. **2** L19 Material discharged from the body, *especially* vomit.

■ An earlier (M19) synonym for sense 1 was *ejectamenta*.

ejido /e'xido/, /eɪ'hi:dəʊ/ *noun* plural **ejidos** /e'xidos/, /eɪ'hi:dəʊz/ L19 Mexican Spanish (from Spanish = common land (on the road leading out of a village), from Latin *exitus* going out). In Mexico: a cooperative farm; a piece of land farmed communally.

ek dum /eɪk 'dʌm/ *adverb phrase* (also **ek dam**) L19 Hindustani (from *ek* one + Urdu *dam* breath). At once, immediately.

élan /er'lɒ̃/, /er'lan/, *foreign* /elɒ̃/ *noun* M19 French. Vivacity, vitality; energy arising from enthusiasm.

1996 *Country Life* Boucher's two canvases with their dramatic *élan* and beautifully painted landscape backgrounds are the best of the series.

élan vital /elɒ̃ vital/, /er'lɒ̃ vi:'ta:l/ *noun phrase* E20 French. An intuitively perceived life-force; any mysterious creative principle.

■ The French philosopher Henri Bergson (1859–1941) posited the *élan vital*, as opposed to inert matter, in *L'Evolution créatrice* (1907); as philosophical concept it has frequently been attacked for its lack of content (see quotation), but the phrase remains current in English in more general use.

1996 *Times* L'évolution créatrice has had much less impact than it deserves. Perhaps, nearly 100 years later, people will now realise that the *élan vital* exists on Mars.

élégante /elegɑ̃t/ *noun* plural pronounced same L18 French (feminine of *élégant* elegant). A fashionable woman.

elenchus /ɪ'lɛŋkəs/ *noun* plural **elenchi** /ɪ'lɛŋkaɪ/ M17 Latin (from Greek *elegkhos* argument of refutation). *Logic* A syllogism in refutation of a syllogistic conclusion; a logical refutation.

elephanta /ɛlɪ'fantə/ *noun* (also **elephanter** /ɛlɪ'fantə/) E18 Portuguese (*elephante*, feminine *elephanta* from Proto-Romance variant of Latin *elephantus*, *elepha(n)s* from Greek *elephas*, elephant-ivory, elephant). A violent storm at the end (or the beginning) of a monsoon.

élite /er'li:t/, /ɪ'li:t/ *noun & adjective* (also **elite**) L18 French (use as noun of feminine of obsolete past participle of *élire*, *eslire* from Proto-Romance variant of Latin *eligere* to elect). **A** *noun* **1** L18 The choice part, the best, (of society, a group of people, etc.); a select group or class. **2** E20 (Usually *elite*.) A size of type used on typewriters, having twelve characters to the inch. **B** *attributive adjective* M19 Of or belonging to an élite; exclusive.

A.1 1996 *Spectator* Gone are the good old days: now only Soho . . . is the resting place of the élite.

El Niño /ɛl 'ni:njəʊ/ *noun phrase* (also **el Niño, El Nino**) L19 Spanish (*El Niño (de Navidad)* the (Christmas) child, with reference to beginning in late December). Formerly, an annual warm southward current off northern Peru. Now, an irregularly occurring southward current in the equatorial Pacific Ocean, associated with weather changes and ecological damage; these associated phenomena.

1992 *Economist* The effects of El Nino are not limited to the countries of the Pacific rim.

éloge /elɔʒ/ *noun* plural pronounced same M16 French (from Latin *elogium* short saying or epitaph, altered from Greek *elegeia* elegy; apparently confused with *eulogium* eulogy). **1** M16-E19 A commendation; an encomium. **2** E18 A discourse in honour of a deceased person; *especially* that pronounced on a member of the French Academy by his successor.

Elysium /ɪ'lɪziəm/ *noun* L16 Latin (from Greek *Elusion* (sc. *pedion* plain)). **1** L16 *Classical Mythology* The home of the blessed after death. **2** L16 A place or state of perfect happiness.

email ombrant /ɛ,meɪl 'ɒmbrənt/, *foreign* /emajɔ̃brɑ̃/ *noun phrase* (also **émail ombrant**) plural **email ombrants**, **émaux**

ombrants /emoz ɔ̃brɑ̃/ L19 French (*émail ombrant*, from *émail* enamel + *ombrer* to shade). A form of decoration in which a coloured glaze is laid over intagliated earthenware or porcelain to give a monochrome picture.

emakimono /ɪˌmakɪˈməʊnəʊ/ *noun* plural same M20 Japanese (from *e* painting, picture + *makimono* scroll). A Japanese scroll containing pictures representing a narrative; a pictorial MAKIMONO.

émaux ombrants plural of EMAIL OMBRANT.

embarcadero /ɛmˌbɑːkəˈdɛːrəʊ/ *noun* plural **embarcaderos** M19 Spanish (from *embarcar* to embark). A wharf, a quay. United States.

embargo /ɛmˈbɑːgəʊ/, /ɪmˈbɑːgəʊ/ *noun & verb* (also formerly **imbargo**) E17 Spanish (from *embargar* to arrest, impede, from Proto-Romance, from Latin *in-* + *barra* bar). **A** *noun* plural **embargoes**. **1** E17 An order prohibiting ships from entering or leaving a country's ports, usually issued in anticipation of war. **2** M17 An official, usually temporary, prohibition of a particular commercial activity, or of trade in general, with another country. **3** L17 *generally* A prohibition, an impediment. **B** *transitive verb* **1** M17 Seize, confiscate; *specifically* seize, requisition, or impound (ships, goods, etc.) for the service of the State. **2** M18 Place (ships, trade, etc.) under an embargo.

embarras /ãbara/ *noun* plural pronounced same M17 French. Embarrassment.

■ Now in English only in phrases below.

embarras de choix /ãbara də ʃwa/ *noun phrase* L19 French (literally, 'embarrassment of choice'). More choices than one knows what to do with.

embarras de richesse /ãbara də riʃɛs/ *noun phrase* (also **embarrass de richesses**) M18 French (literally, 'an embarrassment of riches'). More resources, pleasures, etc., than one knows what to do with.

■ *L'embarras des richesses* (1726) was the title of a work by the Abbé d'Allainval, and the earliest recorded use in English (1751) is in one of Lord Chesterfield's letters. *Richesse* as an independent noun is found earlier (ME–L17) with the meanings 'wealth' or 'richness' and also (L15) 'a group of martens', but it has long been archaic as an independent noun.

1995 *Spectator* There is an *embarras de richesse* of rose gardens to visit in June.

embolus /ˈɛmbələs/ *noun* plural **emboli** /ˈɛmbəlʌɪ/, /ˈɛmbəliː/ M17 Latin (= piston of a pump, from Greek *embolos* peg, stopper). **1** M17–M18 *Mechanical* Something inserted or moving in another; *especially* the piston of a syringe. **2** M19 *Medicine* The blood clot or other object or substance which causes embolism.

embonpoint /ãbɔ̃pwɛ̃/ *noun & adjective* L17 French (phrase *en bon point* in good condition). **A** *noun* L17 Plumpness. **B** *adjective* E19 Plump.

■ In quotation as euphemism for 'cleavage'.

A 1995 *Times* It was Kissinger's bad luck, but our good fortune, that a photographer caught the moment as the learned doctor peered, astonished, at the Princess's embonpoint.

embouchure /ãbuʃyr/, /ˈɒmbʊʃʊə/ *noun* M18 French (from *s'emboucher* reflexive, to discharge itself by a mouth, from *emboucher* put in or to the mouth, from as *em-* + *bouche* mouth). **1** M18 *Music* The manner in which a player's mouth and lips are placed when playing a woodwind or brass instrument. **b** M19 The mouthpiece of a musical instrument, especially of a flute. **2** L18 The mouth of a river; the opening of a valley on to a plain.

1.a 1996 *Times* But my composer friend was right about my trombone-playing. . . . The problem is my *embouchure*, you see: it's just not the same with a false tooth.

embourgeoisé /ãburʒwaze/ *adjective* M20 French (past participle of *embourgeoiser* to make or become BOURGEOIS). That has been bourgeoisified.

embourgeoisement /ãburʒwazmã/ *noun* M20 French (from *embourgeoiser* to make or become BOURGEOIS). Bourgeoisification.

1996 *Spectator* He [sc. Liam Gallagher] is undergoing the same *embourgeoisement* which affected the late John Lennon when he embraced domesticity and started baking his own bread.

embrasure /ɪmˈbreɪʒə/, /ɛmˈbreɪʒə/ *noun* E18 French (from obsolete *embraser* (modern *ébraser*) to widen (a door or window opening), of unknown origin). **1** *Military* E18 An opening in a parapet that widens towards the exterior, made to fire a gun through. **2** M18 A slanting or bevelling of the wall on either side of a door or window opening so as to form a recess; the

area contained between such walls.
3 *Dentistry* M20 The angle between adjacent teeth where their two surfaces curve inwards towards the line of contact.

embusqué /ãbyske/ *noun* plural pronounced same E20 French (past participle of *embusquer* from Old French *embuschier* to ambush). A person who avoids military service by obtaining a post in a government office or the like.

emeritus /ɪ'mɛrɪtəs/ *adjective* M18 Latin (past participle of *emereri* to earn (one's discharge) by service, from *e-* + *mereri* to deserve). Honourably discharged from service; (of a former office-holder, especially a professor) retired but allowed to retain his or her title as an honour.
■ Often postpositive (see quotation).
1995 *Spectator* Sir Michael Richardson, Savoy director emeritus and pastmaster dealmaker, is just the man to go round with the hat.

émeute /emøt/ *noun* L18 French (from Old French *esmote*, from *esmeu* (modern *ému*) past participle of *esmovoir* (modern *émouvoir*), after *meute* crowd, uprising). A popular rising or disturbance.

emigré /'ɛmɪgreɪ/ *noun & adjective* (also **émigré**) L18 French (*émigré*, past participle of *émigrer* from Latin *emigrare* to emigrate). **A** *noun* L18 Originally, a French emigrant, *especially* one from the Revolution of 1789–99. Now, any emigrant, *especially* a political exile. **B** *adjective* E20 That is an emigré; composed of emigrés.

emincé /emɛ̃se/ *noun* E20 French (use as noun of past participle of *émincer* to slice thinly). A dish consisting of thinly sliced meat in sauce.

éminence grise /eminãs griz/ *noun phrase* plural **éminences grises** (pronounced same) M20 French (literally, 'grey eminence'. A person who exercises power or influence though holding no official position. Also, a confidential adviser.
■ Originally applied to the Capuchin Père Joseph, confidential agent of the French statesman Cardinal Richelieu (1585–1642).
1995 *New Scientist* A young researcher talking about her work today would be an invaluable resource for some future investigator about to interview the same person when an elderly *éminence grise* of science.

emir /ɛ'mɪə/ *noun* L16 French (*émir* from Arabic *'amīr*). **1** L16 A male descendant of Muhammad. Now *rare*. **2** M17 A title of certain Muslim rulers; an Arab prince, governor, or commander.

empanada /ɛmpə'nɑːdə/, *foreign* /empa'nada/ *noun* M20 Spanish (use as noun of feminine past participle of *empanar* to bake or roll in pastry, from as *em-* + *pan* bread, from Latin *panis*). *Cookery* A turnover with a filling of meat, cheese, or vegetables.

empiecement /ɪm'piːsm(ə)nt/, /ɛm'piːsm(ə)nt/ *noun* L19 French (*empiècement*, from as *em-* + *piece* piece). A piece of material inserted in a garment for decoration.

emplacement /ɪm'pleɪsm(ə)nt/, /ɛm'pleɪsm(ə)nt/ *noun* E19 French (from as *em-* + *place* place). **1** E19 *Military* A defended or protected position where a gun or missile is placed ready for firing. **2** E19 Situation, position; *specifically* that of a building. **3** M19 The action of putting or settling into place.

employé /ɒm'plɔɪeɪ/, *foreign* /ãplwaje/ (*plural same*) *noun* (feminine **employée**) E19 French (past participial adjective of *employer* to employ). A person who works for an employer.
■ Now naturalized in the later (M19) form *employee*.

emporium /ɛm'pɔːrɪəm/, /ɪm'pɔːrɪəm/ *noun* plural **emporiums, emporia** /ɛm'pɔːrɪə/ L16 Latin (from Greek *emporion*, from *emporos* merchant, from as *em-* + verbal stem *por-, per-* to journey). **1** L16 A centre of commerce; a market. **2** M19 A shop, *especially* one that sells unusual or fancy goods. Chiefly *jocular*.

empressé /ãprɛse/ *adjective* (feminine **empressée**) M19 French (past participial adjective of *empresser* to urge, (reflexive) be eager, (in Old French) to press, crowd in). Eager, zealous; showing EMPRESSEMENT.

empressement /ãprɛsmã/ *noun* E18 French (from *empresser* (see preceding)). Eagerness; effusive friendliness.

enamorata, enamorato variants of INAMORATA, INAMORATO.

en attendant /ã atãdã/ *adverb phrase* M18 French. In the meantime, while waiting.

en avant /ã avã/ *adverb & interjection phrase* E19 French. Forward, onwards.

en beau /ã bo/ *adverb phrase* E19 French. In a favourable manner; in the best light. Cf. EN NOIR.

en bloc /ɑ̃ blɔk/, /ɒn blɒk/ *adverb & adjective phrase* M19 French (literally, 'as a block'). **A** *adverb phrase* M19 As a whole; collectively, all together. **B** *adjective phrase* E20 Performed or made *en bloc*.

> **A 1984** A. G. Lehmann *European Heritage* . . . the civil service moves, *en bloc*, and with no changes, from serving the Kaiser to serving the republic—equally without enthusiasm.

en brosse /ɑ̃ brɔs/ *adverb & adjective phrase* E20 French (literally, 'as a brush'). (Of hair) cut short and bristly.

> **1996** *Times: Weekend* Middle-aged men wore Newcastle United shirts, ear-rings, hair *en brosse* or back-to-front baseball caps.

en cabochon /ɑ̃ kabɔʃɔ̃/ *adverb phrase* E19 French. Of a gem: cut as a CABOCHON, with curved surfaces rather than facets.

enceinte /ɑ̃sɛ̃t/, /ɒ̃'sãt/ *noun* plural pronounced same E18 French (from Latin *incincta* feminine past participle of *incingere* to gird in). The main enclosure or enclosing wall of a fortified place.

enceinte /ɑ̃sɛ̃t/, /ɒ̃'sãt/ *adjective* (also (in legal use) **ensient**) E17 French (from medieval Latin *incincta* ungirded, from Latin *in- + cincta* feminine past participle of *cingere* to gird). Of a woman: pregnant.

■ Now archaic or euphemistic.

enchaînement /ɑ̃ʃɛnmɑ̃/ *noun* plural pronounced same M19 French (literally = a chaining up, a concatenation). *Ballet* A sequence of steps.

enchilada /ɛntʃɪˈlɑːdə/ *noun* M19 American Spanish (feminine of *enchilado* past participle of *enchilar* to season with chili). A usually meat-filled tortilla served with chilli sauce.

enchiridion /ˌɛnkʌɪˈrɪdɪən/ *noun* LME Late Latin (from Greek *egkheiridion*, from as *en- + kheir* hand + diminutive suffix *-idion*). A handbook, a manual.

encierro /enˈsjerro/ *noun* plural **encierros** /enˈsjerros/ M19 Spanish (literally, 'shutting in', from *en-* (from as *in-*) + *cierre* shutting). The driving of bulls through the streets of a Spanish town from a corral to the bullring.

en clair /ɑ̃ klɛr/ *adverb & adjective phrase* L19 French. (Transmitted, written, etc.) in ordinary language, not in code or cipher; also *figurative*.

> *figurative* **1995** *Spectator* Franks worked *en clair*, Goodman in code.

enclave /ˈɛnkleɪv/, *formerly also* /ˈɑ̃klɑv/ *noun* M19 French (from Old and Modern French *enclaver* to enclose, from popular Latin *in- + clavis* key). **1** M19 A region belonging to a country but surrounded by another country as viewed by the latter. **2** M20 A culturally or socially distinct minority group in society or place.

encoignure /ɑ̃kwaɲyr/ *noun* plural pronounced same M19 French (from as *en- + coin* corner). A piece of usually ornamental furniture made with an angle to fit into a corner.

encomium /ɛnˈkəʊmɪəm/ *noun* plural **encomiums**, **encomia** L16 Latin (from Greek *egkōmion* eulogy, use as noun of neuter of adjective (sc. *epos* speech), from as *en- + komos* revel). A formal or high-flown expression of praise; a panegyric.

■ Earlier (M16) Anglicized as *encomy*.

> **1996** *Bookseller* I was miffed, incidentally, not to be among the luminaries asked to provide a 10th birthday encomium for Serpent's Tail.

encore /ˈɒŋkɔː/ *interjection, noun & verb* E18 French. (= still, again). **A** *interjection* E18 Again! **B** *noun* M18 An audience's demand for an item to be performed again or for a further item after the programme finale in a concert, etc. Also an item (to be) performed thus. **C** *transitive verb* M18 Call for a repetition.

■ The origin is uncertain. The Italian equivalent *ancora* 'still' was also formerly used (E18) but neither it nor *encore* occurs in this context in the original languages.

encourager les autres see POUR ENCOURAGER LES AUTRES.

en croûte /ɑ̃ krut/ *adverb & adjective phrase* L20 French. (Cooked) in a pastry crust.

en daube /ɑ̃ dob/ *adverb & adjective phrase* L20 French (cf. DAUBE). Stewed, braised.

en déshabillé /ɒn deɪzaˈbiːjeɪ/, *foreign* /ɑ̃ dezabije/ *adverb & adjective phrase* (also Anglicized as **en déshabille** /ɒn deɪzəˈbiːl/, **en dishabille** /ɒ̃ dɪsəˈbiːl/) L17 French (from preposition *en* + *déshabillé* dishabille). In a state of undress or of partial dress; casually dressed.

en échelon /ɑ̃ eʃlɔ̃/ *adjective & adverb phrase* (also **en echelon**) E19 French. (Arranged) in an ECHELON.

en évidence /ɑ̃n evidɑ̃s/ *adverb phrase* E19 French. In or at the forefront; conspicuously.

en face /ɑ̃ fas/ *adverb phrase* M18 French. **1** M18 With the face to the front, facing forwards. Cf. EN REGARD. **2** M20 *Bibliography* On the facing page.

en famille /ɑ̃ famij/, /ɒn fa'miː/ *adverb phrase* E18 French. At home, with one's family; as one of the family, informally.
1996 Times: Weekend Though mostly in their fifties or sixties, there was a sprinkling of teenagers *en famille.*

enfant gâté /ɑ̃fɑ̃ gate/ *noun phrase* plural **enfants gâtés** (pronounced same) E19 French (= spoilt child). A person given undue flattery or indulgence.

enfantillage /ɑ̃fɑ̃tijaʒ/ *noun* E19 Old and Modern French (from Old French *enfantil* from Latin *infantilis* of an infant). A childish action or prank.

enfant terrible /ɑ̃fɑ̃ tɛribl/ *noun phrase* plural **enfants terribles** (pronounced same) M19 French (= terrible child). A person who causes embarrassment by ill-considered, or unorthodox behaviour or speech; an unconventional person.
1996 Country Life Seven years on, Mr Barr has lost none of his impishness; he remains one of the *enfants terribles*, the young Turks of the wine-writing world, still tweaking the nose of the Establishment . . .

en fête /ɑ̃ fɛt/ *predicative adjective phrase* M19 French. Prepared for or engaged in holiday-making or celebration.

enfilade /ɛnfɪ'leɪd/, /'ɒnfɪlɑːd/ *noun & verb* E18 French (from *enfiler* to thread on a string, pierce or traverse from end to end, from *en-* + *fil* thread). **A** *noun* **1** *Military* **a** The situation of a post such that it commands the whole length of a line. Only in E18. **b** L18 Gunfire directed along a line from end to end (also *enfilade fire*); an act of firing in this way. **2** E18 A suite of rooms with doorways in line with each other; a vista between rows of trees etc. **B** *transitive verb* E18 *Military* Subject to enfilade; cover the whole length of (a target) with a gun or guns.
A.2 *1995 Country Life* Hopetoun's Great Apartment is arranged in a standard enfilade running north from the entrance hall, and incorporating a spectacular five-bay drawing room . . .

engagé /ɑ̃gaʒɛ/, /ˌɒŋgaˈʒeɪ/ *noun & adjective* E19 French (past participle of *engager* to engage). **A** *noun* E19 *History* A boatman hired by a fur-trader or explorer; an engagee. *North American.* **B** *adjective* M20 Of writers, artists, etc., or their works: showing social or political commitment.
1996 Spectator They know where they are with other directors: Truffaut? Wry. Godard? *Engagé.*

en garçon /ɑ̃ garsɔ̃/ *adverb phrase* E19 French. As or in the manner of a boy or a bachelor.

engobe /ɑ̃gɔb/ *noun* M19 French. A mixture of white clay and water applied as a coating to pottery to cover the natural colour or to provide a ground for decoration; a slip.

en grande tenue /ɑ̃ grɑ̃d təny/ *adverb phrase* M19 French. In full dress, *especially* full military dress.

en grand seigneur /ɑ̃ grɑ̃ sɛɲœr/ *adverb phrase* E19 French. In the manner of a nobleman.

engrenage /ɑ̃grənaʒ/ *noun* plural pronounced same E20 French (literally, 'gearing', from *engrener* to feed corn into (a threshing-machine), throw into gear). **1** E20 A set of circumstances that trap one; an organization or society regarded as full of snares. **2** M20 The process of preparing for effective joint action.
2 *1963 Economist* 'Good Europeans' . . . sought consolation in the . . . theory of *engrenage* (getting into gear).

en gros /ɑ̃ gro/ *adverb phrase* E18 French. In general, in broad terms.

en l'air /ɑ̃ lɛr/ *adverb phrase* E18 French (= in the air). **1** E18 *Ballet* While leaping vertically. **2** E19 *Military* While unsupported.

en masse /ɑ̃ mas/, /ɒn mas/ *adverb phrase* L18 French. In a mass; all together, as a group.
1996 Spectator Rereading the stories *en masse* brings out Rose Tremain's strengths as a short story writer . . .

en noir /ɑ̃ nwar/ *adverb phrase* M19 French. On the black side; in the worst light. Cf. EN BEAU.

ennui /ɒn'wiː/, *foreign* /ɑ̃nɥi/ *noun* M18 French (from Latin *in odio* in *mihi in odio est* it is hateful to me). Mental weariness and dissatisfaction arising from lack of occupation or interest; boredom.
1996 Country Life [February] epitomises that rural ennui which is distinguished by its lack of distinguishedness.

ennuyant /ɑ̃nɥijɑ̃/ *adjective* L18 French (present participle of *ennuyer*; see next). That gives rise to ennui; boring, tedious.

ennuyé /ɑ̃nɥije/ *adjective* (feminine **ennuyée**) M18 French (past participial adjective of *ennuyer* to bore, from ENNUI). Affected with ennui; bored.

enosis /ɪˈnəʊsɪs/, /ˈɛnəsɪs/ *noun* M20 Modern Greek (*henōsis*, from *hena* one). Political union, *especially* that proposed between Greece and Cyprus.

en pantoufles /ã pãtufl/ *adverb phrase* E20 French (literally, 'in slippers'). Relaxed, off guard; in a free and easy manner or atmosphere.

en papillote see PAPILLOTE.

en passant /ã pasã/, /ɒ̃ paˈsɒnt/ *adverb phrase* E17 French. In passing, by the way.

1996 *Bookseller* Michael Schwanhauser of Walthari in Freiburg commented almost *en passant* that his twice-weekly orders for British books arrived within four days.

en pension /ã pãsjɔ̃/ *adverb and adjective phrase* E19 French. Living as a boarder, in lodgings.

■ Formerly (L16 onwards) Anglicized as *in* or *on pension*; cf. PENSION.

en permanence /ã pɛrmanãs/ *adverb phrase* M19 French. Permanently.

en place /ã plas/ *adverb phrase* E19 French. In place, in position.

en plein /ã plɛ̃/ *adverb phrase* L19 French (= in full). *Gambling* Entirely on one number or side; with the whole of one's bet.

en plein air /ã plɛn ɛr/ *adverb phrase* L19 French. In the open air.

■ Especially with reference to the working methods of the French Impressionist painters, as compared with their academic *confrères* who worked in studios and from posed models; cf. PLEIN AIR.

1988 K. Adler *Unknown Impressionists* Many of them wished to learn from Pissarro's example, . . . and they watched him at work, often *en plein air,* and discussed ideas about art.

en poste /ã pɔst/ *adverb phrase* M20 French. In an official diplomatic position (at a specified place).

1996 *Spectator* Nathaniel Hawthorne, who actually did get a cushy job as consul, turned out nothing while he was *en poste.*

en primeur /ã primœr/ *adverb & adjective phrase* L20 French. (Of vegetables) fresh, new; (of wine) young, especially before bottling. Cf. PRIMEUR.

1996 *Country Life* If you have not bought *en primeur* before, get as many merchants' lists as you can and compare the tasting notes.

en prince /ã prɛ̃s/ *adverb phrase* L17 French. Like a prince; in a princely or luxurious manner.

en principe /ã prɛ̃sip/ *adverb phrase* E20 French. In principle.

en prise /ã priz/ *adverb phrase* E19 French. *Chess* In a position to be taken.

enragé /ɑ̃raʒe/, /ˌɒnraˈʒeɪ/ *adjective & noun* (also **enrage**) (feminine **enragée**) E18 French (past participle of *enrager* to enrage). **A** *adjective* E18 Furiously angry. **B** *noun* L18 An enraged person; a fanatic.

B 1995 *Spectator* Journalists (and intellectuals in general) have an important responsibility for the creation of a more civilised climate of opinion, so that semi-educated *enrages* do not take to the bomb or the gun each time they grow angry on the basis of undigested gobbets of information.

en rapport /ã rapɔr/ *adjective phrase* E19 French. In (close and harmonious) relationship (*with*); in harmony (*with*). Cf. RAPPORT.

en regard /ã rəgar/ *adverb phrase* E20 French. *Bibliography* On the facing page. Cf. EN FACE.

en règle /ã rɛgl/ *adverb phrase* E19 French. In order, according to form.

en retraite /ã rətrɛt/ *adverb phrase* M19 French. In retirement.

en revanche /ã rəvãʃ/ *adverb phrase* E19 French. In return, as compensation; in revenge.

1996 *Spectator* The best solution would be for you to wait until your friends visit you *en revanche* and then, as they leave, set a trap for them . . .

en route /ã rut/, /ɒn ruːt/ *adverb phrase* L18 French. On the way.

1996 *Spectator* On one occasion, . . . the Prince marched through the meeting in a towel *en route* to the bathroom.

ens /ɛnz/ *noun plural* **entia** /ˈɛntɪə/, /ˈɛnʃɪə/ M16 Late Latin (*ens* use as noun of present participle formed from *esse* to be, on the supposed analogy of *absens* absent, to translate Greek *on* use as noun of present participle of *einai* to be). **1** M16 *Philosophy* etc. Something which has existence; a being, an entity, as opposed to an attribute or quality. **2** L16–M18 The essence; the essential part.

■ Used in various phrases relating especially to Christian medieval theology and scholastic philosophy; thus *ens necessarium* (a necessarily existent being, i.e. God), *ens rationis* (a being having no existence outside the mind), *ens reale* (a being that exists independently of any finite mind), etc.

ensemble /ɒnˈsɒmb(ə)l/, *foreign* /āsābl/
(*plural same*) *noun* M18 Old and Modern
French (from Proto-Romance from Latin
insimul, from *in-* into, in + *simul* at the
same time). **1** M18 (The parts of) a thing
viewed as a whole. **2** E19 The unity of
performaance achieved by a group of artistes. **b** E20 A group of stage artistes who
perform together; *especially* the supporting actors or dancers as opposed to the
principals. **c** E20 A scene on stage in
which the whole cast appears. **d** M20 A
group of singers or musicians, especially
soloists, who perform together. **3** E20 A
set of (usually women's) clothes that har-
monize and are worn together. **4** E20 *Science* A notional collection of systems of
identical constitution but not necessarily
in the same state.

■ Originally (LME) introduced in the adverbial sense of 'together, at the same time',
which it retains in French, but this has
long been rare in English. Sense 1 is found
slightly earlier in the phrase TOUT ENSEM-
BLE.

2.b 1996 *Country Life* Once a small ensemble
of distinct individuals, this company now
resembles a large precision instrument . . .

ensient variant of ENCEINTE.

ensilage /ˈɛnsɪlɪdʒ/, /ɛnˈsʌɪlɪdʒ/ *noun & verb*
L19 French (from *ensiler* from Spanish *ensi-
lar*, from *en-* + *silo* silo). **A** *noun* **1** L19 The
process of making silage. **2** L19 Silage.
B *transitive verb* L19 Treat (fodder) by ensilage; turn into silage.

en suite /ɒn ˈswiːt/, *foreign* /ā sɥit/ *adverb,
adjective, & noun phrase* (also (especially as
adjective & noun phrase) **ensuite**
/ōswiːt/) L18 French. **A** *adverb phrase*
1 L18 In agreement or harmony (*with*).
Now *rare* or *obsolete*. **2** E19 In a row, with
one room leading into another; as part of
the same set of rooms. (Followed by *with*.)
b M20 As part of the same set of objects.
(Followed by *with*.) **B** *adjective phrase* M20
Of a room: that is en suite; forming part
of the same set, immediately adjoining.
C *noun phrase* L20 An en suite room, *especially* an en suite bathroom.

B 1995 D. Lodge *Therapy* She'd already
bagged the master bedroom with the *en suite*
bathroom.

entasis /ˈɛntəsɪs/ *noun plural* **entases**
/ˈɛntəsiːz/ M17 Modern Latin (from Greek,
from *enteinein* to strain). *Architecture* A
slight bowing of the shaft of a column
(introduced to correct the visual illusion
of concavity).

entente /ɒnˈtɒnt/, *foreign* /ātāt/ *noun* M19
French. A friendly understanding, especially between States; a group of States
sharing such an understanding.

1995 *Times* France has its own, largely
German, reasons for wanting a new entente
with Britain; both countries know that a close
bilateral relationship is essential.

entente cordiale /ātāt kɔrdjal/, /ˌɒntɒnt
kɔːdrˈɑːl/ *noun phrase plural* **ententes cor-
diales** (pronounced same) M19 French. An
entente, *specifically* (*historical*) that arrived
at by France and Britain in 1904.

1995 *Times* But the selection of a chap with
such a friendly disposition towards Europe can
only serve to strengthen the new *entente
cordiale* between John Major and Jacques
Chirac.

entia plural of ENS.

entourage /ˈɒntʊrɑːʒ/, /ˌɒntʊ(ə)ˈrɑːʒ/
noun M19 French (from *entourer* to surround, from *entour* surroundings, use as
noun of adverb = 'round about'). A group
of people in attendance on or accompanying someone important. Also, surroundings, environment.

en tout cas /ā tu kɑ/ *noun & adjective
phrase* L19 French (= in any case or emergency). **A** *noun phrase* L19 A parasol which
also serves as an umbrella. **B** *adjective &
noun phrase* M20 (*En-Tout-Cas*) (Proprietary
name designating) a hard tennis-court.

entr'acte /ˈɒntrakt/, *foreign* /ātrakt/ (*plural same*) *noun* M19 French (now obsolete
(modern *entracte*), from *entre* between +
acte act). The interval between two acts of
a play; a performance or entertainment
which takes place during an interval.

entrain /ātrɛ̃/ *noun* M19 French. Enthusiasm, animation.

1954 E. Jenkins *Tortoise and Hare* She
wanted to put her head out of the window, but
that would have shown too much *entrain*.

en train /ā trɛ̃/ *adverb phrase* L18 French.
Afoot, under way; in or into the swing of
something; occupied (*with*).

en travesti /ā travɛsti/ *adverb phrase* M20
pseudo-French. *Theatre* In the dress of the
opposite sex.

■ The phrase is not recorded in French,
and represents the misunderstanding as a
noun of French *travesti*, the past participle
of *travestir* (from Italian *travestire*, from *trans*
(a)cross + *vestire* to clothe).

1996 *Spectator* Carabosse, traditionally
performed by a man *en travesti*, becomes an
unbearable over-gesticulating drag queen.

entrechat /ātrəʃa/ *(plural same)*, /'ɒntrəʃɑ:/ *noun* L18 French (from Italian *(capriola) intrecciata* complicated (caper)). *Ballet* A leap in which a dancer strikes the heels together or crosses the feet a number of times while in the air.

entrecôte /'ɒntrəkəʊt/, *foreign* /ātrəkot/ *(plural same) noun* M19 French (literally = between rib). A boned steak cut off the sirloin. More fully *entrecôte steak.*

entredeux /ātrədø/ *noun* plural pronounced same M19 French (literally = between two). An insertion of lace, linen, etc., in sewing.

entrée /'ɒntreɪ/, *foreign* /ātre/ *(plural same) noun* E18 French. **1** E18 *Music* **a** A piece of instrumental music, usually resembling a march, forming the first part of a suite or divertissement, or introducing a character etc. on stage. **b** L18 A group of dances on one theme in seventeenth- and eighteenth-century French ballet; an act of a seventeenth- or eighteenth-century French opera-ballet. **2** M18 The action or manner of entering. **b** E19 The entrance of the performers in a play, circus, or other large show. **3** M18 The privilege or right of entrance; admission, especially to an exclusive social or professional circle. **4** M18 A dish served between the fish course and the main meat course; *North American* the main dish of a meal.
> **3** 1996 *Times* His upper-class accent and eminently recognisable surname . . . had not only given him an entré to the profession, it had allowed him to land a good royal story . . .

entrée en matière /ātre ā matjɛr/ *noun phrase* M20 French (literally, 'entry into the matter'). An opening remark or statement; the beginning of a literary work.
> **1930** E. F. Thomas *Nevertheless the Duke* 'I have known you before!' . . . As an entrée en matière it was, to say the least, time-worn.

entremet /ātrəmɛ/ *noun* plural **entremets** pronounced same L15 French (*entremets*). **1** L15 In *plural*. Side dishes. **2** M18 *singular* and in *plural* (treated as *singular* or *plural*). A sweet dish; a dessert; *rare* a side dish.

entre nous /ātrə nu/ *adverb phrase* L17 French. Between ourselves; in private.

entrepôt /'ɒntrəpəʊ/, *foreign* /ātrəpo/ *(plural same) noun* E18 French ((earlier *entrepost, entrepos*), from *entreposer* to store, from *entre* among + *poser* to place). **1** E18 A storehouse for the temporary deposit of goods, provisions, etc.; *rare* temporary deposit. **2** M18 A commercial centre to which goods are brought for import and export, and for collection and distribution.

entrepreneur /ˌɒntrəprə'nə:/ *noun* E19 French (from *entreprendre* to undertake). **1 a** E19 A director of a musical institution. **b** M19 A person who organizes entertainments, especially musical performances. **2** M19 A person who undertakes or contols a business or enterprise and bears the risk of profit or loss; a contractor who acts as an intermediary.

entresol /'ɒntrəsɒl/, *foreign* /ātrəsɔl/ *(plural same) noun* (also **entersole, intersole**) E18 French (from Spanish *entresuelo*, from *entre* between + *suelo* storey). A low storey between the ground floor and the first floor of a building; a mezzanine storey.

Entscheidungsproblem /ɛnt'ʃaɪdʊnz 'pro,ble:m/, /ɛnt'ʃʌɪdʊŋgzˌprɒbləm/ *noun* M20 German (= decision problem). *Mathematics* and *Logic* The problem of finding a way to decide whether a formula or class of formulas is true or provable within a given system of axioms.

en ventre sa mère /ā vātr sa mɛr/ *adverb phrase* (also **en ventre sa mere**) L18 French (= in its mother's womb). *Law* In the womb.

environs /ɪn'vʌɪrənz/, /ɛn'vʌɪrənz/, /'ɛnvɪrənz/ *noun* plural M17 French (plural of *environ* surrounding(s)). The district surrounding a place, especially an urban area. (Followed by *of*.)

envoi /'ɛnvɔɪ/ *noun* (also (earlier) **envoy**) LME Old and Modern French (from *envoyer* to send, from phrase *en voie* on the way). The concluding part of a literary work, *especially* a short stanza concluding a ballade; *archaic* an author's concluding words, dedication, etc.; *generally* a conclusion.
> **1996** *Country Life* She ended with a brief piece by Elgar . . . an apt envoi to an evening where landscape, architecture and music met in peculiarly English harmony.

eo ipso /ˌeɪəʊ 'ɪpsəʊ/ *adverb phrase* L17 Latin (ablative of *idipsum* the thing itself). By that very act (or quality); through that alone; thereby. Cf. IPSO FACTO.

eo nomine /ˌeɪəʊ 'nəʊmɪni/, /'nɒmmeɪ/ *adverb phrase* E17 Latin (ablative of *id nomen* that name). Under that name; that is so called; explicitly.

épatant /epatā/ *adjective* E20 French (present participial adjective of *épater* to flabbergast). Shocking (to conventional persons); daring.

épater /epate/ *transitive verb* E20 French (= flabbergast). Startle, shock.

■ Only used in the infinitive, especially in phrase below or English phrases based upon it.

épater les bourgeois /epate lɛ burʒwɑ/ *adverb phrase* (also **épater le bourgeois**) E20 French (= to amaze the bourgeois). To shock the narrow-minded or conventional.

■ 'Je les ai épatés, les bourgeois' is attributed to Alexandre Private d'Anglemont (d. 1859).

1995 *Times* Because it takes more than a urinal to *épater les bourgeois* now, the real things that are being hauled into galleries grow ever more provocative: turds, frozen foetuses and used sanitary towels . . .

épaulement /epolmɑ̃/ *noun* plural pronounced same M19 French (see next). *Ballet* A stance in which one shoulder is turned forward and the other drawn back, with the head facing over the forward shoulder; correct positioning of the shoulders.

epaulette /ˈɛpəlɛt/, /ˈɛpɔːlɛt/, /ɛpəˈlɛt/ *noun* (also **epaulet**) L18 French (*épaulette* diminutive of *épaule* shoulder, from Latin *spatula*, (in Late Latin) shoulder-blade). **1** L18 An ornamental shoulder-piece worn on a military or other uniform, usually as a sign of rank. **b** E19 A military officer; a commission. **2** E19 A small shoulder-plate on a suit of armour. **3** M19 A loop or tab on the shoulder of a coat; a piece of trimming on the shoulder of a dress etc.

épée /ˈeɪpeɪ/, *foreign* /epe/ (*plural same*) *noun* L19 French (= sword, from Old French *espee*). A sharp-pointed duelling-sword used (blunted) for fencing; the art of fencing with this.

ephemera /ɪˈfɛm(ə)rə/, /ɪˈfiːm(ə)rə/, /ɛˈfɛm(ə)rə/ *noun* plural **ephemeras**, **ephemera** /ɪˈfɛm(ə)riː/, /ɪˈfiːm(ə)riː/, /ɛˈfɛm(ə)riː/ L17 Medieval Latin (use as noun of feminine of late Latin *ephemerus* from Greek *ephēmeros* lasting only one day). **1** Originally, a winged insect that lives only one day; an EPHEMERON. Now, a winged insect of the genus *Ephemera*, a mayfly. **2** M18 A person or thing of short-lived usefulness or interest.

ephemeris /ɪˈfɛm(ə)rɪs/, /ɪˈiːm(ə)rɪs/ *noun* plural **ephemerides** /ɛfɪˈmɛrɪdiːz/ E16 Latin (from Greek, from *ephēmeros* lasting only a day. A table or book of tables giving information about celestial bodies on

a daily or regular basis over a particular period; an astronomical almanac.

ephemeron /ɪˈfɛm(ə)rɒn/, /ɪˈfiːm(ə)rɒn/ *noun* plural **ephemerons**, **ephemera** /ɪˈfɛm(ə)rə/, /ɪˈfiːm(ə)rə/ L16 Greek (neuter of *ephēmeros* lasting only one day. **1** L16 A winged insect that lives only one day or spends only one day in its winged form; cf. EPHEMERA 1. **2** L18 A short-lived person, institution, or production. **3** M20 As *ephemera* (*plural*). Printed or written items intended for short-term use, as tickets, posters, etc.

3 1995 *Spectator* The ephemera of rock and roll now plays an important part in the social history of the 20th-century's last half.

épicerie /episri/ *noun* plural pronounced same E20 French. In France: a grocer's shop.

epigramme /ˈɛpɪɡram/ *noun* M18 French (*épigramme*, apparently a fanciful use of *épigramme* = epigram). *Cookery* A small piece of meat, usually lamb, served as an entrée.

epithalamium /ˌɛpɪθəˈleɪmɪəm/ *noun* (also (earlier) **epithalamion** /ˈɛpɪθə ˈleɪmɪən/) plural **epithalamiums**, **epithalamions**, **epithalamia** /ˌɛpɪθəˈleɪmɪə/ L16 Latin (from Greek *epithalamion* use as noun of neuter of *epithalamios* nuptial, from as *epi-* + *thalamos* bridal chamber). A song or poem in celebration of a wedding.

epitome /ɪˈpɪtəmi/, /ɛˈpɪtəmi/ *noun* (also (*non-standard*) **epitomy**) E16 Latin (from Greek *epitomē*, from *epitemnein* to cut into, cut short, from as *epi-* + *temnein* to cut). **1** E16 A summary or abstract of a written work; a condensed account. **2** E16 A thing that represents another in miniature; a person who or thing which embodies a quality etc.; a typical example.

epode /ˈɛpəʊd/ *noun* E17 French (*épode* or Latin *epodos* from Greek *epōidos*, from as *epi-* + *ōidē* ode). **1** E17 A Greek lyric poem composed of couplets in which a long line is followed by a shorter; a serious poem. **2** L17 The part of a Greek lyric ode following the strophe and antistrophe.

éponge /epɔ̃ʒ/ *noun* E20 French (from Latin *spongia* sponge). Sponge cloth.

epos /ˈɛpɒs/ *noun* M19 Latin (from Greek = word, song, from *ep-* stem of *eipein* to say). **1** M19 Epic poetry; an epic poem; *especially* narrative poetry embodying a nation's conception of its past history. **2** M19

Something in real life regarded as a fit subject for an epic poem.

épris /epri/ *adjective* (feminine **éprise** /epriz/) L18 French (past participial adjective of ((*s'*)*éprendre* to become attached or enamoured, from as *es-* + Latin *prehendere* to seize). Enamoured (*of*); taken *with*.
1949 C. Hare *When Wind Blows* As if anybody else could not see that Mr. Ventry is *épris* of Nicola.

epsilon /'ɛpsɪlɒn/, /ɛp'sʌɪlɒn/ *noun* E18 Greek (*e psilon*, literally, 'bare e', short e written ε). **1** E18 The fifth letter (E, ε) of the Greek alphabet; *Astronomy* (preceding the genitive of the Latin name of the constellation) the fifth brightest star in a constellation. **2** E20 An examiner's fifth-class mark; a person of low intelligence.

epyllion /ɪ'pɪlɪən/, /ɛ'pɪlɪən/ *noun* plural **epyllia** /ɪ'pɪlɪə/, /ɛ'pɪlɪə/ L19 Greek (*epullion* diminutive of EPOS). A narrative poem resembling an epic in style or matter but of shorter extent.

équipe /ekip/ *noun* (also **equipe**) plural pronounced same M20 French (= group, team, from as *équiper* to equip (cf. Anglo-Norman *eskipeson*, medieval Latin *eschipare* to man (a vessel)), probably from Old Norse *skipa* to man (a vessel), fit up, from *skip* ship). A motor-racing stable; a team, especially of sports players.

equivoque /'i:kwɪvəʊk/, /'ɛkwɪvəʊk/ *noun* (also **equivoke**) LME Old and Modern French (*équivoque* or late Latin *aequivocus*). **1** L16-M17 A thing which has the same name as something else. **2** E17 An expression capable of more than one meaning; a pun; wordplay, punning. **3** E19 The fact of having more than one meaning or interpretation; ambiguity.
■ Earlier (LME-M17) as an adjective meaning 'equivocal'.

erbswurst /'ə:bzwə:st/ *noun* L19 German (from *Erbse* pea + *Wurst* sausage). *Cookery* Seasoned pease-meal compressed into a sausage shape and used for making soup.

erg /ə:g/ *noun* plural **areg** /'arɛg/ L19 French (from Arabic *'irk̩, 'erg*). An area of shifting desert sand-dunes, especially in the Sahara.

ergo /'ə:gəʊ/ *adverb* LME Latin. Therefore.
■ Later (L16) there was also a nominal sense of *ergo*, meaning 'a use or occurrence of *ergo*, as in a logical conclusion', but this sense has long been rare.

1995 *Spectator* Thus, if the US Federal Government committed a crime (the Waco massacre), everyone who works for the Federal Government shares in its guilt; ergo it is permissible to bomb a Federal Government building because the people in it are by definition guilty.

ergot /'ə:gɒt/ *noun* L17 French (= cock's spur, from Old French *ar(i)got, argoz* of unknown origin). **1** L17 A disease of rye and certain other grasses in which the seeds become replaced by hard black sclerotia of a fungus, giving the appearance of cock's spur: a sclerotium, or sclerotia, of this kind; a fungus causing such a disease. **2** M19 (A preparation or extract of) the dried sclerotia of this fungus used medicinally for the alkaloids they contain, especially to induce contraction of the uterus. **3** L19 A small horny protrusion on the back of the fetlock of most horses.

erh hu /ə: 'hu:/ *noun phrase* (also **erhu**) E20 Chinese (*èrhú*, from *èr* two + *hú* bowed instrument). A Chinese two-stringed musical instrument played with a bow.

Erlebnis /ɛr'le:pnɪs/ *noun* plural **Erlebnisse** /ɛr'le:pnɪsə/ E20 German (literally, 'experience', from *leben* to live). A conscious experience undergone, as opposed to the content or the memory of one.

Eros /'ɪərɒs/, /'ɛrəʊz/ *noun* plural **Erotes** /ɪ'rəʊtɛz/, **Eroses** /'ɪərɒsɪz/, /'ɛrəʊzɪz/ (also **eros**) L17 Latin (from Greek). **1** L17 Love; the god of love, Cupid; earthly or sexual love. **2** E20 In Freudian psychology: the urge for self-preservation and sexual pleasure.

errata /ɛ'rɑːtə/, /ɛ'reɪtə/ *noun* L16 Latin (plural of ERRATUM). **I 1** L16 *plural* of ERRATUM. **II** *singular* plural **errata's, errataes** /ɛ'rɑːtəz/. **2** M17 A list of errors in a text.

erratum /ɛ'rɑːtəm/, /ɛ'reɪtəm/ *noun* plural **errata** /ɛ'rɑːtə/ M16 Latin (= error, use as noun of neuter past participle of *errare* to err). An error in a printed or written text; *especially* one noted in a list appended to a book or published in a subsequent issue of a journal.

ersatz /'ə:sats/, /'ɛ:sats/, *foreign* /ɛr'zats/ *adjective & noun* L19 German (= compensation, replacement). **A** *adjective* L19 Made or used as a (usually inferior) substitute for something else. **B** *noun* L19 An ersatz thing.
A 1996 *Spectator* . . . to judge from recent Australian movies, the old pro-British cringe,

which was at least rooted in historical and cultural reality, has been replaced by an *ersatz* Americanisation, rooted in nothing but commercial calculation.

eruv /ə'rʌv/ *noun* plural **eruvim** /ərʌ'vim/ L20 Hebrew. An area marked out by a community of observant Jews within which they are allowed to move on the Sabbath without contravening the restrictions on Sabbath activity.
1993 *Guardian* Most major American cities now have eruvim—the White House is even in Washington's.

escargot /ɛ'skɑːgəʊ/, /ɪ'skɑːgəʊ/ *noun* plural pronounced same L19 French (from Old French *escargol* from Provençal *escaragol*). A snail as an article of food.

escarole /'ɛskərəʊl/ *noun* E20 French (from Italian *scar(i)ola* from late Latin *(e)scariola*, from Latin *escarius* used as food, from *esca*). A variety of endive with broad undivided leaves, used in salads.
■ Mainly North American.

esclandre /ɛsklãdr/ *noun* plural pronounced same M19 French (from ecclesiastical Latin *scandalum* scandal). Unpleasant notoriety; a scandal, a scene.

escopette /ɛskə(ʊ)'pɛt/ *noun* E19 Spanish (*escopeta* assimilated to French *escopette* from Italian) from Italian *schioppetto* diminutive of *schioppo* carbine, from medieval Latin *sclop(p)us* harquebus). A kind of carbine formerly used in Mexico and the southern United States. *United States History.*

escritoire /ˌɛskriː'twɑː/ *noun* L16 Old French (= study, writing-box (modern *écritoire* writing-desk) from medieval Latin SCRIPTORIUM). A writing-desk with drawers etc., a bureau.

esophagus variant of OESOPHAGUS.

esoterica /ɛsə'tɛrɪkə/, /iːsə'tɛrɪkə/ *noun* plural E20 Greek (*esōterika* neuter plural of *esōterikos* esoteric). Items or publications intended only for the initiated or appropriate only to an inner circle; esoteric details.

espacement /ɪ'speɪsm(ə)nt/, /ɛ'speɪs m(ə)nt/ *noun* M19 French (from *espacer* to space out). **1** M19 The action of spacing, or of placing at suitable intervals. **2** M20 The distance at which trees or crops are set apart when planted.

espada /ɛ'spada/, /ɛ'spɑːdə/ *noun* plural **espadas** /ɛ'spadas/, /ɛ'spɑːdəz/ L19 Spanish (from Latin *spatha* sword). A matador.

■ Although introduced originally (E18) in its literal sense of 'a Spanish sword', the word did not achieve currency and was later reintroduced in its present sense.

espadrille /ɛspə'drɪl/, /'ɛspədrɪl/ *noun* L19 French (from Provençal *espardi(l)hos*, from *espart* esparto). A light canvas shoe with plaited fibre sole, originally worn in the Pyrenees; an ALPARGATA.

espagnole /ɛspaɲɔl/ *noun* M19 French (literally, 'Spanish' (feminine), from Old French *espaignol*, *espaigneul*). A simple brown sauce. In full *espagnole sauce.*

espagnolette /ɪˌspanjə'lɛt/, /ɛˌspanjə'lɛt/ *noun* E19 French (from *espagnol* Spanish; see preceding). A kind of bolt used for fastening French windows, in which a single handle operates fasteners at the top and bottom of the window.

espalier /ɪ'spaljə/, /ɛ'spaljə/ *noun* M17 French (from Italian *spalliera*, from *spalla* shoulder, from Latin *spatula*, (in late Latin) shoulder-blade). **1** M17 A fruit tree or ornamental shrub trained on a lattice or a framework of stakes. **2** A row of trees or shrubs trained in this way. Only in E18. **3** M18 A lattice or framework, or one of the stakes, on which a tree or shrub is trained.

esparto /ɛ'spɑːtəʊ/, /ɪ'spɑːtəʊ/ *noun* plural **espartos** M19 Spanish (from Latin *spartum* from Greek *sparton* rope). A tough grass, *Stipa tenacissima*, growing in Spain and North Africa and used in paper-making. Also *esparto grass.*

espièglerie /ɛspjɛɡləri/ *noun* E19 French (from (*Ul*)*espiegle* frolicsome, from Dutch *Uilenspiegel* (= German *Eulenspiegel*), from *uil* owl + *spiegel* mirror, from Latin *speculum*). Mischievousness; roguishness.
■ Till Eulenspiegel was a mythical fourteenth-century German peasant whose exploits and practical jokes were recounted in a collection of satirical tales first published in the early sixteenth century. The English noun *owlglass* (M16) is also a translation of *Eulenspiegel*.

esplanade /ɛsplə'neɪd/, /ɛsplə'nɑːd/ *noun* L16 French (from Italian *spianata* from feminine of Latin *explanatus* flattened, levelled, past participle of *explanare*). **1** L16 *Fortification* **a** The glacis of a counterscarp. Formerly, an area of flat ground on the top of a rampart. **b** E18 A level open space separating a citadel from the town that it commands. **2** L17 Any level open space, but *especially* one where the public may walk; a road along the sea front of a resort.

espressivo /ˌɛsprɛˈsiːvəʊ/ *adverb & adjective* L19 Italian (from Latin *expressus* distinctly presented, past participle of *exprimere* to express). *Music* (Performed) with expression of feeling.

espresso /ɛˈsprɛsəʊ/ *noun* (also **expresso** /ɛkˈsprɛsəʊ/) plural **espressos** M20 Italian ((*caffè*) *espresso*, from *espresso* squeezed, pressed out, from Latin *expressus* (see preceding)). **1** M20 Coffee made by forcing steam through ground coffee beans. **2** M20 A coffee bar etc. where such coffee is sold. Also *espresso bar, espresso café,* etc.

esprit /ɛspriː/, /ɛˈspriː/, /ˈɛspriː/ *noun* L16 French (from Latin *spiritus* spirit). Vivacity; wit.
1995 *Times* So you walk back to the Rigaud portrait [of Lord Nelson], the slight figure with colourless hair and arched brows and a face full of nervous *esprit* and determination.

esprit de corps /ɛˌspriː də ˈkɔː/, /ˌɛspriː/ *noun phrase* L18 French. Regard for the honour and interests of the group or organization to which one belongs; team spirit.
1995 *Spectator* An *esprit de corps* was emerging fast. As we sped into the Channel Tunnel, the businessman on the next table cracked open a bottle of champagne and handed round paper cups.

esprit de l'escalier /ɛspri də lɛskalje/ *noun phrase* (also **esprit d'escalier**) E20 French (literally, 'wit of the staircase'). A clever remark or rejoinder that only occurs to one after the opportunity for making it is past.
■ The phrase was coined by the French *philosophe* Denis Diderot (1713–84) in *Paradoxe sur le Comédien*. The staircase was the one descending from the salon, and *esprit d'escalier* was the witty saying that came to mind only as one was departing down it.
1995 *Times Magazine* With my usual dunderheaded *esprit d'escalier* I will realise later that the correct response is simply to walk on past . . .

esprit fort /ɛspri fɔr/ *noun phrase* plural **esprits forts** (pronounced same) M18 French (= strong spirit). A strong-minded person, *especially* one who claims independence from conventional thinking on religious or philosophical topics.

esquisse /ɛskis/ *noun* plural pronounced same M18 French (from Italian *schizzo*). A rough or preliminary sketch.

esraj /ɛˈsrɑːʤ/ *noun* E20 Bengali (*esrāj*). A three- or four-stringed Indian musical instrument with added sympathetic strings.

esse /ˈɛsi/ *noun* M16 Latin (use as noun of *esse* to be). Essential nature, essence, especially as opposed to BENE ESSE.

estacade /ɛstakad/ *noun* plural pronounced same E17 French (from Spanish *estacada*, from *estaca*, from Proto-Romance, from Germanic base of *stake*). A dyke made of piles or stakes in water or marshy ground in order to impede an enemy.

estaminet /ɛstaminɛ/ *noun* plural **estaminets** pronounced same E19 French (from Walloon *staminé* byre, from *stamo* pole to which a cow is tethered in a stall, probably from German *Stamm* stem, trunk). Originally, a café where smoking was allowed. Now, a small unpretentious café selling wine, beer, etc.

estancia /ɛˈstansɪə/, *foreign* /eˈstanθia/, /eˈstansia/ *noun* M17 Spanish (literally, 'station' = Old French *estance* dwelling, from medieval Latin *stantia*, from Latin *stant-* present participial stem of *stare* to stand). A cattle-ranch in Latin America or the southern United States.
1996 *Oldie* In the pampas cattle and sheep farmers made their fortunes on huge estancias.

estocada /estoˈkada/, /ɛstəˈkɑːdə/ *noun* E20 Spanish (from *estoque* sword (from Old and Modern French *estoc*) short sword for thrusting + *-ada*). *Bullfighting* The sword-thrust that finally kills the bull.

estouffade /ɛstufad/ *noun* plural pronounced same L19 French (from Italian *stuf(f)ata* past participle of *stufare* to stew, from *stufa* stove, from popular Latin, ultimately from Greek *tuphos* smoke). (A dish of) meat cooked very slowly in its own vapour.

estrade /ɛˈstrɑːd/ *noun* L17 French (from Spanish *estrado*, from Latin STRATUM, literally, 'something spread or laid down', neuter past participle of *sternere* to throw down). Originally, a slightly raised platform or dais for persons of rank to sit or recline on. Later, any dais.
■ The Spanish equivalent *strado* was an earlier introduction into English (L16) than *estrade* and was used with the same two senses, but is now rare.

estrog variant of ETROG.

estrus variant of OESTRUS.

estufa /e'stufa/ noun M19 Spanish (corresponding to Old French *estuve* (modern *étuve*)). **1** M19 An underground chamber in which a fire is kept permanently alight, used as a place of assembly by the Pueblo Indians. **2** L19 A heated chamber in which Madeira is stored and matured.

et /ɛt/ conjunction ME Latin. And.

■ In Modern English only in medieval and Modern Latin phrases; see ET AL., ET CETERA, etc.

eta /'iːtə/ noun LME Greek (*ēta*). **1** LME The seventh letter (H, η) of the Greek alphabet. **2** Frequently written (η). **a** L18 *attributive Astronomy* (Preceding the genitive of the Latin name of the constellation) denoting the seventh brightest star in a constellation. **b** M20 *Physics* A meson with zero isospin and spin and a mass of 549 MeV. In full *eta meson*.

etagere /ɛtə'ʒɛː/ noun (also **étagère**) plural pronounced same M19 French (*étagère*, from *étage* shelf, stage). A piece of furniture with a number of open shelves on which to display ornaments etc.

et al. /ɛt al/ adverb phrase 1 L19 Latin (*et* and + abbreviation of *alii, aliae, alia* masculine, feminine, and neuter plural of *alius* other). And others.

■ Often used in bibliographies in cases of works by several authors; the formula 'Smith et al.' avoids having to list all the authors' names in full.
1996 *Spectator* [There] is a long succession of recreated theatrical 'flats' . . . with original costumes and astonishingly flamboyant designs by Bakst, Benois, Goncharova *et al.*

et al. /ɛt al/ adverb phrase 2 Latin (*et* and + abbreviation of ALIBI elsewhere). And elsewhere.

étalage /etalaʒ/ noun plural pronounced same E20 French (from *étaler* to display). A display, a show.

etamine /'ɛtəmiːn/ noun (also **étamine**) E18 French (*étamine*). A lightweight open-weave fabric of coarse yarn, now usually cotton or worsted.

étang /etɑ̃/ noun plural pronounced same M19 French (from Old French *estanc*, ultimately from base of *stanch*, origin unknown). A shallow pool or small lake, *especially* one resulting from the blocking of streams by sand-dunes along the French Mediterranean coast.

etatism /e'tɑːtɪz(ə)m/ noun (also **étatisme** /etatism/) E20 French (*étatisme*, from *état* state). The extreme authority of the State over the individual citizen.

et cetera /ɛt'sɛt(ə)rə/, /ɪt'sɛt(ə)rə/ adverb, noun, & verb (also **etcetera, et caetera**) ME Latin (from *et* and + *cetera* the rest, neuter plural of *ceterus* remaining over). **A** adverb ME And the rest; and similar things; and so on; and the customary continuation. Also reduplicated. **B** noun **1** L16 (An instance of) the adverb *et cetera*. **2** L16 Something not mentioned explicitly for reasons of propriety. Formerly *specifically* (in *plural*) trousers. **3** M17 A number of unspecified things or persons. **4** (In *plural.*) (The usual) additions, extras, sundries. **C** verb M19 Replacing a suppressed verb.

■ Often abbreviated to *etc* or *&c*.

ethos /'iːθɒs/ noun M19 Greek (*ēthos* nature, disposition). The characteristic spirit of a culture, era, community, institution, etc., as manifested in its attitudes, aspirations, customs, etc.; the character of an individual as represented by his or her values and beliefs; the prevalent tone of a literary work in this respect.
1996 *Country Life: Garden Year* . . . we open six days a week from spring to autumn. This means that the public are very much a part of the ethos in which we live and work.

ethrog variant of ETROG.

etiquette /'ɛtɪkɛt/, /ɛtɪ'kɛt/ noun M18 French (*étiquette* label, etiquette). The conventional rules of personal behaviour in polite society; the prescribed ceremonial of a court; the formalities required in diplomatic intercourse; the order of procedure established by custom in the armed services, Parliament, etc.; the unwritten code restricting professional persons in what concerns the interests of their colleagues or the dignity of their profession.

■ Also formerly (M19) in the primary French sense of 'a label, ticket', but this is rare in English. The sense of 'a rule of etiquette', 'an observance prescribed by etiquette' was also briefly (L18–E19) current in English, generally in the plural. From the word's history in French it is not entirely clear how the transition between between the primary and secondary senses was effected, although the English colloquial expressions 'just the ticket' and 'not quite the ticket' (*ticket* here meaning 'the accepted (or needed) thing') suggest how it could have come about. Modern Romance languages have adapted the word from

French in the secondary sense: Italian *etichetta*, Spanish *etiqueta*.

étourderie /eturdəri/ *noun* M18 French (from next). Thoughtlessness, carelessness; a thoughtless act, a blunder.
> **1958** I. Murdoch *Bell* His love affairs appeared as the *étourderies* of a much younger man.

étourdi /eturdi/ *adjective & noun* (feminine **étourdie**) plural pronounced same L17 French (past participial adjective of *étourdir* to stun, make dizzy). (A person who is) thoughtless or irresponsible.

étrenne /etrɛn/ *noun* plural pronounced same E19 French (from Old French *estreine* ultimately from Latin *strena*). A New Year's gift; a Christmas-box.

étrier /'eɪtrɪə/, *foreign* /etrije/ (*plural same*) *noun* (also **étrier**) M20 French (*étrier* stirrup, etrier). *singular* and in *plural*. A short rope ladder with a few solid rungs, used by climbers.

etrog /'ɛtrɒg/ *noun* (also **ethrog**, **estrog** /'ɛstrɒg/) plural **etrogs**, **etrogim** /'ɛtrɒgɪm/ L19 Hebrew ('eṯrōḡ). A citron fruit as used ritually in the Jewish Feast of Tabernacles.

et seq. /ɛt sɛk/ *noun phrase* plural **et seqq.** (pronounced same) L19 Latin (*et* and + present participle of *sequi* to follow; abbreviation of *et sequentes* (Latin masculine and feminine plural of *sequens*) and *et sequentia* (neuter plural of *sequens*)). And following.

Et tu, Brute /ɛt 'tuː ˌbruːteɪ/ *interjection* L16 Latin (= and you, Brutus). (An expression of) reproach to a friend who has betrayed one's trust and gone over to the enemy.
> ■ The words spoken by Caesar in Shakespeare's *Julius Caesar* (III.i) when he sees his friend Brutus amongst his assassins. Another name is sometimes jocularly substituted for that of Brutus (see quotation 1995(2)).
> **1995** *Times* The cry *Et tu, Brute?* has been the death rattle of many a fallen king.
> **1995** *Times* The penalty shoot-out, the Boland decision, and all such pack-'em-in modifications to a sport . . . betray competition for fun. Each one is a betrayal: a knife in the heart of sport. *Et tu*, Illingworth?

étude /'eɪtjuːd/, /eɪ'tjuːd/, *foreign* /etyd/ (*plural same*) *noun* M19 French (= study). An instrumental piece, especially for the piano, which concentrates on a particular aspect of technique or allows a display of virtuosity.

etui /ɛ'twiː/ *noun* (also **etwee**) E17 French (*étui*, Old French *estui* prison, from Old French *estuier* to shut up, keep, save). A small usually ornamental case for needles etc. Formerly also, a case for surgical instruments.

euchre /'juːkə/ *noun & verb* E19 German (dialect *Jucker(spiel)*). **A** *noun* **1** E19 A card-game for two to four players in which the highest cards are the joker (if used), the jack of trumps, and the other jack of the same colour in a pack with the lower cards removed, the aim being to win at least three of the five tricks played. **2** M19 An instance of euchring or being euchred. **B** *transitive verb* **1** E19 Prevent (a bidder) from winning three or more tricks at euchre, thereby scoring points oneself. **2** M19 Cheat, trick, (*into*, *out of*); deceive, outwit. **3** M20 Exhaust; ruin, finish, do for, (a person). Usually in passive. *Australian*.

eudaimonia /ˌjuːdaɪ'mɒnɪə/ *noun* E20 Greek (from as *eudemon* from as *eu-* good + *daimōn* genius). *Philosophy* Happiness or well-being consisting in the full realization of human potential, *especially* (in Aristotle's ethics) in rational activity exhibiting excellence.

eunomia /juː'nəʊmɪə/ *noun* M19 Greek (from as *eu-* good + *-nomia* state of law). A political condition of good law well administered.

eupepsia /juː'pɛpsɪə/ *noun* E18 Greek (*eupepsia* digestibility, from *eupeptos*, from *eu-* good + *peptein* to digest). Good digestion; absence of indigestion.

euphoria /juː'fɔːrɪə/ *noun* /'juːf(ə)rɪ/ L17 Modern Latin (from Greek, from *euphoros* borne well, healthy, from as *eu-* good + *pherein* to bear). Originally, a state of well-being, especially as produced in a sick person by a medicine. Now, a strong feeling of well-being, cheerfulness, and optimism, *especially* one based on overconfidence or overoptimism; a mood marked by this, as symptomatic of a mental illness or the influence of drugs.
> **1996** *Spectator* After a while one feels a terrific euphoria, and, looking for more, one switches to whiskey or vodka.

eureka /jʊ(ə)'riːkə/ *interjection & noun* (also **Eureka**) E17 Greek (*heurēka*, 1st person singular perfect of *heuriskein* to find). **A** *interjection* E17 Expressive of exultation at a sudden discovery. **B** *noun* **1** M17 A cry of *eureka!* **2** M19 A fortunate discovery. **3** E20 (**Eureka**) (Proprietary name for) an alloy of copper and nickel used for electrical filament and resistance wire.

■ The exclamation supposedly uttered by the Sicilian Greek philosopher Archimedes (c.287–c.212 BC) when he hit upon a method of determining the purity of gold, an inspiration which, according to tradition, occurred to him as he was taking a bath.

euthanasia /juːθəˈneɪzɪə/ *noun* E17 **Greek** (from as *eu-* good + *thanatos* death). **1** E17 A gentle and easy death. **2** M18 A means of bringing about such a death (chiefly *in figurative use*, *of* something). **3** M19 The action of bringing about such a death, especially of a person who requests it as a release from incurable disease.

événement /evenmɑ̃/ *noun* plural pronounced same M20 **French** (= event, happening). Politically motivated civil disorder involving mass demonstrations.

■ Usually plural. The word became current in English with reference to the French strikes and student riots of 1968 and received a further boost from the wave of strikes and demonstrations in France in 1995, though it is no longer necessarily confined to the French political scene (see quotation 1995(2)).
1995 *Times* The French media are full of comparisons with the *événements* of 1968, when students and workers suddenly took to the streets for no very obvious reason.
1995 *Spectator* The next few months will show whether the Ilidza *événements* join the heady days of Belgrade 1941 in the annals of Serb defiance.

évolué /evɔlɥe/ *noun & adjective* plural of noun pronounced same M20 **French** (past participle of *évoluer* to evolve). (Characteristic of or designating) an African who has had a European education or has adopted European ways or attitudes.

Ewigkeit /ˈeːvɪçkaɪt/, /ˈeɪvɪɡkʌɪt/ *noun* (also **ewigkeit**) L19 **German**. Eternity; infinity.

ex /ɛks/ *noun & adjective* plural **exes**, **ex's** /ˈɛksɪz/ E19 **Latin** (from prefix *ex-* former(ly)). **A** *noun* E19 A person who formerly held a position etc. denoted by the context; *specifically*, a former husband or wife. **B** *adjective* E19 Former; outdated.

ex /ɛks/ *preposition* M19 **Latin** (= out of). **1** *Commerce* M19 Of stocks and shares: without, excluding. **2** Of goods: (sold) direct from (a ship, warehouse, etc.) **3** L19 Of an animal: out of (a specified dam).

exacta /ɪɡˈzaktə/, /ɛɡˈzaktə/ *noun* M20 **American Spanish** (*quiniela exacta* exact qui-

nella). *Betting* In North America: a PERFECTA.

exalté /ɛɡzalte/ *adjective & noun* (feminine **exaltée**) plural of noun pronounced same M19 **French** (past participial adjective of *exalter* to exalt, from as *ex-* up(wards) + *altus* high). (A person who is) elated or impassioned.

ex animo /ɛks ˈanɪməʊ/ *adverb phrase* E17 **Latin** (= from the soul, from as *ex* (preposition) + *animo* ablative of *animus* soul). Heartily, sincerely.

ex ante /ɛks ˈanti/ *adjective & adverb phrase* M20 **Modern Latin** (from as *ex* (preposition) + *ante* before). Chiefly *Economics* **A** *adjective phrase* M20 Based on prior assumptions or expectations; predicted, prospective. **B** *adverb phrase* M20 Before the event, in advance, beforehand.

■ The opposite of EX POST.
B 1992 *New York Review of Books Ex ante,* the thing looks dubious. *Ex post* it is, disconcertingly, a surprising success . . .

ex cathedra /ɛks kəˈθiːdrə/, /ɛks ˈkaθɪdrə/ *adverb & adjective* E17 **Latin** (= from the (teacher's) chair, from *ex* (preposition) + *cathedra* chair). **A** *adverb* E17 Authoritatively; as an official pronouncement; *especially* (*Roman Catholic Church*) with the full weight of the Pope's office as divinely appointed guardian of Christian faith and morals. **B** *adjective* E19 Authoritative, official; given *ex cathedra*; dogmatic.

B 1996 *New Scientist* Something of a pattern emerges about deception that will reassure the ex cathedra theoreticians.

excelsior /ɛkˈsɛlsɪɔː/ *interjection & noun* (also **Excelsior**) L18 **Latin** (comparative of *excelsus* from *ex-* + *celsus* lofty). **A** L18 *interjection* Go higher! **B** *noun* **1** M19 Curled shavings of soft wood for stuffing, packing, etc. Originally *United States*. **2** L19 A person who or thing which reaches or aspires to reach higher. **3** E20 A very small size (3 points) of type. Chiefly *United States*.

exceptis excipiendis /ɛkˌsɛptɪs ɛkˌsɪpɪ ˈɛndɪs/ *adverb phrase* L19 **Late Latin** (from ablative plural of Latin *exceptus* past participle, and of *excipiendus* gerundive, of *excipere* to except). With appropriate exceptions.

excreta /ɪkˈskriːtə/, /ɛkˈskriːtə/ *noun plural* M19 **Latin** (use as noun of neuter plural of *excretus* past participle of *excernere* to excrete). Waste matter discharged from the body; *especially* faeces, urine.

excursus /ɪkˈskəːsəs/, /ɛkˈskəːsəs/ *noun* plural **excursuses**, **excursus** /ɪk ˈskəːsuːs/ E19 **Latin** (= excursion, from *excurs-* past participial stem of *excurrere* to run out). **1** E19 A fuller treatment in an appendix of some point in the main text of a book, especially an edition of the classics. **2** M19 A digression within a narrative in which some point is discussed at length.

exeat /ˈɛksɪat/ *noun* E18 **Latin** (= let him or her go out, 3rd person singular present subjunctive of *exire* to go out). **1** E18 A permission for temporary absence from a college or other institution. **2** M18 A permission granted by a bishop to a priest to move to another diocese.

   1 1984 A. Brookner *Hotel du Lac* The tall thin beauty with the dog was never visible in the daytime and it was impossible to imagine her doing anything except eating ice cream and smoking, like a child on an exeat from school.

exedra /ˈɛksɪdrə/, /ɪkˈsiːdrə/, /ɛkˈsɪdrə/ *noun* (also **exhedra** /ˈɛkshɪdrə/, /ɪks ˈhiːdrə/, /ɛksˈhɪdrə/) plural **exedrae** /ˈɛksɪdriː/ E18 **Latin** (from Greek, from *ex-* + *hedra* seat). **1** E18 *Classical History* A hall or arcade with seats, attached to a palaestra or a private house and used for conversation. **b** M19 *generally* An apse, a recess, a large niche. **2** E18 A CATHEDRA.

exegesis /ɛksɪˈdʒiːsɪs/ *noun* plural **exegeses** /ɛksɪˈdʒiːsiːz/ E17 **Greek** (*exēgēsis*, from *exēgeisthai* to interpret). (An) exposition, especially of Scripture; an explanatory note or discourse.

   1996 *Spectator* And his films resist the easy exegesis of critics . . .

exempla plural of EXEMPLUM.

exempli gratia /ɪgˌzɛmpli ˈɡreɪʃə/, /ɛg ˌzɛmpli/ *adverb phrase* M17 **Latin** (from genitive of *exemplum* example + ablative of *gratia* grace). For example; for instance.

   ■ Abbreviated to *e.g. Exempli gratia* and its ubiquitous abbreviation have entirely superseded *exempli causa* (literally, 'by reason of example'), although the latter was the earlier (M16) in English.

exemplum /ɪgˈzɛmpləm/, /ɛgˈzɛmpləm/ *noun* plural **exempla** /ɪgˈzɛmplə/ L19 **Latin**. An example; *especially* an illustrative or moralizing story.

exequatur /ɛksɪˈkweɪtə/ *noun* E17 **Latin** (= let him or her perform, 3rd person singular present subjunctive of *exequi* to carry out, execute). **1** E17 *Roman Catholic Church* A government's authorization for a bishop to exercise his office in its territory, or for any papal enactment to take effect there; a claim by a government that such authorization is required or can be withheld. **2** L18 An official recognition of a consul by a foreign government, authorizing him or her to exercise office.

exergue /ɪkˈsəːɡ/, /ɛkˈsəːɡ/, /ˈɛksəːɡ/ *noun* L17 **French** (from medieval Latin *exergum*, from Greek *ex-* + *ergon* work). *Numismatics* A small space on a coin or medal, usually on the reverse below the principal device, for the date, the engraver's initials, etc.; the inscription placed there.

exeunt /ˈɛksɪʌnt/ *verb & noun* L15 **Latin** (3rd person plural present indicative of *exire* to go out). **A** *intransitive verb* (*defective*) (A stage direction:) (actors, or the characters whose names follow) leave the stage. Cf. EXIT. **B** A collective exit; a departure by more than one person.

   ■ Also in the phrase *exeunt omnes* 'all leave the stage' at the end of a scene or play.

   B 1996 *Times* Usually when the critics slink off to the pub during the last act, their excuse to the paying customers they are forcing to stand up for their exeunt is that they have to catch the early editions.

ex gratia /ɛks ˈɡreɪʃə/ *adverb & adjective phrase* M18 **Latin** (from *ex* from + *gratia* grace). (Done, given, etc.) as a favour or without (especially legal) compulsion.

   1996 *New Scientist* We can only ask that the government provide ex gratia payments to all affected.

exhedra variant of EXEDRA.

ex hypothesi /ˌɛks hʌɪˈpɒθəsʌɪ/ *adverb phrase* E17 **Modern Latin** (from Latin *ex* by + ablative of late Latin HYPOTHESIS). According to the hypothesis (made); supposedly.

exigeant /ɛɡziʒɑ̃/ *adjective* (feminine **exigeante** /ɛɡziʒɑ̃t/) L18 **French** (present participial adjective of *exiger* from Latin *exigere* to exact). Exacting, demanding.

exit /ˈɛksɪt/, /ˈɛɡzɪt/ *noun* L16 **Latin** (*exitus*; cf. EXIT (verb 1)). **1** L16 A departure of an actor etc. from the stage during a scene; *figurative* a person's death. **2** M17 *generally* A departure from any place or situation. Also, freedom or opportunity to depart. **3** L17 A means of egress, especially from a public building; an outlet, a way out. **b** M20 A place where traffic can leave a motorway etc.; a slip-road provided at such a place. **4** M20 *Cards* (especially *Bridge*) The action of deliberately losing the lead; a card enabling one to do this.

exit /'ɛksɪt/, /'ɛgzɪt/ *verb* 1 (*intransitive*) *defective* M16 **Latin** (3rd person singular present indicative of *exire* to go out, from as *ex-* out + *ire* to go). (A stage direction:) (the last speaker, or the character whose name follows) leaves the stage. Cf. EXEUNT.

exit /'ɛksɪt/, /'ɛgzɪt/ *verb* 2 E17 **Latin** (from EXIT (noun)). **1** *intransitive verb* E17 Make one's exit or departure, especially from a stage; leave any place; *figurative* die. **2** *intransitive verb* M20 *Cards* (especially *Bridge*). Lose the lead deliberately. **3** *transitive verb* L20 Leave, get out of.

ex-libris /ɛks'lɪbrɪs/, /ɛks'li:brɪs/, /ɛks 'laɪbrɪs/, /ɛks'li:bri:s/ *noun plural same* L19 **Latin** (literally, 'out of the books *or* library (of —)'). An inscription, label, etc., indicating the owner of a book; *especially* a bookplate.

ex machina see DEUS EX MACHINA.

ex nihilo /ɛks 'ni:hɪləʊ/, /'nʌɪhɪləʊ/ *adverb phrase* L16 **Latin**. Out of nothing.

> **1996** *New Scientist* Atheists are equally alarmed, because the notion of the Universe coming into being from nothing looks suspiciously like the creation, *ex nihilo*, of Christianity.

exodus /'ɛksədəs/ *noun* OE **ecclesiastical Latin** (*Exodus* from Greek *exodos*, from as *ex-* out + *hodos* way). **1** OE (*Exodus*) (The name of) the second book of the Bible, relating the release of the Israelites from their bondage in Egypt and their journey to Canaan. **2** E17 A departure, usually of many people; an emigration; *specifically* the departure of the Israelites from Egypt.

ex officio /,ɛks ə'fɪʃɪəʊ/ *adverb, adjective, & noun* M16 **Latin** (from *officium* duty, office). **A** *adverb* & (usually with hyphen) *adjective* M16 (That is such) by virtue of one's office. **B** *noun* E19 A person serving ex officio.

exordium /ɪg'zɔ:dɪəm/, /ɛg'zɔ:dɪəm/ *noun plural* **exordiums, exordia** /ɪg'zɔ:dɪə/ L16 **Latin** (from *exordiri* to begin). The beginning of anything; *especially* the introductory part of a discourse or treatise.

exotica /ɪg'zɒtɪkə/, /ɛg'zɒtɪkə/ *noun plural* L19 **Latin** (neuter plural of *exoticus* exotic). Exotic things.

> **1995** *Country Life* This year's hot summer is not principally responsible for the increase in insect life . . . The exotica survived because of the mildness of the winter.

ex parte /ɛks 'pɑ:tɪ/ *adverb & adjective phrase* (as adjective frequently **ex-parte**) E17 **Latin** (= from a *or* the side). **A** *adverb phrase* **1** E17 Originally, on the part of. Now (*Law*), on behalf of. **2** L17 *Law* On behalf of or with reference to only one of the parties concerned (and without notice to the adverse party). **B** *adjective phrase* **1** L18 *Law* Of an application, injunction, deposition, etc.: made, issued, etc., by or for only one party in a case. **2** E19 Of a statement etc.: one-sided, partial.

ex pede Herculem /ɛks ˌpɛdi 'hə:kjʊlɛm/ *adverb phrase* M17 **Latin** (= Hercules from his foot). Inferring the whole of something from an insignificant part.

> ■ The ancient Greek mathematician Pythagoras is supposed to have calculated the height of the hero Hercules from the size of his foot.

experimentum crucis /ɪkˌspɛrɪmɛntəm 'kru:sɪs/, /ɛkˌspɛrɪmɛntəm 'kru:kɪs/, *noun phrase* M17 **Modern Latin** (= crucial experiment). A decisive test showing which of several hypotheses is correct.

explication de texte /ɛksplikasjɔ̃ də tɛkst/ *noun phrase plural* **explications de texte** (pronounced same) M20 **French**. A detailed textual examination of a literary work; the making of such examinations.

explicit /'ɛksplɪsɪt/ *noun* M17 **Late Latin** (either = here ends, 3rd person singular indicative of *explicare* to unfold (plural *expliciunt*); or abbreviation of *explicitus est liber* = the book is finished). The end; the conclusion.

> ■ Originally used by medieval scribes to denote the end of a Latin manuscript or work, *explicit* was sometimes also placed (ME–M19) at the end of a printed book, chapter, etc.

exposé /ɪk'spəʊzeɪ/, /ɛk'spəʊzeɪ/, *foreign* /ɛkspoze/ (*plural same*) *noun* (also **expose**) E19 **French** (past participle of *exposer* to set out, display). **1** E19 An orderly statement of facts. **2** E19 A showing up or revelation of something discreditable.

> **2 1996** *Spectator* . . . his relentless research has produced something much more than an exposé of a single rogue . . .

ex post /ɛks 'pəʊst/ *adjective & adverb phrase* M20 **Modern Latin** (from as preposition *ex* + Latin *post* after). Chiefly *Economics*. **A** *adjective phrase* M20 Based on past events or actual results; occurring afterwards; actual rather than predicted; retrospective. **B** *adverb phrase* M20 After the event; retrospectively.

■ The opposite of EX ANTE (see quotation at *ex ante*).

ex post facto /ˌɛks pəʊst ˈfaktəʊ/ *adverb & adjective phrase* M17 Latin (erroneous division of Latin *ex postfacto* in the light of subsequent events, from *ex* from, out of + ablative of *postfactum* that which is done subsequently). **A** *adverb phrase* M17 After the event, after the fact; retrospectively. **B** *adjective phrase* L18 Done after another thing; *especially* (of a law) applied retrospectively.

expresso variant of ESPRESSO.

ex professo /ɛks prəˈfɛsəʊ/ *adverb phrase* L16 Latin (from as preposition *ex* + ablative of *professus* use as noun of past participial stem of *profiteri* to declare). By profession; professedly.

ex proprio motu /ɛks ˌprəʊprɪəʊ ˈməʊtuː/, /ˌprɒprɪəʊ/ *adverb phrase* L17 Late Latin (= by own motion). MOTU PROPRIO; *specifically* in *Law*, by decision of a court without anyone's application.

ex relatione /ɛks rɪˌleɪʃɪˈəʊni/ *prepositional phrase* E17 Latin. *Law* By relation of; according to the report of, as reported by.

ex silentio /ɛks sɪˈlɛntɪəʊ/, /ɛks sɪˈlɛnʃɪəʊ/ *adverb phrase* E20 Latin (= from silence). By or from a lack of evidence to the contrary.

extempore /ɪkˈstɛmp(ə)ri/, /ɛk ˈstɛmp(ə)ri/ *adverb, noun, & adjective* M16 Latin (*ex tempore* on the spur of the moment, from as preposition *ex* + *tempore* ablative of *tempus* time). **A** *adverb* **1** M16 Without premeditation or preparation; impromptu. (Now chiefly of speaking or of performing music.) **2** L16–M17 At once, immediately. **B** *noun* L16–E19 An unprepared improvised speech, composition, or performance. **C** *adjective* **1** E17 Of a speech, musical performance, etc.: spoken or done without preparation, especially without written notes. Of a speaker or performer: performing without preparation. **2** M17 Occasional; sudden, unprepared for. (Now only of personal actions,

with some notion of sense 1.) **3** L17 Makeshift, contrived for the occasion.

extra dictionem /ˌɛkstrə dɪktɪˈəʊnɛm/ *adverb phrase* E19 Latin (translation of Greek *exō tēs lexeōs* outside the wording). Of a logical fallacy: not arising from the wording used to express it.

■ A subdivision of logical fallacy noted by Aristotle in his *Sophistici Elenchi* (ch. 4); it is sometimes also called in Latin *in re* in the matter. Opposed to IN DICTIONE.

extrados /ɪksˈtreɪdɒs/, /ˈɛksˈtreɪdɒs/ *noun* L18 French (from Latin *extra* outside + French *dos* back). *Architecture* The upper or outer curve of an arch; *especially* the upper curve of the voussoirs which form the arch. Cf. INTRADOS.

extraordinaire /ɪkˌstrɔːdɪˈnɛː/, /ˌɛkˌstrɔːdɪ ˈnɛː/, *foreign* /ɛkstraɔrdinɛr/ *postpositive adjective* M20 French. Remarkable, outstanding; (of a person) unusually active or successful in a specified respect.
1996 *Times* This brings up the unfortunate truth that Roger Daltry, trout-farmer extraordinaire, is cooler than Cobain . . .

exuviae /ɪgˈzjuːviː/, /ɛgˈzjuːviː/ *noun plural* M17 Latin (= clothing stripped off, skins of animals, spoils, from *exuere* to divest oneself of). Cast skins, shells, or other shed outer parts of animals, whether recent or fossil; *specifically* (*Zoology*) sloughed skins; *figurative* remnants, remains.

ex vivo /ɛks viːvəʊ/ *adjective & adverb phrase* (also **ex-vivo**) L20 Latin. *Biology* (Performed, obtained, or occurring) outside a living organism.
■ Opposed to IN VIVO.
1995 *New Scientist* Most trials, including the ADA treatments, have relied on the 'ex vivo' approach. Scientists take cells from patients, insert the key gene and return the altered cells to the patient.

ex-voto /ɛksˈvəʊtəʊ/ *noun & adjective* plural of noun **ex-votos** L18 Latin (*ex voto* from *ex* out of, from + *voto* ablative singular of *votum* vow). (Designating) something offered in fulfilment of a vow previously taken.

ezan /ɛˈzʌn/ *noun* M18 Persian and Turkish (pronunciation of Arabic *'aḏān*). The Muslim call to prayer; the AZAN.

F

f abbreviation of FORTE (*musical direction*).

fabliau /ˈfablɪəʊ/, /fablijo/ *noun plural* **fabliaux** /ˈfablɪəʊz/, /fablijo/ E19 **French**. *Literature* A verse tale, often burlesque in character, from the early period of French poetry.
■ The word is also used to denote a similar verse tale of sex and trickery in medieval English, particularly the tales of the Miller, Reeve, Summoner, Merchant, and Shipman in Chaucer's *Canterbury Tales*.

façade d'honneur /fasad dɔnœr/ *noun phrase plural* **façades d'honneur** (pronounced same) M20 **French**. *Architecture* The principal front of a building, esp. of a large formal building.

facetiae /fəˈsiːʃɪiː/ *noun plural* E16 **Latin** (plural of *facetia* jest). **1** E16 Witticisms; humorous sayings. **2** M19 *Bookselling* Pornography.

Fach /fax/ *noun* (also **fach**) M19 **German** (= compartment, division, shelf). A line of business or work; a department of activity.

facia variant of FASCIA senses 4, 5.

faciendum /fakɪˈɛndəm/, /feɪʃɪˈɛndəm/ *noun plural* **facienda** /fakɪˈɛndə/, /feɪʃɪˈɛndə/ M19 **Latin** (= thing to be done, neuter gerundive of *facere* to make, do). *Philosophy* A thing that should be done.

facies /ˈfeɪʃɪiːz/ *noun plural same* E17 **Latin** (= face). **1** L19 *Medicine* The appearance of the face, esp. when characteristic of a particular illness. **2** E18 *Science* A general aspect, appearance, or character. **b** M19 *Geology* The character of a rock formation. **c** E20 *Ecology* The characteristic set of species in a habitat.

facile princeps /ˌfasɪlɪ ˈprɪnsɛps/ *adjective & noun phrase* M19 **Latin** (= easily first). (A person who is) easily first; the acknowledged chief or leader.

facilis descensus Averni /ˌfasɪlɪs deɪˌsɛnsəs aˈvəːnʌɪ/ *noun phrase* E17 **Latin** (= easy (is) the descent to Avernus). The descent to hell is easy.
■ A quotation from Virgil's *Aeneid* (vi.126); Avernus was the name of a deep lake near Puteoli in Italy, reputed to be one of the entrances to the underworld. The subsequent lines state that the difficulty lies in retracing one's steps to the upper air; hence *facilis descensus Averni* is a metaphor for the ease with which one can slide into bad ways, with the implication that it is very hard to recover. The phrase is sometimes abbreviated to simply *facilis descensus*.

façon de parler /fasɔ̃ də parle/ *noun phrase plural* **façons de parler** (pronounced same) E19 **French** (= way of speaking). A manner of speaking; a mere phrase or formula.

façon de Venise /fasɔ̃ də vəniz/ *adjective & noun phrase* L20 **French** (= manner of Venice). (Designating) glassware made according to the technically demanding method and decorative style developed first at Venice during the later Middle Ages.

façonné /fasɔne/ *adjective & noun* (also **faconne**) plural of noun pronounced same L19 **French** (past participial adjective of *façonner* to fashion). (Designating) a fabric into which a design has been woven.

façons de parler plural of FAÇON DE PARLER.

factotum /fakˈtəʊtəm/ *noun* M16 **Medieval Latin** (from *fac* imperative of *facere* to do, make + *totum* the whole). A person who does all kinds of work; a servant or other employee who manages all the employer's affairs.
■ Originally in the now obsolete phrases *dominus factotum* or *magister factotum* (Latin = master) or *Johannes factotum* (Latin = John), now most often in the phrase *general factotum*.

fado /ˈfadu:/, /ˈfɑːdəʊ/ *noun plural* **fados** /ˈfadu:ʃ/, /ˈfɑːdəʊz/ E20 **Portuguese** (literally, 'fate'). A type of popular, frequently melancholy Portuguese song and dance, with a guitar accompaniment.

faena /faˈena/ *noun* E20 **Spanish** (literally, 'task'). *Bullfighting* A series of passes made by a matador with cape and sword, preparatory to the kill.

faenza /fɑːˈɛntsə/ *noun* (also **Faenza**) M19 **Italian** (*Faenza*, city in the northern Italian province of Emilia-Romagna). (Designating) the type of decorated, tin-glazed pottery made in Faenza, especially between *c.*1450 and 1520. See also FAÏENCE.

fagotto /faˈɡɔtto/, /fəˈɡɒtəʊ/ *noun* plural **fagotti** /faˈɡɔtti/, **fagottos** /fəˈɡɒtəʊz/ E18 Italian. A bassoon.

> **1982** G. Jacob *Orchestral Technique* This instrument is usually designated in scores by the abbreviation Fag., its Italian name being Fagotto.

faïence /fʌɪˈɒ̃s/, /feɪˈɒ̃s/, /fʌɪˈɑːns/ *noun & adjective* (also **faience, fayence**) L17 French (from Faïence, Faenza). Ceramics (Designating) tin-glazed pottery (MAJOLICA), usually with elaborate and colourful painted decoration, of a type originally manufactured at the northern Italian town of Faenza; *generally,* any glazed ceramic. See also FAENZA.

> **1980** J. Baines and J. Málek *Atlas of Ancient Egypt* [caption] Small polychrome faience tiles representing lotus flowers, probably from the temple palace of Ramesses III at Tell el-Yahudiya.

faille /feɪl/ *noun* M19 French. A ribbed silk fabric.

■ When originally introduced (M16) it denoted a kind of head-covering worn by women.

fainéant /ˈfeɪneɑ̃/, *foreign* /fɛneɑ̃/ (*plural of noun same*) *noun & adjective* (also **faineant**) E17 French (from *fait* 3rd person singular of *faire* to do + *néant* nothing). A *noun* E17 A person who does nothing; an idler. B *adjective* E19 Indolent, inactive.

fainéantise /feneɑ̃ˈtiːz/, /ˌfeɪneɪɒˈtiːz/ *noun* (also **faineantise**) E17 French. The state or quality of being a FAINÉANT; inactivity.

■ Also (L19) *fainéantism(e).*

faisandé /fəzɑ̃ˈde/ *adjective* E20 French (past participle of *faisander* hang (game) until it is high). Affected, artificial; piquant, improper.

> **1958** *Observer* He plays the part in a faisandé Cockney accent straight out of Bruce Bairnsfather's Old Bill cartoons.

fait accompli /fɛt akɔ̃ˈpli/, /ˌfeɪt əˈkɒpli/, /ˌfeɪt əˈkɒmpli/ *noun phrase* plural **faits accomplis** (pronounced same) M19 French (= accomplished fact). A thing done and irreversible before those affected know of it.

> **1996** *Spectator* He [sc. Konrad Adenauer] governed . . . by a mixture of persuasion, accusation, *faits accomplis* and pressure.

faits divers /ˌfeɪt diːˈvɛː/ *noun phrase plural* L20 French (literally, 'sundry facts'). Short news items, usually trivial in character.

> **1993** *New Yorker* The month of June, 1993, was a good one for those who scrutinize the *faits divers* for clues to this nation's moral state.

faja /ˈfaxa/ *noun* M19 Spanish (cf. FAJITA). A sash.

fajita /fəˈhiːtə/, *foreign* /faˈxita/ *noun* plural **fajitas** /fəˈhiːtəz/, *foreign* /faˈxitas/ L20 Mexican Spanish (literally, 'little belt'). Cookery A small strip of grilled spiced beef or chicken; *plural* a dish made by rolling such strips of meat in a tortilla with vegetables, grated cheese, and other garnishings, topped with sour cream.

faki /ˈfeɪki/, /ˈfaki/ *noun* L16 Arabic. An expert in Islamic law; in parts of Africa, a teacher in a Koran school.

■ Not to be confused with FAKIR.

fakir /ˈfeɪkɪə/; *in sense 1 also* /ˈfakɪə/ *noun* (also formerly **faquir**) E17 Arabic (= poor (man); partly through French *faquir*). **1** E17 A Muslim (or *loosely* Hindu) religious mendicant or ascetic. **2** L19 A faker. *United States* (by popular etymology).

falafel /fəˈlɑːf(ə)l/ *noun* (also **felafel**) plural same M20 Arabic (colloquial Egyptian). Cookery A small ball of spiced minced pulses, fried and usually eaten in bread.

falsetto /fɔːlˈsɛtəʊ/, /fɒlˈsɛtəʊ/ *noun & adjective* L18 Italian. Music A *noun* L18 A voice pitched above its natural register; also, a person who sings in such a voice. B *attributive* or as *adjective* E19 Above the natural register; high-pitched.

falsobordone /ˌfalsoborˈdoːne/ *noun* (also **falso bordone**) plural **falsobordoni** /ˌfalsoborˈdoːni/ M18 Italian (from *falso* false + *bordone* BOURDON; cf. French FAUXBOURDON). Music A technique of singing psalms in harmony, following simple chord progressions.

famille de robe /famij də rɔb/ *noun phrase* plural **familles de robe** (pronounced same) M19 French (literally, 'family of the robe'). In France: a family with a legal tradition or one founded by a lawyer.

famille jaune /famij ʒɔn/ *noun phrase* L19 French (literally, 'yellow family'). A type of Chinese enamelled porcelain of which the predominant colour is yellow, dating from the eighteenth century.

famille noire /famij nwar/ *noun phrase* L19 French (literally, 'black family'). A type of Chinese enamelled porcelain of which the predominant colour is black, dating from the eighteenth century.

famille rose /famij roz/ *noun phrase* L19 French (literally, 'pink family'). A type of Chinese enamelled porcelain of which the predominant colour is pink, dating from the reign of Yongzheng (1723–35).

famille verte /famij vɛrt/ *noun phrase* L19 French (literally, 'green family'). A type of Chinese enamelled porcelain of which the predominant colour is green, dating from the reign of Kangxi (1662–1722).

famulus /'famjʊləs/ *noun plural* **famuli** /'famjʊlʌɪ/, /'famjʊliː/ L19 Latin (= servant). A servant, especially a youth attendant upon a scholar or magician.

fana /fə'nɑː/ *noun* M19 Arabic (= annihilation). *Islam* In Sufism, the obliteration of all human concerns and of consciousness of self and their replacement by pure consciousness of God.

fandango /fan'daŋgəʊ/ *noun plural* **fandangos** or **fandangoes** M18 Spanish. A lively Spanish dance for two in 3/4 or 6/8 time, usually accompanied by guitars and castanets; a piece of music for this dance.

fanfaronade /ˌfanfarə'neɪd/, /ˌfanfarə'nɑːd/ *noun* (also **fanfaronnade**) M17 French (*fanfaronnade* from *fanfaron* a braggart). Ostentation; arrogant, swaggering talk; bluster.

fantaisiste /ˌfantɛ'ziːst/ *noun* E20 French. A person who indulges in extravagant fancies, especially an artist who creates elaborately fantastic works of art.

fantasia /fan'teɪzɪə/, /ˌfantə'ziːə/ *noun* E18 Italian. A musical or other composition in which form is comparatively unimportant; a piece of music based on a familiar tune or tunes.

fantoccini /ˌfantot'tʃiːni/, /ˌfantə'tʃiːni/ *noun* L18 Italian (plural of *fantoccino*, diminutive of *fantoccio* puppet, from *fante* boy). **1** L18 *plural* Mechanically worked puppets; marionettes. **2** L18 *singular* A marionette show.

faquir variant of FAKIR.

farandole /ˌfar(ə)n'dəʊl/, /'far(ə)ndəʊl/ *noun* M19 French (from modern Provençal *farandoulo*. A lively Provençal communal dance, usually in 6/8 time; a piece of music for this dance.

farce /fɑːs/ *noun* E18 French. *Cookery* Forcemeat, stuffing.

■ In medieval cookbooks the word appears in the form *fars*. It was reintroduced into

English in its modern form in Richard Bradley's *Family Dictionary* (1725), which was a translation of Chomel's *Dictionaire oeconomique*.

farceur /farsœr/ (*plural same*), /fɑː'səː/ *noun* (feminine **farceuse**) plural pronounced same L17 French. **1** L17 A joker or buffoon; someone who is not to be taken seriously. **2** L19 A writer or actor of farces.

2 1996 *Country Life* ... it is more than a little odd for British culture to be represented by a detective writer, an actor-producer, a TV mogul, a violinist and a Whitehall *farceur.*

farci /fɑː'si/ *adjective* M20 French (from *farcir* to stuff. *Cookery* Stuffed; filled with forcemeat.

■ Always used postpositively.

farfalle /'farfɑlle/ *noun plural* L20 Italian (plural of *farfalla* butterfly). Pasta in the form of butterflies.

farfel /'fɑːf(ə)l/ *noun* (also **farfal, ferfel**) plural same or **farfels** L19 Yiddish (*farfal, farfil, ferfel* (*plural*), from Middle High German *varveln* noodles, noodle soup). *Cookery* Ground or granulated noodle dough; in *plural* granules of this.

far niente /ˌfar nɪ'ɛnte/ *noun phrase* E19 Italian (= doing nothing). Idleness; DOLCE FAR NIENTE.

farouche /fə'ruːʃ/ *adjective* M18 French (ultimately from Latin *foras* out-of-doors). Unused to company; sullen, shy, ill at ease.

1996 *Country Life* The farouche and unintentionally dangerous colt . . . has become a biddable, lovable and, when handled firmly, quite gentle creature.

farrago /fə'rɑːgəʊ/, /fə'reɪgəʊ/ *noun plural* **farragos**, (chiefly United States) **farragoes** M17 Latin (= mixed fodder for cattle, hence figurative, a medley). A jumble; a hotchpotch; a confused situation.

1995 *Spectator* Only one man, in this entire farrago, appears to have been corrupt in the word's fullest sense, in that he broke the law for the sake of personal financial gain.

farrash /fə'raʃ/ *noun* (also **ferash**) E17 Persian and Urdu (*farrās* from Arabic = a person who spreads out bedding, carpets, etc.). A servant in some Muslim countries, especially one who performs heavy domestic tasks.

farruca /fə'ruːkə/ *noun* E20 Spanish (feminine of *farruco* Galician or Asturian, from *Farruco* pet form of male forename *Francisco*). A type of flamenco dance.

fartlek /ˈfɑːtlɛk/ *noun* M20 Swedish (from *fart* speed + *lek* play). A method of training used by middle- and long-distance runners, alternating fast and slow work in a run across country.

fasces /ˈfasiːz/ *noun plural* L16 Latin (plural of *fascis* bundle). **1** L16 In ancient Rome, rods tied in a bundle with an axe, carried before the leading magistrates as a symbol of power. **2** E17 (Emblems of) power or authority.

> **2 1996** *Times* And our VIPs are at heart no more eager than the Italians to give up their fasces of authority.

Fasching /ˈfaʃɪŋ/ *noun* E20 German. In southern Germany and Austria: the carnival season extending from Epiphany to Shrove Tuesday; a carnival.

fascia /ˈfaʃɪə/, /ˈfeɪʃɪə/, /ˈfaʃə/ *noun* (also (senses 4, 5) **facia**) plural **fasciae** /ˈfeɪʃɪiː/, **fascias** M16 Latin (= band, fillet, casing of a door, etc.). **1** M16 *Architecture* A horizontal band of wood, brick, etc., esp. as used in an architrave. **2** E18 Any object, or arrangement of objects, that gives the appearance of a stripe or band. **3** L18 *Anatomy* Connective tissue; a thin sheet of this enclosing a muscle or other organ. **4** E20 The board or strip over a shop front on which is written the trader's name and line of business. **5** E20 The instrument panel of a motor vehicle; dashboard.

fata morgana /ˌfɑːtə mɔːˈɡɑːnə/ *noun* E19 Italian (= fairy Morgan (Morgan le Fay)). A kind of mirage often seen in the Strait of Messina between Italy and Sicily, formerly attributed to supernatural agency; an illusion.

> ■ According to the northern European Arthurian legends, Morgan le Fay was the sister of Britain's King Arthur and possessed magical powers. Her legend was taken to Sicily by the Normans when they conquered the island in the eleventh century.

fatwa /ˈfatwɑː/ *noun* (also **Fatwa, fetwa,** or **fatwah**) E17 Arabic. A ruling on a point of Islamic law given by a Muslim religious expert (MUFTI).

> ■ Although it was first used in English in the seventeenth century (in the form *fetfa*), the word came into general currency in the English-language media after February 1989, when Ayatollah Khomeini of Iran issued a *fatwa* condemning the Indian-born British writer Salman Rushdie and his publishers to death on account of Rushdie's novel *The Satanic Verses* (1988), which many

Muslims held to be blasphemous and deeply objectionable in its treatment of the Koran. Because of the circumstances of the *fatwa* on Rushdie, the word is sometimes wrongly thought to mean 'a death sentence'. Since its revitalization in English, *fatwa* has moved far beyond its original Islamic context and is often used figuratively to indicate any strong denunciation (see quotation 1995).

> **1989** *Bookseller* The . . . International Committee . . . have capitalized on the outrage felt at the notorious *fatwa* to drive forward . . . the long-nurtured campaign for total abolition of blasphemy laws in this country.
> **1989** *Independent* This Fatwa . . . was written and signed by the Grand Ayatollah of Shia in Iraq, explaining his position regarding the executions of 16 Kuwaiti Pilgrims . . .
> **1995** *Times* That the bishops should choose to intone on a subject as morally trivial as the lottery is itself indicative of that order of priorities which so often flummoxes the Christian on the Clapham omnibus. *Fatwas* against the lottery reveal once more the confusion.

faubourg /ˈfoʊbʊr/ (*plural same*), /ˈfəʊbʊəɡ/ *noun* L15 French (cf. medieval Latin *falsus burgus* not the city proper). A suburb, especially a suburb of Paris; formerly that part of a town or city lying just outside the walls.

fauna /ˈfɔːnə/ *noun* plural **faunae** /ˈfɔːniː/, **faunas** L18 Modern Latin (application of *Fauna*, an ancient Italian rural goddess, sister of the god *Faunus*, who was equated with the Greek god Pan). **1** *collective singular and in plural* L18 The animals and animal life of a particular area, habitat, or epoch; cf. FLORA. **2** L19 A list of or treatise on these.

faute de mieux /fot də mjø/ *adjective & adverb phrase* M18 French. (Used or done) only for want of a more satisfactory alternative.

> **1995** *Times* The dinner party is dead. Enter, faute de mieux, the age of the supper party.

fauteuil /fotœj/ *noun* plural pronounced same M18 French. An armchair; hence, any seat, especially one in a theatre, resembling an armchair.

fauve /fəʊv/ *noun & adjective* (also **Fauve**) plural pronounced same E20 French (literally, 'wild animal'). **A** *noun* E20 An adherent of fauvism, a style of painting notable for its use of brilliant colour, originating in the early twentieth century with the work of Henri Matisse (1869–1954) and his followers; a fauvist(e). **B** *adjective* M20

Of or pertaining to fauvism(e) or fauvist(e)s.

■ The term was coined by the French art critic Louis Vauxcelles at the Autumn Salon in Paris in 1905, who, seeing a traditional Renaissance-type statue exhibited amidst the works of Matisse and his adherents, exclaimed, 'Donatello au milieu des fauves!' **1984** A. G. Lehmann The European Heritage Matisse, even if called a 'fauve', can convey a wonderful serenity . . .

fauvisme, fauviste see under FAUVE.

faux /fəʊ/ adjective L20 French (= false). Fashion and Interior design Imitation, fake.

■ Also faux- as first element in combinations, as in faux-soul, faux-painted, etc. **1993** W. Self My Idea of Fun I ran the length of the new hallway, with its Wilton carpeting, faux hunting prints and brocaded wallpaper. transferred **1996** Spectator The faux egalitarianism of Gap matches the faux illusion of the age of Clinton.

faux amis /ˌfəʊz ˈæmiː/ noun phrase plural M20 French (literally, 'false friends'). Pairs of words in two different languages (especially French and English) that appear the same but which have entirely different meanings.

■ The term derives from Les Faux Amis ou les Trahisons du vocabulaire anglais, the title of a book with a collection of such terms made in 1928 by M. Koessler and J. Derocquigny. An example is English defiance and French défiance 'distrust'.

faux bonhomme /fo bɔnɔm/ noun phrase (also **faux-bonhomme**) plural **faux bonshommes** /fo bɔ̃zɔm/ E20 French (= false good-natured man). A malicious or devious person who pretends to be openhearted and good-natured.

faux-bourdon /foburdɔ̃/ noun plural pronounced same L19 French (= faburden, literally, 'false hum'). A type of improvised polyphony, popular in England from the fifteenth to the mid sixteenth century.

faux marbre /fo ˈmɑrbrə/ noun phrase L20 French (= false marble). Interior design Fake marble; a finish imitating marble.

faux-naïf /fonaif/, /ˌfəʊnɑˈiːf/ noun & adjective (also **faux-naif**) plural pronounced same M20 French (from faux false + naïf ingenuous). **A** noun M20 A person who pretends to be naive. **B** adjective M20 Of a work of art, self-consciously or meretriciously simple; of a person, self-consciously artless.

1996 Times When she attempts the old, cheerful faux-naïf trick, it doesn't work.

faux pas /fo pa/, /ˌfəʊ ˈpɑː/ noun phrase plural same L17 French (from faux false + pas step). An act that offends against social convention; an indiscreet remark or action; a slip.

1995 Times I never gave formal dinner parties and never liked them with their implications that they were to do with somehow showing off at the same time as being a minefield of faux pas.

favela /faˈvɛla/ noun M20 Portuguese. In Brazil: a shack or shanty.

■ Usually in plural favelas 'a slum'. **1961** G. Mikes Tango In the midst of all this beauty and elegance, you discover the favelas . . . A favela is a wretched, ramshackle, filthy hut run up out of sticks, rotting planks, dirty rags and cardboard, as a rule in less than twenty-four hours.

favelado /ˌfavəˈlɑːdəʊ/ noun M20 Portuguese. A person who lives in a FAVELA. **1961** G. Mikes Tango The favelas have no electricity (unless, as frequently happens, an enterprising favelado manages to tap an electric cable).

fazenda /fəˈzɛndə/ noun E19 Portuguese. In Portugal, Brazil, and Portuguese-speaking countries: a large farm or estate; the homestead belonging to such an estate.

■ The equivalent in Spanish-speaking countries is a HACIENDA.

fazendeiro /ˌfazɛnˈdɛːrəʊ/ noun E19 Portuguese. A person who owns or lives on a FAZENDA.

fec. abbreviation of FECIT.

fecit /ˈfeɪkɪt/ verb & noun 19 Latin (3rd person perfect singular of facere to make). Art (A statement:) he (or she) made (it).

■ Always preceded by a personal name, fecit is found inscribed on works of art. Pinxit 'he (or she) painted (it)' and sculpsit 'he (or she) sculpted (it)' are more specific alternatives. Fecit is sometimes abbreviated to fec.

fedai /fəˈdɑːiː/ noun plural (in sense 1) same, **fedais**; (in sense 2) **fedayeen** /ˌfɛdɑrˈjiːn/ L19 Arabic ((or Persian) = one who sacrifices his life for another, from fada ransom). **1** L19 An assassin belonging to the Muslim Ismaili sect. **2** M20 (in plural) Guerrillas in Arab Muslim countries, especially Arab guerrillas operating against the Israelis.

feijão /feɪˈ(d)ʒãʊ/ noun M19 Portuguese (from Latin phaseolus bean). Any edible bean; especially a variety of haricot bean

(*Phaseolus vulgaris*) used as a staple item of diet in Brazil.

feijoada /feɪˈ(d)ʒwada/, /feɪˈ(d)ʒwadə/ *noun* M20 **Portuguese** (from FEIJÃO). A Brazilian stew made with black beans, pork, and sausage and served with rice.

feis /fɛʃ/, /feɪʃ/ *noun* (in sense 1 also **fes(s)**) plural **feiseanna** /fɛʃənə/ L18 **Irish** (= wedding feast, festival). **1** L18 An assembly of kings and chieftains, formerly believed to be a kind of early Celtic parliament. **2** L19 An Irish or Scottish arts festival, similar to the Welsh EISTEDDFOD.

felafel variant of FALAFEL.

feldgrau /ˈfɛltgraʊ/ *noun & adjective* M20 **German** (= field-grey). (Of) a dark grey; hence, a German soldier in a uniform of this colour.

feldsher /ˈfɛldʃə/ *noun* (also **feldscher**) L19 **Russian** (*fel'dsher* from German *Feldscher* a field surgeon). In Russia and the former USSR: a person with practical training in medicine and surgery, but lacking professional medical qualifications; an assistant to a physician or surgeon; a medical auxiliary.

felix culpa /ˌfiːlɪks ˈkʌlpə/, /ˌfeɪlɪks ˈkʊlpɑː/ *noun phrase* M20 **Latin** (literally, 'happy fault'). *Theology* The Fall of Man through the sin of Adam understood as having the blessed outcome of the redemption of mankind by Jesus Christ; *transferred* any fault or disaster with ultimately beneficial consequences.

■ The phrase is taken from the Exultet, which forms part of the Roman Catholic liturgy for Holy Saturday (Easter Eve).
1987 D. Hall *Seasons at Eagle Pond* And, *felix culpa*, Fall is the most beautiful season—at least in New Hampshire.

fellah /ˈfɛlə/ *noun* plural **fellaheen, fellahin** /ˈfɛləhiːn/, **fellahs** M18 **Arabic** (*fallah* colloquial plural *fallahin* tiller of the soil). A peasant in Egypt and other Arabic-speaking countries.

felo de se /ˌfiːləʊ dɪ ˈsiː/, /ˌfɛləʊ də ˈseɪ/ *noun phrase* plural **felones de se** /fɪˌləʊniːz dɪ ˈsiː/, **felos de se** /ˌfɛləʊz də ˈseɪ/ E17 **(Anglo-)Latin** (literally, 'felon of himself'). **1** E17 A person who commits suicide (formerly in the UK a criminal act) or intentionally brings about his or her own death. **2** L18 Suicide.

felsenmeer /ˈfɛlzənmiːr/ *noun* plural **felsenmeere** /ˈfɛlzənmiːrə/ E20 **German** (literally, 'rock-sea'). *Physical Geography* An expanse of angular, frost-riven rocks

which may develop on level terrain in arctic or alpine climates; a boulder-field.

felucca /fɛˈlʌkə/ *noun* E17 **Italian** (*feluc(c)a* perhaps from an Arabic word via Spanish). A small sailing vessel with lateen sails and oars, formerly widely used in the Mediterranean area and still used on the River Nile.

feme covert /fiːm ˈkʌvət/ *noun phrase* (also **femme couverte**) plural **femes coverts** (pronounced same) M16 **Old French**. *Law* A married woman.

■ The technical spelling is *feme*, but the Modern French *femme* is also found.

feme sole /fiːm ˈsəʊl/ *noun phrase* plural **femes soles** (pronounced same) M16 **Old French**. *Law* An unmarried woman, especially a divorcée; *historical* a married woman who carries on a business in her own right, independently of her husband.

femme couverte see FEME COVERT.

femme de chambre /fam də ˈʃɑːbr/, /ˌfɛm də ˈʃɑːmbrə/ *noun phrase* plural **femmes de chambre** (pronounced same) M18 **French** (literally, 'woman of the (bed-) room'). **1** M18 A lady's maid. **2** E19 A chambermaid.

femme de ménage /fam də menaʒ/, /ˌfɛm də meɪˈnɑːʒ/ *noun phrase* (also **femme de menage**) plural **femmes de ménage** (pronounced same) L19 **French** (literally, 'woman of the household'). A domestic help; a charwoman.

femme de trent ans /fam də trãt ã/ *noun phrase* plural **femmes de trent ans** (pronounced same) **French** (literally, 'a woman of thirty'). A woman who has passed the age at which romantic affairs are easily enjoyed.

■ The phrase alludes to the title of a novel published by Balzac in 1834.

femme du monde /fam dy mɔd/, /ˌfɛm du: ˈmɒnd/ *noun phrase* plural **femmes du monde** (pronounced same) L19 **French**. A woman of the world; a sophisticated woman.

femme fatale /fam fatal/, /ˌfɛm faˈtɑːl/ *noun phrase* plural **femmes fatales** (pronounced same) E20 **French** (literally, 'fatal woman'). A dangerously or irresistibly attractive woman.

1995 *Big Issue* Furthermore, the entrance of the femme fatale—embodied by such cat-like sirens as Lauren Bacall and Barbara Stanwyck—exposed male fears of the newly empowered woman . . .

femme incomprise /fɛm ɛ̃kɔ̃priz/ *noun phrase* plural **femmes incomprises** /fɛmz ɛ̃kɔ̃priz/ M19 French. A woman who is misunderstood or unappreciated.

femme savante /fam savɑ̃t/ *noun phrase* plural **femmes savantes** (pronounced same) L19 French. A learned woman.

■ Usually with an implied derogatory allusion to Molière's play *Les Femmes savantes* (1672).

1995 *Times* If the noble art of painting refused to lower itself to the caricaturist's level, it could simply, and decorously, choose to ignore the phenomenon of the *femme savante*.

fenestella /fɛnɪ'stɛlə/ *noun* LME Latin (diminutive of *fenestra* window). **1** LME *Architecture* A small opening in a wall, especially one in the side of an altar that enables relics inside to be seen. **2** L18 A niche in an interior wall of a church, usually on the south side of the altar and containing the PISCINA.

feng-shui /ˌfɛŋ 'ʃuːi/, /ˌfʌŋ 'ʃuːi/ *noun* L18 Chinese (from *feng* wind + *shui* water). *Chinese Mythology* A system of spirit influences, both benign and malignant, which inhabit the natural features of the landscape; a kind of geomancy for dealing with these spirits, employed particularly when selecting the site for a dwelling or a grave.

ferae naturae /ˌfiəri: nə'tʃuəri:/, /ˌfɛrʌɪ nə 'tʃuərʌɪ/ *predicative & postpositive adjective & noun phrase* M17 Latin (= of wild nature). Chiefly *Law* Undomesticated or wild (animals).

ferash variant of FARRASH.

fer-de-lance /ˌfɛː də 'lɑːns/ *noun* plural **fers-de-lance** (pronounced same), fer-de-lances L19 French (= iron (head) of lance). A highly venomous tropical American pit viper, *Bothrops atrox*.

ferfel variant of FARFEL.

feria /'fiəriə/, /'fɛriə/ *noun* LME Latin (= holiday; in sense 2 through Spanish). **1** LME *Ecclesiastical* A weekday, especially one on which no festival falls. **2** M19 In Spain and Spanish-speaking countries: a fair.

2 1996 *Spectator* . . . live television coverage of the [bull]fights at the major *ferias* has become commonplace.

fermata /fə:'mɑːtə/ *noun* plural **fermatas**, **fermate** /fə:'mɑːteɪ/ L19 Italian. *Music* (A sign indicating) an unspecified prolongation of a note or rest.

ferme ornée see under ORNÉ.

ferronnerie /fɛrɔnri/, /fɛ'rɒnəri/ *noun & adjective* (also **ferronerie**) E20 French (= (wrought) iron work). (Designating) decoration with motifs of arabesques and scrolls as used in wrought iron work.

ferronnière /fɛrɔnjɛr/ (*plural same*), /fɛˌrɒnɪ'ɛː/ *noun* (also **ferronière**) M19 French (literally, 'blacksmith's wife'; a frontlet). A piece of jewellery comprising a decorative chain worn around the head with a pendant on the centre of the forehead; a frontlet.

■ The name derives from Leonardo da Vinci's portrait known as *La Belle Ferronnière*, which shows a woman wearing this sort of ornament.

fest /fɛst/ *noun* (also **Fest**) M19 German (= festival). A special occasion; a celebration, a celebratory gathering.

■ Originally United States, it is chiefly used as the second element in a combination, as in *filmfest*, *gabfest* (a gathering for talk; a conference), *glamfest* (= glamourfest), *songfest*, *talkfest*, etc.

1995 *Times* The elegance of the *ancien régime* is taken further in M Saint Laurent's own office, a glamfest of mirrors, gilt and velvet.

1995 *Times* By dawn the *mediafest* which had been gathering outside Westminster on College Green was already setting up its cameras.

festina lente /fɛs'tiːnə ˌlɛnteɪ/ *interjection & noun phrase* L17 Latin (= make haste slowly (imperative singular of *festinare* to hasten + *lente* slowly)). (An expression) urging caution; more haste, less speed!

■ According to Suetonius (*Life of Augustus Caesar* xxv), the Greek form of this tag was a favourite with Augustus with reference to military operations and the qualities he looked for in a commnader.

1996 *Times* Why so long? Must *festina lente* always be the exchange's watchword?

Festschrift /'fɛs(t)ʃrɪft/ *noun* (also **festschrift**) plural **Festschriften** /'fɛs(t)-ʃrɪftən/, **Festschrifts** E20 German (literally, 'celebration-writing'). A volume of writings collected in honour of a scholar, usually presented to mark an occasion in his or her life.

1994 W. D. Hackmann and A. J. Turner *Learning, Language and Invention* The mere existence of a *festschrift* is evidence of esteem for its recipient as it is for his stature in his profession.

figurative **1995** *Spectator* Charm is an underrated quality in public life, as is humour. Goodman had both, as this week's *festschrift* of Goodman stories has indicated.

feta /ˈfɛtə/ *noun* (also **fetta**) M20 Modern Greek. A white salty ewe's milk cheese originally made in Greece.

> *figurative* **1996** *Economist* He should get on well with New York's big fettas, whom he will entertain in the archdiocese's grand building off Fifth Avenue.

fête /feɪt/, /fɛt/ *noun & verb* (also **fete**) LME French (from Old French *feste*). **A** *noun* **1** LME A festival, a fair. **2** L19 A sale or bazaar, often held out of doors, with the object of raising money for charity. **3** E19 A saint's day, a religious festival. **B** *transitive verb* E17 Entertain (a person) with a fête or feast, make much of (a person); give a fête in honour of.

fête champêtre /fɛt ʃãpɛtr/ *noun phrase* plural **fêtes champêtres** (pronounced same) L18 French (= a rural fête). An outdoor or pastoral entertainment, a rural festival.

> **1996** *Spectator* ... no one before had painted prostitutes instead of goddesses, drunks and urban café scenes in the place of *fêtes champêtres*.

fête galante /fɛt galãt/ *noun phrase* plural **fêtes galantes** (pronounced same) E20 French. A rural entertainment, especially as depicted in an eighteenth-century French genre of painting, a fête champêtre; a painting in this genre.

> ■ The subject matter of young ladies and gentlemen in elaborate or theatrical dress making music, flirting, and dancing in Arcadian surroundings is particularly associated with Jean Antoine Watteau (1684–1721).
>
> **1996** *Country Life* It is surprising that rather than call on the talents of the two great animal painters Oudry and Desportes, the artists chosen were history painters or painters of *fêtes galantes*.

fêtes champêtres, fêtes galantes plural of FÊTE CHAMPÊTRE, FÊTE GALANTE.

fetta variant of FETA.

fettucine /fɛtʊˈtʃiːni/ *noun plural* (also **fettucine**) E20 Italian (plural of *fettuccina*, diminutive of *fetta* slice, ribbon). *Cookery* Pasta in the form of ribbons; an Italian dish consisting mainly of this, usually with a sauce.

fetus see FOETUS.

fetwa variant of FATWA.

feu /fø/ *adjective* E19 French. Of a person: deceased, late.

feu d'artifice /fø dartifis/ *noun phrase* plural **feux d'artifice** (pronounced same) L17 French (literally, 'fire of artifice'). A firework show; a firework.

feu de joie /fø də ʒwa/ *noun phrase* plural **feux de joie** (pronounced same) E17 French (literally, 'fire of joy'). **1** E18 A ceremonial or celebratory salute fired with rifles or other small arms. **2** M17 *figurative* A joyful occasion; a celebration.

feu follet /fø fɔlɛ/ *noun phrase* plural **feux follets** (pronounced same) M19 French (literally, 'frolicsome fire'). A will-o'-the-wisp, an IGNIS FATUUS. Usually *figurative*.

feuillemorte /fœjmɔrt/ *adjective* L16 French (= dead leaf). Of the colour of a dead leaf; yellowish brown.

feuilleton /ˈfəːɪtõ/, *foreign* /fœjtõ/ *noun* M19 French (from *feuillet*, diminutive of *feuille* leaf). A section of a newspaper etc. devoted to) fiction, criticism, light reading, etc.; an article or story suitable for or printed in that section.

fez /fɛz/ *noun* plural **fezzes** E19 Turkish (*fes*, perhaps through French *fez*). A flat-topped conical brimless red hat with a tassel, worn by men in some Muslim countries.

> ■ Named after *Fez* (now *Fès*) in Morocco, once the principal place of manufacture, the fez was the national headgear of the Turks until the reforms of Kemal Atatürk in the 1920s.

ff abbreviation of FORTISSIMO (*musical direction*).

fiancé /fɪˈɒnseɪ/, /fɪˈɑːnseɪ/, /fɪˈõseɪ/ *noun* (feminine **fiancée**) M19 French (from (Old) French *fiancer* to betroth). A man engaged to be married; the person to whom one is engaged.

fianchetto /fɪənˈtʃɛtəʊ/, /fɪənˈkɛtəʊ/ *noun & verb* M19 Italian (diminutive of *fianco* flank). *Chess* **A** *noun* plural **fianchettoes** M19 The development of a bishop by moving it one square to a long diagonal of the board. **B** *transitive verb* E20 Develop (a bishop) in this way.

fiasco /fɪˈaskəʊ/ *noun* plural **fiascos** M19 Italian (from phrase *far fiasco*, literally, 'make a bottle'). A complete and ignominious failure, originally of a theatrical or musical performance; an ignominious outcome.

> ■ The allusion in the Italian phrase is unexplained.

fiat /ˈfʌɪat/ *noun & verb* LME Latin (3rd person singular present subjunctive of *fieri* = let it be done, let there be made). **A** *noun*

1 LME A formal authorization for a proposed arrangement, etc.; generally, any authoritative pronouncement, decree. **2** L16 A command by which something is brought into being. **B** *transitive verb* M19 Sanction by (official) pronouncement.

■ In sense A.2 *fiat* is short for or an allusion to *fiat lux* = let there be light (Vulgate Genesis 1:3).

ficelle /fisɛl/ (*plural same*), /fɪ'sɛl/ *noun* L19 French (= string). **1** L19 The off-white colour of undyed string. **2** L19 A (stage) device, an artifice.

■ In sense 1 *ficelle* is used only attributively or in combination as *ficelle-colour(ed)*.

2 1968 *Listener* No Pucelle, Candy's a ficelle; and . . . her fate is to be briefly grabbed by a series of stereotypes.

fiche /fiːʃ/ (*plural same*), /fiːʃ/ *noun* M20 French (short for *fiche de voyageur*). The registration form on which foreign guests must record details of passport etc. when booking into a French hotel.

fichu /'fiːʃuː/ *noun* M18 French (origin unknown). A triangular piece of lace or fine fabric worn by women round the neck or shoulders, and formerly also over the head.

fidalgo /fɪ'dalɡəʊ/ *noun* plural **fidalgos** M17 Portuguese (contraction of *filho de algo* son of something). A Portuguese nobleman.

■ The word is now obsolete except when used historically; cf. HIDALGO.

fides Punica /ˌfɪdeɪs 'pjuːnɪkə/ *noun phrase* (also **Punica fides**) 19 Latin (literally, 'Punic faith'). Treachery.

■ The phrase *Punica fide* 'with Punic (i.e. Carthaginian) faith' occurs in Sallust *Jugurthine War* cviii. It is one of several tags expressing the deep Roman distrust of the Carthaginians, their deadly rivals for control of the Mediterranean world during the initial phase of Roman overseas expansion in the third and second centuries BC.

fidus Achates /ˌfʌɪdəs ə'keɪtiːz/ *noun phrase* L16 Latin (= faithful Achates). A trusted friend.

■ Quotation from Virgil *Aeneid* vi.158. Achates was the loyal and trusted companion of the poem's hero, Aeneas.

fiesta /fɪ'ɛstə/ *noun* M19 Spanish (= feast). In Spain or Spanish America: a religious festival; *generally*, any festivity or holiday.

figura /fɪ'ɡjʊərə/ *noun* plural **figurae** /fɪ'ɡjʊəriː/ M20 Latin (= figure). **1** M20 Theo-

logy A type of a person. **2** M20 In literary use, a person who represents a higher or supervening reality. **b** An act that is representative or symbolic.

figurant /ˈfɪɡyrɑ̃/ (*plural same*), /'fɪɡjʊr(ə)nt/ *noun* (feminine **figurante**) L18 French (present participial adjective of *figurer* to figure). A supernumerary actor with a walk-on role in a theatrical performance.

■ A *figurant* was originally a ballet dancer; in the context of ballet now the term usually denotes a non-dancing performer with a supporting role.

filé /'fiːleɪ/ *noun* M19 French (past participle of *filer* twist). In the United States: powdered or pounded sassafras leaves used to flavour and thicken soup, especially gumbo.

■ Earliest use in *gumbo filé*.

1996 *Times Magazine* If you can get powdered *file*, so much the better. This dried and powdered sassafras is what gives the gumbo its thick and shiny texture.

filet /'fiːleɪ/, /fɪlɪt/, *foreign* /filɛ/ (*plural same*) *noun* L19 French (= net). A kind of net or lace with a square mesh.

filet de boeuf /ˌfiːleɪ də 'bəːf/, *foreign* /filɛ də bœf/ *noun phrase* M19 French. Cookery A fillet of beef; *United States* a tenderloin.

filet mignon /ˌfiːleɪ 'miːnjɒ̃/, *foreign* /filɛ miɲɔ̃/ *noun phrase* plural **filet mignons** (pronounced same) E20 French (= small fillet). Cookery A slice cut from the small end of a fillet of beef.

1995 *Times* Succulent as *filet mignon* but low in fat and cholesterol . . .

filioque /fɪlɪ'əʊkweɪ/ *noun* (also **Filioque**) M19 Latin (= and from the Son). *Christian Church* The statement in the Nicene Creed that the Holy Spirit proceeds not only from God the Father but also from the Son.

■ *Filioque* appeared as an addition to the Creed in the Western Church in the sixth century, possibly originating in Spain. It gradually became a source of contention between the theologians of Rome and Constantinople, since it was accepted in the West but rejected by the Eastern Orthodox Churches. After the failure of attempts to resolve the issue in the period immediately before the conquest of Constantinople by the Ottoman Turks, it remains an issue between Eastern and Western Christendom.

filius nullius /ˌfɪlɪəs 'nʊlɪəs/ *noun phrase* plural **filii nullius** /ˌfɪlɪiː 'nʊlɪəs/ M20 Latin

(= son of nobody). An illegitimate son whose paternity is unacknowledged.

1963 S. M. Brewer *Design for a Gentleman* [Lord Chesterfield's] natural son by Elisabeth du Bouchet . . . was in law *filius nullius* (nobody's son) and was in fact utterly dependent upon his father for everything.

fille de joie /fij də ʒwa/ *noun phrase* plural **filles de joie** (pronounced same) E18 French (literally, 'girl of pleasure'). A prostitute.

fillette /fijɛt/ *noun* plural pronounced same M19 French. A young girl.

film noir /film nwar/, /film 'nwɑ:/ *noun phrase* plural **films noirs** (pronounced same) M20 French (literally, 'black film'). A genre of cinematographic film of a pessimistic, cynical, and sombre character; a film of this type.

■ The typical *film noir* was a black-and-white Hollywood movie of the late 1940s or early 1950s with gloomy lighting, a menacing urban setting, and a fatalistic loner as the anti-hero. The phrase is sometimes abbreviated to simply *noir*, with examples of the revival of the genre in the 1990s being dubbed *neo noir*.

1995 *Big Issue* Film noir was a particular, time-specific genre, a shock antidote to the Technicolor musicals and 'aw-shucks' family dramas that dominated Forties Hollywood.

filo /'fi:ləʊ/ *noun* (also **phyllo**) M20 Modern Greek (*phullo* leaf). Dough that can be stretched into very thin sheets and layered; pastry made from this dough and used in sweet and savoury pastries.

fils /fis/ *noun* L19 French (= the son). The son, the younger, junior.

■ *Fils* is appended to a name to distinguish between father and son of the same name; cf. PÈRE.

1996 *Bookseller* Amis *fils* was believed to have been unhappy about the . . . serialisation of a diary Mr Jacobs had kept of his last meetings with Amis *père*.

filtre /filtr/ *noun* plural pronounced same M20 French. A filtering appliance for making coffee, which allows boiling water to pass through ground coffee beans into a cup or pot; coffee made by this method.

1940 'M. Innes' *Secret Vanguard* Orchard was . . . measuring coffee into a *filtre*.

fin (de) see FIN DE SIÈCLE.

finale /fɪ'nɑ:li/ *noun* M18 Italian (use as noun of adjective from Latin *finalis* from *finis* end). **1** M18 The closing section of a musical, operatic, or dramatic performance. **2** L18 The conclusion.

1 1996 *Country Life* By now, the orchestra in the pit had reached its finale, rending the air with thundering timpani.

finca /'fiŋka/, /'fɪŋkə/ *noun* E20 Spanish (from *fincar* to cultivate). In Spain and Spanish America: a country estate; a ranch.

fin de guerre /fɛ̃ də gɛr/ *noun & adjective phrase* French (= end of war). (Designating or characteristic of) the end of a war.

fin de saison /fɛ̃ də seɪzɔ̃/ *noun & adjective phrase* M20 French (= end of season). (Designating or characteristic of) the end of a season.

1996 *Spectator* There is a *fin de saison* kind of feeling around here, with many friends having returned to London and points elsewhere.

fin de siècle /fɛ̃ də sjɛkl/ *noun phrase* (also **fin-de-siècle**) plural **fins de siècle** (pronounced same) L19 French (= end of century). (Designating or characteristic of) the final years of a century, especially the nineteenth century; decadent. Also *attributive* or as *adjective phrase*.

■ 'Fin de' is sometimes used jocularly in combination with an English word to make a phrase modelled on *fin de siècle*.

1995 *Spectator* Fins de siècle don't have too good a reputation.

attributive **1995** *Spectator* [Isaiah] Berlin is acutely aware of the pathology of nationalism, of the distortions of *fin-de-siècle* Romantic voluntarism that lie at the root of Nazi paganism.

fine /fin/ *noun* plural pronounced same E20 French (abbreviation of FINE CHAMPAGNE). (A) French brandy; specifically, FINE CHAMPAGNE.

fine champagne /fin ʃɑ̃paɲ/ *noun phrase* M19 French (= fine (brandy from) Champagne). Old liqueur brandy from the Grande Champagne and Petite Champagne vineyards in the Charente, France; an example, glass, or drink of this.

■ The abbreviation FINE is also found in English.

fines herbes /finz ɛrb/, /fi:nz 'ɛ:b/ *noun phrase* plural M19 French (= fine herbs). Fresh mixed herbs (usually parsley, tarragon, chervil, and chives) chopped and used in cooking.

■ Frequently used in adjective phrase with *aux*, as in *omelette aux fines herbes*.

finesse /fɪ'nɛs/ *noun & verb* LME French. A *noun* **1** LME Clarity, purity (especially of metals). **2** M16 Delicacy of manipulation or discrimination; refinement. **3** M16

Artfulness; cunning. **4** An artful strata-gem; a ruse, a trick. **b** M19 *Cards* An at-tempt to take a trick with a card lower than but not in sequence with a card of the same suit also held. **B** *verb* **1** M18 *Cards* **a** *intransitive* Attempt to take a trick by a finesse. **b** *transitive* Play (a card) in a finesse. **2** *intransitive* L18 Use artifice or stratagem. **b** *transitive* Achieve by strat-agem; bring about or manage by artful handling.

Fingerspitzengefühl /'fɪŋgəʃpɪtz(ə)ngə ˌfuːl/ *noun* L20 German (= fingertip feel-ing). Intuition; tact, deftness in handling a task or situation.

> **1996** *Spectator* . . . it showed an absurd . . . thickness in, [Sir Anthony] Eden to make a point of wearing a dinner jacket to entertain the khaki-clad Egyptian leader. Not too much *Fingerspitzengefühl* there . . . .

finis /'fiːnɪs/, /'fɪnɪs/, /'fʌnɪs/ *noun* LME Latin (= end). **1** LME At the end of a book: the end. **2** L17 The finish, the conclusion; the end of life, death.

■ In the Latin tag *finis coronat opus* 'the end crowns the work', *finis* is used in sense 2.

fino /'fiːnəʊ/ *noun* plural **finos** M19 Span-ish (= fine *adjective*). A type of pale-col-oured dry sherry; an example, glass, or drink of this.

finocchio /fɪ'nɒkɪəʊ/ *noun* (also **finochio**) E18 Italian (from a popular Latin variant of *faeniculum* fennel). A form of fennel with swollen leaf-bases eaten as a vege-table.

fiord /fjɔːd/, /'fiːɔːd/ *noun* (also **fjord**) L17 Norwegian. A long, narrow, deep inlet of the sea between steep cliffs, as on the Norwegian coast.

fioritura /fɪˌɔːrɪ'tʊərə/ *noun* plural **fiori-ture** /fɪˌɔːrɪ'tʊəri/, /fɪˌɔːrɪ'tʊəreɪ/ M19 Ital-ian (from *fiorire* to flower). *Music* An elaboration or decoration of a melody.

firn /fɪən/ *noun* M19 German ('(snow) of the previous year', from Old High German *firni* old, related to Old Saxon *fern* past, *forn* formerly, Old Norse *forn* ancient). The granular snow on the upper part of a gla-cier which is in the process of being com-pressed into ice. Also called NÉVÉ.

fiumara /fju:'mɑːrə/ *noun* E19 Italian. (The dried bed of) a mountain torrent.

fjeld /fjɛld/ *noun* M19 Norwegian (Bokmål) (from Old Norse *fjall*). A high barren rocky plateau, especially in Scandinavia.

fjord variant of FIORD.

fl. abbreviation of FLORUIT.

flacon /flakɔ̃/ *noun* plural pronounced same. E19 French. A small stoppered bottle, *especially* one used to contain per-fume.

flagellum /flə'dʒɛləm/ *noun* plural **flagella** /flə'dʒɛlə/ E19 Latin (diminutive of *flagrum* scourge). **1** E19 A whip. **2** M19 *Biology* A motile whiplike projection from a cell; also, in botany, a runner, a creeping shoot.

flageolet /flad͡ʒə'lɛt/, /'flad͡ʒəlɪt/ *noun* 1 M17 French. *Music* **1** M17 A small wind instru-ment resembling a recorder, having six principal holes, including two for the thumb, and sometimes keys. **2** M19 An organ-stop having a tone similar to that of this wind instrument.

flageolet /flad͡ʒə'lɛt/, /'flaʒɔlɛ/ (*plural same*) *noun* 2 L19 French (ultimately from Latin *phaseolus* bean). *Cookery* A small kind of (especially French) kidney bean, dried and used in cassoulets. Also *flageolet bean*.

flagrante delicto /fləˌgrantɪ dɪ'lɪktəʊ/ *adverb phrase* E19 Latin. IN FLAGRANTE DE-LICTO.

flambé /flãbe/, /'flɒmbeɪ/ *adjective & verb* L19 French (past participle of *flamber* singe, pass through flame). **A** *adjective* **1** L19 (Of a copper-based glaze) iridescent from the effects of a special firing proc-ess; (of a type of Chinese porcelain) char-acterized by such a glaze. **2** E20 *Cookery* Of food, set alight after being drenched in brandy or other spirit and served while still flaming. **B** *transitive verb* M20 Drench (food) in spirit and set alight.

flambeau /'flambəʊ/ *noun* plural **flam-beaus**, **flambeaux** /'flambəʊz/ M17 French (diminutive of *flambe*, from Latin *flammula*, diminutive of *flamma* flame). **1** M17 A flaming torch. **2** L19 A large (branched) candlestick.

> **1996** *Times* A decade or more ago . . . all the traffic-lights in London used to have *flambeaux*—flaming beacons in cast iron—proudly mounted on top.

flamenco /flə'mɛŋkəʊ/ *noun & adjective* plural **flamencos** L19 Spanish (= Flem-ing). (Designating or pertaining to) a style of music played (especially on a guitar) and sung by Spanish gypsies; (a song or dance) to music in this style.

flâneur /flɑnœr/ *noun* (also **flaneur**) plural pronounced same. M19 French (from *flâ-ner* to lounge, saunter idly). An idler.

1995 *Times* The more Vidal tries to tell us that he is only a *flaneur*, the more real and thorough is his work and life.

flautando /flaʊˈtandəʊ/ *noun & adverb* E19 Italian (present participle of *flautare* to play the flute). *Music* (A direction: with) a flutelike violin tone.

flautato /flaʊˈtɑːtəʊ/ *noun & adverb* M19 Italian (literally, 'fluted'). FLAUTANDO.

flautino /flaʊˈtiːnəʊ/ *noun* plural **flautinos**; in sense 2 also **flautina** E18 Italian (diminutive of *flauto* flute). **1** E18 A small flute or flageolet. **2** M19 A gemshorn organ-stop of 2-ft length and pitch.

flauto /ˈflaʊto/, /ˈflaʊtəʊ/ *noun* plural **flauti** /ˈflaʊti/, **flautos** /ˈflaʊtəʊz/ E18 Italian (= flute). **1** E18 Originally, a recorder; later, a flute; also, the part played by such an instrument. **2** L19 An organ-stop of flute scale.

■ The *flauto piccolo* was likewise formerly a small recorder, now a PICCOLO. Another instrument sometimes known under its Italian name is the side-blown flute, the *flauto traverso*.

flebile /ˈfleɪbɪleɪ/ *adjective* E17 Italian (from Latin *flebilis* that is to be wept for; plaintive). *Music* Mournful.

flèche /flɛʃ/, /fleɪʃ/ *noun* (also **fleche**) ME French (= arrow). **1** E18 *Fortification* A work in communication with the covered way, placed at the salient angle of the GLACIS. **2** M19 *Architecture* A slender spire, often of wood and rising from a roof. **3** M19 Any of the twenty-four points on a backgammon board. **4** E20 *Fencing* A running attack. In full *flèche attack*.

■ First (ME only) in its original French sense; reintroduced in the specialist applications above.

fléchette /fleɪˈʃɛt/ *noun* (also **flechette**) E20 French (diminutive of *flèhe* arrow). *Military* A missile resembling a dart, dropped from an aircraft.

fleur-de-coin /flœrdəkwɛ̃/ *noun phrase* L19 French (= bloom of the minting-die). *Numismatics* Mint or perfect condition of a coin.

fleur-de-lis /ˌflə:dəˈli/ *noun phrase* (also **fleur-de-lys**) plural **fleurs-de-lis** (pronounced same) ME French (Old French *flour de lys*, literally, 'flower of the lily'). (The flower of) any of various plants of the iris family; hence, the heraldic lily composed of three petals bound together near their bases and traditionally supposed to have represented an iris, especially as used as a device on the former royal arms of France.

fleuron /ˈfluərɒn/, /ˈflə:rɒn/, *foreign* /flœrɔ̃/ (*plural same*) *noun* LME French. A decorative motif in the form of a stylized flower, used especially in printing, architecture, or coinage.

flic /flɪk/, *foreign* /flik/ (*plural same*) *noun* L19 French. A French police officer. *slang*.

flicflac /ˈflɪkflak/ *noun* M19 French (imitative of a succession of sharp sounds). *Ballet* A lashing movement of the leg related to the FOUETTÉ.

flor. abbreviation of FLORUIT.

flora /ˈflɔːrə/ *noun* plural **floras**, **florae** /ˈflɔːriː/ E16 Latin (*flos* flower, plural *flora*; *Flora*, an ancient Italian goddess of fertility and flowers). **1** E16 The personification of nature's power to produce flowers. **2** L18 A catalogue of the plants of a given area, with descriptions. **3** L18 The plants or plant life of a particular area, habitat, or epoch; cf. FAUNA.

floreat /ˈflɒreɪat/, /ˈflɔːreɪat/ *noun* Latin (= may he/she/it flourish (3rd person singular present subjunctive of *florere* to flourish)). The expressed wish that someone or something may thrive and prosper; hence, a thriving and prospering.

■ Often used as an interjection, followed by the name of a person, institution, etc., as in *Floreat Etona*! 'May Eton flourish!'
1996 *Bookseller* Why should certain periods produce a floreat of great writers and others be barren for long periods?

flore pleno /ˌflɒrɪ ˈplemaʊ/, /ˌflɔːrɪ ˈpliːnaʊ/ *adjective phrase* L19 Latin (literally, 'with full flower'). Double-flowered.

■ Used after the names of certain garden flowers that exist in both single- and double-flowered versions.

florilegium /flɒrɪˈliːdʒɪəm/, /flɔːrɪˈliːdʒɪəm/ *noun* plural **florilegia** /flɒrɪˈliːdʒɪə/, **florilegiums** E17 Modern Latin (literally, 'bouquet', from Latin *flori-* combining form of *flos* flower + *legere* to gather, translating Greek *anthologion* anthology). A collection of choice extracts from literature; an anthology.

floruit /ˈflɒrʊɪt/, /ˈflɔːrʊɪt/ *noun* M19 Latin (= he/she/it flourished (3rd person singular perfect indicative of *florere* to flourish)). The period during which a person flourished; heyday, period of greatest activity or prosperity.

■ Often abbreviated to *fl.* or *flor.* and used in cases where a person's birth and death dates are unknown or uncertain.

flota /ˈfləʊtə/ *noun* L17 Spanish (= fleet). *History* The Spanish fleet which used regularly to cross the Atlantic during the colonial period to bring back the products of America and the West Indies.

flotilla /fləˈtɪlə/ *noun* E18 Spanish (diminutive of *flota* fleet). A small fleet; a fleet of small vessels.

flügelhorn /ˈfluːɡ(ə)lhɔːn/ *noun* (also **flugelhorn, flugel horn**) M19 German (*Flügelhorn*, from *Flügel* wing + *horn* horn). A brass wind instrument with a cup-shaped mouthpiece and a wide conical bore.

■ Also abbreviated to *flugel.*

focaccia /fɒˈkatʃa/ *noun* plural **focacce** /fɒˈkatʃe/ L20 Italian. Italian bread made with olive oil and sometimes herbs.

> **1996** *Times* Rivals include olive and tomato breads, focaccia and the more established baguette.

focus /ˈfəʊkəs/ *noun & verb* plural **foci** /ˈfəʊsʌɪ/, /ˈfəʊki/, **focuses** M17 Latin (= domestic hearth). **A** *noun* **1** L17 *Physics* The adjustment (of a lens, the eye, etc.) to produce a well-defined image; the state of producing a well-defined image thus. **2** M18 The centre of greatest interest, attraction, activity, or energy. **B1** *transitive verb* L18 Make converge to or as to a focus; bring into focus; concentrate *on.* **2** *intransitive verb* M19 Converge to or as to a focus; come into focus; concentrate *on.*

■ *Focus* was apparently first used in this Modern Latin sense by Kepler in his *Astronomia pars optica,* written in 1604, and it is conjectured that the technical sense of *focus* as 'the burning point of a lens or mirror' (which is easily derived from the literal one) was already current in technical Latin. It was introduced into English in similar technical contexts, first as a term in plane geometry by Hobbes, and then into physics by Boyle in its 'burning point' sense. The plural form *foci* is generally confined to the noun's more technical senses.

foetus /ˈfiːtəs/ *noun* (also **fetus**) LME Latin (*fetus, foetus* pregnancy, giving birth, young offspring). An unborn viviparous animal in the womb, especially an unborn human more than eight weeks after conception; an unhatched oviparous animal in the egg.

■ The American form *fetus* has etymological correctness on its side, but *foetus* is still in general use in British English.

föhn /føːn/ *noun* (also **foehn**) M19 German (in Old High German *phonno*, Middle High German *foenne*, ultimately from Latin (*ventus*) *Favonius* mild west wind). **1** M19 A warm dry south wind which blows down valleys on the north side of the Alps. **2** L19 *Meteorology* A warm dry katabatic wind developing on the lee side of a mountain range as a result of air moving across the range. Also *föhn wind.*

foie gras /fwa: ˈɡra:/ *noun phrase* (also **foie-gras**) E19 French. Abbreviation of PÂTÉ DE FOIE GRAS.

folie /ˈfɒli/, *foreign* /fɔli/ (*plural same*) *noun* E19 French (= madness). Mental illness, mania.

■ Now chiefly in names of pathological mental states (see following entries).

folie à deux /ˌfɒli a: ˈdəː/, *foreign* /fɔli a dø/ *noun phrase* E20 French. An identical mental disorder or illusion affecting two closely associated people; *loosely* a shared act of folly between two people.

folie de grandeur /ˌfɒli də ɡrɒ̃ˈdəː/, *foreign* /fɔli də ɡrãdœr/ *noun phrase* (also **folie des grandeurs**) L19 French. Delusions of grandeur or importance.

> **1995** *Times* . . . either this comet is vast and about to obliterate us; or it is a small comet that has suddenly brightened . . . All experts admit that a diminutive comet with *folie de grandeur* is the likeliest explanation.

folie du doute /ˌfɒli du: ˈduːt/, *foreign* /fɔli dy dut/ *noun phrase* L19 French. Obsessive self-doubt.

fonctionnaire /fɔ̃ksjɔnɛr/ *noun* L20 French. In France: a state or local authority employee; a civil servant.

> **1995** *Spectator* 'Brussels can stay at home, thank you very much,' said Virginia, and how the *fonctionnaires* must have trembled in the Rue de la Loi.

fondant /ˈfɒnd(ə)nt/ *noun* L19 French (use as noun of present participle of *fondre* to melt). *Cookery* A sweet made of a soft paste of flavoured (and usually coloured) sugar; such a paste used in sweets and icings.

fondue /ˈfɒnd(j)uː/ *noun* M19 French (feminine past participle of *fondre;* cf. FONDANT). *Cookery* A dish of flavoured melted cheese, a speciality in the Swiss Alpine region; any dish in which small pieces of food are cooked, usually at table, by being dipped into boiling oil or liquid.

fons et origo /ˌfɒnz ɛt ˈɒrɪgəʊ/, /ˌfɒnz ɛt ɒˈrʌɪgəʊ/ *noun phrase* E19 Latin. The source and origin *of*.

■ Earliest use is in the phrase *fons et origo mali* the source and origin of evil.

1996 *Times Magazine* Half a mile northwest we come to Bedford Park ... the *fons et origo* of every planned suburb between its inception in 1875 and the First World War.

foo yong variant of FU YUNG.

force de frappe /fɔrs də frap/ *noun phrase* plural **forces de frappe** (pronounced same) M20 French. *Military* A striking force; especially, the French independent nuclear capability.

1995 *Times* The French these days seem much more interested in jobs and taxes than in the *force de frappe*.

force majeure /fɔrs maʒœr/ *noun phrase* L19 French (= superior strength). Irresistible force, overwhelming circumstances or opposition; in *Law* or *Commerce* an unforeseeable sequence of events excusing the fulfilment of a contract.

1995 *Times* The oil companies ... realised that their position was untenable. Therefore, they invoked *force majeure* and agreed new contracts with their customers ...

forma pauperis /ˌfɔːmə ˈpɔːpərɪs/ *noun phrase* L16 Latin (literally, 'the form of a poor person'). *Law* (The condition of) a poor person in respect of being able to bring a legal action without payment; figuratively humbly, in supplication.

■ Also frequently in *in forma pauperis* or *sub forma pauperis* as a poor person.

Formgeschichte /ˈfɔːmgəʃɪxtə/ *noun* E20 German (from *Form* form + *Geschichte* history). Textual analysis, especially of the Bible, by tracing the history of its content of proverbs, myths, and other forms; form-criticism.

forte /ˈfɔːteɪ/, /ˈfɔːti/, /ˈfɔːt/ *noun* 1 M17 French (use as noun of feminine of *fort* strong). 1 M17 *Fencing* The stronger part of a sword-blade, from the hilt to the middle. 2 L17 The strong point of a person; the thing in which one excels.

■ The word entered English in its masculine form *fort*, but the feminine form *forte* was later substituted. The modern pronunciation has been influenced by Italian *forte* (see next).

forte /ˈfɔːti/ *adverb, adjective, & noun* 2 E18 Italian (= strong, loud, from Latin *fortis* strong). *Music* **A** *adverb & adjective* E18 (A direction:) loud(ly). **B** *noun* M18 A loud tone or passage.

■ As a direction, usually abbreviated to *f*.

forte-piano /ˌfɔːtɪpɪˈanəʊ/ *noun, adverb, & adjective* M18 Italian. *Music* **A** *noun* M18 An early form of the pianoforte. **B** *adverb & adjective* L19 (A direction:) loud(ly) and then immediately soft(ly).

■ As a musical instrument often aphetized to PIANO (*noun* 2); as a musical direction, usually abbreviated to *fp*.

fortissimo /fɔːˈtɪsɪməʊ/ *adverb, adjective, & noun* E18 Italian (superlative of FORTE loud(ly)). *Music* **A** *adverb & adjective* E18 (A direction:) very loud(ly). **B** *noun* plural **fortissimos, fortissimi** /fɔːˈtɪsɪmi/ M19 A very loud tone or passage.

■ As direction, usually abbreviated to *ff*.

A *transferred* **1995** *Times* Defending himself yesterday, Mr Portillo conceded that his speech had been a 'fortissimo' expression of the Government's newly-sceptical European policy.

forum /ˈfɔːrəm/ *noun* plural **forums, fora**/ˈfɔːrə/ LME Latin (related to *fores* (outside) door, originally an enclosure surrounding a house). 1 LME *Roman Antiquity* The public place or market-place of a city; the place of assembly for judicial and civic business. **b** M18 A place of or meeting for public discussion; a periodical etc. which provides an opportunity for conducting a debate. 2 L17 A court, a tribunal. Also *figurative*.

forzando /fɔːˈtsandəʊ/ *adverb & adjective* E19 Italian (from *forzare* to force). *Music* (A direction:) with force or emphasis; SFORZANDO.

foudroyant /fuːˈdrɔɪənt/, /fudrwajɑ̃/ *adjective* M19 French (present participle of *foudroyer* to strike (as) with lightning, from *foudre* from Latin *fulgur* lightning). 1 M19 Thunderous, noisy. Also, dazzling. 2 L19 Of a disease, beginning suddenly and in a very severe form.

fouetté /fwete/ (*plural same*), /ˈfwɛteɪ/ *noun* M19 French (past participle of *fouetter* to whip). *Ballet* A movement in which a dancer pivots on one *pointe* and executes a rapid whip-like movement with the lower part of free leg.

foulard /ˈfuːlɑː/, /ˈfuːlɑːd/ *noun* M19 French. 1 M19 A lightweight printed or checked material of silk or silk and cotton. 2 L19 A headscarf or neckerchief made from this.

foulé /fule/ *noun* L19 French (= pressed (cloth), past participle of *fouler* to full). A light woollen dress material with a fibrous appearance.

fourchette /fʊə'ʃɛt/ *noun* M18 French.
1 M18 Something forked or resembling a fork. **2** M19 A forked object, device, or instrument; the forked piece between two adjacent fingers of a glove. **3** L19 In any of several card-games, a combination of cards immediately above and immediately below the card led.

fou rire /fu rir/ *noun phrase* E20 French (literally, 'mad laughter'). (A fit of) wild or uncontrollable laughter.

fourreau /'fʊərəʊ/ *noun* plural **fourreaux** (pronounced same) L19 French (literally, 'sheath, scabbard'). A close-fitting dress; an underskirt forming part of a dress.

foyer /'fɔɪeɪ/, *foreign* /fwaje/ (*plural same*) *noun* L18 French (= hearth, home, ultimately from Latin *focus* hearth). **1** L18 A centre of activity; a focus. **2** M19 A large room in a theatre, concert hall, etc., for the use of the audience during intervals; also, the entrance hall of a hotel or other public building.

■ Sense 1 is now uncommon, with *foyer* having been generally superseded by FOCUS in this sense.

fp abbreviation of FORTE-PIANO (musical direction).

fracas /'frakɑ:/ *noun* plural same /'frakɑːz/ E18 French (from *fracasser* from Italian *fracassare* to make an uproar). A disturbance, an uproar, a row.

Fraktur /'fraktʊə/ *noun* (also **fraktur**) L19 German. *Typography* A German style of black-letter type, the normal type used for printing German from the sixteenth to the mid twentieth century.

framboise /frɒm'bwɑːz/ *noun & adjective* L16 French (ultimately from a conflation of Latin *fraga ambrosia* ambrosian strawberry). **A** *adjective* E20 Of raspberry colour. **B** *noun* M20 A shade of pink; raspberry colour.

■ *Framboise* in its original sense of 'raspberry' was current in English only in the sixteenth and seventeenth centuries.

franc fort /frɑ̃ fɔr/ *noun phrase* L20 French (= strong franc). *Economics* The French monetary policy devoted to maintaining the value of the French franc at a high level among international currencies.

1995 *Spectator* Unemployment is, of course, a price paid for the *franc fort*.

franco /'fraŋko/ *adjective & adverb* L19 Italian ((*porto*) *franco* free carriage). Of a foreign business transaction, free of any postal or delivery charge.

franc tireur /frɑ̃ tirœr/ *noun phrase* plural **francs tireurs** (pronounced same) E19 French (= free shooter). An irregular soldier, a guerrilla fighter; *historically* a member of an irregular French light-infantry corps, originating in the Revolutionary wars.

franglais /'frɑ̃glɛ/ *noun* (also **Franglais**) M20 French (blend of *français* French + *anglais* English). A non-standard version of the French language characterized by indiscriminate use of words and phrases taken from British and American English.

■ The problem, as perceived by the French, of their language being sullied by the influx of Anglo-Saxon words was aired under this name in R. Etiemble's *Parlez-vous Franglais* (1964). Despite various campaigns to exclude them, interlopers such as *le week-end* appear firmly entrenched and likely to remain.

frankfurter /'fraŋkfə:tə/ *noun* (also (chiefly *United States*) **frankfurt**) L19 German (*Frankfurter Wurst* Frankfurt sausage). A seasoned sausage made of smoked beef and pork, originally made at Frankfurt am Main in Germany.

frappé /frape/, /'frapeɪ/ *adjective & noun* M19 French (past participle of *frapper* in the sense of 'to ice (drinks)'). **A** *adjective* M19 (Chiefly of wine) iced, chilled; (of a drink) served with crushed ice. **B** *noun* E20 A drink (especially coffee) served with crushed ice or partially frozen to a slushy consistency.

Frau /frau/ *noun* (also **frau**) plural **Frauen** /frauən/, **Fraus** E19 German. A German or Austrian woman.

■ Also used as a title, corresponding to Mrs.

Frauendienst /'frauəndi:nst/ *noun* M20 German (*frauen* women + *dienst* service). Exaggerated chivalry towards women.

■ The word derives from the medieval tradition of courtly love, specifically the title of the mid thirteenth century *Frauendienst* of Ulrich von Lichtenstein (d. *c.*1275), in which the writer describes the extraordinary tasks required of him by his mistress.

1963 W. H. Auden *Dyer's Hand* We find neither outright sexual passion nor sentimental *Frauendienst*.

Fräulein /ˈfrɔɪlʌm/, *foreign* /ˈfrɔɪlam/ *noun* (also **fraulein**) L17 German (diminutive of FRAU). An unmarried German woman; a German governess.

■ Also used as a title, corresponding to *Miss*.

frazil /ˈfreɪz(ə)l/, /frəˈzil/ *noun* L19 Canadian French (*frasil* = snow floating on water; cf. French *fraisil* cinders). Slush consisting of small ice crystals formed in water too turbulent to freeze solid. Also *frazil ice*.

fresco /ˈfrɛskəʊ/ *noun & verb* L16 Italian (= cool, fresh). **A** *noun* plural **frescos, frescoes** L16 A method of painting by which watercolour is applied to damp, freshly laid plaster, so that the colours penetrate and become fixed as the plaster dries. **2** L17 A painting produced by this method. **B** *transitive verb* E19 Paint in fresco.

■ Earliest English use in the phrase *in fresco*, representing Italian *affresco* or *al fresco* 'on the fresh (plaster)'.

fresco buono /ˌfresko ˈbwɔːno/ *noun phrase* M19 Italian (= good fresco). FRESCO sense A. Also *buon fresco* (L19).

fresco secco /ˌfresko ˈsekko/ *noun phrase* M19 Italian (= dry fresco). The process or technique of painting on dry plaster with colours mixed with water.

■ Sometimes abbreviated to *secco* (M19).

fricandeau /ˈfrɪkandəʊ/ *noun & verb* E18 French. **A** *noun* plural **fricandeaux** /ˈfrɪkandəʊz/ E18 Cookery (A slice of) veal or other meat fried or stewed and served with sauce; an escalope; a fricassee of veal. **B** *transitive verb* M18 Make into fricandeaux.

fricassee /ˈfrɪkəsiː/, /frɪkəˈsiː/ *noun & verb* M16 French (*fricassée* feminine past participle of *fricasser* to cut up and stew in sauce). **A** *noun* M16 Cookery Meat sliced and fried or stewed and served with sauce, especially a ragout of game. **B** *transitive verb* M17 Make a fricassee of.

frigidarium /frɪdʒɪˈdɛrɪəm/ *noun* plural **frigidariums, frigidaria** /frɪdʒɪˈdɛrɪə/ E18 Latin (from *frigidus*, from *frigere* to be cold, from *frigus* cold). The room in Roman baths containing the final, cold bath.

frijoles /friˈxoles/, /frɪˈhəʊlɛs/ *noun plural* L16 Spanish (plural of *frijol* bean, ultimately from Latin *phaseolus*). Cookery Especially in Mexico, a dish of beans.

frisé /ˈfriːzeɪ/ *adjective* L19 French (past participle of *friser* to curl). Of or designating a pile fabric with cut and uncut loops forming a pattern, chiefly used in upholstery.

frisée /ˈfriːzeɪ/ *noun* L20 French ((feminine) past participle of *friser* to curl). Curly endive.

■ Abbreviation of French *chicorée frisée*.

frisson /frisɔ̃/, /ˈfrɪsɒn/ *noun* plural pronounced same L18 French (= shiver, thrill). An emotional thrill; a shiver of excitement.

1995 *Country Life* In the 18th century, some followers of the Picturesque movement used to enjoy the frisson of terror experienced when they beheld an unusually 'horrid' landscape; their fear became pleasurable from the knowledge that they were only going to look at the bleak scene before them, not live in it.

frittata /frɪˈtɑːtə/ *noun* L20 Italian. An omelette.

fritto misto /ˌfritto ˈmisto/ *noun phrase* E20 Italian (= mixed fry). Cookery A dish of mixed foods, especially seafood, deep-fried in batter.

froideur /frwadœr/ *noun* L20 French (from *froid* cold). Coldness; lack of warmth.

■ Only in figurative use.
1995 *Times* When one interviewer . . . suggested that she [sc. Catherine Deneuve] seemed a little over-controlled herself, her response was a flash of ironic *froideur* that might have been scripted by Buñuel himself.

fromage blanc /ˌfrɒmaːʒ ˈblɔ̃/, *foreign* /frɔmaʒ blɑ̃/ *noun phrase* L20 French (= white cheese). Cookery A fresh soft white cheese.

fromage frais /ˌfrɒmaːʒ ˈfreɪ/, *foreign* /frɔmaʒ frɛ/ *noun phrase* L20 French (= fresh cheese). Cookery A soft curd cheese, often used as a basis for desserts.

■ In France this type of cheese is generally known as PETIT SUISSE.

fronde /frɔ̃d/ *noun* (usually **Fronde** in sense 1) plural pronounced same L18 French (literally, 'sling'). **1** L18 French History A political party in France during the mid seventeenth century, which initiated violent uprisings against the administration of Cardinal Mazarin during the minority of Louis XIV. **2** E19 *transferred* A malcontent or disaffected party; violent political opposition.

frondeur /frɔdœr/ *noun* (usually **Frondeur** in sense 1) plural pronounced same L18 French (from FRONDE). **1** L18 French

History A participant in the Fronde. **2** M19 *transferred* A malcontent; a political rebel.

fronton /'frʌnt(ə)n/ *noun* L17 French (from Italian *frontone*, augmentative of *fronte* forehead; in sense 2 Spanish *frontón*). **1** L17 *Architecture* A pediment. **2** L19 A building in which pelota is played.

froom variant of FRUM.

frottage /'frɒtɑ:ʒ/, *foreign* /frɔtaʒ/ *noun* M20 French (= rubbing, friction). **1** M20 The practice of rubbing against or touching the (clothed) body of another person (usually in a crowd) as a means of obtaining sexual gratification. **2** M20 *Art* The technique or process of taking a rubbing from an uneven surface, such as grained wood, as a basis for a work of art.

frotteur /frɒ'tə:/, *foreign* /frɔtœr/ *plural same noun* plural pronounced same L19 French. A person who indulges in FROTTAGE (sense 1).

frottola /'frɒtələ/, *foreign* /'frɔttola/ *noun* plural **frottole** /'frɒtəleɪ/, *foreign* /'frɔttole/ M19 Italian (literally, 'fib, tall story'). *Music* A form of Italian comic or amorous song, especially from the fifteenth and sixteenth centuries.

frou-frou /'fru:fru:/ *noun* L19 French (imitative). A continuous soft rustling sound, esp. of skirts; hence, frills and frippery. *verb* E20 Move with a rustle of fabric. Also *attributive*.

> *attributive* **1946** B. Spencer *Aegean Islands* 'Yachts on the Nile' [Yachts] . . . fresh as a girl at her rendezvous, and wearing frou-frou names, Suzy, Yvette or Gaby.

fruits de mer /ˌfrwiːdə'mɛː/ *noun phrase* M20 French (= fruits of the sea). *Cookery* Seafood, especially a dish made up of mixed shellfish.

frum /fru:m/ *adjective* (also **froom**) L19 Yiddish (from Middle High German *vrum* zealous; cf. German *fromm* pious). Pious, religious (used especially of an orthodox Jew).

frustum /'frʌstəm/ *noun* (also **frustrum**) plural **frustums, frusta** /'frʌstə/ M17 Latin (= piece cut off). *Mathematics* The portion of a solid figure, such as a cone, which remains after the upper part has been cut off by a plane parallel to the base.

fuehrer variant of FÜHRER.

fugato /fjuː'ɡɑːtəʊ/ *adverb, adjective, & noun* M19 Italian (= fugued, from *fuga* FUGUE).

Music **A** *adverb & adjective* M19 In the fugue style, but not in strict or complete fugue form. **B** *noun* plural **fugatos** L19 A passage in this style.

fughetta /fjuː'ɡɛtə/ *noun* L19 Italian (diminutive of *fuga* fugue). *Music* A short condensed fugue.

fugu /'fuːɡuː/ *noun* M20 Japanese. A type of puffer fish, renowned as a Japanese delicacy.

fugue /fjuːɡ/ *noun* L16 French (or, its source, Italian *fuga*, from Latin *fuga* flight). **1** L16 *Music* A polyphonic composition in which a short melodic theme, the subject, is introduced by one part or voice, and successively taken up by the others and developed by their interweaving. **2** E20 *Psychiatry* A flight from or loss of awareness of one's own identity, sometimes involving wandering away from home, and often occurring as a reaction to shock or emotional distress.

führer /'fjʊərə/ *noun* (also **fuehrer**) M20 German (= leader). A (ruthless or tyrannical) leader; a dictator.

> ■ Hitler, in his role as leader of the Third Reich, is often alluded to under his assumed title of *the* (or) *die Führer*, and the transferred use of the word in English usually has strongly negative implications.

führerprinzip /'fjʊərəprɪnˌzɪp/ *noun* M20 German (literally, 'leader principle'). The doctrine that a FÜHRER has a right to command and the people a duty to obey.

> ■ Also partially Anglicized as *führer principle*.
> **1995** *Spectator* Vainly they [sc. the Tories] scan the Labour benches for vocal resentment of Mr Blair's *führerprinzip*.

fulcrum /'fʊlkrəm/ *noun* plural **fulcra** /'fʊlkrə/, **fulcrums** L17 Latin (= post or foot of couch, from base of *fulcire* to prop up, support). **1** A prop or support; now specifically, the point against which a lever is placed to get purchase or on which it turns or is supported. **2** L17 *figurative* The means by which or source from which influence etc. is brought to bear.

functus officio /ˌfʌŋktəs ə'fɪʃɪəʊ/ *predicative adjective phrase* plural **functi officio** /ˌfʌŋktaɪ ə'fɪʃɪəʊ/ M19 Latin (= having discharged an office). *Law* Free from further obligations, having discharged its (or their) duty.

fungus /'fʌŋɡəs/ *noun* plural **fungi** /'fʌŋɡiː/, /'fʌŋɡaɪ/, /'fʌndʒi/, /'fʌndʒaɪ/ **fun-**

guses LME Latin (probably from Greek *sphoggos, spoggos* sponge). **1** LME Any of a large division of organisms including mushrooms, which lack chlorophyll and grow on, or obtain nutrients from, organic matter. **b** M18 *figurative* Something growing or spreading rapidly. **2** L17 Soft or spongy diseased tissue. **3** E20 *slang* A growth of facial hair, a beard.

furioso /ˌfjʊərɪˈəʊzəʊ/, *foreign* /furiˈoːso/ *noun, adjective, & adverb* M17 Italian (from Latin *furiosus* enraged, furious). **A** *noun* plural **furiosos** M17 A furious person. **B** *adjective & adverb* E19 Music (A direction:) furious(ly), wild(ly).

furor academicus /ˌfjʊərɔː akəˈdɛmɪkəs/ *noun phrase* M20 Latin. Academic frenzy; excessive excitement provoked by or over an intellectual issue.

furore /fjʊəˈrɔːri/, /fjʊəˈrɔː/ *noun* L18 Italian (from Latin *furor*, from *furere* to rage). **1** L18 Enthusiastic admiration; a craze. **2** M20 (An) uproar, (a) fuss.

furor poeticus /ˌfjʊərɔː pəʊˈɛtɪkəs/ *noun phrase* E20 Latin. Poetic frenzy; emotional over-enthusiasm.

furor scribendi /ˌfjʊərɔː skrɪˈbɛndi/ *noun phrase* M19 Latin (= frenzy of writing). An irresistible urge to write.

> **1975** S. Perelman *Vinegar Puss* The all-consuming urge to create, the *furor scribendi*, is upon him and will not be stilled.

fusain /ˈfjuːzeɪn/, *also foreign* /fyzɛ/ (*plural* same) *noun* L19 French (= spindle tree, charcoal). *Art* Artists' charcoal (made from the wood of the spindle tree); a charcoal drawing.

fusee /fjuːˈziː/ *noun* L16 French (*fusée* spindleful, ultimately from Latin *fusus* spindle). **1** E17 *Horology* A conical pulley onto which a chain is wound so as to equalize the power of the mainspring in a mechanical watch or clock. **2** M17 A detonating device; a fuse. **3** M19 A large-headed match for lighting a cigar or pipe.

fuselage /ˈfjuːzəlɑːʒ/, /ˈfjuːzəlɪʤ/ *noun* E20 French (from *fuseler* to shape like spindle, from *fuseau* spindle). The elongated body section of an aircraft in which the crew and passengers or cargo are carried.

fusillade /fjuːzɪˈleɪd/, /fjuːzɪˈlɑːd/ *noun & verb* E19 French (from *fusiller* to shoot). **A** *noun* E19 (Wholesale slaughter by) asimultaneous or successive discharge of firearms; *figurative* a sustained barrage of criticism, etc. **B** *transitive verb* E19 Assault or shoot down with a fusillade.

fusilli /ˈfusɪli/ *noun plural* L20 Italian. Pasta in the shape of small twists or spirals.

fustanella /fʌstəˈnɛlə/ *noun* M19 Italian (from Modern Greek *phoustani, phoustanela*, Albanian *fustan*, probably from Italian *fustagno* fustian). A stiff white kilt formerly worn by men in Albania and Greece and still part of Greek ceremonial military dress.

futon /ˈfuːtɒn/ *noun* (also **futong**) L19 Japanese. In Japan: a cotton-stuffed mattress rolled over a mat on the floor for use as a bed; more generally, a low-slung Japanese-style bed or mattress.

> ■ The word has occurred in accounts of Japanese culture since the nineteenth century, but its introduction as a fashionable item of Western furniture dates from the 1980s. In modern Western furnishing the futon often includes a slatted wooden base capable of conversion into a seat by day.
> **1996** *Times* Minimalists believe they will be redeemed by the futon, that they can meditate in the kitchen and create the metaphysical from the hygienic.

fu yung /fuː ˈjʌŋ/ *noun phrase* (also **foo yong**) /fuː ˈjɒŋ/ M20 Chinese (Cantonese *foo yung*, literally, 'hibiscus'). *Cookery* A Chinese dish made with eggs mixed and cooked with vegetables and other ingredients.

G

gabelle /gaˈbɛl/ *noun* LME French (from Italian *gabella* corresponding to Spanish *alcavala*). Chiefly *History* A tax, *especially* a foreign tax; *specifically* the salt-tax imposed in France before the Revolution.

gabion /ˈgeɪbɪən/ *noun* M16 French (from Italian *gabbione* augmentative of *gabbia* cage). A cylinder of wicker or woven metal bands to be filled with earth or stones for use in engineering or (*historical*) fortification.

gaffe /gaf/ *noun* (also **gaff**) E20 French. A blunder, a clumsy or indiscreet act or remark.
> **1996** *Times* It's not that Bottomley is alone in making such photographic gaffes—remember John Gummer stuffing a hamburger down his daughter in 1990 to allay fears of mad cow disease affecting humans?

gaga /ˈgɑːgɑː/, /ˈgagə/ *adjective & noun* (also **ga-ga**) E20 French. **A** *adjective* E20 Senile; mad, crazy; foolish, fatuous. **B** *noun* M20 A senile or foolish person. *slang*.

gagaku /ˈgagaku/ *noun* M20 Japanese (from *ga* refined, graceful, noble + *gaku* music). A traditional type of (chiefly ceremonial) Japanese music.

gage d'amour /gaʒ damur/ *noun phrase* plural **gages d'amour** (pronounced same) M18 French. A pledge of love; a love-token.

gaieté de coeur /gete də kœr/ *noun phrase* E18 French. Light-heartedness, playfulness.

gaijin /gʌɪˈdʒɪn/ *noun & adjective* M20 Japanese (contraction of *gaikoku-jin*, from *gaikaku* foreign country + *jin* person). **A** *noun* M20 plural same. In Japan: a foreigner, an alien. **B** M20 *attributive* or as *adjective* Foreign, alien (to the Japanese).
> **A 1995** *Times* The dollars-for-bonds deal is designed to insure both against a collapse, but it is hard to say who is most put out—the Americans, forced to shore up their biggest economic competitor, or the Japanese, coming cap-in-hand to the *gaijin* for financial help.

gala /ˈgɑːlə/, /ˈgeɪlə/ *noun* E17 French (or its source in Italian from Spanish from Old French *gale* merrymaking). **1** E17 Fine or showy dress. Now only in *in gala*. **2** E18–E19 Festivity, rejoicing. **3** M18 A festive occasion; a festival characterized by finery

and display; a special theatrical or other performance.
> **3 1996** *Spectator* Lovers of *Bohème*, those who already know the opera and want a definitive recording, as well as those won over to it by the Gubbay galas, should secure this set.

galabiya /gəˈlɑːbɪjə/, /galəˈbiːjə/ *noun* (also **galabieh, gallabiya**, and many other variants) E18 Arabic (Egyptian variant of Arabic *jallābiyya*). A long loose garment worn in Arabic-speaking Mediterranean countries, especially in Egypt.

galant /galɑ̃/, /gəˈlɑːnt/ *adjective* L19 French and German. **1** L19 *Music* Designating or pertaining to a light and elegant style of eighteenth-century music. **2** L20 Courteous, attentive to women.
> **2 1995** D. Lodge *Therapy* Laurence remains wonderfully *galant*.

galanterie /galɑ̃tri/, (*in sense 1 also*) /ˌgal(ə)ntəˈriː/ *noun* plural **galanteries** (pronounced same), (*in sense 1 also with German plural*) **galanterien** /ˌgal(ə)ntə ˈriːən/ E20 French (or (sense 1) German). **1** E20 *Music* A light non-essential movement in an early eighteenth-century classical suite. **2** E20 Courtesy, politeness, especially to women.
> ■ *Galanterie* in its obsolete sense of 'splendour' or 'a display of magnificence' was introduced earlier (E17), but it did not displace the Anglicized form *gallantry* which was also formerly (L16–E19) used in this sense. The current senses represent a reintroduction.

galère /galɛr/ *noun* plural pronounced same M18 French (= galley). A coterie; a (usually undesirable) group of people; an unpleasant situation.
> ■ The primary literal sense of *galère* as 'a ship powered by oars' in which criminals were condemned to be rowers explains its use as a metaphor for a disagreeable situation or bad company. The figurative use is a reference to Molière's *Scapin* (II xi) 'Que diable allait-il faire dans cette galère?'
> **1995** *Bookseller* I grow a-weary of . . . the whole *galère* of head honchos, smart-alec agents, insanely overpaid writers, etc.

galette /gəˈlɛt/ *noun* L18 French. A broad thin cake usually of pastry.

Galgenhumor /'galgən,hu:mɔr/ *noun* (also **galgenhumor**) E20 German (from *Galgen* gallows + *Humor* humour). Grim, ironical humour.

■ Also (E20) in the English form *gallows-humour*.

1963 W. H. Auden *Dyer's Hand* The gravedigger's song in Hamlet is . . . an expression of the *galgenhumor* which suits his particular mystery.

galipot /'galɪpɒt/ *noun* L18 French (*galipot*, *garipot*: cf. Provençal *garapot* pine-tree resin). A kind of hardened turpentine formed on the stem of the cluster pine.

gallabiya variant of GALABIYA.

galleria /galə'ri:ə/ *noun* L19 Italian. A shopping arcade in an Italian city or designed in imitation of one of these.

■ The idea of the shopping arcade on the Italian *galleria* principle became fashionable among urban architects in the English-speaking world during the 1960s, but the word *galleria* only became a fashionable synonym for 'arcade' in the 1980s. The term is also applied to shops-within-a-shop.

1990 *Times* The winning scheme . . . incorporated the inevitable 'galleria'.

gallinazo /galɪ'neɪzəʊ/ *noun* plural **gallinazos** M18 Spanish (from Latin *gallina* hen). In Latin America: a turkey buzzard or other vulture.

galop /'galəp/, /gə'lɒp/ *noun* M19 French. A lively ballroom dance in 2/4 time; a piece of music for this dance.

galpon /gal'pəʊn/ *noun* L19 American Spanish (*galpón* from Nahuatl *calpulli* large hall). A large building like a barn on a South American farm.

gamba /'gambə/ *noun* 1 (also **gambo**) L16 Italian (= leg; short for VIOLA DA GAMBA). **1** L16 A VIOLA DA GAMBA. **2** M19 An organ-stop resembling a violin or cello in tone. Also *gamba stop*.

gamba /'gambə/ *noun* 2 M20 Spanish. A kind of prawn, *Palaemon serratus*, as an article of food.

gamelan /'gaməlan/ *noun* E19 Javanese. An Indonesian, especially Javanese or Balinese, orchestra consisting mainly of percussion instruments.

gamin /'gamɪn/, /'gamã/, *foreign* /gamɛ̃/ (*plural* same) *noun & adjective* M19 French. **A** *noun* M19 A street urchin, a waif; a street-wise or impudent child. **B** *adjective* M19 Of, pertaining to, resembling, or characteristic of a gamin.

gamine /ga'mi:n/, *foreign* /gamin/ (*plural* same) *noun & adjective* L19 French. **A** *noun* L19 A female gamin; a small, attractively informal, mischievous, or elfish young woman. **B** *adjective* E20 Of, pertaining to, resembling, or characteristic of a gamine.

1984 A. Brookner *Hotel du Lac* In her navy linen trousers and her, perhaps too tight, white jersey, Jennifer was determinedly *gamine*.

gaminerie /gaminri/ *noun* E20 French. The behaviour or characteristics of a gamin or gamine.

gamma /'gamə/ *noun* LME Latin (from Greek). **1** LME The third letter (Γ, γ) of the Greek alphabet. **2** E17–E19 *Music* Gamut. **3** L17 Denoting the third in a numerical sequence: *attributively Science* Frequently written γ, as in *Astronomy* (preceding the genitive of the Latin name of the constellation) denoting the third brightest star in a constellation; *Chemistry* denoting the third of a number of isomeric forms of a compound, or of allotropes of an element, etc.; *Physics* designating high-energy electromagnetic radiation which consists of photons of wavelengths shorter than those of X-rays. **4** M20 A third-class mark in an examination etc. **5** M19 The silver Y, *Plusia gamma*. More fully *gamma moth*. **6** E20 A unit of magnetic field strength equal to 10^{-5} oersted. **b** M20 A unit of mass equal to 10^{-6} gram. **7** E20 *Photography* and *Television* A measure of the contrast of an image compared with that of the scene represented.

gammadion /gə'meɪdɪən/ *noun* M19 Late Greek (from GAMMA). An arrangement of shapes of capital gamma (Γ), especially of four, as a swastika or a hollow Greek cross.

ganbei /gan'beɪ/ *interjection* (also **kan-pei**) M20 Chinese (gānbēi, from gān empty, dry + bēi glass, cup). (A Chinese toast:) a call to drain one's glass.

ganbu /'ganbu:/ *noun* (also **kanpu** /'kanpu:/) M20 Chinese (gànbù). In the People's Republic of China: an office-holder in a military or governmental organization; a CADRE.

gandharva /gan'dɑ:və/ *noun* (also **gandharba** /gan'dɑ:bə/) L18 Sanskrit (gandharvās; perhaps connected with Greek *kentauros* centaur). *Hindu Mythology* Any of a class of minor deities or genii of the sky, often represented as celestial musicians.

gandoura /gan'dʊərə/ noun (also **gandourah, gandura(h)**) M19 Arabic (Algerian *gandūra*, variant of classical Arabic *kandūra*). A long loose gown worn mainly in the Near East and North Africa.

gangue /gaŋ/ noun E19 French (from German *Gang* way, course, vein or lode of metal). The valueless or unwanted components of an ore deposit.

ganja /'gandʒə/, /'gɑːndʒə/ noun (also **ganga**) E19 Hindi (*gãjā*). A strong preparation of marijuana, used chiefly for smoking.

ganosis /gə'nəʊsɪs/ noun E20 Greek (*ganōsis*, from *ganos* brightness, from *ganoun* to polish). The process of applying a wax polish to the white marble surface of a statue or occasionally to some other surface in order to give warmth to its appearance.

gaon /'gɑːəʊn/ noun plural **gaons, geonim** /geɪ'əʊnɪm/ L18 Hebrew (*gā'ōn* excellence, pride). (An honorific for) a head of a Jewish academy in Babylonia, Palestine, Syria, or Egypt, from the sixth to the eleventh centuries. Later, especially in Spain, France, Italy, and Lithuania, an outstanding Talmudic scholar. Also generally, a genius, a prodigy.

garam masala /ˌɡʌrəm mə'sɑːlə/ noun phrase M20 Urdu (*garam maṣāla*). A spice mixture used in Indian cookery.

garbanzo /gɑːˈbanzəʊ/ noun plural **garbanzos** M18 Spanish. A chick-pea.

garçon /garsɔ̃/ noun plural pronounced same E17 French. A waiter, a male servant, especially in a French hotel or restaurant.

garconnière /garsɔnjɛr/ noun plural pronounced same E20 French. A bachelor's set of rooms or flat.

garde champêtre /gard ʃɑ̃pɛtr/ noun phrase plural **gardes champêtres** (pronounced same) E19 French (literally, 'rural guard'). In France: a rural police officer; a gamekeeper.

gare /gar/ noun plural pronounced same M19 French. **1** M19 A dock-basin on a river or canal. Also, a pier, a wharf. **2** L19 In France and French-speaking countries: a railway station.

gare /gar/ intransitive verb (imperative) M17 French (imperative of *garer* to shelter). Look out! Beware! Take care!

gargouillade /gargujad/ noun plural pronounced same M20 French (from *gargouiller* to bubble, gurgle). Ballet A series of steps in which the left leg describes two circular movements in the air, before the left foot is drawn up to the right knee.

garigue /garig/ noun (also **garrigue**) plural pronounced same L19 French. In the south of France: uncultivated land of a calcareous soil overgrown with low scrub; the vegetation found on such land.

garimpeiro /garim'peiru/ noun M19 Portuguese. In Brazil: an independent prospector for diamonds, gold, etc.

garrigue variant of GARIGUE.

garrocha /ga'rrotʃa/ noun M19 Spanish. A goad, especially (in bullfighting) a short-pointed spear.

garuda /'garʊdə/ noun L19 Sanskrit (*garuḍa*). Indian Mythology A fabulous bird, half-eagle, half-man, ridden by the god Vishnu.

garum /'gɛːrəm/ noun L16 Latin (from Greek *garon*, earlier *garos*). History A sauce made from fermented fish, popular in ancient Rome; this sauce used as a medicine for horses.

gaseosa /gase'osa/, /gasɪ'əʊsə/ noun E20 Spanish. A fizzy drink; (a drink of) carbonated (mineral) water.

gaspacho variant of GAZPACHO.

Gastarbeiter /'gast,ɑːrbaɪtər/ noun plural **Gastarbeiters**, same M20 German (from *Gast* guest + *Arbeiter* worker). A person with temporary permission to work in another (especially western European) country.

Gasthaus /'gasthaʊs/ noun plural **Gasthäuser** /'gasthɔyzər/ M19 German (from *Gast* guest + *Haus* house). A small inn or hotel in a German-speaking country.

Gasthof /'gasthoːf/ noun plural **gasthofs, Gasthöfe** /'gasthəːfə/ M19 German (from *Gast* guest + *Hof* hotel, large house). A German hotel, usually larger than a GASTHAUS.

gateau /'gatəʊ/ noun (also **gâteau**) plural **gateaux** /'gatəʊ(z)/, **gateaus** M19 French (*gâteau* cake). A large rich cake, especially one with layers of cream or fruit eaten as a dessert.

■ The word also applies to other recipes, such as a *gâteau de riz* /ˌgatəʊ də 'riːz/ (= of rice) (M19) a rich rice dessert in the shape of a cake, or to meat or fish baked and served in the form of a cake (L19); both usages are now rare.

gauche /ɡəʊʃ/ *adjective* M18 French (literally, 'left(-handed)'). **1** M18 Lacking in tact or ease of manner, awkward, blundering; lacking in subtlety or skill, crude, unsophisticated. **2** L19 *Mathematics* Skew, not plane. *archaic.* **b** M20 *Chemistry* Of a molecular conformation: skew, having two groups staggered along a central axis by (about) 60 degrees.

  1 1995 *Country Life* It was an astounding performance from someone who had once been so gauche as to be an embarrassment before the television cameras.

gaucherie /ˈɡəʊʃ(ə)ri/ *noun* L18 French (from *gauche*; see preceding). Gauche or awkward manner; a gauche action.

gaucho /ˈɡaʊtʃəʊ/ *noun* plural **gauchos** E19 American Spanish (probably from Araucanian *kauču*). A mounted herdsman of the South American pampas, usually of mixed European and American Indian descent.

  1996 *Oldie* The hotel bars would have been lined with gauchos with moustaches and bad teeth much as they are today.

gavotte /ɡəˈvɒt/ *noun* L17 French (from modern Provençal *gavoto*, from *Gavot* an inhabitant of the Alps). **1** L17 A medium-paced dance popular in the eighteenth century. **2** E18 A piece of music for this dance, composed in common time with each phrase beginning on the third beat of the bar; a piece of music in this rhythm, *especially* one which forms a movement of a suite.

gazette /ɡəˈzɛt/ *noun & verb* (also **Gazette**) E17 French (or its source Italian *gazzetta*, originally Venetian *gazeta de la novità* i.e. a 'halfpennyworth of news', so called because sold for a *gazeta*, a Venetian coin of small value). **A** *noun* **1** E17 Originally, a news-sheet; a periodical publication giving an account of current events. Now, a newspaper, *especially* (the title of) the official newspaper of an organization or institution. **2** M17 *specifically* (The title of) an official journal in Britain containing lists of government appointments, bankruptcies, and other public notices; an official journal of any government. **B** *transitive verb* L17 Publish in a gazette. Usually in *passive*, be the subject of an announcement in an official gazette, *especially* be named as appointed *to* a post, command, etc.

gazon coupé /ɡazɔ̃ kupe/ *noun phrase* L20 French (= cut lawn, cut turf). A garden feature comprising an area of grass out of which a design is cut and filled with a contrasting material such as coloured gravel.

  1995 *Country Life* One such garden owner, aching to make a new flowerbed to please next year's pay-at-the-gate visitors, but fearful of the extra maintenance thereafter, has succumbed to the creation of a *gazon coupé.*

gazpacho /ɡəsˈpɑːtʃəʊ/, *foreign* /ɡaθˈpatʃo/, /ɡasˈpatʃo/ *noun* (also **gaspacho**) plural **gazpachos**, /ɡəsˈpɑːtʃəʊz/, *foreign* /ɡaθˈpatʃos/, /ɡasˈpatʃos/ E19 Spanish. A Spanish soup made from tomatoes, peppers, cucumber, garlic, etc., and served cold.

Gebrauchsmusik /ɡəˈbraʊksmuˌziːk/ *noun* M20 German (from *Gebrauch* use + *Musik* music). Music intended primarily for practical use and performance; *especially* music considered suitable for amateur groups and domestic playing.

Gedankenexperiment /ɡəˈdaŋk(ə)n ɛksˌpɛrɪm(ə)nt/ *noun* M20 German (from *Gedanken* thought + *Experiment* experiment). An experiment conducted in the imagination only; a thought-experiment.

gefilte fish /ɡəˈfɪltə fɪʃ/ *noun phrase* (also **gefüllte fish**) L19 Yiddish (= stuffed fish, from *gefilte* inflected past participle of *filn* to fill). A dish either of stewed or baked stuffed fish or of fish cakes boiled in a fish or vegetable broth.

gelato /dʒəˈlɑːtəʊ/ *noun* (also) plural **gelati** /dʒəˈlɑːti/, **gelatos** L20 Italian. An ice-cream.

  ■ Originally in Italy and Italian-speaking countries and now also United States.

Gelehrte /ɡəˈleːrtə/, /ɡəˈlɛːtə/ *noun* (also **Gelehrter** /ɡəˈleːrtə(r)/) plural **Gelehrten** /ɡəˈleːrtn/, /ɡəˈlɛːt(ə)n/ M19 German (from *gelehrt* learned, *lehren* to instruct). A learned (German) person; a scholar; a savant.

Gemeinschaft /ɡəˈmaɪnʃaft/ *noun* M20 German (from *gemein* common, general + -*schaft* -ship). *Sociology* A form of social integration based on personal ties; community. Cf. GESELLSCHAFT.

gemshorn /ˈɡɛmzhɔːn/ *noun* E19 German (literally, 'chamois horn'). *Music* A light-toned organ-stop.

gemütlich /ɡəˈmyːtlɪç/, /ɡəˈmuːtlɪʃ/ *adjective* (also **gemutlich**) M19 German. Pleasant, cheerful; cosy, snug, homely; genial, good-natured.

1996 *Spectator* Austria wins hands down. The people are nicer, the villages more 'gemütlich' . . .

Gemütlichkeit /gə'my:tlıçkaıt/, /gə 'mu:tlıʃkʌıt/ *noun* M19 German (cf. preceding). The quality of being *gemütlich*; geniality; cosiness; cheerfulness.

gendarme /'ʒɒndɑːm/, *foreign* /ʒɑ̃darm/ (*plural same*) *noun* plural **gendarmes**, (now *historical*) **gens d'armes** /ʒɑ̃ darm/ M16 French (a singular from the plural (now *historical*) *gens d'armes* men of arms). **1** M16 In the older French army, a horseman in full armour, having several others under his command; later, a mounted trooper, especially of the royal companies. Usually in *plural*; *obsolete* except *historical*. **2** L18 In France and French-speaking countries: a police officer; originally a member of a military force employed in policing. **b** E20 *generally* A police officer. *slang*.

gendarmerie /ʒɒn'dɑːməri/, *foreign* /ʒɑ̃darməri/ (*plural same*) *noun* (also **gendarmery**) M16 French (from *gendarme*; see preceding). **1** M16 *History* A body of cavalry, especially in the older French army. **2** L18 In France and French-speaking countries: a body of police officers, a police force. **b** M20 A police station.

gêne /ʒɛn/ *noun* E19 French (from Old French *gehine* torture). Constraint, embarrassment, discomfort.

gêné /ʒɛne/ *adjective* (feminine **gênée**) E19 French (past participial adjective of *gêner* to embarrass: related to preceding). Constrained, embarrassed, discomforted.

genera plural of GENUS.

generalia /ˌʤɛn(ə)'reɪlɪə/ *noun plural* M19 Latin (neuter plural of *generalis* general). General principles.

generalissimo /ˌʤɛn(ə)rə'lısıməʊ/ *noun* plural **generalissimos** E17 Italian (superlative of *generale* general). The commander of a combined military, naval, and air force, or of several armies.

genesis /'ʤɛnɪsɪs/ *noun* LOE Latin (from Greek = generation, creation, nativity, horoscope, from base of *gignesthai* to be born or produced). **1** LOE (**Genesis**) (The name of) the first book of the Bible. **2** E17 Origin, mode of formation or generation.

■ *Genesis* is the name given in the Septuagint to the first book of the Old Testament, dealing with the creation of the world; from there it was adopted by the Vulgate

and vernacular Bibles. It was formerly (LME–M17) also an astrological term for 'nativity, horoscope'.

genie /'ʤiːni/ *noun* plural **genii** /'ʤiːnɪʌɪ/, **genis** M17 French (*génie* from Latin GENIUS). **1** M17–E18 A GENIUS (sense 1). **2** M18 A spirit or jinnee (in Arabian stories), especially one inhabiting a bottle, lamp, etc., and capable of granting wishes.

genitor /'ʤɛnɪtə/ *noun* LME Latin (*genitor* (Old French *géniteur*) from base of *gignere* to beget. **1** LME A male parent. **2** M20 *Anthropology* A person's biological as opposed to legal father.

■ Long archaic in the general sense 1, *genitor* in sense 2 was revived in the specific context of the distinction between biological and legal fatherhood; cf. PATER sense 3b.

genius /'ʤiːnəs/ *noun* plural **genii** /'ʤiːnɪʌɪ/, **geniuses** LME Latin (from base of *gignere* to beget, Greek *gignesthai* to be born, come into being). **1** LME The tutelary or attendant spirit in classical pagan belief allotted to every person at their birth, or to a place, institution, etc. **b** L16 Especially as *good* or *evil genius*. Either of the two mutually opposed spirits or angels supposed to attend each person. Hence a person who or thing which for good or bad powerfully influences another. **2** L16 A demon or spirit. **3 a** L16–E19 Characteristic disposition, bent, or inclination. **b** M17 Prevalent feeling, opinion, taste, or character (of a nation, age, etc.). **c** M17 The prevailing character or spirit, or characteristic method (of a law, language, etc.). **d** E19 The body of associations connected with a place; the GENIUS LOCI. **4** E17 Natural ability or tendency; attributes which fit a person for a particular activity. (Passing into sense 5.) **b** M17 Natural aptitude, talent, or inclination *for, to* (something). **5** M17 Inborn exalted intellectual power; instinctive and extraordinary imaginative, creative, or inventive capacity, frequently opposed to *talent*; a person having this.

genius loci /ˌʤiːnɪəs 'ləʊsʌɪ/, /'lɒki:/ *noun phrase* E17 Latin (= genius of the place). The presiding god or spirit of a place. Also = sense 3d above.

1995 *Oldie* Betjeman was a genius in the popular literary sense of the word, but he was also a *genius loci*—a sort of tutelary deity who looked after a particular bit of earth, in his case these poor old islands of ours.

1996 *Spectator* At best, it [sc. a picnic] is as much the product of *genius loci* as the food, drink and company. The best one I have ever had was in Russia on the sprawling meadows of Tolstoy's Yasnaya Polyana estate.

genizah /gɛˈniːzə/ *noun* (also **geniza**) L19 Hebrew (literally, 'a hiding, hiding place', from *gānaz* to set aside, hide). (The contents of) a storeroom for damaged, discarded, or heretical manuscripts and sacred relics, usually attached to a synagogue.

genre /ˈʒãrə/, /ˈʒɒnrə/ *noun* E19 French (= kind). Kind, type; *especially* a style or category of painting, novel, film, etc., characterized by a particular form or purpose; *specifically* a style of painting depicting scenes of ordinary life.

gens /dʒɛnz/ *noun plural* **gentes** /ˈdʒɛntiːz/, /ˈdʒɛnteɪz/ M19 Latin (from base of *gignere* to beget). **1** M19 In ancient Rome: a group of families with a supposed common origin, a common name, and common religious rites. Also, a similar group of families in other cultures. **2** L19 *Anthropology* A kinship group composed of people related through their male ancestors.

gens de la robe /ʒɑ̃ də la rɔb/ *noun phrase* (also **gens de robe**) L17 French (literally, 'folk of the long robe'). Lawyers.

genus /ˈdʒɛnəs/, /ˈdʒiːnəs/ *noun plural* **genera** /ˈdʒɛn(ə)rə/, **genuses** M16 Latin (= birth, family, nation). **1** M16 *Logic* A class of things containing a number of subordinate classes (called species) with certain common attributes. **2** E17 *Biology* A basic taxonomic grouping ranking below family and subfamily. Formerly also used in the classification of minerals, chemical substances, etc. **b** M17 *generally* A category, a kind. **3** M18 In ancient Greek music, each of the three kinds of tetrachord.

georgette /dʒɔːˈdʒɛt/ *noun & adjective* E20 French (from Mme *Georgette* de la Plante (flourished *c.*1900), French modiste). (Made of) a thin plain-woven crêpe dress-material, usually of silk.

germen /ˈdʒəːmən/ *noun* E17 Latin (= seed, sprout). **1** E17 The rudiment of an organism. Now only *figurative*. **2** E17–L18 A shoot, a sprout. **3** M18 *Botany* The rudiment of a seed-vessel.

Gesamtkunstwerk /gəˈzamtkʊnstˌvɛrk/ *noun plural* **Gesamtkunstwerke** /gə ˈzamtkʊnstˌvɛrkə/ M20 German (from *gesamt* total + *Kunstwerk* work of art). An

ideal work of art in which drama, music, and other performing arts are integrated and each is subservient to the whole.

1996 *Spectator* Diaghilev and his friends . . . were fascinated by the notion of the *Gesamtkunstwerk*—total work of art—integrating drama, music and spectacle.

Gesellschaft /gəˈzɛlʃaft/ *noun* (also **gesellschaft**) L19 German (from *Gesell(e)* companion + *-schaft* -ship). *Sociology* A form of social integration based on impersonal ties; association. Cf. GEMEINSCHAFT.

gesso /ˈdʒɛsəʊ/ *noun plural* **gessoes** L16 Italian (from Latin GYPSUM; cf. YESO). Gypsum, plaster of Paris, now only as prepared for use in painting and sculpture; any white substance that can be mixed with water to make a ground.

gestalt /gəˈʃtaːlt/, /gəˈʃtalt/ *noun* (also **Gestalt**) E20 German (= form, shape). Chiefly *Psychology*. An integrated perceptual structure or unity conceived as functionally more than the sum of its parts.

Gestapo /gəˈstɑːpəʊ/ *noun plural* **Gestapos** M20 German (acronym, from *Geheime Staatspolizei* Secret State Police). *History* (An officer of) the secret police of the Nazi regime in Germany; also *transferred*.

1995 *Country Life* . . . one expects nothing better than charred raw meat and discomfort at barbecues. Why the environmental health officers, our wonderful germ gestapo, have not stamped them out long since is a mystery.

gett /gɛt/ *noun* (also **get**) L19 Hebrew. A Jewish bill of divorce, in prescribed form; a divorce by such a bill.

gharana /gəˈrɑːnə/ *noun* M20 Hindustani (*gharānā* family). *Indian Music* A school of players who practise a particular style of interpretation.

ghat /gɑːt/, /gɔːt/ *noun* (also **ghaut**) E17 Hindustani (*ghāt*). **1** E17 *The Ghats* Either of two mountain chains running parallel to the east and west coasts of southern India. **2** L17 In India: a mountain pass. **3** L18 In India: a flight of steps leading to a river-bank; a landing-place. **4** L19 A level place at the top of a river-bank ghat where Hindus cremate their dead. In full *burning-ghat*.

ghazal /ˈgazal/ *noun* (also **ghazel**) L18 Persian (from Arabic *ġazal*). A usually amatory Arabic, Turkish, Urdu, or (especially) Persian lyric poem or song characterized by a limited number of stanzas and the recurrence of the same rhyme.

ghazi /'gɑːzi/ *noun* (also (as a title) **Ghazi**) plural **ghazis** M18 Arabic (*al-ġāzī* active participle of *ġazā* to braid, invade, foray). In the Middle East: a champion, especially of Muslims against non-Muslims; a dedicated Muslim fighter. Frequently as an honorific title.

ghee /giː/ *noun* (also **ghi**) M17 Hindustani (*ghī*, from Sanskrit *ghṛta* past participle of *ghṛ-* to sprinkle). Indian clarified butter made from the milk of a buffalo or cow.

gherao /gɛˈraʊ/ *noun & verb* M20 Hindi (from *ghernā* to surround, besiege). **A** *noun* M20 plural **gheraos**. In India and Pakistan: a form of protest or harassment in labour disputes whereby employers etc. are prevented by workers from leaving the place of work until their claims have been granted. **B** *transitive verb* M20 Detain (a person) in this manner.

ghetto /'gɛtəʊ/ *noun & verb* E17 Italian (origin uncertain: perhaps abbreviation of Italian *borghetto* diminutive of *borgo* borough, or from Italian *getto* foundry, where the first ghetto established in Venice, in 1516, was sited). **A** *noun* plural **ghetto(e)s**. **1** E17 *History* The quarter in a city, originally in Italy, to which Jews were restricted. **2** L19 A densely populated slum area occupied by a minority group or groups, usually as a result of social or economic pressures; an isolated or segregated social group or area.

2 **1996** *Spectator* They did a deal, but Mr Hume has been unable to sell it in the ghetto. The Bogside Residents' Association is an unlovely body.

ghi variant of GHEE.

ghibli /'gɪbli/ *noun* (also **gibli, qibli**) E19 Arabic (*ḳiblī* southern). A hot dry southerly wind of North Africa.

ghilgai variant of GILGAI.

giallo antico /ˌdʒallo anˈtiːko/, /ˌdʒaləʊ anˈtiːkəʊ/ *noun & adjective phrase* M18 Italian (literally, 'ancient yellow'). (Made of) a rich yellow marble found among ruins in Italy, and used as a decoration.

gibber /'gɪbə/ *noun* L18 Aboriginal. In Australia: a boulder, a (large) stone.

gibli variant of GHIBLI.

gigolo /'ʒɪgələʊ/, /'dʒɪgələʊ/ *noun* plural **gigolos** E20 French (formed as masculine of *gigole* dancehall woman). A professional male dancing-partner or escort; a (usually young) man supported by a (usually older) woman in return for his attentions.

gigot /'dʒɪgət/ *noun* E16 French (diminutive of dialect *gigue* leg, from *giguer* to hop, jump, of unknown origin). **1** E16 A leg of mutton etc. **2** M16-M17 A dish made from minced meat, a sausage. **3** E19 A leg-of-mutton sleeve. More fully *gigot sleeve*.

gigue /ʒiːg/ *noun* L17 French. A lively piece of music in duple or triple time, often with dotted rhythms and forming the last movement of a suite; a jig.

gilet /ʒiːlɛ/ *noun* plural pronounced same L19 French. A light often padded waistcoat, usually worn for warmth by women.

gilgai /'gɪlgʌɪ/ *noun* (also **ghilgai**) M19 Aboriginal ((Kamilaroi) *gilgaay*). In Australia: a shallow depression between mounds or ridges, in which rainwater collects.

gimbri /'gɪmbri/ *noun* (also **gunibri** /'guːnɪbri/) L19 Arabic (dialectal variant of *ḳunbura* pomegranate). A small Moorish guitar; a player of this instrument.

ginseng /'dʒɪmsɛŋ/ *noun* M17 Chinese (*rénshēn* (Wade-Giles *jên shên*), from *rén* man + *shēn* kind of herb). **1** M17 A tuberous root credited, especially in the Far East, with valuable tonic properties. **2** L17 The source of this root, any of several plants of the genus *Panax* (family Araliaceae), with palmate leaves and umbels of small greenish flowers.

giocoso /dʒəˈkəʊsəʊ/ *adverb & adjective* E19 Italian (= merry). *Music* (A direction:) merr(il)y, joyous(ly).

girandole /'dʒɪr(ə)ndəʊl/ *noun* (also **girandola** in senses 1 and 2) M17 French (from Italian *girandola*, from *girare* from late Latin *gyrare* to gyrate). **I 1** M17 A kind of revolving firework; a discharge of rockets etc. from a revolving wheel. **2** E19 A revolving jet of water; a series of jets in an ornamental fountain. **II 3** M18 A branched support for candles or other lights which either stands on a surface or projects from a wall. **4** E19 An earring, a pendant, *especially* one which has a large central stone surrounded by smaller ones.

girasol /'dʒɪrəsɒl/, /'dʒɪrəsəʊl/ *noun* (also **girasole** /'dʒɪrəsəʊl/) L16 French (or Italian *girasole*, from *girare* to gyrate + *sole* sun). **1** A sunflower. rare. Only in L16. **2** L16 A variety of opal which reflects a reddish glow, a fire-opal.

giro /'ʤiːro/ *noun 1* plural **giri** /'ʤiːri/ L17 Italian (= round, circuit). A tour, a circuit; a turn.

giro /'ʤʌɪrəʊ/ *noun 2 & verb* L19 **German** (from Italian = circulation (of money)). **A** *noun* plural **giros**. **1** L19 A system of credit transfer between banks, post offices, etc.; *specifically* (frequently **Giro**) a system run by the British Post Office for the banking and transfer of money. Also *giro system.* **2** L20 A cheque or money order issued through the giro system; *specifically* in Britain, such a cheque used for unemployment benefit or social security payments. In full *giro cheque, giro order.* **B** *transitive verb* L20 Pay by giro.

girouette /ʒirwɛt/ *noun* plural pronounced same E19 **French**. A weathercock.

gitana /ʤɪˈtɑːnə/, *foreign* /xiˈtana/ *noun* M19 **Spanish** (feminine of next). A female (Spanish) Gypsy.

gitano /ʤɪˈtɑːnəʊ/, *foreign* /xiˈtano/ *noun* plural **gitanos** /ʤɪˈtɑːnəʊz/, *foreign* /xi ˈtanos/ M19 **Spanish** (representation of popular Latin = Egyptian, from Latin *Aegyptus* Egypt + *-anus*). A male (Spanish) Gypsy.

gîte /ʒit/ *noun* (also **gite**) plural pronounced same L18 **French**. **1** L18 A stopping-place, a lodging. Now *rare.* **2** M20 In France and French-speaking countries: a furnished holiday home usually in a rural district.

Giuoco Piano /ʤuˌəʊkəʊ pɪˈɑːnəʊ/ *noun phrase* E19 **Italian** (= quiet game). *Chess* An initially quiet opening in chess.

gjetost /ˈjɛtɒst/ *noun* E20 **Norwegian** (from *gjet, geit* goat + *ost* cheese). A Norwegian cheese made from goat's milk.

glacé /ˈglaseɪ/ *adjective & noun* M19 **French** (past participle of *glacer* to ice, give a gloss to, from *glace* ice). **A** *adjective* **1** M19 Of cloth, leather, etc.: smooth, highly polished, glossy. **2** L19 Of fruit: covered with icing or sugar. Of icing: made with icing sugar and water. **B** *noun* M19 Glacé silk, glacé leather.

glacis /ˈglasɪs/, /ˈglasi/ *noun* plural same /ˈglasɪz/, /ˈglasiːz/ L17 **French** (from Old French *glacier* to slip, slide, from *glace* ice, from Proto-Romance alteration of Latin *glacies* ice). **1** L17 A gently sloping bank; *specifically* in *Fortification,* a natural or artificial bank sloping down from the covered way of a fort so as to expose ⁻attackers to the defenders' missiles etc. **b** M20 *figurative* A zone or area acting as a protective barrier or buffer between two (potential) enemies. **2** L19 A sloping armour-plate protecting an opening etc. in a ship. In full *glacis-plate.*

glaistig /ˈglastɪk/ *noun* (also **glastick**) E20 **Gaelic**. A fairy with a variety of forms and characters, frequently appearing in the shape of a goat or as half-woman, half-goat, but also as a beautiful watersprite.

glasnost /ˈglaznɒst/, /ˈglɑːsnɒst/ *noun* L20 **Russian** (*glasnost'* the fact of being public). In the former USSR: the policy or practice of more open consultative government and wider dissemination of information. Also *transferred.*

■ *Glasnost* is an old Russian word, but its connotation of 'freedom of information' only evolved in the latter years of the Soviet regime. A debate on the subject started by the state newspaper *Izvestiya* in January 1985 was taken up by Mikhail Gorbachev in his speech in March the same year accepting the post of General Secretary of the Communist Party and expressing his commitment to reform. *Glasnost* was one of the key concepts in the Gorbachev reform programme (see also PERESTROIKA), and English-speaking political commentators, finding that there was no English word exactly equivalent to *glasnost,* opted to use the Russian one. It became widely current in the late 1980s and was soon applied to mean 'openness', in particular 'openness in government', in a variety of situations quite outside its original context.

1986 *New York Times* Exposés of corruption, shortages and economic problems appear virtually daily in the [Soviet] press. It is a change that became evident after Mikhail S. Gorbachev came to office last March and called for more 'glasnost', or openness, in covering domestic affairs.
transferred **1996** *Guardian* 2 For royal correspondents, used to being fobbed off, lied to, and told off like naughty boys, Atkinson and Vulliamy represented a new *glasnost* in Palace PR.

glastick variant of GLAISTIG.

glaucoma /glɔːˈkəʊmə/ *noun* M17 **Greek** (*glaukōma,* from *glaukos* bluish-green, bluish-grey). *Medicine* An eye condition characterized by increased pressure within the eyeball and a gradual impairment or loss of sight.

Gleichschaltung /ˈglaɪçˌʃaltʊŋ/ *noun* (also **gleichschaltung**) M20 **German**. The standardization of political, economic, and cultural institutions in authoritarian States.

glissade /glɪˈsɑːd/, /glɪˈseɪd/ *noun & verb* M19 French (from *glisser* to slip, slide). **A** *noun* **1** M19 *Dancing* A step consisting of a glide or slide in any direction, usually a joining step. **2** M19 *Mountaineering* The action or an act of sliding down a steep slope especially of snow, usually on the feet with the support of an ice-axe etc. **B** *verb* **1** *intransitive & transitive verb* M19 *Dancing* Perform a glissade; progress by glissades. **2** M19 *Mountaineering* Slide down a steep slope especially of snow by means of a glissade.

glissando /glɪˈsandəʊ/ *noun* plural **glissandi** /glɪˈsandi/, **glissandos** L19 Italian (from French *glissant* present participle of *glisser* to slip, slide). *Music* A continuous slide of adjacent notes upwards or downwards.

> **1996** *Times* The hour was late; the booze was strong; the notes on my trombone part seemed very small . . . I felt my *glissandi* getting limper and limper.

glissé /glise/ *noun* plural pronounced same E20 French (past participle of *glisser* to slip, slide). *Ballet* A sliding step in which the flat of the foot is often used. More fully *pas glissé* /pa glise/.

globule /ˈglɒbjuːl/ *noun* M17 French (or Latin *globulus* diminutive of *globus* globe). **1** M17 A small spherical body or globe; a round drop (of liquid). **2** M19 A small pill.

glockenspiel /ˈglɒk(ə)nʃpiːl/, /ˈglɒk(ə)nspiːl/ *noun* E19 German (= bell-play). *Music* **1** E19 An organ-stop imitating the sound of bells. **2** M19 Any of several percussion instruments, *especially* (a) a series of tuned metal bars mounted on a horizontal frame; (b) a series of bells or metal bars in a lyre-shaped frame carried in marching bands (also *lyra glockenspiel*).

glögg /glœg/, /glɒg/ *noun* (also **glugg** /glʌg/) E20 Swedish. A Scandinavian winter drink, consisting of hot sweetened red wine with brandy, almonds, raisins, and spices.

gloire /glwar/ *noun* M19 French. Glory; *specifically* the national glory and prestige of France. In full *la gloire* /la glwar/.

gloria /ˈglɔːrɪə/ *noun & adjective* (in sense 1 **Gloria**) ME Latin (= glory). **A** *noun* **1** ME Any of several Christian liturgical formulae, as *Gloria (Patri)* the doxology 'Glory be

to the Father', *Gloria (tibi)* the response 'Glory be to thee', *Gloria (in excelsis)* the hymn 'Glory be to God on high', forming part of the Mass etc. **b** L16 The music to which any of these is set. **2** L18 An aureole, a nimbus. **3** M19 In France: (a drink of) coffee mixed with brandy or rum. **4** L19 A closely-woven fabric of silk and wool or cotton etc.; a garment made of this. **B** *adjective* E20 Made of the fabric gloria.

gloriette /ˌglɔːrɪˈɛt/ *noun* M19 French. A highly decorated chamber in a castle or other building.

glugg variant of GLÖGG.

glühwein /ˈglyːvam/, /ˈgluːvʌm/ *noun* (also **gluhwein**) L19 German (from *glühen* to mull, glow + *wein* wine). Mulled wine.

gneiss /nʌɪs/ *noun* (also (earlier) **kneiss**) M18 German (from Old High German *gneisto* (= Old English *gnāst*, Old Norse *gneisti*) spark). A foliated usually coarse-grained metamorphic rock in which bands of granular minerals alternate with bands of flaky or prismatic ones, and typically consisting of feldspar, quartz, and mica.

gnocchi /ˈn(j)ɒki/, /ˈgnɒki/, *foreign* /ˈɲokki/ *noun* plural L19 Italian (plural of *gnocco*, from *nocchio* knot in wood). Small dumplings made with flour, semolina, or potato.

gnomon /ˈnəʊmɒn/ *noun* M16 French (or Latin *gnomon*, from Greek *gnōmōn* inspector, indicator, carpenter's square). **1** M16 A pillar, rod, etc., which shows the time of day by casting its shadow on a marked surface; *especially* the pin or triangular plate of a sundial. **b** E17 A column etc. used in observing the meridian altitude of the sun. **2** L16 *Geometry* The part of a parallelogram left after a similar parallelogram is taken away from one of its corners.

■ Various other technical and general uses are now no longer current.

gnosis /ˈnəʊsɪs/ *noun* plural **gnoses** /ˈnəʊsiːz/ L16 Greek (*gnōsis* investigation, knowledge, from *gno-* base of *gignōskein* to know). A special knowledge of spiritual mysteries; *specifically* in *Theology*, the redemptive knowledge that the Gnostics claimed to possess.

go /gəʊ/ *noun* L19 Japanese. A Japanese board game of territorial possession and capture. Cf. WEI CH'I.

gobang /gəʊˈbaŋ/ *noun* L19 Japanese (*goban* board for playing the game of go). A simplified form of the game of GO played on a board marked with squares, each player seeking to place five counters in a row.

godet /gəʊˈdɛt/, /ˈgəʊdeɪ/ *noun* ME Old and Modern French. **1** ME–E17 A drinking-cup. **2** L19 A triangular piece of material inserted into a dress, glove, or other garment. **3** E20 A driven roller or wheel around which the filaments of any of various man-made fibres are drawn during manufacture.

goitre /ˈgɔɪtə/ *noun* (also **goiter**) E17 French (either (i) from Old French *goitron* from Provençal from Proto-Romance, from Latin *guttur* throat, or (ii) back-formation from French *goitreux* goitred, from Latin adjective from *guttur*). *Medicine* A swelling of the neck due to enlargement of the thyroid gland, as caused by disease of the gland, iodine deficiency, etc.

goldwasser /ˈgəʊldvasə/, *foreign* /ˈgɔltvasər/ *noun* E20 German (= gold water). A liqueur containing particles of gold leaf, originally made at Gdańsk in Poland.

golem /ˈgəʊləm/, /ˈgɔɪləm/ *noun* L19 Yiddish (*goylem* from Hebrew *gōlem* shapeless mass). A human figure of clay etc. supernaturally brought to life; an automaton, a robot.

golgotha /ˈgɒlgəθə/ *noun* E17 Late Latin ((Vulgate), from Greek by metathesis from Aramaic *gōgoltâ*, perhaps under influence of Hebrew *gulgōleṭ* skull). A place of interment; a graveyard, a charnel-house.

■ From the explanation in Matthew 27:33 and elsewhere of the name of the site of the Crucifixion as 'a place of a skull', wits at the universities of Oxford and Cambridge formerly (E18–E19) gave the nickname of Golgotha to the meeting place of the heads ('skulls') of university colleges or halls.

gompa /ˈgɒmpə/ *noun* E20 Tibetan (*gōn-pa*, *gōm-pa* a solitary place, a hermitage). A Tibetan temple or monastery.

gondola /ˈgɒndələ/ *noun* M16 Italian ((Venetian) from Rhaeto-Romance *gondolà* to rock). **1** M16 A light asymmetric flat-bottomed boat used on the Venetian canals, having a high pointed prow and stern and usually propelled by a single oar at the stern. **2** L17 A large light flat-bot-

tomed riverboat; a lighter, used also as a gunboat. *United States*. **3** M19 A car or nacelle attached to the underside of a dirigible or airship; something resembling this. **4** L19 An open railway goods wagon with low sides. More fully *gondola-car, gondola-wagon*. *United States*. **5** M20 A car attached to a ski-lift. **6** M20 An island display counter in a self-service shop.

gondolier /ˌgɒndəˈlɪə/ *noun* E17 French (from Italian *gondoliere*, from GONDOLA). A person who rows a Venetian gondola.

gonfalonier /ˌgɒnf(ə)ləˈnɪə/ *noun* L16 French (Old French *gonfanonier*). A standard-bearer; *specifically* (**a**) the Pope's standard-bearer; (**b**) *History* any of various officials or magistrates in the Italian city-states.

gonzo /ˈgɒnzəʊ/ *adjective & noun* L20 Italian (= foolish, or perhaps Spanish *ganso* goose, fool). **A** *adjective* L20 Of, pertaining to, or designating a style of subjective journalism characterized by factual distortion and exaggerated rhetoric; *generally* bizarre, crazy. **B** *noun* plural **gonzos** L20 Gonzo journalism; a journalist writing in this style; *generally* a crazy or foolish person.

■ Originally and chiefly United States slang.

goombah /ˈguːmbɑː/ *noun* (also **goombay** /ˈguːmbeɪ/) L18 West Indian creole (cf. Kikongo [n]*kumbi* a kind of drum, Twi *gumbe* drum music). In the West Indies: any of various types of drum played with the fingers (rather than with sticks).

goonda /ˈguːndə/ *noun* (also **goondah**) E20 Hindi (*guṇḍā* rascal). In the Indian subcontinent: a hired bully.

goondie /ˈguːndi/ *noun* (also **gundy**) L19 Aboriginal ((Kamilaroi) *gunday* stringybark). In Australia: an Aboriginal hut; a GUNYAH.

gooroo variant of GURU.

gopi /ˈgəʊpiː/ *noun* (also **Gopi**) L18 Sanskrit. *Hindu Mythology* Any of the milkmaids of Brindavan, companions of Krishna.

gopura /ˈgəʊpʊrə/ *noun* (also **gopuram** /ˈgəʊpʊrəm/) M19 Sanskrit (*gopura* city gate, from *go* cow, cattle + *pura* city, quarter). In southern India: the great pyramidal tower over the entrance-gate to a temple precinct.

Gorsedd /ˈgɔːsɛð/ *noun* L18 Welsh (= mound, throne, assembly). A meeting of

Welsh bards and druids; *especially* the assembly that meets to announce the next Royal National Eisteddfod and at certain times during this festival.

Götterdämmerung /ˈɡœtərˌdɛmərʊŋ/, /ɡɒtəˈdamərʊŋ/ *noun* E20 German (literally, 'twilight of the gods'). *Germanic mythology* The downfall of the gods; *generally* a cataclysmic collapse of a regime, institution, etc. Cf. RAGNAROK.

■ *Götterdämmerung* is the title of the final opera in Wagner's Ring cycle.

gouache /ɡuːˈɑːʃ/, *foreign* /ɡwaʃ/ *noun* L19 French (from Italian *guazzo*). A method of opaque watercolour painting, in which the pigments are bound by a glue to form a sort of paste; a painting executed in this way; the pigments thus used.

goujon /ˈɡuːdʒ(ə)n/, *in sense 2 foreign* /ɡuʒɔ̃/ (*plural same*) *noun* L19 Old and Modern French (from Latin *gobio(n)*-, from *gobius* goby). **1** L19 In the United States: the flathead catfish, *Pylodictis olivaris*. **2** M20 *Cookery* In *plural*. Narrow strips of fish, especially sole, or of chicken, usually for deep-frying.

goulash /ˈɡuːlaʃ/ *noun* M19 Hungarian (*gulyás(hús)*, from *gulyás* herdsman + *hús* meat). **1** M19 A highly seasoned stew or ragout of meat and vegetables. **2** E20 *Bridge* A fresh deal of unshuffled cards, usually three or more at a time, after the hands have been thrown in without bidding.

gourmand /ˈɡʊəmənd/, /ˈɡɔːmənd/, *foreign* /ɡurmɑ̃/ (*plural same*) *noun & adjective* (occasionally feminine **gourmande** /ˈɡʊəmɒnd/, /ˈɡɔːmɑːnd/, *foreign* /ɡurmɑ̃ːd/, (*plural same*)) LME Old and Modern French (of unknown origin). **A** *noun* **1** LME A person who is overfond of eating; a glutton. **2** M18 A person who is fond of, or a judge of, good food; a GOURMET. **B** *adjective* M16 Gluttonous, greedy; fond of eating.

gourmet /ˈɡʊəmeɪ/, /ˈɡɔːmeɪ/, *foreign* /ɡurmɛ/ (*plural same*) *noun & adjective* E19 French (formerly = wine-merchant's assistant, wine-taster, influenced in sense by GOURMAND). **A** *noun* E19 A connoisseur in eating and drinking; a judge of good food. **B** *attributive* or as *adjective* E20 Of the nature of a gourmet; of a kind or standard suitable for gourmets.

goût /ɡuː/ *noun* (also **gout**) L16 French (earlier *goust* from Latin *gustus* taste). **1** L16 Liking, relish, fondness (*for*). **2** E18 The

ability to perceive and discriminate between flavours, smells, etc.; the faculty of aesthetic appreciation or judgement; (good) taste. **3** E18 Style or manner; *especially* a prevailing or fashionable style. **4** M18 Flavour, savour, taste.

goy /ɡɔɪ/ *noun* plural **goyim** /ˈɡɔɪɪm/, **goys** M19 Hebrew (*gōy* people, nation). Among Jews: a non-Jew, a Gentile.

gradus /ˈɡreɪdəs/ *noun* M18 Latin (*gradus* step(s)). *History* A manual of classical prosody used in schools to help in writing Greek and Latin verse.

■ This category of schoolbook took its name from the title of a manual of Latin prosody, the *Gradus ad Parnassum* 'Step(s) to Parnassus', which appeared in England in many editions from the late seventeenth century onwards and inspired a *Greek Gradus* and other imitations.

Graf /ɡrɑːf/ *noun* M17 German. A German nobleman corresponding in rank to a European count or British earl.

■ Chiefly in titles. The feminine equivalent is *Gräfin*.

graffiti /ɡrəˈfiːti/ *transitive verb* L20 Italian (from plural of next). Apply graffiti to; write as graffiti.

graffito /ɡrəˈfiːtəʊ/ *noun* plural (frequently used as *singular*) **graffiti** /ɡrəˈfiːti/ M19 Italian (from *graffio* scratching). **1** M19 A drawing, writing, or scribbling on a wall etc., originally *specific* on an ancient wall, as at Rome and Pompeii. Usually in *plural*. **2** L19 A method of decoration or design produced by scratching through a plaster layer to reveal a different colour below.

gramdan /ˈɡrɑːmdɑːn/ *noun* M20 Sanskrit (*grāma* village + *dāna* gift). In India: the pooling by villagers of their land for the collective good, especially as advocated by Vinoba Bhave (1895–1982).

grand battement /ɡrɑ̃ batmɑ̃/, /ˈɡrɒ̃ ˈbatmõ/ *noun phrase* plural **grands battements** (pronounced same) M19 French. *Ballet* A BATTEMENT executed with the moving leg stretched out as it is raised.

grand coup /ɡrɑ̃ ku/, /ˈɡrɒ̃ ˈkuː/ plural **grands coups** (pronounced same) E19 French. **1** E19 A bold or important stroke or effort. **2** L19 *Whist* and *Bridge* The deliberate disposal of a superfluous trump by ruffing a winning card from the opposite hand.

grand cru /grã kry/, /grõd 'kru:/ *noun & adjective phrase* plural **grands crus** /grã kry/, **grand crus** /grõd 'kru:z/ E20 French (= great growth). *Wine* (Designating) a wine of superior quality.

1996 *Times Magazine* At the top of the pyramid are those glorious grands crus wines that dreams are made of.

grande amoureuse /grãd amurøz/ plural **grandes amoureuses** /grãdz amurøz/ E20 French. A passionate or amorous woman; a woman skilled in the arts of love.

grande dame /grãd dam/ plural **grandes dames** (pronounced same) M18 French. A woman of high rank or eminence and dignified bearing.

1995 *Times* The latest lifestyle tip from the grandes dames of chic: take your dog to work. The offices of *Tatler* are overrun . . .

grande horizontale /grãd ɔrizõtal/ *noun phrase* plural **grandes horizontales** (pronounced same) L19 French. A courtesan or prostitute.

1970 *New Yorker* He is overshadowed throughout by Aunt Augusta, the still unretired grande horizontale of seventy-three.

grande passion /grãd pasjõ/ plural **grandes passions** (pronounced same) E19 French (= grand passion). An overmastering passion for another person; an engrossing love affair.

grande sonnerie /grãd sɔnri/, /grõd 'sɒnəri/ M20 French. *Horology* A system of chiming in which the hour and the quarter is struck each quarter on different toned bells.

grande tenue see EN GRANDE TENUE.

Grand Guignol /ˌgrõ giːˈnjɒl/, *foreign* /grã giɲɔl/ *noun phrase* E20 French (= Great Punch). A dramatic entertainment in which short horrific or sensational pieces are played successively; a literary work with similar characteristics.

■ In France *Guignol* is a marionette drama equivalent to the English Punch and Judy show. *Grand Guignol* takes its name from a theatre in Paris.

1996 *Spectator* Many novelists who specialise in *grand guignol* . . . might just as well be writing love stories, or crime stories, or something else without the gratuitous details of blood and gore.

grandioso /grandiˈoːso/ *adverb, adjective & noun* L19 Italian. *Music* **A** *adverb & adjective* L19 (A direction:) in a grand or imposing manner. **B** *noun* plural **grandiosi** /grandiˈoːsi/ L20 A movement or passage played in this way.

grand jeté /grã ʒɛte/, /grõ 'ʒəteɪ/ *noun phrase* plural **grands jetés** (pronounced same) M20 French. *Ballet* A JETÉ achieving a high elevation.

grand mal /grõ 'mal/, *foreign* /grã mal/ *noun phrase* L19 French (literally, 'great sickness'). General convulsive epilepsy, with loss of consciousness. Cf. PETIT MAL.

grand monarque /grã mənark/, /ˌgrõ mɔ'nɑːk/ plural **grands monarques** (pronounced same) L17 French. A supreme and absolute ruler; *specifically* an epithet of Louis XIV of France (reigned 1643–1715).

grand monde /grã mõd/, /'grõ 'mɒnd/ E18 French. The BEAU MONDE.

Grand Prix /grõ 'priː/ *noun phrase* plural **Grands Prix** (pronounced same) M19 French (= great prize). **1** M19 An international horse race for three-year-olds run annually in June at Longchamps, Paris. In full *Grand Prix de Paris* /də pa'riː/. **2** L19 The highest prize awarded in a competition or exhibition. **3** E20 Any of a series of motor or motorcycle races forming the World Championship, held in various countries under international rules. Also, a very important competitive event in various other sports.

grand seigneur /grã sɛɲœr/, /ˌgrõ sem'jə:/ plural **grands seigneurs** (pronounced same) E17 French. A great nobleman.

grand siècle /grã sjɛkl/, /ˌgrõ sɪ'ɛk(ə)l/ M19 French (literally, 'great century or age'). A classical or golden age; *especially* the reign of Louis XIV (1643–1715) in France.

granita /gra'niːtə/, *foreign* /gra'nita/ *noun* plural **granite** /gra'niːti/, *foreign* /gra'nite/ M19 Italian. A coarse water-ice or sherbet; a drink made with crushed ice.

gran turismo /gran tu'rizmo/, /ˌgran tʊə'rizməʊ/ *noun & adjective phrase* M20 Italian (literally, 'great touring'). (Designating) a comfortable high-performance model of motor car.

■ Abbreviated to GT.

grappa /'grapə/ *noun* L19 Italian. A brandy distilled from the refuse of grapes after wine-making.

graticule /'gratɪkjuːl/ *noun* L19 French (from medieval Latin *graticula* for (also classical Latin) *craticula* small gridiron, diminutive of Latin *cratis* hurdle). **1** L19 A network of lines representing meridians and parallels, on which a map or plan can be represented. **2** E20 A series of fine lines or fibres incorporated in a telescope or other optical instrument as a measuring scale or an aid in locating objects; a plate etc. bearing this.

gratin /ˈgratɛ̃/, /ˈgratã/ *noun* M17 French (from *gratter*, earlier *grater* to grate). **1** M17 A method of cooking, or a dish cooked, with a crisp brown crust, usually of grated cheese or breadcrumbs. Cf. AU GRATIN. **2** M20 The highest class of society.

■ For sense 2, cf. the English metaphorical phrase 'the upper crust'.

2 1959 *Sunday Times* She belonged to the Edwardo-Georgian *gratin*.

gratiné /gratine/ (*plural same*), /gratɪˈneɪ/ *noun & adjective* (also **gratinée**) E20 French (past participial adjective of *gratiner* to cook *au gratin*). *Cookery* (A dish) cooked with a crisp topping or stuffing of breadcrumbs or grated cheese.

gratis /ˈgratɪs/, /ˈgrɑːtɪs/, /ˈgreɪtɪs/ *adverb & adjective* LME Latin (*gratis* contraction of *gratiis* out of favour or kindness, ablative plural of *gratia* grace, favour). **A** *adverb* **1** LME Freely, for nothing, without return made or expected; without charge, cost, or pay. **2** L16–E19 Without a reason; gratuitously, unjustifiably. **B** *adjective* M17 Given or done for nothing; free; gratuitous.

graupel /ˈgraʊp(ə)l/ *noun* L19 German. *Meteorology* Soft hail, small snow pellets with a fragile ice crust.

gravadlax variant of GRAVLAX.

gravamen /grəˈveɪmɛn/ *noun* plural **gravamens**, **gravamina** /grəˈveɪmɪnə/ E17 Late Latin (*gravamen* physical inconvenience, (in medieval Latin) grievance, from Latin *gravare* to weigh on, oppress, from *gravis* heavy, grave). **1** E17 In the Anglican Church: a memorial from the Lower House of Convocation to the Upper House representing the existence of disorders and grievances within the Church. **b** M17–L19 A formal complaint or accusation. **2** M17 A grievance. **3** M19 The essential or most serious part of an accusation; the part that bears most heavily on the accused.

gravida /ˈgravɪdə/ *noun* M20 Latin (use as noun of feminine of *gravidus* gravid). *Medicine* A woman who is pregnant; (with preceding or following numeral) a woman who had had the specified number of pregnancies, including a present one.

gravitas /ˈgravɪtɑːs/, /ˈgravɪtas/ *noun* E20 Latin. Solemn demeanour; seriousness.

1996 *Times* It [sc. the appointment of a lord to a directorship] may well give added gravitas to the board, but gravitas does not equal competence.

gravlax /ˈgravləks/ *noun* (also **gravlaks**, **gravadlax** /ˌgravadˈləks/) M20 Swedish (from *grav* grave, trench +*lax* salmon (because the process was originally carried out in a hole in the ground)). Raw salmon cured with salt, spices, and especially dill.

grazioso /gratsiˈoːzo/ *adjective & adverb* E19 Italian (= gracious, graceful). *Music* (A direction:) graceful(ly).

grecque /grɛk/ *noun* M19 French (feminine of *grec* Greek). *Architecture* A Greek fret.

grège /grɛʒ/ *adjective & noun* (also **greige** /greɪʒ/) E20 French (in *soie grège* raw silk, from Italian *greggio* raw, crude, unprocessed). (Of) a colour between beige and grey.

grenadine /ˈgrɛnədiːn/ *noun* L19 French ((*sirop de*) *grenadine* from *grenade* pomegranate). A cordial syrup made from pomegranates; a drink of this.

Grenzbegriff /ˈgrɛntsbəˌgrɪf/ *noun* L19 German (from *Grenze* limit, boundary + *Begriff* concept). In Kantian philosophy, a concept showing the limitation of sense-experience, a limiting concept; *generally* a conception of an unattained ideal.

grès /grɛ/ *noun* L19 French. Stoneware.

■ Chiefly in *grès de Flandres* /grɛ də flãdr/, Flemish ware.

grillade /grɪˈleɪd/, /grɪˈjɑːd/, /ˈgriːɑːd/ *noun* M17 French (from *griller* to cook on a grill). (A dish of) grilled food; a grill.

grimoire /grɪmˈwɑː/ *noun* M19 French (alteration of *grammaire* grammar). A manual of black magic supposedly used to cast spells, invoke demons, etc.

gringo /ˈgrɪŋgəʊ/ *noun & adjective* plural **gringos** M19 Spanish (= foreign, foreigner, gibberish). **A** *noun* M19 A (male) foreigner, especially British or American, in a Spanish-speaking country. **B** *adjective* L19 Of or pertaining to a gringo or gringos; foreign.

■ Usually derogatory.

griot /'griːəʊ/ *noun* E19 French. In North and West Africa: a member of a class of travelling poets, musicians, and folk-historians; a praise-singer.

grippe /grɪp/, *foreign* /grip/ *noun* L18 French. Influenza.

grisaille /grɪ'zeɪl/, /grɪ'zeɪli/, *foreign* /gri zaj/ (*plural same*) *noun & adjective* M19 French (from *gris* grey). **A** *noun* M19 A method of painting in grey monochrome, used to represent objects in relief or to decorate stained glass; a stained-glass window or other work of this kind. **B** *adjective* M19 Executed in grisaille.

grisette /grɪ'zɛt/ *noun & adjective* E18 French (from *gris* grey). **A** *noun* **1** E18 A cheap grey dress fabric, formerly worn by working girls in France. **2** E18 A young working-class Frenchwoman. **B** *adjective* E18 Made of grisette.

grissino /gris'siːno/, /grɪ'siːnəʊ/ *noun* plural **grissini** /gris'siːni/ M19 Italian. A long thin stick of crisp bread.
■ Usually in plural.

grognard /grɔɲar/ *noun* plural pronounced same E20 French (literally, 'grumbler'). A member of Napoleon's Old Guard; *transferred* a veteran soldier.

gros /gro/ *noun* plural same M18 French (use as noun of *gros* gross). **1** A heavy silk fabric (*gros du soie*). Only in M18. **2** L18 A silk fabric originally from or associated with a specified city etc., as *gros de Londres* /də lɔ̃dr/, *gros de Lyons* /də ljɔ̃/, *gros de Naples* /də napl/, etc.

gros bleu /gro blø/ *noun & adjective phrase* L19 French (= dark blue). (Of) a deep blue used to paint china.

grosgrain /'grəʊgrem/, *foreign* /grogrɛ̃/ (*plural same*) *noun & adjective* M19 French. (Made of) any of various heavy ribbed fabrics, especially silk or rayon.

gros point /gro pwɛ̃/ *noun phrase* M19 French (= large stitch). **1** M19 A type of lace, originally from Venice, worked in bold relief. More fully *gros point de Venise* /də vəniz/. **2** M20 Any of various embroidery stitches worked over two or more horizontal and vertical threads of the canvas.

grosso modo /ˌgrosso 'moːdo/, /ˌgrɒsəʊ 'məʊdəʊ/ *adverb phrase* M20 Italian. Roughly, approximately.

Grübelsucht /'gryːbəlzʊxt/ *noun* L19 German (from *grübeln* to brood + *Sucht* mania). A form of obsession in which even the simplest facts are compulsively queried.

gruppetto /grup'petto/, /grʊ'pɛtəʊ/ *noun* plural **gruppetti** /grup'petti/, **gruppettos** M19 Italian (diminutive of *gruppo* group). *Music* A melodic ornament consisting of a group of three, four, or five notes, comprising the principal note and the notes one degree above and below it; a turn.

GT abbreviation of GRAN TURISMO.

guaca, **guaco** variants of HUACA, HUACO.

guacamole /gwɑːkə'məʊli/ *noun* (also **guacomole**) E20 American Spanish (from Nahuatl *ahuacamolli*, from *ahuacatl* avocado + *molli* sauce). A Mexican dish made from mashed avocados, onions, tomatoes, chillies, and seasoning.

guaiacum /'gwʌɪəkəm/ *noun* M16 Modern Latin (from Spanish *guayaco*, *guayacan*, from Taino *guayacan*). **1** M16 Any of various trees and shrubs of the genus *Guaiacum* native to the West Indies and tropical America. **2** M16 The hard very heavy wood of such a tree; lignum vitae. **3** M16 A resin obtained from such a tree, formerly used to treat gout and rheumatism, now as a flavouring; a drug prepared from it. Also more fully *gum guaiacum*.

guajira /gwa'xira/ *noun* E20 Cuban Spanish (feminine of next). A Cuban song and dance tune whose rhythm shifts from 6/8 to 3/4 time.

guajiro /gwa'xiro/ *noun* plural **guajiros** /gwa'xiros/ M19 Cuban Spanish (= rustic, rural). A Cuban agricultural worker.

guano /'gwɑːnəʊ/ *noun* plural **guanos** E17 Spanish (or South American Spanish *huano*, from Quechua *huanu* dung). **1** E17 The excrement of sea birds as found especially on the islands off Peru and Chile and used as fertilizer. **2** M19 More fully *fish guano*. An artificial fertilizer resembling natural guano, *especially* one made from fish.

guaracha /gwa'ratʃa/ *noun* M19 Spanish. A lively Cuban song and dance in 3/4 and 6/8, or 2/4, time; a ballroom dance resembling this.

guarache variant of HUARACHE.

guarana /gwə'rɑ:nə/, /'gwɑ:rənə/ *noun* M19 Portuguese (from Tupi *guaraná*). A Brazilian liana, *Paullinia cupana*, of the soapberry family; a paste prepared from the seeds of this shrub, used as a food or medicine and especially to make a drink resembling coffee.

guardia civil /ˌgwardia θiˈbil/, /siˈbil/ *noun phrase* plural **guardias civiles** /ˌgwardias θiˈbiles/, /siˈbiles/ M19 Spanish (= civil guard). (A member of) a police force in Spain organized on military lines.

guêpière /gɛpjɛr/ *noun* M20 French (from *guêpe* wasp). A corset designed to emphasize the slenderness of the waist.
1995 *Oldie* All model girls wore stays—tiny ones called guêpières (wasp-waists).

guéridon /'gɛrɪd(ə)n/, *foreign* /gerɪdɔ̃/ *noun* M19 French. A small ornamental table or stand, usually round, with a single central pedestal, and ornately carved.

guerrilla /gəˈrɪlə/ *noun & adjective* (also **guerilla**) E19 Spanish (diminutive of *guerra* war). **A** *noun* **1** E19 A person taking part in an irregular war waged by small bands operating independently (frequently against a stronger more organized force) with surprise attacks etc. **2** E19 A war waged by guerrillas. Now *rare*. **B** E19 *attributive* or as *adjective* Of fighting: carried on by small irregular bands. Of a person: taking part in such fighting.
■ Introduced into France and England during the Peninsular War (1808–14), when the Spaniards fought such campaigns against the vastly superior invading forces of Napoleon.

gueule de bois /gœl də bwa/ *noun phrase* plural **gueules de bois** (*pronounced same*) L20 French (literally, 'mouth of wood'). A hangover.
■ Colloquial in both French and English.
1995 *Times* As every single drinker who has surged over the alcoholic Maginot Line at a pub or party knows, the thud-thud-thud-thud of the *gueule de bois* is one of the most disagreeable experiences the human head can aspire to.

gueux /gø/ *noun plural* E17 French (plural of *gueux* ragamuffin, beggar). *History* The Dutch nobles who in 1566 petitioned Margaret of Parma on behalf of Protestants; the Dutch and Flemish Protestant partisans who subsequently fought against Spain in the wars of the sixteenth century.
■ Four hundred nobles assembled in Brussels in April 1566 to present a petition to the Habsburg Governess of the Netherlands, Margaret of Parma, against the intolerant edicts being enforced by her administration in the provinces that she was ruling as deputy for her half-brother, the Spanish king Philip II. The president of her council of finance, the Count of Berlaymont, contemptuously dismissed them as *gueux* 'beggars', a sobriquet gleefully seized upon by the disaffected Dutch, who transformed it into a rallying cry for the subsequent revolt against the Habsburgs.

gugelhupf /'gu:gəlhʊpf/ *noun* (also **guglhupf**, **kugelhupf** /'ku:gəlhʊpf/) plural **gugelhupfe** /'gu:gəlhʊpfə/ L19 German (the form with *k* is from dialect). A light Austrian cake baked in a ring-shaped mould.

guichet /'gi:ʃeɪ/ *noun* M19 French. A wicket, a hatch; *especially* one through which tickets are sold.

guidon /'gʌɪd(ə)n/ *noun* M16 French (from Italian *guidone*, from *guida* guide). **1** M16 A pennant narrowing to a point or fork at the free end, especially as used as the standard of a regiment or (*United States*) a troop of cavalry. **2** L16 An officer who carries a guidon.

guilloche /gɪˈləʊʃ/, /gɪˈlɒʃ/ *noun* M19 French (*guillochis* guilloche, or *guilloche* the tool used in making it). An architectural or metalwork ornament imitating braided or twisted ribbons.
1996 *Country Life* . . . the guilloche has a clarity that recalls the appearance of that ornament in borders to the plates in D'Hancarville's *Collection of Etruscan, Greek and Roman Antiquities* . . .

guillotine /'gɪlətiːn/, /gɪləˈtiːn/ *noun & verb* L18 French (from Joseph-Ignace *Guillotin* (1738–1814)). **A** *noun* **1** L18 An instrument for beheading consisting of a heavy blade with a diagonal cutting edge that is allowed to drop between two tall grooved uprights, used in France during the Revolution. **b** M19 *the guillotine* Execution by means of a guillotine. **2** M19 A surgical instrument with a blade that slides in a long groove. **3** L19 A machine with a long blade used for cutting paper etc. **4** L19 A method used in a legislative assembly for preventing obstruction of a bill by fixing times at which its different parts must be voted on. **B** *transitive verb* **1** L18 Behead by means of a guillotine. **2** L19 Cut with a guillotine; *figuratively* cut short.

■ Guillotin suggested the use of this instrument as a means of capital punishment in 1789 on the grounds that executions should be as swift and painless as possible. Such devices had been in operation earlier in England, Scotland (where it was called a 'maiden'), Germany (called a *Diele* or *Hobel*), and Italy (called a *mannaia*), but by the eighteenth century they seem to have fallen out of use until Guillotin's recommendation aroused new interest. There was a period of experimentation using dead bodies, during which the machine was referred to as *La Petite Louison* or the *Louisette*, but after its first public use in April 1792 it speedily and universally became known as *la guillotine*.

guimpe /gɪmp/, *foreign* /gɛ̃p/ *noun* (also **guimp**) M19 French. A high-necked CHEMISETTE; a blouse designed for wearing under a low-necked dress.

guipure /gɪˈpjʊə/ *noun* M19 French (from *guiper* to cover with silk, wool, etc., from Germanic base meaning 'wind round'). A kind of openwork lace in which the motifs are connected by threads.

guiro /ˈgwɪərəʊ/ *noun* L19 Spanish (= gourd). A gourd with an artificially serrated surface which gives a rasping sound when scraped with a stick, used (originally in Latin America) as a musical instrument.

gul /gʊl/ *noun* E19 Persian. **1** E19 A flower; *especially* a rose. **2** E20 A large geometrical motif derived from the shape of the rose that forms part of the design of a Turkoman rug.

■ Sense 1 is poetical, as in the phrase *gardens of gul.*

Gulag /ˈguːlag/, *foreign* /guˈlak/ *noun* (also **gulag**) M20 Russian (acronym, from *Glavnoe upravlenie ispravitel'no-trudovykh lagereĭ* Chief Administration for Corrective Labour Camps). **1** M20 A department of the Soviet secret police that administered corrective labour camps and prisons between 1934 and 1955. *rare.* **2** L20 The Soviet network of labour camps; a camp or prison within it; *figurative* a coercive institution, an oppressive environment.

2 1996 *New Scientist* He [sc. Lysenko] was a shrewd political manipulator, gradually rising in

communist circles as his opponents were exiled to the gulags.

gundy variant of GOONDIE.

gung-ho /gʌŋˈhəʊ/ *adjective* M20 Chinese (*gōnghé*, taken as 'work together'). Enthusiastic, eager.

■ Adopted as a slogan in the war of 1939–45 by the United States Marines.

1996 *Country Life* . . . the banished Duke is neatly played by Robert Demeger as a gung-ho figure cheering up his fellow-exiles during an Arctic winter . . .

gunibri variant of GIMBRI.

gunyah /ˈgʌnjə/ *noun* E19 Aboriginal. In Australia: an Aboriginal hut; a bush hut.

gurdwara /gʊəˈdwɑːrə/, /gəˈdwɑːrə/ *noun* E20 Panjabi (*gurduārā*, from Sanskrit GURU + *dvāra* door). A Sikh temple.

guru /ˈgʊruː/, /ˈguːruː/ *noun* (also **gooroo**) E17 Sanskrit (*guru* elder, teacher). **1** E17 A (Hindu) spiritual teacher. **2** M20 Anyone looked up to as a source of wisdom or knowledge; an influential leader or pundit.

2 1995 *Country Life* Some guru—in Yorkshire, maybe—has warned that we are to have a hard winter.

gusto /ˈgʌstəʊ/ *noun* plural **gusto(e)s** E17 Italian (from Latin *gustus* taste). Keen enjoyment displayed in action or speech, especially in eating or drinking; relish, zest.

■ Often in the phrase *with (great) gusto* (see quotation). The other early (E17) sense of *gusto* as 'an individual fondness or preference' and the art critical sense (M17) of 'the style in which a work of art etc. is executed' (especially in *great* or *grand gusto* (= Italian *gran gusto*)) are both now archaic. ˙
1996 *Spectator* He is not a wild, untempered spirit; he cooks with gusto, but not without formality.

gutta /ˈgʌtə/ *noun* plural **guttae** /ˈgʌtiː/ LME Latin (= drop (of any liquid)). **1** LME–E18 Gum; gum resin, *especially* gamboge. **2** M16 *Architecture* Each of a row of usually conical projections resembling drops underneath the triglyph (and sometimes the mutule) of a Doric capital. **3** M16 *Pharmacology* and *Medicine* A drop of liquid. Now *rare* or *obsolete*. **4** E19 A roundish coloured dot on an insect's wing, *especially* one of a light colour.

gutta-percha /ˌgʌtəˈpəːtʃə/ *noun* M19 Malay (*getah perca*, from *getah* gum + *perca* strips of cloth (which it resembles); assimilated to GUTTA). **1** M19 The coagulated latex of certain Malaysian trees, a hard tough thermoplastic substance consisting chiefly of a hydrocarbon isomeric with rubber and now used especially in dentistry and for electrical insulation. **2** M19 Any of the trees, of the sapote family, which yield gutta-percha.

gymnasium /ʤɪmˈneɪzɪəm/ *noun* plural **gymnasiums, gymnasia** /ʤɪmˈneɪzɪə/ L16 Latin (from Greek *gumnasion*, from *gumnazein* to exercise naked, from *gumnos* naked). **1** L16 A place, room, or building, equipped for gymnastics or for indoor sports. **2** L17 Formerly, a high school, college, or academy in Continental Europe. Now *specifically* in Germany and some other Continental countries, a school of the highest grade, preparing pupils for universities.

gypsum /ˈʤɪpsəm/ *noun & verb* LME Latin (from Greek *gupsos* chalk, gypsum). **A** *noun* LME Hydrated calcium sulphate, a soft mineral that occurs as colourless, white, or grey monoclinic prismatic crystals in many sedimentary rocks and is used for making plaster of Paris and as a fertilizer. **B** *transitive verb* E19 *Agriculture* Dress with gypsum.

gyro /ˈʤʌɪrəʊ/, /ˈʤɪərəʊ/ *noun* plural **gyros** L20 **Modern Greek** (*guros* turning). A sandwich of pitta bread filled with slices of spiced meat cooked on a spit, tomatoes, onions, etc.

■ Mainly United States.

H

habanera /habəˈnɛːrə/, /ˌɑːbəˈnɛːrə/ *noun* L19 **Spanish** (short for *danza habanera* Havanan dance, feminine of *habanero* of Havana the capital of Cuba). A slow Cuban dance and song in duple time.

habeas corpora /ˌheɪbɪəs ˈkɔːpərə/ *noun phrase* LME **Latin** (= thou (shalt) have the bodies (sc. in court)). *Law* (now *historical*). A process formerly issued from the Court of Common Pleas, directing the sheriff to compel the attendance of reluctant jurors.

habeas corpus /ˌheɪbɪəs ˈkɔːpəs/ *noun phrase* LME **Latin** (= thou (shalt) have the body (sc. in court)). *Law* A writ requiring a person to be brought before a judge or into a court; *specifically* such a writ requiring the investigation of the legitimacy of a person's detention, by which his or her release may be secured.
> **1996** *Times* It is ironic that the American President who was most influenced by . . . the values of legalism was compelled by civil war to suspend the writ of habeas corpus and defy Chief Justice Taney.

habitat /ˈhabɪtat/ *noun* L18 **Latin** (literally, 'it inhabits', 3rd person singular present of *habitare* to dwell in). **1** L18 The natural environment characteristically occupied by a particular organism; an area distinguished by the set of organisms which occupy it. Also, such areas collectively. **2** M19 *generally* One's dwelling-place; a habitation; usual surroundings.

habitué /abitɥe/ (*plural same*); /həˈbɪtjʊeɪ/ *noun* E19 **French** (past participle of *habituer* from Latin *habituare* to frequent). A habitual visitor or resident (*of* a place).
> **1996** *Spectator* John became a habitué and, quite literally, sang its praises.

habutai /ˈhɑːbʊtʌɪ/ *noun* L19 **Japanese** (*habutae*). Fine soft silk of a type originally made in Japan. Also called *Japanese* (or *Jap*) *silk*.

háček /ˈhɑːtʃɛk/, /ˈhatʃɛk/ *noun* M20 **Czech** (diminutive of *hák* hook). A diacritic mark (ˇ) used chiefly in Baltic and Slavonic languages, especially to indicate various types of palatalization.

hacendado /asɛnˈdɑːdəʊ/, *foreign* /aθen ˈdado/, /asenˈdado/ *noun* (also **haciendado** /ˌasɪɛnˈdɑːdəʊ/, *foreign* /aθien'dado/, /asjenˈdaðo/ plural **hacendados** /asɛn ˈdɑːdəʊz/, *foreign* /aθenˈdaðos/ M19 **Spanish**. The owner of a HACIENDA.

hachure /haˈʃjʊə/ *noun & verb* M19 **French** (from *hacher* to hatch). *Cartography* **A** *noun* M19 Any of a number of short lines of shading on a map running in the direction of a slope and indicating steepness by their closeness and thickness. Also *hachure line*. Usually in *plural*. **B** *transitive verb* M19 Shade (a map) with hachures.

hacienda /hasɪˈɛndə/, *foreign* /aθiˈenda/, /asiˈenda/ *noun* M18 **Spanish** (from Latin *facienda* things to be done, from *facere* to do). In Spain and Spanish-speaking countries: an estate including a house; a large farm, a plantation; a rural factory.

haciendado variant of HACENDADO.

Hadith /haˈdiːθ/ *noun* E18 **Arabic** (*ḥadīṯ* statement, tradition). The body of tradition concerning the sayings and doings of the Prophet Muhammad, now considered to be second in authority to the Koran and to embody the Sunna; a single such saying.

hadj, hadji variants of HAJJ, HAJJI.

haff /haf/ *noun* M19 **German** (from Middle and Modern Low German *haf* sea, corresponding to Old Norse *haf*, Old English *hæf* sea). A shallow freshwater lagoon found at a river mouth, especially on the Baltic coast.

hafiz /ˈhɑːfɪz/ *noun* M17 **Persian** (from Arabic *ḥāfiẓ* present participle of *ḥafiẓa* to guard, know by heart). A Muslim who knows the Koran by heart.

ha-ha /ˈhɑːhɑː/ *noun* (also **haw-haw** /ˈhɔːhɔː/) E18 **French** (perhaps from the cry of surprise on discovering the obstacle). A ditch with a wall on its inner side below ground level, forming a boundary to a garden or park without interrupting the view from within.

haham /ˈhɑːhəm/ *noun* (also **chacham** /ˈxɑːxəm/ and other variants) L17 **Hebrew** (*ḥākām* wise). A person learned in Jewish law; a wise man; *specifically* among Sephardic Jews, a rabbi; the spiritual head of a Sephardic community.

haiku /'hʌɪkuː/ *noun* plural same, **haikus** L19 Japanese (abbreviation of *haikai no ku* unserious or comic verse). A short Japanese poem in three parts and usually having seventeen syllables; an English imitation of such a poem. Cf. HOKKU.

hajj /hadʒ/ *noun* (also **hadj, haj**) E18 Arabic ((al-) *ḥajj* (the Great) Pilgrimage). The pilgrimage to the Sacred Mosque at Mecca undertaken in the twelfth month of the Muslim year and constituting one of the religious duties of Islam.

> figurative **1995** *Times* The international conference has become a modern form of world pilgrimage, the haj of the leisure classes.

hajji /'hadʒiː/ *noun* (also (feminine) **hajja** /'hadʒə/; **hadji**) E17 Persian (Turkish *ḥājjī, ḥājī* pilgrim, from as preceding). (The title given to) a person who has undertaken the hajj. Cf. ALHAJI.

haka /'hɑːkə/ *noun* M19 Maori. A ceremonial Maori dance accompanied by chanting.

> ■ Best known through its adoption by New Zealand international rugby teams as a pre-match ritual.

hakama /'hakəmə/, /'hɑːkəmə/ *noun* M19 Japanese. Japanese loose trousers with many pleats in the front.

hakeem variant of HAKIM 2.

Hakenkreuz /'hɑːkənkrɔyts/ *noun* (also **hakenkreuz**) plural **Hakenkreuze** /'hɑːkənkrɔytsə/ M20 German (from *Haken* hook + *Kreuz* cross). A swastika, especially as a Nazi symbol.

hakim /'hɑːkɪm/ *noun* 1 E17 Arabic (*ḥākim* ruler, governor, judge from *ḥakama* to pass judgement). A judge, ruler, or governor in a Muslim country.

hakim /ha'kiːm/ *noun* 2 (also **hakeem**) M17 Arabic (*ḥakīm* wise man, philosopher, physician, from as preceding). A physician in a Muslim country.

halal /hə'lɑːl/ *adjective, verb, & noun* (also **hallal**) M19 Arabic (*ḥalāl* according to religious law). **A** *adjective* M19 Killed or prepared in the manner prescribed by Islamic law. **B** *transitive verb* M19 Kill (an animal) in this manner. **C** *noun* M20 An animal killed, or meat prepared, in this manner.

halcyon /'halsɪən/, /'halʃ(ə)n/ *noun & adjective* LME Latin ((h)*alcyon* from Greek *alkuōn* kingfisher (also *halkuōn* by association with *hals* sea and *kuōn* conceiving), related to Latin *alcedo* kingfisher). **A** *noun* 1 LME A bird said by the ancients to breed in a nest floating on the sea around the time of the winter solstice, and to charm the wind and waves so that the sea was calm for this purpose; *poetical* a kingfisher. **b** L18 Any of various brightly coloured tropical kingfishers of the genus *Halcyon*. 2 M17–L18 Calm, quietude. **B** *adjective* 1 L16 Calm, peaceful; happy, prosperous, idyllic. 2 E17 Of or pertaining to the halcyon or kingfisher.

haldi /'hʌldi/ *noun* (also **huldee**) M19 Hindustani (from Sanskrit *haridrā*). The plant *Curcuma longa*, of the ginger family, whose powdered tubers yield turmeric. Also, turmeric itself.

hallal variant of HALAL.

halling /'halɪŋ/ *noun* M19 Norwegian (from *Hallingdal* a valley in southern Norway). A Norwegian country dance in duple rhythm; a piece of music for this dance.

halma /'halmə/ *noun* L19 Greek (= leap). A game played by two or four people on a chequer-board of 256 squares, with pieces advancing from one corner to the opposite corner by being moved over other pieces into vacant squares.

haltere /hal'tɪə/ *noun* plural **halteres** /hal'tɪəriːz/ M16 Greek (*haltēres* plural (sense 1), from *hallesthai* to jump). 1 M16 In *plural*. Weights, like dumb-bells, held in the hand to give an impetus in jumping. 2 E19 *Entomology* Either of the two knobbed filaments which in dipteran insects take the place of posterior wings. Also called *balancer, poiser*. Usually in *plural*.

halutzim /hɑːluː'tsɪm/, /xɑːluː'tsɪm/ *noun* plural (also **haluzim, chalutzim**) E20 Hebrew (*ḥālūṣīm*). *History* Jewish pioneers who entered Palestine from 1917 onwards to build it up as a Jewish State.

halva /'halvɑː/, /'halvə/ *noun* (also **halvah**, (earlier) **hulwa**) M17 Yiddish (*hal(a)va*, modern Hebrew *ḥalbāh*, modern Greek *khalbas*, Turkish *helva*, etc., from) Arabic (and Persian) *ḥalwā* sweetmeat). A Middle Eastern sweet confection made of sesame flour and honey.

> ■ Later (M19) also found in its Arabic form *halawi* /hə'lɑːwi/.

hamada variant of HAMMADA.

hamartia /hə'mɑːtɪə/ *noun* L18 Greek (= fault, failure, guilt). The fault or error leading to the destruction of the tragic hero or heroine of a play, novel, etc.

hamel /'hɑːm(ə)l/ *noun* M19 Afrikaans (= Dutch *hamel*, German *Hammel*, from Old High German *hamal* mutilated). In South Africa: a castrated ram, a wether.

hametz /hɑːˈmɛts/, /ˈxɑːmɛts/ *noun* (also **chametz**, **chometz**) M19 Hebrew (*ḥāmēṣ*). Leaven or food mixed with leaven, prohibited during the Passover.

hammada /həˈmɑːdə/ *noun* (also **hamada**) M19 Arabic (*ḥammāda*). A flat rocky area of desert blown free of sand by the wind, typical of the Sahara.

hammam /ˈhamam/, /həˈmɑːm/, /ˈhʌmʌm/ *noun* (also **hummum** /ˈhʌmʌm/) E17 Turkish (or its source Arabic *ḥammām* bath, from *ḥamma* to heat). An establishment where one may take a Turkish bath.

hamsin variant of KHAMSIN.

hamza /ˈhamzə/ *noun* E19 Arabic (literally, 'compression'). (A symbol in Arabic script representing) the glottal stop.

han variant of KHAN.

haneef variant of HANIF.

hanepoot /ˈhɑːnəpʊət/ *noun* L18 Afrikaans (from Dutch *haan* cock + *poot* foot). **1** L18 A variety of sweet muscat grape, grown in South Africa and used for making wine or raisins. **2** E19 The sweet white wine made from these grapes.

hangi /ˈhaŋi/, /ˈhɑːŋi/ *noun* M19 Maori. An earth-oven in which food is cooked on heated stones; the food cooked in such an oven.
■ Chiefly New Zealand.

hanif /haˈniːf/ *noun* (also **haneef**) M18 Arabic (*ḥanīf*, an epithet applied to Abraham in the Koran). Among Muslims, a follower of the original and true (monotheistic) religion.

haniwa /ˈhanɪwə/ *noun* plural same M20 Japanese (literally, 'rings of clay'). *Archaeology* A clay image based on a cylindrical shape of a type placed outside Japanese tombs of the fifth to seventh century.

Hanse /hans/ *noun* (also **hanse**) ME Middle Low German (*hanshūs* and medieval Latin *hansa* from Old High German *hansa*, Middle and Modern High German *hanse* (whence Middle Low German *hanse*) Gothic *hansa* company, crowd, from Germanic, whence also Finnish *kansa* people,

company). *History* **1** ME A merchant guild. **b** LME *specifically* (A merchant, citizen, or town of) the Hanseatic League. **2** ME A membership fee payable to a merchant guild; a trading fee imposed on non-members of the guild.

haoma variant of HOM.

hapax   legomenon /ˌhapaks lɛ ˈɡɒmənɒn/ *noun phrase* plural **hapax legomena** /ˌhapaks lɛˈɡɒmənə/ M17 Greek (= (a thing) said only once). A word, form, etc., of which only one recorded instance is known.
■ Used in Greek characters until L19 and sometimes abbreviated *hapax*.

harai-goshi /harʌɪˈɡɒʃi/ *noun* M20 Japanese (from *harai* sweep + *koshi* waist, hips). *Judo* A type of sweeping hip throw.

hara-kiri /harəˈkɪri/ *noun* (also (corruptly) **hari-kiri** /harɪˈkɪri/) M19 Japanese (from *hara* belly + *kiri* cutting). In Japan: a ritual form of suicide by disembowelling, formerly prescribed by a feudal superior to disgraced members of the samurai class as an alternative to execution. Also, suicide practised voluntarily from a sense of shame, as a protest, etc.

haram /hɑːˈrɑːm/ *noun & adjective* E17 Arabic (*ḥarām* forbidden; cf. HARAM). **A** *noun* E17 A Muslim sacred place, forbidden to non-Muslims. **B** *adjective* E17 Of food; forbidden under Islamic law. Opposed to HALAL.

haras /ˈarɑː/ *noun* plural same ME Old and Modern French (of unknown origin). An enclosure or establishment in which horses are kept for breeding. Formerly, a herd of such horses.

harem /ˈhɑːriːm/, /hɑːˈriːm/, /ˈhɛːrəm/ *noun* M17 Turkish and Arabic (originally from Turkish *harem*) from Arabic *ḥaram* (that which is) prohibited, (hence) sacred or inviolable place, sanctuary, women's apartments, wives, women; later also from Arabic *ḥarīm* with same meaning, both from *ḥaruma* to be prohibited or unlawful). **1** M17 Separate women's quarters in a Muslim house, designed for the privacy and seclusion of the occupants. **2** L18 The occupants of such quarters collectively; *specifically* a Muslim's wives and concubines. **b** L19 A group of female animals of a single species sharing a mate.

haricot /ˈharɪkəʊ/ *noun* M17 French (in sense 1 in *febves de haricot*, perhaps from Aztec *ayacotli*; in sense 2 Old French *hericoq, hericot* (*de mouton*), probably related

to *harigoter* to cut up). **1** M17 A leguminous plant, *Phaseolus vulgaris*, native to
tropical America but having numerous
widely cultivated varieties; the edible pod
or seed of this plant; *especially* white varieties of the dried seed. More fully *haricot
bean*. **2** M17 A ragout, especially of mutton or lamb.

hari-kiri variant of HARA-KIRI.

harka /'hɑːkə/ *noun* E20 Moroccan Arabic
(*ḥarka*: cf. literary Arabic *ḥaraka* movement, action, military operation). A body
of Moroccan irregular troops.

harmattan /hɑːˈmat(ə)n/ *noun* L17 Twi
(*haramata*). A parching dusty land-wind
on the West African coast from December
to February. Also *harmattan wind*.

haroseth /həˈrəʊsɛθ/ *noun* (also **charo-
seth** /xəˈrəʊsɛθ/, **haroset** /həˈrəʊsɛt/) L19
Hebrew (*ḥărōseṭ* from *ḥeres* earthware). A
mixture of apples, nuts, spices, etc., eaten
at the Passover Seder service to symbolize
the clay mixed by the Israelites during
their slavery in Egypt.

hartal /'hɑːtɑːl/, /'həːtɑːl/ *noun* E20 Hindustani (*harṭāl, hartāl*, for *haṭṭal*, literally,
'locking of shops' (Sanskrit *haṭṭa* shop,
tāla lock, bolt)). In the Indian subcontinent: the organized closing of shops and
offices as a mark of protest or as an act of
mourning.
1920 *Blackwood's Magazine* What I had seen
there of the crowds at the Hartal . . . had made
me nervous.

hashish /'haʃiːʃ/, /'haʃɪʃ/, /haˈʃiːʃ/ *noun*
L16 Arabic (*ḥašīš* dry herb, hay, powdered
hemp-leaves, intoxicant made from this).
Cannabis.

hasid /'hasɪd/ *noun* (also **cha(s)sid**
/'xasɪd/, **hassid**, and with initial capital)
plural **hasidim** /'hasɪdɪm/ E19 Hebrew
(*ḥāsīḏ* pious, pietist). A member of a Jewish sect founded in the eighteenth century by Israel Baal Shem Tov and
emphasizing joy in the service of God.

hasta la vista /ˌasta la 'vista/ *interjection*
M20 Spanish. In Spain: goodbye, *au revoir*.

hatha yoga /ˌhʌtə 'jəʊɡə/, /ˌhatə/ *noun
phrase* E20 Sanskrit (from *haṭha* force +
yoga). A system of physical exercises and
breathing control used in YOGA.

hatha yogi /ˌhʌtə 'jəʊɡi/, /'hatə/ *noun
phrase* M20 Sanskrit (from *haṭha* force +
yogi). A person who practises HATHA
YOGA.

hausfrau /'haʊsfraʊ/ *noun* plural **haus-
fraus, hausfrauen** /'haʊsfraʊən/ L18 German (from *Haus* house + *Frau* wife,
woman). A (German) housewife; a person
who embodies housewifely qualities.
1995 *Times* If you saw her on the street she
could be a *hausfrau*. It's very hard to relate her
to the terrible things you are hearing about.

hausmaler /'haʊsmɑːlə/ *noun* M20 German (from *Haus* house + *Maler* painter). A
person who paints undecorated china at
home or in a private workshop.

haute Bohème /ot bɔɛm/, /ˌəʊt bəʊˈɛm/
noun phrase E20 French (literally, 'high Bo-
hemia'). A fast or upper-class Bohemian
set of people.
■ The phrase was apparently coined by the
English writer Maurice Baring in *Cat's
Cradle* (1925) on the model of HAUTE BOUR-
GEOISIE.

haute bourgeoisie /ot burʒwazi/, /ˌəʊt
bʊəʒwaːˈziː/ *noun phrase* L19 French (literally, 'high bourgeoisie'). The upper
middle class.
1996 *Spectator* There is a thesis to be written
on why all crime stories devised for the haute
bourgeoisie have to present their viewers' class
in a generally unfavourable light.

haute couture /ot kutyr/, /ˌəʊt kʊˈtjʊə/
noun phrase E20 French (literally, 'high
dressmaking'). High fashion; the leading
dressmakers and fashion houses or their
products collectively.
1995 *Times* Here, at the office of Yves Saint
Laurent, is the genuine article, the haute
couture attainable by almost no one, where the
likes of Catherine Deneuve and Elizabeth
Taylor are fitted for dresses which will cost
£25,000.

haute cuisine /ot kɥizin/, /ˌəʊt kwɪˈziːn/
noun phrase E20 French (literally, 'high
cooking'). High-class (French) cooking.
1996 *Times* Haute cuisine was followed by
nouvelle cuisine . . .

haute école /ot ekɔl/, /ˌəʊt eɪˈkɒl/ *noun &
adjective phrase* M19 French (literally, 'high
school'). (Of or pertaining to) the more
difficult feats of horsemanship, or *transferred* of music or other arts.

haute-luxe /ot lyks/, /əʊt 'lʊks/ *adjective*
M20 French (literally, 'high luxury'). Luxurious, opulent.
1995 *Spectator* [A] play demanding incredible
chic and a *haute-luxe* setting has been thrown
onto a studio-stage set which looks as though
it was run up by the cast during a brief break in
rehearsals.

haute noblesse /ot nɔblɛs/, /ˌəʊt nəʊ
'blɛs/ *noun phrase* L18 French (literally,

'high nobility'). The upper stratum of the aristocracy. Cf. PETITE NOBLESSE.

hauteur /əʊˈtəː/, *foreign* /otœr/ *noun* E17 French (from *haut* high). Haughtiness of manner.
1996 *Times* To the dismay of her mother—who held out with an old-fashioned hauteur against her daughter's taking to the stage—Helene Cordot decided to embark upon a career as a cabaret artiste . . .

haute vulgarisation /ot vylɡarizasjɔ̃/, /ˌəʊt vʌlɡərʌɪˈzeɪʃ(ə)n/ *noun phrase* M20 French (literally, 'high vulgarization'). The popularization of abstruse or complex matters.
1995 *Times* This branch of *haute vulgarisation* takes patience, love of getting things shipshape and a tolerance of being thought a spoilsport.

haut-goût /oɡu/, /ˈəʊɡuː/ *noun* M16 French (literally, 'high flavour'). **1** M16 A strong flavour or relish, seasoning (*literally* and *figuratively*). **2** M17-E19 A highly flavoured or seasoned dish. **3** L17 A slightly rotten flavour; a taint.

haut monde /o mɔ̃d/, /əʊ ˈmɒnd/ *noun phrase* M19 French (literally, 'high world'). The fashionable world. Cf. BEAU MONDE.

haut-pas /opa/ *noun plural* same LME French (literally, 'high step'). A dais raised one or more steps above the level of the rest of the floor.

haut-relief /orəljɛf/, /əʊrɪˈliːf/ *noun* M19 French (literally, 'high relief'). ALTO-RE-LIEVO.

haut ton /o tɔ̃/ *noun phrase* E19 French (literally, 'high tone'). (People of) high fashion.
■ Now less common than just 'the TON' in the sense of 'fashionable society'.

havildar /ˈhavɪldɑː/ *noun* L17 Urdu (*hawildār* from Persian *ḥawāl(a)dār* charge holder, from *ḥawāl*, from Arabic *ḥawāl(a)* charge, assignment + Persian *hawāl(a)dār* holding, holder). An Indian non-commissioned officer equivalent to a sergeant.

haw-haw variant of HA-HA.

hazzan /xəˈzɑːn/, /ˈhɑːz(ə)n/ *noun* (also **chaz(z)an, hazan**) plural **hazzanim** /xə ˈzɑːnim/ M17 Hebrew (*ḥazzān* beadle, cantor, probably from Assyrian *hazannu* overseer or governor). A CANTOR in a synagogue.

Hebe /ˈhiːbi/ *noun* E17 Greek (*hēbē* youthful beauty, *Hēbē* the Greek goddess of youth and spring, daughter of Zeus and Hera, and cupbearer of Olympus). **1** E17 A

young woman resembling Hebe; a waitress. **2** M20 (**hebe**) Any of numerous New Zealand evergreen shrubs constituting the genus *Hebe* (formerly included in *Veronica*), with spikes of blue, white, mauve, etc., flowers.

hebra /ˈhɛbrə/ *noun* (also **chevra** /ˈxɛvrə/) plural **hebras, hebroth** /ˈhɛbrəʊt/ L19 Hebrew (*ḥebrāh* association, society). A small group formed by members of a Jewish community for religious and charitable purposes.

heder /ˈhɛdə/, /ˈxɛdə/ *noun* (also **cheder**) plural **hedarim** /hɛˈdɑːrɪm/, **heders** L19 Hebrew (*ḥēḏer* room). A school for Jewish children in which Hebrew and religious knowledge are taught.

Heft /hɛft/ *noun* plural **Hefte** /ˈhɛftə/ L19 German. A number of sheets of paper fastened together to form a book; *specifically* a part of a serial publication, a fascicle.

hegemon /ˈhɛɡɪmɒn/, /ˈhiːɡɪmɒn/, /ˈhɛdʒɪmɒn/ *noun* E20 Greek (*hēgemōn* leader, from *hēgeisthai* to lead). A leading or paramount power; a dominant state or person.

hegira /ˈhɛdʒɪrə/ *noun* (also **Hegira, hejira, hijra** /ˈhɪdʒrə/) L16 Medieval Latin (from Arabic *hijra* departure from one's home and friends, from *hajara* to separate, emigrate). **1** L16 The emigration of Muhammad from Mecca to Medina in 622; the Muslim era reckoned from this. **2** M18 Any exodus or departure.
■ The abbreviation AH (for *anno Hegirae*) is used in Islamic dates.

Heilsgeschichte /ˈhaɪlsɡəˌʃɪçtə/ *noun* M20 German. *Theology* Sacred history; *specifically* the history of the salvation of mankind by God; history seen as the working out of this salvation.

heimisch /ˈhaɪmɪʃ/ *adjective* M20 Yiddish (*heymish* domestic, homelike). In Jewish speech: homely, unpretentious.

Heimweh /ˈhaɪmveː/ *noun* E18 German. Homesickness.

hejira variant of HEGIRA.

hélas /eˈlɑːs/ *interjection* LME French (later form of *ha las*, *a las* alas). Expressing grief, sadness, regret, etc.

Heldentenor /ˌhɛldənteˈnoːr/ *noun* plural **Heldentenöre** /ˌhɛldənteˈnøːrə/ E20 German (= hero tenor). A singer with a powerful tenor voice suited to heroic roles, especially in Wagnerian opera.

helix /'hiːlɪks/ *noun* plural **helices** /'hɛlɪsiːz/, /'hiːlɪsiːz/, **helixes** M16 Latin (*helix, helicis* from Greek *helix*). **1** M16 Chiefly *Architecture.* A spiral ornament, a volute; *specifically* each of the eight smaller volutes under the abacus of a Corinthian capital. **2** E17 An object of coiled form, either round an axis (like a corkscrew) or, less usually, in one plane (like a watchspring); *Geometry* a three-dimensional curve on a (notional) conical or cylindrical surface which becomes a straight line when the surface is unrolled into a plane. **3** L17 *Anatomy* The curved fold which forms the rim of the exterior ear. **4** E19 *Zoology* Any spiral-shelled mollusc of the genus *Helix*.

helot /'hɛlət/ *noun* L16 Latin (*Helotes* plural from Greek *Heilōtes* (plural of *Heilōs*), also *Hilotae* from Greek *Heilōtai* (plural of *Heilōtēs*): usually derived from *Helos* a town in Laconia whose inhabitants were enslaved). *Greek History* **1** L16 (*Helot*) A member of a class of serfs in ancient Sparta, intermediate in status between slaves and citizens. **2** E19 *transferred* and *figurative* A serf, a slave.

hendiadys /hɛn'dʌɪədɪs/ *noun* L16 Medieval Latin (from Greek *hen dia duoin* 'one through two'). A figure of speech in which a single complex idea is expressed by two words usually connected by *and*.

■ An example of *hendiadys* is *nice and warm* for *nicely warm*.

herbarium /həː'bɛːrɪəm/ *noun* L18 Late Latin (*herbarium*, use as noun of adjective represented by Latin *herbarius* botanist, *herbaria* (sc. *ars*) botany). A collection of dried botanical specimens systematically arranged for reference. Also, a room or building housing such a collection.

herem variant of CHEREM.

hermandad /ˌerman'dad/ *noun* plural **hermandades** /ˌerman'dades/ M18 Spanish (= brotherhood). *History* In Spain: a resistance group against oppression by the nobility; *specifically* a voluntary organization later reorganized as regular national police.

heroon /hɪ'rəʊɒn/ *noun* plural **heroa** /hɪ'rəʊə/ (also (earlier) **heroum** /hɪ'rəʊəm/) L18 Latin (*heroum* from Greek *hērōon*, from *hērōios* of a hero, from *hērōs* hero). Originally, a temple dedicated to a hero, often over his supposed tomb. Now, a sepulchral monument in the form of a small temple.

herpes /'həːpiːz/ *noun* LME Latin (= shingles, from Greek, literally, 'creeping', from *herpein* to creep). Originally, any skin disease characterized by the formation of groups of vesicles. Now, (infection with) any of a small group of viruses affecting the skin and nervous system.

Herrenvolk /'hɛːrənfɒlk/, /'hɛr(ə)nfɒlk/, /'hɛːrənfəʊk/ *noun* M20 German (= master-race, from *Herren*, plural of *Herr*, from Old High German *hērro*, comparative of *hēr* exalted + *volk* race). The German nation, viewed (especially by the Nazis) as a race born to mastery; in extended usage, a group regarding itself as innately superior.

hetaera /hɪ'tɪərə/ *noun* (also **hetaira** /hɪ'tʌɪrə/, plural **hetairas**, **hetairai** /hɪ'tʌɪrʌɪ/) plural **hetaeras**, **hetaerae** /hɪ'tɪəriː/ E19 Greek (*hetaira* feminine of *hetairos* companion). Especially in ancient Greece: a mistress, a concubine; a courtesan, a prostitute.

hetman /'hɛtmən/ *noun* M18 Polish (probably from German *Hauptmann* (earlier *Heubtman*) headman, captain). A Cossack military commander. Cf. ATAMAN.

Heurige /'hɔyrɪgə/ *noun* (also **Heuriger** /'hɔyrɪgər/) plural **Heurigen** /'hɔyrɪgən/ M20 German ((southern and Austrian)) new (wine); vintner's establishment). **1** M20 Especially in Austria: wine from the latest harvest. **2** M20 An establishment where such wine is served.

hexapla /'hɛksəplə/ *noun* (also **hexaple** /'hɛksəp(ə)l/) E17 Greek ((ta) *hexapla* (title of Origen's work) neuter plural of *hexaplous* sixfold). A sixfold text in parallel columns, especially of the Old or New Testament.

hiatus /hʌɪ'eɪtəs/ *noun* plural same, **hiatuses** M16 Latin (= gaping, opening, from *hiare* to gape). **1** M16 A physical break in continuity; a gaping chasm; an opening, an aperture. *rare* in *general* sense. **b** L19 *Anatomy* Any of various natural openings or gaps. Usually with specifying word. **2** E17 A gap or break in continuity, especially in a series or an account; a missing link in a chain of events; *especially* in *Geology* (the time value of) a break or unconformity in the stratigraphic sequence. **b** M19 *Logic* A missing link in a chain of argument. **3** E18 *Grammar* and *Prosody* A break between two vowels which come together without an intervening consonant in successive words or syllables.

hibachi /hɪ'batʃi/, /'hɪbətʃi/ *noun* M19 **Japanese** (from *hi* fire + *hachi* bowl, pot). **1** M19 In Japan: a large earthenware pan or brazier in which charcoal is burnt to provide indoor heating. **2** M20 A type of especially outdoor cooking apparatus similar to a barbecue.

hibakusha /'hɪbəku:ʃə/ *noun* plural same M20 **Japanese** (from *hi* suffer + *baku* explosion + *sha* person). A survivor of an atomic explosion, *especially* in *plural*, the survivors of the atomic explosions at Hiroshima and Nagasaki in 1945.

hic jacet /hɪk 'dʒeɪsɛt/, /'jakɛt/ *noun phrase* E17 **Latin** (literally, 'here lies', the first two words of a Latin epitaph). An epitaph.

hidalgo /hɪ'dalgəʊ/ *noun* plural **hidalgos** L16 **Spanish** (formerly also *hijo dalgo* contraction of *hijo de algo*, literally, 'son of something'; cf. FIDALGO). **1** L16 In Spain: a member of the lower nobility. **2** E19 *transferred* A person resembling a hidalgo; *specifically* one who is suited to be or aspires to be a member of the nobility.

hiera picra /ˌhaɪrə 'pɪkrə/ *noun phrase* LME **Medieval Latin** (from Greek, from *hiera* sacred (name of many medicines) + *pikra* feminine of *pikros* bitter). *Pharmacology* A purgative drug composed mainly of aloes and canella bark.
■ Also altered to *hickery-pickery*.

hijab /'hɪdʒab/ *noun* L20 **Arabic**. The headscarf worn by Muslim women.
1995 *Times* Western women observing this rush for the *hijab* (headscarf) tend to stare in disbelief, broadcasting the worst excesses of 'Muslim chauvinism'.

hijra variant of HEGIRA.

hilo /'hi:ləʊ/ *noun* plural **hilos** M19 **Spanish** (= thread, from Latin *filum*). A thin vein of ore.

hippocampus /ˌhɪpə(ʊ)'kampəs/ *noun* plural **hippocampi** /ˌhɪpə(ʊ)'kampʌɪ/ L16 **Latin** (from Greek *hippokampos*, from *hippos* horse + *kampos* sea-monster). **1** L16 A fish of the genus *Hippocampus*; a sea horse. **2** E17 A mythical sea-monster, half horse and half fish or dolphin, represented as drawing the chariot of Neptune etc.; a representation of this. **3** E18 *Anatomy* A swelling on the floor of each lateral ventricle of the brain.

hippodrome /'hɪpədrəʊm/ *noun & verb* L16 **Old and Modern French** (Latin *hippodromus* from Greek *hippodromos*, from *hippos* horse + *dromos* race, course). **A** *noun* **1** L16 In ancient Greece and Rome, a course for chariot- or horse-races. Also, a modern circus. **2** L19 (*Hippodrome*) (The name of) a theatre used for various stage entertainments. **3** L19 A race or contest in which the result is prearranged or fixed. *United States slang.* **B** M19 *intransitive verb* Prearrange or fix the result of a race or contest. Chiefly as *hippodroming* verbal noun, *United States slang.*

hiragana /hɪrə'gɑːnə/ *noun* (also **hirakana** /hɪrə'kɑːnə/) E19 **Japanese** (from *hira* plain + KANA). The form of kana normally used in Japanese, derived from the cursive style of writing. Cf. KATAKANA.

hochgeboren /'hoːxɡəˌboːrən/ *noun & adjective* plural of noun same E20 **German**. (A person who is) high-born.

hogan /'həʊɡ(ə)n/ *noun* L19 **Navajo**. An American Indian (especially Navajo) hut made from logs, earth, etc.

hoi polloi /hɔɪ 'pɒlɔɪ/, /hɔɪ pɒ'lɔɪ/ *noun phrase* M17 **Greek** (= the many). The majority, the masses; the rabble.
■ Frequently with *the* in English, unnecessarily duplicating the Greek definite article *hoi*.
1996 *Spectator* Why do people who can afford to run their businesses from anywhere . . . rush . . . to join city hoi polloi once the Ides of March approach.

hokku /'hɒku:/ *noun* plural same, **hokkus** L19 **Japanese** (= 'opening verse (of a linked sequence of comic verses)'). A HAIKU.

hollandaise /hɒlən'deɪz/, *attributively also* /'hɒləndeɪz/ *noun & adjective* M19 **French** (feminine of *hollandais* Dutch, from *Hollande* Holland). (Designating) a sauce made with butter, egg-yolks, vinegar or white wine, and lemon juice, usually served with fish.

hom /həʊm/ *noun* (also **haoma, homa** /'həʊmə/) M19 **Persian** (obsolete *hōm* (modern *hūm*), Avestan *haoma* = Sanskrit *soma* SOMA). (The juice of) the sacred plant of the ancient Persians and Parsees.

hombre /'ɒmbreɪ/ *noun* M19 **Spanish** (= man, from Latin *homo, homin-* human being). In Spain and Spanish-speaking countries: a man.
■ Also in more general use, chiefly in United States slang.
1996 *Spectator* All newspapers periodically put tough hombres into the accounts department.

homme d'affaires /ɔm dafɛr/ *noun phrase* plural **hommes d'affaires** (*pronounced same*) E18 **French**. A businessman, an agent.

homme moyen sensuel /ɔm mwɑjɛ̃ sɑ̃sɥɛl/ *noun phrase* (also **homme sensuel moyen**) E20 French. The average man; the man in the street.

homo /'həʊməʊ/, /'hɒməʊ/ *noun* plural **homos** L16 Latin (= man). **1** L16 A human being. **2** L18 (**Homo**) The genus to which human beings (HOMO SAPIENS) and certain of their fossil ancestors belong. Also with Latin specific epithets in names of (proposed) species, and with Latin or mock-Latin adjectives (in imitation of zoology nomenclature) in names intended to personify some aspects of human life or behaviour.

2 1961 *Times* Symbolizing . . . this concept of *homo turisticus*, the new Hilton hotel . . . will have 500 rooms—all with a view of the Parthenon.

2 1996 *Times* But as for homo *loquens* [speaking] we seem to be little closer to knowing when, where, why, or how this stage was reached.

homoeoteleuton /hɒˌmiːətɪˈljuːt(ə)n/ *noun* (also **homoioteleuton** /hɒˌmɔɪətɪˈljuːt(ə)n/) L16 Late Latin (from Greek *homoioteleuton* (sc. *rhēma* word), from *homoios* like + *teleutē* ending). **1** L16 A rhetorical figure consisting in the use of a series of words with the same or similar endings. *rare*. **2** M19 (An error in copying caused by) the occurrence of similar endings in two neighbouring words, lines, etc.

Homoiousion /hɒmɔɪˈuːsɪən/, /hɒmˈaʊsɪən/, /hɒmɔɪˈuːzɪən/ *noun* M19 ecclesiastical Greek (neuter of *homoiousios* of like essence, from *homoios* like, similar + *ousia* essence, substance). *Christian Theology* The doctrine that the first and second persons of the Trinity are of like but not identical essence or substance. Cf. HOMOOUSION.

Homoousion /hɒməʊˈuːsɪən/, /hɒmˈaʊsɪən/, /hɒməʊˈuːzɪən/; /həʊməʊˈuːsɪən/ *noun* L18 ecclesiastical Greek (neuter of *homoousios*, from *homos* same + *ousia* essence, substance). *Christian Theology* The doctrine that the first and second persons of the Trinity are of identical essence or substance. Cf. HOMOIOUSION.

■ After a long period of theological and philosophical discussion in the early centuries of the Christian era, this view prevailed at the Council of Chalcedon in 451 against that of the Homoiousian party.

Homo sapiens /ˌhəʊməʊ ˈsapɪɛnz/, /ˌhɒməʊ ˈsapɪɛnz/ *noun phrase* (also **homo sapiens**) E19 Modern Latin (= wise man).

Modern human beings regarded as a species.

■ Term introduced in Linnaeus' *Systema Naturae* (10th edn. 1758), and thence into English via the translation of Linnaeus' book.

1996 *Times* She valuably reviews the anthropological, archaeological, and palaeontological evidence for the emergence of homo sapiens in the Rift Valley.

homunculus /hɒˈmʌŋkjʊləs/ *noun* plural **homunculi** /hɒˈmʌŋkjʊlʌɪ/, /hɒˈmʌŋkjʊliː/ M17 Latin (diminutive of *homo* man). A diminutive person, a dwarf.

■ Formerly also applied to a foetus considered as a fully formed human being.

honcho /'hɒntʃəʊ/ *noun & verb* M20 Japanese (*hanchō* group leader). **A** *noun* M20 plural **honchos**. The leader of a small group or squad; a person who is in a position of power; a strong leader. **B** *transitive verb* M20 Oversee; be in charge of (a situation).

■ Chiefly North American slang. See quotation at GALÈRE.

honda /'hɒndə/ *noun* (also **hondo** /'hɒndəʊ/, plural **hondos**, **hondu** /'hɒndu:/) L19 Spanish (probably from *hondón* eyelet, influenced by Spanish *honda* sling). The eye at the end of a lasso through which the rope passes to form a loop. *United States*.

hong /hɒŋ/ *noun* E18 Chinese (*háng*, (Cantonese) *hòhng* row, trade). **1** E18 In China: a series of rooms or buildings used as a warehouse, factory, etc. *especially* one of the foreign factories formerly maintained at Canton. Also in Hong Kong, a trading establishment. **2** L18 *History* The corporation of Chinese merchants at Canton who had a monopoly of trade with Europeans.

honnête homme /ɔnɛt ɔm/ *noun phrase* plural **honnêtes hommes** (pronounced same) M17 French. A decent, cultivated man of the world.

1960 J. Bayley *Characters of Love* Iago . . . is in many ways a terrible parody of the Augustan *honnête homme*.

honorarium /ɒnəˈrɛːrɪəm/ *noun* plural **honorariums**, **honoraria** /ɒnəˈrɛːrɪə/ M17 Latin (*honorarium* gift made on being admitted to a post of honour, use as noun of neuter of *honorarius* honorary). A (voluntary) fee, especially for professional services nominally rendered without payment.

1996 *Country Life* Mrs Young radiates enjoyment of her job, for which she is paid a reasonable honorarium . . .

honoris causa /ɒˌnɔːrɪs ˈkaʊzə/ *adverb phrase* E17 Latin (= for the sake of honour). As a mark of esteem, especially in reference to an honorary degree at a university.

hookah /ˈhʊkə/ *noun* M18 Urdu (from Arabic ḥuḳḳa small box, container, pot, jar). A pipe of oriental origin for smoking tobacco, marijuana, etc., with a long flexible tube connected to a container of water, through which the smoke is drawn from the tobacco etc.

hoop-la variant of HOUP-LA.

horae /ˈhɔːriː/ *noun* L19 Latin (*horae* plural of *hora* hour). A book of hours.

horchata /orˈtʃata/, /ɔːˈtʃɑːtə/ *noun* (also **orchata**) M19 Spanish. An almond-flavoured soft drink in Spain and Latin American countries.

horizontale /ɔrizɔ̃tal/ *noun slang* plural pronounced same L19 French. A prostitute. More fully GRANDE HORIZONTALE.

horme /ˈhɔːmi/ *noun* (also **hormé**) L17 Greek (*hormē* impulse). **1** L17 A passion, an impulse. *rare*. Only in L17. **2** E20 *Psychology* Vital or purposeful energy.

■ *Horme* was first used in English in the writings of the Cambridge Platonist philosopher Ralph Cudworth (1617–88) but did not achieve currency until its reintroduction as a term in Jungian psychology.

hornito /hɔːˈniːtəʊ/ *noun* plural **hornitos** M19 American Spanish (diminutive of *horno* (from Latin *furnus*) oven, furnace). *Geology* A driblet cone formed by successive ejections through a vent in a lava flow.

horresco referens /hɒˌrɛskəʊ rɛˈfəːrɛnz/ L17 Latin (= I shudder to relate, from *horrescere* to stand on end (of hair) + *referens*, present participle of *referre* to relate). Expressing horror at a memory.

■ The expression comes from Virgil's *Aeneid* (ii. 204), at the point when the hero Aeneas is relating how giant sea serpents killed the priest Laocoon for attempting to warn the Trojans against taking the Greeks' wooden horse into their city.
1995 *Spectator* I ended up bolting down a bowl of spaghetti bolognese the nastiness of which *horresco referens*.

horribile dictu /hɒˌrɪbɪleɪ ˈdɪktuː/, /hɒ ˌriːbɪli/ *adverb phrase* M19 Modern Latin

(by analogy with MIRABILE DICTU). Horrible to relate.

horror vacui /ˌhɒrə ˈvakjuːʌɪ/ *noun phrase* M19 Modern Latin (= the horror of a vacuum). (A) fear or dislike of leaving empty spaces in an artistic composition etc.
1972 E. Lucie-Smith *Eroticism in Western Art* Nudes . . . fill the whole picture-space as if the artist suffered from *horror vacui*.

hors concours /ɔr kɔ̃kur/ *adverb & predicate adjective phrase* L19 French (= out of the competition). Not competing for a prize; *figurative* without a rival, in a class of its own.

■ Both the literal and the figurative senses are also present in modern French.
1941 V. Nabokov *Real Life of Sebastian Knight* Most husbands are fools, but that one was *hors concours*.

hors de combat /ɔr də kɔ̃ba/ *adverb & predicate adjective phrase* M18 French (= out of the fight). Out of the fight; out of the running; in an injured or disabled condition.

hors de question /ɔr də kɛstjɔ̃/ *adverb phrase* L20 French. Out of the question.
1995 *Spectator* As to her father, it was *hors de question* even to ask, enquiries about paternal parents being the modern age's highest form of indelicacy.

hors d'oeuvre /ɔr dœvr/, /ɔː ˈdəːvr(ə)/ *noun phrase* plural same, **hors d'oeuvres** M18 French (literally, 'outside the work'). An extra dish served as an appetizer before or (occasionally) during a meal; a starter; in *plural* also, (usually mixed) items of food served as such a dish. Also *figurative* a preliminary.

horst /hɔːst/ *noun* L19 German (= heap, mass). *Geology* A block of the earth's surface bounded by faults on some or all sides and raised relative to the surrounding land.

horti conclusi, **horti sicci** plurals of HORTUS CONCLUSUS, HORTUS SICCUS.

hortus conclusus /ˌhɔːtəs kənˈkluːsəs/ *noun phrase* plural **horti conclusi** /ˌhɔːtʌɪ kənˈkluːsʌɪ/, /ˌhɔːtiː kənˈkluːsiː/ E17 Latin (= enclosed garden). **1** E17 An enclosed inviolate garden; frequently, in spiritual and exegetical tradition, as symbolic of the soul, the Christian Church, or the virginity of Mary. **2** M19 A painting of the Madonna and Child in an enclosed garden.

1 1996 *Country Life* At the close of the 16th century, it [sc. the garden] is architecturally related to the house, a series of rooms continuing the tradition of the medieval *hortus conclusus* but multiplied . . .

hortus siccus /,hɔ:təs 'sɪkəs/ *noun phrase* plural **horti sicci** /,hɔ:tʌɪ 'sɪkʌɪ/, /,hɔ:ti: 'sɪki:/ L17 Latin (= dry garden). An arranged collection of dried plants; *figurative* a collection of uninteresting facts etc.

hôtel de ville /otɛl də vil/ *noun phrase* plural **hôtels de ville** (pronounced same) M18 French. In France and French-speaking countries: a town-hall.

hôtel-Dieu /otɛl djø/ *noun* plural **hôtels-Dieu** (pronounced same) M17 French. In France and French-speaking countries: a hospital.

hôtel garni /otɛl ɡarni/ *noun phrase* plural **hôtels garnis** (pronounced same) L18 French. In France and French-speaking countries: a lodging-house providing bed and breakfast only; also, a furnished apartment.

hotelier /həʊ'tɛlɪeɪ/, /həʊ'tɛlɪə/ *noun* E20 French (*hôtelier*). A person who owns or runs a hotel or group of hotels.

hotel particulier /otɛl partikyljeɪ/ *noun phrase* plural **hotels particuliers** (pronounced same) M20 French. In France and French-speaking countries: a large privately owned town house or block of flats.

hoummos, houmous variants of HUM-MUS.

houp-la /'hu:plɑ:/ *interjection & noun* (also **hoop-la**) L19 French (*houp-là!*, from *houp* interjection + *là* there). **A** *interjection* L19 Accompanying or drawing attention to a quick or sudden movement. **B** *noun* L19 An exclamation of 'houp-la!'; *slang* a commotion, ballyhoo, pretentious nonsense.

houri /'hʊəri/ *noun* M18 French (from Persian *ḥūrī* from Arabic *ḥūr* plural of *'aḥwar*, feminine *ḥawrā'* having eyes with marked contrast of white and black). Any of the virgins of the Muslim paradise, promised as wives to believers; *transferred* a voluptuously beautiful woman.

howdah /'haʊdə/ *noun* L18 Urdu (*haudah* from Arabic *ḥawdaj* a litter carried by a camel). A seat for two or more, usually with a canopy, carried on an elephant's back.

huaca /'wɑ:kə/ *noun* (also (earlier) **guaca**) E17 Spanish (*huaca, guaca* from Quechua *waca* god of the house). **1** E17 The all-pervading spirit thought by some Peruvian Indians to be disseminated through the whole world; any material object thought to be the abode of such a spirit. **2** M19 A prehistoric Peruvian tomb or temple.

huaco /'wɑ:kəʊ/ *noun* (also **guaco** /'ɡwɑ:kəʊ/) plural **huacos** M20 Spanish (alteration of preceding). In Peru, Bolivia, and Chile: a piece of ancient Indian pottery.

huarache /wa'rɑ:tʃi/ *noun* (also **guarache** /ɡwa'rɑ:tʃi/) L19 Mexican Spanish. A leather-thonged sandal, originally worn by Mexican Indians.

hubris /'hju:brɪs/ *noun* (also **hybris** /'hʌɪbrɪs/) L19 Greek. Presumption, insolence; pride, excessive self-confidence.

■ The earliest instance of *hubris* in a non-specialist English text, a newspaper of 1884, refers to it as 'Academic slang' and defines it as 'a kind of high-flown insolence'. In its original context in ancient Greek literary texts it indicated insolence towards the gods, manifested either in spiritual pride or by behaviour that flouted divine or social law; thus the arrogant and riotous conduct of Penelope's suitors in Homer's *Odyssey* is an instance of hubris that met its due when they were almost all slaughtered by the returned Odysseus. The spelling *hybris* is a slightly later (E20) alternative transliteration of the Greek; both transliterations are current, but *hubris* is marginally more common in general contexts.

1996 *Spectator* Winning is success, and success brings *hybris*, and *hybris* brings disaster.

huerta /'hwɛ:tə/ *noun* M19 Spanish. In Spain and Spanish-speaking countries: a piece of irrigated land; an orchard.

huevos rancheros /,wɛvɒs ran'tʃɛ:rɒs/ *noun phrase* L20 (Mexican) Spanish. A Mexican dish of fried eggs served on tortillas with a spicy sauce.

hui /'hu:i/ *noun* M19 Maori and Hawaiian. In New Zealand: a large social or ceremonial gathering; in Hawaii: a formal club or association.

hula /'hu:lə/ *noun & intransitive verb* (also **hula-hula**) E19 Hawaiian. (Perform) a Hawaiian dance with six basic steps and gestures symbolizing or imitating natural phenomena, historical events, etc. (See quotation at LEI *noun* 1.)

hulan variant of UHLAN.

huldee variant of HALDI.

hulwa variant of HALVA.

hum /hʌm/ *noun* E20 Serbo-Croat. *Physical Geography* A steep-sided hill, of roughly circular cross-section, characteristic of karst topography. Cf. MOGOTE.

huma /ˈhuːmə/ *noun* M19 **Persian and Urdu** (*humā* phoenix). A mythical bird similar to the phoenix, supposed to bring luck to any person over whom it hovers on its restless flights.

humanitas /hjʊˈmanɪtɑːs/ *noun* M20 **Latin**. Humanity.

hummum variant of HAMMAM.

hummus /ˈhʊməs/ *noun* (also **hoummos, h(o)umous**) M20 **Arabic** (*ḥummus*). Ground chick-peas mixed with tahini, garlic, and lemon juice, frequently served as an hors d'oeuvre or dip.

humus /ˈhjuːməs/ *noun* L18 **Latin** (= soil). The organic constituent of soil, formed by the decomposition of plant materials.

hybris variant of HUBRIS.

hydra /ˈhaɪdrə/ *noun & adjective* LME **Old French** (((*h*)*ydre, idre* from) Latin *hydra* from Greek *hudra* water snake). **A** *noun* **1** LME *Greek Mythology* (also **Hydra**) A monster with many heads, which grew again as fast as they were cut off. **2** LME (usually **Hydra**) (The name of) a long faint constellation; the Sea Serpent. **3** L15 A thing or person likened to the mythological hydra in its baneful character, its multifarious aspects, or the difficulty of its extirpation. **4** M16 Any terrible serpent or reptile. *rhetorical*. **5** E17 A water snake. **6** L18 Any of several hydrozoans of the genus *Hydra* that live as solitary polyps attached to pond plants.

> **3 1996** *Oldie* . . . conspiracy mania is a hydra with many heads, and when one is lopped off others appear, even more fantastical.

hydria /ˈhaɪdrɪə/, /ˈhɪdrɪə/ *noun* plural **hydriae** /ˈhaɪdriː/ ME **Old French** (*idr(i)e*, from Latin *hydria*, from Greek *hudria*). Formerly, a water-pot. Now (*Archaeology*), a three-handled pitcher of ancient Greece.

hydrophobia /ˌhaɪdrə(ʊ)ˈfəʊbɪə/ *noun* LME **Late Latin** (*hydrophobia* from Greek *hudrophobia*, from *hudrophobos* water-fearing). **1** LME A strong aversion to or fear of water arising from the spasms that a rabid person suffers when attempting to drink; rabies itself. **2** M18 *generally* A fear or dislike of water; *figurative* madness.

hyle /ˈhaɪliː/ *noun* LME **Late Latin** (from Greek *hulē* wood, timber, material, mat-

ter). Matter, substance; *specifically* the primordial matter of the universe.

hyperbaton /hʌɪˈpəːbətɒn/ *noun* M16 **Latin** (from Greek *huperbaton* overstepping, from *huperbainein*, from as *hyper-* beyond, over + *bainein* to walk). *Grammar* and *Rhetoric* A figure of speech in which the logical order of words or phrases is inverted, especially for the sake of emphasis.

hyperbole /hʌɪˈpəːbəli/ *noun* LME **Latin** (from Greek *huperbolē* excess, exaggeration, from as *hyper-* beyond, over + *ballein* to throw). A figure of speech consisting in exaggerated or extravagant statement, used to express strong feeling or produce a strong impression and not meant to be taken literally; an instance of this; *generally* overstatement.

> **1996** *New Scientist* Hyperbole seems to be the order of the day: this phenomenon is called colossal magnetoresistance.

hyperdulia /ˌhʌɪpədjʊˈlʌɪə/ *noun* M16 **Medieval Latin** (*hyperdulia*, from as *hyper-* beyond + *dulia*). *Roman Catholic Church* The veneration properly given to the Virgin Mary (higher than DULIA but less than LATRIA).

hypogeum /ˌhʌɪpə(ʊ)ˈdʒiːəm/ *noun* (also **hypogaeum**) plural **hypog(a)ea** /ˌhʌɪpə(ʊ)ˈdʒiːə/ M17 **Latin** (*hypogeum, hypogaeum* from Greek *hupogeion, hupogaion* use as noun of neuter singular of *hupogeios* underground). An underground chamber or vault.

hypostasis /hʌɪˈpɒstəsɪs/ *noun* plural **hypostases** /hʌɪˈpɒstəsiːz/ E16 **ecclesiastical Latin** (from Greek *hupostasis* sediment, foundation, subject-matter, (later) substance, existence, essence, personality, from as *hypo-* below + *stasis* standing). **1** E16 *Theology* A person; *specifically* **a** the single person of Christ, as opposed to his two natures, human and divine; **b** each of the three persons of the Trinity. **2** M16 *Medicine* **a** A sediment, especially in urine. Long *rare* or *obsolete*. **b** M19 The accumulation of blood or other fluid in a dependent part of the body. **3 a** L16–E17 A base or foundation on which something abstract rests. **b** *Philosophy* E17 An underlying reality, substance, as opposed to attributes ('accidents') or as distinguished from what is unsubstantial. **c** L17 Essence, essential principle. **4** E20 *Genetics* (Back-formation from *hypostatic*.) Inhibition of the expression of a gene by another at a different locus. **5** M20 *Linguistics* The citing of a word, element, etc., as an example or model; the word etc. so cited.

■ The Anglicized form *hypostasy* is rare.

hypothesis /haɪˈpɒθɪsɪs/ *noun* plural **hypotheses** /haɪˈpɒθɪsiːz/ L16 Late Latin (from Greek *hupothesis* foundation, base, from as *hypo-* + *thesis* placing). **1** L16 A proposition put forward merely as a basis for reasoning or argument, without any assumption of its truth. **2** L16–E18 A subordinate thesis forming part of a more general one; a particular case of a general proposition; a detailed statement. **3** E17 A supposition, an assumption; *especially* one made as a starting-point for further investigation or research from known facts. **4** E17 A groundless assumption; a guess. **5** L18 An actual or possible situation considered as a basis for action.

hysterica passio /hɪˌstɛrɪkə ˈpasɪəʊ/ *noun phrase* E17 Latin (feminine of *hystericus* (from Greek *husterikos* belonging to the uterus) + *passio* passion). Hysteria.

■ Hysteria was formerly held to be a disorder peculiar to women resulting from a disturbance of the uterus.

hysteron proteron /ˌhɪstərɒn ˈprɒtərɒn/ *noun, adverb, & adjective phrase* M16 Late Latin (from Greek *husteron proteron* latter (put in place of) former). **A** *noun phrase* **1** M16 *Rhetoric* A figure of speech in which what should come last is put first. **2** L16 *generally* Position or arrangement of things in the reverse of their natural or rational order. **B** *adverb phrase* In a topsy-turvy way. Only in E17. **C** *adjective phrase* M17 Involving or employing hysteron proteron.

iambus /ʌɪˈambəs/ *noun* plural **iambuses**, **iambi** /ʌɪˈambʌɪ/ L16 Latin (from Greek *iambos* iambus, lampoon, from *iaptein* to assail in words). *Prosody* A metrical foot consisting of one short followed by one long syllable or (in English etc.) of one unstressed followed by one stressed syllable.

■ The metre known as the iambic trimeter was first used by the ancient Greek satirists, hence the connection with lampoons.

ibid /ˈɪbɪd/ *adverb* M17 Latin (abbreviation of next). IBIDEM.

ibidem /ˈɪbɪdɛm/, /ɪˈbʌɪdɛm/ *adverb* M18 Latin (= in the same place, from *ibi* there + demonstrative suffix -*dem*, as in *idem*, *tandem*, etc). In the same book, chapter, passage, etc.

■ The abbreviated form *ibid* is in more general use in bibliographies etc.

ichor /ˈʌɪkɔː/ *noun* M17 Greek (*ikhōr*). **1** M17 Blood; a liquid likened to the blood of animals. Now *literary.* **2** M17 *Medicine* A watery discharge from a wound or sore. *archaic.* **3** L17 Greek *Mythology* A fluid supposed to flow like blood in the veins of the gods. **4** E20 *Geology* An emanation from magma supposed by some to cause granitization.

icon /ˈʌɪkɒn/, /ˈʌɪk(ə)n/ *noun* (also **ikon**) M16 Latin (from Greek *eikōn* likeness, image, similitude). **1** M16–L17 *Rhetoric* A simile. **2 a** L16–E18 A portrait, a picture; *especially* one of an animal or plant in a book of natural history. **b** M19 *Ecclesiastical* An image in traditional Byzantine style of Christ or a holy person that is used ceremonially and venerated in the Orthodox Church. **c** L20 *Computing* A small symbolic picture on a VDU screen, *especially* one that may be selected with a cursor to exercise an option that it represents. **3** L16 A statue. **4** L16 A realistic description in writing. *rare.* **5** E20 *Philosophy* A sign with some factor in common with the object it represents.

iconostasis /ʌɪkəˈnɒstəsɪs/ *noun* plural **iconostases** /ʌɪkəˈnɒstəsiːz/ M19 Modern Greek (*eikonostasis*, from as *icono-* (combining form of) icon + *stasis*, literally, 'standing'). A screen separating the sanctuary or altar from the nave in most Orthodox churches and used to display icons.

id /ɪd/ *noun* E20 Latin (= it, translating German *es*). *Psychoanalysis* The inherited instinctive impulses of the individual, forming part of the unconscious and, in Freudian theory, interacting in the psyche with the ego and the superego.
  1996 *Spectator* . . . talk of leaving Europe is the politics of the id: a regression to infantile fantasy.

id al-fitr variant of ID UL-FITR.

idée fixe /ide fiks/, /ˌiːdeɪ ˈfiːks/ *noun phrase* plural **idées fixes** (pronounced same) M19 French (= fixed idea). An idea that dominates the mind, an obsession.
  1995 *Spectator* I had not realised that Cézanne's numerous bathers were such an *idée fixe*.

idée reçue /ide rəsy/, /ˌiːdeɪ rəˈsjuː/ *noun phrase* plural **idées reçues** (pronounced same) M20 French (= received idea). A generally accepted notion or opinion.

idem /ˈɪdɛm/, /ˈʌɪdɛm/ *noun & adverb* LME Latin. (In) the same author, work, etc.

idem sonans /ˌʌɪdɛm ˈsəʊnanz/ *noun & adjective phrase* M19 Latin (= sounding the same). *Law* chiefly *United States.* **A** *noun* M19 The occurrence in a document of a material word or name misspelt but having the sound of the word or name intended. **B** *adjective* M19 Homophonous with.

Identitätsphilosophie /iˌdɛntiˈtɛːts filozoˌfiː/ *noun* M19 German (= identity-philosophy). *Philosophy* A system or doctrine that assumes the fundamental identity of spirit and nature.

id est /ɪd ˈɛst/ *adverb phrase* L16 Latin (= that is). That is (to say).
  ■ Usually abbreviated to i.e.

idioticon /ɪdɪˈɒtɪk(ə)n/ *noun* M19 German (from Greek *idiōtikon* use as noun of neuter singular of *idiōtikos* uneducated). A dictionary, word-list, etc., of words and phrases peculiar to a dialect, a particular group of people, etc.

idiot savant /idjo savã/ *noun phrase* plural **idiots savants** (pronounced same) L20 French (= learned idiot). A person who in many respects is ignorant or uneducated, but who has an exceptional mastery of one subject or (usually mental) skill. **1995** *New Scientist* She is no idiot savant like the Dustin Hoffman character in *Rain Man* who could memorise a casino-full of cards but could do nothing with the information . . .

idolum /ʌɪˈdəʊləm/ *noun* plural **idola** /ʌɪ ˈdəʊlə/ E17 Latin (from Greek *eidōlon* idol). **1** E17 An image without substance; a phantom; a mental image, an idea. **2** M17 *Philosophy* (now *historical*) A false mental image.

id ul-fitr /ˈiːdʊlfɪtrə/ *noun* (also **id al-fitr** /ˈiːdalfɪtrə/) M18 Arabic (*'īd al-fiṭr*; cf. EID). *Islam* The major festival to celebrate the ending of the Ramadan fast.

i.e. abbreviation of ID EST.

igloo /ˈɪgluː/ *noun* (in sense 2 also **agloo**, **aglu**, /ˈaglu/) M19 Eskimo ((Inuit) *iglu* house). **1** M19 An Eskimo dome-shaped hut, usually one built from blocks of snow. **b** *transferred* M20 Any similarly shaped building or structure used for storage, shelter, etc. **2** M19 A cavity in the snow above a seal's breathing-hole.

ignis fatuus /ˌɪgnɪs ˈfatjʊəs/ *noun phrase* plural **ignes fatui** /ˌɪgniːz ˈfatjʊʌɪ/, /ˌɪgneɪz ˈfatjʊiː/ M16 Modern Latin (= foolish fire, so called from its erratic flitting from place to place). **1** M16 A phosphorescent light seen hovering or floating over marshy ground, perhaps due to the combustion of methane; a will-o'-the-wisp. **2** L16 *figurative* A delusive guiding principle, hope, or aim.

ignoramus /ɪgnəˈreɪməs/ *noun* L16 Latin (= we do not know, (in legal use) we take no notice of (it)). **1** L16 The endorsement formerly made by a grand jury on an indictment which they rejected as not being backed by sufficient evidence. *obsolete* except *historical*. **2** E17 An ignorant person.
 ■ In sense 2 very probably from *Ignoramus*, a comedy by George Ruggle satirizing lawyers, produced before James I in 1615.

ignoratio elenchi /ɪgnəˌreɪʃɪəʊ ɪˈlɛŋkʌɪ/ *noun phrase* plural **ignorationes elenchi** /ˌɪgnəreɪʃˈrəʊniːz/ L16 Medieval Latin (translation of Greek *hē tou elegkou agnoia* ignorance of the conditions of valid proof). A logical fallacy which consists in apparently refuting an opponent while actually disproving something not asserted; *generally* any argument which is irrelevant to its professed purpose.

ignotum per ignotius /ɪgˌnəʊtəm pər ɪgˈnəʊtɪəs/ *noun phrase* LME Late Latin (literally, 'the unknown by means of the more unknown'). An explanation which is harder to understand than what it is meant to explain.

ihram /ɪxˈrɑːm/, /ɪˈrɑːm/ *noun* E18 Arabic (*'iḥrām*, ultimately from *ḥarama* forbid; cf. HAREM). **1** E18 The sacred state into which a Muslim must enter before performing a pilgrimage, during which sexual intercourse, shaving, and several other actions are forbidden. **2** E18 The costume worn by a Muslim in this state, consisting of two lengths of seamless usually white fabric.

ikat /ˈiːkɑːt/ *noun* M20 Malay (literally, 'tie, fasten'). (A fabric made using) an Indonesian technique of textile decoration in which warp or weft threads, or both, are tied at intervals and dyed before weaving.

ikebana /ɪkɪˈbɑːnə/ *noun* E20 Japanese. The art of Japanese flower arrangement, with formal display according to strict rules.

ikon variant of ICON.

ilang-ilang variant of YLANG-YLANG.

illuminato /ɪˌluːmɪˈnɑːtəʊ/, /ɪˌljuːmɪ ˈnɑːtəʊ/ *noun* (also **Illuminato**) usually in plural **illuminati** /ɪˌluːmɪˈnɑːti/ L16 Italian (= enlightened; plural partly from Latin *illuminati* plural of *illuminatus*, but in German context translating German *Illuminaten*). A member of any of various sects or societies claiming special enlightenment. Also *generally*, a person claiming special knowledge on any subject.

illuminé /ilymine/ (*plural same*), /ɪˈluːmmeɪ/, /ɪˈljuːmmeɪ/ *noun* (also **Illuminé**) L18 French (= enlightened). An ILLUMINATO.

imago /ɪˈmeɪgəʊ/ *noun* plural **imagines** /ɪˈmeɪdʒɪniːz/, **imagos** L18 Latin. **1** L18 *Entomology* The final, fully developed form of an insect after passing through all stages of metamorphosis. **2** E20 *Psychoanalysis* An unconscious image of an archetype or of someone (especially a parent) which influences a person's behaviour etc.

imam /ɪˈmɑːm/ *noun* E17 Arabic (*'imām* leader, from *'amma* to lead the way). **1** E17 The leader of prayers in a mosque. **2** M17 (**Imam**) (A title of) any of various Muslim leaders, especially one succeeding Muhammad as the leader of Shiite Islam.

imam bayildi /ɪˌmɑːm 'bɑːjɪldi/ *noun phrase* (also **Imam Bayildi**) M20 Turkish (*imam bayıldı*, literally, 'the imam fainted'). A dish, originating in Turkey, consisting of aubergines stuffed with a garlic-flavoured onion-and-tomato mixture and cooked in oil.
  ▪ Whether the *imam* fainted from pleasure and repletion or because he was overcome by horror at the cost of the dish seems to be a moot point.

imbrex /'ɪmbrɛks/ *noun* plural **imbrices** /'ɪmbrɪsiːz/ M19 Latin (from *imber* rainshower). Archaeology A curved roof-tile used to cover joints in a Roman tiled roof. Cf. TEGULA sense 2.

imbroglio /ɪm'brəʊlɪəʊ/ *noun* (also **embroglio**) plural **imbroglios** M18 Italian (from *imbrogliare* to confuse, corresponding to French *embrouiller* to embroil). **1** M18 A confused heap. *archaic*. **2** E19 A state of great confusion; a complicated or difficult (especially political or dramatic) situation; a confused misunderstanding.
  2 *1996* Spectator If the royal imbroglio does end in a tragedy, Major will have blood on his hands.

immortelle /mɔː'tɛl/ *noun* M19 French (from *fleur immortelle* everlasting flower). An everlasting flower, especially *Xeranthemum annuum*.

immram /'ɪmrɑːm/ *noun* (also **imram, imrama**) plural **immra** /'ɪmrɑː/ L19 Old Irish (*imram* (modern *iomramh*), from *imm-rá* to row around). Any of various stories of fabulous sea voyages written in Ireland between the late eighth and eleventh centuries.

impair /'ɪmpɛː/; *in senses A.2, B.1 foreign* /ɛ̃pɛr/ (*plural same*) *adjective & noun* M19 French (= unequal, from negative *im-* un- + *pair* equal). **A** *adjective* **1** M19 Not paired; not forming one of a pair. **2** M20 Roulette Of or pertaining to an odd number or the odd numbers collectively. **B** *noun* M19 Roulette An odd number; the odd numbers collectively. Cf. PAIR.
  ▪ In the early seventeenth century Shakespeare may have used *impair* in Troilus and Cressida in the sense of 'unfit, inferior', but the reading is doubtful.

impasse /am'pɑːs/, /'ampɑːs/, *foreign* /ɛ̃pɑs/ *noun* M19 French (from negative *im-* not + stem of *passer* to pass). **1** M19 A position from which there is no escape, a deadlock. **2** L19 *literal* A road etc. without an outlet, a blind alley.
  1 *1996* New Scientist . . . the only thing that can help developing countries escape this impasse is a second revolution.

impasto /ɪm'pastəʊ/ *noun* L18 Italian (from *impastare*, from *im-* in + *pasta* paste). **1** L18 The action of painting by laying colour on thickly; this manner of painting. **2** E20 *Ceramics* Enamel etc. colours standing out in relief on a surface.
  1 *transferred* *1996* Spectator As the swirling impasto of adjectives, similes and metaphors becomes increasingly thick and clotted, so the picture becomes less and less distinct.

impayable /ɪm'peɪəb(ə)l/; *in sense 3 foreign* /ɛ̃pɛjabl/ *adjective* ME French (from as *im-* not + *payer* to pay). **1** Implacable, unappeasable. Only in ME. **2** L18 Impossible to pay or discharge. **3** E19 Priceless, invaluable; extraordinary, absurd.

impedimenta /ɪmˌpɛdɪ'mɛntə/ *noun plural* E17 Latin. Travelling equipment, especially of an army etc.; encumbrances; bulky equipment in general.
  1996 Times On the walls and hanging from the ceiling were the impedimenta of many sports: stuffed baseball players in New York Mets shirts, hang gliders, surf boards, caps, bats and gloves.

imperium /ɪm'pɪərɪəm/ *noun* M17 Latin. Command; absolute power; supreme or imperial power; empire.
  ▪ Used especially of the rule of the Roman emperors.

impetus /'ɪmpɪtəs/ *noun* M17 Latin (= assault, force, from *impetere* to assail). **1** M17 The force or energy with which a body moves; impulsion. **2** M17 *figurative* Moving force, (an) impulse, a stimulus.

impi /'ɪmpi/ *noun* M19 Zulu. Chiefly South African History. A body of Zulu warriors or armed tribesmen.

impluvium /ɪm'pluːvɪəm/ *noun* plural **impluvia** /ɪm'pluːvɪə/ E19 Latin (from *impluere* to rain into). Roman Antiquities The square basin in the centre of the atrium of a Roman house, which received rainwater from an opening in the roof.

imponderabilia /ɪmˌpɒnd(ə)rə'bɪlɪə/ *noun plural* E20 Modern Latin (neuter plural of *imponderabilis* that cannot be weighed). Imponderables, imponderable factors.

impresa /ɪm'preɪzə/ *noun* L16 Italian (= undertaking, device, from Proto-Romance verb, from Latin *em-* on + *prendere* to take). **1** L16 An emblem, a device; *especially* one accompanied by a motto. **2** E17 A sentence accompanying an emblem; a motto, a maxim, a proverb. Long *rare*.

impresario /ˌɪmprɪˈsɑːrɪəʊ/ *noun* plural **impresarios** M18 Italian (from as preceding). An organizer or sponsor of public entertainments; a manager of an operatic or a concert company.

1996 *Spectator* [Diaghilev] became an impresario, inspirer and explainer—of Russia to the West and the West to Russia.

imprévu /ɛ̃prevy/ *noun* M19 French (from as *im-* + *prévu* past participle of *prévoir* foresee). *The* unexpected, *the* unforeseen.

imprimatur /ˌɪmprɪˈmeɪtə/, /ˌɪmprɪˈmɑːtə/, /ˌɪmprɪˈmɑːtʊə/ *noun* M17 Latin (= let it be printed, 3rd person singular present subjunctive passive of *imprimere* to imprint). In the Roman Catholic Church: an official licence authorizing the printing of an ecclesiastical or religious work etc.; *generally* official approval, an official sanction.

figurative **1995** *Times* Without America's imprimatur, inward investment to Northern Ireland would wither away.

imprimatura /ˌɪmpriːməˈtʊərə/, foreign /ˌimprimaˈtuːra/ *noun* M20 Italian (*imprimitura*). A usually coloured transparent primer or glaze applied to an artist's canvas or panel.

impromptu /ɪmˈprɒm(p)tjuː/ *adverb, noun, adjective, & verb* M17 French (from Latin *in promptu* at hand, in readiness, from *promptus* readiness). **A** *adverb* M17 Without preparation; on the spur of the moment; extempore. **B** *noun* L17 Something composed, uttered, or done impromptu; an improvisation; *specifically* a musical composition having the character of an improvisation. **C** *adjective* M18 Composed, uttered, or done impromptu; improvised; makeshift. **D** *transitive and intransitive verb* E19 Improvise; extemporize.

imram(a) variants of IMMRAM.

imshi /ˈɪmʃi/ *transitive verb* (*imperative*) (also **imshee**) E20 Arabic ((from colloquial) *'mši* imperative of *miši* to go). Go away!

■ Military slang, recorded (1916) during World War I as being used to street hawkers in Cairo by the Australasian Corps.

in absentia /ɪn abˈsɛntɪə/, /ɪn abˈsɛnʃɪə/ *adverb phrase* L19 Latin. In his, her, or their absence.

■ Almost always in a legal context modifying the verbs 'try' or 'convict' (see quotation).

1996 *Times* The court is trying 71 members of the Dergue, of whom 25 . . . are being tried in absentia.

in abstracto /ɪn abˈstraktəʊ/ *adverb phrase* E17 Latin (= in the abstract). As an abstract thing. Cf. IN CONCRETO.

inamorata /ɪˌnaməˈrɑːtə/ *noun* (also **enamorata**) M17 Italian ((now *innamorata*), feminine of INAMORATO). A female lover.

1996 *Spectator* Paula Yates . . . estranged wife of Bob Geldof, inamorata of rock star has-been Michael Hutchence . . .

inamorato /ɪˌnaməˈrɑːtəʊ/ *noun* (also **enamorato**) plural **inamoratos** L16 Italian (now *innamorato*, past participle of *innamorare* to fall in love with). A male lover.

in antis /ɪn ˈantɪs/ *adjective phrase* M19 Latin. *Classical Architecture* (Of columns) positioned between two antas; (of a building) having walls prolonged beyond the front, with terminating pilasters in line with columns of a façade.

in articulo mortis /ɪn ɑːˌtɪkjʊləʊ ˈmɔːtɪs/ *adverb phrase* L16 Latin (= in the article of death). At the point or moment of death.

in camera /ɪn ˈkam(ə)rə/ *adverb phrase* E19 Late Latin (= in the chamber). In a judge's private chambers, not in open court; *generally* in secret or private session, not in public.

incipit /ˈɪnsɪpɪt/ *noun* L19 Latin (3rd person singular present indicative of *incipere* to begin). The opening words of a manuscript, a printed book (usually an early one), a chanted liturgical text, etc.

■ The word used by medieval scribes to indicate the beginning of a new treatise, poem, division, etc. Cf. EXPLICIT.

incisor /ɪnˈsʌɪzə/ *noun* L17 Medieval Latin (in *dens incisor* incisor tooth, from Latin, literally, 'cutter', from *incis-*, past participial stem of *incidere* to cut). A narrow-edged tooth adapted for cutting; in humans, any of the front four teeth in each jaw. Also *incisor tooth*.

incognita /ˌɪnˈkɒgnɪtə/ *noun* plural M19 Latin (neuter plural of *incognitus* unknown, from as INCOGNITO). Unknown things or places.

incognita /ˌɪnkɒgˈniːtə/, foreign /inˈkɔːɲita/ *adjective & noun* L17 Italian (feminine of *incognito* unknown). **A** *adjective*

L17 Of a woman: disguised; unknown.
B *noun* E18 plural **incognitas, incognite**
/ɪnkɒgˈniːte/. A disguised or unknown
woman, especially one's lover.

incognito /ˌɪnkɒgˈniːtəʊ/, /ɪnˈkɒgnɪtəʊ/ *adjective, adverb, & noun* M17 Italian (from
Latin *incognitus* unknown, from as *in-* un-
+ *cognitus*, past participle of *cognoscere* to
know). **A** *adjective* M17 Of a person: concealed under a disguised or assumed
identity; unknown. **B** *adverb* M17 Under a
disguised or assumed identity. **C** *noun*
plural **incognitos** **1** M17 A person who
conceals his or her identity; an anonymous or unknown person. **2** E19 The condition of being unknown, anonymity;
assumed or pretended identity.

> **B 1996** *Spectator* Surely anyone could see it
> is my duty [as a restaurant critic] to travel
> incognito.

incommunicado /ˌɪnkəmjuːˈnɪˈkɑːdəʊ/
adjective & adverb (also in Spanish form **incomunicado** also *foreign* /ˌinkomuniˈkado/) M19 **Spanish** (*incomunicado* past
participle of *incomunicar* to deprive of
communication). **A** *adjective* M19 Having
no means of communication with others;
especially (of a prisoner) held in solitary
confinement. **B** *adverb* M20 Without
means of communication with others.

in concreto /ɪn kɒnˈkriːtəʊ/ *adverb phrase*
E17 Latin. As a concrete thing. Cf. IN ABSTRACTO.

inconnu /ˈɪŋkənuː/, *foreign* /ɛ̃kɔny/ (*plural
same*) *noun* (in sense 1 feminine **inconnue**, plural (in sense 1) **inconnu(e)s**, (in
sense 2) same) E19 **French** (= unknown).
1 E19 An unknown person, a stranger.
2 E19 A predatory freshwater salmonid
game-fish, *Stenodus leucichthys*, of the Arctic. Originally *Canadian*.

in contumaciam /ɪn ˌkɒntjʊˈmeɪsɪəm/
adverb phrase L19 Latin. While in contempt
of court.

in corpore /ɪn ˈkɔːpəreɪ/ *adjective & adverb
phrase* E20 Latin (literally, 'in the body').
Biology IN VIVO.

incubus /ˈɪŋkjʊbəs/ *noun* plural **incubuses, incubi** /ˈɪŋkjʊbʌɪ/ ME Late Latin (=
Latin *incubo* nightmare, from *incubare* to
lie on). **1** ME An evil spirit supposed to
descend upon sleeping people and especially to have sexual intercourse with
sleeping women. **2** M16 An oppressive
nightmare; a person who or thing which
oppresses or troubles like a nightmare.

> **2 1996** *Times* She has no incubus of
> accumulated policies and attitudes.

incunabulum /ˌɪnkjʊˈnabjʊləm/ *noun*
plural (earlier) **incunabula** /ˌɪnkjʊˈnabjʊlə/ E19 Latin (*incunabula* neuter plural swaddling-clothes, cradle, from as *in-*
in + *cunae* cradle). **1** E19 In *plural* The
early stages of development of a thing.
2 M19 A book printed at an early date; specifically one printed before 1501.

indaba /ɪnˈdɑːbə/ *noun* E19 Zulu (= discussion). **1** E19 A conference between or
with members of southern African Black
peoples. **2** L20 A person's business, problem, or concern. *South African colloquial.*

indecorum /ɪndɪˈkɔːrəm/ *noun* L16 Latin
(use as noun of neuter singular of *indecorus* unseemly). **1** L16 An indecorous action or proceeding; an offence against
recognized standards of behaviour.
2 M17 The quality of being indecorous;
lack of decorum; improper behaviour.

index /ˈɪndɛks/ *noun* plural **indexes**, (especially *in technical use*) **indices** /ˈɪndɪsiːz/
LME Latin (*index, indic-* forefinger, informer, etc., from base represented by *dicere* to say, Greek *deiknunai* to show).
1 LME The finger used in pointing, the
forefinger. Now usually *index finger.* **b** L19
Ornithology The second (occasionally the
first) digit of the manus in a bird's wing.
2 L16 A piece of wood, metal, etc., which
serves as a pointer; specifically (in a scientific instrument) a pointer which moves
along a graduated scale so as to show
movements or quantities. **b** L16 The arm
of a surveying instrument; an alidade.
3 L16 A thing which serves to point *to* a
fact or conclusion; a sign or indication *of.*
4 L16 A list of things in (usually alphabetical) order; especially a list, usually at the
end of a book, giving the names, topics,
etc., mentioned in the book and the
places where they occur. Formerly also, a
table of contents. **5 a** L16-M19 *Music* A
sign placed on the stave at the end of a
page or line to indicate the position of
the next note. **b** E18 *Typography* A hand-shaped symbol with a pointing finger
used to draw attention to a note etc. Also
called *fist.* **6** L17 *Mathematics* A subscript
or superscript symbol denoting some
characteristic of a quantity or function,
as the exponent in x^2, etc. **7** E19 A number or formula expressing a specific property, especially a ratio; especially in
Anatomy, a formula expressing the ratio
between two dimensions (especially of
the skull). **8** L19 *Economics* (A number in)
a scale relating (usually in the form of a
percentage) the level of prices, wages,

etc., at a particular time to those at a date taken as a base.

■ There are also a number of other specialist technical uses of *index* in mathematics, computing, and engineering. In sense 4 the Latin names of various types of index may be used: *index locorum* (index of the passages cited or discussed), *index nominum* (index of the names of people discussed), *index rerum* (index of the subjects and matters treated), *index verborum* (index of the significant words discussed).

index librorum prohibitorum /ˌɪndɛks lɪˌbrɔːrəm prəʊˌhɪbɪˈtɔːrəm/ *noun phrase* (also **Index Librorum Prohibitorum**) M17 Latin (= index of prohibited books). *Roman Catholic Church* The official list of books that Roman Catholics were forbidden to read.

■ The first *Index Librorum Prohibitorum* was published in 1564 as part of the Counter-Reformation programme instituted at the Council of Trent, and the list was not abolished until 1966. It was also referred to simply as *the Index*.

indicium /ɪnˈdɪsɪəm/ *noun plural* **indicia** /ɪnˈdɪsɪə/ E17 Latin (from as INDEX). An indication, a sign; a distinguishing mark. Usually in *plural*.

in dictione /ˌɪn dɪktɪˈəʊnɪ/ *adjective phrase* E19 Latin (translation of Greek *para tēn lexin* in relation to the wording). Of a logical fallacy: arising from the wording used to express it.

■ One of the subdivisions of logical fallacy noted by Aristotle in his *Sophistici Elenchi* (ch. 4), also sometimes referred to in Latin as *in voce* in the voice. Opposed to EXTRA DICTIONEM.

indumentum /ˌɪndjʊˈmɛntəm/ *noun plural* **indumenta** /ˌɪndjʊˈmɛntə/ M19 Latin (= garment, from *induere* to put on). *Botany* The covering of hairs, scales, etc., on (part of) a plant, especially when dense.

induna /ɪnˈduːnə/ *noun* M19 Zulu (from nominal prefix *in-* + *duna* councillor, headman, overseer, captain). **1** M19 A tribal councillor or headman among the Nguni peoples of southern Africa. **2** M20 *transferred* A person, especially a Black person, in authority; a foreman.

inédit /inedi/ *noun plural* pronounced same E20 French (cf. next). An unpublished work; *figurative* something secret or unrevealed.

inedita /ɪnˈɛdɪtə/ *noun plural* L19 Modern Latin (use as noun of neuter plural of Latin *ineditus*, from *in-* not + *editus* past

participle of *edere* to give out, edit). Unpublished writings.

inertia /ɪˈnəːʃə/ *noun* E18 Latin (= inactivity). **1** E18 *Physics* The property of a body, proportional to its mass, by virtue of which it continues in a state of rest or uniform straight motion in the absence of an external force. **b** L19 In other physical properties: the tendency to continue in some state, to resist change. **2** E19 *transferred* Inactivity; disinclination to act or exert oneself; sloth; apathy.

in esse /ɪn ˈɛsi/ *adjective phrase* L16 Latin. In actual existence.

■ Opposed to IN POSSE.

in excelsis /ɪn ɛkˈselsɪs/, /ɛksˈtʃɛlsɪs/ *adverb phrase* LME Latin (= in the highest (places); cf. EXCELSIOR). In the highest.

■ Often in the phrase *Gloria in excelsis Deo* 'Glory to God in the highest!'

in extenso /ɪn ɪkˈstɛnsəʊ/ *adverb phrase* E19 Latin (from *in* in + *extenso* ablative of *extensus* past participle of *extendere* to stretch out). In full, at length.

in extremis /ɪn ɛkˈstriːmɪs/, /ɪn ɪk ˈstriːmɪs/ *adverb phrase* M16 Latin (from *in* in + *extremis* ablative plural of *extremus* last, uttermost). At the point of death; in great difficulty; in a painful or awkward situation.

1996 *Spectator* I can still recall the glorious sight of his headlong dive to the ground and the altogether unexpected knowledge of English he revealed *in extremis.*

infanta /ɪnˈfantə/ *noun* L16 Spanish (Portuguese feminine of INFANTE). *History* A daughter of the King and Queen of Spain or Portugal; *specifically* the eldest daughter who is not heir to the throne. Formerly also *generally*, a girl, a princess.

infante /ɪnˈfanteɪ/ *noun* M16 Spanish and Portuguese (from Latin *infans, infant-* child). *History* A son of the King and Queen of Spain or Portugal other than the heir to the throne; *specifically* the second son.

inferno /ɪnˈfəːnəʊ/ *noun plural* **infernos** M19 Italian (from Christian Latin *infernus* below, subterranean). Hell; *transferred* a scene of horror or distress; *especially* a raging fire.

■ Reference to hell as *the inferno* is generally in allusion to Dante's *Divine Comedy.*

in fine /ɪn ˈfʌmi/, /ˈfiːni/ *adverb phrase* M16 Latin. Finally, in short, to sum up.

1996 *Spectator* Alfred, *in fine*, created a wellspring of instinctive Tory-voting monarchists.

infinitum /ɪnfɪ'nʌɪtəm/ *noun* L16 Latin (use as noun of neuter of *infinitus* unlimited). Infinity; an infinitude, an endless amount or number.
■ Often in the phrase AD INFINITUM.

in flagrante /ɪn flə'grantɪ/ *adverb phrase* E17 Latin (abbreviation of next or similar Latin phrase). In the very act. *colloquial.*
1996 *Oldie* Abby herself attempts to commit suicide on finding her agent *in flagrante* with his secretary.

in flagrante delicto /ɪn flə,grantɪ dɪ'lɪktəʊ/ *adverb phrase* L18 Latin (= in the heat of the crime: cf. preceding). In the very act of committing an offence; *specifically* in the act of adultery or other sexual misconduct.
1996 *Spectator* . . . his sacking as editor . . . was more abrupt since he was caught *in flagrante delicto* with his pretty secretary . . .

influenza /,ɪnflʊ'ɛnzə/ *noun* M18 Italian (literally, 'influence', from medieval Latin *influentia* influence). A highly contagious viral infection of the lining of the trachea and bronchi, often epidemic, and usually marked by fever, weakness, muscular aches, coughing, and watery catarrh. Frequent loosely, any acute respiratory infection accompanied by fever.
■ Generally abbreviated to *flu* in all but the most formal usage.

infra /'ɪnfrə/ *adverb* L19 Latin. Later, further on (in a book or article); below.

infra dig /,ɪnfrə 'dɪg/ *adjective phrase* E19 Latin (abbreviation of Latin *infra dignitatem* beneath (one's) dignity). Beneath the dignity of one's position; undignified. *colloquial.*
1996 *Times* Hoping that this didn't look too infra dig, I duly grasped the mane on our final attempt, all but letting go of the reins . . .

ingenium /ɪn'dʒiːnɪəm/ *noun* plural **ingenia** /ɪn'dʒiːnɪə/ L19 Latin (= mind, intellect). Mental ability, talent; a person possessing this. Also, mental inclination, disposition.
1921 *Glasgow Herald* His scientific ingenium was as keen as ever.

ingénue /,anʒer'njuː/; *foreign* /ɛ̃ʒeny/ (*plural same*) *noun* (also **ingenue**) M19 French (feminine of *ingénu* ingenuous). An artless innocent young woman, especially as a stage role; an actress playing such a role.

1995 *Times* She is 60, that awkward age, too old for ingenues, too young for crones.

ingesta /ɪn'dʒɛstə/ *noun plural* E18 Latin (neuter plural of *ingestus* past participle of *ingerere* to carry in, pour in). Substances introduced into the body as nourishment; food and drink.

in infinitum /ɪn ɪnfɪ'nʌɪtəm/ *adverb phrase* M16 Latin. To infinity, without end.
■ Cf. AD INFINITUM.

injuria /ɪn'dʒʊərɪə/ *noun* plural **injuriae** /ɪn'dʒʊəriː/ L19 Latin. *Law* An invasion of another's rights; an actionable wrong.

inkosi /ɪŋ'kəʊsi/ *noun* M19 Nguni. In South Africa: (the title of) a Zulu ruler, chief, or high official.

in limine /ɪn 'lɪmmi/ *adverb phrase* E19 Latin. On the threshold; at the outset.

in loco parentis /ɪn ,ləʊkəʊ pə'rɛntɪs/ *prepositional phrase* E19 Latin (= in place of a parent). Assuming the responsibilities of a parent.
1995 *Spectator* One of us was in agony and one of us was *in loco parentis*, so it was a very sticky wait.

in medias res /ɪn ,mɛdɪɑːs 'reɪz/, /,miːdɪɑːs/ *adverb phrase* L18 Latin. Into the midst of things; *especially* into the middle of a narrative, without preamble.

in medio /ɪn 'miːdɪəʊ/, /'mɛdɪəʊ/ *adverb phrase* E17 Latin. In the middle; in an undecided state.

in memoriam /ɪn mɪ'mɔːrɪam/ *prepositional & noun phrase* M19 Latin. **A** *prepositional phrase* M19 To the memory of, in memory of. **B** *noun phrase* L19 A poem, notice, etc., in memory of a dead person.
■ The fashion for poems with this title was set by Tennyson's sequence of poems (1850), written in memory of his friend A. H. Hallam, who died in 1833.

in nomine /ɪn 'nəʊmmeɪ/, /ɪn 'nɒmmeɪ/ *noun phrase* M17 Latin (= in the name (of)). An instrumental composition in fugal style (probably originally one set to a Latin text including the words *in nomine*); a free fugue in which the answer does not exactly correspond with the subject.

in nubibus /ɪn 'njuːbɪbəs/ *adverb & adjective phrase* L16 Latin. In the clouds; as yet unsettled; incapable of being carried out.

in nuce /ɪn 'nuːkeɪ/ *adverb phrase* M19 Latin. In a nutshell; in a condensed form.

innuendo /mjʊˈɛndəʊ/ *adverb & noun* M16
Latin (= by nodding at, pointing to, inti-
mating, ablative gerund of *innuere* to nod
to, signify, from as *in-* + *nuere* to nod).
A *adverb* M16 Meaning, that is to say, to
wit, (especially in legal documents, introducing a parenthetical explanation of
the precise reference of a preceding noun
or pronoun). **B** *noun* plural **innuen-
do(e)s**. **1** L17 A parenthetical explanation of, or construction put upon, a word
or expression; *especially* in an action for
libel or slander, the injurious meaning alleged to be conveyed by a word or expression not in itself actionable. **2** L17 An
allusive or oblique remark, hint, or suggestion, usually disparaging; a remark
with a (usually suggestive) double meaning; allusion, hinting, suggestion.

in ovo /m ˈəʊvəʊ/ *adverb phrase* M19 Latin
(= in the egg). In embryo. Also *figurative*.

in pari materia /m ˌpɑːri məˈtɛːrɪə/, /mə
ˈtɪərɪə/ *adverb phrase* M19 Latin. In an
equivalent case or position.

in partibus /m ˈpɑːtɪbəs/ *adverb phrase* L17
Latin (*in partibus* (*infidelium*) in the regions (of the infidels)). *Roman Catholic
Church* In full *in partibus infidelium* /mfɪ
ˈdeɪlɪəm/, /mfɪˈdiːlɪəm/. In heretical territory (with reference to a titular bishop
etc., especially in a Muslim country).

in parvo /m ˈpɑːvəʊ/ *adverb phrase* E20
Latin. In little, in miniature, on a small
scale.

in pectore /m ˈpɛktəri/ *adverb phrase* M19
Latin (= in one's breast). Secretly; IN PETTO
sense 1.

in perpetuum /m pəˈpɛtjʊəm/ *adverb
phrase* M17 Latin. For all time, in perpe-
tuity.

in personam /m pəˈsəʊnam/ *adjective
phrase* L18 Latin (= against a person). *Law*
Made or availing against or affecting a
specific person only; imposing a personal
liability. Frequently *postpositive*. Cf. IN
REM.

in petto /m ˈpɛtəʊ/ *adverb phrase* L17 Italian (= in the breast). **1** L17 In contemplation; undisclosed, secretly (especially of
the appointment of cardinals not named
as such). **2** M19 (By confusion with *petty*
(adjective)). In miniature, on a small
scale; in short.

in pontificalibus /m ˌpɒntɪfɪˈkeɪlɪbəs/, /m
ˌpɒntɪfɪˈkɑːlɪbəs/ *adverb phrase* LME Latin.

In the full vestments of a cardinal, archbishop, etc.; in pontificals.

in posse /m ˈpɒsi/ *adjective phrase* L16
Latin. In the condition of being possible.
Opposed to IN ESSE.

in potentia /m pəˈtɛnʃɪə/ *adverb phrase* E17
Latin. In potentiality.

in propria persona /m ˌprəʊprɪə pə
ˈsəʊnə/ *adverb phrase* M17 Latin. In one's
own person.

in puris naturalibus /m ˌpjʊərɪs natjʊ
ˈrɑːlɪbəs/, /natjʊˈreɪlɪbəs/ *adverb phrase* E17
Latin (cf. PURIS NATURALIBUS). In one's
natural state; stark naked.

in re /m ˈreɪ/ *adverb, adjective, & preposition
phrase* E17 Latin. **A** *adverb phrase* E17 In reality. **B** *adjective phrase* **1** M19 *Logic* EXTRA
DICTIONEM. **2** L19 *Philosophy* Of a universal: existing only in the particulars that
instantiate it. Cf. ANTE REM, POST REM.
C *preposition phrase* L19 In the (legal) case
of; with regard to. Cf. RE.

> **C 1996** *Times Magazine* . . . there are plenty
> of fathers around who feel they've been
> handed the post-marital short straw by the
> judiciary *in re* who gets to keep the children
> and who gets to pay for same.

in rem /m ˈrɛm/ *adjective phrase* M18 Latin
(= against a thing). *Law* Made or availing
against or affecting a thing, and therefore other people generally; imposing a
general liability. Frequently *postpositive*.
Cf. IN PERSONAM.

in rerum natura /m ˌreɪrəm nəˈtjʊərə/ *adverb phrase* L16 Latin. In nature, in the
physical world.

inro /ˈɪnrəʊ/ *noun* plural **inros**, same E17
Japanese (*inrō*, from *in* seal + *rō* basket).
An ornamental box with compartments
for seals, medicines, etc., formerly worn
by Japanese on a girdle.

in saecula saeculorum /m ˌsʌɪkjʊlə
sʌɪkjʊˈlɔːrəm/, /m ˌseɪkjʊlə seɪkjʊˈlɔːrəm/
adverb phrase L16 Late Latin (= to the ages
of ages). To all eternity; for ever.

in se /m ˈseɪ/ *adverb phrase* M19 Latin. *Philosophy* In itself.

inselberg /ˈɪnsəlbəːg/ *noun* plural **insel-
bergs**, **inselberge** /ˈɪnsəlbəːgə/ E20 German (from *Insel* island + *Berg* mountain).
Physical Geography An isolated hill or
mountain which rises abruptly from the
surrounding landscape, especially from
an arid plain.

inshallah /mˈʃalɑː/ *interjection* M19 Arabic
(*in šā' Allāh*). If God wills it.

■ The Muslim equivalent of DEO VOLENTE.

insignia /ɪnˈsɪɡnɪə/ *noun* M17 Latin (plural of *insigne* mark, sign, badge of office, use as noun of neuter of *insignis* distinguished (as by a mark)). **1** *plural* M17 Badges or distinguishing marks (*of* office, honour, etc.); emblems (*of* a nation, person, etc.). **2** *singular* L18 (plural **insignias**) A badge or distinguishing mark (*of* office, honour, etc.); an emblem (*of* a nation, person, etc.). **3** L18 Usually as *plural*. Marks or tokens indicative of something.

in situ /ɪn ˈsɪtjuː/ *adverb phrase* M18 Latin. In its (original) place; in position.

> **1996** *Country Life* Among these are sundry cranesbills . . . whose ends of root, accidentally left *in situ* when a plant is moved, will often sprout and grow anew.

insomnia /ɪnˈsɒmnɪə/ *noun* (also (earlier) **insomnie**, **insomnium** /ɪnˈsɒmnɪəm/) E17 Latin (from *insomnis* sleepless (from as negative *in-* + *somnus* sleep)). Chronic inability to sleep; sleeplessness.

insouciance /ɪnˈsuːsɪəns/, *foreign* /ɛ̃susjɑ̃s/ *noun* L18 French (from as next). Carefreeness, lack of concern.

> **1995** *Times* With each tightening of the regulations to prevent the spread of BSE, it [sc. the British government] has been forced into an almost furtive admission that earlier scare stories had more substance to them than its studied insouciance admitted.

insouciant /ɪnˈsuːsɪənt/, *foreign* /ɛ̃susjɑ̃/ *adjective* E19 French (from as negative *in-* + *souciant* present participle of *soucier* to care, from Latin *sollicitare* to disturb). Carefree, undisturbed.

inspan /ɪnˈspan/ *transitive verb* E19 Afrikaans (from Dutch *inspannen*, from *in-* + *spannen* to span, fasten). **1** E19 Yoke (oxen, horses, etc.) in a team to a vehicle; harness (a wagon). **2** E20 *figurative* Persuade (a person) to give assistance or service; use as a makeshift. *South African.*

> **2** **1971** *Rand Daily Mail* Mrs Barton often gets on the telephone and inspans private householders to help out.

instanter /ɪnˈstantə/ *adverb* L17 Latin. Immediately, at once.

■ Now archaic or jocular.

in statu pupillari /ɪn ˌstatju: pjuːprˈlɑːriː/ *adjective phrase* M19 Latin. Under guardianship; of junior status at a university; not having a master's degree.

in statu quo /ɪn ˌstatju: ˈkwəʊ/ *adjective phrase* E17 Latin. In the same state as formerly. More fully *in statu quo ante*.

insurrecto /ˌɪnsəˈrɛktəʊ/ *noun* plural **insurrectos** E20 Spanish (from Latin *insurrectus* past participle of *insurgere* to rise up). Especially in Spain and Spanish-speaking countries: an insurgent, a rebel; an insurrectionist.

intacta /ɪnˈtaktə/ *adjective* M20 Latin (feminine of *intactus*, extracted from VIRGO INTACTA). Inviolate, unaffected; not spoiled or sullied.

intaglio /ɪnˈtaljəʊ/, /ɪnˈtɑːljəʊ/ *noun & verb* (also **intaglia**) M17 Italian (from *intagliare* to engrave). **A** *noun* plural **intaglios**. **1** M17 A figure or design incised or engraved; a cutting or engraving in a hard material. **2** M17 A thing ornamented with incised work; *especially* a precious stone having a figure or design cut on its surface. **b** E19 A mould of something to be cast or struck in relief. **3** M18 The process or art of engraving or carving in a hard material; printing in which the image is engraved or etched into a metal plate or cylinder so that it lies below the non-printing areas. Also, the condition of being incised. **B** *transitive verb* M19 Engrave with a sunken pattern; execute in intaglio.

intarsia /ɪnˈtɑːsɪə/ *noun* (in senses 1 and 2 also **intarsio** /ɪnˈtɑːsɪəʊ/, plural **intarsios**) M19 Italian (*intarsio*). **1** M19 (A piece of) mosaic woodwork, especially made in fifteenth-century Italy; the art of making this. Also called *tarsia*. **2** M19 (A piece of) similar inlaid work in stone, metal, or glass. **3** M20 A method of knitting with a number of colours in which a separate length or ball of yarn is used for each area of colour (as opposed to the different yarns being carried at the back of the work). Frequently *attributive*.

intelligentsia /ɪnˌtɛlɪˈdʒɛntsɪə/ *noun* E20 Russian (*intelligentsiya*, from Polish *inteligencja*, from Latin *intelligentia* intelligence). The part of a nation (originally in pre-revolutionary Russia) having aspirations to intellectual activity, a section of society regarded as possessing culture and political initiative; *plural* the members of this section of a nation or society, intellectuals.

> **1996** *Country Life* The view that what happens on the screen can influence what happens in life—so long resisted by the liberal intelligentsia—is gaining ground.

intendant /ɪnˈtɛnd(ə)nt/ *noun* (also **intendent**) M17 French (from Latin *intendent-* present participial stem of *intendere* to direst, promote). **1** M17 Chiefly as the title of certain officials: a superintendent, a director; *especially* (in seventeenth- and eighteenth-century France) any of certain agents of the King appointed to supervise the administration of justice, finance, etc., in the provinces on behalf of central government. **2** L19 The administrator of an opera-house or theatre. Also, a musical director, a conductor.

2 1996 *Spectator* He seems incapable of the smarmy two-facedness of the majority of opera house *Intendants* . . .

inter alia /ˌɪntə(r) 'eɪlɪə/, /'alɪə/ *adverb phrase* M17 Latin (from *inter* among + *alia* accusative neuter plural of *alius* another). Among other things.

1996 *Times: Weekend* He recommends, *inter alia*, that sumps should be drained and refilled, fuel tanks should be drained . . . that the spark plug is removed and 'an eggspoon of oil' is dropped on the piston head.

inter alios /ˌɪntə(r) 'eɪlɪəʊs/, /'alɪəʊs/ *adverb phrase* M17 Latin (from *inter* among + *alios* accusative masculine plural of *alius* another). Among other people.

interim /'ɪnt(ə)rɪm/ *noun, adverb, & adjective* M16 Latin ((adverb), from *inter* between + adverbial ending -*im*). **A** *noun* **1** M16 *Ecclesiastical History* (usually *Interim*) A provisional arrangement for the adjustment of religious differences between the German Protestants and the Roman Catholic Church in the mid sixteenth century. **b** M16 *generally* A temporary or provisional arrangement. **2** L16–M17 A thing done in an interval; an interlude. **3** E17 An intervening time; *the* meantime. **4** M20 An interim dividend. **B** *adverb* L16 In the meantime; meanwhile. Now *rare*. **C** *adjective* E17 Done, made, provided, etc., in or for the meantime; provisional, temporary. Formerly (of time), intervening.

Interimsethik /'ɪnterɪmzˌeˑtɪk/ *noun* (also Anglicized as **interim-ethic** /'ɪntərɪm ˌeθɪk/) E20 German (from as INTERIM + *Ethik* ethics). *Theology* The moral principles of Jesus interpreted as meant for people expecting the imminent end of the world; *transferred* a code of behaviour for use in a specific temporary situation.

intermed(i)i plural of INTERMEDIO.

intermedia plural of INTERMEDIUM.

intermedio /ɪntə'mɛdɪəʊ/ *noun* plural **intermed(i)i** /ɪntə'mɛdriː/ L19 Italian (from as INTERMEDIUM). A musical interlude between the acts of a play or an opera. Cf. INTERMEZZO.

intermedium /ɪntə'miːdɪəm/ *noun* plural **intermedia** /ɪntə'miːdɪə/, **intermediums** L16 Late Latin (use as noun of neuter singular of Latin *intermedius* intermediate). **1** L16 An intervening action or performance. Now only *specifically* (*Music*), an INTERMEDIO. **2** E17 An interval of time or space. Now *rare* or *obsolete*. **3** M17 An intermediate agent, an intermediary. **4** L19 *Zoology* (modern Latin *os intermedium*). In tetrapods: a carpal in the centre of the wrist joint; a tarsal in the centre of the ankle joint.

intermezzo /ɪntə'mɛtsəʊ/ *noun* plural **intermezzi** /ɪntə'mɛtsi/, **intermezzos** L18 Italian (from as INTERMEDIUM; cf. MEZZO). **1** L18 A short light dramatic, musical, or other performance inserted between the acts of a play or (formerly) an opera. **2** M19 A short connecting instrumental movement in an opera or other musical work; a similar piece performed independently; a short piece for a solo instrument.

internuncio /ɪntə'nʌnsɪəʊ/ *noun* plural **internuncios** M17 Italian (*internunzio* from Latin *internuntius*, from as *inter-* + *nuntius* messenger). **1** M17 A messenger between two parties; a go-between. **2** L17 An official papal representative or ambassador at a foreign court, ranking below a nuncio. **3** E18 *History* A minister representing a government (especially of Austria) at Constantinople (Istanbul).

inter partes /ˌɪntə 'pɑːtiːz/ *adjective phrase* E19 Latin. *Law* (Of an action) relevant only to the two parties in a particular case; (of a deed etc.) made between two parties.

interreges plural of INTERREX.

interregnum /ɪntə'rɛgnəm/ *noun* plural **interregnums**, **interregna** /ɪntə'rɛgnə/ L16 Latin (from as *inter-* between + *regnum* reign). **1** L16–L18 Temporary authority or rule exercised during a vacancy of the throne or a suspension of the normal government. **2** L16 An interval during which the normal government is suspended, especially during the period between the end of a monarch's rule and the accession of his or her successor; any period of cessation or suspension of rule, authority, etc. **3** M17 An interval, a pause, a break.

interrex /'ɪntərɛks/ *noun* plural **interreges** /ɪntə'riːdʒiːz/ L16 Latin (from as *inter-* between + *rex* king). A person holding the supreme authority in a State during an interregnum.

in terrorem /ɪn tɛ'rɔ:rəm/ *adverb & adjective phrase* E17 Latin (= into a state of terror). (Done) as a warning or to deter.

inter se /ˌɪntə 'seɪ/ *adverb phrase* M19 Latin. Between or among themselves.

interstitium /ɪntə'stɪʃɪəm/ *noun* plural **interstitiums**, **interstitia** /ɪntə'stɪʃɪə/ L16 Latin (from *intersistere* to stand between). **1** L16-E18 An intervening (usually empty) space, an interstice. **b** L16-E18 An intervening space. **2** M20 *Anatomy* and *Zoology* The tissue or region lying between the principal cells, tissues, etc., of a part of the body.

inter vivos /ˌɪntə 'vi:vəʊs/ *adverb & adjective phrase* M19 Latin. (Made) between living people (especially of a gift as opposed to a legacy).

intifada /ɪntɪ'fɑ:də/ *noun* L20 Arabic (*intifāḍa* shaking off). An uprising by Arabs; *specifically* that begun by Palestinians in 1987 against Israeli authority.

■ The word had earlier been current among Islamic groups, for instance in Lebanon, but only began to appear in English-language reports of events on the West Bank in the late 1980s.
1988 *Independent* The Palestinians have succeeded for the first time in bringing the *intifada* into the occupied territories within Israel's pre-1967 boundaries.
1995 *Spectator* Such patterns are common in wars of national liberation, as exemplified . . . by the very high proportion of Palestinian casualties inflicted by their compatriots during the *Intifada*.

intime /ɛ̃tim/ *adjective* E17 French (from Latin *intimus* innermost). Intimate. Now only *specifically* friendly, familiar, cosy.

intimism /'ɪntɪmɪz(ə)m/ *noun* (also **intimisme** /ɛ̃timism/) E20 French (*intimisme*, from as INTIME). A style of intimate domestic genre painting using impressionist techniques.

intimist /'ɪntɪmɪst/ *noun & adjective* (also **intimiste** /ɛ̃timist/ (*plural same*)) E20 French (from *intimisme*, from as INTIME). **A** *noun* E20 A painter following the principles of intimism. **B** *adjective* M20 Of or pertaining to intimism.

intombi /ɪn'tɒmbi/ *noun* E19 Xhosa and Zulu. In southern Africa: a young Black woman who has been ritually prepared for marriage.

intonaco /ɪn'təʊnəkəʊ/ *noun* (also **intonico** /ɪn'təʊnɪkəʊ/) plural **intonacos** E19 Italian (*intonico, intonaco*, from *intonicare* to cover with plaster, ultimately from Latin *tunica* coat, tunic). The final coating of plaster spread upon a wall or other surface, especially for fresco painting.

in toto /ɪn 'təʊtəʊ/ *adverb phrase* L18 Latin. Completely, without exception; altogether, in all.
1995 *Spectator* This does not mean, however, that what the feminists said, *in toto*, was wrong—just as the theory of pure communism contained some benevolent and pertinent points.

intrados /ɪn'treɪdɒs/ *noun* L18 French (from as *intra-* inside + *dos* back). *Architecture* The lower or inner curve of an arch; *especially* the lower curve of the voussoirs which form the arch. Cf. EXTRADOS.

intra vires /ˌɪntrə 'vʌɪri:z/ *adverb phrase* L19 Latin (= within the powers). Chiefly *Law*. Within the powers or legal authority (*of* a corporation or person).
■ Opposed to ULTRA VIRES.

intra vitam /ˌɪntrə 'vi:tam/, /'vʌɪtam/ *adjective phrase* L19 Latin. *Biology* Taking place during life; while still living. Cf. IN VIVO.

intriguant /'ɪntrɪg(ə)nt/, *foreign* /ɛ̃trigɑ̃/ (*plural same*) *noun & adjective* (also **intrigant**) L18 French (present participle of *intriguer* to scheme). **A** *noun* L18 An intriguer. **B** *adjective* E19 Intriguing; scheming.

intriguante /ɛ̃trigɑ̃t/ *noun* (also **intrigante**) plural pronounced same E19 French (feminine of *intriguant*: see preceding). A woman who intrigues.

introit /'ɪntrɔɪt/ *noun* LME Old and Modern French (*introït* from Latin *introitus* entrance, from *introire* to enter, from as *intro-* + *ire* to go). **1** LME The action or an act of going in; (an) entrance. Long *rare*. **2** L15 *Ecclesiastical* An antiphon or psalm sung while the priest approaches the altar to celebrate the Eucharist. Also, the first two or three words of the office of a particular day.

introuvable /ɛ̃truvabl/ *adjective* E19 French (from as negative *in-* + *trouver* to find). Unfindable, undiscoverable.

in utero /ɪn 'ju:tərəʊ/ *adverb & adjective phrase* E18 Latin. In the womb; before birth.
1996 *Times* . . . the study tells us nothing about the route of maternal transmission, which could be *in utero*, at birth or soon after birth.

in vacuo /m ˈvakjʊəʊ/ *adverb phrase* M17 Latin. In a vacuum.

invita Minerva /m͵vʌɪtɑː mɪˈnəːvɑː/, /m'vɪːta/ *adverb phrase* L16 Latin (= Minerva (being) unwilling). When one is not in the mood; without inspiration.

■ Minerva was the Roman goddess of learning and patroness of arts and handicrafts, so her blessing was considered essential to enterprises in these fields.
1954 M. Cost *Invitation from Minerva* It is always a mistake to do anything invita Minerva . . . Briefly, against the grain.

in vitro /m ˈviːtrəʊ/ *adjective & adverb phrase* L19 Latin (literally, 'in glass'). *Biology* (Performed, obtained, or occurring) in a test-tube or elsewhere outside a living organism.
attributive **1995** *New Scientist* A couple from the north of England are hoping that their embryos, conceived by in vitro fertilisation, will be the first to be screened for a gene that could cause cancer in later life.

in vivo /m ˈviːvəʊ/ *adjective & adverb phrase* E20 Latin. *Biology* (Performed, obtained, or occurring) within a living organism.
■ Opposed to EX VIVO; cf. INTRA VITAM.
1996 *New Scientist* . . . it is not possible, at present, to determine directly the impact, in vivo, of Prozac on a particular individual's serotonin receptors.

involucrum /mvəˈl(j)uːkrəm/ *noun* plural **involucra** /mvəˈl(j)uːkrə/ L17 Latin (from *involvere* to involve). **1** L17 An outer covering, an envelope; a covering membrane. **2** M18 *Botany* A whorl or rosette of bracts surrounding an inflorescence or at the base of an umbel; an involucre.

inyanga /mˈjɑːŋə/ *noun* M19 Zulu. In South Africa: a traditional herbalist and medicine man, sometimes acting as diviner or magician.

ion /ˈʌɪən/ *noun* M19 Greek (neuter present participle of *ienai* to go). *Physics* and *Chemistry* Originally, either of the constituents which pass to the electrodes during electrolysis. Now *generally*, any individual atom, molecule, or group having a net electric charge (either positive or negative) due to loss or gain of one or more electrons.

iota /ʌɪˈəʊtə/ *noun* LME Greek (*iōta*, of Phoenician origin; cf. Hebrew *yod*). **1** LME The ninth (and smallest) letter (Ι, ι) of the Greek alphabet. **2** M17 *figurative* The smallest or a very small part or quantity.

■ The English noun *jot* (from Latin *iota*) is a doublet of *iota* in sense 2.
2 1996 *Spectator* In fact, I have never known him change his mind one iota.

ipecacuanha /͵ɪpɪkakjʊˈanə/ *noun* E17 Portuguese (from Tupi-Guarani *ipekaaguéne*, from *ipe* small + *kaa* leaves + *guíne* vomit). **1** E17 The root of *Cephaelis ipecacuanha*, a Brazilian plant of the madder family; an extract or preparation of this, formerly much used as an emetic and expectorant. Also, the plant itself. **2** E18 Any of various other plants with emetic roots; a preparation of such a root.

ippon /ˈɪpɒn/ *noun* M20 Japanese. A score of one full point in judo, karate, etc.

ipse dixit /͵ɪpsi ˈdɪksɪt/, /͵ɪpseɪ/ *noun* plural **ipse dixits** L16 Latin (literally, 'he himself said (it)', translation of Greek *autos epha*). An unproved assertion resting only on the authority of a speaker; a dogmatic statement; a dictum.
■ The Greek expression was used of their master's sayings by the followers of the sage Pythagoras.

ipsissima verba /ɪp͵sɪsɪmə ˈvəːbə/ *noun phrase* E19 Latin (= the very words themselves). The precise words used by a writer or speaker.

ipso facto /͵ɪpsəʊ ˈfaktəʊ/ *adverb phrase* M16 Latin. By that very fact or act; by the fact itself; thereby. Cf. EO IPSO.

ipso jure /͵ɪpsəʊ ˈdʒʊəreɪ/, /ˈdʒʊəriː/ *adverb phrase* L16 Latin. By the operation of the law itself.

irredenta /irreˈdenta/, /ɪrɪˈdɛntə/ *noun* plural **irredente** /irreˈdente/, **irredentas** /ɪrɪˈdɛntəz/ E20 Italian. A region containing people ethnically related to the inhabitants of one State but politically subject to another.
■ Also used postpositively as an adjective (see quotation 1967). Also in TERRA IRREDENTA.
1934 A. Huxley *Beyond Mexique Bay* British Honduras still is regarded by the Guatemalans as an irredenta.
1967 *Punch* They annexed Tibet, but they had argued themselves into the belief that this was ancient Chinese territory, China irredenta.

isangoma variant of SANGOMA.

isba /izˈbɑ/ *noun* (also **izba**) L18 Russia (*izba* (related to Old High German *stuba* from the Germanic base of which modern English *stove* is also ultimately derived)). A Russian hut or log-house.

isblink /'iːsblɪŋk/ *noun* L18 Swedish (or from corresponding words in Danish, German, Dutch). A luminous appearance on the horizon caused by the reflection from ice.

■ Also in Anglicized form as *iceblink*.

ishan /'iːʃaːn/ *noun* E20 Arabic (perhaps from Arabic dialect *īšān* from Persian *nīšān* mark). A prehistoric mound in Iraq.

isolato /iːsəˈlaːtəʊ/ *noun* plural **isolati** /iːsəˈlaːti/, **isolatos** M19 Italian. An isolated person, an outcast.

item /'ʌɪtəm/ *adverb* LME Latin (= just so, similarly, moreover, from *ita* thus, so). Likewise, also.

■ Chiefly used to introduce and draw attention to a new statement, particular, or entry, especially in a list or formal document. From this is derived the fully Anglicized noun meaning 'an individual thing, article, or unit included in a set, list, computation, etc.'.

ius cogens, ius gentium, ius naturae, ius primae noctis variants of JUS COGENS, JUS GENTIUM, JUS NATURAE, JUS PRIMAE NOCTIS.

izar /ɪˈzɑː/ *noun* M19 Arabic ('zār). An enveloping outer garment worn by Muslim women (and, in some countries, Muslim men). Also, the lower garment of the IHRAM (sense 2).

izba variant of ISBA.

izzat /'ɪzʌt/ *noun* (also **izzut**) M19 Persian (Urdu 'izzat, from Arabic 'izza glory). Honour, reputation, credit, prestige.

> **1953** E. M. Forster *Hill of Devi* In every remark and gesture, does not the Indian prince either decrease his own 'izzat' or that of his interlocutor?

J

jabot /'ʒabəʊ/ noun plural pronounced same E19 French (= bird's crop, shirt-frill, probably from a Proto-Romance base meaning 'crop, maw, gullet'). **1** E19 A frill on the front of a man's shirt, edging the opening. Now chiefly *historical*. **2** L19 An ornamental frill on a woman's bodice.

jacal /hə'kɑːl/ noun M19 Mexican Spanish (from Nahuatl *xacalli* contraction of *xamitl calli* adobe house). A hut built of erect stakes filled in with wattle and mud, common in Mexico and the south-western United States; an adobe house. Also, the material or method used in building such a hut.

j'accuse /ʒakyz/ noun M20 French (= I accuse). An accusation, particularly one of injustice against an authority.

■ The opening words of Emile Zola's famous letter to the newspaper *L'Aurore* (13 Jan 1898) denouncing the French military establishment for wrongly condemning the Jewish army officer Alfred Dreyfus for treason in 1894 and then attempting to suppress the facts that proved that a miscarriage of justice had taken place.
1996 *Times* . . . this comes as something of a surprise . . . an authorial disclaimer designed to retract at the last minute what a few pages earlier looked like becoming a grandiloquent *j'accuse.*

jacquard /'dʒakɑːd/, /'dʒakəd/ adjective & noun (also **Jacquard**) M19 French. **A** adjective **1** M19 Designating an attachment to a loom which enables the pattern in the cloth to be produced automatically by means of punched cards. **2** M19 Designating a fabric, article, or pattern made with the aid of this; of an intricate variegated design. **B** noun **1** M19 A jacquard fabric, pattern, or article. **2** L19 A jacquard attachment or loom.

■ The loom attachment is called after its inventor, Joseph-Marie Jacquard (1752–1834).

jacquerie /dʒeɪk(ə)ri/, foreign /ʒakri/ (plural same) noun E16 Old and Modern French (from male forename *Jacques*). A popular rising of the peasantry.

■ The original *jacquerie* was the revolt of the peasants of northern France against the nobles in 1357–8. *Jacques* was the former French name for a villein or peasant.

jadam /'dʒadam/ noun E20 Malay. A type of silver or brass niello ware from the Malay peninsula and Sumatra, used especially for decorating belt buckles.

j'adoube /ʒadub/ interjection E19 French (from *je, j'* I + 1st person singular of *adouber* to repair, mend (ultimate origin unknown)). *Chess* Indicating that a player wishes to touch a piece without making a move.

jäger /'jeɪgə/ noun (also **jaeger**) L18 German (from *jagen* to hunt, pursue). **1** L18 Originally, a marksman in the German or Austrian infantry. Later, a member of a battalion of riflemen in these armies. Now, a member of a regiment using the name as an official title. **2** E19 A (German or Swiss) huntsman or hunter. **3** E19 An attendant wearing a huntsman's costume. Cf. CHASSEUR sense 2a.

■ *Yager* /'jeɪgə/ (or *yager rifle*) (E19), meaning 'a type of short-barrelled large-bore rifle formerly used in the southern United States', is apparently an Anglicized form of *Jäger*.

jai alai /ˌhʌɪ ə'lʌɪ/ noun phrase E20 Spanish (from Basque *jai* festival + *alai* merry). The game of PELOTA.

jalap /'dʒaləp/, /'dʒɒləp/ noun M17 French (from Spanish *jalapa*, in full *purga de Jalapa*, from *Jalapa, Xalapa* a Mexican city). **1** M17 A purgative drug obtained from the tuberous roots of a Mexican climbing plant, *Ipomoea purga*, and from certain other plants of the bindweed family. **2** L17 The plant yielding this drug; (with specifying word) any of certain other plants yielding a similar drug.

jalapeño /hala'pemjəʊ/, /hala'piːnəʊ/ noun plural **jalapeños** M20 Mexican Spanish. A very hot green chilli pepper. Also *jalapeño pepper.*

jalebi /dʒa'leɪbi/ noun M19 Hindustani (*jalebī*). An Indian sweet made by frying a coil of batter and then soaking it in syrup.

jaleo /xa'leo/ noun M19 Spanish (literally, 'halloo'). Clapping to accompany Andalusian dancing; a lively Andalusian dance.

jalousie /ˌʤalʊˈziː/ *noun* M18 French (literally, 'jealousy'; also, a type of blind or shutter). A blind or shutter made from a row of angled slats to exclude sun and rain and control the entry of air and light.
1961 I. Fleming *Thunderball* Inside the small room, the jalousies threw bands of light and shadow over the bed.

jambalaya /ˌʤambəˈleɪə/, /ˌʤambəˈlʌɪə/ *noun* L19 Louisiana French (from Provençal *jambalaia*). A dish composed of rice mixed with shrimps, ham, chicken, turkey, etc.; *figurative* a mixture, a jumble. Originally *United States*.

janitor /ˈʤanɪtə/ *noun* M16 Latin (from *janua* door, entrance). **1** M16 A doorkeeper, a porter; *historically* an ostler. **2** E18 A caretaker of a building, especially a school, responsible for its cleaning, heating, etc.

janken /ˈʤaŋk(ə)n/ *noun* M20 Japanese. A children's game played by using the hands to represent one of three things, paper, scissors, or stone.

japonaiserie /ʒapɔnezri/ *noun* L19 French. Japanese characteristics or fashion; in *plural*, Japanese ornaments or knick-knacks.
■ Cf. CHINOISERIE. The Anglicized form *Japanesery* also dates from the same period (L19) of enthusiasm for Japanese art and artefacts in the West.

jarabe /xaˈrabe/ *noun* (also **jarave**) M19 American Spanish (from Spanish = syrup). A Mexican pair dance in which the man dances the ZAPATEADO steps, performed especially as an exhibition dance in national costume.

jardinière /ˌʤɑːdɪˈnjɛː/ *noun* M19 French (literally, 'female gardener'). **1** M19 An ornamental receptacle, pot, or stand for the display of growing or cut flowers. **2** M19 *Cookery* A garnish made with cooked vegetables.

jargonelle /ˌʤɑːɡəˈnɛl/ *noun* (also **jargonel**) L17 French (diminutive of *jargon* from Italian *giargone*, usually identified ultimately with zircon). An early-ripening (originally inferior) variety of pear.

jaspé /ˈʤaspeɪ/, *foreign* /ʒaspe/ *noun* M19 French (past participle of *jasper* to marble). Marbled, mottled, variegated.

jat /ʤɑːt/ *noun* (also **jati** /ˈʤɑːti/) L19 Hindustani (*jāt*, *jāti* from Sanskrit *jāti* birth). In the Indian subcontinent: a caste, a tribe, a class.

jatha /ˈʤəˈtɑː/ *noun* E20 Panjabi and Hindustani (*jāthā*). In the Indian subcontinent: an armed or organized band of Sikhs.

jati variant of JAT.

jaune /ʒon/ *adjective* LME French (from Latin *galbinum* greenish-yellow). Yellow.
■ Although formerly fully naturalized, *jaune* is now obsolete in English except in the names of pigments, such as *jaune brilliant* cadmium yellow.

jebel /ˈʤɛbɛl/ *noun* M19 Arabic (*jabal*, (colloquial) *jebel*, plural *jibāl*, mountain). In the Middle East and North Africa: a mountain, a range of hills.
■ Frequently in place names.

jehad variant of JIHAD.

jellaba /ˈʤɛləbə/ *noun* (also **djellaba, jellabah**, **jelab** /ˈʤɛləb/, and other variants) E19 Arabic ((Moroccan) *jellāb(a)*, *jellābiyya*: cf. GALABIYA). A loose hooded long-sleeved usually woollen cloak of a kind worn originally by Arab men in North Africa.

je ne sais quoi /ʒənsɛkwa/, /ˌʤə nə seɪ ˈkwɑː/ *noun phrase* M17 French (literally, 'I do not know what'). An indefinable quality, something indescribable or inexpressible.
1996 *Times* Of course, computer-generated images have been a part of movies for several years now . . . But it had always been thought . . . that human actors possessed a certain *je ne sais quoi* that would save them from being consigned to the scrapheap by the relentless advance of the techno-bores.

jet d'eau /ʒedo/ *noun* plural **jets d'eau** (pronounced same) L17 French (= jet of water). An ornamental jet of water rising from a fountain or pipe; a fountain or pipe from which such a jet rises.

jeté /ʒɛˈteɪ/, *foreign* /ʒəte/ (*plural same*) *noun* M19 French (past participle (sc. *pas* step) of *jeter* to throw). *Ballet* A step in which a spring is made from one foot to land on the other, especially with one leg extended forwards and the other backwards. Cf. GRAND JETÉ.

jeté en tournant /ʒɛˈteɪ ɒn ˈtʊənɒ/, *foreign* /ʒəte ɑ̃ turnɑ̃/ *noun phrase* plural **jetés en tournant** /ʒɛˈteɪz ɒn ˈtʊənɒ/, *foreign* /ʒətez ɑ̃ turnɑ̃/ M20 French. *Ballet* A jeté executed with a turning movement. Also called *tour jeté*.

jeton /ˈʤɛtən/, *in sense 2 foreign* /ʒətɔ̃/ (*plural same*) *noun* (also in sense 1 **jetton**) M20 Old and Modern French (from *jeter* to cast up (accounts), calculate). **1** M20 A counter or token used to operate a slot machine. **2** M20 A metal disc used instead of a coin for insertion in a public telephone box, especially in France.

jets d'eau plural of JET D'EAU.

jetton variant of JETON.

jeu /ʒø/ *noun* plural **jeux** /ʒø/ L18 French (from Latin *jocus* joke). Play, game.
■ In English occurs only in various phrases.

jeu de mots /ʒø də mo/ *noun phrase* plural **jeux de mots** /ʒø də mo/ M18 French (literally, 'play of words'). A play on words, a pun.

jeu de paume /ʒø də pom/ *noun phrase* L18 French (literally, 'game of the palm (of the hand)'). Real tennis; a court where this is played.

jeu de société /ʒø də sɔsjete/ *noun phrase* plural **jeux de société** /ʒø də sɔsjete/ E19 French (literally, 'game of society'). A party game or amusement.
■ Used especially in the plural.

jeu d'esprit /ʒø dɛspri/ *noun phrase* plural **jeux d'esprit** /ʒø dɛspri/ E18 French (literally, 'game of wit'). A playful action in which some cleverness is displayed; (now usually) a humorous literary trifle.
1995 *Spectator* When the Stone of Scone was stolen from Westminster Abbey in the 1950s, E. V. Knox in *Punch* in a *jeu d'esprit* confessed that Inspector Lestrade was baffled and injected Sherlock Holmes into the case . . .

jeune fille /ʒœn fij/ *noun & adjective phrase* M19 French. **A** *noun phrase* M19 plural **jeunes filles** (pronounced same). A young girl, an ingénue. **B** *attributive* or as *adjective phrase* L19 Characteristic of an ingénue.

jeune fille bien élevée /ʒœn fij bjɛn ɛlve/ *noun phrase* plural **jeunes filles bien élevées** (*pronounced same*) L20 French. A young girl brought up in a genteel way.
1995 G. Tindall *Célestine* Monsieur Allorent's composition seems redolent of the self-conscious world just being born: that of the *rentier* and the white-collar workers, of the ladylike wife and the *jeune fille bien élevée* . . .

jeune premier /ʒœn prəmje/ *noun phrase* plural **jeunes premiers** (pronounced same) feminine **jeune première** /prəmjɛr/ M19 French (literally, 'first young man (woman)'). An actor who plays the part of a principal lover or young hero (or heroine).

jeunes filles, jeunes filles bien élevées plurals of JEUNE FILLE, JEUNE FILLE BIEN ÉLEVÉE.

jeunes premiers plural of JEUNE PREMIER.

jeunesse /ʒœnɛs/ *noun* L18 French. Young people; the young.

jeunesse dorée /ʒœnɛs dɔre/ *noun phrase* M19 French (literally, 'gilded youth'). Young people of wealth and fashion.
■ The original *jeunesse dorée* was a group of fashionable counter-revolutionaries in France during the Revolution, following the fall of Robespierre.
1996 *Spectator* Sadly, neither *jeunesse dorée*, nor even golden oldies, still flock there.

jheel /dʒiːl/ *noun* (also **jhil**) E19 Hindi (*jhīl*). In the Indian subcontinent: a (large) pool or lake left after a flood.

jibba variant of JUBBA.

jigotai /dʒɪɡəˈtʌɪ/ *noun* M20 Japanese (from *ji* self + *go* defence + *tai* posture). A defensive posture in judo.

jihad /dʒɪˈhɑːd/, /dʒɪˈhad/ *noun* (also **jehad**) M19 Arabic (*jihād*, literally, 'effort'). Religious warfare or a war for the propagation or defence of Islam; *transferred* a fervent campaign in some cause.
1995 *Spectator* The religious impulse, which can no longer attach itself to traditional religions, is satisfied by the taking up of a cause . . . The jihad against the export of veal calves is a case in point.

Jina /ˈdʒmə/ *noun* E19 Sanskrit (*jina*). Jainism A great Jain teacher who has attained liberation from KARMA; a sculptured representation of such a teacher.

jinnee /ˈdʒmiː/ *noun* plural **jinn** (also **jinn**, **djinn**, /dʒm/, plural **jinnees**, same) E19 Arabic (*jinnī* masculine singular, plural *jinn*). In Arabian stories and Muslim mythology: a spirit of an order lower than the angels, able to appear in human or animal form and to exercise supernatural influence.

jinricksha /dʒmˈrɪkʃə/ *noun* (also **jinrikisha** /dʒmˈrɪkɪʃə/) L19 Japanese (*jin-riki-sha*, from *jin* man + *riki* strength, power + *sha* vehicle). A rickshaw.

jiu-jitsu, jiu-jutsu variants of JU-JITSU.

jiva /ˈdʒiːvə/ *noun* E19 Sanskrit (*jīva*). *Hindu and Jain Philosophy* The soul; the embodied self; the vital principle.

joie de vivre /ʒwadəvivr/, /ˌʒwɑː də 'viːvrə/ *noun phrase* L19 French (= joy of living). A feeling of healthy enjoyment of life; exuberance, high spirits.

> **1996** *Times Magazine* ' . . . Is she as proud as she says she is of being a spinster?' It is hard to judge beneath the joie de vivre.

jojoba /həˈhəʊbə/, /həʊˈhəʊbə/ *noun* E20 Mexican Spanish. A desert shrub, *Simmondsia chinensis* (family Simmondsiaceae), of Mexico and the south-western United States, whose seeds yield an oil used as a lubricant and in cosmetics.

■ The word was familiar in the United States long before it became current in British English, which happened only from the mid 1970s onwards, when its value as a substitute for sperm whale oil and its properties as an ingredient in cosmetics and soaps became more widely appreciated.

jolie laide /ʒɔli lɛd/ *noun & adjective phrase* plural **jolies laides** (pronounced same) L19 French (from feminine adjectives *jolie* pretty + *laide* ugly). (An) attractively or fascinatingly ugly (woman).

■ The masculine form *joli laid* is also occasionally found.

> **1996** *Spectator* We passed through unrecommendable, dull Downham Market, whose only points are a Victorian town clock and squat 100-year-old outlying houses in yellow stone which could be called *jolie laide*.

jong /jɒŋ/ *noun* E17 Afrikaans (= young (man)). Originally (*History*), a Coloured male slave or servant. Now, a form of address to a young man or woman.

■ South African colloquial, used especially among young people.

jongleur /ʒɔ̃glœr/ *noun* plural pronounced same L18 French (alteration of *jougleur* (Old French *jogleor* accusative of *joglere*) from Latin *joculator* jester). *History* An itinerant minstrel.

jornada /xorˈnada/ *noun* plural **jornadas** /xorˈnadas/, /jɔːˈnɑːdəz/ M17 Spanish (= Italian *giornata*, French *journée* journey). **1** M17-M19 An act of a play; a book or canto of a poem. **2** E19 In Mexico etc.: a day's journey; *specifically* one across a waterless desert tract with no place to halt.

joruri /ˈdʒoːruri/ *noun* L19 Japanese (*jōruri*, from the name of a character in a popular recitation). **1** L19 A dramatic recitation to music, accompanying a Japanese puppet performance. **2** M20 Japanese puppet drama.

jota /ˈxota/ *noun* M19 Spanish. A northern Spanish folk-dance performed by one or more couples in rapid triple time; a piece of music for this dance.

jotun /ˈjəʊt(ə)n/ *noun* M19 Old Norse (*jǫtunn* = Old English *eoten*, from Germanic). In Scandinavian mythology: a member of a supernatural race of giants.

joual /ʒwal/, /ʒuːˈɑːl/ *noun* M20 Canadian French (dialect form of French *cheval* horse). Demotic Canadian French characterized by non-standard pronunciations and grammar, and influenced by English vocabulary and syntax.

jour /ʒur/ *noun* plural pronounced same LME Old and Modern French (from Latin *diurnum* neuter singular (used as noun in popular Latin) of *diurnus* diurnal). **1** LME-M16 A day. **2** M19 A kind of open stitch used in lace-making. Usually in *plural*.

■ In sense 1 now occurs only in certain phrases used in English, e.g. BONHEUR DU JOUR, PLAT DU JOUR.

jubba /ˈdʒʌbə/, /ˈdʒʊbə/ *noun* (also **jibba(h)** /ˈdʒɪbə/, **jubbah**) M16 Arabic (whence also French JUPE). A type of long open cloth coat with wide sleeves, worn especially by Muslims.

jubilate /ˌdʒuːbɪˈleɪti/, /ˌjuːbɪˈlateɪ/ *noun* (also **Jubilate**) ME Latin (imperative of *jubilare* to call, halloo, (in Christian writers) shout for joy). **1** ME Psalm 100 (90 in the Vulgate) used as a canticle; a musical setting of this. More fully *Jubilate Deo* (the first two words of this psalm). **2** M18 A call to rejoice; an outburst of joyous triumph.

Judenrat /ˈjuːd(ə)nˌrɑːt/ *noun* plural **Judenrate** /ˈjuːd(ə)nˌrɑːtə/ M20 German (= Jewish council). A council representing a Jewish community in a locality controlled by the Germans during the war of 1939–45.

judenrein /ˈjuːd(ə)nˌraɪn/ *adjective* M20 German (= free from Jews). Of a society, organization, etc., *specifically* in Nazi Germany: without Jewish members, out of which Jews have been expelled.

> **1951** H. Arendt *Origins of Totalitarianism* When Hitler came to power, the German banks were already almost *judenrein*.

judo /ˈdʒuːdəʊ/ *noun* L19 Japanese (from *jū* gentle + *dō* way). A refined form of ju-jitsu using principles of movement and balance, practised as a sport or a form of physical exercise.

juge d'instruction /ʒyʒ dɛstryksjɔ̃/ *noun phrase* plural **juges d'instruction** (pronounced same) L19 French. In France: an examining magistrate, a police magistrate.

Jugendstil /'juːɡəntˌʃtiːl/ *noun & adjective* E20 German (from *Jugend* youth + *Stil* style). (Of, pertaining to, or designating) German ART NOUVEAU.

■ *Die Jugend* was the name of an influential German magazine started in 1896 in Munich.

ju-jitsu /dʒuːˈdʒɪtsuː/ *noun* (also **jiu-jitsu, ju-jutsu** /dʒuːˈdʒʌtsuː/) L19 Japanese (*jūjutsu*, from *jū* gentle + *jutsu* skill). A Japanese system of unarmed combat using an opponent's strength and weight to his or her disadvantage, now also practised as physical training. Cf. JUDO.

juju /'dʒuːdʒuː/ *noun* (also **ju-ju**) E17 West African (probably from French *joujou* plaything, reduplicated form from *jouer* to play from Latin *jocare*). A charm, amulet, or cult object in some West African belief systems; the supernatural force believed to be associated with such objects. Also, the system of observances associated with such objects.

jujube /'dʒuːdʒuːb/ *noun* LME French (or medieval French *jujuba*, ultimately from Latin *zizyphum* from Greek *zizuphos, zizuphon zizyphus* (tree)). **1** LME An edible berry-like drupe, the fruit of various trees of the genus *Ziziphus*, of the buckthorn family. **b** M16 Any of the trees which produce this fruit, especially *Ziziphus jujuba*, extending from the Mediterranean to China, and *Z. lotus* of North Africa. Also *jujube tree*. **2** M19 A sweet or confection made of gum arabic, gelatin, etc., originally one flavoured with or tasting like this fruit.

jukskei /'jœkskeɪ/ *noun* E19 Afrikaans (from *juk* yoke + *skei* pin, peg). **1** E19 A wooden peg on an ox-yoke. **2** M20 A game resembling quoits, originally played with yoke-pins; the bottle-shaped peg used in this game.

juku /'dʒuːkuː/ *noun* L20 Japanese. In Japan: a cramming school.

1992 *Economist* The best Japanese *juku* are so hard to get into that there is a booming secondary industry of cramming people to get into cramming schools.

julienne /ˌdʒuːlɪˈɛn/, *foreign* /ʒyljɛn/ (*plural same*) *adjective & noun* E18 French (from male forename *Jules* or *Julien*). **A** *adjective* **1** E18 Designating soup made of various

vegetables (especially carrots), chopped and cooked in meat stock. **2** L19 Designating a small thin strip of a vegetable etc.; (of a vegetable etc.) cut into such strips; (of a dish or garnish) consisting of or containing such strips. **B** *noun* **1** M19 Julienne soup. **2** E20 A julienne strip; a dish of julienne vegetables etc.

jumar /'dʒuːmə/ *noun* M20 **Origin unknown** (originally Swiss). *Mountaineering* A clamp which when attached to a fixed rope automatically tightens when weight is applied and relaxes when it is removed, thus facilitating the climbing of the rope; a climb using such clips.

jumby /'dʒʌmbi/ *noun* (also **jumbie**) E19 Kikongo (*zumbi* fetish; cf. *zombie*). A ghost, an evil spirit. Chiefly *West Indies*.

jumelle /ʒuːˈmɛl/ *adjective* L15 French (feminine (masculine *jumeau*), from Latin *gemellus* diminutive of *geminus* twin). Twinned, paired; made or shaped in couples or pairs, double.

junker /'jʊŋkə/ *noun* M16 German (earlier *Junkher(r)*, from Middle High German *junc* young + *herre* (modern *Herr*) lord). A young German noble; *specifically* a member of the reactionary party of the Prussian aristocracy who aimed to maintain the exclusive privileges of their class; a narrow-minded, overbearing (younger) member of the German aristocracy.

■ Obsolete except in historical contexts.

junta /'dʒʌntə/, /'hʊntə/ *noun* E17 **Spanish and Portuguese** (*junta* (whence French *junte*) from Italian *giunta* from Proto-Romance use as noun of Latin *juncta* feminine past participle of *jungere* to join). **1** E17 A Spanish or Italian deliberative or administrative council or committee. **2** E18 *generally* A body of people combined for a common (especially political) purpose; a self-elected committee or council, a cabal. Now frequently *specifically*, a political or military clique or faction taking power after a revolution or *coup d'état*.

■ The alternative form *junto*, modelled on Spanish nouns in *-o*, has also been current in English in sense 2 from the same period and briefly (E–M18) in sense 1.

jupe /dʒuːp/, *foreign* /ʒyp/ (*plural same*) *noun* ME Old and Modern French (from Arabic JUBBA). **1** ME A man's loose jacket, tunic, or jerkin. Now only *Scottish*. **2** E18–E20 A woman's jacket, gown, or bodice. In *plural*

also, a kind of bodice or stays. *Scottish.* **3** E19 A woman's skirt.

jupon /ˈdʒuːpɒn/, /dʒuːˈpɒn/ *noun* LME **Old French** (*juppon*, (also modern) *jupon*, from JUPE). *History* A close-fitting tunic or doublet; *especially* one worn under a hauberk, sometimes of thick material and padded. Also, a sleeveless surcoat worn outside armour, of rich material and emblazoned with arms.

jure divino /ˌdʒʊərɪ dɪˈviːnəʊ/ *adverb phrase* L16 **Latin.** By divine right or authority.

jus /ʒy/ *noun* M20 **French** (= juice). A thin broth or gravy.

1996 *Country Life* Smooth, creamy bread sauce . . . and a thin *jus*-like gravy flavoured with a little red Burgundy are the classic accompaniments.

jus cogens /ˌdʒʌs ˈkəʊdʒɛnz/ *noun phrase* (also **ius cogens**) L19 **Latin** (= compelling law). A principle of international law which cannot be set aside by agreement or acquiescence; a peremptory norm of general international law.

1996 T. Alexander *Unravelling Global Apartheid* There is no definitive list of laws covered by *jus cogens*, but aggression by one state against another, piracy, war crimes, slavery and genocide are generally accepted as illegal.

jus gentium /ˌdʒʌs ˈdʒɛnʃɪəm/ *noun phrase* (also **ius gentium**) M16 **Latin** (= law of nations). International law.

jus naturae /ˌdʒʌs nəˈtʃʊəriː/, /ˌdʒʌs nəˈtʃʊərʌɪ/ *noun phrase* (also **ius naturae**) M17 **Latin** (= law of nature). Natural law.

1996 *Spectator* . . . it is in his prosecution of Warren Hastings that he appears as the really determined upholder of the *ius naturae*, precisely because there was no other law—Indian or British—under which Hastings could be condemned.

jus primae noctis /ˌdʒʌs ˌprʌɪmiː ˈnɒktɪs/ *noun* (also **ius primae noctis**) L19 **Latin** (= right of the first night). DROIT DU SEIGNEUR.

jusqu'au bout /ʒysko bu/ *adverb phrase* E20 **French** (= up to the end). To the bitter end; until a conclusive victory has been gained.

■ The policy of *jusqu'auboutisme* applied originally in the context of the war of 1914–18.

juste milieu /ʒyst miljø/ *noun phrase* M19 **French** (literally, 'the right mean'). A happy medium, the golden mean; judicious moderation, especially in politics.

juvenilia /ˌdʒuːvəˈnɪlɪə/ *noun plural* E17 **Latin** (neuter plural of *juvenilis* juvenile). Literary or artistic works produced in an author's or artist's youth.

K

kabbala variant of CABBALA.

kabloona /kə'bluːnə/ *noun* L18 Eskimo ((Inuit) *kabluna* big eyebrow). Among Canadian Eskimos: a person who is not an Eskimo; a White person.

kabuki /kə'buːki/ *noun & adjective* L19 Japanese (originally (as verb) to act dissolutely; later interpreted as from *ka* song + *bu* dance + *ki* art, skill). (Of, pertaining to, or characteristic of) a traditional and popular form of Japanese drama with highly stylized song, mime, and dance, performed by male actors only.

kacha variant of KUTCHA.

kachina /kə'tʃiːnə/ *noun* L19 Hopi (*kacína* supernatural, from Keresan). A deified ancestral spirit in North American Pueblo Indian mythology.

Kaddish /'kadɪʃ/ *noun* E17 Aramaic (*qaddīš* holy). An ancient Jewish doxology regularly recited in the synagogue, including brief prayers for the welfare of Israel and concluding with a prayer for universal peace.

kadi variant of CADI.

kafenion /kafə'niːən/ *noun* M20 Greek (*kafeneio(n)*). A Greek coffee-house.

Kaffeeklatsch /'kafeklatʃ/ *noun* (also **kaffee-klatch** /'kafiklatʃ/) L19 German (from *Kaffee* coffee + *Klatsch* gossip; cf. KLATCH). Gossip over coffee cups; a coffee party.

kaffiyeh variant of KEFFIYEH.

kaftan variant of CAFTAN.

kagoule variant of CAGOULE.

kagura /'kaːɡʊrə/ *noun* L19 Japanese. A form of traditional sacred music and dance performed at Shinto festivals.

Kahal /'kaːhal/ *noun* E20 Hebrew (*qāhāl* assembly, community). (The governing body of) any of the former localized Jewish communities in Europe.

kahuna /kə'huːnə/ *noun* L19 Hawaiian. In Hawaii: a priest, a wise man; a minister; a sorcerer.

kai /kʌɪ/ *noun* M19 Maori. Food.

■ New Zealand colloquial. Also in reduplicated form **kaikai** or **kai-kai**, meaning the same or 'feasting'.

kaid /kɑː'iːd/ *noun* (also (*archaic*) **caid**) E19 Arabic (*ḳā'id* leader). An ALCAIDE.

kaikai variant of KAI.

kain /kʌm/ *noun plural* **kains**, same L18 Malay. In Malaysia and Indonesia: (a piece of) cloth, especially for use as clothing; a sarong.

■ Frequently with postpositive adjective (see quotation).
1963 J. Kirkup *Tropic Temper* There are many ways of folding the big starched kerchief in a form of head-dress . . . On the East Coast it is called kain satangan.

kairos /'kʌɪrɒs/ *noun* M20 Greek (= right or proper time). Fullness of time; the propitious moment, especially for decision or action.

■ The word became current in English through the writings of the German-born American theologian Paul Tillich (1886–1965).

Kaiser /'kʌɪzə/ *noun* M19 German (in modern use and in this form; ultimately from Latin *Caesar*, but cf. Old English *cāsere*, Old Frisian *keisar*, Old Saxon *kēsur*, *kēsar*, Old Norse *keisari*, Gothic *kaisar*, Dutch *keizer*). (The title of) an emperor: *specifically* an Austrian or German emperor.

■ Current in various spellings from the OE period, the word in its modern form reflects a Bavarian spelling which supplanted the more usual *keiser* in the seventeenth century. Its use in modern English appears to be because it was the form favoured by the nineteenth-century historian Thomas Carlyle.

k'ai shu /'kʌɪ ʃuː/ *noun phrase* L19 Chinese (*kǎishu*, from *kǎi* model + *shū* write). The usual script used for the Chinese language, suitable for everyday purposes.

kaizen /kʌɪ'zɛn/ *noun* L20 Japanese (= improvement). Continuous improvement of working practices, personal efficiency, etc., as a business philosophy.
1996 *Times* Standard Chartered Bank has decided to teach its executives Japanese kaizen teamwork and continuous self-appraisal.

kakemono /kakɪ'məʊnəʊ/ *noun plural* **kakemonos** L19 Japanese (from *kake-*

hang + *mono* thing). A Japanese unframed wall-picture, usually painted or inscribed on silk or paper.

kalimba /kəˈlɪmbə/ *noun* M20 Bantu. A musical instrument played with the thumbs, consisting of metal strips mounted on a small hollow piece of wood.

kalpa /ˈkalpə/ *noun* L18 Sanskrit. In Indian cosmology: an aeon, a great age of the world, a cycle of YUGAS; *specifically* in *Hinduism*, a period of 4,320 million years.

Kama Sutra /ˌkɑːmə ˈsuːtrə/ *noun & adjective phrase* L19 Sanskrit (from *kāma* love, desire + *sūtra* SUTRA). **A** *noun phrase* L19 (The title of) an ancient Sanskrit treatise on the art of love and sexual technique; a sex manual. **B** *adjective phrase* M20 Sexually explicit; sensual.

> **B 1972** R. Quilty *Tenth Session* He'll be bursting in any minute. Kama Sutra lips—ready for the last waltz.

kameez /kəˈmiːz/ *noun* (also **kameeze**) E19 Arabic (*ḳamīṣ*, perhaps from late Latin *camisia* shirt, nightgown). A loose long-sleeved shirt or tunic worn, especially by Muslims, in the Indian subcontinent, and by some Muslims elsewhere. Cf. SHALWAR.

kamerad /ˈkaməraːd/, *foreign* /kaməˈrɑːt/ *interjection* E20 German (literally, 'comrade', from French *camerade, camarade*). (Expression used by a German-speaking soldier:) notifying to an enemy a wish to surrender.

> ■ The word was current between combatants in this situation during the 1914–18 war and became a cliché of war films.

kami /ˈkami/ *noun* plural same E17 Japanese. A Shinto god or deity. Also, the Japanese emperor.

kamikaze /kamɪˈkɑːzi/ *noun & adjective* L19 Japanese (= divine wind, from as KAMI + *kaze* wind). **A** *noun* **1** L19 In Japanese tradition, the gale that destroyed the fleet of the invading Mongols in 1281. **2** M20 In the war of 1939–45, (a crewman of) a Japanese aircraft, usually loaded with explosives, making a deliberate suicidal crash on an enemy target; a suicide pilot or plane; also *transferred*. **3** M20 *Surfing* A deliberately taken wipe-out. **B** M20 *adjective* Of, pertaining to, or characteristic of a kamikaze; reckless, potentially self-destructive.

> **A.2** *transferred* **1971** *Observer* The stand of the *kamikazes* means that in any critical

division the Government is assured of a working majority.

> **B 1996** *Times Magazine* While these long odds will attract the odd kamikaze punter, . . . the horse cannot be considered a plausible contender for the big race.

kana /ˈkɑːnə/ *noun* plural same E18 Japanese. (A character or syllabary in) Japanese syllabic writing. Cf. HIRAGANA, KATAKANA.

kanat variant of QANAT.

kanban /ˈkanban/ *noun* L20 Japanese (= billboard, sign). **1** L20 A card used for ordering parts etc. in a just-in-time manufacturing system evolved in Japan. **2** L20 A just-in-time manufacturing system in which parts etc. are ordered on cards. In full *kanban-system*.

> **2 1993** *New Scientist* Like most other Japanese businesses, Asahi operates on the Kanban—or just-in-time—principle of stock control, which reduces stockholding to an absolute minimum.

kanga variant of KHANGA.

kanji /ˈkandʒi/, /ˈkɑːndʒi/ *noun* plural same E20 Japanese (from *kan* Chinese + *ji* letter, character). (Any of) the set of borrowed and adapted Chinese ideographs used in the Japanese writing system. Cf. KANA.

kanoon /kəˈnuːn/ *noun* E19 Persian (*ḳānūn* from Arabic, ultimately from Greek *kanōn*). A plucked musical instrument of the dulcimer or psaltery type, in the classic form with seventy-two strings, now with fifty to sixty.

kan-pei variant of GANBEI.

kanpu variant of GANBU.

kantele /ˈkantɪli/ *noun* E20 Finnish. A form of zither used in Finland and the adjoining part of Russia.

kanzu /ˈkanzuː/ *noun* E20 Kiswahili. A long white cotton or linen robe worn by East African men.

kaolin /ˈkeɪəlɪn/ *noun* E18 French (from Chinese *gāolǐng*, literally 'high hill', a place in Jiangxi province where it is found). A fine white clay resulting from the decomposition of feldspar, used to make porcelain and china, as a filler in paper and textiles, and in medicinal adsorbents and poultices. Also (*Mineralogy*), any of a group of clay minerals which typically occur in such clay, *especially* kaolinite.

kapai /ˈkɑːpʌɪ/ *adjective & adverb* M19 Maori (*ka pai*). Good; well, fine.

■ New Zealand. Also used as interjection, expressing pleasure or approval.

kapellmeister /kə'pɛlmʌɪstə/ *noun* M19 German (from *Kapelle* court orchestra, from medieval Latin *capella* chapel + *Meister* master). Chiefly *History* The leader or conductor of a court orchestra, an opera, a choir, etc.

kappa /'kapə/ *noun* LME Greek. **1** LME The tenth letter (K, κ) of the Greek alphabet. **2** M20 *Biology* An infective and independently reproducing particle (now usually regarded as a commensal bacterium) which occurs within cells of some strains of the ciliate *Paramecium aurelia*. Also, such particles collectively.

kappie /'kapi/ *noun* M19 Afrikaans (from Dutch *kapje* diminutive of *kap* hood). In South Africa: a sun-bonnet with a large brim to protect the face.

kapu /'kapu/ *adjective & noun* M20 Hawaiian. TABOO.

kaput /kə'pʊt/ *adjective* (also **kaputt**) L19 German (*kaputt* from French (*être*) *capot* (to be) without tricks in piquet etc.; cf. CAPOT). Finished, worn out; dead, destroyed; rendered useless or unable to function; broken.

■ Slang. The allusion by an English writer in 1914 to *kaputt* as 'the Germans' favourite word about their foe, meaning "done" ' (Duchess of Sutherland *Six Weeks at the War*) indicates the historical background to the word's entrance into the English-speaking consciousness.

karabiner /karə'biːnə/ *noun* M20 German (abbreviation of German *Karabiner-haken* spring-hook). A metal oval or D-shaped coupling link with a closure protected against accidental opening, used in mountaineering.

■ Often further contracted to *krab* in colloquial use.

karaburan /ˌkarə'bjʊər(ə)n/, /ˌkarabʊ'ran/ *noun* E20 Turkish (from *kara* black + *buran* whirlwind). A hot dusty wind which blows in central Asia.

karakul /'karəkʊl/ *noun & adjective* (also **caracul**) M19 Russian (*karakul'*, from the name of an oasis in Uzbekistan and of two lakes in Tadzhikistan, apparently ultimate from Turkic). **A** *noun* **1** M19 (An animal of) a breed of sheep with a coarse wiry fleece. **2** L19 (Cloth or fur resembling) the glossy curled fleece of a young lamb of this breed. Also called *Persian lamb*. **B** L19 *attributive* or as *adjective* Of or pertaining to the karakul or karakul.

karamat variant of KRAMAT.

karana /'kʌrənə/ *noun* M20 Sanskrit (*karaṇa* action, posture). Any of the 108 basic postures in Indian dance.

karanga /'karəŋə/ *noun* E20 Maori. A (Maori) ritual chant of welcome. *New Zealand*.

karaoke /karə'əʊki/, /karɪ'əʊki/ *noun* L20 Japanese (from *kara* empty + *oke* abbreviation of ōkesutora orchestra). A form of entertainment (originating in Japan) in which one or more people sing popular songs as soloists against pre-recorded backing music; (in full *karaoke music*) such pre-recorded backing music.

■ Introduced in both the United States and Britain during the 1980s, *karaoke* became hugely popular. The word is often used attributively, as in *karaoke bar*, an establishment in which the management provides the *karaoke machine* or jukebox that plays the backing music.
1986 J. Melville *Go Gently Gaijin* The hotel people had provided a *karaoke* kit: a microphone and amplifier with backing tapes for amateur songsters.

karate /kə'rɑːti/ *noun* M20 Japanese (from *kara* empty + *te* hand). A Japanese system of unarmed combat using the hands and feet as weapons.

karezza /kə'rɛtsə/ *noun* (also **carezza**) L19 Italian (*carezza* caress). Sexual intercourse in which ejaculation is avoided.

karma /'kɑːmə/, /'kəːmə/ *noun* E19 Sanskrit (*karman* action, effect, fate). Fate or destiny following as effect from cause.

■ *Karma* has specific meanings within the religions of the Indian subcontinent: in Buddhism and Hinduism, it is the sum of a person's actions, especially intentional actions, regarded as determining that person's future states of existence; in Jainism it is subtle physical matter which binds the soul as a result of bad actions.
1996 *Times Magazine* The whole complex will, Spielberg hopes, be imbued with world-beating creative karma.

karoshi /kə'rəʊʃi/ *noun* L20 Japanese. Death through overwork.
1991 *New Age* Thousands of workers have become victims of *karoshi*, or death by overwork.

kaross /kə'rɒs/ *noun* (also **kross**) M18 Afrikaans (*karos*, perhaps from Nama). A cloak or sleeveless jacket like a blanket made of hairy animal skins, worn by the indigenous peoples of southern Africa. Also, a rug of sewn skins used on a bed or on the floor.

Karren /ˈkar(ə)n/ *noun plural* L19 German. *Physical Geography* The furrows or fissures of a KARRENFELD; terrain characterized by these. Cf. LAPIÉS.

Karrenfeld /ˈkar(ə)nfɛlt/, /ˈkar(ə)nfɛld/ *noun plural* **Karrenfelder** /ˈkar(ə)nfɛldə/, **Karrenfelds** /ˈkar(ə)nfɛldz/ L19 German (from preceding + *Feld* field). *Physical Geography* An area or landscape, usually of limestone bare of soil, which has been eroded by solution so as to have an extremely dissected surface with conspicuous furrows and fissures, often separated by knifelike ridges. Cf. LAPIÉS.

karst /kɑːst/ *noun* L19 German (*der Karst* (perhaps related to Slovene *Krâs*) a limestone plateau region in Slovenia). *Physical Geography* A kind of topography characteristic of areas of relatively soluble rock (usually limestone) and mainly underground drainage, marked by numerous abrupt ridges, gorges, fissures, swallowholes, and caverns; a region dominated by such topography.

kasbah /ˈkazbɑː/ *noun* (also **casbah**) M18 French (*casbah* from Maghribi pronunciation of Arab *ḳaṣaba* fortress). (The Arab quarter surrounding) a North African castle or fortress-citadel.

kasha /ˈkaʃə/ *noun* (also (earlier) **casha**) E19 Russian. **1** E19 A porridge made from cooked buckwheat or other grains. **2** M20 A beige colour resembling that of buckwheat groats.

Kashrut /kaʃˈruːt/ *noun* (also **Kashruth** /kaʃˈruːθ/) E20 Hebrew (= legitimacy (in religion), from as KOSHER *adjective*). The body of Jewish religious laws relating to the suitability of food, ritual objects, etc.; the observance of these laws.

kat variant of KHAT.

kata /ˈkɑːtɑː/ *noun* M20 Japanese. A system of basic exercises or postures and movements used to teach and improve the execution of techniques in judo and other martial arts.

katabothron see KATAVOTHRON.

katakana /katəˈkɑːnə/ *noun* (also **katagana**) E18 Japanese (from *kata* side + KANA). An angular form of kana, used in modern Japanese mainly for writing

words of foreign origin and for emphasis. Cf. HIRAGANA.

katavothron /katəˈvɒθrən/ *noun* (also **catavothron, katabothron** /katəˈbɒθrən/, **katavothra** /katəˈvɒθrə/) plural **katavothra** /katəˈvɒθrə/, **katavothrai** /katəˈvɒθrʌɪ/, **katavothrons** E19 Modern Greek (*katabothra*, plural *katabothrai, katabothres*, from Greek *kata* down + *bothros* hole (*katavothron* representing modern Greek pronunciation, *katavothron* from misunderstanding singular as neuter plural)). A subterranean channel or deep hole formed by the action of water; a swallowhole.

■ A feature of the landscape in certain parts of mainland Greece. In general use the word is now usually replaced by swallow-hole.

katel /ˈkɑːt(ə)l/ *noun* (also **kartel**) M19 Afrikaans (apparently from Portuguese *catel, catle* little bed, from Malay *katil* from Tamil *kaṭṭil* bedstead). A lightweight portable bed or hammock, used in an ox-wagon.

■ South African. The Malay word *katil* is used in the Cape Malay community to denote the bier used in funeral ceremonies.

katharevousa /ˌkaθərəˈvuːsə/, /ˌkaθəˈrɛvʊsə/ *noun* E20 Modern Greek (*kathareuousa* feminine of *kathareuōn* present participle of Greek *kathareuein* to be pure, from *katharos* pure). The purist form of modern Greek.

■ At one time (but not since 1976), the archaizing literary version of Greek officially used by the State, as opposed to the popular and spoken demotic.

kathi /ˈkɑːðɪ/ *noun* M20 Malay (*kadi* from Arabic *ḳāḍī* CADI). A judge in Islamic law, who also functions as a registrar of Muslim marriages, divorces, etc.

katsuo /ˈkatswo/ *noun* E18 Japanese. A bonito, *Katsuwonus pelamis*, important as a food fish in Japan, fresh or dried.

katsura /katˈsʊərə/ *noun* E20 Japanese. **1** E20 A type of Japanese wig worn mainly by women. **2** E20 A type of romantic Noh play with a woman as the central character. In full *katsuramono* /katˌsʊərəˈməʊnəʊ/ (*mono* piece, play).

katzenjammer /ˈkats(ə)njamə/ *noun* M19 German (from *Katzen* (combining form of *Katze* cat) + *Jammer* distress, wailing). **1** M19 A hangover; a severe headache. **2** L19 *transferred* and *figurative* Confusion, disorder; clamour, uproar.

■ United States colloquial. The currency of the word has been promoted by the comic strip called *The Katzenjammer Kids*, first drawn in 1897 by Rudolph Dirks for the *New York Journal*.

kava /'kɑːvə/ *noun* L18 Tongan. A shrub, *Piper methysticum*, of the West Pacific islands; a narcotic fermented drink made especially in Fiji from its macerated roots. Cf. YANGGONA.

kavadi /'kɑːvədi/ *noun* M20 Tamil (*kāvaṭi*). In Hindu religious practice, a decorated arch carried on the shoulders as an act of penance or in fulfilment of a vow. Also the festival at which this act is performed.

> **1993** A. Diesel & P. Maxwell *Hinduism in Natal* For those Hindus who 'carry kavadi' today, self-inflicted pain is believed to be another sign of devotion to Maruga.

kayak /'kʌɪak/ *noun* M18 Eskimo ((Inuit) *qayaq*). **A** *noun* **1** M18 An Eskimo canoe, made of a framework of light wood covered with sealskins, and having a small watertight opening in the top to admit a single man. **2** M20 A small covered canoe modelled on this, used for touring or sport. **B** *intransitive verb* L19 Travel by kayak, paddle a kayak.

kazachoc /kazə'tʃɒk/ *noun* (also **kozatchok** and other variants) E20 Russian (diminutive of *kazak* cossack). A Slavonic, chiefly Ukrainian, dance with a fast and usually quickening tempo, and employing the step PRISIADKA.

kebab /kɪ'bab/, /kə'bab/, /kɪ'bɑːb/ *noun* (also (earlier) **cabob** /kə'bɒb/) L17 Arabic (*kabāb* perhaps ultimately from Persian), partly through Urdu, Persian, and Turkish). A dish consisting of pieces of meat (occasionally with vegetables) grilled or roasted on a skewer or spit.

■ The arrangement of the meat pieces on the skewer has given rise (L20) to the use of *kebab* for components of a similar polymer structure in physical chemistry.

kebaya /kə'bɑːjə/ *noun* (also (earlier) **cabaia** and other variants) L16 Arabic (*ḳabāya* representing colloquial pronunciation of *ḳbā'a* feminine of *ḳbā'* tunic, gown, shirt; in early use through Portuguese *cabaya* or Persian, in modern use through Malay *kebaya*). **1** L16 A light loose tunic of a type worn in South-East Asia by women or (formerly) by men. **2** M20 A short tight-fitting long-sleeved jacket, together with a sarong the traditional dress of Malay and Indonesian women.

kef variant of KIEF.

keffiyeh /kə'fiː(j)ə/ *noun* (also **kaffiyeh, kuffiyeh** and other variants) E19 Arabic (*kūfiyya*, (colloquial) *keffiyya*). A kerchief worn as a head-dress by Bedouin Arabs.

keftedes /kɛf'tɛdiːz/ *noun plural* (also **keftedhes**) E20 Modern Greek (*kephtes*, plural *kephtedes* from Turkish *köfte* from Persian KOFTA). In Greek cookery, small meatballs made with herbs and onions.

kehilla /kə'hɪlə/, /ˌkɛhɪ'lɑː/ *noun plural* **kehilloṭ(h)** /ˌkɛhɪ'ləʊt/ L19 Yiddish (*kĕhilĕ* from Hebrew *qĕhillāh* community). The Jewish community in a town or village.

keif variant of KIEF.

keiretsu /'keɪrɛtsu/ *noun* L20 Japanese. A group of closely associated Japanese business companies linked especially by cross-shareholding.

> **1993** *Seattle Times* Some companies seem to be trying to join whatever keiretsu is forming just out of fear that they won't back the right horse.

kelebe /'kɛləbi/ *noun* M19 Greek (*kelebē*). Greek Antiquities A wide-mouthed vessel with a broad flat rim and two handles connecting this to the body but not extending above the rim.

Kelim variant of KILIM.

keller /'kɛlə(r)/ *noun* (also **Keller**) E20 German (= cellar). A beer-cellar in Austria or Germany.

Kempeitai /'kɛmpeɪtʌɪ/ *noun* M20 Japanese (*kenpeitai*). The Japanese military secret service in the period 1931–45.

ken /kɛn/ *noun* L19 Japanese. A Japanese game of forfeits played with the hands and with gestures.

kenaf /kə'naf/ *noun* L19 Persian (variant of *kanab* hemp). The brown fibre of the *Hibiscus cannabinus* plant used to make rope and coarse cloth; ambari hemp.

kendo /'kɛndəʊ/ *noun* E20 Japanese (from *ken* sword + *dō* way). A Japanese sport of fencing with two-handed bamboo staves.

kenosis /kɪ'nəʊsɪs/ *noun* L19 Greek (*kenōsis* an emptying). *Christian Theology* Christ's full or partial renunciation of his divine nature or powers in his Incarnation.

■ The reference is to the Greek New Testament text of Philippians 2:7 *heauton ekenōse*, literally, 'he emptied himself'.

kente /ˈkɛntə/ *noun* (also **Kente**) M20 Twi (= cloth). In Ghana: a brightly coloured banded material; a long garment made from this material, loosely draped on or worn around the shoulders and waist. More fully *kente cloth*.

kepi /ˈkɛpi/, /ˈkeɪpi/ *noun* M19 French (*képi* from Swiss German *Käppi* diminutive of *Kappe* capital). A French military cap with a flat circular top which slopes towards the front and a horizontal peak.

kêrel /ˈkɛːr(ə)l/ *noun* (also **kerel**) L19 Afrikaans (from Dutch from Old High German *kar(a)l* man). A fellow, a chap, a young man; a boyfriend. *South African colloquial*.

kermes /ˈkəːmɪz/ *noun* L16 French (*kermès* from Arabic *ḳirmiz* (= sense 2 below)). **1** L16 A small evergreen oak, *Quercus coccifera*, of the Mediterranean region. More fully *kermes oak*. **2** E17 (The dried bodies of) adult females of the scale insect *Kermes ilicis*, which form hard berry-like galls on the kermes oak, used to make dye and (formerly) medicines; the scarlet dye made from these.

kermesse /kəˈmɛs/ *noun* L19 French (from as next). **1** L19 A KERMIS. **2** M20 *Cycling* A circuit race.

kermis /ˈkəːmɪs/ *noun* (also **kirmess**) L16 Dutch (*kermis, kermisse,* from *kerk* church + *misse* mass). In the Low Countries, parts of Germany, etc.: an annual fair or carnival. Also (*United States*), a similar fair or bazaar, usually for charitable purposes.

■ Originally a *kermis* was a mass held annually on the anniversary of the dedication of a church, when a fair was also held.

kernos /ˈkəːnɒs/ *noun* plural **kernoi** /ˈkəːnɔɪ/ E20 Greek. *Archaeology* An ancient Mediterranean and Near Eastern baked clay vessel having small cups around the rim or fixed in a circle to a central stem.

ketubah /ˌkətuːˈbɑː/ *noun* M19 Hebrew (*kĕṭubbāh* written statement). A formal Jewish marriage contract which includes financial provisions for the wife in the event of the husband's death or of divorce.

khaddar /ˈkadə/ *noun & adjective* (also **khadi** /ˈkadi/) E20 Panjabi (*khaddar,* Hindustani *khādar, khādī*). (Made of) handspun hand-woven cotton (or silk) cloth of the Indian subcontinent.

khaki /ˈkɑːki/ *adjective & noun* M19 Urdu (*ḳākī* dust-coloured, from *ḳāk* dust from Persian). **A** *adjective* M19 Dust-coloured; dull brownish yellow. Also, made of khaki. **B** *noun* **1** M19 Dust-colour; dull brownish yellow. **2** M19 A dull yellowish-brown fabric, originally of stout twilled cotton, later also of wool, etc., used especially for army uniforms. **3** L19 A soldier dressed in khaki; *specifically* (*South African slang*) a British soldier in the Boer War of 1899–1902. **4** M20 In *plural* Khaki trousers; khaki clothes.

khalifa /kəˈliːfə/ *noun* (in sense 2 also **chalifa**) E18 Arabic (*ḳalīfa*). **1** E18 Chiefly *History* The chief civil and religious ruler of the Muslim community, a caliph. **2** M19 A Malay ceremony in which a dancer pierces his person with swords, originally as a demonstration of Islamic faith. *South African*.

khalsa /ˈkɑːlsə/ *noun* (also **khalsah**) L18 Urdu (from Persian *ḳāl(i)ṣa* crown land, revenue department, from feminine of Arabic *ḳāliṣ* pure, free (from), belonging (to)). **1** L18 The governmental revenue department in a State in the Indian subcontinent. **2** L18 The fraternity of warriors into which Sikh males are initiated at puberty.

khamsin /ˈkamsɪn/ *noun* (also **hamsin** /ˈhamsɪn/) L17 Arabic (*ḳamāsīn,* from *ḳamsīn, ḳamsūn* fifty (from the number of days on which it blows)). An oppressive hot southerly wind, which blows in Egypt at intervals for about fifty days in March, April, and May, and fills the air with sand from the desert.

khan /kɑːn/, /kan/ *noun* (also **han** /hɑːn/) LME Persian (*ḳān*). A caravanserai.

khanga /ˈkaŋgə/ *noun* (also **kanga**) M20 Kiswahili. In East Africa: a fabric printed in various colours and designs with borders, used especially for women's clothing.

khanum /ˈkɑːnəm/ *noun* M17 Persian (*ḳānum* from Turkish *hanim,* from *hān* lord + *-im* 1st person singular possessive suffix). In certain parts of the Middle East and the Indian subcontinent: a lady of high rank, *historically* the wife of a khan. Now also used as a polite form of address affixed to a Muslim woman's name.

khat /kɑːt/ *noun* (also **kat, qat**) M19 Arabic (*ḳāt*). A shrub, *Catha edulis*, of the spindle tree family, cultivated in Arabia for its leaves, which are chewed or infused as a stimulant; the narcotic drug obtained from these leaves.

1996 *Oldie* Our own cook was a wild-eyed northerner whose cheeks bulged night and day with qat.

khatun /'kɑːtuːn/ *noun* M19 Turkic (*k̲atūn*, Persian *k̲ātūn* perhaps from Sogdian *k̲wat'yn* queen). In certain parts of the Middle East: a lady of high rank; *historically* a queen. Also used as an honorific title affixed to a Muslim woman's name.

khidmutgar /'kɪdmʌtgɑː/ *noun* (also **khitmutgar** /'kɪtmʌtgɑː/) M18 Urdu (from Persian *k̲idmatgār*, from Arabic *k̲idma(t)* service + Persian agent-suffix *-gār*). In the Indian subcontinent: a male servant who waits at table.

khoja /'kəʊdʒə/ *noun* E17 Turkish ((*hoca* from) Persian *kʷāja*). **1** E17 A teacher in a Muslim school; a Muslim scribe or clerk. **2** L19 (*Khoja*) A member of a Muslim sect found mainly in western India.

khutbah /'kʊtbə/ *noun* E19 Arabic (*k̲uṭba*). A form of sermon, consisting of homily and supplication, delivered in mosques before the midday Friday prayer, at the time of the two main Muslim festivals, and on other exceptional occasions.

ki /kiː/ *noun* M19 Hawaiian. A shrub of the agave family, *Cordyline fruticosa*, found in China and the Pacific islands, the fermented root of which yields an alcoholic drink.

kibbutz /kɪ'bʊts/ *noun* plural **kibbutzim** /kɪ'bʊtsɪm/, (occasionally) **kibbutzes** M20 Modern Hebrew (*qibbūṣ* gathering). A collective (especially farming) settlement in Israel, owned communally by its members, and organized on cooperative principles.

kibbutznik /kɪ'bʊtsnɪk/ *noun* M20 Yiddish (from as KIBBUTZ + Polish and Russian noun suffix *-nik* person connected with (something)). A member of a kibbutz.

kibitz /'kɪbɪts/ *intransitive verb* E20 Yiddish (from German *kiebitzen*, from *Kiebitz* lapwing, pewit, interfering onlooker at cards). Look on at cards, or some other activity, especially offering unwanted advice.

■ Slang, chiefly in North American use.

kiblah /'kɪblə/ *noun* (also **qibla(h)**, **kibla**) M17 Arabic (*k̲ibla* that which is opposite). **1** M17 (The direction of) the place to which Muslims must turn for prayer, now the Kaaba at Mecca. **2** L18 The MIHRAB on an oriental rug.

kiboko /kɪ'bəʊkəʊ/ *noun* plural **kibokos** E20 Kiswahili (= hippopotamus). A strong heavy whip made of hippopotamus hide.

kiddush /'kɪdʊʃ/ *noun* (also **Kiddush**) M18 Hebrew (*qiddūš* sanctification). A ceremony of prayer and blessing over wine, performed by the head of a Jewish household at the meal ushering in the Sabbath (on a Friday night) or a holy day or at the lunch preceding it.

kiddushin /kɪ'duːʃiːn/ *noun* (also **Kiddushin**) L19 Aramaic (*qiddūshīn*). *Judaism* The section of the Mishnah dealing with betrothal and marriage. Also, the Jewish ceremony of betrothal; the gift given by a Jewish groom to effect a betrothal.

kief /kiːf/ *noun* (in sense 1 also **kef** /kɛf/, **keif** /keɪf/; in sense 2 also **kif** /kɪf/) E19 Arabic (representing colloquial pronunciation of *kayf*). **1** E19 A state of drowsiness or dreamy intoxication produced by the use of cannabis etc. Also, the enjoyment of idleness. **2** L19 In Morocco and Algeria: cannabis or some other substance smoked to produce dreamy intoxication.

kielbasa /kiː'lˈbasə/, /kjɛl'basə/ *noun* M20 Polish (*kiełbasa* sausage). A type of highly seasoned Polish sausage, usually containing garlic.

kierie /'kɪri/ *noun* (also (earlier) **kirri**) M18 Nama. A short club or knobbed stick used as a club or missile by indigenous peoples of South Africa.

■ The South African English word *knobkerrie*, by which this weapon is also known, is from Afrikaans *knop* knob + *kierie*.

kif variant of KIEF.

kikoi /kɪ'kɔɪ/ *noun* M20 Kiswahili. In East Africa: a distinctive striped cloth with an end fringe, worn round the waist.

kilim /kɪ'liːm/ *adjective & noun* (also **Kilim**, **Kelim**) L19 Turkish (*Kılım* from Persian *gelīm*). (Designating) a pileless woven carpet, rug, etc., made in Turkey, Kurdistan, and neighbouring areas, and now a fashionable furnishing item in the West.

kimchi /'kɪmtʃi/ *noun* L19 Korean. A raw strongly-flavoured cabbage pickle, the Korean national dish.

kimono /kɪ'məʊnəʊ/ *noun & adjective* M17 Japanese (from *ki* wearing + *mono* thing). A *noun* M17 plural **kimonos**. A long Japanese robe with wide sleeves, tied with a sash. Now also, in Western countries, a garment (especially a dressing-gown) modelled on this. **B** *attributive* or as *adjective* E20 Resembling or characteristic of a kimono.

kinder, kirche, küche /ˌkɪndər ˌkɪrçə ˈkyːçə/ *noun phrase plural* L19 German (literally, 'children, church, kitchen'). The domestic and religious concerns traditionally regarded as appropriate for a woman.

■ Doubly discredited by its association with the Nazi ideal of womanhood and by the agenda of modern feminism, *kinder, kirche, küche* is now most frequently used ironically.
1996 *Times Magazine* But theirs is also the quaintly strident *kinder, kirche, küche* voice of Alf Garnett . . .

kindergarten /ˈkɪndəɡɑːt(ə)n/ *noun* M19 German (literally, 'children's garden'). **1** M19 A nursery school. **2** E20 *History* The group of young men with imperialist ideals recruited by Lord Milner, High Commissioner of South Africa, to help with reconstruction work after the second Boer War of 1899–1902.

■ The term *kindergarten* was coined in 1840 by Friedrich Fröbel (1782–1852) for a school for teaching young children according to his method of stimulating their intelligence by means of interesting objects, exercises with toys, games, singing, etc.

kinderspiel /ˈkɪndəʃpiːl/ *noun* E20 German (literally, 'children's play'). A dramatic piece performed by children.

kinesis /kɪˈniːsɪs/, /kʌɪˈniːsɪs/ *noun plural* **kineses** /kɪˈniːsiːz/ E17 Greek (*kinēsis* movement). **1** E17 *generally* Motion; a kind of movement. *rare.* **2** E20 *Biology* An undirected movement of an organism that occurs in response to a particular kind of stimulus. **3** M20 *Zoology* Mobility of the bones of the skull, as in some birds and reptiles.

kippa /kɪˈpɑː/ *noun* (also **kipa(h)**, **kippah**) M20 Modern Hebrew (*kippāh*). A skullcap, usually of crocheted thread, worn by Orthodox male Jews.

kir /kɪə/, /kə:/ *noun* (also **Kir**) M20 French (personal name). (Proprietary name for) a drink made from dry white wine and cassis.

■ Called after Canon Félix *Kir* (1876–1968), mayor of Dijon in France, who is said to have invented the recipe.

kirin /ˈkɪərɪn/ *noun* (also **Kirin**) E18 Japanese (from as KYLIN). A mythical beast of composite form resembling a unicorn,

frequently portrayed in Japanese pottery and art.

kirmess variant of KERMIS.

kirpan /kəˈpɑːn/ *noun* E20 Panjabi and Hindustani (*kirpān* from Sanskrit *kṛpāṇa* sword). The dagger or sword worn by Sikhs as a religious symbol.

kirri variant of KIERIE.

kirsch /kɪəʃ/ *noun* M19 German (abbreviation of *Kirsch(en)wasser* from *Kirsche* cherry + *Wasser* water). An alcoholic spirit distilled, chiefly in Germany and Switzerland, from the fermented juice of cherries.

■ Earlier (E19) in English in the fuller form *Kirschenwasser*.

kisan /kɪˈsɑːn/ *noun* M20 Hindustani (*kisān* from Sanskrit *kṛṣāṇa* person who ploughs). In the Indian subcontinent: a peasant, an agricultural worker.

kishke /ˈkɪʃkə/ *noun* (also **kishka**, **kishkeh**) M20 Yiddish (from Polish *kiszka* or Ukrainian *kishka*: cf. Russian *kishka*). **1** M20 Beef intestine casing stuffed with a savoury filling. **2** M20 *singular* and in *plural* The guts. *slang.*

kismet /ˈkɪzmɛt/, /ˈkɪzmɪt/, /ˈkɪsmɛt/ *noun* E19 Turkish (*kismet* from Arabic *ḳisma(t)* division, portion, lot, fate). Destiny, fate.

kissel /ˈkɪs(ə)l/, /kɪˈsjɛl/ *noun* E20 Russian (*kisel'*, from same base as *kislyĭ* sour). A dessert dish made from fruit juice or purée boiled with sugar and water and thickened with potato or cornflour.

kist /kɪst/ *noun* ME Old Norse (*kista*; cf. Dutch *kist*). **A** *noun* **1** ME A chest, a trunk, a coffer. **2** ME A coffin; *especially* a stone coffin, a sarcophagus. **b** M19 *Archaeology* A prehistoric burial chamber lined with stone slabs, a cist.

■ The early use of *kist*, mainly in the north of England and Scotland, derives from Old Norse, but its use in South African English in the sense of 'chest' or 'coffer' is derived through Dutch and Afrikaans.

Kitab /kɪˈtɑːb/ *noun* L19 Arabic (*kitāb* piece of writing, record, book). The Koran. Also, among Muslims, the sacred book of any of certain other revealed religions, as Judaism or Christianity.

kithara variant of CITHARA.

kitsch /kɪtʃ/ *noun & adjective* (also **Kitsch**) E20 German. **A** *noun* E20 Art or artefacts perceived as being of poor quality, especially when garish or sentimental; these enjoyed in a perverse or self-conscious way; the qualities associated with ˙such art or artefacts. **B** *adjective* Of the nature of or pertaining to kitsch; garish, tasteless.

A 1995 *Country Life* I'm sorry, but at Christmas I want maximum kitsch, not ghastly good taste.

kittel /'kɪt(ə)l/ *noun* L19 Yiddish ((German = overall, smock), from Middle High German *ki(e)tel* cotton or hempen outer garment). A white cotton or linen robe worn by orthodox Jews on certain holy days; such a robe used as a shroud.

kiva /'kiːvə/ *noun* L19 Hopi (*kíva*). A chamber, built wholly or partly underground, used by male Pueblo Indians for religious rites etc. Cf. ESTUFA.

klaberjass /'klabəjas/ *noun* (also **clobiosh** /'klɒbɪjɒʃ/ and other variants) L19 German (from Dutch *klaverjas*). *Cards* A two-handed card-game distantly related to bezique, in which points are scored for winning value cards in tricks and for declaring combinations.

klatch /klatʃ/ *noun* (also **Klatsch**) M20 German (*Klatsch* gossip). A social gathering. Cf. KAFFEEKLATSCH.

kletterschuh /'klɛtəʃuː/ *noun plural* **kletterschuhe** /'klɛtəʃuːə/ E20 German (literally, 'climbing-shoe'). A cloth- or felt-soled light boot worn especially for rock-climbing. Usually in *plural*.

klezmer /'klɛzmə/ *noun plural same,* **klezmorim** /'klɛzmərɪm/ M20 Yiddish (contraction of Hebrew *kĕlēy zemer* musical instruments). A member of a group of musicians playing traditional eastern European Jewish music; this type of music (in full *klezmer music*).

klippe /'klɪpə/ *noun* E20 German (= partly submerged or buried rock). *Geology* A part of a nappe which has become detached from its parent mass by sliding or by erosion of intervening parts.

klister /'klɪstə/ *noun* M20 Norwegian (= paste). *Skiing* A soft wax for applying to the running surface of skis to facilitate movement, used especially when the temperature is above freezing.

klompie /'klɒmpi/ *noun* (also **klompje**) M19 Afrikaans (from Dutch *klompje* diminutive of *klomp* clump). **1** M19 A group, a cluster, especially of animals or of shrubs or trees. *South African colloquial.* **2** E20 A type of hard yellow brick, originally imported into South Africa from the Netherlands.

klonkie /'klɒŋki/ *noun* M20 Afrikaans (blend of *klein* small, *jong* boy + diminutive suffix -*kie*). In South Africa: a young Black or Coloured boy.

kloof /kluːf/ *noun* M18 Dutch (= cleft). A deep valley, a ravine, a gorge. *South African.*

klops /klɒps/ *noun plural same* **klopse** /'klɒpsə/ M20 German. A type of meatball or meat loaf.

klutz /klʌts/ *noun & verb* (also **klotz**) M20 Yiddish (from German *Klotz* wooden block, from Middle High German *kloz*; cf. Old English *clot(t)*, whence modern English *clot* (in derogatory sense) stupid or awkward person). **A** *noun* M20 A clumsy awkward person, *especially* one considered socially inept; a fool. **B** *intransitive verb* L20 Followed by *about, around*: behave awkwardly or foolishly, move clumsily.

■ North American slang.

1970 *Time* Basically I'm the klutz who makes a terrific entrance to the party and then trips and falls and walks around with food in her hair.

knaidel /'kneɪd(ə)l/ *noun* (also **kneidel**) *plural* **knaidlach** /'kneɪdlax/ M20 Yiddish (*kneydel* from Middle High German, German KNÖDEL). A type of dumpling eaten especially in Jewish households during Passover. Usually in *plural*.

knallgas /'knalgas/ *noun* L19 German (from *Knall* bang, detonation + *Gas* gas). *Chemistry* An explosive mixture of gases, especially one of two volumes of hydrogen with one of oxygen.

kneidel variant of KNAIDEL.

Kneipe /'knaɪpə/ *noun plural* **Kneipen** /'knaɪpən/, **Kneipes** M19 German. In Germany: a lively social gathering of young people, especially students, in a bar or restaurant; a public house, a bar.

knish /knɪʃ/ *noun* M20 Yiddish (from Russian (also *knysh*) kind of bun or dumpling). A baked or fried dumpling made of flaky dough filled with chopped liver, potato, or cheese.

knödel /'knəːd(ə)l/ *noun* (also **knoedel**) E19 German. In South Germany and Austria: a type of dumpling.

knout /naʊt/, /nuːt/ *noun* M17 French (from Russian *knut* from Old Norse *knútr* related to 'knot'). *History* A scourge or whip used in imperial Russia, often causing death.

217

ko | kop

ko /kəʊ/ *noun* plural **kos** M20 Chinese (*gē* (Wade–Giles *ko*) spear, lance). *Chinese Antiquities* A dagger, a halberd.

koan /'kəʊɑːn/ *noun* M20 Japanese (*kōan*, from Chinese *gōngàn* official business). *Zen Buddhism* A riddle without a solution, used to demonstrate the inadequacy of logical reasoning and provoke sudden enlightenment.
1972 *Times Literary Supplement* What he comes up with—his runes and enigmas and impromptu koans—builds gradually into a supplementary creation.

kobold /'kəʊbəld/ *noun* M19 German. In German folklore, a familiar spirit, supposed to haunt houses and help the occupants; a brownie. Also, an underground spirit; a goblin, a gnome.

koeksister /'kʊksɪstə/ *noun* (also **koesister** /'kʊəsɪstə/) E20 Afrikaans (*koe(k)sister*, perhaps from *koek* cake + *sissen* sizzle). In South Africa: a plaited doughnut dipped in syrup, a traditional South African confection.

kofta /'kɒftə/, /'kəʊftə/ *noun* L19 Urdu and Persian (*koftah* pounded meat). A kind of meat or fish rissole, popular in Eastern cookery.

kohl /kəʊl/ *noun* L18 Arabic (*kuḥl*). A powder, usually consisting of antimony sulphide or lead sulphide, used as eye make-up and as eye ointment, especially in Eastern countries.

kohlrabi /kəʊl'rɑːbi/ *noun* E19 German (*Kohlrabi* from (with assimilation to *Kohl* cole) Italian *cauli* or *cavoli rape*, plural of *cavolo rapa* (whence French *chou-rave*), representing medieval Latin *caulorapa*). A variety of cabbage, *Brassica oleracea* var. *gongylodes*, with an edible turnip-shaped base to its stem.

koi /kɔɪ/ *noun* plural same E18 Japanese. A carp (in Japan). Now *especially* a carp of a large ornamental variety bred in Japan. Also *koi carp*.

koine /'kɔɪniː/ *noun* L19 Greek (*koinē* feminine singular of *koinos* common, ordinary). **1** L19 The common literary language of the Greeks from the close of classical Attic to the Byzantine era. **2** L19 *Linguistics* and *Philology* A language or dialect common to a wide area in which different languages or dialects are, or were, used locally; a lingua franca. **3** E20 A set of cultural or other attributes common to various groups.

koinonia /kɔɪ'nəʊnɪə/ *noun* E20 Greek (*koinōnia* communion, fellowship). *Theology* Christian fellowship or communion, with God or, more commonly, with fellow Christians.

kolach /'kɒlətʃ/ *noun* plural **kolache** /'kɒlətʃɪ/, **kolaches** /'kɒlətʃɪz/ E20 Czech (*koláč*, from *kolo* wheel, circle). A small tart or pie popular in the Czech Republic and Slovakia, topped or filled with fruit.

kolkhoz /'kɒlkɒz/, /kʌlk'hɔːz/ *noun* plural same, **kolkhozes** /'kɒlkɒzɪz/, /kʌlk'hɔːzi/ E20 Russian (from *kol(lektivnoe khoz(yaĭstvo* collective farm). In countries of the former USSR: a collective farm.

Kol Nidre /kɒl 'niːdreɪ/ *noun* L19 Aramaic (*kol niḍrē* all the vows (the opening words of the prayer)). An Aramaic prayer annulling vows made before God, sung by Jews at the opening of the Day of Atonement service on the eve of Yom Kippur. Also, the service or the melody at or to which this prayer is sung.

kolo /'kəʊləʊ/ *noun* plural **kolos** L18 Serbo-Croat (= wheel). A Slavonic dance performed in a circle.

kombu /'kɒmbuː/ *noun* L19 Japanese. A brown seaweed of the genus *Laminaria*, used in Japanese cooking, especially as a base for stock.

Kommers /kɔ'mɛrs/ *noun* plural **Kommerse** /kɔ'mɛrsə/ M19 German (from Latin *commercium* communication). A social gathering of German students.

konak /kəʊ'nɑːk/ *noun* M19 Turkish (= halting-place, inn). A large house, palace, or official residence, in Turkey or the former Ottoman Empire.

Konditorei /ˌkɒndɪtɒ'raɪ/ *noun* plural same, **Konditoren** /ˌkɒndɪ'tɔrən/ M20 German (from *Konditor* confectioner). Confectionery; a shop selling confectionery or rich pastries.

konfyt /kɒn'feɪt/ *noun* M19 Afrikaans (= Dutch *konfijt*, probably from French *confiture*). Fruit preserved in sugar; preserve, jam. *South African*.

kop /kɒp/ *noun* M19 Afrikaans (from Dutch *kop* head). **1** M19 A prominent hill or peak. Frequently in place-names. *South African*. **2** E20 *Soccer* (*the Kop*) A high bank of terracing for standing spectators, usually supporting the home side, originally and especially at the ground of Liverpool Football Club; the spectators massed on such terracing.

■ In sense 2, also more fully *Spion Kop* /ˈspʌɪən kɒp/, after a mountain in Natal which was the site of a battle in 1900 during the South African Boer War.

kopje variant of KOPPIE.

koppel /ˈkʌp(ə)l/, /ˈkɒp(ə)l/ *noun* L19 Yiddish. A skullcap worn by male Jews.

koppie /ˈkɒpi/ *noun* (also **kopje**) M19 Afrikaans (from Dutch *kopje* diminutive of *kop* head; cf. KOP). In South Africa: a small hill, *especially* any of the flat-topped or pointed hillocks characteristic of the veld.

koradji /ˈkɒrəʤi/, /kəˈraʤi/ *noun* (also (earlier) **coradgee** and other variants) L18 Aboriginal. In Australia: an Aboriginal medicine man.

kore /ˈkɔːreɪ/ *noun* E20 Greek (*korē* = maiden). *Greek Antiquities* A statue of a clothed young woman. Cf. KOUROS.

korero /ˈkɔːrərəʊ/ *noun plural* **koreros** E19 Maori. In New Zealand: talk, conversation, discussion; a conference.

korma /ˈkɔːmə/ *noun* L19 Urdu (*ḳormā*, *ḳormah* from Turkish *kavurma*). A mildly spiced Indian dish of meat or fish marinated in yoghurt or curds.

koro /ˈkɔːrəʊ/ *noun* E19 Japanese (*kōro* incense-pot, censer). An elaborate Japanese vase, usually of bronze, jade, or porcelain, in which incense is burned.

korrigan /ˈkɒrɪg(ə)n/ *noun* M19 Breton ((Vannes dialect) feminine of *korrig* gnome, diminutive of *korr* dwarf). In Breton folklore, a fairy or witch noted especially for stealing children.

kosher /ˈkəʊʃə/ *adjective & noun* M19 Hebrew (*kāšēr* fit, proper). **A** *adjective* **1** M19 Of food: prepared according to the Jewish law. **2** L19 That sells or prepares such food; where such food is cooked or eaten. **3** L19 Correct, genuine, legitimate. *colloquial*. **B** *noun* **1** L19 *elliptical* Kosher food; a kosher shop. **2** M20 The Jewish law regarding food. Chiefly in *keep kosher*.

koto /ˈkəʊtəʊ/ *noun plural* **kotos** L18 Japanese. A long Japanese zither, now usually having thirteen silk strings, usually played on the floor.

kotow variant of KOWTOW.

koumiss variant of KUMIS.

kouros /ˈkuːrɒs/ *noun plural* **kouroi** /ˈkuːrɔɪ/ E20 Greek (Ionic form of *koros*

boy). *Greek Antiquities* A sculptured representation of a naked youth. Cf. KORE.

kowtow /kaʊˈtaʊ/ *noun & verb* (also **kotow** /kəʊˈtaʊ/) E19 Chinese (*kētóu* (Wade–Giles *k'ot'ou*), from *kē* knock, strike + *tóu* head). **A** *noun* E19 The action or practice, formerly customary in China, of touching the ground with the forehead as a sign of extreme respect, submission, or worship; *figuratively* an act of obsequious respect. **B** *intransitive verb* M19 Perform the kowtow; *figurative* act in an obsequious manner.

kozatchok variant of KAZACHOC.

kraak porselein /ˌkrɑːk ˈpɔːsələm/ *noun phrase* (also **kraak porcelain** /ˈpɔːs(ə)lɪn/) M20 Dutch (from *kraak* carrack (the type of Portuguese ship from which the porcelain was first captured in 1603) + *porselein* porcelain). Blue and white Chinese porcelain of the Wan-li period (1573–1619) or later in the seventeenth century; a European imitation of this.

kraal /krɑːl/ *noun* M18 Afrikaans (from Portuguese *curral* from Nama). **1** M18 In southern Africa: a village of huts enclosed by a fence or stockade, and often having a central space for cattle etc.; the community of such a village. **2** L18 In southern Africa: an enclosure for cattle or sheep, a stockade, a pen, a fold. **3** L19 In Sri Lanka (Ceylon): an enclosure into which wild elephants are driven; the process of capturing elephants by driving them into an enclosure.

krab see KARABINER.

kragdadig /krɑxˈdɑːdɪx/ *adjective* (also (in attributive use) **kragdadige**) M20 Afrikaans (= Dutch *krachtdadig*). Forceful, vigorous in wielding power, unyielding. *South African*.

kraken /ˈkrɑːk(ə)n/ *noun* M18 Norwegian. A mythical sea-monster of enormous size, said to appear off the coast of Norway.

kramat /krɑˈmɑːt/, /ˈkrɑːmət/ *noun & adjective* (also **karamat** /kəˈrɑːmət/) L18 Malay (*keramat* (adjective) sacred, holy, (noun) holy place, holy person, from Arabic *karāma* miracle worked by a saint other than a prophet). **A** *noun* L18 A Muslim holy place or place of pilgrimage. **B** *adjective* M20 Sacred to Muslims.

krans /krɑːns/ *noun* (also **krantz** /krants/) L18 Afrikaans (from Dutch = coronet, chaplet from Old High German, Middle High German, German *Kranz* coronet, circle, encircling ring of mountains, from a base meaning 'ring'). In South Africa: a wall of rock encircling a mountain or summit; a precipitous or overhanging cliff above a river, valley, etc.

kraut /kraʊt/ noun M19 German (= vegetable, cabbage; cf. earlier SAUERKRAUT). **1** M19 Sauerkraut. **2** E20 (usually **Kraut**) A German, especially a German soldier. derogatory slang.

kremlin /'krɛmlɪn/ noun M17 French (from Russian kreml' citadel). A citadel or fortified enclosure within a Russian town or city, especially (Kremlin) that of Moscow; (the Kremlin) the government of the former USSR.

kreplach /'krɛplɑːx/ noun plural L19 Yiddish (kreplech plural of krepel from dialect German Kräppel fritter). Triangular noodles filled with chopped meat or cheese and served with soup.

kriegspiel /'kriːɡʃpiːl/ noun L19 German (from Krieg war + Spiel game). **1** L19 A war-game in which blocks representing troops etc. are moved about on maps. **2** L19 A form of chess with an umpire and two players, in which each player plays at a separate board and has only limited information about the other's moves.

kril /krɪl/ noun (also **krill**) plural same E20 Norwegian (kril small fish fry). A small shrimplike planktonic crustacean of the order Euphausiacea, important as food for fish, and for some whales and seals.
■ Chiefly used as collective plural.

krimmer /'krɪmə/ noun (also **crimmer**) M19 German (from Krim (Russian Krym) Crimea). The grey or black furry fleece of young lambs from the Crimean area; a cloth resembling this. Cf. KARAKUL.

kris /kriːs/ noun (also **creese**) L16 Malay (keris, partly through Dutch kris, German Kris, Spanish, Portuguese cris, French criss, etc.). A Malay or Indonesian dagger with a straight or wavy blade.

kross variant of KAROSS.

krug /krʊɡ/ noun M19 German. In Germany and German-speaking countries: a beer-mug, a tankard.

krummholz /'krʌmhʊlts/ noun E20 German (= elfin-tree, literally, 'crooked wood'). A wood composed of dwarfed and deformed trees, such as is found in alpine regions, an elfin-wood.

krummhorn /'krʌmhɔːn/, /'krʊmhɔːn/ noun (also **crumhorn**) L17 German (from krumm crooked, curved + Horn horn). Music **1** L17 A medieval and Renaissance wind instrument with a double reed and a curved end. **2** L19 An organ reed-stop, usually of 8-ft pitch, suggestive of a krummhorn or clarinet in tone; a CROMORNE.

kuchen /'kuːxən/ noun plural **kuchens** M19 German (= cake). In Germany or among German- or Yiddish-speaking people: a cake; especially a cake taken with coffee.

kudos /'kjuːdɒs/ noun L18 Greek (= praise, renown). Glory, renown. colloquial.
1996 Times . . . the video company ends up with the product, the TV company with first broadcast rights, the opera company with kudos and 'accessibility' brownie points.

kudzu /'kʊdzuː/ noun L19 Japanese (kuzu). A climbing leguminous plant, Pueraria lobata, of China and Japan, cultivated elsewhere for fodder, as an ornamental, and to prevent soil erosion. In full kudzu vine.

kuei /'kuːeɪ/ noun M20 Chinese (gūi (Wade–Giles kūei)). Chinese Antiquities A bronze food-vessel, usually with two handles and often surmounted by animal heads.

kuffiyeh variant of KEFFIYEH.

kugel /'kuːɡ(ə)l/ noun M19 Yiddish (= ball, from Middle High German kugel(e) ball, globe). In Jewish cookery: a kind of pudding; especially a savoury pudding, usually of potatoes or other vegetables, served as a separate course or as a side dish.

kugelhupf variant of GUGELHUPF.

kukri /'kʊkri/ noun E19 Nepali (khukuri). A curved knife broadening towards the point and usually with the sharp edge on the concave side, used by Gurkhas.

kula /'kuːlɑ/ noun E20 Melanesian. In some Pacific communities, especially in the Trobriand Islands: an inter-island system of ceremonial exchange of items as a prelude to or concomitant of regular trading.

kulah /'kuːlɑ/ noun E20 Persian (kulāh cap). A conical cap of felt or lambskin worn by Muslims in the Middle East.

kulak /'kuːlak/ noun L19 Russian (literally, 'fist, tight-fisted person' from Turkic ķol hand). Originally, a well-to-do Russian farmer or trader. Later, a peasant-proprietor working for his own profit in the Soviet Union.

1996 *Times* To suggest that wealthier taxpayers should plan for the worst does not imply that Labour is studying Stalin's treatment of the kulaks as a post-election model.

Kultur /kʊlˈtuːr/ *noun* (also **kultur**) E20 German (*Kultur* from Latin *cultura* or French *culture* culture). German civilization and culture.

▪ Often used in the aftermath of the Nazi era in a derogatory sense to suggest authoritarianism and militarism but also used neutrally as a component in words such as those below.

Kulturgeschichte /kʊlˈtuːrgəˌʃɪçtə/ *noun* (also **kulturgeschichte**) L19 German (*Kultur* culture + *Geschichte* history). The history of the cultural development of a country; history of civilization.

Kulturkampf /kʊlˈtuːrˌkampf/ *noun* (also **kulturkampf**) L19 German (*Kultur* culture + *Kampf* struggle). The conflict in Germany (1872–87) between the government and the Church for control of schools and ecclesiastical appointments; *transferred* a conflict of moral or social issues and ideas.

1996 *Spectator* The great North American *kulturkampf* between classes, between moral codes and between visions of the future has chosen as its latest battlefield a city that was once known, ironically, as Toronto the Good.

kulturny /kʊljˈturnɪj/, /kʊlˈtəːni/ *adjective* M20 Russian (*kulʹturnyĭ*, from *kulʹtur* from Latin *cultura* or French *culture* culture). In countries of the former USSR: cultured, civilized; good mannered, well behaved. Cf. NEKULTURNY.

kumis /ˈkuːmɪs/ *noun* (also **koumiss, kumiss**) L16 French (*koumis*, German *Kumiss*, Polish *kumys*, Russian *kumys* from Tartar *kumiz*). A fermented liquor prepared from mare's or other milk, used as a beverage and medicinally especially by central Asian nomadic tribes; a spirituous liquor distilled from this.

kumkum /ˈkʊmkʊm/ *noun* M20 Sanskrit (*kuṅkuma* saffron). A red powder used ceremonially, especially by Hindu women to make a small distinctive mark on the forehead; the mark so made.

kümmel /ˈkʊm(ə)l/ *noun* M19 German (representative of Middle High German, Old High German *kumil* variant of *kumîn* cumin). A sweet liqueur flavoured with caraway and cumin seeds.

kundalini /ˈkʊndəlmi:/ *noun* L19 Sanskrit (*kuṇḍalinī* literally 'snake'). *Yoga* **1** L19 The latent (female) energy which lies coiled at the base of the spine. **2** M20 A type of meditation which aims to direct and release this energy. In full *Kundalini yoga.*

kung fu /kʊŋˈfuː/, /kʌŋˈfuː/ *noun* L19 Chinese (*gongfu* (Wade–Giles *kung fu*), from *gong* (*kung*) merit + *fu* master). The Chinese form of KARATE.

Kunstforscher /ˈkʊnstˌfɔrʃər/ *noun* plural same L19 Greek (from *Kunst* art + *Forscher* researcher). An art historian.

Kunstgeschichte /ˈkʊnstgəˌʃɪçtə/ *noun* L19 German (from *Kunst* art + *Geschichte* history). The history of art, art history.

Kunsthistoriker /ˈkʊnsthɪˌstoːrikər/ *noun* plural same M20 German (from *Kunst* art + *Historiker* historian). An art historian.

Künstlerroman /ˈkynstlərɔˌmaːn/ *noun* plural **Künstlerromane** /ˈkynstlərɔˌmaːnə/ M20 German (from *Künstler* artist + *Roman* novel). A BILDUNGSROMAN about an artist.

Kunstprosa /ˈkʊnstproːza/ *noun* M20 German (from *Kunst* art + *Prosa* prose). Literary prose, ornate and stylized prose.

Kur /kuːr/ *noun* plural **Kuren** /ˈkuːrən/ L19 German (= a cure). A cure, a medicinal drinking of the waters at a spa in Germany or a German-speaking country; a spa.

kurgan /kʊəˈɡaːn/ *noun* L19 Russian (of Turkic origin: cf. Turkish *kurgan* castle, fortress). A prehistoric sepulchral tumulus or barrow such as is found in Siberia and central Asia.

Kurhaus /ˈkuːrhaʊs/ *noun* plural **Kurhäuser** /ˈkuːrhɔyzər/ M19 German (from *Kur* cure + *Haus* house). In Germany and German-speaking countries: a building at a health resort where medicinal water is dispensed; a pump room.

kuri /ˈkʊri/ *noun* M19 Maori (= dog). In New Zealand: a Maori dog. Also, a mongrel; *slang* an unpleasant or disliked person.

Kurort /ˈkuːrˌɔrt/ *noun* plural **Kurorte** /ˈkuːrˌɔrtə/ M19 German (from *Kur* cure + *Ort* place). In Germany and German-speaking countries: a health-resort, a spa, a watering-place.

kursaal /ˈkuːrsɑːl/ *noun* plural **kursäle** /ˈkuːrsɛːlə/, **kursaals**, /ˈkuːrsɑːlz/ M19 German (from as *Kur* cure + *Saal* hall, room).

Especially in Germany and German-speaking countries: a public building at a health resort, provided for the use and entertainment of visitors.

kurta /ˈkəːtə/ *noun* E20 Urdu and Persian (*kurtah*). A loose shirt or tunic worn by especially Hindu men and women.

kurtosis /kəːˈtəʊsɪs/ *noun* E20 Greek (*kurtōsis* a bulging, convexity, from *kurtos* bulging, convex). *Statistics* The degree of sharpness of the peak of a frequency-distribution curve.

kuru /ˈkʊruː/ *noun* M20 New Guinea. *Medicine* A fatal viral brain disease found among certain peoples of New Guinea.

■ *Kuru* was formerly of mainly anthropological interest as a disease found amongst peoples of New Guinea who practised ritual cannibalism of human brain tissue. It became of interest to the wider medical establishment on account of its similarities to BSE (bovine spongiform encephalopathy) or *mad cow disease* which was identified in cattle in the UK in 1986. In 1990 it was discovered that cats could also contract the disease, maybe as the result of eating contaminated cattle brain or other tissue in pet foods, and the possibility that BSE could be transmitted to humans through cattle offal became the subject of urgent investigations.

kutcha /ˈkʌtʃə/ *adjective & noun* (also **cutcha**, **kacha**) E19 Hindustani (*kaccā* raw, crude, uncooked). **A** *adjective* E19 In the Indian subcontinent: slight, makeshift, unfinished; built of dried mud. **B** *noun* M19 Dried mud used as a building material in the Indian subcontinent.

kuzushi /kʊˈzʊʃi/ *noun* M20 Japanese. *Judo* The fact or state of being unbalanced by one's opponent; a loss of the initiative.

kvass /kvaːs/ *noun* (also **kvas**, **quass**) M16 Russian (*kvas*). In Russia and some neighbouring countries: a fermented beverage, low in alcohol, made from rye flour or bread with malt; rye beer.

kvell /kvɛl/ *intransitive verb* M20 Yiddish (*kveln* from German *quellen* gush, well up). Boast; feel proud or happy; gloat.

■ United States slang.

kvetch /kvɛtʃ/ *noun & verb* M20 Yiddish (as noun from Yiddish *kvetsh*, as verb from Yiddish *kvetshn*, from German *Quetsche* crusher, presser, *quetschen*, crush, press). **A** *noun* M20 An objectionable person; specifically someone who complains a great deal, a fault-finder. **B** *intransitive verb* M20 Complain, whine. Chiefly as *kvetching* verbal noun.

■ North American slang.

kvutza /ˈkvʊtsaː/, /kvʊtˈsaː/ *noun* E20 Modern Hebrew (*qĕbhūṣāh* from Hebrew = group). In Israel: a communal and cooperative settlement, which, with others, may form a kibbutz.

kwai-lo /ˈkwʌɪləʊ/ *noun* M20 Chinese ((Cantonese) (*faan*) *kwaí ló*, literally, '(foreign) devil fellow'). In China, a foreigner, *especially* a European.

■ A derogatory Chinese expression for all non-Chinese.

kwashiorkor /ˌkwɒʃɪˈɔːkɔː/, /ˌkwaʃɪˈɔːkɔː/ *noun* M20 Ghanaian (local name). A form of malnutrition caused by severe protein and energy deficiency, chiefly affecting young (especially newly weaned) children in tropical Africa, and producing apathy, oedema, loss of pigmentation, diarrhoea, and other symptoms.

kwela /ˈkweɪlə/ *noun* M20 Afrikaans (perhaps from Zulu *khwela* climb, mount). A popular dance, and its accompanying music, resembling jazz, of central and southern Africa.

1958 *Time* In the dusty streets, urchins rock to the penny-whistle's fast *kwela* beat.

kya /ˈkʌɪə/ *noun* E20 Zulu (*-khaya* place of abode). In South Africa, Zimbabwe, etc.: an African's hut; the living accommodation of an African servant.

kylin /ˈkiːlɪn/ *noun* M19 Chinese (*qílín*, from *qí* male + *lín* female). A mythical animal of composite form figured on Chinese and Japanese pottery, a Chinese unicorn. Cf. KIRIN.

kylix /ˈkʌɪlɪks/, /ˈkɪlɪks/ *noun* (also **cylix**, plural **cylices** /ˈkʌɪlɪsiːz/) plural **kylikes** /ˈkʌɪlɪkiːz/ M19 Greek (*kulix*). *Greek Antiquities* A shallow cup with a tall stem, a tazza.

kyogen /ˈkjəʊgɛn/ *noun* plural same L19 Japanese (*kyōgen*). A comic interlude presented between performances of Noh plays.

Kyrie eleison /ˌkɪrɪeɪ ɪˈleɪɪzɒn/, /ˌkɪrɪeɪ ɪˈleɪɪsɒn/ *noun phrase* ME Medieval Latin (from Greek *Kuriē eleēson* Lord, have mercy). The words ('Lord, have mercy') of

a short repeated invocation or response used in the Roman Catholic, Greek Orthodox, and Anglican Churches, especially at the beginning of the Eucharist. Also, a musical setting of these words, especially as the first movement of a mass.

kyu /kjuː/ *noun* M20 Japanese (*kyū* class). Each of the (numbered) grades of the less advanced level of proficiency in judo, karate, and other martial (or originally martial) arts, (also *kyu grade*); a person who has reached (a specified grade of) this level. Cf. DAN.

L

La /lɑ/, /lɑː/ *adjective* (*definite article*) (also **la**) M19 French (or Italian feminine definite article, from Latin *illa*, feminine of *ille* that). Used preceding the name of a prima donna, or (frequently *jocular* or *ironical*) the name of any woman.
1996 *Times* The doughty girl has a touch of the Katharine Hepburns about her. *La* Hepburn, 88, still goes swimming in the lake by her house, even if she has to break the ice . . .

laager /'lɑːgə/ *noun* M19 Afrikaans (= German *Lager*, Dutch *leger*). A camp, an encampment; *South African History* a Boer camp marked out and protected by a circle of wagons; *transferred* and *figurative* a defensive position, *especially* one protected by armoured vehicles; an entrenched policy, viewpoint, etc., under attack from opponents.
■ In its figurative sense *laager* was often used attributively in the phrase *laager mentality* to denote the intransigent defensiveness of Afrikaners in their dealings with the outside world during the apartheid era. The noun gave rise (L19) to both transitive and intransitive verbal uses of *laager*, sometimes followed by *up*.
figurative **1996** *Times* The stage appeared to be too big for his four-piece band, whose equipment was drawn up into a laager in the middle.

laban /'laban/ *noun* (also **leban** /'lɛban/, **leben** /'lɛbən/) L17 Arabic (= milk). A drink consisting of coagulated sour milk.

labarum /'labərəm/ *noun* E17 Late Latin (whence Byzantine Greek *labaron*). The imperial standard of Constantine the Great (306–337), with Christian symbols added to Roman military symbols; *generally* a symbolic banner.

labrys /'labrɪs/ *noun* E20 Greek (*labrus*). *Greek Antiquities* The sacred double-headed axe of ancient Crete; a representation of this.

lac /lak/ *noun* (also **lack**, (earlier) **lacca**) LME Medieval Latin (*lac, lac(c)a* from Portuguese *lac(c)a* from Hindustani *lākh*, Persian *lāk*). LME The dark-red resinous incrustation secreted as a protective covering by the females of certain homopteran insects (especially *Laccifer lacca*) parasitic on South-East Asian trees, used (especially in the Indian subcontinent) to make shellac and dye.
■ Formerly (L16–E18) used also for the varnish made from lac or various other resinous wood varnishes (*lacquer*) and (L17–M18) for the crimson colour or pigment derived from lac (*lake*).

lacet /lasɛ/ *noun* plural pronounced same L19 French (= lace, hairpin bend). A hairpin bend in a road.

lachryma Christi /ˌlakrɪmə 'krɪstʌɪ/, /ˌlakrɪmə 'krɪstiː/ *noun phrase* L17 Modern Latin (literally, 'Christ's tear(s)', in Italian *lagrima* (or *-me*) *di Cristo*). A white, red, or pink Italian wine originally from grapes grown near Mount Vesuvius, now also produced elsewhere in Italy.

lachsschinken /'laksˌʃɪŋkən/ *noun* E20 German (from *Lachs* salmon + *Schinken* ham). Cured and smoked loin of pork.

lacrimae rerum /ˌlakrɪmʌɪ 'reɪrəm/, /ˌlakrɪmiː 'rɪərəm/ *noun* (also **lachrymae rerum**) E20 Latin (literally, 'tears (for the nature) of things'). The sadness of life; tears for the sorrows of life.
■ A quotation from Virgil's *Aeneid* (i.462). The etymologically incorrect spelling *lachrymae* is also frequent.
1995 *Oldie* [Critics] wrote off Betjeman as a phoney and a doggerel rhymester. They had not sensed the *lachrymae rerum* in the poems.

lacuna /lə'kjuːnə/ *noun* plural **lacunae** /lə'kjuːniː/, **lacunas** M17 Latin (from *lacus* lake). **1** M17 A hiatus, a blank, a missing portion, especially in a manuscript or text. **2** E18 *in technical use* A gap, a depression; a space or cavity.

ladanum /'ladənəm/ *noun* M16 Latin (*ladanum, ledanum* from Greek *ladanon, lēdanon*, from *lēdon* mastic). A gum resin which exudes from plants of the genus *Cistus*, much used in perfumery and for fumigation.

ladino /lə'diːnəʊ/ *noun* E20 Italian. A large fast-growing variety of white clover (*Trifolium repens*), native to northern Italy and cultivated elsewhere, especially in the United States, as a fodder crop. In full *ladino clover*.

la dolce vita see DOLCE VITA.

l'affaire see AFFAIRE.

lager /'lɑːgə/ *noun* M19 German (*Lager-Bier* beer brewed for keeping, from *Lager* storehouse). A light kind of beer, originally

German or Bohemian, which is stored to mature before use; a drink of this.

lahar /'lɑːhɑː/ *noun* E20 Javanese. *Geology* A mud-flow of volcanic ash mixed with water.

laissez-aller /ˌlɛseɪ'aleɪ/, *foreign* /lɛseale/ *noun* (also **laisser-aller**) E19 French (literally, 'allow to go'). Absence of restraint; unconstrained ease and freedom.

laissez-faire /ˌlɛseɪ'fɛː/, *foreign* /lɛsefɛr/ *noun* (also **laisser-faire**) E19 French (literally, 'allow to do'). Government abstention from interference in the actions of individuals, especially in commerce; *generally* non-interference or indifference.

■ The maxim *laissez faire et laissez passer* is associated particularly with the French free-trade economists of the eighteenth century. See also quotation at DIRIGISME.
1996 *Country Life* The professor's *laissez-faire* philosophy is quite clearly presiding over an impoverishment of English, which is losing not simply its richness but also its comprehensibility.

laissez-passer /ˌlɛseɪ'pɑːseɪ/, *foreign* /lɛsepase/ (*plural same*) *noun* (also **laisser-passer**) E20 French (literally, 'allow to pass'). A permit to travel or to enter a particular place, a pass.
1955 *Times* He has been granted by the Greek Foreign Ministry a laisser-passer to the Greek military zone of the Greek–Bulgarian frontier.

lakh /lak/ *noun* (also **lac**) E17 Hindustani (*lākh* from Sanskrit *lakṣa* mark, token, 100,000). In the Indian subcontinent: one hundred thousand; occasionally, an indefinite large number.

lakoum, lakum variants of LOKUM.

lama /'lɑːmə/ *noun* M17 Tibetan (*bla-ma* (the *b* is silent)). A Buddhist religious teacher of Tibet or Mongolia.

lambada /lam'bɑːdə/ *noun* L20 Brazilian Portuguese (literally, 'beating, lashing'). A fast and erotic dance of Brazilian origin, in which couples dance with their stomachs touching each other; the music for this dance.

■ The *lambada*, danced in Brazil for many years, became a craze in the United States in the late 1980s, and media hype helped spread it to the United Kingdom and Australia. The speed and thoroughness with which this ethnic dance was marketed in the West gave rise to the coinage *lambadazation* for the whole process of taking up and marketing elements of ethnic culture for Western consumers.

1990 *Sun* We danced the lambada face to face and sort of going up and down against each other.

lambda /'lamdə/ *noun* E17 Greek. **1 1** E17 The eleventh letter (Λ, λ) of the Greek alphabet. **ll 2** M20 *Chemistry* A millionth of a litre. Usually written λ. **3** M20 *Nuclear Physics* A neutral hyperon (or its antiparticle) with a mass 2183 times that of the electron; originally also, any of several similar charged hyperons. Frequently written Λ. More fully *lambda particle*. **4** M20 *Microbiology* A bacteriophage originally isolated from *Escherichia coli*, used in genetic research. Frequently written λ.

lamdan /'lʌmdən/ *noun* E20 Hebrew (*lamdān*, literally, 'a person who has learned', from *lāmaḍ* learn). A person learned in Jewish law; a Talmudic scholar.

lamé /'lɑːmeɪ/ *noun & adjective* E20 French (from Old French *lame* from Latin *lamina*, *lamna* thin plate, especially of metal). (Made of) a brocaded fabric consisting of silk or other yarns interwoven with metallic threads.

lamento /la'mento/ *noun* plural **lamenti** /la'menti/ M20 Italian. *Music* An elegiac or mourning song; in Italian opera, a tragic aria.

lamentoso /ˌlamen'toːso/ *adverb & adjective* L19 Italian. *Music* (A direction:) in a mournful style.

lamia /'leɪmɪə/ *noun* plural **lamias, lamiae** /'leɪmiː/ LME Latin (from Greek = mythical monster, carnivorous fish). A mythical monster supposed to have the body of a woman, and to prey on human beings and suck the blood of children. Also, a witch, a she-demon.

lamina /'lamɪnə/ *noun* plural **laminae** /'lamɪniː/ M17 Latin (*la(m)mina*). A thin plate or layer of a metal or other material.

■ Also with technical senses in Anatomy and Biology, Botany (M18), Geology (M19), and Mathematics (M19).

lammergeyer /'laməgʌɪə/ *noun* (also **lammergeier**) E19 German (*Lämmergeier*, from *Lämmer* plural of *Lamm* lamb + *Geier* vulture). A long-winged, long-tailed vulture, *Gypaetus barbatus*, inhabiting lofty mountains in southern Europe, Asia, and Africa. Also called *bearded vulture*.

lammervanger /'laməvaŋə/, /'laməfaŋə/ *noun* M19 Afrikaans (from *lam* lamb + *vanger* catcher). In South Africa: an eagle, especially one believed to prey on lambs. Also, = preceding.

lanai /ləˈnʌɪ/ *noun* (also (earlier) **ranai**) E19 Hawaiian. A porch or veranda, originally in Hawaii; a roofed structure with open sides near a house.

Land /lant/, /land/ *noun* plural **Länder** /ˈlɛndər/, **Lands** /landz/ E20 German. A semi-autonomous unit of local government in Germany and Austria.

> 1996 *Bookseller* The location was chosen to attract booksellers in the reunified Germany's eastern *Länder*, although this did not deter those from Munich and Stuttgart.

landau /ˈlandɔː/, /ˈlandaʊ/ *noun* M18 German (from *Landau* name of town in Germany, where first made). Chiefly *History* A four-wheeled horse-drawn carriage, with folding front and rear hoods enabling it to travel open, half-open, or closed. Also *landau carriage*.

lande /lɑ̃d/ *noun* plural pronounced same L18 French. A tract of wild land, a moor, especially in south-west France.

Länder plural of LAND.

ländler /ˈlɛndlə/ *noun* L19 German. An Austrian peasant dance, similar to a slow waltz; a piece of music for this dance.

landnam /ˈlandnəm/ *noun* M20 Danish (= occupation of land). *Archaeology* The clearance of forested land for (usually short-term) agricultural purposes; evidence of this provided by sudden changes in pollen spectra.

landrace /ˈlandreɪs/ *noun* M20 Danish (= national breed). A breed of large white pig, originally developed in Denmark; an animal of this breed.

landsknecht see LANSQUENET.

landsman /ˈlɒntsmɒn/ *noun* plural **landsleit** /ˈlɒntslʌɪt/ M20 Yiddish (from Middle High German *lantsman, lantman* a native). Among Jews: a fellow Jew; a compatriot.

Landsturm /ˈlantˌʃtʊrm/ *noun* plural **Landstürme** /ˈlantˌʃtyrmə/ E19 German (literally, 'land-storm'). *History* In Germany and German-speaking countries: a general levy in time of war; an auxiliary militia force.

Landwehr /ˈlantveːr/ *noun* E19 German (literally, 'land-defence'). *Military* In Germany and some other countries: that part of the organized land forces of which continuous service is required only in time of war; the army reserve.

langeleik /ˈlaŋələɪk/ *noun* plural **langeleiken** /ˈlaŋəlʌɪkən/ (also **langleik** /ˈlaŋlʌɪk/) E20 Norwegian. An early Norwegian stringed instrument, resembling the zither.

langlauf /ˈlaŋlaʊf/ *noun* (also **Langlauf**) E20 German (literally, 'long run'). Cross-country skiing; a cross-country skiing race.

langleik variant of LANGELEIK.

langosta /laŋˈɡɒstə/ *noun* L19 Spanish (from popular Latin alteration of Latin *locusta* locust). **1** L19 A locust. Now *rare* or *obsolete*. **2** E20 A LANGOUSTE.
■ Chiefly United States.

langostino /laŋɡoˈstino/, /laŋɡəˈstiːnəʊ/ *noun* plural **langostinos** /laŋɡoˈstinos/, /laŋɡəˈstiːnəʊz/ E20 Spanish (from as preceding). A LANGOUSTINE.

langouste /ˈlɒŋɡuːst/, *foreign* /lɑ̃ɡust/ (*plural same*) *noun* M19 French (from Old Provençal *lagosta* from popular Latin alteration of Latin *locusta* locust). A lobster; *especially* the spiny lobster, *Palinurus vulgaris*.

langoustine /ˈlɒŋɡʊstiːn/, *foreign* /lɑ̃ɡustin/ (*plural same*) *noun* M20 French (from as preceding). The Norway lobster, especially as food.

langue /lɑ̃ɡ/ *noun* plural pronounced same ME French (from Latin *lingua* tongue, language). **1** ME–M17 A language. *rare*. **2** L18 A national division or branch of a religious and military Order. Long *rare* except *historical*. **3** E20 *Linguistics* A language viewed as an abstract system used by a speech-community, in contrast to the actual linguistic behaviour of individuals. Opposed to PAROLE sense 3.

langue de chat /lɑ̃ɡ də ʃa/, /ˌlɑːŋ də ˈʃɑː/ *noun phrase* plural **langues de chat** (pronounced same) L19 French (literally, 'cat's tongue'). A long thin piece of chocolate; a long finger-shaped biscuit.

langue d'oc /lɑ̃ɡ dɔk/ *noun phrase* E18 Old and Modern French (from as LANGUE + *de* of + *oc* yes (from Latin *hoc*)). The language of medieval France south of the Loire, generally characterized by the use of *oc* to mean 'yes', and the basis of modern Provençal. Cf. LANGUE D'OÏL.

langue d'oïl /lɑ̃ɡ dɔil/ *noun phrase* (also **langue d'oui** /lɑ̃ɡ dwi/) E18 Old and Modern French (from as LANGUE + *de* of + *oïl* (now *oui*) yes (from Latin *hoc ille*)). The language of medieval France north of the

Loire, generally characterized by the use of *oïl* to mean 'yes', and the basis of standard modern French. Cf. LANGUE D'OC.

langues de chat plural of LANGUE DE CHAT.

lansquenet /'lɑːnskənɛt/, /'lɑnskənɛt/ *noun* (also (in sense 1 now the usual form) **landsknecht** /'lan(d)sknɛkt/) E17 French (from German *Landsknecht*, from genitive of *Land* land + *Knecht* soldier). **1** E17 *History* A member of a class of mercenary soldiers in the German and other Continental armies in the sixteenth and seventeenth centuries. **2** L17 A gambling card-game of German origin.

lanx /laŋks/ *noun* plural **lances** /'lansiːz/ LME Latin. *Antiquities* A large dish or bowl.

lapiés /'lapjez/, /'lapɪeɪz/ *noun* plural (also **lapies**) E20 French (dialectal *lapiaz, lapiés* (singular *lapié*) ultimately from Latin *lapis* stone). *Physical Geography* KARREN. Also (treated as *singular*) KARRENFELD.

lapillus /lə'pɪləs/ *noun* plural **lapilli** /lə'pɪlʌɪ/, /lə'pɪliː/ M18 Latin (diminutive of *lapis* stone; in plural also from Italian *lapilli*, plural of *lapillo*). Originally, a small stone or pebble. Now (*Geology*), a fragment of rock or lava ejected from a volcano, *specifically* one between 2 and 64 mm in size. Usually in *plural*.

lapis /'lapɪs/ *noun* LME Latin. **1** LME Stone; *specifically* the philosopher's stone. *rare* except in phrases. **2** E19 (Abbreviated form of) LAPIS LAZULI.

lapis lazuli /ˌlapɪs 'lazjʊlʌɪ/, /ˌlapɪs 'lazjʊli/ *noun phrase* LME Latin (from Latin *lapis* stone + medieval Latin *lazuli* genitive of *lazulum*, varying with *lazur, lazurius*, from Persian *lāžward* lapis lazuli). A blue semiprecious stone composed chiefly of a sulphur-containing silicate of sodium and aluminium; *History* a pigment consisting of crushed grains of this, the original ultramarine; the colour ultramarine.

lappa /'lapə/ *noun* M20 Hausa (from Arabic *laffa* to wrap up, cover). In West Africa: a woman's shawl, wrap, or skirt.

lapsus /'lapsəs/ *noun* plural same E17 Latin. A lapse, a slip, an error.

■ Chiefly in phrases below.

lapsus calami /ˌlapsəs 'kaləmʌɪ/ *noun phrase* L19 Latin. A slip of the pen.

lapsus linguae /ˌlapsəs 'lɪŋgwiː/ *noun phrase* M17 Latin. A slip of the tongue.

laquear /'lakwɪɑː/ *noun* plural **laquearia** /ˌlakwɪ'ɑːrɪə/ E18 Latin (*laqueare* panelled ceiling). *Architecture* A ceiling consisting of panelled recessed compartments, with bands between the panels.

lar /lɑː/ *noun* (in sense 1 also **Lar**) plural **lars, lares** /'lɑːriːz/ L16 Latin. **1** L16 *Roman History* A household or ancestral god. Frequently in *plural*, the protective gods of a house; household gods; also, the home. Cf. PENATES. **2** E19 The common or white-handed gibbon, *Hylobates lar*, of Thailand and Malaysia. More fully *lar gibbon*.

■ The phrase *lares et penates* (or *lares and penates*) is used figuratively of those components of a household that the owner holds dearest; thus in 1775 Horace Walpole wrote in a letter 'I am returned to my own Lares and Penates—to my dogs and cats'.

lardon /'lɑːdən/ *noun* (also **lardoon** /lɑː'duːn/) LME French (from Old French *lard* bacon, from Latin *lar(i)dum* related to Greek *larinos* fat). *Cookery* A strip of bacon or pork inserted into other meat before cooking to give it flavour and keep it moist.

la recherche du temps perdu see RECHERCHE DU TEMPS PERDU.

lares plural of LAR.

largamente /lɑːgə'mɛnti/ *adverb & adjective* M19 Italian (= broadly). *Music* (A direction:) in a slow dignified style.

largesse /lɑː'ʒɛs/, /lɑː'ʤɛs/ *noun* (also **largess**) ME Old and Modern French (from Proto-Romance, from Latin *largus* liberal in giving). **1** ME Liberality, generosity, munificence. Long *obsolete* except *historical*. **2** ME Liberal bestowal of gifts, especially by a person in a high position on some special occasion. **b** M16 An act of such giving; a free gift of money etc. **3** LME–L16 Freedom, liberty.

2.b 1995 D. Lodge *Therapy* The youth came back soon afterwards, hoping for more *largesse*.

larghetto /lɑː'gɛtəʊ/ *adverb, adjective, & noun* E18 Italian (diminutive of LARGO). *Music* **A** *adverb & adjective* E18 (A direction:) in fairly slow time. **B** *noun* plural **larghettos** L19 A movement or passage (to be) played in this way.

largo /'lɑːgəʊ/ *adverb, adjective, & noun* L17 Italian (= broad). *Music* **A** *adverb & adjective* L17 (A direction:) in slow time and

227

larmoyant | laudator temporis acti

with a broad dignified treatment.
B *noun* plural **largos** M18 A movement or
passage (to be) played in this way.

larmoyant /lɑːˈmɔɪənt/ *adjective* E19
French (present participle of *larmoyer* to
be tearful). Given to tears, lachrymose.
1972 P. Porter *'Preaching to the Converted'*
Calling down the funnel of your mind News the
charnel chords make *larmoyant*, The
Pretenders come . . .

larnax /ˈlɑːnaks/ *noun* plural **larnakes**
/ˈlɑːnəkiːz/ L19 Greek. *Greek Antiquities* A
chest, ossuary, urn, or coffin, usually of
terracotta and frequently ornamented
with designs.

larva /ˈlɑːvə/ *noun* plural **larvae** /ˈlɑːviː/
M17 Latin (= ghost, mask). **1** M17 A disem-
bodied spirit; a ghost, a spectre. *obsolete
except historical.* **2** M18 An insect in a
state of development (displaying little or
no similarity to the adult) lasting from
the time of its leaving the egg until its
transformation into a pupa; a grub, a caterpillar. Also, an immature form in other
animals that undergo some sort of metamorphosis, e.g. amphibians, tapeworms,
etc.

larynx /ˈlarɪŋks/ *noun* plural **larynges** /ləˈrɪndʒiːz/,
larynxes L16 Modern Latin
(from Greek *larugx, larugg-*). *Anatomy* and
Zoology A hollow cartilaginous and muscular organ forming the upper part of
the trachea or windpipe, and holding the
vocal cords in humans and most mammals.

lasagne /ləˈzanjə/, /ləˈsanjə/, /ləˈsɑːnjə/,
/ləˈzɑːnjə/ *noun* (also **lasagna**) M19 Italian
(plural of *lasagna*, ultimately from Latin
lasanum chamber-pot, perhaps also cooking-pot). Pasta in the form of long wide
strips; an Italian dish consisting largely
of this, usually with a sauce.

lassi /ˈlʌsi/, /ˈlasi/ *noun* L19 Hindustani
(*lassī*). In the Indian subcontinent: a drink
made from a buttermilk or yoghurt base
with water.

lasya /ˈlɑːsjə/ *noun* M20 Sanskrit (*lāsya*). A
graceful Indian style of female dancing.

latex /ˈleɪtɛks/ *noun* plural **latexes, lati-
ces** /ˈleɪtɪsiːz/ M17 Latin (= liquid, fluid).
1 M17–M18 *Medicine* Any of various body
fluids. **2** M19 *Botany* A milky liquid found
in many plants; *specifically* that of *Hevea
brasiliensis* or other plants used to produce rubber. **3** M20 A dispersion in water
of particles of a polymer that is formed

during polymerization and is used to
make paints, coatings, etc.

lathi /ˈlɑːti/ *noun* (also **lathee**) M19 Hindustani (*lāṭhī*). In the Indian subcontinent: a long heavy iron-bound stick,
usually of bamboo, used as a weapon.

latifundium /lɑːtɪˈfʌndɪəm/, /latɪ-
ˈfʌndɪəm/, /leɪtɪˈfʌndɪəm/ *noun* plural **lat-
ifundia** /lɑːtɪˈfʌndɪə/ M19 Latin (from *latus*
broad + *fundus* landed estate; partly from
Spanish *latifundio* from Latin). A large
landed estate or ranch, frequently
worked by slaves or people of semiservile
status; *especially* one in Spain or Latin
America or in ancient Rome.
▪ Now usually occurring in the plural, *latifundium* was originally (M17) Anglicized as
latifund. Its opposite is a MINIFUNDIUM.

latigo /ˈlatɪɡəʊ/ *noun* plural **latigo(e)s** L19
Spanish. A strap for tightening a cinch.
United States.

Latino sine flexione /ˌlatməʊ ˌsɪnɪ flɛksɪ
ˈəʊni/ *noun phrase* E20 Latin ((*Latino* ablative of adjective *Latinus* Latin) = in Latin
without inflection). The language Inter-
lingua, in which nouns are taken from
the ablative case of Latin nouns.

latke /ˈlʌtkə/ *noun* E20 Yiddish (from Russian *latka* earthenware cooking vessel,
(dialect) dish cooked in such a vessel). In
Jewish cookery: a pancake, *especially* one
made with grated potato.

latria /ləˈtrʌɪə/ *noun* E16 Late Latin (from
Greek *latreia*, from *latreuein* to wait on,
serve with prayer). *Roman Catholic Church*
The highest form of worship, due to God
alone; the veneration properly given to
God. Cf. DULIA, HYPERDULIA.

latticinio /latɪˈtʃiːnjo/, /latɪˈtʃiːnjəʊ/ *noun*
Also written **latticino** /latɪˈtʃiːno/, /latɪ
ˈtʃiːnəʊ/ M19 Italian (literally, 'dairy produce', from medieval Latin *lacticinium*).
An opaque white glass used in threads to
decorate clear Venetian glass.

laúd /laˈud/ *noun* plural **laúdes** /laˈudes/
L19 Spanish (*laúd* from Arabic *al-'ūd*). A
Spanish lute.

laudator temporis acti /lɔːˌdeɪtə
ˌtɛmp(ə)rɪs ˈaktʌɪ/ *noun phrase* plural **lau-
datores temporis acti** /lɔːdəˌtɔːriːz/ M18
Latin (= a praiser of times past). A person
who holds up the past as a golden age.
▪ *Laudator temporis acti se puero* 'a praiser of
former times when he himself was a boy' is
a quotation from a passage in Horace's *Ars*

Poetica (173–4) on the tiresome traits that tend to accompany old age.

laulau /'laʊlaʊ/ *noun* M20 Hawaiian (reduplication of *lau* leaf). A portion of a Hawaiian dish of meat or fish wrapped in leaves and steamed or baked. Also, the wrapping of leaves for this dish.

laura /'lɔːrə/ *noun* (also **lavra** /'lavrə/) E18 Greek (= lane, passage, alley). *Christian Church* A group of huts or cells inhabited by reclusive monks in Egypt and the Middle East. In the Orthodox Church, a monastery consisting of separate cells; a large monastery.

lavabo /lə'veɪbəʊ/, *in sense 2* /'lavəbəʊ/ *noun plural* **lavabo(e)s** M18 Latin (= I will wash). **1** M18 *Ecclesiastical* In the Eucharist, the ritual washing of a celebrant's hands at the offertory; also the small towel or the basin used for the washing. **2 a** L19 A washing-trough used in some medieval monasteries. **b** E20 A wash-hand basin. **c** M20 A lavatory; washroom.

lavage /'lavɪdʒ/, /la'vɑːʒ/ *noun & verb* L18 French (from *laver* to wash). **A** *noun* **1** L18 An act of washing, a wash. **2** L19 *Medicine* The irrigation of an organ, either to cleanse it or to allow its contents to be examined. **B** *transitive verb* M20 *Medicine* Cleanse, irrigate, (an organ).

lava-lava /'lɑːvəlɑːvə/ *noun* L19 Samoan. In Samoa and some other Pacific islands: a wrap-around skirtlike garment worn by either sex.

lavaliere /lə'valjɛː/ *noun* (also **lava(l)lière**, **lavalier** /lə'valɪə/, **Lavaliere**) L19 French (proper name). **1** L19 Used *attributively* to designate any of various items of women's clothing in styles associated with the reign of Louis XIV of France. **2** E20 A pendent necklace. **3** M20 A loosely tied cravat. **4** M20 A small microphone worn hanging around the neck. Also *lavaliere microphone*.

■ Louise de *la Vallière* (1644–1710) was mistress to the French king Louis XIV. In French the most frequent context is *une cravate lavallière*.

lavolta /lə'vɒltə/ *noun* L16 Italian (from *la* the + *volta* turn). *History* A lively dance for couples in 3/4 time, in which each partner lifts the other clear of the ground in turn.

lavra variant of LAURA.

layette /leɪ'ɛt/ *noun* M19 French (diminutive of Old French *laie* drawer, box, from

Middle Dutch *laege*). A set of clothing, toilet articles, and bedclothing for a newborn child.

lazaretto /lazə'rɛtəʊ/ *noun plural* **lazarettos** M16 Italian (diminutive of LAZZARO). **1** M16 A hospital for diseased people, especially those with leprosy. **2** E17 A building or ship for quarantine. **3** E18 *Nautical* The after part of a ship's hold, used for stores.

■ Less common, but also used in all three senses, is the French word *lazaret* (E17 in sense 1), derived from the Italian.

lazzaro /'lazərəʊ/ *noun* (also plural **lazzari** /'lazəri/) M17 Italian. A LAZZARONE.

lazzarone /lazə'rəʊneɪ/ *noun plural* **lazzaroni** /lazə'rəʊni/ L18 Italian (augmentative of LAZZARO). In Naples and other Italian cities: a person who subsists on the proceeds of odd jobs, an idler, a beggar.

leban, leben variants of LABAN.

Lebensform /'leːbənsfɔrm/, /'leɪbənfɔːm/ *noun plural* **Lebensformen** /'leːbəns fɔrmən/ M20 German (literally, 'form of life'). A sphere of human social activity involving values; a style or aspect of life.

Lebenslust /'leːbənslʊst/, /'leɪbənzlʊst/ *noun* L19 German. Zest for life, *joie de vivre*.

1958 P. De Vries *Mackeral Plaza* Security he could give her, yes, but not, I'm afraid, something else demanded by her *Lebenslust*.

lebensraum /'leːbənsraʊm/, /'leɪbənraʊm/ *noun* Also written **Lebensraum** E20 German (= living room). Space for living, room to exist and function freely; *specifically* territory which many German nationalists in the mid twentieth century claimed was needed for the survival and healthy development of the nation.

■ Originally the biological concept of a space inhabited, or habitable, by a particular organism, *Lebensraum* was developed by the nineteenth-century German geographer Friedrich Ratzel to mean the space sufficient both for a people's material needs and for the evolution of its particular social and cultural identity. The concept was subsequently hijacked by the Nazis to justify the racist and expansionist policies of the Third Reich.

1995 *Spectator* The sub-text is that if the united Germany . . . can be closely bound into the Community she will never again be tempted to fight for *lebensraum*.

transferred **1996** *Spectator* My liver obviously needed *lebensraum* and was heavily leaning on its neighbours.

lebensspur /'le:bəns,ʃpuːr/, /'leɪbənz ,ʃpʊə/ *noun plural* **lebensspuren** /'le:bəns ,ʃpuːrən/ (also **Lebensspur**) M20 German (from *Leben* life + *Spur* trace, track). *Geology* A small track, burrow, cast, etc., left in sediment by a living organism; *especially* one preserved in fossil form in sedimentary rock, a trace fossil.

■ Usually in the plural, the term was apparently first used in German by O. Abel in 1912.

1973 *Nature* In a recently completed series of laboratory studies, lebensspuren were produced by individual macrobenthic organisms on a variety of marine sand and mud substrates ...

Lebenswelt /'le:bənsvɛlt/, /'leɪbənzvɛlt/ *noun plural* **Lebenswelten** /'le:bəns vɛltən/ M20 German. *Philosophy* All the immediate experiences, activities, and contacts that make up the world of an individual, or of a corporate, life.

■ A term particularly associated with the German philosopher E. G. A. Husserl (1859–1938), it is often translated into English as 'life-world'.

leberwurst /'leɪbəwəːst/, /'leɪbəvʊəst/ *noun* M19 German. (A) liver sausage.

lebes /'lɛbiːz/ *noun* M19 Greek (*lebēs*). *Greek Antiquities* A deep round-bottomed bowl for holding wine.

lechayim /lə'xajim/ *interjection* (also **lechaim** /lə'xʌɪm/ and other variants) M20 Hebrew (*lĕ-ḥayyīm*). (A drinking toast:) to life!

lectio difficilior /,lɛktɪəʊ dɪfɪ'kɪlɪɔː/ *noun phrase plural* **lectiones difficiliores** /lɛktɪ ,əʊneɪz dɪfɪkɪlɪ'ɔːreɪz/ M20 Latin. (Word-order variant of) DIFFICILIOR LECTIO.

lector /'lɛktɔː/ *noun* LME Latin (from *lect-* past participial stem of *legere* to read). **1** LME *Ecclesiastical* A person commissioned as, or ordained to the office of, a liturgical reader. **2** LME A person who reads; *specifically* a reader or lecturer in a college or university, now especially one in a Continental country, as Germany or France, or in a foreign country teaching his or her native language.

lectrice /lɛk'triːs/, /'lɛktriːs/ *noun* L19 French (from Latin *lectrix* feminine of Latin LECTOR). **1** L19 A woman engaged as

an attendant or companion to read aloud. **2** M20 A female lecturer.

lecythus see LEKYTHOS.

lederhosen /'leɪdəhəʊz(ə)n/ *noun plural* M20 German (from *Leder* leather + *Hosen* plural of *Hose* trouser). Leather shorts, especially as traditionally worn in Alpine regions of Bavaria etc.

legato /lɪ'gɑːtəʊ/ *adjective, adverb, & noun* M18 Italian (past participle of *legare* to bind, from Latin *ligare*). *Music* **A** *adjective & adverb* M18 (A direction:) smooth(ly) and connected(ly), with no breaks between successive notes. **B** *noun* L19 A legato style of performance; a piece or passage (to be) played legato.

legator /lɪ'geɪtə/ *noun* M17 Latin (from *legat-* past participial stem of *legare* to bequeath). A person who gives something by will, a testator.

legerdemain /,lɛdʒədə'meɪn/ *noun* LME French (*léger de main*, from *léger* light + *de* of + *main* hand). **1** LME Sleight of hand; juggling; conjuring. **2** M16 *transferred* and *figurative* Trickery, deception. **3** M16–M17 An instance of legerdemain.

leggiero /lɛ'dʒɛːrəʊ/, *foreign* /lɛd'dʒɛːro/ *adjective & adverb* (also **leggero**) L19 Italian. *Music* (A direction:) light(ly) and graceful(ly).

legionnaire /,liːdʒə'nɛː/ *noun* (also **legionaire**) E19 French (*légionnaire*, from *légion* legion). A member of a legion; *especially* (usually *Legionnaire*) a member of a named legion, as the American Legion, the Royal British Legion, or the French Foreign Legion.

legong /lɛ'gɒŋ/ *noun* E20 Indonesian. (A participant in) a stylized Balinese dance performed especially by young girls.

legume /'lɛgjuːm/ *noun* M17 French (*légume* from Latin *legumen*, from *legere* to gather: so called because the fruit may be gathered by hand). **1** M17 The fruit or edible portion of any leguminous plant (bean, pea, etc.) grown for food; any vegetable used as food. Usually in *plural*. **2** L17 A leguminous plant. **3** L18 The pod or seed-vessel of a leguminous plant.

■ The Latin word *legumen* was used earlier (LME) in English and is found, though not so commonly, in all three senses above.

Lehrjahr /'leːrjaːr/ *noun plural* **Lehrjahre** /'leːrjaːrə/ M19 German (from *lehr(en)*) teach + *Jahr* years). A year of apprenticeship or learning.

■ Usually in the plural, the word is also often used figuratively for one's apprenticeship to life. Cf. WANDERJAHR.

lei /leɪ/ *noun* 1 M19 Hawaiian. A Polynesian garland made of flowers, feathers, shells, etc., often given as a symbol of affection.

1996 *Times* The lure of the lei, that garland of welcome traditionally bestowed on visitors by bare-bosomed young hula dancers, is considerable.

lei /leɪ/ *noun* 2 E20 Chinese (*léi*). *Chinese Antiquities* An urn-shaped bronze wine-vessel of the Shang period (*c.* 250 BC).

leitmotiv /'lʌɪtməʊtiːf/ *noun* (also **leitmotif**) L19 German (from *leit-* leading + *Motiv* motive). **1** L19 *Music* A theme associated throughout a work with a particular person, situation, or sentiment. **2** L19 *generally* A recurrent idea or image in a literary work etc.

1995 *Spectator* Gray finds in Berlin's 'value pluralism' the *leitmotif* of all his writings.

lekach /'lɛkax/ *noun* M20 Yiddish. A Jewish cake traditionally made with honey.

lekane /lɛ'kɑːni/ *noun* E20 Greek (*lekanē* a bowl, a dish). *Greek Antiquities* A shallow bowl, usually with handles and a cover.

lekker /'lɛkə/ *adjective* E20 Afrikaans (from Dutch (cf. German *lecker*) related to Dutch *likken* to lick). Pleasant, sweet, nice; good, excellent.

■ South African colloquial, used as a general term of approbation.

lekythos /'liːkɪθɒs/, /'lɛkɪθɒs/ *noun plural* **lekythoi** /'liːkɪθɔɪ/ M19 Greek (*lēkuthos*). *Greek Antiquities* A vase or flask with a narrow neck.

■ Also in the Late Latin form *lecythus* (M19).

lemma /'lɛmə/ *noun plural* **lemmas, lemmata** /'lɛmətə/ L16 Latin (from Greek *lēmma*, plural *lēmmata*, something taken for granted or assumed, theme, argument, title, from base also of *lambanein* to take). **1** L16 An axiom or demonstrated proposition used in an argument or proof. **2** E17 The argument or subject of a literary work, prefixed as a heading. Also, a motto attached to a picture etc. **3** M20 A word or phrase defined in a dictionary, glossed in a glossary, entered in a wordlist, etc.

lemur /'liːmə/ *noun plural* (in sense 1) **lemures** /'lɛmjʊriːz/, (in sense 2) **lemurs**

M16 Modern Latin (from Latin *lemures* (plural) shades of the dead). **1** M16 Chiefly *Roman Mythology* In plural, the spirits of the dead, ghosts. Now occasionally *singular*, a ghost. **2** L18 *Zoology* Any mammal of the prosimian family Lemuridae, comprising long-tailed, sharp-muzzled, arboreal animals found chiefly in Madagascar. Also, any related primate, as the indri and the loris.

lentamente /lɛntə'mɛnti/ *adverb* M18 Italian (from *lento* from Latin *lentus* slow). *Music* Slowly, in slow time.

lente /'lɛnti/ *adjective* M20 Latin (= slowly). *Medicine* Of a substance, especially insulin: that is metabolized or absorbed gradually when introduced into the body.

lento /'lɛntəʊ/ *adverb & adjective* E18 Italian. **1** *adverb & adjective* E18 *Music* (A direction:) in slow time, slower than adagio. **2** *adjective* M20 Pronounced more slowly than in normal speech.

leprechaun /'lɛprəkɔːn/ *noun* E17 Irish (*leipreachán* alteration of Middle Irish *luchrupán* alteration of Old Irish *luchorpán*, from *lu* small + *corp* body). In Irish folklore, a small, usually mischievous being of human form, often associated with shoemaking or buried treasure.

lèse-majesté /lɛzmaʒɛste/ *noun* (also **lese-majesty** /liːz'madʒɪsti/) LME French (from Latin *laesa majestas* hurt or violated majesty (i.e. of the sovereign people), from *laesa* feminine past participle of *laedere* to injure, hurt, *majestas* majesty). **1** LME The insulting of a monarch or other ruler. Also, treason. **2** M17 *transferred* Presumptuous behaviour, disrespect.

■ *Lese-* or *lèse-* is also used with other French or English words in jocular imitation of *lese-majesty* or *lèse-majesté* (see quotation 1995 (2)).

1 **1995** *Times* [Wei Jingsheng] was brazen enough to write to Mr Deng and denounce him as a man 'who will be laughed at and condemned by history'. Such lèse-majesté is deeply wounding.

2 **1996** *Times* Les Enfants [du Paradis] really is one of the best movies ever made . . . So the stage version got a panning for *lèse-majesté* . . .

2 **1995** *Spectator* To suppress or control such emotions is to be guilty of absurd and psychologically unhealthy stiff-upper-lippism; it is to commit the terrible crime of *lese-psychotherapie*.

le tout /lə tu/ *adjective phrase* E20 French. The whole of, everyone in, all, (a place).

■ Frequently used in a context of making fun of social pretensions. The word(s) defined by *le tout* may be French, on the analogy of (*le*) *tout Paris* all Paris (meaning 'Parisian society') or, in jocular use, more often English (see quotations). Cf. TOUT.

1995 *Spectator* I look forward to the day when *le tout Londres* goes to a lecture once a week as a matter of course . . .
1996 *Oldie* When *Cav* and *Pag* were given by the Moldavian State Opera, *le tout* gentrified Hackney and Islington attended.

lettre /lɛtr/ *noun* plural pronounced same E18 French (from Latin *littera* letter of the alphabet, (*in plural*) epistle, document). A letter.

■ Occurs in English only in various phrases mainly designating styles of handwriting: e.g. *lettre bâtard* a kind of cursive Gothic script originating in France in the late Middle Ages (also known as *bastarda*), *lettre de forme* a kind of formal, angular handwriting on which some typefaces for early printed books were based (also known as *textura*), and *lettre de somme* a kind of rounded Gothic script originating in thirteenth-century Italy on which some typefaces for early printed books were based (also known as *rotunda*).

lettre de cachet /lɛtr də kaʃe/ *noun phrase* plural **lettres de cachet** (pronounced same) E18 French (literally, 'letter of seal'). **1** *History* In France under the *ancien régime*, a warrant for the imprisonment of a person without trial at the pleasure of the monarch. **2** An (arbitrary) official order for imprisonment, exile, etc.

lettrisme /lɛtrism/ *noun* (also in Anglicized form **lettrism** /'lɛtrɪz(ə)m/) M20 French (from as LETTRE). A movement in French art and literature characterized by a repudiation of meaning and the use of letters (sometimes invented) as isolated units.

levade /lə'vɑːd/ *noun* M20 French (from *lever* to raise). A dressage movement (superseding the *pesade*) in which the horse raises its forequarters with the forelegs drawn up, and balances on its hind legs which are placed well forward under the body and deeply bent.

levee /'lɛvi/, /'lɛveɪ/ *noun* 1 L17 French (*levé* variant of *lever* rising, use as noun of *lever* to rise). **1 a** L17 *History* A reception of visitors on rising from bed; a morning assembly held by a person of distinction. **b** M18 *History* An afternoon assembly for men only held by (a representative of) the

British monarch. **c** M18 A reception or assembly at any time of day. Now *archaic* except in *North America*. **2** The company assembled at a levee. Only in 18. **3** E18-E19 The action of rising, *specifically* from one's bed.

■ The less fashionable evening equivalent of sense 1 was the COUCHEE.

levee /'lɛvi/, /lɪ'viː/ *noun* 2 & *verb* E18 French (*levée* feminine of *levé* past participle of *lever* to raise). A *noun* **1** E18 An embankment to prevent the overflow of a river. **b** L19 *Physical Geography* A low broad ridge of sediment running alongside a river channel. Also, any similar natural embankment, as one formed by a mud flow, lava flow, or submarine current. **2** M19 A landing-place, a pier, a quay. **B** *transitive verb* M19 Raise a levee or embankment along (a river) or in (a district). Also, shut or keep *off* by means of a levee.

levée en masse /ləve ã mas/ *noun phrase* plural **levées en masse** (pronounced same) E19 French. A mass mobilization (originally in Revolutionary France) in response to the threat of invasion.

lever de rideau /ləve də rido/ *noun phrase* plural **levers de rideau** (pronounced same) M19 French (= curtain-raiser). A short opening piece before the main performance; a preliminary event.

lex domicilii /ˌlɛks dɒmɪ'sɪlɪaɪ/ *noun phrase* E19 Latin (= law of the domicile). *Law* The law of the country in which a person is domiciled, as determining the right to make a will, succeed to property, etc.

lex fori /lɛks 'fɔːraɪ/ *noun phrase* E19 Latin (= law of the court). *Law* The law of the country in which an action is brought, as regulating procedure, evidence, execution of judgements, etc.

lexis /'lɛksɪs/ *noun* M20 Greek (= a word, phrase, from *legein* to speak). **1** M20 The diction or wording, in contrast to other elements, of a piece of writing. **2** M20 *Linguistics* Items of lexical, as opposed especially to grammatical, meaning; the total word-stock of a language. Also, the branch of knowledge that deals with words as lexical items.

lex loci /lɛks 'ləʊsaɪ/ *noun phrase* L18 Latin (= law of the place). *Law* The law of the country in which some event material to a case took place.

■ Frequently followed by a defining word or phrase, as in *lex loci contractus* the law of the country in which a contract was made or *lex loci delicti* the law of the country in which an offence was committed.

lex talionis /ˌlɛks talɪ'əʊnɪs/ *noun phrase* M17 Latin (from *lex* law + *talionis* genitive of *talio(n)* recompense). The (supposed) law of retaliation; the retributive theory of punishment, based on the Mosaic principle 'an eye for an eye, a tooth for a tooth'.

li /liː/ *noun* 1 L17 Chinese (lǐ). In Neo-Confucianism: correct observance of the rules governing behaviour to others, regarded as needed to maintain a person's harmony with the moral principles of nature.

li /liː/ *noun* 2 plural same M20 Chinese (lì). *Chinese Antiquities* A bronze or pottery cooking vessel, with (usually three) hollow legs.

liaison /lɪ'eɪz(ə)n/, /lɪ'eɪzɒn/, /lɪ'eɪzɔ̃/ *noun* M17 French (from *lier* to bind, from Latin *ligare*). **1** M17 *Cookery* A binding or thickening agent for sauces, consisting chiefly of the yolks of eggs. Formerly, the process of binding or thickening. **2** E19 An intimate relation or connection; *specifically* an illicit sexual relationship, especially between a man and a married woman. **3** E19 Communication and cooperation, original *specifically* between military forces or units, especially during a battle or campaign. **4** L19 *Phonetics* The pronunciation of a normally silent final consonant before a vowel (or mute *h*) beginning the following word, especially in French.

■ In sense 2 sometimes in the phrase *liaison dangereuse* (literally, 'dangerous acquaintance'), an allusion to the brilliant and scandalous epistolary novel *Les Liaisons dangereuses* (1782) by Pierre Laclos.
1996 *Times* The Auld Alliance is the Sunday name for the long flirtation between France and Scotland which, like all *liaisons dangereuses*, has provided the spice to keep the main marriage successful.

libero /'liːbero/ *noun* plural **liberi** /'liːberi/ M20 Italian (literally, 'free'). *Soccer* A defending player positioned near the goal, a sweeper.

liberum arbitrium /ˌliːbərʊm ɑː'bɪtrɪəm/, /ˌlʌɪbərəm/ *noun phrase* M17 Latin (= free judgement, free will). Full power to decide; freedom of action.

■ A quotation from Livy's history of Rome (iv.43.5).

libido /lɪ'biːdəʊ/, /lɪ'bʌɪdəʊ/ *noun* E20 Latin (= desire, lust). *Psychoanalysis* Psychic drive or energy, *especially* that associated with the sexual instinct.
1996 *Times* Loss of libido is only one cause of failing potency. More often the spirit is willing but the mechanism has failed naturally.

libretto /lɪ'brɛtəʊ/ *noun* plural **librettos**, **libretti** /lɪ'brɛti/ M18 Italian (diminutive of *libro* book). The text of an opera or other long vocal composition.

lidia /'lidja/ *noun* L19 Spanish (literally, 'fight'). A bullfight, especially the earlier stages in which the CUADRILLA prepares the bull for the FAENA.

lidiador /ˌlidja'dor/ *noun* plural **lidiadores** /ˌlidja'dores/ L19 Spanish. A bullfighter.

lido /'liːdəʊ/, /'lʌɪdəʊ/ *noun* plural **lidos** L17 Italian (= shore, beach, from Latin *litus*). A bathing beach; a resort; a public open-air swimming pool.

■ Originally specifically *the Lido*, a bathing beach near Venice.

lié /lje/, /'liːeɪ/ *predicative adjective* M19 French (past participle of *lier* to bind). Connected (*with*), intimately acquainted (*with*).

liebchen /'liːpçən/, /'liːtʃ(ə)n/ *noun* (also **Liebchen**) L19 German. A person who is very dear to another; a sweetheart, a pet, a darling.

■ Frequently used as a term of endearment.

Liebestod /'liːbəstoːt/ *noun* (also **liebestod**) L19 German (literally, 'love's death'). An aria or a duet in an opera etc. proclaiming the suicide of lovers; such a suicide.

liebling /'liːplɪŋ/, /'liːblɪŋ/ *noun* (also **Liebling**) M19 German. A sweetheart. Cf. LIEBCHEN.

lied /liːd/, /liːt/ *noun* plural **lieder** /'liːdə/ (also **Lied**) M19 German. A song; *especially* a song characteristic of the German Romantic period, usually for solo voice with piano accompaniment.

lien /liːn/, /'liːn/, /'lʌɪən/ *noun* M16 French (from Old French *loien* from Latin *ligamen* bond, from *ligare* to tie). *Law* A right to retain possession of property belonging to another person until a debt due by that person is discharged.

■ Often in the expression *have a lien on* (*something*), used both literally and figuratively.

lierne /lɪ'ɜːn/ *noun* LME French (perhaps transferred use of *lierne* clematis, dialectal variant of *liane*). *Architecture* A short rib connecting the bosses and intersections of vaulting-ribs.

lieu /lju:/, /lu:/ *noun* ME French (from Latin *locus* place). Place, stead.
■ Only in *in lieu* 'in the place, instead, (of)'.

lignum vitae /ˌlɪɡnəm 'vaɪtiː/, /'viːtaɪ/ *noun* L16 Latin (= wood of life). GUAIACUM (senses 1–3).

limaçon /'lɪməsɒn/ *noun* (also **limacon**) L16 French (= snail shell, spiral staircase, etc., from Old and modern French *limace* from Latin *limax, limac-* slug, snail). **1** A kind of spiral military manoeuvre. Only in L16. **2** L19 *Mathematics* A type of heart-shaped curve.

limbo /'lɪmbəʊ/ *noun* plural **limbos** LME Latin (ablative singular of *limbus* edge, border (in medieval Latin, border of Hell), in phrases like *in limbo, e* (= out of) *limbo*). **1** LME *Christian Church* A region supposed in some beliefs to exist on the border of Hell as the abode of the just who died before Christ's coming and of unbaptized infants. **b** L16–M17 Hell, Hades. **2** L16 Prison, confinement. *slang.* **3** M17 An unfavourable place or condition, likened to limbo; *especially* a condition of neglect or oblivion to which people or things are consigned when regarded as superseded, useless, or absurd; an intermediate or indeterminate condition; a state of inaction or inattention pending some future event.

limes /'laɪmiːz/ *noun* plural **limites** /'laɪmɪtiːz/ M16 Latin (= limit). Now *Archaeology* A boundary; *specifically* the boundary of the Roman Empire, especially in the north of Europe.

linctus /'lɪŋktəs/ *noun* L17 Medieval Latin ((classical Latin = licking, from *lingere* to lick), after late Latin *electuarium* electuary). A syrupy liquid medicine, now *especially* a soothing cough mixture.

linga /'lɪŋɡə/ *noun* (also **lingam** /'lɪŋɡam/) E18 Sanskrit (*liṅga* sign, (sexual) characteristic; variant influenced by Tamil *iliṅkam*). A Hindu sacred object constituting

a symbol of the god Siva, *specifically* (the representation of) a phallus.

ling chih /'lɪŋ dʒə/ *noun phrase* E20 Chinese (*língzhī* (Wade–Giles ling chih), from ling divine + zhī fungus). A motif on Chinese ceramic ware, especially a representation of the fungus *Polyporus lucidus*, symbolizing longevity or immortality.

lingerie /'lãʒ(ə)ri/, *foreign* /lɛ̃ʒri/ *noun* M19 French (from *linge* linen). Originally, linen articles collectively; all the articles of linen, lace, etc., in a woman's wardrobe or trousseau. Now, women's underwear and nightclothes.

lingoa geral variant of LINGUA GERAL.

lingua franca /ˌlɪŋɡwə 'fraŋkə/ *noun phrase* plural **lingua francas, lingue franche** /ˌlɪŋɡwɪ 'fraŋki/ L17 Italian (= Frankish tongue). A mixture of Italian with French, Greek, Arabic, Turkish, and Spanish, used in the Levant (now *historical*). Also, any language serving as a medium between different nations etc. whose own languages are not the same; a system of communication providing mutual understanding.
■ 'Frank', in many local variants, was the word generally used by the inhabitants of the eastern Mediterranean region for a person of western or northern European origin—not only a Frenchman.

lingua geral /ˌlɪŋɡwə dʒə'rɑːl/ *noun phrase* (also **lingoa geral**) M19 Portuguese (*língua geral* general language). A trade language based on Tupi and used as a LINGUA FRANCA in Brazil.

lingue franche plural of LINGUA FRANCA.

linguine /lɪŋ'ɡwiːni/ *noun plural* M20 Italian (plural of *linguina* diminutive of *lingua* tongue, from Latin). Pasta in the form of tongue-shaped ribbons; an Italian dish consisting largely of this and usually a sauce.

Linzertorte /'lɪntsərtɔːtə/, /'lɪntsətɔːtə/ *noun plural* **Linzertorten** /'lɪntsərtɔːt(ə)n/ E20 German (from *Linzer* adjective of the Austrian city Linz + *Torte* tart, pastry, cake). A kind of pastry with a jam filling, decorated on top with strips of pastry in a lattice pattern.

liqueur /lɪ'kjʊə/ *noun* M18 French (= liquor). **1** M18 Any of various strong sweet alcoholic spirits flavoured with aromatic substances, usually drunk after a meal.

Also, a glass of such a drink. **2** E20 *elliptically* A liqueur-glass; a liqueur chocolate.

lisse /li:s/ *(plural same) noun & adjective* M19 French (= smooth (in *crêpe lisse*)). (Of) a kind of silk or cotton gauze.

lissoir /'li:swa:/, *foreign* /liswar/ *(plural same) noun* E20 French (from *lisser* to smooth). *Archaeology* A smoothing, polishing tool.

literae humaniores /ˌlɪtərʌɪ hjuːˌmanɪ 'ɔːriːz/ *noun phrase* (also **litterae humaniores**) M18 Latin (= more humane letters). The humanities, secular learning as opposed to divinity; *especially* at Oxford University, the school or subject of Greek and Roman classical literature, philosophy, and ancient history.

▪ Abbreviated as *lit. hum.*

litera scripta /ˌlɪtərə 'skrɪptə/ *noun phrase* M19 Latin. The written word.

literati /lɪtə'rɑːtiː/ *noun plural* E17 Latin (*lit-(t)erati* plural of *lit(t)eratus* literate). Men of letters; the learned class as a whole.

  1996 *Spectator* . . . much of his [sc. Larbaud's] best writing is taken up with the subject of getting away from France, a variant on the theme currently much canvassed by American campus literati under the label 'otherness'.

literatim /lɪtə'reɪtɪm/, /lɪtə'rɑːtɪm/ *adverb* M17 Medieval Latin (*lit(t)eratim*, from *lit-(t)era* letter, after *gradatim* step by step; cf. VERBATIM). Letter for letter; literally.

literato /lɪtə'rɑːtəʊ/ *noun singular* (corresponding plural LITERATI) E18 Italian (*litterato* (now usually *letterati*) from as Latin *lit(t)eratus* literate). A member of the literati; a man of letters.

litotes /lʌɪ'təʊtiːz/ *noun* L16 Late Latin (from Greek *litotēs*, from *litos* single, simple, meagre). *Rhetoric* Ironical understatement, *specifically* in which an affirmative is expressed by the negative of the contrary.

▪ Examples of this figure of speech are 'no small amount' and 'no mean feat'. It is also called, less commonly, MEIOSIS.

litterae humaniores variant of LITERAE HUMANIORES.

littérateur /ˌlɪtərɑː'tə:/, *foreign* /literatœr/ *(plural same) noun* E19 French (from Latin *litterator*). A writer of literary or critical works, a literary person.

litzendraht /'lɪtsəndrɑːt/ *noun* E20 German (from *Litze* braid, cord, lace, strand + *Draht* wire). Wire composed of many fine strands twisted together and individually insulated.

▪ Also partially translated as Litz wire.

livraison /livrɛzɔ̃/ *noun plural* pronounced same E19 French (from Latin *liberatio(n-)* liberation). A part, number, or fascicle of a work published by instalments.

livre de chevet /livrə də ʃəvɛ/ *noun phrase* plural **livres de chevet** (pronounced same) E20 French (literally, 'book of the bed-head'). A bedside book; a favourite book.

  1958 L. Durrell *Mountolive* It was Darley . . . who introduced me to the current Alexandrian *livre de chevet* which is a French novel called *Moeurs*.

livre de circonstance /livrə də sirkɔ̃stɑ̃s/ *noun phrase* plural **livres de circonstance** (pronounced same) M20 French. A book composed or adapted for the occasion.

  1957 C. Vereker *Development of Political Theory* Begun as a *livre de circonstance*, Hooker's great work raised most of the abiding problems of political authority.

llanero /(l)ja'nero/, /lja:'nɛːrəʊ/ *noun* plural **llaneros** E19 South American Spanish (from next). An inhabitant of a llano.

llano /'(l)jano/, /'lja:nəʊ/ *noun plural* **llanos** E17 Spanish (from Latin *planum* level ground). A level treeless plain in the south-western United States and the northern parts of South America.

loa /'ləʊə/ *noun plural same*, **loas** M20 Haitian (creole *lwa*, from Yoruba *oluwa* lord, owner). A god in the voodoo cult of Haiti.

lobo /'ləʊbəʊ/ *noun plural* **lobos** M19 Spanish (from Latin *lupus* wolf). A large grey wolf of the south-western United States. Also called *loafer (wolf)*.

lobola /lə'bəʊlə/ *noun* (also **lobolo** /lə 'bəʊləʊ/) M19 Bantu (cf. Xhosa *lobola* to give a bride-price). The bride-price, usually in cattle, given by many Black grooms in southern Africa to the parent or guardian of the bride; the custom of paying such a bride-price.

locale /ləʊ'kɑːl/ *noun* (also **local**) L18 French (*local* (noun), respelt to indicate stress; cf. MORALE). A place, a locality, especially with reference to some event or circumstances connected with it; a venue.

loc. cit. /ˌlɒk ˈsɪt/ *adverb phrase* M19 Latin (abbreviation of Latin *loco citato* or *locus citatus* (in) the place cited). In the book etc. that has previously been quoted, in the passage already cited.

loch /lɒk/, /lɒx/ *noun* LME Gaelic. In Scotland: a lake; (more fully *sea loch*) an arm of the sea, especially when narrow or partially land-locked.

loci classici, loci desperati etc. plurals of LOCUS CLASSICUS, LOCUS DESPERATUS, etc.

loco /ˈləʊkəʊ/ *noun & adjective* L19 Spanish (= insane). **A** *noun* plural **loco(e)s**. **1** L19 Any of several leguminous plants (chiefly species of *Astragalus*) found in the western and south-western United States which cause loco disease when eaten by cattle, horses, etc. **2** L19 Loco disease.

loco citato see LOC. CIT.

locoum variant of LOKUM.

locum /ˈləʊkəm/ *noun* 1 E20 Latin (abbreviation of medieval Latin *locum tenens* from Latin *locum* accusative of *locus* place + *tenens* present participle of *tenere* to hold). **1** E20 A person (especially a physician or priest) who undertakes the professional duties of someone else or stands in for someone else during his or her absence. **2** E20 The situation of a locum; a post as a locum.
■ *Locum tenens*, now entirely superseded in everyday English usage, antedated *locum* in both sense 1 (from M17) and sense 2 (from L19).

locum noun 2 variant of LOKUM.

locus /ˈləʊkəs/, /ˈlɒkəs/ *noun* plural **loci** /ˈləʊsʌɪ/, /ˈlɒkiː/ E18 Latin (= place). **1** E18 A place, a site; a position, a point, especially in a text. **b** E20 *Genetics* A position on a chromosome at which a particular gene is located; a gene. **2** E18 *Mathematics* The curve or other figure composed of all the points which satisfy a particular equation or are generated by a point, line, or surface moving in accordance with defined conditions. **3** M18 A subject, a topic. **4** E20 LOCUS STANDI.

locus citatus see LOC. CIT.

locus classicus /ˌləʊkəs ˈklasɪkəs/, /ˌlɒkəs/ *noun phrase* plural **loci classici** /ˌləʊsʌɪ ˈklasɪsʌɪ/, /ˌlɒki: ˈklasɪkiː/ M19 Latin (= classical place). A passage regarded as the principal authority on a subject or the origin of a quotation or saying; the best-known occurrence of an idea or theme.
1996 *Times* You would certainly not suspect from this . . . production . . . that Strindberg's preface to *Miss Julie* is a *locus classicus* of naturalist theory.

locus desperatus /ˌləʊkəs dɛspəˈreɪtəs/, /ˌlɒkəs dɛspəˈrɑːtəs/ *noun phrase* plural **loci desperati** /ˌləʊsʌɪ dɛspəˈreɪtʌɪ/, /ˌlɒkiː dɛspəˈrɑːtiː/ E20 Latin (= hopeless place). A corrupt manuscript reading that defies interpretation.
1969 R. Renehan *Greek Textual Criticism* The textual critic . . . must decide in each case whether the original reading . . . has been or can be recovered by modern conjecture or whether the passage is a *locus desperatus*.

locus poenitentiae /ˌləʊkəs piːnɪˈtɛnʃiː/, /ˌlɒkəs piːnɪˈtɛnʃɪʌɪ/ *noun phrase* plural **loci poenitentiae** /ˌləʊsʌɪ piːnɪˈtɛnʃiː/, /ˌlɒkiː piːnɪˈtɛnʃɪʌɪ/ M18 Latin (= place of penitence). A place of repentance; *Law* an opportunity for a person to withdraw from a commitment or contract, especially an illegal one, so long as some particular step has not been taken.

locus standi /ˌləʊkəs ˈstandʌɪ/, /ˌlɒkəs ˈstandiː/ *noun phrase* plural **loci standi** /ˌləʊsʌɪ ˈstandʌɪ/, /ˌlɒkiː ˈstandiː/ E19 Latin (= place of standing). A recognized or identifiable status, especially in law; the right to be heard in a court of law.
1974 *Times* The power of the Department [sc. of Trade and Industry] should of course be discretionary but the Panel should be given a *locus standi* with the Department.

loden /ˈləʊd(ə)n/ *noun & adjective* (also **Loden**) E20 German. **A** *noun* **1** E20 A heavy waterproof woollen cloth. **2** M20 A coat or cloak made of this. **3** M20 A dark green colour in which the cloth is often made. **B** *adjective* E20 Made of this cloth.

loess /ˈləʊɪs/, /ˈləːs/ *noun* M19 German (*Löss* from Swiss German *lösch* loose, from *lösen* to loosen). *Geology* A fine yellowish-grey loam composed of material transported by the wind during and after the glacial period which forms extensive deposits from north central Europe to eastern China, in the American Midwest, and elsewhere.

loge /lɔʒ/ (plural same), /ləʊʒ/ *noun* M18 French. **1 a** M18 A booth, a stall. **b** M20 A concierge's lodge. **2** M18 A box in a theatre, opera-house, etc.

loggia /'ləʊdʒə/, /'lɒdʒə/, /'ləʊdʒɪə/ noun M18 Italian (= lodge). **1** M18 A gallery or arcade having one or both of its sides open to the air. **2** E20 An open-sided extension to a house, a veranda.

Logos /'lɒgɒs/ noun L16 Greek (= account, relation, ratio, reason(ing), argument, discourse, saying, speech, word, related to *legein* to choose, collect, gather, say). **1** L16 *Philosophy* and *Christian Theology* The Word of God, the second person of the Trinity. **2** M17 A pervading cosmic idea or spirit of creativity or rationality.

■ Used in a mystic sense by Hellenistic and Neoplatonist philosophers, *Logos* entered Christian discourse primarily through its use in the opening passage of St John's Gospel.

Lohan /'ləʊhɑːn/ noun M19 Chinese (*luóhàn* (Wade–Giles *Lo-han*)). An ARHAT.

lokoum variant of LOKUM.

lokshen /'lɒkʃ(ə)n/ noun plural L19 Yiddish (plural of *loksh* noodle). Noodles (in Jewish cookery).

lokum /lɒ'kuːm/ noun (also **lokoum, loc(o)um, lakum** /lə'kuːm/) E20 Turkish (abbreviation of Turkish RAHAT *lokum*). Turkish delight.

loma /'ləʊmə/ noun M19 Spanish (from *lomo* back, loin, ridge). In the south-western United States: a broad-topped hill or ridge.

longeron /'lɒndʒərɒn/ noun E20 French. *Aeronautics* A frame member running lengthways along a fuselage.

longo intervallo /ˌlɒŋgəʊ ɪntə'valəʊ/ adverb phrase L17 Latin (= at a distance). At some remove; in spite of the gulf between.

■ Virgil uses the phrase in the spatial sense (*Aeneid* v.320), but other Roman writers (e.g. Cicero) also used it in the temporal sense 'after a long time'.

1935 J. C. Masterman *Fate Cannot Harm Me* I remember asking him once . . . who were his literary idols among the moderns.'Well,' he said, 'Max Beerbohm of course . . . and then, but *longo intervallo* P. G. Wodehouse.'

longueur /lɔ̃gœr/ (plural same), /lɒ̃(ŋ)'gəː/ noun L18 French (= length). A lengthy or tedious passage of writing, music, etc.; a tedious stretch of time.

1995 *Spectator* Looking back, *The Name of the Rose* bears up pretty well, although the

longueurs seem much more like inexperience in pacing a novel than an engaging, wacky academic wanting to share an odd bit of information with the reader.

loofah /'luːfə/ noun (also **luffa** /'lʌfə/) L19 Arabic (*lūfa* the plant, *lūf* the species). A coarse sponge made from the bleached vascular system of the fruit of a tropical gourd, *Luffa aegyptiaca*, used to cleanse and scrub the skin. Also, the gourd itself.

loquitur /'lɒkwɪtə/ intransitive verb M19 Latin (3rd person singular present of *loquor* to speak). Speaks.

■ Used with the speaker's name added, as a stage-direction or to inform a reader. Abbreviated as *loq*.

lorgnette /lɔːn'jɛt/, foreign /lɔrɲɛt/ (plural same) noun E19 French (from *lorgner* to squint, ogle). *singular* and in *plural* A pair of eyeglasses to be held in the hand, usually by a long handle. Also, a pair of opera-glasses.

■ *Lorgnon(s)* (M19), meaning 'a single eyeglass' as well as the above, is rather less common.

louche /luʃ/, /luːʃ/ adjective E19 French (= cross-eyed, squinting). Not straightforward. Now usually, dubious, shifty, disreputable.

1996 *Times* Enter that figure so beloved of late-Victorian dramatists, the siren with the louche past.

loup /lu/ noun plural pronounced same. M18 French (= wolf, from Latin *lupus*). **1** M18 The sea-bass, *Dicentrachus labrax*, found off the western European coast and in the Mediterranean. **2** M19 A light mask or half-mask for a woman's face.

■ In sense 2 the word was known earlier (L17) in the form *loo* or more fully *loomask*.

loup-garou /'luːgəruː/ noun L16 French (from *loup* wolf + *garou* (from Old High German antecedent of Middle High German *werwolf*) werewolf). A werewolf.

luau /'luːaʊ/ noun M19 Hawaiian (*lū'au*). A Hawaiian party or feast usually accompanied by some form of entertainment.

lucus a non lucendo /ˌluːkʊs ɑ nɒn luːˈkendəʊ/, /ˌl(j)uːkʊs eɪ nɒnl(j)uːˈsendəʊ/ noun phrase E18 Latin (literally, 'a grove from its not shining', i.e. *lucus* (a grove) is derived from *lucere* (to shine) because there is no light there). A paradoxical or otherwise absurd derivation; something of which the qualities are the opposite of what its name suggests.

■ Also abbreviated *lucus a non*. The phrase is discussed by the Roman rhetorician Quintilian in his *Institutio Oratoria* (i.6.34).

1958 R. Liddell *Morea* Was its name Hydraea (watery), a *lucus a non lucendo*—it is singularly waterless today.

ludo /'luːdəʊ/, /'ljuːdəʊ/ *noun* L19 Latin (= I play). A simple board game played with dice and counters.

lues /'luːiːz/, /'ljuːiːz/ *noun* M17 Latin (= plague). Syphilis (also more fully *lues venerea* /vəˈnɪərɪə/). Formerly also, a plague, a pestilence.

■ *Lues* also appears in a modern Latin phrase apparently coined by Macaulay who in 1834 wrote in the *Edinburgh Review* of the *Lues Boswellianae* or 'disease of admiration' that tends to afflict biographers writing uncritically about their subjects—as James Boswell did in his life of Dr Johnson.

luffa variant of LOOFAH.

luftmensch /'lʊftmɛnʃ/ *noun* (also **luftmensh**) plural **luftmens(c)hen** /'lʊft mɛnʃ(ə)n/ E20 Yiddish (*luftmensh*, from *luft* (German *Luft*) air + *mensh* (German *Mensch*) person). An impractical visionary.

1966 *New Society* Americans, children of the soil, have become traders in air, advertising men, *luftmenschen*.

luge /luːʒ/ *verb & noun* L19 Swiss French. **A** *intransitive verb* L19 Toboggan; ride or race on a luge. **B** *noun* E20 A light toboggan for one or two people usually ridden in a supine position; the sport in which these are raced.

lulav /'luːlɑːv/, /'lʊləv/ *noun* (also **lulab**) plural **lulavs**, **lulavim** /'luːlɑːvɪm/ L19 Hebrew (*lūlāḇ* branch). A palm branch traditionally carried at the Jewish festival of Succoth.

lumbago /lʌmˈbeɪɡəʊ/ *noun* L17 Latin (*lumbago*, *lumbagino*, from *lumbus* loin). Rheumatic pain in the lower muscles of the back.

lumen siccum /ˌluːmɛn ˈsɪkəm/, /ˌljuːmɛn ˈsɪkəm/ *noun phrase* E17 Latin (literally, 'dry light'). The objective light of rational knowledge or thought.

■ Francis Bacon characterized rational knowledge as *lumen siccum* in 1605 in his *Advancement of Learning* (II.f.48), and the metaphor has been in intermittent use, especially among English philosophers, since then.

lumpenproletariat /ˌlʌmpənprəʊlɪ ˈtɛːrɪət/ *noun derogatory* E20 German (from *Lumpen* rag + PROLETARIAT). The poorest and least cohesive section of the proletariat, making no contribution to the workers' cause; the ignorantly contented lower orders of society uninterested in revolutionary advancement. *derogatory*.

■ Originally used by Karl Marx in *Die Klassenkämpfe in Frankreich* (1850).

1995 *Times* Which is preferable, to patronise 'ordinary people' with string quartets, or exploit them, treat them as a lumpenproletariat and ensure that they remain lumpen by depriving them of anything better?

lundum /'lʊndəm/ *noun* M20 Portuguese. A simple Portuguese song and dance originating from Africa, probably one of the sources from which the FADO developed.

lunette /luːˈnɛt/, /ljuːˈnɛt/ *noun* L16 French (diminutive of *lune* moon, from Latin *luna*). **1** L16 *Farriery* A semicircular horseshoe for the front of the hoof only. Also *lunette-shoe*. **2** E17 *Architecture* **a** An arched aperture in a concave ceiling for the admission of light. **b** E18 A crescent-shaped or semicircular space in a ceiling, dome, etc., decorated with paintings or sculptures; a piece of decoration filling such a space. **3** M17 A blinker for a horse. **4** L17 In *plural* Spectacles. Now *rare*. **5** E18 *Fortification* A work larger than a redan, consisting of two faces forming a salient angle and two flanks. **6** L18 The figure or shape of a crescent moon. **7** M19 A watch-glass of flattened shape. Also *lunette (watch-)glass*. **8** M19 In the guillotine, the circular hole which receives the neck of the victim. **9** M19 Any of the flues connecting a glass furnace and its arch. (Earlier in the form *linnet-hole*.) **10** M19 A crescent-shaped ornament. **11** L19 A ring or forked plate to or by which a field-gun carriage or other vehicle for towing is attached. **12** L19 *Roman Catholic Church* A circular case, fitting into an aperture in a monstrance, for holding the consecrated host. **13** M20 *Physical Geography* A broad shallow mound of wind-blown material along the leeward side of a lake or dry lake basin, especially in arid parts of Australia, and typically crescent-shaped with the concave edge along the lake shore.

lunula /'luːnjʊlə/ *noun* plural **lunulae** /'luːnjʊliː/ L16 Latin (diminutive of *luna* moon). **1** L16 *Geometry* A figure formed on a plane by arcs of two circles intersecting at two points, a lune. **2** E18 *Archaeology* A gold crescent-shaped neck ornament of the early Bronze Age. **3** E19 *Anatomy, Zoology,* and *Botany* A crescent-shaped mark or spot, *specifically* the pale area at the base of a fingernail, a lunule. **b** M19 *Anatomy* A crescent-shaped region of thin tissue on each side of the nodule on each cusp of a valve in the heart or aorta. **4** M19 *Conchology* The crescent-shaped depression in front of the umbo of a shell, a lunule.

lupara /luˈpɑːra/, /luːˈpɑːrə/ *noun* M20 Italian ((slang), from *lupa* she-wolf). A sawn-off shotgun as used by the Mafia.

lustrum /ˈlʌstrəm/ *noun* plural **lustra** /ˈlʌstrə/, **lustrums** L16 Latin (originally, a purificatory sacrifice after a quinquennial census, later also, a period of five years: ultimate origin unknown). A period of five years.

lusus /ˈluːsəs/, /ˈljuːsəs/ *noun* plural same /ˈluːsuːs/, **lususes** E17 Latin (*lusus naturae* a sport of nature). A freak of nature, an abnormal formation, a natural curiosity. In full *lusus naturae* /nəˈtjʊəriː/, /nə ˈtjʊərʌɪ/.

luthier /ˈluːtɪə/, /ˈljuːtɪə/ *noun* L19 French (from *luth* lute). A maker of stringed instruments, *specifically* of the violin family.

luxe /lʌks/, /lʊks/ *noun* M16 French (from Latin *luxus* luxury). (A) luxury. Cf. DE LUXE.

lycée /lise/ (*plural same*), /ˈliːseɪ/ *noun* M19 French (from Latin LYCEUM). A State secondary school in France.

Lyceum /lʌɪˈsiːəm/ *noun* L16 Latin (from Greek *Lukeion* (sc. *gumnasion* gymnasium) neuter of *Lukeios* epithet of Apollo (from whose neighbouring temple the Lyceum was named)). **1** L16 The garden at Athens in which Aristotle taught his philosophy; Aristotelian philosophy and its adherents. **2** E19 A LYCÉE. **3** E19 *United States History* (**lyceum**) An institution in which popular lectures were delivered on literary and scientific subjects. **4** L19 *Theatre* A theatre near the Strand in London, England. Used *attributively* to denote a melodramatic performance or style, formerly characteristic of this theatre.

Lyonnais /liːəˈneɪ/, *foreign* /ljɔnɛ/ *adjective* (feminine **Lyonnaise** /liːəˈneɪz/, *foreign* /ljɔnɛz/) E19 French (from *Lyon* the name of a city in south-east France). Of, pertaining to, or characteristic of the city of Lyons (Lyon) or the former province of Lyonnais, in France; *specifically* (*Lyonnaise*) in *Cookery*, designating food, especially sliced potatoes, cooked with onions or with white wine and onion sauce.

M

maar /mɑ:/ *noun* plural **maars, maare** /'mɑ:rə/ E19 **German** (dialect). **1** E19 (Usually **Maar**) A crater-lake in the Eifel district of Germany. **2** L19 *Geology* A broad low-rimmed usually lake-filled volcanic crater of a kind exemplified by the Eifel Maars.

maas /mɑ:s/ *noun* (also in Zulu form **amasi** /ə'mɑ:si/) E19 **Afrikaans** (from Zulu (plural) *amasi* curdled milk). In South Africa: thick sour milk.

mabele /mə'bi:li/ *noun* E19 **Bantu** (cf. Zulu, Xhosa *ibele*, plural *amabele*). In South Africa: kaffir corn, *Sorghum bicolor* var. *caffrorum*; meal or porridge made from this.

macabre /mə'kɑ:br(ə)/, *foreign* /makabr/ *adjective* M19 **French** (Old French *macabré* adjective (modern *macabre*), perhaps alteration of *Macabé* Maccabaeus, Maccabee, with reference to a miracle play containing the slaughter of the Maccabees). Grim, gruesome.

■ In early use perhaps regarded as a proper name and introduced into English as a noun; the earliest (LME) instance of the phrase *daunce of Machabree* is in the title of one of Lydgate's works, but this usage has long been obsolete. The modern adjectival sense likewise originated in the phrase *dance macabre*, an Anglicized version of the French DANSE MACABRE. The deaths of seven Jewish brothers and their mother, tortured to death for their religion under Hellenistic rule in the second century BC, are narrated in the Apocrypha (2 Maccabees 7); the Western Christian Church honoured them as martyrs, with a feast day celebrated on 1 August.

macaroni /makə'rəʊni/ *noun* plural **macaronies** L16 **Italian** (*mac(c)aroni*, later *maccheroni*, plural of *mac(c)arone*, *maccherone* from late Greek *makaria* barley food). **1** L16 Pasta in the form of tubes. **2** M18 A fop, a dandy. *obsolete except historical*. **3** E19 *History* A West Indian coin worth a quarter of a dollar or (later) one shilling. **4** M19 In full *macaroni penguin*. A penguin, *Eudyptes chrysolophus*, apparently so called from its orange crest. **5** M19 An Italian. *slang*. *derogatory*. **6** E20 Nonsense, meaningless talk. *slang* (chiefly *Australian*).

macchia /'mɑ:kɪə/ *noun* E20 **Corsican Italian** (from Latin *macula* spot). **1** E20 MAQUIS vegetation. **2** *Art* In painting, a fleck or touch of paint. (See quotation.)

2 1988 K. Adler *Unknown Impressionists* The Macchiaioli were so named because of the extensive use they made of 'macchia' (or, in French, the 'tache'), the patch or touch which was seen in France in the 1860s to be a distinguishing feature of anti-academic painting.

macédoine /'masɪdwɑ:n/ *noun* E19 **French** (from *Macédoine* Macedonia, with reference to the diversity of peoples in the empire of Alexander the Great, King of Macedon). Mixed fruit or vegetables cut up into small pieces; *figurative* a medley, a mixture.

machair /'makə, 'maxə/ *noun* L17 **Gaelic**. In Scotland: a flat or low-lying coastal strip of arable or grassland; land of this nature.

1996 *Country Life* Stand with your back to the sea on South Uist, where the most spectacular machair is to be found, and look inland across the vast, fenceless expanses . . .

mâche /mɑ:ʃ/ *noun* L17 **French**. Lamb's lettuce, corn-salad.

■ Originally Anglicized (only in plural) in the now obsolete form of *maches*.

macher /'maxə/ *noun* M20 **Yiddish** (from German = maker, doer). A man of importance, a bigwig; a braggart. *United States*, frequently *derogatory*.

machete /mə'tʃɛti/, /mə'ʃɛti/ *noun* (also **matchet** /'matʃɪt/ and other variants) L16 **Spanish** (from *macho* hammer, from Latin *marcus*). A broad and heavy knife or cutlass, used, especially in Central America and the West Indies, as a tool or a weapon.

■ *Machete* has gained general currency in English in the twentieth century, superseding the Anglicized *matchet* and the other variants.

machismo /mə'tʃɪzməʊ/, /mə'kɪzməʊ/ *noun* M20 **Mexican Spanish** (from as MACHO). The quality of being macho; male virility, masculine pride; a show of this.

1996 *Times* Spanish Man seems to have changed as well, at a pace remarkable for a society which was once so steeped in machismo.

macho /'matʃəʊ/ *noun & adjective* E20 **Mexican Spanish** (= male animal or plant, (as adjective) masculine, vigorous). **A** *noun* plural **machos** **1** E20 A man; *specifically* an assertively vigorous man. **2** M20 MACHISMO. **B** *adjective* Ostentatiously masculine, virile.

■ Originally United States.

B 1996 *Times* There is no merit in adopting a macho attitude regardless of its efficacy.

Macht-politik /'maxtpɔlɪˌtiːk/ *noun* E20 **German** (from *Macht* power, strength + *Politik* policy, politics). Power politics; strength as a potential factor to use in gaining a desired result.

macramé /mə'krɑːmi/ *noun & adjective* M19 **Turkish** (*makrama* handkerchief, tablecloth, towel from Arabic *miḵrama* bedcover, bedspread). **A** *noun* M19 A fringe, trimming, or lace of knotted thread or cord; knotted-work; the art of making this. **B** *attributive* or as *adjective* L19 Made of or by macramé.

macro /'makrəʊ/ *noun & adjective* M20 **Greek** (*makro-* combining form of *makros* large, long). **A** *noun* plural **macros**. **1** M20 *Computing* A macro-instruction. **2** M20 *Photography* Macrophotography; a macro lens. **B** *adjective* M20 Macroscopic, large-scale; overall, comprehensive; *Chemistry* of macroanalysis; *Photography* pertaining to or used in macrophotography.

■ An independent use of the combining form found in numerous English words derived from Greek, particularly in scientific terminology; cf. MEGA. *Macro* is frequently contrasted, either explicitly or implicitly, with MICRO.

macron /'makrɒn/ *noun* M19 **Greek** (*makron* neuter of *makros* long). A straight horizontal line (ˉ) written or printed over a vowel to indicate length or stress.

macula /'makjʊlə/ *noun* plural **maculae** /'makjʊliː/, **maculas** LME **Latin**. **1** LME Chiefly *Science* A spot, a stain; *Medicine* a permanent spot or stain in the skin. **2** M19 *Anatomy* Any of various structures which have the appearance of a spot.

■ The French word *macule* deriving from *macula* was also found in English in sense 1 (from L15).

Madame /madam/, /mə'dɑːm/, /'madəm/ *noun* (also **madame**, **madam**) plural **Mesdames** /medam/, /mɛ'dam/, /mer'dam/ ME **Old French**. **I 1** ME Madam, my lady. **II 2 a** M16 Used as a title (preceding the surname) of or as a respectful form of address to a French married woman or (more widely) a married woman of any non-British nationality (corresponding to English *Mrs*, *Lady*, etc.), or in literal renderings of French speech. **b** L16 *French History* (A title of) a female member of the French royal family, *specifically* the eldest daughter of the French king or the dauphin (cf. MADEMOISELLE 3). **c** M19 Used as a title (preceding a name) by a businesswoman, fortune-teller, etc., especially to imply skill and sophistication, or foreign origin. **3** L16–M18 A woman usually addressed or referred to as 'Madame'; a French married woman; a Frenchman's wife.

■ As a title, usually abbreviated to *Mme*. The plural *Mesdames* (abbreviation *Mmes*) is also used as the plural of *Mrs*. The usual Anglicized version *madam* has also been current since the Middle Ages and is most generally used as a respectful form of address to a woman, although it has also evolved some derogatory associations (e.g. 'a spoilt or affected woman' (L16), 'a female brothel-keeper' (L19)).

madeleine /'madlem/ *noun* M19 **French** (probably from *Madeleine* Paulmier, nineteenth-century French pastry-cook). A (kind of) small rich cake, in French cookery baked in a fluted tin, and in English cookery usually baked in a dariole mould and decorated with coconut and jam.

Mademoiselle /madmwazɛl/, /ˌmadəm wə'zɛl/ *noun* (also **mademoiselle**) plural **Mesdemoiselles** /medmwazɛl/, /ˌmɛdm wa'zɛl/, /ˌmeɪdəmwə'zɛl/, **Mademoiselles** /madmwazɛl/, /ˌmadəmwə'zɛlz/ LME **Old French**. **1** LME Used as a title (preceding a name) of or as a respectful form of address to an unmarried Frenchwoman or (more widely) an unmarried woman of any non-British nationality (corresponding to English *Miss*), or in literal renderings of French speech. Also used as a respectful form of address to a French governess or a female French teacher in an English-speaking school. **2** M17 A woman usually addressed or referred to as 'Mademoiselle'; an unmarried Frenchwoman; a French governess. **3** L17 *French History* (A title of) the eldest daughter of the eldest brother (known as '*Monsieur*') of the French king. Later, (a title of) the French king's eldest daughter or (if he had no daughter) the unmarried princess most closely related to him (cf. MADAME 2b). **4** L19 A croaker (fish), *Bairdiella chrysoura*, of the southern United States. Also called *silver perch, yellowtail*. *United States*.

■ As a title, usually abbreviated to *Mlle*.

madérisé /maderize/ *adjective* M20 French (past participle of *madériser*). Of wine: affected with the brown discoloration that afflicts white wines that have been stored too long or under unsuitable conditions.

Madonna /məˈdɒnə/ *noun* (also **madonna**) L16 Italian (from *ma* old unstressed form of *mia* my (from Latin *mea*) + *donna* lady (from Latin *domina*)). **1 a** L16 Used as a respectful form of address to an Italian woman, or in literal renderings of Italian speech. **b** E17 An Italian woman. *rare.* **2** M17 The or the Virgin Mary; a picture or statue of the Virgin Mary. **3** M19 A hairstyle in which the hair is parted in the centre and arranged smoothly on either side of the face, as in certain Italian representations of the Virgin Mary. More fully *Madonna braid*.

madrasah /məˈdrasə/ *noun* (also **medresseh** /mɛˈdrɛseɪ/ and other variants) M17 Arabian (*madrasa*, noun of place from *darasa* to study). A Muslim college.

madrigal /ˈmadrɪɡ(ə)l/ *noun* L16 Italian (from medieval Latin *matricalis* mother: cf. medieval Latin *ecclesia matrix* mother church). **1** L16 A short lyrical love poem. **2** L16 *Music* A part-song for several voices, specifically one of a sixteenth- or seventeenth-century Italian style, arranged in elaborate counterpoint, and sung without instrumental accompaniment. Also, a fourteenth-century Italian pastoral song of several stanzas. **3** L16 *generally* A song, a ditty.

madrilene /madrɪˈliːn/, /madrɪˈlɛn/ *noun* E20 French ((*consommé à la*) *madrilène*, of or pertaining to Madrid). A clear soup usually served cold.

maelstrom /ˈmeɪlstrəm/ *noun* L17 Early Modern Dutch ((now *maalstroom*), from *maalen* to grind, whirl round + *stroom* stream whence the Scandinavian forms (e.g. Swedish *malström*, Danish *malstrøm*). **1** L17 A great whirlpool, originally one in the Arctic Ocean off the west coast of Norway, formerly supposed to suck in and destroy all vessels that ventured near it. **2** M19 *figurative* A state of turbulence or confusion.

maestoso /mʌɪˈstəʊsəʊ/ *adverb, adjective, & noun* E18 Italian (= majestic, from *maestà* from Latin *majestas, majestatis* majesty). *Music* **A** *adverb & adjective* E18 (A direction:) majestic(ally). **B** *noun* plural **maestosos** L19 A majestic piece or movement.

maestrale /mʌɪˈstrɑːleɪ/ *noun* M18 Italian (from Latin *magistralis* (sc. *ventus* wind) from *magister* master; cf. MISTRAL). Any of several mainly north-westerly winds which blow in the Mediterranean, especially a summer wind in the Adriatic, and a winter wind, milder than a mistral, in the west.

maestria /mʌɪˈstriːə/ *noun* L19 Italian (from Latin *magisterium*, from *magister* master). Skill, mastery.

maestro /ˈmʌɪstrəʊ/, *foreign* /maˈɛstro/ *noun* plural **maestri** /ˈmʌɪstri/, *foreign* /maˈɛstri/, **maestros** E18 Italian (from Latin *magister* master). **1 a** E18 An expert in music; a great musical composer, teacher, or conductor. **b** M20 *transferred* A great performer or leader in any art, profession, etc. **2** E20 The MAESTRALE.

> **1.a** 1996 *Spectator* I had some reservations about Bernard Haitink's conducting—unusually for him (normally the most cushioning of maestros) he seemed at times to be pushing too hard . . .

Mafia /ˈmafɪə/ *noun* (also **mafia, maffia**) M19 Italian ((Sicilian) = bragging, specifically hostility towards the law and its upholders, frequently as manifested in vindictive crimes). **1** M19 *the Mafia*, an organized secret society of criminals, originating in Sicily but now operating internationally, especially in the United States. **2** M20 *generally* Any group regarded as exerting a secret and often sinister influence.

> **2** 1995 *Private Eye* Crofton himself is now in trouble with the council's race relations mafia having accused a black colleague . . . of failing to deal with these allegations.

Mafioso /mafɪˈəʊsəʊ/ *noun* plural **Mafiosi** /mafɪˈəʊsi/, **Mafiosa** feminine **Mafiosa** /mafɪˈəʊsə/ (also **mafioso, maffioso**) L19 Italian (from as MAFIA). A member or supporter of the Mafia or a mafia.

> 1996 *Times: Weekend* Adams's new thriller . . . is heavily laced with all the paraphernalia of the genre in the new world order, including post-Soviet Russian female mafiosi, a few mad generals . . .

Magen David /mɑːˌɡɛn dɑːˈviːd/ *noun phrase* E20 Hebrew (literally, 'shield of David' (king of Israel from *c.*1000 BC)). The Star of David, a six-pointed figure consisting of two interlaced equilateral triangles, used as a Jewish and Israeli symbol.

magi plural of MAGUS.

magma /'magmə/ *noun* LME Latin (from Greek, from base of *massein* to knead). **1** LME–M19 The dregs remaining after a semi-liquid substance has been pressed or evaporated. **2** L17 A mixture of mineral or organic substances having the consistency of paste. Now *rare*. **3** M19 *Geology* A hot fluid or semifluid material beneath the crust of the earth or other planet, from which igneous rocks are formed by cooling and which erupts as lava.

Magna Carta /ˌmagnə 'kɑːtə/ *noun phrase* (also **Magna Charta**) L15 Medieval Latin (literally, 'great charter'). The charter of English personal and political liberty obtained from King John in 1215; *transferred* any similar document establishing rights.

magna cum laude /ˌmagnə kʌm 'lɔːdiː/, /ˌmagnə: kʊm 'laʊdeɪ/ *adverb & adjective phrase* L19 Latin (literally, 'with great praise'). With or of great distinction; *specifically* (of a degree, diploma, etc.) of a higher standard than the average (though not the highest). ■ Chiefly North American; cf. CUM LAUDE, SUMMA CUM LAUDE.

magna mater /ˌmagnə 'meɪtə/, /ˌmɑːtə/ *noun phrase* plural **magnae matres** /ˌmagni: 'meɪtriːz/, /ˌmagnʌɪ 'mɑːtreɪz/ E18 Latin (literally, 'great mother'). A mother-goddess; a fertility goddess.

magna opera see MAGNUM OPUS.

magnificat /mag'nɪfɪkat/ *noun* ME Latin (2nd person singular present indicative of *magnificare* to magnify. **1** ME (the *Magnificat*) A canticle forming part of the Christian liturgy at evensong and vespers, and comprising the hymn of the Virgin Mary in Luke 1:46–55 (in the Vulgate beginning *Magnificat anima mea Dominum*). Also, the music to which this is set. **2** E17 *transferred* A song of praise.

magnifico /mag'nɪfɪkəʊ/ *noun* plural **magnifico(e)s** L16 Italian ((adjective) = magnificent). A magnate (originally a Venetian one); a grandee.

magnum /'magnəm/ *noun & adjective* L18 Latin (use as noun of neuter singular of *magnus* large). **A** *noun* **1** L18 A bottle for wine, spirits, etc., twice the standard size, now usually containing 1.5 litres; the quantity of liquor held by such a bottle. **2** M20 (Also *Magnum*) A Magnum revolver or cartridge (see sense **B** below). **3** M20 *Zoology* The section of a bird's oviduct which secretes albumen. **B** *attributively*

or as *adjective* **1** M20 (Also *Magnum*) Of a cartridge: adapted so as to be more powerful than its calibre suggests. Of a gun: designed to fire such cartridges. **2** L20 Large, oversized. ■ In the United States, senses A.2 and B.1 are proprietary names. **B.2** 1996 *New Scientist* All this, and much more, Lord Justice Scott relates in his magnum Arms-to-Iraq report published last month.

magnum opus /ˌmagnəm 'əʊpəs/, /'ɒpəs/ *noun phrase* (also **opus magnum**) plural **magnum opuses**, **magna opera** /ˌmagnə 'əʊpərə/, /ˌmagnə 'ɒpərə/ L18 Latin (= great work). A great and usually large work of art, literature, etc.; *specifically* the most important work of an artist, writer, etc.

magus /'meɪgəs/ *noun* (also **Magus**) plural **magi** /'meɪdʒʌɪ/ ME Latin (from Greek *magos* from Old Persian *maguš*). **1** ME *History* A member of an ancient Persian priestly caste; *transferred* a magician, a sorcerer. **2** LME *the* (*three*) *Magi*, the three 'wise men' from the East who brought gifts to the infant Jesus (Matthew 2:1), a representation of these.

maharaja /ˌmɑː(h)ə'rɑːdʒə/, /ˌməhɑː'rɑːdʒə/ *noun* (also **maharajah**, **maharaj** /ˌmɑː(h)ə 'rɑːdʒ/, **Maharaja**) L17 Sanskrit (*mahārājā*, from *mahā* great + *rājān* RAJA). (The title of) an Indian prince of high rank.

maharani /ˌmɑː(h)ə'rɑːni/, /ˌməhɑː'rɑːni:/ *noun* (also **maharanee**, **Maharani**) M19 Hindustani (*mahārānī*, from Sanskrit *mahā* great + *rājñī* RANEE). (The title of) the wife or widow of a maharaja.

maharishi /ˌmɑː(h)ə'rɪʃi/ *noun* (also **Maharishi**) L18 Sanskrit (alteration of Sanskrit *maharṣi*, from *mahā* great + *r̥ṣi* holy man). (The title of) a Hindu sage; *generally* (the title of) a popular leader of spiritual thought. Cf. GURU.

mahatma /mə'hatmə/, /mə'hɑːtmə/ *noun* L19 Sanskrit *mahātman*, from *mahā* great + *ātman* soul). **1** L19 In the Esoteric Buddhism of members of the Theosophical Society: any of a class of people with preternatural powers, supposed to exist in the Indian subcontinent and Tibet; *transferred* a sage, an adept. **2** M20 (*Mahatma*) In the Indian subcontinent: (the title of) a revered person regarded with love and respect.

Mahdi /'mɑːdi/ *noun* E19 Arabic ((al-)*mahdī*, literally, 'he who is rightly guided', from passive participle of *hadā* to lead on the right way, guide aright). In Muslim belief:

the restorer of religion and justice who will rule before the end of the world; a claimant of this title.

■ The *Mahdi* best known to history was Muhammad Ahmad of Dongola in Sudan who proclaimed himself such in 1881 and launched a political and revolutionary movement which overthrew the Turco-Egyptian regime.

mah-jong /mɑ:'dʒɒŋ/ *noun* (also **mah-jongg**) E20 Chinese (dialect *ma jiang* sparrows). A game (originally Chinese) for four, played with 136 or 144 pieces called tiles, divided into five or six suits.

maillot /majo/ *noun* plural pronounced same L19 French. **1** L19 Tights. **2** E20 A tight-fitting, usually one-piece, swimsuit. **3** M20 A jersey, a top.

maiolica variant of MAJOLICA.

maison /mɛzɔ̃/ *noun* plural pronounced same M16 French. In France and French-speaking countries: a house; now usually a business (especially a fashion) house or firm.

■ See phrases below and PÂTÉ MAISON.

maison clos /mɛzɔ̃ kloz/ *noun phrase* M20 French (literally, 'closed house'). A brothel.

> **1939** E. Ambler *Mask of Dimitrios* Your *maison close* must have proved disappointing. The inevitable Armenian girls, of course.

maison de couture /mɛzɔ̃ də kutyr/ *noun phrase* E20 French. A fashion house.

> **1970** S. J. Perelman *Baby, it's Cold Inside* The rigors of squiring her through a score of *maisons de couture*, jewelers, and millinery shops were . . . unimaginable.

maison de passe /mɛzɔ̃ də pas/ *noun phrase* (also **maison-de-passe**) M20 French (literally, 'house of passage'). A house to which prostitutes can take clients.

> **1960** B. Marshall *Divided Lady* The hotel we drew up at eventually reminded me of a *maison-de-passe* I used to know in Barcelona.

maison de santé /mɛzɔ̃ də sɑ̃te/ *noun phrase* M19 French (literally, 'house of health'). A nursing home, *especially* one for the mentally ill.

> **1942** A. Bridge *Frontier Passage* We don't want him shut up in a *maison de santé* for spy mania.

maisonette /meɪzə'nɛt/ *noun* L18 French (*maisonnette* diminutive of *maison* house). **1** L18 A small house. **2** E20 A part of a residential building which is occupied separately, usually on more than one floor.

maison tolérée /mɛzɔ̃ tɔlere/ *noun phrase* L19 French (literally, 'tolerated house'). A licensed brothel.

> **1970** K. Chesney *Victorian Underworld* Conditioned by her existence in a *maison tolérée*, . . . she was very much in the hands of the bawd to whom she was consigned.

maître /mɛ:tr(ə)/ *noun* plural pronounced same L19 French (literally, 'master'). The title of or form of address to a French lawyer.

■ Also with the sense of 'instructor' in the phrases MAÎTRE D'ARMES and MAÎTRE DE BALLET; see also CHER MAÎTRE, MAÎTRE D'HÔTEL.

maître d' /mɛtr(ə) də/; /ˌmeɪtrə 'də/, /'di:/ *noun phrase* (also **maître de**, /'də/) plural **maîtres d'**, **maîtres de**, (pronounced same) L19 French (colloquial abbreviation of MAÎTRE D'HÔTEL). The manager of a hotel dining-room or restaurant, a head waiter.

> **1996** *Times* [Flowers] conducted with small, effete waves of his baton, like the maître d' of an upmarket restaurant waving his clients towards their table.

maître d'armes /mɛtr(ə) darm/ *noun phrase* L19 French (literally, 'master of arms'). A fencing instructor.

maître de ballet /mɛtr(ə) də balɛ/ *noun phrase* E19 French. *Ballet* Originally, the composer of a ballet who superintended its production and performance; now, a trainer of ballet dancers.

maître d'hôtel /mɛtr(ə) dotɛl/, /ˌmeɪtrə dəʊ'tɛl/ *noun phrase* plural **maîtres d'hôtel** (pronounced same) M16 French (literally, 'master of house'). **1** M16 A major-domo, a steward, a butler. **2** L19 A hotel manager. Now usually the manager of a hotel dining-room or restaurant, a head waiter.

maîtres d', **maîtres d'armes**, etc. plurals of MAÎTRE D', MAÎTRE D'ARMES, etc.

maîtresse en titre /mɛtrɛs ɑ̃ titr/ *noun phrase* (also **maîtresse-en-titre**, **maitresse en titre**) plural **maîtresses en titre** (pronounced same) M19 French (literally, 'mistress in name'). An official or acknowledged mistress.

> **1973** D. Chandler *Marlborough* Arabella [Churchill] was . . . combining the roles of maid-of-honour to the Duchess and *maîtresse-en-titre* to the Duke, to whom she bore several children.

maîtresse femme /mɛtrɛs fam/ *noun phrase* M19 French. A strong-willed or domineering woman.

1973 E. Hyams *Final Agenda* The widow was a *maîtresse femme* whose place in the hierarchy was three steps higher than that of her . . . husband.

maja /'maxa/ *noun* M19 Spanish. In Spain and Spanish-speaking countries: a woman who dresses gaily.

■ Best known in English in the titles of two of Goya's paintings, the *Naked Maja* and the *Clothed Maja*. The equivalent male term *majo* (M19) is less common.

Majlis /madʒ'lɪs/ *noun* (also **majlis**) E19 Arabic (= place of session, from *jalasa* to be seated). An assembly for discussion, a council; *specifically* the Parliament of any of various North African or Middle Eastern countries, especially Iran. Also, a reception room.

majolica /mə'jɒlɪkə/, /mə'dʒɒlɪkə/ *noun &* *adjective* (also **maiolica** /mə'jɒlɪkə/) M16 Italian (from the former name of the island of Majorca). **A** *noun* M16 A fine kind of Renaissance Italian earthenware with coloured decoration on an opaque white glaze; any of various other kinds of glazed Italian ware. Also, a modern imitation of this. **B** *attributive* or as *adjective* M19 Made of majolica.

majuscule /'madʒəskju:l/ *adjective &* *noun* E18 French (from Latin *majuscula* (*littera*) diminutive of *major* major). **A** *adjective* **1** E18 *Typography* Of a letter: capital. *rare*. **2** M19 *Palaeography* Of a letter: large (whether capital or uncial); pertaining to, of, or written in large lettering; designating or pertaining to a script having every letter bounded by the same two (imaginary) lines. **B** *noun* **1** E19 *Typography* A capital letter. *rare*. **2** M19 *Palaeography* A large letter, whether capital or uncial; (a manuscript in) large lettering or majuscule script.

makai /mə'kʌɪ/ *adverb &* *adjective* M20 Hawaiian (from *ma* toward + *kai* the sea). In Hawaii: in the direction of the sea, seaward.

makimono /makɪ'mono/, /makɪ'məʊnəʊ/ *noun* plural same, **makimonos** L19 Japanese (= something rolled up, a scroll). A Japanese scroll containing a narrative, usually in pictures with explanatory writing, designed to be examined progressively from right to left as it is unrolled. Cf. EMAKIMONO.

malade imaginaire /malad imaʒinɛr/ *noun phrase* plural **malades imaginaires** (pronounced same) E19 French. A person with an imaginary illness.

■ After the title of a play by Molière (1673).

maladif /maladif/ *adjective* M19 French (from *malade* sick, ill, from Proto-Romance, from Latin *male* badly + *habitus*, past participle of *habere* to have, hold). Sickly.

maladresse /maladrɛs/, /malə'drɛs/ *noun* E19 French (from *mal-* bad, ill + *adresse* skill, dexterity). Lack of dexterity or tact; awkwardness.

maladroit /'malədrɔɪt/ *adjective* L17 French (from *mal-* bad(ly) + *adroit* skilful). Lacking in adroitness or dexterity; awkward, bungling, clumsy.

1996 *Spectator* He has tried to introduce a sense of fun, though sometimes the tone is childishly maladroit . . .

mala fide /ˌmeɪlə 'fʌɪdi:/, /ˌmalə 'fi:deɪ/ *adverb &* *adjective phrase* E17 Latin (= with bad faith (ablative of next)). (Acting or done) in bad faith; insincere(ly), not genuine(ly).

mala fides /ˌmeɪlə 'fʌɪdi:z/, /ˌmalə 'fi:deɪz/ *noun phrase* L17 Latin (= bad faith). Chiefly *Law* Bad faith, intent to deceive.

mala in se plural of MALUM IN SE.

malaise /ma'leɪz/ *noun* M18 French (from Old French *mal* bad, ill (from Latin *malus*) + *aise* ease). A condition of bodily discomfort, *especially* one without the development of specific disease; a feeling of uneasiness. Frequently *figurative*.

1996 *Country Life* In his opening analysis of the Grecian malaise he describes how their cause is ruined by 'so many factions' . . .

malapropos /ˌmalaprə'pəʊ/ *adverb, adjective, &* *noun* (also **mal-à-propos** and other variants) M17 French (*mal à propos*, from *mal* ill + *à* to + *propos* purpose). **A** *adverb* M17 In an inopportune or awkward manner; at an inopportune or awkward time; inappropriately. **B** *adjective* E18 Inopportune, inappropriate. **C** *noun* M19 An inopportune or inappropriate thing.

malaria /mə'lɛːrɪə/ *noun* M18 Italian (*mal' aria = mala aria* bad air). Originally, an unwholesome condition of the atmosphere in hot countries due to the exhalations of marshes, to which fevers were ascribed. Now (also *malaria fever*), any of a class of intermittent and remittent febrile diseases formerly supposed to result from this cause, but now known to be due to infection with parasitic protozoans of the genus *Plasmodium*, transmitted by the bite of a mosquito of the genus *Anopheles*.

mal de mer /mal də mɛr/ *noun phrase* L18 French. Seasickness.

mal du siècle /mal dy sjɛkl/ *noun phrase* E20 French. World-weariness, weariness of life, deep melancholy because of the condition of the world.

malebolge /malɪˈbɒlʤeɪ/, *foreign* /male ˈbɒlʤe/ *noun* M19 Italian (*Malebolge*, from *male* feminine plural of *malo* evil + *bolge* plural of *bolgia* literally 'sack, bag'). A pool of filth; a hellish place or condition.

■ In literary use only. Malebolge was the name given in Dante's *Inferno* to the eighth circle in hell, consisting of ten rock-bound concentric circular trenches (see especially Canto xviii).

maleesh /ˈmɑːliːʃ/ *interjection & noun* E20 Arabic (colloquial) (*mā ʿalē-š* never mind). **A** *interjection* E20 No matter! never mind! **B** *noun* M20 Indifference, slackness.

mal élevé /mal el(ə)ve/ *adjective phrase* (feminine **mal élevée**) L19 French (= badly brought up). Bad-mannered, ill-bred.

mal-entendu /malãtãdy/ *adjective & noun* E17 French (from *mal* ill + *entendu* past participle of *entendre* to hear, understand). **A** *adjective* Mistaken, misapprehended. Only in E17. **B** *noun* (plural pronounced same) L18 A misunderstanding.

malerisch /ˈmɑːlərɪʃ/ *adjective* M20 German (= painterly, from *Maler* painter). (Of painting) characterized more by the merging of colours than by a formal linear style; painterly.

■ A term used by Heinrich Wölfflin in his *Kunstgeschichtliche Grundbegriffe* (1915). **1955** *Times* This is . . . a resuscitation of the great malerisch tradition, which was rejected by those who thought they were following Cézanne.

malgré /malgre/ *preposition* E16 French. In spite of, notwithstanding.

mallee /ˈmaliː/ *noun* M19 Aboriginal. Any of various low-growing eucalypts which have many slender stems rising from a large underground stock; scrub or thicket formed by such trees, typical of some arid parts of Australia.

malpais /ˌmalpɑːˈiːs/ *noun* M19 Spanish (from *malo* bad + *país* country, region). Rugged or difficult country of volcanic origin. United States.

malum in se /ˌmaləm m ˈsiː/, /ˈseɪ/ *noun & adjective phrase* plural of noun **mala in se**

/ˈmalə/ E17 Medieval Latin (= bad in itself). (A thing) intrinsically evil or wicked. *especially in legal contexts.*

mal vu /mal vy/ *adjective phrase* E20 French (literally, 'badly seen'). Held in low esteem, looked down on.
1958 L. Durrell *Mountolive* He is . . . rather an old-fashioned reactionary in his outlook, and is consequently rather *mal vu* by his brother craftsmen.

mamaloi /ˈmam(ə)lwɑː/ *noun* plural **mamalois**, same L19 Haitian (creole *mamalwa*, from *mama* mother + *lwa* LOA). A voodoo priestess. Cf. PAPALOI.

mama-san /ˈmaməsan/ *noun* plural **mama-sans**, same M20 Japanese (from *mama* mother + SAN). In Japan and the Far East: a woman in a position of authority, *specifically* one in charge of a geisha-house; the mistress of a bar.

mambo /ˈmambəʊ/ *noun* plural **mambos** M20 American Spanish (probably from Haitian creole, from Yoruba, literally, 'to talk'). **1** M20 A kind of rumba, a ballroom dance of Latin American origin; a piece of music for this dance. **2** M20 A voodoo priestess.

mamzer /ˈmʌmzə/ *noun* (also **momser**, **momzer**, /ˈmɒmzə/) plural **mamzerim** /ˈmʌmzərɪm/, **mamzers** M16 Late Latin (from Hebrew *mamzēr*). A person conceived in a forbidden sexual union, especially as defined by rabbinical tradition.

■ In contemporary colloquial speech often used, like 'bastard', as a term of abuse or familiarity.

mana /ˈmɑːnə/ *noun* M19 Maori. Power, authority, prestige; *Anthropology* an impersonal supernatural power which can be associated with people or with objects and which can be transmitted or inherited.

■ Originally New Zealand. **1995** D. Lodge *Therapy* Actresses and production assistants and publicity girls and secretaries—all susceptible to the *mana* of a successful writer.

mañana /maˈɲana/, /manˈjɑːnə/ *adverb & noun* M19 Spanish (= morning, tomorrow (in this sense from Old Spanish *cras mañana*, literally, 'tomorrow early') ultimately from Latin *mane* in the morning). Tomorrow, (on) the day after today; (in) the indefinite future (from the supposed easy-going procrastination of Spain and Spanish-speaking countries).
1995 *Oldie* And . . . of course the damage would be paid for . . . *mañana*.

mancala /man'kɑːlə/ *noun* M19 Arabic ((colloquial) *mankala*, from *nakala* to remove, take away). A board game for two players, originally Arabic but now common throughout Africa and Asia, played on a special board with rows of holes or hollows.

mancando /man'kando/, /man'kandəʊ/ *adjective & adverb* E19 Italian (= lacking, failing). *Music* (A direction:) becoming even softer, dying away.

mandala /'mandələ/, /'mʌndələ/ *noun* M19 Sanskrit (*mándala* disc, circle). A symbolic circular figure, usually with symmetrical divisions and figures of deities, etc., in the centre, used in Buddhism and other religions as a representation of the universe; *Jungian Psychology* an archetype of a similar circle, held to symbolize a striving for unity of self and completeness.

mandat /mãda/ (*plural same*), /'mandat/ *noun* M19 French (from Latin *mandatum* use as noun of neuter past participle of *mandare* to command, enjoin, entrust, from *manus* hand). **1** M19 *History* A paper money issued by the revolutionary government of France from 1796 to 1797. **2** L19 In France: a money order.
> 1939 E. Ambler *Mask of Dimitrios* I received here a letter from him enclosing a *mandat* for the three thousand francs.

mandolin /'mandəlɪn/ *noun* (also (the usual form in sense 2) **mandoline**) E18 French (*mandoline* from Italian *mandolino* diminutive of *mandola*). **1** E18 A musical instrument of the lute kind having from four to six paired metal strings stretched on a deeply-rounded body, usually played with a plectrum. **2** M20 A kitchen utensil fitted with cutting blades and used for slicing vegetables.

mandorla /man'dɔːlə/ *noun* L19 Italian (= almond). An almond-shaped panel or decorative space in religious art.

manège /ma'neɪʒ/ *noun* (also **manege**) M17 French (from Italian *maneggio* from *maneggiare* from Proto-Romance from Latin *manus* hand). **1** M17 A riding-school. **2** L18 The movements in which a horse is trained in a riding-school; the art or practice of training and managing horses; horsemanship.

manes /'mɑːneɪz/, /'meɪmiːz/ *noun* LME Latin. **1** LME *plural* The deified souls of dead ancestors (as beneficent spirits). **2** L17 *singular* The spirit or shade of a dead person, considered as an object of reverence or as demanding to be propitiated.

manga /'maŋgə/ *noun* 1 E19 Spanish (literally, 'sleeve', from Latin *manica*). A Mexican and Spanish-American cloak or poncho.

manga /'maŋgə/ *noun* 2 L20 Japanese. A Japanese comic book or strip.
> 1996 *Independent* The biggest trend, though, is the continual advance of the Japanese manga, and lately, the first co-operations between Japanese publishers and western artists.

mange-tout /'mãʒtuː/, /mãʒ'tuː/ *noun* plural same, **mange-touts** (pronounced same) E19 French (literally, 'eat-all'). A variety of pea of which the pods are eaten whole with the seeds they contain. Also *mange-tout pea*. Also called *sugar pea* or *sugar snap*.

manicotti /manɪ'kɒti/ *noun plural* M20 Italian (plural of *manicotto* sleeve, muff). Large tubular pasta shells; an Italian dish consisting largely of these and usually a sauce.

maniéré /manjere/ *adjective* M18 French. Affected or characterized by mannerism, mannered.

manière criblée /manjɛr krible/ *noun phrase* E20 French. CRIBLÉ engraving.

manifesto /manɪ'fɛstəʊ/ *noun* plural **manifestos**, **manifestoes** M17 Italian (from *manifestare* to show, display, from Latin *manifestus* from *manus* hand + *-festus* struck). A public declaration or proclamation; *especially* a printed declaration or explanation of policy (past, present, or future) issued by a monarch, State, political party or candidate, or any other individual or body of individuals of public relevance.

manna /'manə/ *noun* OE Late Latin (from Hellenistic Greek from Aramaic *mannā* from Hebrew *mān* corresponding to Arabic *mann* exudation of the tamarisk *Tamarix mannifera*). **I 1** OE The edible substance described as miraculously supplied to the Israelites in the wilderness (Exodus 16). **2** ME Spiritual nourishment, *especially* the Eucharist; something beneficial provided unexpectedly (frequently *manna from heaven*). **II 3** LME A sweet hardened flaky exudation obtained from the manna-ash and used as a mild laxative. Also, a similar exudation from other plants and certain insects. **4** LME-M18 (A grain of) frankincense. **5** L17-E18 *Chemistry* A fine white precipitate. **6** L18 The seeds of the floating sweet-grass, *Glyceria* *fluitans*, used as food. In full *Polish manna*.

mannequin /'manɪkɪn/, /'manɪkwɪn/ *noun* M18 French (from Dutch *manneken* diminutive of *man* man). **1** M18 A model of a human figure; an artist's lay figure; a dummy for the display of clothes etc. **2** E20 A woman (or occasionally a man) employed by a dressmaker, costumier, etc., to display clothes by wearing them; a model.

mano /'mano/, /'mɑːnəʊ/ *noun* plural **manos** /'manos/, /'mɑːnəʊz/ E20 Spanish (= hand). *Anthropology* A primitive handheld stone implement, used in the Americas for grinding cereals etc.

mano a mano /ˌmɑːnəʊ ə 'mɑːnəʊ/ *foreign* /ˌmano a 'mano/ *adjective, adverb, & noun phrase* (also **mano-a-mano**) L20 Spanish (= hand to hand). **A** *adjective & adverb phrase* L20 Hand to hand; one to one; face to face. **B** *noun phrase* L20 A confrontation, a duel.

manoir /manwɑr/ *noun* plural pronounced same M19 French. A French manor-house; a country house built in the style of a French manor-house.

manqué /mãke/, /'mɒŋkeɪ/ *adjective* (feminine **manquée**) L18 French (past participial adjective of *manquer* to lack). **1** *postpositive* L18 That might have been but is not, that has missed being. **2** *predicative* L18 Defective, spoilt, missing, lacking.

> **1 1996** *Times Magazine* The subway genius is probably . . . a writer manqué, since many of his chosen citations deal with creating literature.

manso /'manso/ *noun & adjective* plural **mansos** /'mansos/ M19 Spanish. (A person who or animal which is) meek, tame, or cowardly.

■ Especially in the context of bullfighting.

manta /'mantə/ *noun* L17 Spanish (= blanket). **1** L17 In Spain and Spanish-speaking countries: a wrap, a cloak. **2** M18 A very large tropical ray of the genus *Manta* or the family Mobulidae. More fully *manta ray*. Also called *devilfish*.

mantelletta /mantɪ'lɛtə/ *noun* plural **mantellettas**, **mantellette** /mantɪ'lɛti/ M19 Italian (probably from medieval Latin *mantelletum* from Latin *mantellum* mantle). *Roman Catholic Church* A sleeveless vestment reaching to the knees, worn by cardinals, bishops, and other high-ranking ecclesiastics.

mantilla /man'tɪlə/ *noun* E18 Spanish (diminutive of *manta* mantle). **1** E18 A light scarf, frequently of black lace, worn over the head and shoulders, especially by Spanish women. **2** M19 A small cape or mantle.

mantra /'mantrə/ *noun* (also (*rare*) **mantram** /'mantrəm/) L18 Sanskrit (literally, 'thought', from *man* to think). A sacred Hindu text or passage, *especially* one from the Vedas used as a prayer or incantation; in Hinduism and Buddhism, a holy name or word, for inward meditation; *transferred* and *figurative* a repeated phrase or sentence, a formula, a refrain.

> **1995** *Spectator* The Princess 'just wants to be happy'. She wants everyone to be happy. We know this because she has said it time and time again, like a mantra.

manyatta /man'jatə/ *noun* E20 Masai. Among certain African peoples, especially the Masai: a group of huts forming a unit within a common fence.

manzanilla /manzə'nɪlə/, /manzə'niːljə/; *foreign* /manθa'ni(l)ja/, /mansa'ni(l)ja/ *noun* M19 Spanish (literally, 'camomile'). **1** M19 A kind of pale very dry sherry; a drink or glass of this. **2** E20 A variety of olive, distinguished by small thinskinned fruit.

maquereau /makro/ *noun* plural **maquereaux** /makro/ L19 French (literally, 'mackerel'). A pimp.

■ Colloquial, also used as a term of abuse.

> **1971** D. Wallis *Bad Luck Girl* No girl . . . goes on ship these days. They . . . lead you to some place where her *maquer[e]au* can slug you.

maquette /ma'kɛt/ *noun* E20 French (from Italian *macchietta* speck, diminutive of *macchia* spot, from *macchiare* to spot, from Latin *maculare* to stain). A small preliminary sketch or wax or clay model from which a sculpture is elaborated.

maquiladora /ˌmakila'dora/ *noun* L20 Mexican Spanish (from *maquilar* to assemble). A factory in Mexico run by a foreign company and exporting its products to the country of that company.

> *attributive* **1996** M. Anderson *Frontiers* The 1965 maquiladora programme to attract US industry into the frontier region of Mexico explicitly stated that in northern Mexico US firms would face both lower labour costs and less exacting health and environmental regulations.

maquillage /makijaʒ/ noun L19 French (from *maquiller* to make up one's face, from Old French *masquiller* to stain, alteration of *mascurer* to darken). Make-up, cosmetics; the application of this.
> **1959** R. Graves *Collected Poems* Confirming hazardous relationships By kindly maquillage of Truth's pale lips.

maquillé /makije/ adjective (feminine **maquillée**) E20 French. Wearing cosmetics, made up.

maquis /'mɑːkiː/ noun plural same M19 French (from as MACCHIA). **1** M19 The dense scrub characteristic of certain Mediterranean coastal regions, especially in Corsica. **2** M20 *History* (usually **Maquis**) A member of the French resistance movement during the German occupation (1940–5). **b** M20 A member of any resistance group or army.
> ■ The maquis scrub was the traditional hiding place for fugitives, hence the connection between senses 1 and 2.

maquisard /ˌmɑːkiːˈsɑː/ noun M20 French. A member of the Maquis.

marabou /'marəbuː/ noun & adjective (also **maribou** /'marɪbuː/, **marabout**) E19 French (from Arabic *murābit* holy man (see next), the stork being regarded as holy). **A** noun **1** E19 A tropical African stork, *Leptoptilus crumeniferus*. Also *marabou stork*. **2** E19 A tuft of soft white down from the wings or tail of this stork, used for trimming hats etc.; *collectively* trimming made of this down. **3** M19 An exceptionally white kind of raw silk which can be dyed without first removing the natural gum and is used in crêpe weaving. **B** adjective E19 Made of marabou.

marabout /'marəbuːt/ noun E17 French (from Portuguese *marabuto* from Arabic *murābit*, from *ribāṭ* frontier station, where merit could be acquired by combat against the infidel). **1** E17 A Muslim holy man or mystic, especially in North Africa. **2** M19 A shrine marking the burial place of a marabout.

maraca /məˈrakə/ noun (also **maracca**) E17 Portuguese (*maracá* from Tupi *maráka*). A Latin American percussion instrument made from a hollow gourd or gourd-shaped container filled with beans etc., and usually shaken in pairs. Usually in *plural*.

maranatha /marəˈnaθə/ adverb, noun, & interjection (also **Maranatha**) LME Greek (from Aramaic *māran 'tā* our Lord has come, or *māranā tā* O Lord, come). **A** adverb LME In translations of 1 Corinthians 16:22: at the coming of the Lord. **B** noun M17 (By a misunderstanding of 1 Corinthians 16:22:) a portentously intensified anathema; a terrible curse. More fully *anathema maranatha*. **C** interjection L19 In the early Church: expressing a deep longing for the coming of the Lord.

maraschino /marəˈskiːnəʊ/, /marəˈʃiːnəʊ/ noun plural **maraschinos** L18 Italian. A strong sweet red liqueur distilled from the marasca cherry.
> *figurative* **1995** *Times* God, what would those of us cursed with wen and crow's-foot and blackhead and the maraschino mappings of bust capillaries not give for the secrets of Douglas's posset-pot!

marc /mɑːk/ noun E17 French (from *marcher* to walk (originally, to tread, trample, ultimately from late Latin *marcus* hammer)). **1** E17 The refuse of processed grapes etc. **2** M19 A brandy made from this. Also *marc brandy*.

marcato /mɑːˈkɑːtəʊ/ adverb & adjective M19 Italian (past participle of *marcare* to mark, accent, of Germanic origin). *Music* (With each note) emphasized.

Märchen /'mɛːrçən/ noun plural same (also **märchen**) L19 German (= fairy tale from Middle High German *merechyn* short verse narrative, from Middle High German *mære* (Old High German *mārī*) news, famous, ultimately from Germanic). A folk-tale, a fairy tale.

marcottage /mɑːkʊˈtɑːʒ/, /mɑːˈkʊtɪdʒ/ noun E20 French (= layering). *Horticulture* A method of propagating plants in which an incision is made below a joint or node and covered with a thick layer of moss etc., into which new roots grow.

Mardi gras /ˌmɑːdɪ ˈgrɑː/ noun phrase L17 French (literally, 'fat Tuesday'). Shrove Tuesday, celebrated in some Roman Catholic countries with a carnival; the last day of a carnival etc., especially in France; *Australia* a carnival or fair at any time.

maréchaussée /mareʃose/ noun (also **Maréchaussée**) plural pronounced same L18 French (from Old French *mareschaucie*). *History* A French military force under the command of a marshal. Now (*jocular* and *colloquial*), the French police, the gendarmerie.

mare clausum /ˌmɑːreɪ ˈklaʊsʊm/, /ˌmɛːrɪ ˈklɔːzəm/ noun phrase plural **maria clausa** /ˌmɑːrɪə ˈklaʊsə/, /ˌmɛːrɪə ˈklɔːzə/

M17 Latin (= closed sea). A sea under the jurisdiction of a particular country.

■ The title of a work published in 1635 by the English jurist John Selden (1584–1654), in answer to Grotius (see MARE LIBERUM). The terms *mare clausum* and *mare liberum* both originated in the struggle between the Dutch and English maritime empires in the seventeenth century.

mare liberum /ˌmɑːreɪ ˈliːbərʊm/, /ˌmɛːri ˈlaɪbərəm/ *noun phrase* plural **maria libera** /ˌmɑːrɪə ˈliːbərə/, /ˌmɛːrɪə ˈlaɪbərə/ M17 Latin (= free sea). A sea open to all nations. Cf. MARE CLAUSUM.

■ The title of a treatise (1609) by Hugo Grotius (1583–1645), Dutch jurist.

maremma /məˈrɛmə/ *noun* plural **maremme** /məˈrɛmi/ M19 Italian (from Latin *maritima* feminine of *maritimus* maritime). In Italy: low marshy unhealthy country by the seashore; an area of this.

mariachi /mærɪˈɑːtʃi/ *noun* M20 Mexican Spanish (*mariache, mariachi*). An itinerant Mexican folk band (also *mariachi band*); a member of such a band.

maria clausa plural of MARE CLAUSUM.

mariage blanc /marjaʒ blɑ̃/ *noun phrase* plural **mariages blancs** (pronounced same) E20 French (literally, 'white marriage'). An unconsummated marriage.

> 1975 *Listener* Opal . . . suggested a *mariage blanc* between Natalie and Bosie that would enable Opal and Bosie to have a lasting liaison.

mariage de convenance /marjaʒ də kɔ̃vnɑ̃s/ *noun phrase* plural **mariages de convenance** (pronounced same) M19 French. A marriage of convenience.

> 1995 *Country Life* The following year, she [sc. Sonia Delaunay] entered a brief *mariage de convenance* with the homosexual art dealer Wilhelm Uhde . . .

maria libera plural of MARE LIBERUM.

maribou(t) variant of MARABOU.

mari complaisant /mari kɔ̃plɛzɑ̃/ *noun phrase* plural **maris complaisants** (pronounced same) L19 French. A husband tolerant of his wife's adultery.

> 1958 L. Durrell *Justine* She was reputed to have had many lovers, and Nessim was regarded as a *mari complaisant*.

marijuana /mærɪˈhwɑːnə/, /ˌmɑːrjʊˈɑːnə/ *noun* (also **marihuana**) L19 American Spanish. **1** L19 Cannabis, *especially* in a form for smoking. **2** E20 Indian hemp, cannabis plant.

marimba /məˈrɪmbə/ *noun* E18 Congolese. A kind of deep-toned xylophone, originating in Africa and consisting of wooden keys on a frame with a tuned resonator beneath each key.

marina /məˈriːnə/ *noun* E19 Italian and Spanish (feminine of *marino* from Latin *marinus* marine). A harbour, usually specially designed or located, with moorings for yachts and other small craft.

marinade /marɪˈneɪd/ *noun* E18 French (from Spanish *marinada*, from *marinar* to pickle in brine (= Italian *marinare*, French *mariner*), from *marino*, from Latin *marinus* marine). A flavouring and tenderizing mixture of wine, vinegar or other acidic liquid, with oil, herbs, spices, etc., in which meat, fish, etc., may be soaked before cooking; the meat, fish, etc., thus soaked.

marinara /mɑːrɪˈnɑːrə/, /marɪˈnɑːrə/ *adjective* M20 Italian (*alla marinara* sailor-fashion, from feminine of *marinero* seafaring). Designating a sauce made from tomatoes, onions, herbs, etc., usually served with pasta.

marinera /marɪˈnerə/ *noun* E20 Spanish (feminine of *marinero* marine, seafaring). A lively South American dance. Also called *cueca*.

marionette /ˌmarɪəˈnɛt/ *noun* E17 French (*marionnette*, from *Marion* diminutive of *Marie* Mary). A puppet with jointed limbs operated by strings.

maris complaisants plural of MARI COMPLAISANT.

marivaudage /marivodaʒ/ *noun* M18 French (from P. C. de *Marivaux* (1688–1763), French novelist and dramatist). Exaggeratedly sentimental or affected style, language, etc., characteristic of Marivaux.

> 1969 *Observer* It [sc. lesbianism] is a tricky subject, poised on the brink of either tiresome *marivaudage* or tasteless titillation.

marmite /ˈmɑːmʌɪt/, *in sense 1 also foreign* /marmit/ (*plural same*) *noun* E19 French. **1** E19 An earthenware cooking-vessel. **2** E20 (also **Marmite**) (Proprietary name for) a savoury extract made from fresh brewer's yeast, used especially in sandwiches and for flavouring.

marocain /marəˈkeɪm/ *noun & adjective* E20 French (from *Maroc* Morocco). **A** *noun* E20 (A garment made from) a crêpe fabric of silk or wool or both. **B** *adjective* L20 Made of marocain.

maror /mɑːˈrɔː/ *noun* L19 Hebrew (*mārōr*). Bitter herbs eaten at the Passover Seder service as a reminder of the bitterness of the Israelites' captivity in Egypt.

marque /mɑːk/ *noun* E20 French (back-formation from *marquer* to mark or brand, alteration of Old French *merchier*, from *merc* limit, of Scandinavian origin (cf. Old High German *marc(h)a* mark)). A make or brand of something, especially a motor vehicle.

> **1996** *Country Life* All this might give the impression that Rafael Gonzalez is an ancient and noble marque . . .

marquise /mɑːˈkiːz/, *foreign* /markiz/ (*plural same*) *noun* E17 French (feminine of *marquis* marquess, from Old French *marchis* (later altered to *marquis* after Provençal *marques*, Spanish *marqués*) from Proto-Romance base of *march* border). **1** E17 (The title of) a marchioness in Continental Europe or (formerly) Britain. **2** E18 A variety of pear. **3a** L18 A marquee. Now *rare* or *obsolete*. **b** L19 A permanent canopy projecting over the entrance to a hotel, theatre, etc. Also called *marquee*. **4** L19 A finger-ring set with a pointed oval gem or cluster of gems. Also more fully *marquise ring*.

marquisette /mɑːkɪˈzɛt/ *noun & adjective* E20 French (diminutive of MARQUISE). (Of) a plain gauze dress fabric originally made from silk, later from cotton.

marron /ˈmarɒn/, *foreign* /marɔ̃/ *noun* L16 French. A large and particularly sweet kind of chestnut.

■ Now chiefly in MARRON GLACÉ.

marron glacé /ˌmarɒn ˈɡlaseɪ/, *foreign* /marɔ̃ ɡlase/ *noun phrase* plural **marrons glacés** (pronounced same) L19 French. A chestnut preserved in syrup as a sweet.

martelé /ˈmɑːt(ə)leɪ/ *adjective, adverb, & noun* L19 French (past participle of *marteler* to hammer). *Music* Martellato.

■ Used only with reference to bowed stringed instruments (cf. MARTELLATO).

martellato /mɑːtɪˈlɑːtəʊ/ *adjective, adverb, & noun* L19 Italian (past participle of *martellare* to hammer). *Music* **A** *adjective & adverb* L19 (Played) with notes heavily accented and left before their full time has expired. **B** *noun* E20 Martellato playing.

martyrion /mɑːˈtɪrɪən/ *noun* (also in Latin form **martyrium** /mɑːˈtɪrɪəm/) plural of both **martyria** /mɑːˈtɪrɪə/ E18 Greek. A shrine, oratory, or church built in mem-

ory of a martyr; a building marking the place of a martyrdom or the site of a martyr's relics.

Marxisant /marksizɑ̃/ *adjective* (also **marxisant**) M20 French (from *Marxiste* Marxist). Having Marxist leanings.

marzacotto /mɑːtsəˈkɒtəʊ/, /mɑːzə ˈkɒtəʊ/ *noun* plural **marzacottos** L19 Italian. A transparent glaze used by Italian majolica workers.

mas /mɑ/ *noun* plural same E20 Provençal. A farm, house, or cottage in the south of France.

> **1996** *Times Magazine* . . . the houses themselves, no longer dilapidated, but restored through lavish investment of care and understanding—centuries-old village houses, abandoned *mas* or farmhouses, grand *bastides*, dressed up for today's tastes but retaining their nobility.

masa /ˈmasa/ *noun* E20 Spanish. In Central and South American cuisine, a type of dough made from cornmeal and used to make tortillas etc.

masala /məˈsɑːlə/ *noun* L18 Urdu (*maṣālah* from Persian and Urdu *masālih* from Arabic *maṣālih*). Any of various spice mixtures ground into a paste or powder for use in Indian cookery; a dish flavoured with this. Cf. GARAM MASALA.

mascara /maˈskɑːrə/ *noun & verb* L19 Italian (*mascara, maschera* mask). **A** *noun* L19 A cosmetic for darkening and colouring the eyelashes. **B** *transitive verb* M20 Put mascara on.

mascaron /maskarɔ̃/ (*plural same*), /ˈmaskər(ə)n/ *noun* M17 French (from Italian *mascherone*, from *maschera* mask). *Decorative Arts* A grotesque face or mask.

mascarpone /ˌmaskarˈpoːne/ *noun* M20 Italian. A soft mild Italian cream cheese.

mashallah /maˈʃalə/, /ˌmɑːʃɑːˈlɑː/ *interjection* E19 Arabic (*mā šāʾllāh* (This is) what God wills).

■ Used as an expression of praise or resignation.

masjid /ˈmʌsdʒɪd/, /ˈmasdʒɪd/ *noun* M19 Arabic. A mosque.

Masorah /masəˈrɑː/, /məˈsɔːrə/ *noun* (also **Massorah, Masora**) E17 Hebrew (variant of *māsōret* bond (Ezekiel 20:37), from *ʾāsar* to bind (later interpreted as 'tradition' as if from *māsar* to hand down)). The body of traditional information and comment relating to the text of the Hebrew Scriptures, compiled by Jewish scholars in the tenth century and earlier; the collection of critical notes in which this information is preserved.

massage /'masɑːʒ/, /'maˈsɑːʒ/, /'masɑːdʒ/ *noun & verb* L19 French (from *masser* to apply massage to, perhaps from Portuguese *amassar* to knead). **A** *noun* **1** L19 The application (usually with the hands) of pressure and strain on the muscles and joints of the body by rubbing, kneading, etc., in order to stimulate their action and increase their suppleness; an instance or spell of such manipulation. **2** E20 *euphemistic* The services of prostitutes. Chiefly in *massage parlour*. **B** *transitive verb* **1** L19 Apply massage to; treat by means of massage. **b** L20 Rub (lotion etc.) *into* by means of massage. **2** M20 Manipulate (data, figures, etc.), especially in order to give a more acceptable result.

massé /'maseɪ/ *adjective & noun* L19 French (past participle of *masser* to play a massé stroke, from *masse* mace). *Billiards* etc. (Designating) a stroke made with the cue more or less vertical, so as to impart extra swerve to the cue-ball.

massecuite /masˈkwiːt/ *noun* L19 French (literally, 'cooked mass'). The juice of sugar cane after concentration by boiling.

masseur /maˈsəː/ *noun* (feminine **masseuse** /maˈsəːz/) L19 French (from *masser* to apply massage to). A person who provides massage (professionally).

massif /'masɪf/, /maˈsiːf/, *foreign* /masif/ (*plural same*) *noun* E16 French (use as noun of *massif* massive). **1** E16 A block of building. Passing into *figurative* use of sense 2. **2** L19 A large mountain-mass; a compact group of mountain heights. **3** L19 *Horticulture* A mass or clump of plants.

Massorah variant of MASORAH.

mastaba /'mastəbə/ *noun* (also **mastabah**) E17 Arabic (*miṣṭaba, maṣ-*). **1** E17 In Islamic countries: a (stone) bench or seat attached to a house. **2** L19 *Archaeology* An ancient Egyptian flat-topped tomb, rectangular or square in plan and with sides sloping outward to the base. Also *mastaba tomb*.

mastika /maˈstiːkə/ *noun* E20 Modern Greek (*mastikha*). A liquor flavoured with mastic gum.

matador /'matədɔː/ *noun* (also (especially senses 2, 3) **matadore**) L17 Spanish (from *matar* to kill). **1** L17 A bullfighter whose task is to kill the bull. **2** L17 In some card-games (as quadrille, ombre, solo): any of the highest trumps so designated by the rules of the game. **3** M19 A domino game in which halves are matched so as to make a total of seven; any of the dominoes which have seven spots altogether, together with the double blank.

matchet variant of MACHETE.

maté /'mateɪ/ *noun* E18 Spanish (*mate* from Quechua *mati*). **1** E18 A gourd, calabash, etc., in which the leaves of the shrub maté are infused. Also *maté-cup*. **2** M18 (An infusion of) the leaves of a South American shrub, *Ilex paraguariensis*; the shrub itself. Also more fully *yerba maté*.

matelassé /mat(ə)ˈlaseɪ/, *foreign* /matlase/ (*plural same*) *noun & adjective* (also **matelasse**) L19 French (past participle of *matelasser* to quilt, from *matelas* mattress). **A** *noun* L19 A silk or wool fabric with a raised design. **B** *adjective* L19 Having a raised design like quilting.

matelot /'matləʊ/ *noun* E20 French (= sailor). **1** E20 A sailor. *nautical slang*. **2** E20 A shade of blue.

1 1995 *Spectator* When Floyd cooks for, say, a crew of matelots, you never know whether they really enjoyed his bouillabaisse or whether they are just doing it to please him.

matelote /'mat(ə)ləʊt/, *foreign* /matlɔt/ (*plural same*) *noun* E18 French (from as preceding). A dish of fish etc. served in a sauce of wine, onions, etc.

mater /'meɪtə/ *noun* L16 Latin (literally, 'mother'). **1** L16 The thickest plate of an astrolabe. **2** M19 Mother.

■ Sense 2 is chiefly jocular or in school slang; cf. PATER.

Mater Dolorosa /ˌmeɪtə dɒləˈrəʊsə/ *noun phrase plural* **Matres Dolorosae** /ˌmeɪtriːz dɒləˈrəʊsiː/ E19 Medieval Latin (literally, 'sorrowful mother'). (A title of) the Virgin Mary, as having a role in the Passion of Christ; a representation, in painting or sculpture, of the Virgin Mary sorrowing; *transferred* a woman resembling the sorrowful Virgin in appearance, manner, etc.

materfamilias /ˌmeɪtəfəˈmɪlɪəs/ *noun* M18 Latin (from MATER + *familias* old genitive of *familia* family). The female head of a family or household.

materia medica /məˌtɪərɪə ˈmɛdɪkə/ *noun phrase plural* L17 Modern Latin (translation of Greek *hulē iatrikē* healing material). The remedial substances used in the practice of medicine; (treated as *singular*) the branch of medicine that deals with their origins and properties.

materia prima /məˌtɪərɪə ˈprʌɪmə/ *noun phrase* M16 Latin (= first matter). The primordial substance formerly considered to be the original material of the universe.

matériel /materjɛl/, /məˌtɪərɪˈɛl/ *noun* E19 French (use as noun of adjective). **1** E19 Available means or resources. Also (*rare*), technique. **2** E19 The equipment, supplies, etc., used in an army, navy, or business. Opposed to *personnel*.

matière /matjɛr/ *noun* E20 French. The quality an artist gives to the pigment used.

matinée /ˈmatɪneɪ/, *foreign* /matine/ (*plural same*) *noun* (also **matinee**) M19 French (= morning, what occupies a morning, from *matin*). **1** M19 An afternoon performance at a theatre, cinema, or concert hall. **2** L19 A woman's lingerie jacket.

matje /ˈmatjə/ *noun* (also **matjes** /ˈmatjəs/) L19 Dutch (*maatjes*). A young herring, especially salted or pickled. More fully *matje herring*.

■ In the form *matie, mattie* or other variants the word was known much earlier (E18), chiefly in Scotland. The form with 'j' represents a reintroduction from Dutch.

matraca /məˈtrɑːkə/ *noun* E20 Spanish. In Spain: a mechanical wooden rattle used instead of church bells on Good Friday.

Matres Dolorosae plural of MATER DOLOROSA.

matrix /ˈmeɪtrɪks/ *noun plural* **matrixes**, **matrices** /ˈmeɪtrɪsiːz/ LME Latin (= breeding-female, register, (in Late Latin) womb, from *mater, matr-* mother). **1** LME The uterus, the womb. *archaic* **2** M16 A place or medium in which something is bred, produced, or developed; a setting or environment in which a particular activity or process occurs or develops; a place or point of origin and growth. **3** L16 A mould in which something is cast or shaped. **4** M17 The rock material in which a fossil, gem, etc., is embedded.

■ *Matrix* has also been adopted as a specialist technical term in a whole range of disciplines including Anatomy and Zoology

(M19), Botany (M19), Mathematics (M19), and Computing (M20).

matzo /ˈmʌtsə/, /ˈmatsəʊ/ *noun* (also **matzah** /ˈmʌtsə/) plural **matzos**, **matzoth** /ˈmʌtsəʊt/ M19 Yiddish (*matse* from Hebrew *maṣṣāh*). (A wafer of) unleavened bread for Passover.

maudit /modi/ *noun & adjective* M20 French (literally, 'cursed', from *maudire* to curse). **A** *noun* M20 plural pronounced same. A person who is cursed; a despicable or deeply unpleasant person. **B** *adjective* L20 Cursed; (of an artist etc.) insufficiently appreciated, forgotten.

■ The adjective is usually postpositive. Cf. POÈTE MAUDIT.

Maulana /maʊˈlɑːnə/ *noun* M19 Arabic (*mawlānā* our master). (A title given to) a Muslim man revered for his religious learning or piety.

maulvi variant of MOULVI.

mau-mau /ˈmaʊmaʊ/ *transitive verb* L20 Kikuyu (*Mau Mau*, a secret society dedicated to the expulsion of British settlers from Kenya in the 1950s). Terrorize, threaten.

■ United States slang.

mausoleum /mɔːsəˈlɪəm/ *noun plural* **mausolea** /mɔːsəˈlɪə/, **mausoleums** LME Latin (from Greek *Mausōleion*, from *Mausōlos* Mausolos). **1** LME The magnificent tomb of Mausolus, King of Caria, erected in the 4th century BC at Halicarnassus by his queen Artemisia. **2** LME *generally* A large and magnificent place of burial.

mauvais /mɔvɛ/ *adjective* E18 French. Bad.

■ In English only in the following French phrases.

mauvais coucheur /mɔvɛ kuʃœr/ *noun phrase* plural **mauvais coucheurs** (pronounced same) M20 French (literally, 'bad bedfellow'). A difficult, uncooperative, or unsociable person.

1963 *Times Literary Supplement* Goddard was a man of talent but he was obviously a *mauvais coucheur*.

mauvaise foi /mɔvɛz fwa/ *noun phrase* M20 French. Bad faith.

1995 *Spectator* They accept the general futility of life and take corruption and *mauvaise foi* in anyone 'important' for granted.

mauvaise langue /mɔvɛz lãg/ *noun phrase* plural **mauvaises langues** (pronounced same) L19 French (literally, 'bad tongue'). A venomous tongue; a scandalmonger.

1936 R. West *Thinking Reed* In another moment that couple of *mauvaises langues* would have something to wag about.

mauvais pas /mɔvɛ pa/ *noun phrase* plural same E19 French (literally, 'bad step'). *Mountaineering* A place that is difficult or dangerous to negotiate.
1940 F. S. Chapman *Helvellyn to Himalaya* We decided to return once more to the couloir . . . thus short-circuiting the *mauvais pas* we had seen in our reconnaisance.

mauvais quart d'heure /mɔvɛ kar dœr/ *noun phrase* plural **mauvais quarts d'heure** (pronounced same) M19 French (literally, 'bad quarter of an hour'). An unpleasant but brief period of time; an unnerving experience.
1965 *Economist* John Kennedy had his *mauvais quart d'heure* between April and June, 1961.

mauvais sujet /mɔvɛ syʒɛ/ *noun phrase* plural **mauvais sujets** (pronounced same) L18 French (literally, 'bad subject'). A worthless person, a scoundrel.
1975 A. Christie *Curtain* The *mauvais sujet*—always women are attracted to him.

maven /'meɪv(ə)n/ *noun* M20 Hebrew (*mēḇîn* understanding). An expert, a connoisseur. *North American.*
1975 *New York Times* Mama, who had managed to support herself by becoming a local real estate *maven*, negotiated the purchase.

mavrodaphne /ˌmavrə'dafni/ *noun* E20 Modern Greek (from late Greek *mauros* dark (Greek *amauros*) + *daphnē* laurel). A dark-red sweet Greek wine; the grape from which this is made.

maxixe /mak'si:ks/, *foreign* /mə'ʃiʃə/ *noun* E20 Portuguese. A dance for couples, of Brazilian origin, resembling the polka and the local tango.
1995 *Spectator* From Brazil in the 20s there came a dance called the maxixe—a challenge to those not confident of their Portuguese pronunciation—followed by the samba and the more primitive baiao.

maya /'mɑ:jə/ *noun* L18 Sanskrit (*māyā*, from *mā* create). In *Hindu Philosophy*, illusion, magic, the supernatural power wielded by gods and demons. In *Hindu and Buddhist Philosophy*, the power by which the universe becomes manifest, the illusion or appearance of the phenomenal world.

mayonnaise /meɪə'neɪz/ *noun* E19 French (also *magnonaise, mahonnaise,* perhaps feminine of *mahonnais* adjective, from *Mahon* capital of Minorca). A thick sauce consisting of yolk of egg beaten up with oil and vinegar and seasoned with salt etc., used as a dressing especially for salad, eggs, cold meat, or fish; a dish (of meat etc.) having this sauce as a dressing.

mazar /mə'zɑ:/ *noun* E20 Arabic (*mazār* place visited, from *zāra* to visit). A Muslim tomb revered as a shrine.

mazel tov /'maz(ə)l to:v/, /tɒf/ *interjection* M19 Modern Hebrew (*mazzāl ṭōḇ*, literally, 'good star', from Hebrew *mazzāl* star). Among Jews: good luck, congratulations.

mazout variant of MAZUT.

mazuma /mə'zu:mə/ *noun* E20 Yiddish (from Hebrew *mēzummān*, from *zimmēn* to prepare). Money, cash; *especially* betting money. *United States and Australian slang.*

mazurka /mə'zə:kə/, /mə'zʊəkə/ *noun* E19 French (or from German *masurka* from Polish *mazurka* woman of the province Mazovia). **1** E19 A Polish dance in triple time, usually with a slide and hop. **2** M19 A piece of music for this dance or composed in its rhythm, usually with accentuation of the second or third beat.

mazut /mə'zu:t/ *noun* (also **mazout**) L19 Russian. A viscous liquid left as residue after the distillation of petroleum, used in Russia as a fuel oil and coarse lubricant.

mbira /(ə)m'bɪərə/ *noun* L19 Bantu. A musical instrument of southern Africa consisting of a set of keys or tongues attached to a resonator, which are plucked with the thumb and forefingers. Also called *sansa.*

mea culpa /ˌmeɪə 'kʊlpə/, /ˌmi:ə 'kʌlpə/ *interjection & noun phrase* LME Latin (literally, '(through) my own fault'). **A** *interjection* LME Acknowledging one's guilt or responsibility for an error. **B** *noun phrase* E19 An utterance of '*mea culpa*'; an acknowledgement of one's guilt or responsibility for an error.
■ Taken from the prayer of confession in the Latin liturgy of the Church. Also sometimes *mea maxima culpa* '(through) my own great fault'. As an interjection, now often jocular.
B 1996 *Times* In fact, Mr de Klerk's statement was far from the *mea culpa* many had hoped for and was a masterfully bland performance.

mealie /'mi:li/ *noun* (also **mielie**) E19 Afrikaans (*mielie* from Portuguese *milho* maize, millet, from Latin *milium*). In

South Africa: maize; a corn-cob (usually in *plural*).

mebos /'mi:bɒs/, *foreign* /'me:bɔs/ *noun* L18 Afrikaans (probably from Japanese *ume-boshi* dried and salted plums). A South African confection made from dried flattened apricots, preserved in salt and sugar.

mecate /meɪ'kɑːteɪ/ *noun* M19 Mexican Spanish (from Nahuatl *mecatl*). A rope made of horsehair or of maguey fibre, used especially to tether or lead a horse. Chiefly *United States*.

méchant /meʃɑ̃/ *adjective* (feminine **méchante** /meʃɑ̃t/) E19 French. Malicious, spiteful.

médaillon /medajɔ̃/ *noun* plural pronounced same E20 French (from Italian *medaglione*, augmentative of *medaglia* medal). A small, flat, round or oval cut of meat or fish.

■ The cognate *medallion*, in the sense of 'large medal', was established in English much earlier (M17).

media /'miːdɪə/ *noun* E20 Latin (plural of MEDIUM (noun)). **1** E20 *plural and collective singular* The main means of mass communication (also *mass media*), *especially* newspapers, radio, and television; the reporters, journalists, etc., working for organizations engaged in such communication. **2** E20 *singular* A means of mass communication, a MEDIUM.

medina /mɪ'diːnə/ *noun* (also **Medina**) E20 Arabic (literally, 'town'). The old Arab or non-European quarter of a North African town.

medium /'miːdɪəm/ *noun & adjective* plural of noun **media** /'miːdɪə/, **mediums** (see also MEDIA) L16 Latin (literally, 'middle, midst', medieval Latin 'means', use as noun of *medius* mid). **A** *noun* **1** L16 A middle quality, degree, or condition; something intermediate in nature or degree. **2** L16 An intervening substance through which a force acts on objects at a distance or through which impressions are conveyed to the senses, as air, water, etc. **b** M19 A pervading or enveloping substance; the substance in which an organism lives or is cultured; *figurative* one's environment, one's usual social setting. **3** E17 An intermediate agency, instrument, or channel; a means; *specifically* a channel of mass communication, as newspapers, radio, television, etc. See also MEDIA. **4 a** E19 A person acting as an intermediary, a mediator. *rare*. **b** M19 (plural **mediums**) A person thought to be in contact with the spirits of the dead and to communicate between the living and the dead. **5** M19 A liquid substance with which a pigment is mixed for use in painting. Also, anything used as a raw material by an artist etc.; a style or variety of art, as determined by the materials or artistic form used. **B** *adjective* **1** L17–E19 Average, mean. **2** E18 Intermediate between two or more degrees in size, character, amount, quality, etc.

■ There also are or have been numerous technical applications of the noun *medium*, as in Logic (L16–E19) 'the middle term of a syllogism', Geometry and Arithmetic (E17–E19) 'a mean; an average', and Photography (L19) 'a varnish used in retouching'.

medresseh variant of MADRASAH.

medusa /mɪ'djuːzə/, /mɪ'djuːsə/ *noun* (in sense 1 usually **Medusa**) plural **medusae** /mɪ'djuːziː/, /mɪ'djuːsiː/, **medusas** LME Latin (from Greek *Medousa* the only mortal one of the three Gorgons in Greek mythology, with snakes for hair and a gaze which turned any beholder to stone: in sense 2 originally as modern Latin genus name). **1** LME A terrifying or ugly woman, a gorgon. **2** M18 A jellyfish; *specifically* in Zoology, a coelenterate in the medusoid stage of its life cycle.

mee /miː/ *noun* M20 Chinese (*miàn* (Wade–Giles *mien*) flour). A Chinese dish made with noodles and other ingredients, popular in Malaysia.

meerschaum /'mɪəʃɔːm/, /'mɪəʃəm/ *noun* L18 German (from *Meer* sea + *Schaum* foam, translation of Persian *kef-i-daryā* foam of sea, with reference to its frothiness). A tobacco-pipe with a bowl made from speiolite or hydrated magnesium silicate occurring as a soft white or yellowish claylike mineral.

méfiance /mefjɑ̃s/ *noun* L19 French. Mistrust.

mega /'mɛɡə/ *adjective* L20 Greek (*mega-* combining form of *megas* great) Large, great. Also, brilliant, excellent.

■ Originating in the United States, this is an independent colloquial use of a combining form, similar to that of MACRO.

megaron /'mɛɡər(ə)n/ *noun* L19 Greek. In ancient Greece: the great central hall of a type of house characteristic especially of the Mycenaean period.

Megillah /məˈgɪlə/ noun (also **megillah**) M17 Hebrew (měğillāh, literally, 'roll, scroll'). **1** M17 Each of five books of the Hebrew Scriptures (the Song of Solomon, Ruth, Lamentations, Ecclesiastes, and Esther) appointed to be read on certain Jewish notable days; especially the Book of Esther, read at the festival of Purim. Also, a copy of all, or any, of these books. **2** M20 A long, tedious, or complicated story. Frequently in a or the whole megillah. slang.
> **1970** S. Sheldon Naked Face 'Do you know the most peculiar thing about this whole megillah?' queried Moody thoughtfully.

meiosis /mʌɪˈəʊsɪs/ noun plural **meioses**, /mʌɪˈəʊsiːz/ M16 Modern Latin (from Greek meiōsis, from meioun to lessen, from meiōn less). **1** M16 Rhetoric **a** A figure of speech by which something is intentionally presented as smaller, less important, etc., than it really is. Now rare. **b** M17 LITOTES. **2** E20 Biology A particular kind of cell division.

mei ping /ˌmeɪ ˈpɪŋ/ noun phrase E20 Chinese (méi píng prunus vase). A kind of Chinese porcelain vase with a narrow neck designed to hold a single spray of flowers.

meisie /ˈmeɪsi/ noun L19 Afrikaans (from Dutch meisje). In South Africa: a girl, a young woman.

melamed /mɪˈlɑːməd/ noun L19 Hebrew (mělammēd). A teacher of elementary Hebrew.

melancholia /mɛlənˈkəʊlɪə/ noun L17 late Latin (from Greek melankholia from melan-, melas black + kholē bile). Medicine A pathological state of depression. Also (generally), melancholy, depression.

mélange /melɑ̃ʒ/ (plural same), /meɪˈlɒ̃ʒ/ noun M17 French (from mêler to mix). **1** M17 A mixture; a collection of heterogeneous items or elements, a medley. **2** L19 Yarn, especially woollen yarn, to which dye has been applied unevenly so as to leave some areas undyed; a fabric of such a yarn. **3** E20 Coffee made with sugar and whipped cream; a drink of this.
> **1** **1995** Times Davenport-Hines denounces the usual biographical mélange of gossip, scandal and 'sexual tale-telling'.

mêlée /ˈmɛleɪ/ noun (also **melée**, **melee**) M17 French (from Old French mellée past participial adjective of meller variant of mesler to meddle; sense 2 probably a different word). **1** M17 A battle at close quarters, a hand-to-hand fight; a confused struggle or skirmish, especially involving many people; a crush, turmoil; a muddle. **2** E20 collectively Small diamonds less than about a carat in weight.
> **1** **1996** Times He continued to kick and punch at officers as he was led away after the two-minute mêlée.

melisma /mɪˈlɪzmə/ noun plural **melismata**, /mɪˈlɪzmətə/, **melismas** L19 Greek (literally, 'song'). Music Originally, a melodic tune, melodic music. Now, in singing, the prolongation of one syllable over a number of notes.
> **1996** Times Ray Charles is the name that invariably comes to mind in any discussion of Feliciano—not simply for the trite reason that they are both blind and fond of gospel melismata ...

melktert /ˈmɛlktɛːt/ noun M20 Afrikaans (from melk milk + tert tart, pie). In South Africa: a kind of open tart with a custard filling sprinkled with cinnamon.

melos /ˈmɛlɒs/, /ˈmiːlɒs/ noun M18 Greek (= song, music). Music Song, melody; specifically the succession of tones considered apart from rhythm; an uninterrupted flow of melody.

meltemi /mɛlˈtɛmi/ noun E20 Modern Greek (meltémi, Turkish meltem). A dry north wind blowing over the eastern Mediterranean region in summer; an Etesian wind.

melusine /ˌmɛl(j)ʊˈsiːn/ noun & adjective (also **Melusine**) E20 French (mélusine, perhaps connected with Mélusine, a fairy in French folklore). **A** noun E20 A silky long-haired felt, used for making hats. **B** attributive or as adjective M20 Made of this material.

membra disiecta, **membra disjecta** variants of DISJECTA MEMBRA.

membrillo /mɛmˈbriːljo/, /mɛmˈbriːljəʊ/ noun E20 Spanish (= quince). A Spanish preserve of quinces.

membrum virile /ˌmɛmbrəm vɪˈriːli/ noun phrase M19 Latin (= male member). The penis. Archaic or euphemistic.

memento /mɪˈmɛntəʊ/ noun plural **memento(e)s** LME Latin (imperative of meminisse to remember). **1** LME Christian Church Either of the two prayers (beginning with Memento) in the canon of the Mass, in which the living and the dead are respectively commemorated; the commemoration of the living or the dead in these prayers. **2** L16 A reminder, warning, or hint as to future conduct or events. Now *especially* an object serving as such a reminder or warning. Cf. MEMENTO MORI, MEMENTO VIVERE. **3** M18 A reminder of a past event or condition, of an absent person, or something that once existed. Now *especially* an object kept as a memorial of some person or event, a souvenir.

memento mori /mɪˌmɛntəʊ ˈmɔːrʌɪ/, /mɪ ˌmɛntəʊ ˈmɔːri/ *noun phrase* Latin (= remember that you have to die). A warning or reminder of death, *especially* a skull or other symbolical object.

> **1996** *Country Life* ... it explores the theme of life among the ruins ... a powerful memento mori of departed grandeur.

memento vivere /mɪˌmɛntəʊ ˈviːvəri/ *noun phrase* E20 Latin (= remember that you have to live). A reminder of (the pleasures of) life.

■ Formed as the opposite of MEMENTO MORI.

> **1928** E. Blunden *Undertones of War* Sitting in the headquarters dugout with 'La Vie Parisienne' as a *memento vivere*.

memo abbreviation of MEMORANDUM.

memorabilia /ˌmɛm(ə)rəˈbɪlɪə/ *noun plural* L18 Latin (use as noun of neuter plural of *memorabilis* from *memorare* to bring to mind). **1** L18 Memorable or noteworthy things. **2** L19 Souvenirs.

> **1 1996** D. Chambers *Stonyground* As the museum of the house, this parlour of my childhood was filled with memorabilia: a loon, now stuffed, that my grandmother had rescued from a ditch and nursed to tameness; my great-uncle Hugh's bayonet from the First World War ...

memorandum /mɛməˈrandəm/ *noun* plural **memoranda** /mɛməˈrandə/, **memorandums** L15 Latin (neuter singular of *memorandus* gerundive of *memorare* to bring to mind, from *memor* mindful). **1** L15 A note to help the memory, a record of events or of observations on a particular subject, especially for future consideration or use. **2** L16 *Law* A writing or document summarizing or embodying the terms of a transaction, contract, agreement, establishment of a company etc. **3** E17 A record of a money transaction. **4** M17 An informal diplomatic message, especially summarizing the state of a question or justifying a decision. **5** L19 An informal written communication of a kind conventionally not requiring a signature, as within a business or organization, usually written on paper headed 'Memorandum' or 'Memo'.

■ *Memorandum* was first introduced (LME) as an adjective meaning 'to be remembered' and placed at the beginning of a note of something to be remembered or a record (for future reference) of something done, but this usage is now confined to legal contexts. In sense 5 *memorandum* is now generally abbreviated to *memo*, which also functions attributively (as in *memo pad*) and as a transitive verb meaning 'to make a memorandum of'.

memoria technica /mɪˌmɔːrɪə ˈtɛknɪkə/ *noun phrase* M18 Modern Latin ((= technical memory) represented Greek to *mnēmonikon tekhnēma*). A method of assisting the memory by artificial contrivances; a system of mnemonics, a mnemonic aid.

memsahib /ˈmɛmsɑːb/ *noun* M19 Anglo-Indian (from *mem* representing a pronunciation of 'ma'am' + SAHIB). A European married woman as spoken of or to by Indians.

ménage /meɪˈnɑːʒ/, *foreign* /menaʒ/ (*plural same*) *noun* (also **menage**) ME French (Old French *menaige, manaige* (modern *ménage*) from Proto-Romance, from Latin *mansio* station, abiding-place, from *mans-* past participial stem of *manere* to stay, remain). **1** ME A domestic establishment, a household. Formerly also, the members of a household. **b** M20 A sexual relationship; an affair. **2** E19 The management of a household, housekeeping. **3** E19 A benefit society or savings club of which every member pays in a fixed sum weekly; an arrangement for paying for goods by instalments. *Scottish and northern dialect.*

■ In sense 1 also occasionally found in the phrases *ménage à deux* 'household of two' and *ménage à quatre* 'household of four', but by far the most frequent is MÉNAGE À TROIS. The related French word *menagerie* (introduced L17) meaning 'a collection of wild animals kept in cages' is now completely Anglicized in pronunciation (/mə ˈnadʒ(ə)ri/).

ménage à trois /menaʒ a trwɑ/, /meɪ ˌnɑːʒ a trwɑː/ (*plural same*) *noun phrase* (also **ménage-à-trois**) L19 French (= household of three). An arrangement or relationship in which three people live together, usually consisting of a husband and wife and the lover of one of them.

> **1996** *Spectator* He seemed saddened by some people's view that 'I might be having my cake and eating it', referring to his *ménage-à-trois* with wife Rosie and mistress Morrigan.

menhaden /mɛnˈheɪd(ə)n/ *noun* L18 Algonquian (perhaps from a base meaning 'fertilize'). A fish of the herring family, *Brevoortia tyrannus*, of the Atlantic coast of North America, an important source of fish guano and oil.

menhir /ˈmɛnhɪə/ *noun* M19 Breton (*maenhir* (*maen* stone, *hir* long) = Welsh *maen hir*, Cornish *mênhere*). *Archaeology* A single tall upright monumental stone, especially of prehistoric times.

meniscus /mɪˈnɪskəs/ *noun plural* **menisci** /mɪˈnɪskʌɪ/ L17 Modern Latin (from Greek *mēniskos* crescent, diminutive of *mēnē* moon). **1** L17 A lens convex on one side and concave on the other; *especially* a convexo-concave lens (i.e. one thickest in the middle, with a crescent-shaped section). **2** E18 A crescent moon. *rare.* **3** E19 The convex or concave upper surface of a column of liquid in a tube, caused by surface tension or capillarity. **4** M19 *Anatomy* A disclike fibrocartilage situated between the articular surfaces of certain joints, as those of the wrist and knee. **5** L19 A figure in the form of a crescent.

meno /ˈmɛnəʊ/, /ˈmeɪnəʊ/ *adverb* L19 Italian. *Music* Less.
■ Used in directions, as *meno mosso* 'less rapidly'.

menologium /ˌmɛnə(ʊ)ˈləʊʤɪəm/ *noun* (also **menology** /mɪˈnɒlədʒi/) *plural* **menologia** /ˌmɛnə(ʊ)ˈləʊʤɪə/, **menologiums** E18 Modern Latin (from ecclesiastical Greek *mēnologion*, from *mēn* month + *logos* account). An ecclesiastical calendar of the months.
■ The English form *menology* was introduced earlier (E17), but the form *menologium* is used in parallel with it, in particular with reference to the Old English metrical church calendar first published in 1705. The Greek form is also used specifically to mean a calendar of the Orthodox Church containing biographies of the saints in the order of the dates on which they are commemorated.

menorah /mɪˈnɔːrə/ *noun* L19 Hebrew (*mĕnōrāh* candlestick). A holy candelabrum with seven branches that was used in the temple in Jerusalem; a candelabrum having any number of branches, but usually eight, used in Jewish worship, especially during Hanukkah; a representation of either as a symbol of Judaism.

mensch /mɛnʃ/ *noun* M20 Yiddish (from German = person). A person of integrity or rectitude; a just, honest, or honourable person.

> 1972 *New Yorker* What is a *mensch*? . . . It means you're a substantial human being.

menses /ˈmɛnsiːz/ *noun plural* L16 Latin (plural of *mensis* month). The menstrual discharge. Also, the time of menstruation.

mens rea /ˌmɛnz ˈriːə/ *noun phrase* M19 Latin (= guilty mind). *Law* The state of mind accompanying an illegal act which makes the act a crime; criminal state of mind.

> 1992 P. Manning *Erving Goffman and Modern Sociology* The law encourages this defense strategy by requiring prosecution lawyers to demonstrate *mens rea* on the part of the accused; that is, it requires proof that the accused intended to commit the crime.

mens sana in corpore sano /mɛns ˌsɑːnə ɪn ˌkɔːpəreɪ ˈsɑːnəʊ/ *noun phrase* E17 Latin. A sound mind in a sound body, especially regarded as the ideal of education.
■ Also elliptical as *mens sana* (see quotation 1967). The quotation is from the *Satires* (x.356) of the Roman poet Juvenal.

> 1967 S. Johnson *Gold Drain* 'They' accused him of suffering from the effects of a public-school education, from the *mens sana* approach.

mensur /mɛnˈzuːr/, /mɛnˈsʊə/ *noun plural* **mensuren** /mɛnˈzuːrən/, **mensurs** E20 German (literally, 'measure'). Chiefly *History* In Germany: a fencing duel between students fought with partially blunted weapons.

> 1970 M. Hebden *Mask of Violence* Anarchical young men of . . . the older universities . . . were already shouting the old *Mensur* wish before the commencement of a fight: 'Waffenschein!'

mentor /ˈmɛntɔː/ *noun* M18 French (from Latin *Mentor* from Greek *Mentōr* the guide and adviser of Odysseus' son Telemachus (probably chosen as a name as from base meaning 'remember, think, counsel')). An experienced and trusted adviser or guide; a teacher, a tutor.

menudo /mɪˈn(j)uːdəʊ/ *noun* M20 Mexican Spanish (use as noun of adjective = small from Latin *minutus* very small). A spicy Mexican soup made from tripe.

menus plaisirs /məny plɛzir/ *noun phrase plural* L17 French (= small pleasures). Simple pleasures; small personal expenses or gratifications; fanciful or trifling objects bought with pocket money.

> 1966 M. Innes *Change of Heir* 'It's in her letter. The bit about . . . *menus frais*.' 'What's that?'

'The same as *menus plaisirs.* Pocket-money on the scale appropriate to an English gentleman.'

mercado /mə:'kɑ:dəʊ/, *foreign* /merˈkado/ *noun* plural **mercados** /mə:'kɑ:dəʊz/, *foreign* /merˈkados/ M19 Spanish (from Latin *mercatus* market). In Spain and Spanish-speaking countries: a market.

merde /mɛrd/ *noun* M20 French (from Latin *merda*). Excrement, dung.

■ Also in slang use as an interjection, expressing annoyance, exasperation, surprise, etc. Cf. MOT DE CAMBRONNE.

merdeka /mə:'deɪkə/ *noun* M20 Malay. In Malaysia and Indonesia: freedom, independence.

mère /mɛr/, /mɛː/ *noun* M19 French (= mother). The mother, elder.

■ *Mère* is appended to a name especially to distinguish between a mother and daughter of the same name (see quotation).
1968 J. Haythorne *None of Us Cared for Kate* Prentice *mère* has been bombarding the Secretary of State with letters.

merengue /məˈrɛŋgeɪ/ *noun* (also **meringue** /məˈraŋ/) M20 American Spanish (from Haitian creole *méringue* literally, 'meringue' from French). A dance of Dominican and Haitian origin, with alternating long and short stiff-legged steps; a piece of music for this dance, usually in duple and triple time.

meridional /məˈrɪdɪən(ə)l/ *adjective & noun* (also **meridianal**) LME Old and Modern French (*méridional* from late Latin *meridionalis*, irregularly from *meridies* after *septentrionalis* septentrional). **A** *adjective* **1** LME Of or pertaining to the south; situated in the south; southern, southerly. **b** M19 *specifically* Pertaining to or characteristic of the inhabitants of southern Europe. **2** LME–M19 Of or pertaining to the position of the sun at midday; pertaining to or characteristic of midday. **3** M16 Of, pertaining to, or aligned with a meridian. **4** M17 Of a marking or structure on a roundish body: lying in a plane with the axis of the body. **B** *noun* L16 A native or inhabitant of the south. Now *specifically* a native or inhabitant of the south of France.

meringue /məˈraŋ/, *foreign* /mərɛ̃g/ (*plural same*) *noun* E18 French (of unknown origin). A confection made chiefly of sugar and whites of eggs whipped together and baked crisp; a small cake or shell of this, usually decorated or filled with cream.

merino /məˈriːnəʊ/ *noun & adjective* plural of noun **merinos** L18 Spanish (of unknown origin). **1** L18 (Designating or pertaining to) a breed of sheep prized for the fineness of its wool, originating in Spain; (designating) a sheep of this breed. **b** E19 *pure merino*, (i) an early immigrant to Australia with no convict origins, a member of a leading family in Australian society, a person of fine breeding or good character; (ii) *attributively* first-class, well-bred, excellent. *Australian slang*. **2** E19 (Of) a soft fine material resembling cashmere, made of wool (originally merino wool) or wool and cotton. **b** M19 A garment, especially a dress or shawl, made of this; *West Indies* a vest. **3** L19 (Of) a fine woollen yarn used in the manufacture of hosiery and knitwear.

mesa /'meɪsə/ *noun* M18 Spanish (= table, from Latin *mensa*). A high rocky tableland or plateau; a flat-topped hill with precipitous sides.

■ The earliest occurrences are in the names of particular plateaux or hills in the United States.

mésalliance /mezaljɑ̃s/ (*plural same*), /mɛ'zalɪəns/ *noun* L18 French (from *més-* mis- + *alliance* alliance). A marriage with a person thought to be of inferior social position; an unsuitable union.

■ The English form *misalliance* (M18) is also current for an inappropriate marital or sexual union, but it is also used more generally.

mes ami(e)s plural of MON AMI(E).

mescal /'mɛskal/, /mɛ'skal/ *noun* E18 Spanish (*mezcal* from Nahuatl *mexcalli*). **1** E18 Any of several plants of the genus *Agave* found in Mexico and the southwestern United States, used as sources of fermented liquor, food, or fibre. **2** E19 A strong intoxicating spirit distilled from the fermented sap of the American aloe or allied species. Cf. TEQUILA. **3** L19 A small desert cactus, *Lophophora williamsii*, of Mexico and Texas; a preparation of this used as a hallucinogenic drug. Cf. PEYOTE.

Mesdames plural of MADAME.

Mesdemoiselles plural of MADEMOISELLE.

meseta /meˈseta/ *noun* E20 Spanish (diminutive of MESA). In Spain and Spanish-speaking countries: a plateau; specifically *the* high plateau of central Spain.

meshuga /mɪˈʃʊgə/ *adjective* (also **me-shugga(h)** and other variants) L19 Yiddish (*meshuge* from Hebrew *mĕshuggā'*; cf. German *meschugge* crazy). Mad, crazy; stupid.

■ Slang. *Meshuga* is chiefly used predicatively, in contrast to MESHUGENER.

meshugaas /mɪˈʃʊgɑːs/ *noun* (also **mishugas** and other variants) E20 Yiddish (from Hebrew *mĕshuggā'*: see MESHUGA). Madness, craziness; nonsense, foolishness. *slang*.

meshugener /mɪˈʃʊgənə/ *attributive adjective & noun slang* (also **meshuggener**, **meshugenah**, and other variants) E20 Yiddish (from Hebrew *mĕshuggā'*: see MESHUGA). (A person who is) mad, crazy, or stupid.

■ Slang. It is a positional variant of *meshuga* in that it precedes its noun.

meshugga(h) variant of MESHUGA.

meshuggenah, **meshuggener** variants of MESHUGENER.

meshumad /mɪˈʃʊmad/ *noun* (also **meshummad**) plural **meshumadim** /mɪˈʃʊmadɪm/ L19 Yiddish (from Hebrew *mĕshummād*, literally, 'a person who is destroyed', or *mĕshuˈmād* baptized, from Aramaic *'mad* to be baptized). An apostate from Judaism.

meson /ˈmeɪsɒn/ *noun* E19 Spanish (*mesón*). In Mexico or the south-western United States: an inn or lodging-house.

messa di voce /ˌmessa di ˈvotʃe/, /ˌmɛsə dɪ ˈvəʊtʃi/ *noun phrase* plural **messe di voce** /ˌmesse/, /ˌmɛseɪ/ L18 Italian (literally, 'placing of the voice'). In singing, a gradual crescendo and diminuendo on a long-held note.

messagerie /mesaʒri/ *noun* plural pronounced same L18 French. The transportation or delivery of goods, messages, or people; a conveyance for these. In *plural* also, goods, messages, or people for transportation or delivery.

messaline /ˈmɛsəliːn/ *noun & adjective* E20 French. (Made of) a soft lightweight and lustrous silk or rayon fabric.

messe di voce plural of MESSA DI VOCE.

Messiah /mɪˈsʌɪə/ *noun* (also **messiah**, (earlier) **Messias**) ME Old and Modern French (*Messie* from popular Latin *Messias* from Greek *Messias* from Aramaic *mĕšīḥā*, Hebrew *māšîāḥ* anointed, from *māšaḥ* to anoint). The promised deliverer of the Jewish nation prophesied in the Hebrew Scriptures; Jesus regarded as the saviour of humankind. Also (*transferred*), an actual or expected liberator of an oppressed people or country etc.; a leader or saviour of a specified group, cause, etc.

■ The modern form *Messiah* was created by the Geneva translators of the Bible of 1560 as looking more Hebraic than *Messias*.
transferred **1996** *New Scientist* Shoko Asahara, the self-styled messiah who convinced his followers that Armageddon was coming . . . , is accused of masterminding a nerve-gas attack in the Tokyo underground . . .

mestizo /mɛˈstiːzəʊ/ *noun & adjective* plural of noun **mestizos** (feminine **mestiza** /mɛˈstiːzə/) L16 Spanish (from Proto-Romance from Latin *mixtus* past participle of *miscere* to mix). **A** *noun* L16 A Spanish or Portuguese person with parents of different races, *specifically* one with a Spaniard as one parent and an American Indian as the other; *generally* any person of mixed blood. Also, a Central or South American Indian who has adopted European culture. **B** *attributive* or as *adjective* E17 That is a mestizo or mestiza.

mesto /ˈmɛsto/ *adverb & adjective* E19 Italian (from Latin *maestus* sad). *Music* (A direction:) sad(ly), mournful(ly).

métairie /meteri/ *noun* plural pronounced same E19 French (from as MÉTAYER). A farm held on the MÉTAYAGE system.

metamorphosis /mɛtəˈmɔːfəsɪs/, /ˌmɛtə mɔːˈfəʊsɪs/ *noun* plural **metamorphoses** /mɛtəˈmɔːfəsiːz/, /ˌmɛtəmɔːˈfəʊsiːz/ M16 Latin (from Greek *metamorphōsis*, from *metamorphoun* to transform, from as *meta-* + *morphē* a form). **1** M16 The action or process of changing in form, shape, or substance; *especially* transformation by supernatural means. **b** L16 A metamorphosed form. **2** M16 A complete change in appearance, circumstances, condition, or character. **3** M17 *Biology* Normal change of form of a living organism, part, or tissue; *specifically* the transformation that some animals undergo in the course of becoming adult (e.g. from tadpole to frog), in which there is a complete alteration of form and habit.

metanoia /mɛtəˈnɔɪə/ *noun* L19 Greek (from *metanoein* to change one's mind, repent). Penitence; reorientation of one's way of life, spiritual conversion.

metastasis /mɪˈtastəsɪs/ noun plural **metastases** /mɪˈtastəsiːz/ L16 Late Latin (from Greek = removal, change, from *methistanai* to remove, change). **1** L16 *Rhetoric* A rapid transition from one point to another. Long *rare*. **2** M17 *Medicine* The transference of a bodily function, pain, or disease, or of diseased matter, from one site to another; *specifically* the occurrence or development of secondary foci of disease at a distance from the primary site, as in many cancers.

metate /məˈtɑːteɪ/ noun E17 American Spanish (from Nahuatl *métatl*). In Central America: a flat or somewhat hollowed oblong stone on which grain, cocoa, etc., are ground by means of a smaller stone. Also *metate-stone*.

metathesis /mɛˈtaθɪsɪs/, /mɪˈtaθɪsɪs/ noun plural **metatheses** /mɛˈtaθɪsiːz/ L16 Late Latin (from Greek, from *metatithenai* transpose, change, from as *meta-* + *tithenai* to put, place). **1** L16 *Linguistics* The transposition of sounds or letters in a word; the result of such a transposition. Formerly also, the transposition of words. **2** L17-M19 *Medicine* Spread of a disease within the body, METASTASIS; movement of diseased matter to another part of the body. **3** E18 *generally* Change or reversal of condition. **4** L19 *Chemistry* (An) interchange of an atom or atoms between two different molecules; *especially* double decomposition.

métayage /metɛjɑːʒ/ (plural same) noun (also **metayage**) L19 French (from as MÉTAYER). A system of land tenure in Europe and the United States, in which the farmer pays the owner a proportion (usually half) of the produce as rent, and the owner normally provides the stock and seeds.

métayer /metɛje/ noun plural pronounced same L18 French (from medieval Latin *medietarius*, from *medietas* half). A farmer who holds land on the MÉTAYAGE system.

metempsychosis /ˌmɛtɛm(p)sʌɪˈkəʊsɪs/ noun plural **metempsychoses** /ˌmɛtɛm(p)sʌɪˈkəʊsiːz/ L16 Late Latin (from Greek *metempsukhōsis*, from as *meta-* + *en* in + *psukhē* soul). Transmigration of the soul; *especially* the passage of the soul of a person or animal at or after death into a new body of the same or a different species.

■ Belief in *metempsychosis* was a feature of the ancient sect of Pythagoreans and is also a tenet in some Eastern religions.

méthode champenoise /metɔd ʃãpənwaz/ noun phrase E20 French (literally, 'champagne method'). The method of introducing a sparkle into wine by allowing the last stage of fermentation to take place in the bottle; a sparkling wine made in this way.

1995 *Country Life* And, thanks to Napoleon's sister and the introduction of the *méthode champenoise*, bottles of the modest, local, sparkling brew, Malvasia.

Methodenstreit /meˈtoːdənˌʃtraɪt/ noun plural **Methodenstreite** /meˈtoːdən ˌʃtraɪtə/ M20 German (literally, 'methods struggle'). (A) discussion or dispute concerning the methodology of a field of study.

Methuselah /mɪˈθ(j)uːz(ə)lə/ noun (also **Methuselem** /mɪˈθ(j)uːz(ə)ləm/) LME Hebrew (*mĕṯûšelaḥ*, a pre-Noachian patriarch, stated to have lived 969 years (Genesis 5:27)). **1** LME A very old person or thing, especially as a type or representation of extreme longevity. **2** M20 (Usually **methuselah**) A very large wine bottle, equivalent to eight ordinary bottles.

métier /metje/, /ˈmeɪtɪeɪ/ noun L18 French (from Proto-Romance alteration of Latin *ministerium* service, ministry, probably influenced by *mysterium* mystery). One's occupation or department of activity. Now usually, a field in which one has special skill or ability; one's forte.

1995 *Spectator* Louisa Alcott was to find her true métier as a chronicler of family life . . . .

metif /meɪˈtiːf/ noun E19 French (*métif*, alteration of *métis*: see METIS). A person with one White and one quarter Black parent.

metis /meɪˈtiːs/ *Canadian* /meɪˈtiː/, /ˈmeɪti/ noun plural same /meɪˈtiː(s)/, /ˈmeɪti/, /ˈmeɪtɪz/ (feminine **métisse** /meɪˈtiːs/, *Canadian also* /ˈmeɪtiːs/, plural **métisses**) E19 French (*métis* from Old French *mestis* from Proto-Romance, from Latin *mixtus* past participle of *miscere* to mix). A person of mixed descent; *especially* (in Canada) a person with one White and one American Indian parent.

metope /ˈmɛtəʊp/, /ˈmɛtəpɪ/ noun M16 Latin (*metopa* from Greek *metopē*, from *meta* between + *opē* hole in a frieze for a beam-end). *Architecture* A square space between triglyphs in a Doric frieze.

metro /'mɛtrəʊ, /'meɪtrəʊ/ *noun colloquial* (also **Metro**) plural **metros** E20 French (*métro* abbreviation of (*Chemin de Fer*) *Métropolitain* Metropolitan (Railway)). An underground railway system in a city, *especially* that in Paris.

metteur en scène /mɛtœr ɑ̃ sɛn/ *noun phrase* plural **metteurs en scène** (pronounced same) E20 French (literally, 'a person who puts on the stage'; cf. MISE EN SCÈNE). A producer of a play; a director of a film.

Mettwurst /'mɛtvʊrst/ *noun* L19 German. A type of smoked German sausage.

meum /'miːəm/, /'meɪəm/ *noun archaic* L16 Latin (neuter of *meus* mine). The principle that a person has sole rights to his or her own property and no rights to another's.

■ Chiefly in *meum and tuum*, '(the distinction between) what is mine or one's own and what is yours or another's'.

meunière /məːˈnjɛː/, *foreign* /mønjɛr/ *adjective* M19 French ((*à la*) *meunière*, literally, '(in the manner of) a miller's wife'). *Cookery* Especially of fish: cooked or served in lightly browned butter with lemon juice and parsley.

■ Usually postpositive, as in *trout meunière*.

mézair /meɪˈzɛː/, *foreign* /mezɛr/ (*plural same*) *noun* M18 French (from Italian *mezzaria* middle gait). *Horsemanship* A movement involving a series of levades with a short step between each.

meze /'meɪzeɪ/ *noun* (also **mezé**) plural same, **mezes** E20 Turkish (= snack, appetizer, from Persian *maza* to taste, relish). (Any of) a selection of hot and cold dishes served as an hors d'oeuvre in the Middle East and eastern Mediterranean region.

mezuza /məˈzuːzə/ *noun* (also **mezuzah**) plural **mezuzoth** /məˈzuːzəʊt/ M17 Hebrew (*mĕzūzāh*, literally 'doorpost'). A piece of parchment inscribed with Pentateuchal texts enclosed in a case and attached to the doorpost of a Jewish house in fulfilment of religious law.

■ The practice is based upon the injunction in Deuteronomy 6:9.

mezzani /mɛtˈsɑːni/ *noun* L19 Italian (plural of *mezzano*: see next). Pasta in the form of medium-sized tubes; an Italian dish consisting largely of this and usually a sauce.

mezzanine /'mɛzəniːn/ *noun & adjective* E18 French (from Italian *mezzanino* diminutive of *mezzano* middle, medium, from Latin *medianus* median). **A** *noun* **1** E18 A low storey between two others in a building, usually between the ground floor and the floor above. **b** M19 *Theatre* A floor beneath the stage, from which the traps are worked. **c** E20 The lowest gallery in a theatre or cinema; a dress circle. *North American*. **2** M18 A small window at the level of a mezzanine or attic. **B** *adjective* **1** M19 Designating an intermediate floor, storey, etc. **2** L20 *Commerce* Designating unsecured, higher-yielding loans that are subordinate to bank loans and secured loans but rank above equity.

B 1 1996 *Times Magazine* Even when the overall area is divided into smaller units, the tall ceilings provide an opportunity for horizontal divisions such as mezzanine floors.

mezza voce /ˌmɛtsə ˈvɒtʃi/ *adverb, noun, & adjective phrase* L18 Italian (*mezza* feminine of *mezzo* middle, half, *voce* voice). *Music* (With) half of the possible vocal or instrumental power; restrained.

mezzo /'mɛtsəʊ/ *adverb* M18 Italian (= middle, half, from Latin *medius* medium). *Music* (Qualifying a direction:) half, moderately, fairly.

mezzo *noun* abbreviation of MEZZO-SOPRANO.

mezzo-relievo /ˌmɛtsəʊrɪˈliːvəʊ/ *noun* (also **mezzo-rilievo** /ˌmɛtsəʊrɪˈljervəʊ/) plural **mezzo-relievos** L16 Italian (*mezzo* half + *relievo* relief). (A sculpture, moulding, carving, etc., in) half-relief.

mezzo-soprano /ˌmɛtsəʊsəˈprɑːnəʊ/ *noun & adjective* M18 Italian (*mezzo* middle + SOPRANO). *Music* **A** *noun* M18 plural **mezzo-sopranos**. A female voice intermediate in compass between soprano and contralto; a singer with such a voice; a part written for such a voice. **B** *adjective* E19 Designating, pertaining to, or intended for a mezzo-soprano.

■ In informal contexts often abbreviated to *mezzo*.

mezzo termine /ˌmɛtso ˈtɛrmine/ *noun phrase* plural **mezzo termini** /ˈtɛrmini/ M18 Italian (*mezzo* half, *termine* term). A middle term, measure, or period.

miasma /mɪˈazmə/, /mʌɪˈazmə/ *noun* plural **miasmas**, **miasmata** /mɪˈazmətə/ M17 Greek (*miasma(t-)* defilement, pollution, related to *miainein* to pollute). **1** M17 (An) infectious or noxious vapour, especially from putrescent organic matter, which pollutes the atmosphere. **2** M19 *figurative* A polluting, oppressive, or foreboding atmosphere; a polluting or oppressive influence.

micro /'mʌɪkrəʊ/ *noun & adjective* M19 Greek (combining form *mikr-* from *mikros* small) **A** *noun* plural **micros**. **1** M19 *Entomology* A moth belonging to the Microlepidoptera. **2** M20 A microskirt. **3** L20 A microcomputer; a microprocessor. **4** L20 A microwave oven. **B** *adjective* **1** E20 Microscopic; very small; small-scale; *Chemistry* of microanalysis. **2** M20 Microeconomic.

■ A colloquial, independent use of the combining form found in many English words derived from Greek and other sources, particularly in technical terminology; cf. MEGA. *Micro*, particularly in its chemical sense, is often contrasted, either explicitly or implicitly, with MACRO.

midinette /mɪdɪ'nɛt/, *foreign* /midinɛt/ (*plural same*) *noun* E20 French (from *midi* midday + *dînette* light dinner). A French, especially a Parisian, shop-girl; *especially* a milliner's assistant.

mielie variant of MEALIE.

migma /'mɪgmə/ *noun* M20 Greek (= mixture). *Geology* (A) MAGMA containing solid material.

mignon /'miːnjɒn/, *foreign* /miɲɔ̃/ (*plural same*) *adjective & noun* (feminine **mignonne** /'miːnjɒn/, *foreign* /miɲɔn/) M16 French. **A** *adjective* M16 Delicately formed; prettily small or delicate. **B** *noun* E19 A pretty child or young person.

mignonette /mɪnjə'nɛt/ *noun* E18 French (*mignonnette* diminutive of MIGNON). **1** E18 A kind of light fine narrow pillow-lace. Also *mignonette lace*. **2** L18 Any of several plants of the genus *Reseda*, with small greenish or whitish flowers; specifically *R. odorata*, cultivated for its fragrant flowers. **b** L19 A colour resembling that of the flowers of the mignonette; greyish green or greenish white. **c** L19 A perfume derived from or resembling that of the flowers of the mignonette.

migraine /'miːgreɪn/, /'mʌɪgreɪn/ *noun* LME Old and Modern French (from late Latin *hemicrania* from Greek *hēmikrania*, from *hēmi-* half + *kranion* skull). A recurrent throbbing headache, usually affecting one side of the head, often accompanied by nausea or disturbed vision; the

illness or condition characterized by such headaches.

mihrab /'miːrɑːb/ *noun* E19 Arabic (*miḥ-rāb*). **1** E19 A niche, chamber, or slab in a mosque, indicating the direction of Mecca. **2** E20 A niche motif on an oriental prayer rug, resembling the shape of a mihrab in a mosque.

mikva /'mɪkvə/ *noun* (also **mikvah, mikveh**) M19 Yiddish (*mikve* from Hebrew *miqweh*, literally, 'collection, mass, especially of water'). A bath in which certain Jewish ritual purifications are performed; the action of taking such a bath.

miles gloriosus /ˌmiːleɪz glɔːrɪ'əʊsəs/, /ˌmʌɪliːz/ *noun* plural **milites gloriosi** /ˌmiːlɪteɪz glɔːrɪ'əʊsiː/, /ˌmʌɪliːtiːz glɔːrɪ'əʊsʌɪ/ E20 Latin (= boastful soldier). A vainglorious soldier who boasts about his military exploits.

■ *Miles gloriosus* is the title of a comedy by the Roman playwright Plautus (*c.*250–184 BC). The *miles gloriosus* became a stock character of Renaissance comedy— Shakespeare's Parolles in *All's Well That Ends Well* is an example—and the phrase generally occurs in literary contexts.

milieu /'miːljəː/, /mɪ'ljəː/, *foreign* /miljø/ *noun* plural **milieus, milieux** /'miːljəːz/, *foreign* /miljø/ M19 French (from *mi* (from Latin *medius* mid) + *lieu* place). **1** M19 An environment; (especially social) surroundings. **2** M20 *transferred* A group of people with a shared (cultural) outlook; a social class or set. **b** L20 (also **Milieu**) In France: (a group or organization belonging to) the criminal underworld.

1 1996 *Spectator* She sketches in the Surrealist milieu of Twenties Paris.

milites gloriosi plural of MILES GLORIOSUS.

militia /mɪ'lɪʃə/ *noun* L16 Latin (= military service, warfare, war, from *miles, milit-* soldier). **1** L16-L17 A system of military discipline, organization, and tactics; a manner or means of conducting warfare. **2** L16 A military force, a body of soldiers; *specifically* a military force raised from the civilian population, as distinguished from mercenaries or professional soldiers; an auxiliary military force drawn from the civilian population in order to supplement the regular forces in an emergency; *collectively* the members of such a militia. **3** L18 The body of people, usually men, legally liable to military service, without enlistment. *United States*.

millefeuille /milfœj/, /ˈmiːlfəːj/ *noun* plural pronounced same L19 French (literally, 'a thousand leaves'). A rich confection of thin layers of puff pastry and a filling of jam, cream, etc.

millefiore /ˌmiːlfiˈɔːri/ *noun* M19 Italian (from *mille* thousand + *fiore* flowers). A kind of ornamental glass made by fusing together a number of glass rods of different sizes and colours and cutting the mass into sections which exhibit ornamental figures of varying pattern. Also *millefiore glass*.

mille-fleurs /milflœr/ *noun* M19 French (literally, 'a thousand flowers'). **1** M19 A perfume distilled from flowers of different kinds. **2** E20 A pattern of flowers and leaves used in tapestry, on porcelain, etc.

∎ Usually attributive (see quotation).

2 1996 *Country Life* The enclosed garden in which she is sitting is chequered with tiny daisies and small birds like a *mille-fleurs* tapestry.

millegrain /ˈmiligrem/ *noun & adjective* (also **milligrain**) M20 French (*mille* thousand + *grain* grain). (Designating) a gem setting of beaded or crenellated metal.

millennium /mrˈlɛnɪəm/ *noun* plural **millenniums**, **millennia** /mrˈlɛnɪə/ M17 Modern Latin (from Latin *mille* thousand, after BIENNIUM). **1** M17 A period of one thousand years. Also, a thousandth anniversary. **2** M17 *Christian Church* The period of one thousand years during which (according to one interpretation of Revelation 20:1–5) Christ will reign in person on earth. **3** E19 A period of peace, happiness, prosperity, and ideal government.

millet /ˈmilɛt/ *noun* E20 Turkish (= nation, group of co-religionists, from Arabic *milla(t)* religion). *History* A part of the population of the Ottoman Empire that owed allegiance to a particular religious leader, especially a non-Muslim one.

milpa /ˈmilpə/ *noun* M19 Mexican Spanish. In Central America and Mexico: a small cultivated field, usually of corn or maize.

mimbar /ˈmimbɑː/ *noun* (also **minbar** /ˈmɪmbɑː/) M19 Arabic (*minbar*, from *nabara* to raise). A small set of steps in a mosque from which the KHUTBAH is delivered.

mimesis /mɪˈmiːsɪs/, /mɪˈmʌɪsɪs/ *noun* M16 Greek (*mimēsis*, from *mimeisthai* to imitate, from *mimos* mime). **1** M16 Chiefly *Rhetoric* Imitation of another person's words or actions. **b** M20 The representation of the real world in art, poetry, etc. **2** M19 *Biology* Mimicry by one organism of another. Now *rare*. **3** M20 *Sociology* The deliberate imitation of the behaviour of one group of people by another as a factor in social change.

minaret /ˈmɪnərɛt/, /mɪnəˈrɛt/ *noun* L17 French (or Spanish *minarete*, Italian *minaretto*, from Turkish *minâre* from Arabic *manâra* lighthouse, minaret, from *nâra* to shine). **1** L17 A tall tower or turret connected with a mosque and surrounded by one or more projecting balconies from which a muezzin calls at hours of prayer. **2** M19 *transferred* An object or structure shaped like this.

minaudière /minodjɛr/ *noun* plural pronounced same E18 French (from *minauder* to simper, flirt, from *mine* mien). **1** E18–E19 A coquettish woman. **2** M20 A small handbag without a handle, a clutch-bag.

minbar variant of MIMBAR.

minerval /mɪˈnəːv(ə)l/ *noun* E17 Latin (from *Minerva* (earlier *Menerva*) the Roman goddess of handicrafts, wisdom (cf. Sanskrit *manasvin* wise), and later also of war, from earlier form related to Sanskrit *manas* mind, Greek *menos* courage, fury). A gift given in gratitude by a pupil to a teacher.

minestra /mɪˈnɛstrə/ *noun* L17 Italian. In Italy: soup, *especially* MINESTRONE.

minestrone /mɪnɪˈstrəʊni/ *noun* L19 Italian. A thick soup containing vegetables, beans, and pasta.

mingei /mɪŋˈɡeɪ/ *noun* M20 Japanese (from *min* people + *gei* arts). Japanese folk-art; traditional Japanese handicraft.

minifundium /mɪnɪˈfʌndɪəm/ *noun* plural **minifundia** /mɪnɪˈfʌndɪə/ (also **minifundio** /mɪnɪˈfʌndɪəʊ/, plural **minifundios**) M20 Modern Latin (or Spanish *minifundio* smallholding: cf. LATIFUNDIUM). In Latin America: a small farm or property, *especially* one that is too small to support a single family. Usually in *plural*.

minimus /ˈmɪnɪməs/ *noun & adjective* L16 Latin. **A** *noun* plural **minimi** /ˈmɪnɪmʌɪ/, /ˈmɪnɪmiː/. L16 A very small or insignificant creature. **B** *adjective* L18 Designating the youngest of several pupils with the same surname or the last to enter a school.

∎ As an adjective appended to a surname, the usage is found especially in public schools; thus the eldest and middle brothers of the three of which Smith *minimus* was the youngest would be known respectively as Smith *major* and Smith *minor*. Cf. PRIMUS.

Minnelied /'mɪnəli:d/ *noun* plural **Minnelieder** /'mɪnəli:də(r)/ L19 German (from *Minne* love + *Lied* song). A love-song written by a minnesinger, or in the style of the minnesingers.

Minnesinger /'mɪnəsɪŋə/ *noun* (also **minnesinger**) E19 German (from *Minne* love + *Singer* (modern *Sänger*) singer). A German lyric poet or singer of the twelfth to fourteenth centuries.

minuetto /minu'etto/, /ˌmɪnjʊ'ɛtəʊ/ *noun* plural **minuetti** /minu'etti/, **minuettos** /ˌmɪnjʊ'ɛtəʊz/ E18 Italian. A minuet.

minuterie /mɪ'nju:t(ə)ri/ *noun* M20 French (= clockwork, timing mechanism, from *minute* minute). (An electric light controlled by) a light switch incorporating a timing mechanism to turn it off automatically after a short time.

> **1955** W. Gaddis *Recognitions* Crémer opened the door, and the light of the minuterie threw his flat shadow across the sill.

minutia /mɪ'nju:ʃɪə/, /mʌɪ'nju:ʃɪə/ *noun* plural **minutiae** /mɪ'nju:ʃiː/, /mɪ'nju:ʃʌɪ/ M18 Latin (= smallness (in plural, trifles), from *minutus* small). A precise detail; a small or trivial matter or object.

■ Almost always used in the plural.

minyan /'mɪnjan/ *noun* plural **minyanim** /'mɪnjanɪm/ M18 Hebrew (*minyān*, literally, 'count, reckoning'). The quorum of ten males over thirteen years of age required for traditional Jewish public worship.

mirabelle /'mɪrəbɛl/ *noun* E18 French. **1** E18 (A fruit from) a European variety of plum tree. **2** M20 (A) liqueur distilled from mirabelles, especially those grown in Alsace, France.

mirabile dictu /mɪˌrɑ:bɪleɪ 'dɪktu:/ *interjection* M19 Latin (*mirabile* neuter of *mirabilis* wonderful + *dictu* supine of *dicere* to say). Wonderful to relate.

■ Generally used sarcastically (see quotation).

> **1996** *New Scientist* 'Mirabile dictu!' one might exclaim, though few people did. Most used an Anglo-Saxon term: hogwash.

mirabilia /mɪrə'bɪlɪə/ *noun* plural M20 Latin (use as noun of neuter plural of *mirabilis* wonderful). Wonders, marvels, miracles.

mirador /mira'ðor/ *noun* L17 Spanish (from *mirar* to look, observe). In Spain: a watch-tower. Also, a turret or belvedere on the top of a Spanish house.

mirage /'mɪrɑːʒ/, /mɪ'rɑːʒ/ *noun & adjective* E19 French (from *se mirer* to be reflected or mirrored, from Latin *mirare*). **A** *noun* **1** E19 An optical illusion caused by atmospheric conditions (usually the refraction of light in heated air); *especially* the false appearance of a distant sheet of water in a desert or on a hot road. Also, the appearance in the sky of a reflected image of a distant object, a wavelike appearance of warmed air just above the ground. **2** E19 *figuratively* An illusion, a fantasy. **3** E20 Any of various pale fashion colours; *especially* pale blue, grey, or turquoise. **B** *adjective* **1** E20 Resembling a mirage. **2** M20 Of a pale colour, especially blue, grey, or turquoise.

mirepoix /'mirpwa/ *noun* plural same L19 French (from the Duc de *Mirepoix* (1699–1757), French diplomat and general). *Cookery* A mixture of sautéed diced vegetables used in sauces etc. or served as a separate dish.

mirliton /'mə:lɪtɒn/ *noun* E19 French (= reed pipe, of imitative origin). **1** E19 A musical instrument resembling a kazoo; any instrument in which a sound is given a nasal quality by means of a vibrating membrane. **2** E20 A CHAYOTE. *United States.*

miscellanea /mɪsə'leɪnɪə/ *noun* L16 Latin (neuter plural of Latin *miscellaneus* from *miscellus* mixed). As *plural*, miscellaneous items, especially literary compositions, collected together. As *singular*, a miscellaneous collection, especially of literary compositions; a miscellany.

Mischsprache /'mɪʃˌʃprɑːxə/ *noun* plural **Mischsprachen** /'mɪʃˌʃprɑːxən/ M20 German (= mixed language). A language made up of elements of two or more languages.

mise au point /miz o pwẽ/ *noun phrase* plural **mises au point** (pronounced same) M20 French. A focusing or clarification of an obscure subject or problem.

> **1946** *Word* A general mise au point of the linguistic side of semantic problems is thus overdue.

mise-en-page /mizɑ̃paʒ/ *noun* plural **mises-en-page** (pronounced same) E20 French (*mise en pages* page-setting, imposition). The design of a printed page etc., including the layout of text and illustrations. Also, the composition of a picture.

1968 *Listener* Television cannot emphasise in the manner of a newspaper's *mise-en-page*.

mise en scène /miz ã sɛn/ *noun phrase* (also **mise-en-scène**) plural **mises en scène** (pronounced same) M19 French (cf. METTEUR EN SCÈNE). **1** M19 The staging of a play; the scenery and properties of a stage production. **2** L19 The setting or surroundings of an event or action.

1 1996 *Spectator* Covent Garden has really done it proud, . . . with a stupendously gorgeous staging by that genius of *mise-en-scène* Philip Prowse . . .

2 1995 *Observer Review* . . . the way the book imports real-life VIPs . . . and restaurants . . . into its narrative suggests the *mise en scène* isn't to be taken as entirely fantastical.

misère /mɪˈzɛː/, *foreign* /mizɛr/ (*plural same*) *noun* E19 French (= poverty, misery). **1** E19 *Cards* A declaration by which the caller undertakes not to win any tricks. **2** L19 Misery; a miserable condition or circumstance.

1 1995 *New Scientist* Many games exist in a 'misère' version, where the aim is to lose, not win. The misère version of dividing economic goods is dividing economic 'bads' such as unemployment, responsibility for pollution or responsibility for crime.

miserere /mɪzəˈrɪəri/, /mɪzəˈrɛːri/ *noun* ME Latin (imperative singular of *misereri* to have pity, have mercy, from *miser* wretched). **1 a** ME Psalm 51 (50 in the Vulgate), beginning *Miserere mei Deus* 'Have mercy upon me, O God', one of the penitential psalms. **b** L18 A musical setting of this psalm. **2** E17 *transferred* A cry for mercy; a prayer in which mercy is sought. **3** L18 A misericord seat.

mises au point plural of MISE AU POINT.

mises-en-page, mises en scène plurals of MISE-EN-PAGE, MISE EN SCÈNE.

miso /ˈmiːsəʊ/ *noun* E18 Japanese. Paste made from fermented soya beans and barley or rice malt, used in Japanese cookery.

mistral /ˈmɪstr(ə)l/, /mɪˈstrɑːl/ *noun* E17 French (from Provençal from Latin *magistralis* (sc. *ventus* wind)). A strong cold north-west wind which blows through the Rhône valley and southern France into the Mediterranean, mainly in winter.

1996 *Times Magazine* Overtones of Africa must be cheering in mid-winter when the

mistral sweeps down the Rhône Valley from Siberia.

mit /mɪt/ *preposition & adverb* L19 German (= with). With (me, us, etc.). *jocular* and *colloquial*.

Mitbestimmung /ˈmɪtbəˌʃtɪmʊŋ/ *noun* M20 German (= co-determination). In Germany: the policy in industry of involving both workers and management in decision-making.

1996 *Independent* And the other way round: no Ernest Bevin, no *Mitbestimmung*—the great postwar understanding between German unions and the bosses which still, just about, lasts.

Mitnagged /mɪtˈnagɛd/ *noun* plural **Mitnaggim** /mɪtˈnagɪm/ E20 Hebrew (*miṯnaggēḏ* opponent). A religious opponent of the Hasidim; any Jew who is not a Hasid.

Mitsein /ˈmɪtzʌɪn/ *noun* M20 German (use as noun of infinitive *mitsein*, from *mit* with + *sein* to be). *Philosophy* The concept of a person's being in its relationship with others.

1966 A. Manser *Sartre* The essence of relations between consciousnesses is not Mitsein (being together), it is conflict.

Mittelschmerz /ˈmɪtəlˌʃmɛrts/ *noun* L19 German (= middle pain). *Medicine* Pain in the lower abdomen regularly experienced by some women midway between successive menstrual periods and often thought to coincide with ovulation.

Mittelstand /ˈmɪtəlstand/ *noun* L20 German (= middle class). Something between extremes of size; middling size range.

1994 *Guardian* The problems facing smaller firms in growing into the Mittelstand are also highlighted . . .

mittimus /ˈmɪtɪməs/ *noun & verb* LME Latin (literally, 'we send', the first word of the writ in Latin). **A** *noun* **1** *Law* **a** LME–E18 A writ to transfer records from one court to another. **b** L16 A warrant committing a person to prison. **2** L16 A dismissal from office; a notice to quit.

▪ Sense 2 is chiefly used colloquially and in dialect in *get one's mittimus*, that is, 'be dismissed'.

mitzvah /ˈmɪtsvə/ *noun* plural **mitzvoth** /ˈmɪtsvəʊt/ M17 Hebrew (*miṣwāh* commandment). *Judaism* A precept; a duty, an obligation. Also, a good deed. Cf. BAR MITZVAH, BAT MITZVAH.

mixte /mikst/ *adjective & noun* plural of noun pronounced same L20 French (= mixed). (Designating) a bicycle or bicycle frame having no crossbar but instead two thin tubes running from the head of the steering column to either side of the rear axle.

Mizpah /'mɪzpə/ *adjective* L19 Hebrew (*Miṣpah* place-name in ancient Palestine). Designating a ring, locket, etc., given as an expression or token of association or remembrance, originally and especially one with 'Mizpah' inscribed on it.

▪ The allusion is to the cairn of stones made in token of the covenant between Jacob and Laban (Genesis 31:43–55), which was called Mizpah 'for he said, The Lord watch between me and thee, when we are absent one from another' (verse 49).

moccasin /'mɒkəsɪn/ *noun* E17 Virginia Algonquian (*mockasin*, and in other North American Indian languages). **1 a** E17 A kind of soft leather shoe, worn by North American Indians, trappers, etc. **b** L19 A soft informal shoe resembling this. **2** L18 A venomous North American snake.

mochi /'mɒtʃi/ *noun* plural same E17 Japanese. A cake made from glutinous rice, steamed and pounded.

modello /mɒ'dɛləʊ/, *foreign* /mo'dɛllo/ *noun* plural **modelli** /mo'dɛlli/, **modellos** M20 Italian. A detailed sketch for a larger painting, prepared for a patron's approval. Also, a small model for a larger sculpture.

moderato /mɒdə'rɑːtəʊ/ *adverb* E18 Italian (= moderate). *Music* (A direction:) at a moderate pace or tempo.

moderne /mə'dəːn/, *foreign* /mɔdɛrn/ *adjective & noun* M20 French (= modern). (Designating or characterized by) a popularization of the art deco style marked by bright colours and austere geometric shapes, or (frequently *derogatory*) any ultra-modern style.

Modernismus /modɛr'nɪsmʊs/, /mɒdə'nɪzməs/ *noun* M20 German (= modernism). Modernism in architecture, art, etc.

▪ Frequently derogatory.

modi plural of MODUS.

modicum /'mɒdɪkəm/ *noun* L15 Latin (= little way, short time, neuter singular of *modicus* moderate, from *modus* mode). A small quantity or portion; a limited amount.

▪ Usually followed by *of* in contexts in which *modicum* means 'a decent or necessary minimum amount' (see quotation).

1996 *Spectator* . . . there seems no reason why an editor, if he has to be sacked, cannot be despatched with a modicum of courtesy.

modiste /mɒ'diːst/, *foreign* /mɔdist/ (*plural* same) *noun* M19 French (from *mode* fashion, mode). A person who makes, designs, or deals in articles of fashion; *especially* a fashionable milliner or dressmaker.

1996 *Spectator* The result can be seen in the glorious 'Milliner's Shop' . . . in which the *modiste* can be seen nestling behind her stock as if sheltering beneath brilliantly coloured tropical flowers.

modulus /'mɒdjʊləs/ *noun* plural **moduli** /'mɒdjʊlʌɪ/, /'mɒdjʊliː/, **moduluses** M16 Latin (diminutive of *modus* mode). **1** M16–M17 *Architecture* A unit of length by which proportions are expressed. **2** *Mathematics* **a** M18 A number by which logarithms to one base must be multiplied in order to obtain the corresponding logarithms to another base. **b** M19 A constant multiplier, coefficient, or parameter. **c** M19 A measure of a quantity which depends on two or more other quantities. **d** M19 A number by which another number may be divided leaving a remainder. **3** E19 *Physics* and *Engineering* A numerical quantity representing some property of a substance, and equal to the ratio of the magnitude of a (usually mechanical) cause to the magnitude of its effect on the substance; *specifically* = modulus of elasticity.

modus /'məʊdəs/ *noun* plural **modi** /'məʊdʌɪ/, **moduses** L16 Latin. A mode; *especially* the way in which something is done; a mode or manner of operation.

▪ Now chiefly in Latin phrases (see following entries) or used elliptically for MODUS OPERANDI.

modus operandi /ˌməʊdəs ɒpə'randiː/, /ˌməʊdəs ɒpə'randʌɪ/ *noun phrase* M17 Modern Latin (= mode of operating). **1** M17 The way in which something operates. **2** L19 The way in which a person sets about a task.

2 1995 *Spectator* Certainly, as the last *NoW* editor to benefit from the narks, Mr Morgan would be familiar with their *modus operandi*.

modus vivendi /ˌməʊdəs vɪ'vɛndiː/, /ˌməʊdəs vɪ'vɛndʌɪ/ *noun phrase* L19 Modern Latin (= mode of living). A way of living or coping; *especially* a working arrangement between parties in dispute pending a final settlement.

1996 *Times* It is the modus vivendi of Christianity which underpins European thought.

moellon /ˈmwɛlɒn/ *noun* L19 French. DE-GRAS sense 1.

moeurs /məːz/, /mœr/ *noun plural* E20 French (from Latin MORES, plural of *mos* custom). The behaviour, customs, or habits of a people or a group of people.

1996 *Spectator* The director Stefano Vizioli and his designer Susanna Rossi Just present this sharp satire of marital *moeurs* with a light touch . . .

mofette /mɒˈfɛt/ *noun* E19 French (from Neapolitan Italian *mofetta* = Spanish *mofeta*). (An exhalation of gas from) a fumarole.

mofussil /məʊˈfʌsɪl/ *noun & adjective* (also **Mofussil, mofusil**) L18 Urdu (*mufassil* from Persian and Urdu *mufassal* from Arabic *mufaṣṣal* passive participle of *faṣṣala* to divide, separate). **A** *noun* L18 In the Indian subcontinent: the rural localities of a district as distinguished from the chief station or the town. **B** *attributive* or as *adjective* Of the mofussil; remote, provincial.

1996 *Spectator* Whether from across the sea or the Indian *mofusil*, immigrants come to these island cities to escape not only from poverty but also from the social constraints that held them back in their old worlds.

mogote /məˈɡəʊti/ *noun* E20 Spanish (= hillock, heap, haystack). *Physical Geography* A steep-sided hill of roughly circular cross-section characteristic of karst topography, especially in Cuba. Cf. HUM.

mohel /ˈməʊ(h)(ə)l/ *noun* M17 Hebrew (*mōhēl*). A Jew who performs the rite of circumcision.

moi /mwa/ *personal pronoun* L20 French (= me). Me; I, myself.

■ Since the late 1970s in jocular use as a pretentious reference to oneself. Chief popularizer of the expression was the character Miss Piggy in the television series *The Muppets*, the children's puppet show created by Jim Henson, and it was then also taken up by adult shows.
1996 *Times: Weekend* But naturally. Why do anything by halves? Cynical, moi? Not at all.

moire /mwɑː/ *noun* M17 French (later form of *mouaire* mohair). A watered fabric (originally mohair, now usually silk). Also *moire antique*.

moiré /ˈmwɑːreɪ/ *adjective & noun* E19 French (past participle of *moirer* to give a watered appearance to, from as preceding). **A** *adjective* **1** E19 Of silk: watered. Also, (of metal etc.) having a clouded appearance like watered silk. **2** M20 Designating or pertaining to a pattern of light and dark fringes observed when a pattern of lines, dots, etc., is visually superimposed on another similar pattern, or on an identical one slightly out of alignment with the first. **B** *noun* **1** E19 A variegated or clouded appearance like that of watered silk, especially as an ornamental finish applied to metal; a moiré pattern or effect. **2** M19 MOIRE.

A.1 *figurative* 1995 *Spectator* . . . it is very long, at times a shade too fluid, too gorgeously moiré.

moksha /ˈmɒkʃə/ *noun* L18 Sanskrit (*mokṣa*, from *muc* to set free, release). *Hinduism and Jainism* The final release of the soul from a cycle of incarnations; the bliss so attained. Also called *mukti*.

mola /ˈməʊlə/ *noun* M20 Cuna. A square of brightly coloured appliquéd cloth worn as a blouse by Cuna Indian women of the San Blas Islands, Panama.

1977 A. Jeffs (ed.) *Creative Crafts* Originally, when the Indians moved to the islands in the mid-19th century, these molas were simple garments made from dark blue fabric with just a narrow single band of color around the bottom.

molcajete /molkaˈxete/, /mɒlkəˈheɪtɛr/ *noun* L20 Mexican Spanish (from Spanish *moler* to grind + *cajete* pot, bowl). A mortar for grinding spices and small seeds in.

mole /ˈmoli/, /ˈməʊli/ *noun* M20 Mexican Spanish (from Nahuatl *molli* sauce, stew). A highly spiced Mexican sauce made chiefly from chilli and chocolate, served with meat.

molleton /ˈmɒlɪtɒn/ *noun* L18 French (from *mollet* diminutive of *mol* soft). Swanskin (flannel).

moloch /ˈməʊlɒk/ *noun* (in sense 1 usually **Moloch**) E17 Late Latin (from Greek *Molokh* from Hebrew *mōlek*, a Canaanite idol to whom children were sacrificed as burnt offerings (Leviticus 18:21), held to be alteration of *melek* king, by substitution of the vowels of *bōšeṯ* shame). **1** E17 An object to which horrible sacrifices are made. **2** M19 A slow-moving spiny Australian lizard, *Moloch horridus*, of grotesque appearance. Also called *mountain devil*, *spiny lizard*, *thorny devil*. **3** L19 A forest monkey of tropical America, a dusky titi.

molossus /məˈlɒsəs/ *noun plural* **molossi** /məˈlɒsʌɪ/ L16 Latin (= Greek *Molossos*). **1** L16 *Prosody* A metrical foot consisting of three long syllables. **2** E17 *History* A mastiff dog from the region of ancient Molossia, in north-western Greece. More fully *molossus dog.*

molto /'mɒltəʊ/ *adverb* E19 Italian (from Latin *multus* much). *Music* Very.

■ Usually in directions modifying adjectives from Italian.

momentum /mə'mɛntəm/ *noun* plural **momenta** /mə'mɛntə/ E17 Latin (see MOMENT). **1** E17–M19 A turning motion. **2 a** L17 *Physics* The quantity of motion of a moving body, equal to the product of the mass and the velocity of the body. **b** L18 The effect of inertia in the continuance of motion; impetus gained by movement; *figuratively* strength or continuity derived from an initial effort. **3** *Mathematics* An infinitesimal increment. Only in M18. **4** M18–E19 Force of movement. **5** E19 An element of a complex conceptual identity, a moment.

mompei /'mɒmpeɪ/ *noun* *plural* (also **mompe**) M20 Japanese (*monpe*). Baggy working trousers worn in Japan.

momser, momzer variants of MAMZER.

monad /'mɒnad/, /'məʊnad/ *noun & adjective* (in sense 1 also (earlier) in Latin form **monas** /'mɒnas/, plural **monades** /'mɒnədiːz/ M16 French (*monade* or its source late Latin *monas*, *monad-* from Greek, from *monos* alone). **1** M16 (**Monad**) The Deity, God. **b** E17 The number one, unity; a unit. Now chiefly *Historical*, with reference to ancient Greek philosophy, in which the numbers were regarded as being generated from the unitary one. **2** M18 *Philosophy* Especially in the philosophy of Leibniz: an indivisible unit of being (as a soul, an atom); an absolutely simple entity. **3** M19 *Biology* A hypothetical simple organism, *especially* one assumed as the first term in the genealogy of living beings, or regarded as associated with others to form an animal or vegetable body.

mon ami /mɒn ami/ *noun phrase* (also (feminine) **mon amie**) plural **mes amis** (feminine **mes amies**) /mez ami/ L18 French. (As a form of address:) my friend.

monas see MONAD.

mon cher /mɔ̃ ʃɛr/ *noun phrase* L17 French. (As a form of address to a male:) my dear, my dear fellow.

mondain /mɔ̃dɛ̃/ *noun & adjective* (feminine **mondaine** /mɔ̃dɛn/) L19 French. A *noun* L19 plural pronounced same. A worldly or fashionable person. Cf. DEMI-MONDAINE. **B** *adjective* L19 Of the fashionable world; worldly.

monde /mɔ̃d/, /mɒnd/ *noun* M18 French (= world). The world of fashionable or aristocratic people; such people collectively. Also, a person's particular circle or set.

■ Earlier in BEAU MONDE.

mondo /'mɒndəʊ/ *noun* plural **mondos** E20 Japanese (from *mon* asking + *dō* answering). An instructional technique of Zen Buddhism consisting of rapid dialogue of questions and answers between teacher and pupil.

mondo /'mɒndəʊ/ *adjective & adverb* M20 Italian (= world). **A** *adjective* **1** M20 Anarchic and tasteless. **2** L20 As an intensifier: considerable, much; huge. **B** *adverb* L20 Very, extremely.

■ Slang use of *mondo* derives ultimately from *Mondo Cane*, the title of an Italian film (1961) showing bizarre behaviour (released in 1963 in the English-speaking world as *A Dog's Life*). The film became a cult and was imitated in similar titles such as *Mondo Bizarro* (1966). The adjectival and adverbial uses arose through the interpretation of, for instance, *mondo bizarro* as 'very bizarre'. In the 1980s *mondo* became simply an intensifier in American slang. It was taken up in this way by the children's comic-book characters the Teenage Mutant Ninja Turtles (in Britain, the Teenage Mutant Hero Turtles) in phrases such as *mondo cool* to express approval, and the usage spread to Britain during the Turtlemania of 1989–90.

mondongo /mɒn'dɒŋgəʊ/ *noun* plural **mondongos** E17 Spanish (= tripe, black pudding). A Latin American or West Indian dish composed of tripe.

monocoque /'mɒnə(ʊ)kɒk/ *noun & adjective* E20 French (from *mono-* mono- + *coque* eggshell). **A** *noun* **1** E20 An aircraft fuselage or other structure having an outer covering in the form of a rigid load-bearing shell, usually without longerons or stringers. **2** M20 A motor vehicle underframe and body built as a single rigid structure (or in racing cars as a number of boxlike sections) throughout which the stresses are distributed. **B** *attributive* or as *adjective* E20 Designating or based on a structure of this type.

monosabio /mono'sabjo/, /mɒnəʊ'sabɪəʊ/ noun plural **monosabios** /mono'sabjos/, /mɒnəʊ'sabɪəʊz/ L19 Spanish (from *mono* monkey + *sabio* wise, trained). *Bullfighting* A picador's assistant in the ring.

monsoon /mɒn'suːn/ noun L16 Early Modern Dutch (*monssoen* (modern *moesson*, influenced by French forms) from Portuguese *monção* (cf. Old Spanish *monzon*) from Arabic *mawsim* season, fixed period, from *wasama* to brand, mark). **1** L16 A seasonal wind which blows in southern Asia, especially in the Indian Ocean, approximately from the south-west from April to October (in full *south-west, summer, wet,* or *rainy monsoon*), and from the north-east from October to April (in full *north-east, winter,* or *dry monsoon*). **b** M18 The rainfall which accompanies the south-west or summer monsoon; the rainy season. **2** L17 Any wind which reverses its direction seasonally, as the temperature varies between two areas, especially between land and ocean.

mons pubis /mɒnz 'pjuːbɪs/ noun phrase L19 Latin (= mount of the pubes). *Anatomy* The rounded mass of fatty tissue on the lower abdomen, over the joint of the pubic bones; *especially* that of a female (= MONS VENERIS sense 2).

monstre sacré /mɔ̃str sakre/ noun phrase plural **monstres sacrés** (pronounced same) M20 French (literally, 'sacred monster'). A striking, eccentric, or controversial public figure.

> **1995** *Spectator* Since Scruton was demolishing the claims of much of the painting and sculpture featured in the Tate, its director, Nicholas Serota, the *monstre sacré* of London's modern art establishment, found it convenient to be in New York.

mons Veneris /mɒnz 'vɛnərɪs/ noun phrase E17 Latin (= mount of Venus). **1** E17 *Palmistry* The ball of the thumb. **2** L17 *Anatomy* The rounded mass of fatty tissue on a female's lower abdomen, above the vulva. Cf. MONS PUBIS.

montage /mɒn'taːʒ/, /'mɒntaːʒ/ noun E20 French (from *monter* to mount). **1** E20 *Cinematography* and *Television* The selection and arrangement of separate sections of film as a consecutive whole; the blending (by superimposition) of separate shots to form a single picture; a sequence or picture resulting from such a process. **2** *generally* M20 The process or technique of producing a composite whole by combining several different pictures, pieces of music, or other elements, so that they blend with or into one another; the result of such a process.

montagnard /mɔ̃tanar/, /mɒntə'njaːd/ (plural same) adjective & noun M19 French (from *montagne* mountain). **A** adjective M19 Inhabiting a mountain region; of or pertaining to montagnards. **B** noun M20 A native or inhabitant of a mountain region; a highlander.

montagne russe /mɔ̃tan rys/ noun phrase plural **montagnes russes** (pronounced same) M19 French (literally, 'Russian mountain'). A switchback, a scenic railway, a roller coaster. *Canadian.*

Montaña /mon'taɲa/ noun M19 Spanish (= mountain). In Spanish-American countries: a forest of considerable extent; *specifically* the forested eastern foothills of the Andes in Peru etc.

mont de piété /mɔ̃ də pjete/ noun phrase plural **monts de piété** (pronounced same) M19 French (= mount of piety). A State pawnbroking organization in France providing loans to the poor at low rates of interest.

> ■ The term 'mount' for a financial institution was formerly (E17–M18) current in English. Cf. Italian MONTE DI PIETÀ.

monte /'mɒnti/ noun (in branch I (especially sense 2) also **monty** E19 Spanish (= mountain, pile of cards left after dealing). **I 1** E19 A Spanish and Spanish-American gambling game usually played with a pack of forty cards. Also (in full *three-card monte*), a form of three-card trick. **2** L19 A certainty; *specifically* a horse considered a safe bet to win a race. *Australian and New Zealand colloquial.* **II 3** M19 In Spanish-American countries: a small wooded tract; (a region of) chaparral or scrub.

monte di pietà /ˌmonte di pje'ta/ noun phrase plural **monti di pietà** /ˌmonti/ M17 Italian (= mount of piety). A State pawnbroking organization in Italy providing loans to the poor at low rates of interest. Cf. French MONT DE PIÉTÉ.

montera /mon'tera/ noun (also (now rare) **montero** /mon'tero/, plural **monteros** /mon'teros/) E17 Spanish (from *montero* mountaineer, hunter, from *monte* mount). A Spanish cap, originally worn for hunting, with a spherical crown and flaps able to be drawn over the ears. Now usually *specifically*, the black hat worn by a bullfighter.

monti di pietà, monts de piété plurals of MONTE DI PIETÀ, MONT DE PIÉTÉ.

montuno /mɒnˈtuːnəʊ/ *noun* plural **montunos** M20 American Spanish (= native to mountains, wild, untamed). **1** M20 A traditional male costume worn in Panama, consisting of white cotton short trousers and an embroidered shirt. **2** M20 An improvised passage in a rumba.

mon vieux /mɔ̃ vjø/ *noun phrase* L19 French. (As an affectionate form of address:) old friend, old man.

moolvi(e) variant of MOULVI.

moquette /mɒˈkɛt/ *noun* M19 French (perhaps from obsolete Italian *mocaiardo* mohair). A heavy piled fabric used for carpets and upholstery.
1996 *Times The Virgin in the Garden* supplies the interior decor of a Fifties lower middle-class home in such evocative detail that you can feel the texture of the uncut moquette.

mor /mɔː/ *noun* M20 **Danish** (= humus). *Soil Science* Humus forming a discrete layer on top of the soil with little mineral soil mixed with it, characteristic of coniferous forests and generally strongly acid.

moraine /məˈreɪn/ *noun* L18 French (from Savoyard Italian *morena*, from southern French *mor(re)* muzzle, snout, from Proto-Romance word). **1** L18 An area or bank of debris that a glacier or ice sheet has carried down and deposited; the material forming such a deposit. **2** E20 *Gardening* A bed made largely of stones covered with fine chippings, designed to produce suitable conditions for alpine plants.

morale /məˈrɑːl/ *noun* M18 French (*moral*, respelt to indicate stress; cf. LOCALE). **1** M18 Morality; moral teaching. Now *rare*. **2** M19 The mental and emotional attitude of a group or individual with regard to confidence, willingness, hope, etc.; degree of contentment with one's lot or situation.

moratorium /mɒrəˈtɔːrɪəm/ *noun* plural **moratoriums, moratoria** /mɒrəˈtɔːrɪə/ L19 Modern Latin (use as noun of neuter singular of late Latin *moratorius* that delays, from *morat-* past participial stem of *morari* to delay). **1** L19 *Law* A legal authorization to a debtor to postpone payment for a certain time; the period of such a postponement. **2** M20 A postponement or deliberate temporary suspension of some activity etc.
2 1995 *New Scientist* . . . there are plenty of grey whales migrating past Vancouver Island these days, after a decade-long moratorium on commercial whaling.

morbidezza /mɔrbiˈdɛddza/, /ˌmɔːbɪˈdɛtsə/ *noun* E17 Italian (from *morbido* morbid). **1** E17 *Painting* Lifelike delicacy in flesh tints. **2** L19 Delicacy, softness, especially in musical performance; sensibility, smoothness; sickliness.

morbilli /mɔːˈbɪlʌɪ/ *noun* plural M16 Medieval Latin (plural of *morbillus* pustule, spot characteristic of measles, diminutive of Latin *morbus* disease). *Medicine* (The spots characteristic of) measles.

morceau /mɔːˈsəʊ/, *foreign* /mɔrso/ *noun* plural **morceaux** /mɔːˈsəʊz/, *foreign* /mɔrso/ M18 French (Old French *morsel*, *morcel* diminutive of *mors* from Latin *morsus* bite, from *mors-* past participial stem of *mordere* to bite). A short literary or musical composition.

mordent /ˈmɔːd(ə)nt/ *noun* E19 German (from Italian *mordente* use as noun of verbal adjective from *mordere* to bite, from Proto-Romance alteration of Latin *mordere*). *Music* An ornament consisting of the rapid alternation of the note written with the one immediately below it. Cf. PRALLTRILLER.

mordida /morˈdida/ *noun* M20 **Central American and Mexican Spanish**. In Mexico and Central America: a bribe, an illegal exaction.

mordoré /mɔrdɔre/ *noun* L18 French (from Old French *More* (modern *Maure*) Moor + *doré* past participle of *dorer* to gild). A colour between brown and red; russet.

more /ˈmɔːreɪ/ *noun* E17 Latin (ablative of *mos, mor-* custom). In the fashion *of*, according to the custom *of*.
■ Only in Latin adverbial phrases (see following entries).

more hispanico /ˌmɔːreɪ hɪˈspanɪkəʊ/ *adverb phrase* M20 Latin. In accordance with Spanish custom.

more majorum /ˌmɔːreɪ məˈdʒɔːrəm/ *adverb phrase* E17 Latin (*majorum*, genitive plural of *majores* ancestors). In traditional manner.

more meo /ˌmɔːreɪ ˈmeɪəʊ/ *adverb phrase* E19 Latin. In my own fashion.

mores /ˈmɔːreɪz/, /ˈmɔːriːz/ *noun* plural L19 Latin (plural of *mos* manner, custom). **1** L19 The acquired customs and moral assumptions which give cohesion to a com-

munity, social group, or period. Cf. O TEM-
PORA, O MORES. **2** E20 *Zoology* The habits,
behaviour, etc., of a group of animals of
the same kind.

> **1** 1996 *Times* By posthumously according his
> official and unofficial families equal status, the
> former President held up a strange mirror to
> French *mores.*

Moresca /məˈrɛskə/ *noun* M19 Italian
(feminine of *Moresco* from *Moro* Moor; cf.
MORISCA). An Italian folk-dance related to
the English morris dance.

more suo /ˌmɔːreɪ ˈsuːəʊ/ *adverb phrase*
M19 Latin. In his own fashion.

morgue /mɔːg/ *noun* M19 French (proper
name of a Paris mortuary). **1** M19 A mortuary. **2a** E20 In a newspaper office, the
collection of material assembled for the
future obituaries of people still living. *colloquial.* **b** E20 A repository of cuttings,
photographs, and information in a newspaper office, film studio, etc. *colloquial.*

Morisca /məˈrɪskə/ *noun* M20 Spanish
(feminine of next; cf. MORESCA). A Spanish
folk-dance related to the English morris
dance.

Morisco /məˈrɪskəʊ/ *adjective & noun* M16
Spanish (from *Moro* Moor). **A** *adjective*
M16 Of or pertaining to the Moors; Moorish. **B** *noun plural* **Morisco(e)s. 1** M16 A
Moor, especially in Spain. **2** M16 Originally, a dance with Moorish elements and
sharing some features with the morris
dance. Now usually = MORISCA. **3** E18 Arabesque art, ornament, etc.

morituri te salutamus /mɒrɪˌtʊri teɪ
salʊˈtɑːməs/ *interjection* (also **morituri te
salutant** and other variants) E18 Latin (=
we who are about to die salute you).
Roman History The words addressed by
gladiators to the Roman emperor as they
entered the arena.

> ■ Quoted from Suetonius *Life of Claudius*
> xxi.6. Used allusively in English in many
> variant forms by people facing danger or
> difficulty.

moron /ˈmɔːrɒn/ *noun* E20 Greek (*mōron*
neuter of *mōros* foolish). **1** E20 *Medicine*
An adult with a mental age of between
about eight and twelve. **2** E20 A stupid or
slow-witted person; a fool. *colloquial.*

mortadella /mɔːtəˈdɛlə/ *noun plural* **mor-
tadellas, mortadelle** /mɔːtəˈdɛli/ E17 Italian (irregular from Latin *murtatum*
(sausage) seasoned with myrtle berries). A
large spiced pork sausage; Bologna sausage.

moscato /məˈskɑːtəʊ/ *noun plural* **mo-
scatos** E20 Italian. A sweet Italian dessert
wine.

moshav /ˈməʊʃɑːv/ *noun plural* **mosha-
vim** /ˈməʊʃɑːvɪm/ M20 Modern Hebrew
(*mōšāḇ* dwelling, colony). In Israel: a
group of agricultural smallholdings
worked partly on a cooperative and partly
on an individual basis.

mosso /ˈmɒsəʊ/ *adverb* L19 Italian (past
participle of *muovere* to move). *Music* (A direction:) rapidly, with animation.

mot /mo/, /məʊ/, (*plural same*), *in sense 1*
/mɒt/ *noun* L16 French (= word, saying,
from Proto-Gallo-Romance alteration of
popular Latin *muttum* related to Latin
muttire to murmur; cf. MOTTO). **1** L16
Originally, a motto. Later (now *dialectal*) a
word, an opinion. **2** E19 A witty saying.
Cf. BON MOT.

> **2** 1996 *Country Life* If I should leave my
> notebook open on the kitchen seat, I may find
> that some priceless thought, some *mot,* or
> maybe merely some item on a shopping list,
> has been eaten off the page.

motard /mɒtar/ *noun plural* pronounced
same M20 French (from *moto-* combining
form of *moteur*). A member of the French
motor cycle police.

> **1963** B. Abro *July 14 Assassination* Two
> motards were by the door . . . They . . . kicked
> their machines into life.

mot de Cambronne /mo də kambrɒn/,
/ˌməʊ də kamˈbrɒn/, *noun phrase* French
(literally, 'Cambronne's word'). The
French expletive *merde!*

> ■ The reputed reply of General Pierre Cam-
> bronne (1770–1842) when called upon to
> surrender at the Battle of Waterloo. The of-
> ficial version of what he said—*La garde
> meurt mais ne se rend pas* 'The Guard dies,
> but does not surrender'—seems to have
> been a happy journalistic invention, since
> the general himself denied saying it.

mot d'ordre /mo dɔrdr/, /məʊ ˈdɔːdrə/,
noun phrase plural **mots d'ordres** (*pronounced same*) M19 French (= word of command). A political slogan; a statement of
policy; an oral directive.

> **1930** *Observer* The official *mot d'ordre* is that
> Mr. Gandhi's salt campaign must be treated
> with a sense of humour.

motif /məʊˈtiːf/ *noun* M19 French. **1** M19 A
distinctive, significant, or dominant idea
or theme; *specifically* (**a**) *Art* a distinctive
feature, subject, or structural principle in
a composition or design; (**b**) in literature
or folklore, a particular or recurrent

event, situation, theme, character, etc.;
(c) *Music* a figure, a leitmotiv. **2** L19 An
ornamental design or piece of decoration; *specifically* (**a**) an ornament of lace,
braid, etc., sewn separately on a garment;
(**b**) an ornament on a vehicle identifying
the maker, model, etc. **3** L19 A motivation, a basis, (for an idea etc.).

motivi plural of MOTIVO.

motiviert /moti'viːrt/ *adjective* E19 German. Motivated.

motivo /moˈtiːvo/ *noun* plural **motivi** /mo
ˈtiːvi/ M18 Italian. *Music* A motif.

mot juste /mo ʒyst/, /məʊ ˈʒuːst/ *noun
phrase* plural **mots justes** (*pronounced
same*) E20 French (= exact word). The precisely appropriate expression.

moto /ˈməʊtəʊ/ *noun* M18 Italian. *Music*
Movement, pace.
■ In various musical directions; cf. CON
MOTO.

moto perpetuo /ˌməʊtəʊ pəˈpɛtjʊəʊ/
noun phrase plural **moti perpetui** /ˌməʊtiː
pəˈpɛtjuːi/ L19 Italian (= perpetual motion). A rapid instrumental composition
consisting mainly of notes of equal
value.

motte /mɒt/ *noun* L19 French (= mound).
Antiquities A large man-made earthen
mound with a flattened top, usually surmounted by a fort, castle, etc.

motto /ˈmɒtəʊ/ *noun* plural **mottos, mottoes** L16 Italian (from Proto-Gallo-
Romance word whence also MOT). **1** L16
Originally, a sentence or phrase attached
to an emblematical design to explain its
significance. Later, a short sentence or
phrase inscribed on an object, expressing
a reflection or sentiment considered appropriate to its purpose or destination.
Also, a maxim adopted as a rule of conduct. **b** E17 *Heraldry* A significant word or
sentence usually placed on a scroll, either
below an achievement of arms or above
the crest. **c** M19 A verse or saying in a
paper cracker etc. **2** E18 A short quotation or epigram placed at the beginning
of a book, chapter, etc.; an epigraph.
3 M19 A sweet wrapped in fancy paper together with a saying or scrap of verse.
Also *motto-kiss. United States.* **4** L19 *Music* A
recurrent phrase having some symbolical
significance.

motu proprio /ˌməʊtuː ˈprəʊprɪəʊ/,
/ˌməʊtuː ˈprɒprɪəʊ/ *adverb & noun phrase*
E17 Latin. **A** *adverb phrase* E17 Of one's

own volition, on one's own initiative,
spontaneously. **B** *noun phrase* plural
motu proprios. M19 An edict issued by
the Pope personally to the Roman Catholic Church, or to a part of it.

mouche /muːʃ/ *noun* L17 French (literally,
'a fly', from Latin *musca*). **1** L17 *History* A
small patch of black plaster worn on the
face as an ornament or to conceal a blemish. **2** M19 A natural mark on the face
resembling such a patch; a beauty spot.

mouchette /muːˈʃɛt/ *noun* E20 French.
Architecture A motif in curvilinear tracery
shaped like a curved dagger.

moue /muː/ *noun* M19 French. A pouting
expression, a pout.

moujik variant of MUZHIK.

moulage /ˈmuːlɑːʒ/ *noun* E20 French (=
moulding, moulded reproduction, from
mouler to mould). A cast or impression of
a (part of a) person or thing; the material
used for or the process of making a cast
or taking an impression.

moule /mul/ *noun* plural pronounced
same L19 French. *Cookery* A mussel.
■ Usually in plural in names of dishes, as
in *moules marinières.*

moulin /ˈmuːlɪn/, *foreign* /mulɛ̃/ (*plural
same*) *noun* M19 French (literally, 'mill').
1 M19 A deep, nearly vertical shaft in a
glacier, formed by falling water. Also
called *glacier mill.* **2** M20 A type of kitchen
utensil for grinding or puréeing food.

moulvi /ˈmuːlvi/ *noun* (also **maulvi**
/ˈmaʊlvi/, **moolvi(e)**) E17 Urdu (*maulvī*
from Arabic *mawlawī* judicial (used as
noun), from *mawlā* mullah). A Muslim
doctor of the law, an imam; *generally* (especially in the Indian subcontinent, used
as a form of address to) a learned person
or teacher.

mousaka variant of MOUSSAKA.

mousquetaire /ˌmuːskəˈtɛː/ *noun & adjective* E18 French (= musketeer, from *mousquet* musket). **A** *noun* **1** E18 *History* A
French musketeer. **2** L19 A glove with a
long loose wrist. More fully *mousquetaire
glove.* **B** *attributive* or as *adjective* M19 Of
an article of clothing: in the style of that
of a French musketeer.

moussaka /muːˈsɑːkə/, /muːsəˈkɑː/ *noun*
(also **mousaka**) M20 Turkish (*musakka*, ultimately from Arabic *musaḳḳā*; cf. modern
Greek *mousakas*, Romanian *musaca*, Albanian, Bulgarian *musaka*, etc.). An eastern

Mediterranean dish made with minced beef or lamb, aubergine, etc., with a cheese sauce.

mousse /muːs/ *noun* M19 French (= moss, froth). **1** M19 The aggregation of tiny bubbles in sparkling wine, as champagne etc. **2** L19 *Cookery* A sweet or savoury dish made from a purée or other base stiffened with whipped cream, gelatin, egg whites, etc., and usually served chilled. Frequently with specifying word. **3** M20 A brown emulsion of seawater and oil produced by the weathering of oil spills and resistant to dispersal; a mass of this substance. More fully *chocolate mousse*. **4** L20 *Hairdressing* A frothy preparation for applying to the hair to facilitate setting or colouring.

mousseline /ˈmuːsliːn/ *noun* L17 French. **1** L17 French muslin; a dress of this material. Also *mousseline-de-laine*. **2** M19 (A wineglass of) a very thin blown glassware with ornamentation resembling muslin or lace. More fully *mousseline glass*. **3** E20 *Cookery* A rich frothy sauce of seasoned or sweetened eggs or cream. More fully *mousseline sauce*. **b** E20 Any of various dishes with a light frothy texture and usually prepared by whipping or beating; a mousse.

mousseux /musø/, /muːˈsə/ *adjective & noun* E19 French (from as MOUSSE). **A** *adjective* E19 Of wine: sparkling. **B** *noun* M20 plural same. A sparkling wine, a VIN MOUSSEUX.

moustache /məˈstɑːʃ/ *noun* (also **mustache**) L16 French (from Italian *mostaccio*, *mostacchio* from medieval Latin *mustacia*, ultimately from Greek *mustax*, *mustak-* upper lip, moustache). **1** L16 A (cultivated) growth of hair above the whole or either half (frequently in *plural*, especially in *pair of moustaches*) of a man's lip or extending from this on either side of the lip; a growth of hair above a woman's lip. Also, an artificial strip of hair worn in imitation of this. **2** E17 A growth of hairs or bristles, or a marking resembling a man's moustache, round the mouth of certain animals or birds.

mouton enragé /mutɔ̃ ɑ̃raʒe/ *noun phrase* plural **moutons enragés** (pronounced same) M20 French (literally, 'angry sheep'). A normally placid person who has become suddenly enraged or violent.

moutonné(e) see ROCHE MOUTONNÉE.

mouvementé /muvmɑ̃te/ *adjective* E20 French. Animated, agitated, bustling, full of variety; *specifically* (of music) lively.
> **1965** *Guardian* Her life has been unusually mouvementé—and erratic.

moyen-âge /ˌmwɑːjənˈɑːʒ/ *adjective* (also **moyen-age** and with capital initials) M19 French (= the Middle Ages). Of or pertaining to the Middle Ages, medieval.

moyen sensuel /mwajɛ̃ sɑ̃sɥɛl/ *adjective phrase* (also **moyen-sensuel**) E20 French. Of an average sensual and materialistic character.
■ Generally in the phrase HOMME MOYEN SENSUEL.
> **1996** *Spectator* He is told to 'go and sell that thou hast, and give to the poor', but with the proviso: 'If thou wilt be perfect . . . and . . . have treasure in heaven'—to which the *moyen sensuel* capitalist could reply: 'who is talking about perfection, and surely any place in Heaven is treasure?'

mozetta variant of MOZZETTA.

mozzarella /ˌmɒtsəˈrɛlə/ *noun* E20 Italian (diminutive of *mozza* a kind of cheese, from *mozzare* to cut off). A white Italian cheese originally made in the Naples area from buffalo milk. More fully *mozzarella cheese*.

mozzetta /məʊˈzetə/, /məʊˈtsetə/ *noun* (also **mozetta**) L18 Italian (aphetized from *almozzetta*, from medieval Latin *almucia* amice). *Roman Catholic Church* A short cape with a hood, worn by the Pope, cardinals, and some other ecclesiastics.

mu /mjuː/ *noun* ME Greek. **1** ME The twelfth letter (M, μ) of the Greek alphabet. **2** L19 Plural same. One micrometre (micron). Usually denoted by μ. **3** E20 *Electronics* The amplification factor of a valve.

muchacha /muˈtʃɑːtʃə/ *noun* L19 Spanish (feminine of next). In Spain and Spanish-speaking countries: a girl, a young woman; a female servant.

muchacho /muˈtʃɑːtʃəʊ/ *noun* plural **muchachos** L16 Spanish. In Spain and Spanish-speaking countries: a boy, a young man; a male servant.

mudra /ˈmʌdrə/, /ˈmuːdrə/ *noun* E19 Sanskrit (*mudrā* seal, sign, token). Any of a large number of symbolic hand gestures used in Hindu religious ceremonies and in Indian dance. Also, a movement or pose in yoga.

muesli /ˈmuːzli/, /ˈmjuːzli/ noun M20 Swiss German. A dish, originating in Switzerland, consisting of a cereal (usually oats), fruit, nuts, etc., eaten with milk or cream, especially for breakfast.

muezzin /muːˈɛzɪn/ noun L16 Arabic (dialectal variant of Arabic muʾaḏḏin active participle of ʾaḏḏana to call to prayer, from ʾuḏn ear). A Muslim crier who proclaims the hours of prayer from a minaret or the roof of a mosque.

mufti /ˈmʌfti/ noun L16 Arabic (muftī active participle of ʾaftā to decide a point of law (related to FATWA)). A Muslim cleric or legal expert empowered to give rulings on religious matters; in the Ottoman Empire, a chief legal authority, especially of a large city (also Grand Mufti).

■ Mufti in the sense of 'plain or informal clothes worn by a person who has the right to wear a uniform of some kind' (E19) may be a facetious use of this word, but its origins are uncertain.

muguet /mygɛ/ noun L16 French (from medieval Latin muscatum musk-scented, from muscus musk). 1 L16–M17 Any of certain fragrant plants; specifically woodruff, Galium odoratum. 2 L16 Lily of the valley, Convallaria majalis; a scent made from or resembling it.

mukhtar /ˈmʊktɑː/ noun E20 Turkish (muhtar from Arabic muḵtār passive participle of iḵtāra to choose, elect). In Turkey and some Arab countries: the head of the local government of a town or village; a minor provincial official.

mukti /ˈmʌkti/, /ˈmʊkti/ noun L18 Sanskrit (= release, from muc to set free, release). Hinduism and Jainism MOKSHA.

mulatta /mjuːˈlatə/ noun E17 Spanish (mulata feminine of mulato mulatto). A female mulatto.

mulatto /mjuːˈlatəʊ/ noun & adjective plural mulatto(e)s L16 Spanish and Portuguese (mulato young mule, mulatto, irregularly from mulo mule). A noun L16 A person having one White and one Black parent; a person of mixed White and Black parentage. B adjective 1 E17 Of the colour of the skin of a mulatto; tawny. 2 L17 That is a mulatto; of or pertaining to mulattos. 3 M18 Designating a kind of mid-brown fertile soil. United States.

muleta /məˈleɪtə/ noun M19 Spanish. Bullfighting A red cloth fixed to a stick used by a matador during the FAENA.

1996 Spectator Because some of the bulls tired quickly, opportunities for assessing performances with the muleta were limited.

mulga /ˈmʌlgə/ noun M19 Aboriginal. 1 M19 Any of several small acacia, forming dense scrub in dry inland areas of Australia and sometimes used for fodder (also mulga tree); the land covered with such vegetation, (colloquial) the outback. 2 M19 A thing made of the wood of a mulga tree, especially a club or shield. 3 L19 A rumour, a message, a (false) report; the grapevine. In full mulga wire. Australian slang.

mullah /ˈmʌlə/, /ˈmʊlə/ noun E17 Persian (Urdu mullā, Turkish molla from Arabic mawlā). (A title given to) a Muslim learned in Islamic theology and sacred law.

multum in parvo /ˌmʌltəm m ˈpɑːvəʊ/ noun phrase M18 Latin (= much in little). A great deal in a small compass.

mumpsimus /ˈmʌmpsɪməs/ noun M16 pseudo-Latin (erroneously for Latin sumpsimus in the passage in the Eucharistic service that runs quod in ore sumpsimus 'which we have taken into our mouth'). 1 M16 An obstinate adherent of old ways, in spite of clear evidence of their error; an ignorant and bigoted opponent of reform. Formerly also loosely, an old fogey. 2 M16 A traditional custom or notion obstinately adhered to although shown to be unreasonable.

■ The origin is Richard Pace's anecdote in De Fructu (1517) of an illiterate English priest who garbled the passage in the Mass quoted above by substituting the nonsense word mumpsimus. When corrected, he replied 'I will not change my old mumpsimus for your new sumpsimus'. Now only in literary use. Cf. SUMPSIMUS.

mu-mu variant of MUU-MUU.

mung /mʌŋ/, /muːŋ/ noun E19 Hindi (mūng). (The seed of) either of two widely cultivated tropical legumes.

municipio /mjuːnɪˈsɪpɪəʊ/, /mjuːnɪˈtʃɪpɪəʊ/ noun plural **municipios** L19 Spanish and Italian (from Latin municipium). A Spanish, Latin American, or Italian municipality.

munshi /ˈmuːnʃiː/ noun (also **moonshee**) L18 Persian and Urdu (munšī from Arabic munšiʾ writer, author, active participle of ʾanšaʾa to write (a book)). In the Indian subcontinent: a secretary, an assistant; a language-teacher.

murex /'mjʊərɛks/ *noun* plural **murices** /'mjʊərɪsiːz/, **murexes** L16 Latin (perhaps related to Greek *muax* sea-mussel). Any of various spiny-shelled predatory gastropod molluscs of the genus *Murex* and related genera, of tropical and temperate seas, from some of which the dye Tyrian purple was formerly obtained. Also *murex shell.*

murus gallicus /ˌmjʊərəs 'galɪkəs/ *noun phrase* plural **muri gallici** /ˌmjʊəri: 'galɪki:/ M20 Latin (from *murus* wall + *gallicus* Gallic). *Archaeology* A type of late Iron Age Celtic fort having stone walls bound by horizontally placed timber frames.

muscadel variant of MUSCATEL.

muscae /'mʌsi:/ *noun* plural M18 Latin (plural of *musca* fly). Chiefly *Medicine* Specks which appear to float before the eyes, frequently due to particles in the vitreous humour of the eye. In full *muscae volitantes* /vɒlɪ'tanti:z/ (present participle of *volitare* to fly about).

muscat /'mʌskat/ *noun* M16 Old and Modern French (from Provençal (= Italian MOSCATO), from *musc* musk). **1** M16 MUSCATEL wine. In full *muscat wine.* **2** M17 Any of several varieties of grape with a musky taste or smell; a vine bearing a variety of such a grape. In full *muscat grape.* **3** M17–M18 A kind of peach or pear with a musky taste or smell.

muscatel /mʌskə'tɛl/ *noun* (also **muscadel** /mʌskə'dɛl/) LME Old French (*muscadel, muscatel* (= Italian *moscatello*) from Provençal diminutive of MUSCAT). **1** LME (A) strong sweet wine made from the muscat or similar grape; a drink of this. **2** E16 A muscat grape. In full *muscatel grape.* **3** M16–M18 A variety of pear with a musky taste or smell. **4** M17 A raisin from the muscatel grape. In full *muscatel raisin.* Usually in *plural.*

museau /myzo/ *noun* plural **museaux** /myzo/ E19 French (colloquial, literally, 'muzzle, snout'). A person's face.

musée /myze/ (*plural same*), /'mju:zeɪ/ *noun* M17 French (from Latin *mus(a)eum* library, study, from Greek *mouseion* seat of the Muses). In France and French-speaking countries: a museum.

musette /mju:'zɛt/ *noun* LME Old and Modern French (diminutive of *muse* bagpipe). **1** LME A kind of small bagpipe, *especially* a small French bagpipe of the eighteenth century with a soft tone. **2** E18 A soft pastoral air imitating the sound of the musette; a dance performed to such music. **3** E19 A reed-stop in an organ producing a soft tone resembling that of the musette. **4** L19 A small and simple variety of oboe without a reed-cap. **5** E20 A type of lightweight knapsack used especially by the military and by racing cyclists. More fully *musette bag.*

> **5** 1965 *Sun* The musette, or featherweight knapsack from the Continent, has largely replaced the saddlebag.

musica /'mju:zɪkə/ *noun* Latin (= music). Occurring in various phrases used in English, especially with reference to early music (see entries below).

musica ficta /ˌmju:zɪkə 'fɪktə/ *noun phrase* E19 Latin (literally, 'feigned music'). (Early contrapuntal music characterized by) the introduction by a singer of conventional chromatically altered tones to avoid unacceptable intervals.

musica figurata /ˌmju:zɪkə fɪgjʊ'rɑ:tə/ *noun phrase* M18 Latin (literally, 'figured music'). **1** Contrapuntal music in which the different melodic strands move more or less independently. **2** M20 Plainsong with decorated melody.

musica plana /ˌmju:zɪkə 'plɑ:nə/ *noun phrase* M20.Latin (literally, 'plain music'). Plainsong, canto fermo.

musica reservata /ˌmju:zɪkə rɛzə'vɑ:tə/ *nounb phrase* M20 Latin (literally, 'reserved music'). Early music characterized by clarity, balance, restraint, and expressiveness.

musicale /mju:zɪ'kɑ:l/ *noun* L19 French ((*soirée*) *musicale* musical evening). A musical party; a concert, especially at a private address.

■ United States; cf. SOIRÉE MUSICALE.

musique concrète /myzik kɔ̃krɛt/, /ˌmju:ziːk kɒn'krɛt/ *noun phrase* M20 French (= concrete music). Electronic music constructed by the rearrangement of recorded natural sounds.

mustache variant of MOUSTACHE.

mustafina /mʌstə'fi:nə/ *noun* E19 Spanish (apparently from *mustee*, abbreviation of Spanish MESTIZO). A person with one parent a mestizo and the other a White.

muta /'mju:tə/ *intransitive verb* L19 Italian (imperative of *mutare* to change). *Music* (A direction:) change instrument or tuning.

mutatis mutandis /mju:'tɑ:tɪs mju:'tandɪs/, /mu:ˌtɑ:tɪs/, /mju:'tandɪs/ *adverb* *phrase* L15 **Latin** (literally, 'things being changed that have to be changed'). Making the necessary changes; with due alteration of details.

> **1962** S. E. Finer *Man on Horseback* What is said of the army here is to be taken also to apply, *mutatis mutandis*, to the air force and the navy.

mutato nomine /mjuːˌtɑːtəʊ ˈnəʊmmeɪ/, /muːˌtɑːtəʊ ˈnɒmmeɪ/ *adverb phrase* E17 **Latin**. The name being changed, with a change of name or names.

■ Earliest in English as a quotation from Horace's *Satires* (I.i.69): *Quid rides? mutato nomine de te / Fabula narratur* 'Laughing are you? Just change the name and the tale is told about you.'

mutuel /ˈmjuːtʃʊəl/, /ˈmjuːtjʊəl/, *foreign* /mytɥɛl/ (*plural same*) *noun* E20 **French** (abbreviation of PARI-MUTUEL). A totalizator, a *pari-mutuel*. Chiefly *North American*.

muu-muu /ˈmuːmuː/ *noun* (also **mu-mu**) E20 **Hawaiian** (*muʻu muʻu*, literally, 'cut off' from the original absence of a yoke). A woman's usually brightly coloured and patterned loose-fitting dress, (as) worn in Hawaii.

muzhik /muːˈʒɪk/ *noun* (also **moujik**) M16 **Russian**. *History* A Russian peasant.

mystae plural of MYSTES.

mystagogue /ˈmɪstəɡɒɡ/ *noun* M16 **French** (Latin *mystagogus* from Greek *mustagōgos*, from *mustēs* MYSTES + *agōgos* leading, from *agein* to lead). In ancient Greece, a person who gave preparatory instruction to candidates for initiation into the Eleusinian or other mysteries; *generally* a person who introduces others to religious mysteries, a teacher of mystical

doctrines, a creator or disseminator of mystical doctrines.

mysterioso /mɪˌstɪərɪˈəʊzəʊ/ *adjective* M20 **Italian** (= mysterious). *Music* Executed in a mysterious manner.

mysterium tremendum /mɪˌstɪərɪəm trɪˈmɛndəm/ *noun phrase* E20 **Latin** (= tremendous mystery). A great or overwhelming mystery, *especially* the great or overwhelming mystery of God or of existence.

mystes /ˈmɪstiːz/ *noun* plural **mystae** /ˈmɪstiː/ L17 **Latin** (from Greek *mustēs*). A person initiated into mysteries.

mystique /mɪˈstiːk/ *noun* L19 **French**. The atmosphere of mystery and veneration investing some doctrines, arts, professions, or people; a mysterious attraction; any professional skill or technique designed or able to mystify and impress the lay person.

mythoi plural of MYTHOS.

mythopoeia /ˌmɪθə(ʊ)ˈpiːə/ *noun* M20 **Greek** (*muthopoiía*). The creation of a myth or myths.

mythos /ˈmʌɪθɒs/ *noun* plural **mythoi** /ˈmʌɪθɔɪ/ M18 **Greek** (*muthos* myth). **1** M18 A traditional story, either wholly or partly fictitious, a myth; a body of myths. **2** M20 A traditional or recurrent narrative theme or pattern; a standard plot in literature.

■ *Mythos* and its Latin derivative *mythus* (E19), both now used solely in literary contexts, were current before the Anglicized *myth* (M19), which is now the form used in all general contexts for sense 1.

N

naan variant of NAN.

naartjie /ˈnɑːtʃɪ/, /ˈnɑːki/ *noun* (also **naartje** and other variants) L18 **Afrikaans** (from Tamil *nārattai* citrus). In South Africa: a soft loose-skinned tangerine or mandarin orange.

naat /nɑːt/ *noun* M20 **Afrikaans** (= seam, from Dutch *naad*). An irregularity in the structure of a diamond caused by a change in direction in the grain; a diamond containing such an irregularity.

nabi /ˈnɑːbiː/ *noun* plural (in sense 1) **nebiᶜim** /nɛˈbɪɪm/, (in sense 2) **nabis** (also **Nabi**) L19 **Hebrew** (*nābī* prophet). **1** L19 *Theology* A person inspired to speak the word of God; a prophet; *specifically* a prophetical writer of the Old Testament and Hebrew Scriptures. Also (in *plural*) = *the Prophets*. **2** M20 A member of a group of late nineteenth-century French post-impressionists following the artistic theories of the French painter Paul Gauguin (1848–1903).

nabla /ˈnablə/ *noun* L19 **Greek** (= a kind of harp, probably of Semitic origin). *Mathematics* The symbolic differential operator in the shape of the inverted Greek capital letter delta Δ (hence often known under the abbreviation *del*).

nabob /ˈneɪbɒb/ *noun* E17 **Portuguese** (*nababo* or Spanish *nabab* from Urdu *nawwāb*, *nawāb* deputy governor: cf. NAWAB). **1** E17 *History* (The title of) any of certain Muslim officials acting as deputy governors of provinces or districts in the Mughal Empire; a governor of an Indian town or district. **2** M18 A person of great wealth or (formerly) high rank; *specifically* a European returning from India with a large fortune acquired there.

nacarat /ˈnakərat/ *noun* M18 **French** (perhaps from Spanish and Portuguese *nacarado*, from *nacar* nacre). **1** M18 A bright orange-red colour. **2** M19 A fine linen fabric dyed in this colour.

nacelle /nəˈsɛl/ *noun* E20 **French** (from late Latin *navicella*, diminutive of Latin *navis* ship). **1** E20 The basket or car of a balloon or airship. **2** E20 Originally, the cockpit of an aeroplane. Now, a streamlined bulge on an aircraft's wing or fuselage enclosing an engine etc. **3** M20 A similarly shaped structure on or in a motor vehicle.

■ In the core sense of 'a small boat', *nacelle* appears in Caxton's *Golden Legend* (1483), but it never achieved much currency in this sense, and seems not to have been used in English between the late fifteenth century and its modern reintroduction.

naches /ˈnʌxəs/ *noun* (also **nachas**) E20 **Yiddish** (*nakhes* from Hebrew *naḵaṯ* contentment). A sense of pleasure or pride, especially at the achievements of one's children; joy, gratification. *United States.*

Nachlass /ˈnɑːxlas/ *noun* plural **Nachlasse** /ˈnɑːxlasə/, **Nachlässe** /ˈnɑːxlɛsə/ M19 **German**. *singular* and (*rare*) in *plural*. Unpublished material left by an author after his or her death.

nacho /ˈnatʃəʊ/ *noun* plural **nachos** M20 (Mexican) **Spanish** (origin uncertain: perhaps from Mexican Spanish *Nacho* pet-form of male forename *Ignacio*, but cf. Spanish *nacho* flat-nosed). A snack or appetizer consisting of fried tortilla chips covered in melted cheese, peppers, spices, etc.

■ Perhaps the invention of a Mexican chef, Ignacio Anaya, who worked in the Piedras Niegras area in the 1940s, the dish was originally found only in the northern Mexico–Texas area and did not spread much beyond there until the 1970s. Taken up by the fast-food chains in the 1980s, it is now a popular food item in Europe too. *Nacho* is always used in the plural except when attributive (see quotation).
1983 *Fortune* The chain of Mexican fast-food restaurants is busily expanding its product line to include . . . a nacho side dish, and a salad.

Nachschlag /ˈnɑːxʃlaːk/ *noun* plural **Nachschläge** /ˈnɑːxʃlɛːgə/ L19 **German** (from *nach* after + *Schlag* blow, note). *Music* A grace-note taking its value from that of the note preceding it.

Nachtmaal variant of NAGMAAL.

Nacht und Nebel /ˌnaxt ʊnt ˈneːb(ə)l/ *noun phrase* M20 **German** (literally, 'night and fog'). A situation characterized by mystery or obscurity, especially as associated with Nazi Germany between 1941 and 1945.

nacre /'neɪkə/ *noun* L16 French (probably ultimately of oriental origin). Mother-of-pearl.

nada /'nɑːda/ *noun* 1 E20 Sanskrit (*nāda* sound). *Hinduism* Inchoate or elemental sound considered as the source of all sounds and as a source of creation.

nada /'nada/, /'nadə/ *noun* 2 M20 Spanish (= nothing, from Latin (*res*) *nata* thing born, insignificant thing). Nothing; nothingness, non-existence.

nadir /'neɪdɪə/ *noun* LME Old and Modern French ((also Spanish, Italian) from Arabic *naẓīr* (*as-samt*) opposite (the zenith)). **1** LME–E18 *Astronomy* A point in the heavens diametrically opposite to some other point, especially to the sun. Followed by *of*, *to*. **2** L15 *Astronomy* The point of the heavens diametrically opposite to the zenith; the point directly below an observer. **3** L18 The lowest point (*of* something); the place or time of greatest depression or degradation.

naevus /'niːvəs/ *noun* (also **nevus**) plural **naevi** /'niːvʌɪ/ M19 Latin. *Medicine* A congenital reddish or brown mark or (usually) raised blemish on the skin, *especially* a haemangioma; a birthmark, a mole.

naga /'nɑːɡə/ *noun* L18 Sanskrit (*nāga* serpent, snake). *Indian Mythology* A member of a race of semi-divine creatures, half-snake and half-human, that are the genii of rain, rivers, etc.

nagana /nə'ɡɑːnə/ *noun* L19 Zulu (*nakane*). A disease of cattle, antelope, etc., in southern Africa, characterized by fever, lethargy, and oedema caused by trypanosomes transmitted by tsetse-flies.

Nagmaal /'naxmɑːl/ *noun* (also (earlier) **Nachtmaal** /'naxtmɑːl/) M19 Afrikaans (*nagmaal* (Dutch *nachtmaal*), from *nag* (Dutch *nacht*) night + *maal* meal). In South Africa: the usually quarterly celebration of the Eucharist in the Dutch Reformed Church (an occasion of family reunions and celebration).

nahal /nə'hɑːl/ *noun* M20 Hebrew (from initials of the name of the organization, *Nŏ^car Ḥălūtzī Lōḥēm* Pioneer Military Youth). A military youth organization in Israel; an agricultural settlement manned by members of this organization.

naïf /nʌɪ'iːf/, /nɑː'iːf/ *adjective & noun* plural of noun pronounced same L16 French (see NAIVE). **A** *adjective* **1** L16 NAIVE sense 1.

b M20 NAIVE sense 1b. **2** M–L17 Of a diamond: without an imperfection, flawless. *rare*. **B** *noun* L19 A naive person.

naive /nʌɪ'iːv/, /nɑː'iːv/ *adjective* (also **naïve**) M17 Old and Modern French (*naïve*, feminine of *naïf* from Latin *nativus* native; cf. NAÏF). **1** M17 Unaffected, unconsciously artless. Also, foolishly credulous, simple. **b** M20 Of art etc.: straightforward in style, eschewing subtlety or conventional technique. **2** M20 *Biology* and *Psychology* Not having had a particular experience before, or been the subject of a particular experiment; lacking the knowledge to guess the purpose of an experiment; *especially* not having taken or received a particular drug. (Followed by *to*.)

naïveté /naivte/, /nʌɪ'iːvteɪ/ *noun* plural pronounced same L17 French (from as preceding). **1** L17 A naive action, remark, etc. **2** E18 The state or quality of being naive.

namaskar /ˌnʌməs'kɑː/ *noun* M20 Hindi (from Sanskrit *namaskāra*, from *namas* (see next) + *kāra* action). A traditional Hindu gesture of greeting made by bringing the palms together before the face or chest and bowing.

■ In Thailand a similar gesture is called *wai*.

namaste /'nʌməsteɪ/ *noun, interjection, & verb* M20 Hindi (from Sanskrit *namas* bowing, obeisance + *te* dative of *tvam* you (singular)). **A** *noun* M20 A traditional Hindu greeting, a NAMASKAR. **B** *interjection* M20 Expressing respectful greeting (said when giving a namaskar). **C** *intransitive verb* M20 Give a namaste.

nan /nɑːn/ *noun* (also **naan**) E20 Persian and Urdu (*nān*). In Indian cookery, a type of leavened bread cooked especially in a clay oven.

naos /'neɪɒs/ *noun* L18 Greek (= temple). (The inner cell or sanctuary of) a temple; also *Christian Church*, the main part of an Orthodox church where the congregation assembles (cf. BEMA, NARTHEX).

nappe /nap/ *noun* L19 French (literally, 'tablecloth'). **1** L19 A sheet of water falling over a weir or similar obstacle. **2** E20 *Geology* A sheet of rock which has moved horizontally over neighbouring strata, as a result of overthrusting or recumbent folding.

narcosis /nɑː'kəʊsɪs/ *noun* plural **narcoses** /nɑː'kəʊsiːz/ L17 Greek (*narkōsis*, from *narkoun* to make numb). *Medicine* The operation or effects of narcotics on the body; a state of insensibility or stupor, especially as induced by a drug; the production of this state. Also, therapeutic sleep artificially prolonged by the use of drugs.

narghile /'nɑːɡɪleɪ/ *noun* (also **narghileh**) M18 Persian (*nārgīl* coconut, hookah, from Sanskrit *nārikela* coconut; partly through French *nargileh, narguilé* from Turkish *nargile* from Persian *nārgīl*). A hookah.

narikin /'narɪkɪn/ *noun* E20 Japanese. In Japan: a wealthy parvenu.

narod /na'rod/ *noun* M20 Russian. In countries of the former USSR: the people; *specifically* the common people seen (in some ideologies) as the bearers of national culture.

■ The Narodnik movement was a type of socialism originating among the Russian intelligentsia in the nineteenth century which looked on the peasants and intelligentsia as revolutionary forces, rather than the urban working class. Supporters (*Narodniki*) endeavoured to give political education to a community of rural or urban poor while sharing its living conditions.

narrischkeit /'nɑːrɪʃkʌɪt/ *noun slang* L19 Yiddish (*naarishkeit, narrishkeit* from German *Närrischkeit*, from *närrisch* foolish, from *Narr* fool). Foolishness, nonsense.

narthex /'nɑːθɛks/ *noun* L17 Latin (from Greek *narthēx* giant fennel, stick, casket, narthex). An antechamber at the western end of some (especially early and Orthodox) churches, separate from the NAOS.

nasi /'nɑːsi/ *noun* L19 Malay. In Malaysian and Indonesian cookery: cooked rice.

naskhi /'naski/ *noun & adjective* (also **neskhi** /'nɛski/) L18 Arabic (*naskī* (plural), from *nasaḳa* to copy). (Designating) the standard Arabic script.

natatorium /ˌneɪtə'tɔːrɪəm/ *noun* L19 Late Latin (use as noun of *natatorius* of a swimmer). A swimming pool, *especially* an indoor swimming pool. *North American.*

natura naturans /naˌtjʊərə 'natjʊranz/ *noun phrase* E19 Latin (Latin *natura* nature + medieval Latin *naturans* (present participle) creating, from *naturare*). *Philosophy* Nature as creative; the essential creative power or act. Cf. next.

natura naturata /naˌtjʊərə natjʊ'rɑːtə/ *noun phrase* E19 Latin (Latin *natura* nature + medieval Latin *naturata* (past participle) created, from *naturare*). *Philosophy* Nature as created; the natural phenomena and forces in which creation is manifested. Cf. preceding.

naturelle /ˌnatʃʊ'rɛl/, *foreign* /natyrɛl/ *adjective & noun* L19 French (feminine of *naturel* natural). (Of) a pale pink or beige colour; skin-colour(ed).

nature morte /natyr mɔrt/ *noun phrase* plural **natures mortes** (pronounced same) E20 French. A still life.

■ Used as a descriptive term in French art since the eighteenth century.

Naturphilosophie /na'tuːrfɪlozoˌfiː/ *noun* E19 German (from *Natur* nature + *Philosophie* philosophy). The theory put forward, especially by Schelling (1775–1854) and other German philosophers, that there is an eternal and unchanging law of nature, proceeding from the absolute, from which all laws governing natural phenomena and forces derive.

naumachia /nɔː'meɪkɪə/ *noun* plural **naumachiae** /nɔː'meɪkɪiː/, **naumachias** L16 Latin (from Greek *naumachia*, from *naus* ship + *makhē* fight). *Roman History* An imitation sea battle staged for entertainment; a place, especially a building enclosing a stretch of water, specially constructed for such a battle.

navarin /'nav(ə)rm/, *foreign* /navarɛ̃/ (plural same) *noun* L19 French. A casserole of mutton or lamb with (especially root) vegetables.

navarin printanier /navarɛ̃ prɛ̃tanje/ *noun phrase* plural **navarins printaniers** (pronounced same) E20 French (= spring navarin). A navarin made with spring vegetables.

navette /na'vɛt/ *noun* E20 French (= little boat, shuttle, from medieval Latin *naveta* diminutive of Latin *navis* ship). **1** E20 A cut of jewel in the shape of a pointed oval; a jewel cut in such a shape. **2** L20 A railway truck designed to shuttle cars through a tunnel under the sea, *specifically* through the Channel Tunnel.

navicula /nə'vɪkjʊlə/ *noun* plural **naviculae** /nə'vɪkjʊliː/, /nə'vɪkjʊlʌɪ/, **naviculas** M19 Latin (diminutive of *navis* ship). *Ecclesiastical* An incense-holder shaped like a boat.

nawab /nə'wɑːb/, /nə'wɔːb/ *noun* (also (as a title) **Nawab**) M18 Urdu (*nawāb* from Urdu, Persian *nawwāb* variant of *nuwwāb* plural (used as singular) of (Arabic) *nā'ib* deputy; cf. NABOB). (The title of) a governor or nobleman in the Indian subcontinent (*historical*); (the title of) a distinguished Muslim in the Indian subcontinent.

NB abbreviation of NOTA BENE.

né /neɪ/, *foreign* /ne/ *adjective* M20 French (= born, masculine past participle of *naître* to be born). Born with the name, originally called: placed before the name by which a man was originally known.
■ Much more usual in the feminine NÉE.

nebbish /'nɛbɪʃ/ *noun & adjective* (also **nebbich**) L19 Yiddish (*nebech* poor thing). **A** *noun* L19 A nobody, a nonentity, a submissive timid person. Also as *interjection*, expressing commiseration, dismay, etc. **B** *adjective* M20 Of a person: innocuous, ineffectual; timid, submissive. *colloquial.*

nebelwerfer /'nɛːb(ə)lˈvɛrfər/, /'nɛb(ə)l ˌwəːfə/ *noun* M20 German (from *Nebel* mist, fog + *Werfer* thrower, mortar, from *werfen* to throw). A six-barrelled rocket mortar used by the German forces in the war of 1939–45.

nebula /'nɛbjʊlə/ *noun* plural **nebulae** /'nɛbjʊliː/, **nebulas** M17 Latin (= mist, vapour). **1 a** M17 A film or clouded spot on or over the cornea of the eye. Now only *Medicine*. **b** M18 A cloud, (a) cloudlike appearance; an indistinct, insubstantial, or nebulous thing or (*figurative*) person. **2** E18 *Astronomy* A hazy or indistinct luminous area in the night sky representing a distant cluster of stars. Now usually *specifically*, a cloud of gas, dust, etc., in deep space.

nebulé /'nɛbjʊleɪ/ *adjective* (also **nebuly** /'nɛbjʊli/) M16 French (*nébulé* from medieval Latin *nebulatus* past participle of *nebulare* to cloud). **1** M16 *Heraldry* Of a particular wavy form, used to represent clouds. **2** M19 *Architecture* Of a moulding: of a wavy form.

nécessaire /nesɛsɛr/ *noun* plural pronounced same E19 French. A small usually ornamental case for pencils, scissors, tweezers, etc.

necessarium /nɛsəˈsɛːrɪəm/ *noun* plural **necessaria** /nɛsəˈsɛːrɪə/, **necessariums** M19 Medieval Latin (use as noun of neuter singular of *necessarius* (probably after accusative (*locum*) *necessarium* necessary (place)) from Latin *necessarius*). A privy, a lavatory, especially in a monastic building.

necrosis /nɛˈkrəʊsɪs/ *noun* plural **necroses** /nɛˈkrəʊsiːz/ M17 Modern Latin (from Greek *nekrōsis* state of death, from *nekroun* to kill, mortify). *Medicine* and *Biology* The death or decay of (part of) an organ or tissue due to disease, injury, or deficiency of nutrients; mortification.

née /neɪ/, *foreign* /ne/ *adjective* (also **nee**) M18 French (= born, feminine past participle of *naître* be born; cf. NÉ). **1** M18 Born with the name. **2** M20 *transferred* Formerly called.
■ Normally follows a woman's married name to indicate her family name before she married, as in 'Julia Smith *née* Jones'.

negligée /'nɛglɪʒeɪ/ *noun* (also **negligee**, **négligé** also *foreign* /negliʒe/ (*plural same*)) M18 French (*négligé* past participle of *négliger* neglect). **1** M18 *History* A kind of loose gown worn by women in the eighteenth century. **2** M19 *Informal*, unceremonious, or incomplete attire. **3** E20 A shroud. *United States.* **4** M20 A woman's light dressing-gown, *especially* one of flimsy semi-transparent fabric trimmed with ruffles, lace, etc.
> **4** 1996 *Times* There were crocheted tops suited to a chilly English summer worn over ankle-length négligés.

négociant /negɔsjɑ̃/ *noun* plural pronounced same E20 French (= merchant (sc. *des vins*), from *négoce*, from Latin *negotium* business). A wine merchant.
> 1995 *Country Life* We put this to the test . . . recently, with a tasting of growers' and small *négociant's* champagnes compared with three non-vintage, benchmark *grandes marques* . . .

Negritude /'nɛgrɪtjuːd/ *noun* (also **Négritude** /negrityd/, **negritude**) M20 French (*négritude* from Latin *nigritudo*, from *niger*, *nigr-* black). The quality or characteristic of being a Negro (Black); affirmation of the value of Black or African culture, identity, etc.

nekulturny /nikʊlʲˈturnɪj/, /nɛkʊlˈtəːni/ *adjective* M20 Russian (*nekul'turnyǐ* uncivilized, from *ne-* not + KULTURNY). In countries of the former USSR: not having cultured manners, uncivilized, boorish.

nembutsu /nɛmˈbʊtsuː/ *noun* M20 Japanese (from *nen* thought + *butsu* Buddha). In Japanese Buddhism, the invocation and repetition of the name of the Buddha Amida for the purpose of salvation and spiritual unity; this invocation.

nem. con. /nɛm ˈkɒn/ *adverb phrase* L16 Latin (abbreviation of *nemine contradicente*). With no one contradicting.

■ *Nemine contradicente* (M17) is very seldom found in English.

nem. diss. /nɛm 'dɪs/ *adverb phrase* L18 Latin (abbreviation of *nemine dissentiente*). With no one dissenting.

■ *Nemine dissentiente* is not used in English in its full form.

nemesis /'nɛmɪsɪs/ *noun* (also **Nemesis**) plural **nemeses** /'nɛmɪsiːz/ L16 Greek (= righteous indignation, personified as the goddess of retribution or vengeance, from *nemein* to deal out what is due, related to *nomos* custom, law). **1** L16 An agent of retribution; a person who avenges or punishes. **b** M20 A persistent tormentor; a long-standing rival or enemy. *United States.* **2** L16 (An instance of) retributive justice.

1.b 1996 *New Scientist* . . . Mallon's nemeses, Dr George Soper and S. Josephine Baker, were reasonable and humane public health officials who took the actions they and their colleagues felt were best . . .

nemine contradicente see NEM. CON.

nemine dissentiente see NEM. DISS.

nepenthes /nɪ'pɛnθiːz/ *noun* L16 Latin (from Greek *nēpenthes* neuter of *nēpenthēs* banishing pain (qualifying *pharmakon* drug), from *nē-* not + *penthos* grief). **1** L16 A drug mentioned in Homer's *Odyssey* (iv.221) as liberating the mind from grief or trouble; any drug or potion bringing welcome forgetfulness. Also, a plant yielding such a drug. **2** M18 Any of various frequently climbing pitcher plants of the genus *Nepenthes*, chiefly of South East Asia.

ne plus ultra /ˌniː plʌs 'ʌltrə/, /ˌneɪ plʊs 'ʊltrɑː/ *noun phrase* M17 Latin (= not further beyond). **1** M17 A prohibition of further advance or action; an impassable obstacle or limitation. **2** L17 The furthest limit reached or attainable; *especially* the point of highest attainment, the acme or highest point *of* a quality etc.

■ The inscription imagined by the inhabitants of the ancient Mediterranean world to be on the Pillars of Hercules (Strait of Gibraltar), prohibiting further westward passage by ships.

2 1996 *Country Life* . . . in the United States, where Cuban cigars are not available, Davidoff cigars are regarded as the *ne plus ultra*.

neroli /'nɪərəli/ *noun* L17 French (*néroli*, from Italian *neroli* after an Italian prin-cess of that name, to whom its discovery is attributed). An essential oil distilled from the flowers of the Seville orange and used in perfumery. Also *neroli oil*, *oil of neroli*.

neskhi variant of NASKHI.

netsuke /'nɛtski/, /'nɛtsʊki/ *noun* plural **netsukes**, same. L19 Japanese. A small piece of ivory, wood, or other material, carved or otherwise decorated, formerly worn by Japanese on a cord suspending articles from a girdle.

Neue Sachlichkeit /ˌnɔyə 'zaxlɪçkʌɪt/ *noun phrase* E20 German (literally, 'new objectivity'). A movement in the fine arts, music, and literature, which developed in Germany during the 1920s and was characterized by realism and a deliberate rejection of romantic attitudes. Cf. SACHLICHKEIT.

neurosis /njʊə'rəʊsɪs/ *noun* plural **neuroses** /njʊə'rəʊsiːz/ M18 Modern Latin (from Greek *neuron* nerve). **1** M18 *Psychology* (A) mild mental illness, not attributable to organic disease, characterized by symptoms of stress such as anxiety, depression, obsessive behaviour, hypochondria, etc., without loss of contact with reality. **2** E20 Any more or less specific anxiety or malaise experienced by an individual, group, nation, etc.

névé /neve/ *noun* plural pronounced same M19 Swiss French (from Latin *nix*, *niv-* snow). The crystalline or granular snow on the upper part of a glacier, which has not yet been compressed into ice. Also, a field or bed of this. Also called FIRN.

nevus variant of NAEVUS.

nexus /'nɛksəs/ *noun* plural same, **nexes** /'nɛksiːz/ M17 Latin (from *nex-* past participial stem of *nectere* to bind). **1** M17 A connection; a bond, a link. **b** E20 *Grammar* A group of words (with or without a verb) expressing a predicative relation. **2** M19 A connected group or series; a network.

2 1996 *Spectator* But most of their successes were due to social control: the nexus of family life, religion and working-class self-help groups which enabled bourgeois values to permeate society.

ngoma /(ə)ŋ'gəʊmə/ *noun* E20 Kiswahili ((also *goma*) drum, dance, music). In East Africa: a dance; a night of dancing.

nibbana /nɪˈbɑːnə/ noun E20 Pali (nibbāna, Sanskrit nirvāṇa nirvana). Buddhism NIRVANA.

niche /nɪtʃ/, /niːʃ/ noun E17 Old and Modern French (from Old French nichier (modern nicher) to make a nest, nestle, from Proto-Romance from Latin nidus nest). **1** E17 An artificially constructed wall recess; specifically a shallow ornamental recess for a statue, urn, etc. **b** M19 A natural hollow in a rock or hill. **c** E20 A MIHRAB motif on an oriental prayer rug. More fully prayer niche. **2** figurative **a** E18 A place or position suited to or intended for a person's capabilities, occupation, or status. **b** E18 A place of safety or retreat. **c** E20 Ecology A position or role taken by a kind of organism within its community. **d** M20 Commerce A position from which an opening in a market etc. can be exploited; especially a specialized but profitable segment of a commercial market.

nicht wahr /nɪçt vɑːr/ interjection E20 German (literally, 'not true'). Is it not true? Isn't that so?

Niçois /niswa/, /niːˈswɑː/ adjective (feminine **Niçoise** /niswaz/, /niˈswɑːz/) L19 French (= of Nice, a city in southern France). Of, pertaining to, or characteristic of Nice or its inhabitants; specifically in Cookery, designating food, especially garnished with tomatoes, capers, anchovies, etc., characteristic of Nice or the surrounding region.
■ Generally postpositive, as in salade Niçoise.

niello /nɪˈɛləʊ/ noun plural **nielli** /nɪˈɛli/, **niellos** E19 Italian (from Latin nigellus diminutive of niger black). **1** A black composition of sulphur with silver, lead, or copper, for filling engraved designs on silver or other metals. **2** M19 (A specimen of) such ornamental work; an article decorated with niello. **3** M19 An impression on paper of a design to be filled with niello. **b** transitive verb M19 Inlay with niello. Chiefly as nielloed participial adjective.

nien hao /ˈnɪən haʊ/ noun plural same, **nien haos** L19 Chinese (niánhào, literally, 'reign year'). A title given to (part of) the reign of a Chinese emperor, used in imperial China as a system of dating. Also, a mark (signifying the reign of a particular emperor) used on Chinese pottery or porcelain to indicate an object's period of manufacture.

niente /niˈɛnte/, /nɪˈenti/ noun, adverb, & adjective E19 Italian. **A** noun E19 Nothing. **B** adverb & adjective E20 Music (A direction:) with gradual fading away of the sound or tone to nothing.
■ In nineteenth-century use the noun apparently existed in English only in the phrase (DOLCE) FAR NIENTE.

niet /ˈnjɛt/ adverb & noun (also **nyet**) E20 Russian (net no). **A** adverb E20 In Russian: no, especially expressing a blunt refusal. **B** noun E20 An utterance of 'niet'.

nihil obstat /ˌnʌɪhɪl ˈɒbstat/, /ˌnɪhɪl/ noun phrase M20 Latin (literally, 'nothing hinders' (the censor's formula of approval)). A certificate or statement recording that a work has been approved by the Roman Catholic Church as free of doctrinal or moral error; a statement of official approval, authorization.

nil admirari /ˌnɪl admɪˈrɑːri/ noun M18 Latin (= to wonder at nothing). An attitude of imperturbability or indifference to the distractions of the outside world.
■ A stance advocated by the Roman poet Horace in the opening lines of one of his Epistles (I.vi.1): nil admirari prope res est una ... solaque quae possit facere et servare beatum 'to wonder at nothing is just about the only way a man can become contented and remain so.'

nilas /ˈniːlas/ noun M20 Russian. Partly refrozen ice forming a thin flexible layer on the surface of water.

nil desperandum /ˌnɪl dɛspəˈrandəm/ interjection E17 Latin (= no need to despair). Do not despair, never despair.
■ From Horace Odes I.vii.27: nil desperandum Teucro duce et auspice Teucro 'no need to despair with Teucer as your leader and Teucer to protect you'.

nimbi plural of NIMBUS.

nimbu-pani /ˈnɪmbuːˌpɑːni/ noun M20 Hindustani (nimbū lime, lemon + pānī water). A drink of the Indian subcontinent consisting of lemon juice or lime juice with sugar and ice or water.

nimbus /ˈnɪmbəs/ noun plural **nimbi** /ˈnɪmbʌɪ/, /ˈnɪmbiː/, **nimbuses** E17 Latin (= cloud, rain, aureole). **1** E17 A bright or luminous cloud or cloudlike formation investing a god etc.; transferred a cloud of fine particles or other matter surrounding a person or thing. **2** E18 (A representation of) a halo surrounding the head of Jesus, a saint, etc. **3** E19 Meteorology A rain-cloud. Now rare.

ninja /ˈnɪndʒə/ *noun* plural same M20 Japanese (= spy). A person, especially a Japanese samurai, expert in NINJUTSU.

■ The word was little known in the West until the rise of interest in oriental martial arts in 1970s. *Ninjas* then began to play a role in fantasy and computer games but it was the huge popular and commercial success of the children's comic-book characters the Teenage Mutant Ninja Turtles in the United States at the end of the 1980s that brought the word into a wider circulation.

ninjutsu /nɪnˈdʒʌtsuː/ *noun* M20 Japanese (from *nin* stealth, invisibility + *jutsu* art, science). The traditional Japanese technique of espionage, developed in feudal times for military purposes and subsequently used in the training of samurai.

Niño, el see EL NIÑO.

ninon /ˈniːnɒn/, *foreign* /ninɔ̃/ *noun & adjective* E20 French. **A** *noun* E20 A lightweight dress fabric of silk, nylon, etc. **B** *attributive* or as *adjective* E20 Made of ninon.

nirvana /nɪəˈvɑːnə/ *noun* M19 Sanskrit (*nirvāṇa* use as noun of past participle of *nirvā-* to be extinguished, from *nis-* out + *vā-* to blow). In *Buddhism*, the experience that comes to a person in life when greed, hatred, and delusion are extinguished and enlightenment gained; the release from the effects of KARMA and the cycle of death and rebirth that comes when an enlightened person dies. In *Hinduism* and *Jainism*, liberation of the soul from the effects of karma and from bodily existence. Also *figurative* a state of bliss, an ideal state.

figurative **1996** *New Scientist* Without patents on extracted human material, . . . investment in biotechnology will drain out of Europe and into the patent nirvanas of the US and Japan . . .

nisei /ˈniːseɪ/ *noun* plural same M20 Japanese (from *ni-* second + *sei* generation). An American whose parents were immigrants from Japan. Cf. SANSEI.

nisi /ˈnʌɪsʌɪ/ *postpositive adjective* M19 Latin (= unless). *Law* That takes effect only on certain conditions, not final.

■ Generally in the phrase *decree nisi* 'a provisional order for divorce that will be made absolute unless cause to the contrary can be shown within a fixed period'.

nitchevo /ˌniːtʃʼɪˈvəʊ/ *interjection & noun* E20 Russian (*nichego*). **A** *interjection* E20 In Russian: Never mind! It does not matter! **B** *noun* M20 The use of the word 'nitch-

evo'; an attitude of resignation or fatalism.

noblesse /nəʊˈblɛs/, *foreign* /nɔblɛs/ *noun* ME Old and Modern French (from Latin *nobilis*). **1** ME Noble birth or rank; nobility, nobleness. **2** L15 *The* nobility; a class of people of noble rank, now especially in a foreign country.

■ The most usual occurrence in English is of sense 1 in NOBLESSE OBLIGE; *petite noblesse* (sense 2) is used of the minor nobility of France.

noblesse oblige /nɔblɛs ɔbliːʒ/, /nəʊˌblɛs ɒˈbliːʒ/ *noun phrase* M19 French. (The principle that) noble ancestry and privilege entail responsibility.

1995 *Spectator* But then I decided they were victims of *noblesse oblige*, considering it incumbent upon themselves as dukes to supply any reasonable favour requested of them.

noceur /nɔsœr/ *noun* plural pronounced same E20 French. A reveller, a rake, a libertine; a person who stays up late at night.

nockerl /ˈnɔkərl/ *noun* plural **nockerln** /ˈnɔkərln/ M19 Austrian German (= little dumpling). A small light Austrian and Bavarian dumpling, made with a batter including eggs, and usually semolina.

■ A *Salzburger nockerl* is a sweetened version eaten as a pudding.

nocturne /ˈnɒktəːn/ *noun* M19 French. **1** M19 A musical composition of a dreamy character. **2** L19 A painting of a night scene, a night-piece.

noel /nəʊˈɛl/ *noun* (also **noël**) E19 French (*noël*). A Christmas carol.

noema /nəʊˈiːmə/, /nəʊˈeɪmə/ *noun* plural **noemata** /nəʊˈiːmətə/ E20 Greek (*noēma* thought). *Philosophy* An object of perception or thought, as opposed to a process or aspect of perceiving or thinking. Cf. NOESIS 3.

noesis /nəʊˈiːsɪs/ *noun* plural **noeses** /nəʊˈiːsiːz/ L19 Greek (*noēsis*, from *noein* to think, perceive). **1** L19 Mental capacity or action. *rare*. **2** L19 An intellectual view of the moral and physical world. *rare*. **3** M20 *Philosophy*. A process or aspect of perceiving or thinking, as opposed to an object of perception or thought. Cf. NOEMA.

nogaku /ˈnɔːɡaku/, /ˈnəʊɡakuː/ *noun* E20 Japanese (*nōgaku*, from *nō* Noh + *gaku* music). Noh as a dramatic form or genre.

Noh /nəʊ/ noun (also **No**) L19 Japanese (nō (also = talent, accomplishment)). The traditional Japanese masked drama with dance and song, evolved from Shinto rites.

noia /'nɔɪə/ noun M20 Italian (ultimately from Latin in odio; cf. ENNUI). Boredom, weariness, ennui.

noir /nwɑ:/ adjective & noun LME French. **1** LME Black. **2** L18 Black as one of the two colours of divisions in rouge-et-noir and roulette. Earliest in rouge-et-noir.

■ Sense 1 is rare in English except in or with reference to the cinematic genre of FILM NOIR or, by extension, black humour in other media (see quotations below and ROMAN NOIR). It occurs in its literal meaning in a few phrases such as pinot noir (a variety of black grape) and figuratively in EN NOIR.

1996 Times Magazine More noir than knockabout, thriller than caper, it is an effort to transport the [Dr Who] series in time and imbue it with the values of a new television era.
1996 Bookseller Higson . . . says that he is more conscious of the influence of the American noir writer Jim Thompson.

noisette /nwɑ:'zɛt/ noun L19 French (diminutive of NOIX nut). A small round piece of meat.

noix /nwa/ noun plural same M19 French (literally, 'nut'; cf. NOISETTE). A piece of veal cut from the rump. Also noix de veau /nwa də vo/.

nolens volens /ˌnəʊlɛnz 'vəʊlɛnz/ adverb phrase L16 Latin (present participles of nolo, nolle to be unwilling, and volo, velle to be willing). Willing or unwilling, whether willing or not, willy-nilly.

noli me tangere /ˌnəʊlʌɪ mi: 'tan(d)ʒəri/, /ˌnəʊlɪ meɪ 'taŋ(ə)ri/ noun LME Latin (= do not touch me). **1** LME Medicine An ulcerous condition attacking bone and soft tissues especially of the face: specifically lupus. Now rare or obsolete. **2** LME A person who or thing which must not be touched or interfered with. **3** M16–M18 Botany A balsam or impatiens the seed capsules of which burst open on a touch; specifically Impatiens noli-tangere, touch-me-not. **4** M17 A warning or prohibition against meddling or interference. **5** L17 A painting representing the appearance of Jesus to Mary Magdalen at the sepulchre (John 20:17).

■ The original injunction is the Vulgate version of the risen Christ's warning to Mary Magdalen when He appears to her outside the sepulchre (John 20:17).

nolle prosequi /ˌnɒlɪ 'prɒsɪkwʌɪ/ noun L17 Latin (= be unwilling to pursue). Law (Originally, now United States) the relinquishment by a plaintiff or prosecutor of part or all of his or her suit or prosecution; (later) a procedure by which the Attorney General can terminate criminal proceedings. Also, an entry of this in a court record.

■ Also abbreviated to nolle in the United States (L19).

nolo contendere /ˌnəʊləʊ kɒn'tɛndəri/ noun L19 Latin (= I do not wish to contend). United States Law A plea by which a defendant in a criminal prosecution accepts conviction as in the case of a plea of guilty but does not admit guilt.

nom de guerre /nɔ̃ də gɛr/, /ˌnɒm də 'gɛ:/ noun phrase plural **noms de guerre** (pronounced same) L17 French (= war-name). An assumed name under which a person fights or engages in some other action or enterprise.

1995 Spectator . . . Avraham Stern of the eponymous gang took the nom de guerre 'Yair' after the commander of the Sicarii garrison at Masada.

nom de plume /ˌnɒm də 'plu:m/, foreign /nɔ̃ də plym/ noun phrase plural **noms de plume** (pronounced same) E19 pseudo-French (formed from nom name, de of, plume pen, after nom de guerre). An assumed name under which a person writes, a pen-name.

1996 Times . . . Elytis was the nom de plume he chose to use in place of his family name . . .

nom de théâtre /nɔ̃ də teatr/, /ˌnɒm də ter'ɑ:tr/ noun phrase plural **noms de théâtre** (pronounced same) L19 French (= theatre-name). An assumed name under which a person performs on stage.

nomen dubium /ˌnəʊmən 'dju:bɪəm/ noun phrase plural **nomina dubia** /ˌnɒmɪnə 'dju:bɪə/ E20 Latin (= doubtful name). Taxonomy A Latin name the correct application of which is vague or uncertain.

nomenklatura /nɑˌmjɛnklaˈtura/, /nɒ ˌmɛnkləˈtjʊərə/ noun M20 Russian (from Latin nomenclatura list of names). In the former Soviet Union: a list of influential posts in government and industry to be filled by Party appointees; collectively the holders of these posts, the Soviet élite; also transferred.

1995 Spectator Naturally, the BBC's higher nomenklatura—all those Controllers and Heads of This and That—will reply that the two [sc. high ratings and public service broadcasting] are not incompatible.

nomen nudum /ˌnəʊmən ˈnjuːdəm/ *noun phrase* plural **nomina nuda** /ˌnɒmɪnə ˈnjuːdə/ E20 Latin (= naked name). *Taxonomy* A Latin name which has no standing because it was not validly published.

nominata plural of NOMINATUM.

nominatim /nɒmɪˈneɪtɪm/ *adverb* M19 Latin (from *nomen, nomin-* name). Chiefly *Law* By name; particularly, expressly.

nominatum /nɒmɪˈnɑːtəm/, /nɒmɪˈneɪtəm/ *noun* plural **nominata** /nɒmɪˈnɑːtə/ M20 Latin (neuter of *nominatus*). The thing named by a sign or expression.

nominis umbra /ˌnɒmmɪs ˈʌmbrə/ *noun phrase* M19 Latin (literally, 'the shadow or appearance of a name'). A name without substance; a thing which is not what the name implies.

▪ The phrase comes from Lucan's *Pharsalia* (i. 135): *Stat magni nominis umbra* 'he stands the mere shadow of a mighty name'.

nomos /ˈnɒmɒs/ *noun* M20 Greek (= usage, custom, law). *Theology* The law; the law of life.

noms de guerre, noms de plume, etc. plurals of NOM DE GUERRE, NOM DE PLUME, etc.

non /nɔ̃/ *noun* plural pronounced same L20 French (= no). In France and French-speaking countries: an utterance of 'non', an absolute refusal or veto.

nonchalance /ˈnɒnʃ(ə)l(ə)ns/ *noun* L17 Old and Modern French (see next). The state of being nonchalant; lack of enthusiasm or interest; casual indifference, unconcern.

nonchalant /ˈnɒnʃ(ə)l(ə)nt/ *adjective* M18 Old and Modern French (from *non* + *chalant* present participle of *chaloir* to be concerned). Calm and casual; lacking or showing no enthusiasm or interest.

non compos mentis /nɒn ˌkɒmpɒs ˈmɛntɪs/ *adjective phrase* E17 Latin. Not in one's right mind. Cf. COMPOS MENTIS.

▪ Almost always predicative and often shortened to *non compos* (also E17).

non est /nɒn ˈɛst/ *adjective phrase* L19 Latin (abbreviated from *non est inventus* he was not found). Non-existent, absent.

▪ *Non est inventus* (L15) was the legal name formerly given to a sheriff's statement in returning a writ, to the effect that the defendant was not to be found within the sheriff's jurisdiction.

non est factum /ˌnɒn ɛst ˈfaktəm/ *noun phrase* E17 Latin (= it was not done). *Law* A plea that a written agreement is invalid because the defendant was mistaken about its character when signing it. Long chiefly *United States*.

non nobis /nɒn ˈnəʊbɪs/ *interjection* E19 Latin (= not to us). Expressing humble gratitude or thanksgiving; disclaiming credit for a success or benefit.

▪ In the Vulgate *Non nobis, Domine, non nobis* 'Not to us, O Lord, not to us' is part of a verse of Psalm 113; in the English Bible the words form the opening of Psalm 115.

non-obstante /ˌnɒnɒbˈstanti/ *noun* (also **non obstante**) LME Medieval Latin (*non obstante* not being in the way, from *non* not + *obstante* ablative present participle of *obstare* to be in the way (originally in ablative absolute, as *non obstante veredicto* notwithstanding the verdict)). **1** LME *History* A clause in a statute or letter patent, beginning 'non obstante', and conveying a dispensation from a monarch to perform an action despite any statute to the contrary. Also, a similar clause issued by the Pope. In full *clause of non-obstante*. **2** E17-M18 *generally* A dispensation from or relaxation of a law or rule (followed by *on, of, to*). Also, an exception to a rule.

nonpareil /ˌnɒnpəˈreɪl/ *adjective & noun* LME French (from *non-* + *pareil* like, equal, from popular Latin *pariculus* diminutive of Latin *par*). **A** *adjective* LME Having no equal; unrivalled, unique. **B** *noun* **1** L15 A person or thing having no equal; an unrivalled or unique person or thing. **2** M18 An old variety of apple. **3 a** M18 The painted bunting, *Passerina ciris*. **b** M18 The eastern rosella, *Platycercus eximius*. More fully *nonpareil parrot*. Chiefly *Australian*. **4** M18 Any of several attractively patterned moths.

▪ Formerly also a size of type roughly equivalent to modern 6 point (L17) and a kind of sweet (L17).

B 1 1996 *Spectator* She's a genius, an inspirational revolutionary, a great designer, a nonpareil . . .

non placet /ˌnɒn ˈpleɪsɛt/ *noun & verb phrase* (as verb also **non-placet**) L16 Latin (= it does not please). **A** *noun* L16 Originally, an expression of dissent or disapproval. Later, a negative vote in a university or Church assembly. **B** *transitive verb* E19 Give a negative vote on (a proposition); reject (a measure).

■ A formula used especially in university and Church assemblies in giving a negative vote on a proposition.

nonplus /nɒn'plʌs/ *noun & verb* L16 **Latin** (from *non plus* not more, no further). **A** *noun* L16 A state in which no more can be said or done; inability to proceed in speech or action; a state of perplexity; a standstill. Chiefly in *at a nonplus*, *bring* or *reduce to a nonplus*. **B** *transitive verb* L16 (inflected *-ss-*) Bring (a person etc.) to a nonplus; perplex; make (a thing) ineffective or inoperative. Frequently as *nonplussed* participial adjective.

non plus ultra /ˌnɒn plʌs 'ʌltrə/ *noun phrase* L17 **Latin** (= not more beyond). A NE PLUS ULTRA, the highest point or culmination *of*.

non sequitur /nɒn 'sɛkwɪtə/ *noun* M16 **Latin** (literally, 'it does not follow'). An inference or conclusion not logically following from the premisses; a response, remark, etc., not logically following from what has gone before.

■ Earliest in a rare and obsolete use (only LME) for part of the collar of a shirt etc.; an unfastened collar.
1996 *Spectator* There are one or two odd slips and non sequiturs in the book, which may be attributed to inexpert editing . . .

nori /'nɔːri/ *noun* L19 **Japanese**. Edible seaweed of the genus *Porphyra*, eaten especially by the Japanese either fresh or dried in sheets.

noria /'nɔːrɪə/ *noun* L18 **Spanish** (from Arabic *nāy'ūra*). Especially in Spain and the East: a device for raising water from a stream etc., consisting of a chain of pots or buckets, revolving round a wheel driven by the water current.

norte /'nɔrte/ *noun* M19 **Spanish** (= north). Any of the violent gales from the north prevailing in the Gulf of Mexico from September to March. Usually in *plural*.

norteamericano /ˌnorteameri'kano/ *noun & adjective* plural of *noun* **norteamericanos** /ˌnorteameri'kanos/ (also **Norteamericano**, feminine **norteamericana** /ˌnorteameri'kana/) E20 **Spanish and Portuguese** (from *norte* north + *americano* American). Especially in Latin America, (a native or inhabitant) of North America, a North American.

nosh /nɒʃ/ *noun & verb* E20 **Yiddish** (cf. German *naschen* to nibble). **A** *noun* **1** E20 A restaurant; a snack bar. More fully *nosh bar*, *nosh-house*. **2** M20 Food, a meal.

3 M20 A snack eaten between meals, a titbit. Chiefly *North American*. **B** *transitive and intransitive verb* **1** M20 Nibble or eat (a snack) (chiefly *North American*); eat (food), especially heartily or greedily. **2** M20 Practise fellatio (with). *slang*.

nostalgie de la boue /nɔstalʒi də la bu/ *noun phrase* L19 **French** (literally, 'yearning for mud'). A desire for degradation and depravity.
1995 *Spectator* Feinstein allows Mellors' inherent misogyny, fascism and *nostalgie de la boue* to overwhelm him, and permits Connie to be reclaimed by her own well-heeled bohemian class.

nostos /'nɒstɒs/ *noun* plural **nostoi** /'nɒstɔɪ/ L19 **Greek**. A homecoming, a homeward journey, *specifically* of Odysseus and the other heroes from Troy. Also, an account of such a homecoming or homeward journey, especially as the conclusion of a literary work. *literary*.

■ *Nost(o)i* was the title of an ancient Greek poem, now lost, dealing with the homecomings of the Greek heroes after the Trojan War.

nostrum /'nɒstrəm/ *noun* plural **nostrums**, **nostra** /'nɒstrə/ E17 **Latin** (neuter singular of *noster* our). **1** E17 A quack remedy, a patent medicine, *especially* one prepared by the person recommending it. **2** M18 A pet scheme, a favourite remedy, especially for bringing about social or political reform or improvement.
2 1995 *Times* Every age has its prevailing fallacies, and most of them from a similar origin: the insensitive overuse of an apparently commonsense nostrum.

nota bene /ˌnəʊtə 'bɛneɪ/ *verb phrase transitive & intransitive* (*imperative*) E18 **Latin** (from *nota* note + *bene* well). Mark well, observe particularly (usually drawing attention to a following qualification of what has preceded).

■ In general use in the abbreviated form NB.

notabilia /ˌnəʊtə'bɪlɪə/ *noun* plural M19 **Latin** (neuter plural of *notabilis* notable, after MEMORABILIA). Things worthy of note.

notes inégales /nɔts inegal/ *noun phrase plural* E20 **French** (literally, 'unequal notes'). *Music* In baroque music, notes performed by convention in a rhythm different from that shown in the score.

note verbale /nɔt vɛrbal/ *noun phrase* plural **notes verbales** (pronounced same) M19 **French** (literally, 'verbal note').

An unsigned diplomatic note, of the nature of a memorandum, written in the third person.

notitia /nəʊˈtɪʃɪə/, /nəʊˈtɪʃə/ *noun* E18 Latin (= knowledge, (in late Latin) list, account, etc., from *notus* known). **1** Knowledge, detailed information. *rare.* Only in E18. **2** L18 An account, a list; *specifically* a register or list of ecclesiastical sees or districts.

nougat /ˈnuːɡɑː/, /ˈnʌɡət/ *noun* (also (earlier) **nogat**) E19 French (from Provençal *nogat*, from *noga* nut, from Latin *nux*). (A sweet made from) egg-white sweetened with sugar or honey and mixed with nuts and sometimes pieces of fruit.

nouille /nuːj/ *noun* plural pronounced same M19 French. Noodle. Usually in *plural.*

noumenon /ˈnaʊmənɒn/, /ˈnuːmənɒn/ *noun* plural **noumena** /ˈnaʊmənə/ L18 German (from Greek, use as noun of neuter present participle passive of *noien* to apprehend, conceive). An object of purely intellectual intuition, devoid of all phenomenal attributes.

■ Chiefly in the philosophy of Immanuel Kant (1724–1804); cf. DING AN SICH.

nous /naʊs/ *noun* (also **nouse**) L17 Greek. **1** L17 *Greek Philosophy* Intuitive apprehension, intelligence; mind, intellect. **2** E18 Common sense, practical intelligence, gumption. *colloquial.*

> **2 1996** *Times* Taxpayers who follow them blindly, without using their nous, are fools.

nous autres /nuz otr/ *personal pronoun* (*1st plural*) M19 French (literally 'we others'). We as opposed to somebody or anybody else.

nouveau /ˈnuːvəʊ/, /nuːˈvəʊ/, *foreign* /nuvo/ *adjective & noun* E20 French (= new). **A** *adjective* **1** E20 *Nouveau art* = ART NOUVEAU. **2** M20 Of a person: possessing recently acquired wealth, NOUVEAU RICHE; ostentatiously displaying such wealth. Of wealth etc.: recently acquired. **b** L20 *Nouveau poor* = NOUVEAU PAUVRE. **3** L20 Modern, up to date. **B** *noun* plural **nouveaus**, **nouveaux** /ˈnuːvəʊ/, /ˈnuːvəʊz/, *foreign* /nuvo/. **1** L20 A *nouveau riche.* Usually in *plural.* **2** L20 BEAUJOLAIS NOUVEAU. *colloquial.*

■ *Nouveau* seldom occurs independently in English, but is used elliptically and colloquially for such phrases as *Beaujolais nouveau* etc., the context making plain the meaning intended.

nouveau pauvre /nuvo povr/, /ˌnuːvəʊ ˈpɔːvrə/ *adjective & noun phrase* plural **nouveaux pauvres** (pronounced same) M20 French (literally, 'new poor', after NOUVEAU RICHE). **A** *adjective* M20 Of a person: newly impoverished. **B** *noun* L20 A person who has recently become poor.

> **A 1995** *Times* Far better, for a *nouveau pauvre* hostess, to take advantage of the national mood of exhaustion among thirty-to-forty somethings . . . and issue instead a more casual invitation.

nouveau riche /nuvo riʃ/, /ˌnuːvəʊ ˈriːʃ/ *noun & adjective phrase* plural **nouveaux riches** (pronounced same) E19 French (literally, 'new rich'). **A** *noun* E19 A person who has recently acquired wealth, *especially* one who displays the fact ostentatiously or vulgarly. **B** *attributive* or as *adjective* L19 Of, pertaining to, or characteristic of a *nouveau riche*; that has recently acquired wealth.

> **B 1995** *Spectator* Throughout last week I had to endure the roar of *nouveaux riches* engines as their hideous-looking children gunned them to impress.

nouveau roman /nuvo rɔmɑ̃/ *noun phrase* M20 French (literally, 'new novel'). A type of (especially French) novel characterized by precise descriptions of characters' mental states and absence of interpretation of or comment on them.

> **1974** *Times Literary Supplement* The sources of Mr Gordon's off-the-peg technique are fairly clear: some Kafka; the Burroughs scissors; but mostly the *nouveau roman*. The novel, so this modish dogma asserts, is a 'vision of things', and the universe no more than the sum of the author's sensations.

nouveaux plural of NOUVEAU.

nouveaux arrivés /nuvoz arive/ *noun phrase* plural L19 French (literally, 'new arrivals'). People who have recently acquired a higher financial and social standing.

nouveaux pauvres, nouveaux riches plurals of NOUVEAU PAUVRE, NOUVEAU RICHE.

nouvelle /nuvɛl/ *noun* plural pronounced same L17 French. A short fictitious narrative, a short novel, *especially* one dealing with a single situation or a single aspect of a character or characters.

nouvelle /nuːˈvɛl/, *foreign* /nuvɛl/ *adjective* L18 French (feminine of NOUVEAU; in sense 2 elliptical for NOUVELLE CUISINE). **1** L18 *generally* New, novel. Now rare. **2** L20

Of, pertaining to, or characteristic of *nouvelle cuisine*.

nouvelle cuisine /nuvɛl kɥizin/, /ˌnuːvɛl kwɪˈziːn/ *noun phrase* L20 French (literally, 'new cooking'). A style of (especially French) cooking that avoids traditional rich sauces and emphasizes the freshness of the ingredients and attractive presentation.

■ The fashion for *nouvelle cuisine* spread beyond France in the 1970s and early 1980s, and its characteristics of lightness, short cooking times, and small helpings continued to endear it to the healthy eating lobby. In the hands of pretentious practitioners, however, the fashionable extremes of artistic presentation and meagreness of quantity have incurred considerable ridicule (see quotation).
1990 *Country Living* One establishment we visited served every dish flanked by the same ludicrously inappropriate clutter: a frilly lettuce leaf pinned down by a couple of hefty spring onions, a pallid slice of kiwi fruit and a strawberry. Oh nouvelle cuisine, what have you spawned!

nouvelles plural of NOUVELLE.

nouvelle vague /nuvɛl vag/ *noun phrase* M20 French (literally, 'new wave'; cf. VAGUE). A new movement or trend; *specifically* that in film-making originating in France in the late 1950s.
attributive **1996** *Times* As a young man at the Amsterdam Film Academy in the early Sixties, Jan De Bont ... would make a regular pilgrimage to Paris to sit at the feet of the *nouvelle vague* guru Jean-Luc Goddard.

nova /ˈnəʊvə/ *noun* plural **novae** /ˈnəʊviː/, **novas** L19 Latin (feminine singular of *novus* new). Astronomy Originally, a new star or nebula. Now *specifically* a star whose brightness suddenly increases by several magnitudes, with violent ejection of gaseous material, and then decreases more or less gradually. Formerly also, a supernova.

■ The present astronomical term is a reintroduction, as *nova* was originally (L17) used in the rare and obsolete sense of 'a thick ring or roll of tobacco'.

novella /nəˈvɛlə/ *noun* E20 Italian. A short fictitious prose narrative, a short novel, a long short story.

■ The word was particularly applied to the tales in Boccaccio's *Decameron* and its Italian imitators before being transferred to a work in any language midway in length between a full-scale novel and a short story.

novena /nəˈ(ʊ)viːnə/ *noun* plural **novenae** /nəˈ(ʊ)viːniː/, **novenas** M19 Medieval Latin (from *novem* nine, after Latin *novenarius* of nine days). *Roman Catholic Church* A devotion consisting of special prayers or services on nine successive days.

novi homines plural of NOVUS HOMO.

novillada /noviˈ(l)jada/, /nɒvɪˈljaːdə/ *noun* plural **novilladas** /noviˈ(l)jadas/, /nɒvɪˈljaːdəz/ L19 Spanish (from NOVILLO). A bullfight in which three-year-old bulls are fought by novice matadors.

novillero /noviˈ(l)jero/, /nɒvɪˈljɛːrəʊ/ *noun* plural **novilleros** /noviˈ(l)jeros/, /nɒvɪˈljɛrəʊz/ E20 Spanish (from NOVILLO). An apprentice matador who has fought only in NOVILLADAS.

novillo /noˈvi(l)jo/, /nɒˈviːljəʊ/ *noun* plural **novillos** /noˈvi(l)jos/, /nɒˈviːljəʊz/ M19 Spanish (from Latin *novellus* new). A young bull; *specifically* a fighting bull not more than three years old.

novio /ˈnovjo/ *noun* plural **novios** /ˈnovjos/ E20 Spanish. In Spain and Spanish-speaking countries: a boyfriend, a lover.

novus homo /ˌnəʊvəs ˈhɒməʊ/ *noun phrase* plural **novi homines** /ˌnəʊvʌɪ ˈhɒmmiːz/ L16 Latin (literally, 'new man'). A man who has recently risen to a position of importance from insignificance; an upstart.

■ In ancient Rome, the phrase was specifically applied to the first man in a particular family to rise to the office of a magistrate.

noxa /ˈnɒksə/ *noun* plural **noxae** /ˈnɒksiː/ L19 Latin (= hurt, damage). *Medicine* A thing harmful to the body.

noyade /nwaːˈjaːd/, *foreign* /nwajad/ *noun* plural **noyades** /nwaːˈjaːdz/, *foreign* /nwajad/) E19 French (from *noyer* to drown, from Latin *necare* kill without a weapon, (later) drown, from *nex, nec-* slaughter). An execution carried out by drowning, especially a mass one as in France in 1794.

noyau /nwaːˈjəʊ/, *foreign* /nwajo/ *noun* plural **noyaux** /nwaːˈjəʊz/, *foreign* /nwajo/ L18 French (earlier *noiel* kernel, from Proto-Romance use as noun of neuter of late Latin *nucalis*, from *nux, nuc-* nut). **1** L18 A liqueur made of brandy flavoured with the kernels of certain fruits. **2** E20 A type of sweet similar to nougat.

nritta /ˈ(ə)nrɪtə/ *noun* E20 Sanskrit (*nṛtta* dancing). A type of Indian dance with abstract patterns of movement and neutral facial expressions.

nritya /ˈ(ə)nrɪtjə/ *noun* L19 Sanskrit (*nrtya* dance, mime). A type of Indian dance through which ideas or emotions are expressed.

nuance /ˈnjuːɑːns/ *noun & verb* L18 French (from *nuerto* show cloudlike variations in colour, from *nue* cloud, from popular Latin variant of Latin *nubes*). **A** *noun* L18 A slight or subtle variation in or shade of meaning, expression, colour, etc. **B** *transitive verb* L19 Give a nuance or nuances to.

nuancé /nɥɑ̃se/ *adjective* M20 French (from as preceding). Having or characterized by nuances.

nucleus /ˈnjuːklɪəs/ *noun* plural **nuclei** /ˈnjuːklɪʌɪ/, **nucleuses** E18 Latin (= nut, kernel, inner part, variant of *nuculeus*, from *nucula* diminutive of *nux*, *nuc-* nut). **1** E18 *Astronomy* The dense core of the head of a comet. **b** L18 A dense, usually bright, central part in a galaxy or nebula. **2** M18 The central part or thing around which others are grouped or collected; the centre or kernel of an aggregate or mass; an initial part or collection of things to which others may be added.

■ Besides its initial astronomical sense, *nucleus* has acquired a large number of specialist senses in a variety of subject fields: Anatomy (E19), Archaeology (M19), Biology (M19), Chemistry (M19), Bee-keeping (L19), Physics (E20), and Linguistics (E20).

nudnik /ˈnʊdnɪk/ *noun* (also **nudnick**) M20 Yiddish (from Russian *nudnyĭ* tedious, boring + noun suffix *-nik* person connected with (something)). A pestering, nagging, or irritating person; a bore. *United States slang.*

attributive **1972** *New York* Too many of our nudnik moviegoers . . . dread the prospect of sharing their pleasures with the plain folks.

nuée ardente /nɥe ardɑ̃t/ *noun phrase* plural **nuées ardentes** (pronounced same) E20 French (literally, 'burning cloud'). *Geology* A hot dense cloud of ash and fragmented lava suspended in a mass of gas, typically ejected from the side of the dome of certain volcanoes and flowing downhill like an avalanche.

■ The phrase was introduced into formal vulcanology in 1903 by A. Lacroix, who subsequently observed (in *La Montagne Pelée et ses eruptions* (1904)) that the expression had earlier been in use amongst the inhabitants of San Jorge in the Azores. While La-

croix said that by *nuée ardente* he meant *brulant* 'burning' rather than *incandescent* 'glowing', the phrase is nonetheless usually rendered in English as 'glowing cloud'.

nugae /ˈnjuːdʒiː/, /ˈnuːɡʌɪ/ *noun* plural E18 Latin. Trifles.

■ Chiefly in NUGAE DIFFICILES.

nugae difficiles /ˌnjuːdʒiː ˈdɪfɪkɪleɪz/ *noun* plural phrase E18 Latin (= difficult trifles). *Philosophy* Matters of trifling importance occupying a disproportionate amount of time owing to their difficulty.

nuit blanche /nɥi blɑ̃ʃ/ *noun phrase* plural **nuits blanches** (pronounced same) M19 French (literally, 'white night'). A sleepless night.

nulla bona /ˌnʌlə ˈbəʊnə/ *noun phrase* E19 Latin (= no goods). The return made by a sheriff upon an execution when the party has no goods to be distrained.

nulli secundus /ˌnʌlɪ sɪˈkʌndəs/ *adjective phrase* (also **nulli secundum** /ˌnʌlɪ sɪ ˈkʌndəm/) M19 Latin. Second to none.

numdah /ˈnʌmdə/ *noun* E19 Urdu (*namdā* from Persian *namad* felt, carpet, rug). **1** E19 In the Indian subcontinent and the Middle East: a kind of felt or coarse woollen cloth, frequently embroidered; a rug or carpet made from this (also *numdah rug*). **2** L19 A NUMNAH.

numen /ˈnjuːmən/ *noun* plural **numina** /ˈnjuːmnə/ E17 Latin (related to *nuere* to nod, Greek *neuein* to incline the head). Divinity; a local or presiding god.

numéro /nymero/ *noun* plural **numéros** /nymero/ E20 French. A person or thing having a place in a series, a number. Also, a remarkable or strange person.

numero uno /ˌnjuːmərəʊ ˈuːnəʊ/ *noun phrase* plural **numero unos** L20 Italian and Spanish (= number one). The best or most important person.

1996 *Spectator* Then there is Enrique Ponce, acclaimed as numero uno and already being spoken of as the matador of the century.

numerus clausus /ˌnjuːmərəs ˈklaʊsəs/ *noun phrase* E20 Latin (literally, 'closed number'). A fixed maximum number of entrants admissible to an academic institution.

numina plural of NUMEN.

numnah /ˈnʌmnə/ *noun* M19 Urdu (*namdā* from Persian *namad* felt, carpet, rug; a variant of NUMDAH). A saddle-cloth; a pad placed under a saddle to prevent soreness.

nunatak /'nʌnətak/ *noun* L19 Eskimo ((Greenlandic) *nunataq*). An isolated peak of rock projecting above a surface of inland ice or snow in Greenland, Norway, etc.

nunc dimittis /ˌnʌŋk dɪˈmɪtɪs/ *noun phrase* M16 Latin (= now you let (your servant) depart). **1** M16 A canticle forming part of the Christian liturgy at evensong and compline, comprising the song of Simeon in Luke 2:29–32 (in the Vulgate beginning *Nunc dimittis, Domine*). **2** L16 Permission to depart; dismissal.

nunchaku /nʌnˈtʃaku:/ *noun* L20 Japanese (from Okinawa dialect). A Japanese martial arts weapon consisting of two hardwood sticks joined together by a strap, chain, etc. More fully *nunchaku stick*. Usually in *plural*.

nuncio /'nʌnsɪəʊ/, /'nʌnʃɪəʊ/ *noun* plural **nuncios** E16 Italian (*nuncio, nuntio* (now *nunzio*) from Latin *nuncius, nuntius* messenger). **1** E16 *Roman Catholic Church* A papal ambassador to a foreign court or government. **2** E17 A person bearing a message; a messenger. **3** L17 *History* A member of the Polish diet.

nuntius /'nʌnʃɪəs/, /'nʌnʃəs/ *noun* plural **nuntii** /'nʌnʃɪAɪ/ E17 Latin (variant of *nuncius* messenger). A NUNCIO.

nuoc mam /nwɒk 'mɑːm/ *noun phrase* E20 Vietnamese. A spicy Vietnamese fish sauce.

nuragh /'nʊərag/ *noun* plural **nuraghi** /'nʊəragi/ E19 Sardinian. *Archaeology* A type of massive stone tower found in Sardinia, dating from the Bronze and Iron Ages. Cf. TALAYOT.

nux vomica /ˌnʌks 'vɒmɪkə/ *noun phrase* LME Medieval Latin (literally, 'emetic nut', from Latin *nux* nut + adjective from *vomere* to vomit). The highly poisonous seeds of the tree *Strychnos nux-vomica*, used as a major source of strychnine and in homoeopathic remedies; this tree, a native of southern Asia.

nyet variant of NIET.

nymphaeum /nɪmˈfiːəm/ *noun archaic* plural **nymphaea** /nɪmˈfiːə/ (also **nympheum**, plural **nymphea**) L18 Latin (from Greek *numphaion, -eion* temple or shrine of the nymphs, neuter of *numphaios, -eios* sacred to the nymphs, from *numphē* nymph). *Classical Antiquities* A grotto or shrine dedicated to a nymph or nymphs; (a part of) a building built to represent this.

O

ob. abbreviation of OBIIT.

obbligato /ɒblɪˈgɑːtəʊ/ adjective and noun (also **obligato**) L18 Italian (= obliged, obligatory). Music **A** adjective L18 Indispensable; that cannot be omitted: designating a part or accompaniment forming an integral part of a composition, and the instrument on which it is played. **B** noun M19 plural **obbligatos**. An obbligato part or accompaniment, *especially* one of particular prominence in a piece.

obelus /ˈɒb(ə)ləs/ noun plural **obeli** /ˈɒb(ə)lʌɪ/, /ˈɒb(ə)liː/ LME Latin (= spit, critical obelus, from Greek *obelos*). A straight horizontal stroke (-), sometimes with a dot above and below (÷), used in ancient manuscripts to mark a word, passage, etc., especially as spurious. Also, a dagger-shaped reference mark (†) used in printed matter as a reference to a footnote etc., and in some dictionaries to denote obsoleteness. Also called *obelisk*.

oberek /ə(ʊ)ˈbɛrɪk/ noun M20 Polish. A lively Polish dance in triple time, related to the mazurka but usually faster.

obi /ˈəʊbi/ noun E19 Japanese (= belt). A sash worn round the waist with Japanese clothing.

obiit /ˈɒbɪɪt/ verb Latin. He, she, or it died.
■ Frequently on epitaphs, followed by the date of death; also abbreviated to *ob*.

obiit sine prole /ˌɒbɪɪt ˌsɪneɪ ˈprəʊleɪ/ phrase L19 Latin. He, she, or it died without offspring.
■ Frequently in genealogies, usually abbreviated to *ob.s.p.* or *o.s.p.*

obit /ˈɒbɪt/, /ˈəʊbɪt/ noun LME Old and Modern French (from Latin *obitus* going down, setting, death, from *obit-* past participial stem of *obire* to perish, die (from *mortem obire* to meet death); in sense 3 partly abbreviation of *obituary*). **1** LME-L17 Departure from life, death, decease. **2 a** LME-E18 A ceremony performed at the burial of a deceased person; a funeral service. **b** LME History A ceremony (usually a mass) commemorating, or commending to God, a deceased person, especially a founder or benefactor of an institution on the anniversary of his or her death; an annual or other regular memorial service. **3** LME Originally, a record or notice of (the date of) a person's death. Later (*colloquial*), an obituary.

obiter /ˈɒbɪtə/ adverb, noun, & adjective L16 Latin (originally two words, *ob itur* by the way). **A** adverb L16 By the way, in passing, incidentally. **B** noun E17 A thing said, done, or occurring by the way; an incidental matter. Also, an OBITER DICTUM. **C** adjective M18 Made or said by the way; incidental.

obiter dictum /ˌɒbɪtə ˈdɪktəm/ noun phrase plural **obiter dicta** /ˌɒbɪtə ˈdɪktə/ E19 Latin (from as preceding + DICTUM). A judge's expression of opinion uttered in discussing a point of law or in giving judgement, but not essential to the decision and so without binding authority; *generally* an incidental remark.
1996 *Spectator* The *obiter dicta* of earlier scientific materialists, all of them in their own day at least as eminent and confident as Dawkins, make hilarious reading today.

objet /ɔbʒɛ/, /ˈɒbʒeɪ/ noun plural pronounced same M19 French. **1** M19 An object displayed as an ornament. **2** M19 A person forming the object of another's attentions or affection. *rare*.
1 1996 *Country Life* Occasionally, a composition is enriched by other *objets* such as shells, a jewel, even a skull.

objet d'art /ɔbʒɛ dar/, /ˌɒbʒeɪ ˈdɑː/ noun phrase plural **objets d'art** (pronounced same) M19 French (literally, 'object of art'; cf. preceding). A small decorative object.

oblietjie /ʊˈbliːki/ noun L19 Afrikaans (from French *oublie* (from ecclesiastical Latin *oblata* use as noun of feminine of past participle of *offerre* to offer) + diminutive suffix *-tjie*). In South Africa: a rolled wafer-thin teacake.

obligato variant of OBBLIGATO.

oboe da caccia /ˌəʊbəʊ da ˈkatʃa/ noun phrase plural **oboi da caccia** /ˈəʊbɔɪ/ L19 Italian (literally, 'hunting oboe'). Chiefly History An obsolete type of tenor oboe with a pitch a fifth lower than the ordinary oboe.

oboe d'amore /ˌəʊbəʊ daˈmɔːreɪ/ noun phrase plural **oboes d'amore, oboi d'amore** /ˈəʊbɔɪ/ L19 Italian (literally, 'oboe of love'). A type of alto oboe with a pear-shaped bell and a pitch a minor third below that of the ordinary oboe, now used especially in baroque music.

oboi da caccia, oboi d'amore plurals of OBOE DA CACCIA, OBOE D'AMORE.

obscurum per obscurius /əb͵skjʊərəm pər əbˈskjʊərɪəs/ *noun phrase* L19 Late Latin (literally, 'the obscure by the still more obscure'). An explanation that is more difficult to understand than that which it purports to explain. Cf. IGNOTUM PER IGNOTIUS.

ob.s.p. abbreviation of OBIIT SINE PROLE.

ocarina /ɒkəˈriːnə/ *noun* L19 Italian (from *oca* goose (with reference to its shape)). A simple wind instrument in the form of a hollow egg-shaped body with finger-holes and a hole to blow at.

occupatio /ɒkjʊˈpeɪʃɪəʊ/, /ɒkjʊˈpɑːtɪəʊ/ *noun* L16 Latin. *Rhetoric* (The device of making) mention of a thing by pretending to omit to mention it.

octapla /ˈɒktəplə/ *noun* (also **octaple** /ˈɒktəp(ə)l/) L17 Greek (*oktapla* neuter plural of *oktaplous* eightfold, after HEXAPLA). A text consisting of eight versions in parallel columns, especially of the Old or New Testament.

octli /ˈəʊktli/ *noun* M19 Mexican Spanish. PULQUE.

oculus /ˈɒkjʊləs/ *noun* plural **oculi** /ˈɒkjʊlʌɪ/, /ˈɒkjʊliː/ M19 Latin (= eye). *Architecture* A round or eyelike opening or design; *specifically* a circular window (especially in a church); the central boss of a volute; an opening at the apex of a dome.

■ Previously also in the phrases *oculus Christi* (literally, 'of Christ'), wild clary (a plant reputed to be good for the eyes) (LME–M17), and *oculus mundi* (literally, 'of the world') a white variety of opal, hydrophane (L17–L18).

odalisque /ˈəʊd(ə)lɪsk/ *noun* L17 French (from Turkish *ōdahk*, from *ōda* chamber + *hk* suffix expressing function). A female slave or concubine in an Eastern harem, especially in the seraglio of the Sultan of Turkey (now *historical*); *transferred* an exotic sexually attractive woman.

odeon /ˈəʊdɪən/ *noun* (also in sense 1 **odeion**; in sense 2 **Odeon**) M19 Greek (*ōdeion*; see ODEUM). **1** M19 An ODEUM. **2** M20 Any of a chain of large, lavish cine-

mas in a chain built by Oscar Deutsch in the 1930s; *generally* a luxurious cinema.

odeum /ˈəʊdɪəm/ *noun* plural **odeums, odea** /ˈəʊdɪə/ E17 French (*odéum* or Latin *odeum* from Greek *ōideion* from *ōidē* Attic form of *aoidē* song, singing, from *aeidein* to sing). A building for the performance of vocal and instrumental music, especially among the ancient Greeks and Romans.

odium /ˈəʊdɪəm/ *noun* E17 Latin (= hatred, from *odi* I hate). The fact or state of being hated; general or widespread unpopularity or opprobrium.

oedema /ɪˈdiːmə/ *noun* plural **oedemata** /ɪˈdiːmətə/, **oedemas** LME Late Latin (from Greek *oidēma*, from *oidein* to swell). *Medicine* (A) local or general swelling produced by the accumulation of fluid in the body tissues or cavities; dropsy.

oeil-de-boeuf /œjdəbœf/ *noun* plural **oeils-de-boeuf** (pronounced same) M18 French (literally, 'ox-eye'). **1** M18 A small round window. **2** L18 A small vestibule or antechamber in a palace (*specifically* one in Versailles lighted by a small round window); *transferred* (a part of) a monarch's court.

■ Sense 1 appears later (M19) in English form as 'bull's-eye'.

1 1996 *Country Life* He added a new range of three rooms . . . , with a symmetrical, Classical façade, the pediment containing an *œil-de-bœuf* window. . . . They [sc. the stables] have old-fashioned mullion and transom windows and an *œil-de-bœuf* in the east façade.

oeil-de-perdrix /œjdəpɛrdri/ *noun* M19 French (literally, 'partridge-eye'). **1** M19 In French pottery and porcelain, a design of dotted circles, usually on a coloured background, frequently used on Sèvres porcelain. Also *oeil-de-perdrix pattern* etc. **b** L19 A similar design used as a ground in lace-making. **2** L19 Pink or pale red wine or champagne. In full *oeil-de-perdrix wine*, *champagne*.

oeils-de-boeuf plural of OEIL-DE-BOEUF.

oenochoe /iːˈnɒkəʊi/ *noun* (also **oino-choe** /iːˈnɒkəʊi/, /ɔɪˈnɒkəʊi/) L19 Greek (*oinokhoē*, from *oeno-* combining form of *oinos* wine + *khoas*, *khoē* pouring). *Greek Antiquities* A vessel used for ladling wine from a bowl into a cup.

oesophagus /ɪˈsɒfəgəs/ *noun* (also **esophagus**) LME Medieval Latin (*ysophagus*, *iso-* from Greek *oisophagos*, from obscure first element + (apparently) -*phagos* eating, eater; current spelling after modern Latin). *Anatomy* and *Zoology* The canal leading from the back of the mouth, through which food and drink pass to the stomach; the gullet.

oestrus /'iːstrəs/, /'ɛstrəs/ *noun* (also **estrus**) L17 Latin (from Greek *oistros* gadfly, breeze, sting, frenzy). **1** L17 A parasitic insect; now *specifically* a biting fly of the genus *Oestrus* or the family Oestridae whose larvae are parasitic on various animals; a botfly. Now chiefly as modern Latin genus name. **2** E19 *figurative* A sharp stimulus; a passion, a frenzy. Now *rare*. **3** L19 *Zoology* and *Physiology* (The period of) a female animal's readiness to mate, accompanied by certain physiological changes; the rut, heat.

oeufs en cocotte /øf ɑ̃ kɔkɔt/ *noun phrase plural* E20 French (= eggs in a cocotte). A French dish of eggs in butter baked and served in individual cocottes or ramekins.

œuvre /œvr/, /'əːvrə/ *noun* (also **oeuvre**) plural pronounced same L19 French (= work). A work of art, music, literature, etc.; the whole body of work produced by an artist, composer, etc. Cf. CHEF-D'ŒUVRE.

1996 *Oldie* . . . that he has been able to keep both aspects of his oeuvre alive and developing with such élan is in itself remarkable.

œvre de vulgarisation /œvr də vylgarizasjɔ̃/, /'əːvrə də ˌvʊlgarɪ'zasjɔ̃(ŋ)/ *noun phrase* (also **oeuvre de vulgarisation**) M20 French (= work of popularization). A work which attempts to make an academic or esoteric subject accessible to the general public.

officina /ɒfɪ'sʌmə/, /ɒfɪ'siːnə/ *noun plural* **officinae** /ɒfɪ'sʌmiː/, /ɒfɪ'sʌmʌɪ/ E19 Latin (= workshop etc., contraction of *opificina*, from *opifex* workman). A workshop; a place of production, (frequently *figurative*).

oficina /ɒfɪ'siːnə/ *noun* L19 Spanish (from Latin OFFICINA). In Spanish-speaking South America or Mexico: a factory.

ogham /'ɒɡəm/ *noun* (also **ogam, Ogham**) E18 Old Irish (*ogam, ogum* (genitive *oguim*), modern Irish *ogham*, plural **oghaim**, Gaelic *oghum*, connected with its mythical inventor *Ogma*). An ancient British and Irish system of writing using an alphabet of twenty or twenty-five characters; any of these characters, consisting of a line or stroke, or a group of two to five

parallel strokes, arranged alongside or across a continuous line or the edge of a stone (usually in *plural*). Also, an inscription in this alphabet.

oinochoe variant of OENOCHOE.

ojime /'əʊdʒɪmeɪ/, *foreign* /'ɔːdʒime/ *noun* plural same, **ojimes** L19 Japanese (from *o* string + *shime* fastening, fastener). A bead or beadlike object, often very elaborate, used in Japan as a sliding fastener on the strings of a bag, pouch, or INRO.

ole /'ole/ *noun* M19 Spanish. A Spanish folk-dance which is accompanied by castanets and singing.

olé /o'le/, /əʊ'leɪ/ *interjection & noun* E20 Spanish. **A** *interjection* E20 Bravo! **B** *noun* M20 A cry of '*olé!*'

olim /əʊ'lɪm/ *noun plural* M20 Hebrew ('ōlīm plural of 'ōleh person who ascends). Jewish immigrants who settle in the State of Israel.

olim /'əʊlɪm/ *adverb* M17 Latin. At one time; formerly.

olla /'ɒlə/ *noun plural* **ollas**, (in sense 3) **ollae** /'ɒliː/, /'ɒlʌɪ/ E17 Spanish ((Portuguese *olha*) from Proto-Romance variant of Latin *olla* pot; in sense 3, from Latin). **1** E17 In Spain and Spanish-speaking countries: an earthen jar or pot used for cooking etc.; a dish of (especially stewed) meat and vegetables cooked in this. Cf. OLLA PODRIDA sense 1. **2** M19 In Spanish America: a large porous earthen jar for keeping drinking-water cool by evaporation from its outer surface. **3** M19 An ancient cinerary urn.

■ *Olio* (M17) is an alteration of *olla* used in sense 1 and also figuratively for a hotch-potch, medley, or miscellany.

olla podrida /ˌɒlə pə(ʊ)'driːdə/ *noun phrase* L16 Spanish (literally 'rotten pot', from as OLLA *noun* + *podrida* putrid). **1** L16 A highly spiced stew of various meats and vegetables, of Spanish and Portuguese origin; *generally* any dish containing a great variety of ingredients. **2** M17 *figurative* Any mixture of heterogeneous things or elements; a hotchpotch, a medley.

2 1996 *Spectator* . . . the RSC, so careful of Shakespeare on our behalf, long ago decided to commit this olla podrida of Bardic tricks [sc. Cymbeline] to the scrapheap for scholars to pick over . . .

oloroso /ɒlə'rəʊsəʊ/ *noun plural* **olorosos** L19 Spanish (= fragrant). A heavy, dark, medium-sweet sherry; a glass of this.

olpe /ˈɒlpeɪ/ *noun* L19 Greek (*olpē*). *Greek Antiquities* A leather flask for oil, wine, etc. Also, a pear-shaped jug with a handle.

om /əʊm/ *interjection & noun* L18 Sanskrit (*oṃ, om,* sometimes regarded as composed of three sounds, *a-u-m,* symbolizing the three major Hindu deities: see also OM MANI PADME HUM). *Hinduism* and *Tibetan Buddhism* **A** *interjection* L18 Used as a mantra or auspicious formula at the beginning of prayers etc. **B** *noun* L19 An utterance of 'om'.

ombré /ˈɔ̃bre/ *noun & adjective* L19 French (past participle of *ombrer* to shade). (A fabric or design) having gradual shading of colour from light to dark.

ombrellino /ˌɒmbrelˈliːno/, /ˌɒmbrɛ ˈliːnəʊ/ *noun* plural **ombrellini** /ˌɒmbrel ˈliːni/, **ombrellinos** /ˌɒmbrɛˈliːnəʊz/ M19 Italian. *Roman Catholic Church* A small umbrella-like canopy held over the sacraments when they are moved from one place to another.

ombres chinoises /ɔ̃br ʃinwaz/ *noun phrase plural* L18 French (= Chinese shadows). *History* A European version of Chinese shadow-puppets, used in a galanty show.

ombudsman /ˈɒmbʊdzmən/ *noun* plural **ombudsmen** M20 Swedish (from *ombud* commissioner, agent, representing Old Norse *umboð* charge, commission, *umboðsmaðr* commissary, manager). An official appointed to investigate complaints by individuals against maladministration by public authorities; *especially* a British official of this kind (officially called the Parliamentary Commissioner for Administration), first appointed in 1967.

omega /ˈəʊmɪgə/ *noun* E16 Greek (*ō mega,* literally, 'great O', opposed to *o mikron* omicron). **1** E16 The last letter (Ω, ω) of the Greek alphabet, having originally the value of a long open o; *figurative* the last of a series; the last word, the final development. **2** M20 *Particle Physics* Either of two subatomic particles: *omega meson* and *omega minus*.

■ In the figurative use of sense 1, often in the phrase 'the alpha and the omega' (see under ALPHA).

omertà /omerˈta:/ *noun* L19 Italian (dialectal variant of *umiltà* humility). A code of silence observed by members or associates of the Mafia or (*transferred*) others engaged in clandestine activities.

■ The Italian sense of 'humility' originally referred to the Mafia code which enjoins submission of the group to its leader.
1996 Times Pressed time and again on quarantine by baffled Members of Parliament, she preserved the ministry *omertà* towards the kennel owners and referred only to her 'veterinary advisers'.

om mani padme hum /əʊm ˌmʌni pʌdmeɪ ˈhuːm/ *noun phrase & interjection* L18 Sanskrit (*Oṃ maṇipadme hūṃ* literally, 'oh (goddess) Manipadma', reinterpreted as 'oh jewel in the lotus', from *maṇi* jewel, *padma* lotus; cf. OM). *Tibetan Buddhism* (Used as) a mantra or auspicious formula in prayer and meditation.

omnium /ˈɒmnɪəm/ *noun* M18 Latin (literally, 'of all (things, sorts)', genitive plural of *omnis* all: cf. next). **1** *Stock Exchange* **a** M18 *History* The total value of the stock and other interests offered to the Government to each subscriber when raising a loan. **b** L19 Any combined stock the constituents of which can be dealt with separately. *colloquial.* **2** M18 The sum of what one values; one's all. **3** M19 A piece of furniture with open shelves for ornaments; a whatnot.

omnium gatherum /ˌɒmnɪəm ˈgaðərəm/ *noun phrase* plural **omnium gatherums**, (*rare*) **omnium gathera** /ˌɒmnɪəm ˈgaðərə/ M16 pseudo-Latin (from Latin OMNIUM + English *gather*). A gathering or collection of all sorts of persons or things; a confused medley. *colloquial.*

omphalos /ˈɒmfəlɒs/ *noun* M19 Greek (literally, 'navel'). **1** M19 *Greek Antiquities* **a** A boss on a shield etc. **b** M19 A stone, in the temple of Apollo at Delphi, reputed to mark the central point of the earth. **2** M19 *figurative* A central point, a centre.

on dit /ɔ̃ di/ *noun* plural **on dits** (pronounced same) E19 French (= they say). An item of gossip; something reported on hearsay.

onnagata /ɒnəˈgɑːtə/ *noun* plural same E20 Japanese (from *onna* woman + *kata* figure). In Japanese *kabuki* theatre, a man who plays female roles. Also called *oyama*.

onomasticon /ɒnə(ʊ)ˈmastɪkɒn/ *noun* E18 Greek (use as noun (sc. *biblion* book) of neuter of *onomastikos* pertaining to naming, from *onoma* name). A vocabulary or alphabetic list of (especially personal) proper names. Also, a vocabulary of nouns; a general lexicon.

onomatopoeia /ˌɒnə(ʊ)matə'piːə/ *noun* L16 Late Latin (from Greek *onomatopoiia* making of words, from *onomatopoios*, from *onomato-* combining form of *onoma* name + -*poios* making, from *poiein* to make, create). **1** L16 The formation of a word by an imitation of the sound associated with the thing or action designated; the principle or practice of forming words by this process. **2** M19 A word formed by this process. **3** M19 *Rhetoric* The use of naturally suggestive language for rhetorical effect.

onus /'əʊnəs/ *noun* M17 Latin (= load, burden). A burden, a responsibility, a duty.
> **1996** *Times* The onus will now be on the many producers who make some claim to eco-friendly status . . . to prove to consumers that their products really are all that they claim.

oom /ʊəm/ *noun* E19 Afrikaans (from Dutch *oom*). Uncle.
> ■ Frequently used by children or young people in South Africa as a respectful form of address to any older or elderly man.

oomiak variant of UMIAK.

op. abbreviation of OPUS.

op. cit. /ɒp 'sɪt/ *noun & adverb phrase* L19 Latin (abbreviation of *opus citatum* the work quoted, or *opere citato* in the work quoted). (In) the work already quoted.

opera plural of OPUS.

opéra bouffe /ɔpera buf/, /ˌɒp(ə)rə 'buːf/ *noun phrase* plural **opéras bouffe(s)** (pronounced same) L19 French (from as next). OPERA BUFFA; (an example of) French comic opera.
> *figurative* **1995** *Times* Eventually their relationship turned into an *opera bouffe* of the most debilitating, if diverting, kind.

opera buffa /ˌɒp(ə)rə 'buːfə/, *foreign* /ˌopera 'buffa/ *noun phrase* plural **operas buffa**, **opere buffe** /'opere 'buffe/ E19 Italian (= comic opera). (Italian) comic opera, with dialogue in recitative and characters drawn from everyday life; an example of this.
> **1995** *Spectator* Yet much of this power is dissipated by the preceding *opera buffa* with the disguises. Those who wear Armani suits must behave like Armani suit-wearers.

opéra comique /ɔpera kɔmik/, /ˌɒp(ə)rə kɒ'miːk/ *noun phrase* plural **opéras comiques** (pronounced same) M18 French (= comic opera). A type of opera (originally humorous, later romantic) characterized by spoken dialogue; an example of this.

opéras bouffe(s), operas buffa, etc. plurals of OPÉRA BOUFFE, OPERA BUFFA, etc.

opera seria /ˌɒp(ə)rə 'sɪərɪə/, *foreign* /ˌopera 'sɛːrja/ *noun phrase* plural **operas seria, opere serie** /ˌopere 'sɛːrje/ L19 Italian (= serious opera). A type of opera prevalent in the eighteenth century, with elaborate arias and usually based on mythological themes; an example of this. Cf. TRAGÉDIE LYRIQUE.

opere buffe, opere serie plurals of OPERA BUFFA, OPERA SERIA.

operetta /ɒpə'rɛtə/ *noun* L18 Italian (diminutive of *opera*). A short, originally one-act, opera on a light or humorous theme.
> ■ *Opérette*, the French word derived from *operetta* and Anglicized as *operette*, is a more recent introduction (L19), but *operetta* remains the more generally used term.

opprobrium /ə'prəʊbrɪəm/ *noun* plural **opprobria** /ə'prəʊbrɪə/ M17 Latin (= infamy, reproach, from *ob-* towards + *probrum* shameful deed, disgrace, use as noun of neuter of *probus* disgraceful). **1** M17 An occasion or cause of reproach; shameful conduct; something that brings disgrace. **2** L17 Disgrace attached to conduct considered shameful; the expression of this disgrace; shame, reproach.
> **2 1996** *Spectator* The German translation has not yet been published here, but it has already managed to attract relentless opprobrium.

optime /'ɒptɪmeɪ/ *noun* M18 Latin (= best, very well, from *optime disputasti* you have disputed very well). In the mathematical tripos at Cambridge University, a student placed in the second or third division. Also (respectively) *senior, junior optime*.

optimum /'ɒptɪməm/ *noun & adjective* L19 Latin (use as noun of neuter of *optimus* best). Originally *Biology*. **A** *noun* L19 The conditions most favourable for growth, reproduction, or other vital process; *generally* the best, a level, condition, etc., regarded as the best or most favourable. Opposed to PESSIMUM. **B** *adjective* L19 Best, most favourable, especially under a particular set of circumstances; optimal.

opus /'əʊpəs/, /'ɒpəs/ *noun* plural **opuses** /'əʊpəsɪz/, /'ɒpəsɪz/, **opera** /'ɒp(ə)rə/ E18 Latin (= work). An artistic work, a composition; *especially* a musical composition or set of compositions as numbered among the works of a composer in order of publication.

■ In bibliographies and catalogues usually abbreviated to *op.* Cf. OP. CIT.

opus Alexandrinum /ˌɒpəs ˌalɛksɑːnˈdriːnəm/ *noun phrase* M19 Medieval Latin (literally, 'Alexandrian work'). A pavement mosaic work widely used in Byzantium in the ninth century and later in Italy, consisting of coloured stone, glass, and semiprecious stones arranged in intricate geometric patterns.

opus anglicanum /ˌɒpəs aŋɡlɪˈkɑːnəm/ *noun phrase* (also **opus Anglicanum**) M19 Medieval Latin (literally, 'English work'). Fine pictorial embroidery produced in England in the Middle Ages and used especially on ecclesiastical vestments.

opus araneum /ˌɒpəs aˈrɑːnɪəm/ *noun phrase* M19 Medieval Latin (literally, 'spider's work'). Darned netting; delicate embroidery done on a net and resembling a spider's web. Also called *spider-work*.

opus citatum see OP. CIT.

opus consutum /ˌɒpəs kɒnˈsuːtəm/ *noun phrase* L19 Medieval Latin (literally, 'work sewn together'). APPLIQUÉ work.

opuscule /əˈpʌskjuːl/ *noun plural* **opuscules** (also in Latin form **opusculum** /əˈpʌskjʊləm/, plural **opuscula** /əˈpʌskjuːlə/) M17 Old and Modern French (from Latin *opusculum* diminutive of *opus* work). A minor (especially literary or musical) work.

opus Dei /ˌɒpəs ˈdeɪiː/ *noun phrase* L19 Medieval Latin. **1** L19 *Ecclesiastical* The work of God; *specifically* liturgical worship regarded as man's primary duty to God. **2** L19 (*Opus Dei*) A Roman Catholic organization of priests and lay people founded in Spain in 1928 with the aim of re-establishing Christian ideals in society.

opus magnum variant of MAGNUM OPUS.

opus sectile /ˌɒpəs ˈsɛktɪleɪ/ *noun phrase* M19 Latin (literally, 'cut work'). An originally Roman floor decoration made up of pieces shaped individually to fit the pattern or design, as distinct from mosaic which uses regularly shaped pieces.

opus signinum /ˌɒpəs sɪɡˈniːnəm/ *noun phrase* M18 Latin (literally, 'work of Signia'). An originally Roman flooring material consisting of broken tiles etc. mixed with lime mortar.

■ The town of Signia (now Segni) in Central Italy was famous for its tiles.

or /ɔː/ *noun* LME Old and Modern French (ultimately from Latin *aurum* gold). Originally, gold. Later (*Heraldry*), the tincture gold or yellow in armorial bearings.

orangerie /ˈɒrɪndʒ(ə)ri/ *noun* (also **orangery**) M17 French (from French *oranger* orange tree). A place, especially a special protective structure, where orange trees are cultivated.

orans /ˈɔːrənz/ *noun* E20 Latin (*orans, orantem* present participle of *orare* to pray). *Art* A representation of a person in a kneeling or praying position.

■ Often postpositive, as in *Virgin orans*.

oratio obliqua /ɒˌrɑːtɪəʊ ɒˈbliːkwə/, /ɒˌreɪʃ(ɪ)əʊ əˈblʌɪkwə/ *noun phrase* M19 Latin (*oratio* speech + *obliqua* feminine of *obliquus* oblique). Indirect speech.

oratio recta /ɒˌrɑːtɪəʊ ˈrɛktə/, /ɒˌreɪʃ(ɪ)əʊ ˈrɛktə/ *noun phrase* M19 Latin (from *oratio* speech + *recta* feminine of *rectus* straight, direct). Direct speech.

oratorio /ɒrəˈtɔːrɪəʊ/ *noun plural* **oratorios** E18 Italian (from ecclesiastical Latin *oratorium* oratory). **1** E18 A semi-dramatic extended musical composition, usually based on a Scriptural theme, performed by a choir with soloists and a full orchestra, without costume, action, or scenery. **2** L19 The genre of musical composition or drama characterized by such a theme and such performance.

■ Originally (M17) in English in its more literal sense of 'a pulpit', but this is rare and became obsolete before its reintroduction in its modern senses, which derive from the musical services in the church of the Oratory of St Philip Neri in Rome.

orchata variant of HORCHATA.

ordinaire abbreviation of VIN ORDINAIRE.

ordonnance /ˈɔːdənəns/, *foreign* /ɔrdɔnɑ̃s/ (*plural same*) *noun* M17 French (alteration of Old French *ordenance* after Old and Modern French *ordonner* to arrange). **1** M17 Systematic arrangement, especially of literary material or architectural parts; a plan or method of literary or artistic composition; an architectural order. **2** M18 In various European countries, especially France, an ordinance, a decree, a law. **3** M18 *French History* Any of those organized companies of men-at-arms who formed the beginnings of a standing army in France. In full *company of ordonnance*.

oregano /ɒrɪˈgɑːnəʊ/, /əˈrɛɡənəʊ/ *noun* L18 Spanish and American Spanish (variant of ORIGANUM). A seasoning prepared from the (usually dried) leaves of wild marjoram, *Origanum vulgare*, or, especially in Central and South America, of shrubs of the genus *Lippia*, especially *Lippia graveolens*.

ore rotundo /ˌɔːrɪ rəˈtʌndəʊ/ *adverb phrase* E18 Latin (literally, 'with round mouth', from ablative of *os* mouth + ablative of *rotundus* round). With round, well-turned speech.

orfèvrerie /ɔrfɛvrəri/ *noun* ME French (from *orfèvre* from popular Latin *aurifabrum* worker in gold, goldsmith). Goldsmiths' work.

■ Formerly also the goldsmiths' quarter in London.

organon /ˈɔːɡ(ə)nɒn/ *noun* L16 Greek (= instrument, organ). **1** L16–E17 A bodily organ, especially as an instrument of the soul. **2** E17 An instrument of thought or knowledge; a means of reasoning; *specifically* a system of logical rules of investigation or demonstration.

■ The *Organon* is the collective title of the logical treatises of Aristotle.

orgeat /ˈɔːdʒɪət/ *foreign* /ɔrʒa/ (*plural same*) *noun* LME French (from Provençal *orjat*, from *ordi* barley from Latin *hordeum*). A syrup or cooling drink made from barley (later from almonds) and orange-flower water.

orientalia /ˌɔːrɪɛnˈteɪlɪə/, /ˌɒrɪɛnˈteɪlɪə/ *noun plural* E20 Latin (neuter plural of *orientalis* oriental). Things, especially books, relating to or characteristic of the Orient.

oriflamme /ˈɒrɪflam/ *noun* LME Old and Modern French (*oriflambe, oriflamme*, in medieval Latin *auriflamma*, from *aurum* gold + *flamma* flame). **1** LME *History* The sacred red or orange-red silk banner of St Denis, given to early kings of France by the abbot of St Denis on setting out for war. **2** E17 *transferred* and *figurative* **a** A banner, principle, ideal, etc., that serves as a rallying point in a struggle. **b** M19 A bright conspicuous object, colour, etc.

origami /ɒrɪˈgɑːmi/ *noun* M20 Japanese (from *oru, -ori* fold + *kami* paper). The Japanese art of folding paper into decorative shapes and objects. Also *figurative*.

figurative **1996** *Spectator* . . . any information about the songs has been left to rot in the unfathomable origami of CD booklets.

origanum /ɒˈrɪɡ(ə)nəm/ *noun* ME Latin (from Greek *origanon*, perhaps from *oros* mountain + *ganos* brightness, joy; cf. OREGANO). Any of various aromatic labiate plants of the genus *Origanum*, much grown as herbs; *especially* wild marjoram, *O. vulgare*.

orihon /ˈɒrɪhɒn/ *noun* E20 Japanese (from *ori* fold + *hon* book). A book formed by folding a printed roll alternately backwards and forwards between the columns, and usually fastening it with cord down one side.

orlo /ˈɔːləʊ/ *noun plural* **orlos** M17 Italian (= border, hem, etc., from Latin *ora* edge, border). *Architecture* **1** M17 The fillet under the ovolo of a capital. **2** E18 The plinth under the base of a column.

orné /ˈɔːneɪ/ *adjective* (feminine **ornée**) L18 French (= ornate, past participle of *orner* from Latin *ornare* to adorn). Decorated, ornate.

■ Usually in English in the noun phrases *cottage orné* and *ferme ornée* (see quotations). Despite its appearance, *cottage orné* ('a rural dwelling in the form of a cottage with a decorative appearance') is an Anglo-French hybrid, as *cottage* derives from Old English *cot*, via Anglo-Latin *cotagium* and Anglo-Norman *cotage*. *Cottage*, identified in the *Encyclopédie* in 1754 as a *mot anglais* was indeed borrowed into French in the nineteenth century, but the English phrase (L18) antedates this borrowing. A *ferme ornée* is 'a farm designed for aesthetic pleasure as well as practical purposes'.

1995 G. Tindall *Célestine* A handyman, he had embellished the classic French exterior with a veranda and a blue-painted trellis, so that it now resembled an English *cottage orné* of the Edwardian era.

1996 D. Chambers *Stonyground* . . . Philip Southcote . . . first created . . . what came to be known as a *ferme ornée*—Wooburn Farm in Surrey: a modest farm around and through which went walks planted with trees and shrubs and flowers, so that one could stroll through a farm in a garden and enjoy the beauties of horticulture and agriculture together.

orterde /ˈɔːtɛːdə/ *noun* M20 German (from *Ort* place + *Erde* earth). *Soil Science* A dark sandy layer in soil containing redeposited materials from the upper layers, but not cemented into a hardpan. Cf. ORTSTEIN.

orthosis /ɔːˈθəʊsɪs/ *noun plural* **orthoses** /ɔːˈθəʊsiːz/ M20 Greek (*orthōsis* making straight, from *orthoun* to set straight). *Medicine* An artificial external device, as a brace or splint, serving to prevent or assist relative movement in the limbs or the spine.

ortolan /'ɔ:t(ə)lən/ *noun* M17 French (from Provençal = gardener, from Latin *hortulanus*, from *hortulus* diminutive of *hortus* garden). A bunting, *Emberiza hortulana*, found throughout much of the western Palaearctic, formerly esteemed as a delicacy (also *ortolan bunting*). Also (*United States* and *West Indies*, *rare*) any of certain other birds of similar gastronomic reputation.

■ Earlier (but only E16) in its original sense of 'gardener'.

ortstein /'ɔ:tstʌn/ *noun* E20 German (from *Ort* place + *Stein* stone). *Soil Science* A hardpan; *especially* an iron pan in a podzol. Cf. ORTERDE.

orzo /'ordzo/ *noun* L20 Italian (= barley). Pasta in the shape of grains of rice.

o.s.p. abbreviation of OBIIT SINE PROLE.

ossia /ɒ'si:ə/, /'ɒsjə/ *conjunction* L19 Italian. *Music* In directions: or, alternatively.

■ Indicating an alternative and usually easier way of playing a passage.

osso bucco /ˌɒsəʊ 'bu:kəʊ/ *noun phrase* M20 Italian (= marrowbone). (An Italian dish of) shin of veal containing marrowbone stewed in wine with vegetables.

ostinato /ɒstɪ'nɑːtəʊ/ *adjective & noun* L19 Italian (= obstinate, persistent). *Music* **A** *adjective* L19 Recurring; frequently repeated. **B** *noun* E20 plural **ostinati** /ɒstɪ 'nɑːti/, **ostinatos**. A melodic phrase repeated through all or part of a piece.

B 1996 *Country Life* Matthew Richardson's short film, which told of the beginning of Lulu's downfall, was perfectly tailored to the catastrophic progress of the central orchestral *ostinato*.

Ostpolitik /'ɒstpɒlɪˌtiːk/ *noun* M20 German (from *Ost* east + *Politik* policy). *History* The foreign policy of a western country (*specifically* of the Federal Republic of Germany) with reference to the Communist States. Cf. WESTPOLITIK.

ostracon /'ɒstrəkɒn/ *noun* plural **ostraca** /'ɒstrəkə/ (also **ostrakon**, plural **ostraka**) L19 Greek (*ostrakon* hard shell, potsherd). *Archaeology* A potsherd used as a writing surface. Usually in *plural*.

o tempora, o mores! /əʊ 'tɛmpərə əʊ ˌmɔ:reɪz/ *interjection* M16 Latin (= o times, o manners!). What times, what ways!

■ Originally quoted from the Roman orator Cicero's impeachment of the conspirator Catiline (*In Catilinam* I.1) in 63 BC; now a general expression of alarm, contempt, amusement, etc., about behaviour in contemporary society.

1996 *Times* 'Even in the age of Aids, . . . self-styled vampires drink blood—but from monogamous donors.' Sexually responsible vampires? *O tempora! O mores!*

otium /'əʊʃɪəm/ *noun* E18 Latin. Leisure, ease, idleness.

■ Chiefly in *otium cum dignitate* or *cum dignitate otium* 'dignified leisure', quoting from one of Cicero's letters *Ad Familiares* (I.ix.21).

ottava rima /ɒtˌtɑːva 'ri:ma/, /ɒˌtɑ:və 'ri:mə/ *noun* L18 Italian (= eighth rhyme). A stanza of eight lines, 11-syllabled in Italian, 10-syllabled in English, rhyming as *ababbcc*.

ottocento /ɒtəʊ'tʃɛntəʊ/ *noun* (also **Ottocento**) E20 Italian (= eight hundred). The nineteenth century in Italy; the style of Italian art, architecture, music, etc., of this period.

ou /əʊ/ *adjective & noun* M19 Afrikaans (from Dutch *oud* old). **A** *adjective* M19 Old, elder. **B** *noun* plural **ouens** /'əʊənz/, **ous** M20 A man, a fellow. Cf. OUTJIE.

■ In South African colloquial speech, frequently used in terms of affection or casual reference.

oubaas /'əʊbɑ:s/ *noun* M19 Afrikaans (from OU + BAAS). A head of a family; an elderly man.

■ In South Africa, a colloquial form of address to an older man.

oubliette /u:blɪ'ɛt/ *noun* L18 French (from *oublier* to forget). A secret dungeon accessible only through a trapdoor.

oudstryder /'əʊtstreɪdə/ *noun* M20 Afrikaans (= ex-soldier). In South Africa: a veteran of the South African War (1899–1902) who fought on the side of the Boer republics; *generally* any war veteran.

oued see under WADI.

ouens plural of OU.

oukha variant of UKHA.

ouma /'əʊmə/ *noun* E20 Afrikaans (= grandmother, from OU old + *ma* mother). A grandmother; an elderly woman.

■ In South Africa, chiefly as a respectful or affectionate form of address or reference.

oupa /'əʊpə/ *noun* E20 **Afrikaans** (= grandfather, from **ou** old + *pa* father). A grandfather; an elderly man.

■ In South Africa, chiefly as a respectful or affectionate form of address or reference.

oursin /'ɔːsan/, *foreign* /ursɛ̃/ *noun* E20 **French**. A sea urchin, *especially* an edible one.

outjie /'əʊki/, /'əʊtʃi/ *noun* M20 **Afrikaans** (from as **ou** + diminutive suffix -*tjie*). A child, a little fellow.

■ In South African colloquial speech can also be used jocularly or derogatively of an adult.

outré /utre/, /'uːtreɪ/ *adjective* E18 **French** (past participle of *outrer* to exaggerate). Beyond the bounds of what is usual or proper; eccentric, unusual, out-of-the-way.

> **1996** *Country Life* Peter York celebrates some of the artefacts which still shine forth as emblems of the British soul, be they as conservative as the Bath Oliver biscuit or as outré as a Vivienne Westwood frock.

ouvert /uvɛr/ *noun* plural pronounced same E20 **French** (= open). *Ballet* An open position of the feet.

ouvrier /uvrije/ *noun* (feminine **ouvrière** /uvrijɛr/) plural pronounced same M19 **French**. In France: a manual or industrial worker; a labourer.

> **1996** *Times Magazine* Most of this non-village comprises formerly humble ouvrier dwellings of two storeys plus semi-basement for burglar access.

ouzo /'uːzəʊ/ *noun* plural **ouzos** L19 **Modern Greek**. (A glass of) an aniseed-flavoured spirit from Greece.

ova plural of OVUM.

ovolo /'əʊvələʊ/ *noun* plural **ovoli** /'əʊvəli/ M17 **Italian** (diminutive of *uovo, ovo* from Latin *ovum* egg). *Architecture* A rounded convex moulding.

ovum /'əʊvəm/ *noun* plural **ova** /'əʊvə/ E17 **Latin** (= egg). **1** E17 *Roman History* Any of a number of egg-shaped objects used in the circus to indicate the number of laps in a race. Usually in *plural*. **2** E18 *Biology* The female gamete or reproductive cell in animals; an egg, an egg cell. **b** M18 *Botany* Originally (*rare*), the ovule or seed of a plant. Now, the egg cell in the nucellus of an ovule. **3** E18 *Architecture* An egg-shaped ornament or carving.

oy /ɔɪ/ *interjection* (also **oi**) L19 **Yiddish**. Used by Yiddish-speakers as an exclamation of dismay, grief, etc.

■ Also in *oy vay, oy vey* /ɔɪ veɪ/ (Yiddish *vey* = woe).

oyama /əʊˈjaːmə/ *noun* plural same M20 **Japanese**. An ONNAGATA.

oyer /'ɔɪə/ *noun* LME **Anglo-Norman** (= Old French *oïr*: see next). *Law* **1** LME The hearing of a case. **2** LME A criminal trial held under the commission of oyer and terminer. **3** E17 *History* The hearing of a document read in court, especially an instrument in writing pleaded by one party in a suit.

■ Sense 1 exists only in the phrase *oyer and terminer* (formerly also *oyer (and) determiner*) 'a commission authorizing a judge on circuit to hold courts'.

oyez /əʊˈjɛs/, /əʊˈjɛz/, /əʊˈjeɪ/ *verb & noun* (also **oyes** /əʊˈjɛs/) LME **Anglo-Norman** (Old French (also *oiez*) imperative plural of *oïr* (modern *ouïr*) from Latin *audire* to hear). **A** *intransitive verb* LME (*imperative*) Listen! **B** *noun* LME plural same **oyesses**. A call or cry of 'oyez!'.

■ Uttered (usually three times) by a public crier or a court officer to command silence and attention.

P

p.a. abbreviation of PER ANNUM.

pabulum /'pabjələm/ *noun* M17 Latin (from stem of *pascere* to feed). **1** M17 Food, nutriment, especially for plants or animals or their tissues. **2** L17 That which feeds a fire. **3** M18 That which nourishes and sustains the mind or soul. **4** L20 Bland intellectual fare; an insipid or undemanding diet of words, entertainment, etc.

> **4 1996** *Spectator* The dons who supply these masses with pabulum are not allowed to feel job-secure unless they are also engaged upon their own 'work'.

pace /'pɑːʧeɪ/, /'peɪsɪ/ *preposition* L18 Latin (ablative singular of *pax* peace, as in *pace tua* by your leave). With due deference to (a person named).

■ Used especially as a courteous or ironical apology for a contradiction or difference of opinion (see quotation). Normally italicized to distinguish it from the English verb or noun 'pace'.

> **1996** *Spectator* Had he read the magnificent Turing biography by Andrew Hodges, which remains the best work on Bletchley Park to date (*pace* Robert Harris and his marvellous book), the hapless Volkman could have provided us with the theologically resonant denouement.

pacha variant of PASHA.

pachalic variant of PASHALIC.

pachinko /pə'ʧɪŋkəʊ/ *noun* M20 Japanese. A variety of pinball popular in Japan.

pachisi /pə'ʧiːzi/ *noun* (also **parcheesi** /pɑː'ʧiːzi/, **Pachisi**) E19 Hindustani (*pac(c.)īsī* (throw of) twenty-five (the highest in the game), ultimately from Sanskrit *pañcaviṃśati* twenty-five). A four-handed Indian board game with six cowries for dice.

pachuco /pə'ʧuːkəʊ/, *foreign* /pa'ʧuko/ *noun plural* **pachucos** /pə'ʧuːkəʊz/, *foreign* /pa'ʧukos/ M20 Mexican Spanish (literally, 'flashily dressed'). A juvenile delinquent of Mexican-American descent, especially in the Los Angeles area; *derogatory* any Mexican-American. Also the argot spoken by pachucos.

> **1972** J. Wambaugh *Blue Knight* 'Órale, panzón,' he said, like a pachuco, which he put on for me. He spoke beautiful Spanish . . . but the barrios of El Paso Texas died hard.

pacifico /pə'sɪfɪkəʊ/ *noun plural* **pacificos** L19 Spanish. A person of peaceful character; *specifically* (*historical*) a native or inhabitant of Cuba or the Philippines who submitted without active opposition to Spanish occupation.

paco /'pɑːkəʊ/, *foreign* /'pako/ *noun plural* **pacos** /'pɑːkəʊz/, *foreign* /'pakos/ E17 Spanish ((in sense 2 with reference to the brown and white colour) from Quechua *pako* red, reddish yellow). **1** E17 An alpaca. **2** M19 *Mineralogy* An earthy brown oxide of iron, containing particles of silver.

padma /'pʌdmə/ *noun* M19 Sanskrit (= lotus). (The flower of) the lotus-plant; an emblematic representation of this.

padmasana /pʌd'mɑːsənə/ *noun* L19 Sanskrit (*padmāsana*, from *padma* lotus + *āsana* seat, posture). *Yoga* A bodily position with legs crossed and feet resting on the opposite thighs, said to resemble the flower of a lotus.

padre /'pɑːdri/, /'pɑːdreɪ/ *noun* L16 Italian ((also Spanish, Portuguese) from Latin *pater, patr-* father). In Italy, Spain, Portugal, Latin America, and other areas of Spanish influence: (a title of) a Christian clergyman, especially a Roman Catholic priest. Now chiefly (*colloquial*), a chaplain in the armed services.

padrone /pa'drəʊni/, *foreign* /pa'drone/ *noun plural* **padrones** /pa'drəʊnɪz/, **padroni** /pa'droni/ (feminine (especially in sense (b)) **padrona** /pa'drəʊnə/, *foreign* /pa'drona/, plural **padronas** /pa'drəʊnɑːz/, **padrone** /pa'drone/) L17 Italian. A patron, a master; *specifically* (a) (now chiefly *United States colloquial*) an employer, a manager; *especially* an exploitative employer of unskilled immigrant workers; (b) the proprietor of an inn or hotel in Italy.

paedeia variant of PAIDEIA.

paella /pʌɪ'ɛlə/, /pa'e(l)jɑ/ *noun* L19 Catalan (from Old French *paele* (modern *paêle*), from Latin *patella* pan, dish). A Spanish dish of rice, saffron, chicken, seafood, vegetables, etc., cooked and served in a large shallow pan.

> *figurative* **1996** *Times* He is a full 20 seats short [of a parliamentary majority], compelling

him to rely for survival . . . on a *paella* of regional parties.

pagoda /pə'gəʊdə/ *noun* L16 Portuguese (*pagode*, probably ultimately from Persian *butkada* idol temple, from *but* idol + *kada* habitation, alteration by association with Prakrit *bhagodī* divine, holy). **1** A Hindu or Buddhist temple or sacred building, usually in the form of a many-tiered tower with storeys of diminishing size, each with an ornamented projecting roof, in China, India, Japan, and elsewhere in the Far East. **2** L18 An ornamental structure built in imitation of such a temple.

pagri variant of PUGGAREE.

pahit /'pɑːhɪt/ *noun* E20 Malay (= bitter). In South East Asia: gin and bitters. More fully *gin pahit*.

pahoehoe /pə'həʊɪhəʊi/ *noun* M19 Hawaiian. *Geology* Smooth, undulating or corded lava. Cf. AA.

paideia /pʌɪ'dʌɪə/ *noun* (also **paedeia**) M20 Greek. *Greek History* Education, upbringing; the ideal result of this; a society's culture.

pai-hua /'pʌɪhwɑː/ *noun* E20 Chinese (*báihuà* (Wade–Giles *pai-hua*), from *bái* white, clear, plain + *huà* language, speech). The standard written form of modern Chinese, based on the northern dialects, especially that of Peking (Beijing). Cf. PUTONGHUA.

paillette /pal'jɛt, /pʌɪ'jɛt/ *noun* M19 French (diminutive of *paille* straw, chaff). **1** M19 A small piece of glittering foil, shell, etc., used to decorate a garment; a spangle. **2** L19 A decorative piece of coloured foil or bright metal used in enamel painting.

pain /pɛ̃/ *noun* LME Old and Modern French (from Latin *panis*, *pan-*). Bread, *specifically* in French bakery.

■ Formerly naturalized, it now occurs only in *pain perdu* (toasted stale bread, usually sweetened and flavoured with cinnamon) and in names of specialty breads.

pair /pɛr/ *noun & adjective* plural of noun same M19 French (= equal). *Roulette* (Of) an even number; (of) the even numbers collectively.

paisano /pʌɪ'sɑːnəʊ/, *foreign* /pai'sano/ *noun* plural **paisanos** /pʌɪ'sɑːnəʊz/, *foreign* /pai'sanos/ M19 Spanish (= peasant, rustic). **1** M19 In Spain and Spanish-speaking areas, especially in the south-

western United States: a fellow-countryman; a peasant. **2** L19 In Mexico and the south-western United States: a road-runner.

pakapoo /'pakəpuː/, /pakə'puː/ *noun* (also **pakapu** and other variants) E20 Chinese (*bái gē piào* (Wade–Giles *pai ko p'iao*) literally, 'white pigeon ticket', perhaps referring to a Cantonese competition which involved releasing pigeons and predicting the distance they would fly and the numbers expected to return). A Chinese form of lottery played with slips of paper marked with columns of characters.

■ Chiefly Australian, and in the phrase *like a pakapoo ticket*, meaning 'disordered, unintelligible'.

pak-choi /pak'tʃɔɪ/ *noun* M19 Chinese ((Cantonese) *paåk ts' oi* white vegetable: cf. PE-TSAI). Chinese cabbage.

pakeha /'pɑːkɪhɑː/ *noun & adjective* E19 Maori. **A** *noun* E19 A White person (as opposed to a Maori). **B** *adjective* M19 Of, pertaining to, or designating a pakeha. *New Zealand*.

pakora /pə'kɔːrə/ *noun* M20 Hindustani (*pakoṛā* a dish of vegetables in gram-flour). A savoury Indian dish consisting of diced or chopped vegetables coated in batter and deep fried.

pa-kua /pɑː'kwɑː/ *noun* L19 Chinese (*bāguà* (Wade–Giles *pà-kua*), from *bā* eight + *guà* divinatory symbols). **1** L19 *Art* Any of various decorative and religious motifs incorporating the eight trigrams of *I Ching*; *specifically* an arrangement of these trigrams in a circle round the yin-yang symbol. **2** M20 A Chinese martial art in which fighters are arranged around a circle according to the trigram sequence in positions which they must defend.

palacio /pa'laθjo/, /pa'lasjo/, /pə'lasɪəʊ/ *noun* plural **palacios** /pa'laθjos/, /pa'lasjos/, /pə'lasɪəʊz/ M19 Spanish (from Latin *palatium*). In Spain and Spanish-speaking countries: a palace, a country seat, an imposing official building.

paladin /'paladɪn/ *noun* L16 French (from Italian *paladino*, from Latin *palatinus* officer of the palace). Each of the twelve bravest and most famous warriors of Charlemagne's court. Also, a knight errant, a champion.

palaestra /pə'liːstrə/, /pə'lʌɪstrə/ *noun* (also **palestra** /pə'liːstrə/, /pə'lɛstrə/) LME Latin (from Greek *palaistra*, from *palaiein* wrestle). *Classical History* **1** LME A place devoted to the public teaching and practice of wrestling and athletics. **2** LME Wrestling, athletics.

palais /'paleɪ/ *noun* plural same /'paleɪz/ E20 French (literally, 'palace') Abbreviation of PALAIS DE DANSE.

■ Frequently used attributively, as in *palais glide* a form of ballroom dance.

palais de danse /ˌpaleɪ də 'dɒs/ *noun phrase* plural same E20 French. A public hall for dancing.

Palais Royal /ˌpaleɪ 'rɔ(ə)l/, *foreign* /palɛ rwajal/ *adjective phrase* L19 French Designating a type of indelicate farce said to be typical of the Palais Royal theatre, Paris.

palapa /pə'lapə/ *noun* L20 Mexican Spanish (= (the leaves and branches of) the palm *Orbignya cohune*). A traditional Mexican shelter roofed with palm leaves or branches. Also, any structure imitating this, especially on a beach. *United States.*

palatschinken /ˌpalat'ʃɪŋkən/ *noun* plural E20 Austrian German (from Hungarian *palacsinta* from Proto-Romance *placinta* from Latin *placenta* cake). Austrian (stuffed) pancakes.

palazzo /pə'latsəʊ/ *noun & adjective* M17 Italian (from Latin *palatium* palace). **A** *noun* plural **palazzos**, (in sense 1) **palazzi** /pə'latsi/. **1** M17 A palatial mansion; a large imposing building. **2** L20 *singular* and (usually) in *plural* Loose wide-legged trousers worn by women. **B** *attributive* or as *adjective* M20 Designating a loose wide-legged garment, outfit, etc.

> **1 1996** *Spectator* Of course, not everyone could afford imitation *palazzi* of their own.

palestra variant of PALAESTRA.

paletot /'palətəʊ/ *noun* M19 French (of unknown origin). A short loose outer garment, coat, or cloak. Also, a fitted jacket worn by women in the nineteenth century.

palette /'palɪt/ *noun* L18 French. **1** L18 A thin (oval) board or slab, usually with a hole for the thumb, on which an artist lays and mixes colours. **b** L19 *transferred* The range of colours used by a particular artist or in a particular picture. **c** M20 The range or variety of tonal or instrumental colour in a musical piece, composer's work, etc.; the verbal range of a writer etc. **d** L20 *Computing* In computer graphics, the range of colours or shapes available to the user. **2** M19 *Zoology* A disc-

like structure. **3** M20 A device used by the banker in certain card-games to move cards and money.

pali /'pɑːli/ *noun* E19 Hawaiian. In Hawaii: a steep cliff.

■ *The Pali* is a precipice on the island of Oahu.

palio /'pɑːlio/, /'palɪəʊ/ *noun* L17 Italian (from Latin *pallium* covering, cover). A traditional horse-race held in Italy, especially in Siena, every July and August. Also, the cloth or banner of velvet, silk, etc., given as the prize for winning this race.

paliotto /pali'ɒtto/, /palɪ'ɒtəʊ/ *noun* plural **paliotti** /pali'ɒt(t)i/, **paliottos** /palɪ'ɒtəʊz/ M20 Italian. The frontal painting on an altarpiece.

palladium /pə'leɪdɪəm/ *noun* plural **palladia** /pə'leɪdɪə/ LME Latin (from Greek *palladion*, from *Pallas*, *Pallad-* epithet of the goddess Athene). **1** LME *Classical Mythology* An image of the goddess Pallas (Athene), in the citadel of Troy, on which the safety of the city was supposed to depend, later reputed to have been taken to Rome. **2** E17 *transferred* and *figurative* A thing on which the safety of a nation, institution, etc., is believed to depend; a safeguard.

> **2 1989** R. Milner-Gulland *Cultural Atlas of Russia* The icon of the 'Virgin of Vladimir,' the palladium of Vladimir and Moscow Grand Principalities, is of the iconographic type known as 'Tenderness' . . .

pallium /'palɪəm/ *noun* plural **pallia** /'palɪə/, **palliums** ME Latin (= covering, mantle). **1** ME *Ecclesiastical* A woollen vestment conferred by the Pope on an archbishop in the Latin Church, consisting of a narrow circular band placed round the shoulders with a short lappet hanging from front and back. Also (*transferred*), the office or dignity of an archbishop. **2** M16 *Antiquities* A man's large rectangular cloak, worn especially by Greek philosophical and religious teachers. **3a** L19 *Zoology* The mantle of a mollusc or brachiopod. **b** L19 *Anatomy* and *Zoology* The outer wall of the cerebrum.

pallone /pal'lone/ *noun* L19 Italian (augmentative of *palla* ball). An Italian game, partially resembling tennis, in which a large ball is struck with a cylindrical wooden guard, worn over the hand and wrist.

palmette /pal'mɛt/ *noun* M19 French (diminutive of *palme* palm leaf). *Archaeology*

An ornament (in sculpture or painting) with radiating petals like a palm leaf.

palmier /palmje/ *noun* plural pronounced same. E20 French (literally, 'palm tree'). A small crisp cake shaped like a palm leaf, made from puff pastry and sugar.

palomino /palə'mi:nəʊ/ *noun* plural **palominos** E20 American Spanish (from Spanish from Latin *palumbinus* of or resembling a dove). **1** E20 A horse with light golden-brown coat and white or pale mane and tail. Also *palomino horse*. **2** M20 A pale golden-brown colour.
■ Originally United States.

palsa /'palsə/ *noun* M20 Swedish (*palse*, *pals* (plural *palsar*) from Finnish and Lappish *palsa*). A landform of subarctic regions, consisting of a mound or ridge of peat covered with vegetation and containing a core of frozen peat or mineral soil in which are numerous ice lenses.

pampas /'pampəs/, /'pampəz/ *noun plural*, also used as *singular* (also in singular form **pampa** E18 Spanish (plural of *pampa* from Quechua = a plain). **1** E18 *plural* (treated as *singular* or *plural*). The extensive treeless plains of South America south of the Amazon. Also in *singular*, these plains considered collectively; any one of these plains. **2** L20 *plural* (treated as *singular*). A yellowy-green colour. Usually *attributive*.

pan /pɑːn/ *noun* E17 Hindustani (*pān* betel leaf, from Sanskrit *parṇa* feather, leaf). In the Indian subcontinent: the leaf of the betel, especially as used to enclose slices of areca nut mixed with lime for chewing; the mixture for chewing so formed.

p'an /pan/ *noun* M20 Chinese (*pán*). *Chinese Antiquities* A kind of shallow dish-shaped ritual vessel.

panacea /panə'si:ə/ *noun* M16 Latin (from Greek *panakeia*, from *panakēs* all-healing, from *pan-* all + base of *akos* remedy). A remedy for all diseases; a thing for solving all difficulties or adopted in every case of difficulty.

panache /pə'naʃ/ *noun* M16 French (from Italian *pennacchio* from late Latin *pinnaculum* diminutive of *pinna* feather). **1** M16 A tuft or plume of feathers, especially as a head-dress or a decoration for a helmet. Formerly also, a decoration like a plume of feathers, e.g. a tassel. **2** L19 Flamboyantly or stylishly confident behaviour; a manner marked by this.

2 1996 *Country Life* Lord Petersham drove his Cumberland cobs with considerable panache through the marathon obstacles in the horse pairs class . . .

panada /pə'nɑːdə/ *noun* (also **panade** /pə'neɪd/) L16 Spanish ((also Portuguese) = Italian *panata*, represented a Proto-Romance derivation of Latin *panis* bread). Bread boiled in water to a pulp and flavoured. Also, a paste of flour, water, etc., used for thickening.

panatela /panə'tɛlə/ *noun* M19 American Spanish (= long thin biscuit, sponge cake from Spanish from Italian *panatello* small loaf, diminutive of *panata* (as PANADA)). **1** M19 A long slender cigar, *especially* one tapering at the sealed end. Also more fully *panatela cigar*. **2** M20 *transferred* A cigarette made of Central or South American marijuana. *slang*.

pancetta /pan'(t)ʃetə/, *foreign* /pan'tʃetta/ *noun* M20 Italian (diminutive of *pancio* belly from Proto-Romance word (whence also 'paunch'). Italian cured belly of pork.

panchshila /pɑːn'ʃiːlə/, /pan'ʃiːlə/ *noun* M20 Sanskrit (*pañcaśīla*, from *pañca* five + *śīla* moral principle). The five principles of peaceful relations formulated between India and China (and, by extension, other Communist countries) and set out in the preamble of a treaty signed in April 1954.

pancratium /pan'kreɪʃɪəm/ *noun* (also in Greek form **pancration** /pan'kreɪʃɪən/, /pan'kreɪtɪən/) E17 Latin (from Greek *pagkration*, from *pan-* all + *kratos* strength). **1** E17 *Greek History* An athletic contest combining both wrestling and boxing. **2** M17 *Botany* Any of various bulbous African and Mediterranean plants; *especially* the sea daffodil, *P. maritimum*.

panem et circenses /ˌpanɛm ɛt sə: 'kɛnziːz/, /kə:'kɛnseɪz/ *noun phrase* L18 Latin (= bread and circuses). State provision of popular entertainment and distribution of food to win popularity with the people.
■ Originally, the hand-outs and gladiatorial games provided by Roman statesmen and emperors in the Circus of ancient Rome to assuage the city's notoriously volatile populace.
1961 D. L. Munby *God and Rich Society* Leaders . . . win votes by offering panem et circenses to those they despise.

panettone /panɪ'təʊni/, *foreign* /panet 'toni/ *noun* (also **panetone** /panɪ'təʊni/, *foreign* /pane'tone/) plural **panettoni** /panet'toni/ E20 Italian (from *panetto* cake, bar, diminutive of *pane* bread, from Latin *panis*). A rich Italian bread made with eggs, fruit, and butter.

panforte /pan'fɔːti/, *foreign* /pan'forte/ *noun* L19 Italian (from *pane* bread + *forte* strong). A hard spicy Sienese cake containing nuts, candied peel, and honey.

panga /'pɑːŋgə/ *noun* 1 (also **ponga**) E20 American Spanish. A flat-bottomed boat with rising stem and stern used especially in Latin America.

panga /'paŋgə/ *noun* 2 M20 Kiswahili. In East Africa: a large knife used either as a tool or a weapon.

panier de crabes /panje də krab/ *noun phrase* plural **paniers de crabes** (pronounced same) M20 French (literally, 'basket of crabs'). A competitive struggle.
1963 *Economist* The visitor is ... not able to move around in this communist *panier de crabes*.

panino /pa'niːno/ *noun* plural **panini** /pa'niːni/ M20 Italian. An Italian bread roll or sandwich.

panne /pan/ *noun* L18 French (of unknown origin). A soft silk or rayon fabric with a flattened pile, resembling velvet. Also *panne velvet*.

panocha, panoche variants of PEN-UCHE.

pansala /'pʌnsələ/ *noun* M19 Sinhalese (from *pan* leaf + *sala* dwelling) from Sanskrit *parṇaśālā*, Pali *pannasālā*). A Buddhist temple or monastery; the home of a Buddhist religious teacher.

panthea see SIGNUM PANTHEUM.

panzanella /ˌpantsə'nɛlə/ *noun* L20 Italian. Bread salad made with olive oil and chopped vegetables.

panzer /'panzə/, *foreign* /'pantsər/ *noun & adjective* (also **Panzer**) M20 German (= mail, coat of mail). A *noun* M20 (A member of) a German armoured unit. Also, a German tank. B *attributive* or as *adjective* M20 Of, pertaining to, or designating a panzer; *transferred* heavily armoured.
A *figurative* 1996 *Times Magazine* ... the story was also swiftly turned into a television comedy, ... the starring role being given to 'Wanda', a panzer among other cheerleader moms.
B 1995 *Spectator* [The opposition's informants] were subsequently invited to leave instantly, unless they wanted their departures assisted

by the steel-capped boot of a management which has proved over the past three years that it can make a panzer division look positively benign.

papabile /papa'biːle/, /pə'pɑːbɪli/ *adjective & noun* (also (as adjective) **papabili** /papa'biːli/) M20 Italian (from *papa* Pope). A *adjective* M20 (Of a prelate) worthy of or eligible to be elected Pope; *generally* suitable for high office. B M20 *absolutely* as *noun* plural **papabili** /papa'biːli/. A prelate regarded as eligible to be elected Pope; *generally* one regarded as suitable for high office. Usually in *plural*.
A 1964 *Spectator* He [sc. Harold Macmillan] thought that three of the members of his Cabinet who were in the House of Commons, apart from Butler, were *papabile* and of sufficient seniority to be considered: Maudling, Heath and myself [sc. Iain Macleod].

papaloi /'pap(ə)lwɑː/ *noun* plural **papalois**, same L19 Haitian (creole *papalwa*, from *papa* father + *lwa* LOA). A voodoo priest. Cf. MAMALOI.

paparazzo /papə'ratsəʊ/ *noun* plural **paparazzi** /papə'ratsi/ M20 Italian. A (freelance) photographer who pursues celebrities in order to take their pictures.
1995 *Times* Video paparazzi, who sell their film to downmarket television shows, are viewed as the vultures of the celebrity market, sometimes seeking to pick fights with the famous to secure pictures.

paperasserie /paprasri/ *noun* E20 French. Excessive official paperwork or routine; bureaucracy.

papeterie /pap(ə)tri/ (*plural same*), /'papətri/ *noun* M19 French (= paper manufacture, stationer's shop, writing-case, from *papetier* paper-maker). A (usually ornamental) case or box for paper and other writing materials.

papier collé /papje kɔle/ *noun phrase* plural **papiers collés** (*pronounced same*) M20 French (= glued paper). A collage made from paper; the use of paper for collage.

papier déchiré /papje deʃire/ *noun phrase* plural **papiers déchirés** (*pronounced same*) M20 French (= torn paper). Paper torn haphazardly for use in collage; a collage made of such paper.

papier mâché /ˌpapɪeɪ 'maʃeɪ/, *foreign* /papje maʃe/ *noun & adjective phrase* M18 French (*papier* paper + *mâché* past participle of *mâcher* to chew, from Latin *masticare*). A *noun* M18 Material made from pulped paper; paper reduced to a pulp mixed with glue etc. or (for fine work) sheets of paper pasted together, used for making moulded boxes, jars, trays, etc. **B** *adjective* M18 Made of papier mâché.

B 1996 *Times Magazine* A visit to the set of *Dr Who* conjures up images of papier-mâché monstrosities, nightmares in latex.

papier poudré /papje pudre/ *noun phrase* plural **papiers poudrés** (*pronounced same*) E20 French (= powdered paper). A paper impregnated with face-powder.

papillote /'papɪləʊt/, /ˌpapɪlɒt/, *in sense 2 usually* /'papɪjɒt/ *noun* M18 French. **1** M18 A curl-paper. *obsolete except historical.* **2** E19 A usually greased paper wrapper in which a fillet etc. of meat or fish is cooked.

■ Frequently in *en papillote* /ɒ̃/, in a paper wrapper.

1996 *Times* Usually it comes between the aubergine caviar and the salmon *en papillote*, though sometimes it can be staved off until the moment of decision between coffee and camomile tea.

pappardelle /papɑːˈdɛli/ *noun plural* L20 Italian. Pasta made in wider strips than TAGLIATELLE and served especially with meat sauces.

1996 *Spectator* Pappardelle with tender little broad beans and dark shards of rocket were good as well . . .

paprika /'paprɪkə/, /pəˈpriːkə/ *noun & adjective* L19 Hungarian. **A** *noun* **1** L19 A condiment made from the dried ground fruits of certain (especially red) varieties of the sweet pepper, *Capsicum annuum*. **b** M20 The bright orange-red colour of this. **2** E20 Any of several European varieties of the sweet pepper bearing mildly flavoured fruits. **B** *adjective* **1** M20 Of a dish: flavoured with (especially the condiment) paprika. Often *postpositive*. **2** M20 Of the colour of paprika.

papyrus /pəˈpʌɪrəs/ *noun* plural **papyri** /pəˈpʌɪrʌɪ/, /pəˈpʌɪriː/ LME Latin (from Greek *papuros* paper reed, of unknown origin). **1** LME An aquatic plant of the sedge family, formerly abundant in Egypt and the source of the writing material papyrus. **2** E18 Material in the forms of fine strips of the stem of the papyrus plant, soaked in water, pressed together, and dried, to form a writing surface, used by the ancient Egyptians, Romans, etc. **3** E19 A manuscript or document written on this.

par /par/, /pɑː/ *preposition* ME Old and Modern French (from Proto-Romance combination of Latin *per* through + *ad* to). Through, by.

■ Occurring in various phrases used in English: see PAR ÉMINENCE, PAR EXCELLENCE, PAR EXEMPLE.

parador /'parədɔː/ *noun* plural **paradores** /'parədɔːrɛz/, **paradors** M19 Spanish. In Spain: a hotel owned and administered by the government. Formerly, any Spanish hotel or inn.

1995 D. Lodge *Therapy* It's now a five-star *parador*, one of the grandest hotels in Spain.

parados /'parədɒs/, *foreign* /parado/ *noun* plural **paradoses** /'parədɒsɪz/, same M19 French (from *para*- protector of + *dos* back). An elevation of earth behind a defended place as a protection against attack from the rear; the mound along the back of a trench.

paramo /'parəməʊ/ *noun* plural **paramos** M18 Spanish ((also Portuguese) *páramo* from Spanish Latin *paramus* bare plain). A high plateau in the tropical parts of South America, bare of trees and exposed to wind and thick cold fogs.

parang /'pɑːraŋ/ *noun* M19 Malay. A large heavy knife used in Malaysia for clearing vegetation etc.

paraphernalia /ˌparəfəˈneɪlɪə/ *noun plural* M17 Medieval Latin (use as noun of neuter plural of *paraphernalis*, from Latin *parapherna* from Greek, from *para*- beside, beyond + *phernē* dowry). **1** M17 *History* Those articles of personal property which the law allowed a married woman to keep and deal with as her own, when most of her personal or movable property vested in her husband. **2** M18 Personal belongings, especially of dress or adornment; the miscellaneous objects that go to make up a thing or are associated with it; trappings, bits and pieces. Also treated as *singular*.

paratha /pəˈrɑːtə/ *noun* M20 Hindustani (*parāṭhā*). In Indian cookery, a flat piece of unleavened bread fried in butter, ghee, etc., on a griddle.

paratonnerre /paratɔnɛr/ *noun* plural pronounced same E19 French (from *para*-protection against + *tonnerre* thunder). A lightning-conductor.

parc fermé /ˌpɑːk ˈfɛːmeɪ/ *noun phrase* (also **parc ferme**) M20 French (literally, 'enclosed area'). In motor sports, an enclosure or paddock used by vehicles before or after a race.

parcheesi variant of PACHISI.

par éminence /par eminãs/, /pɑ:(r) 'ɛmɪnəns/ *adverb phrase* L19 French. Pre-eminently.

parens patriae /ˌparɛnz 'patrɪi:/ *noun phrase* M18 Modern Latin (literally, 'parent of the country'). *Law* The monarch, or any other authority, regarded as the legal protector of citizens unable to protect themselves.

parergon /pəˈrɜ:gɒn/ *noun plural* **parerga** /pəˈrɜ:gə/ E17 Latin (from Greek, from *para-* beyond, beside + *ergon* work). **1** E17–E18 An ornamental accessory or addition, especially in a painting; an embellishment. **2** E17 Subsidiary work or business, apart from one's ordinary employment. Also, a work, composition, etc., that is supplementary to or a by-product of a larger work.

par excellence /par ɛkslãs/, /pɑ:(r) 'ɛks(ə)ləns/ *adverb phrase* L17 French (from Latin *per excellentiam* by virtue of excellence). Pre-eminently; supremely, above all.

1996 *Country Life* Miss Guest is an Edwards pasticheur *par excellence* . . .

par exemple /par əgzãpl/, /pɑ:r əg 'zɒmp(ə)l/ *adverb phrase* M19 French. For example.

parfait /'pɑ:feɪ/ *noun* L19 French (literally, 'perfect'). A rich iced pudding of whipped cream, eggs, etc. Also, a sweet consisting of layers of ice-cream, fruit, syrup, whipped cream, etc., served in a tall glass.

parfleche /'pɑ:flɛʃ/ *noun & adjective* E19 Canadian French (*parflèche*, from French *parer* + *flèche* arrow). **A** *noun* E19 (A) depilated (especially buffalo's) hide dried by stretching on a frame; an article made from this. **B** *attributive* or as *adjective* M19 Made of parfleche.

parfumerie /parfymri/ *noun plural* pronounced same M19 French. A shop or department which sells perfume. Also, a perfume factory.

pariah /pəˈrʌɪə/ *noun* E17 Tamil (*paraiyar* plural of *paraiyan*, literally, 'hereditary drummer', from *parai* drum). **1** E17 Originally, a member of a very extensive low caste in southern India. Later, a member of a low caste or of no Hindu caste. *obso-*

lete except *historical*. **2** E19 *transferred* A member of a despised social class; an outcast. **3** E19 A half-wild stray dog. Also *pariah-dog* or *pye-dog*.

2 1996 *Times* Nothing seems to boost a dictator so much as to be . . . ostracised. The world's longest established rulers—Castro, Gaddafi, Assad, Saddam Hussein, the Ayatollahs—have all benefited from such pariah status.

pari-mutuel /parimytɥɛl/ (*plural same*); /ˌpɑ:rɪˈmju:tʃʊəl/ *noun* L19 French (= mutual stake or wager). **1** L19 A form of betting in which those backing the first three places divide the losers' stakes. **2** E20 A booth for placing bets under this system; a totalizator.

■ Often abbreviated to MUTUEL.

pari passu /ˌpɑ:ri: 'pasu:/, /'pari/ *adverb phrase* M16 Latin (literally, 'with equal step'). With equal speed; side by side; simultaneously and equally. Also, on an equal footing, without preference.

1997 *Spectator* . . . these blunders in public relations moved *pari passu* with the growth of the media . . .

parka /'pɑ:kə/ *noun* L18 Aleut (from Russian = skin jacket). A long hooded skin jacket worn by Eskimos; a similar garment, usually of windproof fabric, worn especially by mountaineers.

parlando /pɑ:'landəu/ *adverb, adjective, & noun* L19 Italian. *Music* **A** *adverb & adjective* L19 (A direction:) in an expressive or declamatory manner, as if speaking. **B** *noun* M20 plural **parlandos, parlandi** /pɑ:'landi/ An expressive or declamatory passage or piece.

parlementaire /ˌpɑ:ləmɛn'tɛ:/ *noun* E20 French (from *parlementer* to discuss terms, parley). A person deputed to parley with an enemy.

parloir /parlwar/ *noun plural* pronounced same E18 French. A conversation room in a monastery or convent; a parlour. Also, a similar room in a prison.

parmigiana /ˌpɑ:mɪ'dʒɑ:nə/ *adjective* L19 Italian (feminine of *parmigiano* of or pertaining to the city and province of Parma in northern Italy). *Cookery* Made or served with Parmesan cheese.

■ Chiefly used postpositively in names of dishes, as in *veal parmigiana*.

parnas /pɑ:'nas/ *noun* (also **parnass**) plural **parnassim** /pɑ:'nasɪm/ M19 Hebrew (from Greek *pronous* provident). The lay leader of the congregation of a synagogue.

parochet /paˈroxet/ noun (also **parocheth** and other variants) plural **parochot** /paˈroxɒt/ L19 Hebrew (pārōḵeṯ curtain; cf. Akkadian parāku to shut off). A richly decorated curtain which hangs in front of the Ark in a synagogue.

parole /pəˈrəʊl/, in sense 3 usually foreign /parɔl/ noun & verb L15 Old and Modern French (from Proto-Romance, from Latin parabola parable, from Greek parabolē comparison, analogy, proverb, from paraballein to put alongside, compare). **A** noun **1** L15 A person's word of honour; specifically (a) a prisoner of war's promise to abide by the specific terms of a conditional release; (b) a prisoner's promise of good behaviour in return for release before the expiry of a custodial sentence. Also, the granting to or acceptance by a prisoner of a conditional release on the basis of such a promise; the system or practice of granting or accepting such a conditional release. **2** L18 Military The password used by an officer or inspector of the guard. **3** M20 Linguistics The actual linguistic behaviour or performance of an individual, in contrast to the linguistic system. Opposed to LANGUE sense 3. **B** transitive verb M17 Put on parole; release on parole.

paroli /ˈpɑːrəli/ noun E18 French (from Italian, from paro like, from Latin par equality). In a gambling card-game (especially faro), the staking of double the sum previously staked.

paronomasia /ˌparənəˈmeɪzɪə/ noun L16 Latin (from Greek, from as para- beside. beyond + onomasia naming). A play on words, a pun; punning.

parquet /ˈpɑːki/, /ˈpɑːkeɪ/, in sense 3 foreign /parkɛ/ noun E19 Old and Modern French (= small marked-off space etc., diminutive of parc park). **1** E19 A flooring, especially one composed of blocks of various woods arranged in a geometric pattern. Also parquet floor. **2** M19 (The front part of) the ground floor of a theatre or auditorium. Chiefly United States. **3** L19 In France and French-speaking countries: the branch of the administration of the law that deals with the prosecution of crime.

parroco /ˈparɒkəʊ/ noun plural **parrocos** M19 Italian (parroco, Spanish párroco = parish priest). In Italian- and Spanish-speaking countries: a priest, especially a parish priest.

parsemé /parsəme/, /ˈpɑːsəmeɪ/ adjective E19 French (past participle of parsemer to

sprinkle, strew). Especially of a fabric, garment, etc.: decorated with embroidered motifs, beads, etc., sprinkled over a background.
■ Usually postpositive.

pars pro toto /ˌpɑːz prəʊ ˈtəʊtəʊ/ noun phrase E18 Latin. A part taken as representative of the whole.
■ Frequently attributive.

parterre /pɑːˈtɛː/ noun E17 French (use as noun of parterre on or along the ground). **1** E17 A level space in a garden occupied by an ornamental arrangement of flowerbeds. **2** L17 A level space on which a house or village stands. **3** E18 The part of the ground-floor of the auditorium of a theatre behind the orchestra; United States the part beneath the galleries; the occupants of this.

parti /parti/ (plural same) noun L18 French (= choice, from Old French partie part, share, side in a contest, from Proto-Romance use as noun of Latin partita feminine past participle of partiri to part). A person (especially a man) considered in terms of eligibility for marriage on grounds of wealth, social status, etc.

partie /parti/ noun plural pronounced same L17 French (cf. PARTI). A match in a game; a game.

partie carrée /parti kare/ noun phrase plural **parties carrées** (pronounced same) M18 French (from as PARTI + carrée square). A party of four, especially comprising two men and two women.

partigiano /ˌpartiˈdʒiano/ noun (also **Partigiano**) plural **partigiani** /ˌpartiˈdʒiani/ M20 Italian (Tuscan). History A member of the Italian resistance during the war of 1939–45, an Italian partisan.

parti pris /parti pri/, /ˌpɑːtɪ ˈpriː/ noun & adjective phrase M19 French (literally, 'side taken', from as PARTI + pris past participle of prendre to take). **A** noun phrase M19 plural **partis pris** (pronounced same). A preconceived view, a prejudice; bias. **B** adjective phrase E20 Prejudiced, biased; on the side of a particular party.

> **B 1995** Spectator He doesn't attempt to hide the fact that he is parti pris.

partita /pɑːˈtiːtə/ noun plural **partite** /pɑːˈtiːteɪ/, **partitas** L19 Italian (feminine past participle of partire to divide from Latin partiri to part). Music A suite, especially one for a solo instrument or a chamber ensemble; a variation in early modern music.

partouse /partuz/ *noun* (also **partouze**) plural pronounced same M20 French (from as *parti* party + pejorative slang suffix *-ouse*). **1** M20 A party at which there is indiscriminate and collective sexual activity. **2** L20 A nightclub etc. noted for the licentiousness of its entertainment.

parure /pəˈrʊə/ *noun* ME Old and Modern French (from *parer* to adorn, arrange, peel (fruit), from Latin *parare* to prepare). **1** ME–E16 An ornament for an alb or amice. **2** LME–L16 A paring, a peeling. **3** E19 A set of jewels or other ornaments intended to be worn together.

parvenu /ˈpɑːvənuː/, /ˈpɑːvənjuː/ *noun & adjective* E19 French (use as noun of past participle of *parvenir* to arrive from Latin *pervenire*, from *per-* through + *venire* to come). **A** *noun* E19 (feminine **parvenue**) A person of humble origin who has gained wealth or position and risen in society, *especially* one regarded as unfitted for the position achieved in this way, or as lacking the accomplishments appropriate to it; an upstart. **B** *adjective* E19 That has recently risen to wealth or position; resembling or characteristic of a parvenu.

> **A 1996** *Spectator* There are also several female whores . . . , a witch, and the famous *parvenu*, Trimalchio, who gives a Lucullan banquet with perverse and ingenious cookery . . .

> **B 1996** *Spectator* As a rule, though, the [Jockey] club has been happier cracking down on some flat-hatted trainer or parvenu owner who would never be allowed in.

pas /pa/, /pɑː/ *noun* plural same E18 French. **1** E18 The right of going first; precedence. **2** L18 A step in dancing; a kind of dance, especially in classical ballet.
■ In sense 2 chiefly with qualifying word or phrase.

pas ciseaux variant of PAS DE CISEAUX.

pas d'action /padaksjɔ̃/ *noun phrase* M20 French. *Ballet* A dance expressing a theme or narrative.

pas d'âne /padan/ *noun* L19 French (literally, 'donkey's step'). *Fencing* Two rings below the cross-guard of some old swords for protecting the fingers.

pas de basque /pa də bask/ *noun phrase* E19 French. A dance step in three beats similar to a waltz step, but with a circular movement of the right leg on the second beat.

pas de bourrée /pa də bure/ *noun phrase* E20 French. A BOURRÉE step.

pas de chat /pa də ʃa/ *noun phrase* E20 French (literally, 'step of cat'). *Ballet* A springing step in which each foot in turn is raised to the opposite knee.

pas de cheval /pa də ʃəval/ *noun phrase* E20 French (literaly, 'step of horse'). *Ballet* A step in which a pawing movement is executed with one foot.

pas de ciseaux /pa də sizo/ *noun phrase* (also **pas ciseaux**) L19 French (literally, 'step of scissors'). *Ballet* A jump in which the legs are opened wide apart in the air.

pas de deux /pa də dø/, /ˌpa də ˈdəː/ *noun phrase* M18 French. A dance for two people, especially in classical ballet.

> **1995** *Times* Stuart Cassidy and Muriel Valtat, dressed in vaporous white, . . . swirl and float through their romantic pas de deux.

pas de quatre /pa də katr/ *noun phrase* L19 French. A dance for four people, especially in classical ballet.

pas de trois /pa də trwa/ *noun phrase* M18 French. A dance for three people, especially in classical ballet.

pas devant /pa dəvɑ̃/ *interjection* M20 French (= not in front of). Of a statement, action, etc.: not appropriate or proper for the present company.
■ *Pas devant* is an elliptical version of the warning expression *pas devant les enfants* /lɛz ɑ̃fɑ̃/ 'not in front of the children'. The assumption is that the children will not understand a warning given in French. Other nouns are substituted, as appropriate, for *les enfants*.

pas du tout /pa dy tu/ E19 French. Not at all.

pasear /paserˈɑː/ *intransitive verb & noun* M19 Spanish (= to take a walk; cf. PASEO). (Take) a walk. *United States slang and dialect.*

paseo /paˈseɪəʊ/, *foreign* /paˈseo/ *noun* plural **paseos** /paˈseɪəʊz/, *foreign* /paˈseos/ M19 Spanish. In Spain, Spanish-speaking parts of America, and the south-western United States: a leisurely walk or stroll; a parade or procession, *especially* at a bullfight; also, a road, an avenue.

pasha /ˈpɑːʃə/ *noun* (also **pacha**) M17 Turkish (*paşa*, from Persian *pād(i)šhāh*, Pahlavi *pati* lord + SHAH). *History* (The title of) a Turkish officer of high rank, as a military commander, provincial governor, etc.

pashalic /'pɑːʃəlɪk/, /pə'ʃɑːlɪk/ *noun & adjective* (also **pachalic**) L17 Turkish (*paşalık*, from as PASHA + suffix indicating quality or condition -*lık*). *History* **A** *noun* L17 The jurisdiction of a pasha; the district governed by a pasha. **B** *adjective* M19 Of or pertaining to a pasha.

paskha /'pasxə/, /'paskə/ *noun* (also **paska**) E20 Russian (= Easter). A rich Russian dessert made with curd cheese, dried fruit, nuts, spices, etc., set in a mould and traditionally eaten at Easter.

paso /'paso/, /'pasəʊ/ *noun plural* **pasos** /'pasos/, /'pasəʊz/ E20 Spanish. An image or group of images representing Passion scenes, carried in procession as part of Holy Week observances in Spain.

paso doble /ˌpasə(ʊ) 'dəʊbleɪ/ *noun phrase* plural **paso dobles** E20 Spanish (= double step). A quick ballroom dance based on a Latin American style of marching; a piece of music for this dance, usually in 2/4 time.
■ See quotation at CHA-CHA.

pasquinade /ˌpaskwɪ'neɪd/ *noun & verb* (originally **pasquinadata**) L16 Italian (*pasquinata*, French *pasquinade*, from *Pasquin* the name of a statue in Rome on which abusive Latin verses were annually posted during the sixteenth century). **A** *noun* L16 A lampoon, a satire, originally one exhibited in a public place. **B** *transitive verb* L18 Satirize or libel in a pasquinade.

passacaglia /pasə'kɑːlɪə/ *noun* M17 Italian (from Spanish *pasacalle*, from *pasar* to pass + *calle* street (originally often played in the streets)). A slow musical composition usually with a ground bass and in triple time; an early kind of dance to this music.

passacaille /pasə'kʌɪ/ *noun* (also **passecaille**) E18 French (from Spanish *pasacalle*). A PASSACAGLIA.

passade /pə'seɪd/, *in sense 2* /pa'sɑːd/, *foreign* /pasad/ (*plural same*) *noun* M17 French (from Italian *passata* or Provençal *passada*, from medieval Latin *passare* to pass). **1** M17 *Horsemanship* A forwards or backwards turn performed on the spot. *rare*. **2** E19 A transitory love affair; a passing romance.

passe /pas/ *noun* M19 French (from *passer* to pass). In roulette: the section of the cloth covering the numbers 19 to 36; a bet placed on this section.

passé /'paseɪ/, *foreign* /pase/ *adjective & noun* (feminine **passée**) L18 French (past participial adjective of *passer* to pass). **A** *adjective* **1** L18 Past one's prime. *archaic*. **2** E19 No longer fashionable; out of date, behind the times. **B** *noun* M20 *Ballet* The transitional movement of the leg from one position to the next.
A.2 1996 *Bookseller* European publishers who went to Milia last week to display their latest CD-ROM products with pride must have been more than a little put out to hear American visitors saying that CD-ROMs are passé.

passecaille variant of PASSACAILLE.

passée see PASSÉ.

passeggiata /ˌpassed'dʒiata/ *noun* plural **passeggiate** /ˌpassed'dʒiate/ M20 Italian. A stroll, a promenade.
■ Usually referring to the evening stroll for relaxation and socializing habitually taken by citizens of many Mediterranean countries (see quotation); the equivalent of the Greek *volta*.
1971 N. Fisher *Rise at Dawn* We drove into Viareggio one evening. It was the hour of the *passeggiata* . . . The pavements thronged with strolling families.

passéisme /paseism/ *noun* M20 French. Adherence to and regard for the traditions and values of the past, especially in the arts.

passementerie /'pasm(ə)ntri/, *foreign* /pasmɑ̃tri/ *noun* E17 French (from *passement* from *passer* to pass; the connection with Spanish and Italian *passamano* (apparently from *passare* to pass + *mano* hand) and the reason for this name are both obscure). Decorative trimming consisting of gold or silver lace, gimp, or braid.

passe-partout /ˌpaspɑː'tuː/, /ˌpɑːspɑː'tuː/ *noun* L17 French (from *passer* to pass + *partout* everywhere). **1** L17 A thing which goes or provides a means of going everywhere; *specifically* a master-key. **2** M19 A frame or border into which a picture of suitable size may be inserted for display; a frame for displaying mounted photographs etc., consisting of two sheets of transparent material (or one sheet with a card backing) stuck together at the edges with adhesive tape. Also, adhesive tape used in such framing.

pas seul /pa sœl/ *noun phrase* plural **pas seuls** (*pronounced same*) E19 French. A dance for one person, especially in classical ballet.

passim /'pasɪm/ *adverb & adjective* E19 Latin (literally, 'scatteredly', from *passus* scattered, past participle of *pandere* to spread out). Of an allusion or reference in a published work: (to be found) at various places throughout the text. Also *transferred* and *figurative*.

1996 *Country Life* . . . a minister's life—see Tristan Garel-Jones *passim*—can and does include a certain salty lack of political correctness when it comes to dealing with foreigners.

passus /'pasəs/ *noun* plural same L16 Latin (= step, pace). A section, division, or canto of a (medieval) story or poem.

pasta /'pastə/ *noun* L19 Italian (from late Latin *pasta* a small square piece of medicinal preparation, from Greek *pastē*). 1 L19 A type of dough made from durum wheat flour and water and extruded or stamped into particular shapes (and often dried if not for immediate use). Also, an Italian dish consisting largely of this and usually a sauce. 2 L20 Marijuana. *slang*.

pasticcio /pa'stɪtʃɪəʊ/ *noun* plural **pasticcios** M18 Italian (= pie, pasty, from Proto-Romance, from late Latin *pasta* paste). A PASTICHE.

pastiche /pa'stiːʃ/ *noun & verb* L19 French (from as PASTICCIO). **A** *noun* L19 A medley of various things; *specifically* (a) a picture or a musical composition made up of pieces derived from or imitating various sources; (b) a literary or other work of art composed in the style of a well-known author, artist, etc. **B** *transitive & intransitive verb* M20 Copy or imitate the style of (an artist, author, etc.).

A.b *transferred* 1996 *Times Magazine* It's a pastiche of a fashionable London restaurant of the moment.

pasticheur /ˌpasti:'ʃəː/ *noun* E20 French (from PASTICHE). An artist who imitates the style of another artist.

1996 *Country Life* Miss Guest is an Edwards pasticheur . . . , creating wide-screen images of hounds in full cry and horses streaming across open country.

pastiglia /pa'stiːlja/, /pa'stiːlɪə/ *noun* E20 Italian (= paste). Intricately moulded gesso used in the decoration of furniture, caskets, etc., in Renaissance Italy.

pastille /'past(ə)l/, /'pastɪl/ *noun* (also **pastil**) M17 French (from Latin *pastillus* little loaf or roll, lozenge, diminutive of *panis* loaf). 1 M17 A small pellet of aromatic

paste burnt as a perfume or as a fumigator, deodorizer, or disinfectant. 2 M17 A small flat, usually round, sweet, often coated with sugar and sometimes medicated; a lozenge. **b** E20 *Medicine* A small disc of barium platinocyanide whose gradual change of colour when exposed to X-rays was formerly used as an indication of the dose delivered.

pastis /'pastɪs/, /pa'stiːs/ *noun* E20 French. (A drink of) a liqueur flavoured with aniseed.

pastorale /pastə'rɑːl/, /pastə'rɑːleɪ/ *noun* plural **pastorales**, **pastorali** /pastə'rɑːli/ E18 Italian (use as noun of *pastorale* pastoral, from Latin *pastoralis* from *pastor* shepherd, from *past-* past participial stem of *pascere* to feed, graze). *Music* 1 E18 A slow instrumental composition in compound time, often with drone notes in the bass suggestive of a shepherd's bagpipes. 2 L19 A simple musical play with a rural subject.

pastoralia /pɑːstə'reɪlɪə/ *noun* plural E18 Latin (neuter plural of *pastoralis* pastoral). Spiritual care or guidance as a subject of theological study; the duties of a pastor.

pastourelle /pasturɛl/ (*plural same*), /pastʊ'rɛl/ *noun* L19 French (feminine of *pastoureau* shepherd). A medieval lyric whose theme is love for a shepherdess.

■ The Provençal or Portuguese word *pastorela* (L19) is also used.

pastrami /pa'strɑːmi/ *noun* M20 Yiddish (from Romanian *pastramă*, probably of Turkish origin). Highly seasoned smoked beef, usually, served in thin slices.

pata /'pʌtə/ *noun* M20 Sanskrit (*paṭa*). Cloth, canvas; *especially* (an example of) an ancient form of Indian painting typically executed on a strip of cloth or scroll of canvas.

patchouli /'patʃʊli/, /pə'tʃuːli/ *noun* (also **patchouly**) M19 Tamil (*paccuḷi*). 1 M19 Either of two Indo-Malayan labiate shrubs, *Pogostemon cablin* and *P. heyneanus*, whose leaves yield an essential oil much used in perfumery. 2 M19 Perfume prepared from this plant.

pâte /pɑt/ *noun* M19 French. Paste.

■ Occurs in English with a defining word or phrase, usually indicating a substance or process.

pâte brisée /pɑt brizeː/ *noun phrase* M19 French (literally, 'broken paste'). *Cookery* A type of sweet shortcrust pastry.

pâte de verre /pɑt də vɛʁ/ *noun phrase* E20 French (literally, 'paste of glass'). Powdered glass that has been fired a second time.

pâte dure /pɑt dyr/ *noun phrase* M19 French (literally, 'hard paste'). (Porcelain made from) hard clay.

pâte-sur-pâte /pɑtsyrpɑt/ *noun phrase* L19 French (literally, 'paste on paste'). A method of relief decoration formed by applying layers of white slip on unfired porcelain.

pâte tendre /pɑt tɑ̃dr/ *noun phrase* M19 French (literally, 'tender paste'). (Porcelain made from) soft clay.

pâté /ˈpateɪ/ *noun* E18 French (from Old French *pasté*). **1** E18 A pie, a pasty. Now *rare*. **2** L19 A rich paste or spread made from finely minced or pounded meat, fish, herbs, etc.

■ In sense 2 often with a qualifying word or phrase indicating a particular recipe, such as *rough pâté*, *Strasbourg pâté* (see also phrases below).

pâté de campagne /ˌpateɪ də kɒm ˈpɑːnjə/ *noun phrase* M20 French (= country pâté). A coarse pork and liver pâté.

pâté de foie gras /ˈpateɪ də fwɑ ˌɡrɑː/ *noun phrase* E19 French. A smooth rich pâté of fatted goose liver.

■ Originally a pie filled with this paste, also known as a 'Strasbourg pie'; now applied just to the filling served as a separate dish.

pâté en croûte /ˌpateɪ ɑ̃ ˈkruːt/ *noun phrase* M20 French. Pâté baked in a pastry case.

pâté maison /ˈpateɪ ˌmɛzɔ̃/ *noun phrase* M20 French (= house pâté). Pâté made to the recipe of a particular restaurant.

patella /pəˈtɛlə/ *noun plural* **patellae** /pəˈtɛliː/ (originally Anglicized as **patel**) L15 Latin (diminutive of PATERA). **1 a** *generally* A pan. Only in L15. **b** M19 *Archaeology* A small pan or shallow vessel, *especially* a Roman one. **2** L16 *Anatomy* The kneecap. **3** L17 A natural structure in the form of a shallow cup or pan. **4** L17 *Zoology* A univalve mollusc of the genus *Patella*, which includes the common limpet. Chiefly as modern Latin genus name.

pater /ˈpeɪtə/, *in sense 1 also* /ˈpɑːtə/ *noun* ME Latin. **1** ME The Lord's Prayer, the PATERNOSTER. **2** E17-M19 An ecclesiastical or spiritual father. **3** E18 Father. Cf. MATER sense 2. Chiefly *jocular* and *school slang*.

b M20 *Anthropology* A person's legal as opposed to biological father. Cf. GENITOR.

patera /ˈpat(ə)rə/ *noun plural* **paterae** /ˈpat(ə)riː/ M17 Latin (from *patere* to be open). **1** M17 *Roman Antiquities* A broad shallow dish used especially for pouring libations. **2** L18 *Architecture* An ornament resembling a shallow dish; any flat round ornament in bas-relief.

paterfamilias /ˌpeɪtəfəˈmɪlɪas/, /ˌpatəfə ˈmɪlɪas/ *noun plural* **patresfamilias** /ˌpeɪtriːzfəˈmɪlɪas/, /ˌpatriːzfəˈmɪlɪas/ L15 Latin (from *pater* father + archaic genitive of *familia* family). **1** L15 A male head of a family or household. **2** M19 *Roman Law* The male head of a family or household having authority over its members. Also, any male legally independent and free from parental control.

paternoster /patəˈnɒstə/, /ˌpɑːtəˈnɒstə/ *noun* OE Latin (*paternoster* literally, 'our father', the first two words of the Lord's Prayer in Latin). **1** OE The Lord's Prayer, especially in the Latin version. **b** ME A repetition or recital of this as an act of worship. **c** LME *transferred* A form of words repeated as or like a prayer, imprecation, or charm. Also, a nonsensical or tedious recital. **2** ME Any of several special beads occurring at regular intervals in a rosary to indicate that a paternoster is to be said. Also, the whole rosary. **3** M19 A fishing line with hooks or weights attached at intervals. More fully *paternoster line*. **4** E20 A lift consisting of a series of doorless compartments moving continuously on an endless belt. Also more fully *paternoster elevator*, *paternoster lift*.

patha patha /ˌpatə ˈpatə/ *noun phrase* M20 Xhosa (*phathphatha* to feel with the hands). **1** M20 In South Africa: a sensuous Black African dance; music for this dance. **2** L20 Sexual intercourse. *South African slang*.

pathos /ˈpeɪθɒs/ *noun* L16 Greek (= suffering, feeling, related to *paskhein* to suffer, *penthos* grief). **1** L16 A pathetic expression or utterance. *rare*. **2** M17 A quality in speech, writing, events, persons, etc., which excites pity or sadness; the power of stirring tender or melancholy emotion. **3** L17 Physical or mental suffering. *rare*.

2 1996 *Country Life* . . . the work's humour served deeply serious ends and was flecked with darker moments and a touchingly lyrical pathos.

patina /ˈpatmə/ *noun* M18 Italian (from Latin = shallow dish or pan). A usually green film produced by oxidation on the surface of old bronze; a similar alteration of the surface of coins, flint, etc. Also, a gloss on wooden furniture produced by age, polishing, etc; an acquired change in the appearance of a surface, *especially* one suggestive of age.

> *transferred* **1996** *Country Life* In keeping with this patina of elder statesmanship, the tone is disconcertingly formal by today's standards . . .

patio /ˈpatɪəʊ/ *noun* plural **patios** E19 Spanish (= court of a house). **1** E19 Originally, an inner court, open to the sky, in a Spanish or Spanish-American house. Now also, a usually roofless paved area adjoining and belonging to a house. **2** M19 *Mining* A yard or floor where ores are cleaned, sorted, or amalgamated.

patisserie /pəˈtiːs(ə)ri/ *noun* (also **pâtisserie**) L16 French (*pâtisserie* from medieval Latin *pasticium*, from *pasta* paste). **1** L16 *singular* and in *plural* Articles of food made by a pastry-cook, pastries collectively. **2** E20 A shop which sells pastries.

patissier /pəˈtiːsɪə/, *foreign* /pɑtisje/ *noun* (also **pâtissier**, feminine **patissiere, patissière** /pəˈtiːsɪɛː/, *foreign* /pɑtisjɛr/) E20 French. A pastry-cook.

> **1995** *Times Magazine* If I were seriously rich and had a large kitchen, I sometimes think I would like to employ a pâtissier.

patois /ˈpatwɑː/ *noun & adjective* M17 Old and Modern French (= rough speech, perhaps from Old French *patoier* to handle roughly, trample, from *patte* paw, of unknown origin). **A** *noun* plural same /ˈpatwɑːz/. **1** M17 A dialect (originally in France) of the common people in a particular area, differing fundamentally from the literary language; any nonstandard local dialect. **2** L18 *transferred* A social dialect; jargon. **3** M20 The creole of the English-speaking Caribbean, especially Jamaica. **B** *attributive* or as *adjective* L18 Of, pertaining to, or of the nature of a patois.

> **A.1 1995** G. Tindall *Célestine* In . . . age he had become hard of hearing and had reverted in his own speech to the patois of long ago.
> **B 1996** *Spectator* One needs to speak Swahili or Urdu to be understood, although at times patois French will do.

patresfamilias plural of PATERFAMILIAS.

patria /ˈpatrɪə/, /ˈpeɪtrɪə/ *noun* E20 Latin. One's native country; one's homeland.

patrin /ˈpatrɪn/ *noun* M19 Romany. A trail left by Gypsies, using arrangements of grass, leaves, twigs, etc., to indicate the direction taken.

patron /paˈtrɒn/, *foreign* /patrɔ̃/, *foreign* /paˈtron/ *noun* ME Old and Modern French (from Latin *patronus* protector of clients, advocate, defender, from *pater*, *patr-* father). **1** LME The captain or master of a Mediterranean galley or coaster (now *rare* or *obsolete*); in North American waters, the captain or steersman of a longboat, barge, etc. **2** M16 A case for pistol cartridges; a cartridge. Now *obsolete* except *historical*. **3** E17–E18 A master or owner of slaves in countries bordering the eastern and southern Mediterranean. **4** M19 A manager or boss of a hacienda; in New Mexico, the master or head of a family. (From *Spanish*). **5** L19 The proprietor of an inn or restaurant, especially in France and Spain. Cf. Italian PADRONE.

■ The above senses represent only modern Romance uses, as *patron*, with the pronunciation /ˈpeɪtr(ə)n/, has also been fully Anglicized (ME onwards), in senses derived from ecclesiastical and classical Latin.

patronat /patrɔna/ *noun* M20 French. An organization of industrial employers in France; French employers collectively.

patronne /patrɔn/ *noun* plural pronounced same L18 French (feminine of PATRON). A woman who is the owner, or the wife of the owner, of a business, especially a café, hotel, or restaurant.

patte /pat/ *noun* L18 French (of unknown origin). **1** L18 A paw; *jocularly* a hand. Now only in PATTE DE VELOURS. **2** M19 A short band or strap sewn on a dress as a trimming, or used to fasten a coat, hold a belt in place, etc.

patte de velours /pat də vlur/ *noun phrase* M19 French (= paw of velvet). A cat's paw with the claws retracted, as symbolic of ruthlessness or inflexibility hidden beneath apparent softness.

paupiette /pɔːpˈjɛt/ *noun* (originally **poupiets**) E18 French (perhaps from Italian *polpetta*, from Latin *pulpa* pulp). *Cookery* A long thin slice of fish, meat, etc., especially rolled and stuffed with a filling.

■ Usually in plural in names of dishes, as in *paupiettes de veau*. A dish of this sort is also sometimes called *alouettes sans tête* '(sky)larks without heads'. An alternative etymology perhaps connects with French *poupée* 'doll'; cf. the minced-meat dish called in modern Greek *koukla*, also meaning 'doll'.

pavane /pə'van/, /ˌpə'vɑːn/ *noun* (also **pavan**, /ˈpav(ə)n/) M16 French (probably from Italian dialect *pavana* feminine of *pavano* of Padua, from *Pavo* dialect name of Padua (Italian *Padova*)). **1** M16 *History* A grave and stately dance in slow duple time, performed in elaborate clothing and popular in the sixteenth century. **2** M16 A piece of music for this dance or in its rhythm.

pavé /ˈpaveɪ/, *foreign* /pave/ (*plural same*) *noun* (also (earlier) Anglicized as **pave** /peɪv/) LME French (use as noun of past participle of *paver* to pave). **1** LME A paved road or path. **2** L19 A setting of jewels placed close together so that no metal is visible.

> **2 1996** *Country Life* The brooch ... is a geometric platinum-set design of baguette and brilliant cut diamonds with *pavé*-set terminals ...

pavillon /pavijɔ̃/ *noun* L19 French (literally 'pavilion'). **1** L19 The bell-shaped mouth of a trumpet or similar musical instrument. **2** L19 A percussion instrument similar to a Turkish crescent, consisting of a stick having transverse brass plates from which hang a number of small bells which jingle. More fully *pavillon chinois* /pavijɔ̃ ʃinwa/ 'Chinese pavillon'. Also called *jingling Johnny*.

pax /paks/ *noun* LME Latin (= peace). **1** LME *Ecclesiastical* (also **Pax**) The ceremonial exchange of greetings as part of a church service to signify Christian concord. **2** LME *Ecclesiastical History* A tablet of gold, silver, ivory, glass, etc., with a projecting handle, depicting the Crucifixion or other sacred subject, which was kissed by all participants at mass. Also called *osculatory*. **3** L15 Peace, tranquillity, concord; *especially* peace between nations. Cf. PAX ROMANA. **4** L18 A friend; good friends. *School slang*. **5** M19 As *interjection* A call for quiet or (a) truce. *school slang*.

pax Romana /ˌpaks rəʊˈmɑːnə/ *noun phrase* L19 Latin (= Roman peace). The peace which existed between nationalities under the Roman Empire.

■ Originally from Pliny's *Natural History* (xxvii.3), *pax Romana* has been the model for other phrases with a Latin or modern Latin adjective referring to the dominant influence of a State, empire, etc. (see quotation 1996).

> **1993** G. Fowden *Empire to Commonwealth* They [sc. the Jews] benefited from the *pax Romana* to develop their communities, build impressive synagogues, and assert a claim to social esteem.
>
> **1996** *Times* They [sc. the Serbs] will fight, fight and fight again for this, long after the Americans lose interest in their *pax Americana*, as it becomes a desert ...

paysage /peizaʒ/ *noun* plural pronounced same E17 French (from *pays* country). (A representation of) a rural scene or landscape.

paysan /peizɑ̃/ *noun & adjective* E19 French (from Old French *païsant*, *païsent*, alteration of earlier *païsenc*, from *païs* (modern *pays*) country, from Proto-Romance alteration of Latin *pagus* rural district). **A** *noun* E19 plural pronounced same. A peasant, a countryman, especially in France. **B** *adjective* L19 Of a style of art, dress, etc: resembling that of peasants.

paysanne /peizan/ *noun* plural pronounced same M18 French (feminine of PAYSAN). A peasant-woman, a country-woman, especially in France.

peag /piːɡ/ *noun* (also **peak** /piːk/) M17 American Indian. WAMPUM.

péage /ˈpeɪɑːʒ/, *in sense 2 also foreign* /peaʒ/ (*plural same*) *noun* (in sense 1 also **payage**) LME Old and Modern French (from medieval Latin *pedaticum*, from Latin *pes, ped-* foot; in sense 2 from modern French). **1** LME Toll paid for passing through a place or country. *obsolete in general sense*. **2** L20 Toll paid to travel on a French motorway; a gate or barrier where this is paid.

peau-de-soie /podəswa/, /ˌpəʊdə'swɑː/ *noun* M19 French (literally, 'silk skin'). A close-woven heavy satin silk; an (especially rayon) imitation of this.

peau d'Espagne /po dɛspaɲ/ *noun phrase* (also **Peau d'Espagne**) M19 French (literally, 'skin of Spain'). **1** M19 Perfumed leather. **2** L19 A scent suggestive of the aroma of this leather.

peccadillo /pɛkə'dɪləʊ/ *noun* plural **peccadilloes**, **peccadillos** L16 Spanish (*pecadillo* diminutive of *pecado* sin). A small fault, a venial sin; a trifling offence.

peccavi /pɛˈkɑːviː/ *interjection & noun* E16 Latin (= I have sinned). **A** *interjection* E16 Acknowledging guilt. **B** *noun* L16 An acknowledgement or confession of guilt.

■ As an interjection, now usually jocular; cf. MEA CULPA.

pecorino /pɛkəˈriːnəʊ/ noun M20 Italian (from *pecora* sheep). A hard Italian cheese made from ewe's milk.

pedregal /pɛdrɪˈɡɑːl/, /ˈpɛdrɪɡ(ə)l/ noun M19 Spanish (from *piedra* stone, from Latin *petra*). In Mexico and the south-western United States: a rocky tract, especially in a volcanic region; an old lava-field.

peignoir /ˈpeɪnwɑː/ noun M19 French (from *peigner* to comb). A woman's loose dressing-gown or bathrobe.

peineta /peiˈneta/ noun M20 Spanish. A woman's ornamental comb traditionally worn with a mantilla.

pelmeny /pɛlˈmɛni/ noun plural M20 Russian (*pelʹmeni*). Small pasta cases stuffed with seasoned meat etc. as a Russian dish.

pelota /pɪˈlɒtə/, /pɪˈləʊtə/ noun E19 Spanish (= ball, augmentative of *pella* from Latin *pila* ball). **1** E19 A Basque or Spanish ball game played in a walled court using basket-like wicker rackets attached to gloves. **2** E20 The ball used in pelota.

peloton /ˈpɛlətɒn/ noun M20 French (from *pelote* from Proto-Romance diminutive of Latin *pila* ball). *Cycling* The main field, group, or pack of cyclists in a race.

■ The original senses in which *peloton* was introduced (both E18) are now rare or obsolete: 'a small ball or pellet' and (its modern French sense) 'a platoon'.

1996 *Times* Riis . . . has grown up in the peloton, the toughest school of all, and has no time for niceties.

pelouse /pəˈluz/ noun plural pronounced same E20 French. Especially in France: an area of grass; *specifically* a public enclosure at a racecourse.

pelta /ˈpɛltə/ noun plural **peltae** /ˈpɛltiː/ (also Anglicized as **pelt**) E17 Latin (from Greek *peltē* a small light leather shield). **1** E17 *Classical Antiquities* A small light shield; a buckler. **2** M18 *Botany* Any of various shieldlike structures. **3** E20 An ornamental motif resembling a shield in architecture, metalwork, etc.

pelure /pɛlˈjʊə/ noun L19 French (literally, 'peeling', from *peler* to peel). Especially *Philately*. A kind of very thin paper. Also *pelure-paper*.

pelure d'oignon /p(ə)lyr dɔɲɔ̃/ noun & adjective phrase M20 French (literally, 'onion peel'). **A** noun phrase M20 plural **pelures d'oignons** (pronounced same). A tawny colour characteristic of some aged red wines; a wine of this colour. **B** adjective phrase M20 (Designating a wine) of this colour.

pemmican /ˈpɛmɪk(ə)n/ noun L18 Cree (*pimihkan*, from *pimiy* grease). A lightweight, highly nutritious food of pounded dried meat mixed to a paste with melted fat and berries, used originally by North American Indians, now also by explorers, hikers, etc.

penates /pɪˈnɑːtiːz/, /pɪˈneɪtiːz/ noun plural E16 Latin (*Penates* (plural), from *penus* provision of food, related to *penes* within). *Roman History* The protective gods of a house, especially of its storeroom; household gods. Cf. LAR.

■ Often in English in the phrase *lares and penates*.

penchant /ˈpɒ̃ʃ/ noun L17 French (use as noun of present participle of *pencher* to incline, lean). An inclination, a (strong or habitual) liking.

1996 *Spectator* She had a penchant for younger men, on whom she squandered much of her money . . .

penchée /ˈpɒ̃ʃeɪ/, /ˈpɒnʃeɪ/ adjective M20 French (feminine of *penché* past participle of *pencher* to lean, incline). *Ballet* Especially of an arabesque: performed while leaning forward.

■ Usually postpositive.

pendeloque /ˈpɒnd(ə)lɒk/, foreign /pɑ̃dlɔk/ (plural of noun same) adjective & noun M19 French (from Old French *pendeler* to dangle). (A gem, especially a diamond) cut in the shape of a drop.

pendente lite /pɛnˌdɛntɪ ˈlʌɪti/ adverb phrase E18 Latin (literally, 'with the lawsuit pending'). *Law* During the progress of a suit; during litigation.

penetralia /pɛnɪˈtreɪlɪə/ noun plural M17 Latin (use as noun of *penetralia* neuter plural of *penetrālis* innermost). The innermost parts of a building etc.; *especially* the sanctuary or innermost shrine of a temple; *figurative* secret parts, mysteries.

penne /ˈpɛneɪ/ noun plural L20 Italian (literally, 'quills, pens'). Pasta in the form of short tubes cut diagonally at both ends.

pensée /ˈpɑ̃se/ noun (also (in sense 1) **pensee**) plural pronounced same LME Old French (*pensee*; in sense 2 reintroduced from French). **1** LME–L15 Thoughtfulness, anxiety, care; a thought, an idea. **2** L19 A poem or prose composition expressing a single thought or reflection. Also, an aphorism.

penseroso /pɛnsəˈrəʊsəʊ/, *foreign* /pense
ˈrozo/ *noun & adjective* L18 Italian (obsolete
form of *pensieroso*, from (obsolete) *pensiere*
thought, from Provençal *pensier*, from
Proto-Romance variant of Latin *pensare* to
weigh, ponder, consider). **A** *noun* L18 plural **penserosos** /pɛnsəˈrəʊsəʊz/, **penser-
osi** /penseˈrozi/. (A person having) a
brooding or melancholy character. **B** *adjective* E19 Pensive, brooding, melancholy.

■ John Milton's classic depiction of the
melancholy character in his poem 'Il Penseroso' (1632) was responsible for the wider
use of the word in English.

pensiero /penˈsjɛːro/ *noun* plural **pen-
sieri** /penˈsjɛːri/ E20 Italian. **1** E20 A
thought, an idea; an anxiety. **2** M20 *Art* A
sketch.

pension /pɑ̃sjɔ̃/ (*plural same*) *noun* M17
French (Old French *pension* from Latin
pensio(n-) payment, rent, from *pens-* past
participial stem of *pendere* to weigh, pay).
A usually fixed-rate boarding-house or
(formerly) a boarding-school in France or
another European country. Cf. EN PEN-
SION.

■ *Pension* was first introduced in the LME
period and, with the pronunciation
/ˈpɛnʃ(ə)n/, is now wholly Anglicized in its
numerous senses deriving from Old French
and Latin, almost all of which contain the
idea of 'a fixed regular payment'. The sense
above was also formerly Anglicized.

pensionnaire /pɑ̃sjɔnɛr/ *noun* plural pronounced same L16 French (from medieval
Latin *pensionarius*). **1** L16 A person receiving a pension; a pensioner, a paid retainer. *rare*. **2** L18 A person who boards in
a French lodging-house or institution, or
with a French family.

pentathlon /pɛnˈtaθlɒn/, /pɛnˈtaθlən/
noun (also formerly in Latin form **pen-
tathlum**) E17 Greek (from *penta-* five + *ath-
lon* contest). **1** E17 *Classical History* An
athletic contest in which competitors engaged in five different events (leaping,
running, discus-throwing, spear-throw-
ing, and wrestling). **2** E20 An athletic or
sporting contest in which competitors engage in five different events (especially (in
full *modern pentathlon*) fencing, shooting,
swimming, riding, and cross-country
running).

pentimento /pɛntɪˈmɛntəʊ/ *noun* plural
pentimenti /pɛntɪˈmɛnti/ E20 Italian (literally, 'repentance'). *Art* A visible trace of
(an) earlier painting beneath a layer or

layers of paint; (a) painting revealed by
such traces.

penuche /pɛˈnuːʧi/ *noun* (also **panocha**
/pəˈnɒʧə/, **panoche** /pəˈnɒʧi/, and other
variants) M19 American Spanish (*panoche*).
1 M19 A kind of coarse brown sugar used
in Mexico. **2** L19 A kind of sweet resembling fudge, made with brown sugar, butter, milk or cream, and often nuts. *North
American*.

peon /ˈpiːən/, *in branch* I *also* /pjuːn/, *in
branch* II *also* /perˈɒn/, *foreign* /peˈon/ *noun*
plural **peons**, (*in sense* 3 *also*) **peones**
/ˈpiːəniz/, *foreign* /peˈones/ E17 Portuguese
and Spanish (in sense 1 from Portuguese
peão; in senses 2 and 3 from Spanish *peón*
peasant, from medieval Latin *pedo(n-)*
foot-soldier). **I 1** E17 In the Indian subcontinent and South East Asia: a person
of low rank; *specifically* (*a*) a foot-soldier;
(*b*) an orderly; (*c*) an office boy. **II 2** E19 A
Spanish-American day labourer or farm
worker, *especially* one in poor circumstances. Also (*historical*), a debtor held in
servitude by a creditor, especially in the
southern United States and Mexico.
3 M20 A BANDERILLERO.

peperoni variant of PEPPERONI.

peplos /ˈpɛplɒs/ *noun* L18 Greek. *Greek Antiquities* A (usually rich) outer robe or
shawl worn by women in ancient Greece,
hanging in loose folds and sometimes
drawn over the head; *specifically* the one
woven for the statue of the goddess
Athene at Athens, and carried in procession to her temple at the greater Pana-
thenaea.

peplum /ˈpɛpləm/ *noun* L17 Latin (from
Greek PEPLOS). **1** L17 A PEPLOS. **2** M19 Formerly, a kind of overskirt, in supposed
imitation of the ancient peplum. Now
also, a usually short flounce on a jacket,
blouse, or tunic, hanging from the waist
over a skirt; a jacket etc. incorporating
this.

pepperoni /pɛpəˈrəʊni/ *noun* (also **peperoni**) M20 Italian (*peperone* chilli, from
peper-, *pepe* pepper, from Latin *piper* + augmentative suffix *-one*). Beef and pork sausage seasoned with pepper.

per /pə/ *preposition* LME Latin (whence Old
French and Italian *per*, French *par*
through). **1** LME Through, by; by means
of: (*a*) in Latin and modern Latin (also medieval Latin and Italian) phrases, as PER
SE; (*b*) in Old French phrases and words
derived therefrom. **2** M16 *Heraldry* In the

direction of (a specified ordinary). **3** L16 By means of, by the instrumentality of; in accordance with (usually as *per*); *Law* as laid down by (a judge) in a specified case. **4** L16 For each, for every, as *per cent*, *per mil*, etc. **b** L19 With ellipsis of following noun: per hour, per cent, etc. Chiefly *United States*.

per accidens /pə:(r) 'aksɪdɛnz/ *adverb phrase* E16 Modern Latin (from as PER + Latin *accidens*, *accident-* present participial stem of *accidere* to happen). **1** E16 By virtue of some non-essential circumstance; contingently, indirectly. Opposed to PER SE. **2** L16 *Logic* By which the quantity of the proposition is changed from universal to particular in a conversion. Opposed to *simply*.

per annum /pə(r) 'anəm/ *adverb phrase* E17 Modern Latin (from as PER + accusative of Latin *annus* year). For or in each year.

■ Abbreviated to *p.a.*

percale /pə'keɪl/, *foreign* /pɛrkal/ *noun* E17 French (in modern use, but origin unknown (= Spanish *percal*, Italian *percalle*)). Originally, a fabric imported from India in the seventeenth and eighteenth centuries. Later, a light fine cotton fabric without gloss.

per capita /pə 'kapɪtə/ *adverb & adjective phrase* L17 Modern Latin (from as PER + accusative plural of Latin *caput* head). **A** *adverb phrase* **1** L17 *Law* (Divided, shared, etc.) equally among or by individuals, on an individual basis. Opposed to PER STIRPES. **2** E20 For each person or head of population. **B** *adjective phrase* M20 Possessed, performed, etc., by each person when averaged over a population etc.

A.2 1996 *Times* Government expenditure in Scotland is nearly one-third higher *per capita* than that for England.

per centum /pə 'sɛntəm/ *adverb phrase* M17 Modern Latin (Latinized form of *per cent*). Per cent.

■ Frequently in legal contexts.

perceptum /pə'sɛptəm/ *noun* plural **percepta** /pə'sɛptə/ L19 Latin (neuter of *perceptus* past participle of *percipere* to perceive). An object of perception, a percept.

per contra /pə: 'kɒntrə/ *adverb & noun phrase* M16 Italian. **A** *adverb phrase* M16 On the opposite side (of an account, assessment, etc.); on the other hand. **B** *noun phrase* E19 The opposite side.

1996 *Times* . . . a mass exit by the City herd would make AIM shares even more volatile than they are by nature. *Per contra*, AIM could become too respectable.

per diem /pə: 'di:ɛm/, /'dʌɪɛm/ *adverb, noun, & adjective phrase* E16 Modern Latin (from as PER + accusative of Latin *dies* day). **A** *adverb phrase* E16 For or in each day. **B** *noun phrase* E19 An amount or allowance of so much each day. Chiefly *North American*. **C** *adjective phrase* E19 Daily. Chiefly *North American*.

B 1996 *Spectator* . . . Hollywood doesn't help at all and he goes crackers *con brio* with vanishing agents, certifiable producers, grotty hotels, stingy *per diems* and lurking rewrite men.

perdu /pə:'dju:/, *foreign* /pɛrdy/ *adjective* (also **perdue**) L16 Old and Modern French (past participle of *perdre* to lose, from Latin *perdere*). **A** *adjective* **1** L16-L17 Posted in, or designating, a sentinel's position that is so dangerous that death is almost inevitable. Only in *sentinel perdue*, *perdue sentinel*. **b** E-M17 Placed in a very hazardous situation; (of a case) desperate. **2** E17 Hidden and on the watch; lying in ambush. Chiefly in *lie, set, stand*, etc., *perdu*. **3** E18 Concealed, hidden; out of sight; disguised.

■ Also formerly a noun (E17-M18), meaning principally 'soldier(s) posted in a very hazardous situation', but now obsolete in all nominal senses.

père /pɛr/, /pɛː/ *noun* E17 French (= father). **1** E17 Father: used in France and French-speaking countries as a title preceding the name of a priest. **2** E19 The father, senior.

■ *Père* in sense 2 is appended to a name to distinguish between a father and son of the same name (see quotations). Cf. FILS; also in phrase *père et fils* 'father and son'.

1995 *Spectator* And yet—another irony—Forte *père* remained, well beyond normal retirement age, a fiercely combative entrepreneur . . .

père de famille /pɛ də famij/, /ˌpɛː də fa 'mi:/ *noun phrase* E19 French. A father of a family, a family man.

perestroika /pɛrɪ'strɔɪkə/ *noun* L20 Russian (*perestroĭka* restructuring). The reform of the economic and political system of the former USSR, first proposed by Leonid Brezhnev in 1979 and actively promoted under the leadership of Mikhail Gorbachev from 1985; *transferred* any programme of fundamental reform.

1996 *Spectator* Ostensibly, it's to pay for digital technology in radio and television, . . . but I don't accept that this is the main reason for such *perestroika*.

perfecta /pə'fɛktə/ *noun* L20 American Spanish (shortened from *quiniela perfecta* perfect quinella). *Betting* A bet in which the first and second finishers of a race must be predicted in the correct order.

perfecto /pə'fɛktəʊ/ *noun* plural **perfectos** L19 Spanish (= perfect). A large thick cigar tapered at each end.

perfide Albion /pɛrfid albjɔ̃/ *noun phrase* M19 French (= perfidious Albion). England (with reference to its alleged habitual treachery towards other nations); an (untrustworthy) Englishman.

pergola /'pə:gələ/ *noun* L17 Italian (from Latin *pergula* projecting roof, vine arbour, from *pergere* to come or go forward). An arbour or covered walk, formed of growing plants trained over trellis-work.

■ First (M17 only) in the sense of 'an elevated stand or balcony', but this never passed into general currency.

peri /'pɪəri/ *noun* L18 Persian (*perī*). In Iranian mythology, one of a race of superhuman beings, originally represented as evil but subsequently as good and graceful; *transferred* a graceful or beautiful person.

peridot /'pɛrɪdɒt/ *noun* ME Old French (*peritot* (modern *peridot*) = medieval Latin *peridotus*, of unknown origin; in sense 2 readopted from French). **1** A green gemstone. Only in ME. **2** E18 Olivine (chrysolite), especially as used as gem.

periegesis /ˌpɛrɪ'dʒiːsɪs/ *noun* plural **periegeses** /ˌpɛrɪ'dʒiːsiːz/ E17 Greek (*periēgēsis* from *peri-* around + *hēgēsis*, from *hēgeisthai* to lead, guide). A description of a place or region.

per impossibile /ˌpə:(r) ɪmpɒ'sɪbɪli/ *adverb phrase* M19 Latin. As is impossible.

1995 *Spectator* Una Woodruff . . . will go to infinite trouble to choose brushes for a particular task, and then soak them in warm water so that she can identify and pull out any slightly loose hair which might, *per impossibile*, threaten a perfectly smooth wash.

peripeteia /ˌpɛrɪpɪ'tʌɪə/, /ˌpɛrɪpɪ'tiːə/ *noun* (also **peripetia** /ˌpɛrɪpɪ'tiːə/) L16 Greek (ultimately from *peri-* around + stem *pet-* of *piptein* to fall). A sudden change of fortune or reverse of circumstances (fictional or real).

■ Used by Aristotle in his *Poetics* as a technical term for the sequence of events in the plot of a drama which, in the case of a tragic hero, takes the protagonist from happiness to misfortune.

1984 A.G. Lehmann *European Heritage* The insidious flatteries of the 'mirror' stage—the symmetrical throne-room scenes, the hero revolving great dilemmas, the god descending, the wonderful *peripeteia*—become lessons in style to haunt the prince's dream and shape his acts.

periphrasis /pə'rɪfrəsɪs/ *noun* plural **periphrases** /pə'rɪfrəsiːz/ M16 Latin (from Greek, from *periphrazein*, from *peri-* + *phrazein* to declare). The figure of speech which consists in expressing a meaning by many or several words instead of by few or one; a roundabout way of speaking or writing; (a) circumlocution.

periplus /'pɛrɪplʌs/ *noun* L18 Latin (from Greek *periplous*, from *peri-* around + *plous* voyage). (A) circumnavigation; a voyage (or journey) round a coastline etc.; a narrative of such a voyage.

peristyle /'pɛrɪstʌɪl/ *noun* E17 French (*péristyle* from Latin *peristylum* from Greek *peristulon* use as noun of neuter of *peristulos* having pillars all round, from *peri-* + *stulos* column). *Architecture* **1** E17 A row of columns surrounding a building, court, cloister, etc.; the court etc. surrounded by the columns. **2** L17 The columned porch of a church or other large building; a pillared verandah.

per mensem /pə: 'mɛnsɛm/ *adverb phrase* M17 Modern Latin (from as PER + accusative singular of Latin *mensis* month). For or in each month.

permis de séjour /pɛrmi də seʒur/ *noun phrase* plural same L19 French. Permission to stay in a country; a residence permit.

perpetuum mobile /pə:ˌpɛtjʊəm 'məʊbɪli/, /pə:ˌpɛtjʊʊm/, /'məʊbɪleɪ/ *noun phrase* L17 Latin (from *perpetuus* perpetual + *mobilis* movable, mobile, after PRIMUM MOBILE). **1** L17 Motion that continues forever; *specifically* that of a hypothetical machine that runs forever; such a machine. **2** L19 *Music* A MOTO PERPETUO.

perruquier /pɛ'ruːkɪeɪ/ *noun* M18 French (from *perruque* peruke). A person who makes, dresses, or sells wigs.

per se /pə: seɪ/ *adverb phrase* L16 Latin. By or in itself; intrinsically. Opposed to PER ACCIDENS 1.

persiennes /pɛːsɪ'ɛnz/ *noun plural* M19
French (use as noun of feminine plural
of *persien* Persian). Window-shutters or
outside blinds made of light movable
slats fastened horizontally in a frame.

persiflage /'pɛːsɪflɑːʒ/ *noun* M18 French
(from *persifler* to banter, from as PER- + *siffler* to whistle). Light banter or raillery;
frivolous talk.

persona /pə'səʊnə/ *noun plural* **perso-
nas, personae** /pə'səʊniː/ E20 Latin (originally = the mask worn by actors in
ancient Greek and Roman drama). **1** E20
A character assumed by an author, performer, etc., in his or her writing, work,
etc. **2** E20 An aspect of the personality as
displayed to others. Cf. ANIMA.

persona designata /pə,səʊnə dɛzɪg
'nɑːtə/ *noun phrase* plural **personae desig-
natae** /pə,səʊni: dɛzɪg'nɑːti:/ L19 Law Latin
(from as PERSONA + Latin *designata* feminine of *designatus* past participle of *desig-
nare* to mark out, elect). A person
individually specified in a legal action, as
opposed to one included in a category.

**personae gratae, personae non gra-
tae** plurals of PERSONA GRATA, PERSONA
NON GRATA.

persona grata /pə,səʊnə 'grɑːtə/ *noun
phrase* plural **personae gratae** /pə,səʊni:
'grɑːti:/ L19 Late Latin (from as PERSONA +
Latin *grata* feminine of *gratus* pleasing). A
person, especially a diplomat, acceptable
to certain others.

personalia /pə:sə'neɪlɪə/ *noun plural* E20
Latin (neuter plural of *personalis* personal). Personal matters; personal me-
mentoes.

persona non grata /pə,səʊnə nɒn
'grɑːtə/, /nəʊn/ *noun phrase* plural **personae non gratae** /pə,səʊni:/, /'grɑːti:/ E20
Late Latin (from as PERSONA GRATA + Latin
non not). An unacceptable or unwelcome
person.

personnel /pə:sə'nɛl/ *noun* E19 French
(use as noun of adjective, as contrasted
with MATÉRIEL). **1** E19 The body of people
employed in an organization etc. or engaged in a service or undertaking, especially a military one. Opposed to *matériel*.
2 M20 *specifically* The members of an orchestra or band. **3** M20 The department
in an organization etc. concerned with
the appointment, welfare, records, etc.,
of employees. Also more fully *personnel
department*.

per stirpes /pə: 'stə:pi:z/ *adverb phrase* L17
Modern Latin (from as PER + accusative
plural of Latin *stirps* family, stem). *Law* (Divided, shared, etc.) equally among the
branches of a family (and then each share
among the members of one branch). Opposed to PER CAPITA sense A.1.

pervenche /pɛ:'vɑːnʃ/ *noun* L19 French (=
periwinkle). A shade of light blue resembling the colour of the flowers of the periwinkle. More fully *pervenche blue*.

peshmerga /pɛʃ'mə:gə/ *noun* plural
peshmergas, same M20 Kurdish (*pêsh-
merge* from *pêsh* before, in front of + *merg*
death). A member of a Kurdish nationalist guerrilla organization.

pessimum /'pɛsɪməm/ *noun* M20 Latin
(neuter singular of *pessimus* worst). The
most unfavourable condition (original especially, in the habitat of an animal or
plant). Frequently *attributive*. Opposed to
OPTIMUM.

pesto /'pɛstəʊ/ *noun* M20 Italian (contraction of *pestato* past participle of *pestare* to
pound, crush). A sauce of crushed basil,
nuts (especially pine nuts), cheese, garlic,
and olive oil, served with pasta and other
foods. Cf. PISTOU.

pétanque /petɑ̃k/, /pə'tɑŋk/ *noun* M20
French. A game similar to BOULE noun 2
sense 2.

pétillant /petijɑ̃/, /'peɪtɪjɒ̃/ *adjective* L19
French. Sparkling, lively. Of wine: slightly
sparkling.

petit /pəti/, /pə'ti:/, /'pɛti/; *same in plural
collocations adjective* LME French (cf. feminine PETITE). Little, small.

■ Occurs in various phrases used in English, and until the seventeenth century was
in common use alongside the English form
petty.

petit battement /pəti batmã/ *noun phrase* plural **petits battements** (*pronounced same*) E20 French. *Ballet* A BATTE-MENT executed with the moving leg bent.

petit beurre /pəti bœr/ *noun phrase* plural **petits beurres** (*pronounced same*) E20 French. A sweet butter biscuit.

petit bourgeois /ˌpɛtɪ 'buəʒwaː/, /ˌpəˌtiː/; *foreign* /pəti burʒwa/ *noun & adjective phrase* plural **petits bourgeois** (pronounced same); (feminine **petite bourgeoise** /pəˌtiːt 'buəʒwaːz/, *foreign* /pətit burʒwaz/, plural **petites bourgeoises** (pronounced same)) M19 French (literally, 'little citizen'). **A** *noun phrase* M19 A member of the lower middle classes; *derogatory* a person judged to have conventional or conservative attitudes. **B** *adjective phrase* L19 Pertaining to or characteristic of the PETITE BOURGEOISIE; lower middle class; conventional.

■ Also partially Anglicized (L19 onwards) as *petty bourgeois*.

B 1996 *Spectator* Mr Volkman rails about the CIA's petit bourgeois ignorance of foreign cultures in his account of a disastrous operation in Cuba . . .

petite /pə'tiːt/, *foreign* /pətit/ *adjective & noun* M16 French (feminine of PETIT). **A** *adjective* **1 a** M16–L17 Of a small size or importance. **b** L18 Of small stature. Now chiefly of a woman or girl. **c** E20 Designating a small size in women's clothing. **2** E18 The French (feminine) for 'little, small', occurring in various phrases used in English. **3** M20 *Microbiology* Designating mutant strains of yeast that are characterized by defective mitochondrial DNA and tend to form small colonies. **B** *noun* **1** M20 A petite woman or girl. **2** M20 A petite size in women's clothing. **3** M20 A petite strain of yeast.

A.b 1996 *Country Life* She is as bright and charming as she is petite and beautiful.

petite amie /pətit ami/ *noun phrase* plural **petites amies** M20 French (= little (female) friend). A young mistress.

1978 W. Garner *Möbius Trip* His *petite amie* . . . had raised the subject of marriage.

petite bourgeoise see PETIT BOURGEOIS.

petite bourgeoisie /pəˌtiːt buəʒwaːziː/, *foreign* /pətit burʒwazi/ *noun phrase* E20 French. The lower middle classes collectively.

■ Also partially Anglicized (M19, but mainly 20) as *petty bourgeoisie*.

1995 *Spectator* Lack of a belief in the social explanation of crime is thought to be a failing of the petite bourgeoisie.

petite noblesse /pətit nɔblɛs/ *noun phrase* L19 French. The lesser nobility in France. Cf. HAUTE NOBLESSE.

petites amies, petites marmites, etc. plurals of PETITE AMIE, PETITE MARMITE, etc.

petit four /ˌpɛtɪ 'fɔː/, *foreign* /pəti fur/ *noun phrase* plural **petits fours** /ˌpɛtɪ 'fɔːz/, *foreign* /pəti fur/ L19 French (literally, 'little oven'). A small cake or biscuit usually served with the coffee after a meal.

petitio principii /pɪˌtɪʃɪəʊ prɪn'sɪpɪaɪ/, /prɪŋ'kɪpɪaɪ/ *noun phrase* M16 Latin (= assuming a principle, from *petitio* laying claim to + genitive of PRINCIPIUM). *Logic* A fallacy in which a conclusion is taken for granted in a premiss; begging the question.

petit-maître /pətimɛtr/ *noun phrase* plural **petits-maîtres** (*pronounced same*) E18 French (literally, 'little master'). **1** E18 A dandy, a fop. **2** M19 An artist, writer, etc., of minor importance.

■ In sense 2 sometimes translated as *little masters* with reference to practitioners of the minor arts, such as the engravers of late medieval Germany.

1996 *Spectator* These are the pictures that have earned him [sc. William Nicholson] the title of *petit maître*, a French expression for a rather English virtue of recognising one's limits and sticking within them.

petit mal /ˌpɛtɪ 'mal/, /pəti mal/ *noun phrase* L19 French (literally, 'little sickness'). Mild epilepsy, with only momentary loss of consciousness. Cf. GRAND MAL.

petit marmite /pətit marmˈit/ *noun phrase* plural **petits marmites** (*pronounced same*) E20 French. Soup served in the (individual serving sized) MARMITE in which it has been cooked.

petit pain /pəti pɛ̃/ *noun phrase* plural **petits pains** (*pronounced same*) M18 French. A small bread roll.

petit point /pəti pwɛ̃/, /ˌpɛtɪ 'pɔɪnt/ *noun phrase* L19 French. **1** L19 Embroidery on canvas using small stitches. **2** L19 Tent-stitch.

petit poussin /pəti pusɛ̃/ *noun phrase* plural **petits poussins** (*pronounced same*) E20 French. A young chicken for eating.

■ Now rare, being almost entirely superseded by POUSSIN.

petits battements, petits beurres, etc. plurals of PETIT BATTEMENT, PETIT BEURRE, etc.

petits chevaux /pəti ʃəvo/ *noun phrase plural* L19 French (literally, 'little horses'). A gambling game in which bets are placed on mechanical horses made to spin round a flag at the centre of a special table.

petits fours, petits pains plurals of PETIT FOUR, PETIT PAIN.

petits pois /ˌpetɪ ˈpwɑː/, *foreign* /pəti pwa/ *noun phrase plural* E19 French (literally, 'small peas'). Small young green peas.

petits poussins plural of PETIT POUSSIN.

petits soins /pəti swɛ̃/ *noun phrase plural* E19 French. Small attentions or services.

petit suisse /pəti sɥis/, /ˌpetɪ ˈswiːs/ *noun phrase* E20 French. A small cream cheese. Cf. FROMAGE FRAIS.

petit tranchet /pəti trɑ̃ʃɛ/, /ˌpetɪ ˈtrɑːnʃɪt/ *noun phrase* M20 French (= little knife). *Archaeology* A small stone artefact of mesolithic and neolithic cultures with the end made into a broad cutting edge.

petit verre /pəti vɛr/ *noun phrase plural* **petits verres** (*pronounced same*) M19 French. A glass of liqueur.

> 1995 *Spectator* Instead of some monumental goddess at the dawn of time, . . . you see only a sagging model of the *quartier,* longing for a *petit verre* and the regained dignity of her corsets.

pétrissage /petrisaʒ/ *noun* L19 French (from *pétrir, pétriss-* to knead). A kneading process used in massage.

pétroleur /pɛtrɔlœr/ *noun* (feminine **pétroleuse** /pɛtrɔləz/) plural pronounced same L19 French (from *pétrole* petrol). An arsonist who uses petrol.

pe-tsai /peɪˈtsʌɪ/ *noun* L18 Chinese ((Pekingese) *báicài* (Wade-Giles *pê ts'ai*), literally, 'white vegetable': cf. PAK-CHOI). A kind of Chinese cabbage, *Brassica pekinensis,* with leaves in a loose head, grown as a winter vegetable.

peyote /peɪˈəʊti/ *noun* M19 American Spanish (from Nahuatl *peyotl*). MESCAL sense 3.

phaeton /ˈfeɪt(ə)n/ *noun* L16 French (*phaéton* from Latin *Phaethon* from Greek *Phae-*thōn (*phaethōn* shining), in Greek mythology the son of Helios and Clymene, who was allowed to drive the sun's chariot for a day, with disastrous results). **1** L16–M18 A rash or adventurous charioteer like Phaethon; any charioteer; a thing that, like Phaethon, sets the world on fire. **2** M18 Chiefly *History* A light four-wheeled open carriage, usually drawn by a pair of horses, and with one or two forward-facing seats. **3** E20 A touring car. *United States.*

phallus /ˈfaləs/ *noun* plural **phalli** /ˈfalʌɪ, /ˈfaliː/, **phalluses** E17 Late Latin (from Greek *phallos*). **1** E17 An image of the erect penis, symbolizing the generative power in nature; *specifically* that carried in solemn procession in the Dionysiac festivals in ancient Greece. **2** E20 The penis, especially as an organ of symbolic significance; an erect penis.

phantasma /fanˈtazmə/ *noun* plural **phantasmas, phantasmata** /fanˈtazmətə/ L16 Italian (*fantasma* from Latin *phantasma* from Greek, from *phantazein* to make visible). An illusion, a vision, a dream; an apparition, a ghost.

pharmacopoeia /ˌfɑːməkəˈpiːə/ *noun* (also **pharmacopeia**) E17 Modern Latin (from Greek *pharmakopoiia* art of preparing drugs, from *pharmakopoios* of drugs, from *pharmaco-* combining form of *pharmakon* drug + *-poios* making, maker). **1** E17 A book containing a list of drugs with their effects and directions for their use (and, formerly, their preparation and identification); *specifically* such a book officially published and revised periodically. **2** E18 A collection or stock of drugs.

phenomenon /fɪˈnɒmmən/ *noun* (also **phaenomenon, phainomenon**) plural **phenomena** /fɪˈnɒmmə/, also (*non-standard*) used as singular, **phenomenas** L16 Late Latin (*phaenomenon* from Greek *phainomenon* use as noun of neuter present participle passive of *phainein* to show, (in passive) be seen, appear). **1** L16 A fact or event that appears or is perceived by one of the senses or by the mind; *especially* one whose cause or explanation is in question. **2** L17 *Philosophy* An immediate object of perception (as distinguished from substance, or a thing in itself). **3** E18 A very notable, extraordinary, or exceptional fact or occurrence; *colloquial* a thing, person, or animal remarkable for some unusual quality.

Phi Beta Kappa /ˌfʌɪ ˌbiːtə ˈkapə/ *noun phrase* M19 Greek (from the initial letters *phi, beta, kappa,* of *philosophia biou kubernētēs* philosophy the guide of life). (A member of) an intercollegiate society to which distinguished (usually undergraduate) scholars may be elected as an honour. Frequently *attributive*. United States.

philia /ˈfɪlɪə/ *noun* M20 Greek. Amity, friendship, liking.

philosophe /ˌfɪlə(ʊ)ˈzɒf/ *noun* OE French (from Latin *philosophus* from Greek *philosophos* lover of wisdom, from *philo-* from *philein* to love + *sophos* wise). A (sceptical) philosopher, *specifically* a member of the French rationalist group associated with the production of the *Encyclopédie* in the mid eighteenth century.

■ *Philosophe,* which was also occasionally found in Anglicized form as *philosoph,* appears in Old English in the general sense of *philosopher,* and during the Middle Ages the form *philosophe* was reinforced by Old French *philosophe* or *filosophe.* Since the Enlightenment, the word is mainly used in English for the French Encyclopedists or, derogatively, for those who emulate their sceptical stance or fall into similar errors.
1995 *Spectator* Diderot once complained to David Hume that *philosophes* 'preach wisdom to the deaf'.

philosophia perennis /ˌfɪləˌsɒfɪə pəˈrɛnɪs/ *noun phrase* M19 Latin (= perennial philosophy). A posited core of philosophical truths independent of and unaffected by time or place, frequently taken to be exemplified in the writings of Aristotle and St Thomas Aquinas.

philosophia prima /ˌfɪləˌsɒfɪə ˈpriːmə/ *noun phrase* E17 Latin (= first philosophy). (The branch of inquiry that deals with) the most general truths of philosophy; *specifically* (the branch of inquiry that deals with) the divine and the eternal.

phobia /ˈfəʊbɪə/ *noun* L18 Latin (independent use of the Latin suffix *-phobia* from Greek *-phobos* fearing, from *phobos* fear). (A) fear, (a) horror, (an) aversion; *especially* an abnormal and irrational fear or dread aroused by a particular object or circumstance.

■ *Phobia* as a suffix also appears in numerous abstract nouns, especially in modern coinages after the Greek denoting states in clinical psychology, such as AGORAPHOBIA, *arachnophobia* (E20) 'fear of spiders', etc., and in other (often jocular or nonce) formations such as *Anglophobia* (L18), *Francophobia* (L19), etc.

physique /fɪˈziːk/ *noun* E19 French (use as noun of adjective = physical). The form, size, and development of a person's body.

pi /pʌɪ/ *noun* LME Greek (in sense 2 representative of initial letter of Greek *periphereia* periphery; in sense 3 after the shape; in sense 4 after *pi-orbital* etc.). **1** LME The sixteenth letter (Π, π) of the Greek alphabet. **2** E18 *Mathematics* The ratio of the circumference of a circle to its diameter. Usually written π.

■ More recently (E20) pi (generally written π or Π and used attributively) has also become part of the technical vocabulary of Electricity (as *pi-network* etc.) and Physics and Chemistry (as π electron or Π molecule).

piaffe /pjaf/ *verb & noun* M18 French (*piaffer* to strut, make a show). *Horsemanship* **A** *intransitive verb* M18 Move (especially on the spot) with a high slow trotting step. **B** *noun* L19 An act of piaffing.

pianissimo /pɪəˈnɪsɪməʊ/ *adverb, adjective, & noun* E18 Italian (superlative of PIANO). *Music* **A** *adverb & adjective* E18 (A direction:) very soft(ly). **B** *noun* L19 plural **pianissimos, pianissimi** /pɪəˈnɪsɪmi/ A very soft passage.

■ As a musical direction abbreviated to *pp* or *ppp*.
B 1996 *Times* And on top is that 'brilliant technique', . . . and floating pianissimos to melt the sternest critical heart.

piano /ˈpjɑːnəʊ/ *noun* 1 plural **pianos, piani** /ˈpjɑːni/ M18 Italian (from Latin *planus* flat, (later of sound) soft, low). **1** M18 *Music* A soft or quiet passage. **2** M19 A flat or storey in an Italian building. Cf. PIANO NOBILE.

piano /prˈanəʊ/ *noun* 2 plural **pianos** E19 Italian (abbreviation of PIANOFORTE or aphetized from FORTE-PIANO). **1** E19 A large keyboard musical instrument having metal strings struck by hammers and stopped by dampers, with two or three pedals to regulate the volume or length of the notes. **2** M20 The playing of this instrument.

piano /ˈpjɑːnəʊ/ *adverb & adjective* L17 Italian (from Latin *planus* flat, (later of sound) soft, low). **1** *adverb & adjective* L17 *Music* (A direction:) soft(ly), quiet(ly). **2** *adjective* E19 Of a person: quiet, subdued.

■ As a musical direction usually abbreviated to *p*.

pianoforte /pɪˌanəʊ'fɔːti/ *noun* M18 Italian (earlier *pian(o) e forte*, literally, 'soft and loud' (with reference to its capacity for gradation of tone); cf. FORTE-PIANO). A PIANO noun 2 sense 1.

piano nobile /ˌpjano 'nobile/ *noun* L19 Italian (from *piano* floor, storey + *nobile* noble, great). *Architecture* The main (usually first-floor) storey of a large house, containing the principal rooms.
1995 *Spectator* To let in Bishopsgate is the lavish modern mansion built for Standard Chartered, complete with *piano nobile*.

piano piano /'pjano 'pjano/ *adverb phrase* (also (earlier) **pian piano**) E17 Italian (= softly, softly). In a quiet leisurely manner; little by little.

piazza /pɪ'atsə/ *noun* L16 Italian (= French *place* (town) square). **1** L16 A public square or market-place, *especially* one in an Italian town. Formerly also, any open space surrounded by buildings. **2 a** M17 A covered gallery or walk surrounding an open square; a single such gallery or walk in front of a building. Now *rare*. **b** E18 The veranda of a house. Chiefly *United States*.

pibroch /'piːbrɒk/, /'piːbrɒx/ *noun* E18 Gaelic (*piobaireachd* the art of playing the bagpipe, from *piobair* piper (from *piob* pipe, from English *pipe*) + suffix of function *-achd*). A series of variations on a theme for the bagpipes, usually of a martial or funerary character.

picador /'pɪkədɔː/ *noun* L18 Spanish (from *picar* to prick, pierce). *Bullfighting* A person mounted on horseback who goads the bull with a lance.

picaresque /pɪkə'rɛsk/ *adjective & noun* E19 French (from Spanish *picaresco*, from *pícaro* roguish, knavish, (noun) rogue; cf. next). **A** *adjective* **1** E19 Of or pertaining to rogues, knaves, or urchins; *especially* (of a style of especially Spanish fiction) dealing with the episodic adventures of such characters. **2** M20 Drifting; wandering.

picaro /'pɪkərəʊ/ *noun* plural **picaros** E17 Spanish (see PICARESQUE). A rogue, a scoundrel.

picayune /pɪkə'juːn/ *noun & adjective* E19 French (*picaillon* old copper coin of Piedmont, halfpence, cash from Provençal *picaioun*, of unknown origin). **A** *noun* E19 Originally (in the southern United States), a Spanish half-real, worth 6¼

cents. Now, a five-cent piece or other coin of small value; *colloquial* an insignificant or mean person or thing. **B** *adjective* E19 Mean, contemptible, insignificant. *North American colloquial*.

piccolo /'pɪkələʊ/ *noun & adjective* M19 Italian (= small). **A** *noun* plural **piccolos** **1** M19 A small flute sounding an octave higher than the ordinary flute; a player on this in an orchestra etc. **b** L19 An organ-stop having the tone of a piccolo. **2** M19 A small upright piano. **3** E20 A waiter's assistant in a hotel, restaurant, etc.; a page at a hotel. **4** M20 A jukebox. *United States slang*. **B** *adjective* M19 Designating the highest-pitched member of a family of musical instruments.

pickelhaube /'pɪk(ə)l,(h)aʊbə/ *noun* plural **pickelhaubes, pickelhauben** /'pɪk(ə)l ,(h)aʊbən/ L19 German. *History* A spiked helmet worn by German soldiers, especially before and during the war of 1914–18.
1996 *Times* Their [sc. British policemen's] helmets were modelled on the Prussian pickelhaube . . .

picot /'piːkəʊ/ *noun* E17 French (diminutive of *pic* peak, point, prick). Any of a series of small loops worked in lace or embroidery, used to form an ornamental edging, buttonhole, etc.

picotee /pɪkə'tiː/ *noun & adjective* E18 French (*picoté(e)* past participle of *picoter* to mark with points, prick, from as PICOT). **A** *noun* E18 A variety of carnation, having light petals marked or edged with a darker colour. **B** *adjective* L19 Of a colour, pattern, etc.: resembling that of the picotee.
B 1996 *Country Life* The last variant [of busy lizzie] was the picotee type . . . and the next will have speckled flowers.

picquet variant of PIQUET.

pièce à thèse /pjɛs a tɛz/ *noun phrase* plural **pièces à thèse** (pronounced same) M20 French. A play written with the aim of supporting a thesis or proposition. Also called *thesis-play*.

pièce de circonstance /pjɛs də sirkɔ̃stɑ̃s/ *noun phrase* plural **pièces de circonstance** (pronounced same) M19 French. A literary composition, theory, etc., arising out of a particular situation.

pièce de résistance /pjɛs də rezistɑ̃s/, /pɪˌɛs də rɛ'zɪstɑ̃s/, /'rɛzɪstɒ̃s/ *noun phrase* plural **pièces de résistance** (pronounced same) L18 French. **1** L18 The

most important or outstanding item.
2 M19 The main dish of a meal.

1 **1996** *Country Life* The *pièce de résistance* was Thomas Cooper's enormous canvas, *The Monarch of the Meadows* . . .

pièce d'occasion /pjɛs dɔ̃kazjɔ̃/ *noun phrase* plural **pièces d'occasion** (pronounced same) L19 French. A literary or musical work written for a special occasion.

1996 *Country Life* Another *pièce d'occasion*, created for San Francisco's United We Dance festival which, in 1995, celebrated the 50th anniversary of the United Nations Charter, Bruce's *Meeting Point* overcomes its Nyman score . . . with far greater success.

pièce noire /pjɛs nwar/ *noun phrase* plural **pièces noires** (pronounced same) M20 French (literally, 'black play'). A play or film with a tragic or macabre theme.

■ The phrase originated with French dramatist Jean Anouilh (1910–87); see PIÈCE ROSE.

pièce rose /pjɛs roz/ *noun phrase* plural **pièces roses** (pronounced same) M20 French (literally, 'pink play'). A play or film with a pleasantly entertaining theme; a comedy.

■ *Pièces roses* and *Pièces noires* were the titles given by Anouilh to collections of his plays published in 1942, roughly analogous to George Bernard Shaw's *Plays: Pleasant and Unpleasant.*

pièces à thèse, pièces de circonstance etc. plurals of PIÈCE À THÈSE, PIÈCE DE CIRCONSTANCE, etc.

pied-à-terre /ˌpjeɪdɑːˈtɛː/ *noun* plural **pieds-à-terre** (pronounced same) E19 French (literally, 'foot to earth'). A small town house, flat, or room used for short periods of residence; a home base.

1995 *Country Life* The ideal pied-à-terre should be compact, easy and economical to run, well placed for the City, the West End or escape routes to the country, and secure without being claustrophobic.

pied d'éléphant /pje deləfɑ̃/ *noun phrase* plural **pieds d'éléphant** (pronounced same) M20 French (literally, 'elephant's foot'). A padded sack used to protect the lower part of the body on a bivouac when mountaineering etc.

pied noir /pje nwar/ *noun phrase* plural **pieds noirs** (pronounced same) M20 French (literally, 'black foot'). A person of European origin who lived in Algeria during French rule.

■ Competing explanations of the sobriquet are based either on the black shoes worn by Europeans but not by native Algerians or on the traditional employment of barefooted Algerians as stokers on French steamers.

pieds-à-terre, pieds d'éléphant, etc. plurals of PIED-À-TERRE, PIED D'ÉLÉPHANT, etc.

pierrette /pɪəˈrɛt/, /pjɛˈrɛt/ *noun* L19 French (feminine diminutive of *Pierre* Peter, corresponding to next). A female member of a company of pierrots.

pierrot /ˈpɪərəʊ/, /ˈpjɛrəʊ/ *noun* (also **Pierrot**) M18 French (appellative use of petform of *Pierre* Peter). A typical character in French pantomime. Now also, a musical entertainer with a whitened face and a loose white costume.

Pietà /pɪɛrˈtɑː/, *foreign* /pjeˈtɑː/ *noun* M17 Italian (from Latin *pietas* piety). A painting or sculpture representing the Virgin Mary holding the dead body of Jesus on her lap or in her arms.

pietas /piːˈeɪtɑːs/ *noun* E20 Latin. An attitude of respect towards an ancestor, institution, etc.

pietra commessa /piˌetra komˈmessa/ *noun phrase* plural **pietre commesse** /piˌetre komˈmesse/ M17 Italian (literally, 'stone fitted together'). (An example of) mosaic work.

pietra dura /piˌetra ˈdura/ *noun phrase* plural **pietre dure** /piˌetre ˈdure/ E19 Italian (literally, 'hard stone'). Semiprecious stones; *singular* and in *plural*, mosaic work of such stones.

pietre commesse, pietre dure plurals of PIETRA COMMESSA, PIETRA DURA.

pignon /piɲɔ̃/ *noun* plural pronounced same E17 French (= Spanish *piñon*, Portuguese *pinhão*, all from late Latin derivation of Latin *pinea* pine cone). The edible seed of the stone pine, *Pinus pinea*, of southern Europe.

pikau /ˈpiːkaʊ/ *noun & verb* M19 Maori. **A** *noun* M19 A pack for carrying on the back, a knapsack. **B** *transitive verb* L19 Carry (a load or pack) on the back. *New Zealand.*

piki /ˈpiːki/ *noun* L19 Hopi (*píːki*). Maizemeal bread in the form of very thin sheets, made by the Hopi Indians of the south-western United States.

pilau /prˈlaʊ/, /ˈpiːlaʊ/ *noun* (also **pilaff** /prˈlaf/, **pilaw** /prˈlɔː/, **pulao** /pəˈlaʊ/, and other variants) E17 Turkish (*pílâv* cooked rice = Persian *pīlaw* boiled rice and meat). An Indian or Middle Eastern dish of rice (or occasionally other grain) cooked in stock with spices and often meat, fish, vegetables, etc.

pileus /'pʌɪlɪəs/ *noun* plural **pilei** /'pʌɪlɪʌɪ/ M18 Latin (= felt cap). **1** M18 *Botany* The spore-bearing circular structure surmounting the stipe in a mushroom or toadstool, which has an undersurface composed of radiating plates or gills. Also called *cap*. **2** L18 *Classical Antiquities* L18 A felt cap without a brim.

pilón /pi'lon/, /pi:'ləʊn/ *noun* plural **pilones** /pi'lones/, /pi:'ləʊnɪz/ L19 **Mexican Spanish** (from Spanish = sugar loaf, pillar, post). In Mexico and the south-western United States: a small gift given to a customer making a purchase etc.

pilotis /piloti/ *noun* plural M20 **French**. *Architecture* A series of columns or piles, used to raise the base of a building above ground level.

pilpul /'pɪlp(ə)l/ *noun* L19 **Hebrew** (from *pilpēl* to search, debate hotly). (An instance of) subtle or keen rabbinical disputation; *transferred* unprofitable argument, hairsplitting.

pimento /pɪ'mɛntəʊ/ *noun & adjective* L17 **Spanish** (PIMIENTO). **A** *noun* plural **mentos** **1** Cayenne pepper. Only in L17. **2** L17 The spice allspice; (more fully *pimento tree*) the West Indian tree, *Pimenta dioica*, of the myrtle family, from which allspice is obtained. Now *West Indies*. **3** E20 A sweet (especially a red) pepper, a capsicum. **B** *adjective* M20 Pimento red.

pimiento /pɪmɪ'ɛntəʊ/, /pɪm'jɛntəʊ/ *noun* plural **pimientos** (also written **pimienta** /pɪmɪ'ɛntə/) M17 **Spanish** (from Latin *pigmentum* paint, colour). **1** M17 PIMENTO sense 2. *West Indies*. **2** M19 PIMENTO sense 3.

pina colada /ˌpiːnə kə'lɑːdə/ *noun* (also **piña colada** /ˌpiːnjə kə'lɑːdə/, *foreign* /ˌpiɲa ko'laa/ E20 **South American Spanish** (literally, 'strained pineapple' from *piña* (Portuguese *pinha*) pineapple, (originally pine cone, from Latin *pinea* pine cone). A drink made with pineapple juice, rum, and coconut (milk).

> 1975 P. Moyes *Black Widower* In the bar itself, ice tinkled merrily into tall glasses of rum punch and *pina colada* . . .

pinard /pinar/ *noun* (also **Pinard**) plural pronounced same E20 **French**. Rough red wine; *generally* any wine; a glass of this.

piñata /pɪ'njɑːtə/ *noun* L19 **Spanish** (= jug, pot). In Mexico and the south-western United States: a decorated container filled with sweets or small gifts, which is opened (especially by breaking) by a blindfolded person at a festive celebration.

pinax /'pɪnaks/ *noun* plural **pinaces** /'pɪnəsiːz/ L17 **Latin** (from Greek = board, plank, tablet, picture). **1** L17 A tablet; a list inscribed on this; a catalogue, an index. Now *rare* or *obsolete*. **2** M19 *Antiquities* A (painted or engraved) plate, platter, or dish.

pince-nez /pans'neɪ/, *foreign* /pɛ̃sne/ *noun* (treated as *singular* or *plural*) L19 **French** (from *pincer* to pinch + *nez* nose). A pair of eyeglasses kept in position by a spring clipping the nose rather than by earpieces.

pinetum /pʌɪ'niːtəm/ *noun* plural **pineta**, /pʌɪ'niːtə/ M19 **Latin** (from *pinus* pine). A plantation or collection of pines or other conifers, for scientific or ornamental purposes.

pinga /'piŋa/ *noun* M20 **Portuguese** (literally, 'drop (of water)'). A raw white rum distilled from sugar cane in Brazil; a drink of this.

pingo /'pɪŋgəʊ/ *noun* plural **pingo(e)s** M20 **Eskimo** ((Inuit) *pinguq* NUNATAK). *Physical Geography* A persistent low conical or dome-shaped mound, often with a crater on top, formed in regions with thin or discontinuous permafrost; a round depression in temperate regions thought to be the remains of such a mound.

pinole /pɪ'nəʊleɪ/ *noun* M19 **American Spanish** (from Aztec *pinolli*). Parched cornflour mixed with the flour of mesquite beans, sugar, and spice. *United States*.

piñon /pɪ'njɒn/, /'pɪnjən/ *noun* plural **piñons**, **piñones** /pɪ'njəʊnɪz/ M19 **Spanish** (cf. French PIGNON). (The edible seed of) any of a group of small pines of southwestern North America. Also, the wood of these trees.

pinto /'pɪntəʊ/ *adjective & noun* plural **pintos** M19 **Spanish** (= painted, mottled, from Proto-Romance). **A** *adjective*. **1** M19 Of a horse: piebald; skewbald. **2** E20 *pinto bean*, a variety of kidney bean with mottled seeds, widely cultivated in Central America and the south-western United States; the seed of this. **B** *noun* M19 A piebald horse.

■ With reference to horses, chiefly North American.

piob mhor /piːp ˈvɔːr/, /piːəb/ *noun phrase* M19 Gaelic (*piob mhòr*, literally, 'big pipe'). A kind of bagpipes traditionally played in the Scottish Highlands.

piolet /pjəʊˈleɪ/ *noun* M19 French ((Savoy dialect) diminutive of *piolo*, apparently cognate with *pioche*, *pic* pickaxe). A two-headed ice-axe used by mountaineers.

piperade /pɪpəˈrɑːd/, *foreign* /pipərad/ (*plural same*) *noun* M20 French. A dish originating in the Basque country, consisting of eggs scrambled with tomatoes and peppers.

pipette /pɪˈpɛt/ *noun & verb* (also **pipet**) M19 French (diminutive of *pipe* pipe). **A** *noun* M19 A frequently tubular device for transferring or measuring small quantities of a liquid or gas by means of aspiration and dispensation, used especially in scientific laboratories. **B** M19 *transitive verb* inflected *pipetted*, **pipete**. Transfer, measure, draw *off* or *out*, (a liquid or gas) with a pipette.

pipkrake /ˈpɪpkreɪk/, /ˈpɪpkrɑːkə/ *noun* plural **pipkrakes**, **pipkraker** /ˈpɪpkrɑːkə/ M20 Swedish ((dialect) from *pip* pipe + *krake* variant of *klake* frozen ground). *Physical Geography* An ice-needle; needle ice.

piquant /ˈpiːk(ə)nt/, /ˈpiːkɑːnt/ *adjective* (in senses 2 and 3 also **piquante** /pɪˈkɑːnt/) E16 French (present participial adjective of *piquer* to prick, sting). **1** E16 Sharp or stinging to the feelings; severe, bitter. Long *archaic*. **2** M17 Of food etc.: agreeably pungent, sharp-tasting; spicy; savoury, appetizing. **3** M17 Pleasantly stimulating to the mind; racy, spicy; fascinating, charming.

pique /piːk/ *noun* M16 French (literally, 'pike', figuratively, 'cutting remark', from *piquer* to prick, pierce, sting, irritate, *se piquer* take offence, from Proto-Romance, origin uncertain). **1** M16 A quarrel or feeling of enmity between two or more people; ill feeling, animosity. **2** L16 (A feeling of) anger or resentment resulting from a slight or injury, especially to one's pride; offence taken.
■ Also early (M17) in English use as verb.

piqué /ˈpiːkeɪ/ *noun, adjective, & verb* (also **pique** M19 French (use as noun of past participle of *piquer* to backstitch). **A** *noun* **1** M19 A stiff fabric woven in a strongly ribbed or raised pattern (originally in imitation of hand quilting); the raised pattern (characteristic) of such a fabric. **2** L19 Work inlaid with gold etc. dots. **3** M20 *Ballet* A step directly on to the point of the leading foot without bending the knee. **B** *adjective* **1** M19 *Cookery* Larded. *rare.* **2** L19 Made of piqué; having the pattern of piqué. **3** L19 Inlaid with gold etc. dots. **4** *Ballet* E20 Stepping directly on to the point of the leading foot without bending the knee. **C** *transitive verb* M19 *Cookery* Lard.

piquet /pɪˈkɛt/ *noun* (also **picquet**) M17 French (of unknown origin). A card-game for two players with a pack of 32 cards, the cards from the two to the six being excluded.

piqûre /pikyr/ *noun* (also **piqure**) plural pronounced same E20 French (from *piquer*; see PIQUE). A hypodermic injection; a puncture made in the skin by such an injection.

piranha /pɪˈrɑːnə/, /pɪˈrɑːnjə/ *noun* M18 Portuguese (from Tupi *piránʼe*, *piráya*, from *pirá* fish + *sainha* tooth). Any of several gregarious predatory freshwater fishes of South America, noted for their aggressiveness and voracity.

piri-piri /ˈpɪrɪpɪrɪ/ *noun* M20 Ronga (= pepper). A sauce made with red peppers. Also *piri-piri sauce.*

pirog /pɪˈrɒg/ *noun* plural **pirogi** /pɪˈrɒgi/, **pirogen** /pɪˈrɒgən/ M19 Russian. A large Russian pie. Cf. PIROSHKI.

pirogue /pɪˈrəʊg/ *noun* E17 French (probably from Carib). A long narrow canoe. Also, any canoe or open boat.

piroshki /pɪˈrɒʃki/ *noun plural* (also **pirotchki** /pɪˈrɒtʃki/, **pirozhki** /pɪˈrɒzki/) E20 Russian (*pirozhki* plural of *pirozhok* diminutive of PIROG). Small Russian pastries or patties filled with meat, fish, rice, etc.

pirouette /pɪrʊˈɛt/ *noun & verb* M17 French (ultimate origin unknown). **A** *noun* **1** M17 *Horsemanship* A full circle made by pivoting on a hind leg while walking or cantering. **2** E18 An act of spinning round on one foot or on the points of the toes by a ballet dancer etc.; *generally* a rapid whirl of the body. **3** L19 *Music* A form of mouthpiece used with a shawm, rackett, etc. **B** *intransitive verb* E19 Perform a pirouette.

pirozhki variant of PIROSHKI.

pis aller /pizale/ (*plural same*), /piːz ˈaleɪ/ *noun* L17 French (from *pis* worse + *aller* to go). The worst that can be or happen; a last resort.

piscina /pɪˈsiːnə/, /pɪˈsʌmə/ *noun* plural **piscinas, piscinae** /pɪˈsiːniː/ L16 Latin (= fish-pond, in medieval Latin in sense 2, from *piscis* fish). **1** L16 A fish-pond. Also (*historical*), a pool or pond for bathing or swimming. **2** L18 *Ecclesiastical* A stone basin for draining water used in the Mass.

pisé /pize/, /ˈpiːzeɪ/ *noun & adjective* (also **pisée**) L18 French (use as noun of past participle of *piser* to beat, pound, stamp (earth), from Latin *pinsere*). **A** *noun* L18 A building material of stiff clay or earth, sometimes mixed with gravel, forced between boards which are removed as it hardens; building with this material. Also *pisé de terre* /də tɛr/, /də tɛː/ (= of earth). Also called *terre pisée*. **B** *attributive* or as *adjective* M19 Made with or using *pisé*.

pissaladière /pisaladjɛr/ *noun* (also **pissaladiera** /pisaladjera/) M20 French (from Provençal *pissaladiero*, from *pissala* salt fish). A Provençal open tart similar to pizza, usually with onions, anchovies, and black olives.

pissoir /piswar/ (*plural same*), /piːˈswaː/, /ˈpɪswɑː/ *noun* E20 French. A public urinal, especially in France.

1996 *Bookseller* If I call this *pissoir* a great work of art and sign it, who are you to disprove that?

piste /piːst/ *noun* E18 French (= track, from Latin *pista* (sc. *via*) beaten track, from feminine past participle of *pinsere* to pound, stamp). **1** E18 A trail or track beaten by a horse or other animal; the track of a race-course or training ground. **2** E20 The specially marked-out rectangular playing area in fencing. **3** E20 A specially prepared or marked slope or trail of compacted snow used as a ski-run.

pistou /pistu/, /ˈpiːstuː/ *noun* M20 Provençal (= Italian PESTO). A sauce or paste made from crushed basil, garlic, cheese, etc., used especially in Provençal dishes; a thick vegetable soup made with this.

pita variant of PITTA.

pithos /ˈpɪθɒs/ *noun* plural **pithoi** /ˈpɪθɔɪ/ L19 Greek. *Archaeology* A large spherical wide-mouthed earthenware jar used for holding wine, oil, food, etc.

piton /ˈpiːtɒn/ *noun* L19 French (= eye-bolt). **1** L19 *Mountaineering* A metal spike which is hammered into rock or ice and used to

secure a rope through an eye at one end. **2** E20 A (steep-sided) volcanic peak, especially in the West Indies.

pitta /ˈpɪtə/ *noun* (also **pita**) M20 Modern Greek (*pētta*, *pit(t)a* bread, cake, pie; cf. Turkish *pide*, Aramaic *pittā* in similar sense). A flat unleavened bread of Mediterranean and Arab countries, which can be cut open to receive a filling.

più /pju:/ *adverb* E18 Italian. *Music* More.
■ Used in directions, as in *più mosso* more animated(ly).

pizza /ˈpiːtsə/ *noun* L19 Italian (= pie). A flat usually round base of dough baked with a topping of tomatoes, cheese, meat, olives, etc.

pizzeria /ˌpiːtsəˈriːə/ *noun* M20 Italian. A place where pizzas are made or sold.

pizzicato /ˌpɪtsɪˈkɑːtəʊ/ *noun, adjective, & adverb* M19 Italian (past participle of *pizzicare* to pinch, twitch, from *pizzare*, from Old and Modern Italian *pizza* point, edge). *Music* **A** *noun* plural **pizzicati** /ˌpɪtsɪˈkɑːti/, **pizzicatos**. M19 A note or passage played on a violin, cello, etc., by plucking a string with the finger instead of bowing. **B** *adjective & adverb* L19 (Played) by plucking a string instead of bowing.

placebo /pləˈsiːbəʊ/ *noun* plural **placebo(e)s** ME Latin (= I shall please or be acceptable (first word of Psalm 114:9), 1st person singular future indicative of *placere* to please). **1** ME *Roman Catholic Church* The vespers for the dead, from the initial word of the antiphon formerly used to open the office. **2** LME-L18 A flatterer, a sycophant. **3** L18 A pill, medicine, procedure, etc., prescribed more for the psychological benefit to the patient of being given a prescription than for any physiological effect. Also, a substance with no therapeutic effect used as a control in testing new drugs etc.; a blank sample in a test.

3 1996 *New Scientist* However, the day when the placebo effect becomes a respectable medical tool is still some way off.

place d'armes /plas darm/ *noun phrase* plural **places d'armes** (pronounced same) E18 French (= place of arms). An assembly point for troops, weapons, or ammunition; a parade ground; an arsenal.

placement /plasmã/ *noun* M19 French (from *placer* to place, seat (guests)). The allocation of places to people at a dining-table etc. Also *place à table*.

■ Also fully naturalized, with pronunciation /'pleɪsm(ə)nt/, in the sense of 'the action or an act of placing or positioning a thing or person', especially '(a period of) attachment to a workplace or educational establishment other than one's own'.

1962 J. Le Carré *Murder of Quality* If you . . . make a fault in the *placement* of your dinner guests . . . D'Arcy will find you out.

places d'armes plural of PLACE D'ARMES.

placet /'pleɪsɛt/, /'plakɛt/ *interjection & noun* L16 Latin (= it pleases, 3rd person singular present indicative of *placere* to please). A *interjection* L16 Expressing assent to a vote in a council or assembly of a university, Church, etc. B *noun* L16 Assent or sanction (as) by an utterance of '*placet*'.

plafond /plafɔ̃/ (*plural same*) *noun* M17 French (from *plat* flat + *fond* bottom). **1** M17 *Architecture* An ornately decorated ceiling, either flat or vaulted; painting or decoration on a ceiling. Also, a soffit. **2** M20 *Cards* An early form of contract bridge.

plage /plaʒ/, *in sense 4* /pleɪdʒ/ *noun* LME Old French (= region, (modern) beach (from Italian *piaggia*) from medieval Latin *plaga* open space). **1** LME–E17 A region, a district; a zone. **2** LME–M17 Each of the four principal directions or quarters of the compass; a direction, a side. **3** L19 A beach or promenade at a seaside resort, especially at a fashionable one; a seaside resort. **4** M20 *Astronomy* A bright region of the sun's chromosphere, usually associated with sunspots. Also *plage region*.

planche /plɑːnʃ/ *noun* E20 French (literally, 'plank'). *Gymnastics* A position in which the body is held parallel to the ground, especially by the arms (as on the parallel bars etc.).

planchette /plɑːnˈʃɛt/ *noun* M19 French (diminutive of *planche* plank, (wooden) board). **1** M19 A small usually heart-shaped board, supported by two castors and a vertical pencil, which, when one or more people rest their fingers lightly on the board, supposedly writes automatic messages under spirit guidance. **2** M20 A small shallow dish used to hold a sample while its radioactivity is measured.

planctus /'plaŋktəs/ *noun* plural same /'plaŋktuːs/ E20 Latin (= beating of the breast, lamentation). A medieval poem or song of lament.

plastique /plaˈstiːk/, *foreign* /plastik/ (*plural same*) *noun* L19 French (use as noun of adjective = plastic, from Latin *plasticus* from Greek *plastikos* from *plastos* past participle of *plassein* to mould, form). **1** L19 *Dance* Statuesque poses or slow graceful movements; the art or technique of performing these. **2** E20 A plastic substance used for modelling. **3** M20 Plastic explosive; a plastic bomb.

plastiqueur /plastikœr/, /'plastɪkə/ (*plural same*) *noun* M20 French (from as PLASTIQUE). A person who plants or detonates a plastic bomb.

plat /pla/ *noun* plural pronounced same M18 French. A dish of food.

plat du jour /pla dy ʒur/ *noun phrase* plural pronounced same E20 French (= dish of the day). A dish specially featured on a restaurant's menu for a particular day.

1996 *Spectator* Another *plat du jour* was breast of pheasant in a port wine sauce . . .

plateau /'platəʊ/ *noun & adjective* plural **plateaux** /'platəʊz/, **plateaus** L18 French (Old French *platel*, from *plat* wide, flat, from popular Latin, from Greek *platus* broad, flat). A *noun* **1** L18 *Physical Geography* An elevated tract of comparatively flat or level land; a tableland. **b** L19 *transferred* A more or less level portion of a graph or trace (originally of the pulse) adjacent to a lower sloping portion; a stage, condition, or period when there is neither an increase nor a decrease in something. **2** L18 An ornamented tray or dish for table-service. B E20 *attributive* or as *adjective* Of the nature of or pertaining to a plateau.

platteland /'platəland/ *noun* M20 Afrikaans (from Dutch *plat* flat + *land* country). The remote rural inland part of South Africa.

■ In South Africa often used attributively with derogatory connotations of backwardness and reaction, as in 'platteland mentality'.

platzel /'plats(ə)l/ *noun* M20 Yiddish (perhaps related to German *Plätzchen* fancy biscuit). A flat crisp bread roll.

playa /'plʌɪə/ *noun* M19 Spanish (= shore, beach, coast, from late Latin *plagia* open space). **1** M19 A flat area of silt or sand, free of vegetation and usually salty, lying at the bottom of a desert basin and dry except after rain; (more fully *playa lake*) a temporary lake formed in such an area. **2** M19 In Spain and Spanish-speaking countries: a beach. **3** L19 *Geography* Flat alluvial coastland.

■ Originally United States.

plaza /'plɑːzə/ *noun* L17 Spanish (from Proto-Romance source of *place*). A marketplace, square, or open public space, originally in Spain and Spanish-speaking countries; (chiefly *North America*) a large paved area surrounded by or adjacent to buildings, especially as a feature of a shopping complex.

plectrum /'plɛktrəm/ *noun* plural **plectrums, plectra** /'plɛktrə/ LME Latin (from Greek *plēktron* anything to strike with, from *plēssein* to strike). **1** LME Originally (*rare*), a device for tightening the strings of a harp. Now, a thin flat piece of horn, metal, plastic, etc., held in the hand and used to pluck the strings of a guitar, lyre, etc. Also, the corresponding mechanical part of a harpsichord etc. **2** E19 *Anatomy* and *Zoology* A small process, a single thick bristle.

plein-air /plɛnɛr/ *adjective* L19 French (from EN PLEIN AIR (literally, 'in full air')). Designating a style or school of impressionist painting originating in France during the late 1860s, which sought to represent the transient effects of atmosphere and light by direct observation from nature. Also, designating a work painted out of doors or representing an outdoor scene and painted with a spontaneous technique.

■ Also as a noun phrase *plein air*.
1995 *Spectator* . . . most of the Impressionist canvases on show smell of lamp-oil rather than *plein air*.

plein-airisme /plɛnɛrism/ *noun* M20 French (from as PLEIN-AIR). The theories and practices of the *plein-air* school of painters.

plein-airiste /plɛnɛrist/ *noun* L19 French (from as PLEIN-AIR). A painter of the *plein-air* school.

plein jeu /plɛ̃ ʒø/ *adverb, adjective, & noun phrase* M19 French (= full play). *Music* **A** *adverb & adjective phrase* M19 (A direction:) with full power; *specifically* without reeds in organ playing. **B** *noun* M19 A type of mixture stop in an organ; music written for the full organ.

plenum /'pliːnəm/ *noun & adjective* L17 Latin (neuter of *plenus* full (sc. *spatium* space); in sense 2 later influenced by Russian *plenum* plenary session). **A** *noun* **1** L17 *Physics* A space completely filled with

matter; *specifically* the whole of space regarded as being so filled. **b** L18 *transferred* A condition of fullness; a full place. **2** L18 A full assembly; a meeting of a legislative body, conference, association, etc., at which all the members are expected to be present; *specifically* a meeting of all the members of a Communist Party committee. **3** M20 (The air in) a plenum chamber in a ventilation system etc. **B** *attributive* or as *adjective* E20 Pertaining to or designating an artificial ventilation system in which fresh air is forced into a building and drives out the stale air.

pleroma /plə'rəʊmə/ *noun* M18 Greek (*plērōma* that which fills, from *plēroun* to make full, from *plērēs* full). *Theology* **1** M18 In Gnosticism, the spiritual universe as the abode of God and of the totality of the divine powers and emanations. **2** E19 The totality of the Godhead which dwells in Christ; completeness, fullness (with allusion to Colossians 2:9).

plethora /'plɛθ(ə)rə/ *noun* M16 Late Latin (from Greek *plēthōrē* fullness, repletion, from *plēthein* to be full). **1** M16 *Medicine* Originally a condition characterized by an excess of blood or a bodily humour; later, an excess of red blood cells. **2** E18 Overfullness, oversupply; a glut.

■ Sense 2 is now the only current sense, as sense 1, except in historical contexts, is rare or obsolete.
2 1996 *Times Magazine* . . . I read the plethora of faxes detailing where and whither I am to be sent . . .

plié /plije/ *noun* plural pronounced same L19 French (past participle of *plier* to bend). *Ballet* A movement in which the knees are bent outwards in line with the out-turned feet.

plique à jour /plik a ʒur/ *noun* L19 French (literally, 'braid that lets in the daylight'). A technique in enamelling in which small areas of translucent enamel are fused into the spaces of a wire framework to give an effect similar to stained glass.

plissé /'pliːseɪ/, *foreign* /plise/, (*plural of noun same*) *noun & adjective* L19 French (past participle of *plisser* to pleat). **A** *noun* L19 Originally, a piece of fabric shirred or gathered into narrow pleats; a gathering of pleats. Now usually, fabric with a wrinkled or puckered finish produced by chemical treatment. **B** *adjective* L19 Formed into small pleats; treated so as to give a wrinkled or puckered effect.

plombière /ˌplɒmbɪˈɛː/ noun M19 French (*Plombières*-les-Bains, a village in the Vosges department of eastern France). A kind of dessert made with ice-cream and glacé fruits.

plongeur /plɔ̃ʒœr/ noun plural pronounced same M20 French (from *plonger* to plunge, immerse in liquid). A person employed as a menial in a restaurant or hotel, especially to wash dishes.

■ The word entered English via George Orwell's account of menial labour in *Down and Out in Paris and London* (1933).

plumeau /plymo/ noun plural **plumeaux** /plymo/ L19 French (from *plume* from Latin *pluma* small soft feather). A duvet.

plus ça change /ply sa ʃɑ̃ʒ/ interjection & noun phrase E20 French (shortened form of *plus ça change, plus c'est la même chose*). The more things change, the more they remain the same.

■ The observation was originally made by the French author and satirical journalist Alphonse Karr (1808–90) writing in *Les Guêpes* (January 1849).
1995 *Times* Both have printed reams of photographs through the decades. The pictures are shockingly similar—a serious case of *plus ça change*.

Pluvius /ˈpluːvɪəs/ adjective E20 Latin (= rainy, causing or bringing rain). Designating the insurance of holidays, outdoor sports and events, etc., against disruption by bad weather.

■ Frequently in the phrase *Pluvius policy*.

p.m. abbreviation of POST MERIDIEM.

pneuma /ˈnjuːmə/ noun L19 Greek (= wind, breath, spirit, that which is blown or breathed, from *pneein, pnein* to blow, breathe). The spirit of a person, as opposed to the soul; the breath of life.

■ In Stoic and Epicurean philosophy the *pneuma* was a person's vital force or energy, but modern usage takes its cue from the New Testament distinction between the spirit and the soul or PSYCHE (cf. 1 Thessalonians 5.23).

poblador /ˌpɒblaˈdor/ noun plural **pobladores** /ˌpɒblaˈdores/ M20 Spanish. In Spanish America: a settler, a colonist; *specifically* a country person who moves to settle or squat in a town.

pochade /pɔʃad/ (plural same), /pɒˈʃaːd/ noun L19 French (from *pocher* to sketch (roughly), blur). A rough, smudgy, or blurred sketch.

poché /ˈpɒʃeɪ/, foreign /pɔʃe/ noun E20 French (use as noun of past participle of *pocher* to sketch). *Architecture* Shading on an architectural plan representing the solid parts of a building; the use of such shading.

pochette /pɒˈʃɛt/ noun L19 French. **1** L19 A small violin, as used by French dancing-masters. **2** E20 A small pocket. **3** E20 A handbag shaped like an envelope. Also *pochette bag*.

pochismo /pɒˈtʃizmo/ noun plural **pochismos** /pɒˈtʃizmos/ M20 Mexican Spanish (from as POCHO). A form of slang consisting of English words given a Mexican Spanish form or pronunciation; a word of this sort.

■ An example of a *pochismo* is *lonche* for 'lunch'.

pocho /ˈpɒtʃo/ noun & adjective plural of noun **pochos** /ˈpɒtʃos/ M20 Mexican Spanish (= Spanish *pocho* discoloured, pale, faded). (Designating or pertaining to) a citizen of the United States of Mexican origin or a culturally Americanized Mexican. Often *derogatory*.

pochoir /pɔʃwar/ noun plural pronounced same M20 French (= stencil). A process used in book illustration, especially for limited editions, in which a monochrome print is coloured by hand, using a series of stencils; a print made by this process.

pococurante /ˌpəʊkəʊkjʊˈranteɪ/ noun & adjective M18 Italian (from *poco* little + *curante* caring). **A** noun M18 A careless, indifferent, or nonchalant person. Now *rare*. **B** adjective E19 Caring little; careless, indifferent, nonchalant.

pocosin /pəˈkəʊsɪn/ noun (also **poquosin**) M17 Algonquian (probably from Algonquian *poquosin*). In the southern United States: a tract of low swampy ground, usually wooded; a marsh, a swamp.

podium /ˈpəʊdɪəm/ noun plural **podia** /ˈpəʊdɪə/, (in branch I also) **podiums** M18 Latin (= elevated place, balcony from Greek *podion* diminutive of *pous, podfoot*). **I 1** M18 A raised platform surrounding the arena in an ancient amphitheatre. **2** L18 *Architecture* **a** A continuous projecting base or pedestal, a stylobate. **b** M20 A projecting lower structure around the base of a tower block. **3** M20 A raised platform or dais at the front of a hall or stage; *specifically* one occupied by the conductor of an orchestra. **‖ 4** M19 Zoology A foot; an organ acting as a foot.

podzol /'pɒdzɒl/ noun (also **podsol** /'pɒdsɒl/) E20 Russian (from pod- under + zola ash; variant altered after -sol from Latin solum soil). Soil Science An acidic, generally infertile soil characterized by a white or grey subsurface layer resembling ash, and occurring especially under coniferous woods or heaths in moist, usually temperate climates.

poêlée /pwale/ noun M19 French (literally, 'panful', from poêler to cook in a pan). A broth or stock made with bacon and vegetables.

poète maudit /pɔɛt modi/ noun phrase plural **poètes maudits** (pronounced same) M20 French (literally, 'cursed poet'). A poet or other creative artist who is insufficiently appreciated by his or her contemporaries.

■ Les Poètes maudits (1884) was the title of a study of several such poets by the French Symbolist poet Paul Verlaine (1844–96).
1977 Time Once the ignored art, photography now stands robed in puffery, and . . . like painting, . . . has acquired its cast of heroes and poètes maudits.

poffertje /'pɒfərtjə/ noun (also **poffertjie** /'pɒfərtʃə/) L19 Dutch (poffertje, Afrikaans poffertjie, from French pouffer to blow up). A small light doughnut or fritter dusted with sugar, as made in the Low Countries and South Africa.

pogrom /'pɒgrəm/, /'pɒgrɒm/, /pə'grɒm/ noun & verb E20 Russian (= devastation, from gromit' to destroy by violent means). **A** noun **1** E20 An organized massacre in Russia, originally and especially of Jews. **2** E20 generally An organized, officially tolerated, attack on any community or group. **B** transitive verb E20 Massacre or destroy in a pogrom.

poi /pɔɪ/ noun E19 Polynesian (cf. POIPOI). A Hawaiian dish made from the fermented root of the taro. Also = POIPOI.

poilu /'pwɑːluː/, foreign /pwaly/ (plural same) noun E20 French (= hairy, virile, from Latin pilus hair). A soldier in the French army. especially one who fought in the war of 1914–18.

■ Slang, alluding to the unkempt appearance.

point /pwɛ̃/ noun plural pronounced same M17 French (= stitch). Needle-lace.)

■ Chiefly in point de (or d') /d(ə)/ (of), specifying a real or supposed place of manufac-

ture, as point d'Alençon, point d'Angleterre, point de France, point de Paris, point de Venise, etc. Cf. PETIT POINT.

point d'appui /pwɛ̃ dapɥi/ noun phrase E19 French (= point of support). A fulcrum; a strategic point.

point de départ /pwɛ̃ də depar/ noun phrase E20 French. A point of departure.

point de repère /pwɛ̃ də rəper/ noun phrase L19 French. A point of reference.

point d'orgue /pwɛ̃ dɔrg/ noun phrase L19 French. An organ-point, a pedal-point.

pointe /pwɛ̃t/ noun plural pronounced same M19 French. Dancing The tip of the toe. Also, a dance movement executed on the tips of the toes.

pointillé /pwɛ̃tije/ adjective E20 French (past participle of pointiller to mark with dots). Ornamented with designs engraved or drawn with a sharp-pointed tool or style.

pointillisme /pwɛ̃tijism/ noun (also **pointillism** /'pwantɪlɪz(ə)m/) E20 French (pointillisme, from pointiller to mark with dots, from pointille from Italian puntiglio diminutive of punto point). **1** E20 A technique of impressionist painting in which luminous effects are produced by tiny dots of various pure colours, which become blended in the viewer's eye. **2** M20 Music The breaking up of musical texture into thematic, rhythmic, and tonal fragments.

poipoi /'pɔɪpɔɪ/ noun E19 Polynesian (reduplication of POI). A Polynesian dish made from fermented fruit, especially breadfruit.

poivrade /pwavrad/ noun L17 French (from poivre pepper). Pepper sauce.

polder /'pəʊldə/ noun E17 Dutch (from Middle Dutch polre). A piece of low-lying land reclaimed from the sea, a lake, etc., and protected by dykes, originally and especially in the Netherlands.

polenta /pə(ʊ)'lɛntə/, foreign /po'lenta/ noun OE Latin (in later use directly from Italian from Latin = pearl barley). Originally, pearl barley, (porridge made from) barley meal. Later, maize flour as used in Italian cookery; a paste or dough made from this boiled and then often fried or baked.

policier /pɔlisje/ noun plural pronounced same L20 French (literally, 'detective

polis | pomme

novel'). A film based on a police novel. Cf.
ROMAN POLICIER.

1977 *Time* Not so in *Man on the Roof*, the
Swedish-made *policier* based on one of the
Martin Beck novels.

polis /'pɒlɪs/ *noun* plural **poleis** /'pɒleɪs/
L19 Greek (= city). *History* A city-State, especially in ancient Greece; *specifically* such
a State considered in its ideal form.

1996 *Spectator* We are also political in that
nearly everything that happens is looked at for
the effect it is likely to have on the *polis*—or
what politics graduates call 'the political
process'.

polisson /pɔlisɔ̃/ *noun* plural pronounced
same M19 French. An urchin, a scamp; an
ill-bred and uncouth person.

Politbureau /'pɒlɪtˌbjʊərəʊ/ *noun* (also
politburo, plural **politburos**) E20 Russian
(*politbyuro*, from *polit(icheskii* political +
byuro bureau). The highest policy-making
committee of a Communist country or
party, especially of the former USSR. Also
transferred and *figurative*.

politesse /pɔlitɛs/ *noun* E18 French (from
Italian *politezza*, *pulitezza*, from *pulito*
from Latin *politus* past participle of *polire*
to smooth, polish). Formal politeness.

politique /pɔlitik/ *noun* plural pronounced same E17 French (use as noun of
adjective = political). 1 *History* E17 A
member or supporter of a French oppor-
tunist and moderate party, founded in
c.1573, which regarded peace and reform
as more important than the continuing
civil war between Catholics and Hugue-
nots. Also, an indifferentist, a temporizer.
2 M20 A political concept or doctrine; an
expression of political ideas.

polka /'pəʊlkə/ *noun & verb* M19 German
(French from Czech, perhaps related to
Polka feminine of *Polák* a Pole). A *noun*
1 M19 A lively dance of Bohemian origin
in duple time. 2 M19 A piece of music for
this dance or in its rhythm. 3 M19 A
woman's tight-fitting jacket, usually knitted. Now *rare*. B *intransitive verb* M19
Dance the polka.

■ The nineteenth-century craze for the
polka led to the word's being attached a variety of commercial articles; hence *polka
dot* for a pattern of dots of uniform size and
distribution.

pollo /'pɒləʊ/ *noun* plural **pollos** M19 Spanish (Italian = chicken). *Cookery* Chicken, a
chicken dish, *especially* one cooked in an
Italian or (Mexican-)Spanish fashion.

polloi /pɒ'lɔɪ/ *noun* M20 Greek (= many). A
crowd, a mob.

■ Slang, shortened from HOI POLLOI.

polonaise /pɒlə'neɪz/ *noun, adjective, &
verb* M18 French (use as noun of feminine
of *polonais* Polish, from medieval Latin *Po-
lonia* Poland). A *noun* 1 M18 A slow
dance of Polish origin, consisting chiefly
of an intricate march or procession, in
triple time; a piece of music for this
dance or in its time or rhythm. 2 L18 A
kind of dress or overdress, with the skirt
open at the front and looped up at the
back, originally resembling a garment
worn by Polish women. b L19 A fabric
made from a silk and cotton mixture.
3 L19 *Cookery* A dish cooked in a Polish
style. 4 M20 A polonaise rug or carpet.
B *adjective* 1 E20 Designating a kind of
rug or carpet made in Persia during the
sixteenth and seventeenth centuries,
using silver and gold warp threads.
2 *Cookery* M20 Of a dish: cooked in a Polish
style. C *intransitive verb* E19 Dance a polonaise; move in a stately manner.

polska /'pɒlskə/ *noun* L19 Swedish (from
Polsk Polish). A processional Scandinavian
folk-dance of Polish origin, usually in 3/4
time; a piece of music for this dance.

poltergeist /'pɒltəɡaɪst/ *noun* M19 German (from *poltern* to make a noise, create
a disturbance + *Geist* ghost). A spirit believed to manifest itself by making noises
and moving physical objects.

polynya /pəʊ'lɪmjə/ *noun* (also **polynia**)
M19 Russian (from base of *pole*, *polyana*
field). A space of open water in the midst
of ice, especially in Arctic seas.

pomade /pə'meɪd/, /pə'mɑːd/ *noun & verb*
M16 French (*pommade* from Italian *pomata*
from modern Latin POMATUM). A *noun*
M16 A scented ointment (in which apples
were perhaps originally an ingredient)
for the skin, now especially for the skin of
the head and for the hair. B *transitive
verb* L19 Anoint with pomade. Chiefly as
pomaded participial adjective.

pomatum /pə(ʊ)'meɪtəm/ *noun & verb* M16
Modern Latin (from Latin *pomum* apple).
A *noun* M16 Hair ointment, pomade.
B *transitive verb* M17 Anoint with poma-
tum. Chiefly as *pomatumed* participial
adjective.

pomme /pɔm/ *noun* plural pronounced
same E20 French (short for POMME DE
TERRE). *Cookery* A potato.

■ Chiefly plural and in phrases designating ways of cooking potatoes, as in *pommes allumettes* (matchstick-thin potato chips) and *pommes frites* (fried potato chips).

pomme de terre /pɒm də tɛr/ *noun* plural **pommes de terre** (pronounced same) E19 French (literally, 'apple of the earth'). *Cookery* A potato.

pompadour /'pɒmpədʊə/ *noun & adjective* M18 French (Jeanne-Antoinette Poisson, Marquise de *Pompadour* (1721–64), mistress of Louis XV of France). **A** *noun* **1** M18 Any of various items of costume fashionable in the time of the Marquise de Pompadour or resembling these. **2** M18 A shade of crimson or pink; a fabric of this colour. **3** M18 A South American cotinga with brilliant crimson-purple plumage. Also *pompadour cotinga*. **4a** L19 A style of dressing men's hair, in which it is combed back from the forehead without a parting. *United States*. **b** L19 A style of arranging women's hair, in which it is turned back off the forehead in a roll, sometimes over a pad. **B** *attributive* or as *adjective* M18 (Of dress, furniture, etc.) in the style prevalent in the time of the Marquise de Pompadour; *specifically* (*a*) of a crimson colour or fabric; (*b*) patterned with sprigs of (usually pink and blue) flowers on a white ground; (*c*) (of hair) arranged in a pompadour.

pompier /pɔ̃pje/ (*plural same*), /'pɒmpɪə/ *noun* M19 French (from *pompe* pump). **1** M19 In France, a fireman. **2** E20 An artist regarded as painting in an academic, imitative, vulgarly neoclassical style.

■ The designation of late nineteenth-century French academic artists as *pompiers* is probably based on their fondness for showing the Greek and Roman heroes in their pictures wearing helmets that put the viewer in mind of the helmets worn by Parisian firefighters.

pompon /'pɒmpɒn/, *foreign* /pɔ̃pɔ̃/ (*plural same*) *noun* (also (in senses 2 and 3) **pompom** /'pɒmpɒm/, (in sense 1) **pompoon**) M18 French (of unknown origin). **1** M18 A bunch of ribbon, feathers, flowers, silk threads, etc., formerly worn by women in the hair, or on the cap or dress. *obsolete except historical*. **2** M19 A variety of chrysanthemum, dahlia, or cabbage rose, bearing small globular flowers. **3** L19 An ornamental ball of wool, silk, ribbons, etc., on a woman's hat, a slipper, etc.; the round tuft on a sailor's cap, on the front of a shako, etc.

pomposo /pɒm'pəʊzəʊ/ *adverb & noun* E19 Italian (from Latin *pomposus* from *pompa* solemn procession, from Greek *pompē* from *pempein* to send). **A** *adverb* E19 *Music* A direction:) in a stately manner. **B** *noun* **1** M20 An affected, self-important person. **2** M20 *Music* A stately movement or passage.

poncho /'pɒntʃəʊ/ *noun* plural **ponchos** E18 South American Spanish (from Araucanian). A South American cloak made of a piece of cloth like a blanket with a slit in the middle for the head; any garment in this style.

poncif /pɔ̃sif/ *noun* E20 French (literally, 'pounced design'). Stereotyped literary ideas, plot, character, etc.

pondok /'pɒndɒk/ *noun* (also **pondokkie** /pɒn'dɒki/) E19 Afrikaans (probably from Malay, ultimately from Arabic *funduq* hotel). A shack or shanty made of oddments of wood, corrugated iron, etc.; *transferred* a house etc. in a poor state of repair. *South African*.

pons asinorum /ˌpɒnz asɪ'nɔːrəm/ *noun phrase* M18 Latin (= bridge of asses). The fifth proposition of the first book of Euclid, so called from the difficulty which beginners find in 'getting over' it.

ponticello /ˌpɒntɪ'tʃɛləʊ/ *noun, adverb, & adjective* M18 Italian (= little bridge). *Music* **A** *noun* plural **ponticellos**. M18 The bridge of a stringed instrument. **B** *adverb & adjective* M19 (A direction:) with the bowing close to the bridge.

pontifex /'pɒntɪfɛks/ *noun* (also **Pontifex**) plural **pontifices** /pɒn'tɪfɪsiːz/ L16 Latin (from *pons, pontis* bridge + *-fex* from *facere* to make). **1** L16 *Roman History* A member of the principal college of priests in ancient Rome. **2** M17 The Pope.

pontificalia /ˌpɒntɪfɪ'keɪlɪə/, /ˌpɒntɪfɪ'kaːlɪə/ *noun* plural L16 Latin (use as noun of neuter plural of *pontificalis* pontifical). The vestments and insignia of a bishop, cardinal, or abbot; pontificals.

pontil /'pɒntɪl/ *noun* M19 French (apparently from Italian *pontello, puntello* diminutive of *punto* point). *Glass-making* An iron rod used to hold or shape soft glass (also *pontil rod*). Also called *punty*.

pooja variant of PUJA.

poort /pʊət/ *noun* L18 Dutch (*poort* gate, port). In South Africa: a narrow mountain pass, *especially* one cut by a stream or river.

popadam variant of POPPADAM.

popote /pɔpɔt/ *noun* plural pronounced same E20 French. A French military kitchen or canteen.

poppadam /'pɒpədəm/ *noun* (also **popadam, poppadom**, and other variants) E19 Tamil (*pappaṭam*, perhaps from *paruppa aṭam* lentil cake). A (flat cake of) thin crisp spiced bread usually eaten with curry or other Indian food.

poquosin variant of POCOSIN.

port-a-beul /ˌpɔːʃtə'biːəl/ *noun* (also **puirt-a-beul** /ˌpʊəʃtə'biːəl/) plural **puirt-a-beul** E20 Gaelic (literally, 'music from mouth'). A quick lively tune of Lowland Scottish origin to which Gaelic words of a quick repetitive nature have been added.

portail /'pɔːteɪl/ *noun* L15 French (literally, 'façade of a church', alteration of Old French *portal* from medieval Latin *portale*). A door or gateway.

■ Confused with *portal* in both French and English.

portamento /pɔːtə'mɛntəʊ/ *noun* plural **portamenti** /pɔːtə'mɛnti/ L18 Italian (literally, 'a carrying'). *Music* Gliding or moving from one note to another without a break in singing or in playing a trombone or a bowed stringed instrument, as a violin. Also, piano-playing of a style between legato and staccato.

port-crayon /pɔː't'kreɪən/ *noun* (also **porte-crayon** /pɔːt(ə)krɛjɔ̃/ (*plural same*)) E18 French (*porte-crayon*, from *porte-* stem of *porter* to carry + *crayon* crayon). An instrument used to hold a crayon for drawing, usually a metal tube split at the end with a sliding ring so as to secure the crayon.

port de bras /pɔr də bra/ *noun phrase* plural **ports de bras** (pronounced same) E20 French (literally, 'carriage of the arms'). *Ballet* The action or manner of moving and posing the arms; any of a series of exercises designed to develop graceful movement and disposition of the arms.

port de voix /pɔr də vwa/ *noun* plural **ports de voix** (pronounced same) M18 French (literally, 'carrying of the voice'). *Music* Originally, a kind of APPOGGIATURA. Now, a vocal PORTAMENTO.

porte-bouquet /'pɔːtbʊkeɪ, /'pɔːtbəʊkeɪ/ *noun* M19 French (from *porte-* stem of *porter* to carry + *bouquet* bouquet). A device for holding a bouquet.

porte-cochère /ˌpɔːtkəʊ'ʃɛ:/, *foreign* /pɔrtkɔʃɛr/ (*plural same*) *noun* (originally **port-cocher**; also **porte cochère**) L17 French (from *porte* port + *cochère* feminine adjective from *coche* coach). **1** L17 A gateway for carriages, leading into a courtyard. **2** L19 A covered area at the entrance to a building into which vehicles can be driven. Chiefly *United States*.

2 1996 *Times Magazine* ... the view from the west corner is lost, as is something of the drama and excitement of being dropped off under the glittering lights of the porte cochère.

porte-crayon variant of PORT-CRAYON.

portée /'pɔːteɪ/, *foreign* /pɔrte/ (*plural same*) *noun* (also **portee** /'pɔːtiː/) L19 French (from *porter* to carry, from Latin *portare*). **1** L19 The importance or weight of a theory, an argument, etc.; the (far-reaching) consequences of an action or event. **2** E20 In handloom weaving, a specified number of threads grouped together to form the warp. **3** M20 *Military* A self-propelled vehicle on which an anti-tank gun can be mounted.

porte-monnaie /'pɔːtmʊneɪ/ *noun* M19 French (from *porte-* stem of *porter* to carry + *monnaie* money). A flat purse or pocketbook, especially of leather.

porteur /pɔrtœr/ *noun* plural pronounced same M20 French (literally, 'a person who carries'). *Ballet* A male dancer whose role is (only) to lift and support a ballerina when she performs leaping or jumping movements.

portico /'pɔːtɪkəʊ/ *noun* plural **portico(e)s** E17 Italian (from Latin *porticus* porch). *Architecture* A formal entrance to a classical temple, church, or other building, consisting of columns at regular intervals supporting a roof often in the form of a pediment; a covered walkway in this style; a colonnade.

portière /pɔrtjɛr/ *noun* plural pronounced same M19 French (from *porte* door). A curtain hung over a door or doorway, as a screen or for ornament, or to prevent draughts.

portmanteau /pɔː't'mantəʊ/ *noun & adjective* M16 French (*portemanteau* from *porte-* stem of *porter* to carry + *manteau* mantle). **A** *noun* plural **portmanteaus, portmanteaux** /pɔː't'mantəʊz/ **1** M16 A case or bag for carrying clothing etc. when travelling, *especially* one made of stiff leather and hinged at the back so as to open into two equal parts. **2** E18 A rack or arrangement of pegs for hanging clothes on. Now *rare.* **B** *attributive* or as *adjective* L19 Of a word, expression, etc.: consisting of a blend, both in spelling and meaning, of two other words. Of a description, expression, etc.: of general or widespread application.

portrait parlé /pɔrtrɛ parle/ *noun phrase* plural **portraits parlés** (pronounced same) E20 French (= spoken portrait). A detailed chiefly anthropometric description of a person's physical characteristics, especially of the type invented by Bertillon and used in the identification of criminals.

ports de bras, ports de voix plurals of PORT DE BRAS, PORT DE VOIX.

posada /pəˈsɑːdə/, *foreign* /poˈsada/ *noun* M18 **Spanish** (from *posar* to lodge). **1** M18 In Spain and Spanish-speaking countries: an inn or place of accommodation for travellers. **2** M20 In Mexico: each of a series of visits traditionally paid to different friends before Christmas, representing Mary's and Joseph's search for a lodging in Bethlehem.

posaune /pəˈzaʊnə/ *noun* plural **posaunen** /pəˈzaʊnən/, **posaunes** /pəˈzaʊnɪz/ E18 **German** (ultimately from Old French *buisine* from Latin *buccina* trumpet). *Music* **1** E18 A trombone. **2** M19 An organ reed-stop resembling a trombone in tone.

posé /ˈpəʊzeɪ/, *foreign* /poze/ (*plural same*) *adjective & noun* E18 **French** (past participle of *poser* to place, pose). **A** *adjective* **1** E18 *Heraldry* Of an animal: standing still. **2** M19 Composed, poised, self-possessed. **3** M20 *Ballet* Of a position: held, prolonged. **4** M20 Adopted as a pose. *rare.* **B** *noun* **1** E20 *Ballet* A movement in which a dancer steps with a straight leg on to the full or half point. **2** M20 *North American History* A resting-place on a portage.

pose plastique /poz plastik/ *noun phrase* plural **poses plastiques** (pronounced same) M19 **French** (literally, 'flexible pose'). A type of *tableau vivant*, usually one featuring near-naked women.
    1969 V. G. Kiernan *Lords of Human Kind* There was a vogue of *poses plastiques*, and tableaux such as 'The Sultan's favourite returning from the bath' were popular.

poseur /pəʊˈzə:/ *noun* (feminine **poseuse** /pəʊˈzə:z/) L19 **French** (from *poser* to pose). A person who poses for effect or attitudinizes; one who adopts an affected style or demeanour.
    1996 *Times* His full, florid voice, face, wig and cravat all seem designed to evoke Wilde

himself; but, as it turns out, less Wilde the poseur and paradoxist than Wilde the enemy of the rigid and frigid.

post-bellum /pəʊs(t)ˈbɛləm/ *adjective* (also **Post-bellum, post-Bellum**) L19 Latin (from *post* after + *bellum* war). Existing, occurring, etc., after a (particular) war, especially (*United States*) the American Civil War. Opposed to ANTE-BELLUM.
    1996 *Spectator* . . . it was for the rural post-Bellum Virginia of her birth and her innate American roots she . . . yearned.

post coitum /pəʊs(t) ˈkəʊɪtəm/ *adjective, adverb & noun phrase* E20 **Latin** (from *post* after + *coitum* accusative of COITUS). (Condition) following sexual intercourse; post-coital(ly) (state).
    ■ Used especially with reference to the saying *post coitum omne animal triste est* 'after sexual intercourse every animal is sad'. The saying itself is not known from classical Latin, although the idea can be traced back to passages in Aristotle and Pliny.
    transferred **1975** M. Bradbury *History Man* He is in that flat state of literary post coitum that affects those who spend too much time with their own lonely structures and plots.

poste restante /pəʊst ˈrɛstɒt/, *foreign* /pɔst rɛstɑ̃t/ *adverb & noun phrase* M18 **French** (= letter(s) remaining). **1** *adverb & noun phrase* M18 (A direction written on a letter indicating that it is) to remain at the post office specified until called for by the addressee. **2** *noun* M19 The department in a post office where such letters are kept.

post eventum /pəʊst ɪˈvɛntəm/ *adverb phrase* M19 **Latin** (= after the event). POST FACTUM.

post factum /pəʊs(t) ˈfaktəm/ *adverb phrase* L17 **Latin** (= after the fact). After the event; with hindsight.

post festum /pəʊs(t) ˈfɛstəm/ *adverb phrase* L19 **Latin** (= after the festival). After the event.

post hoc /pəʊst ˈhɒk/ *adverb & adjective phrase* M19 **Latin**. After this; after the event; consequent(ly).
    ■ Chiefly with reference to the fallacy *post hoc, ergo propter hoc* 'after this, therefore because of this'.

postiche /pɒˈstiːʃ/ *adjective & noun* (as adjective also (earlier) **postique**) E18 **French** (from Italian *posticcio* counterfeit, feigned). **A** *adjective* E18 Artificial; (of a decoration in architecture etc.) added to a finished work, especially inappropriately or superfluously. *rare*. **B** *noun* **1** L19 An imitation substituted for the real thing; *especially* a piece of false hair worn as an adornment. **2** L19 Imitation, pretence. *rare*.

post meridiem /pəʊs(t) məˈrɪdɪəm/ *adjective & adverb phrase* M17 Latin. After midday; between noon and midnight.
■ Abbreviated to *p.m.*

post-mortem /pəʊs(t)ˈmɔːtəm/ *adverb, adjective, noun, & verb* (also especially as adverb) **post mortem**) M18 Latin. **A** *adverb* M18 After death. **B** *adjective* M18 Taking place, formed, or done after death or (*colloquial*) after the conclusion of a matter (cf. sense C.2 below). **C** *noun* **1** M19 An examination of a body performed after death especially in order to determine the cause of death; an autopsy. **2** E20 An analysis or discussion conducted after the conclusion of a game, examination, or other event. *colloquial*. **D** *transitive verb* L19 Conduct a post-mortem examination of.

post-partum /pəʊs(t)ˈpɑːtəm/ *adjective & adverb* M19 Latin (*post partum* after childbirth). *Medicine* (Occurring, existing, etc.) after childbirth; postnatal(ly).

post rem /pəʊst ˈrɛm/ *adjective & adverb phrase* E20 Medieval Latin (= after the thing). *Philosophy* Subsequent to the existence of something else; (of a universal) existing only as a mental concept or as an abstract word after the fact of being experienced from particulars. Cf. ANTE REM, IN RE.

postscriptum /pəʊs(t)ˈskrɪptəm/ *noun* plural **postscripta** /pəʊs(t)ˈskrɪptə/ E16 Latin (use as noun of neuter past participle of *postscribere* to write after, from *post* after + *scribere* to write). Additional matter appended to any text, a postscript.

potage /pɒtaʒ/ (*plural same*), /pɒˈtɑːʒ/ *noun* ME Old and Modern French (literally, 'what is put in a pot', from *pot* pot). (A) soup, *especially* (a) thick (vegetable) soup.
■ Originally from Old French, the word was Anglicized in the form *pottage*; it was later reintroduced from French first in Scotland and later (M17) in England with reference to dishes of French provenance.

potager /ˈpɒtədʒə/, *foreign* /pɒtaʒe/ (*plural same*) (also **potagère**) *noun* M17 French (in

(*jardin*) *potager* (garden) for the kitchen). A kitchen garden.
■ The original sense of *potager* as 'one who makes pot(t)ages' is long obsolete. The seventeenth-century garden writer John Evelyn introduced the word with its present sense in the form *potagere*.
1996 *Country Life* Chinese chives . . . are worthy of a prominent place in a perennial border or potager.

pot-au-feu /pɔtofø/ *noun* plural **pot-au-feux** /pɔtofø/ L18 French (literally, 'pot on the fire'). A large cooking pot of a kind common in France; the (traditional) soup cooked in this.

pot de chambre /po də ʃɑ̃br/ *noun phrase* plural **pots de chambre** (pronounced same) L18 French. A chamber-pot.
1995 *Spectator* [He] mainly reviews films made by Americans, who luckily do not refer to *pots de chambre* as 'chambers', 'jerries', 'goesunders' or—when placed on dreaming spires—'articles'.

pot-et-fleur /pɔteflœr/ (*plural same*), /ˌpɒteɪˈflə:/ *noun* M20 French (literally, 'pot and flower'). A style of floral decoration using pot plants together with cut flowers.

potiche /pɒtiʃ/ *noun* plural pronounced same L19 French. A large (especially Chinese) porcelain jar or vase with a rounded bulging shape and a wide mouth, frequently having a lid.

pot-pourri /pəʊˈpʊəri/, /pəʊˈpʊəriː/, /pɒt ˈpʊəri/ *noun* (also **potpourri**) E17 French (literally, 'rotten pot', from *pot* pot + *pourri* past participle of *pourrir* to rot (translating Spanish OLLA PODRIDA). **1** E17-E18 A stew made of different kinds of meat. **2** M18 Dried flower petals, leaves, etc., mixed with spices and kept in a jar or bowl to scent the air. Also, a container for holding this. **3** M19 *figurative* A medley, *especially* a musical or literary one.

potrero /pɒˈtrɛːrəʊ/ *noun* plural **potreros** M19 Spanish (from as next). **1** M19 In South America and the south-western United States, a paddock or pasture for horses or cattle. **2** L19 In the south-western United States, a narrow steep-sided plateau.

potro /ˈpɒtrəʊ/ *noun* plural **potros** L19 Spanish. A colt, a pony. *United States*.

pots de chambre plural of POT DE CHAMBRE.

poudre /'puːdrə/ *noun* L18 French (= powder, earlier *pol(d)re* from Latin *pulvis, pulver-* dust). Light powdery snow. *Canadian*.

poudré /pudre/, /puːˈdreɪ/ *adjective* (feminine **poudrée**) E19 French (past participial adjective of *poudrer* to powder). Of the hair, a wig, etc.: powdered.

poudreuse /pudrøz/ *noun* plural pronounced same E20 French (from as POUDRE). A lady's dressing table of a kind made in France in the time of Louis XV.

pouf /puːf/ *noun* (in sense 3 usually **pouffe**) E19 French (ultimately imitative). **1** E19 An elaborate female head-dress fashionable in the late eighteenth century; (*History*) a high roll or pad of hair worn by women. **2** M19 *Dressmaking* A part of a dress gathered up to form a soft projecting mass of material. **3** L19 A large firm cushion with a stable base, used as a low seat or footstool. Also, a soft stuffed ottoman or couch.

poule /pul/ *noun* plural pronounced same E20 French (literally, 'hen'). A young woman, *especially* a promiscuous one. *slang*.
1955 D. Barton *Glorious Life* 'If I had thought she would have understood,' said Swindlehurst, 'I would have called her to her face "the typing *poule*".'

poule au pot /pul o po/ *noun phrase* plural **poules au pot** (pronounced same) L19 French. A boiled chicken.

poule de luxe /pul də lyks/ *noun phrase* plural **poules de luxe** (pronounced same) M20 French (= 'poule' of luxury). A prostitute.
1976 *Times Literary Supplement* . . . his wife has remarried and . . . his daughter is in business as a *poule de luxe* and doing very well.

poulet /pulɛ/ (*plural same*), /'puːleɪ/ *noun* M19 French. **1** M19 A chicken; a chicken dish. **2** M19 A (neatly-folded) billet-doux.
■ In sense 1 especially with reference to French cooking, usually with a qualifying adjective, as in *poulet Provençal* (Provençal chicken), *poulet rôti* (roast chicken), etc.

poulette /'puːlɛt/ *noun* E19 French. *Cookery* A (French) sauce made with butter, cream, and egg-yolks. More fully *poulette sauce*.

poult-de-soie /puːdə'swɑː/ *noun & adjective* M19 French (alteration of *pou-de-soie* of unknown origin). (Made of) a fine corded silk or taffeta, usually coloured.

poupée /pupe/ *noun* plural pronounced same L18 French (= doll, puppet, wax figure). A figure used in making and displaying dresses, wigs, and other items of dress.

pourboire /purbwar/ *noun* plural pronounced same E19 French (literally, 'for drinking'). A gratuity, a tip.

pour encourager les autres /pur ãkuraʒe lez otr/ *adverb phrase* E19 French (literally, 'to encourage the others'). As an example to others; to encourage others.
■ The source is a witticism of Voltaire's in *Candide* (1759) concerning the execution in 1757 of Admiral John Byng for failing to relieve Minorca when the island came under attack by the French in 1756: *Dans ce pays-ci il est bon de tuer de temps en temps un amiral pour encourager les autres* (In this country [sc. England] it is thought a good idea to kill an admiral from time to time to encourage the others).
1995 *Spectator* The only thing that could be said in its [sc. the hospital's] favour was that it was better than Addenbrookes [Hospital], in Cambridge, with its giant crematorium chimney next to the entrance, *pour encourager les autres*, I suppose.

pour le sport /pur lə spɔr/ *adverb phrase* E20 French. For fun, amusement, or sport.
1973 L. Meynell *Thirteen Trumpeters* Lucian had automatically made tentative exploratory investigations as to her readiness *pour le sport* and bedworthiness.

pourparler /purparle/ *noun* plural pronounced same E18 French (use as noun of Old French *po(u)rparler* discuss, from *po(u)r-* pro- + *parler* to speak). An informal discussion or conference preliminary to actual negotiation.

pour passer le temps /pur pase lə tã/ *adverb phrase* L17 French. To pass the time; to amuse oneself.
1976 M. Birmingham *Heat of the Sun* Cynthia asked if she could go too: 'Pour passer le temps,' she said . . . 'I love riding in cars at night.'

pour rire /pur rir/ *adjective & adverb phrase* L19 French (literally, 'in order to laugh'). (In a manner) that causes amusement or suggests jocular pretence; not serious(ly).
1980 *Country Life* The jokes about such jargon . . . have long ceased to be *pour rire*.

pourriture noble /purityr nɔbl/ *noun phrase* E20 French (= noble rot). A common

grey mould, *Botrytis cinerea*, as deliberately cultivated on grapes to perfect certain French and German wines and
Tokay; the condition of being affected by
this mould; noble rot.

pour-soi /purswa/ *noun* M20 French (literally, 'for itself, for oneself'). *Philosophy* In
the thought of J.-P. Sartre, the spontaneous free being of consciousness; being for
itself.

■ Contrasted with *en-soi* ((being) in itself) in
Sartre's *L'Être et le néant* (1943).

pousada /pəʊˈsɑːdə/ *noun* M20 Portuguese
(literally, 'resting-place', from *pausar* to
rest). An inn or hotel in Portugal, *especially*
one of a chain of hotels administered by
the State.

pousse-café /puskafe/ *noun* plural pronounced same L19 French (literally, 'push
coffee'). A glass of various liqueurs or cor-
dials poured in successive layers, taken
immediately after coffee.

poussin /ˈpuːsã̃/, *foreign* /pusɛ̃/ (*plural
same*) *noun* M20 French. A young chicken
for eating.

■ Earlier in PETIT POUSSIN.

pou sto /paʊ ˈstəʊ/, /puː ˈstɔː/ *noun* M19
Greek (*pou stō* where I may stand). A place
to stand on, a standing-place; *figuratively* a
basis of operation.

■ *Dos moi pou stō kai kinō tēn gēn* (Give me a
place where I may stand and I will move
the earth), a saying attributed to the ancient Greek sage Archimedes (died *c*.212
BC).

powwow /ˈpaʊwaʊ/ *noun & verb* (also
pow-wow) E17 Narragansett (*powah, pow-
waw* shaman). A *noun* **1** E17 A North American Indian priest, sorcerer, or
medicine man, a shaman. **b** M19 The art
of a powwow, especialiy as used in healing. **2** E17 A North American Indian ceremony, *especially* one involving magic,
feasting, and dancing. Also, a council or
conference of or with Indians. **3** E19
transferred Any meeting for discussion; a
conference, congress, or consultation, especially among friends or colleagues.
Also, noisy bustle or activity. Originally
United States. **B** *verb* **1** *intransitive verb*
M17 Of North American Indians: practise
powwow; hold a powwow. **2** *transitive
verb* E18 Treat with powwow. **3** *intransitive
verb* L18 *transferred* Confer, discuss, deliberate. Chiefly *North American*.

praecognitum /priːˈkɒɡnɪtəm/ *noun* plural **praecognita** /priːˈkɒɡnɪtə/ E17 Latin
(neuter past participle of *praecognoscere* to
know beforehand). A thing known beforehand; *especially* a thing needed or assumed to be known in order to infer or
ascertain something else. Usually in *plural*.

praenomen /priːˈnəʊmɛn/ *noun* E17 Latin
(= forename, from *prae* pre- + *nomen*
name). An ancient Roman's first or personal name preceding the nomen and
cognomen (as *Marcus* Tullius Cicero); *generally* a first name, a forename.

Praesidium variant of PRESIDIUM.

praetorium /priːˈtɔːrɪəm/ *noun* (also **pretorium**) plural **praetoria** /priːˈtɔːrɪə/ E17
Latin (use as noun of adjective *praetorius*
belonging to a praetor). *Roman History*
1 E17 The tent of the commanding general in a Roman camp; the space where
this was placed. **2** E17 The court or palace of the governor of a Roman province;
transferred an official building, *especially*
the court or palace of an ancient king.
3 L17 The quarters of the praetorian guard
in Rome.

Prägnanz /prɛɡˈnants/ *noun* E20 German
(= conciseness, definiteness). *Psychology* In
gestalt theory, the tendency of every perceptual or mental form to be integrated
into a whole and become coherent and
simple.

■ Also Anglicized as *pregnance* (M20).

praire /prɛr/ *noun* plural pronounced
same E20 French. The European clam or
the North American hard-shell clam especially as an item of food.

praline /ˈprɑːliːn/ *noun* E18 French (from
Marshal de Plessis-Praslin (1598–1675), the
French general whose cook invented the
technique). A confection made by heating
together chopped almonds or other nuts
with sugar until the sugar liquefies and
turns brown and then letting the mixture cool, used especially as a filling for
chocolates.

1996 *Spectator* A real plantsman's border is as
bitty as a chocolate praline.

pralltriller /ˈpraltrɪlə/ *noun* plural same,
pralltrillers M19 German (from *prallen* to
bounce + *Triller* trill). *Music* An ornament
consisting of rapid alternation of the
note written with the one immediately
above it. Cf. MORDENT.

pratiquant /pratikã/ *adjective* E20 French. Observant of religious duties or practices.

1965 *New Statesman* After lapsing for 15 years, she had recently tried to become *pratiquant* again.

pratique /ˈpratiːk/, *foreign* /pratik/ *noun* E17 Old and Modern French (= practice, intercourse, corresponding to or from Italian *pratica* from medieval Latin *practica* use as noun (sc. *ars* art) of *practicus* from Greek *praktikos* from *prattein* to do). Permission granted to a ship to use a port after quarantine or on showing a clean bill of health.

praxis /ˈpraksɪs/ *noun* L16 Medieval Latin (from Greek, from *prattein* to do). 1 a L16 Action, practice; *specifically* the practice of a technical subject or art, as opposed to or arising out of the theory of it. b L19 Habitual action, accepted practice, custom. c M20 In Marxism, the willed action by which a theory or philosophy becomes a practical social activity. 2 E17 An example or collection of examples used for practice in a subject, especially in grammar; a practical specimen.

1.a 1996 *Oldie* He recalls that the lecturing, as opposed to praxis, was deficient and that most students went over to the Architectural Association for intellectual stimulus.

précieux /presjø/ *noun & adjective* (feminine **précieuse** /presjøz/) E18 French (= precious). A *noun* E18 plural same /presjøz/ A person affecting an over-refined delicacy of language and taste. B *adjective* L18 Overrefined, affectedly fastidious in taste etc.

■ Use of *précieux* (or *précieuse*) in English is under the influence of *Les Précieuses ridicules* (1659), Molière's famous comedy of manners satirizing the circle of people surrounding the Marquise de Rambouillet; thus the feminine form of the French noun and adjective was current in English earlier than the masculine (M20 and L19 respectively). The English word 'precious' as an adjective had long been in use (LME onwards) in the sense of 'overrefined', 'affected'. However, as a noun (L16) it is used only as an endearment and the derogatory sense is confined to the French word.

precipitato /pre,tʃipiˈtato/, /prɪˌtʃɪpɪˈtɑːtəʊ/ *adjective & adverb* L19 Italian. *Music* (A direction:) in a hurried or headlong manner; (to be) played in this manner.

précis /ˈpreɪsiː/ *noun & verb* M18 French (use as noun of *précis*). A *noun* plural same /ˈpreɪsiːz/. 1 M18 A summary or ab-

stract, especially of a text or speech. 2 L19 The action or practice of précis-writing. B *transitive verb* M19 Make a précis of; summarize.

B 1996 *Times* A glance at the subtitles which every few seconds précis the disorder in question . . . will testify to that . . .

predella /prɪˈdɛlə/ *noun* M19 Italian (= stool). 1 M19 A step or platform on which an altar is placed, an altar-step; a painting or sculpture on the vertical face of this. 2 M19 A raised shelf at the back of an altar; a painting or sculpture on the front of this, forming an appendage to an altarpiece above; any painting that is subsidiary to another painting.

premier cru /prəmje kry/, /ˌprɛmɪə ˈkruː/ *noun phrase* plural **premiers crus** (pronounced same) M19 French (literally, 'first growth'). A wine of the best quality.

premier danseur /prəmje dɑ̃sœr/ *noun phrase* plural **premiers danseurs** (pronounced same) E19 French (literally, 'first dancer'). A leading male dancer in a ballet company. Cf. PREMIÈRE DANSEUSE.

première /ˈprɛmɪɛː/, *foreign* /prəmjɛr/ (*plural same*) *noun & adjective* (also **premiere**) L19 French (feminine of *premier*; as noun short for *première représentation* first representation). A *noun* L19 A first performance or showing of a play, film, etc.; a first night. B *adjective* L19 First in order or importance; leading, foremost.

■ *Première* as a transitive and intransitive verb is a more recent (M20) development.

A 1996 *Spectator* La Bohème was not an instant success . . . at its Turin première on 1 February 1896 . . .

première danseuse /prəmjɛr dɑ̃søz/ *noun phrase* plural **premières danseuses** (pronounced same) E19 French (feminine of PREMIER DANSEUR). A leading female dancer in a ballet company; a ballerina.

premiers crus, premiers danseurs plurals of PREMIER CRU, PREMIER DANSEUR.

pre-mortem /priːˈmɔːtəm/ *adjective & noun* L19 Latin (*prae mortem* before death). A *adjective* L19 Taking place or performed before death (opposed to *post-mortem*). B *noun* L20 A discussion or analysis of a presumed future death. Chiefly *figurative*.

pré-salé /presale/ *noun* M19 French (= salt meadow). In France: seashore meadow or marshland, *especially* one on which sheep are reared; the flesh of sheep reared on such a meadow.

presidio /prɪˈsɪdɪəʊ/, *foreign* /preˈsidjo/ *noun* plural **presidios** /prɪˈsɪdɪəʊz/, *foreign* /preˈsidjos/ M18 Spanish (from Latin *praesidium* garrison, fort). In Spain and Spanish America: a fort, a fortified settlement, a garrison town. Also, a Spanish penal settlement in a foreign country.

Presidium /prɪˈsɪdɪʌm/, /prɪˈzɪdɪʌm/ *noun* (also **Praesidium**) plural **Presidia** /prɪˈsɪdɪə/, **Presidiums** E20 Russian (*prezidium* from Latin *praesidium*). The presiding body or standing committee in a Communist organization, *especially* (*historical*) that in the Supreme Soviet.

prestissimo /preˈstɪsɪməʊ/ *adverb, adjective, & noun* E18 Italian (superlative of PRESTO). *Music* **A** *adverb & adjective* E18 (A direction:) very rapid(ly). **B** *noun* E20 plural **prestissimos, prestissimi** /preˈstɪsɪmi/ A very rapid movement or passage.

presto /ˈprestəʊ/ *adverb, interjection, noun, & adjective* L16 Italian (= quick, quickly, from late Latin *praestus* ready, for Latin *praesto* at hand). **A** *adverb & interjection* **1** L16 In various commands used by conjurors: quickly, at once. Also as *interjection*, announcing the climax of a trick or a surprising dénouement. Frequently in *hey presto*. **2** L17 *Music* (A direction:) rapidly. **B** *noun* plural **prestos** **1** E17 An exclamation of 'presto!' **2** M19 *Music* A rapid movement or passage. **C** *attributive* or as *adjective* **1** M17 Originally, in readiness. Now, rapid, instantaneous; of the nature of a magical transformation. **2** M20 *Music* In a rapid tempo.

> **A.1** 1996 *Spectator* A ghetto upbringing, a broken home, an abusive parent and, presto, the criminal is 'emoting his feelings' as he maims, robs or even kills his victim.

prêt-à-porter /prɛtəˈpɔːteɪ/, *foreign* /prɛtaporte/ *adjective & noun* M20 French. **A** *adjective* M20 Of clothes: sold ready to wear. **B** *noun* M20 Ready-to-wear clothes.

> **A** 1996 *Times Magazine* No Anglo-Saxon squeamishness here—animals are either prêt-à-manger or prêt-à-porter.
> **B** 1995 *Times* Paris, in October, goes *prêt à porter* mad.

pretorium variant of PRAETORIUM.

pretzel /ˈprets(ə)l/ *noun* (also (now *rare* or *obsolete*) **bretzel** /ˈbrets(ə)l/) M19 German (South German dialect form of *Brezel* from Old High German *brizzila* (Italian *bracciello* usually taken as adaptation of

medieval Latin *bracellus* bracelet). A hard salted biscuit usually in the form of a knot, eaten originally in Germany.

preux chevalier /prø ʃəvalje/ *noun phrase* L18 French. A gallant knight, *especially* a man who behaves chivalrously towards women.

> ■ The Old French adjective *preu*, from which the modern *preux* derives, was current in the Middle English period but became obsolete in the sixteenth century. Revived in the phrase *preux chevalier*, *preux* now exists in English only in this context.

Priapus /prʌɪˈeɪpəs/ *noun* (also **priapus**) plural **Priapi** /prʌɪˈeɪpʌɪ/, /prʌɪˈeɪpiː/, **Priapuses** LME Latin (from Greek *Priapos*, the Greek and Roman god of procreation whose symbol was the phallus, later adopted as a god of gardens). **1** LME A statue or image of the god Priapus, especially characterized by having large genitals. **2** L16 *transferred* (A representation of) the penis, especially when erect.

prie-dieu /priːˈdjə/, *foreign* /pridjø/ *noun* plural **prie-dieux** (pronounced same), same M18 French (literally, 'pray God'). A desk for prayer consisting of a kneeling surface and a narrow upright front surmounted by a ledge for books etc. Also, (more fully *prie-dieu chair*) a chair with a low seat and a tall sloping back, used especially as a prayer seat or stool and fashionable in the mid nineteenth century.

prima /ˈpriːmə/ *noun* M18 Italian (feminine of PRIMO). A first or most important female; a prima donna, a prima ballerina.

prima ballerina /ˌpriːmə baləˈriːnə/ *noun phrase* L19 Italian (from as PRIMA + BALLERINA). The principal female dancer in a ballet or ballet company; a ballerina of the highest accomplishment or rank.

prima donna /ˌpriːmə ˈdɒnə/ *noun phrase* L18 Italian (from as PRIMA + *donna* lady). **1** L18 The principal female singer in an opera or opera company; a female opera singer of the highest accomplishment or rank. **2** M19 Originally, *transferred* a person of high standing in a particular field of activity. Now chiefly, a temperamentally self-important person.

prima facie /ˌprʌɪmə ˈfeɪʃiː/ *adverb & adjective phrase* L15 Latin (= at first sight, from feminine ablative of *primus* first and of *facies* face). **A** *adverb* L15 At first sight; from a first impression. **B** *adjective* E19

Arising at first sight; based on a first impression.

adjective phrase **1996** *Spectator* ... the widespread acceptance of the phrase 'couch potato' is good *prima facie* evidence of the direction of that influence [of commercial television].

prima inter pares see PRIMUS INTER PARES.

prima materia /ˌprʌɪmə məˈtɪərɪə/ *noun phrase* E20 **Latin** (literally, 'first matter'). A supposed formless primordial matter out of which the universe was created.

prima vista /ˌprima ˈvista/ *adverb phrase* M19 **Italian** (literally, 'first sight'). *Music* At first sight.

primeur /primœr/ *noun* plural pronounced same L19 **French** (= newness, something quite new, from as *prime* first). A new or early thing; *specifically* (a) in plural, fruit or vegetables grown to be available very early in the season; (b) new wine. Cf. EN PRIMEUR.

primo /ˈpriːməʊ/ *adjective & noun* plural (in senses A.1, B) **primi** /ˈpriːmi/, (in sense B) **primos** M18 **Italian** (= first; cf. PRIMA). **A** *adjective* **1** M18 *Music* Of a musician, performer, role, etc.: principal, chief; of highest quality or importance. **2** L20 First-class, first-rate; of top quality. *slang* (chiefly *United States*). **B** *noun* L18 *Music* (The pianist who plays) the upper part in a piano duet.

primum mobile /ˌpriːməm ˈməʊbɪli/, /ˌprʌɪməm ˈməʊbɪli/ *noun phrase* plural **primum mobiles** L15 **Medieval Latin** (literally, 'first moving thing', from Latin neuter of *primus* first + *mobilis* mobile). **1** L15 In the medieval version of the Ptolemaic system, an outermost sphere supposed to revolve round the earth in twenty-four hours, carrying with it the inner spheres. **2** E17 *transferred* An initiator of a course of action, events, etc.

primus /ˈpriːməs/, /ˈprʌɪməs/ *adjective* L16 **Latin** (= first). **1** L16 First, original, principal. Originally and chiefly in Latin phrases. **2** L18 Designating the first of several pupils with the same surname to enter a school. Cf. SECUNDUS, TERTIUS.

primus inter pares /ˌpriːməs mtə ˈpɑːriːz/, /ˌprʌɪməs/ *adjective & noun phrase* (feminine **prima inter pares** /ˌpriːmə/, /ˌprʌɪmə/) E19 **Latin**. (The) first among equals, (the) senior in a group.

1996 *Economist* A predecessor who made the mistake of behaving too much like an ordinary

boss ... and too little as *primus inter pares* did not last long.

princesse lointaine /prɛ̃sɛs lwɛ̃tɛn/ *noun phrase* plural **princesses lointaines** (pronounced same) E20 **French** (literally, 'distant princess'). An idealized unattainable woman.

■ The title of a play (1895) by Edmond Rostand (1868–1918), based on the theme of the love of the twelfth-century troubadour poet Rudel for the Lady of Tripoli.

principium /prɪnˈkɪpɪəm/, /prɪnˈsɪpɪəm/ *noun* plural **principia** /prɪnˈkɪpɪə/ L16 **Latin** (from *princip-*). **1** L16 *Roman History* In plural The general's quarters in an army camp. **2** E17 A fundamental cause or basis of something; a principle.

■ In scholastic philosophy the *principium individuationis* ('principle of individuation') was the criterion by which any individual was uniquely distinguished from any other. In sense 2 *Principia* occurs as the abbreviated title of either of two major works by English philosophers: the *Philosophiae Naturalis Principia Mathematica* (1687) of Isaac Newton and the *Principia Mathematica* (1910–13) of Bertrand Russell and A. N. Whitehead.

printanier /prɛ̃tanje/ *adjective & noun* (feminine **printanière** /prɛ̃tanjɛr/) M19 **French** (literally, 'of springtime', from *printemps* spring, from Latin *primus* first + *tempus* time). (A soup) made from or garnished with spring vegetables.

prisiadka /prjiˈsjatkə/ *noun* M20 **Russian** (*prisyadka*). A dance step in which a squatting male dancer kicks out each leg alternately to the front; the dance which uses this step. Cf. KAZACHOC.

prix fixe /pri fiks/ *noun phrase* L19 **French** (literally, 'fixed price'). A meal consisting of several courses served at a total fixed price. Cf. À LA CARTE.

1996 *Spectator* Thus, taramasalata is there, and moussaka on the lunchtime *prix fixe* ...

pro /prəʊ/ *preposition, adverb, noun & adjective* LME **Latin** (= before, in front of, for, on behalf of, in return for). **A** *preposition* **1** LME For. In Latin phrases (cf. PRO BONO PUBLICO, PRO FORMA). **2** M19 In favour of. **B** *adverb* LME In favour (of a proposition etc.). **C** *noun* **pros** LME A reason, argument, or arguer in favour of something. **D** *adjective* E18 Favourable, supportive.

■ As an adverb, chiefly in the phrase *pro and contra* or *pro and con* ('for and against'), and as a noun chiefly in the phrase *pros and cons* ('(the points) for and against').

B 1996 *Times* . . . the famous Christian name eggs on a studio audience to put in its frenzied two penn'orth, pro and con, until some kind of conclusion is arrived at . . .

problematique /ˌprɒbləməˈtiːk/, *foreign* /prɔbləmatik/ *noun* (also **problématique** /prɔbləmatik/) L20 French. The problematic area of a subject etc.; *specifically* environmental and other global problems collectively.

■ Earlier in sociological terminology in Anglicized form *problematic* (M20).

pro   bono   publico /prəʊ ˌbɒnəʊ ˈpʊblɪkəʊ/, /prəʊ ˌbəʊnəʊ ˈpʌblɪkəʊ/ *adverb & adjective phrase* E18 Latin. For the public good.

■ In colloquial use often shortened to *pro bono*. This has given rise, originally in United States usage, to the adjective *pro-bono* (or *pro bono*), designating legal work undertaken at no charge for a person unable to pay legal fees, also a lawyer who undertakes such work (see quotation 1995 (2)).
1995 *Times* Mr Goldsmith made his promise as he launched a Bar Council *pro bono publico* scheme . . . to co-ordinate the provision of free services by barristers.
1995 *Times* It is hoped that it may prompt lawyers to dig into their pockets or do more *pro bono* work.

procédé /prɔsede/ *noun* plural pronounced same L19 French. Manner of proceeding; a method, a procedure, a process.
1962 *Listener* All the familiar *procédés* of opera have vanished, whether set numbers or Wagnerian leading-motives.

procès-verbal /prɔsɛvɛrbal/, /ˌprɒsɛɪvaˈbaːl/ *noun* plural **procès-verbaux** /prɔsɛvɛrbo/, /ˌprɒsɛɪvaːˈbəʊ/ M17 French. A detailed written report of proceedings; minutes; an authenticated written statement of facts in support of a charge.

proconsul /prəʊˈkɒns(ə)l/ *noun* LME Latin (from earlier *pro consule* (person acting) for the consul). **1** LME *History* In the Roman Republic, an officer, usually an ex-consul, who acted as governor or military commander of a province; in the Roman Empire, the governor of a senatorial province. **2** L17 A governor of a modern dependency, colony, or province.

proferens /prəˈfɛrɛnz/ *noun* plural **proferentes** /prɒfəˈrɛntiːz/ M20 Latin (present participle of *proferre* to bring forth). *Law* The party which proposes or adduces a contract or a condition in a contract.

profil perdu /profil pɛrdy/ *noun phrase* plural **profils perdus** (pronounced same) M20 French (literally, 'lost profile'). A profile in which the head is more than half turned away from the onlooker.
1967 E. Wymark *As Good as Gold* She . . . stood gazing down the street, her figure a *profil perdu* against a grey sky.

profiterole /prəˈfɪtərəʊl/ *noun* L19 French (diminutive of *profit* profit). A small hollow case of choux pastry usually filled with cream and covered with chocolate sauce.

■ Earlier (E16-E18) evidence exists in English for the word in the sense of some kind of cooked food; the literal etymological sense of 'small gains', meaning the gratuities or tips that a servant can pick up, is attested in Cotgrave's French–English dictionary of 1611.

pro forma /prəʊ ˈfɔːmə/ *adverb, adjective, & noun phrase* E16 Latin. **A** *adverb phrase* E16 As a matter of form. **B** *adjective phrase* M19 Done or produced as a matter of form; designating a model or standard document or form; *specifically* (of an invoice) sent in advance of goods supplied or with goods sent on approval. **C** *noun* plural **pro formas** E20 A pro forma invoice or form.
B 1996 *Times* Somerfield is now being sold on a multiple of only 6.5 times its pro forma earnings to the end of April.

prognosis /prɒgˈnəʊsɪs/ *noun* plural **prognoses** /prɒgˈnəʊsiːz/ M17 Late Latin (from Greek *prognōsis*, from *progignōskein* to know beforehand, from *pro-* before + *gignōskein* to know). **1** M17 *Medicine* (A prediction of) the likely outcome of a disease (in general or in a particular case). **2** E18 *generally* (A) prognostication.

projet /prɔʒɛ/ *noun* plural pronounced same E19 French (from Latin from *projectum* from *project-* past participial stem of *pro(j)icere* to throw out). A proposal or a draft, especially of a treaty.

prolegomenon /prəʊlɪˈgɒmmən/ *noun* plural **prolegomena** /prəʊlɪˈgɒmmə/ M17 Latin (from Greek, use as noun of neuter present participle of *prolegein* to say beforehand). A critical or discursive introduction prefaced to a literary work; *transferred* a preliminary remark; *figurative* an event, action, etc., serving as an introduction *to* something. Frequently in *plural* (treated as *singular* or *plural*).

proletariat /ˌprəʊlɪˈtɛːrɪət/ *noun* M19 French (*prolétariat*, from Latin *proletarius* a Roman citizen of the lowest class, from *proles* offspring (since such citizens were considered capable of serving the State only by producing offspring)). **1** M19 The lowest classs of any community, especially when regarded as uncultured. **2** M19 The working class(es); wage-earners collectively.

proletkult /prəʊ'lɛtkʊlt/ *noun* (also **proletcult**) E20 Russian (contraction of *proletarskaya kul'tura* proletarian culture). Especially in the former USSR, (the advocacy of) cultural activities designed to reflect or encourage a purely proletarian ethos.

prominenti /prɒmɪ'nɛnti/ *noun plural* M20 Italian (plural of noun from *prominente* adjective, from Latin *prominent-* present participial stem of *prominere* to jut out). Prominent or eminent people; leading personages.

pronaos /prəʊ'neɪɒs/ *noun plural* **pronaoi** /prəʊ'neɪɔɪ/ E17 Latin (from Greek, from *pro-* before + NAOS). *Classical Antiquities* The space in front of the body of a temple, enclosed by a portico and projecting sidewalls. Also, a narthex.

prononcé /prɒnɔ̃se/ *adjective* M19 French (past participle of *prononcer* to pronounce, from Latin *pronuntiare* to proclaim, narrate). Pronounced; strongly marked; conspicuous.

pronto /'prɒntəʊ/ *adverb 1 & adjective* M18 Italian (from Latin *promptus* prompt; cf. next). *Music* (A direction:) quick(ly), prompt(ly).

pronto /'prɒntəʊ/ *adverb 2* E20 Spanish (from Latin *promptus* prompt; cf. preceding). Quickly; promptly, at once.

■ Colloquial, originally United States.
1976 P. Cave *High Flying Birds* You tell that bastard to come and see me . . . Pronto.

pronunciamento /prə,nʌnsɪə'mɛntəʊ/ *noun plural* **pronunciamentos** M19 Spanish (*pronunciamiento*, from *pronunciar* (from Latin *pronuntiare* to pronounce). Especially in Spain and Spanish-speaking countries: a pronouncement, proclamation, or manifesto, *especially* a political one.

1995 *Oldie* The book keeps trumpeting such pseudo-omniscient *pronunciamentos* as that 'there is no reciprocity in love, harmony is not the human condition, and the thing sung will always be the unenjoyed ideal'.

pro-nuncio /prəʊ'nʌnsɪəʊ/, /prəʊ'nʌnʃɪəʊ/ *noun* M20 Italian (*pro-nunzio*,

from *pro-* + *nunzio* nuncio). *Roman Catholic Church* A papal ambassador to a country which does not accord the Pope's ambassador automatic precedence over other ambassadors.

propaganda /prɒpə'gandə/ *noun* E18 Italian (from modern Latin *congregatio de propaganda fide* congregation for propagating the faith). **1** E18 *Roman Catholic Church* (Also **Propaganda**) A committee of cardinals responsible for foreign missions, founded in 1622 by Pope Gregory XV. Also more fully *Congregation* or *College of the Propaganda*. **2** L18 An organization or concerted movement for the propagation of a particular doctrine, practice, etc. Now *rare*. **3** E20 The systematic dissemination of doctrine, rumour, or selected information to propagate or promote a particular doctrine, view, practice, etc.; ideas, information, etc., disseminated thus (frequently *derogatory*).

proprium /'prəʊprɪəm/ *noun plural* **propria** /'prəʊprɪə/ M16 Latin (use as noun of neuter singular of *proprius* proper). **1** M16 *Logic* A non-essential characteristic common to all, and only, the members of a class, a property. **2** L18 Chiefly *Theology*. An essential attribute of something, a distinctive characteristic; essential nature, selfhood.

propugnaculum /,prəʊpʌg'nakjʊləm/ *noun* L18 Latin. A bulwark, a rampart; *figurative* a defence, a protection.

propylaeum /prɒpɪ'liːəm/ *noun plural* **propylaea** /prɒpɪ'liːə/ E18 Latin (from Greek *propulaion* use as noun of neuter of adjective *propulaios* before the gate, from *pro-* before + *pulē* gate). The entrance to a temple or other sacred enclosure; *specifically* (**Propylaeum**) *the* entrance to the Acropolis at Athens; *generally* a gateway, a porch.

■ The Greek word is represented in English in the form *propylon* (M19); both are current, although the Latin word is perhaps more common.

pro rata /prəʊ 'rɑːtə/, /'reɪtə/ *adverb & adjective phrase* L16 Latin (= according to the rate). **A** *adverb* L16 In proportion, proportionally. **B** *adjective* M19 Proportional.

proscenium /prə'siːnɪəm/, /prəʊ'siːnɪəm/ *noun plural* **prosceniums**, **proscenia** /prə'siːnɪə/ E17 Latin (from Greek *proskēnion*, from *pro-* before + *skēnē* scene). **1** E17 *Classical Antiquities* The performance area between the background and the orchestra of a theatre; the stage. **b** E19 The part of the stage of a modern theatre between the curtain or drop-scene and the auditorium, often including the curtain itself and the enclosing arch. Frequently *attributive.* **2** *transferred* and *figurative* M17 The front, the foreground.

prosciutto /prɒˈʃuːtəʊ/ *noun* M20 Italian (= ham). Italian cured ham, usually served raw and thinly sliced as an hors d'oeuvre.

prosit /ˈproːzɪt/ *interjection & noun* (also **prost** /proːst/, (as noun) **Prosit**) M19 German (from Latin = may it benefit). (An utterance of the exclamation) wishing a person good health, success, etc., especially in drinking a toast.

prospectus /prəˈspɛktəs/ *noun* M18 Latin (= view, prospect, use as noun of past participle of *prospicere* to look forward). A printed document giving advance notification of the chief features of a forthcoming publication, issue of shares for a commercial enterprise, etc. Also, a brochure or pamphlet detailing the courses, facilities, etc., of an educational institution.

prosthesis /ˈprɒsθɪsɪs/, *in sense 2 usually* /prɒsˈθiːsɪs/ *noun plural* **prostheses** /ˈprɒsθɪsiːz/, *in sense 2 usually* /prɒsˈθiːsiːz/ M16 Late Latin (from Greek, from *prostithenai* to add, from *pros* to + *tithenai* to place). **1** M16 *Grammar* The addition of a letter or syllable at the beginning of a word. **2 a** E18 The branch of surgery that deals with artificial replacements for defective or absent parts of the body. Now *rare.* **b** E20 An artificial replacement for a part of the body.

protégé /ˈprɒtɪʒeɪ/, /ˈprɒtɛʒeɪ/, /ˈprəʊtɪʒeɪ/, *noun* (feminine **protégée**) L18 French (past participial adjective of *protéger* from Latin *protegere* to protect). A person under the protection, care, or patronage of another, especially of a person of superior position or influence.

> **1996** *Spectator* I do so with [sc. doff my cap to] Mr Preston, even though he was rather rude about me . . . after I had elsewhere written some disobliging comments about his newly appointed protégé, Mr Jaspan.

pro tem abbreviation of PRO TEMPORE.

pro tempore /prəʊ ˈtɛmpəri/ *adverb & adjective phrase* LME Latin (= for the time). **A** *adverb phrase* LME For the time being, temporarily. **B** *adjective phrase* M18 Temporary.

■ Also colloquially in abbreviated form *pro tem* (E19).

protocolaire /prɒtɔkɔlɛr/ *adjective* M20 French (from *protocole* protocol). Characterized by a strict regard for protocol; formal, ceremonial.

> **1979** H. Wilson *Final Term* Duncan Sandys . . . said that even in pre-Amin days he had always insisted on the title 'Britain' despite protocolaire objections.

protome /ˈprɒtəmi/ *noun* M18 Greek (*protomē* the foremost or upper part of a thing, from *protoenein* to cut off in front). Chiefly *Classical Antiquities.* A bust; a piece of sculpture representing the forepart of an animal.

proviso /prəˈvaɪzəʊ/ *noun plural* **proviso(e)s** LME Latin (neuter ablative singular of past participle of *providere* to provide, as in medieval Latin *proviso quod* (or *ut*) it being provided that). A clause in a legal or formal document, making some condition, stipulation, exception; or limitation, or on the observance of which the operation or validity of the instrument depends; *generally* a condition, a qualification, a stipulation, a provision.

provocateur /prɒvɔkatœr/ *noun plural* pronounced same E20 French (= provoker). A person who provokes a disturbance; an agitator. Cf. AGENT PROVOCATEUR.

provolone /prɒvəˈləʊni/ *noun* M20 Italian (from *provola* buffalo's milk cheese). An Italian smoked cheese, often made in a variety of shapes. Also *provolone cheese.*

prox. abbreviation of PROXIMO.

proxime accessit /ˌprɒksɪmeɪ akˈsɛsɪt/ *noun phrase* L19 Latin (literally, '(he or she) came very near'). Second place in merit to the actual winner of a prize, scholarship, etc.; a person gaining this.

> **1995** *Spectator* As Herbert Morrison found out, to be *proxime accessit* in Labour's class list is not much fun.

proximo /ˈprɒksɪməʊ/ *adjective* M19 Latin (= in the next (sc. *mense* month)). Chiefly *Commerce* Of next month.

■ Often abbreviated to *prox.,* it is used following the ordinal number denoting the day, as in *1st proximo.*

prunelle /prynɛl/ *noun* E20 French (literally, 'sloe', diminutive of *prune* ultimately from Latin *prunum* plum; cf. PRUNELLO). A French brandy-based liqueur flavoured with sloes.

prunello /pruˈnɛləʊ/ *noun plural* **prunello(e)s** E17 Italian (alteration of obsolete Italian *prunella* diminutive of *pruna* (now *prugna*) plum, prune). Originally, a variety of plum or prune. Now, a fine kind of prune, *especially* one made from a greengage.

pruritus /prʊəˈrʌɪtəs/ *noun* M17 Latin (from *prurire* to itch). Itching of the skin, with or (especially) without visible eruption.

■ Frequently with modern Latin specifying word.

pseudepigrapha /ˌsjuːdɪˈpɪɡrəfə/ *noun plural* L17 Greek (use as noun of neuter plural of *pseudepigraphos* with false title, from *pseudo-* false + *epigraphein* to inscribe). Books or writings collectively wrongly titled or attributed; spurious writings; *specifically* Jewish writings ascribed to various biblical patriarchs and prophets but composed *c.*200 BC–AD 200.

pseudo /ˈsjuːdəʊ/ *adjective & noun* LME Greek (independent use of *pseudo-* false). **A** *adjective* **1** LME False, counterfeit, pretended, spurious. **2** M20 Intellectually or socially pretentious; insincere, affected; meaningless. **B** *noun plural* **pseudo(e)s**. **1** LME–M19 A false person, a pretender. **2** M20 An intellectually or socially pretentious person; an insincere person. Abbreviated to *pseud* (*slang*).

psi /psʌɪ/, /sʌɪ/ *noun* LME Greek (*psei*). **1** LME The twenty-third letter (Ψ, ψ) of the Greek alphabet. **2** M20 Paranormal phenomena or faculties collectively; the psychic force supposed to be manifested by these. Frequently *attributive*, as *psi powers* etc. **3** L20 *Nuclear Physics* A neutral, relatively long-lived strongly interacting particle, produced by high-energy collisions.

psyche /ˈsʌɪki/ *noun* M17 Latin (from Greek *psukhē* breath, life, soul, mind (also butterfly, moth), related to *psukhein* to breathe; in some uses with allusion to *Psukhē* Psyche, in Greek mythology the beloved of Eros (Cupid), the god of love). **I 1** M17 The soul, the spirit. Formerly also (*rare*), the animating principle of the universe. Now chiefly *historical*. **2** E20 The mind, especially in its spiritual, emotional, and motivational aspects; the collective mental or psychological characteristics of a nation, people, etc. **II 3** E19 (After Greek). A butterfly, a moth. *rare*. **III 4** M19 (Said to be after Raphael's painting of Psyche.) A cheval-glass. Also *psyche-glass*. *archaic*.

psychomachia /ˌsʌɪkə(ʊ)ˈmeɪkɪə/ *noun* (also occasionally Anglicized as **psycho-**

machy /sʌɪˈkʌməki/) E17 Late Latin ((title of a poem by Prudentius *c.* 400) from Greek *psukhē* psyche + *makhē* fight). Conflict of the soul; the battle between spirit and flesh, or virtue and vice.

psychopompos /ˌsʌɪkə(ʊ)ˈpɒmpɒs/ *noun* (also in English form **psychopomp** /ˈsʌɪkə(ʊ)pɒmp/) M19 Greek (*psukhopompos*, from *psukhē* psyche + *pompos* conductor). A mythical conductor of souls to the place of the dead. Also, the spiritual guide of a (living) person's soul.

pteroma /təˈrəʊmə/ *noun plural* **pteromata** /təˈrəʊmətə/ M19 Latin (from Greek *pterōma*). *Architecture* The space between the cella of a Greek temple and the surrounding colonnade (peristyle).

pubes /ˈpjuːbiːz/, /ˈpjuːbz/ *noun plural* same L16 Latin (= the pubic hair, the groin, the genitals). **1** L16 The pubic hair. Now *colloquial*. **2** L17 The lower part of the abdomen at the front of the pelvis, which becomes covered with hair from the time of puberty.

puchero /pʊˈtʃɛrəʊ/ *noun plural* **pucheros** M19 Spanish (= pot, from Latin *pultarius* cooking- or drinking-vessel, from *puls*, *pult-* a kind of thick porridge). **1** M19 A glazed earthenware cooking-pot. *rare*. **2** M19 A Latin American stew of beef, sausage, bacon, and various vegetables.

pucka variant of PUKKA.

pudendum /pjuːˈdɛndəm/ *noun plural* **pudenda** /pjuːˈdɛndə/ M17 Latin (*pudenda* use as noun of neuter plural of *pudendus* gerundive of *pudere* to be ashamed). In *plural* and (occasionally) *singular*. The genitals, *especially* the female external genitals.

pudeur /pydœr/ *noun* M20 French (from Latin PUDOR). A sense of shame or embarrassment, especially with regard to matters of a sexual or personal nature; modesty.

> **1995** D. Lodge *Therapy* A kind of *pudeur* restrained me.

pudor /ˈpjuːdɔː/ *noun* E17 Latin (= shame, modesty, from *pudere* to be ashamed). Due sense of shame; bashfulness, modesty.

pueblo /ˈpwɛbləʊ/ *noun & adjective plural* **pueblos** E19 Spanish (from Latin *populus* people). **A** *noun* **1** E19 A town or village in Latin America or the south-western United States; *especially* an Indian settlement. **2** M19 (**Pueblo**) A member of the Pueblo Indians. **B** *attributive* or as *adjec-*

tive M19 Of or pertaining to a pueblo; (usually **Pueblo**) designating or pertaining to a group of North American Indians living in pueblos chiefly in New Mexico and Arizona.

puggaree /'pʌg(ə)ri:/ *noun* (also **pagri** /'pagri/, **puggree** /'pʌgri:/) M17 Hindustani (*pagrī* turban). **1** M17 A turban, as worn in the Indian subcontinent. **2** M19 A thin scarf wound round the crown of a sun-helmet or hat so that the ends of the scarf form a shade for the neck.

> **2 1996** *Spectator* We are shown, above a wood engraving . . . of the two explorers doffing their headgear to one another at Ujiji, Stanley's helmet with its red check pagri and Livingstone's cap.

puisne /'pju:ni/ *noun & adjective* L16 Old French ((modern *puîne*), from *puis* (from Latin *postea* afterwards) + *né* (from Latin *natus* born)). **A** *noun* **1** L16–M17 A junior; an inferior; a novice. **2** E19 A puisne judge (see sense B.1 below). **B** *adjective* **1** E17 Younger, junior. Now *rare* or *obsolete* except in *Law*, designating an ordinary judge of the High Court. **2** E17–L18 Small, insignificant, petty. **3** M17 Later, more recent, of subsequent date. Now chiefly in *puisne mortgage*.

puissance /'pju:ɪs(ə)ns/, /'pwi:s(ə)ns/, /'pwɪs(ə)ns/, (*especially in sense* 1b) /'pwi:sõs/ *noun* LME Old and Modern French (from Proto-Gallo-Romance from Latin *posse* to be able). **1** LME Power, strength, force, might; influence. Chiefly *archaic* and *poetical*. **b** M20 A showjumping competition testing a horse's ability to jump large obstacles. **2** LME–L16 An armed force. Also, a number or crowd of people.

puja /'pu:dʒə/ *noun* (also **pooja**, **pujah**) L17 Sanskrit (*pūjā* worship). A Hindu religious ceremony or rite.

pukka /'pʌkə/ *adjective* (also **pukkah**, **pucka**) L17 Hindi (*pakkā* cooked, ripe, substantial). **1** L17 Of full weight, full; genuine. **2** L18 Certain, reliable; authentic, true; proper, socially acceptable. **3** L18 Permanent; (of a building) solidly built. Cf. KUTCHA.

■ Originally Anglo-Indian, often in phrases such as *pukka sahib*, a true gentleman; now colloquial or slang. The spelling *pucka* was the one in most frequent use prior to the twentieth century. *Pukka* was also formerly used in nominal and other adjectival senses that are now rare or obsolete.

> **2 1996** *Times Magazine* . . . foreign literature, nevertheless, dominates—the study of indigenous Indian-language writers is not regarded as pukka by renowned institutions of learning.

pulao variant of PILAU.

pullus /'pʊləs/ *noun* plural **pulli** /'pʊlʌɪ/ L18 Latin (= young chick). A young bird or nestling prior to fledging (especially with reference to ringed birds and museum specimens).

pulperia /ˌpʊlpəˈri:ə/, *foreign* /ˌpulpeˈria/ *noun* E19 American Spanish. In Spanish-speaking America: a grocery; a tavern.

pulpitum /'pʊlpɪtəm/ *noun* M19 Latin. A stone screen in a church separating the choir from the nave, frequently surmounted by an organ-loft.

pulque /'pʊlkeɪ/, /'pʊlki/ *noun* L17 American Spanish (from Nahuatl *puliúhki* decomposed). A Mexican and Central American fermented drink made from the sap of any of several agaves.

pulvino /pʌlˈvi:nəʊ/ *noun* plural **pulvini** /pʌlˈvi:ni/, **pulvinos** E20 Italian (from Latin *pulvinus* cushion, pillow). *Architecture* A dosseret resembling a cushion pressed down by a weight.

pumpernickel /'pʊmpəˌnɪk(ə)l/, /'pʌmpəˌnɪk(ə)l/ *noun* M18 German (transferred use of earlier sense 'lout', ultimate origin unknown). Dark German bread made from coarsely ground wholemeal rye.

puna /'pu:nə/ *noun* E17 American Spanish (from Quechua). **1** E17 A high bleak plateau in the Peruvian Andes. **2** M19 Difficulty of breathing, nausea, etc., caused by climbing to high altitudes; mountain sickness.

punctum /'pʌŋ(k)təm/ *noun* plural **puncta** /'pʌŋ(k)tə/ L16 Latin (originally neuter of *punctus* past participle of *pungere* to prick). **1** L16 A point. *obsolete* except in phrases; cf. PUNCTUM INDIFFERENS. **2** M17 *Zoology, Botany, Medicine*, etc. A minute rounded speck, dot, or spot of colour, or a small elevation or depression on a surface. **3** L18 *Anatomy* The orifice of either of the two lacrimal canals, at the corner of the eye. More fully *punctum lachrymale*. **4** M20 *Palaeography* A punctuation mark consisting of a point in a medieval manuscript.

punctum indifferens /ˌpʌŋ(k)təm ɪnˈdɪfərɛnz/ *noun phrase* E20 Latin (= not differing point). A neutral point.

> **1976** J. Davey *Treasury Alarm* Things may rearrange themselves around me just because I'm there—as a *punctum indifferens*.

punctus /'pʌŋktəs/ *noun* plural **puncti** /'pʌŋktʌɪ/, /'pʌŋkti:/ M20 Latin (see PUNC-TUM). *Palaeography* A punctuation mark in a medieval manuscript.

pundonor /ˌpundo'nor/ *noun* plural **pun-donores** M17 Spanish (contraction of *punto de honor* point of honour). In Spain: (originally, with *plural*) a point of honour; (now) one's sense of honour, dignity, self-respect, pride.

Punica fides variant of FIDES PUNICA.

punkah /'pʌŋkə/, /'pʌŋkɑ:/ *noun* (also **punka**) L17 Hindustani (*paṅkhā* fan, from Sanskrit *pakṣaka*, from *pakṣa* wing). In the Indian subcontinent: a large fan to cool a room etc.; *specifically* (a) a large portable fan made especially from a palmyra leaf; (b) a large swinging cloth fan on a frame worked manually by a cord operated by a punkah-WALLAH or by electricity.

punto /'pʌntəʊ/, *foreign* /'punto/ *noun* (in sense 3 also **ponto** /'pɒntəʊ/) plural **pun-tos** /'pʌntəʊz/, *foreign* /'puntos/ L16 Italian or Spanish (= Latin *punctum* point). **1** L16–E18 A small point or detail; a particle, a jot. Also, a moment, an instant. **b** L16–M18 A small point of behaviour, (a) punctilio. **2** L16–E17 *Fencing* A stroke or thrust with the point of the sword or foil. **3** L17 *Cards* In quadrille, the ace of trumps when trumps are either diamonds or hearts. **4** M19 *Lace-making* Lace, embroidery. Only in phrases *punto a rilievo*, a type of lace worked in bold relief, and *punto in aria*, an early form of needlepoint lace originally made in Venice.

punto banco /ˌpuntəʊ 'baŋkəʊ/ *noun phrase* L20 Italian or Spanish (probably from as PUNTO + BANCO). A form of baccarat.

purdah /'pə:də/ *noun* E19 Persian and Urdu (*parda* veil, curtain). **1** E19 In the Indian subcontinent and South East Asia, a curtain, a veil; *especially* one used to screen women from men or strangers. **2** M19 A system in certain Muslim and Hindu societies, especially in the Indian subcontinent, of screening women from men or strangers by means of a veil or curtain. **b** E20 *transferred* Seclusion; (medical) isolation or quarantine; secrecy. Chiefly in *in, into, out of, purdah*.

1977 D. Bagley *Enemy* When I came out of purdah, but before I was discharged, I went to see her.

purée /'pjʊəreɪ/, *as noun also foreign* /pyre/ (*plural same*) *noun & verb* E18 Old and Modern French (in form feminine past par-

ticiple of *purer* from medieval Latin *purare* to refine (metal), from *purus* pure). **A** *noun* E18 A pulp of vegetables, fruit, etc., reduced to the consistency of cream. **B** *transitive verb* M20 Reduce (food) to a purée.

pur et simple /pyr e sɛ̃pl/ *adjective phrase* M19 French (= pure and simple). Taken absolutely by itself, nothing short of.

■ Follows a noun, as does its much more common English equivalent 'pure and simple'.

puri /'pu:ri/ *noun* M20 Hindustani (*pūrī* from Sanskrit *pūrikā*). In Indian cookery, a small round cake of unleavened wheat flour deep-fried in ghee or oil.

puris naturalibus /ˌpjʊərɪs natjʊ 'rɑ:lɪbəs/, /ˌpjʊərɪs natjʊ'reɪlɪbəs/ *adverb phrase* E20 Latin (cf. earlier IN PURIS NAT-URALIBUS). In one's natural state; stark naked.

puro /'puro/ *noun* plural **puros** /'puros/ M19 Spanish (literally, 'pure'). In Spain and Spanish-speaking countries: a cigar.

pur sang /pyr sɑ̃/ *adjective & adverb phrase* M19 French (*pur-sang* thoroughbred animal, from *pur* pure + *sang* blood). Without admixture, genuine(ly).

purusha /'purʊʃə/ *noun* L18 Sanskrit (*pur-uṣa* literally 'man', plural 'mankind'; in Hindu mythology, a being sacrificed by the gods in order to create the universe). *Hinduism* The universal spirit or soul; spirit or consciousness as opposed to matter; *specifically* in Sankya philosophy, the active or animating principle (personified as male) which with the passive (female) principle produces the universe.

puta /'puta/ *noun* M20 Spanish. A prostitute, a slut. *slang*.

putonghua /pu:'tʊŋhwɑ:/ *noun* M20 Chinese (*pŭtōnghuà*, from *pŭtōng* common + *huà* spoken language; cf. PAI-HUA). The standard spoken form of modern Chinese, based on the northern dialects, especially that of Peking (Beijing).

putsch /pʊtʃ/ *noun* E20 Swiss German (= thrust, blow). **1** E20 An attempt at (political) revolution; a violent uprising. **2** M20 A sudden vigorous effort or campaign. *colloquial*.

transferred **1** 1996 *Times* [Chris Evans] boasts about how he is famous enough to leave for six

weeks in Barbados while wimpier DJs clutch
their headphones for fear of a putsch.

putto /'pʊtəʊ/, *foreign* /'putto/ *noun* plural
putti /'pʊti/, *foreign* /'putti/ M17 **Italian**
(from Latin *putus* boy). A representation
of a (boy) child, naked or in swaddling
clothes, in (especially Renaissance and
baroque) art, a cherub, a cupid.

putz /pʊts/, /pʌts/ *noun* E20 **German** (= decoration, finery; in sense 2 from Yiddish).

1 E20 In Pennsylvanian Dutch homes, a
representation of the Nativity scene traditionally placed under a Christmas tree.
United States. **2** M20 The penis. *United
States slang.* **b** M20 A fool; a stupid or objectionable person. *North American slang.*

puy /pwiː/ *noun* plural pronounced same
M19 **French** (= hill, from Latin PODIUM). A
small extinct volcanic cone; originally
and *specifically* any of those in the Au-
vergne, France.

Q

qadi variant of CADI.

qanat /kə'nɑ:t/ *noun* (also **kanat**) M19 Persian (from Arabic *ḳanāt* reed, lance, pipe, channel). A gently sloping underground channel or tunnel, *especially* one constructed to lead water from the interior of a hill to a village below.

qat variant of KHAT.

QED abbreviation of QUOD ERAT DEMONSTRANDUM.

QEF abbreviation of QUOD ERAT FACIENDUM.

qibla(h) variants of KIBLAH.

qinghaosu /ˌtʃɪŋhaʊ'suː/ *noun* L20 Chinese (*qīnghāosū*, from *qinghao* artemisia (plant) + suffix *-su* 'active principle'). *Medicine* A naturally occurring compound extracted from the Chinese plant *Artemisia annua* for use against malaria, artemisium.

■ Used for centuries against fever in traditional Chinese medicine, *qinghaosu* became an object of study by Western researchers seeking for a compound with which to treat strains of malaria that were resistant to standard anti-malarial drugs.

qiviut /'kɪvɪət/ *noun* M20 Eskimo ((Inuit) plural of *qiviuq*). The underwool of the musk ox; fibre made from this.

qq.v. see QUOD VIDE.

qua /kweɪ, /kwɑː/ *adverb* M17 Latin (ablative singular feminine of *qui* who). In so far as; in the capacity of.
    1996 *Spectator* So can the historian *qua* historian give any sort of credence to *any* of this?

quadra /'kwɒdrə/ *noun* M17 Latin (= a square). *Architecture* The plinth of a podium. Also, a platband, a fillet, *especially* one above or below the scotia in an Ionic base.

quadrennium /kwɒ'drɛnɪəm/ *noun* (also (earlier) **quadriennium** /kwɒdrɪ'ɛnɪəm/) plural **quadrenniums**, **quadrennia** /kwɒ'drɛnɪə/ E19 Latin (*quadriennium*, from *quadri-* combining form of *quottuor* four + *annus* year). A period of four years.

quadriga /kwɒd'riːgə/, /kwɒd'rʌɪgə/ *noun* plural **quadrigae** /kwɒd'riːgiː/ E17 Latin (singular form of plural *quadrigae* contraction of *quadrijugae*, from *quadri-* combining form of *quottuor* four + *jugum* yoke). *Roman Antiquities* A chariot drawn by four horses harnessed abreast; *especially* a representation of this in sculpture or on a coin.

quadrille /kwə'drɪl/ *noun* 1 M18 French (from Spanish *cuadrilla*, Italian *quadriglia* troop, company, from *cuadro*, *quadro* square). **1** M18 Each of four groups of riders taking part in a tournament or carousel; *generally* a riding display. **2** L18 A square dance usually performed by four couples and containing five figures, each of which is a complete dance in itself; a piece of music for such a dance.

quadrille /kwə'drɪl/ *adjective & noun* 2 (also **quadrillé** /kwɒ'drɪleɪ/) L19 French (*quadrillé*, from *quadrille* small square from Spanish *cuadrillo* square block). (Something, especially paper) marked with small squares.

quadrivium /kwɒ'drɪvɪəm/ *noun* E19 Latin (= place where four ways meet, from *quadri-* combining form of *quottuor* four + *via* way). In the Middle Ages, the higher division of a course of study of seven sciences, comprising arithmetic, geometry, astronomy, and music. Cf. TRIVIUM.

quaere /'kwɪəri/ *verb & noun* (also (earlier) **quere**) M16 Latin (imperative singular of *quaerere* to inquire, seek). **1** *transitive verb* M16 (in *imperative* now also interpreted as *noun*) Ask, inquire, query. Chiefly and now only in *imperative* introducing a question. **2** *noun* L16 A question, a query.

quaesitum /kwiː'sʌɪtəm/ *noun* plural **quaesita** /kwiː'sʌɪtə/ M18 Latin (neuter singular of *quaesitus* past participle of *quaerere* to inquire, seek). That which is sought; the answer to a problem.

quae vide plural of QUOD VIDE.

quai /keɪ, foreign /ke/ (plural same) *noun* L19 French. **1** L19 A public street or path along the embankment of a stretch of navigable water, usually having buildings on the land side; *specifically* such a street on either bank of the Seine in Paris. **2** E20 The French Foreign Office. In full *Quai d'Orsay* /'dɔːseɪ/, foreign /dɔrsɛ/ (the quai on the south bank of the Seine where the French Foreign Office is situated).

quaich /kweɪk/, /kweɪx/ *noun* (also **quaigh**) M16 Gaelic (*cuach* cup, perhaps from *cua* hollow; cf. Latin *caucus* (Greek *kauka*), Welsh *caurg* bowl). In Scotland: a shallow cup, usually made of wooden staves hooped together and having two handles, but sometimes made of silver or fitted with a silver rim.

quand même /kɑ̃ mɛm/ *adverb phrase* E19 French. All the same, even so, nevertheless.

quanta see QUANTUM.

quantité négligeable /kɑ̃tite negliʒabl/ *noun phrase* plural **quantités négligeables** (pronounced same) L19 French (= negligible quantity). A factor of no account, something insignificant.

quantum /ˈkwɒntəm/ *noun & adjective* M16 Latin (neuter of *quantus* how much). A *noun* plural **quanta** /ˈkwɒntə/, **quantums**. **1** M16 Quantity; a quantity. Now *especially* in *Law*, an amount of or *of* money payable in damages etc. **2** M17 One's (required or allowed) share or portion. **3** E20 *Physics* A discrete quantity of electromagnetic energy proportional in magnitude to the frequency of the radiation it represents. **b** M20 *transferred* and *figurative* A small discrete quantity of anything. **4** M20 *Physiology* The unit quantity of acetylcholine which is released at a neuromuscular junction by each single synaptic vesicle, corresponding to a certain small voltage. **B** *attributive* or as *adjective* E20 *Physics* etc. Involving quanta or quantum theory; quantized.

quantum meruit /ˌkwɒntəm ˈmɛruɪt/ *noun phrase* M17 Latin (= as much as he has deserved). *Law* A reasonable sum of money to be paid for services rendered or work done, when the amount due is not stipulated in a legally enforceable contract.

quantum sufficit /ˌkwɒntəm ˈsʌfɪsɪt/ *adverb & noun phrase* L17 Latin. As much as suffices; (in) a sufficient quantity; (to) a sufficient extent.

quark /kwɑːk/, /kvɑːk/ *noun* M20 German (= curd(s), cottage or curd cheese). A low-fat soft cheese of German origin.

quartier /kartje/ *noun* plural pronounced same E19 French (from Latin *quartarius* fourth part of a measure, from *quartus* fourth). A district or area, originally of a French city; *elliptical* for *Quartier Latin* the Latin Quarter of Paris on the left bank of the Seine, where students and artists live.

> **1995** *Spectator* Twenty years ago, Covent Garden was a deserted no-man's-land at weekends. On Saturday night, a quarter of a million people must have been carousing through this now gilded *quartier.*

quasi in rem /ˌkweɪzaɪ ɪn ˈrɛm/, /ˈkweɪsaɪ ɪn ˈrɛm/ *adjective phrase* L19 Latin (literally, 'as if against a thing'). *United States Law* Brought against a person in respect of his or her interest in a property within the jurisdiction of the court. Frequently *postpositive.*

quatorze /kəˈtɔːz/ *noun* E18 French (from Latin *quattuordecim* fourteen). **1** E18 In piquet, a set of four aces, kings, queens, or jacks held by one player, scoring fourteen. **2** M20 In full *Quatorze Juillet* /ˈʒwiːjeɪ/. In France, Bastille Day (14 July).

quatre-couleur /ˌkatrəkuˈləː/ *adjective* (also **quatre-couleurs** /ˌkatrəkuˈləː/) M20 French (*quatre-couleurs*, from *quatre* four + *couleurs* colours). Of an *objet d'art*: made of or decorated with carved gold of several (especially four) different colours.

quatsch /kvatʃ/ *noun* E20 German. Nonsense, rubbish.

> ■ Frequently used as an interjection.
> **1979** N. Freeling *Widow* 'Oh Quatsch,' she said. 'I . . . know how to look after myself.'

quattrocento /ˌkwatrə(ʊ)ˈtʃɛntəʊ/ *noun & adjective* L19 Italian (= four hundred). A *noun* L19 The fifteenth century in Italy; the Italian style of art, architecture, etc., of this period. **B** *attributive* or as *adjective* E20 Of or pertaining to the quattrocento.

quebrada /keˈbrada/, /kɪˈbrɑːdə/ *noun* plural **quebradas** /keˈbradas/, /kɪˈbrɑːdəz/ M19 Spanish (feminine of *quebrado* past participle of *quebrar* to break). A mountain stream or ravine in South America.

quel /kɛl/ *adjective* plural **quels** (feminine **quelle**, plural **quelles**) L19 French. What (a) (with following noun).

> ■ Only in French phrases and in English phrases imitating them.
> **1996** *Spectator* 'Arnie! *Quelle surprise! What are you doing here?'

Quellenforschung /ˈkvɛlənˌfɔrʃʊŋ/ *noun* M20 German (from *Quelle* source + *Forschung* research). The investigation of the sources of, or influences on, a literary work.

quenelle /kə'nɛl/ *noun* M19 French (of unknown origin). A seasoned ball or roll of meat or fish ground to a paste.

quere variant of QUAERE.

querencia /ke'renθja/, /ke'rensia/ *noun* M20 Spanish (= lair, haunt, home ground, from *querer* to desire, love). **1** M20 *Bullfighting* The part of the arena where the bull takes its stand. **2** M20 *figurative* A person's home ground, a refuge.

> **2 1952** R. Campbell *Lorca* Andalusia is Lorca's *querencia*.

quesadilla /kesa'di(l)ja/, /keɪsa'di:ljə/ *noun* plural **quesadillas** /kesa'di(l)jas/, /keɪsa'di:ljəz/ M20 Spanish. A tortilla stuffed with cheese (or occasionally other filling) and heated.

questionnaire /kwɛstʃə'nɛː/, /kɛstjə'nɛː/ *noun* L19 French (from *questionner* to question). A formulated series of questions by which information is sought from a selected group, usually for statistical analysis; a document containing these.

quête /kɛt/ *noun* E20 French (= quest). The traditional act of begging for food or alms to the accompaniment of folksong.

quia timet /ˌkwiːə 'tɪmɛt/ *adverb & adjective phrase* E17 Latin (literally, 'because he or she fears'). *Law* **A** *adverb phrase* E17 So as to prevent a possible future injury. **B** *adjective phrase* L17 Of an injunction: brought for this purpose.

quiche /kiːʃ/ *noun* M20 French (from Alsatian dialect *Küchen* (German *Kuchen* cake)). An open flan consisting of a pastry case filled with a savoury mixture of milk, eggs, and other ingredients, and baked until firm.

quid /kwɪd/ *noun* L16 Latin (= what, anything, something, neuter singular of *quis* who, anyone, etc.; in sense 3 abbreviation of TERTIUM QUID). **1** A nicety in argument, a quibble. *rare.* Only in L16. **2** E17 The nature of something; that which a thing is. **3** E19 *United States History* A section formed within the Republican Party, 1805–11.

quid pro quo /ˌkwɪd prəʊ 'kwəʊ/ *noun phrase* M16 Latin (= something for something). **1** M16 A thing (originally a medicine) given or used in place of another; a substitute. **b** L17 The action or fact of substituting one thing for another. Also, a mistake or blunder arising from such substitution. **2** L16 An action performed or thing given in return or exchange for another.

> **2 1996** *Spectator* Mr Major's error was to let the Chancellor pocket a concession without extracting a quid pro quo.

quieta non movere /kwiːˌeɪtə nəʊn məʊ'vɛːri/ *verb phrase* L18 Latin (literally, 'not to move settled things'). Let sleeping dogs lie.

> **1960** *Encounter* Quieta non movere is the motto of many once aggressive . . . radicals.

quietus /kwʌɪ'iːtəs/ *noun* LME Latin (abbreviation of medieval Latin *quietus est*, literally, 'he is quit'). **1 a** LME An acquittance granted on payment of a debt; a receipt. Originally more fully *quietus est*. **b** L16-L18 A discharge or release from office or duty. **2** M16 *figurative* Death regarded as a release from life; something which causes death. **b** E19 A final settlement, an ending. **3** M18 (By association with *quiet*). A sedative, a salve; a state of quiet or repose, a lull.

quincaillerie /kɛ̃kajri/ *noun* plural pronounced same L19 French. **1** L19 Metalwork; metal artefacts. *rare.* **2** M20 In France: a hardware or ironmonger's shop.

quinella /kwɪ'nɛlə/ *noun* (also (earlier) **quiniela** /kwɪnɪ'ɛlə/) E20 American Spanish (*quiniela*). A form of betting in which the punter must select the first two place-winners in a race etc., not necessarily in the correct order. Originally *United States*.

quinquennium /kwɪŋ'kwɛnɪəm/ *noun* plural **quinquenniums**, **quinquennia** /kwɪŋ'kwɛnɪə/ E17 Latin (from *quinque* five + *annus* year). **1** E17 A fifth anniversary. **2** M17 A period of five years.

quinta /'kinta/, /'kwɪntə/ *noun* M18 Spanish and Portuguese (from *quinta parte* fifth part, originally the amount of a farm's produce paid as rent). In Spain, Portugal, and Latin America: a large house or villa in the country or on the outskirts of a town; a country estate; *specifically* a wine-growing estate in Portugal.

quipu /'kiːpuː/, /'kwɪpuː/ *noun* (also **quipo**) E18 Quechua (*khípu* knot). An ancient Peruvian device for recording information, events, etc., consisting of variously coloured cords arranged and knotted in different ways.

qui vive /kiː 'viːv/, *foreign* /ki viv/ *noun phrase* L16 French (literally, '(long) live who?'). An alert or watchful state or condition. Chiefly in *on the qui vive*, on the alert or lookout.

■ Originating in a sentry's challenge to a person approaching his post in order to ascertain to whom that person is loyal.
1996 *Spectator* Ever on the *qui vive* for the bore of the party, when sheep replace cows in the fields nearby he comments approvingly: 'Sheep have a more active, at least more interesting, social life than cows.'

quoad /'kwəʊad/ *preposition* E17 Latin (= so far as, as much as, as to, from *quo* where, whither + *ad* to). To the extent of, as regards, with respect to.

quod erat demonstrandum /kwɒd ə ˌrat dɛmən'strandəm/ *noun phrase* M17 Latin (translating Greek *hoti edei deixai*). (Which is) what it was necessary to prove.

■ Generally abbreviated to QED and used to emphasize the clinching point in an argument or to conclude a mathematical proof. Like the less widely used QUOD ERAT FACIENDUM, the phrase and its use are derived from the Greek mathematician Euclid (early 3rd century BC).

quod erat faciendum /kwɒd əˌrat faʃɪ 'ɛndəm/, /kwɒd əˌrat fakɪ'ɛndəm/ *noun phrase* L17 Latin (translating *hoti edei poiein*). (Which is) what it was necessary to construct.

■ Abbreviated to QEF and appended to a geometrical proof.

quodlibet /'kwɒdlɪbɛt/ *noun* LME Medieval Latin (*quodlibet(um)* from Latin *quodlibet*, from *quod* what + *libet* it pleases). **1** LME *History* A question proposed as an exercise in philosophical or theological debate; a scholastic debate, thesis, or exercise. **2** E19 *Music* A light-hearted combination of several tunes; a medley.

quod vide /kwɒd 'viːdeɪ/ *noun phrase* plural **quae vide** /kwʌɪ 'viːdeɪ/ M18 Latin (*quod* which + imperative singular of *videre* to see). Which see.

■ Abbreviated to *q.v.* (plural *qq.v.*) and used to direct a reader to further information under the reference cited.

quondam /'kwɒndəm/, /'kwɒndam/ *adverb, noun, & adjective* M16 Latin (= formerly). **A** *adverb* M16 At one time, formerly. *rare*. **B** *noun* M16 The former holder of an office or position; *derogatory* a person who has been deposed or ejected. **C** *adjective* L16 That once was or existed; former.

quorum /'kwɔːrəm/ *noun* LME Latin (literally, 'of whom (we wish that you be one, two, etc.)' in the wording of commissions for members of bodies, committees, etc.). **1** LME Originally, certain (usually eminent) justices of the peace whose presence was necessary to constitute a deciding body. Later *generally*, all justices collectively. **b** L16 *transferred* Distinguished or essential members of any body; a select company. **2** E17 A fixed minimum number of members whose presence is necessary to make the proceedings of an assembly, society, etc., valid.

quota /'kwəʊtə/ *noun* E17 Medieval Latin (*quota* sc. *pars*) how great (a part), feminine of *quotus*, from Latin *quot* how many). **1** E17 The share which an individual or group is obliged to contribute to a total; the minimum number or quantity of a particular product which under official regulations must be produced, exported, imported, etc. **b** M19 In a system of proportional representation, the minimum number of votes required to elect a candidate. **2** L17 The share of a total or the maximum number or quantity belonging, due, given, or permitted to an individual or group. **b** E20 The maximum number (of immigrants or imports) allowed to enter a country within a set period; (a) regulation imposing such a restriction on entry to a country. Also, the number of students allowed to enrol for a course, at a college, etc.

quot homines, tot sententiae /kwɒt ˌhɒmmeɪz tɒt sɛn'tɛntɪʌɪ/ *noun phrase & interjection* M16 Latin. (There are) as many opinions as (there are) men.

■ From the comedy *Phormio* (line 454) by the Roman playwright Plautus (died 184 BC).
1996 *Oldie* As then, so now: *quot homines, tot sententiae*, there are as many opinions as there are people.

quotum /'kwəʊtəm/ *noun* M17 Latin (neuter singular of *quotus*). A number or quantity considered in proportion to a larger number or amount of which it forms part; a quota.

q.v. abbreviation of QUOD VIDE.

R

rabat /ra'bat/ *noun* M20 French (= collar). A false shirt-front, a stock.

■ Earlier (L16–M17) a *rabat* (also called a *rabato*) was a stiff collar but the word has long been obsolete in this sense.

rabbi /'rabʌɪ/ *noun* LOE ecclesiastical Latin and Greek (from Hebrew *rabbī* my master, from *raḇ* master). **1** LOE A Jewish scholar or teacher having authority on law and doctrine; now *specifically* one authorized by ordination to deal with questions of law and ritual and to perform certain functions. Also as a title of respect and form of address (usually with following personal name). **2** M16 *transferred* A person whose learning, authority, or status is comparable to that of a Jewish rabbi; *specifically* (*United States slang*) a senior official who exerts influence or patronage on behalf of a person.

■ The French word *rabbin* is now rare in English but was formerly used in both senses (sense 1 from L16, sense 2 M16–M17). The ending -*n* may be due to a Semitic plural form.

raccourci /rakursi/ *noun* plural pronounced same M20 French (use as noun of past participle of *raccourcir* to shorten). *Ballet* A movement in which the toe is made to touch the bent knee of the other leg.

rackett /'rakɪt/ *noun* (also **racket, ranket** /'raŋkɪt/) L19 German (*Rackett, Rankett*). *Music* A Renaissance wind instrument related to the oboe.

raclette *in sense 1* /ra'klɛt/, *in sense 2 foreign* /raklɛt/ (*plural same*) *noun* M20 French (= small scraper). **1** M20 *Archaeology* A stone tool of the scraper type discovered in the valley of the Vézère in south-west France, dating from the early Magdalenian period. **2** M20 A dish of cheese melted before an open fire, scraped on to a plate, and served with potatoes.

racloir /raklwɑː/ *noun* L19 French (= scraper). *Archaeology* A prehistoric flint instrument with one broad side shaped for scraping.

raconteur /ˌrakɒn'təː/ *noun* E19 French (from *raconter* to relate). A (usually skilled) teller of anecdotes.

raconteuse /ˌrakɒn'təːz/ *noun* M19 French (feminine of RACONTEUR). A female teller of anecdotes.

> **1995** *Spectator* Freely is not an incisive polemicist, but she's an excellent raconteuse, and one who has knocked around enough to have a good fund of stories.

radeau /ra'dəʊ/ *noun* M18 French (from Provençal *radel*, from Latin diminutive of *ratis* raft). A raft; *specifically* (*Military*) a floating battery.

radicchio /ra'diːkɪəʊ/ *noun* plural **radicchios** L20 Italian (= chicory). A variety of chicory from Italy, with reddish-purple white-veined leaves.

radius /'reɪdɪəs/ *noun* plural **radii** /'reɪdɪʌɪ/ L16 Latin (= staff, spoke, ray). **1** L16–M18 A straight object such as a staff or bar. **2** L16 *Anatomy* and *Zoology* One of the two bones of the forearm; the corresponding bone of a tetrapod's foreleg or a bird's wing. **3** E17 A straight line from the centre of a circle or sphere to the circumference. **4** E18 Any of a set of lines, rods, spokes, etc., diverging from a point like the radii of a circle; a radiating part. **5** M19 A circular area of which the extent is measured by the length of the radius of the circle which bounds it.

radix /'radɪks, 'reɪdɪks/ *noun* plural **radices** /'radɪsiːz/, **radixes** L16 Latin (*radix, radic-* root of a plant). **1 a** L16–E18 *Mathematics* A root of a number. **b** L18 *Mathematics* and *Computing* The number from whose various powers a system of counting, logarithms, etc., proceeds, a base. **2** E17–L18 *Astrology* and *Astronomy* A fact used as a basis of calculation. **3** E17 A thing in which something originates; a source.

■ Sometimes in the phrase *radix malorum* 'the root of evil', with allusion to 1 Timothy 6:10 (Vulgate version). In the Bible it is 'love of money' (*cupiditas*) which is 'the root of all evil', while in popular use it is frequently just 'money'.

rafale /rafal/ *noun* plural pronounced same E20 French (literally, 'gust of wind'). Repeated bursts of gunfire; a drum roll.

raffia /'rafɪə/ *noun* (in sense 1 also **raphia**, (earliest) **rofia**) E18 Malagasy. **1** E18 A palm of the African genus *Raphia*, especially *R. farinifera* of Madagascar. **2** L19 The soft fibre from the leaves of such a palm, used as garden twine, in basketwork, etc.

raffiné /rafine/ *adjective* L19 French. Of manners or judgement: refined.

raga /'rɑːgə/ *noun* (also **rag** /rɑːg/) L18 Sanskrit (*rāga* colour, passion, melody). In Indian music: a pattern of notes used as a basis for melodies and improvisations; a piece of music based on a particular raga.

Ragnarok /'ragnarɒk/ *noun* (also **Ragnarök**) L18 Old Norse (*ragnarǫk, ragnarøkkr* (Icelandic *Ragnarök*), from *ragna* genitive of *regin* the gods + *rǫk* destined end or (later) *røkr, røkkr* twilight). *Scandinavian Mythology* The destruction of the gods; *specifically* the defeat of gods and men by monsters in a final battle. Cf. GÖTTERDÄMMERUNG.

ragout /ra'guː/ *noun* M17 French (*ragoût*, from *ragoûter* to revive the taste of, from as GOÛT). **1** M17 A highly seasoned dish of meat cut into small pieces and stewed with vegetables. **2** L17–M18 A sauce, a relish.

rahat /'rɑːhat/ *noun* M19 Turkish (*rahat* (*lokum*) from Arabic *rāḥat* (*al-ḥulḳūm*) ease (of the throat); cf. LOKUM). Turkish delight. In full *rahat lokum* /lɒ'kuːm/.

rais variant of REIS.

raison d'état /rɛzɔ̃ deta/ *noun phrase* plural **raisons d'état** (pronounced same) M19 French (= reason of State). A reason having to do with the security or interests of a State.
> **1996** *Spectator* This must be conducted on the basis of *raison d'état*, which includes secrecy.

raison d'être /rɛzɔ̃ dɛtr/, /'reɪzɔ̃ ˌdɛtrə/ *noun* plural **raisons d'être** (pronounced same) M19 French (= reason for being). A purpose or reason accounting for or justifying the existence of a thing.
> **1996** *Spectator* . . . it had the bad luck to be the first big British company to become caught up in a lurching shift in society's perceptions of the rights, responsibilities and *raison d'être* of business.

raisonné /rɛzɔne/ *adjective* L18 French (past participle of *raisonner* to reason, from *raison* reason). Reasoned out, systematic. Chiefly in CATALOGUE RAISONNÉ.

raisonneur /rɛzɔnœr/ *noun* plural pronounced same E20 French (literally 'a person who reasons or argues'). A character

in a play etc. who expresses the author's message or standpoint.

raisons d'état, raisons d'être plurals of RAISON D'ÉTAT, RAISON D'ÊTRE.

raita /rɑːˈiːtə/ *noun* M20 Hindustani (*rāytā*). An Indian dish consisting of chopped vegetables (or fruit) in curd or yoghurt.

raj /rɑː(d)ʒ/ *noun* E19 Hindustani (*rāj* from Sanskrit *rājya*; cf. RAJA). **1** E19 Sovereignty, rule; kingdom. **2** M19 *History* (the *Raj*) (The period of) British rule in the Indian subcontinent before 1947. In full *British Raj*.

raja /'rɑːdʒə/ *noun* (also **rajah**, (as a title) **Raja**) M16 Sanskrit (*rājan* king, from *rāj* to reign or rule; probably through Portuguese and related to Latin *rex, regis*, Old Irish *rí, ríg* king). *History* Originally, an Indian king or prince. Later also, a petty dignitary or noble in India; a Malay or Javanese ruler or chief.

raja yoga /ˌrɑːdʒə 'jəʊgə/ *noun phrase* L19 Sanskrit (from *rājan* king + YOGA). A form of yoga aimed at gaining control over the mind and emotions.

raki /rəˈkiː/, /'raki/ *noun* L17 Turkish (*rāqī* (now *rakı* whence also modern Greek *rhakē, rhaki*) brandy, spirits). Originally, an aromatic liquor made from grain-spirit or grape juice in Greece, Turkey, and the Middle East. Now also, a liquor made from various other ingredients in eastern Europe and the Middle East; a drink of this.

rakshasa /'rɑːkʃasa/ *noun* (also **raksasa**) M19 Sanskrit (*rākṣasa* demon). *Hindu Mythology* A malignant demon, *especially* any of a band at war with Rama and Hanuman; a representation of such a demon.

raku /'rɑːkuː/ *noun & adjective* L19 Japanese (literally 'ease, relaxed state, enjoyment'). (Designating) a kind of usually lead-glazed Japanese pottery, often used as tea-bowls and similar utensils.

rallentando /ˌralən'tandəʊ/ *adverb, adjective, & noun* E19 Italian (present participle of *rallentare* to slow down). *Music* **A** *adverb & adjective* E19 (A direction:) with gradual decrease of speed. **B** *noun* M19 plural **rallentandos, rallentandi** /ˌralən'tandi/. A gradual decrease of speed; a passage (to be) played with a gradual decrease of speed.

ramada /rəˈmɑːdə/ *noun* M19 Spanish. An arbour, a porch. *United States*.

rambutan /ram'buːt(ə)n/ *noun* (also **rambootan**) E18 Malay (from *rambut* hair, in reference to the covering of the fruit). A Malaysian tree, *Nephelium lappaceum* (family Sapindaceae); the fruit of this tree, resembling a lychee and covered with soft bright red spines or prickles.

ramen /'rɑːmɛn/ *noun* (treated as *singular* or *plural*) L20 Japanese (from Chinese *lā* to pull + *miàn* noodles). Quick-cooking Chinese noodles, usually served in a broth with meat and vegetables.

rancheria /ˌrɑːn(t)ʃəˈriːə/ *noun* E17 Spanish (*ranchería*, from as RANCHO). In Spanish America and the western United States: a collection of Indian huts; a place or house where a number of rancheros live.

ranchero /rɑːnˈtʃɛːrəʊ/ *noun* plural **rancheros** E19 Spanish (from as RANCHO). A rancher or ranchman, especially in Mexico.

ranchito /rɑːnˈtʃiːtəʊ/ *noun* plural **ranchitos** M19 Spanish (diminutive of RANCHO). In the western United States: a small ranch or farm.

rancho /'rɑːn(t)ʃəʊ/ *noun* plural **ranchos** E19 Spanish (= a group of people who eat together). **1** E19 In Latin America: a hut, a hovel, a very simple building; a group of these, a small village; *especially* one put up to accommodate travellers. Later also, a roadhouse, an inn; a meal at such a place. **2** M19 In the western United States: a cattle-farm, a ranch.

rancio /'rɑːnsɪəʊ/ *adjective & noun* M19 Spanish (literally, 'rancid', from Latin *rancidus* stinking). **A** *adjective* M19 Of wine: having the distinctive bouquet, nutty flavour, or tawny colour characteristic of certain well-matured, fortified, or dessert wines. **B** *noun* M20 plural **rancios** /'rɑːnsɪəʊz/. A rancio wine.

rand /rand/, /rant/ *noun* plural **rands**, (in sense 2 also) same M19 Afrikaans (from Dutch *rand* edge). **1** M19 In South Africa: a rocky ridge or area of high sloping ground, especially overlooking a river-valley; *specifically* (*the Rand*), the Witwatersrand, the chief gold-mining area of the Transvaal. **2** M20 The basic monetary unit of South Africa since 1961.

randkluft /'rantklʊft/ *noun* plural **randklufts**, **randklüfte** /'rantklyftə/ E20 German (literally, 'edge, crevice'). A crevasse between the head of a glacier and a surrounding rock wall.

randori /ranˈdɔːri/ *noun* E20 Japanese (from *ran* disorder + *tori* bout, participation). Free or informal judo practice.

ranee /'rɑːniː/ *noun* (also **rani**, (as a title) **Ranee**) L17 Hindustani (*rānī* from Prakrit from Sanskrit *rājñī* feminine of *rājan* RAJA). History A Hindu queen; a raja's wife or widow.

rangé /rɑ̃ʒe/ *adjective* (feminine **rangée**) L19 French (past participial adjective of *ranger* to range). Of a person, lifestyle, etc.: orderly, regular, settled.

 ■ Earlier (L18) in dictionaries in a heraldic sense describing charges 'placed in a row' or 'set within a band', but this sense seems never to have gained wider circulation.

rangoli /raŋˈgəʊli/ *noun* M20 Marathi (*rãgolī*). A Hindu symbolic design painted in coloured powdered stone, rice, etc.

rani variant of RANEE.

ranz-des-vaches /rɑ̃devaʃ/ *noun* plural same L18 Swiss French dialect (from unknown first element + 'of the cows'). A melody played especially by Swiss cowherds, consisting of irregular phrases formed from the harmonic notes of the Alpine horn.

rapide /rapid/, /raˈpiːd/ *noun* plural pronounced same E20 French. In France: an express train.

rapido /'rapɪdəʊ/, *foreign* /'rapido/ *adverb, adjective, & noun* L19 Italian. **A** *adverb and adjective* L19 Music (A direction:) in rapid time. **B** *noun* M20 plural **rapidi** /'rapɪdi/, **rapidos** /'rapɪdəʊz/. In Italy: an express train.

rappel /raˈpɛl/ *noun* M19 French (from *rappeler* to recall). **1** M19 A drum roll calling soldiers to arms. *rare*. **2** M20 *Mountaineering*. An abseil.

rapport /raˈpɔː/ *noun* M17 French (from *rapporter* to bring back). **1** M17 Relationship, *especially* a relationship characterized by harmonious accord. **2** M19 A posited state of deep spiritual, emotional, or mental connection between people.

 ■ Originally (M16) introduced in the sense of 'report' or 'talk', but this was never widely current and has been totally ousted by the current sense. Cf. EN RAPPORT.

 1 1996 *Times* The 'jungle fighter' boss, who rules by fear and manipulation, gets less out of the workforce than the manager who sets out to establish a close rapport with the employees.

rapportage /rapɔrtaʒ/, /ˌrapɔːˈtɑːʒ/ *noun* E20 French (literally, 'tale-telling', influenced by *reportage*). The reporting or describing of events in writing; mere description, uncreative recounting.

rapporteur /ˌrapɔːˈtəː/ *noun* L18 French (from *rapporter* to bring back). A person who makes a report of the proceedings of a committee etc. for a higher body.

■ Introduced earlier (but used only L15) from Old French in the general sense of 'a reporter, a recounter', *rapporteur* is now used in English only in the very specific sense above.

1996 *Times* How many emuwonks does it take to change a light-bulb? Five hundred and one. One to hold the bulb, 250 to revolve the room around him, and another 250 to act as *rapporteurs* for the ghastly documentation with 94 subsections.

rapprochement /raprɔʃmã/, /raˈprɒʃmã/ *noun* E19 French (from *rapprocher* to bring closer together, from *re-* + *approcher* to approach). (An) establishment or resumption of harmonious relations, especially between foreign States.

1996 *Country Life* . . . the shooting down of two light planes by the Cuban airforce has reversed the rapprochement with the United States . . .

raptus /ˈraptəs/ *noun* M19 Latin. **1** M19 A state of rapture. **2** M19 *Medicine* A sudden violent attack. Usually with modern Latin specifying word.

rara avis /ˌrɛːrə ˈeɪvɪs/, /ˌrɑːrə ˈavɪs/ *noun phrase* plural **rarae aves** /ˌrɛːriː ˈeɪviːz/, /ˌrɑːriː/, /ˌrɑːreɪ ˈaviːz/ E17 Latin (= rare bird). **1** E17 A kind of person rarely encountered; an unusual or exceptional person. **2** L19 A rarity; an unusual or exceptional occurrence or thing.

rariora /ˌrɛːrɪˈɔːrə/, /ˌrarɪˈɔːrə/ *noun plural* M19 Latin (neuter plural comparative of *rarus* rare *adjective*). Rare books.

rarissime /ˌrɛːˈrɪsɪmeɪ/, /raˈrɪsɪmeɪ/ *adjective* E20 Latin (literally, 'very rarely (sc. found)'). Extremely rare.

rasa /ˈrʌsə/ *noun* 1 (also **ras** /rʌs/) L18 Sanskrit (literally, 'juice, essence, flavour'). The mood or aesthetic impression of an artistic work.

rasa /ˈrɑːsə/ *noun* 2 (also **ras** /rɑːs/) E19 Sanskrit (*rāsa*). A traditional Indian dance (commemorating that) performed by Krishna and the gopis in Hindu mythology; a festival celebrating this.

rasant /ˈreɪz(ə)nt/ *adjective* (also **razant**) L17 Old and Modern French (present participle of *raser* to shave close). *Military* Of a line of defence: sweeping; long and curving (originally so that the shot would graze the target).

rasgado /rasˈɡado/, /razˈɡɑːdəʊ/ *noun* plural **rasgados** /rasˈɡados/, /razˈɡɑːdəʊz/ M19 Spanish (past participle of *rasgar* to strum, make a flourish). *Music* (An arpeggio produced by) the act of sweeping the strings of a guitar with the fingertips.

Raskolnik /rʌˈskɒlnɪk/ *noun* (also **raskolnik**) E18 Russian (*raskol'nik*, from *raskol* separation, schism + *noun* suffix *-nik* person connected with (something)). *Ecclesiastical History* A member of a Russian Orthodox group which refused to accept the liturgical reforms of the patriarch Nikon (1605–81); an Old Believer.

rassolnik /rʌsˈsoljnjik/ *noun* (also **rasolnik**) E20 Russian (*rassol'nik* from *rassol* brine + *-nik*). A Russian soup of brine, salted dill cucumbers, and pickled vegetables, meat, or fish, served chilled.

rasta /rasta/ *noun* plural pronounced same E20 French. Abbreviation of RASTAQUOUÈRE.

rastaquouère /rastakwɛr/ *noun & adjective* plural pronounced same L19 French (from South American Spanish *rastacuero* tycoon in the hide trade, upstart). **A** *noun* L19 A person (especially from a Mediterranean or South American country) intruding into a particular social group and having an exaggerated manner or style of dress; a dashing but untrustworthy foreigner. **B** *attributive* or as *adjective* E20 Of, pertaining to, or characteristic of *rastaquouères*; of the nature of a *rastaquouère*.

ratafia /ratəˈfiə/ *noun* L17 French. **1** L17 A liqueur flavoured with almonds or kernels of peach, apricot, or cherry. **2** M19 A kind of small macaroon.

rataplan /ratəˈplan/ *noun* M19 French (of imitative origin). A drumming or beating noise; a tattoo.

ratatouille /ratəˈtuːi/, /ratəˈtwiː/ *noun* L19 French ((dialect) cf. French *touiller* to stir up). **1** A ragout. Only in L19. **2** M20 A vegetable dish of aubergines, courgettes, tomatoes, onions, and peppers fried and stewed in oil.

raté /rate/ *adjective & noun* plural pronounced same E20 French. **A** *adjective* E20

Ineffective; unsuccessful. **B** *noun* E20 A person who has failed in his or her vocation.

A 1977 *Times* They are failures . . . They will all be *ratés* and hopeless when they are 30.

ratelier /ratəlje/ *noun* plural pronounced same M17 French (*râtelier*). **1** A stand for arms. *rare*. Only in M17. **2** M19 A set of (especially false) teeth.

ratine /rə'ti:n/ *noun & adjective* (also **ratiné** /rə'ti:neɪ/) E20 French (*ratiné* past participle of *ratiner* to put a nap on (cloth), from *ratine* ratteen). (Made of) a plain-woven (usually cotton) fabric with a loose open weave and rough surface, used for linings, furniture covers, etc.

rauschpfeife /'rauʃ,(p)fʌɪfə/ *noun* plural **rauschpfeifen** /'rauʃ,(p)fʌɪf(ə)n/ L19 German (= reed-pipe; cf. SCHREIERPFEIFE). *Music* **1** L19 A low-pitched mixture stop in an organ. **2** M20 A reed-cap shawm of the Renaissance period.

ravalement /ravalmã/ *noun* plural pronounced same M20 French (from *ravaler* to bring down, reduce). *Music* The action or an instance of modifying and extending the range of a keyboard instrument by rebuilding; an instrument modified in this way.

ravelin /'ravlɪn/ *noun* L16 French (from Italian *ravellina* (now *rivellino*), of unknown origin). *History* An outwork of fortifications, consisting of two faces forming a salient angle, constructed beyond the main ditch and in front of the curtain.

ravigote /ravigɒt/ *noun* M19 French (from *ravigoter* to invigorate). A mixture of chopped chervil, chives, tarragon, and shallots, used to give piquancy to a sauce, as a base for a herb butter, etc.; a vinaigrette dressing containing capers and chopped hard-boiled egg flavoured with such a mixture; a velouté sauce containing such a herb butter.

ravinement /rə'vi:nm(ə)nt/ *noun* E20 French (from *raviner* to furrow). *Physical Geography* Erosion of ravines or gullies in soil or soft rock by running water. Also, an unconformity in river or shallow marine sediments caused by interruption of deposition by erosion.

ravioli /ravɪ'əʊli/ *noun* M19 Italian (plural of *raviolo*). Pasta in the form of small square cases filled with minced meat, vegetables, etc.

ravissant /ravisã/ *adjective* (also (feminine) **ravissante** /ravisãt/) M17 French (present participial adjective of *ravir* (formerly) to seize, carry off, (now) to enchant). Ravishing, delightful.

■ Originally (ME–M16) used in English of an animal and reflecting the older French sense of *ravir*, hence 'ravening'; it also had a specific heraldic sense (E18) meaning 'in the half-raised posture of a wolf beginning to spring on its prey'.

rayah /'rʌɪə/ *noun* E19 Turkish (*râya* from Arabic *ra'āyā* plural of *ra'iyya(t)*). Under the Ottoman Empire, a non-Muslim subject of the Sultan of Turkey, liable to a poll tax.

rayonnant /rɛjɒnã/ *adjective* (feminine **rayonnante** /rɛjɒnãt/) E19 French (present participial adjective of *rayonner* to shine forth). Of a person: beaming, radiant.

razant variant of RASANT.

razet /razɛ/ *noun* plural pronounced same M20 French (from Provençal *raset*). *Bullfighting* In southern France, a contest in which teams compete to snatch a rosette from between the bull's horns.

razeteur /razətœr/ *noun* M20 French. A member of a team competing in a *razet*.

razzia /'razɪə/ *noun* M19 French (from Algerian Arabic *ġāziya* raid, from Arabic *ġazā* to go forth to fight, make a raid). A raid, a foray; *specifically* (*historical*) a hostile Moorish incursion for purposes of conquest, plunder, capture of slaves, etc.

re /reɪ/, /ri:/ *preposition* E18 Latin (ablative of *res* thing). In the matter of, concerning, about.

realia /reɪˈɑːlɪə/, /rɪˈeɪlɪə/ *noun* plural M20 Late Latin (use as noun of neuter plural of *realis* real). **1** M20 Objects which may be used as teaching aids but were not made for the purpose. *North American*. **2** M20 Real things, actual facts, especially as distinct from theories about them.

realpolitik /reˌɑːlpɒliˈtiːk/, /reɪˈɑːlpɒlɪtiːk/ *noun* E20 German (*real* real + *Politik* politics). Politics based on practical, rather than moral or ideological, considerations; practical politics.

1995 *Spectator* The Defence Secretary, Michael Portillo, was at last moved by the spectacle of the Balkan tragedy to go beyond considerations of *realpolitik* to true moral indignation.

Realpolitiker /reˌɑːlpɒliˈtiːkə/, /reɪˈɑːlpɒ ˌlɪtiːkə/ *noun* M20 German. A person who believes in, advocates, or practises REAL-POLITIK.

1995 *Spectator* Machiavelli . . . is not a mere *realpolitiker* writing a handbook counselling princes how to achieve and maintain themselves in power.

reata variant of RIATA.

reb /rɛb/ *noun* L19 Yiddish (from as REBBE). A traditional Jewish courtesy title used preceding a man's forename or surname.

rebab /rɪˈbab/ *noun* M18 Arabic (*rabāb*). A bowed or (occasionally) plucked stringed instrument of Arab origin, used especially in North Africa, the Middle East, and the Indian subcontinent.

rebbe /ˈrɛbə/ *noun* L19 Yiddish (from Hebrew *rabbī* rabbi). A rabbi; *specifically* a Hasidic religious leader.

rebbitzin /ˈrɛbɪtsɪn/ *noun* L19 Yiddish (feminine of REBBE). The wife of a rabbi.

rebec /ˈriːbɛk/ *noun* (also **rebeck**) LME French (alteration of Old French *rebebe*, *rubebe*). Chiefly *History* A medieval musical instrument with usually three strings and played with a bow; a player on this in an orchestra etc.

reblochon /rəblɔʃɔ̃/ *noun* E20 French. A soft French cheese made originally and chiefly in Savoy.

reboso variant of REBOZO.

rebours see À REBOURS.

rebozo /rɪˈbəʊzəʊ/, /rɪˈbəʊsəʊ/ *noun* (also **reboso**) plural **rebozos** E19 Spanish. A long scarf covering the head and shoulders, traditionally worn by Spanish-American women.

rebus /ˈriːbəs/ *noun* E17 French (*rébus* from Latin *rebus* ablative plural of *res* thing). A representation of a word or phrase by pictures, symbols, arrangement of letters, etc., which suggest the word or phrase, or the syllables of which it is made up; *specifically* a device, often of heraldic appearance, suggesting the name of its bearer.

■ This usage originated in *De rebus quae geruntur* (literally, 'concerning the things that are taking place'), the title given in sixteenth-century Picardy to satirical pieces containing riddles in picture form.

rebus sic stantibus /ˌreɪbəs sɪk ˈstantɪbəs/ *noun & adverb phrase* E17 Modern Latin (literally, 'things standing thus'). *International Law* (According to) the principle that a treaty is subject to an implied condition that if circumstances are substantially different from those obtaining when it was concluded, then a party to the treaty is entitled to be released from it.

recado /reˈkado/, /rɪˈkɑːdəʊ/ *noun* plural **recados** /reˈkados/, /rɪˈkɑːdəʊz/ E17 Spanish and Portuguese (= gift, of unknown origin). **1** A present; a message of goodwill. Only in 17. **2** E19 A South American saddle or saddle-cloth.

Récamier /reɪˈkamjeɪ/, *foreign* /rekamje/ (*plural same*) *noun & adjective* (also **récamier**) E20 French (from the name of Jeanne *Récamier* (1777–1849), society hostess, depicted reclining on a chaise longue in a famous portrait by Jacques Louis David). (Designating) a style of chaise longue.

1979 *New York Times Magazine* The smaller studio . . . is more formal, primarily because of the major furnishings—a matching pair of *récamiers* (Empire-style lounges).

réchaud /reʃo/ *noun* plural pronounced same E20 French (from *réchauffer* to reheat, warm up again). A dish in which food is warmed or kept warm.

réchauffé /reʃofe/, /reɪˈʃəʊfeɪ/ *noun & adjective* E19 French (past participle of *réchauffer* to reheat, from *re-* again + *échauffer* to warm (up), from Proto-Romance variation of Latin *cal(e)facere* to make warm, from *calere* to be warm + *facere* to make). **A** *noun* E19 A warmed-up dish; *figurative* a rehash. **B** *adjective* E20 (Of food) reheated; *figurative* rehashed.

recherché /rəˈʃɛːʃeɪ/ *adjective* L17 French (past participle of *rechercher* to seek out, look for). Carefully sought out; rare, exotic; far-fetched, obscure.

1995 *Observer Review* Now there's nothing wrong with using *recherché* words—Nabokov did it all the time—and the inquisitive need only consult a dictionary.

recherche du temps perdu /rəʃɛrʃ dy tɑ̃ pɛrdy/ *noun phrase* M20 French (*à la recherche du temps perdu*, literally, 'in search of the lost time', title of novel by Marcel Proust (1871–1922)). A narration or evocation of one's early life.

1996 *Spectator* Marcel Proust was never one of the great rugby players, but the entire impetus of the French rugby union team springs from *la recherche du temps perdu*.

Rechtsstaat /ˈrɛçtsˌʃtɑːt/ *noun* M20 German (from *Recht* right + genitive suffix *-s* +

Staat State). A country in which the rule of law prevails.

récit /resi/ *noun* plural pronounced same L19 French. **1** L19 *Music* A passage or composition for a solo voice or instrument. Also, a division of the classical French organ. **2** M20 The narrative of a book as opposed to the dialogue; a book or passage consisting largely of this.

recitativo /ˌretʃita'tiːvo/, /ˌrɛsɪtə'tiːvəʊ/ *noun* plural **recitativi** /ˌretʃita'tiːvi/, **recitativos** /ˌrɛsɪtə'tiːvəʊz/ M17 Italian (from Latin *recitat-* past participial stem of *recitare* to recite). *Music* A style of musical declamation between singing and ordinary speech; a passage in a musical score or libretto (intended to be) delivered in this style; (a) recitative.

■ *Recitativo* may be accompanied either by the full orchestra (*recitativo accompagnato* or *recitativo stromentato* (literally, 'instrumented')) or by continuo instruments only (*recitativo secco*).

réclame /reklam/ *noun* plural pronounced same L19 French (from *réclamer* to ask for). (An) advertisement; self-publicity; public acclaim or notoriety.

1996 *Spectator* It is difficult for people today to realise the extraordinary *réclame* that T. E. Lawrence . . . had in those years between the wars.

récolte /rekɔlt/ *noun* plural pronounced same (also (earlier) **recolt**) L18 French. In France: a harvest, a crop.

recta plural of RECTUM.

recte /'rɛkteɪ/ *adverb* M19 Latin (literally, 'in a straight line, rightly'). Correctly.

■ Used when introducing a word or phrase as a correct version of that just given, as in 'Jane Blundell *recte* Blunden'.

recti plural of RECTUS.

rectius /'rɛktɪəs/ *adverb* M20 Latin (comparative of RECTE). More correctly: introducing a word or phrase as a more correct version of that just given.

recto /'rɛktəʊ/ *noun* plural **rectos** E19 Latin ((sc. *folio*) ablative of *rectus* right). The right-hand page of an open book; the front of a leaf in a manuscript or printed book, as opposed to the back or VERSO.

rectum /'rɛktəm/ *noun* plural **rectums**, **recta** /'rɛktə/ M16 Latin (neuter of *rectus* straight, short for *intestinum rectum* straight gut). The final section of the large intestine leading to the anus.

rectus /'rɛktəs/ *noun* plural **recti** /'rɛktʌɪ/ E18 Latin ((sc. *musculus* muscle) see preceding). **1** E18 *Anatomy* Any of several straight muscles, especially of the abdomen, thigh, neck, and eye. Frequently with modern Latin specifying word. Also *rectus muscle*. **2** M20 *Music* In a fugal composition, the version of a theme performed in the original, as opposed to the reversed or inverted, order.

recueil /rəkœj/ *noun* L15 Old and Modern French (from *recueillir* to gather up, from Latin *recolligere*, from as re- + *colligere* to collect). **1** L15 A literary compilation. **2** L15-L16 Reception, welcome; succour.

recueillement /rəkœjmã/ *noun* M19 French (from as RECUEIL). Serious concentration of thought.

reculer pour mieux sauter /rəkyle pur mjø sote/ *noun phrase* E19 French (literally, 'to draw back in order to leap better'). The use of a withdrawal or setback as a basis for further advance or success.

1996 *Country Life* Hostility towards mobiles runs high in the world of commuters for the train has traditionally provided a brief capsule of immunity from the real world, an opportunity to *reculer pour mieux sauter*.

redingote /'rɛdɪŋɡəʊt/ *noun* L18 French (from English *riding-coat*). Originally, a man's double-breasted greatcoat with long plain skirts not cut away in the front. Now usually, a woman's long coat with a cut-away front or a contrasting piece on the front.

redivivus /rɛdɪ'viːvəs/ *postpositive adjective* (feminine **rediviva** /rɛdɪ'viːvə/; occasionally (earlier) Anglicized as **redivive** /rɛdɪ'vʌɪv/) L16 Latin (from re- again + *vivus* living, alive). Come back to life; reborn; renewed.

■ Always postpositive (see quotation). The Latin form first appeared (L17) in book titles, e.g. R. Head's *Proteus redivivus: or the art of wheedling* (1675). Cf. REDUX.

1975 *Times* Some still believe in Stormont Redivivus.

redowa /'rɛdəvə/ *noun* M19 French (or German, from Czech *rejdovák*, from *rejdovat* to turn or whirl round). A Bohemian folk-dance; a ballroom dance in relatively quick triple time resembling this; a piece of music for such a dance.

reductio ad absurdum /rɪˌdʌktɪəʊ ad əb'sɜːdəm/ *noun phrase* M18 Latin (literally, 'reduction to the absurd'). *Logic* A method of proving the falsity of a premiss by showing that the logical consequence is absurd.

> **1995** *Times* Making criminal the carrying of all knives in public places could—and this is the *reductio ad absurdum*—lead to the prosecution of people going on a picnic.

reductio ad impossibile /rɪˌdʌktɪəʊ ad ɪmpɒˈsɪbɪli/ *noun phrase* M16 Latin (literally, 'reduction to the impossible'). A method of proving a proposition by drawing an absurd or impossible conclusion from its contradictory.

redux /ˈriːdʌks/ *adjective* L19 Latin (from *reducere* to bring back). **1** L19 *Medicine* Of crepitation etc.: indicating the return of the lungs to a healthy state. Now *rare*. **2** L19 Brought back, revived, restored.

■ Usually postpositive and often in titles, from John Dryden's poem on the restoration of King Charles II *Astraea Redux* (1662) to John Updike's novel *Rabbit Redux* (1971); cf. REDIVIVUS.

Reeperbahn /ˈriːpəbɑːn/ *noun* L20 German (a street in Hamburg, Germany, literally, 'rope-walk', from *Reeper* ropemaker + *Bahn* road, way). (The principal street in) the red-light district of a city etc.

referendum /rɛfəˈrɛndəm/ *noun plural* **referendums, referenda** /rɛfəˈrɛndə/ M19 Latin (gerund or neuter gerundive of *referre* to refer). The process or principle of referring an important political question, e.g. a proposed constitutional change, to the entire electorate to be decided by a general vote; a vote taken by referendum.

reflet /rəflɛ/ *noun plural* pronounced same M19 French. Colour due to reflection; lustre, iridescence; *specifically* a metallic lustre on pottery.

refugium /rɪˈfjuːdʒɪəm/ *noun plural* **refugia** /rɪˈfjuːdʒɪə/ M20 Latin (= place of refuge). *Biology* A refuge, *specifically* one in which a species survived a period of glaciation.

> **1996** *New Scientist* . . . during the last ice ages . . . less rain fell over Amazonia. As a result, the rainforest shrunk into isolated pockets, or refugia, in the wettest parts of the region.

reg /rɛg/ *noun* E20 Arabic (colloquial). *Physical Geography* A desert plain covered with small rounded pebbles; a stony desert.

> **1976** L. Deighton *Twinkle, Twinkle, Little Spy* The going changed to the gravelly surface of the 'reg' and then to rough 'washboard'.

regalia /rɪˈgeɪlɪə/ *noun* **1** *plural and collective singular* M16 Medieval Latin (= royal residence, royal rights, use as noun of neuter plural of *regalis* regal). **1** M16 Rights belonging to a king or queen; royal powers or privileges. **2** The emblems or insignia of royalty. Also *transferred*, the decorations or insignia of an order; any distinctive or elaborate clothes.

> **2 1996** *Times Magazine* Just as no one who lives in London has ever been . . . to see the crown jewels, so I had never been to Edinburgh Castle to see the Scottish regalia.

regalia /rɪˈgeɪlɪə/ *noun* **2** E19 Spanish (= royal privilege). A Cuban or other large high-quality cigar.

regardant /rɪˈgɑːd(ə)nt/ *adjective & noun* LME Old and Modern French ((also Anglo-Norman) present participle of *regarder* to look at). **1** LME *Heraldry* Usually of a lion: looking backwards over the shoulder. Usually *postpositive*. **2** L16 Observant, watchful, contemplative.

■ In feudal usage also with reference to a serf attached to a manor, as in *villein regardant*.

regatta /rɪˈgatə/ *noun* E17 Italian (Venetian dialect *regatta, rigatta, regata* a fight, a struggle, a contest). **1** E17 Any of certain boat races held on the Grand Canal in Venice. **2** L18 An organized series of boat or yacht races. **3** M19 A cotton fabric, usually made in twill; a striped garment made in this fabric.

régie /reʒi/ *noun plural* pronounced same L18 French (feminine past participle of *régir* to rule). In some European countries, a government department that controls an industry or service; *specifically* (*historical*) one with complete control of the importation, manufacture, and taxation of tobacco, salt, etc.

regime /reɪˈʒiːm/ *noun* (also **régime**) L15 French (*régime* from Latin REGIMEN). **1** L15 A lifestyle adopted for health reasons; a REGIMEN 2. **2** L18 A method or system of rule or government; a system or institution having widespread influence or prevalence. Now frequently (usually *derogatory*), a particular government. **3** *Physical Geography* **a** M19 The condition of a watercourse with regard to changes in its form or bed; *especially* an equilibrium between erosion and deposition. **b** L19 The condition of a body of water with regard to the rates at which water enters and leaves it. **4** L19 *Science and Engineering* The set of conditions under which a system occurs or is maintained.

regimen /ˈrɛdʒɪmən/ *noun* LME Latin (from *regere* to rule). **1** LME The action of governing; government, rule. Later also, a particular system of government; a regime. *archaic*. **2** LME Chiefly *Medicine* A prescribed course of exercise, way of life, or diet, especially for the promotion or restoration of one's health. **3** M16 *Grammar* The government of one word by another; the relationship between one word and another dependent word. Now *rare*. **4** E19 *Physical Geography* REGIME sense 3a.

régisseur /reʒisœr/ *noun* plural pronounced same E19 French. *Theatre* and *Ballet* A stage-manager, an artistic director.

Regius /ˈriːdʒəs/ *adjective* E17 Latin (= royal, from *rex, reg-* king). Designating (a professor holding) a university chair founded by a monarch or filled by Crown appointment.

reglement /rɛɡləmã/ *noun* plural pronounced same L16 French (*règlement, reiglement,* from Old and Modern French *regler, reigler* to rule, from late Latin *regulare* to regulate). **1** L16–M18 The action of regulating or controlling something. **2** M17 A regulation.

règlement de compte /rɛɡləmã də kɔ̃t/ *noun phrase* L20 French. Settlement of an account; the settling of a score.
1995 *Spectator* The summer of dirt and treachery will be followed by a *règlement des comptes* in the autumn.

Reich /raɪk/, /raɪx/ *noun* plural **Reiche** /raɪkə/ E20 German (= kingdom, empire, State). Chiefly *History* The former German State or commonwealth, *especially* the Third Reich (the Nazi regime 1933–45).

reine /rɛn/ *noun* M19 French (= queen). *Cookery* Chiefly in *à la reine* (literally, 'in the fashion of a queen'), designating a dish prepared in some special way.

reinette /reɪˈnɛt/ *noun* LME French (*reinette, rainette,* perhaps from *raine* tree frog (from Latin *rana* frog), from the spots in certain varieties). Any of several eating apples of French origin, chiefly small and late-ripening, with dry skin and firm juicy flesh.

reis /reɪs/ *noun* (also **rais** /raɪs/) L16 Arabic (*ra'īs* chief from *ra's* head). **1** L16 The captain of a boat or ship. **2** L17 A chief, a governor.

2 1996 *Times* On January 20, the Palestinian people will vote to elect their *rais,* or 'leader', and an 88-member national council.

reja /ˈrexa/ *noun* M19 Spanish. In Spain: a wrought-iron screen or grille used to protect windows, chapel tombs, etc.

relâche /rəlaʃ/ *noun* plural pronounced same M19 French. A period of rest, an interval; a break *from* something.

relais /rəlɛ/ *noun* plural pronounced same M20 French. In France: a café, a restaurant, sometimes also providing overnight accommodation.

relance /rəlãs/ *noun* plural pronounced same L20 French. *Politics* A relaunch, a revival, especially of a policy.

relevé /rələˈveɪ/ *noun* E19 French (= raised up). **1** E19 A course of a meal; a remove. *archaic*. **2** M20 *Ballet* A step in which the body is raised on half or full point. **3** M20 *Ecology* An enumeration of the species and environmental factors in a small stand of vegetation, taken as a sample of a wider area; the stand of vegetation itself.

relievo /rɪˈliːvəʊ/ *noun* plural **relievos** (also **rilievo** /rɪˈljeɪvəʊ/) E17 Italian (*rilievo* from *rilevare* to raise, ultimately from Latin *relevare* to raise again). **1** A method of moulding, carving, etc., in which the design stands out from the plane surface. Cf. ALTO-RELIEVO, BASSO-RELIEVO, MEZZO-RELIEVO. **2** The appearance of solidity given to a composition on a plane surface; *figurative* vividness or distinctness due to artistic presentation.

religieuse /rəliʒjøz/ *noun* plural pronounced same L17 French (feminine of next). **1** L17 A woman bound by religious vows; a nun. **2** M20 A confection consisting of two round cakes of choux pastry sandwiched together with cream and decorated with icing.

religieux /rəliʒjø/ *noun* plural same M17 French. A man bound by religious vows; a monk.

religioso /reˌliːdʒiˈoːzo/, /rɪˌlɪdʒɪˈəʊzəʊ/ *adverb & adjective* M19 Italian (= religious). *Music* (A direction:) with a devotional quality.

reliquiae /rɪˈlɪkwiː/ *noun plural* M17 Latin (use as noun of feminine plural of *reliquus* remaining, from as *re* + *liq-* stem of *linquere* to leave). Remains; *specifically* (a) *Geology* fossilized remains of animals or plants; (b) literary remains, unpublished or uncollected writings.

relleno abbreviation of CHILLI RELLENO.

remanié /rəmanje/ adjective L19 French (past participle of remanier to rehandle, reshape). Geology Derived from an older stratum or structure.

remaniement /rəmanimɑ̃/ noun plural pronounced same E20 French (from as preceding). A rearrangement, a reconstruction.

remarque /rɪˈmɑːk/, foreign /rəmark/ (plural same) noun (also **remark**) L19 French. Engraving A distinguishing feature indicating the state of the plate, frequently taking the form of a sketch in the margin.

remboîtage /rɑ̃bwataʒ/ noun plural pronounced same M20 French (from remboîter to re-case (a book)). The action or an act of transferring a book into new binding, especially of superior quality.

remittitur /rɪˈmɪtɪtə/ noun L18 Latin (3rd person singular passive of remittere to remit). Law 1 L18 The remission of excessive damages awarded to a plaintiff; a formal statement of this. 2 L18 The action of sending the transcript of a case back from an appellate to a trial court; a formal notice of this.

remontoir /ˌrɛmənˈtwɑː/ noun (also **remontoire**) E19 French (from remonter to remount). Horology A device by which a uniform impulse is given to the pendulum or balance at regular intervals.

remora /ˈrɛmərə/ noun M16 Latin (= delay, hindrance, from re- + mora delay). 1 M16 Any of various slender marine fishes of the family Echeneidae, with the dorsal fin modified to form a large sucker for attachment to sharks etc., formerly believed to hinder the progress of any sailing ship to which it attached itself. 2 E17 An obstacle, a hindrance, an impediment.

rémoulade /ˈrɛmʊlɑːd/, foreign /remulad/ (plural same) noun (also **remoulade**) M19 French (from Italian remolata, of unknown origin). A salad dressing made with hard-boiled egg-yolks, oil, vinegar, herbs, etc.

remplaçant /rɑ̃plasɑ̃/ noun (feminine **remplaçante** /rɑ̃plasɑ̃t/) plural pronounced same M19 French (present participial adjective of remplacer to replace). A person who replaces another.

remskoen /ˈrɛmskʊn/ noun (also **riemskoen** /riːmskʊn/ and other variants) plural **remskoene** /ˈrɛmskʊnə/ E19 Afrikaans (from Dutch remschoen, from rem brake + schoen shoe). South African History A wooden or metal shoe used to prevent a wheel from revolving; figurative an impediment to progress.

remuage /rəmɥaʒ/, /ˌrɛmjʊˈɑː/ noun E20 French (literally, 'moving about'). The periodic turning or shaking of bottled wine, especially champagne, to move sediment towards the cork.

remuda /rəˈmuːdə/ noun L19 American Spanish (from Spanish = exchange, replacement). A collection of saddle-horses kept for remounts.

remueur /rəmɥœr/ noun plural pronounced same E20 French (literally, 'mover'). A person who engages in REMUAGE.

Renaissance /rɪˈneɪs(ə)ns/, foreign /rənɛsɑ̃s/ noun (also (especially in sense 2) **renaissance**) M19 French ((in specific use short for renaissance des arts, renaissance des lettres), from as re- + naissance birth from Latin nascentia, from nasci be born, or from French naiss- present stem of naître from Proto-Romance). 1 a M19 The revival of art and literature under the influence of classical models between the fourteenth and sixteenth centuries, begun in Italy; the period of this movement. b M19 The style of art, architecture, etc., developed in and characteristic of this period. 2 L19 Any revival or period of significant improvement and new life in cultural, scientific, economic, or other areas of activity.

rendezvous /ˈrɒndɪvuː/, /ˈrɒndeɪvuː/ noun (also **rendez-vous**) plural same /ˈrɒndɪvuːz/ L16 French (use as noun of imperative rendez-vous 'present yourselves', from rendre from Proto-Romance alteration of Latin reddere to give back). 1 Military a L16 A place appointed for the assembling of troops or armed forces. b E17 A place or port used or suitable for the assembling of a fleet or number of ships. Also, instructions concerning such a place. 2 L16 generally Any appointed or habitual meeting-place. 3 E17 A meeting or assembly held by appointment or arrangement. Formerly also, a group of people thus assembled. b M-L17 An assemblage of things. c M20 The prearranged meeting in space between a spacecraft and another spacecraft or a celestial body; an instance of this.

> **2 1996** *Spectator* . . . we had both been the recipients of mysterious notes from Richard, establishing the rendez-vous for lunch and insisting upon the most absolute secrecy.

rendu /rɑ̃dy/ *adjective* M20 French (= rendered, delivered). Designating a price on imported goods which includes tariffs and delivery costs.

rendzina /rɛndˈziːnə/ *noun* E20 Russian (from Polish *rędzina*). *Soil Science* A fertile lime-rich soil characterized by a dark friable humus-rich surface layer above a softer pale calcareous layer.

renga /ˈrɛŋɡə/ *noun* plural same, **rengas** L19 Japanese (from *ren* linking + *ga* from *ka* poetry). A Japanese poem consisting of a series of half-tanka contributed by different poets in turn.

renseignement /rɑ̃sɛɲəmɑ̃/ *noun* plural pronounced same M19 French. (A piece of) information. Also, a letter of introduction.

rente /rɑ̃t/ *noun* plural pronounced same L19 French. Stock, *especially* French government stock; the interest or income accruing from such stock.

rentier /rɑ̃tje/, /ˈrɒntɪeɪ/ *noun* plural pronounced same M19 French (from RENTE). A person who makes an income from property or investment.

> **1995** G. Tindall *Célestine* [The] composition seems redolent of the self-conscious world just being born: that of the *rentier* and the white-collar workers, . . . of trains and newspapers and morning coffee . . .

rentrée /ˈrɒntreɪ/, *foreign* /rɑ̃tre/ (*plural same*) *noun* L19 French. A return, *especially* a return home after an annual holiday.

renvers /rɑ̃vɛrs/, /ˈrɛnvəs/ *noun* plural same L19 French (from *renverser*, from as *re-* + *enverser* to overturn). *Horsemanship* A movement in which a horse walks parallel to a wall with its head and neck facing forward and its hindquarters curved towards the wall.

renversement /rɑ̃vɛrsəmɑ̃/ (*plural same*), /rɒnˈvəːs(ə)m(ə)nt/ *noun* E17 French (from as RENVERS). Originally, the action of reversing or inverting; the result of this. Now usually *specifically*, an aeroplane manoeuvre consisting of a half-loop effected simultaneously with a half-turn.

repêchage /ˈrɛpəʃɑːʒ/ *noun* E20 French (from *repêcher*, literally, 'to fish out, rescue'). An extra contest, especially in rowing and cycling, in which the runners-up in the eliminating heats compete for a place in the final.

> **1996** *Times* . . . an unsettlingly sportless lull between the recorded highlights of, as I recall, the men's synchronised triple frisbee and the repechage of the women's 80m coxless egg-and-spoon . . .

répétiteur /repetitœr/ (*plural same*), /rɛˌpɛtɪˈtə:/ *noun* M20 French (= tutor, coach). **1** M20 A person who teaches musicians and singers, especially opera singers, their parts. **2** M20 A person who supervises ballet rehearsals etc.

> **1 1996** *Times* Maybe Savonlinna should beef up its team of répétiteurs; the raw material is marvellous, and could be further refined.

réplique /replik/ *noun* (also **replique**) plural pronounced same L15 French (from *répliquer* from Latin *replicare* to unfold, (later) reply). A reply, a rejoinder.

> ■ Formerly fully Anglicized.

repoussé /rəˈpuːseɪ/ *adjective & noun* M19 French (past participle of *repousser*, from *re-* + *pousser* to push). **A** *adjective* M19 Of metalwork: raised into or ornamented in relief by means of hammering from the reverse side. **B** *noun* M19 Ornamental metalwork fashioned by the repoussé method; the process of hammering into relief.

repoussoir /rəpuswar/ *noun* plural pronounced same L19 French (from REPOUSSÉ). An object in the foreground of a painting serving to emphasize the principal figure or scene.

reprise /rɪˈprʌɪz/, *chiefly in sense 6* /rɪˈpriːz/ *noun* LME Old and Modern French (use as noun of past participle feminine of *reprendre* to take back, take again). **I 1** The fact of taking back something for one's own advantage; an amount taken back; loss, expense, cost. Only in LME. **2** LME A charge or payment falling due annually from a manor or estate. Usually in *plural*. **3a** M16–M18 Compensation. **b** M17–E18 The action of taking something by way of retaliation. **4** L17 A renewal or repetition of an action; a separate occasion of doing something. **II 5** E16 *Architecture* A return of mouldings etc. in an internal angle. **6a** E18 *Music* The repetition of the first theme of a movement after the close of the development. Formerly also, a refrain. **b** M20 *Linguistics* The repetition of a word or word group occurring in a preceding phrase. **c** M20 A repetition of a theatrical performance; a restaging or rewriting of a play; a replay. Also more widely, a further performance of any kind.

requiem /'rɛkwɪəm/, /'rɛkwɪɛm/ *noun* ME Latin (accusative of *requies* rest, first word of the introit in the mass for the dead, *Requiem aeternam dona eis, Domine* Give them eternal rest, O Lord). **1** ME (frequently **Requiem**) *Roman Catholic Church* A special mass said or sung for the repose of the soul of a dead person. Also *mass of requiem, requiem mass.* **b** L18 A musical setting of a mass for the dead. **2** E17 Any dirge, solemn chant, etc., for the repose of the dead; *figurative* a memorial, a commemoration. **3** E17 Rest, peace, quiet; a period of this. Now *rare*.

requiescat /rɛkwɪ'ɛskat/ *noun* E19 Latin (from *requiescat in pace* may he or she rest in peace). A wish for the repose of a dead person.

res /reɪz/ *noun plural* same E17 Latin (= thing). A thing, a matter.

▪ Originally in legal terminology and still chiefly in Latin legal phrases, e.g. *res communis* 'common property', *res integra* 'a matter that has not been covered', *res judicata* 'a matter that has been adjudicated', *res nullius* 'no one's property'. Used alone, *res* can now also have the more general senses of 'the condition of something; the matter in hand, the point at issue, the crux' (see quotation).
1966 P. G. Wodehouse *Plum Pie* I saw that I had better come to the *res* without delay.

res cogitans /reɪz 'kɒgɪtanz/, /reɪz 'kɒdʒɪtanz/ *noun phrase* E20 Latin (= thinking thing). *Philosophy* The concept of a human as a thinking being.

▪ The concept originated with Descartes in his *Meditationes* (1641): *Sed quid igitur sum? res cogitans* 'But what therefore am I? A thinking being' (ii.23).

réseau /'reɪzəʊ/, *foreign* /rezo/ *noun plural* **réseaux** /'reɪzəʊ/, *foreign* /rezo/ (also **rézel** /'reɪzɛl/, *foreign* /rezɛl/ (*plural* same)) L16 French (= net, web) **1** L16 A plain net ground used in lace-making. **2** E20 A network, a grid, *especially* one superimposed as a reference marking on a photograph in astronomy, surveying, etc. **3** M20 A spy or intelligence network, especially in the French resistance movement during the German occupation (1940–5).

res extensa /reɪz ɪk'stɛnsə/ *noun phrase plural* **res extensae** /reɪz 'ɪkstɛnsiː/ M20 Latin (= extended thing). *Philosophy* A material thing considered as material substance.

res gestae /reɪz 'gɛstʌɪ/, /reɪz 'dʒɛstiː/ *noun phrase plural* E17 Latin (= things done). (An account of) things done; (a person's) achievements; events in the past; in *Law* the facts of the case.
1969 *North Dakota Law Review* What they [sc. children] say when pressures of emotion and strangeness are absent is more apt to be true, somewhat analogous to *res gestae*.

residentura /ˌrɪzɪdɛn'tʊrə/, /ˌrɛzɪdɛn'tʊərə/ *noun* M20 Russian (*rezidentura*). A group or organization of intelligence agents in a foreign country.

residuum /rɪ'zɪdjʊəm/ *noun plural* **residua** /rɪ'zɪdjʊə/ L17 Latin (use as noun of neuter of *residuus* remaining, from *residere* to reside). **1** L17 That which remains; a residue. **b** M19 The masses; the poor. **2** M18 *Law* The residue of an estate. **3** M18 *Chemistry* etc. A substance left after combustion, evaporation, etc., a residue.

résistant /rezistɑ̃/ *noun plural* pronounced same M20 French. A member of the French Resistance movement in the war of 1939–45.
1996 *Spectator* In 1994, the then President Mitterand, whilst claiming to have been a *résistant*, under the patronage of Marshal Pétain, stated that in 1942 he knew nothing about the anti-Jewish laws that Pétain's government had passed in 1940 and 1941.

res non verba /ˌreɪz nɒn 'vəːbə/ *noun phrase plural* M20 Latin (= things not words). Action rather than talk.

▪ Also as a motto, sometimes with the addition *crux non vis* 'the Cross not force'.

respondentia /ˌrɪspɒn'dɛnʃə/ *noun* E18 Modern Latin (from *respondent-* present participial stem of Latin *respondere* from *re-* + *spondere* to pledge). A loan on the cargo of a vessel, to be repaid (with maritime interest) only if the goods arrive safe at their destination.

responsum /rɪ'spɒnsəm/ *noun plural* **responsa** /rɪ'spɒnsə/ L19 Latin (= reply). A written reply by a rabbi or Talmudic scholar to an inquiry on some matter of Jewish law.

ressentiment /rəsɑ̃timɑ̃/ *noun* M20 German (*Ressentiment* from French *ressentiment*, from *ressentir* to resent). *Social Psychology* A negative attitude towards society or authority arising from repressed hostility, feelings of inadequacy, etc.

▪ The term is particularly associated with the philosophy of Friedrich Nietzsche (1844–1900) (see quotation).

1994 I. M. Zeitlin *Nietzche Ressentiment* entails a negation and repudiation of the master's values, a saying of No!, which eventually becomes the creative act of inverting those values and substituting new ones for them.

restaurant /'rɛst(ə)rɒnt/, /'rɛst(ə)r(ə)nt/, /'rɛst(ə)rɔ̃:/, /'rɛst(ə)rɔ̃/, /'rɛst(ə)rɑ̃:/ *noun* E19 French (use as noun of present participle of *restaurer* to restore). A public establishment where meals or refreshments may be obtained.

restaurateur /rɛst(ə)rə'tə:/, /ˌrɛstɒrə'tə:/ *noun* L18 French (from *restaurer* to restore). A keeper of a restaurant.

restitutio in integrum /rɛstɪˌtju:tɪəʊ ɪn m'tɛgrəm/ *noun phrase* E18 Latin (= restoration to the uninjured state). *Law* Placement of an injured party in the situation which would have prevailed had no injury been sustained; restoration of the STATUS QUO ANTE.

résumé /'rɛzjʊmeɪ/ *noun* (also **resumé**, in sense 2 **resume**) E19 French (past participle of *résumer* to resume). **1** E19 A summary, an epitome. **2** M20 A CURRICULUM VITAE. Chiefly *North American*.

1 1996 *Times* His 'quest' is in reality a literary convention: what Johnson has written is an excellent résumé of a traditional Catholic's faith.

2 1996 *Spectator* Only incidentals on the résumé are different—Stanton missed Vietnam because of a crocked knee.

resurgam /rɪ'sə:gam/ *interjection* M17 Latin (literally, 'I shall rise again'). Proclaiming one's Christian faith in the resurrection of the dead. Usually *transferred* and *figurative*.

retable /rɪ'teɪb(ə)l/ *noun* E19 French (*rétable, retable* from Spanish *retablo* from medieval Latin *retrotabulum*, from Latin *retro-* behind + *tabula* table). A frame enclosing painted or decorated panels or a shelf or ledge for ornaments, raised above the back of an altar.

retablo /rɪ'tɑːbləʊ/ *noun* plural **retablos** M19 Spanish (see preceding). A RETABLE. Also, a votive picture displayed in a church.

retardataire /rətardatɛr/ *noun & adjective* plural of noun pronounced same E20 French. Chiefly *Art*. **A** *noun* E20 A work of art executed in the style of an earlier period. **B** *adjective* M20 Behind the times; characterized by the style of an earlier period.

B 1977 *Times Literary Supplement* The *retardataire* appearance of much colonial architecture is derived from the poor, often secondhand knowledge of contemporary architectectual practice as well as from a conservatism in patrons' tastes.

retiarius /rɛtɪ'ɑːrɪəs/, /rɛtɪ'ɛːrɪəs/ *noun* plural **retiarii** /rɛtɪ'ɑːrɪɪ/, /rɛtɪ'ɛːriː/ M17 Latin (from *rete* net). *Roman History* A gladiator who fought using a net with which to entangle his adversary.

reticella /rɛtɪ'tʃɛlə/ *noun & adjective* M19 Italian (diminutive of *rete* net). **A** *noun* M19 A lacelike fabric with a characteristic geometric pattern produced especially in Venice from the fifteenth to the seventeenth century. **B** M20 *attributive* or as *adjective* Of, pertaining to, or characteristic of reticella.

reticello /rɛtɪ'tʃɛləʊ/ *noun* plural **reticelli** /rɛtɪ'tʃɛli/ L19 Italian (from as preceding). A network of fine glass threads embedded in some Venetian glass. Also (more fully *reticello glass*), glass made with this type of decoration.

reticule /'rɛtɪkjuːl/ *noun* E18 French (*réticule* from Latin *reticulum* diminutive of *rete* net). **1** E18 A grid of fine lines or threads set in the focal plane or eyepiece of an optical instrument, a reticle. **2** E19 A woman's small netted or other bag, especially with a drawstring, carried or worn to serve the purpose of a pocket.

retina /'rɛtɪnə/ *noun* LME Medieval Latin (from Latin *rete* net). The light-sensitive layer which lines much of the inside of the eyeball, in which nerve impulses are triggered and pass via the optic nerve to the brain where a visual image is formed.

retiré /rətire/ *noun* plural pronounced same M20 French (past participle of *retirer* to withdraw). *Ballet* A movement in which one leg is raised at right angles to the body until the toe is in line with the knee of the supporting leg.

retornado /ˌretur'nadu/ *noun* plural **retornados** /ˌretur'naduʃ/ L20 Portuguese (from past participle of *retornar* to return). A Portuguese citizen returning to settle in Portugal after living in a Portuguese colony.

retraite /rətrɛt/ *noun* plural pronounced same M19 French (from Old French *retraite* retreat). **1** M19 Retirement, seclusion, retreat. **2** L19 *Military* The signal for retreating.

retroussage /rətruːsaʒ/ *noun* M20 **French** (from as *retroussé:* see next). In etching, the action of drawing a fine cloth across an inked plate to draw out some ink and smear it irregularly across the plate.

retroussé /rə'truːseɪ/, *foreign* /rətruse/ *adjective* E19 **French** (past participle of *retrousser* to turn up, from *re-* + *trousser* from Old French *trusser*, medieval Latin *trossare*, probably from late Latin *tors-* past participial stem of *torquere* to twist). Usually of the nose: turned up at the tip.

retsina /rɛt'siːnə/ *noun* E20 **Modern Greek** (from *retsini* from Greek *rētinē* pine resin). A Greek white wine flavoured with resin.

réussi /reysi/ *adjective* M20 **French** (past participle of *réuss* to turn out, result, succeed). Fine, excellent, successful.

revanche /rəvɑ̃ʃ/ *noun* M19 **French** (earlier *revenche*, from Old French *revencher* from late Latin *revindicare* to avenge, claim). Revenge; retaliation; *specifically* a nation's policy of seeking the return of lost territory.

◼ The policy of *revanchisme* was particularly associated with France's determination to recover Alsace-Lorraine after losing the territory to Germany in the Franco-Prussian War of 1870, but in other contexts the word is now generally Anglicized as *revanchism*.

reveille /rɪ'vali/ *noun* (also (now *rare*) **reveillé** /rɪ'valeɪ/) M17 **French** (*réveillez* imperative plural of *réveiller* to awaken, from *ré-* + *veiller* from Latin *vigilare* to keep watch). A signal given in the morning, usually on a drum or bugle, to waken soldiers and indicate that it is time to rise; (the time of) the sounding of this signal.

réveillon /revɛjɔ̃/ *noun* plural pronounced same E19 **French** (from *réveiller* (see preceding)). In France: a night-time feast or celebration, originally one after midnight on Christmas morning.

revenant /'rɛv(ə)nənt/, *foreign* /rəvənɑ̃/ (*plural of noun* same) *noun & adjective* E19 **French** (present participle of *revenir* to return). **A** *noun* E19 A person who has returned, especially supposedly from the dead; a ghost. **B** *adjective* E20 Returned, especially supposedly from the dead.

> **B 1996** *Spectator* Evidently a revenant, a returning spirit, ... really wants only to be allowed to die and stay dead.

reverdie /rəvɛrdi/ *noun* plural pronounced same M20 **French** (use as noun of feminine past participle of *reverdir* to grow, turn green again). A medieval French song celebrating the return of spring.

reverie /'rɛv(ə)ri/ *noun* (also **revery**) ME **French** (in branch I from Old French *reverie* rejoicing, revelry, from *rever* to be delirious (modern *rêver* to dream), of unknown origin; in branch II from later French *resverie* (now *rêverie*)). **I 1** ME–M16 Joy, delight; revelry; wantonness, wildness. *rare*. **II 2** E17 A fantastic, fanciful, or unpractical notion; a delusion. *archaic*. **3** M17 A fit of abstracted musing; a daydream. **b** L19 *Music* An instrumental composition suggestive of a dreamy or musing state. **4** M18 The fact, state, or condition of being lost in thought or engaged in musing.

revers /rɪ'vɪə/ *noun* plural same /rɪ'vɪəz/ M19 **French**. A turned-back edge of a garment revealing the undersurface; the material covering such an edge. Usually *plural*.

revirement /rəvirmɑ̃/ *noun* plural pronounced same E20 **French**. An alteration of one's plans; a complete change of attitude or opinion.

revolte /reɪ'vəʊlteɪ/ *noun* (also **révolté**, (feminine) **révoltée**, /revolte/ (*plural* same)) L19 **French**. A person who revolts; a rebel; a nonconformist.

revue /rɪ'vjuː/ *noun* L19 **French** (= review). A light theatrical entertainment consisting of a series of short (usually satirical) sketches, comic turns, songs, etc. Also, the genre comprising such entertainments.

rezident /rɛzɪ'dɛnt/ *noun* plural **rezidenty** /rɛzɪ'dɛnti/ M20 **Russian**. An intelligence agent in a foreign country.

rhagades /'ragədiːz/ *noun* plural OE **Latin** (from Greek, plural of *rhagas* fissure). *Medicine* Cracks, fissures, or thin scars in the skin, especially around the mouth or anus.

rho /rəʊ/ *noun* LME **Greek** (*rhō*). **1** LME The seventeenth letter (Ρ, ρ) of the Greek alphabet. **2** M20 *Statistics* A correlation coefficient. **3** M20 *Physics* A meson with isospin and spin of one and a mass of 770 MeV. In full *rho meson*.

rhodomontade variant of RODOMONTADE.

rhombus /'rɒmbəs/ *noun* plural **rhombuses, rhombi** /'rɒmbʌɪ/ M16 **Latin** (from

Greek *rhombos*). **1** M16 *Geometry* A plane figure having four equal sides and equal opposite angles (two acute and two obtuse); an oblique equilateral parallelogram. **2** E17 A lozenge-shaped object, part, marking, etc.

rhumba variant of RUMBA.

rhyton /ˈrʌɪtɒn/, /ˈrɪtɒn/ *noun* plural **rhytons**, **rhyta** /ˈrʌɪtə/ M19 Greek (*rhuton* neuter of *rhutos* flowing, related to *rhein* to flow). *Greek Antiquities* A type of drinking-vessel, often in the form of an animal's head, with one or more holes at the bottom through which liquid can flow.

ria /ˈriːə/ *noun* L19 Spanish (*ría* estuary). *Physical Geography* A long narrow inlet of the sea formed by partial submergence of an unglaciated river valley.

Rialto /rɪˈaltəʊ/ *noun* (also **rialto**) M16 Italian (name of district of Venice in which the Exchange was situated). A market, an exchange.

riata /rɪˈɑːtə/ *noun* (also **reata**) M19 Spanish (*reata*). A lariat.

richesse /riːˈʃɛs/, /ˈrɪtʃɛs/ *noun* ME Old French (*richeise*, *richesce* (modern *richesse*), from *riche* rich). **1** ME–L17 *singular* and in *plural* Wealth; richness; riches. **2** L15 A number or group of martens.

■ Long archaic, but cf. EMBARRAS DE RICHESSE.

ricochet /ˈrɪkəʃeɪ/, /ˈrɪkəʃɛt/ *noun* M18 French (= the skipping of a shot or of a flat stone on water, of unknown origin). Originally *Military* The action of a projectile, especially a bullet or shell, in rebounding at an angle off a surface or surfaces after being fired; a hit made after such a rebound.

1996 *New Scientist* The fax messages are sent by someone living in 2024. Because of some ricochet of the arrow of time they are received by a present-day and startled Brazilian.

ricordo /riˈkordo/ *noun* plural **ricordi** /riˈkordi/ E20 Italian (literally, 'memory'). A token of remembrance, a souvenir; *Art* a copy made by a painter of another's composition.

ricotta /rɪˈkɒtə/ *noun* L19 Italian (= re-cooked, from Latin *recocta* feminine past participle of *recoquere*, from as re- + *coquere* cook). A kind of soft white unsalted Italian cheese. Also *ricotta cheese.*

rictus /ˈrɪktəs/ *noun* M18 Latin (literally, 'open mouth', from *rict-* past participial

stem of *ringi* to gape). **1** M18 *Botany* The throat of a two-lipped corolla. **2** E19 The expanse or gape of the mouth, or of the beak or jaws of a bird, fish, etc.; *transferred* a fixed grin or grimace.

riegel /ˈriːɡ(ə)l/ *noun* E20 German (from Middle High German *rigel* crossbar, Old High German *rigil* bar). *Physical Geography* A low transverse ridge of resistant bedrock on the floor of a glacial valley, a rock bar.

riem /rɪm/, /riːm/ *noun* E19 Dutch (from Middle Dutch *rieme*). A long strip or thong of dressed softened leather. *South African.*

riempie /ˈrɪmpi/, /ˈriːmpi/ *noun* & *adjective* (also **riempje**) M19 Dutch (*riempje*, from as RIEM + Afrikaans diminutive suffix -*ie*). **A** *noun* M19 A fine narrow *riem* or leather thong. **B** E20 *attributive* or as *adjective* Of furniture: having a seat or bottom of criss-crossed fine narrow leather thongs, as a *riempie chair* (Afrikaans *riempiestoel*). *South African.*

rien ne va plus /rjɛ̃ nə va ply/ *interjection* (also **rien n'va plus**) L19 French. In roulette, the call made by the croupier while the wheel is spinning: no more bets!

rifacimento /rɪˌfatʃɪˈmɛntəʊ/, *foreign* /rifatʃiˈmento/ *noun* plural **rifacimenti** /rɪˌfatʃɪˈmɛnti/ L18 Italian (from *rifacimento* stem of *rifare* to remake). A remodelling or recasting of a literary work.

rigadoon /rɪɡəˈduːn/ *noun* (also **rigaudon** /rɪɡodɔ̃/ (plural same)) L17 French (*rigodon*, *rigaudon* said to be from *Rigaud* a dancing-master who devised it). **1** L17 A lively dance for couples, in duple or quadruple time, of Provençal origin. **2** M18 A piece of music for this dance.

rigatoni /rɪɡəˈtəʊni/ *noun* M20 Italian (from *rigato* past participle of *rigare* to draw a line, make fluting, from *riga* a line). Pasta in the form of short hollow fluted tubes; an Italian dish consisting largely of this and usually a sauce.

rijsttafel /ˈrʌɪsˌtɑːf(ə)l/ *noun* L19 Dutch (from *rijst* rice + *tafel* table). A South East Asian meal consisting of a selection of different foods (such as eggs, meat, fish, fruit, curry, etc.) mixed with rice and served in separate dishes.

rikka /ˈrika/ *noun* L19 Japanese (literally, 'standing flowers', from *ritsu* stand + *ka* flower(s)). A traditional and formal style of Japanese flower arrangement, used especially to decorate Buddhist temples.

rillettes /'riːjɛt/ *noun* (treated as *singular* or *plural*) L19 French. Pâté made of minced pork, chicken, etc., seasoned and combined with fat.

rimaye /riːˈmeɪ/ *noun* E20 French (from Latin *rima* fissure + French collective suffix *-aye*). A BERGSCHRUND.

rimmon /riˈmoːn/ *noun* (also **rimon**) plural **rimmonim** /riˈmoːnɪm/ M20 Hebrew (*rimmōn*, literally, 'pomegranate'). A pomegranate-shaped ornament or decorative cover for each of the bars at either end of a Jewish law-scroll.

rinceau /rɛ̃so/ *noun* plural **rinceaux** /rɛ̃so/ L18 French. A moulded, carved, or painted decoration on furniture etc., often in the form of scrolls or acanthus leaves.

rinderpest /'rɪndəpɛst/ *noun* M19 German (from *Rinder* cattle (plural of *Rind*) + *Pest* plague). An infectious disease of ruminants, especially oxen; cattle-plague.

rinforzando /ˌrɪnfɔːtˈsandəʊ/ *adverb, adjective, & noun* E19 Italian (present participle of *rinforzare* to strengthen). *Music* **A** *adverb & adjective* E19 (A direction:) with a sudden stress or crescendo. **B** *noun* M19 plural **rinforzandos, rinforzandi** /ˌrɪnfɔːtˈsandi/ A sudden stress or crescendo made on a short phrase.

ripieno /rɪpɪˈeməʊ/ *adjective & noun* E18 Italian (from *ri-* re- + *pieno* full). *Music* **A** *attributive adjective* E18 Originally, supplementary, re-enforcing. Now chiefly, of or pertaining to a ripieno. **B** *noun* M18 plural **ripienos, ripieni** /rɪpɪˈemi/ Originally, a supplementary player or instrument. Now chiefly, the body of instruments accompanying the concertino in baroque concerto music.

riposte /rɪˈpɒst/ *noun* E18 French ((earlier *risposte*) from Italian *risposta* use as noun of feminine past participle of *rispondere*, from Latin *respondere* from *re-* + *spondere* to pledge). **1** E18 *Fencing* A quick thrust given after parrying a lunge; a return thrust. **2** M19 A retaliatory action; a quick sharp reply or retort.

    2 1996 *Spectator* Unfortunately, a witty riposte invariably escaped me.

ripresa /riˈpresa/ *noun* plural **riprese** /riˈprese/ M18 Italian. *Music* A repeat; a refrain.

ris de veau /ri də vo/ *noun phrase* E19 French. Sweetbread of veal prepared as a dish.

risoluto /rɪzəˈluːtəʊ/ *adjective & adverb* M18 Italian. *Music* **A** *adjective* Resolved into a concord. Only in M18. **B** *adverb* M19 (A direction:) with resolution or emphasis.

Risorgimento /rɪˌsɔːdʒɪˈmɛntəʊ/ *noun* plural **Risorgimenti** /rɪˌsɔːdʒɪˈmɛnti/, **Risorgimentos** L19 Italian (= renewal, renaissance). **1** L19 *History* The movement which led to the unification of Italy as an independent State in 1870. **2** M20 A revitalization or renewal of activity in any sphere.

risotto /rɪˈzɒtəʊ/ *noun* plural **risottos** M19 Italian (from *riso* rice). An Italian dish of rice cooked in stock with various other ingredients, as meat, onions, etc.

risqué /'riːskeɪ/ /'rɪskeɪ/, /rɪˈskeɪ/ *adjective* (feminine **risquée**) M19 French (past participle of *risquer* to risk). Slightly indecent, liable to shock slightly.

    1996 *Spectator* The erotic poetry of the 17th and 18th centuries and the libertinism of Restoration drama, however risqué, lead you down a garden path with carefully laid out grassy borders.
    1996 *Times* Nowadays, Vivienne [Westwood] is still considered *risquée*.

rissole /'rɪsəʊl/ *noun* E18 French (later form of Old French *ruissole* dialectal variant of *roisole, roussole* from Proto-Romance use as noun of feminine of late Latin *russeolus* reddish, from Latin *russus* red). A ball or small cake of chopped meat etc. coated with breadcrumbs, cooked by frying.

risus sardonicus /ˌrʌɪsəs saːˈdɒnɪkəs/ *noun phrase* L17 Modern Latin (from Latin *risus* laugh (from *ridere* to laugh) + medieval or modern Latin *sardonicus* sardonic). *Medicine* An involuntary grinning expression resulting from chronic abnormal contraction of the facial muscles, as in tetanus.

ritardando /riːtaːˈdandəʊ/ *adverb, adjective, & noun* plural of noun **ritardandos, ritardandi** /riːtaːˈdandi/ E19 Italian (present participle of *ritardare* to slow down). *Music* RALLENTANDO.

rite de passage /rit də pɑsaʒ/, /ˌriːt də paˈsɑːʒ/ *noun phrase* plural **rites de passage** (pronounced same) E20 French. *Anthropology* A formal procedure or act marking the beginning of a new defined stage in a person's life, a rite of passage.

■ The phrase was coined by Arnold van Gennep in the title of his book *Les Rites de passage* (1909). In English use, the translation *rite of passage* appeared in the same year as van Gennep's book; the 1960 translators of *Les Rites de passage* suggested that *rites of transition* would have been a better rendering, but acknowledged that *rites of passage* had become too firmly established in general usage to dislodge. Although less frequent than the English version, *rite de passage* is still found.

1977 *Times* The [Newfoundland] seal hunt is . . . a necessary *rite de passage* for all young men.

ritenuto /rɪtə'nuːtəʊ/ *adverb, adjective, & noun* E19 **Italian** (past participle of *ritenere* from Latin *retinere* to hold back). *Music* **A** *adverb & adjective* E19 (A direction:) with immediate reduction of speed, restrained, held back in tempo. **B** *noun* E19 plural **ritenuti** /rɪtə'nuːti/, **ritenutos** A ritenuto phrase or passage.

rites de passage plural of RITE DE PASSAGE.

ritornello /rɪtɔː'nɛləʊ/ *noun* plural **ritornellos**, **ritornelli** /rɪtɔː'nɛli/ L17 **Italian** (diminutive of *ritorno* return). *Music* An instrumental refrain, interlude, or prelude, especially in a vocal work.

ritournelle /ˌrɪtʊə'nɛl/ *noun* M19 **French** (from as preceding). *Music* A RITORNELLO.

ritter /'rɪtə/ *noun* E19 **German** (variant of *reiter* rider). A German or Austrian knight or mounted warrior; a member of the German or Austrian minor nobility.

■ Obsolete except in historical contexts.

riu variant of RYU.

riverain /'rɪvəreɪn/ *adjective & noun* M19 **French** (from *rivière* river). **A** *adjective* M19 Riverine. **B** *noun* M19 A person who lives beside or near a river.

riviera /rɪvɪ'ɛːrə/ *noun* (also **Riviera**) M18 **Italian** (= seashore, coast). A coastal region with a warm climate and popularity as a holiday resort, originally *specifically* one around Genoa in Italy, later also the Mediterranean coast from Marseilles in France to La Spezia in Italy.

rivière /rivjɛr/ (*plural same*), /ˌrɪvɪ'ɛː/ *noun* M19 **French**. **1** M19 *Needlework* A row of openwork. **2** L19 A necklace of diamonds or other gems, *especially* one consisting of more than one string.

riza /'riːzə/ *noun* E20 **Russian** (from Old Church Slavonic = garment). A metal shield or plaque framing the painted face and other features of a Russian icon, and engraved with the lines of the completed picture.

robe de chambre /rɔb də ʃɑ̃br/ *noun phrase* plural **robes de chambre** (pronounced same) M18 **French**. A dressing-gown, a negligée.

robe de nuit /rɔb də nɥi/ *noun phrase* plural **robes de nuit** (pronounced same) M19 **French**. A nightdress.

robe de style /rɔb də stil/ *noun phrase* plural **robes de style** (pronounced same) E20 **French**. A woman's formal dress with a tight bodice and a long bouffant skirt.

robes de chambre, **robes de nuit**, etc. plurals of ROBE DE CHAMBRE, ROBE DE NUIT, etc.

rocaille /rə(ʊ)'kʌɪ/, *foreign* /rɔkaj/ *noun* M19 **French**. An artistic or architectural style of decoration characterized by ornate rock- and shell-work; a rococo style.

roche moutonnée /rɔʃ mutɔne/, /ˌʃɑ̃ mu:tɒ'neɪ/ *noun phrase* plural **roches moutonnées** (pronounced same) M19 **French** (*roche* rock (from medieval Latin *rocca*, *rocha* of unknown origin) + *moutonnée* (from *mouton* sheep, from medieval Latin *multo(n)-*, probably of Gaulish origin). *Physical Geography* A bare rock outcrop which has been shaped by glacial erosion, characteristically smoothed and rounded by abrasion but often displaying one side which is rougher and steeper.

1977 A. Hallam *Planet Earth* Many valleys are very deeply incised, with U-shaped cross-profiles and floors composed of smoothed, striated and streamlined rock hummocks (called roches moutonées).

rococo /rə'kəʊkəʊ/ *adjective & noun* M19 **French** (fanciful alteration of *rocaille* pebble- or shell-work from *roc* rock). **A** *adjective* **1** M19 Old-fashioned, antiquated. **2** M19 (Of furniture or architecture) of or characterized by an elaborately ornamental late baroque style of decoration prevalent in eighteenth-century Continental Europe, with asymmetrical patterns involving motifs, scroll-work, etc.; (of music, literature, etc.) highly ornamented, florid; *generally* extravagantly or excessively ornate. **B** *noun* M19 The rococo style of art, decoration, etc.

rodeo /'rəʊdɪəʊ/, /rə'deɪəʊ/ *noun* plural **rodeos** M19 **Spanish** (from *rodear* to go round, based on Latin *rotare* to rotate). **1** M19 A round-up of cattle for counting, inspecting, branding, etc.; a place where cattle are rounded up. **2** E20 A display or competition exhibiting the skills of riding broncos, roping calves, wrestling steers, etc. **b** E20 *transferred* A similar (usually competitive) exhibition of other skills, as motorcycle riding, fishing, etc.

■ Originally United States.

rodomontade /ˌrɒdə(ʊ)mɒnˈteɪd/ *noun, verb, & adjective* (also **rhodomontade**) E17 French (from Italian *rodomontada, rodomontata,* from *Rodomonte* the name of a boastful character in the Renaissance *Orlando* epics). **A** *noun* **1** E17 A brag, a boast; an extravagantly boastful or arrogant remark or speech. **2** M17 Boastful or inflated language or behaviour; extravagant bragging. **B** *intransitive verb* L17 Boast, brag; rant. **C** *adjective* M18 Bragging, boastful; ranting.

roemer /ˈrømə/ *noun* L19 Dutch (or German *Römer*). A type of decorated German or Dutch wineglass with knobs or prunts on the stem.

■ The English *rummer* or *rummer-glass* is cognate with *roemer* and its other Continental variants and has nothing to do with the liquor rum. The ultimate origin may be 'Roman glass'.

roesti /ˈrɒsti/ *noun plural* (treated as *singular* or *plural*) (also **rösti**) M20 Swiss German. A Swiss dish of grated potatoes, formed into a pancake and fried.

rofia see RAFFIA.

rogan josh /ˌrəʊg(ə)n ˈdʒəʊʃ/ *noun phrase* (also **roghan josh**) M20 Urdu (*roġan još, rauġan-još* (preparation of mutton) stewed in ghee, from Urdu *roġan, rauġan* from Persian *rauġan* oil, ghee + Urdu, Persian *roġan još* act of braising or stewing). A dish of curried meat (usually lamb) cooked in a rich sauce.

rognon /rəɲɔ̃/ *noun plural* pronounced same E19 French. **1** E19 A kidney, used as food. Usually in *plural*. **2** M20 *Mountaineering* A rounded outcrop of rock or stones surrounded by a glacier or an ice-field.

roi fainéant /rwa fɛneɑ̃/ *noun phrase* plural **rois fainéants** (pronounced same) M19 French (literally, 'sluggard king'; cf. FAINÉANT). Any person with merely nominal power.

■ Originally applied to any of the later Merovingian kings of France, whose power was merely nominal.

1966 *Economist* The launching of the Sputnik in 1957, in the reign of the *roi fainéant,* President Eisenhower, seemed to justify Khrushchevian boasts that America's days of . . . supremacy were numbered.

roi soleil /rwa sɔlɛj/ *noun phrase* plural **rois soleils** (pronounced same) L19 French (literally, 'sun king', (the heraldic device of) Louis XIV of France). A pre-eminent person or thing.

romaine /rə(ʊ)ˈmem/ *noun* E20 French (feminine of *romain* Roman). **1** E20 A cos lettuce. Also more fully *romaine lettuce.* Chiefly *North American.* **2** E20 Any of various crêpe fabrics.

■ *Romaine crêpe* (a proprietary name in the United States) is a semi-sheer crêpe fabric of silk, rayon, or acetate.

roman-à-clef /rɔmɑ̃ a kle/, /ˌrəʊˌmɑːn ɑː ˈkleɪ/ *noun phrase* (also **roman à clef**) plural **romans-à-clef** (pronounced same) L19 French (literally, 'novel with a key'). A novel in which actual people or events appear under fictitious names.

1996 *Times: Weekend* Anonymous's novel is more than a political *roman à clef* . . .

roman à thèse /rɔmɑ̃ a tɛz/ *noun phrase* plural **romans à thèse** (pronounced same) M19 French (literally, 'novel with a thesis'). A novel that seeks to expound or promote a theory.

romancé /rɔmɑ̃se/ *adjective* M20 French (from *romancer* to fictionalize). Especially of a biography: fictionalized, written in the form of a novel.

roman de geste /rɔmɑ̃ də ʒɛst/ *noun phrase* plural **romans de geste** (pronounced same) M19 French (literally, 'romance of heroic deeds'). A CHANSON DE GESTE.

roman-fleuve /rɔmɑ̃ flœv/ *noun phrase* plural **romans-fleuves** (pronounced same) M20 French (literally, 'river novel'). A novel featuring the leisurely description of the lives and members of a family; a sequence of self-contained novels.

1996 *Times* The *roman fleuve* is a courageous undertaking.

romanità /roˌmaniˈtɑː/ *noun* E20 Italian (from next). **1** E20 ROMANITAS. **2** M20 The spirit or influence of the central Roman Catholic authorities; acceptance of papal policy.

romanitas /rəʊˈmɑːnɪtɑːs/, /rəʊˈmanɪtɑːs/ *noun* M20 Late Latin (from Latin *Romanus*). The spirit or ideals of ancient Rome.

roman noir /rɔmɑ̃ nwar/ *noun phrase* plural **romans noirs** (pronounced same) M20 French (literally, 'black novel'). A Gothic novel, a thriller.

■ See quotation 1996(2) at NOIR.

roman policier /rɔmɑ̃ pɔlisje/ *noun phrase* plural **romans policiers** (pronounced same) E20 French. A detective novel or story.

> **1995** *Times* French *romans policiers*, and crime procedural novels from John Creasey to Nicholas Freeling, have brought in chippy police heroes instead of private detectives.

romanza /ro'mansa/, /ro'mantsa/, /ro 'manza/ *noun* M19 Spanish (or Italian, from popular Latin adverb formed on Latin *Romanicus* from *Romanus* Roman). *Music* A romantic song or melody; a lyrical piece of music; a romance.

Romanze /ro'mantsə/ *noun* plural **Romanzen** /ro'mantsən/ L19 German (literally, 'romance'). *Music* A composition of a tender or lyrical character; *specifically* a slow romantic instrumental piece or movement.

rondavel /rɒn'dɑ:v(ə)l/ *noun* L19 Afrikaans (*rondawel*). A round tribal hut usually with a thatched conical roof. Also, a similar building used especially as a holiday cottage or an outbuilding on a farm. *South African*.

rond de cuir /rɔ̃ də kɥir/ *noun phrase* plural **ronds de cuir** (pronounced same) E20 French (literally, 'circle of leather'). A round leather cushion, often used on office chairs in France. Also *transferred*, a bureaucrat.

ronde /rɒnd/ *noun* M19 French (feminine of *rond* round). **1** M19 A style of script with gothic characteristics used in France from the eighteenth century; printing type imitating or based on this writing. **2** M20 A dance in which the participants move in a circle or ring. **3** M20 A round or course of talk, activity, etc.; *figurative* a treadmill.

> **3 1977** *Times Literary Supplement* Heinz already represented the first step away from what was ultimately unbearable about the homosexual *ronde*.

rondeau /'rɒndəʊ/ *noun* plural **rondeaux** /'rɒndəʊ/, /'rɒndəʊz/ E16 Old and Modern French (later form of *rondel* from *rond* round). **1** E16 A poem of ten or thirteen lines with only two rhymes throughout and with the opening words used twice as a refrain. **2** L18 *Music* A RONDO sense 1.

rondelle /rɒn'dɛl/ *noun* M19 French (from *rond* round). A circular piece of something.

rondo /'rɒndəʊ/ *noun* plural **rondos** L18 Italian (from French RONDEAU). **1** L18 A piece of music with a recurring leading theme, often as the final movement of a concerto, sonata, etc. **2** M19 A game of chance played with balls on a table.

rond-point /rɔ̃pwɛ̃/ *noun* plural **ronds-points** (pronounced same) L19 French (from *rond* round + *point* centre). A circular space in a garden whence paths radiate; a roundabout where roads converge.

ronds de cuir plural of ROND DE CUIR.

rongeur /rɔ̃ʒœr/ *noun* L19 French (= gnawing, a rodent, from *ronger* to gnaw). *Surgery* Strong surgical forceps with a biting action, used for removing small pieces from bone. Also *rongeur forceps*.

ronin /'rəʊnɪn/ *noun* plural same, **ronins** L19 Japanese. In feudal Japan: a lordless wandering samurai; an outlaw. Now also *transferred*, a Japanese student who has failed and is permitted to retake a university (entrance) examination.

rooinek /'rɔɪnɛk/ *noun* L19 Afrikaans (from *rooi* red + *nek* neck). A British or English-speaking South African.

■ In derogatory or jocular use in South African slang, the term was especially associated with the British troops in South Africa during the Boer War (1899–1902).

roquette /rɒ'kɛt/ *noun* E20 French. A cruciferous plant eaten as a salad, rocket.

rosalia /rəʊ'zɑ:lɪə/ *noun* E19 Italian (female forename in *Rosalia, mia cara* title of an Italian song using this device). *Music* The repetition of a phrase or melody one note higher, with the retention of the same intervals and a consequent change of key.

rosé /'rəʊzeɪ/, *foreign* /roze/ *noun & adjective* L19 French (= pink). (Designating) any light red or pink wine, coloured by brief contact with red grape skins.

rosemaling /'rəʊsə,mɑ:lɪŋ/, /'rəʊsə ,mɔ:lɪŋ/ *noun* M20 Norwegian (= rose-painting). The art of painting (wooden objects) with flower motifs; flower motifs, especially painted on wood.

rosolio /rəʊ'zəʊlɪəʊ/ *noun* (also **rosoglio**) plural **rosolios** E19 Italian (variant of *ro-*

soli, from Latin *ros* dew + *solis* genitive of *sol* sun). A sweet cordial made especially in Italy from alcohol, raisins, sugar, rosepetals, cloves, cinnamon, etc.

rosso antico /ˌrɒsəʊ anˈtiːkəʊ/ *noun phrase* L18 **Italian** (literally, 'ancient red'). **1** L18 A red stoneware produced at Josiah Wedgwood's Staffordshire factories. **2** L19 A rich red Italian marble used for decoration.

rösti variant of ROESTI.

rostrum /ˈrɒstrəm/ *noun* plural **rostra** /ˈrɒstrə/, *(rare)* **rostrums** M16 **Latin** (= beak, beak-head, from *rodere* to gnaw). **1** M16 *Roman Antiquities* A platform or stand for speakers in the Forum of ancient Rome, decorated with the beakheads of captured warships. **b** M18 *transferred* A platform, stage, stand, etc., especially for public speaking; *specifically* (*a*) a pulpit; (*b*) a conductor's platform facing the orchestra; (*c*) a platform for supporting a film or television camera. **2** E17 *Roman Antiquities* A beaklike projection from the prow of a warship. **3** *Anatomy and Zoology* **a** M18 A beak, a snout; an anterior prolongation of the head, as in a weevil. **b** E19 A process or formation resembling a beak. **4** M19 *Botany* A beaklike process.

rota /ˈrəʊtə/ *noun* L17 **Latin** (= wheel). A rotational order of people, duties to be done; a list of these.

■ *Rota* occurs first (E17) as the name of the supreme court of the Roman Catholic Church, then (M17) as the name of a political club. The above is the only sense generally used in English.

roti /ˈrəʊtiː/ *noun* E20 **Hindustani** (*roṭī*). A type of unleavened bread originally from the Indian subcontinent.

rôti /roti/ *noun & postpositive adjective* plural of noun pronounced same L18 **French** (from *rôtir* to roast). *Cookery* **A** *noun* L18 A dish or main course of roasted meat. **B** *postpositive adjective* M19 Of food: roasted.

rotisserie /rə(ʊ)ˈtɪs(ə)ri/ *noun* M19 **French** (*rôtisserie*, from *rôtir* to roast). **1** M19 A restaurant or shop specializing in roasted or barbecued meat etc. **2** M20 A type of roasting oven with a power-driven rotating spit. Also *rotisserie oven*.

2 1996 *Times: Weekend* A few weeks ago I wrote that the demise of the spit (or rotisserie, if you prefer) had robbed us of roast meat . . .

rôtisseur /rotisœr/ *noun* plural pronounced same M18 **French** (from *rôtir* to roast). A chef in charge of all roasting, and usually grilling and frying, in a restaurant etc.

roué /ˈruːeɪ/ *noun* E19 **French** (use as noun of past participle of *rouer* to break on the wheel (the punishment said to be deserved by such a person)). A debauchee, a rake.

1996 *Times* . . . I got hopelessly lost in the Casanova papers themselves, mainly because they assumed some knowledge of the old roué's life.

rouge /ruːʒ/ *noun & adjective* LME **Old and Modern French** (from Latin *rubeus* red). **A** *adjective* LME Red. obsolete except in certain heraldic contexts. **B** *noun* **1** The colour red. rare. Only in LME. **2** M18 A red powder or cream used as a cosmetic to add colour to the lips or especially the cheeks. **3** L18 Red as one of the two colours of divisions in rouge-et-noir and roulette. Earliest in ROUGE-ET-NOIR. **4** E19 A radical; a republican; a socialist. Now chiefly (*Canadian*), a member of the Quebec Liberal Party. **5** M19 Any of various metallic oxides etc. used as polishing powders; *especially* (in full *jeweller's rouge*) a fine preparation of ferric oxide used as a metal polish. Usually with specifying word. **6** M20 French red wine.

rouge de fer /ˌruːʒ də ˈfɛː/ *noun phrase* E20 **French** (literally, 'red of iron'). An orangered enamel used on Chinese porcelain, made from a ferric oxide base.

rouge-et-noir /ˌruːʒeɪˈnwɑː/ *noun phrase* L18 **French** (= red and black). A gambling game in which stakes are placed on a table marked with red and black diamonds.

rouge flambé /ruːʒ ˈflɒmbeɪ/ *noun phrase* E20 **French**. A bright red Chinese porcelain glaze, made from copper oxide.

rouget /ruːʒɛ/ *noun* plural pronounced same L19 **French**. A red mullet, especially as used in cooking.

rouille /ruj/ *noun* M20 **French** (literally, 'rust'). A Provençal sauce made from pounded red chillies, garlic, breadcrumbs, etc., blended with stock, frequently added to bouillabaisse.

roulade /rʊˈlɑːd/ *noun* E18 **French** (from *rouler* to roll). **1** E18 *Music* A florid passage of runs etc. in solo vocal music, *especially* one sung to one syllable. **2** L19 Any of various dishes prepared by spreading a filling on to a base of meat, sponge, etc., which is then rolled up and frequently served sliced.

rouleau /rʊˈləʊ/ *noun* plural **rouleaux** /rʊ ˈləʊ/, **rouleaus** L17 French (from *rôle*, originally, a roll or paper containing an actor's part). **1** L17 A cylindrical packet of gold coins. **b** M19 A stack of disc-shaped objects, especially red blood cells. **2** L18 A roll or a coil *of* something, especially hair. **3** E19 A turned tube or length of rolled fabric used as trimming or to form a belt on a garment etc. **4** E20 A type of narrow-necked cylindrical vase originally made in China in the late seventeenth century. In full *rouleau vase*.

roulement /rulmɑ̃/ *noun* plural pronounced same E20 French (literally, 'roll, roster'). *Military* (A) movement of troops or equipment, especially from a reserve force to provide relief.

roulette /rʊˈlɛt/ *noun* M18 French (diminutive of *rouelle* wheel, from late Latin *rotella* diminutive of *rota* wheel). **1** *generally* A small wheel. *rare*. Only in M18. **2** M18 A gambling game in which a ball is dropped on to a revolving wheel with numbered compartments in the centre of a table, players betting on (the colour, height, or parity of) the number at which the ball comes to rest. **3** M19 A revolving toothed wheel; *specifically* (*a*) one for making dotted lines in etching and engraving; (*b*) one for perforating a sheet of paper.

■ Other senses are now rare or obsolete. A transferred use of sense 2 is in the phrase 'Russian roulette' (the act of bravado involving spinning the cylinder of a revolver, one chamber of which is loaded, and then pulling the trigger while pointing it at one's head); hence figuratively, *playing Russian roulette* means taking dangerous risks.

routier /rutje/ *noun* plural pronounced same M17 French (from Old French *rute* from Proto-Romance use as noun (sc. *via* way) of feminine of Latin *ruptus* past participle of *rumpere* to break). **1** M17 *History* A mariner's guide to sea routes, a rutter. **2** M19 *History* A member of any of numerous bands of mercenaries active in France during the later Middle Ages. **3** M20 In France: a long-distance lorry driver.

routinier /rutinje/ *noun* plural pronounced same E19 French. A person who adheres to (a) routine; *especially* (*Music*) a conductor who performs in a mechanically correct but uninspiring way.

roux /ru:/ *noun* E19 French (= browned (sc. butter)). *Cookery* A blend of melted fat (especially butter) and flour used as a thickener in making sauces.

ruana /rʊˈɑ:nə/ *noun* M20 American Spanish (from Spanish (*manta*) *ruana*, literally, 'poor man's cloak', from *rúa* street, from late Latin *ruga* furrow, street, from Latin *ruga* wrinkle). A South American cape or poncho, worn especially in Colombia and Peru.

rubato /rʊˈbɑ:təʊ/ *adjective & noun* L18 Italian (literally, 'robbed'). *Music* **A** *adjective* L18 *tempo rubato*, rubato. **B** *noun* plural **rubatos**, **rubati** /rʊˈbɑ:ti/ L19 The action or practice of temporarily disregarding strict tempo during performance; an instance of this.

rubella /rʊˈbɛlə/ *noun* L19 Latin (use as noun of neuter plural of Latin *rubellus* reddish, from *rubeus* red). German measles.

ruche /ru:ʃ/ *noun* E19 Old and Modern French (from medieval Latin *rusca* tree bark, of Celtic origin). A frill of gathered ribbon, lace, etc., used especially as a trimming on a garment.

rucola /ˈrʊkəʊlə/ *noun* L20 Italian. A vegetable the leaves of which are used for salads.

rumba /ˈrʌmbə/ *noun* (also **rhumba**) E20 American Spanish. An Afro-Cuban dance; a ballroom dance imitative of this, danced on the spot with a pronounced movement of the hips; the dance rhythm of this, usually in 2/4 time; a piece of music with this rhythm.

rusé /ryze/ *adjective* (feminine **rusée**) M18 French. Inclined to use ruses; deceitful, sly, cunning.

> **1973** C. M. Woodhouse *Capodistria* They constantly used of him [sc. Capodistria] the conventional epithets which seemed to fit his nationality—wily, *rusé*, supple, crafty.

ruse de guerre /ryz də gɛr/ *noun phrase* plural **ruses de guerre** (pronounced same) E19 French (literally, 'ruse of war'). A stratagem intended to deceive an enemy in war; *transferred* a justifiable trick.

rusée see RUSÉ.

ruses de guerre plural of RUSE DE GUERRE.

rus in urbe /ˌruːs m ˈəːbeɪ/ *noun phrase* M18 Latin (literally, 'country in city'). An illusion of countryside created by a building, garden, etc., within a city; an urban building etc. which has this effect.

1976 *Times* Two foxes . . . live in a corner of the allotments—which seems to be taking *rus in urbe* too far.

rya /ˈriːə/ *noun* M20 Swedish. A Scandinavian type of knotted pile rug. In full *rya rug*.

ryu /rɪˈuː/ *noun* (also **riu**) plural same L19 Japanese (*-ryū* school, style, system). Any Japanese school or style of art.

S

sabayon /'sabʌjɒn/ *noun* E20 French (from Italian *zabaione* variant of ZABA-GLIONE). Zabaglione.

sabha /sə'bɑː/ *noun* E20 Sanskrit (*sabhā*). In the Indian subcontinent: an assembly; a council; a society.
■ Hence the *Lok Sabha* and the *Rajya Sabha* are respectively the lower and the upper houses of the Indian parliament.

sabi /'sabi/ *noun* M20 Japanese (literally, 'loneliness'). In Japanese art, a quality of simple and mellow beauty expressing a mood of spiritual solitude recognized in Zen Buddhist philosophy. Cf. WABI.

sabkha /'sabkə/, /'sabxə/ *noun* (also **seb-kha** /'sɛbkə/) L19 Arabic (*sabk̲a* a saline in-filtration, salt flat). *Geography* An area of coastal flats subject to periodic flooding and evaporation, found especially in North Africa and Arabia.

sabot /'sabəʊ/ *noun* E17 French (from Old French *çabot* blend of *çavate* (modern SA-VATE) and *bote* (modern *botte*) boot). **1 a** E17 A shoe made of a single piece of wood shaped and hollowed out to fit the foot. **b** M19 A heavy shoe with a thick wooden sole. **c** M20 A decorative metal foot-cover for a piece of wooden furni-ture. **2** *Military* **a** M19 A wooden disc at-tached to a spherical projectile to keep it in place in the bore when discharged. **b** M19 A metal cup or ring fixed to a con-ical projectile to make it conform to the grooves of the rifling. **c** M20 A device fit-ted inside the muzzle of a gun to hold the projectile to be fired. **3** M20 In baccarat and chemin de fer, a box for dealing the cards, a shoe. **4** M20 A small snub-nosed yacht. *Australian.*

sabotage /'sabətɑːʒ/ *noun & verb* E20 French (from *saboter* to make a noise with sabots, execute badly, destroy, from as preceding). **A** *noun* E20 Deliberate dam-age to or destruction of property, espe-cially in order to disrupt the production of goods or as a political or military act. **B** *transitive verb* E20 Commit sabotage on; destroy; make useless.

saboteur /ˌsabə'təː/ *noun* E20 French (from *saboter* (see SABOTAGE)). A person who commits sabotage.

sabra /'sabrə/ *noun* (also **Sabra**) M20 Mod-ern Hebrew (*ṣabbār* or its source Arabic *ṣabr* prickly pear). A Jew born in the re-gion of the modern State of Israel.
attributive **1995** *Times* Yitzhak Rabin was . . . the first *sabra*, or native-born, leader of his country.

sabreur /sa'brəː/ *noun* M19 French (from *sabrer* to sabre). **1** M19 A person, espe-cially a cavalry soldier, who fights with a sabre. **2** E20 A person who fences using a sabre.

saccade /sə'kɑːd/ *noun* E18 French. **1** E18 A jerking movement. Now *rare* except as passing into sense 2. **2** M20 A brief rapid movement of the eye from one position of rest to another, whether voluntary or involuntary.

Sachertorte /'zaxər,tɔrtə/ *noun* plural **Sachertorten** /'zaxər,tɔrt(ə)n/ E20 Ger-man (from Franz *Sacher* Viennese pastry-chef, its creator + *Torte* tart, pastry, cake). A chocolate gateau with apricot jam fill-ing and chocolate icing.

sachet /'saʃeɪ/ *noun* L15 Old and Modern French (diminutive of *sac*). **1** A small car-rying bag. *rare* Only in L15. **2 a** M19 A small scented bag, especially for holding handkerchiefs. **b** M19 (A small bag or packet containing) dry perfume for plac-ing among clothing etc. **3** E20 A small sealed bag or packet, now frequently of plastic, containing a small portion of a substance, especially shampoo.

Sachlichkeit /'zaxlıçkaıt/ *noun* M20 Ger-man (literally, 'objectivity'). Objectivism, realism. Also *specifically* NEUE SACHLICH-KEIT.
1984 A. G. Lehmann *European Heritage* George Lukács calls *Sachlichkeit* 'mere reportage', instead of an interpretation of reality.

sacro egoismo /ˌsakro ego'izmo/ *noun phrase* M20 Italian (literally, 'sacred ego-ism'). Egocentric nationalism, especially in dealing with foreign States.
■ Usually derogatory, the phrase was coined (1914) by the Italian statesman An-tonio Salandra (1853–1931) who, on the outbreak of World War I, first proclaimed Italy's neutrality in defiance of treaty obli-gations to Germany and Austria-Hungary

and then brought Italy into the war on the side of the Allies.

1996 *Spectator* It is the law of nations that countries are driven by *sacro egoismo*—each one, naturally, wishes to defend its own interests.

sacrum /'seɪkrəm/ *noun* plural **sacrums**, **sacra** /'seɪkrə/ M18 Latin (short for late Latin *os sacrum*, translation of Greek *hieron osteon* sacred bone (from the belief that the soul resides in it)). *Anatomy* A triangular bone which is wedged between the two hip-bones, forming the back of the pelvis and resulting from the fusing of (usually five) vertebrae.

sadhu /'sɑːdhuː/ *noun* (also **Sadhu**) M19 Sanskrit (*sādhu* adjective, good, (as noun) good man, holy man). *Hinduism* A holy man, a sage.

saeva indignatio /ˌsʌɪvə ɪndɪgˈnɑːtɪəʊ/ *noun phrase* M19 Latin (literally, 'savage indignation'). An intense feeling of contemptuous anger at human folly.

▪ The phrase is particularly associated with the satirist Jonathan Swift (1667–1745), appearing in the epitaph that he composed for his tomb in St Patrick's, Dublin.

1969 *Punch* Solzhenitsyn's *The First Circle* . . . fell short of greatness because it was too docile. It lacked *saeva indignatio*.

safari /səˈfɑːri/ *noun, verb, & adjective* L19 Kiswahili (from Arabic *safar* journey, trip, tour). **A** *noun* **1** L19 A hunter's or traveller's party or caravan, especially in East Africa. **2** E20 A journey; a cross-country expedition on foot or in vehicles, originally and especially in East Africa, for hunting, tourism, or scientific investigation. Frequently in *on safari*. **B** *intransitive verb* E20 Go on safari. **C** *attributive* or as *adjective* L20 Sandy brown or beige; of the colour of clothes traditionally worn on safari.

saga /'sɑːgə/ *noun* E18 Old Norse ((Icelandic); cf. Old English *sagu* (modern *saw*), German *Sage*). **1** E18 An Old Norse prose narrative of Iceland or Norway, *especially* one which recounts the traditional history of Icelandic families or of the kings of Norway. **b** *transferred* M19 A narrative regarded as having the traditional characteristics of the Icelandic sagas; a story of heroic achievement. Also, a novel or series of novels recounting the history of a family through several generations; *loosely* a long and complicated account of a series of events. **2** M19 (partly after German *Sage*) A story which has been handed down by oral tradition and added to or adapted in the course of time; historical or heroic legend.

sagamité /səˌgɑːmɪˈteɪ/ *noun* M17 French (representing Cree *kisa:kamite:w*, literally, 'it is a hot liquid'). Gruel or porridge made from coarse hominy.

saganaki /sagəˈnɑːki/ *noun* M20 Modern Greek (= small two-handled frying-pan (traditionally used to prepare the dish)). A Greek dish consisting of breaded or floured cheese fried in butter, often with lemon juice, served as an appetiser.

sahib /'sɑː(h)ɪb/, /'sɑːb/ *noun* (also **saab** /sɑːb/) L17 Urdu (through Persian from Arabic *ṣāḥib* friend, lord, master). **1** L17 An Englishman or other European as addressed or spoken of by Indians. **2** E20 *transferred* A gentleman; a person considered socially acceptable. See also PUKKA.

▪ Anglo-Indian. Also as a title affixed to a person's name or office, as in *Malarao Sahib*, *the inspector sahib*.

sainfoin /'semfɔɪn/, /'sanfɔɪn/ *noun* (also **sanfoin**) M17 French (*saintfoin* (modern *sainfoin*), originally 'lucerne', from modern Latin *sanctum foenum*, literally, 'holy hay', alteration of *sanum foenum* wholesome hay, which was based on Latin *herba medica* erroneous alteration of *herba Medica*, literally, 'Median grass', translation of Greek *Mēdikē poa*). A leguminous plant, *Onobrychis viciifolia*, with pinnate leaves and bright pink flowers in dense racemes, formerly much grown for fodder.

sais variant of SYCE.

sake /'sɑːki/, /'sakeɪ/ *noun* (also **saké**, **saki**) L17 Japanese. A Japanese alcoholic drink made from fermented rice.

sakia /'sɑːkɪə/ *noun* L17 Arabic (*sāḳiya* use as noun of feminine active participle of *saḳā* to irrigate). A machine for drawing water for irrigation, consisting of a large vertical wheel to which earthen pots are attached and moved by means of a horizontal wheel turned by oxen or asses.

salaam /səˈlɑːm/ *noun* E17 Arabic (*salām* = Hebrew *šālōm*). **1** E17 An oriental greeting, meaning 'Peace', used chiefly in Muslim countries; a ceremonial obeisance sometimes accompanying this salutation, consisting in the Indian subcontinent of a low bow with the right palm on the forehead. **2** L18 In *plural* Respectful compliments.

salade niçoise /salad niswaz/ *noun phrase* plural **salades niçoises** (pronounced same) E20 French (= salad from Nice (in southern France)). A salad usually made from hard-boiled eggs, anchovies, black olives, tomatoes, etc.

saladero /salə'dɛːrəʊ/ *foreign* /sala'dero/ *noun* plural **saladeros** /salə'dɛːrəʊz/, *foreign* /sala'deros/ L19 Spanish. In Spain and Latin America: a slaughterhouse where meat is also prepared by drying or salting.

salades niçoises plural of SALADE NIÇOISE.

salami /sə'lɑːmi/ *noun* M19 Italian (plural of *salame*, representing popular Latin word from verb meaning 'to salt'). **1** M19 An original Italian variety of sausage, highly seasoned and often flavoured with garlic. **2** L20 A way of carrying out a plan by means of a series of small or imperceptible steps; *specifically* computer fraud in which small amounts of money are transferred from numerous customer accounts into another account. In full *salami technique* or *salami tactics*.

salariat /sə'lɛːrɪət/ *noun* E20 French (from *salaire* salary, after *prolétariat* PROLETARIAT). The salaried class; salary-earners collectively.

salaud /salo/ *noun* plural pronounced same M20 French (from *sale* dirty). As a term of abuse: a contemptible or objectionable person.

salep /'saləp/ *noun* M18 French (from Turkish *sālep* from Arabic *ṭa'lab* fox, shortening of *ḳuṣā 'ṭ-ṭa'lab* orchid (literally, 'fox's testicles')). A starchy preparation of the dried tubers of various orchids, used in cookery and formerly as a tonic.

salina /sə'lʌɪnə/ *noun* L16 Spanish (from medieval Latin = salt pit; in Latin only as plural *salinae* salt-pans). A salt lake, spring, or marsh; a salt-pan, a salt-works. Also (originally *Jamaican*), a low marshy area of land near the coast.

salle /sal/ *noun* plural pronounced same M18 French. A hall; a large room

■ Generally as an element in one of the following phrases, but also sometimes as the abbreviation of one of them.

salle-à-manger /salamɑ̃ʒe/ *noun phrase* M18 French. A dining-hall, a dining-room.

salle d'armes /sal darm/ *noun phrase* L19 French. A fencing hall or school.

salle d'attente /sal datɑ̃t/ *noun* M19 French. A waiting-room, especially at a station.

salle d'eau /sal do/ *noun phrase* M20 French. A washroom, a shower-room.

salle de jeux /sal də ʒø/ *noun phrase* M20 French. A gambling house or room.

salle des pas perdus /sal de pa pɛrdy/ *noun phrase* M19 French (literally, 'of the lost footsteps'). A waiting-hall at a court of law, station, etc.; a lobby.

salle privée /sal prive/ *noun phrase* M20 French. A private gambling room in a casino.

salmi /'salmi/ *noun* (also **salmis**) plural pronounced same M18 French (abbreviation of French *salmigondis* salmagundi). A game stew with a rich sauce.

salon /'salɒn/, *foreign* /salɔ̃/ (plural same) *noun & adjective* L17 French (from Italian *salone* augmentative of *sala* hall). **A** *noun* **1** L17 A reception room in a palace or large house, especially in France or other Continental country; a drawing-room. **2** E19 *specifically* The reception room of a lady of fashion, especially in Paris; a social gathering of eminent people in such a room. **3** E20 An establishment in which the business of hairdresser, beautician, etc., is conducted.

salon des refusés /salɔ̃ de rəfyze/ *noun phrase* L19 French (= exhibition of rejected works). An exhibition ordered by Napoleon III in 1863 to display pictures rejected by the Salon; also *transferred*.

■ The Salon, the annual exhibition in Paris of painting, sculpture, etc., by living artists, was notoriously hostile to the works of impressionist artists.

salonnière /sə.lɒnɪ'ɛː/ *noun* (also **salonière**) E20 French (from as SALON). A woman who holds a salon; a society hostess.

1995 *Times* . . . apart from the ever-present George Sand, Flaubert's mistress Louise Colet and a few *salonières*, the thinking-woman-in-oils is striking by her absence.

salopette /salə'pɛt/ *noun* L20 French. *singular* and (usually) in *plural* Trousers with a high waist and shoulder-straps, worn especially as a skiing garment and as a Frenchman's overalls.

salpicon /'salpɪkɒn/ *noun* E18 French (from Spanish, from *salpicar* to sprinkle (with salt)). *Cookery* A stuffing for veal, beef, or mutton, also used as a garnish.

salsa /'salsə/ *noun* M19 Spanish (= sauce; in sense 2 American Spanish). **1** M19 *Cookery* A sauce served with meat. **2** L20 Contemporary dance music of Caribbean origin which incorporates jazz and rock elements; a dance to this music.
2 1996 *Country Life* Over the road, a salsa band blared out in raunchy competition.

saltarello /saltə'rɛləʊ/ *noun* plural **saltarellos**, **saltarelli** /saltə'rɛli/ L16 Italian (*salterello*, Spanish *salterelo* related to Italian *saltare*, Spanish *saltar* to leap, dance, from Latin *saltare*). **1** L16 The jack of a spinet or harpsichord. *rare.* **2** E18 *History* An animated Italian and Spanish dance for a couple involving numerous sudden skips or jumps; a piece of music for this dance or in its rhythm.

salti plural of SALTO.

saltimbocca /ˌsaltɪm'bɒkə/ *noun* M20 Italian (from *saltare* to leap + *in* in, into + *bocca* mouth). *Cookery* A dish consisting of rolled pieces of veal and ham cooked with herbs.

salto /'saltəʊ/, *in sense 1 also foreign* /'saltɔ/ *noun* plural **saltos**, (in sense 1) **salti** /'salti/ L19 Italian (= leap, from Latin *saltus*). **1** L19 *salto mortale* /mɔː'taːleɪ/, *foreign* /mor'taːle/ (= fatal leap), a daring or flying leap; *figurative* a risky step, an unjustified inference, a leap of faith. **2** L20 A somersault.

salumeria /ˌsalume'riːa/, /ˌsal(j)uːmə'riːə/ *noun* E20 Italian (= grocer's, or pork-butcher's shop, from *salume* salted meat, from *sale* from Latin *sal* salt). A delicatessen.

salve /'salveɪ/, /'salviː/ *noun* LME Latin (= hail, greetings, imperative of *salvere* be well; in sense 1 from the opening words of the antiphon *salve regina* hail (holy) queen). **1** LME *Roman Catholic Church* (usually **Salve**) More fully *Salve Regina* /rə'dʒiːnə/. A popular Marian antiphon, now said or sung especially after compline. Also, a musical setting for this. **2** L16 An utterance of 'salve'; a greeting or salutation on meeting. Now *rare* or *obsolete*.

salvo /'salvəʊ/ *noun* plural **salvos** E17 Latin (ablative neuter singular of *salvus* safe, as in medieval Latin law phrases like *salvo jure* without prejudice to the right of (a specified person) etc.). **1** E17 A saving clause; a provision that a certain ordinance shall not be binding where it would interfere with a specified right or duty; a reservation, a qualification. (Followed by *of*, *for*, *to*.) **2** M17 A dishonest

mental reservation; an evasion, an excuse. Now *rare*. **3** M17–L18 A solution of a difficulty, an answer to an objection. **4** M18 A thing intended to save a person's reputation or soothe offended pride or conscience.

sal volatile /ˌsal və'latɪli/ *noun phrase* M17 Modern Latin (= volatile salt). Ammonium carbonate, especially in the form of an aromatic solution in alcohol to be sniffed as a restorative in faintness etc.; smelling-salts.

salwar variant of SHALWAR.

samadhi /sə'mɑːdi/ *noun* L18 Sanskrit (*samādhi* contemplation, literally, 'a putting together, joining'). *Hinduism* and *Buddhism* **1** L18 The state of union with creation into which a perfected yogi or holy man is said to pass at the time of apparent death. **2** E19 A state of intense concentration induced by meditation, in which union with creation is attained; the last stage of yoga.

samba /'sambə/ *noun* L19 Portuguese (of African origin). A Brazilian dance of African origin; a Latin American and ballroom dance imitative of this; a piece of music for this dance, usually in 2/4 or 4/4 time.

sambal /'sambal/ *noun* E19 Malay. In Malayan and Indonesian cookery, a relish consisting of raw vegetables or fruit prepared with spices and vinegar.

sambar /'sambɑː/ *noun* M20 Tamil (*campār* from Marathi *sāb(h)ar* from Sanskrit *sambhāra* collection, materials). In southern Indian cookery, a highly seasoned lentil and vegetable dish.

sambo /'sambəʊ/ *noun* M20 Russian (acronym, from *samozashchita bez oruzhiya*, literally, 'unarmed self-defence'). A type of wrestling resembling judo, originating in the former USSR. Also more fully *sambo wrestling*.

sambok variant of SJAMBOK.

samfu /'samfuː/ *noun* M20 Chinese ((Cantonese) *shaam foò*, from *shaam* coat + *foò* trousers). A suit consisting of jacket and trousers worn by Chinese women and occasionally men.

samisen /'samɪsɛn/ *noun* (also **shamisen** /'ʃamɪsɛn/) E17 Japanese (from Chinese *sānxián* (Wade–Giles *sān-hsien*), from *sān* three + *xián* string). A long-necked three-stringed Japanese lute, played with a plectrum. Cf. SAN-HSIEN.

samizdat /'samɪzdat/, /ˌsamɪz'dat/ *noun* (also **Samizdat**) M20 Russian (from *sam*(o- self + *izdat*(*el*'*stvo* publishing house). The clandestine or illegal copying and distribution of literature, especially in the former USSR; an underground press; a text or texts produced by this.
1980 *Times Literary Supplement* The strongest works to have come out since 1962 . . . have appeared, and could only appear, in *samizdat*.

samosa /sə'məʊsə/ *noun* M20 Persian and Urdu (*samosa*(h)). A triangular pastry fried in ghee or oil, containing spiced vegetables or meat.

samovar /'saməvɑː/, /samə'vɑː/ *noun* M19 Russian (from *samo*- self + *varit'* to boil). A Russian tea urn, with an internal heating device to keep the water at boiling point.

sampan /'sampan/ *noun* E17 Chinese (*sān-ban* (Wade–Giles *san-pan*) boat, from *sān* three + *bǎn* board). A small boat used in the Far East, usually with a stern-oar or stern-oars.

samsara /səm'sɑːrə/ *noun* L19 Sanskrit (*saṃsāra* a wandering through). *Hinduism* and *Buddhism* The endless cycle of death and rebirth to which life in the material world is bound.

samskara /səm'skɑːrə/ *noun* E19 Sanskrit (*saṃskāra* preparation, a making perfect). **1** E19 *Hinduism* A purificatory ceremony or rite marking a stage or an event in life. **2** E19 *Buddhism* A mental impression, instinct, or memory.

samurai /'samʊrʌɪ/, /'samjʊrʌɪ/ *noun & adjective* E18 Japanese. **A** *noun* E18 plural same. In feudal Japan, a member of a military caste, *especially* a member of the class of military retainers of the daimyos. Now also more widely, a Japanese army officer. **B** *attributive* or as *adjective* **1** L19 Of or pertaining to the samurai. **2** L20 *Samurai bond*, a bond in yen in the Japanese market, issued by a foreigner.

samyama /'samjəmə/ *noun* E19 Sanskrit (*saṃyama* restraint, control of the senses). *Hinduism* and *Buddhism* Collectively, the three final stages of meditation in yoga, which lead to SAMADHI.

san /san/ *noun* L19 Japanese (contraction of more formal *sama*). In Japan: an honorific title used after a personal or family name as a mark of politeness. Also (*collo-quially*), used after other names or titles (cf. MAMA-SAN).

sanatarium /sanə'tɛːrɪəm/ *noun* plural **sanataria** /sanə'tɛːrɪə/, **sanatariums** M19 Modern Latin (from as SANATORIUM). = SANATORIUM senses 1, 2. Chiefly *United States*.

sanatorium /sanə'tɔːrɪəm/ *noun* plural **sanatoriums**, **sanatoria** /sanə'tɔːrɪə/ M19 Modern Latin (from *sanat*- past participial stem of *sanare* to heal). **1** M19 An establishment for the medical treatment and recuperation of invalids, especially convalescents or the chronically sick. **2** M19 A health resort. **3** M19 A room or building for sick people in a school etc. Often abbreviated in school slang to *san*.

sanbenito /ˌsanbə'niːtəʊ/ *noun* plural **sanbenitos** M16 Spanish (*sambenito*, from *San Benito* St Benedict, so called ironically from its resemblance to the Benedictine scapular). In the Spanish Inquisition, a yellow scapular-shaped garment, with a red St Andrew's cross before and behind, worn by a confessed and penitent heretic. Also, a similar black garment with flames, devils, and other devices, worn by an impenitent confessed heretic at an auto-da-fé.

sancocho /san'kotʃo/ *noun* M20 American Spanish (from Spanish = half-cooked meal, from *sancochar* to parboil). In South America and the Caribbean: a rich soup or stew of meat, fish, and vegetables.

sancta plural of SANCTUM.

sancta sanctorum plural of SANCTUM SANCTORUM.

sancta simplicitas /ˌsaŋ(k)tə sɪm'plɪsɪtɑːs/ *interjection* M19 Latin (literally, 'holy simplicity'). Expressing astonishment at a person's naivety.
■ These are said to have been the last words of the Bohemian religious reformer John Huss, burnt at the stake in 1415, on seeing a simple peasant bringing wood to add to the fire.

sanctum /'saŋ(k)təm/ *noun* plural **sanctums**, **sancta** /'saŋ(k)tə/ L16 Latin (neuter of *sanctus* holy; cf. next). **1** L16 A sacred place or shrine in a temple or church. **2** E19 A place where a person can be alone and free from intrusion; a private room, study, etc.

sanctum sanctorum /ˌsaŋ(k)təm saŋ(k)'tɔːrəm/ *noun phrase* plural **sancta sanctorum** /ˌsaŋ(k)tə/ LME Latin (neuter singular and neuter genitive plural of *sanctus* holy, translation of Hebrew *qōḏeš haq-qōḏāšīm* holy of holies). **1** LME *Jewish Antiquities* The holy of holies in the Jewish Temple. **2** L16 A SANCTUM sense 1. **3** E18 A SANCTUM sense 2.

sanctus /'saŋ(k)təs/ *noun* LME Latin (= holy, the first word of the hymn). *Christian Church* (also **Sanctus**) The hymn beginning *Sanctus, sanctus, sanctus* 'Holy, holy, holy', which forms the conclusion of the Eucharistic preface; a musical setting of this.

sandur /'sandə/, /'sandə:/ *noun* plural **sandar**, **sandurs** (also **sandr**, plural same, **sandurs**) L19 Icelandic (*sandur*, plural *sandar*, (Old Norse *sandr*), sand). *Physical Geography* A broad, flat or gently sloping plain of glacial outwash.

sanfoin variant of SAINFOIN.

sang-de-boeuf /sãdəbœf/ *noun* L19 French (literally, 'ox's blood'). A deep red colour found on old Chinese porcelain; (porcelain bearing) a ceramic glaze of this colour.

Sängerfest /'sɛŋərfɛst/ *noun* (also **Saengerfest**) M19 German (from *Sänger* singer + FEST). A choral festival. *United States.*

sang-froid /sɒŋ'frwɑ:/ *noun* M18 French (literally, 'cold blood'). Coolness, self-possession, especially in the face of danger or disturbing circumstances.

> **1996** *Spectator* Thanks to our sang-froid, we have only once fallen into the hands of idiotic optimists—the grim Puritans of the Commonwealth.

sangha /'saŋgə/ *noun* M19 Sanskrit (*saṃgha*, from *sam* together + *han* to come in contact). *Buddhism* The Buddhist community, the Buddhist order of monks, nuns, and novices.

sanglier /sãglije/ *noun* plural pronounced same LME Old French (*sengler*, (also modern) *sanglier* from Latin *singularis* solitary, singular, used as noun in late Latin = a boar separated from the herd, in medieval Latin = wild boar). A wild boar. Formerly *specifically*, one that is fully grown.

sangoma /saŋ'gɔ:ma/ *noun* (also **isangoma** /ɪsaŋ'gɔ:ma/) L19 Nguni. In southern Africa: a witch-doctor, usually a woman, claiming supernatural powers of divination and healing.

sangre azul /ˌsangre a'θul/, /ˌa'sul/ *noun phrase* M19 Spanish (= blue blood). The

purity of blood claimed by certain ancient Castilian families, which professed to be free from Moorish or Jewish ancestry.

sangria /saŋ'gri:ə/ *noun* (also **Sangria**) M20 Spanish (*sangría*, literally, 'bleeding'). A Spanish drink made of sweetened diluted red wine with spices and fruit.

san-hsien /san'ʃjɛn/ *noun* (also **sanxian**) M19 Chinese (*sānxián* (Wade–Giles *sān-hsien*), from *sān* three + *xián* string). *Music* A Chinese three-stringed lute. Cf. SAMISEN.

sannyasi /sən'jɑ:si/ *noun* (also **sanyasi**, **sannyasin** /sən'jɑ:sm/) E17 Sanskrit (*saṃnyāsī* nominative singular of *saṃnyāsin* laying aside, abandoning, ascetic, from *saṃ* together + *ni* down + *as* throw). A brahmin in the fourth stage of his life; a wandering Hindu fakir.

sanpaku /san'paku/ *noun* M20 Japanese (literally, 'three white', from *san* three + *haku* white). Visibility of the white of the eye below the iris as well as on either side.

sans /sɑ̃(z)/, /san(z)/ *preposition* ME Old French (*san, sanz* (modern *sans*), earlier *sen(s)* from Proto-Romance variation of Latin *sine* without, partly influenced by Latin *absentia* absence). Without.

■ Although formerly fully naturalized, *sans* is now, apart from use in heraldic terminology, mainly literary and often jocular—especially with reference to Shakespeare's line on second childhood: 'Sans teeth, sans eyes, sans taste, sans everything' (*As You Like It* II.vii). It also occurs in a number of phrases borrowed from French.

> **1996** *Times* Ms Thompson is not allowed to leave her house in a track-suit *sans* make-up without being pilloried by the press.

sans blague /sɑ̃ blag/ *interjection* E20 Old French (literally, 'without joking'). You don't say! I don't believe it!

sans cérémonie /sɑ̃ seremɔni/ *adverb phrase* M17 Old French. Unceremoniously; without the usual ceremony or formality.

sansculotte /ˌsanzkju:'lɒt/, *foreign* /sãkylɔt/ (*plural same*) *noun* (also **sans culottes**) L18 French (from *sans* without + *culotte* knee-breeches). **1** L18 *History* A lower-class Parisian republican in the French Revolution; *generally* an extreme republican or revolutionary. **2** E19 *transferred* A shabbily dressed person, a ragamuffin.

> **1 1996** *Times* After my election . . . I warned my council colleagues that if I were seen to be obstructed, it would not be long before *sans culottes* to the left of me emerged.

sansei /'sanseɪ/ *noun* plural same M20 Japanese (from *san* three, third + *sei* generation). An American whose grandparents were immigrants from Japan. Cf. NISEI.

sanserif variant of SANS SERIF.

sans façon /sã fasɔ̃/ *adverb phrase* L17 Old French (literally, 'without manner'). Without the customary formality; SANS CÉRÉMONIE.

sans-gêne /sã ʒɛn/ *noun phrase* L19 Old French (literally, 'without embarrassment'). Disregard of the ordinary forms of civility or politeness.

sans pareil /sã parɛj/ *adjective phrase* Old French (literally, 'not having its like'). Unique, unequalled.

> ▪ Earlier (M18) current as a noun meaning 'smelling salts' or some other kind of perfume.
> **1996** *Times* Not for nothing is Mr Gordon considered an agent *sans pareil*.

sans peur /sã pœr/ *adjective phrase* E19 Old French. Without fear, fearless.

> ▪ Especially in the phrase *sans peur et sans reproche*, which was applied to the Chevalier de Bayard (1476–1524), a renowned soldier in the Italian wars of Charles VIII of France.
> **1995** *Spectator* Whether for religious reasons or because it hasn't got a licence, there's no alcohol in the place, though you can bring your own with you *sans peur et sans reprôche* [*sic*].

sans phrase /sanz 'frɑːz/ *adjective phrase* E19 Old French. Without more words, without exceptions or qualifications.

> ▪ After *La mort sans phrase* ('death, without more words'), the expression allegedly used by the Abbé Sieyès (1748–1836) in giving his vote for the execution of Louis XVI.

sans recours /sã r(ə)kur/, /ˌsanz rə'kə:/ *noun phrase* L19 Old French (literally, 'without recourse'). *Law* An endorsement on a bill of exchange absolving the endorser or any other party from liability.

sans reproche /sanz rə'prɔʃ/ *adjective phrase* M19 Old French. Without reproach, blameless.

> ▪ Earlier (E19), and especially, in *sans peur et sans reproche*; cf. SANS PEUR.

sans serif /san 'sɛrɪf/ *noun & adjective* (also **sanserif**) M19 French (apparently from SANS + *serif* cross-stroke of a letter (origin uncertain, but possibly from Dutch *schreef* dash, line)). *Typography* **A** *noun* M19 A letterform, especially a typeface, without serifs. **B** *adjective* L19 Having no serifs.

santeria /ˌsante'ria/ *noun* M20 Spanish (*santería*, literally, 'holiness, sanctity'). An Afro-Cuban religious cult with many Yoruba elements.

santero /san'tero/ *noun* plural **santeros** /san'teros/ M20 Spanish. **1** M20 In Mexico and Spanish-speaking areas of the southwestern United States: a maker of religious images. **2** M20 A priest of a religious cult, especially of *santeria*.

santir /san'tɪə/ *noun* (also **santoor, santour** /san'tʊə/) M19 Arabic (*santīr, sintīr, santūr* (Persian *santūr*, Turkish *santur*), alteration of Greek *psaltērion* psaltery). A dulcimer of Arab and Persian origin.

santo /'santəʊ/ *noun* plural **santos** M17 Spanish (or Italian). **1** M17 A SANTON sense 1. **2** M19 A wooden representation of a saint or other religious symbol from Mexico or the south-western United States.

santon /'santɒn/ *noun* L16 French (from Spanish, from *santo* saint). **1** L16 A Muslim hermit or holy man, a marabout. Formerly also, a yogi, a Hindu ascetic. **2** E20 Chiefly in Provence: a figurine adorning a representation of the manger in which Jesus was laid.

santoor, santour variants of SANTIR.

san ts'ai /'san tsʌɪ/ *noun phrase* E20 Chinese (*sāncǎi* (Wade–Giles *sān-ts'ai*), from *sān* three + *cǎi* colour). Chinese pottery, especially of the Tang dynasty, decorated in three colours; decoration in three enamel colours applied to pottery and porcelain.

sanyasi variant of SANNYASI.

saphir d'eau /safir do/ *noun* E19 French (literally 'sapphire of water'). An intense blue variety of cordierite occurring mainly in Sri Lanka; a water sapphire.

sarabande /sarə'bɑːnd/ *noun* (also **saraband** /'sarəband/) E17 French (from Spanish or Italian *zarabanda*). A slow and stately Spanish dance in triple time; a piece of music for this dance or in its rhythm.

sarang variant of SERANG.

sarangi /sə'raŋgi/, /saː'rʌŋgi/ *noun* M19 Sanskrit (*sāraṅgī*). An Indian bowed stringed instrument.

sarape variant of SERAPE.

sarcoma /saː'kəʊmə/ *noun* plural **sarcomas**, **sarcomata** /saː'kəʊmətə/ M17 Modern Latin (from Greek *sarkōma*, from *sarkoun* to become fleshy, from *sarx*, *sark-* flesh). *Medicine* **1** M17–M18 A fleshy excrescence. **2** E19 A malignant tumour of connective or other non-epithelial tissue.

sarcophagus /saː'kɒfəgəs/ *noun* plural **sarcophagi** /saː'kɒfəgʌɪ/, /saː'kɒfədʒʌɪ/ LME Latin (from Greek *sarkophagos* (adjective & noun), from *sarx*, *sark-* flesh + *-phagos* eating). **1** A stone coffin, *especially* one adorned with sculpture, an inscription, etc. **2** E17 *Greek Antiquities* A stone fabled to be able to consume the flesh of dead bodies deposited in it, and used for coffins. Now *rare*. **3** E17–M19 A flesh-eater; a cannibal. *rare*.

sardana /sar'dana/ *noun* E20 Catalan and Spanish. A Catalan dance performed to pipes and drum.

sari /'saːri/ *noun* (also **saree**) L18 Hindi (*sārī* from Sanskrit *śāṭikā*). A traditional garment of Indian women, worn over a CHOLI and an underskirt, consisting of a length of cotton, silk, or other cloth wrapped around the waist and draped over one shoulder.

sarmale /sar'male/ *noun* plural M20 Romanian. A Romanian dish of forcemeat and other ingredients wrapped in especially cabbage or vine leaves.

sarod /sə'rəʊd/ *noun* M19 Urdu (from Persian *surod* song, melody). An Indian stringed musical instrument.

saron /'saːrɒn/ *noun* E19 Javanese. An Indonesian musical instrument, normally having seven bronze bars which are struck with a mallet.

sarong /sə'rɒŋ/ *noun* M19 Malay (literally, 'sheath, quiver'). A traditional skirtlike garment of the Malay archipelago, Java, and some Pacific islands, consisting of a long strip of (often striped) cloth worn tucked round the waist or under the armpits by both sexes; a woman's garment resembling this, worn especially on the beach.

sarsaparilla /ˌsaːs(ə)pə'rɪlə/ *noun* L16 Spanish (*zarzaparilla*, from *zarza* bramble + diminutive of Spanish *parra* vine, twining plant). **1** L16 Any of several tropical American kinds of smilax used medicinally; the dried root of such a plant, used to treat rheumatism, skin complaints, and formerly also syphilis. Also, a carbonated drink flavoured with this root. **2** M19 Any of several plants of other genera which resemble sarsaparilla or have a root used similarly. Chiefly with specifying word.

sartage /'saːtɪdʒ/ *noun* L19 French (from *sarter* to clear ground). The clearing of woodland by setting fire to trees. *United States*.

sashimi /'saʃɪmi/ *noun* L19 Japanese (from *sashi* pierce + *mi* flesh). A Japanese dish of slices of raw fish served with grated horseradish and soy sauce.

sassafras /'sasəfras/ *noun* L16 Spanish (*sasafrás*, perhaps ultimately from Latin *saxifraga* saxifrage). **1** L16 A tree of the genus *Sassafras*, of the laurel family, especially *S. albidum* native to the eastern United States; also, the wood of this tree. **b** L16 The dried bark of this tree, used as a medicine and flavouring and for infusing. **c** M18 An oil extracted from (the bark of) the sassafras, used medicinally and in perfumery. In full *sassafras oil*, also *oil of sassafras*. **2** E19 Any of various similarly aromatic and medicinal trees of other genera and families; also, the wood or bark of such a tree.

sastruga /sa'struːgə/ *noun* (also **zastruga** /za'struːgə/) plural **sastrugi** /sa'struːgi/ M19 German (from Russian *zastruga* small ridge, furrow in snow, from *zastrugat'* to plane or smooth, from *strug* plane (the tool)). Any of a series of low irregular ridges formed on a level snow surface by wind erosion, often aligned parallel to the wind direction. Usually in *plural* (see quotation).

> **1975** E. Hillary *Nothing Venture, Nothing Win* The surface, which had appeared so smooth from above, was . . . liberally peppered with large sastrugi—some of them up to three feet in height.

satay /'sateɪ/ *noun* (also **satai**, **saté**) M20 Malay (*satai*, *sate*, Indonesian *sate*; cf. SO-SATIE). An Indonesian and Malaysian dish consisting of small pieces of meat grilled on a skewer and usually served with a spiced peanut sauce.

sati variant of SUTTEE.

satori /sə'tɔːri/ *noun* E18 Japanese (= awakening). *Zen Buddhism* A sudden inner experience of enlightenment.

satranji /ʃə'trandʒi/ *noun* (also **sitringee** /sɪ'trɪndʒiː/ and other variants) E17 **Persian and Urdu** (šhaṭranjī from Persian šaṭranj chess, ultimately from Sanskrit caturaṅga army, chess, with reference to the original chequered pattern). A carpet or floor-rug made of coloured cotton, now usually with a striped pattern.

satsuma /sat'suːmə/, in sense 1 also /'satsjʊmə/ *noun* (also (especially in sense 1) **Satsuma**) L19 Japanese (name of a province in the island of Kiusiu, Japan). **1** L19 A kind of cream-coloured Japanese pottery. In full *Satsuma ware*. **2** L19 A variety of tangerine, originally from Japan, with a sharper taste and frequently seedless or with undeveloped seeds; the tree bearing this fruit.

Saturnalia /satə'neɪlɪə/ *noun* (treated as *singular* or *plural*) (in sense 2 also **saturnalia**) L16 Latin (use as noun of neuter plural of *Saturnalis* of or pertaining to *Saturnus* Saturn, the Roman god of agriculture and ruler of the gods until deposed by his son Jupiter). **1** L16 *Roman History* The festival of Saturn, held in mid December and characterized by general unrestrained merrymaking, the precursor of Christmas. **2** L18 *transferred* and *figurative* A period of unrestrained tumult and revelry; an orgy.

satyagraha /sʌ'tjɑːgrəhɑː/ *noun* E20 Sanskrit (satyāgraha force born of truth, from satya truth + āgraha pertinacity). **1** E20 *History* A policy of passive resistance to British rule in India formulated by M. K. Gandhi. **2** E20 *generally* Any policy of nonviolent resistance.

saucier /sosje/ *noun* plural pronounced same M20 French. A sauce cook.

saucisson /sosisɔ̃/ *noun* plural pronounced same M17 French (augmentative of *saucisse* sausage). **1a** M17 A firework consisting of a tube packed with gunpowder. **b** E19 *History* A long tube packed with gunpowder, formerly used as a fuse for firing a mine. **2** E18 *Military* A large fascine. **3** M18 A large thick sausage.

saudade /sau'dadʒi/ *noun* E20 Portuguese. Longing, melancholy, nostalgia, as a supposed characteristic of the Portuguese or Brazilian temperament.

sauerbraten /'sauəbrɑːt(ə)n/ *noun* L19 German (from *sauer* sour + *Braten* roast meat). A dish of German origin consisting of beef marinaded in vinegar with peppercorns, onions, and other seasonings and then cooked. *North American*.

sauerkraut /'sauəkraut/ *noun* M17 German ((whence French *choucroute*), from *sauer* sour + *Kraut* vegetable, cabbage). Finely chopped pickled cabbage, a typical German dish.

■ In United States slang *Sauerkraut* was in use earlier (M19) as a derogatory word for 'a German' than its British equivalent KRAUT.

sauna /'sɔːnə/ *noun* L19 Finnish. A Finnish-style hot steam bath; a room or building in which such a bath is taken. Also *sauna bath*.

saut /so/ *noun* plural pronounced same L19 French (= leap). **1** L19 *Saut Basque*, a dance of the French Basque provinces. **2** L19 *Ballet* A leap in dancing. Especially in *saut de Basque*, a leap made while turning, holding one leg straight and the other at right angles to the body.

sauté /'səʊteɪ/ *noun, adjective, & verb* E19 French (past participle of *sauter* to leap). *Cookery* **A** *noun* E19 A dish cooked by frying quickly in a little hot fat. **B** *adjective* M19 Of meat, vegetables, etc.: fried quickly in a little hot fat. **C** *transitive verb* M19 (past tense and participle *sautéd, sautéed*) Fry (food) quickly in a little hot fat.

sautoir /'səʊtwɑː/ *noun* M20 French (Old French *saut(e)our, sau(l)toir* stirrup cord). A long necklace consisting of a fine gold chain usually set with jewels.

1980 *Times* Sautoirs, or long neckchains . . . were very popular at the beginning of the century.

sauve qui peut /sovkipø/ *noun & verb phrase* E19 French (literally, 'save-who-can'). **A** *noun phrase* E19 A general stampede, a complete rout; panic, disorder. **B** *verb phrase intransitive* M20 Stampede or scatter in flight.

A 1980 *Guardian* It is in those hallowed halls of the UN . . . that I feel most keenly the theatre of anarchy, of sauve-qui-peut.

savannah /sə'vanə/ *noun* (also **savanna**) M16 Spanish (zavana, çavana, (now sabana) from Taino zavana). **1** M16 Originally, a treeless plain, especially in tropical America. Now, an open grassy plain with few or no trees in a tropical or subtropical region; grassland or vegetation of this kind. **2** L17 A tract of low-lying damp or marshy ground. *United States*.

savant /'sav(ə)nt/, *foreign* /savɑ̃/ (*plural same*) *noun* E18 French (use as noun of adjective, originally present participle of *savoir* to know). A learned person, *especially* a distinguished scientist.

savante /'sav(ə)nt/, *foreign* /savɑ̃:t/ (*plural same*) *noun* M18 French (feminine of preceding). A learned (French) woman. Cf. FEMME SAVANTE.

savarin /'savərɪn/, *foreign* /savarɛ̃/ (*plural same*) *noun* L19 French (Anthelme Brillat-Savarin (1755–1826), French gastronome). A light ring-shaped cake made with yeast and soaked in liqueur-flavoured syrup.

savate /sə'vɑ:t/, *foreign* /savat/ (*plural same*) *noun* M19 French (originally, a kind of shoe (cf. SABOT)). A form of boxing in which the feet and fists are used.

savoir /savwar/ *noun* E19 French (literally, 'know'). Knowledge.
▪ Also used elliptically for SAVOIR FAIRE and SAVOIR VIVRE.

savoir faire /savwar fɛr/ *noun* (also **savoir-faire**) E19 French (literally, 'to know how to do'). The instinctive ability to act suitably in any situation; tact.
1996 *Spectator* Others who had some political savoir-faire (such as Fitzroy Maclean, who had been a diplomat in Moscow before the war) had no special knowledge of the Balkans.

savoir vivre /savwar vivr/ *noun* M18 French (literally, 'know how to live'). Knowledge of the world and the ways of society, ability to conduct oneself well; worldly wisdom, sophistication.

savonette /'savɒnɛt/ *noun* E18 French ((now *savonnette*), diminutive of *savon* soap). Soap, especially in the form of a ball.

sayonara /sʌɪə'nɑ:rə/ *interjection* & *noun* L19 Japanese (literally, 'if it be so'). (The Japanese word for) goodbye.

sayyid /'seɪjɪd/ *noun* (also **saiyid, syed,** and other variants, **Sayyid**) M17 Arabic (= lord, prince). (A title of respect for) a Muslim claiming descent from Muhammad through Husain, the prophet's elder grandson.
▪ In Muslim countries, also as a respectful form of address.

sc. abbreviation of SCILICET.

scaglia /'skɑ:ljə/ *noun* L18 Italian (= scale, chip of marble, from Germanic base from which modern English *scale* (noun)). *Geology* A dark fine-grained shale found in the Alps and Apennines.

scagliola /skal'jəʊlə/ *noun* L16 Italian *scagli(u)ola* diminutive of SCAGLIA). **1** L16–L18 SCAGLIA. **2** M18 Plasterwork of Italian origin, designed to imitate marble and other kinds of stone.

scala mobile /ˌskala 'mo:bile/ *noun phrase* L20 Italian (literally, 'moving stair, escalator'). In Italy: a system of wage indexation by which earnings are linked by a sliding scale to the retail price index.

scald variant of SKALD.

scaloppine /ˌskalə(ʊ)'pi:neɪ/ *noun* (also Anglicized as **scallopini** /ˌskalə(ʊ)'pi:ni/) M20 Italian (plural of *scaloppina* diminutive of *scaloppa* escalope). A dish consisting of escalopes of meat (especially veal) sautéed or fried.

scampi /'skampi/ *noun plural* (also treated as *singular*; in sense 1 singular **scampo** /'skampəʊ/) E19 Italian (plural of *scampo*). **1** E19 Norway lobsters. Also (*rare*) *singular,* a Norway lobster. **2** M20 A dish of these lobsters, usually fried in breadcrumbs or in a sauce. Usually treated as *singular.*
▪ In both senses also called *Dublin Bay prawn(s).*

scandalon variant of SKANDALON.

scarabaeus /ˌskarə'bi:əs/ *noun plural* **scarabaei** /ˌskarə'bi:ʌɪ/ L16 Latin (= beetle: cf. Greek *karabos* horned beetle). **1** L16 *Entomology* A scarabaeid beetle. Now only as modern Latin genus name. **2** L18 *Antiquities* An ancient Egyptian amulet or seal in the form of a beetle with symbols on its flat underside, a scarab.

scarpetti /skɑː'pɛti/ *noun plural* L19 Italian (plural of *scarpetto* small shoe, from *scarpa* shoe). Rope-soled shoes worn for rock-climbing, especially in the North Italian Alps.

scenario /sɪ'nɑ:rɪəʊ/ *noun* & *verb* L19 Italian (from Latin *scena* scene). **A** *noun* plural **scenarios**. **1a** L19 A sketch or outline of the plot of a play, ballet, novel, etc., with details of the scenes and situations. **b** E20 *Cinematography* A film script with all the details of scenes, stage-directions, etc., necessary for shooting the film. **2** M20 A description of an imagined situation or a postulated sequence of events; an outline of an intended course of action; *specifically* a scientific description or speculative model intended to account for observable facts. Also *loosely,* a situation, a sequence of events. **B** *transitive verb* M20 Make a scenario of (a book, idea, etc.); sketch *out.*

2 1996 *New Scientist* Once the current crisis is over, the most important question for the government will be why it never planned for a worst-case scenario when the risks of BSE were first raised in 1986.

scène à faire /sɛn a fɛr/ *noun phrase* plural **scènes à faire** (pronounced same) L19 French (literally, 'scene for action'). *Theatrical* The most important scene in a play or opera.

Schadenfreude /ˈʃɑːd(ə)nfrɔɪdə/ *noun* (also **schadenfreude**) L19 German (from *Schaden* harm + *Freude* joy). Malicious enjoyment of another's misfortune.

1995 *Times* In a lifelong personal effort not to become a sour old besom, I fight very hard against *Schadenfreude* and its complement, Saki's 'natural displeasure at the good fortune of a friend'.

schalet /ˈʃalɪt/, /ʃaˈlɛt/ *noun* M20 Yiddish (*shalent, shalet* variant of *tsholnt* cholent). **1** M20 CHOLENT. **2** M20 A Jewish baked fruit pudding.

schappe /ʃap/, /ˈʃapə/ *noun* L19 German (= silk waste). A fabric or yarn made from waste silk.

schema /ˈskiːmə/ *noun* plural **schemata** /ˈskiːmətə/, **schemas** L18 German (from Greek *skhēma, skhēmat-*). **1** L18 In Kantian philosophy, a rule or procedure of the imagination enabling the understanding to apply a concept, especially a category, to what is given in sense-perception. **2** M19 *Ecclesiastical* A draft canon or decree for discussion. **3** L19 A schematic representation of something; a hypothetical outline or plan; a draft, a synopsis, a design. **4** E20 *Psychology* An (unconscious) organized mental model of something in terms of which new information can be interpreted or an appropriate response made.

schemozzle variant of SHEMOZZLE.

scherzando /skɛːˈtsandəʊ/ *adverb, adjective, & noun* E19 Italian (from *scherzare* to joke, from SCHERZO). *Music* **A** *adverb & adjective* E19 (A direction:) playful(ly). **B** *noun* L19 plural **scherzandos, scherzandi** /skɛːˈtsandi/. A movement or passage (to be) played playfully.

scherzo /ˈskɛːtsəʊ/ *noun* plural **scherzos, scherzi** /ˈskɛːtsiː/ M19 Italian (literally, 'sport, jest'). *Music* A vigorous, light, or playful composition, especially as a movement in a symphony or sonata.

attributive **1996** *Times* This is not to say that Ozick doesn't go at all her subjects with

anything less energetic than a scherzo tempo . . .

schiacciato variant of STIACCIATO.

schiller /ˈʃɪlə/ *adjective & noun* E19 German (= play of colours). *Geology* **A** E19 *attributive adjective* Designating minerals or rocks having a shining surface. **B** *noun* M19 An iridescent lustre, *specifically* that characteristic of certain minerals.

Schimpfwort /ˈʃɪmpfˌvɔrt/ *noun* plural **Schimpfwörter** /ˈʃɪmpfˌvœrtər/ M20 German (from *Schimpf* insult + *Wort* word). An insulting epithet, a term of abuse.

schinken /ˈʃɪŋkən/ *noun* M19 German. German ham.

schlag /ʃlɑːk/ *noun* M20 German (abbreviation). **1** SCHLAGOBERS. **2** SCHLAGSAHNE.

Schlagobers /ˈʃlɑːkˈoːbərs/ *noun* M20 German ((dialect) from *schlagen* to beat + *Obers* cream). (Coffee with) whipped cream.

schlagsahne /ˈʃlɑːkzɑːnə/ *noun* E20 German (from *schlagen* to beat + *Sahne* cream). Whipped cream.

Schlamperei /ˈʃlampəraɪ/ *noun* M20 German. Indolent slovenliness, muddle-headedness.

■ In its original German context, used derogatorily to designate the supposed sloppiness of the south Germans and Austrians.

schlemiel /ʃləˈmiːl/ *noun* (also **schlemihl, Shlemihl**) L19 German (*Shlemihl*). An awkward or clumsy person; a foolish or unlucky person. *colloquial*.

■ The word may ultimately be connected with the biblical *Shelumiel*, head of the tribe of Simeon (Numbers 1:6), who, according to the Talmud, came to an unfortunate end. Modern use of *schlemiel* is influenced by Adelbert von Chamisso's famous tale *Peter Schlemihls wundersame Geschichte* (1814), the eponymous hero of which sells his shadow.

schlenter /ˈʃlɛntə/ *noun & adjective* (also (*Australia* and *New Zealand*) **slanter** /ˈslantə/ and other variants) M19 Afrikaans (or Dutch possibly from Dutch *slenter* knavery, trick). **A** *noun* **1** M19 A trick. *Australian* and *New Zealand colloquial*. **2** L19 A counterfeit diamond. *South African*. **B** *adjective* L19 Dishonest, crooked; counterfeit, fake. *Australian, New Zealand, and South African colloquial*.

■ The history of this word is obscure; the likelihood is that the Australian and New Zealand usages derive from South African English, but the route of the borrowing is uncertain. In Australia and New Zealand the most common spelling is now *slanter*, presumably under the influence of *slant* (i.e. crooked).

schlep /ʃlɛp/ *noun* 1 M20 Yiddish (abbreviation). A SCHLEPPER. *United States colloquial.*

schlep /ʃlɛp/ *noun* 2 M20 Yiddish (probably from German *schleppen* to drag). A troublesome business, (a piece of) hard work. Chiefly *United States colloquial.*

schlep /ʃlɛp/ *verb* (also **schlepp**; inflected -*pp*-) E20 Yiddish (*shelpn* from German *schleppen* to drag). **1** *transitive verb* E20 Haul, carry, drag. **2** *intransitive verb* M20 Toil; move or go slowly or awkwardly. *colloquial.*

schlepper /ˈʃlɛpə/ *noun* M20 Yiddish (as preceding). A person of little worth; a fool; a hanger-on. *United States colloquial.*

schlimazel /ʃlɪˈmɒz(ə)l/ *noun* (also **shlimazel**, **schlimazl**) M20 Yiddish (from Middle High German *slim* crooked + Hebrew *mazzāl* luck). A consistently unlucky and accident-prone person. Chiefly *United States colloquial.*

schlock /ʃlɒk/ *noun & adjective* E20 Yiddish (apparently from *shlak* apoplectic stroke, *shlog* wretch, untidy person, apoplectic stroke, from *shlogn* to strike). **A** *noun* E20 Cheap, shoddy, or defective goods; inferior material, trash. **B** *adjective* E20 Cheap, inferior, trashy.

■ Colloquial and chiefly North American (but see quotation).

A 1996 *Times Silver Lake* is a fascinating hybrid: certainly not an opera, but . . . not quite a musical either, at least not the escapist schlock that the term 'musical' so often suggests nowadays.

schlong /ʃlɒŋ/ *noun* M20 Yiddish (*shlang*, from Middle High German *slange* (German *Schlange*) snake). The penis. Also, a contemptible person. *United States slang.*

schloss /ʃlɒs/ *noun* E19 German. A castle, *especially*, one in Germany or Austria.
1995 *Spectator* On the way we had a glimpse of Glamis Castle . . . [a] charming *schloss*, turreted and stucco'd . . .

schlub variant of SHLUB.

schmaltz /ʃmɔːlts/, /ʃmalts/ *noun & verb* M20 Yiddish (from German *Schmalz* dripping, lard). **A** *noun* **1** M20 Melted

chicken fat. Chiefly in *schmaltz herring*, a form of pickled herring. **2** M20 Sentimentality, emotionalism; excessively sentimental music, writing, drama, etc. *colloquial.* **B** *transitive verb* M20 Impart a sentimental atmosphere to; play (music) in a sentimental manner. Frequently followed by *up*. *colloquial.*

A.2 1995 *Spectator* This orgy of smug schmalz starts with Doris's dad dropping dead in church, presumably having seen the rest of the show in rehearsal . . .

schmatte variant of SHMATTE.

schmear, **schmeer** variants of SHMEAR.

schmelz /ʃmɛlts/ *noun* M19 German (= enamel). Any of several varieties of decorative glass; *especially* one coloured red with a metallic salt, used to flash white glass.

Schmelzglas /ˈʃmɛlts,glaːs/ *noun* M20 German. SCHMELZ.

Schmerz /ʃmɛrts/ *noun* E20 German (= pain). Grief, sorrow, regret, pain.

schmierkäse /ˈʃmiːr,kɛːzə/ *noun* E20 German (from *schmieren* to smear + *Käse* cheese). A soft cheese, *specifically* cottage cheese.

schmooze /ʃmuːz/, /ʃmuːs/ *noun* M20 Yiddish (*schmues* chat, gossip from Hebrew *šĕmūʿōṯ* plural of *šĕmūʿāh* rumour). Chat; gossip; a long and intimate conversation. *North American colloquial.*

schmuck /ʃmʌk/ *noun* L19 Yiddish (*shmok* penis). A contemptible or objectionable person; an idiot.

■ North American slang. *Schmo* is a more recent (M20) alternative.

schmutz /ʃmʊts/ *noun* M20 Yiddish or German. Dirt, filth, rubbish. *slang.*

schnapps /ʃnaps/ *noun* (also **schnaps**) E19 German (*Schnaps* dram of drink, liquor (especially gin) from Low German, Dutch *snaps* gulp, mouthful, from *snappen* to seize, snatch, snap). Any of various strong spirits resembling genever.

■ The Dutch, Danish, and Swedish word *snaps* (M19) is less common in English.

schnitzel /ˈʃnɪts(ə)l/ *noun* M19 German. A veal cutlet.

■ Especially in *Wiener* (or Vienna) *schnitzel*, a veal cutlet coated with egg and breadcrumbs and fried.

schnook /ʃnʊk/ *noun* M20 German or Yiddish (perhaps from German *Schnucke* a small sheep, or Yiddish *shnuk* snout). A dupe, a sucker; a simpleton. *North American colloquial.*

schnorrer /ˈʃnɒrə/ *noun* L19 Yiddish (variant of German *Schnurrer*, from *schnurren* (slang) go begging). Originally (*specifically*) a Jewish beggar. Now (*generally*), a beggar, a layabout, a scrounger. Chiefly *United States*.

schnozz /ʃnɒz/ *noun* M20 Yiddish (*shnoytz* from German *Schnauze* snout. The nose; a nostril.

■ North American slang. The Yiddish diminutive form of *shnoytz*, *shnoytzl*, has given rise to *schnozzle* /ˈʃnɒz(ə)l/ (M20), also a slang word for 'nose'.

schola cantorum /ˌskəʊlə kanˈtɔːrəm/ *noun phrase* plural **scholae cantorum** /ˌskəʊliː/, /ˌskəʊlʌɪ/ L18 Medieval Latin (= school of singers). **1** L18 A choir school attached to a cathedral or monastery; originally, the papal choir at Rome, established by Gregory the Great (*c.*540–604). **2** E20 *generally* A group of singers. Frequently as the title of such a group.

scholium /ˈskəʊlɪəm/ *noun* plural **scholia** /ˈskəʊlɪə/ M16 Modern Latin (from Greek *skholion* from *skholē* learned discussion). An explanatory note or comment, *especially* one made by an ancient commentator on a classical text.

■ Generally used in the plural, but in the singular the Greek ending -*ion* (L16) is also found.

schottische /ʃɒˈtiːʃ/, /ˈʃɒtɪʃ/ *noun* M19 German ((*der*) *Schottische(tanz)* (the) Scottish (dance)). **1** M19 A dance resembling a slow polka; a piece of music for this dance. **2** L19 (*Highland Schottische*) A lively dance resembling the Highland fling.

Schrecklichkeit /ˈʃrɛklɪçˌkaɪt/ *noun* (also **schrecklichkeit**) E20 German (= frightfulness). Originally *specific*, a deliberate military policy of terrorizing an enemy, especially the civilian population. Now *generally*, frightfulness, awfulness, an atmosphere of dread or fear.

1972 K. Bonfiglioli *Don't Point that Thing at Me* I embarked on the quotidian *schrecklichkeit* of getting up.

schreierpfeife /ˈʃrʌɪə(p)fʌɪfə/ *noun* plural **schreierpfeifen** /ˈʃrʌɪə(p)faɪf(ə)n/ M20 German (literally, 'screamer pipe'; cf. RAUSCHPFEIFE). *Music* A kind of shawm used in the sixteenth and seventeenth centuries.

■ This instrument is also called a *schryari* (M20), a word the origin of which is uncer-

tain but which may be related to *schreier-pfeife*.

schrund /ʃrʊnt/ *noun* L19 German (= cleft, crevice). A crevasse; *specifically* a BERGSCHRUND.

schtoom variant of SHTOOM.

Schuhplattler /ˈʃuːˌplatlər/ *noun* L19 German (from *Schuh* shoe + southern German dialect *Plattler* (from *platteln* to slap)). A lively Bavarian and Austrian folk-dance, characterized by the slapping of the thighs and heels.

schuss /ʃʊs/ *noun & verb* M20 German (literally, 'a shot'). **A** *noun* M20 A straight downhill run on skis; the slope on which such a run is executed. Also *transferred*, a rapid downward slide. **B** *verb* **1** *transitive verb* M20 Ski straight down (a slope etc.); cover (a certain distance) by means of a schuss. **2** *intransitive verb* M20 Ski straight down a slope. Also *transferred*, move rapidly (especially downwards).

schvartze, schvartzer see SCHWARTZE.

schwa /ʃwɑː/ *noun* (also **shwa**) L19 German. *Phonetics* The neutral central vowel sound /ə/, typically occurring in unstressed syllables, as the final syllable of 'sofa' and the first syllable of 'along'. Also, the symbol '/ə/' representing this sound, as in the International Phonetic Alphabet. Also called SHEVA.

schwarm /ʃvarm/ *noun* E20 German. An enthusiasm, a craze, an infatuation.

■ Followed by *for* (see quotation).

1968 N. Marsh *Clutch of Constables* The wretched woman . . . had developed a *schwarm* for Troy herself.

schwärmerei /ˌʃvɛrməˈraɪ/, /ˈʃvɛrməraɪ/ *noun* plural **schwärmereien** /ˌʃvɛrmə ˈraɪən/ M19 German (from *schwärmen* to swarm, display enthusiasm, rave). Enthusiastic or fervent devotion to a person or a cause; a juvenile attachment, especially to a person of the same sex; (an) infatuation, a crush.

schwartze /ˈʃvɑːtsə/ *noun* (also **schvartze, schwartzer**, and other variants) M20 Yiddish (*shvartser* (masculine), *shvartse* (feminine), from *shvarts* black, from German *schwarz* from Old High German *swarz* from Germanic). A Black person. *slang, generally derogatory.*

Schweinerei /ˌʃvaɪnəˈraɪ/, /ˈʃvaɪnəraɪ/ *noun* (also **schweinerei**) plural **Schweinereien** /ˌʃvaɪnəˈraɪən/ E20 German (literally, 'piggishness'). Obnoxious behaviour, an instance of this; a repulsive incident or object, a scandal.

> 1965 *Economist* Some Japanese producers were recently discovered selling out of line at the recent Canton Fair. But this *schweinerei* was swiftly stamped on.

schwerpunkt /ˈʃvɛːrpʊŋkt/ *noun* M20 German (= centre of gravity, focal point, from *schwer* hard, weighty + *Punkt* point). Focus, emphasis; strong point; area of concentrated (especially military) effort.

Schwung /ʃvʊŋ/ *noun* M20 German (literally, 'swinging motion'). Energy, verve, panache.

scilicet /ˈsʌɪlɪsɛt/, /ˈskiːlɪkɛt/ *adverb & noun* LME Latin (from *scire licet* one may understand or know; cf. VIDELICET). **A** *adverb* LME To wit; that is to say; namely. **B** *noun* M17 The word 'scilicet' or its equivalent, introducing a specifying clause.

▪ As an adverb, used to introduce a word to be supplied or an explanation of an ambiguity and generally abbreviated to *scil.* or *sc.*

scintilla /sɪnˈtɪlə/ *noun* L17 Latin. A spark; a trace, a tiny piece or amount.

> 1996 *Times* ... serious thinkers in sharp suits ... convene around shiny rosewood tables, on both sides of the Atlantic, to thrash out the last scintilla of marketing policy.

scirocco variant of SIROCCO.

scordatura /ˌskɔrdaˈtura/ *noun* plural **scordature** /ˌskɔrdaˈture/ L19 Italian (from *scordare* to be out of tune). *Music* Alteration of the normal tuning of a stringed instrument so as to produce particular effects for certain pieces or passages; an instance of this.

scoria /ˈskɔːrɪə/ *noun* plural **scoriae** /ˈskɔːriiː/, (*rare*) **scorias** LME Latin (from Greek *skōria* refuse, from *skōr* dung). **1** LME The slag or dross remaining after the smelting out of a metal from its ore. **2** L18 *Geology* Rough masses resembling clinker, formed by the cooling of volcanic ejecta, and of a light aerated texture.

scorzonera /ˌskɔːzə(ʊ)ˈnɪərə/ *noun* E17 Italian (from *scorzone* from Proto-Romance alteration of medieval Latin *curtio(n)* poisonous snake, against whose venom the plant may have been regarded as an antidote). Any of various plants constituting the genus *Scorzonera*; especially *S. hispanica*, cultivated in Europe for its tapering purple-brown root. Also, the root of *S. hispanica*, eaten as a vegetable.

scotia /ˈskəʊʃə/ *noun* M16 Latin (from Greek *skotia* from *skotos* darkness (with reference to the dark shadow within the cavity)). *Architecture* A concave moulding, especially at the base of a column; a casement.

scriptorium /skrɪpˈtɔːrɪəm/ *noun* plural **scriptoria** /skrɪpˈtɔːrɪə/, **scriptoriums** L18 Medieval Latin (from *script-* past participial stem of *scribere* to write). A room set apart for writing; *especially* a room in a monastery where manuscripts were copied.

scrutator /skruːˈteɪtə/ *noun* L16 Latin (from *scrutat-* past participial stem of *scrutari*). **1** L16 A person who examines or investigates something or someone. **2** E17 A person whose official duty it is to examine or investigate something closely; *especially*, a scrutineer at an election.

scungille /skunˈdʒille/ *noun* plural **scungilli** /skunˈdʒilli/ M20 Italian (dialect *scunciglio*, probably alteration of Italian *conchiglia* seashell, shellfish). A mollusc, a conch; *especially* the meat of a mollusc eaten as a delicacy.

scuola /ˈskwola/ *noun* plural **scuole** /ˈskwole/ M19 Italian (= school). In Venice: any of the buildings in which the medieval religious confraternities or guilds used to meet, a guildhall; *History* any of these guilds.

sebkha variant of SABKHA.

sebum /ˈsiːbəm/ *noun* L19 Modern Latin (use of Latin *sebum* suet, grease, tallow). *Physiology* The oily secretion of the sebaceous glands which lubricates and protects the hair and skin.

sec /sɛk/ *adjective & noun* ME French (from Latin *siccus*). Dry (wine); a drink of this.

secateur /sɛkəˈtəː/, /ˈsɛkətəː/ *noun* M19 French (*sécateur*, irregularly from Latin *secare* to cut + *-ateur*). *singular* and (usually) in *plural* A pair of pruning clippers with crossed blades, for use with one hand. Also *pair of secateurs*.

secco /ˈsɛko/ *noun & adjective* M19 Italian (from Latin *siccus* dry; in sense A.1 elliptical for *fresco secco*, literally, 'dry fresco'). **A** *noun* plural **seccos** **1** M19 The process or technique of painting on dry plaster with colours mixed with water. **2** M20 *Music* (A) RECITATIVO secco. **B** *adjective* L19

Music Of recitative: plain, lacking or having only sparse instrumental accompaniment.

secretaire /ˌsɛkrɪ'tɛː/ *noun* L18 French (*secrétaire* from late Latin *secretarius* confidential officer, use as noun of adjective from Latin *secretum* secret). A writing-desk with drawers and pigeon-holes; a bureau.

secretariat /ˌsɛkrə'tɛːrɪət/ *noun* (also **Secretariat**) E19 French (*secrétariat* from medieval Latin *secretariatus*, from as SECRETAIRE). The official position of secretary; the place where a secretary works, preserves records, etc. Also, the administrative and executive department of a government or similar organization; such a department's staff or premises.

secret de Polichinelle /səkrɛ də poliʃinɛl/ *noun phrase* M19 French (= Punchinello's secret). An apparent secret which is generally known; an open secret.

secundus /sɪ'kʌndəs/ *adjective* E19 Latin (= second). Designating the second of two or more pupils of the same surname to enter the school. Cf. PRIMUS adjective 2, TERTIUS.

sederunt /sɪ'dɪərənt/ *noun* E17 Latin (= there were sitting (sc. the following persons), use as noun of 3rd person plural perfect indicative of *sedere* to sit). **1** E17 A sitting of a deliberative or judicial body, especially an ecclesiastical assembly. Also *generally* (now *rare*), a (period of) sitting, especially for discussion or talk. **2** E18 The list of people present at such a sitting. Also in *plural*, the people named on such a list.

sede vacante /ˌsiːdi vəˈkanti:/, /ˌseɪdeɪ vəˈkanti:/ *adverb phrase* LME Latin (= the seat being vacant). *Ecclesiastical* During the vacancy of an episcopal see.

sedile /sɪ'dʌɪli/ *noun plural* **sedilia** /sɪ'dɪlɪə/ LME Latin (= seat, from *sedere* to sit). **1** *generally* A seat. Only in LME. **2** L18 *Ecclesiastical* Each of a series of usually canopied and decorated stone seats, usually three in number, placed on or recessed into the south side of the choir near the altar for use by the clergy. Usually in *plural*.

segue /'sɛgweɪ/ *adverb, verb, & noun* M18 Italian (3rd person singular present indicative of *seguire* to follow). *Music* **A** *adverb* M18 (A direction:) proceed to the next movement without a break; continue

with an indicated formula. **B** *intransitive verb* M20 Of a person or music: move without interruption from one (live or prerecorded) song or melody to another. Frequently followed by *into*. **C** *noun* M20 An uninterrupted transition from one song or melody to another.

Sehnsucht /'zeːnzʊxt/ *noun* M19 German. Yearning, wistful longing.

seicento /seɪ'tʃɛntəʊ/ *noun* (also **Seicento**) E20 Italian (= six hundred). The seventeenth century in Italy; the Italian style of art, literature, etc., of this period.

seiche /seɪʃ/ *noun* M19 Swiss French (perhaps from German *Seiche* sinking (of water)). *Physical Geography* A short-lived standing oscillation of a lake or other body of water (as a bay or basin of the sea), resembling a tide, caused especially by abrupt changes in atmospheric conditions or by small earth tremors.

seif /siːf/, /seɪf/ *noun* (also **sif**) E20 Arabic (*sayf*, literally, 'sword'). *Physical Geography* A sand-dune in the form of a long narrow ridge parallel to the direction of the prevailing wind. Also **seif dune**.

seigneur /seɪ'njə:/, *foreign* /sɛɲœr/ (*plural* same) *noun* (also **Seigneur**) L16 Old and Modern French (from Latin *senior* comparative of *senex* old). Especially in France and Canada, a feudal lord, the lord of a manor, (chiefly *historical* except in the Channel Islands, *specifically* Sark). Now *generally*, a lord, a person exercising (feudal) authority.

seigneurie /sɛɲœri/ *noun* (also **seigneury** /'semjəri/) plural pronounced same L17 French ((Old French *seignorie*) from preceding; cf. SIGNORIA). **1** L17 *History* Especially in France and Canada, a landed estate held by feudal tenure, the territory or domain of a seigneur. **2** L19 Especially in the Channel Islands and Canada, the residence or mansion of a seigneur.

Seilbahn /'zaɪlbɑːn/ *noun* M20 German (from *Seil* cable, rope + *Bahn* road, way). A cable railway, an aerial cableway.

seiza /'seɪzə/ *noun* M20 Japanese (from *sei* correct + *za* sitting). An upright kneeling position which is the Japanese traditional formal way of sitting and is used in meditation and as part of the preparation in martial arts.

séjour /seʒur/ *noun* plural pronounced same M18 French (from *séjourner* to sojourn). **1** M18 The action of staying or sojourning in a place. **2** M18 A place of sojourn or residence.

Sekt /zɛkt/ *noun* E20 German. A German sparkling white wine; a drink of this.

selon les règles /səlɔ̃ le rɛgl/ *adverb phrase* E19 French. According to the rules (of polite society).

selva /ˈsɛlvə/ *noun* M19 Spanish or Portuguese (from Latin *silva* wood). *Physical Geography* (A tract of land covered by) dense equatorial forest, especially in the Amazon basin. Usually in *plural*.

semiosis /ˌsiːmɪˈəʊsɪs/, /ˌsɛmɪˈəʊsɪs/ *noun* (also **semeiosis**) E20 Greek (*sēmeiosis* (inference from) a sign, from *sēmeion* sign, from *sēma* sign, mark). The process of signification, especially in language or literature.

semis /səmi/, /səˈmiː/ *noun* E20 French (literally, 'sowing', from *semer* to sow). A form of decoration used in bookbinding, in which small ornaments are repeated regularly.

sempervivum /ˌsɛmpəˈvʌɪvəm/ *noun* (formerly Anglicized as **sempervive**) L16 Latin (neuter of *sempervivus* ever-living). Any of various succulent plants constituting the genus Sempervivum, of the stonecrop family; *especially* houseleek, *S. tectorum*.

semplice /ˈsɛmplɪtʃi/ *adverb & adjective* M18 Italian (= simple). *Music* (A direction:) simply, simple.

sempre /ˈsɛmpreɪ/ *adverb* E19 Italian. *Music* (A direction:) always, still, throughout.

senex /ˈsɛnɛks/ *noun* plural **senes** /ˈsɛneɪs/ L19 Latin (= old man). In literature (especially comedy), an old man as a stock figure.

senhor /sɛnˈjɔː/, *foreign* /seˈɲor/ *noun* L18 Portuguese (from Latin *senior* comparative of *senex* old). Used as a title (preceding the surname or other designation) of or as a respectful form of address to a Portuguese or Brazilian man (corresponding to English *Mr* or *Sir*); a Portuguese or Brazilian man.

senhora /sɛnˈjɔːrə/, *foreign* /seˈɲora/ *noun* E19 Portuguese (feminine of SENHOR). Used as a title (preceding the surname or other designation) of or as a respectful form of address to a Portuguese or Brazilian woman, especially a married one (corresponding to English *Mrs* or *madam*); such a woman.

senhorita /sɛnjəˈriːtə/, /seɲoˈrita/ *noun* L19 Portuguese (diminutive of preceding). Used as a title (preceding the surname or other designation) of or as a respectful form of address to a young especially unmarried Portuguese or Brazilian woman (corresponding to English *Miss*); such a woman.

sennachie /ˈsɛnəxi/ *noun* (also **shenachie** /ˈʃɛnəxi/ and other variants) LME Gaelic (*seanachaidh* (= Old Irish *senchaid*), from *sean* old (Old Irish *sen*)). In Ireland and the Scottish Highlands: a professional recorder and reciter of family or traditional history and genealogy, attached to the household of a clan chieftain or person of noble rank. Now, a teller of traditional Gaelic heroic tales (chiefly in Scotland).

sennin /ˈsɛnm/ *noun* (also **sennen**) plural same L19 Japanese (= wizard, sage, recluse, from Chinese *Xi'anren* immortal man). In oriental mythology (originally in Taoism): an elderly recluse who has achieved immortality through meditation and self-discipline; a human being with supernatural powers, a reclusive mystic or teacher.

señor /sɛnˈjɔː/ *foreign* /seˈɲor/ *noun* plural **señores** /sɛnˈjɔːrɪz/, *foreign* /seˈɲores/ **1** E17 Spanish (from Latin *senior* comparative of *senex* old). Used as a title (preceding the surname or other designation) of or as a respectful form of address to a Spanish or Spanish-speaking man (corresponding to English *Mr* or *Sir*). **2** M19 A Spanish or Spanish-speaking man.

señora /sɛnˈjɔːrə/, *foreign* /seˈɲora/ *noun* L16 Spanish (feminine of SEÑOR). Used as a title (preceding the surname or other designation) of or as a respectful form of address to a Spanish or Spanish-speaking woman, especially a married one (corresponding to English *Mrs* or *madam*; such a woman.

señorita /sɛnjəˈriːtə/, *foreign* /seɲoˈrita/ *noun* E19 Spanish (diminutive of preceding). **1** E19 Used as a title (preceding the surname or other designating) of or as a respectful form of address to a young especially unmarried Spanish or Spanish-speaking woman (corresponding to English *Miss*); such a woman. **2** L19 A small labroid fish, *Oxyjulis californica*, of the eastern Pacific. Also *señorita-fish*.

señorito /seɲoˈrito/ *noun plural* **señoritos** /seɲoˈritos/ E20 Spanish (diminutive of SEÑOR). Used as a title (preceding the surname or other designation) or as a respectful form of address to a young man; a young man, *especially* (frequently *derogative*) a noble or rich one regarded as leading an ostentatious or frivolous existence.

sensei /sɛnˈseɪ/ *noun* L19 Japanese (from *sen* previous + *sei* birth). In Japan: a teacher, an instructor, frequently of martial or other arts; a professor, a scholar.

sensibile /sɛnˈsɪbɪleɪ/ *noun plural* **sensibilia** /ˌsɛnsɪˈbɪlɪə/ M19 Latin (neuter of *sensibilis* sensible). *Philosophy* The kind of thing which, if sensed, is a sense-datum.

sensibilité /sɑ̃sibilite/ *noun* E20 French. Sensibility; sensitivity.

> **1995** *Times* Not since Ronald Reagan's Bonzo went to college have American chimpanzees been treated with such *sensibilité*.

sensiblerie /sɑ̃siblǝri/ *noun* M20 French. Sentimentality; exaggerated or superficial sensitivity.

sensorium /sɛnˈsɔːrɪəm/ *noun plural* **sensoria** /sɛnˈsɔːrɪə/, **sensoriums** M17 Late Latin (from Latin *sens-* past participial stem of *sentire* to feel). The seat of sensation in the brain of humans and animals; the percipient centre to which sensory impulses are transmitted by the nerves; the whole sensory apparatus (including the sensory nerves). Formerly also, the brain regarded as centre of consciousness and nervous energy. Also *common sensorium*.

sensu lato /ˌsɛnsu: ˈlɑːtəʊ/ *adverb & adjective phrase* M20 Latin. (Of a scientific etc. term) In the broad sense. Opposite of SENSU STRICTO.

sensu stricto /ˌsɛnsu: ˈstrɪktəʊ/ *adverb & adjective phrase* M19 Latin (= in the restricted sense). (Of a scientific etc. term) Strictly speaking, in the narrow sense. Opposite of SENSU LATO.

■ Also latterly (M20) as STRICTO SENSU.

sententia /sɛnˈtɛnʃɪə/ *noun plural* **sententiae** /sɛnˈtɛnʃiː/ E20 Latin (= mental feeling, opinion, philosophical judgement, from *sentire* to feel). A pithy or memorable saying, a maxim, an aphorism, an epigram; a thought, a reflection.

senza /ˈsɛntsa/ *preposition* E18 Italian (probably from Latin *absentia* absence, with influence of Latin *sine* without; cf. SANS). *Music* (In directions:) without.

separatum /sɛpəˈreɪtəm/ *noun plural* **separata** /sɛpəˈreɪtə/ L19 Latin (use as noun of neuter, singular of *separatus* past participle of *separare* to separate). An offprint.

sephira /ˈsɛfɪrɑː/ *noun plural* **sephiroth** /ˈsɛfɪrəʊθ/ M16 Hebrew (*sĕp̄īrāh* (plural *sĕp̄īrōt*), from *sāp̄ar* to number). In the philosophy of the Jewish cabbala, each of the ten hypostatized attributes or emanations surrounding the Infinite, by means of which the Infinite enters into relation with the finite. Usually in *plural*.

sepia /ˈsiːpɪə/ *noun & adjective* LME Latin (from Greek *sēpia* cuttlefish; in sense 2 (as French *sépia*) probably immediately from Italian *seppia*). **A** *noun* **1** LME A cuttlefish. Now chiefly as modern Latin genus name. **2** E19 A rich brown pigment prepared from the black secretion of the cuttlefish, used in monochrome drawing and watercolour painting; the dark reddish-brown colour of this pigment. Also, a brown tint used in photography. **b** L19 The black secretion itself. **3** M19 *elliptical* A sepia photograph or drawing. **B** *adjective* E19 Of the colour of sepia; drawn or tinted in sepia.

■ The adjective was also used as an euphemism in the 1940s in the United States to denote skin colour amongst American Blacks.

seppuku /sɛˈpuːkuː/ *noun* L19 Japanese (from *setsu* to cut + *fuku* abdomen). HARA-KIRI.

sepsis /ˈsɛpsɪs/ *noun* L19 Greek (*sēpsis*, from *sēpein* to make rotten). *Medicine* The state of being septic; blood-poisoning, especially through infection of a wound.

septennium /sɛpˈtɛnɪəm/ *noun plural* **septennia** /sɛpˈtɛnɪə/, **septenniums** M19 Late Latin (for classical Latin *septuennium*, from Latin *septem* seven + *annus* year). A period of seven years.

septum /ˈsɛptəm/ *noun plural* **septa** /ˈsɛptə/ M17 Latin ((also *saeptum*), from *sepire*, *saepire* to enclose, from *sepes*, *saepes* hedge). **1** M17 *generally* A partition; a dividing wall, layer, membrane, etc., especially in a living organism. **2** L17 *specifically* in *Anatomy* A thin layer of tissue forming a partition in a cavity, organ, etc. **3** E18 *Geology* A thin sheet of material filling a crack. **4** M20 *Electronics* A metal plate placed transversely across a waveguide and attached to the walls by conducting joints.

sequela /sɪ'kwi:lə/ *noun* plural **sequelae** /sɪ'kwi:lə/ L18 Latin (*sequel(l)ae*, from *sequi* to follow). **1** L18 *Medicine* A disease or condition occurring as the result of a previous disease or condition. Usually in *plural*. **2** L19 A consequence or result.

sequin /'si:kwɪn/ *noun* (in sense 1 also (earlier) **chequeen** /tʃɪ'ki:n/) L16 French (from Italian *zecchino*, from *zecca* mint, from Arabic *sikka* a die for coining, a coin). **1** L16 *History* Any of various Italian and Turkish gold coins. **2** L19 A small shiny usually circular piece of material for attaching to garments as a decoration.

sequitur /'sɛkwɪtə/ *noun* M19 Latin (= it follows). An inference or conclusion which follows logically from the premisses; a logical deduction, a logical remark. Cf. NON SEQUITUR.

sera plural of SERUM.

serac /'sɛrak/, /sə'rak/ *noun* M19 Swiss French (*sérac*, originally the name of a compact white cheese, probably from Latin *serum* whey). A pinnacle or ridge of ice on the surface of a glacier where crevasses intersect.

seraglio /sɛ'rɑ:lɪəʊ/, /sɪ'reɪlɪəʊ/ *noun* plural **seraglios** L16 Italian (*serraglio*, from Turkish *saray* palace, mansion, from Persian, with assimilation to Italian *serraglio* cage (from medieval Latin *serraculum* diminutive of Latin *sera* bolt)). **1** L16 A harem, *especially* one in a palace. **b** M17 The women of a harem. **c** M-L17 *generally* An enclosure; a place of confinement. **2** L16 *History* A Turkish palace, *especially* that of the Sultan in Istanbul.

serai /sə'rʌɪ/ *noun* E17 Turkish (*saray* palace, mansion, from Persian: cf. preceding). **1** E17 In various South West Asian countries: a building for the accommodation of travellers, a caravanserai. **2** E17 *History* A SERAGLIO sense 2.

serang /sə'raŋ/ *noun* (also **sarang**) L18 Anglo-Indian (Persian and Urdu *sar-hang* commander, from *sar* head + *hang* authority. **1** A headman among Lascars. **2** E20 A person in authority, a person in charge. More fully *head serang*. *Australian slang*.

serape /sɛ'rɑ:peɪ/, *foreign* /se'rape/ *noun* (also **sarape** /sa'rɑ:peɪ/, **zarape** /sa'rape/) E19 **Mexican Spanish**. A shawl or blanket worn as a cloak by Spanish-Americans.

serdab /sə'dɑ:b/ *noun* M19 Arabic (*sirdāb* cellar, underground vault; or directly from Persian *sardāb* grotto, cellar for ice, from *sard* cold + *āb* water). **1** M19 In the Middle East: a cellar, an underground chamber. **2** L19 *Egyptology* A secret passage or chamber in an ancient tomb.

serein /sərɛ̃/ *noun* L19 Old and Modern French (from Proto-Gallo-Romance, from Latin *serum* evening, use as noun of *serus* late). *Meteorology* A fine rain (apparently) falling from a cloudless sky.

sereno /sɛ'remaʊ/, *foreign* /se'reno/ *noun* plural **serenos** /sɛ'remaʊz/, *foreign* /se'renos/ L19 **Spanish**. In Spain and Spanish-speaking parts of America: a nightwatchman.

seriatim /ˌsɪərɪ'eɪtɪm/ *adverb & adjective* L15 Medieval Latin (from as Latin *series* chain, row, series (from *serere* to join, connect) + *-atim* after Latin *gradatim*, *literatim*). **A** *adverb* L15 One after another, one by one in succession. **B** *adjective* L19 Following one after the other. *rare*.

serin /'sɛrɪn/ *noun* M16 French (= canary, of unknown origin). Originally, a canary. Now, any bird of the same genus, *especially* (more fully *serin finch*) *Serinus serinus*, a small yellow European finch.

seron /'sɪərən/ *noun* (also **ceroon**, **seroon** /sɪ'ru:n/) M16 Spanish (= hamper, crate (from *sera* large basket), partly through French *serron*). A bale or package (especially of tropical plant products) bound with hide.

serra /'sɛrə/ *noun* M19 Portuguese (from Latin *serra* saw; cf. SIERRA). In Portuguese-speaking regions: a ridge of mountains or hills.

serré /sɛre/ *adjective* M19 French. Tightly compact; *figurative* constricted by grief or emotion.

sertão /'sɛ:tɑ̃:ʊ/ *noun* plural **sertãos** /'sɛ:tɑ̃:ʊʃ/ E19 Portuguese. *Geography* An arid barren region of Brazil; the remote interior of Brazil.

serum /'sɪərəm/ *noun* plural **sera** /'sɪərə/, **serums** L17 Latin (= whey, watery fluid). **1** L17 Watery fluid, as a normal or pathological constituent of animal tissues; *specifically* the yellowish protein-rich liquid which separates from coagulated blood.

2 L19 *Medicine* The blood serum of an animal used as a therapeutic or diagnostic agent.

servante /sɛrvãt/ *noun* plural pronounced same L19 French (= side-table). An extra table or concealed shelf used in conjuring tricks.

serviette /sə:vɪ'ɛt/ *noun* L15 Old and Modern French (= towel, napkin, from *servir* to serve). A table-napkin, now *especially* a paper one.

sestina /sɛ'sti:nə/ *noun* M19 Italian (from *sesto* from Latin *sextus* sixth). A form of rhymed or unrhymed poem of six stanzas of six lines and a concluding triplet in which the same six words at the line-ends occur in each stanza in six different sequences.

se-tenant /sətənã/ *adjective* E20 French (literally, 'holding together'). *Philately* Of postage stamps, especially of different denominations or designs: joined together as when printed.

settecento /sɛtɪ'tʃɛntəʊ/ *noun* E20 Italian (= seven hundred). The eighteenth century in Italy; the style of Italian art, architecture, music, etc., of this period.

sève /sɛv/ *noun* M18 French (= sap). The quality and flavour appropriate to a specified wine; liveliness, savour.

seviche /sɛ'vi:tʃeɪ/ *noun* (also **ceviche**) M20 South American Spanish (*seviche, cebiche*). A South American dish of marinaded raw fish or seafood, usually garnished and served as a starter.

sévigné /seviɲe/ *noun* (also **sevigné**) plural pronounced same E19 French (probably from Mme de *Sévigné* (1626–96), French letter-writer). *History* A kind of bandeau, especially for the hair; a jewel or ornament for decorating a head-dress.

sevruga /sɛv'ru:gə/ *noun* L16 Russian (*sevryuga*). (Caviar from) the sturgeon, of the Caspian and Black Seas.

Sezession /ze,tsɛ'sio:n/ *noun* plural **Sezessien** /ze'tsɛsiən/ E20 German. *Art* A radical art movement that started in Vienna and was contemporaneous with and related to ART NOUVEAU; SEZESSIONS-STIL.

Sezessionsstil /ze,tsɛsi'o:ns,ʃti:l/ *noun* L20 German. *Art* The style of the SEZESSION.

sf abbreviation of SFORZANDO (*musical direction*).

sforzando /sfɔ:'tsandəʊ/ *adjective, adverb, & noun* E19 Italian (present participle of *sforzare* to use force). *Music* **A** *adjective & adverb* E19 (A direction:) with special emphasis or sudden loudness. Abbreviated to *sf, sfz.* **B** *noun* M19 plural **sforzandi** /sfɔ:'tsandi/, **sforzandos**. A note or group of notes specially emphasized; an increase in emphasis and loudness.

sforzato /sfɔ:'tsɑ:təʊ/ *adjective, adverb, & noun* plural of noun **sforzati** /sfɔ:'tsɑ:ti/, **sforzatos** E19 Italian (past participle of *sforzare* to use force). *Music* SFORZANDO.

sfumato /sfu'mato/, /sfʊ'mɑ:təʊ/ *adjective & noun* M19 Italian (past participle of *sfumare* to shade off, from *s-* ex- + *fumare* to smoke). *Painting* **A** *adjective* M19 Painted with or using indistinct outlines, depicting hazy forms. **B** *noun* E20 The technique of softening outlines and allowing tones and colours to shade gradually into one another; an indistinct outline or hazy form produced in this way.

sfz abbreviation of SFORZANDO (musical direction).

sgraffiato /zgraffi'ato/ *noun* plural **sgraffiati** /zgraffi'ati/ M19 Italian (past participle of *sgraffiare* to scratch away; see next). SGRAFFITO.

sgraffito /sgra'fi:təʊ/ *noun* plural **sgraffiti** /sgra'fi:ti/ M18 Italian (from *sgraffiare* to scratch away: *s-* representing Latin ex- ex- + (later) GRAFFITO). A form of decoration or design made by scratching through wet plaster on a wall or through slip on pottery to reveal a different colour below.

shabti /'ʃabti/ *noun* plural **shabtiu** /'ʃabtɪu/, **shabtis** M19 Egyptian (*šbty*). *Egyptology* A USHABTI. Cf. SHAWABTI.

shabu-shabu /,ʃabu:'ʃabu:/ *noun* L20 Japanese. A Japanese dish of pieces of thinly sliced beef or pork cooked quickly with vegetables in boiling water.

shadoof /ʃə'du:f/ *noun* (also **shaduf**) M19 Arabic ((Egyptian) *šādūf*). A device consisting of a pivoted rod or pole with a bucket at one end and a counterbalancing weight at the other, used especially in Egypt for raising water.

shaganappi /,ʃagə'napi/ *noun & adjective* M18 Ojibwa. **A** *noun* M18 Thread, cord, or thong made from rawhide, rawhide cut into strips; a strip of rawhide. Also, a rough pony. **B** *adjective* E19 Made of a strip or strips of rawhide; *figurative* tough, rough; cheap, inferior, makeshift. *North American.*

shagetz, shagitz variants of SHEGETZ.

shah /ʃɑː/ *noun* (also (as title) **Shah**) M16 Persian (*šāh* from Old Persian *xšāyaθiya* king). *History* (A title of) the monarch of Iran (Persia).

shahada /ʃəˈhɑːdə/ *noun* L19 Arabic (*šahāda* testimony, evidence). The Muslim profession of faith.

■ The *shahada—Lā ilāha illā* (A)*llāh, Muḥammadun rasūl Allāh* 'there is no God but Allah, [and] Muhammad is the messenger of Allah'—forms part of the regular call to prayer.

shahid /ʃəˈhiːd/ *noun* (also **shaheed**) L19 Arabic (*šahīd* witness, martyr). A Muslim martyr.

shaikh, Shaikha variants of SHEIKH, SHEIKHA.

shako /ˈʃeɪkəʊ/, /ˈʃakəʊ/ *noun* plural **shakos** E19 French (*schako* from Hungarian *csákó* probably from German *Zacken* peak, point, spike). A cylindrical military hat with a peak and a plume or pompon.

shakudo /ˈʃakudəʊ/ *noun & adjective* M19 Japanese (from *shaku* red + *dō* copper). (Made of) a Japanese alloy of copper and gold.

shakuhachi /ˌʃakuˈhɑːtʃi/ *noun* L19 Japanese. An end-blown Japanese flute, made of bamboo.

shalom /ʃəˈlɒm/, *foreign* /ʃaˈlɔm/ *interjection & noun* L19 Hebrew (*šālōm* peace). In Jewish society, used as a salutation at meeting or parting; an utterance of 'shalom'.

shalwar /ˈʃʌlvɑː/ *noun* (also **salwar, shalvar**) E19 Persian and Urdu (*šalwār*). *singular* and in *plural* Loose trousers worn in some South Asian countries and by some Muslims elsewhere, *especially* those worn by women together with a KAMEEZ.

■ Often in the combination *shalwar-kameez*, describing a woman's matching outfit.

1996 *Times* Shalwar kameez tunics were layered over tiered bloomers.

shaman /ˈʃamən/ *noun* L17 German (*Schamane*, Russian *shaman* from Tungusian *šaman*). A priest among certain peoples of northern Asia, regarded as one with heal-

ing and magical powers and influence over the spirits who bring about good and evil; a healer among North American Indians, regarded as possessing magical powers. Now also, a person regarded as having powers of spiritual guidance and healing through direct access to and influence in the spirit world.

shamba /ˈʃambə/ *noun* L19 Kiswahili. In East Africa: a cultivated plot of ground. Also, a farm, a plantation.

shambok variant of SJAMBOK.

shamisen variant of SAMISEN.

shanachie variant of SENNACHIE.

shanti /ˈʃanti/ *interjection & noun* L19 Sanskrit (*śānti* peace, tranquillity). *Hinduism* (A prayer for) peace; peace be with you.

■ Usually repeated three times at the end of an Upanishad for the peace of the soul.

sharif /ʃəˈriːf/ *noun* (also **shareef, shereef, sherif**) L16 Arabic (*šarīf* noble, highborn). **1** L16 A descendant of Muhammad through his daughter Fatima. **2** E17 (frequently **Sharif**) (The title of) any of various Arab rulers, magistrates, or religious leaders; *specifically* (*a*) the ruler of Morocco; (*b*) the governor of Mecca.

sharifa /ʃəˈriːfə/ *noun* (also **shereefa, sherifa, Sharifa**) E20 Arabic (*šarīfa* feminine of *šarīf* SHARIF). The wife of a Moroccan sharif.

shashlik /ˈʃaʃlɪk/ *noun* E20 Russian (*shashlyk* from Crimean Turkish *šišlik* from *šiš* skewer; cf. SHISH KEBAB). An eastern European and Asian kebab of mutton and garnishings, frequently served on a skewer.

shauri /ˈʃaʊri/ *noun* plural **shauri(e)s** E20 Kiswahili (from Arabic *šūrā* consultation, deliberation, counsel). In East Africa: counsel, debate; a problem.

1970 *Kenya Farmer* Often he can solve a problem by calling a meeting of the staff and obtaining their views and suggestions, not only on their personal *shauris*, but also on improvements in sales and service.

shawabti /ʃəˈwabti/ *noun* plural **shawabtiu** /ʃəˈwabtruː/, **shawabtis** E20 Egyptian (*šwзbt(y)*, probably from *šwзb* persea wood, perhaps the original material). *Egyptology* An USHABTI. Cf. SHABTI.

shchi /ʃtʃi/ *noun* E19 Russian. A Russian cabbage soup.

shebeen /ʃɪˈbiːn/ *noun* L18 Irish ((Anglo-Irish form) of *síbín*, of unknown origin).

An unlicensed house or shop selling alcoholic liquor; a disreputable public house.

■ Originally meaning an illicit liquor outlet in Ireland, *shebeen* is now commonly used in South African English for a Black-run establishment where alcohol is illegally brewed and sold.

shechita /ʃɛˈxita/ *noun* L19 Hebrew (*šĕḥîṭāh*, from *šāḥaṭ* to slaughter). The method of slaughtering animals that fulfils the requirements of Jewish law.

sheesh kebab variant of SHISH KEBAB.

shegetz /ˈʃeɪɡɪts/ *noun* (also **shagetz, shagitz**) plural **shkotsim** /ˈʃkɔːtsɪm/ E20 Yiddish (*sheygets, sheyhets* from Hebrew *sheqeṣ* detested thing; cf. SHIKSA). Among Jewish people, a Gentile boy; a Jewish boy not observing traditional Jewish behaviour.

■ Originally and chiefly United States, and usually derogatory.

sheikh /ʃeɪk/, /ʃiːk/ *noun* (also **shaikh, sheik**) L16 Arabic (ultimately from Arabic *šayḵ* sheikh, old man, elder, from *šāḵa* to be or grow old). **1a** L16 (also **Sheikh**) Originally, an Eastern governor, prince, or king. Later *especially*, a chief or head of an Arab family, people, or village. Also, a title of respect. **b** E20 A strong, romantic, or dashing male lover. **2** L16 A leader of a Muslim religious order or community; a great religious doctor or preacher; now *especially*, a saint with a localized cult. **3** L19 In the Indian subcontinent, a Hindu convert to Islam.

■ In sense 1b from *The Sheik*, a novel by E. M. Hull (1919) made into a film (1921) starring Rudolph Valentino.

sheikha /ˈʃeɪkə/ *noun* (also **Sheik(h)a, Shaikha**) M19 Arabic (*šayḵa*). An Arab lady of good family; the (chief) wife of a sheikh. Also, a title of respect.

shekel /ˈʃek(ə)l/ *noun* M16 Hebrew (*šeqel*, from *šāqal* to weigh). **1** *History* A unit of weight and silver coin used in the ancient Middle East. **2** In *plural* Money; riches. *colloquial*. **3** The basic unit of currency in modern Israel.

■ In sense 2 often in colloquial phrases such as *bringing* (or *raking*) *in the shekels* meaning 'making a lot of money quickly and easily' (see quotation).

2 1996 *Spectator* They [sc. oysters] are sold all year round for some reason, which I think is a mistake, but doubtless it brings in the shekels.

shemozzle /ʃɪˈmɒz(ə)l/ *noun & verb slang* (also **schemozzle**) L19 Yiddish (probably from as SCHLIMAZEL). **A** *noun* L19 A muddle, a complicated situation; a quarrel, a brawl, a mêlée. **B** *intransitive verb* E20 Make one's escape, leave hastily.

shenachie variant of SENNACHIE.

shenzi /ˈʃɛnzi/ *noun* E20 Kiswahili. In East Africa: an uncivilized African; a barbarian, a person outside one's cultural group. Chiefly *derogatory*.

1970 K. Thackeray *Crownbird* The Chinese face was impassive . . . That he should be . . . involved with this bunch of shenzis . . . was very confusing.

sherbet /ˈʃəːbət/ *noun* E17 Turkish (*şerbet*, Persian *šerbet* from Arabic *šarba(t)* draught, drink, from *šariba* to drink). **1** E17 A cooling drink made of sweetened and diluted fruit juice, drunk especially in Arab countries. Now also, an effervescing drink made of sherbet powder (see sense 2). **2** M19 A flavoured sweet powder containing bicarbonate of soda, tartaric acid, etc., eaten as a confection or used to make an effervescing drink. Also more fully *sherbet powder*. **3a** L19 A water-ice. *North American*. **b** L19 (A glass of) alcoholic liquor, especially (*specifically* in Australia) beer. *slang*.

shereef, shereefa variants of SHARIF, SHARIFA.

sherif, sherifa variants of SHARIF, SHARIFA.

sherpa /ˈʃəːpə/ *noun, adjective, & verb* M19 Tibetan (*sharpa* inhabitant of an eastern country). **A** *noun* plural **sherpas**, same **1** M19 (*Sherpa*) A member of a Tibetan people inhabiting the southern slopes of the Himalayas, renowned for their skill in mountaineering. **2** M20 (*sherpa*) *transferred* and *figurative* A mountain guide or porter; an official making preparations for a summit conference. **B** E20 *attributive* or as *adjective* Of, pertaining to, or designating the Sherpas and their language. **C** L20 *intransitive verb* Act as or like a sherpa.

C 1996 *Spectator* In the weeks before their principals meet, hundreds of officials are sherpa-ing all over Europe.

sheshbesh /ˈʃɛʃbɛʃ/ *noun* L20 Turkish (*şeşbeş*, from Persian *šaš* six + Turkish *beş* five). A variety of backgammon played in the Middle East.

sheva /ʃəˈvɑː/ *noun* (also **shewa**) L16 Hebrew *šĕwāʾ*, apparently arbitrary alteration of *šāw'* emptiness, vanity, spelt in German books *Schwa*, whence SCHWA. **1** L16 *Hebrew Grammar* The sign ꞉ placed under a consonant to express the absence of a following vowel sound, having in certain positions no sound (*quiescent sheva*) but in others sounding as a schwa /ə/ (*movable sheva*); the sound of movable sheva. **2** *Phonetics* E19 A SCHWA.

shiatsu /ʃɪˈatsuː/ *noun* M20 Japanese (literally, 'finger pressure'). A kind of therapy of Japanese origin, in which pressure is applied with the thumbs and palms to certain points of the body.

▪ Imported under this name into the West in the 1960s, *shiatsu* has, since the late 1970s, become more generally referred to as *acupressure*.

shibboleth /ˈʃɪbəlɛθ/ *noun* M17 Hebrew (*šibbōleṯ* ear of corn, stream in flood, used as a test of nationality for the difficulty for foreigners of pronouncing /θ/ (see Judges 12:4–6)). **1** M17 A word used as a test for detecting people from another district or country by their pronunciation; a word or sound very difficult for foreigners to pronounce correctly. **b** M17 A peculiarity of pronunciation or accent indicative of a person's origin; the distinctive mode of speech of a profession, class, etc. **c** E19 A custom, habit, style of dressing, etc., distinguishing a particular class or group of people. **2** M17 A long-standing formula, idea, phrase, etc., held (especially unreflectingly) by or associated with a group, class, etc.; a catchword, a slogan; a taboo. Also, a received wisdom; a truism, a platitude.

shibui /ˈʃɪbuɪ/ *adjective & noun* (also **shibu** /ˈʃɪbuː/) M20 Japanese (= astringent, from *shibu* an astringent substance). **A** M20 *adjective* Tasteful in a quiet, profound, or unostentatious way. **B** *noun* M20 Tastefulness, refinement; appreciation of elegant simplicity.

shidduch /ˈʃɪdəx/ *noun* L19 Yiddish (from Hebrew *šiddūḵ* negotiation, especially of an arranged marriage). An arranged marriage, a (good) match.

shifta /ˈʃɪftə/ *noun* plural same, **shiftas** M20 Somali (*shúfto* bandit, from Amharic). A Somali bandit or guerrilla, operating mainly in northern Kenya.

shiitake /ʃɪˈtaːkeɪ, /ˈʃiːtaːkeɪ/ *noun* L19 Japanese (from *shii* a kind of oak + *take* mushroom). An edible agaric (mushroom), *Lentinus edodes*, cultivated in Japan

and China on logs of various oaks and allied trees. Also *shiitake mushroom*.

shikar /ʃɪˈkaː/ *noun & verb* E17 Persian and Urdu (*šikār*). **A** *noun* E17 Hunting, shooting; game. **B** *verb* Inflected -rr-. **1** *intransitive verb* L19 Hunt animals for sport. **2** *transitive verb* L19 Hunt (animals).

▪ Originating and used almost solely in the Indian subcontinent, the word often occurs in the phrase *on shikar* 'on a hunting expedition'.

shikari /ʃɪˈkaːriː/ *noun* E19 Urdu (from Persian *šikārī*: see SHIKAR). In the Indian subcontinent: a hunter (either European or Indian); an expert guide or tracker.

shikhara /ˈʃɪkhərə/ *noun* (also **sikhara**) E19 Sanskrit (*śikhara* peak, spire). A pyramidal tower on a Hindu temple, sometimes having convexly curved sides.

shiksa /ˈʃɪksə/ *noun & adjective* L19 Yiddish (*shikse* from Hebrew *šiqṣāh* from *šeqeṣ* detested thing + feminine suffix -*āh*). **A** *noun* L19 A Gentile girl or woman. **B** *attributive* or as *adjective* M20 Of a girl or woman: Gentile. *derogatory*.

shippo /ˈʃiːpəʊ/ *noun & adjective* (also **shipo**) L19 Japanese (*shippō* seven precious things, from *shichi* seven + *hō* jewel). (Made of) Japanese cloisonné-enamel ware.

shisha /ˈʃiːʃə/ *noun* (also **shi-sha** M20 Urdu (*šīša(h)*, Persian *šīša* glass, mirror). (Used *attributively* to designate) mirror-work and items connected with it.

1977 A. Jeffs *Creative Crafts* Though India and Pakistan are known for many different forms of embroidery, the one style that is considered to be unique is the mirror embroidery known as 'Shishakari' or 'Shi-sha', which originated many centuries ago in the arid plateaux of Sind and Baluchistan in Pakistan.

shish kebab /ʃɪʃ kɪˈbab/ *noun* (also **sheesh kebab** /ʃiːʃ/) E20 Turkish (*şiş kebab*, from *şiş* skewer + *kebab* roast meat; cf. SHASHLIK). A dish consisting of pieces of marinated meat (usually lamb) and vegetables grilled and served on skewers.

shiva /ˈʃɪvə/ *noun* (also **shivah**) L19 Hebrew (*šiḇ'āh* seven). *Judaism* A period of seven days' formal mourning for the dead, beginning immediately after the funeral. Frequently in *sit shiva*, observe this period.

shivaree variant of CHARIVARI.

shkotsim plural of SHEGETZ.

shlub /ʃlʌb/ *noun* (also **schlub**) M20 Yiddish (perhaps from Poland *żłób* blockhead). A worthless person, an oaf. *United States slang.*

shmatte /ˈʃmatə/ *noun* (also **schmatte**) L20 Yiddish (*schmatte*, from Poland *szmata* rag). A rag; a garment, *especially* a ragged one. *United States colloquial.*

shmear /ʃmɪə/ *noun* (also **schmear, schmeer**) M20 Yiddish (*schmirn* to flatter, grease, smear: cf. German *schmieren* smear). Bribery, corruption, flattery.

■ North American colloquial. Often in the phrase *the whole shmear* meaning 'everything (possible)'.
1969 E. Stewart *Heads* Why couldn't you burrow around and ferret out the whole shmear yourself?

shochet /ˈʃɒxɛt/ *noun plural* **shochetim** /ˈʃɒxɛtɪm/ L19 Hebrew (*šōḥēṭ* present participle of *šāḥaṭ* to slaughter). A person officially certified as competent to kill cattle and poultry in the manner prescribed by Jewish law.

shofar /ˈʃəʊfə/ *noun plural* **shofroth** /ˈʃəʊfrəʊt/ M19 Hebrew (*šōpār*, plural *šōpārōṯ*). A ram's-horn trumpet used in Jewish religious services and in biblical times as a war-trumpet.

shogi /ˈʃəʊɡi/ *noun* M19 Japanese (*shōgi*). A Japanese board game resembling chess.

shogun /ˈʃəʊɡʊn/ *noun* E17 Japanese (*shōgun*, from Chinese *jiàng jūn* general). *History* Any of a succession of hereditary commanders-in-chief of the Japanese army, before 1868 the virtual rulers of Japan.

shomer /ˈʃəʊmə/ *noun plural* **shomerim** /ˈʃəʊmərɪm/ E20 Hebrew (*šōmēr* watchman). **1** E20 A watchman, a guard, now especially in Israel. **2** E20 An inspector who verifies that food is prepared in accordance with Jewish religious laws.

shonda /ˈʃɒndə/ *noun* M20 Yiddish (*shande* from Middle High German *schande*). A disgrace. *colloquial, chiefly United States.*

shosagoto /ˌʃɒsəˈɡəʊtəʊ/ *noun plural* same E20 Japanese (from *shosa* acting, conduct + *koto* matter, affair). In Japanese kabuki theatre: a dance play, a mime performed to music.

shosha /ˈʃəʊʃə/ *noun plural* same L20 Japanese (*shōsha* business firm, from *shō* mercantile + *sha* society, company). A SOGO SHOSHA.

shott /ʃɒt/ *noun* (also **chott**) L19 Arabic (*šaṭṭ* shore, strand; (in North Africa) salt lake; (in Iraq) waterway, river). A shallow brackish lake or marsh especially in Algeria and southern Tunisia, usually dry in summer and covered with saline deposits. Cf. SABKHA.

shoyu /ˈʃəʊjuː/ *noun* E18 Japanese (*shōyu* from Chinese *jiàngyóu* (Wade-Giles *chiangyu*) from *jiàng* bean paste + *yóu* oil). A sauce made from fermented soya beans; soy sauce. Also *shoyu sauce.*

shrikhand /ˈʃriːkand/ *noun* M20 Sanskrit (*śrīkhaṇḍa* sandalwood). An Indian sweet dish made from curd, sugar, almonds, and spices.

shtetl /ˈʃtɛt(ə)l/, /ˈʃteɪt(ə)l/ *noun plural* **shtetlach** /ˈʃtɛt(ə)lɑːx/, **shtetls** M20 Yiddish (= little town, from German *Stadt* town). *History* A small Jewish town or village in eastern Europe.
1996 *Times* Wiesenthal was born in a *shtetl* in Buczacz in Galicia.

shtibl /ˈʃtiːb(ə)l/ *noun* (also **shtiebel**) plural **shtiblach** /ˈʃtiːb(ə)lɑːx/ E20 Yiddish (diminutive of *shtub* room, house; cf. German dialect *Stüberl* small room). A small synagogue.

shtick /ʃtɪk/ *noun* (also **shtik**) M20 Yiddish (from German *Stück* piece, play). **1** M20 A (comedian's) stage routine; a joke; *transferred* a patter, a gimmick. **2** M20 A particular area of activity or interest. *slang, chiefly North American.*

1 1996 *Spectator* Yes, as critics have pointed out, a lot of Carrey's shtick dies even as he utters it . . .

shtiebel variant of SHTIBL.

shtik variant of SHTICK.

shtoom /ʃtʊm/ *adjective & verb* (also **s(h)tumm** /ʃtʌm/, **schtoom**) M20 Yiddish (from German *stumm* silent). **A** *adjective* M20 Silent, mute. Chiefly in *keep* (or *stay*) *shtoom*, refrain from disclosing information etc. **B** *intransitive verb* M20 Become silent, shut *up*.

shufti /ˈʃʊfti/ *noun* (also **shufty**) M20 Arabic (from colloquial Arabic *šuftī* have you seen?, from *šāfa* to see). A look; a glance.

■ Especially in *take* (or *have*) *a shufti*. Originally military slang, but also more generally used in dated colloquial speech (see quotation). The verbal use from which the noun derives is rare in English.
1980 R. Adams *Girl in a Swing* Good idea, old boy. I'm game. Let's 'ave a crafty shufti round with that in mind, shall we?

shul /ʃuːl/ *noun* L19 Yiddish (from German *Schule* school). A synagogue.

shunga /ˈʃuːŋɡɑ:/ *noun* plural same M20 Japanese (from *shun* spring + *ga* picture). An example of Japanese erotic art.

shura /ˈʃʊərə/ *noun* M20 Arabic (*šūrā* consultation). The Islamic principle of (rule by) consultation; an Islamic consultative council.

shuriken /ˈʃʊərɪkɛn/ *noun* L20 Japanese (*shuri-ken*, literally, 'dagger in the hand', from *shu* hand + *ri* inside + *ken* sword, blade). A weapon in the form of a star with projecting blades or points, used in some martial arts.

sic /sɪk/ *adverb & noun* L19 Latin (= so, thus). **A** L19 *adverb* Used or spelt as written. **B** *noun* M20 An instance of using 'sic'.

■ As an adverb used parenthetically after a quoted word etc. to call attention to an anomalous or erroneous form or to prevent the supposition of misquotation.

sic et non /ˈsɪk ɛt ˌnɒn/ *noun phrase* E20 Latin (literally, 'yes and no'). *Theology* A method of argument used by medieval theologians, in which contradictory passages of scripture are presented without commentary in order to stimulate readers to resolve the contradictions themselves. Frequently *attributive*.

■ *Sic et non* was the title of a work by the twelfth-century French theologian and philosopher Peter Abelard, in which he employed this method, later imitated by other Scholastic philosophers.

Sicherheitsdienst /ˈzɪçərhaɪtsˌdiːnst/ *noun* M20 German (from *Sicherheit* security + *dienst* service). *History* The security branch of the Nazi Schutzstaffel (SS), set up in 1931–2. Abbreviated to *SD*.

siciliana /sɪtʃiˈljana/, /sɪˌtʃɪlɪˈɑːnə/ *noun* plural **siciliane** /sɪtʃiˈljane/, /sɪˌtʃɪlɪˈɑːneɪ/ (also **siciliano** /sɪtʃiˈljano/, /sɪˌtʃɪlɪˈɑːnəʊ/, plural **sicilianos** /sɪˌtʃɪlɪˈɑːnəʊz/, **siciliani** /sɪtʃiˈljani/) E18 Italian (feminine of *Siciliano* Sicilian). *Music* A piece of music for a Sicilian peasant dance, resembling a slow jig; *transferred* a composition in 6/8 or 12/8 time, frequently in a minor key and evoking a pastoral mood.

sicilienne /sɪˌsɪlɪˈɛn/ *noun* L19 French (feminine of *sicilien* Sicilian). **1** L19 A fine poplin of silk and wool. **2** L19 *Music* A SICILIANA.

siddha /ˈsɪdhə/ *noun* M19 Sanskrit. In Indian religions: a person who has attained perfection, a saint, a semi-divine being; *specifically* in Jainism, a perfected bodyless being freed from the cycle of rebirths.

Sieg Heil /ziːk ˈhaɪl/ *noun phrase & interjection* M20 German (literally, 'Hail victory'). (An exclamation of) a victory salute used especially at a political rally originally during the Nazi regime in Germany.

sierozem /ˈsɪərə(ʊ)zɛm/ *noun* M20 Russian (*serozëm*, from *seryĭ* grey + Slavonic base *zem-* (cf. Russian *zemlya* earth, soil)). *Soil Science* A soil, usually calcareous and humus-poor, characterized by a brownish-grey surface and developed typically under mixed shrub vegetation in arid climates.

sierra /sɪˈɛrə/, /sɪˈɛːrə/ *noun* plural **sierras** M16 Spanish (from Latin *serra* saw; cf. SERRA). A long mountain range rising in jagged peaks, especially in Spain and Latin America.

siesta /sɪˈɛstə/ *noun & verb* M17 Spanish (from Latin *sexta (hora)* sixth hour of the day). **A** *noun* M17 An afternoon rest or nap; *especially* one taken during the hottest hours of the day in a hot country. **B** *intransitive verb* M19 Take a siesta.

siffleur /siːˈfləː/ *noun* (feminine (sense 2) **si'ffleuse** /siːˈfləːz/) E18 French (from *siffler* to whistle). **1** E18 Any of various animals that make a whistling noise. **2** E19 A person who entertains professionally by whistling.

sigilla plural of SIGILLUM.

sigillata /sɪdʒɪˈleɪtə/, /sɪɡɪˈlɑːtə/ *noun* E20 Latin (= sealed). *Archaeology* TERRA SIGILLATA sense 3.

sigillum /sɪˈdʒɪləm/ *noun* plural **sigilla** /sɪˈdʒɪlə/ M17 Late Latin (= sign, trace, impress, (in medieval Latin) seal (classical Latin *sigilla* (plural) little images, seal), diminutive of Latin *signum* sign). **1** In *plural* Small human images. *rare*. Only in M17. **2** E20 *Roman Catholic Church* The seal of confession. **3** M20 A sign, a symbol; an abbreviation.

siglum /ˈsɪɡləm/ *noun* plural **sigla** /ˈsɪɡlə/ E18 Late Latin (*sigla* plural, perhaps for *singula* neuter plural of *singulus* single). A letter (especially an initial) or other symbol used as an abbreviation for a word, proper name, etc., in a printed text; *Bibliography* such a letter or symbol used to designate a particular version of a literary text.

sigma /'sɪgmə/ noun LME Latin (from Greek). **1** LME The eighteenth letter (Σ, σ, or, when final, s), of the Greek alphabet represented in English by S, s. **2** E20 *Physics* and *Chemistry* **a** Used. *attributively* to designate an electron, orbital, molecular state, etc., possessing zero angular momentum about an internuclear axis. **b** M20 *Particle Physics* Used (usually *attributive*), to denote each of a triplet of hyperons (and their antiparticles). **3** L20 *Biochemistry* A component of RNA polymerase which determines where transcription begins. In full *sigma factor*. **4** L20 *Statistics* A (unit of) standard deviation.

signa, **signa panthea** plurals of SIGNUM, SIGNUM PANTHEUM.

significacio /sɪg,nɪfɪˈkɑːsɪəʊ/ noun (also **significatio** /sɪg,nɪfɪˈkɑːtɪəʊ/) plural **significaciones** /sɪg,nɪfɪˌkɑːsɪˈəʊniːz/ M20 Medieval Latin (from Latin significatio(n)-). A parallel or second meaning not directly stated in a text; the deeper or implied meaning of an allegory, emblem, symbol, etc.

signor /'siːnjɔː/ noun plural **signori** /siːˈnjɔːri/ L16 Italian (reduced form of *signore*, from Latin *senior*). **1** L16 Used as a title (preceding the surname or other designation) of or as a respectful form of address to an Italian or Italian-speaking man (corresponding to English Mr or sir). **b** L18 An Italian man, especially a singer. **2** L16 A man of distinction, rank, or authority; a gentleman or nobleman.

signora /siːˈnjɔːrə/ noun M17 Italian (feminine of SIGNORE). Used as a title (preceding the surname or other designation) of or as a respectful form of address to an Italian or Italian-speaking (especially married) woman (corresponding to English Mrs or madam). Also, an Italian (especially married) woman.

signoria /ˌsiːnjəˈriːə/ noun M16 Italian (from as SIGNOR). *History* The governing body of any of various medieval Italian republics, especially Venice.

signorina /ˌsiːnjəˈriːnə/ noun E19 Italian (diminutive of SIGNORA). Used as a title (used preceding the surname or other designation) of or as a respectful form of address to a young (especially unmarried) Italian or Italian-speaking woman (corresponding to English Miss). Also, a young (especially unmarried) Italian woman.

signum /'sɪgnəm/ noun plural **signa** /'sɪgnə/ M19 Latin. A mark, a sign.

signum pantheum /ˌsɪgnəm panˈθiːəm/ noun phrase plural **signa panthea** /ˌsɪgnə panˈθiːə/ E18 Latin (= divine statue, from *signum* statue + *pantheus* from Greek *pantheios* dedicated to all the gods (from *pan-* all + *theios* divine)). *Classical Antiquities* A statue combining the figures, symbols, or attributes of several gods.

sikhara variant of SHIKHARA.

silenus /saɪˈliːnəs/ noun (also **Silenus**) plural **sileni** /saɪˈliːnaɪ/ E17 Latin (*Silenus* from Greek *Seilēnos* foster-father of Bacchus and leader of the satyrs). *Greek Mythology* A wood-god, a satyr, *especially* one represented as a bearded old man with the tail and legs of a horse.

■ Earlier (L16) in the Anglicized form *silen*.

silhouette /sɪluˈɛt/ noun & verb L18 French (from Étienne de *Silhouette* (1709–67), French author and politician). **A** noun **1** L18 A portrait obtained by tracing the outline of a profile, head, or figure, especially by means of its shadow, and filling in the whole with black or cutting the shape out of black paper; a figure or picture drawn or printed in solid black. **b** *figuratively* E19 A brief verbal description of a person etc. **2 a** M19 An object seen as a dark outline against a lighter background; a dark shadow of something. **b** E20 The contour or outline of a garment or a person's body. **B** verb **1** *transitive verb* L19 Represent in silhouette, throw up the outline of. Usually in *passive* (followed by *against*, *on*). **2** *intransitive verb* L19 Show up as a silhouette.

sillar /siːˈlja:/ noun M20 Spanish. *Geology* A kind of volcanic tuff.

silo /'saɪləʊ/ noun plural **silos** M19 Spanish (from Latin *sirus* from Greek *siros* pit). **1** M19 A pit or underground chamber used for storing grain, roots, etc.; *specifically* one in which green crops are compressed and preserved for fodder as silage. Also, a cylindrical tower or other structure built above ground for the same purpose. **2** E20 *transferred* A large bin used for storing loose materials etc. **3** M20 An underground structure in which a guided missile is stored and from which it may be fired.

silva variant of SYLVA.

simba /ˈsɪmbə/ noun E20 Kiswahili. A lion; figurative a warrior. Chiefly East African.

simchah /ˈsɪmtʃə/, /ˈsɪmtʃxa/ noun M20 Hebrew (śimḥāh rejoicing). A Jewish private party or celebration.

simi /ˈsmi/ noun M20 Kiswahili (sime). In East Africa: a large two-edged knife.

simoom /sɪˈmuːm/ noun (also **simoon** /sɪˈmuːn/) L18 Arabic (samūm, from samma to poison). A hot dry dust-laden wind blowing at intervals in the African and Asian (especially Arabian) deserts.

simpatico /simˈpatiko/, /sɪmˈpatɪkəʊ/ adjective (feminine **simpatica** /simˈpatika/, /sɪmˈpatɪkə/) M19 Spanish (simpático, from simpatía, or Italian simpatico from simpatia, both from Latin sympathia from Greek sumpatheia from sumpathēs having a fellow-feeling). Pleasing, likeable; congenial.

> 1995 Oldie And Fangio was so charming and so simpatico, and of course the damage would be paid for . . .

simplex /ˈsɪmplɛks/ adjective & noun L16 Latin (= single, variant of simplus simple, with second element as in duplex, multiplex, etc.). **A** adjective 1 L16 Composed of or characterized by a single part or structure. 2 Telecommunications and Computing L19 Designating a system, circuit, etc., along which signals can be sent in only one direction at a time. 3 Genetics E20 Of a polyploid individual: having the dominant allele of a particular gene represented once. **B** noun 1 L19 A word without an affix; a simple uncompounded word. 2 E20 Geometry The figure, in any given number of dimensions, that is bounded by the least possible number of hyperplanes (e.g. the simplex in two dimensions is a triangle). 3 M20 Linguistics In early transformational grammar, a basic or core sentence, a kernel sentence.

simplex munditiis /ˌsɪmplɛks mʊn ˈdɪtiːs/ noun & adjective phrase M18 Latin (literally, 'simple in your adornments'). **A** noun phrase M18 Beauty without adornment or ostentation. **B** adjective phrase L19 Unostentatiously beautiful.

■ A quotation from Horace Odes I.v.

simulacrum /ˌsɪmjʊˈleɪkrəm/ noun plural **simulacrums**, **simulacra** /ˌsɪmjʊˈleɪkrə/ L16 Latin (from simulare to simulate). 1 L16 A material image or representation of a person or thing, especially a god. 2 E19 A thing having the appearance but not the substance or proper qualities of

something; a deceptive imitation or substitute; a pretence.

> 2 1996 Times The effort to turn the whole continent into the economic simulacrum of Germany . . . has instilled pessimism and depression into the peoples of all Europe.

simurg /sɪˈməːg/ noun (also **simurgh**) L18 Persian (sīmurǧ, from Pahlavi sēn eagle + murǧ bird). Iranian Mythology A giant bird believed to have the power of speech and reasoning and to be of great age.

sindicato /sindiˈkato/ noun plural **sindicatos** /sindiˈkatos/ M20 Spanish (= syndicate, trade union). In Spain and Spanish-speaking countries: a trade union.

sine die /ˌsʌɪni ˈdʌɪiː/, /ˌsmeɪ ˈdiːeɪ/ adverb phrase E17 Latin (= without day, from sine without + die ablative singular of dies day). With reference to adjourned business etc.: without any day being appointed for resumption; indefinitely.

sine qua non /ˌsʌɪni kweɪ ˈnɒn/, /ˌsmeɪ kwɑː ˈnəʊn/ adjective & noun phrase (also in Latin plural form **sine quibus non** /ˌsʌɪni kwiːbəs ˈnɒn/, /ˌsmeɪ kwiːbəs ˈnəʊn/, (chiefly Scottish Law) Latin masculine form **sine quo non** /ˌsʌɪni kweɪ ˈnɒn/, /ˌsmeɪ kwəʊ ˈnəʊn/) E17 Latin ((causa) sine qua non literally, '(cause) without which not', from sine without + qua ablative singular feminine of qui with + non not). **A** adjective phrase E17 Indispensable, absolutely essential. Also postpositive. **B** noun phrase 1 E17 An indispensable person or thing; especially an essential condition or element. 2 L17 Scottish Law (sine quo non) A curator, a trustee, archaic.

> B.1 1996 Times A merchant banker in London . . . told me that at one stage an Eton and Oxbridge education was almost a sine qua non in his organisation . . .

sinfonia /smfəˈniːə/, /sɪnˈfəʊnɪə/ noun L18 Italian (from Latin symphonia instrumental harmony, voices in concert, from Greek sumphōnia from sumphōnos harmonious). Music 1 L18 In baroque music, an orchestral piece used as an introduction to an opera, cantata, or suite; an overture. 2 (Sinfonia) (The title of) a small symphony orchestra.

sinfonietta /ˌsmfəʊnɪˈɛtə/ noun E20 Italian (diminutive of SINFONIA). Music 1 E20 A short or simple symphony. 2 E20 (Sinfonietta) A SINFONIA sense 2.

singerie /sɛ̃ʒri/ noun plural pronounced same E20 French (from singe monkey). A painting depicting monkeys in human roles and attitudes; a piece of porcelain decorated with such paintings; work done in this style.

Singspiel /'zɪŋʃpiːl/ noun plural **Singspiele** /'zɪŋʃpiːlə/ L19 German (from singen to sing + Spiel play). Music A dramatic performance alternating between song and dialogue, popular especially in late eighteenth-century Germany; (a) comic opera.

sinopia /sɪ'nəʊpɪə/ noun plural **sinopie** /sɪ'nəʊpɪeɪ/ M19 Italian. **1** M19 A red pigment containing sinopite or similar-coloured minerals. **2** M20 transferred A preliminary rough sketch for a fresco, covered by the final work.

sinter /'sɪntə/ noun L18 German (= cinder). **1** L18 A hard incrustation formed on rocks etc. by precipitation from mineral waters. **2** E20 Material which has been coalesced into a solid or porous mass under the influence of heat or pressure without liquefaction, especially after compression in a shaped die.

sirocco /sɪ'rɒkəʊ/ noun (also **scirocco**) plural **siroccos** E17 Italian (scirocco ultimately from Spanish Arabic šalūk, šulūk, šalūk south-east wind, perhaps of Romance origin). **1** E17 A hot, oppressive, and often dusty or rainy wind which blows from the north coast of Africa over the Mediterranean and parts of southern Europe; generally any hot southerly wind. **2** figurative M19 A blighting influence; a fiery storm. **3** L19 A machine or oven for drying hops or tea leaves by means of a hot, moist current of air. Also more fully sirocco drying-machine, sirocco oven.

sirop /siro/ noun plural pronounced same L19 French. (A drink made from) a syrupy preparation of sweetened fruit-juice.

sissonne /si:sɒn/, foreign /sisɔn/ (plural same) noun E18 French. Ballet A jump in the air from fifth position, landing on one foot with the other leg extended.

sistrum /'sɪstrəm/ noun plural **sistra** /'sɪstrə/, **sistrums** LME Latin (from Greek seistron, from seiein to shake). A musical instrument of ancient Egyptian origin, consisting of a metal frame with transverse metal rods which rattled when the instrument was shaken.

sitar /'sɪtɑː/, /sɪ'tɑː/ noun M19 Persian and Urdu (sitār from sih three + tār string). A stringed Indian musical instrument, resembling a lute, with a long neck and

(usually) seven principal strings which the player plucks.

situla /'sɪtjʊlə/ noun plural **situlae** /'sɪtjʊliː/, **situlas** L19 Latin (= bucket). Archaeology A vessel resembling a bucket in shape.

situs /'sʌɪtəs/ noun E18 Latin. **1** E18 Situation, position rare. **2** Law a E19 The place to which for purposes of legal jurisdiction or taxation a property belongs. Chiefly United States. **b** M20 A work-site, especially (in full common situs) one occupied by two or more employers. United States.

Sitzfleisch /'zɪts,flaɪʃ/ noun (also written **sitzfleisch**) E20 German (from sitzen to sit + Fleisch flesh). The ability to persist in or endure an activity.

> **1975** Harpers & Queen Lenny hadn't got the patience, the concentration, the sitzfleisch.

Sitz im Leben /,zɪts ɪm 'leːbən/ noun phrase M20 German (literally, 'place in life'). Theology In biblical criticism, the determining circumstances in which a tradition developed.

sitzkrieg /'sɪtskriːg/ noun M20 pseudo-German (after BLITZKRIEG, as if from German sitzen to sit + krieg war). (A part of) a war marked by a (relative) absence of active hostilities.

sjambok /'ʃambɒk/ noun (also **sambok**, **shambok**) L18 Afrikaans (from Malay sambuk, chambuk from Persian and Urdu chābuk horsewhip). In South Africa: a heavy whip made of rhinoceros or hippopotamus hide.

skald /skɔːld/, /skald/ noun (also **scald**) M18 Old Norse (skáld, of unknown origin). History An (itinerant or court) oral poet, a bard, originally and especially in ancient Scandinavia.

skandalon /'skandəlɒn/ noun (also **scandalon**) M20 Greek. Theology A stumbling-block; a cause of offence; a scandal.

skat /skɑːt/ noun M19 German (from Italian scarto (= French écart) cards laid aside, from scartare to discard; cf. ÉCARTÉ). A three-handed card-game with bidding for contract, originating in Germany; collective the two cards dealt to the table in this game.

skaz /skaz/ noun E20 Russian. First-person narrative in which the author assumes a persona.

skene /'skiːni/ noun L19 Greek (skēnē hut, tent). Theatre In ancient Greek theatre, a three-dimensional structure forming part of the stage or set and able to be decorated according to the current play's theme.

skepsel /ˈskɛps(ə)l/ *noun* M19 Afrikaans (*skepsel*, Dutch *schepsel* creature, from *scheppen* to create). A creature, a villain, a rascal.

■ In South African colloquial speech frequently used as a derogatory and offensive form of address to a Black or Coloured person.

ski-joring /ˈskiːdʒɔːrɪŋ/, /ˈʃiːˈjəːrɪŋ/ *noun* (also **skikjøring** E20 Norwegian (*skikjøring*, from *ski* ski + *kjøring* driving). A winter sport in which a skier is towed by a horse or vehicle.
1996 *Country Life* Racing on ice has a long history in St Moritz, and skikjøring races started in 1906.

skoff /skɔf/ *noun* L18 Afrikaans (*skof* from Dutch *schoft* quarter of the day, each of the four meals of a day). A stage of a journey; a period of travel between outspans. Also, a period of work, a shift. *South African colloquial.*

slainte /ˈslɑːntʃə/ *interjection* E19 Gaelic (*slàinte* (*mhór*) = '(good) health'). Expressing good wishes, especially before drinking.

slalom /ˈslɑːləm/ *noun & verb* E20 Norwegian (*slalåm*, from *sla* sloping + *låm* track). **A** *noun* **1** E20 A downhill ski race on a zigzag course marked by artificial obstacles, usually flags, and descended singly by each competitor in turn. **2** M20 A similar obstacle race for canoeists, waterskiers, skateboarders, etc. **B** *intransitive verb* M20 Perform or compete in a slalom; make frequent sharp turns (as) in a slalom.

slivovitz /ˈslɪvəvɪts/ *noun* (also **slivovic**) L19 Serbo-Croat (*šljivovica* from *šljiva* plum). A plum brandy made chiefly in Romania, Serbia, and neighbouring States.

smetana /ˈsmɛtənə/ *noun* E20 Russian (from *smetat'* to sweep together, collect). Sour cream. Frequently in *smetana sauce*.

smørbrød /ˈsməːbrɔːd/ *noun* M20 Norwegian (from *smøre* butter + *brød* bread: cf. next). In Norway: an open sandwich; food consisting of open sandwiches.

smorgasbord /ˈsmɔːɡəsbɔːd/ *noun* L19 Swedish (*smörgåsbord*, from *smörgås* (slice of) bread and butter (from *smör* butter, *gås* goose, lump of butter) + *bord* board, table). **1** L19 Open sandwiches served with delicacies as hors d'oeuvres or a buffet, originally and especially in Scandinavia. **2** M20 *figurative* A medley, a miscellany, a variety.
2 1996 *Times* This being Dead Can Dance, there was a whole *smorgasbord* of musical styles on show . . .

smørrebrød /ˈsmaːrəbrəːd/, /ˈsmaːrə brəːð/ *noun* E20 Danish (from *smør* butter + *brød* bread: cf. preceding). In Denmark: an open sandwich; food consisting of open sandwiches.

smorzando /smɔːˈtsandəʊ/ *adverb, adjective, & noun* E19 Italian (present participle of *smorzare* to extinguish). *Music* **A** *adverb & adjective* E19 (A direction:) dying away. **B** *noun* E19 plural **smorzandos, smorzandi** /smɔːˈtsandi/. A smorzando passage.

snobisme /snobism/ *noun* E20 French. Snobbishness.

snoek /snuːk/, /snʊk/ *noun* plural same L18 Dutch (= pike). A long slender food fish of southern oceans, a barracouta. Chiefly *South African.*

soba /ˈsəʊbə/ *noun* (treated as *singular* or *plural*) L19 Japanese. Japanese noodles made from buckwheat flour.

sobornost /soˈbɔrnost/ *noun* M20 Russian (*sobornost'* conciliarism, catholicity). *Theology* A unity of people in a loving fellowship in which each member retains freedom and integrity without excessive individualism.

sobriquet /ˈsəʊbrɪkeɪ/ *noun* M17 French (of unknown origin). An epithet, a nickname.
■ The older French form SOUBRIQUET is also found in English.

socle /ˈsəʊk(ə)l/, /ˈsɒk(ə)l/ *noun* E18 French (from Italian *zoccolo* wooden shoe, socle, representing Latin *socculus* diminutive of *soccus* sock). A low plinth serving as a pedestal for a statue, column, vase, etc.

sogo shosha /ˌsəʊɡəʊ ˈʃəʊʃə/ *noun phrase* plural same, **sogo shoshas** M20 Japanese (*sōgō shōsha*, from *sōgō* comprehensive + SHOSHA). A very large Japanese company that trades internationally in a wide range of goods and services.

soi-disant /swadizã/ *adjective* (also **soi disant**) M18 French (from *soi* oneself + *disant* present participle of *dire* to say). **1** M18 Of a person: self-styled, would-be. **2** M19 Of a thing: so-called, pretended.

1 1995 *Times* A French *soi-disant* sexual scientist claims that women who are worried about being pestered by men on the beach this summer should go topless.

soigné /swaɲe/, /ˈswɑːnjeɪ/ *adjective* (feminine **soignée**) E19 French (past participial adjective of *soigner* to care for, from *soin* care). Meticulously dressed, prepared, or arranged; well-groomed.

> **1996** *Times* What could be more classic than a soigné tuxedo suit or an understated little black dress . . . ?

soigneur /swaɲœr/ *noun* plural pronounced same L20 French (from *soigner* to care for). In cycling, a person who gives training, massage, and other assistance to a team.

soirée /ˈswɑːreɪ/, *foreign* /sware/ (*plural* same) *noun* L18 French (from *soir* evening). An evening party, gathering, or social meeting, especially in a private house.

soirée dansante /sware dɑ̃sɑ̃t/ *noun phrase* plural **soirées dansantes** (pronounced same) M19 French (from as SOIRÉE + *dansante* feminine of present participle of *danser* to dance). An evening party with dancing.

soirée musicale /ˌswɑːreɪ mjuːzɪˈkɑːl/ *noun phrase* plural **soirées musicales** (pronounced same) M19 French (from as SOIRÉE + MUSICALE). An evening party to perform or listen to music.

soit /swa/ *interjection* L19 French (3rd person singular present subjunctive of *être* be). So be it.

soixante-neuf /swasɑ̃t nœf/ *noun* L19 French (= sixty-nine, after the position of the couple involved). Sexual activity between two people involving mutual oral stimulation of the genitals; a position enabling this.

> **1973** M. Amis *Rachel Papers* The other couple were writhing about still, now seemingly poised for a session of fully robed soixante-neuf.

sokaiya /ˈsəʊkʌɪjə/ *noun* plural same L20 Japanese (from *sōkai* general meeting + -*ya* dealer). A holder of shares in a company who tries to extort money from it by threatening to cause trouble for executives at a general meeting of the shareholders.

sola /ˈsəʊlə/ *adverb & adjective* M18 Latin (feminine of *solus* alone, or Italian, feminine of *solo* alone). **1** *adverb & predicative adjective* M18 Of a woman: solitary; alone. **2** *adjective* M18 Commerce Of a bill of exchange: single (as opposed to one of a set).

solarium /səˈlɛːrɪəm/ *noun* plural **solaria** /səˈlɛːrɪə/, **solariums** M19 Latin (from *sol* sun). **1** M19 A sundial. Now *rare* or *obsolete*. **2a** A room etc usually with large areas of glass designed to maximize exposure to the sun's rays. **2b** M20 A room equipped with sun-lamps for inducing an artificial suntan; an establishment providing sun-lamps.

solatium /səˈleɪʃɪəm/ *noun* plural **solatia** /səˈleɪʃɪə/ E19 Latin. A sum of money or other compensation given to a person to make up for loss, inconvenience, injured feelings, etc.; *specifically* in *Law*, such an amount awarded to a litigant over and above the actual loss.

sola topi see under TOPI.

solera /səˈlɛːrə/, *foreign* /soˈlera/ *noun* M19 Spanish (literally, 'crossbeam, stone base' from *suelo* ground, floor, dregs, from Latin *solum* soil). **1** M19 A blend of sherry or Malaga wine produced by the Spanish solera system (see sense 3 below). Also *solera wine*. **2** M19 A wine-cask, usually with a capacity of four hogsheads; a set of such casks arranged in tiers so as to produce wine by the solera system. **3** M20 (*solera system*) A method of producing wine, especially sherry and Madeira, whereby small amounts of younger wines stored in an upper tier of casks are systematically blended with the more mature wine in the casks below.

solfatara /sɒlfəˈtɑːrə/ *noun* (also earlier **solfaterra** /sɒlfəˈtɛrə/) L18 Italian (originally, a sulphurous volcano near Naples, from Italian *solfo* sulphur). *Geology* A fumarole which emits sulphurous gases, encrusting the edge with sulphur etc. Cf. SOUFRIÈRE.

solfège /sɒlfɛʒ/ *noun* plural pronounced same E20 French. *Music* SOLFEGGIO. Also (*generally*), rudimentary musical instruction, especially using textless exercises for the voice.

solfeggio /sɒlˈfɛdʒɪəʊ/ *noun* plural **solfeggi** /sɒlˈfɛdʒi/, **solfeggios** L18 Italian (from *sol-fa* sol-fa). *Music* An exercise for the voice (formerly also for a musical instrument), using the sol-fa syllables. Also, solmization.

solidus /ˈsɒlɪdəs/ *noun* plural **solidi** /ˈsɒlɪdʌɪ/ ME Latin (*solidus* solid used as noun; in branch I from Latin *solidus* (*nummus*) a gold coin). **I 1** ME History A gold coin of the later Roman Empire, originally worth about 25 denarii. Formerly also, in medieval England, a shilling. **2** L19 An oblique stroke formerly written to separate shillings from pence, and now used in writing fractions, to separate figures and letters, or to denote alternatives or ratios. Cf. VIRGULE sense 1. ‖ **3** E20 A line or surface in a binary or ternary phase diagram respectively, or a temperature (corresponding to a point on the line or surface), below which a mixture is entirely solid and above which it consists of solid and liquid in equilibrium.

solitaire /'sɒlɪtɛː/, /ˌsɒlɪ'tɛː/ *noun* E18 French (from Latin *solitarius* solitary. **1** E18 A person who lives in solitude; a recluse. **2** E18 (A ring with) a diamond or other gem set by itself. **3** M18 A card or board game for one player. **4** M18 *History* A man's loose necktie of black silk or broad ribbon. **5** L18 Either of two extinct flightless birds related to the dodo.

solod /'sɒlət/ *noun* (also **soloth** /'sɒləθ/) plural **solodi** /'sɒlədi/, **soloti** /'sɒləti/, **solods** /'sɒləts/ E20 Russian (*solod'* from *sol'* salt). *Soil Science* A type of soil derived from a SOLONETZ by leaching of saline or alkaline constituents, occurring in arid regions.

solonchak /'sɒləntʃak/ *noun* E20 Russian (= salt-marsh, salt lake, from *sol'* salt). *Soil Science* A type of salty alkaline soil that has little or no structure, is typically pale in colour, and occurs in poorly drained regions.

solonetz /'sɒlənɛts/ *noun* E20 Russian (*solonets* salt-marsh, salt lake, from *sol'* salt). *Soil Science* A type of alkaline soil that is rich in carbonates, has a thin friable surface layer, and occurs in better-drained areas than a SOLONCHAK.

solus /'səʊləs/ *adverb & adjective* L16 Latin (cf. SOLA). **1** *adverb & predicative adjective* L16 Of a male (occasionally a female) person: alone, by oneself. Frequently as a stage direction. **2** *adjective* **a** M20 Of an advertisement: standing alone on a page etc.; dealing with one item only. Also, of or pertaining to such an advertisement. **b** M20 *Commerce* Of a petrol station etc.: selling the products of one company only. Also, of or pertaining to such an arrangement.

solyanka /sə'ljankə/ *noun* M20 Russian. A soup made of vegetables and meat or fish.

sol y sombra /ˌsɒl i 'sɒmbra/ *noun* M20 Spanish (literally, 'sun and shade'). A drink of brandy mixed with anisette or gin.

soma /'səʊmə/ *noun* L18 Sanskrit. A plant the juice of which was used in India to prepare an intoxicating liquor; the liquor itself, used in Vedic ritual. Cf. HOM.

■ In his novel *Brave New World* (1932), Aldous Huxley gave the name *soma* to the narcotic drug distributed by the State to keep people happy and acquiescent.

sombrero /sɒm'brɛːrəʊ/ *noun* plural **sombreros** L16 Spanish (from *sombra* shade). **1** L16–E18 An oriental umbrella or parasol. **2** L18 A broad-brimmed hat of felt or other soft material, of a type common in Mexico and the south-western United States.

sommelier /'sɒm(ə)ljeɪ/, /sə'mɛljeɪ/; *foreign* /sɔməlje/ (*plural same*) *noun* E19 French. A wine waiter.

1996 *Times: Weekend* For fun, we asked for the wine list, and irritated the sommelier by pondering a Pétrus 1955 Pomerol at £1,307 before settling for a glass of house white.

sommité /sɔmite/ *noun* plural pronounced same M19 French (= summit, top, tip). A person of great eminence or influence.

son /sɔn/ *noun* M20 Spanish (= sound). A slow Cuban dance and song in 2/4 time.

sonata /sə'nɑːtə/ *noun* L17 Italian (feminine past participle of *sonare* to sound). A musical composition for one or two instruments (one usually being the piano), usually in several movements with one (especially the first) or more in sonata form.

■ Varieties of *sonata* popular in the seventeenth and eighteenth centuries were the *sonata da camera* (literally, 'chamber sonata'), for one or more solo instruments and continuo and usually consisting of a suite of dance movements, and the *sonata da chiesa* (literally, 'church sonata'), likewise for one or more solo instruments and continuo, but usually consisting of four alternately slow and fast movements. Both phrases were introduced into English somewhat later (E19).

sonatina /sɒnə'tiːnə/ *noun* M18 Italian (diminutive of SONATA). A short or simple sonata.

sondage /sɒn'dɑːʒ/ *noun* plural **sondages** /sɒn'dɑːʒɪz/ M20 French (= sounding, borehole). *Archaeology* A trench dug to investigate the stratigraphy of a site.

sonde /sɒnd/ *noun* E20 French (= sounding-line, sounding). **1** E20 A radiosonde or similar device that is sent aloft to transmit or record information on conditions in the atmosphere. Originally only in combination with specifying word, as *ballon-sonde* etc. **2** M20 An instrument probe for transmitting information about its surroundings underground or under water.

son et lumière /ˌsɒn eɪ ˈluːmjɛː/, *foreign* /sɔn e lymjɛr/ *noun phrase* plural **son et lumières** /ˈluːmjɛːz/, *foreign* /lymjɛr/ M20 French (literally, 'sound and light'). **1** M20 An entertainment using recorded sound and lighting effects, usually presented at night at a historic building or other site to give a dramatic narrative of its history. **2** M20 *figurative* Writing or behaviour resembling a son et lumière presentation, especially in its dramatic qualities.

sons bouchés /sɔ̃ buʃe/ *noun plural* E20 French (literally, 'blocked sounds'). In horn-playing, notes stopped by the insertion of the hand into the bell of the instrument; a direction indicating this.

sopaipilla /sopaiˈpiljɑ/, /ˌsəʊpʌɪˈpiːljə/ *noun* plural **sopaipillas** /sopaiˈpiljɑs/, /ˌsəʊpʌɪˈpiːljəz/ M20 American Spanish (diminutive of Spanish *sopaipa* a kind of sweet fritter). Especially in New Mexico, a deep-fried usually square pastry eaten with honey or sugar or as a bread.

sopra bianco /ˌsopra ˈbjanko/ *noun phrase* M19 Italian (elliptical for BIANCO SOPRA BIANCO). Bianco sopra bianco.

soprani see SOPRANO.

sopranino /sɒprəˈniːnəʊ/ *noun & adjective* plural **sopraninos** E20 Italian (diminutive of SOPRANO). (Designating) an instrument (usually wind) of higher pitch than a soprano instrument.

soprano /səˈprɑːnəʊ/ *noun & adjective* M18 Italian (from *sopra* above, from Latin *supra*). **A** *noun* plural **sopranos**, **soprani** /səˈprɑːni/. **1** M18 The highest singing voice; the quality or range of this voice. **b** E19 A part for or sung by such a voice. **2** M18 A female or boy singer having such a voice; a person singing a soprano part. **b** L19 (The player of) an instrument of a high pitch, *specifically* of the highest pitch in a family. **B** *attributive* or as *adjective* M18 Of, pertaining to, or designating the highest singing voice or instrumental pitch.

A.1 1996 *Spectator* Musetta and Mimì are both written for lyric sopranos, the commonest voices . . .

sorbet /ˈsɔːbeɪ/, /ˈsɔːbɪt/ *noun* L16 French (from Italian *sorbetto* from as SHERBET). Originally, an Eastern sherbet. Now usually, a water-ice.

sorbetière /sɔːˈbɛtɪɛː/, *foreign* /sɔrbətjɛr/ *noun* M20 French (from as SORBET). A domestic ice-cream-making machine, in which the mixture is stirred as it is being frozen.

sordino /sɔːˈdinəʊ/ *noun* plural **sordini** /sɔːˈdiːni/ (also **sordine** /sɔːˈdiːn/) L16 Italian (from *sordo*, from Latin *surdus* deaf, mute). A mute for a wind or bowed instrument; a damper for a piano. Cf. CON SORDINO.

sortes /ˈsɔːtiːz/, /ˈsɔːteɪz/ *noun plural* also treated as *singular* L16 Latin (plural of *sors* lot, chance). Divination, or the seeking of guidance, by chance selection of a passage in a book.

■ The authorities traditionally consulted in this way are Virgil (in full *sortes Virgilianae* /ˌvəˈdʒɪlˈrɑːniː/), Homer (in full *sortes Homericae* /həʊˈmɛrɪkiː/), and the Bible (in full *sortes Biblicae* /ˈbɪblɪkiː/).

sosatie /sɔˈsɑːti/, /səˈsɑːti/ *noun* M19 Afrikaans (ultimately from Malay *sesate*; cf. SATAY). In South Africa: marinaded spiced meat grilled on a skewer.

soshi /ˈsəʊʃi/ *noun* plural same L19 Japanese (*sōshi*, literally, 'strong man'). A mercenary political agitator.

sostenuto /ˌsɒstəˈn(j)uːtəʊ/ *adverb, adjective, & noun* E18 Italian (past participle of *sostenere* to sustain). Music **A** *adverb & adjective* E18 (A direction) in a sustained or prolonged manner. **B** *noun* plural **sostenutos**. A passage (to be) played in a sustained or prolonged manner. Also, a sustained sound or note.

sottise /sɔˈtiːz/ *noun* plural pronounced same L17 French (from *sot* fool, from medieval Latin *sottus*). A foolish remark or action.

1977 *Times* The *Daily Mail* Diary . . . is not slow to criticize errors and *sottises* in rival newspapers.

sottisier /sɔtizje/ *noun* plural pronounced same E20 French (from as SOTTISE). A collection or (especially) a written list of *sottises*.

sottoportico /sottoˈportiko/, /ˌsɒtəʊˈpɔːtɪkəʊ/ *noun* plural **sottoportichi**

/sotto'portiki/, **sottoporticos** (also **sotto-portego** /sotto'portego/, /ˌsɒtəʊ'pɔːteɪgəʊ/, plural **sottoportighi** /sotto'portigi/, **sottoportigos**) E20 Italian (from *sotto* under + PORTICO). *Architecture* The passage formed by a portico.

sotto voce /ˌsotto 'votʃe/, /ˌsɒtəʊ 'vəʊtʃi/ *adverb & adjective phrase* M18 Italian (*sotto* under + *voce* voice). **A** *adverb* M18 In an undertone or aside. **B** *adjective* E19 Uttered in an undertone; *transferred* muted, understated.

> **B 1995** *Spectator* Sir Edward [Heath] is not so rude (at least to foreigners) as to suggest that he believes today's apologetic and democratic Germany is a potential threat to European peace, but that is the *sotto voce* message nonetheless.

sou /suː/ *noun* L15 French (singular form deduced from *sous*, *soux* plural of Old French *sout*, from Latin *solidus* (sc. *nummus* coin) use as noun of *solidus* solid). *History* A French coin, formerly a twentieth of a livre, later a five-centime piece.

> ■ In English mainly used in one or other form of the colloquial expression *haven't a sou*, i.e. 'have absolutely no money at all'. Cf. SOU MARKEE.

Soubise /subiz/ *noun* plural pronounced same L18 French (Charles de Rohan *Soubise* (1715–87), French general and courtier). **1** A kind of cravat. Only in L18. **2** E19 A white onion sauce. Also *sauce Soubise*.

soubresaut /subrəso/ *noun* plural pronounced same M19 French. **1** M19 A jumping motion seen in some liquids when boiling. Now *rare* or *obsolete*. **2** E20 *Ballet* A straight-legged jump from both feet with the toes pointed and feet together, one behind the other.

soubrette /suːˈbrɛt/ *noun* M18 French (from modern Provençal *soubreto* feminine of *soubret* coy, from *soubra* (Provençal *sobrar*) from Latin *superare* to be above). **1** M18 A maidservant or lady's maid as a character in a play or opera, *especially* one of a pert or coquettish character; an actress or singer playing the role of a pert or coquettish female in any light entertainment. **2** E19 A lady's maid; a maidservant.

> **1 1996** *Spectator* . . . she . . . can toss her auburn curls with the wily femininity of a soubrette from Offenbach.

soubriquet /ˈsuːbrɪkeɪ/ *noun* E19 French (older variant of *sobriquet*). A nickname, a SOBRIQUET.

souchong /ˈsuːʃɒŋ/ *noun* M18 Chinese ((Cantonese) *siù chúng* small sort). A fine black variety of China tea.

soucouyant /ˌsuːkuːˈjõ/ *noun West Indies* (also **soucriant** /ˌsuːkriˈjõ/ and other variants) M20 West Indian creole (probably related to Fulah *sukunyadyo* sorcerer, witch). In eastern Caribbean folklore, a malignant witch believed to shed her skin by night and suck the blood of her victims.

soufflé /ˈsuːfleɪ/, *foreign* /sufle/ (*plural same*) *noun & adjective* E19 French (past participle of *souffler* from Latin *sufflare*, from *sub* under + *flare* to blow). **A** *noun* E19 A light spongy dish made by mixing eggyolks and other ingredients with stiffly beaten egg-whites, usually baked in an oven until puffy. **B** *adjective* L19 Of ceramic ware: having liquid colour applied by means of blowing.

souffrante /sufrɑ̃t/ *adjective* E19 French (feminine singular present participial adjective of *souffrir* to suffer). Of a woman: delicate; prone to illness, anxiety, or depression.

souffre-douleur /sufrədulœr/ *noun* plural pronounced same M19 French (literally, 'to suffer sorrow'). A person who is in a subservient position and must listen to or share another's troubles; *specifically* a woman who acts as a paid companion to an older woman.

soufrière /ˌsuːfrɪˈɛː/ *noun* M19 French (from *soufre* sulphur). A SOLFATARA.

souk /suːk/ *noun* (also **suk, sukh, suq**) E19 Arabic (*sūḳ* market, probably through French *souk*). An Arab market or marketplace, a bazaar.

soukous /ˈsuːkuːs/ *noun* L20 African (from French *secouer* to shake). Zairean popular dance music.

sou markee /ˌsuː mɑːˈkiː/ *noun* M17 French (*sou marqué*, literally, 'marked sou'). A small eighteenth-century French coin issued for the colonies and circulating especially in the West Indies and North America (*historical*); *generally* something of little value.

soupçon /ˈsuːpsɒn/, *foreign* /supsɔ̃/ *noun* M18 French (from Old French *sous(s)peçon*, from medieval Latin *suspectio(n-)*). A suspicion, a suggestion; a very small quantity, a trace.

> **1996** *Spectator* The bomb had had little effect on the markets—except for a *soupçon* of

trouble for leisure groups with Northern Ireland interests.

soupe /sup/ *noun* M18 **French**. Soup, especially in French cooking.

■ Chiefly in phrases designating particular kinds of soup, as *soupe à l'oignon* onion soup.

soupirant /supirɑ̃/ *noun* M19 **French** (present participle of *soupirer* to sigh). A male admirer, a suitor.

souple /supl/ *noun* L19 **French**. A fabric made of partially degummed silk. More fully *souple silk*.

sous- /su/, /suz/ *prefix* ME **Old and Modern French** (*sous*, from Latin *subtus* under). Under-, sub-.

■ Used in words adopted from French such as *sous-chef*, *sous-lieutenant*, etc.

sous-entendu /suzɑ̃tɑ̃dy/ *noun* plural pronounced same M19 **French**. Something implied or understood but not expressed.

sous vide /su vid/, /su: 'vi:d/ *adjective & adverb phrase* L20 **French** (from *sous* under + *vide* vacuum). Of food: (prepared) by partial cooking followed by vacuum-sealing and chilling.

soutache /su:'taʃ/ *noun* M19 **French** (from Hungarian *sujtás*). A narrow flat ornamental braid used for decorative trimming. More fully *soutache braid*. Also called *Russia braid*.

soutane /su:'tɑ:n/ *noun* M19 **French** (from Italian *sottana*, from *sotto* from Latin *subtus* under). *Roman Catholic Church* A cassock, *especially* a cassock with scarf and cincture worn by a priest.

souteneur /sutənœr/ *noun* plural pronounced same E20 **French** (= protector, from *soutenir* to sustain). A pimp.

soutenu /sutəny/ *adjective & noun* M20 **French** (past participle of *soutenir* to sustain). *Ballet* **A** *adjective* M20 Of a movement: sustained, performed slowly. **B** *noun* M20 plural pronounced same. A sustained or slow movement; *especially* a complete turn on point or half point.

souterrain /'su:tərem/ *noun* M18 **French** (from *sous* under + *terre* earth, after Latin *subterraneus*). Chiefly *Archaeology* An underground chamber or passage.

souvenir /ˌsu:və'nɪə/ *noun* L18 **French** (use as noun of verb = to remember, from Latin *subvenire* to come into the mind, from *sub-* + *venire* to come). **1** L18 A remembrance, a memory. Now *rare*. **2** L18 A token of remembrance; *especially* an article given or purchased as a reminder *of* a particular person, place, or event; a keepsake. **b** E19 *specifically* A usually illustrated publication designed to be purchased as a gift. **c** E20 In the war of 1914–18, a bullet, a shell. *Military slang*.

souvlaki /su:'vlɑ:ki/ *noun* plural **souvlakia** /su:'vlɑ:kɪə/ M20 **Modern Greek** (*soublaki* from *soubla* skewer). A Greek dish of small pieces of meat grilled on a skewer.

sovkhoz /'sɒvkɒz/, /sʌv'kɔ:z/ *noun* plural same, **sovkhozes** /'sɒvkɒzɪz/, **sovkhozy** /'sɒvkɒzi/ E20 **Russian** (from *sov(etskoe khoz(yaĭstvo* Soviet farm). A State-owned farm in countries of the former USSR.

soya /'sɔɪə/ *noun* L17 **Dutch** (*soja* from Japanese *shōyu*; cf. SHOYU). Soy sauce.

■ Also used as short for *soya bean*, the leguminous plant grown as a vegetable or for its protein-rich seeds that yield an edible oil.

spaghetti /spə'gɛti/ *noun* M19 **Italian** (plural of diminutive of *spago* string). **1** M19 Pasta in the form of long solid threads, between MACARONI and VERMICELLI in thickness. **2** M20 Complex roadways forming a multi-level junction, especially on a motorway. In full *spaghetti junction*. *colloquial*.

spaghettini /ˌspagɛ'ti:ni/ *noun* M20 **Italian** (diminutive of preceding). Pasta in the form of strings of thin spaghetti.

Spätlese /'ʃpɛtle:zə/ *noun* plural **Spätlesen** /'ʃpɛtle:zən/, **Spätleses** M20 **German** (from *spät* late + *Lese* picking, vintage). A white wine made (especially in Germany) from grapes picked later than the general harvest.

Spätzle /'ʃpɛtslə/, /'ʃpɛts(ə)l/ *noun plural* L19 **German** ((dialect) literally, 'little sparrows'). Noodles of a type made in southern Germany.

spécialité /spesjalite/ *noun* (also **specialité**) M19 **French** (Old French *especialité* from late Latin *specialitas*, from Latin *specialis* special, particular). **1** M19 An article or service specially characteristic of, dealt in, or produced by, a particular place, firm, etc. **2** M19 An unusual or distinctive thing.

■ *Speciality* in the sense of 'the quality of being special, distinctive, or limited in some respect' was adopted from Old French in the late medieval period and

quickly Anglicized, and the Anglicized version of *spécialité* (and of closely related (e)*specialté*) is used in most general senses. In sense 1, *spécialité* is often used in the phrase *spécialité de la maison* 'special(i)ty of the house', to mean a dish on which a particular restaurant prides itself.

specie /'spiːʃiː/, /'spiːʃi/ *noun* E17 Latin (ablative singular of *species* kind, originally (M16) in phrase *in specie* in the real, precise, or actual form). Coin money as opposed to paper money. Frequently *attributive*.

spectrum /'spɛktrəm/ *noun* plural **spectra** /'spɛktrə/, **spectrums** E17 Latin (= image of a thing, apparition). **1** E17 An apparition, a spectre. *archaic.* **2** L17 An image. *rare.* **3 a** L17 The coloured band into which a beam of light is split by means of a prism or diffraction grating. **b** L19 (Any part of) the entire range of wavelengths of electromagnetic radiation. **c** L19 An actual or notional arrangement of the component parts of any phenomenon according to frequency, energy, mass, etc. **d** M20 *figurative* The entire or a wide range of something arranged by degree, quality, etc.

speculum /'spɛkjʊləm/ *noun* plural **specula** /'spɛkjʊlə/, **speculums** LME Latin (from base of *specere* to look, see). **1** LME *Medicine* An instrument, usually of metal, used to dilate an orifice or canal in the body to allow inspection. **2** M17 *Chiefly Science* A mirror or reflector of glass or metal. **3** E19 *Ornithology* A bright patch of plumage on the wings of certain birds. **4** E20 An alloy of copper and tin in a ratio of around 2:1, formerly used to make mirrors for scientific instruments. Also more fully *speculum metal*.

spermaceti /ˌspɜːməˈsiːti/, /ˌspɜːməˈsɛti/ *noun* L15 Medieval Latin (from late Latin *sperma* (from Greek = sperm, seed, from base of *speirein* to sow) + *ceti* genitive of *cetus*, Greek *kētos* whale (from its appearance or the belief that it represents whale-spawn)). A soft white waxy substance used in the manufacture of candles, ointments, etc., found in the sperm whale and some other cetaceans, chiefly in a rounded organ in the head which focuses acoustic signals and aids control of buoyancy.

sphendone /'sfɛndəni/ *noun* M19 Greek (*sphendonē*). *Archaeology* **1** M19 A headband or fillet shaped like a form of sling, worn by women in ancient Greece. **2** M19 An area composed of elongated sloping sides with a rounded end.

sphincter /'sfɪŋ(k)tə/ *noun* L16 Latin (from Greek *sphigktēr* band, contractile muscle, from *sphiggein* to draw tight). *Anatomy* A contractile muscular ring by which an orifice of the body is normally kept closed.

■ Often with modern Latin specifying word, as *sphincter ani* 'sphincter of the anus'.

sphinx /sfɪŋks/ *noun* plural **sphinxes**, **sphinges** /'sfɪndʒiːz/ LME Latin (from Greek *Sphigx*, *Sphigg-*, apparently from *sphiggein* to draw tight). **1** LME *Greek Mythology* (*Sphinx*) A hybrid monster, usually described as having a woman's head and a (winged) lion's body, which plagued the Greek city of Thebes until Oedipus solved its riddle. Also, any monster resembling this. **b** E17 *figurative* An inscrutable or enigmatic person or thing; a mystery. **2** L16 Any of several ancient Greek or (especially) Egyptian stone figures of a creature with a human or animal head and a lion's body. **3** M18 A moth of the genus *Sphinx*, or of the family Sphingidae, so called from the typical attitude of the caterpillar; a hawkmoth. Also *sphinx-moth*. Chiefly *United States*.

spianato /spɪəˈnɑːtəʊ/ *adjective & adverb* L19 Italian. *Music* (Played) in a smooth, even, level-toned style.

spiccato /spɪˈkɑːtəʊ/ *adjective, adverb, & noun* E18 Italian (= detailed, distinct). *Music* **A** *adjective & adverb* E18 (Played) in a staccato style performed by bouncing the bow on the strings of a violin etc. **B** *noun* L19 Spiccato playing; a passage played in this style.

Spielraum /'ʃpiːlraʊm/ *noun* plural **Spielräume** /'ʃpiːlrɔʏmə/ E20 German (from *Spiel* game, play + *Raum* room). *Philosophy* The range of possibilities within which the probability of an outcome or likelihood of a hypothesis is to be assessed.

1969 P. Geach *God and Soul* There has to be this element of chance in things if human choices are to have any *Spielraum*.

spinto /'spɪntəʊ/ *noun & adjective* plural of noun **spintos** M20 Italian (past participle of *spingere* to push). *Music* (Designating) a lyric soprano or tenor voice of powerful dramatic quality; (designating) a singer with such a voice.

spirituel /ˌspirityɛl/, /ˌspɪrɪtjuˈɛl/ *adjective* (also **spirituelle**) L17 French. Highly refined and lively; witty.

spiritus rector /ˌspɪrɪtʊs ˈrɛktɔː/ *noun phrase* E20 Latin. A ruling or directing spirit.
1980 *Encounter* More than fifteen years ago he was the *spiritus rector* of the European *Journal of Sociology.*

sporran /ˈspɒr(ə)n/ *noun* M18 Gaelic (*sporan* = Irish *sparán* purse, Middle Irish *sboran* from Latin *bursa* purse). A pouch or large purse usually made of leather or sealskin covered with fur and with ornamental tassels etc., worn by a Scottish Highlander in front of the kilt.

sportif /spɔrtif/ *adjective* M20 French. Sportive; active or interested in athletic sports; (of a garment) suitable for sport or informal wear.
1996 *Oldie* . . . her sneering references to his game attempts to take up water-skiing on their honeymoon when he was a mere sixty-two have proved equally irritating to more *sportif* oldies.

Sprechgesang /ˈʃprɛçgəˌzaŋ/ *noun* E20 German (literally, 'speech song'). *Music* A style of dramatic vocalization intermediate between speech and song.

Sprechstimme /ˈʃprɛçˌʃtɪmə/ *noun* E20 German (literally, 'speech voice'). *Music* SPRECHGESANG.

sprezzatura /ˌsprettsaˈtura/ *noun* M20 Italian. Ease of manner, studied carelessness, nonchalance, especially in art or literature.
1973 *Times Literary Supplement* Literary fashion and his own aristocratic *sprezzatura* demanded that he affect an unconcern.

springar /ˈsprɪŋə/ *noun* M20 Norwegian. (A piece of music for) a Norwegian country dance in 3/4 time.

springbok /ˈsprɪŋbɒk/ *noun* (in sense 1 also **Springbok**, in sense 1 also Anglicized as **springbuck** /ˈsprɪŋbʌk/) L18 Afrikaans (from Dutch *springen* to spring + *bok* goat, antelope). 1 L18 A common and gregarious southern African gazelle, characterized by the habit of leaping (pronking) when excited or disturbed. 2 E20 A South African.
■ *Springboks* (often abbreviated to *Boks*) was formerly the name given to South African national sporting (especially rugby) teams.

spritzer /ˈsprɪtsə/ *noun* M20 German (= a splash). A mixture of (usually white) wine and soda water; a drink or glass of this.

spritzig /ˈsprɪtsɪç/ *adjective & noun* M20 German (from *spritzen* to squirt, splash). **A** *adjective* M20 Of wine: sparkling. **B** *noun* M20 Sparkle in wine.

spruit /spreɪt/, *foreign* /sprœyt/ *noun* M19 Dutch (= sprout). In South Africa: a small watercourse that is usually dry except in the rainy season.

spumante /spuˈmanti/ *noun* E20 Italian (= sparkling). A sparkling white wine, especially from the Italian province of Asti (in full *Asti spumante*).

spumoni /spuˈməʊni/ *noun* E20 Italian (*spumone*, from *spuma* foam). A rich dessert consisting of layered ice-cream with candied fruits, nuts, and sometimes brandy. *North American.*

spurlos /ˈʃpuːrlɔːs/ *adjective* E20 German (= (sunk) without trace). (Sunk) without trace. Chiefly *figurative*, lost from sight, ruined. In full *spurlos versenkt* /ˌʃpuːrlɔːs fərˈsɛŋkt/.
■ The phrase became widely used in English as the result of the publication of a notorious secret telegram sent in May 1917 by the German minister in Buenos Aires, Count Luxburg, to Berlin, in which he recommended that Argentine shipping should either be turned back or sunk without trace.
1963 *Oxford Medical School Gazette* Many distinguished research workers have ceased production when they have become professors and like submarines in dangerous waters have been *spurlos versenkt*.

sputa plural of SPUTUM.

sputnik /ˈspʊtnɪk/, /ˈspʌtnɪk/ *noun* (also **Sputnik**) M20 Russian (literally, 'travelling companion', from *s* with + *put'* way, journey + noun suffix *-nik* person connected with (something)). 1 M20 An unmanned artificial earth satellite, especially a Russian one; *specifically* each of a series of such satellites launched by the Soviet Union between 1957 and 1961. 2 M20 *Bridge* A take-out double of a suit overcall of one's partner's opening bid. In full *Sputnik double*.

sputum /ˈspjuːtəm/ *noun* plural **sputa** /ˈspjuːtə/ L17 Latin (use as noun of neuter past participle of *spuere* to spit). *Medicine* Thick mucus coughed up from the respiratory tract especially in certain diseases of the lungs, chest, or throat; a mass or quantity of this.

staccato /stəˈkɑːtəʊ/ *adjective, adverb, noun, & verb* E18 Italian (past participle of *staccare* aphetic from *distaccare* to detach). **A** *adjective & adverb* E18 With each note or sound sharply separated or detached from the next, with a clipped style. Opposed to LEGATO. **B** *noun* L18 A succession of disconnected notes or sounds; a staccato passage in music etc.; staccato delivery, playing, or speech. **C** *transitive verb* E19 Play or utter in a staccato manner.

stadium /ˈsteɪdɪəm/ *noun* plural **stadiums**; **stadia** /ˈsteɪdɪə/ LME Latin (from Greek *stadion*). **I 1** LME *Classical Antiquities* A unit of length, usually equal to 600 Greek or Roman feet, or one-eighth of a Roman mile (c.185 m.). **2** E17 *Classical Antiquities* A course (originally a stadium in length) for foot-racing or chariot-racing; a race on such a course. **3** M19 An athletic or sports ground or arena with tiered seats or terraces for spectators. **II 4** M17 A stage of a process, disease, etc. **b** L19 *Zoology* An interval between moults in the growth of an insect, crustacean, etc. **5** M19 Any of various instruments for measuring distance; a levelling rod.

Stadthaus /ˈʃtathaʊs/ *noun* plural **Stadthauser** /ˈʃtathɔyzər/ M19 German (from *Stadt* town + *Haus* house). A town hall in a German-speaking country.
■ The partially Anglicized form *stadthouse* derives either from *stadthaus* or from Dutch *stadhuis* and is used of a town hall in a German-speaking or (especially) a Dutch-speaking country.

staffage /stəˈfɑːʒ/ *noun* L19 German (pseudo-French form from *staffieren* to fit out, decorate, perhaps from Old French *estoffer*, from *estoffe* stuff). Accessory items in a painting, especially figures or animals in a landscape picture.

stagione /staˈdʒone/ *noun* plural **stagioni** /staˈdʒoni/ M20 Italian (= season). An opera or ballet season, *especially* an opera season in which one work is performed on several occasions in a limited period with no change of cast.

stanza /ˈstanzə/, (in sense 2 also) /ˈstantsə/ *noun* plural **stanzas**, (in sense 2 also) **stanze** /ˈstantsi/ L16 Italian (= standing, stopping-place, room, strophe, from Proto-Romance, from Latin *stant-* present participial stem of *stare* to stand). **1** L16 A group of (usually between four and twelve) lines of verse occurring as the basic metrical unit of a song or poem consisting of a series of such groups; a

verse. **2** M17 In Italy: an apartment, a chamber, a room; *specifically* a room in the Vatican (usually in *plural*). **3** M20 A half or other session of a game or sporting contest.

starets /ˈstarjɛts/ *noun* (also **startz**) plural **startsy, startzy,** /ˈstartsi/ E20 Russian (= (venerable) old man, elder). A spiritual leader or counsellor in the Russian Orthodox Church.

starover /starəˈvjɛr/, /starəˈvjɛː/ *noun* plural **starovery** /starəˈvjɛri/, **starovers** E19 Russian. *Ecclesiastical History* An Old Believer, a RASKOLNIK.

startsy, startz see STARETS.

stasis /ˈsteɪsɪs/, /ˈstasɪs/ *noun* plural **stases** /ˈsteɪsiːz/, /ˈstasɪs/ M18 Modern Latin (from Greek, literally, 'standing, stoppage; party, faction', from *sta-* base of *histanai* to stand). **1** M18 *Medicine* A stagnation or stoppage of flow due usually to obstruction, as of the blood or lymph, or of the intestinal contents. **2** E20 *generally* Inactivity; stagnation; a state of equilibrium. **3** M20 *Psychoanalysis* The presence of high energy or excitement in the libido caused especially by repression and thought to produce neurosis. **4** M20 Party faction, civil strife.

status /ˈsteɪtəs/ *noun* plural **statuses**, (rare) same L17 Latin (from *stat-* past participial stem of *stare* to stand). **1** *Medicine* **a** The crisis of a disease. rare. Only in L17. **b** L19 A state, a condition. Only with modern Latin specifying word (e.g. *status epilepticus* a condition in which epileptic fits follow one another without pause). **2** L18 Chiefly *Law* A person's standing or position such as determines his or her legal rights or limitations; condition in respect of marriage or celibacy, minority or majority, etc. **3** E19 Position or standing in society; rank, profession; relative importance; *specifically* (a) superior social etc. position. Also *social status*. **4** M19 Condition or position of a thing, especially with regard to importance.

status quo /ˌsteɪtəs ˈkwəʊ/ *noun phrase* M19 Latin (= the state in which). The existing state of affairs.
1996 *Times* This was the *status quo*, and it was a brave Tory who dared to challenge it.

status quo ante /ˌsteɪtəs ˌkwəʊ ˈanti/ *noun phrase* L19 Latin (= the state in which before). The previously existing state of affairs.

1996 *Spectator* Those who framed the peace treaties had objectives far beyond restoring the *status quo ante*, which would in most cases have been impossible.

stela /ˈstiːlə/ *noun* plural **stelae** /ˈstiːliː/ L18 Latin (from as STELE). *Antiquities* An upright slab or pillar, usually bearing a commemorative inscription or sculptured design and often serving as a gravestone.

stele /stiːl/, /ˈstiːli/ *noun* plural **steles**, (especially in sense 1) **stelae** /ˈstiːliː/ E19 Greek (*stēlē* standing block; cf. STELA). **1** E19 *Antiquities* A stela. Also *loosely*, any prepared surface on the face of a building, rock, etc., bearing an inscription. **2** L19 *Botany* The central core of the stem and root of a vascular plant.

stelline /stɛˈliːni/ *noun* plural (also **stellini**) M20 Italian (from *stellina* diminutive of *stella* star). Small star-shaped pieces of pasta.

stelling /ˈstɛlɪŋ/ *noun* M19 Dutch (from *stellen* to place). In Guyana and the Caribbean: a wooden pier or landing-stage.

stemma /ˈstɛmə/ *noun* plural **stemmata** /ˈstɛmətə/ M17 Latin (from Greek (= garland), from *stephein* to crown). **1a** M17 A recorded genealogy of a family, a family tree; a pedigree. **b** M20 A diagram representing a reconstruction of the interrelationships between surviving witnesses in the (especially manuscript) tradition of a text. **2** E19 *Zoology* In arthropods, a simple eye, an ocellus.

steppe /stɛp/ *noun* L17 Russian (*step'*). Any of the vast level grassy usually treeless plains of South East Europe and Siberia. Also, any similar plain elsewhere.

stet /stɛt/ *noun & verb* M18 Latin (3rd person singular present subjunctive of *stare* = let it stand). **A** *noun* M18 A direction in the margin of a proof-sheet etc. indicating that a correction or deletion should be ignored and that the original matter is to be retained. **B** *transitive verb* L19 (inflected -tt) Cancel the correction or deletion of; write 'stet' against (an accidental deletion, miscorrection, etc.).

stiacciato /stjaˈtʃɑːtəʊ/ *noun* (also **schiacciato** /skjaˈtʃɑːtəʊ/) M19 Italian (*schiacciato*, *stiacciato* past participle of *schiacciare*, *stiacciare* to flatten). *Sculpture* Very low relief. Also more fully *stiacciato-relievo*, *relievo stiacciato*.

stifado /stɪˈfɑːdəʊ/ *noun* plural **stifados** M20 Modern Greek (*stiphado* probably from Italian *stufato*). A Greek dish of meat stewed with onions and sometimes tomatoes.

stigma /ˈstɪɡmə/ *noun* plural **stigmas**, **stigmata** /ˈstɪɡmətə/, /stɪɡˈmɑːtə/ L16 Latin (from Greek *stigma*, *stigmat-*, from base of *stizein* to prick). **1** L16 A mark made on the skin by pricking, cutting, or (especially) branding, as a sign of disgrace or subjection. **b** M17 (in *plural*) Marks resembling the wounds on Jesus' crucified body, said to have appeared on the bodies of certain saints etc. **2a** E17 A mark or sign of disgrace or discredit, regarded as impressed on or carried by a person or thing. **b** M19 A visible or apparent characteristic indicative of some (especially undesirable or discreditable) quality, action, or circumstance (followed by *of*); *Medicine* a visible sign *of* a disease or condition. **3** M18 *Zoology* **a** A small external opening or pore. **b** E19 A natural spot or mark. **4** M18 *Botany* That part of the pistil in flowering plants which receives the pollen in impregnation.

2.a 1996 *Country Life* But generally it can be said that divorce has lost most, if not all, of its social stigma.

stile antico /ˌstiːle anˈtiko/ *noun phrase* M20 Italian (= old style). *Music* The strict contrapuntal style of the sixteenth century, especially as exemplified in the works of Palestrina.

stile concitato /ˌstiːle kɒntʃiˈtato/ *noun phrase* E20 Italian (= excited style). *Music* A baroque style developed by Monteverdi, emphasizing dramatic expression and excitement.

stile rappresentativo /ˌstiːle ˌrapprezenˈtativo/ *noun phrase* L19 Italian (= representative style). *Music* The vocal style of recitative used by Italian musicians of the early seventeenth century.

stiletto /stɪˈlɛtəʊ/ *noun* E17 Italian (diminutive of *stilo* dagger, ultimately from Latin *stilus* stylus). **A** *noun* plural **stiletto(e)s**. **1** E17 A short dagger with a thick blade. **2** E19 A small pointed instrument for making eyelet-holes. **3** M20 A very high tapering heel on a woman's shoe; a shoe with such a heel. In full *stiletto heel*.

Stimmung /ˈʃtɪmʊŋ/ *noun* E20 German. Mood, spirit, atmosphere, feeling.

stimulus /ˈstɪmjʊləs/ *noun* plural **stimuli** /ˈstɪmjʊlʌɪ/, /ˈstɪmjʊliː/ L17 Latin (= goad, spur, incentive, probably from base also of *stilus* stylus). **1** L17 A thing that provokes, increases, or quickens bodily activity. **b** L18 *generally* An agency or influence that rouses or spurs something or someone to action or quickens an activity or process; a spur, an incentive (followed by *to* an action etc.) **c** L19 *Psychology* Any change or event which excites a nerve impulse and gives rise to a response or reaction. **2** L17 The effect or property of producing such a reaction; stimulation; an instance of this.

stoa /'stəʊə/ *noun* plural **stoas, stoai** /'stəʊʌɪ/ E17 Greek. **1** E17 ῾(*the Stoa*) The great hall in ancient Athens in which the philosopher Zeno lectured; the Stoic school of philosophy. **2** L18 A portico, a roofed colonnade.

■ The followers of Zeno (335–263 BC) were accordingly called Stoics.

stoep /stuːp/ *noun* L18 Afrikaans (from Dutch, related to *step*, from West Germanic; cf. STOOP). In South Africa: a raised platform or veranda running along the front and sometimes round the sides of a house.

stollen /'stɒlən/, /'ʃtɒlən/ *noun* E20 German. A rich fruit loaf, often with nuts added.

stoop /stuːp/ *noun* M18 Dutch (cf. STOEP). A small raised platform at the entrance door of a house; a set of steps approaching this; a small porch or veranda. *North American.*

stoss /stɒs/, *foreign* /ʃtoːs/ *adjective* L19 German (= thrust, push). *Geology* Designating the side of an object that faces a flow of ice or water.

strabismus /strə'bɪzməs/ *noun* L17 Modern Latin (from Greek *strabismos*, from *strabizein* to squint, from *strabos* squinting). **1** L17 *Medicine* A disorder of the eye-muscles resulting in an inability to direct the gaze of both eyes to the same object simultaneously; squinting, a squint. **2** M19 *figurative* Perversity of intellectual perception.

stracchino /stra'kiːnəʊ/ *noun* M19 Italian. A variety of soft cheese made in the north of Italy. In full *stracchino cheese*.

stracciatella /ˌstratʃə'tɛlə/ *noun* M20 Italian. An Italian soup made with stock, eggs, and cheese.

strapontin /strapɔ̃tɛ̃/ *noun* plural pronounced same E20 French. A tip-up seat, usually additional to the ordinary seat-ing in a theatre, taxi, etc., especially in France.

strata plural of STRATUM.

strath /straθ/ *noun* M16 Gaelic (*Scottish s(t)rath* = Old Irish *srath* (modern *sraith*)). A broad river valley bounded by hills or high ground. Formerly also, a stretch of flat land by the waterside.

stratum /'strɑːtəm/, /'streɪtəm/ *noun* plural **strata** /'strɑːtə/, /'streɪtə/ L16 Modern Latin (use of Latin *stratum*, literally, 'something spread or laid down', neuter past participle of *sternere* to lay down, throw down). **1** L16 *generally* A quantity of a substance or material spread over a nearly horizontal surface to a more or less uniform thickness; *especially* each of two or more parallel layers or coats successively superposed one upon another. **2** L17 A bed of sedimentary rock, usually consisting of a series of layers of the same kind. **3** M18 *Anatomy* and *Biology* Each of a number of layers composing an animal or plant tissue or structure (frequently with modern Latin specifying word). Also *Ecology*, a layer of vegetation in a plant community. **4** L18 A region of the atmosphere, of the sea, or of a quantity of fluid, assumed for purposes of calculation to be bounded by horizontal planes. **5** E19 *figurative* **a** A portion of a body of institutions, a set of traditions, an artist's work, etc., originating from one historical period, or representing one stage of development or level of analysis. **b** M19 (Part of a population belonging to) a particular level or grade in social status, education, etc. **6** E20 *Statistics* Each of the groups into which a population is divided in the technique of stratified sampling.

strepitoso /strɛpɪ'təʊsəʊ/ *adverb, adjective, & noun* E19 Italian (literally, 'noisy, loud'). *Music* **A** *adverb & adjective* E19 (A direction:) spirited(ly), boisterous(ly). **B** *noun* M20 A spirited or boisterous piece or passage.

stretta /'strɛtə/ *noun* plural **strette** /'strɛti/, **strettas** L19 Italian (feminine of STRETTO). *Music* A final passage played at a (gradually) faster tempo.

stretto /'strɛtəʊ/ *adverb & noun* M18 Italian (literally, 'narrow'). *Music* **A** *adverb* M18 (A direction:) with gradually increasing speed (especially in a final passage). **B** *noun* M19 A fugal device in which subject entries follow closely in succession.

streusel /'strɔɪz(ə)l/, /'struːz(ə)l/ *noun* E20 German (from *streuen* to sprinkle). (A cake or pastry with) a crumbly topping or filling made from fat, flour, cinnamon, and sugar.

■ Chiefly North American and frequently attributive as in *streusel cake*.

stria /'strʌɪə/ *noun plural* **striae** /'strʌɪiː/ M16 Latin (= furrow, grooving). **1** M16 *Architecture* A fillet between the flutes of a column, pilaster, etc. **2** L17 Chiefly *Science* A small groove, channel, or ridge; a narrow streak, stripe, or band of distinctive colour, structure, or texture; *especially* each of two or more.

stricto sensu /ˌstrɪktəʊ 'sɛnsuː/ *adverb & adjective phrase* M20 Latin (= in the restricted sense). SENSU STRICTO.

striges /'strʌɪdʒiːz/ *noun plural* M16 Latin. *Architecture* The fillets of a fluted column.

■ Deriving from the writings of the Roman architectural authority Vitruvius (c.50–26BC), *striges* is perhaps a misreading of *striae* (see STRIA) or *strigae* 'row, strip'.

stringendo /strɪn'dʒɛndəʊ/ *adverb, adjective, & noun* M19 Italian (present participle of *stringere* to press, squeeze, bind together, from Latin *stringere* to bind). *Music* **A** *adverb & adjective* M19 (A direction:) with increasing *speed and excitement*. **B** *noun* M20 plural **stringendos**, **stringendi** /strɪn'dʒɛndi/. An increase of speed and excitement; a passage (to be) played with such an increase.

strophe /'strəʊfi/ *noun plural* **strophes** /'strəʊfiz/, **strophae** /'strəʊfiː/ E17 Greek (*strophē* (whence late Latin *stropha*), literally, 'turning', from *stroph-* ablaut variant of base of *strephein* to turn). Originally, a movement from right to left in Greek choruses and dances, answered by an ANTISTROPHE; the lines of choral song recited during this movement. Also (*Prosody*), a metrically structured section of a usually Greek choral ode or lyric verse, the structure of which is repeated in an antistrophe. More widely, a group of lines forming a section of a lyric poem.

strudel /'struːd(ə)l/, /'ʃtruːd(ə)l/ *noun* L19 German (literally, 'eddy, whirlpool'). A confection of thin layers of flaky pastry rolled up round a usually fruit filling and baked.

Stube /'ʃtuːbə/ *noun plural* **Stuben** /'ʃtuːbən/ M20 German (= room). A BIERSTUBE.

stucco /'stʌkəʊ/ *noun plural* **stuccoes** L16 Italian (ultimately from Germanic). **1a** L16 A fine plaster, especially made from gypsum and pulverized marble, for covering walls, ceilings, etc., and making cornices and other architectural decorations. **b** M18 A coarse plaster or calcareous cement especially for covering a rough exterior surface to give the appearance of stone. **c** M19 Plaster of Paris. **2** L17 The process of ornamenting walls, ceilings, etc. with stucco; work or ornamentation produced by this process. **b** L20 A building plastered with stucco.

studiolo /studi'olo/ *noun plural* **studioli** /studi'oli/ E20 Italian (= small study). In Italy: a private study hung with paintings.

1996 *Country Life* ... apart from the building's splendid chimneypieces, two overdoors in the Queen's apartment and the panelling in François I's *studiolo*, there was no original decoration left.

studium generale /ˌstjuːdɪəm dʒɛnə'reɪleɪ/, /ˌstjuːdɪəm dʒɛnə'rɑːleɪ/ *noun phrase* plural **studia generalia** /ˌstjuːdɪə dʒɛnə'reɪlɪə/, /ˌstjuːdɪə dʒɛnə'rɑːlɪə/ M19 Latin (*studium* zeal, application (to learning) + neuter singular of *generalis* general). *History* In the Middle Ages, a university attended by students from outside as well as within its own locality.

stupa /'stuːpə/ *noun* L19 Sanskrit (*stūpa*). A round usually domed structure erected as a Buddhist shrine.

Sturm und Drang /ˌʃtʊrm ʊnt 'draŋ/ *noun phrase* M19 German (literally, 'storm and stress'). (The period of) a radical movement in German literature in the late 1770s characterized by the violent expression of emotion and the rejection of neoclassical literary norms; *transferred* (a period of) emotion, stress, or turbulence.

■ *Sturm und Drang* was the title of a 1776 play by Friedrich Maximilian Klinger (1752–1831).

transferred **1996** *Times* There are effective supporting performances from Paul Jesson as an implacable Burleigh, Ben Miles as a *Sturm und Drang* hero who wants simultaneously to rape and rescue Mary ...

stylus /'stʌɪləs/ *noun plural* **styli** /'stʌɪlʌɪ/, /'stʌɪliː/, **styluses** E18 Latin (erroneous spelling of Latin *stilus* writing implement (influenced by the spelling of Greek *stulos* column)). **1** E18 *Botany* A projection of the ovary bearing the stigma. Now *rare*. **2** E19 An ancient implement for incising letters on wax. **3** M19 *Zoology* A small slender pointed process or part. **4** L19 A tracing-point used to produce a written record in a chart recorder, telegraph receiver, etc. **b** L19 A hard (especially diamond or sapphire) point following a groove in a record and transmitting the recorded sound for reproduction; a similar point used to make such a groove when producing a record; a needle.

■ Senses 1–3 are also found in the English form *style*.

subbotnik /suːˈbɒtnɪk/ *noun* plural **subbotniki** /suːˈbɒtnɪki/, **subbotniks** E20 Russian (from *subbota* Saturday + noun suffix *-ník* person connected with (something)). In countries of the former USSR: the practice or an act of working voluntarily on a Saturday, for the benefit of the national economy.

subgum /ˈsʌbɡʌm/ *noun* (also **sub gum**, **sup gum** /ˈsʌpɡʌm/ E20 Chinese ((Cantonese) *shâp kám*, from *shâp* mixed + *kám* brocade). A Chinese dish of mixed vegetables, as water chestnuts, mushrooms, bean sprouts, etc.

subito /ˈsuːbɪtəʊ/ *adverb* E18 Italian. *Music* (A direction:) suddenly, quickly.

sub judice /sʌb ˈdʒuːdɪsi/, /sʊb ˈjuːdɪkeɪ/ *adjective phrase* E17 Latin (literally, 'under a judge'). *Law* Under the consideration of a judge or court and therefore prohibited from public discussion elsewhere.

sub rosa /sʌb ˈrəʊzə/ *adjective & adverb phrase* M17 Latin (literally, 'under the rose'). Of communication, consultation, etc.: (given, told, etc.) in secrecy or confidence.

■ The concept of the rose as a symbol of confidentiality or secrecy may have originated in Germany and is enshrined in the German phrase *unter der rose* (cf. Early Modern Dutch *onder de roose*).

sub silentio /sʌb sɪˈlɛntɪəʊ/, /sʌb sɪˈlɛnʃɪəʊ/ *adverb phrase* E17 Latin (literally, 'under silence'). In silence, without remark.

sub specie aeternitatis /sʌb ˈspiːʃiː ɪˌtəːnɪˈtɑːtɪs/ *adverb phrase* L19 Latin (literally, 'under the aspect of eternity'). Viewed in relation to the eternal; in a universal perspective.

■ In Spinoza's *Ethices* (*Posthuma Opera* (1677) V.xxix.254). The opposite of SUB SPECIE TEMPORIS.

sub specie temporis /sʌb ˌspiːʃiː ˈtɛm pɔːrɪs/ *adverb phrase* L19 Latin (literally 'under the aspect of time'). Viewed in relation to time rather than eternity.

> **1960** *Encounter Sub specie temporis* his Combination Rooms say more to us than Beckett's wet and windy plains.

substratum /sʌbˈstrɑːtəm/, /sʌb ˈstreɪtəm/ *noun* plural **substrata** /sʌb ˈstrɑːtə/, (*rare*) **substratums** M17 Modern Latin (use as noun of neuter past participle of Latin *substernere*, from *sub-* under + *sternere* to lay down, throw down). **1** M17 *Metaphysics* That which is regarded as supporting attributes or accidents; the substance in which qualities inhere. **2** M17 An underlying layer or substance; the basis or foundation of a structure, condition, activity, etc. **3** M18 An underlayer of soil or earth. **4** E20 *Linguistics* Elements or features of a language identified as being relics of, or due to the influence of, an earlier extinct language.

sub verbo /sʌb ˈvəːbəʊ/ *adverb phrase* E20 Latin. SUB VOCE.

sub voce /sʌb ˈvəʊsi/, /ˈvəʊtʃi/ *adverb phrase* M19 Latin. (As a direction in a text:) under the word or heading given; SUB VERBO.

■ Abbreviated to *s.v.*.

succah /ˈsʊkə/ *noun* **succoth** /ˈsʊkɒt/ L19 Hebrew (*sukkāh*, literally, 'hut'). Any of the booths in which a practising Jew spends part of the feast of Tabernacles (Succoth).

succedaneum /sʌksɪˈdeɪnɪəm/ *noun* plural **succedanea** /sʌksɪˈdeɪnɪə/, **succedaneums** E17 Modern Latin (neuter singular of Latin *succedaneus* from *succedere* to come close after). **1** E17 A thing which takes the place of another; a substitute; *specifically* a medicine or drug substituted for another. (Followed by *for, of, to*.) **2** M-L18 A remedy, a cure.

succès d'estime /syksɛ dɛstim/ *noun phrase* M19 French (= success of opinion or regard). A critical as opposed to a popular or commercial success.

> **1996** *Spectator* Being a *succès d'estime* is not enough for a mid-market newspaper which must rely on a much wider constituency than the chattering classes.

succès de scandale /sʏksɛ də skɑ̃dal/ *noun phrase* L19 French (= success of scandal). Success due to notoriety or scandalous character.

> **1996** *Spectator* His book had achieved a notable *succès de scandale* in this town, particularly amongst the Society's older members who remembered many of the characters mentioned.

succès fou /sʏksɛ fu/ *noun phrase* L19 French (= mad success). A success marked by wild enthusiasm.

> **1996** *Times* I picked Newell because he had used my drawing-room to shoot a scene of a previous *succès fou* of his, *Enchanted April*.

succi plural of SUCCUS.

succuba /'sʌkjʊbə/ *noun* plural **succubae** /'sʌkjʊbiː/ L16 Late Latin (= prostitute, from *succubare* from *sub-* under + *cubare* to lie. A SUCCUBUS.

succubus /'sʌkjʊbəs/ *noun* plural **succubi** /'sʌkjʊbʌɪ/ LME Medieval Latin (masculine form (with feminine meaning) corresponding to SUCCUBA, after INCUBUS). **1** LME A demon in female form supposed to have sexual intercourse with sleeping men. **b** E17 *generally* A demon, an evil spirit. **2** E17 A prostitute, a whore. *archaic* and *derogatory*.

succus /'sʌkəs/ *noun* plural **succi** /'sʌk(s)ʌɪ/, /'sʌk(s)iː/ L18 Latin. A juice; a fluid secretion in an animal or plant.

sucrier /'suːkrɪeɪ/, *foreign* /sykrie/ (*plural* same) *noun* M19 French (from *sucre* sugar). A sugar bowl, usually made of porcelain and with a cover.

sudarium /suːˈdɛːrɪəm/, /sjuːˈdɛːrɪəm/ *noun* plural **sudaria** /suːˈdɛːrɪə/ E17 Latin (from *sudor* sweat). **1** E17 A cloth for wiping the face. **2** E17 A cloth with a likeness of Christ's face on it, a veronica. **3** M19 Chiefly *Roman Antiquities* A steam or hot air bath.

sudd /sʌd/ *noun* L19 Arabic (= obstruction, dam, from *sadda* to obstruct, block, congest). **1** L19 An area of floating vegetation which impedes navigation on the White Nile. **2** L19 *transferred* A temporary dam across a river.

suede /sweɪd/ *noun & adjective* (also **suède**) M17 French (*Suède* Sweden). **A** *noun* M17 Leather, originally especially kidskin, with the flesh side rubbed to make a velvety nap; a shoe or other article made of this. **B** *attributive or as adjective* L19 Made of suede.

■ The French phrase *gants de Suède* 'gloves of Sweden' was misunderstood as referring to the material rather than to the country of origin.

suggestio falsi /sə.dʒɛstɪəʊ ˈfalsʌɪ/ *noun phrase* plural **suggestiones falsi** /sə.dʒɛstɪˌəʊniːz/ E19 Modern Latin (literally, 'suggestion of what is false'). A misrepresentation of the truth whereby something incorrect is implied to be true.

■ Often in contexts with the associated verbal stratagem of SUPPRESSIO VERI (see quotation).

> **1980** D. Newsome *On Edge of Paradise* There are undoubted cases of *suppressio veri*; on the other hand, he appears to eschew *suggestio falsi*.

suiboku /'suːɪbəʊkuː/ *noun* E20 Japanese (literally, 'liquid ink', from *sui* water + *boku* ink stick). A style of Japanese painting, using black ink on a white surface and characterized by bold brush-work and subtle tones.

sui generis /suːʌɪ ˈdʒɛn(ə)rɪs/, /suːiː/; /sjuːʌɪ ˈdʒɛn(ə)rɪs/ *adjective phrase* L18 Latin. Of its own kind; peculiar, unique.

> **1996** *Spectator* Major's rhinocerine obstinacy in putting his personal political survival before any other consideration is *sui generis* . . .

sui juris /suːʌɪ ˈdʒʊərɪs/, /suːiː ˈdʒʊərɪs/, /sjuːiː ˈdʒʊərɪs/ *adjective phrase* E17 Latin (literally, 'of one's own right'). *Law* **1** E17 *Roman History* Of the status of a person who was not subject to paternal authority. **2** L17 Of full age and capacity.

suite /swiːt/ *noun* L17 French. **1** L17 A set of people in attendance; a retinue. **2** E18 A succession, a series; a set of things belonging together. **3** E18 *specifically* **a** A set of rooms in a hotel etc. for use by one person or group of people. **b** M18 *Music* Originally, a set or series of lessons etc. Later, a set of instrumental compositions, in dance style, to be played in succession; a set of selected pieces from an opera, ballet, etc., arranged to be played as one instrumental work. **c** E19 A set of furniture, especially a sofa and armchairs, of the same design. **d** M19 *Geology* A group of associated minerals, rocks, or fossils, especially from the same place; an associated sequence of strata etc. that is repeated at different localities.

suk, sukh variants of SOUK.

sukiya /sʊˈkiːyə/ *noun* E20 Japanese (literally, 'room of fantasy, room of refined taste'). **1** E20 A room in which the tea ceremony is held, a tea-house. **2** M20 *Archi-*

tecture A style of Japanese architecture inspired by a certain type of tea-house, characterized by functionality of design and the use of wood and other natural materials. Frequently *attributive*.

sukiyaki /sʊkɪˈjaki/, /sʊkɪˈjaːki/ *noun* E20 Japanese. A Japanese dish consisting of thin slices of beef fried with vegetables in sugar, stock, and soy sauce.

sultan /ˈsʌlt(ə)n/ *noun* M16 French (or medieval Latin *sultanus*, from Arabic *sulṭān* power, ruler). **1** M16 The monarch or chief ruler of a Muslim country. **b** M17 An absolute ruler; a despot, a tyrant. **2** M17 A plant of the Near East grown for its sweet-scented purple, pink, white, or yellow flowers. Originally more fully *sultan's flower*; now usually *sweet sultan*. **3** M19 A small white-crested variety of domestic fowl, originally brought from Turkey.

sultana /sʌlˈtaːnə/, *in sense 5 also* /s(ə)lˈtaːnə/ *noun* L16 Italian (feminine of *sultano* sultan). **1** L16 A wife or concubine of a sultan; the queen mother or any other woman of a sultan's family. **2** E18 A mistress, a concubine. **3** E18 A Turkish warship. *obsolete* except *historical*. **4** M19 Any of various gallinules, *especially* the purple gallinule. Now *rare*. **5** M19 A kind of small seedless raisin used in puddings, cakes, etc. **6** M20 The plant Busy Lizzie, *Impatiens walleriana*.

sulu /ˈsuːluː/ *noun* M19 Fijian. In Fiji: a length of cotton or other light fabric wrapped about the body as a sarong; a type of sarong worn from the waist by men and full-length by women; a similar fashion garment worn by women.

sumi /ˈsuːmi/ *noun* E20 Japanese (= ink, blacking). A carbon-based pigment used for painting and writing.

summa /ˈsʊmə/, /ˈsʌmə/ *noun & adverb* plural **summae** /ˈsʊmiː/, **summa(e)s** LME Latin. **1** LME–L18 A sum total. **2** L15–E16 The quantity or number *of* something. **3** E18 A treatise, a manual; a compendium of knowledge. **4** L20 A degree SUMMA CUM LAUDE.

> **3** 1996 *Country Life* Bach's artistic last will and testament, *The Art of Fugue*, is a musical *summa* which demonstrates the expressive power of his beloved counterpoint.

summa bona plural of SUMMUM BONUM.

summa cum laude /ˌsʌmə kʌm ˈlɔːdi/, /ˌsʊmə kʊm ˈlaʊdeɪ/ *adverb & adjective* *phrase* L19 Latin (literally, 'with the highest praise'). With or of highest distinction; *specifically* (of a degree, diploma, etc.) of the highest standard.

■ Chiefly North American; cf. CUM LAUDE, MAGNA CUM LAUDE.

summae see SUMMA.

summa genera plural of SUMMUM GENUS.

summum bonum /ˌsʊməm ˈbɒnəm/, /ˌsʌməm ˈbəʊnəm/ *noun* *phrase* plural **summa bona** /ˌsʊmə ˈbɒnə, ˌsʌmə ˈbəʊnə/ M16 Latin (= highest good). The chief or a supreme good; *specifically* (*Ethics*) the highest good as the end or determining principle in an ethical system.

summum genus /ˌsʊməm ˈdʒɛnəs/, /ˌsʌməm ˈdʒiːnəs/ *noun* plural **summa genera** /ˌsʊmə ˈdʒɛn(ə)rə/, /ˌsʌmə/ L16 Latin (= highest kind). The highest or most comprehensive class in a classification; *specifically* (*Logic*) a genus not considered as a species of a higher genus.

summum jus /ˌsʊməm ˈjuːs/, /ˌsʌməm ˈdʒʌs/ *noun* L16 Latin (= highest law). The utmost rigour of the law, extreme severity.

sumo /ˈsuːməʊ/ *noun* plural **sumos**, same L19 Japanese (*sūmo*). A Japanese form of heavyweight wrestling in which a wrestler wins a bout by forcing his opponent outside a circle or making him touch the ground with any part of the body except the soles of the feet. Also, a sumo wrestler.

sumotori /ˌsuːməʊˈtɔːri/ *noun* L20 Japanese (*sūmotori*, from as preceding + *tori* taking). A sumo wrestler.

sumpsimus /ˈsʌm(p)sɪməs/ *noun* M16 Latin (1st person plural perfect indicative of *sumere* to take). A correct expression taking the place of an incorrect but popular one.

■ Cf. MUMPSIMUS. The expressions usually occur together in contexts contrasting obtuse conservatism with a more enlightened attitude.

sunyata /ˈʃuːnjətaː/, /ˈsuːnjətaː/ *noun* E20 Sanskrit (*śūnyatā* emptiness, from *śūnya* empty, void). *Buddhism* The doctrine that phenomena are devoid of an immutable or determinate intrinsic nature, often regarded as a means of gaining an intuition of ultimate reality.

superficies /ˌsuːpəˈfɪʃiːz/, /ˌsjuːpəˈfɪʃɪiːz/ *noun* plural same M16 Latin (from *super-*

above + *facies* face). **1** M16 *Geometry* A magnitude of two dimensions, having only length and breadth; a surface. **2 a** L16 The outer surface of an object. **b** E17 A surface layer. Now *rare*. **3a** L16–L18 A thing likened to a surface; the outward form or aspect. **b** L16 The outward appearance as distinct from the real nature. **4** M17 Superficial area or extent. **5** M19 *Roman Law* A structure in or on the surface of a piece of land which is so closely connected with it as to form part of it.

suppositum /səˈpɒzɪtəm/ *noun* plural **supposita** /səˈpɒzɪtə/ M17 Medieval Latin (use as noun of neuter singular of *suppositus* past participle of *supponere* to place under). **1** M17 *Metaphysics* A being that subsists by itself, an individual thing or person; occasionally, a being in relation to its attributes. Long *rare* or *obsolete*. **2** M19 *Logic* An assumption.

suppressio veri /səˌprɛʃɪəʊ ˈvɪərʌɪ/ *noun phrase* plural **suppressiones veri** /səˌprɛʃɪˌəʊniːz/ M18 Modern Latin (literally, 'suppression of what is true'). A misrepresentation of the truth by concealing facts which ought to be made known.

■ In use often linked with SUGGESTIO FALSI (at which see quotation).

supra /ˈsuːprə/, /ˈsjuːprə/ *adverb & adjective* E16 Latin. **A** *adverb* **1** E16 Earlier in a book or article; above. Cf. UT SUPRA. **2** L16–L18 In addition, besides. **B** *adjective* L16–L18 Additional, extra.

suprême /syprɛm/, /suːˈprɛm/ *noun* E19 French. A rich cream sauce; a dish of especially chicken breasts cooked in this sauce.

■ Latterly (M20) often Anglicized as *supreme*, as in *chicken supreme*.

supremo /suːˈpriːməʊ/, /suːˈpreɪməʊ/, /sjuːˈpriːməʊ/ *noun* plural **supremos** M20 Spanish ((*generalísimo*) *supremo* supreme general). **1** M20 A supreme leader or ruler. **2** M20 *transferred* A person in overall charge of something.

■ *Supremo* was the nickname given to Earl Mountbatten of Burma during his time as Supreme Allied Commander, South East Asia.

2 1983 *Private Eye* A short list of possible replacements . . . included . . . the ruthless supremo of the Royal Philharmonic Orchestra.

suq variant of SOUK.

sura /ˈsʊərə/ *noun* E17 Arabic (*sūra*, (with definite article) *as-sūra*, probably from Syriac *ṣūrtā* scripture). Any of the sections of the Koran.

■ *Sura* (M17) supplanted the now obsolete form *assura* (incorporating the Arabic definite article, in which the word was first used in English.

surah /ˈsʊərə/, /ˈsjʊərə/ *noun & adjective* L19 French (representing French pronunciation of *Surat* a port in India). (Of) a soft twilled silk fabric.

surbahar /ˈsʊəbəhɑː/ *noun* L19 Bengali (*surbāhār*). A mellow-toned Indian stringed instrument, a bass sitar.

surimono /ˌsʊərɪˈməʊnəʊ/ *noun* plural same L19 Japanese (from *suri* printing + *mono* thing). A print; *specifically* a small Japanese colour print used to convey greetings or to mark a special occasion.

sur place /syr plas/ *adverb phrase* E20 French. **1** E20 At the place in question; on the spot. **2** M20 *Ballet* Without leaving the place where one has been standing.

Sursum corda /ˌsəːsʊ(ə)m ˈkɔːdə/ *noun phrase* M16 Latin (from *sursum* upwards + *corda* plural of *cor* heart). *Christian Church* In Latin Eucharistic liturgies, the words addressed by the celebrant to the congregation at the beginning of the Eucharistic Prayer; in English rites, the corresponding versicle, 'Lift up your hearts'.

surveillant /syrvɛjɑ̃/, /səˈveɪl(ə)nt/ *noun & adjective* (also (feminine) **surveillante** /syrvɛjɑ̃t/, /ˌsəːverˈjɑːnt/) E19 French ((use as noun of) present participle of *surveiller* to watch over, from as *sur-* over + *veiller* to keep watch, from Latin *vigilare*). **A** *noun* **1** E19 A person who exercises surveillance. **2** M19 A teacher on non-teaching duty. **B** *adjective* M19 Exercising surveillance.

■ The corresponding noun *surveillance* (E19) is now fully Anglicized.

sushi /ˈsuːʃi/, /ˈsʊʃi/ *noun* L19 Japanese. A Japanese dish consisting of rolls of cold boiled rice flavoured with vinegar and garnished with raw fish.

1996 *Times* From the earliest records, fish have had a fried deal from chippers and a raw deal from sushi-eaters.

susurrus /sjuːˈsʌrəs/, /suːˈsʌrəs/ *noun* LME Latin (= a whisper, humming, muttering, of imitative origin). **1** Malicious whispering. Only in LME. **2** E19 A low soft whispering or rustling sound.

■ Only in literary use.

sutra /ˈsuːtrə/ *noun* E19 Sanskrit (*sūtra* thread, string, rule). **1** E19 In Sanskrit lit-

417 · **suttee | symposium**

erature, a rule or aphorism, or a set of these, on grammar, or Hindu law or philosophy, expressed with maximum brevity. **2** L19 A Buddhist scripture, usually doctrinal in content. Also, the Jain scriptures.

suttee /sʌˈtiː/, /ˈsʌti/ *noun* (also **sati**) L18 Sanskrit (*satī* faithful wife, feminine of *sat* good). Chiefly *History* **1** L18 A Hindu widow who immolates herself on her husband's funeral pyre. **2** E19 The immolation of a Hindu widow in this way.

suzuribako /səˌzʊərɪˈbɑːkəʊ/ *noun* plural same M20 Japanese (from *suzuri* slab for ink + *hako* box). A box, often of finely-wrought lacquer-work, for holding Japanese writing implements.

s.v. abbreviation of SUB VOCE.

svelte /svɛlt/ *adjective* E19 French (from Italian *svelto*). **1** E19 Slender, willowy. **2** E20 *transferred* Elegant, graceful.

swami /ˈswɑːmi/ *noun* (also **swamy**) L18 Sanskrit (*svāmin*, nominative *svāmī*, master, prince). **1** L18 A Hindu image or temple. **2** E20 A male Hindu religious teacher.

swart gevaar /ˌswart xəˈfɑːr/ *noun phrase* M20 Afrikaans (literally, 'black peril', from Dutch *zwart* black + *gevaar* danger). The threat to the Western way of life and White supremacy in South Africa believed by some to be posed by the Blacks. *South African.*
> **1996** T. Alexander *Unravelling Global Apartheid Die swart gevaar*—the black danger—united the white minority after their savage conflict in the Boer War.

swastika /ˈswɒstɪkə/ *noun* L19 Sanskrit (*svastika* from *svasti* well-being, luck, from *su* good + *asti* being). **1** L19 An ancient symbol in the form of a cross with equal arms with a limb of the same length projecting at right angles from the end of each arm, all in the same direction and (usually) clockwise. **2** M20 This symbol (with clockwise projecting limbs) used as the emblem of the German and other Nazi parties; a HAKENKREUZ. Also, a flag bearing this emblem.

syce /sʌɪs/ *noun* (also **sais**) M17 Persian and Urdu (*sāʾis* from Arabic). In parts of Africa and Asia, and especially in the Indian subcontinent: a groom, a servant who attends to horses, drives carriages, etc.; a chauffeur. Also, an attendant following on foot a mounted rider or a carriage.

sylva /ˈsɪlvə/ *noun* (also **silva**) plural **sylvae** /ˈsɪlviː/, **sylvas** M17 Latin (*silva* a wood, woodland (misspelt *sylva* after synonymous Greek *hulē* wood); in sense 2, after the title (*Silvae*) of Statius' collection of occasional poems). **1** M17 A treatise on forest trees; (a descriptive catalogue of) the trees of a particular region. Cf. FLORA sense 2. **2** M17-L18 A collection of pieces, especially of poems.
> ■ The spelling *sylva* in English treatises on arboriculture is a tribute to the authority of John Evelyn's *Sylva; or a discourse of Forest Trees and the propagation of timber* (1664), which for many years remained the standard English text in its field.

symbiosis /ˌsɪmbɪˈəʊsɪs/, /ˌsɪmbʌɪˈəʊsɪs/ *noun* plural **symbioses** /ˌsɪmbɪˈəʊsiːz/ E17 Modern Latin (from Greek *sumbiōsis* a living together, from *sumbioun* to live together, from *sumbios* (adjective) living together, (noun) companion, partner, from *sym* together + *bios* life). **1** E17 Living together, communal living. *rare.* **2** L19 *Biology* An interaction between two dissimilar organisms living in close physical association; *especially* one in which each benefits the other. **3** E20 *transferred* and *figurative* A relationship or association of mutual advantage between people, organizations, etc.

sympathique /sɛ̃patik/ *adjective* M19 French. Of a thing, a place, etc.: agreeable, to one's taste, suitable. Of a person: likeable, in tune with or responsive to one's personality or moods.
> **1996** *Times Magazine* I answer sometimes indiscreetly, which I tend to do when I find the interviewer intelligent and *sympathique*.

sympathisch /zymˈpaːtɪʃ/ *adjective* E20 German. SYMPATHIQUE.

symposium /sɪmˈpəʊzɪəm/ *noun* plural **symposia** /sɪmˈpəʊzɪə/, **symposiums** L16 Latin (from Greek *sumposion*, from *sumpotēs* fellow-drinker, from *sym-* together + *potēs* drinker). **1** L16 A drinking-party; a convivial meeting, *especially* (*historical*) one held by the ancient Greeks for drinking, conversation, philosophical discussion, etc.; *History* an account of such a meeting or the conversation at it. **2a** L18 A meeting or conference for the discussion of a particular subject; a collection of opinions delivered or a series of articles contributed at such a meeting or conference. **b** L19 A collection of essays or papers on various aspects of a particular subject by a number of contributors.

syncope /ˈsɪŋkəpi/ *noun* LME **Late Latin** (from Greek *sugkopē*, from *sun-* with + *kop-* stem of *koptein* to strike, cut off). **1** LME Fainting; temporary loss of consciousness caused by an insufficient flow of blood to the brain, frequently due to blood loss, shock, long standing, overheating, etc. **2** M16 Shortening of a word by omission of one or more syllables or letters in the middle; a word so shortened. **3** M17–L18 *Music* Syncopation. **4** M17 *generally* A cutting short of something; sudden cessation or interruption. *rare*.

synecdoche /sɪˈnɛkdəki/ *noun* LME **Latin** (from Greek *sunekdokhē*, from *sunekdekhesthai*, literally, 'to take with something else', from *sun-* with + *ekdekhesthai* take, take up). *Grammar* and *Rhetoric* A figure of speech in which a more inclusive term is used for a less inclusive one or vice versa, as a whole for a part or a part for a whole.

   1996 *Country Life* It is a remarkable thing that, now that the very synecdoche of these islands—Land's End and John o'Groats—have come up for sale, no national body . . . appears to be formulating a plan to buy them on behalf of the nation.

synthesis /ˈsɪnθɪsɪs/ *noun* plural **syntheses** /ˈsɪnθɪsiːz/ LME **Latin** (from Greek *sunthesis*, from *suntithenai*, from *sun-* with + *tithenai* to put, place). **I 1** *Grammar* **a** Apposition. Only in LME. **b** E17–E18 The construction of a sentence according to sense, in violation of strict syntax. **II 2** E17 *Logic* and *Philosophy* **a** The action of proceeding in thought from causes to effects, or from laws or principles to their consequences. **3** E18 *Medicine* The joining of divided parts in surgery. Now *rare* or *obsolete*. **4** M18 *Chemistry* Formation of a compound by combination of its elements or constituents. **b** M19 *Physics* Production of white or other compound light by combination of its constituent colours, or of a complex musical sound by combination of its component simple tones. **5** M19 *Linguistics* The tendency of a language to mark categories by inflections rather than by (groups of) distinct words. Also, the process of making compound and derivative words. **6** M19 *generally* The action or an act of putting together parts or elements to make up a complex whole. Also, a complex whole made up of a number of united parts or elements. **III 7** E17 *Roman Antiquities* A loose flowing robe worn at meals and festivities.

   ■ Sense 2 also occurs in specialized uses in Kantian and Hegelian philosophy.

système D /sistɛm de/ *noun phrase* L20 **French** (contraction of *système débrouillard* (or *système débrouiller*), literally, 'resourceful system'). A policy or practice for coping with difficult circumstances.

   ■ Apparently originating in France as a response to conditions during the 1939–45 war, the phrase returned to currency during the French public transport strikes of 1995.

   1995 *Times* The French have a phrase for the survivalist spirit: *Système-D*, which stands for *débrouiller*—manage, sort yourself out, muddle through by making do.

T

taal /tɑ:l/ *noun* (also **Taal**) L19 Dutch (= language, speech, from Middle Dutch *tāle* = Old English *talu* tale). Afrikaans.

■ In colloquial South African English *die* (or *the*) *taal* is often a mildly contemptuous way of referring to Afrikaans.

tabac /taba/ *noun* plural pronounced same E20 French. In French-speaking countries: a tobacconist's shop.

tabbouleh /tə'bu:leɪ/ *noun* M20 Arabic (*tabbūla*). A Syrian and Lebanese salad made with bulgur, parsley, onion, mint, lemon juice, oil, and spices.

tabi /'tɑ:bi/ *noun* plural same **tabis** E17 Japanese. A thick-soled Japanese ankle sock with a separate stall for the big toe.

tabla /'tʌblə/, /'tʌblɑ:/ *noun* M19 Persian and Urdu (*tabla(h)*, Hindustani *tablā* from Arabic *ṭabl*). A pair of small hand drums of unequal size used in Indian music; the smaller of these drums.

tableau /'tabləʊ/, *foreign* /tablo/ *noun* plural **tableaux** /'tabləʊz/, *foreign* /tablo/ L17 French (from Old French *tablel* diminutive of *table* from Latin *tabula* plank, tablet, list). **1** L17 A picture; *figurative* a picturesque presentation or description. **2** L18 A table, a schedule; an official list. **b** M20 *Mathematics* In full *simplex tableau*. A table displaying the constraints in problems of the type soluble by the simplex method. **3 a** E19 A group of people etc. forming a picturesque scene. **b** E19 A TABLEAU VIVANT. **c** M19 *Theatre* A motionless representation of the action at some (especially critical) stage in a play; a stage direction for this. Also (*transferred*), the sudden creation of a striking or dramatic situation. **4** L19 *Cards* The arrangement of the cards as laid out in a game of patience.

tableau vivant /ˌtabləʊ 'vi:vɒ̃/, *foreign* /tablo vivɑ̃/ *noun* plural **tableaux vivants** (pronounced same) E19 French (literally, 'living picture'). A silent and motionless representation of a character, scene, incident, etc., by a person or group of people; *transferred* a picturesque actual scene.

> **1996** *Spectator* But viewed as the sequence of one glittering plastic set after another, . . . and a series of fantastically elaborate, dizzying

tableaux vivants, no one could resist its poisoned brilliant intensity.

table d'hôte /ˌtɑ:b(ə)l 'dəʊt/, *foreign* /tablə dot/ *noun phrase* E17 French (= host's table). Originally, a common table for guests at a hotel or eating-house. Now usually, a meal at a hotel, restaurant, etc., consisting of a set menu at a fixed price.

tablier /'tablieɪ/, *foreign* /tablje/ (*plural same*) *noun* (in sense 1 also (earlier) **tabler** ME Old and Modern French (ultimately from Latin *tabula* plank, tablet, list). **1** ME–L15 A backgammon board or chessboard. Also, backgammon. **2** M19 *History* A part of a woman's dress resembling an apron; the front of a skirt having the form of an apron. **3** L19 *Anthropology* An extension of the labia minora characteristic of Khoisan women.

taboo /tə'bu:/ *adjective & noun* (also **tabu**, (chiefly *New Zealand*) **tapu** /'tɑ:pu:/) L18 Tongan (*tabu*). A *adjective* **1** L18 Set apart for or consecrated to a special use or purpose; forbidden to general use or to a particular person or class of people; sacred; forbidden. **2** E19 *transferred* and *figurative* Especially of a word, topic, or activity: avoided or prohibited, especially by social custom. B *noun* L18 The putting of a person or thing under temporary or permanent prohibition or interdict, especially as a social custom; the fact or condition of being taboo; a customary prohibition or interdict. **2** M19 *transferred* and *figurative* Prohibition or interdiction of the use or practice of anything; ostracism; *specifically* a prohibition of the use of certain words, topics, etc., especially in social conversation.

tabouret /'tabərɛt/, /'tabəreɪ/ *noun* M17 French (diminutive of Old French *tabour* (also *tanbor*, *tamb(o)ur*), apparently of oriental origin; cf. Persian *tabīra*, *tabūrāk* drum). **1** M17 A low backless seat or stool for one person. **2** E20 A small table, especially one used as a stand for houseplants; a bedside table. *United States*.

tabula gratulatoria /ˌtabjʊlə ˌgratjʊlə 'tɔ:rɪə/ *noun* Late Latin (*tabula* list + feminine of *gratulatorius* congratulatory). L20 A list in a FESTSCHRIFT of the people and institutions who have subscribed to the publication.

tabula rasa /ˌtabjʊlə 'rɑːzə/ *noun phrase* Latin (literally, 'scraped tablet'). A tablet from which the writing has been erased, ready to be written on again; a blank tablet; *figurative* a clean slate; a mind having no innate ideas (as in some views of the human mind at birth).

> **1995** J. D. Barrow *Artful Universe* No mind was ever a *tabula rasa*. We enter the world with minds that possess an innate ability to learn.

tac-au-tac /'takəʊtak/ *noun* E20 French (literally, 'clash for clash', from *tac* (imitative)). *Fencing* A parry combined with a riposte.

tacenda /təˈsɛndə/ *noun plural* M19 Latin (plural of *tacendum*, use as noun of neuter of gerundive of *tacere* to be silent). Things to be passed over in silence; matters not to be mentioned or made public, *especially* those of an embarrassing nature.

tacet /'teɪsɛt/, /'tasɪt/ *adverb & noun* E18 Latin (= is silent, from *tacere* to be silent). *Music* **A** *adverb* E18 (A direction:) be silent for a time; pause. **B** *noun* L18 A pause.

tache /taːʃ/, /taʃ/ *noun* ME Old French (*teche*, (also modern) *tache*, ultimately from Frankish = a token). **1 a** ME A spot, a blotch, a blot. *obsolete* except *Scottish.* **b** L19 *Medicine* A blemish on the skin, an organ, etc. Usually with French specifying word. **c** *Art* M20 A dab or dash of colour. **2** *figurative* **a** ME–E17 A moral spot or blemish. **b** E17 An imputation of fault or disgrace; a stain or blot on one's character. *Scottish.* **3** LME A distinctive mark, quality, or habit. *obsolete* except *dialect.*

> **1.c** 1978 G. Greene *Human Factor* The simple precise words, with the single tache of colour reminded Castle of the local background so often to be found in primitive paintings.

taco /'taːkəʊ/, /'takəʊ/ *noun plural* **tacos** M20 Mexican Spanish. A Mexican dish comprising a tortilla or cornmeal pancake rolled or folded and filled with various mixtures, such as seasoned mincemeat, chicken, beans, etc.

taedium vitae /ˌtʌɪdɪəm 'viːtʌɪ/, /ˌtiːdɪəm 'vʌɪtiː/ *noun phrase* M18 Latin (*taedium* weariness, disgust + *vitae* genitive of *vita* life). Weariness of life; extreme ennui or inertia, often as a pathological state with a tendency to suicide.

tae kwon do /ˌtʌɪ kwɒn 'dəʊ/ /ˌteɪ kwɒn 'dəʊ/ *noun phrase* M20 Korean (literally, 'art of hand and foot fighting'). A modern Korean system of unarmed combat developed chiefly in the mid twentieth century, combining elements of KARATE, ancient Korean martial art, and KUNG FU, differing from karate in its wide range of kicking techniques and its emphasis on different methods of breaking objects.

taele variant of TJAELE.

taenia /'tiːnɪə/ *noun* (also **tenia**) plural **taeniae** /'tiːniː/, **taenias** M16 Latin (from Greek *tainia* band, fillet, ribbon). **1** M19 *Architecture* A fillet or band between a Doric architrave and frieze. **2** E18 *Zoology* A tapeworm. Now only as modern Latin genus name. **3** M19 *Greek Antiquities* A headband, ribbon, or fillet. **4** L19 *Anatomy* A ribbon-like structure. Usually with specifying word.

Tafelmusik /'taːfəlmuˌziːk/ *noun* L19 German (literally, 'table music'). **1** L19 *Music* so printed as to enable the same page to be read by two or more people seated on opposite sides of a table. **2** L19 *Music* intended to be performed at a banquet or a convivial meal, especially popular in the eighteenth century.

Tafelwein /'taːfəlvaɪn/ *noun* L20 German (literally, 'table wine'). Ordinary German wine of mediocre quality, suitable for drinking with a meal.

tafia /'tafɪə/ *noun* M18 French (from West Indian creole, alteration of RATAFIA). In the West Indies: a liquor resembling rum distilled from the lower grades of molasses, refuse brown sugar, etc.

tafone /taˈfəʊni/ *noun* plural **tafoni** /taˈfəʊni/ M20 Corsican (dialect *tafóne* hole, hollow). *Geology* A shallow rounded cavity in rock produced by weathering. Usually in *plural.*

tagliarini /taljəˈriːni/ *noun* M19 Italian (*taglierini* plural, from *tagliare* to cut). Pasta made in very narrow strips.

tagliatelle /taljəˈtɛli/ *noun* L19 Italian (from *tagliare* to cut; cf. preceding). Pasta made in narrow strips.

tahina /taːˈhiːnə/ *noun* (also **tahini** /taːˈhiːni/) M20 Modern Greek (*takhini* from Arabic *ṭaḥīnā* from *ṭaḥana* to grind, crush, pulverize). A Middle Eastern paste or sauce made from sesame seeds.

T'ai Chi /tʌɪ 'tʃiː/ *noun* M18 Chinese (*tàijí* (Wade–Giles *t'ai chi*), from *tài* extreme + *jí* limit). **1** M18 In Taoism and Neo-Confucianism, the ultimate point, constituting both source and limit, of the life-force. Also, the symbol representing this.

2 M20 A Chinese martial art and system of callisthenics consisting of sequences of very slow controlled movements, believed to have been devised by a Taoist priest in the Song dynasty (960–1279). In full *T'ai Chi Ch'uan* /'ʧwaːn/ (Chinese *quán* fist).

taiga /'tʌɪgə/ *noun* L19 Russian (*taïga* from Mongolian). The swampy coniferous forest of high northern latitudes, *especially* that between the tundra and steppes of Siberia.

taiglach variant of TEIGLACH.

taihoa /tʌɪ'həʊə/ *interjection* M19 Maori. Wait a bit; by and by; presently. *New Zealand.*

taiko /'tʌɪkəʊ/ *noun* plural same, **taikos** L19 Japanese. A Japanese drum; *specifically* any of a class of barrel-shaped drums.

taille /taːj/, /taj/ *noun* plural pronounced same M16 French (from Old French *taillier* (modern *tailler* from Proto-Romance (medieval Latin *tailliare*) from Latin *talea* rod, twig, cutting). **1** M16 In France, a tax levied on the common people. *obsolete* except *historical*. **2** M17 Cut, shape, form; shape of the bust from the shoulders to the waist; figure, build. **3** M19 *Music* (now *historical*). The register of a tenor or similar voice; an instrument of this register.

taille-douce /tajdus/ *noun* M17 French (= soft cutting, from TAILLE + *douce* soft). Engraving on a metal plate with a graver or burin as opposed to a dry-point or etching needle.

tailleur /tajœr/ *noun* plural pronounced same E20 French (from TAILLE). A woman's tailor-made suit.

> **1982** T. Fitzgibbon *With Love* I pressed the black *tailleur*, bought a gay scarf . . . and went off to look for a job.

taipan /'tʌɪpan/ *noun* M19 Chinese ((Cantonese) *daaihbāan*). Originally, a foreign merchant or businessman in China. Now *especially*, the head of a foreign business in China.

taisch /tʌɪʃ/ *noun* (also **taish**) L18 Gaelic (*taibhse* from Old Irish *taidbse* phantasm). In Scottish folklore, the apparition of a living person who is about to die; *generally* something perceived by second sight.

takamakie /ˌtaːkəmaːkɪ'jɛ/ *noun* (also **takamakiye** and other variants) E20 Japanese. Decorative Japanese lacquer-work done in relief, especially in gold.

takhaar /'takhaː/ *noun* plural **takhare** /'takhaːri/, **takhaars** L19 Afrikaans (from Dutch *tak* branch + *haar* hair). In South Africa: an unkempt, unsophisticated person, especially from a rural area. *colloquial* and *derogatory*.

takht /taːkt/ *noun* L20 Persian (*taḵt*). In Eastern countries: a sofa, a bed.

talak /təˈlaːk/ *noun* (also **talaq**) L18 Arabic (*ṭalaḳ*, from *ṭalaḳat*, *ṭaluḳat* be repudiated). In Islamic law: divorce, especially by the husband's verbal repudiation of his wife in the presence of witnesses.

talaq variant of TALAK.

talaria /təˈlɛːrɪə/ *noun* plural L16 Latin (neuter plural of *talaris* from *talus* ankle). *Roman Mythology* Winged sandals or small wings attached to the ankles of some gods and goddesses, especially Mercury.

talayot /təˈlaːjɒt/ *noun* L19 Catalan (*talaiot* small watch-tower, from Arabic (Muslim Spain) *ṭāliʿāt* plural of *ṭāliʿa* watch-tower). *Archaeology* A Bronze Age stone tower characteristic of the Balearic Islands, usually circular with a large central pillar supporting the roof. Cf. NURAGH.

taleggio /taˈlɛdʒɪəʊ/ *noun* L20 Italian. A rinded semi-soft cheese.

talik /'talɪk/ *noun* M20 Russian (from *tayat'* to melt). *Physical Geography* An area of unfrozen ground surrounded by permafrost.

talio /'talɪəʊ/ *noun* E17 Latin. (A) retaliation.

tallith /'talɪθ/ *noun* E17 Hebrew (rabbinical Hebrew *ṭallīt*, from biblical Hebrew *ṭillel* to cover). The shawl with fringed corners traditionally worn by male Jews at prayer.

talus /'teɪləs/ *noun* plural **taluses** M17 French (of unknown origin). **1** M17 A slope; *specifically* (*Fortification*) the sloping side of a wall or earthwork. **2** M19 *Geology* A scree slope, consisting of material which has fallen from the face of the cliff above. **b** *generally* M19 The slope of a mountain, hill, or iceberg. Now *rare*.

tamagotchi /ˌtaməˈɡɒtʃi/ *noun* (also **Tamagotchi, tamagocchi**) L20 Japanese (= lovable egg). (Proprietary name for) a small, portable electronic device which can be programmed to mimic the demands for food, attention, etc. of a pet bird or animal.

> **1997** *Weekend Telegraph* . . . the record Tamagotchi lifespan is less than a month . . .

tamale /təˈmɑːli/ *noun* L17 Mexican Spanish (*tamal*, plural *tamales*, from Nahuatl *tamalli*). A Mexican dish of seasoned meat and maize flour steamed or baked in maize husks.

tamari /təˈmɑːri/ *noun* L20 Japanese. A Japanese variety of rich wheat-free soy sauce. Also *tamari sauce*.

tamasha /təˈmɑːʃə/ *noun* (also (earlier) **tomasha**) E17 Persian and Urdu (*tamāšā* (for *tamāšī*) walking about for amusement, entertainment, from Arabic *tamāšā* walk about together, from *mašā* walk). **1** E17 In the Indian subcontinent: an entertainment, a show, a spectacle, a public function. **2** L19 A fuss, a commotion. *colloquial*.

> **2** 1981 S. Rushdie *Midnight's Children* Enough of this tamasha! No more of this . . . tomfoolery!

tambour /ˈtambʊə/ *noun* L15 French (Old French *tabour* (also *tanbor*, *tamb(o)ur*), apparently of oriental origin (cf. Persian *tabīra*, *tabūrāk* drum), spelling perhaps influenced by Arabic *ṭunbūr* a kind of lute or lyre). **1** L15 A drum; now *especially* a small drum with a deep tone. **2** E18 *Architecture* **a** The part of a Corinthian or composite capital around which the foliage and volutes are arranged, a bell. **b** E18 Any of the courses forming the shaft of a cylindrical column. **c** E18 A lobby with a ceiling and folding doors serving to obviate draughts, especially in a church porch. **d** E19 A wall of circular plan, as one supporting a dome or surrounded by a colonnade. **3** E18 A projecting part of the main wall of a real tennis or fives court, with a sloping end face. **4 a** A circular frame formed of one hoop fitting inside another, in which fabric is held taut for embroidering. **b** M19 Material embroidered or embroidery done using such a frame. **5** M19 *Military* A small redan defending an entrance or passage. **6** L19 *Medicine* A stretched membrane forming part of an instrument for recording arterial pulsations, respiratory movements, etc., by slight changes in air pressure. **7** M20 A sliding flexible shutter or door on a desk, cabinet, etc., made of strips of wood attached to a canvas backing.

tameletjie /taməˈlɛki/, /taməˈlɛtʃi/ *noun* M19 Afrikaans (perhaps from *tabletje* small cake). In South Africa: (a piece of) hard toffee often containing almonds or pine nuts. Now also, a sweet consisting of a roll of compressed and sweetened dried fruit (also more fully *tameletjie-roll*).

tandoor /ˈtandʊə/, /tanˈdʊə/ *noun* (also (in sense 1 usually) **tandour**, and other variants) M17 French or Urdu (sense 1 from French *tandour* from Turkish *tandır* variant of Persian, Arabic *tannūr* oven, furnace; sense 2 from Urdu, *tandūr*, Persian *tanūr* ultimately from Arabic *tannūr*). **1** M17 A square table with a brazier under it, round which people sit for warmth in cold weather in Persia, Turkey, and adjacent countries. Now *rare*. **2** M19 A clay oven of a kind used originally in northern India and Pakistan; a shop selling food cooked in such an oven.

tandoori /tanˈdʊəri/ *adjective & noun* M20 Persian and Urdu (from *tandūr*: see preceding). **A** *adjective* M20 Designating, pertaining to, or using a style of Indian cooking based on the use of a tandoor. **B** *noun* M20 Tandoori cooking or food; a tandoori dish.

tandour see TANDOOR.

tanga /ˈtaŋgə/ *noun* E20 Portuguese (ultimately of Bantu origin). **1** E20 *Anthropology* A triangular loincloth or pubic covering worn by indigenous peoples in tropical America. **2** L20 A very brief bikini made of triangles of material connected by thin ties.

tango /ˈtaŋgəʊ/ *noun & verb* plural **tangos**, (now *rare*) **tangoes** L19 American Spanish (perhaps of African origin). **A** *noun* **1** L19 A kind of Spanish flamenco dance. **2** L19 A syncopated ballroom dance in 2/4 or 4/4 time, of South American origin, characterized by slow gliding movements and abrupt pauses; a piece of music intended to accompany or in the rhythm of this dance. **B** *intransitive verb* E20 Dance a tango.

tanka /ˈtaŋkə/ *noun* plural same, **tankas** L19 Japanese (from *tan* short + *ka* song). A Japanese poem consisting of thirty-one syllables in five lines, the first and third lines having five and the others seven syllables. Also called *uta*.

tant bien que mal /tɑ̃ bjɛ̃ kə mal/ *adverb phrase* M19 French (literally, 'as well as badly'). With indifferent success; moderately well, after a fashion.

tant mieux /tɑ̃ mjø/ *interjection* M18 French. So much the better. Cf. TANT PIS.

1972 M. Kaye *Lively Game of Death* If your boss can pin his death on somebody, *tant mieux*.

tanto /ˈtantəʊ/ *adverb* L19 Italian (from Latin *tantum* so much). *Music* So, so much.

■ Used to modify adjectives from Italian, as in *allegro non tanto*, meaning 'fast, but not too much so'.

tant pis /tã pi/ *interjection* L18 French. So much the worse. Cf. TANT MIEUX.
1995 D. Lodge *Therapy* I hope that Laurence and I can go back to our chaste, companionable relationship, but if we can't, *tant pis*.

tantra /ˈtantrə/ *noun* (also **Tantra**) L18 Sanskrit (= loom, warp, groundwork, system, doctrine). **1** L18 Any of a class of Hindu or Buddhist religious writings of the late medieval period, often of a magical, erotic, or mystical nature. **2** M20 Tantrism.

tapa /ˈtapa/ *noun* M20 Spanish (literally, 'cover, lid'). In a bar or café, especially one providing Spanish food, a savoury snack to accompany a glass of wine.
■ Usually in plural *tapas*, which is often treated as singular (see quotation).
1996 *Spectator* Tapas in the town square—*tortilla de patatas, rinones al Jerez, caracoles, albondigas, calamares*—was followed by a swim and a siesta.

tapadero /tapəˈdɛːrəʊ/ *noun* plural **tapaderos** (also **tapadera** /tapəˈdɛːrə/) M19 Spanish (= cover, lid, stopper, from *tapar* to stop up, cover). In the western United States: a leather hood for the front of a stirrup, to hold and protect the foot especially when riding through brush.

tapénade /tapenad/ *noun* M20 French (from Provençal *tapeno*). A Provençal dish, usually served as an hors d'oeuvre, made mainly from black olives, capers, and anchovies.

tapette /tapɛt/ *noun & adjective* M20 French ((slang) = pederast, homosexual, from *taper* hit, tap). **A** *noun* M20 Plural pronounced same. A passive male homosexual; an effeminate man. **B** *adjective* M20 Of a man: effeminate; like a *tapette*.
B 1978 J. Sherwood *Limericks of Lachasse* My mother . . . wondered if you were perhaps *tapette*, but my brothers assured her that . . . you were perfectly masculine.

tapia /ˈtapɪə/ *noun* M18 Spanish (= mudwall). Clay or mud puddled, compressed, and dried, as a material for walls.

tapis /ˈtapi/ *noun* plural same L15 French (= carpet, tablecloth, from Old French *tapiz* (also modern *tapis*) from late Latin *tapetium* from Greek *tapētion* diminutive of *tapēs, tapēt-* tapestry). A cloth, especially of a decorated oriental fabric of a type exported to France in the eighteenth century, worked with artistic designs in colours, used as a curtain, tablecloth, etc.; a tapestry.
■ The phrase (*up*)*on the tapis* (L17) meaning 'under discussion (*or* consideration)', is a partial translation of French *sur le tapis* (literally, 'on the tablecloth'), also occasionally used in English.

tapis vert /tapi vɛr/ *noun phrase* plural **tapis verts** (pronounced same) M20 French (= green carpet). A long strip of grass.
1965 (Mrs) L. B. Johnson *White House Diary* He wants to . . . preserve the tapis vert, the long green ribbon that stretches . . . from the Capitol to the Lincoln Memorial.

tapotement /təˈpəʊtm(ə)nt/ *noun* L19 French (from *tapoter* to tap). A percussive technique used in massage, consisting of hacking, clapping, and pounding actions.

taqueria /ˌtɑːkəˈriːə/ *noun* L20 Mexican Spanish (from TACO). In the United States: a restaurant specializing in tacos.

taqueté /takte/ *adjective* M20 French (from *taquet* wedge, peg). *Ballet* Designating or pertaining to a style of point-work accentuated with quick precise short steps.

tarantella /ˌtar(ə)nˈtɛlə/ *noun* (also **tarantelle** /ˌtar(ə)nˈtɛl/) L18 Italian (diminutive of *Taranto* (Latin *Tarentum*), a town in southern Italy: popularly associated with *tarantola* tarantula). **1** L18 A rapid whirling South Italian dance popular since the fifteenth century, when it was supposed to be the most effective cure for tarantism. **2** M19 A piece of music for such a dance or composed in its triplet rhythm, with abrupt transitions from the major to the minor.

tarboosh /tɑːˈbuːʃ/ *noun* (also **tarbush**) E18 Arabic ((Egyptian) *ṭarbūš* from Ottoman Turkish *terpōş*, Turkish *tarbuş* from Persian *sarpūš*, from *sar* head + *pūš* cover). A cap similar to a fez, usually of red felt with a tassel at the top, worn by Muslim men either alone or as part of a turban.

targa /ˈtɑːgə/ *adjective & noun* L20 Italian (= plate, shield; the name of a model of Porsche motor car (introduced in 1965) with a detachable hood (see below), probably after the *Targa Florio* (= Florio Shield), a motor time-trial held annually in Sicily). **A** *adjective* L20 Designating a type of detachable roof hood or panelling on a convertible sports car, *especially* one which when removed leaves a central roll-bar for passenger safety. **B** *noun* L20 A car having this feature.

tarkashi /taːˈkaʃiː/ *noun* L19 Urdu ((and Persian) *tār-kašī*, literally, 'wire-drawing'). Especially in the Indian subcontinent: the craft of inlaying wood with brass wire; the artefacts so produced.

tarot /ˈtarəʊ/ *noun* L16 French (from Italian *tarocchi* plural of *tarocco*, of unknown origin). **1** L16 In *singular* or *plural* Any of various games played with a pack of tarot cards (see sense 2). **2** L19 Any of a pack of 78 playing-cards having five suits, the last of which is a set of permanent trumps, first used in Italy in the fifteenth century and now also used for fortune-telling. Also, any of the trump cards in such a pack. Also *tarot card*.

tarsia /ˈtaːsɪə/ *noun* L17 Italian. INTARSIA.

tartine /taːˈtiːn/ *noun* E19 French (from *tarte* tart). A slice of (usually toasted) bread spread with butter or jam.

tasajo /təˈsaːhəʊ/, *foreign* /taˈsaxo/ *noun* L18 Spanish (= slice of dried meat, of unknown origin). Buffalo meat cut into strips and dried in the sun.

■ Chiefly North American. The synonymous *tasso* is perhaps a derivation from *tasajo*, but cf. Louisiana French *tasseau* (jerked beef).

tastevin /tastəvɛ̃/ *noun* plural pronounced same M20 French (*tastevin*, *tâtevin* wine-taster). A small shallow (especially silver) cup for tasting wines, of a type used in France. Also (**Tastevin**), a member of a French order or guild of wine-tasters.

tasto /ˈtastəʊ/ *noun* plural **tastos** M18 Italian (= touch, key). *Music* A key of a piano or other keyboard instrument; the fingerboard of a stringed instrument.

tatami /təˈtaːmi/ *noun* E17 Japanese. **1** E17 A rush-covered straw mat forming the standard floor-covering in Japan. Also *tatami mat*. **2** E20 A standard unit in room measurement in Japan, approximately 1.83 by 0.91 metres.

tathata /tatəˈtaː/, /taθəˈtaː/ *noun* M20 Pali (*tathatā* true state of things, from *tathā* in

that manner, so). *Buddhism* The ultimate nature of all things, as expressed in phenomena but inexpressible in language.

tâtonnement /tatɔnmã/ *noun* plural pronounced same M19 French (from *tâtonner* feel one's way, proceed cautiously). Experimentation, tentative procedure; an instance of this.

tau /tɔː/, /taʊ/ *noun* (also **taw**) ME Greek (from Hebrew *tāw* final letter of Hebrew alphabet). **1** ME The nineteenth (originally the final) letter (T, τ) of the Greek alphabet, corresponding in form to the letter T. **2** ME A T-shaped mark, sign, or object; *specifically* (a) the sign of the cross as made with the hand; (b) (more fully *tau cross*) a cross in which the transverse piece surmounts the upright piece (also called *St Anthony's cross*); (c) An ANKH; (d) A T-shaped pastoral staff. (more fully *tau-staff*) **3** M20 *Particle Physics* Frequently written τ. **a** A meson that decays into three pions, now identified as a kaon. **b** L20 An unstable heavy charged lepton. Also *tau lepton*, *tau particle*.

taula /ˈtaʊlə/ *noun* L19 Catalan (from Latin *tabula* table). *Archaeology* A megalithic Bronze Age structure found on Minorca, consisting of two slabs forming a T-shaped column, frequently enclosed by a horseshoe-shaped wall.

taupe /təʊp/ *noun & adjective* E20 French (from Latin *talpa* mole). (Of) a brownish shade of grey resembling the colour of moleskin.

taverna /təˈvəːnə/ *noun* E20 Modern Greek (from Latin *taberna* tavern). A Greek eating-house.

taxe de séjour /taks də seʒur/ *noun phrase* plural **taxes de séjour** (pronounced same) E20 French (literally, 'tax of visit'). In France and French-speaking countries: a tax imposed on visitors to spas or tourist resorts.

tazia /taˈziːə/ *noun* E19 Arabic (*ta'ziya* consolation, mourning). *Islam* **1** E19 A representation, often made of paper and elaborately decorated, of the tomb of Husain (grandson of Muhammad) carried in procession during Muharram. **2** L19 A play commemorating the suffering and death of Husain, performed especially on the anniversary of the event each year.

tazza /ˈtatsə/ *noun* plural **tazze** /ˈtatseɪ/, **tazzas** E19 Italian (from Arabic *ṭasa*). A shallow ornamental wine-cup or vase, *especially* one mounted on a foot.

tchin /tʃɪn/ *noun* (also **chin**) M19 Russian (*chin* = rank). Rank; person or persons of quality.

tchotchke variant of TSATSKE.

te /teɪ/ *noun* L19 Chinese (*dé* virtue (Wade–Giles *te*)). (In Taoism) the essence of Tao inherent in all beings; (in Confucianism and in extended use) moral virtue.

tecbir variant of TEKBIR.

tedesco /te'desko/ *noun & adjective* plural **tedeschi** /te'deski/ E19 Italian (= German, from medieval Latin *theodiscus*, ultimately from Germanic base of *Dutch*). (An instance of) German influence in Italian art or literature; showing such influence.

Te Deum /ti: 'di:əm/, /teɪ 'deɪəm/ *noun phrase* OE Latin. **1** OE An ancient Latin hymn of praise beginning *Te deum laudamus* 'We praise you, O God', sung as an expression of thanksgiving on special occasions, and sung or recited regularly at Roman Catholic matins and (in translation) at Anglican matins. **2** L17 A recital of this; any (public) expression of thanksgiving or exultation. **3** M19 A musical setting of this hymn.

teepee variant of TEPEE.

tefillin /tiːˈfɪliːn/ *noun plural* E17 Aramaic (*těpillīn* prayers). Jewish phylacteries; the texts inscribed on these.

tegula /ˈtɛɡjʊlə/ *noun* plural **tegulae** /ˈtɛɡjʊliː/ E19 Latin (= tile, from *tegere* to cover). **1** E19 *Entomology* A small scalelike sclerite covering the base of the forewing in the orders Lepidoptera, Hymenoptera, Diptera, etc. **2** L19 *Archaeology* A flat rooftile, used especially in Roman roofs. Cf. IMBREX.

teiglach /ˈteɪɡləx/ *noun plural* (also **taiglach** and other variants) E20 Yiddish (*teiglekh* plural of *teigl* dough pellet, from *teig* dough, ultimately from Old High German *teic* from Germanic from Indo-European base meaning 'smear, knead'). A Jewish confection made of pellets of dough boiled in honey.

tekbir /ˈtɛkbɪə/ *noun* (also **tecbir**) E18 Arabic (*tekbīr*, colloquial pronunciation of *takbīr* to proclaim the greatness of, from base also of *kabīr* great, *'akbar* greater, greatest). A cry of *Allāhu 'akbar* 'Allah is most great', uttered by Muslims.

tekke /ˈtɛkeɪ/ *noun* M17 Turkish (*tekke*, Arabic *takiyya*, Persian *takya* place of repose, pillow, abode of a dervish or fakir, per-

haps ultimately from Arabic *ittaka'a* to lean on). A monastery of dervishes, especially in Ottoman Turkey.

telamon /ˈtɛləmən/, /ˈtɛləmaʊn/ *noun* plural **telamones** /tɛləˈmaʊniːz/ E17 Latin (*telamones* (plural) from Greek *telamōnes* plural of *Telamōn* Telamon, a mythical hero). *Architecture* A male figure used as a pillar to support an entablature or other structure.

■ The female equivalent is a *caryatid*.

téléphérique /teleferik/ *noun* (also **teleferic** /tɛlɪˈfɛrɪk/, **téléférique** /teleferik/ (*plural same*), **telepherique**, /ˌtɛlɪfɛ'riːk/) plural pronounced same E20 French (Italian *teleferica*, from Greek *tēle-* far + *pherein* to carry). A cableway.

telos /ˈtɛlɒs/ *noun* plural **teloi** /ˈtɛlɔɪ/ M16 Greek (= end). **1** M16 FINIS sense 1. *rare*. **2** L19 End, purpose, (an) ultimate object or aim.

> **2** 1995 *Spectator* The *telos* of society became increasing amounts of health, wealth and happiness.

tel quel /tɛl 'kɛl/ *adjective phrase* L19 French. Just as it is; without improvement or modification.

temblor /tɛm'blɔ:/ *noun* L19 American Spanish. An earthquake. *South-western United States.*

temenos /ˈtɛmənɒs/ *noun* plural **temene** /ˈtɛməni/ E19 Greek (from stem of *temnein* to cut off, sever). Chiefly *Archaeology* A piece of ground surrounding or adjacent to a temple; a sacred enclosure or precinct.

temmoku /ˈtɛməʊkuː/ *noun* (also **tenmoku** /ˈtɛnməʊkuː/) L19 Japanese (from Chinese *tiān mù* eye of heaven). A type of Chinese porcelain or stoneware with lustrous black or dark brown glaze; the glaze used on such porcelain or stoneware.

témoignage /temwaɲaʒ/ *noun* M20 French (from *témoigner* to bear witness). Testimony, witness; *especially* testimony regarding the character or beliefs of a person.

tempeh /ˈtɛmpeɪ/ *noun* M20 Indonesian (*tempe*). An Indonesian dish made by deep-frying fermented soya beans.

tempera /ˈtɛmp(ə)rə/ *noun* M19 Italian (in *pingere a tempera* paint in distemper). A method of painting using especially an emulsion e.g. of pigment with egg, especially as a fine art technique on canvas.

Also, the emulsion etc. used in this method.

tempête /tɛm'pɛt/, *foreign* /tɑ̃pɛt/ *noun* L19 French. A country dance popular in England in the late nineteenth century; a piece of music for this dance.

tempi plural of TEMPO.

tempietto /ˌtɛmpɪ'ɛtəʊ/ *noun* plural **tempietti** /ˌtɛmpɪ'ɛti/ L19 Italian (literally, 'little temple'). A small usually circular building resembling a miniature temple.

tempo /'tɛmpəʊ/ *noun* plural **tempi** /'tɛmpi/, **tempos** M17 Italian (from Latin *tempus* time). **1** M17 The timing of an attack in fencing so that one's opponent is within reach. *rare.* **2** L17 *Music* Relative speed or rate of movement; pace; time; *specifically* the (especially characteristic) speed at which music for a dance etc. is or should be played. **3** L19 The rate of motion or activity (*of* someone or something).

tempo giusto /ˌtɛmpəʊ 'dʒuːstəʊ/ *noun phrase* M18 Italian (literally, 'strict time'). The speed at which a particular style of music is or should be played.

temporale /ˌtɛmpə'rɑːl/ *noun* M19 Spanish (*temporal* storm, spell of rainy weather). A weather condition on the Pacific coast of Central America consisting of strong south-west winds bringing heavy rain.

tempo rubato /ˌtɛmpəʊ rʊ'bɑːtəʊ/ *noun phrase* L18 Italian (literally, 'stolen time'). Cf. RUBATO.

temps /tɑ̃/ *noun* plural same L19 French (literally, 'time'). *Ballet* **1** L19 A movement in which there is no transfer of weight from one foot to the other. **2** E20 A movement forming one part of a step.

temps perdu /tɑ̃ pɛrdy/ *noun phrase* M20 French (literally, 'time lost'). The past, contemplated with nostalgia and a sense of irretrievability. Cf. RECHERCHE DU TEMPS PERDU.

tempura /'tɛmpʊrə/ *noun* E20 Japanese (probably from Portuguese *têmpero* seasoning). A Japanese dish consisting of shellfish or whitefish and often vegetables, fried in batter.

temura /ˌtəmʊ'rɑː/ *noun* (also **temurah**) E20 Hebrew (*těmūrāh* exchange). A cabbalistic method of interpreting the Hebrew scriptures by the systematic replacement of the letters of a word with other letters.

tendenz /tɛn'dɛnts/ *noun* L19 German (from English *tendence* or French *tendance*). Drift or aim of a story; purpose of a novel, etc.

Tendenzroman /tɛn'dɛntsrəˌmɑːn/ *noun* M19 German (TENDENZ + *Roman* novel). A novel with a purpose; a ROMAN À THÈSE.
    1975 *Listener* Humphrey House, the eminent Dickens critic, said that it [sc. *Oliver Twist*] was the closest thing to a *tendenzroman* that Dicken ever wrote . . .

tendido /ten'dido/ *noun* plural **tendidos** /ten'didos/ M19 Spanish (past participle of *tender* to stretch). An open tier of seats above the barrera in a bullring.

tendresse /tɑ̃drɛs/ *noun* plural pronounced same LME French (from *tendre* tender). (A) fondness, (an) affection.
    1996 *Bookseller* . . . he played a shy landowner, struggling with the *tendresse* he felt for Ted . . . , his estate manager.

tendu /tɑ̃dy/ *adjective* E20 French (past participle of *tendre* to stretch). *Ballet* Stretched out or held tautly.

tenebroso /tene'broso/ *noun & adjective* L19 Italian (= dark, from Latin *tenebrosus* dark, gloomy). **A** *noun* L19 plural **tenebrosi** /tene'brosi/ A member of a group of early seventeenth-century Italian painters influenced by Caravaggio, whose work is characterized by dramatic contrasts of light and shade. **B** *adjective* L19 Designating the style of this group of painters.

tenendum /tɪ'nɛndəm/ *noun* E17 Latin (literally, 'to be held' neuter gerundive of *tenere* to hold). *Law* (now *historical* except *United States*) That part of a deed defining the tenure by which the things granted are to be held.

tenet /'tɛnɪt/, /'tiːnɛt/ *noun* L16 Latin (literally, 'he holds', 3rd person present singular of *tenere* to hold). A doctrine, dogma, principle, or opinion, in religion, philosophy, politics, etc., held by a group or person. Also *loosely,* any opinion held.
    ■ Since E18 has entirely superseded the earlier form *tenent* (M16).

teniente /te'njente/ *noun* L18 Spanish. A lieutenant.

tenmoku variant of TEMMOKU.

tenore /te'noːre/ *noun* M18 Italian. An adult male voice intermediate between a bass and counter-tenor or alto, a tenor voice; a singer having such a voice.

tenore di forza /te‚noːre di ˈfɔrtsa/ *noun phrase* L19 **Italian** (literally, 'tenor of power'). A singer with a powerful tenor voice.

> **1996** *Spectator* Unnecessarily pleading indulgence for a throat infection, he [sc. José Cura] sounded excitingly like a true *tenore di forza*, a Mario del Monaco for the Millennium, and an Otello in the making.

tenore di grazia /te‚noːre di ˈɡratsia/ *noun phrase* L19 **Italian** (literally, 'tenor of grace'). A light or lyric tenor.

tenore robusto /te‚noːre roˈbusto/ *noun phrase* L19 **Italian** (= strong tenor). A dramatic tenor.

tenorino /tɛnəˈriːnəʊ/ *noun* plural **tenorini** /tɛnəˈriːni/ M19 **Italian** (diminutive of TENORE). A high tenor.

tenue /təny/ *noun* E19 **French** (use as noun of feminine past participle of *tenir* to hold, keep). Deportment, bearing; propriety, manners; dress.

> **1996** *Spectator* . . . there is a photograph, taken in 1914, of Wallis wearing this bizarre *tenue* [sc. monocle and spats] in Michael Bloch's newest book on the Duchess.

tenuto /təˈnuːtəʊ/ *adverb, adjective & noun* M18 **Italian** (past participle of *tenere* to hold). *Music* **A** *adverb & adjective* M18 (A direction:) giving the note its full time-value; sustained(ly). Abbreviated to *ten.* **B** *noun* M20 plural **tenutos, tenuti** /təˈnuːti/ A note or chord played tenuto.

teocalli /tiːəˈkali/ *noun* E17 **American Spanish** (from Nahuatl *teoːkalli*, from *teoːtl* god + *kalli* house). An ancient Mexican or Central American place of worship, usually consisting of a truncated pyramid surmounted by a temple.

tepache /teˈpatʃe/ *noun* E20 **Mexican Spanish** (from Nahuatl *tepiatl*). Any of several Mexican drinks of varying degrees of fermentation, typically made with pineapple, water, and brown sugar.

tepee /ˈtiːpiː/ *noun* (also **teepee, tipi**) M18 **Sioux** (tʰípi dwelling). A conical tent of the North American Indians, made of skins, cloth, canvas, etc., stretched over a frame of poles fastened together at the top. Now also, a structure imitating or resembling such a tent.

tephra /ˈtɛfrə/ *noun* M20 **Greek** (= ashes). *Geology* Dust and rock fragments that have been ejected into the air by a volcanic eruption.

tepidarium /tɛpɪˈdɛːrɪəm/ *noun* plural **tepidaria** /tɛpɪˈdɛːrɪə/ E19 **Latin**. In an an-cient Roman bath, the warm room between the frigidarium and the caldarium. Also, a similar room in a Turkish bath.

teppan-yaki /ˈtɛpanjaki/ *noun* L20 **Japanese** (from *teppan* steel plate + *yaki* fry). A Japanese dish of meat, fish, or both, fried with vegetables on a hot steel plate forming the centre of the dining-table.

tequila /tɛˈkiːlə/ *noun* M19 **Mexican Spanish** (from the name of a town producing the drink). A Mexican spirit made by distilling the fermented sap of a maguey, *Agave tequilana*. Cf. MESCAL sense 2.

terai /təˈrʌɪ/ *noun* L19 **Hindustani** (*tarāī* marshy lowlands). A wide-brimmed felt hat with a double-layered crown and a vent, worn by travellers etc. in subtropical regions. In full **terai hat**.

> ■ The *terai* is a belt of marshy jungle lying between the southern foothills of the Himalayas and the plains.

tercet /ˈtəːsɪt/ *noun* L16 **French** (from Italian *terzetto*, from *terzo* from Latin *tertius* third). *Prosody* A set or group of three lines rhyming together, or bound by double or triple rhyme with the adjacent triplet or triplets.

tercio /ˈtəːsɪəʊ/, /ˈtəːʃɪəʊ/ *noun* plural **tercios** /ˈtəːsɪəʊz/, /ˈtəːʃɪəʊz/ (in sense 1 also **tertio**) L16 **Spanish** (Latin *tertio*, *terzo*, Portuguese *têrço* a regiment, from Latin *tertium* a third). **1** L16 A regiment of Spanish (or, formerly, Italian) infantry, originally of the sixteenth and seventeenth centuries. Also *generally*, a body of infantry forming a main division of an army. **2** M20 Each of the three parts of a bullfight. **b** M20 Each of the three concentric circular areas into which a bullring is considered to be divided.

teriyaki /tɛrɪˈjɑːki/ *noun* M20 **Japanese** (from *teri* gloss, lustre + *yaki* grill). A Japanese dish consisting of fish or meat marinated in soy sauce and grilled.

terminus ad quem /‚təːmməs ad ˈkwɛm/ *noun phrase* M16 **Latin** (= end to which; cf. TERMINUS A QUO). The finishing-point of an argument, policy, period, etc.

terminus ante quem /‚təːmməs antɪ ˈkwɛm/ *noun phrase* M20 **Latin** (= end before which). The finishing-point of a period, the latest possible date for something.

> ■ Also elliptically as *terminus ante*.

terminus a quo /ˌtəːmməs ɑː ˈkwəʊ/ *noun phrase* M16 Latin (= end from which). The starting-point of an argument, policy, period, etc.

■ Like TERMINUS AD QUEM, originally part of the technical vocabulary of the thirteenth-century scholastic philosophers (Albertus Magnus, Thomas Aquinas, etc.).

terminus post quem /ˌtəːmməs pəʊst ˈkwɛm/ *noun phrase* M20 Latin (= end after which). The starting-point of a period, the earliest possible date for something.

■ Also elliptically as *terminus post*.

terra alba /ˌtɛrə ˈalbə/ *noun phrase* E20 Latin (*terra* earth + feminine of *albus* white). Any of various white earths, as pipeclay, kaolin, etc.; now *specifically* white pulverized gypsum used in the manufacture of paper, paint, etc.

terra cognita /ˌtɛrə kɒɡˈniːtə/ *noun phrase* M20 Latin (*terra* land + feminine of *cognitus* known). *figurative* Familiar territory. Opposite of TERRA INCOGNITA.

1962 E. Snow *Other Side of River* My last remark had put them back on terra cognita and it would have been an appropriate moment to leave.

terracotta /ˌtɛrəˈkɒtə/ *noun & adjective* E18 Italian (*terra cotta* baked earth from Latin *terra cocta*). **A** *noun* **1** E18 Hard unglazed usually brownish-red earthenware, used chiefly for decorative tiles and bricks and in modelling. **b** E19 A statuette or figurine made of this substance. **2** L19 The typical brownish-red colour of this earthenware. **B** *attributive* or as *adjective* M19 Of or pertaining to terracotta; made of terracotta; of the typical colour of terracotta, brownish red.

terrae filius /ˌtɛriː ˈfiliəs/, /ˌtɛrʌɪ/ *noun phrase* plural **terrae filii** /ˈfiliʌɪ/, /ˈfiliːi/ L16 Latin (= a son of the earth, a man of unknown origin). **1** L16 A person of doubtful or obscure parentage. **2** M17 At Oxford University, an orator who made a humorous and satirical speech during the Act or public defence of candidates' theses. *obsolete* except *historical*.

terra firma /ˌtɛrə ˈfəːmə/ *noun phrase* M17 Latin (= firm land). **1** M17–E18 A mainland or continent, as distinct from an island etc. **2** L17 The land as distinguished from the sea; dry land; firm ground. **3** L17–E18 Landed estate; land. *jocular* and *colloquial*.

■ Originally (E17) in English as the name of the territories on the Italian mainland which were subject to the State of Venice.

Then later (M18–E19) used for the northern coastland of South America (Colombia), as distinguished from the West Indies. Also, the isthmus of Panama. Sense 2 is now the only one in common use.

terraglia /tɛrˈɑːlɪə/ *noun* M19 Italian (= earthenware, china, from Latin *terra* earth). *Ceramics* An Italian cream-coloured earthenware.

terra ignota /ˌtɛrə ɪɡˈnəʊtə/ *noun phrase* E20 Latin (*terra* land + feminine of *ignotus* unknown). TERRA INCOGNITA.

terra incognita /ˌtɛrə ɪnˈkɒɡnɪtə/, /ɪnkɒɡ ˈniːtə/ *noun phrase* E17 Latin (= unknown land). An unknown or unexplored territory, land, or region; *figurative* an unknown or unexplored area of study, knowledge, or experience.

■ Frequently without article.

1996 *New Scientist* . . . sequencing the yeast genome has revealed a vast *terra incognita*. Biologists have no clue as to the function of 40 per cent of the genes they have identified . . .

terrain vague /tɛrɛ̃ vag/ *noun phrase* E20 French (colloquial, literally 'waste ground'). Wasteland, no man's land; a grey area.

1984 *Sunday Times* Alastair Reid occupies a *terrain vague* between reportage and *belles lettres*.

terra irredenta /ˌtɛrə ɪrɪˈdɛntə/ *noun phrase* M20 Italian. IRREDENTA.

terra rosa /ˌtɛrə ˈrəʊzə/ *noun phrase* L19 Italian (literally, 'rose-coloured earth'). A light red pigment produced from iron oxide and used in oil and watercolour painting; the light red colour of this pigment, similar to Venetian red.

terra rossa /ˌtɛrə ˈrɒsə/ *noun phrase* L19 Italian (*terra* earth + feminine of *rosso* red). *Soil Science* A reddish soil occurring on limestone in Mediterranean climates.

terra sigillata /ˌtɛrə sɪdʒɪˈleɪtə/ *noun phrase* LME Medieval Latin (= sealed earth). **1** LME An astringent bole, of fatty consistency and reddish colour, originally obtained from the Aegean island of Lemnos, formerly valued as a medicine and antidote. *obsolete* except *historical*. **2** M16–E17 Red pigment; ruddle. **3** E20 *Archaeology* A type of fine Roman earthenware, especially Samian ware, made from this or a similar earth from the first century BC to the third century AD in Gaul (also Italy and Germany), usually red in colour and sometimes decorated with stamped figures or patterns. **b** M20 A ware made in imitation of this.

429

terrasse | tessera

terrasse /tɛras/ *noun* plural pronounced same L19 French. Originally in France, a flat, paved area outside a building, especially a café, where people sit to take refreshments.

terrazzo /təˈratsəʊ/ *noun* plural **terrazzos** E20 Italian (= terrace, balcony). A flooring-material made of chips of marble or granite set in concrete and polished to give a smooth surface.

terre-à-terre /tɛratɛr/ *adjective & adverb phrase* E18 French (from Italian *terra a terra* level with the ground). *Ballet* Of a step or manner of dancing: in which the feet remain on or close to the ground. Also *transferred*, without elevation of style; down-to-earth, realistic; pedestrian, unimaginative.

terre cuite /tɛr kɥit/ *noun phrase* M19 French (literally, 'baked (cooked) earth'). TERRACOTTA sense 1.

terre pisée /tɛr pize/ *noun phrase* M20 French (literally, 'beaten earth'). PISÉ.

terreplein /ˈtɛːplɛm/, *foreign* /tɛrplɛ̃/ (*plural same*) *noun* L16 French (*terre-plein* from Italian *terrapieno*, from *terrapienare* to fill with earth, from *terra* earth + *pieno* (from Latin *plenus*) full). **1** L16 Originally, a talus or sloping bank of earth behind a wall or rampart. Later, the surface of a rampart behind a parapet. **2** M17 The level base (above, on, or below the natural surface of the ground) on which a battery of guns is mounted in field fortifications. Also, the natural surface of the ground around a fortification.

terre-verte /tɛːˈvɛːt/ *noun* M17 French (= green earth). A soft green earth of varying composition used as a pigment, *especially* a variety of glauconite obtained from Italy, Cyprus, and France; the colour of this pigment, a soft greyish green.

terribilità /ˌtɛrribiliˈta/ *noun* (also **terribiltà** /ˌterˌribilˈta/) L19 Italian. **1** L19 *Art* Awesomeness or emotional intensity of conception and execution in an artist or work of art; originally a quality attributed to Michelangelo by his contemporaries. **2** M20 *generally* Terrifying or awesome quality.
2 1975 *New Yorker* Fathers have voices, and each voice has a *terribilità* of its own.

terrine /təˈriːn/ *noun* E18 French (= large earthenware pot, feminine of Old French *terrin* earthen, from Latin *terra* earth). **1** E18 Originally a tureen. Now, an earthenware or similar fireproof vessel, especially one in which a terrine or pâté is cooked or sold. **2** E18 Originally, a dish of meat, game, poultry, etc., stewed in a tureen or covered earthenware vessel. Now, a kind of pâté, usually coarse-textured, cooked in and often served from a terrine or earthenware vessel.

terroir /tɛrwar/ *noun* L20 French (= soil). *Viticulture* The soil and other local conditions especially as seen as giving a particular character to a wine.
1995 *Country Life* The world of still wine continues to preach the 'small is beautiful' message, the importance of the individual grower and winemaker, the influence of *terroir* (that elusive mix of soil and climate) and the effect of both on wines.

tertium comparationis /ˈtəːʃɪəm ˌkɒmpareɪʃɪˈəʊnɪs/, /ˈtəːtɪəm ˌkɒmparaːtɪˈəʊnɪs/ *noun phrase* E20 Latin (= the third element in comparison). The factor which links or is the common ground between two elements in comparison.

tertium quid /ˌtəːʃɪəm ˈkwɪd/, /ˌtəːtɪəm ˈkwɪd/ *noun phrase* E18 Late Latin (translation of Greek *triton ti* some third thing). Something indefinite or left undefined related in some way to two definite or known things, but distinct from both.

tertius /ˈtəːʃɪəs/, /ˈtəːtɪəs/ *adjective* E19 Latin (= third). Designating the youngest (in age or standing) of three people, especially pupils, with the same surname.
■ Appended to a surname and used especially in public schools. Cf. PRIMUS adjective 2, SECUNDUS.

tertius gaudens /ˌtəːʃɪəs ˈɡaʊdɛnz/, /ˌtəːtɪəs ˈɡaʊdɛnz/ *noun phrase* L19 Latin (from *tertius* third + *gaudens* present participle of *gaudere* rejoice). A third party benefiting by the conflict or estrangement of two others.
1980 D. Newsome *On Edge of Paradise* It would be better for them both to withdraw to allow the election of a *tertium gaudens*.

terza rima /ˌtɛːtsə ˈriːmə/ *noun phrase* E19 Italian (= third rhyme). *Prosody* A form of iambic verse of Italian origin, consisting of triplets in which the middle line of each triplet rhymes with the first and third of the next.
■ Best known as the metre of Dante's *Divina Commedia*.

terzetto /tɛːtˈsɛtəʊ/, /təːtˈsɛtəʊ/ *noun* plural **terzettos**, **terzetti** /tɛːtˈsɛti/ E18 Italian. *Music* A vocal or (occasionally) instrumental trio.

tessera /ˈtɛs(ə)rə/ *noun* plural **tesserae** /ˈtɛs(ə)riː/ M17 Latin (from Greek, neuter of *tesseres* variant of *tessares* four). **1a** M17 *Classical Antiquities* A small quadrilateral tablet of wood, bone, etc., used as a token, tally, ticket, etc. **b** M17 *figurative* A distinguishing sign or token; a watchword. **2** L18 A small square block of marble, glass, tile, etc., used in mosaic. **3** E20 *Zoology* Each of the plates of an armadillo's carapace.

tessitura /tɛsɪˈtʊərə/ *noun* L19 Italian. *Music* The range within which most tones of a voice part or melody lie.
> **1978** *Early Music* He chose singers for whom the resulting tessituras did not mean any strain.

teste /ˈtɛstiː/, /ˈtɛsteɪ/ *noun & preposition* LME Latin (ablative of *testis* witness, in the formula of authentication *teste meipso*, literally, 'I myself being a witness'). **A** *noun* LME *Law* (now *historical*). Originally, the final clause in a royal writ naming the person who authenticates the monarch's seal. Later, the concluding part of any duly attested writ, giving the date and place of issue. **B** *preposition* M19 On the authority or testimony of (a specified person).

testimonium /tɛstɪˈməʊnɪəm/ *noun* plural **testimonia** /tɛstɪˈməʊnɪə/ L17 Latin (from *testis* witness). **1** L17 A letter testifying to the suitability of a candidate for holy orders; a certificate of proficiency awarded by a university, college, etc. **2** M19 *Law* A concluding part of a document stating the manner of its execution. In full *testimonium clause*.
> *transferred* **1996** *Spectator* The testimonia collected by his widow [sc. R. A. Butler's] . . . are further reminders of the loss.

testo /ˈtɛsto/ *noun* plural **testi** /ˈtɛsti/ E18 Italian (from Latin *textus* text). *Music* **1** E18 The words of a song; the libretto of an opera; the text or theme of a composition. **2** M20 The narrator in an oratorio or similar work.

tête-à-tête /ˌteɪtɑːˈteɪt/, /ˌtɛtaˈtɛt/ *noun, adverb, adjective, & verb* (also **tête à tête**) L17 French (literally, 'head to head'). **A** *noun* **1** L17 A private conversation or interview, especially between two people. **2** M19 An S-shaped sofa, enabling two people to sit face to face. **B** *adverb* E18 Together in private; face to face. **C** *attributive* or as *adjective* E18 Private, confidential; involving or attended by only two people. **D** *intransitive verb* M19 Engage in private conversation (*with* another person).
> **A.1** **1995** D. Lodge *Therapy* I knew I was in for a long, harrowing *tête à tête*.

tête-bêche /tɛtbɛʃ/; /tɛtˈbɛʃ/, /teɪtˈbɛʃ/ *noun & adjective* plural of noun pronounced same L19 French (from *tête* head + *bêche* (reduced from *béchevet*), literally, 'double bed-head'). *Philately* (A postage stamp) printed upside down relative to the next stamp in the same row or column.

tête de boeuf /tɛt də bœf/ *adjective phrase* L19 French (literally, 'ox's head'). *Embroidery* Designating an embroidery stitch involving two slanting stitches in the form of a vee.

tête de cuvée /tɛt də kyve/ *noun phrase* plural **têtes de cuvées** (pronounced same) E20 French (literally, 'head of the vatful'). (Wine from) a vineyard producing the best wine in the locality of a village.

tête de nègre /tɛt də nɛgr/ *adjective phrase* E20 French (literally, 'negro's head'). Of a dark brown colour approaching black.

tête montée /tɛt mõte/ *adjective & noun phrase* E19 French (literally, 'excited head'). **A** *adjective phrase* E19 Overexcited, agitated, worked up. **B** *noun phrase* M19 plural pronounced same. Such a state of mind.

têtes de cuvées plural of TÊTE DE CUVÉE.

textura /tɛkˈstjʊərə/ *noun & adjective* E20 German ((also *Textur*) from Latin *textura* texture). (Designating or pertaining to) any of a group of typefaces first used in the earliest printed books, distinguished by narrow, angular letters and a strong vertical emphasis. Also, (designating or pertaining to) the formal manuscript hand on which these typefaces were based.

textus receptus /ˌtɛkstəs rɪˈsɛptəs/ *noun* plural same M19 Latin (literally, 'received text' (medieval Latin *textus* the Gospel)). A text accepted as authoritative; *specifically* (usually with capital initials) the received text of the Greek New Testament.

thali /ˈtɑːli/ *noun* M20 Hindustani (*thālī* from Sanskrit *sthālī*). A metal platter or flat dish on which Indian food is served; an Indian meal comprising a selection of assorted dishes, especially served on such a platter.

thalweg /ˈtɑːlvɛg/, /ˈθɑːlwɛg/ *noun* (also **talweg**) M19 German (from *thal* (now *Tal*) valley + *Weg* way). *Physical Geography* The line of fastest descent from any point on land; *especially* one connecting the deepest points along a river channel or the lowest points along a valley floor.

1996 M. Anderson *Frontiers* According to the 1913 Protocol of Constantinople, part of the frontier was to follow the *Thalweg*, but the waters of the lower part of the river and the estuary remained Turkish.

theatrum mundi /teɪˌɑːtrəm ˈmʌndʌɪ/, /teɪˌɑːtrəm ˈmʊndiː/ *noun phrase* M16 Latin (literally, 'theatre of the world'). The world thought of as a theatrical presentation of all aspects of human life.

thé complet /te kɔ̃plɛ/ *noun phrase* plural **thés complets** (pronounced same) M20 French (literally, 'complete tea'). A light meal including tea and usually bread and cake. Cf. CAFÉ COMPLET.

thé dansant /te dɑ̃sɑ̃/ *noun phrase* plural **thés dansants** (pronounced same) E19 French (literally, 'dancing tea'). An afternoon entertainment at which there is dancing and tea is served.

1995 *Spectator* One afternoon I went to Hatchett's to observe a typical afternoon *thé dansant*. What a strange thing to have done.

thermae /ˈθəːmiː/ *noun plural* M16 Latin (from Greek *thermai* hot baths). *Classical Antiquities* Public baths.

■ The Anglicized singular form, *therm*, is seldom found.

thesaurus /θɪˈsɔːrəs/ *noun plural* **thesauri** /θɪˈsɔːrʌɪ/, **thesauruses** L16 Latin (from Greek *thesauros* store, treasure, storehouse). **1** L16 A dictionary; an encyclopedia. **b** M19 A collection of words arranged in lists or groups according to sense. Also (chiefly *North American*), a dictionary of synonyms (and occasionally of antonyms). **c** M20 A classified list of terms, especially keywords, in a particular field, for use in indexing and information retrieval. **2** E19 A treasury, especially of a temple.

thesis /ˈθiːsɪs/; *in branch I also* /ˈθɛsɪs/ *noun* plural **theses** /ˈθiːsiːz/ LME Late Latin (from Greek = putting, placing; a proposition, an affirmation, from *the-* base of *tithenai* to put, place). **I 1** LME The syllable or part of a metrical foot that is unstressed (originally, *Classical Prosody*, by lowered pitch or volume); the stressed beat in barred music. Opposed to ARSIS. **II 2** L16 A proposition laid down or stated, *especially* one maintained or put forward as a premise in an argument, or to be proved; a statement, an assertion, a tenet. **3** L16 A dissertation to maintain and prove a thesis or proposition; *especially* one written or submitted by a candidate as the sole or principal requirement for a university degree.

theta /ˈθiːtə/ *noun* LME Greek (*thêta*). **1** LME The eighth letter (Θ, θ) of the Greek alphabet, also used in transliterating other languages. Also, the phonetic symbol θ, used *specifically* in the International Phonetic Alphabet to represent a voiceless dental fricative. **2** M20 *Chemistry* Used *attributively* to designate the temperature of a polymer solution at which it behaves ideally as regards its osmotic pressure (also θ, Θ *temperature*), and the conditions, solvent, etc., associated with such behaviour. **3** M20 *Particle Physics* A meson that decays into two pions, now identified as a kaon. Also *theta meson*, θ-*meson*.

■ In a transferred use of sense 1, *theta* is a sign of doom or a death sentence, in allusion to the custom of using θ as standing for *thanatos* 'death' on the ballots used in voting on a sentence of life or death in ancient Greece.

tholos /ˈθɒlɒs/ *noun* plural **tholoi** /ˈθɒlɔɪ/ (also (especially in sense 1) **tholus** /ˈθəʊləs/, plural **tholi** /ˈθəʊlʌɪ/) M17 Latin (*tholus*, Greek *tholos*). **1** M17 *Architecture* A circular domed building or structure; a dome, a cupola. **2** L19 *Greek Antiquities* A dome-shaped tomb, especially of the Mycenaean period. Also *tholos tomb*.

thorax /ˈθɔːraks/ *noun* plural **thoraces** /ˈθɔːrəsiːz/, **thoraxes** LME Latin (from Greek *thōrax*, *thōrak-*). **1** LME *Anatomy* and *Zoology* The part of the body of a mammal between the neck and the abdomen; the chest. Also, the corresponding part of a bird, reptile, amphibian, or fish. **2** M18 *Zoology* The middle section of the body of an arthropod, between the head and the abdomen. **3** M19 *Greek Antiquities* A breastplate, a cuirass.

threnos /ˈθriːnɒs/ plural **threnoi** /ˈθriːnɔɪ/ E17 Greek (*thrēnos* funeral lament). A song of lamentation; a dirge, a threnody.

■ The Anglicized form *threne* (cf. Old French *thrène*) was in use earlier (LME), but is now chiefly poetic. *Threnos* was the heading given by Shakespeare to the lament in his *Phoenix and Turtle* (1601), but in modern usage it is generally used with reference to a ritualized funeral lamentation as practised in the ancient Mediterranean world.

Thule /ˈθjuːli/, *in sense 2* /θuːl/, /ˈθjuːl/ *noun* OE Latin (*Thule*, *Thyle* from Greek *Thoulē*,

Thulē, of unknown origin; in sense 2, from *Thule* (now Dundas), a settlement in North West Greenland). **1a** OE *Antiquities* A land (variously conjectured to be the Shetland Islands, Iceland, or part of Denmark or Norway) to the north of Britain, believed by ancient Greek and Roman geographers to be the most northerly region in the world. **b** L18 *transferred* ULTIMA THULE. **2** E20 *Archaeology* A prehistoric Eskimo culture. Frequently *attributive*.

Thummim /'θʌmɪm/ *noun* M16 Hebrew (*tummīm* plural of *tōm* completeness). One of the two objects of a now unknown nature worn on the breastplate of a Jewish high priest (Exodus 28:30). Chiefly in *Urim and Thummim*. See URIM.

thuringer /'θjʊərmə/ *noun* M20 German (*Thüringer Wurst* Thuringian sausage). A mildly seasoned summer sausage. Chiefly *United States*.

thyrsus /'θəːsəs/ *noun* plural **thyrsi** /'θəːsʌɪ/, /'θəːsiː/ L16 Latin (from Greek *thursos* stalk of a plant, Bacchic staff). **1** L16 *Classical Antiquities* A staff or spear tipped with an ornament like a pine cone, carried by Bacchus and his followers. **2** E18 *Botany* Any of several forms of inflorescence.

tian /tjã/ *noun* plural pronounced same M20 Provençal (ultimately from Greek *tēganon* frying-pan, saucepan). A large oval earthenware cooking-pot traditionally used in Provence; a dish of finely chopped vegetables cooked in olive oil and then baked *au gratin*.

tiara /tɪ'ɑːrə/ *noun* M16 Latin (from Greek, partly through Italian). **1** M16 *History* Any of various head-dresses formerly worn in (the region of) ancient Persia. **2** M17 A richly ornamental three-crowned diadem formerly worn by popes; *figurative* the office of pope. Also more fully *triple tiara*. **b** L18 *Heraldry* A charge in the form of a triple crown, representing the papal tiara. **3** E18 A woman's (usually jewelled) ornamental coronet or headband worn on the front of the hair. **4** M19 The headdress of the Jewish high priest.

tic /tɪk/ *noun* E19 French (from Italian *ticchio*). **1** E19 (A disorder characterized by) a repeated habitual spasmodic twitching of one or more muscles, especially of the face, largely involuntary and accentuated under stress. **2** E19 TIC DOULOUREUX. **3** L19 A whim, a spontaneous reaction, an idiosyncrasy.

1978 C. P. Snow *Realists* He had the tic, common to many writers, of insisting that the table be kept pernicketily tidy.

tic douloureux /ˌtɪk duːlə'ruː/, /ˌtɪk duːlə 'rəː/ *noun phrase* E19 French (= painful tic). Trigeminal neuralgia, in which spasms of pain are frequently accompanied by twitching of the facial muscles.

tiens /tjɛ̃/ *interjection* M20 French (imperative singular of *tenir* hold). Expressing surprise.

tienta /'tjenta/ *noun* E20 Spanish (literally, 'probe'). In Spain: an occasion at which young bulls are tested for qualities suitable for stud and fighting bulls.

tiercé /'tjəːseɪ/, *foreign* /tjɛrse/ *noun* (also **tierce** /tɪəs/) M20 French (past participle of Old and Modern French *tiercer* to divide into three parts). Especially in France, a method of betting requiring the first three horses in a race to be named in the correct order; a horse-race at which this method prevails.

tierceron /'tɪəsərɒn/ *noun* M19 French (from *tiers* third). *Architecture* A subordinate rib springing from the point of intersection of two main ribs of a vault.

tiers état /tjɛrz eta/ *noun phrase* L18 French. Chiefly *History* The Third Estate, the commons in the National Assembly of pre-Revolutionary France.

tiers monde /tjɛr mõd/ *noun phrase* M20 French. The Third World; the developing nations.

tignon /'tiːjɒn/ *noun* L19 Louisiana French (from French *tigne* dialectal variant of *teigne* moth). A handkerchief worn as a turban head-dress especially in Louisiana by Creole women.

tika /'tiːkɑː/, /'tɪkɑː/ *noun* (also **tikka**) L19 Hindustani (*ṭīkā*, Panjabi *ṭikkā*). Among Hindus, a mark on the forehead (especially of a woman) indicating caste, status, etc., or worn by both sexes as an ornament. Also *tika dot, mark*. Cf. TILAK.

tiki /'tɪki/ *noun* L18 Maori (= image). A large wooden or small ornamental greenstone image of an ancestor or any human figure.

tikka /'tɪkə/, /'tiːkə/ *noun* M20 Panjabi (*ṭikkā*). *Indian Cookery* (A dish of) small pieces of meat or vegetable marinated in spices and cooked on a skewer. Frequently with qualifying word, as *chicken tikka, lamb tikka*.

tilak /'tɪlək/ noun L19 Sanskrit (*tilaka*). Among Hindus, a mark or large symbol on the forehead indicating caste, status, etc., or worn as an ornament. Cf. TIKA.

tilde /'tɪldə/ noun M19 Spanish (from (with metathesis) Latin *titulus* title). **1** M19 The diacritic mark ~ placed in Spanish above *n* to indicate the palatalized sound /ɲ/, as in *señor*; a similar mark in Portuguese above *a* and *o* and in some phonetic transcriptions to indicate nasality. **b** M20 *Palaeography* and *Printing* The diacritic mark ~ placed above a letter to indicate contraction of a following *n* or *m*. **2** M20 This mark used as a symbol in mathematics and logic, chiefly to indicate negation.

tilleul /tɪ'jəːl/ noun & adjective M16 French (from Latin diminutive form from *tilia* linden). **A** noun **1** M16 A lime or linden tree. **2** L19 A pale yellowish-green colour. Also *tilleul green*. **B** adjective L19 Of a pale yellowish-green colour.

tilma /'tɪlmə/ noun M19 Mexican Spanish (from Nahuatl *tílmatli*). A simple cloak or blanket secured with a knot, worn by Mexican Indians.

timbale /tam'bɑːl/, /'tɛbal/ (plural same); in sense 3 /tɪm'bɑːli/ noun E19 French (in sense 3, perhaps from Spanish *timbal*, plural *timbales* of same origin). **1** E19 A drum-shaped dish made of finely minced meat, fish, etc., cooked in a pastry crust or a mould. Also (in full *timbale mould*), the mould or crust in which this dish is served. **2** M19 *Entomology* A membrane which forms part of the sound-producing organ in various insects, as the cicada. **3** E20 In plural Two single-headed drums played as a pair with drumsticks.

tinaja /tɪ'nɑːhə/, foreign /ti'naxa/ noun plural **tinajas** /tɪ'nɑːhəz/, foreign /ti'naxas/ L16 Spanish (augmentative of *tina*, *tino* vat from Latin *tina*). **1** L16 In Spain: a large earthenware jar for holding wine, oil, olives, or salted fish or meat. In parts of Latin America: such a jar used for storing water. **2** M19 In the south-western United States: a rock hollow where water is retained; any temporary or intermittent pool.

t'ing /tɪŋ/ noun M19 Chinese (*tíng* (Wade–Giles *t'ing*)). In China: a small open pavilion used as a place to rest or view the landscape.

tinnitus /tɪ'nʌɪtəs/, /'tɪnɪtəs/ noun M19 Latin (from *tinnire* to ring, tinkle, of imi-tative origin). *Medicine* A sensation of ringing or buzzing in the ears.

tinto /'tɪntəʊ/ noun L16 Spanish (= tinted, dark-coloured). A sweet deep-red wine. Now also *generally*, (a drink of) any red wine.

tiorba /'tjɔrba/ noun plural **tiorbe** /'tjɔrbe/ M20 Italian. A theorbo.

tipi variant of TEPEE.

tirade /tʌɪ'reɪd/, /'tɪreɪd/ noun & verb E19 French (from Italian *tirata* volley, from *tirare* Proto-Romance verb meaning 'draw'). **A** noun **1** E19 A long vehement speech on some subject; a declamation, a denunciation. **2** E19 A passage of a poem dealing with a single theme or idea. **3** L19 *Music* An ornamental run or flourish filling an interval between two notes. **B** intransitive verb L19 Utter or write a tirade; declaim vehemently.

tirage /tɪ'rɑːʒ/, foreign /tiraʒ/ noun plural pronounced same L19 French (= drawing, bringing out, printing, from *tirer* to draw). A reprint of a book from the same type; an impression.

tirailleur /ˌtɪrʌɪ'jəː/ noun L18 French (from *tirailler* to fire in skirmishing order, from *tirer* to draw, shoot). *French History* Any of a body of skirmishers employed in the French Revolutionary War in 1792; a skirmisher, a sharpshooter.

tiramisu /ˌtiːrəmɪ'suː/ noun L20 Italian (from phrase *tira mi sù* pick me up). An Italian dessert consisting of layers of sponge cake soaked in coffee and brandy or liqueur and powdered chocolate and mascarpone cheese.

tiro /'tʌɪrəʊ/ noun (also **tyro**) plural **tiro(e)s** LME Latin (= young soldier, recruit). A beginner, a learner, a novice.

■ The medieval Latin spelling *tyro* is also very widely used.

1996 *Spectator* . . . all the business people . . . , whether tyros or managing directors of major corporations, were unanimous about their value.

tirocinium /ˌtʌɪrəʊ'sɪnɪəm/ noun (also **tyrocinium**) plural **tirocinia** /ˌtʌɪrəʊ'sɪnɪə/ E17 Latin (= first military service on campaign, young troops, from preceding). **1** E17 First experience of anything; training, apprenticeship; *transferred* inexperience, rawness. **2** M17 A band of novices or recruits.

tisane /tɪ'zan/ noun LME Old and Modern French (*tisane*, also formerly *ptisane*, from

Latin (p)*tisana* from Greek *ptisanē* peeled barley, barley-water, related to *ptissein* to peel). A wholesome or medicinal drink or infusion, originally *specifically* made with barley; now (*especially*), a herbal tea.

titre /ˈtʌɪtə/, /ˈtiːtə/ *noun* (also (*United States*) **titer**) M19 French. **1** M19 Originally, the fineness of gold or silver. Now (*Chemistry*), the concentration of a solution as determined by titration; *Medicine* the concentration of an antibody, as measured by the extent to which it can be diluted before ceasing to give a positive reaction with antigen. **2** L19 *Chemistry* The highest temperature reached during controlled crystallization of free insoluble fatty acids in an oil.

titulus /ˈtɪtjʊləs/ *noun* plural **tituli** /ˈtɪtjʊlʌɪ/, /ˈtɪtjʊliː/ E20 Latin. An inscription on or over something; *especially* the inscription on the Cross.

ti-tzu /ˈtiːtsuː/ *noun* L19 Chinese (*dízi* (Wade–Giles *ti-tzu*)). *Music* A Chinese bamboo transverse flute.

tjaele /ˈʧeɪlə/, /ˈʃeɪlə/ *noun* (also **taele** /ˈteɪlə/) E20 Swedish (*tjäle* ice in frozen ground). A frozen surface at the base of the active layer in a periglacial environment, which moves downwards as thaw occurs. Frequently *attributive*.

tjurunga /ʧəˈrʊŋgə/ *noun* (also **churinga** /ʧəˈrɪŋgə/) plural **tjurungas**, same L19 Aranda (*tywerrenge*). Among Australian Aborigines, a sacred object, *specifically* an amulet.

tmesis /ˈtmiːsɪs/ *noun* plural **tmeses** /ˈtmiːsiːz/ M16 Greek (*tmēsis* cutting, from *temnein* to cut). *Grammar* and *Rhetoric* The separation of the elements of a compound word by the interposition of another word or words.

toccata /təˈkɑːtə/ *noun* E18 Italian (use as noun of feminine past participle of *toccare* to touch). *Music* A composition for a keyboard instrument, intended to exhibit the performer's touch and technique and having the air of an improvisation. Also, a fanfare for brass instruments.

toccatina /tɒkəˈtiːnə/ *noun* M18 Italian (diminutive of TOCCATA). *Music* A short toccata.

tochis variant of TOKUS.

tofu /ˈtəʊfuː/ *noun* L18 Japanese (*tōfu* from Chinese *dòufu*, from *dòu* beans + *fǔ* rot, turn sour). A curd made from mashed soya beans; bean curd.

toga /ˈtəʊgə/ *noun* E17 Latin (related to *tegere* to cover). **1** E17 *Roman History* A loose flowing outer garment worn by a Roman citizen, made of a single piece of cloth and covering the whole body apart from the right arm. **2** M18 *transferred* and *figurative* A robe of office; a professional gown; a mantle of responsibility etc.

togidashi /tɒgɪˈdaʃi/ *noun & adjective* L19 Japanese (from *togu* whet, grind + *dasu* produce, let appear). (Made of) a kind of Japanese lacquer in which gold or silver designs are overlaid with several coats of lacquer which are then rubbed and ground down, revealing the underlying design as if floating below the lacquer surface.

togt /tɒxt/ *noun* M19 Afrikaans (from Dutch *tocht* expedition, journey). **1** A trading expedition or venture. Only in M19. **2** E20 In South Africa: casual labour, hired for a specific job.

tohu-bohu /ˌtəʊhuːˈbəʊhuː/ *noun* E17 Hebrew (*tōhū wa-bhōhū* emptiness and desolation (Genesis 1:2)). That which is empty and formless; chaos; utter confusion.

toile /twɑːl/ *noun* LME French. **1 a** LME–L16 Cloth; cloth or canvas used for painting on. *rare*. **b** E20 A painting on canvas. **2** L18 Any of various linen or cotton fabrics. Frequently with French specifying word(s), as in *toile de Jouy*. **3** M20 A reproduction of a fashion garment made up in muslin or other cheap material so that fitting alterations or copies can be made.

> **3** 1982 *Times* I spent seven months of a two-year couture course *just* making toiles for skirts.

toison d'or /twazɔ̃ dɔr/ *noun phrase* E17 French (= fleece of gold). *Heraldry* and *Greek Mythology* The Golden Fleece.

tokamak /ˈtəʊkəmak/ *noun* M20 Russian (from *toroidal'naya kamera s magnitnym polem*, toroidal chamber with magnetic field). *Physics* A toroidal apparatus for producing controlled fusion reactions in a hot plasma, in which the controlling magnetic field is the sum of a toroidal field and a poloidal field.

tokoloshe /tɒkəˈlɒʃi/ *noun* M19 Sesotho (*thokolosi*, *t(h)koloshi*, Xhosa *uThikoloshe*, Zulu *utokoloshe*). In southern African folklore, a mischievous and lascivious hairy manlike creature of short stature.

tokus /ˈtəʊkəs/ *noun* (also **tochis** /ˈtəʊkɪs/, /ˈtɒkɪs/, **tuchis** /ˈtuːkɪs/) E20 Yiddish (*tokhes* from Hebrew *taḥaṭ* beneath). The buttocks; the anus. *North American slang.*

toldo /'toldo/ *noun* plural **toldos** /'toldos/ M19 Spanish (= awning, canopy, penthouse). **1** M19 In Spanish-speaking countries: a canopy. **2** M19 A South American Indian tent, hut, or other simple dwelling.

tole /təʊl/ *noun & adjective* (also **tôle** /to:l/) M20 French (*tôle* sheet iron, from dialect *taule* table, from Latin *tabula* a flat board). **A** *noun* M20 Enamelled or lacquered tin-plated sheet iron used for making decorative metalwork. Also *tôle peinte.* **B** *attributive* or as *adjective* M20 Made of tole.

> **1996** *Country Life* . . . a decorative feature was the use of locally made *tôle peinte*, or japanned tinware, in imitation of porcelain . . . a splendid pair of *tôle* vases on red lacquer, pagoda-shaped stands . . .

tolkach /'tolkatʃ/ *noun* plural **tolkachi** /'tolkatʃi/ M20 Russian (from *tolkat'* to push, jostle). In countries of the former USSR: a person who negotiates difficulties or arranges things, a fixer.

toman /'təʊmən/ *noun* E19 Gaelic (diminutive of *tom* hill). A hillock; a mound, *especially* one formed of glacial moraine.

tomatillo /'tomatɪləʊ/ *noun* L20 Mexican Spanish (= small tomato). A small green berry used in Mexican cooking.

tombac /'tombak/ *noun* E17 French (from Portuguese *tambaca* from Malay *tembaga* copper, brass, perhaps from Sanskrit *tāmraka* copper; cf. TUMBAGA). *Metallurgy* A brittle brass alloy originally produced in Indo-China, containing from 72 to 99 per cent of copper and from 1 to 28 per cent of zinc, used in the east for gongs and bells, and in the west for cheap jewellery etc. Also called *red brass.*

tombarolo /tomba'ro:lo/ *noun* plural **tombaroli** /tomba'ro:li/ L20 Italian (from *tomba* tomb, grave). A grave-robber.

tombola /tom'bəʊlə/ *noun* L19 French (or Italian, from Italian *tombolare* to turn a somersault, tumble). A kind of lottery with tickets usually drawn from a turning drum-shaped container, especially at a fête or fair.

tombolo /'tombələʊ/ *noun* plural **tombolos** L19 Italian (= sand-dune). *Physical Geography* A bar of shingle, sand, etc., joining an island to the mainland.

tomme /tom/ *noun* plural pronounced same M20 French. Any of various cheeses made in Savoy, a region of south-east France.

ton /tɔ̃/ *noun* M18 French (from Latin *tonus* tone). **1** M18 *The* fashion, *the* vogue; fashionableness, style. **2** M18 Fashionable people collectively; the fashionable world. Treated as *singular* or *plural.* Cf. HAUT TON.

> **2 1969** H. Elsna *Abbot's House* A waste, when all the *ton* will flock here for this event.

tonadilla /tona'di(l)ja/, /tɒnə'di:ljə/ *noun* plural **tonadillas** /tɒnə'di(l)jas/, /tɒnə'di:ljəz/ M19 Spanish (diminutive of *tonada* tune, song). A light operatic interlude performed originally as an intermezzo but later independently.

tondi plural of TONDO.

tondino /ton'di:no/ *noun* plural **tondini** /ton'di:ni/ E18 Italian (diminutive of TONDO). **1** E18 *Architecture* A round moulding resembling a ring. **2** L19 *Ceramics* A majolica plate with a wide flat rim and deep centre.

tondo /'tondəʊ/ *noun* plural **tondi** /'tondi/, **tondos** L19 Italian (= a round, a circle, a compass, shortened from *rotondo* round). An easel painting of circular form; a carving in relief within a circular space.

tong /tɒŋ/ *noun* L19 Chinese ((Cantonese) *t'ŏng* (= Mandarin *táng*) hall, meeting place). An association or secret society of Chinese in the United States, originally formed as a benevolent or protective society but frequently associated with underworld criminal activity.

tonneau /'tɒnəʊ/ *noun* plural **tonneaus**, in sense 1 also **tonneaux** L18 French (= barrel, cask). **1** L18 A unit of capacity for French (especially Bordeaux) wine, usually equal to 900 litres (198 gallons). **2** E20 The rounded rear body of some vintage motor-cars (originally with the door at the back); the rear part of a car with front and rear compartments, or of an open car or carriage. Also, a car having a tonneau.

tonnelle /tɒnɛl/ *noun* plural pronounced same M19 French (= tunnel). An arbour.

tontine /tɒn'ti:n/ *noun & adjective* M18 French (from Lorenzo *Tonti* (1630–95), Neapolitan banker, who started such a scheme to raise government loans in France around 1653). **A** *noun* **1** M18 A financial scheme by which subscribers to a loan or common fund each receive an annuity for life, the amount increasing as each dies, till the last survivor enjoys the whole income. Also, the share or right of each subscriber in such a scheme; the subscribers collectively; the fund so established. **2** L19 A scheme for life assurance in which the beneficiaries are those who survive and maintain a policy to the end of a given period. **B** *attributive* or as *adjective* L18 Of, pertaining to, or of the nature of a tontine.

tonto /ˈtɒntəʊ/ *noun & adjective* L20 Spanish. **A** *noun* L20 plural **tontos**. A foolish or stupid person. **B** *adjective* L20 Foolish, crazy; mad.
  ■ Colloquial, originally United States.

topi /ˈtəʊpi/ *noun* (also **topee**) M19 Anglo-Indian (Hindustani *ṭopī* hat). A hat; *specifically* a pith helmet, a sola topi.
  ■ *Sola topi* has no etymological connection with the sun or *solar*, but refers to the tropical Asian swamp plants (Bengali *solā*, Hindustani *śolā*) from the lightweight pith of which the sun-helmets were made.

topinambour /tɒpɪˈnambʊə/ *noun* (also (earlier) **topinambou**) M17 French (*topinambou*, now *topinambour*, from Portuguese *tupinambo(r)* alteration of *tupinamba* (sc. *batata* potato)). The Jerusalem artichoke, *Helianthus tuberosus*.

topos /ˈtɒpɒs/ *noun* plural **topoi** /ˈtɒpɔɪ/ M20 Greek. A traditional theme in a literary composition; a rhetorical or literary formula.

toque /təʊk/ *noun* E16 French (corresponding obscurely to Italian *tocca*, *tocco*, Spanish *toca*, Portuguese *touca* cap, woman's head-dress, of unknown origin). **1** E16 Originally, a type of hat with a full pouched crown and a narrow closely turned-up brim, fashionable amongst both sexes in the sixteenth century. Now, a small hat without a projecting brim, or with a very small or closely turned-up brim. **b** E19 *History* A pad used in hairdressing to give additional height. *rare*. **2** L19 A TUQUE. *Canadian*. **3** M20 A tall white hat with a full pouched crown, worn by chefs.

torana /ˈtɔːrana/ *noun* L19 Sanskrit (*toraṇa* gate, arched portal). In the Indian subcontinent: a sacred Buddhist gateway, consisting of a pair of uprights with one or more (usually three) crosspieces and elaborate carving.

torc variant of TORQUE.

torchère /tɔːˈʃɛː/, *foreign* /tɔrʃɛr/ *noun* plural pronounced same E20 French (from Old and Modern French *torche* torch, from Proto-Romance, from Latin *torqua* variant of *torques* necklace, wreath, from *torquere* to twist). A tall ornamental flat-topped stand for a candlestick.
  1995 *Country Life* A detail of a painting of the interior . . . shows in the niches . . . gilt metal torchères in tripod form . . .

torchon /ˈtɔːʃ(ə)n/, *foreign* /tɔrʃɔ̃/ *noun* M19 French (= duster, dish-cloth, from *torcher* to wipe). A coarse loose-textured kind of bobbin lace with geometrical designs. In full *torchon lace*.

toreador /ˈtɒrɪədɔː/, /ˌtɒrɪəˈdɔː/ *noun* plural **toreadors**, **toreadores** /ˈtɒrɪədɔːrɪz/ E17 Spanish (from *torear* to fight bulls, from TORO). A bullfighter, *especially* one on horseback. Cf. TORERO.

torero /tɒˈrɛːrəʊ/, *foreign* /toˈrero/ *noun* plural **toreros** /tɒˈrɛːrəʊz/, *foreign* /toˈreros/ E18 Spanish (from TORO). A bullfighter, *especially* one on foot. Cf. TOREADOR.

tori plural of TORUS.

torii /ˈtɔːriː/ *noun* plural same E18 Japanese (from *tori* bird + *i* sit, perch). A ceremonial gateway of a Japanese Shinto shrine, with two uprights and two crosspieces.

toril /toˈril/ *noun* plural **toriles** /toˈriles/ L19 Spanish. *Bull-fighting* Any of a series of pens confining the bull before a fight, *especially* the last pen leading to the ring.

toro /ˈtɔːrəʊ/, *foreign* /ˈtoro/ *noun* plural **toros** /ˈtɔːrəʊz/, *foreign* /ˈtoros/ M17 Spanish (from Latin *taurus* bull). A bull used in bullfighting.

torque /tɔːk/ *noun* (also **torc**) M19 French (from Latin *torques* necklace, wreath, from *torquere* to twist). *History* A neck ornament formed from a twisted band of (usually precious) metal, worn especially by the ancient Celts.

torsade /tɔːˈseɪd/ *noun* L19 French (from Latin *tors-* past participial stem of *torquere* to twist). A decorative twisted braid, ribbon, etc., used as trimming; an artificial plait of hair.

Torschlusspanik /ˈtɔːrʃlʊsˌpaːnɪk/ *noun* M20 German (= last-minute panic (literally, 'shut door (or gate) panic')). A sense of alarm or anxiety at the passing of life's opportunities, said to be experienced in middle age.

torso /ˈtɔːsəʊ/ *noun* plural **torsos** L18 Italian (= stalk, stump, trunk of a statue, from as THYRSUS). **1** L18 The trunk of a statue, without or considered independently of head and limbs. Also, the trunk of the human body. **2** E19 *figurative* An incomplete or mutilated thing.

torte /'tɔːt/ *noun* plural **tortes, torten** /'tɔːt(ə)n/ M18 German (*Torte* tart, pastry, cake, from Italian *torta* from late Latin; cf. TOURTE). An elaborate sweet cake or tart.

■ Originally (ME–M16) used in English in the sense of 'round loaf of bread', probably deriving directly from late Latin *torta* meaning 'round loaf or cake', but the sense derived from German is now the only one current. Cf. LINZERTORTE, SACHERTORTE.

tortellini /tɔːtɪ'liːni/ *noun* plural M20 Italian (plural of *tortellino* diminutive of *tortello* small cake, fritter). Small squares of pasta stuffed with meat, cheese, etc., rolled and shaped into rings; an Italian dish consisting largely of this and usually a sauce.

torticollis /tɔːtɪ'kɒlɪs/ *noun* E19 Modern Latin (from Latin *tortus* crooked, twisted + *collum* neck). *Medicine* A condition in which the head is persistently or intermittently turned or twisted to one side.

tortilla /tɔː'tiːjə/ *noun* L17 Spanish (diminutive of *torta* cake, from late Latin; see TORTE). Especially in Mexican cookery, a thin round cake made with either cornmeal or wheat flour and frequently filled with meat, cheese, beans, etc. Also, in Spanish cookery, a thick flat omelette frequently eaten cold in wedges.

tortillon /tɔː'tɪljən/ *noun* L19 French (from *tortiller* to twist, twirl). An instrument with tapered ends used for softening the edges of a drawing and for making tints uniform, a stump.

torus /'tɔːrəs/ *noun* plural **tori** /'tɔːrʌɪ/, **toruses** M16 Latin (= swelling, bolster, round moulding). **1** M16 *Architecture* A large convex moulding, especially at the base of a column. **2** E19 *Botany* The receptacle of a flower. **3** L19 *Zoology* A protuberant part or organ; *Anatomy* a smooth rounded ridge. **4** L19 *Geometry* Originally, a surface or solid generated by the revolution of a circle or other conic about any axis. Now *specifically* a surface or solid generated by the circular motion of a circle about an axis outside itself but lying in its plane; a solid ring of circular cross-section; a body topologically equivalent to this, having one hole in it but not necessarily circular in form or cross-section.

tostada /tɒ'stɑːdə/ *noun* (also **tostado** /tɒ'stɑːdəʊ/, plural **tostados**) M20 Spanish (past participle of *tostar* to toast). A deep-fried cornmeal pancake topped with a seasoned mixture of beans, mincemeat, and vegetables.

Totentanz /'tɔːtəntants/ *noun* plural **Totentänze** /'tɔːtəntentsə/ L18 German (literally, 'death dance'). A representation of Death leading people of all ranks in a dance towards the grave; the Dance of Death. Cf. DANSE MACABRE.

totidem verbis /ˌtɒtɪdɛm 'vəːbiːs/ *adverb phrase* M17 Latin. In so many words.

toties quoties /ˌtɒtɪeɪz 'kwɒtɪeɪz/, /ˌtəʊʃiːz 'kwəʊʃiːz/ *adverb phrase* LME Latin (= so often as often). As often as something happens or occasion demands.

toto /'təʊtəʊ/ *noun* plural **totos** E20 Kiswahili (*mtoto* offspring, child). In East Africa: a child; a baby; a young animal; a young servant.

toto caelo /ˌtəʊtəʊ 'siːləʊ/, /ˈkʌɪləʊ/ *adverb phrase* L17 Latin (literally, 'by the whole heaven'). Entirely, utterly.

tot siens /tɒt 'sɪns/, /tɒt 'siːns/ *interjection & noun* M20 Afrikaans (*tot* (*weer*)*siens* until we meet again, from Dutch *tot* until + *zien* see). In South Africa: (goodbye) until we meet again; an utterance of this.

touché /'tuːʃeɪ/ *interjection* E20 French (past participle of *toucher* to touch). **1** E20 *Fencing* Expressing acknowledgement of a hit by one's opponent. **2** E20 Expressing good-humoured acknowledgement of a valid point or justified accusation made by another person.
> **2** 1981 A. Price *Soldier no More* 'Touché . . . ' he nodded, accepting the rebuke.

toughra variant of TUGHRA.

toujours gai /tuʒur ge/ *adverb* E18 French. Always cheerful, cheerful under all circumstances.

■ Now generally with reference to its use as the slogan of mehitabel the cat in Don Marquis' *archy and mehitabel* (1927).

toujours perdrix /tuʒur pɛrdri/ *adverb* E18 French (literally, 'always partridge'). (Implying that one can have) too much of a good thing.

toupet /'tuːpeɪ/, /'tuːpɪt/, *foreign* /tupɛ/ (*plural same*) *noun* E18 French. A patch of false hair or a small wig to cover a bald spot.

■ Originally, a curl or artificial lock of hair worn on the top of the head, especially as part of a wig, or a wig or natural hair dressed to create such a topknot. Formerly also, a wearer of a toupee or topknot, hence a fashionable person.

tourbillion /tʊəˈbɪljən/ *noun* (also (especially in sense 3) **tourbillon** /tʊəˈbɪlən/, /tʊəˈbrjən/, *foreign* /turbijɔ̃/ (*plural same*)) L15 French (*tourbillon* from Old French *torbeillon*, from Latin *turbellae* bustle, stir, blended with *turbo* whirlwind). **1** L15 A whirlwind, a whirling storm. Now usually *transferred* and *figurative*, a vortex, a whirl; an eddy, a whirlpool. **2** M18 A kind of firework which spins as it rises. **3** L19 *Watchmaking* A revolving carriage in which the escapement is fitted to counteract position errors.

tour de force /ˌtʊə də ˈfɔːs/, *foreign* /turdəfɔrs/ *noun phrase* plural **tours de force** (pronounced same) E19 French. A feat of strength or skill; an impressive achievement or performance.
> **1995** *New Scientist* The book is a *tour de force* by nearly 40 contributing authors . . .

tour d'horizon /tur dɔrizɔ̃/ *noun phrase* plural **tours d'horizon** (pronounced same) M20 French (literally, 'tour of the horizon'). An extensive tour. Chiefly *figurative*, a broad general survey.
> **1995** *Times* His [sc. the Foreign Secretary's] aim, after a *tour d'horizon* of world affairs, was to press against the Opposition the charge of inconsistency and on Europe, abdication.

tour jeté see JETÉ EN TOURNANT.

tourmente /turmɑ̃t/ *noun* plural pronounced same M19 French. A whirling storm or eddy of snow.

tournasin /ˈtʊənəsɪn/ *noun* M19 French (*tournas(s)in*, from *tournas(s)er* to turn pottery on a wheel, from *tourner* to turn). A knife or spatula used to remove partially dried excess slip from decorated pottery.

tournedos /ˈtʊənədəʊ/, *foreign* /turnədo/ *noun* plural same /ˈtʊənədəʊz/, *foreign* /turnədo/ L19 French (from *tourner* to turn + *dos* back). A small round thick cut from a fillet of beef, with a surrounding strip of fat.

tournee /ˈtʊəni/ *noun* (also **tournée** /turne/ (*plural same*)) L18 French. A round, a circuit, a tour.

tournette /tʊəˈnɛt/ *noun* E20 French (from *tourner* to turn). *Archaeology* A rotating disc resembling a simple form of potter's wheel.

tourniquet /ˈtʊənɪkeɪ/ *noun* L17 French (perhaps alteration of Old French *tournicle* variant of *tounicle*, *tunicle* coat of mail, tunicle, by association with *tourner* to turn). A device for stopping or slowing the flow of blood through an artery by compression.

tournure /ˈtʊənjʊə/, *foreign* /turnyr/ (*plural same*) *noun* M18 French (from Old French *torneure* from popular Latin *tornatura*, from Latin *tornare* to turn). **1** M18 Graceful manner or bearing, deportment. **2** E19 The turning of a phrase, mode of expression. *rare*. **3** E19 The contour or shape of a limb etc. **4** M19 *History* A bustle. Also, a kind of corset.

tours de force, **tours d'horizon** plurals of TOUR DE FORCE, TOUR D'HORIZON.

tourte /tʊət/, *foreign* /turt/ (*plural same*) *noun* M17 French (from late Latin *torta* round loaf, cake; cf. TORTE). A pie, a tart, a flan.

tourtière /tʊətɪˈɛ/, *foreign* /turtjɛr/ (*plural same*) *noun* M20 French (from as TOURTE). **1** M20 A kind of meat pie traditionally eaten at Christmas in Canada. **2** M20 A tin or round baking-sheet for tarts and pies.

tout /tu/ *adjective, noun, & adverb* E18 French. All, everything; quite entirely.
■ Mainly in following phrases, but see also LE TOUT, which may be shortened to *tout*, with similar high society connotations, as in *tout Paris* 'all Paris'.
> **1996** *Country Life Tout* Shropshire (and Hereford) were invited to drinks . . .

tout au contraire /tut o kɔ̃trɛr/ *adverb phrase* E18 French. Quite the contrary. Cf. AU CONTRAIRE.

tout compris /tu kɔ̃pri/ *adverb & adjective phrase* E18 French. All included, inclusive.

tout court /tu kur/ *adverb phrase* E18 French. In short, simply, without qualification or addition.
> **1995** *Spectator* Unlike Selwyn Lloyd, who was sacked *tout court*, Mr Lamont was offered another job . . .

tout de suite /tu də sɥit/ *adverb phrase* E18 French. At once, immediately.
> **1995** D. Lodge *Therapy* I chipped in *tout de suite* to say that I quite understood.

tout ensemble /tut ɑ̃sɑ̃mbl/ *noun phrase* E18 French (from TOUT + ENSEMBLE *noun*). (The parts of) a thing viewed as a whole.

■ Independent use of *ensemble* in this sense is slightly later (M18).

tout le monde /tu lə mɔ̃d/ *noun phrase* E18 French. All the world, everyone.

tout Paris see under LE TOUT, TOUT.

tou ts'ai /tuː 'tsʌɪ/ *noun & adjective* M20 Chinese (*dǒucǎi* (Wade–Giles *tou ts'ai*), literally, 'contrasting colours'). *Ceramics* (Designating) a kind of Chinese porcelain delicately decorated with a blue underglaze overlaid with coloured enamels, developed in the reign of Ch'êng Hua (1465–87); (of or designating) this style of decoration.

tout seul /tu sœl/ *adverb phrase* E18 French. Quite alone, on one's own.

tout simple /tu sɛ̃pl/ *adverb phrase* M20 French. Quite simply, just that.

tovarish /tɒˈvɑːrɪʃ/ *noun* (also **tovarich**) E20 Russian (*tovarishch* from Turkic, perhaps Tatar). In the former USSR: comrade.

■ Frequently as a form of address.

tracasserie /trəˈkas(ə)ri/ *noun* M17 French (from *tracasser* to bustle, worry oneself). A state of disturbance or annoyance; a fuss; a petty quarrel.

■ Usually in plural.

tragédie lyrique /traʒedi lirik/ *noun phrase* plural **tragédies lyriques** (pronounced same) E20 French (literally, 'lyric tragedy'). A type of serious French opera of the seventeenth and eighteenth centuries making use of tragic mythological or epic subjects; an example of this. Cf. OPERA SERIA.

tragédienne /trəˌʤiːdɪˈɛn/ *noun* M19 French (feminine of *tragédien* tragedian). A tragic actress.

tragédies lyriques plural of TRAGÉDIE LYRIQUE.

tragedietta /trəˌʤiːdɪˈɛtə/ *noun* L19 Italian (from *tragedia* tragedy). A slight or short tragedy; a dramatic sketch of tragic character.

trahison des clercs /traizɔ̃ de klɛr/ *noun phrase* M20 French (literally, 'the treachery of the clerks'). A compromise of intellectual integrity or betrayal of standards by writers, artists, and thinkers.

■ From *La Trahison des Clercs*, the title of a work by Julien Benda (1927).

1978 *Listener* Look, they say, terrorism is a phenomenon of our times. Let us . . .

acknowledge that a diplomat . . . is fair game . . . I find this *trahison des clercs*.

traineau /trɛrˈnəʊ/, *foreign* /trɛno/ *noun* plural **traineaux** (pronounced same) M17 French (*traîneau*, from *traîner*). A sledge, a sleigh, *especially* one drawn by one or more horses or dogs over snow or ice.

trait d'union /trɛ dynjɔ̃/ *noun phrase* plural **traits d'union** (pronounced same) E20 French (literally, 'hyphen'). A link or point of contact between or amongst otherwise unconnected characteristics or parties.

traiteur /trɛtœr/ *noun* plural pronounced same M18 French (from *traiter* to treat, supply with food for money). Originally, (a person running) a restaurant in France, Italy, etc., supplying or sending out meals to order. Now, a caterer; (a person who runs) a delicatessen selling prepared meals.

traits d'union plural of TRAIT D'UNION.

trajet /ˈtraʤɪt/, *foreign* /traʒɛ/ (*plural same*) *noun* M18 French (from Latin *trajectus* place for crossing). **1** M18 A crossing, a passage. **2** M19 The course of a nerve, blood-vessel, etc. *rare*.

tramontana /ˌtramɒnˈtɑːnə/ *adjective & noun* ME Italian (*tramontana* north wind, polestar, *tramontani* dwellers beyond the mountains, from Latin *transmontanus*, from *trans-* across + *mons*, *mont-* mount). **A** *noun* **1** ME–M17 The polestar (originally so called because visible beyond the Alps from Italy); *figurative* a guiding star. **2** L16 A person living or originating from beyond the mountains, especially the Alps as seen from Italy; (especially from the Italian point of view) a foreigner. **3** E17 In the Mediterranean and especially in Italy, the north wind (as coming from beyond the Alps). More widely, a cold wind from across a mountain range. **B** *adjective* **1** L16 Living, situated, or originating from beyond the mountains, especially the Alps as seen from Italy. Also (especially from the Italian point of view), foreign; barbarous. **2** E18 Of wind: coming across or from beyond the mountains (especially the Alps).

tranche /trɑːnʃ/, /trɑ̃ːʃ/ *noun* plural pronounced same or /trɑːnʃɪz/ L15 Old and Modern French (from *trancher* to cut, ultimately from Latin *truncare*). **1** L15 A cutting, a cut; a piece cut off, a slice. **2** M20 Chiefly *Economics* A portion of something, especially of income; an instalment of a loan; a block of shares or of government stock.

2 1995 *Spectator* The initial tranche of applications has been remarkably evenly spread.

tranche de vie /ˌtrɑːnʃ də ˈviː/ *noun phrase* M20 French (literally, 'slice of life'). A representation of daily life, especially in literature or painting.

tranchet /ˈtrɑːnʃɪt/, *foreign* /trɑ̃ʃɛ/ (*plural same*) *noun* M19 French (from *trancher* to cut: cf. TRANCHE). **1** A cobbler's knife. Only in M19. **2** L19 *Archaeology* A chisel-shaped flint implement of some mesolithic and neolithic cultures.

tranchette /trɑːnˈʃɛt/ *noun* L20 French (from as TRANCHE). *Economics* A small tranche; *especially* a limited issue of government stocks.

tranquillo /tranˈkwɪləʊ/ *adverb, adjective, & noun* M19 Italian (from Latin *tranquillus*). *Music* **A** *adverb & adjective* M19 (A direction:) in a tranquil style or tempo; tranquil(ly). **B** *noun* M19 plural **tranquillos, tranquilli** /tranˈkwɪli/. A movement or piece in a tranquil style or tempo.

transire /tranˈzʌɪə/, /trɑːnˈzʌɪə/, /tranˈsʌɪə/, /tranˈzʌɪri/ *noun* L16 Latin (= to go across). *Law* A customs permit for the passage of goods.

trapezium /trəˈpiːzɪəm/ *noun* plural **trapezia** /trəˈpiːzɪə/, **trapeziums** L16 Late Latin (from Greek *trapezion* from *trapeza* table). **1** *Geometry* **a** L16 Any quadrilateral that is not a parallelogram. Now *rare*. **b** L17 A quadrilateral having one pair of opposite sides parallel. **c** L18 An irregular quadrilateral having neither pair of opposite sides parallel, a trapezoid. Now chiefly *North American*. **2** M19 *Anatomy* and *Zoology* The first distal carpal bone of the wrist; the corresponding bone in other mammals. Also *trapezium bone*. **3** M19 *Astronomy* An asterism in the form of a trapezium; *specifically* the multiple star θ Orionis in the Great Nebula of Orion.

trapiche /traˈpitʃe/ *noun* M17 American Spanish (from Latin *trapetum* oil-press). A sugar cane mill.

trapunto /trəˈpʊntəʊ/, /trəˈpʌntəʊ/ *noun* E20 Italian (use as noun of past participle of *trapungere* to embroider). A kind of quilting in which the design is padded by pulling or cutting the threads of the underlying fabric to insert stuffing.

attributive **1977** A. Jeffs *Creative Crafts* Trapunto quilting lends itself particularly well to pictorial use because of its interesting three-dimensional effect.

trascinando /traʃɪˈnandəʊ/ *adverb & adjective* L19 Italian (present participle of *trascinare* to drag, pull). *Music* RALLENTANDO *adverb & adjective*.

trasformismo /ˌtrasforˈmizmo/ *noun* E20 Italian (from *trasformare* to change, transform). In Italy: a system of shifting political alliances to form a stable administration or a workable policy.

trauma /ˈtrɔːmə/, /ˈtraʊmə/ *noun* plural **traumas, traumata** /ˈtrɔːmətə/, /ˈtraʊmətə/ L17 Greek (= wound). **1** L17 *Medicine* Originally, physical wound. Now, external or internal injury; a state or condition resulting from this, e.g. shock. **2** L19 *Psychoanalysis* and *Psychiatry* A psychic injury, especially one caused by emotional shock; a state or condition resulting from this. **3** L20 *generally* Distress; (a) disturbance.

travaux préparatoires /travo prɛparatwar/ *noun phrase plural* M20 French (literally, 'preparatory works'). *Law* Drafts, records of discussions, etc., relating to legislation or a treaty under consideration.

travers /travɛr/, /ˈtravəs/ *noun* plural same L19 French (*pied de travers* foot askew, from *travers* breadth, irregularity, from *traverser* to traverse). *Horsemanship* A movement in which a horse walks parallel to a wall with its head and neck facing forward and its hindquarters curved out from the wall.

traverso /traˈvəːsəʊ/ *noun* plural **traversos** E19 Italian. *Music* A transverse flute.

travois /traˈvɔɪ/ *noun* plural same /traˈvɔɪz/ M19 North American French (alteration of French *travail*). A traditional North American Indian vehicle consisting of two joined poles pulled by a horse etc.

trebuchet /ˈtrɛbjʊʃɛt/, /ˈtrɛbəʃɛt/, *foreign* /trebyʃɛ/ (*plural same*) *noun* (also **trebucket** /ˈtriːbʌkɪt/, /ˈtrɛbʌkɪt/) ME Old and Modern French (*trébuchet* (medieval Latin *trebuchetum, trabuchetum*), from *trébucher* to overturn, overthrow, stumble, fall, ultimately from *tra-, tres-* (from Latin *trans-* expressing displacement) + *buc* trunk (of the body), bulk, from Frankish *būk* belly). **1** ME *History* A medieval military machine used in siege warfare for hurling heavy stones and other missiles. **2** M16 A small delicately poised balance or pair of scales. **3** M17 *History* A ducking-stool.

trecento /treɪˈtʃɛntəʊ/ *noun* M19 Italian (= three hundred). The fourteenth century as a period of Italian art, architecture, literature, etc.; the style of the art etc. of this period.

tre corde /ˌtreɪ ˈkɔːdeɪ/ *adverb & adjective phrase* M20 Italian (= three strings). (A direction in music for the piano:) with release of the soft pedal; (to be) played with such release. Cf. UNA CORDA.

trefa /ˈtreɪfə/ *noun & adjective* (also **trifa** /ˈtrʌɪfə/, **tref** /treɪf/, and other variants) M19 Hebrew (*ṭĕrēpāh* flesh of an animal torn or mauled, from *ṭārap* to tear, rend). **A** *noun* M19 Meat forbidden to Jews because of coming from an animal not slaughtered according to Jewish law; *generally* any food that is not kosher. **B** *attributive* or as *adjective* M19 Of food: not prepared according to Jewish law, forbidden to Jews, not kosher.

> **B** 1966 H. Kemelman *Saturday the Rabbi went Hungry* When a utensil becomes tref, the way you cleanse it is to bury it in the earth.

treff /trɛf/ *noun* M20 German (*Treff* meeting(-place), *Treffpunkt* rendezvous, from *treffen* to meet, strike). In espionage, a secret meeting or meeting-place, especially for the transfer of goods or information. *slang.*

treillage /ˈtreɪlɪdʒ/ *noun* L17 French (from Old French *treille* from Latin *trichila* arbour, bower). A trellis; trellis-work.

> *attributive* 1996 *Country Life* The treillage obelisks are engulfed and obscured by climbers and hedges . . .

trek /trɛk/ *noun* M19 Afrikaans (from Dutch *trekken* to pull). **1** M19 Travel by ox-wagon; a journey, especially an organized migration or expedition, made in this way; a stage of such a journey. *South African*, chiefly *historical*. **2** L19 *generally* A long and arduous journey or expedition, *especially* one made on foot or by inconvenient means.

tremblement /ˈtrɛmb(ə)lm(ə)nt/, *in sense 3 foreign* /trɑ̃bləmɑ̃/ (*plural same*) *noun* L17 French. **1** L17 A tremor; the act of trembling. **2** L17 A cause of trembling; a terror. *rare.* **3** L19 *Music* A trill.

trembleuse /trɛmˈbləːz/ *noun* M19 French (feminine of *trembleur* trembler). A cup having a saucer with a well into which it fits. More fully *trembleuse cup.*

tremendum /trɪˈmɛndəm/ *noun* E20 Latin (neuter of *tremendus* fearful, terrible, from *tremere* to tremble). Elliptical form of MYSTERIUM TREMENDUM.

tremie /ˈtrɛmi/ *noun* E20 French (*trémie* from Old French *tremuie* (mill-)hopper, from Latin *trimodia* a three-peck measure, from *tri-* three + *modius* peck). *Engineering* A movable metal tube, widening at its upper end into a large hopper, for depositing concrete under water.

tremolando /trɛməˈlandəʊ/ *noun, adverb, & adjective* M19 Italian (present participle of *tremolare* to tremble). *Music* **A** *noun* M19 plural **tremolandos, tremolandi** /trɛməˈlandi/ A TREMOLO senses 1, 2a. **B** *adverb & adjective* M19 (A direction:) with tremolo.

tremolant /ˈtrɛm(ə)l(ə)nt/ *noun* M19 German (from Italian *tremolante* tremulant). A TREMOLO sense 2a.

tremolo /ˈtrɛm(ə)ləʊ/ *noun, adjective, & adverb* M18 Italian (from Latin *tremulus* from *tremere* to tremble). *Music* **A** *noun* plural **tremolos** **1** M18 A tremulous or vibrating effect produced on musical instruments or in singing by rapid reiteration of a single note (especially on a stringed instrument) or rapid alternation between two notes. Cf. VIBRATO. **2a** M19 A mechanical device fitted in an organ to produce such an effect; a tremulant. Also *tremolo stop.* **b** M20 A device, especially a lever, fitted to an electric guitar to produce a similar effect (also *tremolo arm*); an electrical device of similar effect in an amplifier etc. **B** *adjective & adverb* L19 (A musical direction:) with tremolo.

trente-et-quarante /trɑ̃tɛkarɑ̃t/, /trɑ̃t eɪkaˈrɑ̃t/ *noun* L17 French (literally, 'thirty-and-forty'). = ROUGE-ET-NOIR.

très /trɛ/, /treɪ/ *adverb* E19 French. Very.

> ■ Colloquial, usually with reference to a fashionable or modishly superior quality.

triage /ˈtrɪɑːʒ/, *in senses* A.2 *and* B *also* /trɪˈɑːʒ/, *foreign* /trijaʒ/ *noun & verb* E18 Old and Modern French (from *trier* to sort out). **A** *noun* **1** E18 The action of sorting samples of a commodity according to quality. **2** M20 *Medicine* The assignment of degrees of urgency of need in order to decide the order of treatment of a large number of injured or ill patients. **b** L20 *generally* Prioritization. **B** *transitive & intransitive verb* L20 Assign a degree of urgency of need to (a casualty); separate out by triage.

2 1995 *Times Magazine* With so many girls arriving every week, only the strongest are put up for adoption, and the orphanages are forced to practise a sort of triage.

tribade /ˈtrɪbəd/ *noun* E17 French (or its source Latin *tribas, tribad-* from Greek *tribas*, from *tribein* to rub). A lesbian.

triclinium /trʌɪˈklɪnɪəm/, /trʌɪˈklʌɪnɪəm/ *noun* plural **triclinia** /trʌɪˈklɪnɪə/ M17 Latin (from Greek *triklinion* diminutive of *triklinos* dining-room with three couches, from *tri-* combining form of *treis* three + *klinē* couch, bed). *Roman Antiquities* A couch, running round three sides of a table, on which to recline at meals. Also, a dining-room.

tricorne /ˈtrʌɪkɔːn/ *adjective & noun* (also **tricorn**) M18 French (*tricorne* or Latin *tricornis* three-horned, from *tri-* combining form of *tris* three + *cornu* horn). **A** *noun* **1** M18 An imaginary creature with three horns. **2** L19 A hat with the brim turned up on three sides. **B** *adjective* M19 Having three horns; (of a cocked hat) having the brim turned up on three sides.

tricot /ˈtrɪkəʊ/, /ˈtriːkəʊ/ *noun* L18 French (from *tricoter* to knit). A fine warp knitted fabric made of a natural or man-made fibre, produced in any of various designs.

tricoteuse /trikɔtøz/ *noun* plural pronounced same M19 French (from *tricoter* knit). **1** M19 *History* A woman who, during the French Revolution, sat and knitted at meetings of the Convention or at executions by guillotine. **2** M20 A small table with a gallery used for sewing.

2 1996 *Country Life* Until about that date [1848], the term *tricoteuse* would presumably not have been popular in France for a lady's tray-top worktable. Marie Antoinette had had one, but after that, the word would have been painful to Royalists.

tric-trac /triktrak/ *noun* L17 French (from the clicking sound made by the pieces in the playing of the game). Chiefly *History* A form of backgammon.

triduo /ˈtrɪdjʊəʊ/, /ˈtrʌɪdjʊəʊ/ *noun* plural **triduos** M19 Italian and Spanish (from Latin TRIDUUM). *Roman Catholic Church* A three days' prayer or festal celebration.

triduum /ˈtrɪdjʊəm/, /ˈtrʌɪdjʊəm/ *noun* E18 Latin (use as noun of adjective (sc. *spatium* space), from *tri-* combining form of *tres* three + *dies* day). A period of three days; *especially* (*Roman Catholic Church*) the last three days of Lent.

triennium /trʌɪˈɛnɪəm/ *noun* plural **trienniums, triennia** /trʌɪˈɛnɪə/ M19 Latin (from *tri-* combining form of *tres* three + *annus* year). A space or period of three years.

trifa variant of TREFA.

triforium /trʌɪˈfɔːrɪəm/ *noun* plural **triforia** /trʌɪˈfɔːrɪə/ E18 (Anglo-)Latin (of unknown origin). *Architecture* A gallery or arcade above the arches at the sides of the nave, choir, and sometimes transepts of some large churches, originally *specifically* of Canterbury Cathedral.

Trinkhalle /ˈtrɪŋkˌhalə/ *noun* L19 German (literally, 'drinking-hall'). In German-speaking countries: a place at a spa where medicinal water is dispensed for drinking; a pump room. Also, an establishment at which alcoholic drink is served.

trio /ˈtriːəʊ/ *noun* E18 Italian (from Latin *tres, tria* three, after DUO). **1** *Music* **a** E18 A composition for three voices or instruments. Also, a group or company of three performers. **b** M19 The central section of a minuet, scherzo, or march, frequently in a different key and style from the preceding and following main division. **2** L18 A group or set of three things or people.

tripot /tripo/ *noun* plural pronounced same M19 French. In France: a gaming-house, a gambling-den.

tripotage /tripotaʒ/ *noun* L18 French. Underhand dealings, intrigue.

triptyque /trɪpˈtiːk/, *foreign* /triptik/ (*plural same*) E20 French. A customs permit (originally in three sections) serving as a passport for a motor vehicle.

triquetra /trʌɪˈkwɛtrə/, /trʌɪˈkwiːtrə/ *noun* plural **triquetrae** /trʌɪˈkwɛtriː/, **triquetras** L16 Latin (feminine of *triquetrus* three-cornered). Originally, a triangle. Now *specifically* a symmetrical triangular ornament formed of three interlaced arcs or lobes.

triste /triːst/ *adjective* (originally Anglicized as **trist**) LME Old and Modern French (from Latin *tristis* sad). **1** LME Feeling or expressing sorrow; sad, melancholy; causing sorrow, lamentable. **2** M18 Not lively or cheerful; dull, dreary.

2 1996 *Country Life* When the photographs and descriptions are truly breath-taking . . . , I get the particulars. As my purchasing power is nil, this may seem a triste activity.

tristesse /trɪ'stɛs/ *noun* LME Old French (*tristesce* (modern *tristesse*) from Latin *tristitia*, from *tristis* sad). Sadness, sorrow; melancholy.

tristeza /trɪ'steɪzə/ *noun* E20 Portuguese (and Spanish) literally, 'sadness', cognate with preceding). **1** E20 *Veterinary Medicine* In South America: Texas fever of cattle. Now *rare*. **2** M20 *Agriculture* A viral disease affecting some citrus plants, causing yellowing of the leaves, stunting, and death.

triumvir /trʌɪ'ʌmvə/ *noun* plural **triumvirs, triumviri** /trʌɪ'ʌmvɪrʌɪ/ LME Latin (from *triumviri* plural, back-form from *trium virorum* genitive plural of *tres viri* three men). **1** LME *Roman History* Each of three public officers forming a committee overseeing any of the administrative departments. Also *specifically*, each member of the first or second triumvirate. **2** E17 *transferred* In *plural* Any group of three persons or things in a joint position of power or authority.

trivia /'trɪvɪə/ *noun plural* E20 Modern Latin (plural of TRIVIUM, influenced in sense by *trivial*). Trivialities, trifles; *specifically* unimportant factual information (as used in the game of Trivial Pursuit).
> **1996** *Times* But the message is surely universal: lift your eyes to the hills, to the greater questions, away from the trivia that clutter our frantic modern lives.

trivium /'trɪvɪəm/ *noun* E19 Latin (= place where three ways meet, from *tri-* combining form of *tres* three + *via* way). *History* In the Middle Ages, the lower division of a university course of study, comprising grammar, rhetoric, and logic. Cf. QUADRIVIUM.

trochilus /'trɒkɪləs/ *noun* M16 Latin (apparently from Greek *trokhilos*, from *trekhein* to run). *Architecture* A SCOTIA.

Trockenbeerenauslese /'trɒkənbeːrən,aʊslɛːzə/ *noun* (also **trockenbeerenauslese**) plural **Trockenbeerenauslesen** /'trɒkənbeːrən,aʊslɛːzən/, **Trockenbeerenausleses** M20 German (from *trocken* dry + as BEERENAUSLESE). A sweet white wine of superior quality made (especially in Germany) from selected individual grapes picked later than the general harvest and affected by noble rot.

troika /'trɔɪkə/ *noun* M19 Russian (*troĭka*, from *troe* a set of three). **1** M19 A Russian vehicle drawn by three horses abreast; the team of horses for such a vehicle. **2** M20 A group of three people or things

working together, especially in an administrative or managerial capacity.
> **2 1996** *Spectator* . . . the terrible troika of Steven Spielberg, Jeffrey Katzenberg and David Geffen announced they were setting up a billion dollar entertainment company . . .

trombenik /'trɒmb(ə)nɪk/ *noun* M20 Yiddish (from *tromba* trumpet, horn + noun suffix *-nik* person connected with (something)). A boaster, a bragger; an idle or dissolute person. *United States slang*.

trompe l'oeil /trɔ̃p lœj/ *noun phrase* plural **trompe l'oeils** (pronounced same) L19 French (literally, 'deceives the eye'). Deception of the eye; (an) optical illusion; *especially* a painting or object intended to give an illusion of reality.
> **1995** *Times Magazine* Barnes's most recent favourite downstairs cloakroom was a trompe l'oeil potting shed: 'I painted three of the walls as glasshouse walls, with views to the garden beyond, and a brick wall on the fourth wall with shelves covered in garden equipment, such as gloves and watering cans.'

tronc /trɒŋk/ *noun* E20 French (= collecting box). In a hotel or restaurant, a common fund into which tips and service charges are paid for distribution to the staff.
> *attributive* **1981** *Times* The money was massaged by managements and distributed on their behalf to staff . . . or paid into an independent tronc fund.

troppo /'trɒpəʊ/ *adverb* E20 Italian. *Music* (In directions:) too much.
> ■ Especially in adverb phrase *ma non troppo* 'but not too much'.

trotteur /trɒtə:/ *noun* E20 French (from as next). *History* An ankle-length skirt, usually flared at the back for ease of walking.

trottoir /'trɒtwɑː/; *foreign* /trɔtwar/ (*plural* same) *noun* L18 French (from *trotter* to trot). Especially in France and French-speaking countries: a pavement.

troubadour /'truːbədɔː/ *noun* E18 French (from Provençal *trobador* (= Old French *troveor*), from *trobar* (= Old French *trover*) to find, compose in verse, invent, ultimate origin unknown; cf. TROUVÈRE. **1** E18 *History* Any of a class of French medieval lyric poets composing and singing in Provençal especially on the themes of chivalry and courtly love, living in southern France, eastern Spain, and northern Italy between the eleventh and thirteenth centuries. **2** E19 A person who composes or sings verses.

■ The northern French equivalent of the *troubadour* was the TROUVÈRE.

trousseau /ˈtruːsəʊ/ *noun* plural **trousseaus, trousseaux** /ˈtruːsəʊz/ M19 French (from Old French *troussel* diminutive of *trousse* truss). The clothes etc. collected by a bride in preparation for her marriage.

■ Originally (ME) in the sense of 'a bundle or package', later 'a bunch', but long rare or obsolete with this meaning. Old French *troussel* in this sense was also represented in English as *trussell* (LME only).

trouvaille /truvɑj/ *noun* plural pronounced same M19 French (from *trouver* to find). A lucky find; a windfall.
1996 *Spectator* It is not only the curious *trouvailles* that make this travel book a special pleasure.

trouvère /truːˈvɛː/, *foreign* /truvɛr/ (*plural same*) *noun* (also **trouveur** /truːˈvəː/, *foreign* /truvœr/ (*plural same*)) L18 French (Old French (*trovere* (modern *trouvère, trouveur*) from *troveor,* from *trover* (modern *trouver* to find) to compose in verse, invent, find, ultimate origin unknown; cf. TROUBADOUR). *History* Any of a class of French medieval epic poets composing especially *chansons de geste* and fabliaux, living in northern France between the eleventh and fourteenth centuries.

truite au bleu /trᵿit o blø/ *noun phrase* M20 French (literally, 'trout in the blue'). A dish consisting of trout cooked with vinegar, which turns the fish blue.

■ Also earlier (E20) as *truite bleue* /trᵿit blø/, literally, 'blue trout'.

trullo /ˈtrʊlloʊ/ *noun* plural **trulli** /ˈtrʊlli/ E20 Italian. In Apulia in southern Italy: a small round house built of stone, with a conical roof.

trumeau /truːˈməʊ/ *noun* plural **trumeaux** /truːˈməʊz/ L19 French (literally, 'calf of the leg'). **1** L19 A pier-glass. Also *trumeau mirror.* **2** L19 *Architecture* A section of wall or a pillar between two openings, *especially* a pillar supporting the middle of the tympanum of a church doorway.

tsaddik /ˈtsadɪk/ *noun* (also **tzaddik**) plural **tsaddikim** /ˈtsadɪkɪm/, **tsaddiks** L19 Hebrew (*ṣaddîq* just, righteous). In Judaism, a man of exemplary righteousness; a Hasidic spiritual leader or sage.

tsar /zɑː/, /tsɑː/ *noun* (also **czar**; also especially in titles) with capital initial) M16 Russian (*tsar'* Old Church Slavonic *cěsarĭ* ultimately representing Latin *Caesar,*

probably through Germanic; the spelling with *cz-* is not Slavonic). **1** *History* (The title of) the former emperor of Russia; (the title of) certain other eastern European rulers. **2** M19 *transferred* A person with great authority or power; a despot.

tsarevich /ˈzɑːrɪvɪtʃ/, /tsɑːˈrjɛɪvɪtʃ/ *noun* (also **czarevich**; also (especially in titles) with capital initial) E18 Russian (from as TSAR + patronymic *-evich*). *History* The eldest son of the former emperor of Russia; the (male) heir of a tsar.

tsarevna /zɑːˈrɛvnə/, /tsɑːˈrɛvnə/ *noun* (also **czarevna**; also (especially in titles) with capital initial) L19 Russian. *History* A daughter of a tsar.

tsarina /zɑːˈriːnə/, /tsɑːˈriːnə/ *noun* (also **czarina**; also (especially in titles) with capital initial) E18 Italian and Spanish (*tzarina (c)zarina,* French *tsarine, czarine,* from German *Zarin, Czarin* feminine of *Zar, Czar*). The wife of a tsar; *History* (the title of) the former empress of Russia.

tsaritsa /zɑːˈrɪtsə/, /tsɑːˈrɪtsə/ *noun* (also **czaritsa**; also (especially in titles) with capital initial) L17 Russian. *History* (The title of) the former empress of Russia.

tsatske /ˈtsɒtskə/ *noun* (also **tchotchke** /ˈtʃɒtʃkə/) M20 Yiddish (from Slavonic: cf. Russian *tsatska*). A trinket; *transferred* a pretty girl or woman. *United States colloquial.*
1977 *New Yorker* ... stocked with a careful selection of New York's best tchotchkes. These include thirteen-inch-long matchbooks.

tsimmes variant of TZIMMES.

tsipouro /ˈtsɪpʊrəʊ/ *noun* M20 Modern Greek. A rough Greek liquor resembling RAKI, sometimes flavoured with mastic gum.

tsitsith /ˈtsɪtsɪt/ *noun* (treated as *singular* or *plural*) (also **tzitzit(h)**) L17 Hebrew (ṣîṣît). The tassels on the corners of the Jewish tallith or prayer-shawl. Also, (the tassels on each corner of) a small tasselled rectangular garment with a large hole in the middle, worn under the shirt by orthodox male Jews.

tsores /ˈtsɒrəs/ *noun* plural E20 Yiddish (plural of *tsore* trouble, woe, from Hebrew *ṣārāh*). Troubles, worries; (treated as *singular*) trouble, worry. *United States colloquial.*

tsotsi /ˈtsɒtsi/ *noun* M20 Bantu (perhaps from Nguni *-tsotsa* dress in exaggerated clothing). In South Africa: a hoodlum, *es-*

pecially a member of a Black African street gang wearing clothing of exaggerated cut.

tsuba /'tsuːba/ *noun* plural same, **tsubas** L19 Japanese. A Japanese sword-guard.

tsugi ashi /ˌtsuːgɪ 'aʃi/ *noun phrase* M20 Japanese (from *tsugi* next, following + *ashi* foot). *Judo* A method of moving in which the same foot always leads rather than both feet alternating. Also in other martial arts.

tsuica /'tsuːɪkə/ *noun* (also **tuica** /'tuːɪkə/) E20 Romanian (*tuică*). A Romanian plum brandy.

tsukemono /tsuːkɪ'moːno/, /tsuːkɪ'məʊnəʊ/ *noun* L19 Japanese (from *tsukeru* pickle + *mono* thing). A Japanese side dish of pickled vegetables, usually served with rice.

tsunami /tsuːˈnɑːmi/ *noun* plural **tsunamis**, same L19 Japanese (from *tsu* harbour + *nami* wave). A long high undulation or series of undulations of the surface of the sea caused by an earthquake or similar underwater disturbance, travelling at great speed and in shallow waters often building up enough height and force to flood the land.

> **1995** *New Scientist* A tsunami—a series of mountainous waves—is generated when a section of the ocean floor lurches upwards during an earthquake and lofts a vast body of water with it.

tsutsumu /tsʊ'tsuːmuː/ *noun* L20 Japanese (= wrap). The Japanese art of wrapping items in an attractive and appropriate way.

tuan /tuːˈɑːn/ *noun* L18 Malay. In Malaysia and Indonesia: a master, a lord. Also used as a respectful form of address corresponding to *Mr* or *sir*.

tuchis variant of TOKUS.

tufa /'tuːfə/, /'tjuːfə/ *noun* L18 Italian (obsolete local variant of *tufo*, from late Latin *tofus*). *Geology* Originally, a friable porous stone formed of consolidated, often stratified material; tuff, tophus. Now usually *specifically*, a soft porous calcium carbonate rock formed by deposition around mineral springs.

tughra /'tʊgrə/ *noun* (also **toughra, tugra**) M19 Turkish (*tuğra*). *History* A Turkish ornamental monogram incorporating the name and title of the Sultan.

tuica variant of TSUICA.

tuile /twiːl/, *in sense 2 also foreign* /tɥil/ (*plural same*) *noun* (in sense 1 also **tuille**) LME French (or from Old French *tieule* from Latin *tegula* tile). **1** LME *History* In medieval armour, any of two or more steel plates hanging below or forming the lowest part of the tasses, and covering the front of the thighs. **2** M20 A thin curved biscuit, usually made with almonds.

tule /'tuːli/ *noun* M19 Spanish (from Nahuatl *tollin, tullin*). Either of two species of bulrush, *Scirpus lacustris* and *S. acutus*, abundant in flooded marshy areas in south-west North America, especially in California; an area of low-lying ground in the United States dominated by such a plant.

> ■ The plural, *tules*, has given rise to the Canadian word *toolies* (M20) meaning 'the backwoods'.

tulle /t(j)uːl/ *noun & adjective* E19 French (*Tulle*, a town in south-west France where originally made). **A 1** E19 A fine soft silk bobbin-net used for women's dresses, veils, etc. **2** M20 *tulle gras* /grɑː/ (= fatty), a gauze dressing for the skin impregnated with petroleum jelly. **B** *attributive* or as *adjective* M19 Made of tulle.

tumbaga /tʊm'bɑːgə/ *noun* (also **tombaga, tumbago** /tʊm'bɑːgəʊ/, plural **tumbagos**) E17 Spanish (from Malay *tembaga* copper, brass). **1** E17–L18 TOMBAC. **2** M20 Chiefly *Archaeology* An alloy of gold and copper commonly used in pre-Columbian South and Central America.

tu-mo /'tjuːməʊ/ *noun* L20 Chinese (*dū mài* (Wade–Giles *tu mai*)). In Chinese medical theory, the chief passage through which vital energy circulates, located in the spine.

tumulus /'tjuːmjʊləs/ *noun* plural **tumuli** /'tjuːmjʊlaɪ/, /'tjuːmjʊli/ LME Latin (related to *tumere* to swell). An ancient sepulchral mound, a barrow.

tundra /'tʌndrə/ *noun* L16 Lappish. A vast, nearly level, treeless Arctic region usually with a marshy surface and underlying permafrost.

tunku /'tʊŋkuː/ *noun* (also (especially in titles) **Tunku**) L18 Malay. A male title of rank in certain states of Western Malaysia; prince.

tupik /'tuːpɪk/ *noun* M19 Eskimo ((Inuit) *tupiq*). A hut or tent of skins used by Eskimos as a summer residence. Also called *summer lodge*.

tuque /tuːk/ *noun* L19 Canadian French (from French *toque*). In Canada: a close-fitting knitted cap, *especially* a knitted stocking cap sealed at both ends, one end being tucked into the other to form a cap.

tu quoque /tuː ˈkwəʊkwiː/, /tjuː ˈkwɒkweɪ/ *noun phrase* L17 Latin (literally, 'thou also' = English slang 'you're another'). An argument which consists of turning an accusation back on the accuser.

turba /ˈtʊəbə/ *noun* plural **turbae** /ˈtʊəbiː/ L19 Latin (= crowd). *Music* The chorus in passion-plays and other religious oratorios in which crowds participate in the action.

turbeh /ˈtəːbeɪ/, /ˈtʊəbeɪ/ *noun* L17 Turkish (*türbe* from Arabic *turba* tomb). A small building, resembling a mosque, erected over the tomb of a Muslim, especially a person of sanctity or rank.

turlough /ˈtʊələʊx/ *noun* L17 Irish (*turloch*, from *tur* dry + *loch* lake). In Ireland: a low-lying area on limestone which becomes flooded in wet weather through the welling up of groundwater from the rock.

turnverein /ˈtəːnvərʌɪn/, /ˈtəːnfərʌɪn/ *noun* M19 German (from *turnen* to do gymnastic exercises + *Verein* society, club). In the United States: a gymnastics club, originally for German immigrants.

turron /tʊˈrɒn/ *noun* plural **turrones** /tʊˈrɒneɪs/, **turrons** E20 Spanish (*turrón*). A kind of Spanish confectionery resembling nougat, made from almonds and honey; a piece of this.

tusche /ˈtʊʃə/ *noun* L19 German (back-formation from *tuschen* from French *toucher* to touch). A greasy black composition, in liquid form or to be mixed with liquids, used for making lithographic drawings; lithographic drawing ink.

tutoyer /tʊˈtwaːjeɪ/ *transitive verb* inflected *tutoy-*, past tense also written **tutoyered** /tʊˈtwaːjeɪd/ L17 French (from the singular pronoun *tu*, *toi*, *te*). In French, address with the singular and more familiar pronoun *tu*, *toi*, *te* rather than the plural and more formal *vous*; *generally* treat or address with familiarity.

tutti-frutti /tuːtɪˈfruːti/ *noun* (also (especially sense 2) **Tutti-frutti** and as two words) M19 Italian (= all fruits). **1** M19 A confection of mixed fruits; *specifically* a mixture of chopped preserved fruits, nuts, etc., used to flavour ice-cream; ice-cream so flavoured. **2** M19 (Proprietary name for) a chewing-gum with a mixed fruit flavouring.

tutti quanti /ˌtuːtɪ ˈkwanti/ *noun phrase* L18 Italian. Everyone, everything; all the people or things of this or that kind.

tutu /ˈtuːtuː/ *noun* E20 French (childish alteration of *cucu* diminutive of *cul* buttocks). *Ballet* A skirt made up of layers of stiffened frills that stand out from the dancer's legs (*classic tutu*) or extend to mid-calf (*romantic tutu*).

tuyère /twiːˈjɛː/, /tuːˈjɛː/ *noun* (also **tuyere**, **twyer** /ˈtwʌɪə/) L18 French (from *tuyau* pipe). *Metallurgy* A nozzle through which the air is forced into a forge or furnace.

tvorog /ˈtvɔːrək/ *noun* E20 Russian. A soft Russian cheese similar to cottage or curd cheese.

tycoon /tʌɪˈkuːn/ *noun* M19 Japanese (*taikun* great lord or prince, from Chinese *dà* great + *jūn* prince). **1** M19 *History* A title applied by foreigners to the shogun of Japan in power between 1854 and 1868. **2** M19 A business magnate.

tympanum /ˈtɪmpənəm/ *noun* plural **tympanums**, **tympana** /ˈtɪmpənə/ E16 Latin (from Greek *tumpanon* drum, from nasalized variant of base of *tuptein* to strike). **1** *Medicine* Severe distension of the abdomen by gas in the intestine, tympanites. *rare*. Only in E16. **2** E17 *Anatomy* and *Zoology* The tympanic membrane or eardrum. Also, a membrane in any animal which is thought to form part of a hearing organ. **b** L19 *Ornithology* Either of the two inflatable air-sacs at the sides of the neck in certain birds, such as grouse. *rare*. **3** M17 *Architecture* **a** The die or dado of a pedestal. **b** L17 A vertical recessed area within a pediment; a similar area over a door between the lintel and the arch; a carving on this. **4** L17 A drum, *especially* a hand drum of ancient Greece and Rome. *archaic*. **5** L19 A kind of wheel (originally drum-shaped) with curved radial partitions, used for raising water from a stream.

typhoon /tʌɪˈfuːn/ *noun* L16 Portuguese (partly from Portuguese *tufão* from Urdu *ṭūfān* hurricane, tornado, from Arabic, perhaps from Greek *tuphōn*; partly from Chinese dialect *tai fung* big wind, from Chinese *dà* big + *fēng* wind). A violent storm occurring in or around the Indian subcontinent; *especially* a tropical cyclone occurring in the region of the Indian or western Pacific oceans.

tyro, tyrocinium variants of TIRO, TIRO-CINIUM.

tzatziki /tsat'siːki/ *noun* M20 Modern Greek (from Turkish *cacık*). A Greek side dish made with yoghurt, cucumber, garlic, and usually mint.

tzedaka /tse'dɔka/ *noun* (also **tzedakah**) M20 Hebrew (*sĕḏāqāh* righteousness). The obligation to help fellow Jews; *generally* charity.

tzigane /tsɪ'gaːn/ *noun & adjective* M18 French (from Hungarian *czigany, cigány*). **A** *noun* M18 A Hungarian Gypsy. **B** *adjective* L19 That is a tzigane; consisting of tziganes; characteristic of the tziganes or especially their music.

tzimmes /'tsɪmǝs/ *noun* (also **tsimmes, tzimmis** and other variants) plural same L19 Yiddish (*tsimes*, of unknown origin). A Jewish stew of sweetened vegetables or vegetables and fruit, sometimes with meat; *figurative* a fuss, a confusion.

   1974 R. L. Simon *Wild Turkey* Why are you making such a *tsimmis*? Hecht is dead.

tzitzit(h) variant of TSITSITH.

U

U-bahn /'uːbɑːn/, /'juːbɑːn/ *noun* M20 German (from *U* (abbreviation of *Untergrund*) underground + *Bahn* railway). In Germany and Austria: the underground railway in various major cities.

über alles /ˌyːbər 'aləs/ *adjective & adverb phrase* M20 German (from *über* over + *alles* all). Above all else.

■ Generally used with implicit reference to the opening words of the German national anthem *Deutschland über alles*, misunderstood to mean 'Germany supreme'.

Überfremdung /ˌyːbərˈfrɛmdʊŋ/ *noun* M20 German (from *überfremden* to give foreign character to (from *über* over + *fremd* foreign)). The admission or presence of too many foreigners.

■ Used particularly by right-wing politicians in Switzerland protesting against immigrant workers.

überhaupt /ˌyːbərˈhaʊpt/ *adverb* L19 German (from *über* over + *Haupt* head, (in compounds) main). In general, (taken) as a whole; par excellence.

Übermensch /'yːbərmɛnʃ/ *noun* plural **Übermenschen** /'yːbərmɛnʃən/ L19 German (back-formation from *übermenschlich* superhuman, from *über* over + *menschlich* human, from *Mensch* person). The highest type of human being, superman.

■ The concept was important in the philosophy of Friedrich Nietzsche (1844–1900), from whom George Bernard Shaw borrowed it for his comedy *Man and Superman* (1903). It—and its opposite UNTERMENSCH—subsequently became part of the vocabulary of the Nazi ideology of the master race. In English translations of Nietzsche, Übermensch is often translated as 'Overman', thus sidestepping the cartoon associations of 'Superman'. In jocular use *über* may be attached to an English noun (see quotation).

1996 *Times Magazine* . . . the nadir came with whispers that *Baywatch*'s uber-babe Pamela Anderson was being lined up to star with Eric Idle's Doctor.

uberrima fides /juːˌbɛrɪmə 'fʌɪdiːz/ *noun phrase* M19 Latin. *Law* The utmost good faith.

ubi sunt /ˌʊbɪ 'sʊnt/ *adjective phrase* E20 Latin (= 'where are', the opening words or refrain of certain medieval Latin works). *Literary Criticism* Designating or characterizing a literary theme or passage lamenting the mutability of things.

attributive **1996** *Spectator* The whole thing is in fact a subtle homage to all the classic '*ubi sunt*' poems ever written about deserted places where human life once reverberated . . .

uchiwa /'uːtʃiwa/ *noun* L19 Japanese. A flat Japanese fan that does not fold.

udon /'uːdɒn/ *noun* E20 Japanese. In Japanese cookery: a thick strip of pasta made from wheat flour; pasta in this form.

uhlan /'uːlɑːn/, /'juːlɑːn/, /ʊˈlɑːn/ *noun* (also **hulan** /'h(j)uːlən/) M18 French (*uhlan*, German *U(h)lan* from Polish *ułan*, *hułan* from Turkish *oğlan* youth, servant). *History* A type of cavalryman or lancer in certain European armies, especially that of Poland or (later) Germany.

uhuru /ʊˈhuːruː/ *noun* (also **Uhuru**) M20 Kiswahili (= freedom). National independence of an African country, *specifically* Kenya.

1984 *Listener* An entire continent has seemed hell-bent on self-destruction, despite uhuru, despite the bright hopes of the many thousands who died seeking it.

Uitlander /'eɪtlandə/, /'ɔɪtlandə/, *foreign* /'œytlandər/ *noun* L19 Afrikaans (from Dutch *uit* out + *land* land). In South Africa: a foreigner, an alien; *specifically* a British person who went to South Africa before the Boer War of 1899–1902.

ujamaa /ˌʊʤaˈmɑː/ *noun* M20 Kiswahili (= consanguinity, brotherhood, from *jamaa* family, from Arabic *jamāʿa* group (of people), community). A kind of socialism introduced in Tanzania by President Nyerere in the 1960s, in which self-help village cooperatives were established.

ukase /juːˈkeɪz/ *noun* E18 Russian (*ukaz* ordinance, edict, from *ukazat'* show, order, decree). **1** E18 A decree or edict, having legal force, issued by the tsarist Russian government. **2** E19 *generally* Any proclamation or decree; an order, an arbitrary command.

2 1995 *Times* . . . when I am made Emperor of the Universe, my first ukase will be to make it a capital offence to complain about anyone's dead relatives . . .

ukeke /uːˈkeɪkeɪ/ *noun* L19 Hawaiian ('*ūkēkē*). A Hawaiian stringed instrument consisting of a strip of wood with two or three strings that are played with the fingers and mouth.

ukelele variant of UKULELE.

ukemi /ˈuːkeɪmi/ *noun* M20 Japanese (from *uke* person held or thrown + *mi* body). *Judo* The art of falling safely.

ukha /ʊˈxa/ *noun* (also **oukha**) E20 Russian. A Russian fish soup.

uki /ˈuːki/ *noun* E20 Japanese (= floating). *Judo* Used in the names of various techniques involving a controlled throw in which the opponent's feet and body leave the ground.

ukiyo-e /ˌukijoˈjeː/, /ˌuːkɪjəʊˈjeɪ/ *noun* L19 Japanese (from *ukiyo* fleeting world (from *uku* float, go by fleetingly + *yo* world) + *e* picture). A Japanese art-form in which everyday subjects are treated simply in woodblock prints or paintings; a work in this art-form.

ukulele /juːkəˈleɪli/ *noun* (also **ukelele**) L19 Hawaiian (literally, 'jumping flea'). A small four-stringed guitar originating in Hawaii but developed from an earlier Portuguese instrument.
■ Colloquially abbreviated to *uke*.

ulema /ˈʊləmə/, /ˈuːlmə/, /uːləˈmɑː/ *noun* (also **ulama** /ˈʊləmə/, /uːləˈmɑː/) L17 Arabic (Turkish, Persian) ('*ulamā*', plural of '*ālim*, '*alīm* learned, from '*alima* to have (religious) knowledge). **1** L17 *collectively* or in *plural* The members of a Muslim society or country who are recognized as having specialist knowledge of Islamic sacred law and theology. **2** M19 A person who belongs to a *ulema*.

ulpan /ʊlˈpan/ *noun* plural **ulpanim** /ˌʊlpaˈniːm/ M20 Modern Hebrew (*ulpān*, from Aramaic *allēp* to teach). An intensive course in the Hebrew language, originally for immigrants to the State of Israel; a centre providing such a course; *transferred* any intensive language course.

ult. abbreviation of ULTIMO.

ultima ratio /ˌʊltmə ˈreɪʃɪəʊ/ *noun phrase* M19 Latin. The final sanction.

ultimata plural of ULTIMATUM.

ultima Thule /ˌʊltmə ˈtjuːli/ *noun phrase* (also **ultima thule**) L18 Latin (= farthest Thule). The type of the extreme limit of travel and discovery; *figurative* the highest or uttermost point or degree attained or attainable, the (lowest) limit, the nadir. Cf. THULE.

ultimatum /ˌʊltɪˈmeɪtəm/ *noun* plural **ultimatums**, **ultimata** /ˌʊltɪˈmeɪtə/ M18 Latin (use as noun of neuter of late Latin *ultimatus* in the medieval Latin senses 'final, completed'). **1** M18 The final terms presented by one party in a dispute etc. to another, the rejection of which could cause a breakdown in relations, a declaration of war, an end of cooperation, etc. **2** M18 The final point, the extreme limit; an ultimate end or aim. (Followed by *of*.) **3** M19 A primary element beyond which advance or analysis is impossible; something fundamental.

ultimo /ˈʊltɪməʊ/ *adjective* L16 Latin ((sc. *die* or *mense*) ablative singular masculine of *ultimus* last, final). **1** L16–L17 Designating the last day (of a specified month). **2** E17 Of last month. Frequently written *ult.*, *ulto.*

ultra /ˈʊltrə/ *adjective* & *noun* E19 Latin (independent use of *ultra-* lying beyond). **A** *adjective* **1** E19 Of a person or party: holding extreme views in politics or other matters of opinion. **2** E19 Going beyond what is normal or ordinary; excessive, extreme. **B** *noun* **1** E19 A person holding extreme views. **2** L20 A long-distance run of great length. *colloquial*.
■ Originally introduced as an abbreviation for French *ultra-royaliste*, referring to a political party in early nineteenth-century France.
B.1 1996 *Spectator* He hopes to encourage the Thatcherite ultras to continue undermining Mr Major . . .

ultra crepidam /ˌʊltrə ˈkrɛpɪdam/ *preposition* L19 Latin. On matters beyond a person's knowledge.

ultra vires /ˌʊltrə ˈvʌɪriːz/, /ˌʊltrɑː ˈviːreɪz/ *adverb phrase* L18 Latin (= beyond the powers). Chiefly *Law*. Beyond the powers or legal authority of a corporation or person.
■ Opposed to INTRA VIRES.
1996 *Times* The only possible challenge would be to claim Mr Lang's block for the . . . merger was *ultra vires*, that it was not in Mr Lang's power to make such a decision.

ultreya /ulˈtreja/, /ʊlˈtreɪə/ *noun* M20 Spanish (apparently recalling the medieval cry (E)*ultreya* 'onward!', 'forward!' in the hymn sung by pilgrims to Compostela). *Roman Catholic Church* A regular discussion group held by participants in a CUR-SILLO.

umbilicus /ʌmˈbɪlɪkəs/, /ˌʌmbrˈlʌɪkəs/ *noun* plural **umbilici** /ʌmˈbɪlɪsʌɪ/, **umbilicuses** L17 Latin (from base of UMBO, related to Greek *omphalos* and Indo-European base of navel). **1** L17 *Anatomy* A navel. **b** M19 *Botany* The scar on a seed marking its separation from the placenta; the hilum. Now *rare*. **2** *Mathematics* A focus of an ellipse. Only in E18. **b** M19 An umbilical point. **3** E19 *Biology* A small usually central depression or hole suggestive of a navel.

umbo /ˈʌmbəʊ/ *noun* plural **umbones** /ʌmˈbəʊniːz/, **umbos** E18 Latin (= shield-boss, knob). **1** E18 The boss of a shield. **2** M18 A rounded or conical projection or knob, especially in the centre of a rounded natural structure.

umbra /ˈʌmbrə/ *noun* plural **umbras, umbrae** /ˈʌmbriː/ L16 Latin. **1** L16 A phantom, a ghost. **2** M17 A shadow; *especially* (*Astronomy*) the shadow cast by the moon or earth during an eclipse. **3** An inseparable companion, a hanger-on.

umfaan /ˈʊmfɑːn/ *noun* M19 Zulu (*umFana* small boy). In South Africa: a young African boy, *especially* one employed in domestic service.

umfundisi /ʊmˈfʊndisi/, /ˌʊmfʊnˈdiːzi/ *noun* E19 Xhosa and Zulu (*umFundisi*). In South Africa: a teacher, a minister, a missionary. Also used as a respectful form of address.

umiak /ˈuːmɪak/ *noun* (also **umiaq, oomiak**) M18 Eskimo ((Inuit) *umiaq*). A large Eskimo canoe with a wooden frame covered in skins, *especially* one paddled by women.

umlaut /ˈʊmlaʊt/ *noun* M19 German (from *um-* about + *Laut* sound). **1** M19 *Philology* Vowel change arising historically by partial assimilation to an adjacent sound, usually a vowel or semivowel in a following syllable (often now lost), as in German *Mann, Männer,* or English *man, men.* Also called (*vowel*) *mutation.* **2** M20 A diacritical sign (¨) placed over a vowel, especially in Germanic languages, to indicate such a change.

> **2** *figurative* **1995** *Spectator* The colour nude photos of her [sc. Mimi Papandreou's] spectacular umlauts have 'graced' the Athenian front pages non-stop . . .

umma /ˈʊmə/ *noun* L19 Arabic (= people, community, nation). The Muslim commu-

nity, originally founded by Muhammad at Medina, comprising individuals bound to one another predominantly by religious ties.

umrah /ˈʊmrɑː/ *noun* E19 Arabic ('umra). Islam A lesser pilgrimage to Mecca made independently of or at the same time as the HAJJ, and consisting of a number of devotional rituals performed within the city.

Umwelt /ˈʊmvɛlt/ *noun* plural **Umwelten** /ˈʊmvɛltən/ M20 German (= environment). The outer world as it affects and is perceived by the organisms inhabiting it; the environment.

una corda /ˌuːnə ˈkɔːdə/ *adverb & adjective phrase* M19 Italian (= one string). *Music* (A direction:) using the soft pedal of the piano.

una voce /ˌjuːneɪ ˈvəʊsiː/, /ˌuːnə ˈvəʊkeɪ/ *adverb phrase* M16 Latin (*una* ablative singular feminine of *unus* one + *voce* ablative singular of *vox* voice). With one voice; unanimously.

unberufen /ˌʊnbəˈruːfən/ *interjection* M19 German (= unauthorized, gratuitous). Touch wood! (to avert ill luck).

unda maris /ˌʌndə ˈmɑːrɪs/ *noun phrase* E19 Latin (literally, 'wave of the sea'). *Music* A type of organ-stop, usually consisting of two ranks of pipes, one of which is tuned slightly sharp or flat, together producing a slowly undulating tone.

Unding /ˈʊndɪŋ/ *noun* M20 German (= absurdity). A non-existent thing, a vague abstraction, a concept having no properties.

und so weiter /ˌʊnt zo ˈvaɪtər/ *adverb phrase* L19 German. And so forth.

unheimlich /ʊnˈhaɪmlɪç/ *adjective* L19 German. Uncanny, weird.

unicum /ˈjuːnɪkəm/ *noun* plural **unica** /ˈjuːnɪkə/ L19 Latin (neuter singular of *unicus* unique). A unique example, specimen, or thing.

Untergang /ˈʊntərɡaŋ/ *noun* M20 German (= decline, downfall). An irreversible decline, especially leading to the destruction of culture or civilization.

> ■ Often used with implicit allusion to Oswald Spengler's *Der Untergang des Abendlandes* (1918), translated as *The Decline of the West.*

Untermensch /ˈʊntərˌmɛnʃ/ *noun* plural **Untermenschen** /ˈʊntərˌmɛnʃən/ M20

German. Especially in Nazi Germany, a person regarded or classified as racially inferior.

1996 *Country Life* Himmler believed that their [sc. the Austrians'] historical involvement with other races made them more suitable than pure Germans for dealing with the *Untermensch.*

unum necessarium /ˌjuːnəm nɛsɪ ˈsɛːrɪəm/ *noun phrase* M20 **Modern Latin** (from (Vulgate) Latin *unum est necessarium* one thing is necessary (Luke 10:42)). The one or only necessary thing, the essential element.

uomo universale /ˌwoːmo univerˈsɑːle/ *noun phrase* plural **uomini universali** /ˌwoː mini univerˈsɑːli/ M20 **Italian** (literally, 'universal man'). A man who excels in the major fields of learning and action. Also called *Renaissance man.*

upsara variant of APSARA.

upsilon /ʌpˈsʌɪlɒn/, /ˈʊpsɪlɒn/, /juːp ˈsʌɪlən/ *noun* M17 **Greek** (*u psilon* simple or slender u, from *psilos* slender, with reference to the need to distinguish upsilon from the diphthong οι, with which upsilon shared a pronunciation in late Greek). **1** M17 The twentieth letter (Υ, υ) of the Greek alphabet. **2** L20 *Particle Physics* A meson with a mass of about 9.4 GeV. Also *upsilon particle.*

ur- /ʊə/ M19 **German** (combining form). Forming words with the sense 'primitive, original, earliest'.

1983 *Sunday Telegraph* Russell Hoban is an ur-novelist, a maverick voice that is like no other.

uraeus /jʊˈriːəs/ *noun* plural **uraei** /jʊ ˈriːʌɪ/ M19 **Modern Latin** (from Greek *ouraios* (perhaps from *oura* tail), representing Egyptian word for 'cobra'). *Egyptian Antiquities* A representation of the sacred asp or snake, symbolizing supreme power, especially worn on the head-dresses of ancient Egyptian divinities and sovereigns.

urbi et orbi /ˌəːbɪ ɛt ˈɔːbi/ *adverb phrase* M19 **Latin.** (Of a papal proclamation etc.) To the city (of Rome) and to the world; *transferred* for general information or acceptance, to everyone.

1973 M. Bence-Jones *Palaces of Raj* One of the nobles, whose bard would, every two hours of the night, proclaim *urbi et orbi . . . his* titles and honours.

urbs /əːbz/ *noun* M20 **Latin** (= city). The city, especially as a symbol of harsh or busy modern life.

Urfirnis /ˈʊəfəːnɪs/ *noun & adjective* E20 **German** (from UR- + *firnis* varnish, veneer). *Greek Archaeology* (Designating) an early form of Greek pottery characterized by the use of dark lustrous paint.

Urheimat /ˈuːrˌhaɪmat/ *noun* M20 **German** (from UR- + *Heimat* home, homeland). The place of origin of a people or language.

Urim /ˈjʊərɪm/ *noun* M16 **Hebrew** ('*ūrīm* plural of '*ōr*). One of the two objects of a now unknown nature worn on the breastplate of a Jewish high priest. Chiefly in *Urim and Thummim.* Cf. THUMMIM.

figurative **1996** *Oldie* Everybody has to have a say nowadays, and the practitioner who can hit the media headlines becomes a pundit, a Urim and Thummim.

urinoir /yrinwar/ *noun* plural pronounced same M20 **French**. In France: a public urinal.

urlar /ˈʊələ/ *noun* L19 **Gaelic** (*ùrlar* ground, floor). *Music* The ground theme in a pibroch.

urs /ʊəs/ *noun* M19 **Arabic** ('*urs,* literally, 'wedding, wedding feast'). Especially in the Indian subcontinent: a ceremony celebrating the anniversary of the death of a Muslim saint.

Ursprache /ˈuːrˌʃprɑːxə/ *noun* plural **Ursprachen** /ˈuːrˌʃprɑːxən/ E20 **German** (from UR- + *Sprache* speech). A hypothetical early language from which actual languages are derived, a proto-language.

Urtext /ˈuːrtɛkst/ *noun* plural **Urtexte** /ˈuːrtɛkstə/ M20 **German** (from UR- + *Text* text (ultimately from Latin *textus*)). An original or the earliest version of a text.

1983 *London Review of Books* Elaborate versions often point back to the gospel of Mark as a kind of cryptic *Urtext.*

ushabti /uːˈʃabti/ *noun* plural **ushabtiu** /uːˈʃabtuː/, **ushabtis** L19 **Egyptian** (*wšbty* answerer, replacing *šwbt(y)* SHAWABTI). *Egyptology* A figurine of a dead person, made of faience, stone, wood, etc., and placed with the body in the tomb to substitute for the dead person in any work required in the afterlife. Also *ushabti-figure.*

usine /juːˈziːn/ *noun* L18 **French** (= factory, (in early use) water-mill). **1** Material used or suitable for a furnace or foundry. Only in L18. **2** M19 A factory; *especially* a West Indian sugar factory.

usque ad nauseam earlier variant of AD NAUSEAM.

uti possidetis /ˌjuːtʌɪ pɒsɪˈdiːtɪs/, /ˌjuːtʌɪ pɒsɪˈdeɪtɪs/ *noun phrase* L17 Late Latin (= as you possess). *Law* A principle whereby property or territory not expressly disposed of in a treaty remains in the hands of the party holding it at the end of hostilities.

1996 M. Anderson *Frontiers* . . . the Organization of African Unity . . . in a . . . 1964 resolution on border disputes accepted the principle of *uti possidetis ita possideatis* (that which you possess, you continue to possess) . . .

utopia /juːˈtəʊpɪə/ *noun* (also **Utopia**) M16 Modern Latin (= no-place, from Greek *ou* not + *topos* place). **1** M16 An imaginary place or state of things considered to be perfect; a condition of (ideal) social perfection. **2** M18 An impossibly ideal scheme, especially for social improvement.

■ The origin of the name and of all subsequent *utopias* was the political fable *Utopia* (1516) written in Latin by Sir Thomas More (1477–1535) and translated into English in 1551. The antithesis of a *utopia* is a *dystopia* (modern Latin from Greek *dys-* bad + *topos*), a nightmare society of the kind depicted in, for example, Aldous Huxley's *Brave New World* (1932). The word *dystopia* (M19) was coined originally by J. S. Mill but it has only gained currency since the mid twentieth century, especially in sociological contexts.

1 1996 *Spectator* The narrator, the 'Black Widow', Brady and Chico hope to take the fast lane into that middle-class utopia by robbing a bank.

ut supra /ʊt ˈsuːprə/ *adverb phrase* LME Latin (from *ut* as + *supra* above). In a book etc.: as previously, as before, as above. Frequently abbreviated *ut sup.*

uvala /ˈuːvələ/ *noun* E20 Serbo-Croat (= hollow, depression). *Physical Geography* A large depression in the ground surface occurring in karstic regions, resulting from the collapse of an underground watercourse.

V

v. abbreviation of VERSUS.

vaaljapie /ˈfɑːljɑːpi/ noun M20 Afrikaans (literally, 'tawny Jake', from Dutch *vaal* pale + *japie* diminutive of male forename Jaap from Jakob Jacob). In South Africa: rough young wine, cheap or inferior wine.

va banque /va bɑ̃k/ interjection M20 French (literally, 'go bank'). In baccarat: expressing a player's willingness to bet against the banker's whole stake. Cf. BANCO.

vacherin /vaʃrɛ̃/ noun M20 French. **1** M20 A soft French or Swiss cheese made from cow's milk. **2** M20 A dessert of a meringue shell filled with whipped cream, fruit, etc.

vade-mecum /ˌvɑːdɪˈmeɪkəm/, /ˌveɪdɪ ˈmiːkəm/ noun E17 French (from modern Latin use as noun of Latin *vade mecum* go with me). **1** E17 A small book or manual carried on one's person for ready reference; a handbook, a guidebook. **2** M17 Anything useful commonly carried about or kept available for use by a person.

vae victis /ˌvʌɪ ˈvɪktɪs/ interjection & noun E17 Latin (= woe to the conquered). (A cry noting or calling for) the humiliation of the vanquished by their conquerors.

■ *Vae* was formerly (M16–M17) used on its own as a denunciation, calling down a curse on someone. *Vae victis* is a quotation from Livy (V. xlviii.9) and is chiefly used as an interjection.

vagantes /vəˈgantiːz/, /vəˈganteɪz/ noun plural E20 Latin (nominative plural of *vagans* present participle of *vagari* to wander). Itinerant medieval scholar monks.

vagitus /vəˈdʒʌɪtəs/ noun M17 Latin (from *vagire* to wail). A cry, a wail, *specifically* that of a newborn child.

vague /vag/ noun plural pronounced same M20 French (literally, 'wave'). A movement, a trend. Cf. NOUVELLE VAGUE.

vahana /ˈvɑːhənə/ noun (also **vahan** /ˈvɑːhən/) E19 Sanskrit (*vāhana*, literally, 'conveyance'). *Indian Mythology* The mount or vehicle of a god.

vahine /vaˈhine/, /vɑːˈhiːni/ noun M20 Tahitian (cf. WAHINE). A Tahitian woman or wife.

vajra /ˈvʌdʒrə/ noun L18 Sanskrit. *Hinduism* and *Buddhism* (A representation of) a thunderbolt or mythical weapon, *especially* one wielded by the god Indra.

vale /ˈvɑːleɪ/ interjection & noun M16 Latin (imperative singular of *valere* to be well). **A** interjection M16 Farewell. Cf. AVE ATQUE VALE. **B** noun L16 A written or spoken farewell.

valet /ˈvalɪt/, /ˈvaleɪ/ noun & verb L15 Old and Modern French ((also *vaslet*, *varlet* varlet), ultimately related to *vassal* from medieval Latin *vassallus* man-servant, retainer). **A** noun **1** L15 *Military* A footman acting as attendant or servant to a horseman. Now *rare* or *obsolete*. **2** M16 A man's personal (usually male) attendant, responsible for his or her master's clothes, appearance, etc. Now also, a hotel employee performing similar duties for guests. **3** M20 A rack on which clothing may be hung to retain its shape. Chiefly *United States*. **B** verb **1** *transitive & intransitive verb* M19 Act as a valet (to). **2** *transitive verb* M20 Look after (clothes etc.). **3** *transitive verb* L20 Clean (a motor vehicle).

valeta variant of VELETA.

valet-de-chambre /valɛ də ʃɑ̃br/, /ˌvaleɪ də ˈʃɒmbrə/ noun plural **valets-de-chambre** (pronounced same) M17 French (literally 'chamber-valet'). A VALET (noun) sense 2.

Valhalla /valˈhalə/ noun L17 Modern Latin (from Old Norse *Valhall-*, *Valhǫll*, from *valr* those slain in battle (= Old English *wæl*, Old Saxon, Old High German *wal*) + *hǫll* hall). **1** L17 In Scandinavian mythology, the hall in which the souls of those who have died in battle feast with Odin for eternity. **2** M19 *transferred* and *figurative* A place or sphere assigned to a person or thing worthy of special honour. Also, paradise; a place or state of perfect bliss.

valise /vəˈliːz/ noun E17 French (from Italian *valigia* corresponding to medieval Latin *valesia*, of unknown origin). **1** E17 A

travelling case or portmanteau, now usually made of leather and of a size suitable
for carrying by hand, formerly also for
strapping to a horse's saddle. Now chiefly
United States. **2** M19 *Military* A soldier's
cloth or leather kitbag.

vallum /'valəm/ *noun* E17 Latin (collectively from *vallus* stake, palisade). **1** E17 A
defensive wall or rampart of earth, sods,
or stone; *especially* one constructed by the
Romans in northern England and central
Scotland. **2** E19 *Archaeology* A palisaded
bank or rampart, formed of the earth dug
up from the ditch or fosse around a
Roman military camp.

valse /vɑːls/, /vɔːls/ *noun* L18 French (from
German *Walzer* waltz). A waltz; a piece of
music for this dance or in its rhythm.

valuta /və'ljuːtə/, /və'luːtə/ *noun* L19 Italian (= value). The value of one currency in
respect of its exchange rate with another;
a currency considered in this way.

Vanitas /'vanɪtɑːs/ *noun* (also **vanitas**) E20
Latin (= vanity). *Art* A still-life painting of
a seventeenth-century Dutch genre incorporating symbols of mortality or mutability.

vanitas vanitatum /ˌvanɪtɑːs vanɪ
'tɑːtəm/ *noun phrase* M16 Late Latin (= vanity of vanities). Futility.

■ Quotation from the Vulgate version of
Ecclesiastes 1:2, often as an exclamation of
disillusionment or pessimism.

vaporetto /vapə'rɛtəʊ/ *noun plural* **va-
poretti** /vapə'rɛti/, **vaporettos** E20 Italian (= small steamboat, diminutive of
vapore from Latin *vapor* steam). In Venice:
a canal boat (originally a steamboat, now
a motor-boat) used for public transport.

vaquero /və'kɛːrəʊ/ *noun plural* **vaque-
ros** E19 Spanish (from *vaca* cow; cf. Portuguese *vaqueiro*). In Spanish-speaking parts
of America: a cowboy, a cowherd; a cattle-
driver.

■ *Buckaroo*, a now archaic term used (from
E19) in the United States for 'a cowboy', was
an alteration of *vaquero*.

vardo /'vɑːdəʊ/ *noun plural* **vardos** (also
varda /'vɑːdə/) E19 Romany. A wagon.
Now *specifically* a Gypsy caravan. Originally *slang*.

vargueño /vɑː'ɡemjəʊ/ *noun* E20 Spanish
(*bargueño*, *vargueño* adjective of Bargas, a
village near Toledo, the former place of
manufacture). A kind of cabinet made in
Spain in the sixteenth and seventeenth

centuries, with numerous small compartments and drawers behind a fall-front
which opens out to form a writing surface.

varia lectio /ˌvɛːrɪə 'lɛktɪəʊ/ *noun phrase*
plural **variae lectiones** /ˌvɛːrɪaɪ lɛktɪ
'əʊniːz/ M17 Latin. A variant reading in a
text.

variorum /ˌvɛːrɪ'ɔːrəm/ *noun & adjective*
E18 Latin (literally, 'of various (people)',
genitive plural of *varius* various, especially in phrase *editio cum notis variorum*
edition with the notes of various (commentators)). **A** *noun* **1 a** E18 An edition,
especially of the complete works of a classical author, containing the notes of various commentators or editors. Also
variorum edition. **b** M20 An edition, usually of an author's complete works, containing variant readings from
manuscripts or earlier editions. Also *variorum edition.* **2** L18 Variation; (a) novelty;
a source of variety. Also, an unnecessary
decoration or flourish. *Scottish.* **B** *attributive* or as *adjective* E18 Of, pertaining to, or
designating a variorum; (of matter in a
book etc.) obtained or collected from various sources. Also, (of a reading in a text)
variant.

varna /'vɑːnə/, /'vʌrnə/ *noun* M19 Sanskrit
(*varṇa*, literally, 'appearance, aspect, colour'). Each of the four original castes of
Hindu society; the system or basis of this
division.

varve /vɑːv/ *noun* E20 Swedish (= layer,
turn). *Physical Geography* A pair of thin layers of clay and silt of contrasting colour
and texture which represent the deposit
of a single year (summer and winter) in
still water at some time in the past (especially in a lake formed by a retreating ice
sheet).

Vaterland /'fɑːtərlant/ *noun* M19 German.
Germany as the fatherland.

vates /'veɪtiːz/ *noun* E17 Latin (= seer, poet,
related to Greek *ouateis* (plural) ovate,
representing a Gaulish word). A poet,
especially one divinely inspired; a prophet-
poet.

vaudeville /'vɔːdəvɪl/, /'vəʊdəvɪl/ *noun*
M18 French (earlier *vau* (plural *vaux*) *de
ville, vau de vire,* and in full *chanson du Vau
de Vire* song of the valley of Vire (in Normandy, north-west France)). **1** M18 A satirical or topical song; *specifically* one sung
on the stage. Now *rare.* **2** E19 A light stage
play or comedy with interspersed songs.

Also, such plays as a genre; *United States* variety theatre, music hall. Frequently *attributive*.

vedette /vɪ'dɛt/ *noun* L17 French (from Italian *vedetta*, alteration (after *vedere* to see) of southern Italian *veletta*, perhaps from Spanish *vela* watch, from *velar* to keep watch, from Latin *vigilare*). **1** L17 *Military* A mounted sentry placed in advance of an army's outposts to observe the movements of the enemy; a scout. **2** L19 In full *vedette boat*. A small vessel used for scouting purposes in naval warfare. Also *generally*, a small motor launch or patrol-boat. **3** M20 A leading star of stage or screen.

veduta /ve'duːta/ *noun* plural **vedute** /ve'duːte/ E20 Italian (= a view, from *vedere* to see). In Italian art: a detailed, factually accurate landscape, usually a townscape showing buildings of interest.

veena /'viːnə/ *noun* (also **vina**) L18 Sanskrit and Hindi (*vīṇā*). In the Indian subcontinent: a plucked musical instrument with a gourd at one or either end of a fretted finger-board and seven strings.

vega /'veɪgə/ *noun* M17 Spanish and Catalan (*vega* = Portuguese *veiga*). **1** M17 In Spain and Spanish America: an extensive, usually fertile and grass-covered, plain or valley. **2** L19 In Cuba: a tobacco field.

veilleuse /vɛjøz/ *noun* plural pronounced same E19 French. A small and usually highly decorated night-light or night-lamp. Also, a small decorative bedside food-warmer, usually with an enclosed burner under a bowl or teapot, and made of pottery or porcelain so as to give out some light.

veld /vɛlt/ *noun* (also **veldt**) L18 Afrikaans (from Dutch = field). Unenclosed country; open grassland.

■ South African; frequently with specifying word, as in *bushveld, sandveld*.

veldskoen /'fɛltskʊn/, /'fɛlskʊn/ *noun* E19 Afrikaans (= field-shoe, ultimately by assimilation to VELD of earlier *velschoen*, from *fel* skin, + *schoen* shoe). Formerly, a light shoe made of untanned hide. Now, a strong but usually soft leather or suede boot or shoe for walking etc.

veldt variant of VELD.

veleta /və'liːtə/ *noun* (also **valeta**) E20 Spanish (= weather-vane). An old-time round dance for couples in triple time, faster than a waltz and with partners side by side.

velours /və'lʊə/ *noun* (also **velour**) E18 French (= velvet, from Old French *velour*, *velous* from Latin *villosus* hairy, from *villus* hair). **1** E18 A silk or velvet pad for smoothing hats. **2** L18 Any of various plush or pile fabrics similar to velvet and used for hats, garments, upholstery, etc.

■ Cf. PATTE DE VELOURS. The French phrase *velours croché* 'hooked velvet' has given rise to the proprietary name Velcro (M20) for a form of fastening widely used for fabrics, consisting of two strips of nylon with complementary meshed and hooked surfaces which adhere to each other when pressed together.

velouté /və'luːteɪ/ *noun* M19 French (= velvety). A rich white sauce made with chicken, veal, or fish stock, and often thickened with cream and egg-yolks. More fully *velouté sauce*.

vendange /vɑ̃dɑ̃ʒ/ *noun* plural pronounced same M18 **Old and Modern** French (cf. VENDEMMIA, VENDIMIA). In France: the grape-harvest; the vintage or grapes harvested; a particular vintage of wine.

vendangeur /vɑ̃dɑ̃ʒœr/ *noun* plural pronounced same L19 French. In France: a grape-picker.

1995 *Times* I have travelled the world for half a century gobbling bacteria on biscuits . . . washed down . . . with plonk contaminated by everything from insecticide and cork-mould to *vendangeur's* widdle and Austrian anti-freeze.

vendemmia /ven'demmja/ *noun* plural **vendemmie** /ven'demmje/ E19 Italian (from Latin *vindemia*; cf. VENDANGE, VENDIMIA). In Italy: the grape-harvest; the vintage or grapes harvested; a particular vintage of wine.

vendetta /vɛn'dɛtə/ *noun* M19 Italian (from Latin *vindicta* vengeance). **1** M19 A blood feud in which the family of a murdered person seeks vengeance on the murderer or the murderer's family, especially as customary in Corsica and Sicily. **2** M19 A similar blood feud, or prosecution of private revenge. Also, a prolonged bitter quarrel with or campaign against a person etc.

vendeuse /vɑ̃døz/ *noun* plural pronounced same E20 French (from *vendre* to sell). A saleswoman; *specifically* one employed in a fashion house.

1996 *Times Magazine* Abandoning the stage, she worked as a *vendeuse* for the fashion house Worth.

vendimia /ven'dimja/ *noun* M20 Spanish (from Latin *vindemia*; cf. VENDANGE, VENDEMMIA). In Spain: the grape-harvest; the vintage or grapes harvested; a particular vintage of wine. Also, a festival celebrating the vintage.

vendue /vɛn'dju:/ *noun* L17 Dutch (*vendu*, *vendue* from Old and Modern French (now dialect) *vendue* sale, from *vendre* to sell). A public sale; an auction. *United States* and *West Indies*.

veni, vidi, vici /'vemi 'vi:di 'vi:ki/ *interjection* L16 Latin. I came, I saw, I conquered.

■ According to the ancient biographer Plutarch, the words in which Julius Caesar reported his victory at Zela over Pharnaces, king of Pontus in Asia Minor, in 47 BC. Used with reference to any swift and overwhelming success.

venire /vɪ'nʌɪri:/ *noun* M17 Latin (= to come). **1** M17 *Law* (now *historical*) Elliptically for VENIRE FACIAS sense 1. **2** M20 *United States Law* A panel of people available for jury service.

venire facias /vɪ,nʌɪri: 'feɪʃɪas/ *noun phrase* LME Latin (literally, 'to make or cause to come'). *Law* **1** LME A judicial writ directing a sheriff to summon a jury. Now *historical* except *United States*. **2** LME–M18 A writ issuing a summons to appear before a court.

ventre à terre /vãtr a tɛr/ *adverb phrase* M19 French (literally, 'belly to the ground'). **1** M19 Of an animal, especially a horse: represented in a painting etc. with legs stretched out in line with the belly; moving at full speed. **2** M20 Lying on the stomach; prone.

1 1977 E. Crispin *Glimpses of Moon* Man and horse . . . went on to gallop almost *ventre à terre* in the direction of the hedge.

venue /'vɛnju:/ *noun* ME Old and Modern French (use as noun of feminine past participle of *venir* to come, from Latin *venire*). **1** ME A sally in order to assault someone, an attack. *rare*. Only in ME. **2** *Law* (now *historical*) The locality within which a cause must be tried. **b** The scene of a real or supposed action or event. **c** An appointed meeting-place, especially for a sporting match or competition; a rendezvous.

■ Also formerly in sense 1 with now obsolete uses in fencing terminology.

vera causa /,vɛːrə 'kaʊzə/ *noun phrase* M19 Latin (= real cause). *Philosophy* A true cause which brings about an effect as a minimum independent agency.

vera copula /,vɛːrə 'kɒpjʊlə/ *noun phrase* M19 Latin (= true union). *Law* Sexual intercourse with erection and penetration.

veranda /və'randə/ *noun* (also **verandah**; **viranda**, **virando**) E18 Hindustani (*varaṇḍā* from Portuguese *varanda* railing, balustrade, balcony, of unknown origin). **1** E18 A usually roofed open portico or gallery extending along a wall of a house or building. **2** M19 A roof or canopy extending over the pavement outside a shop or business establishment. *Australia* and *New Zealand*.

verbatim /və'beɪtɪm/ *adverb, adjective, & noun* L15 Medieval Latin (from Latin *verbum* word; cf. LITERATIM). **A** *adverb* **1** L15 Word for word; in exactly the same words. **2** E16–M17 In so many words; exactly, precisely. **B** *adjective* M18 Corresponding with or following an original word for word. **C** *noun* L19 A full or word-for-word report of a speech etc.

verboten /fɛr'boːtən/ *adjective* E20 German. Forbidden, not allowed.

verbum sapienti /,və:bəm sap,ɪɛnti 'sat ɛst/ *interjection* E19 Latin (*verbum sapienti sat est* a word is sufficient for a wise person). A word to the wise (implying that any further explanation or comment is unnecessary or inadvisable).

■ The expression in its full form is virtually never found; by far the most common variant is *verb. sap.* /və:b 'sap/ (E19), but *verbum sap.* /və:bəm 'sap/ or *verbum sat* /,və:bəm 'sat/ 'a word (is) enough' (M17) are also used.

verd-antique /,və:dan'ti:k/ *noun & adjective* M18 French (*verd* (now *vert*) green + *antique* antique). **A 1** M18 An ornamental variety of marble, consisting chiefly of serpentine mixed with calcite and dolomite. **2** M19 A greenish patina or incrustation on brass or copper; verdigris. **3** M19 Greenstone. More fully *oriental verd-antique*, *verd-antique porphyry*. **B** *attributive* or as *adjective* E19 Made or consisting of verd-antique.

verde antico /,verde 'antiko/ *noun phrase* M18 Italian. VERD-ANTIQUE sense 1.

Verfremdung /fɛr'frɛmdʊŋ/ *noun* M20 German. Chiefly *Theatre* Distancing, alienation, especially of a theatrical audience.

■ Also *Verfremdungseffekt* /fɛr'frɛmduŋsɛ
ˌfɛkt/ (= alienation effect). The term was
coined by the German dramatist and theatrical producer Bertold Brecht (1898–1956)
for his theory of theatrical alienation.

verglas /'vɛːglɑː/ *noun* E19 French (from
verre glass + *glas* (now *glace*) ice). A glassy
coating of ice formed on the ground or
an exposed surface by rain freezing on
impact or the refreezing of thawed ice.

verismo /vɛ'rɪzməʊ/ *noun* E20 Italian. Realism or naturalism in the arts, especially
with reference to late nineteenth-century
Italian opera.
> **1996** *Times Verismo* is a bogus and self-contradictory term—all theatre is illusion—but
> there is abundant, near-unbearable human
> truth in these episodes [of *La Bohème*].

vérité /verite/ *noun* M20 French (= truth).
Realism or naturalism, especially in cinema, radio, and television; documentary
method. Cf. CINÉMA-VÉRITÉ.

verkrampte /fer'krɑmptə/ *adjective* &
noun (also (as predicative adjective) **ver-
kramp** /fer'krɑmp/) M20 Afrikaans (= narrow, cramped). **A** *adjective* M20 Politically
or socially conservative or reactionary, especially in racial matters. **B** *noun* M20
Such a conservative or reactionary person.

■ Originally used in South Africa of politicians on the conservative wing of the Nationalist Party, but now more generally of
any die-hard reactionary, especially a hardline segregationist Afrikaner. The word
often appears in contexts in which it is explicitly or implicitly contrasted with VER-
LIGTE.

verligte /fer'lɪxtə/ *adjective* & *noun* (also
(as predicative adjective) **verlig** /fer'lɪx/)
M20 Afrikaans (= enlightened). **A** *adjec-
tive* M20 Progressive, enlightened, especially in racial matters. **B** *noun* M20 Such
a progressive or enlightened person.

■ In South Africa, the opposite of VER-
KRAMPTE (see quotation).
> **1981** *Observer* Like most black African
> Muslims, Edvis favours a liberal interpretation
> of the Koran, being *verligte* rather than
> *verkrampte* in that regard.

vermicelli /ˌvəːmɪ'(t)sɛli/ *noun* M17 Italian
(plural of *vermicello* diminutive of *verme*
worm, from Latin *vermis*). Pasta in the
form of long slender threads, often added
to soups. Now also (*transferred*), shreds of
chocolate used as cake decoration etc.

vernaccia /və'natʃə/ *noun* E19 Italian. A
strong (usually dry white) wine produced
in the San Gimignano area of Italy and in
Sardinia; the grape from which this is
made.

vernis martin /ˌvɛːniː 'mɑːtan/, *foreign*
/vɛrni martɛ̃/ *noun* & *adjective phrase* L19
French (from *vernis* varnish + family
name *Martin* of French brothers noted for
using the lacquer). **A** *noun phrase* L19 A
lacquer or varnish imitating oriental lacquer, used in the eighteenth century.
B *adjective phrase* L19 Finished in vernis
martin.

vernissage /vɛrnisaʒ/ *noun* plural pronounced same E20 French (literally, 'varnishing'). Originally, a day before an
exhibition of paintings on which exhibitors could retouch and varnish pictures
already hung. Now usually, a private view
of paintings before public exhibition.

veronique /vɛrə'niːk/, *foreign* /verɔnik/
postpositive adjective also **Véronique** E20
French (*Véronique* Veronica). *Cookery* Designating a dish, especially of fish or
chicken, prepared or garnished with
grapes.

verre églomisé /vɛr eglɔmize/ *noun
phrase* E20 French (*verre* glass + ÉGLOMISÉ).
Glass decorated with a layer of engraved
gold.
> **1996** *Country Life* The pair of mirrors with red
> and gold *verre églomisé* frames . . . are in the
> arched alcoves above.

versant /'vəːs(ə)nt/ *noun* M19 French (use
as noun of present participle of *verser*
from Latin *versare* to turn hither and
thither). The slope, side, or descent of a
mountain or mountain chain; the general slope of an area or region.

vers de société /vɛr də sɔsjete/ *noun
phrase* L18 French (literally, 'verse of society'). Verse treating topics provided by polite society in a light, often witty style.

vers d'occasion /vɛr dɔkazjɔ̃/ *noun
phrase* M19 French. Light verse written for
a special occasion.

vers libre /vɛr libr/ *noun phrase* plural
vers libres (pronounced same) E20
French (literally, 'free verse'). Unrhymed
verse which disregards the traditional
rules of prosody; an example of this.

verso /'vəːsəʊ/ *noun* plural **versos** M19
Latin (*verso* (sc. *folio*) = (the leaf) being
turned, ablative singular neuter of *versus*
past participle of *vertere* to turn). **1** M19
The left-hand page of an open book; the

back of a leaf in a manuscript or printed book, as opposed to the front or RECTO. **2** L19 The reverse side, especially of a coin or medal.

Versöhnung /fɛrˈzøːnʊŋ/ *noun* plural **Versöhnungen** /fɛrˈzøːnʊŋən/ M19 German (= conciliation, propitiation). A reconciliation of opposites.
1976 G. Talbot *Permission to Speak* It was a jarring note in an evening of festive international *versöhnung*.

Verstandesmensch /fɛrˈʃtandəsˌmɛnʃ/ *noun* plural **Verstandesmenschen** /fɛr ˈʃtandəsˌmɛnʃən/ L19 German. A matter-of-fact person; a realist.

Verstehen /fɛrˈʃteːən/ *noun* M20 German (= understanding, comprehension). (The use of empathy in) the sociological or historical understanding of human action and behaviour.

versus /ˈvəːsəs/ *preposition* LME Medieval Latin (use of Latin *versus* towards, in sense of *adversus* against). Against, in opposition to.
■ Used especially in legal or sporting contexts, where it is generally abbreviated *v.* or *vs*, as in *Rovers v. Wolves*.

vertex /ˈvəːtɛks/ *noun* plural **vertices** /ˈvəːtiːsiːz/, **vertexes** LME Latin (= whirl, vortex, crown of the head, highest point, from *vertere* to turn). **1** LME *Anatomy* and *Zoology* The crown or top of the head or skull. **b** E19 *Entomology* The top of the head of an insect. **2** L16 *Geometry* The point opposite to the base of a (plane or solid) figure; the point in a curve or surface at which the axis meets it; an angular point of a triangle, polygon, etc. **b** E18 *Optics* The point where the optical axis intersects the surface of a lens. **c** L19 *Astronomy* The point on the limb of a celestial object where it is intersected by a circle passing through the zenith and the centre of the object. Now also, the point to which a group of stars appears to converge, or from which a shower of meteors appears to radiate. **d** M20 *Mathematics* A junction of two or more lines in a network or graph; a node. **3** M17 The point in the sky directly above a given place; the zenith. **4** M17 The top or highest point of a thing.

vertigo /ˈvəːtɪɡəʊ/ *noun* LME Latin ((stem *vertigin-*) = whirling about, giddiness, from *vertere* to turn). **1** LME *Medicine* A sensation of whirling motion, tending to result in a loss of balance and sometimes of consciousness; giddiness, dizziness.

2 M17 *figurative* A disordered state of mind or things.

vertu variant of VIRTU.

vesica /ˈvɛsɪkə/, /ˈviːsɪkə/ *noun* M17 Latin (= bladder, blister). **1** M17 *Anatomy* A bladder. Usually with Latin specifying word. *rare*. **2** E19 Elliptical for VESICA PISCIS.

vesica piscis /ˌvɛsɪkə ˈpɪskɪs/, /ˌviːsɪkə ˈpɪskɪs/ *noun phrase* (also **vesica piscium** /ˌvɛsɪkə ˈpɪskɪʌm/) E19 Latin (= fish's (or fishes') bladder). A pointed oval figure used as an architectural feature and as an aureole enclosing figures of Christ, the Virgin, etc., in medieval painting and sculpture.
■ The origin of the name is uncertain; one nineteenth-century writer objected that it was not a bladder belonging to a fish but a bladder which, when filled, would be in the shape of a fish. Another attributed the invention of the term to the German artist Albrecht Dürer (1471–1528).

vespasienne /vɛspazjɛn/ *noun* plural pronounced same E20 French (abbreviation of *colonne vespasienne* Vespasian column). In France: a public lavatory.
■ The allusion is to the Roman emperor Vespasian, who introduced a tax on public lavatories.

vestigium /vɛˈstɪdʒɪəm/ *noun* plural **vestigia** /vɛˈstɪdʒɪə/ M17 Latin. A vestige, a trace. Usually followed by *of*.

veto /ˈviːtəʊ/ *noun* & *verb* E17 Latin (= I forbid, used by Roman tribunes of the people to oppose measures of the Senate or actions of the magistrates). **A** *noun* E17 plural **vetoes** A prohibition of a proposed or intended act, especially a legislative enactment; the right or power of preventing an act in this way. Frequently in *apply*, *place*, or *put a veto on* or *to*. **B** *transitive verb* E18 Put a veto on (a measure etc.), refuse consent to, forbid authoritatively; refuse to admit or accept (a person).

ve-tsin /verˈtsɪn/ *noun* M20 Chinese (*wèijīng*, from *wèi* taste, ingredient + *jīng* refined, essence, extract). Monosodium glutamate, as used in Chinese cookery.

veuve /vəːv/, *foreign* /vœv/ *noun* L18 French. In France: a widow.
■ Frequently as a title prefixed to a woman's surname and perhaps most familiar as part of a proprietary name of a brand of champagne: *Veuve Clicquot*.

vexata quaestio /vɛkˌsɑːtə ˈkwʌɪstɪəʊ/, /vɛkˌseɪtə ˈkwiːstɪəʊ/ *noun phrase* plural

vexatae quaestiones /vɛkˌsɑːtiː ˌkwʌɪstɪ
ˈəʊniːz/ E19 Latin. A vexed question.

vexillum /vɛkˈsɪləm/ noun plural **vexilla**
/vɛkˈsɪlə/ E18 Latin (= flag, banner, from
vex-, vect-, vehere to carry, convey). 1 E18
Roman History A military standard or banner; a body of soldiers grouped under
this. b L19 Ecclesiastical A small piece of
linen or silk attached to the upper part of
a crozier. 2 E18 Botany The standard or
large uppermost petal of a papiliona-
ceous flower. 3 M19 Ornithology The vane
of a feather.

via /ˈvʌɪə/, /ˈviːə/ preposition L18 Latin (ablative singular of via way). 1 By way of;
by a route passing through or over. 2 M20
By means of; with the aid of.

via affirmativa /ˌviːə əfəˈmɑːtʌɪvə/ noun
phrase M19 Modern Latin (= affirmative
way). Theology The approach to God
through positive statements about his nature. Cf. VIA NEGATIVA.

Via Crucis /ˌviːə ˈkruːʧɪs/ noun phrase M19
Latin (= way of the cross). The route followed by Christ to Calvary; Christian
Church the Way of the Cross as a series of
devotions or, especially in the Roman Catholic Church, a series of 'stations' or
shrines set around a church interior for
devotion and meditation; figurative an extremely painful experience requiring
strength or courage to bear.

Via Dolorosa /ˌviːə dɒləˈrəʊzə/ noun
phrase L19 Latin (literally, 'sorrowing
way'). 1 L19 The route believed to have
been taken by Christ through Jerusalem
to Calvary. 2 E20 figurative A prolonged
ordeal.

2 1996 C. Lis and H. Soly Disordered Lives
Married life for him was a via dolorosa: his wife
beat him till the blood flowed, killed their cat
and dog, set the household furniture on fire
and threw burning embers at passers-by . . .

via media /ˌviːə ˈmiːdɪə/ noun phrase M19
Latin A middle way; an intermediate
course, a compromise.

1996 Spectator The Anglican via media was
almost always Burke's way . . .

via negativa /ˌviːə nɛɡəˈtʌɪvə/ noun phrase
M19 Modern Latin (= negative way). Theology The approach to God believing no
positive statements can be made about
his nature; transferred a way of denial.

viaticum /vʌɪˈatɪkəm/ noun plural **viatica**
/vʌɪˈatɪkə/ (formerly also Anglicized as
viatic) M16 Latin (use as noun of neuter of
viaticus pertaining to a road or journey,

from via road). 1 M16 Christian Church The
Eucharist as administered to a person
near or in danger of death. 2 L16 A supply or official allowance of money for a
journey: travelling expenses. b M17 A
supply of food for a journey.

vibrato /vɪˈbrɑːtəʊ/ adverb & noun M19 Italian (past participle of vibrare vibrate).
Music A adverb M19 With a rapid slight
variation in pitch. B noun L19 plural **vibratos** A rapid slight variation in pitch in
the singing or playing of a note. Cf. TREM-
OLO noun 1.

B 1996 Times The real weight lies in the
middle of the voice, with the sweetest of
vibratos . . .

vice anglais /vis ɑ̃glɛ/ noun phrase M20
French (literally, 'English vice'). A vice
considered characteristic of the English;
especially the use of corporal punishment
for sexual stimulation.

vicereine /ˈvʌɪsrɛm/ noun E19 French
(from vice- vice- + reine queen). The wife of
a viceroy. Also, a female viceroy.

vice versa /ˌvʌɪsə ˈvəːsə/, /ˌvʌɪs/ adverb
phrase E17 Latin (literally, 'the position
being reversed', from as vice ablative of vix
change, place, stead + versa ablative feminine singular of versus past participle of
vertere to turn). With a reversal of the
order of terms or conditions mentioned;
contrariwise, conversely.

1996 Spectator The medium seems to have
chosen him rather than vice versa.

vichyssoise /ˌviːʃiːˈswɑːz/ noun M20
French (crême vichyssoise glacée, literally,
'iced cream soup of Vichy'). A soup made
with potatoes, leeks, and cream, and usually served cold.

victor ludorum /ˌvɪktə luːˈdɔːrəm/ noun
phrase E20 Latin (= victor of the games).
The overall champion in a sports competition, especially at a school or college; the
sports competition itself.

figurative 1996 Times Though his former
teacher Brunetto Latini is condemned to run
forever on the burning marl among the
sodomites, Dante treats him as a father figure,
and as an intellectual victor ludorum.

vicuña /vɪˈkjuːnjə/, /vɪˈkuːnjə/ noun (also
vicugna, **vicuna** /vɪˈkjuːnə/) E17 Spanish
(from Quechua wikúña). 1 E17 A hoofed
mammal of the high Andes, Vicugna vicugna, which is related to the llama and
guanaco and has a fine silky coat used for
textile fabrics. 2 M19 A fine fabric made
from the wool of the vicuña (also more

fully *vicuña cloth*). Also, a garment made of this fabric.

vicus /'vʌɪkəs/, /'viːkəs/ *noun* plural **vici** /'vʌɪkiː/ M19 Latin (= village, group of dwellings). *Archaeology* In the Roman Empire, a village, a settlement; *specifically* the smallest unit of ancient Roman municipal administration, consisting of a village, part of a town, etc. Also, a medieval European township.

vide /'vʌɪdi/, /'vɪdeɪ/ *transitive verb* (*imperative*) M16 Latin (imperative singular of *videre* to see). See, refer to, consult.

■ Used as a direction in a text referring the reader to a specified passage, work, etc., for fuller or further information. Also abbreviated to *vid*.

1996 *Spectator* . . . English intellectuals like to define themselves by their philistinism about sport. This is not true of intellectuals elsewhere: *vide* my prized collection of Renaissance goalkeepers, which includes Albert Camus, Vladimir Nabokov, . . .

videlicet /vɪ'dɛlɪsɛt/, /vʌɪ'dɛlɪsɛt/, /vɪ'dɛlɪkɛt/ *adverb & noun* LME Latin (from *vide-* stem of *videre* to see + *licet* it is permissible; cf. SCILICET). **A** *adverb* LME Usually introducing an amplification or explanation of a previous statement or word; that is to say, namely. **B** *noun* M17 The word 'videlicet' introducing an explanation or amplification, especially in a legal document.

■ Frequently abbreviated to *viz*(.) (M16), the *z* representing the usual medieval Latin symbol of contraction for *-et*.

vidimus /'vʌɪdɪməs/ *noun* LME Latin (= we have seen, from *videre* to see). **1** LME A copy of a document bearing an attestation of its authenticity or accuracy. **b** M19 An inspection of accounts.

vie de Bohème /vi də bɔɛm/ *noun phrase* L19 French. A Bohemian way of life.

vie de château /vi də ʃɑto/ *noun phrase* E20 French. The way of life of a large country house; aristocratic social life.

vie d'intérieur /vi dēterjœr/ *noun phrase* L19 French. Private or domestic life.

vie en rose /vi ã roz/ *noun phrase* M20 French. A life seen through rose-coloured spectacles.

■ A phrase popularized by the French singer Edith Piaf (1915–63), one of whose songs was called 'La Vie en rose'.

1974 M. Cecil *Heroines in Love* So many hopes had tumbled that magazine writers were reluctant to present an unending *vie en rose*.

vie intérieure /vi ēterjœr/ *noun phrase* E20 French. One's inner life, the life of the spirit.

vie intime /vi ētim/ *noun phrase* L19 French. The intimate private life of a person.

vie romancée /vi rɔmãse/ *noun phrase* plural **vies romancées** (pronounced same) M20 French. A fictionalized biography.

vi et armis /ˌviː ɛt 'ɑːmiːs/ *adverb phrase* E17 Latin (= with force and arms). Violently, forcibly, by compulsion; *specifically* in *Law* (now *historical*), with unlawful violence.

vieux jeu /vjø ʒø/ *noun & adjective* plural of noun **vieux jeux** (pronounced same) L19 French (literally, 'old game'). (Something or someone) old-fashioned, outmoded, passé.

vieux marcheur /vjø marʃœr/ plural **vieux marcheurs** (pronounced same) E20 French (literally, 'old campaigner'). An elderly womanizer.

■ From the title of a play *Le Vieux Marcheur* (1909) by Henri Lavedon.

vieux rose /vjø roz/ *noun & adjective* L19 French. (Of) a deep pink colour, old rose.

viga /'viːgə/ *noun* M19 Spanish. In United States: a rough-hewn roof timber or rafter, especially in a Pueblo building.

vigia /'vɪdʒɪə/ *noun* M19 Portuguese (= lookout, from *vigiar*, from Latin *vigilia* wakefulness, from *vigil* awake, alert). A warning on a sea chart to denote a reported but as yet unverified danger.

vigilante /vɪdʒɪ'lanti/ *noun* M19 Spanish (from Latin *vigilant-* present participial stem of *vigilare* to keep awake). A member of a vigilance committee; any person executing summary justice in the absence or breakdown of legally constituted law enforcement bodies. Now also, a member of a self-appointed group undertaking law enforcement but without legal authority, operating in addition to an existing police force to protect property etc. within a localized area. Originally *United States*.

attributive **1995** *New Scientist* . . . the California-based Sea Shepherd Conservation Society—a kind of marine vigilante squad—threatens to halt the Makah hunt by force.

vigneron /'viːnjərɒn/, *foreign* /viɲərɔ̃/ (*plural same*) *noun* LME French (from *vigne*

vine). A person who cultivates grapevines; a vine-grower.

vignette /viːˈnjɛt/, /vɪˈnjɛt/ *noun & verb* LME Old and Modern French (diminutive of *vigne* vine). **A** *noun* **1** LME A usually small decorative design or illustration on a blank space in a book etc., especially at the beginning or end of a chapter or on the title page; *specifically* one not enclosed in a border, or with the edges shading off into the surrounding paper. **2** LME *Architecture* A carved decoration representing the trailing tendrils, branches, or leaves of a vine. **3** M19 A photographic portrait showing only the head or the head and shoulders and with the edges gradually shading into the background. **4** L19 A brief descriptive account, anecdote, or essay; a character sketch; a short evocative episode in a play etc. **B** *transitive verb* **1** M19 Make a vignette of; *specifically* produce (a photograph) in the style of a vignette by softening away or shading off the edges of the subject. **2** M20 *Optics* Cause vignetting of an image.

  A.4 1996 *Spectator* The minor characters seem alive; the incidental vignettes are as well told as the climaxes . . .

vignoble /ˈviːnjəʊb(ə)l/ *noun* L15 Old and Modern French (from popular Latin, from Latin *vinea* vineyard). A vineyard.

vihara /vɪˈhɑːrə/ *noun* L17 Sanskrit (*vihāra*). A Buddhist monastery or nunnery.

villa /ˈvɪlə/ *noun* E17 Italian and Latin (partly from Latin *villa* country house, farm, partly from Italian *villa* from Latin). **1** E17 *Roman Antiquities* A large country house with an estate. Now, a country residence; *specifically* a rented or privately owned holiday home, especially abroad. **2** M18 A detached or semi-detached house in a suburban or residential district.

  ■ In sense 2 often in proper names, as *Villa Ariadne*.

villancico /ˌvɪ(l)janˈθiːko/, /ˌvɪ(l)janˈsiːko/ *noun* plural **villancicos** /ˌvɪ(l)janˈθiːkos/, /ˌvɪ(l)janˈsiːkos/ E19 Spanish (diminutive of *villano* peasant, rustic, from medieval Latin *villanus* villager, from Latin *villa* (sense 1)). *Music* A form of Spanish and Portuguese song consisting of short stanzas separated by a refrain, originally a kind of folk-song but later used in sacred music; now *especially* a Christmas carol.

villanella /vɪləˈnɛlə/ *noun* plural **villanelle** /vɪləˈnɛleɪ/, **villanellas** L16 Italian (see next). *Music* A form of Italian part-song having a rustic character and a vigorous rhythm.

villanelle /vɪləˈnɛl/ *noun* L16 French (from Italian *villanella* feminine of *villanello* rural, rustic, from *villano* peasant, rustic, from medieval Latin *villanus* villager, from Latin *villa* (sense 1)). **1** L16–L17 *Music* A VILLANELLA. **2** L19 A usually pastoral or lyric poem consisting normally of five three-line stanzas and a final quatrain, with only two rhymes throughout and some lines repeated.

ville /vɪl/, /vʌɪl/ *noun* M19 French (= town). A town, a village.

  ■ Colloquial, chiefly United States, where *-ville* occurs in the names of many towns (e.g. *Louisville*). Hence used jocularly as a suffix to form the name of a fictitious place that epitomizes the quality concerned (see quotation 1972).

  1972 *Publishers' Weekly* There are some who will simply not get the fun of it out there in mass-marketville.
  1977 M. Herr *Dispatches* Once we fanned over a little ville that had just been airstruck.

villeggiatura /ˌvilledʤaˈtuːra/ *noun* plural **villeggiature** /ˌvilledʤaˈtuːrə/ M18 Italian (from *villeggiare* to live at a villa or in the country, from *villa* villa). Residence at a country villa or in the country, especially in Italy; a holiday spent in this way.

ville lumière /vil lymjɛr/ *noun* E20 French (= town or city of light(s)). A brightly lit city or town; an exciting modern city or town; *specifically* (*la Ville Lumière*), Paris.

vim /vɪm/ *noun* M19 Latin (probably from *vim* accusative singular of *vis* strength, energy). Vigour, energy, spirit. Originally *United States*.

vimana /vɪˈmɑːnə/ *noun* M19 Sanskrit. In the Indian subcontinent: the central tower enclosing the shrine in a temple; *Mythology* a heavenly chariot.

vin /vɛ̃/ *noun* L17 French. French wine.

vina variant of VEENA.

vinaigrette /ˌvɪnerˈgrɛt/, /ˌvɪnɪˈgrɛt/ *noun* LME French (from *vinaigre* vinegar). **1** A stew, sauce, or other dish made with vinegar. Only in LME. **b** A condiment prepared with vinegar. Only in L17. **2** L17 *History* A small two-wheeled carriage drawn or pushed by people, formerly used in France. **3** E19 A small ornamental bottle or box for holding a sponge saturated with smelling-salts etc. **4** L19 A salad dressing of oil and wine vinegar with seasoning. Also more fully *vinaigrette dressing, vinaigrette sauce.*

vin blanc /vɛ̃ blɑ̃/ *noun phrase* L18 French. White wine.

vin compris /vɛ̃ kɔ̃pri/ *noun phrase* L19 French. Wine included in the price of a meal or other entertainment.

vin cuit /vɛ̃ kɥi/ *noun phrase* M19 French (literally 'cooked, boiled'). **1** M19 Grape juice boiled to a syrup and used to fortify or sweeten other wine. Cf. VINO COTTO. **2** M20 A sweet aperitif wine.

vinculum /'vɪŋkjʊləm/ *noun plural* **vincula** /'vɪŋkjʊlə/ M17 Latin (from *vincire* to bind). **1** M17 A bond, a tie. Chiefly *figurative.* **2** E18 *Mathematics* A horizontal line over two or more terms, denoting that they are to be treated as a unit in the following operation. **3** M19 *Anatomy* A connecting band or bandlike structure; *especially* a narrow tendon.

vindaloo /vɪndə'lu:/ *noun* L19 Portuguese (probably from Portuguese *vin d'alho* wine and garlic sauce, from *vinho* wine + *alho* garlic). A highly spiced hot Indian curry dish made with meat, fish, or poultry. Also *vindaloo curry.*

vin de paille /vɛ̃ də pɑj/ *noun phrase* M19 French (= straw wine). Wine made from grapes that have been dried on straw mats before being pressed.

vin de table /vɛ̃ də tabl/ *noun phrase* M20 French. Wine suitable for drinking with a meal, usually one that is not fortified or sparkling.

■ The English phrase *table wine* (L17) is also used, especially of non-French wines; the German equivalent is TAFELWEIN.

vin d'honneur /vɛ̃ dɔnœr/ *noun phrase* E20 French. A wine formally offered in honour of a person or persons; the reception at which the wine is offered.

vin doux (naturel) /vɛ̃ du natyrel/ *noun phrase* M20 French (literally, 'sweet (natural)'). A sweet fortified wine.

vin du pays /vɛ̃ dy pe(j)i/ *noun phrase* L18 French (literally, 'of the country'). A local wine.

vin fou /vɛ̃ fu/ *noun phrase* M19 French (literally, 'mad'). A white or rosé sparkling wine from the Jura.

vin gris /vɛ̃ gri/ *noun phrase* M19 French (literally, 'grey'). A rosé wine of eastern France.

vingt-et-un /vɛ̃t e œ̃/ *noun* Also written **vingt-un** L18 French (= twenty-one). The card-game pontoon.

vinho /'viɲu/, /'vi:nəʊ/ *noun* M19 Portuguese. Portuguese wine.

vinho branco /ˌviɲu 'braŋku/, /ˌviɲu 'braŋkəʊ/ *noun phrase* M19 Portuguese. White wine.

vinho corrente /ˌviɲu kɔ'rrentə/ *noun phrase* L20 Portuguese (literally, 'common wine'). Cheap wine equivalent to VIN ORDINAIRE.

vinho da casa /ˌviɲu da 'kaza/ *noun phrase* M20 Portuguese (literally, 'wine of the house'). House wine.

vinho de consumo /ˌviɲu də kɔ̃'sumu/ *noun phrase* L20 Portuguese (literally, 'wine for consumption'). VINHO CORRENTE.

vinho tinto /ˌviɲu 'tintu/, /ˌvi:nəʊ 'tɪntəʊ/ *noun phrase* M19 Portuguese. Red wine.

vinho verde /ˌviɲu 'verdə/, /ˌviɲu 'və:di/ *noun phrase* M20 Portuguese (literally, 'green wine'). Young wine not allowed to mature.

vin jaune /vɛ̃ ʒon/ *noun phrase* M19 French (literally, 'yellow'). A yellowish wine from the Jura region of eastern France.

vin mousseux /vɛ̃ musø/ *noun phrase* L18 French. A sparkling wine. Also called MOUSSEUX.

vino /'vinʊ/, *especially in sense 3* /ˌvɪ:nəʊ/ *noun* L17 Spanish and Italian (= wine). **1** L17 Spanish or Italian wine. **2** E20 An alcoholic liquor distilled from nipa-palm sap drunk in the Philippines. **3** E20 Wine, especially of an inferior kind. *colloquial, often jocular.*

3 1976 P. Cave *High Flying Birds* I was far too stoned to take much notice of Lloyd's vino-inspired ramblings.

vino blanco /ˌvino 'blaŋko/ *noun phrase* L20 Spanish. White wine.

vino corriente /ˌvino ko'rrjente/ *noun phrase* M20 Spanish (literally, 'common wine'). Cheap wine equivalent to VIN ORDINAIRE.

vino cotto /ˌvino 'kɔtto/ *noun phrase* M19 Italian (literally 'cooked'). Grape juice boiled to a syrup and used to fortify or sweeten other wine, especially marsala. Cf. VIN CUIT.

■ The opposite is *vino crudo* /ˌvino 'kru:do/ (literally, 'raw wine') or 'wine in its natural state'. The distinction is first mentioned in English by the seventeenth-century English botanist John Ray: 'The boil'd wine, which they call *Vin Cotto*, seemed to us much stronger than the wine unboil'd, which they call *Vin Crudo*' (*Observations . . .* , 1673).

vino de color /ˌvino de koˈlor/ *noun phrase* M19 **Spanish**. A rich sweet wine, used in the blending of sherry and other fortified wines.

vino de pasto /ˌvino de ˈpasto/ *noun phrase* L19 **Spanish** (literally, 'pasture wine'). **1** L19 A pale and fairly dry sherry. **2** M20 A table wine for everyday consumption.

vino dolce /ˌvino ˈdoltʃe/ *noun phrase* E20 **Italian**. Sweet Italian wine.

vino dulce /ˌvino ˈdulθe/, /ˈdulse/ *noun phrase* E20 **Spanish**. Sweet Spanish wine.

vino maestro /ˌvino maˈestro/ *noun phrase* E20 **Spanish** (literally, 'master wine'). A sweet and strong wine used to fortify or sweeten other wines.

vino nero /ˌvino ˈneːro/ *noun phrase* M20 **Italian** (literally, 'black wine'). Dark red wine.

vin ordinaire /vɛ̃ ɔrdinɛr/ *noun phrase* E19 **French** (literally, 'ordinary wine'). Simple (usually red) table wine for everyday use.

■ Also referred to elliptically as ORDINAIRE (M19).

vino rosso /ˌvino ˈrosso/ *noun phrase* M20 **Italian**. Red wine.

vino santo /ˌvino ˈsanto/ *noun phrase* L17 **Italian** (literally, 'holy wine'). VINSANTO.

vino secco /ˌvino ˈsekko/ *noun phrase* E20 **Italian**. Dry wine.

vino tierno /ˌvino ˈtjerno/ *noun phrase* E20 **Spanish** (literally, 'tender'). Wine made from partially dried grapes, used especially for fortifying malaga.

vino tinto /ˌvino ˈtinto/ *noun phrase* L17 **Spanish**. Red wine.

vin rosé /vɛ̃ roze/, /ˈrəʊzeɪ/ *noun phrase* M20 **French**. Rosé wine.

vin rouge /vɛ̃ ruʒ/ E20 **French**. Red wine.

vinsanto /vinˈsanto/, /vɪnˈsantəʊ/ *noun* M20 **Italian** (from *vino santo* holy wine). A sweet white Italian dessert wine.

viola bastarda /vɪˌəʊlə baˈstɑːdə/ *noun phrase* E18 **Italian** (literally, 'bastard viol'). *Music* A bass viol tuned and played according to a system of tablature. Also called *lyra viol*.

viola da braccio /vɪˈəʊlə da ˌbratʃə/ *noun phrase* M19 **Italian** (literally, 'viol of the arm'). Any member of the violin family, as opposed to a viola da gamba; *specifically* a viol corresponding to the modern viola.

viola da gamba /vɪˌəʊlə də ˈgambə/ *noun phrase* (also (earlier) **viol da gamba** /ˌvaɪəl də ˈgambə/) L16 **Italian** (literally, 'leg viol'). **1** L16 A viol held between the player's legs, *especially* one corresponding to the modern cello. **2** M19 An organ-stop resembling this instrument in tone.

viola d'amore /vɪˈəʊlə daˌmɔːre/ *noun phrase* E18 **Italian** (literally, 'viol of love'). A kind of tenor viol usually having sympathetic strings and no frets.

violetta /vioˈlɛtta/ *noun* plural **violette** /vioˈlɛtte/ M18 **Italian** (diminutive of *viola* viola). *Music* A small viol.

violette de Parme /vjɔlɛt də parm/ *noun phrase* plural **violettes de Parme** (pronounced same) E20 **French**. Any of various cultivated violets with double, scented, usually light purple flowers, used for perfume or crystallized for food decoration, a Parma violet.

violon /ˈvaɪələn/ *noun* M16 **French**. **1** M16–E17 A violin. Also, a violinist. **2** M19 A kind of organ-stop resembling a double bass in tone.

violoncello /ˌvaɪələnˈtʃɛləʊ/, /ˌviːələn ˈtʃɛləʊ/ *noun* E18 **Italian** (diminutive of *violone*). **1** E18 A cello. **b** M19 A cellist. **2** L19 An organ-stop similar in tone to a cello.

violon d'Ingres /vjɔlɔ̃ dɛgr/ *noun phrase* plural **violons d'Ingres** (pronounced same) M20 **French** (literally, 'Ingres' violin'). An interest or activity other than that for which a person is best known; an occasional pastime.

■ The allusion is to the French painter J.-A.-D. Ingres (1780–1867), who was a keen amateur violinist and said to have been more proud of his violin-playing than of his highly acclaimed pictures.

virage /viraʒ/ *noun* plural pronounced same M20 **French**. A hairpin bend; a sharp turn made in negotiating such a bend.

virago /vɪˈrɑːgəʊ/, /vɪˈreɪgəʊ/ *noun & adjective* LME Latin (from *vir* man). **A** *noun* plural **viragos**. **1** LME A woman of masculine strength or spirit; a female warrior, an amazon. *archaic.* **2** LME A domineering woman; a fierce or abusive woman. **B** *adjective* L16 That is a virago; of or pertaining to a virago or viragos.

■ Earlier (OE–L16) meaning 'woman', but only in biblical allusions with reference to the name given by Adam to Eve.

vires plural of VIS.

virga /ˈvəːgə/ *noun* plural **virgae** /ˈvəːgiː/ E20 Latin (= rod). **1** E20 *Music* (A symbol designating) a note used in plainsong. **2** M20 *Meteorology, singular* and in *plural* Streaks of precipitation that appear to hang from the undersurface of a cloud and usually evaporate before reaching the ground.

virgo intacta /ˌvəːgəʊ ɪnˈtaktə/ *noun phrase* E18 Latin (literally, 'untouched virgin'). Chiefly *Law* A girl or woman who has never had sexual intercourse.

virgule /ˈvəːgjuːl/ *noun* M19 French (= comma, from Latin *virgula* diminutive of *virga* rod). **1** M19 A slanting or upright line used especially in medieval manuscripts to mark a caesura, or as a punctuation mark equivalent to a comma. Now also a SOLIDUS sense 2. **2** L19 *Watchmaking* A type of escapement in which the teeth of the wheel have the shape of a comma. More fully *virgule escapement*.

virtu /vəːˈtuː/ *noun* (also **vertu, virtù**) E18 Italian (*virtù* virtue; the form *vertu* altered as if from French). **1** E18 A love of or interest in works of art; a knowledge of or expertise in the fine arts; the fine arts as a subject of study or interest. **2** M18 *collective* Objects of art; curios. **3** M20 The strength or worth inherent in a person or thing; *especially* inherent moral worth or virtue.

virtuoso /vəːtjʊˈəʊsəʊ/, /vəːtjʊˈəʊzəʊ/ *noun & adjective* E17 Italian (= learned, skilful, from late Latin *virtuosus*). **A** *noun* plural **virtuosi** /vəːtjʊˈəʊsiː/, **virtuosos** **1** E17–L18 A person who has a general interest in arts and sciences, or who pursues special investigations in one or more of these; a learned person. **2** M17 A person who has a special knowledge of or interest in the fine arts; a connoisseur, *especially* a person pursuing these interests in a dilettante manner. **3** M18 A person who has special knowledge or skill in the technique of a fine art, especially

music. Also, a person with outstanding technical skill in any sphere. **B** *attributive* or as *adjective* M17 Of or pertaining to a virtuoso; displaying the skills of a virtuoso; characterized by virtuosity.

A.3 1996 *Times* The virtuoso in interpersonal skills is the corporate future.

virtute officii /vəːˌtjuːti ɒˈfɪʃiː/ *adverb phrase* E19 Latin. *Law* By virtue of (one's) office.

vis /vɪs/ *noun* plural **vires** /ˈvʌɪriːz/ E17 Latin. **1** E17 Strength, force, energy, vigour. **2** L20 *Law* In *plural* Legal validity; legal authority or power.

■ Chiefly now in various phrases; in the legal sense *vires* occurs earlier in INTRA VIRES and ULTRA VIRES.

visa /ˈviːzə/ *noun* M19 French (from Latin = things seen, neuter plural of past participle of *videre* to see). An endorsement on a passport etc. indicating that it has been examined and found correct, especially as permitting the holder to enter or leave a country.

vis a fronte /ˌvɪs ɑː ˈfrɒnteɪ/ *noun phrase* E19 Latin. A force operating from in front, as in attraction or suction. Opposite of VIS A TERGO.

visagiste /ˌviːzɑːˈʒiːst/ *noun* (also **visagist** /ˈvɪzədʒɪst/) M20 French. A make-up artist.

vis a tergo /ˌvɪs ɑː ˈtəːgəʊ/ *noun phrase* E19 Latin. A force operating from behind; a propulsive force. Opposite of VIS A FRONTE.

vis-à-vis /ˌviːzɑːˈviː/ *noun, preposition & adverb* M18 Old and Modern French (literally, 'face to face', from Old French *vis* visage + *à* to + *vis*). **A** *noun* plural same. **1** M18 A light horse-drawn carriage for two people sitting face to face. *obsolete* except *historical*. **2** M18 A person or thing facing or situated opposite to another, especially in certain dances. **b** E20 A counterpart, an opposite number. Also (*United States*), a social partner. **3** M19 A face-to-face meeting. **B** *preposition* M18 Regarding, in relation to. Also, opposite to, face to face with. **C** *adverb* E19 Opposite; facing one another.

B 1996 *Times* But the Foreign Office must accept that its own obsessive secrecy . . . has ensured a climate of deep suspicion about anything involving its own role *vis-à-vis* the Jews and their treatment at the hands of the Nazis.

vis comica /ˌvɪs ˈkɒmɪkə/ *noun phrase* M18 Latin. Humorous energy; comic force or effect.

visibilia /ˌvɪzɪˈbɪlɪə/ *noun plural* M20 Latin (neuter plural of *visibilis* visible). Visible things; visual images.

vis inertiae /ˌvɪs ɪˈnɜːʃɪaɪ/ *noun phrase* E18 Latin. *Mechanics* The resistance offered by matter to any force tending to alter its state of rest or motion; *transferred* a tendency to remain inactive or unprogressive.

visitant /ˈvɪzɪt(ə)nt/ *noun & adjective* L16 French (present participle of *visiter* to visit, or Latin *visitant-* present participial stem of *visitare*). **A** *noun* **1** L16 A person who visits a place, another person, etc.; a visitor, now *especially* a supernatural one. **2** M18 A thing which affects or comes to a person, especially for a temporary period. **3** L18 A migratory bird or animal that frequents a certain locality only at particular times of year. **B** *adjective* M17 Of the nature of a visitant.

visite de digestion /vizit də diʒɛstjɔ̃/ *noun phrase* E20 French (literally, 'visit of digestion'). A formal call paid in return for hospitality received, especially after a dinner party.

vis major /ˌvɪs ˈmeɪdʒə/ *noun phrase* E17 Latin. *Law* Overpowering force, especially of nature (used as a reason for damage done to, or loss of, property).

vis medicatrix naturae /ˌvɪs mɛdɪˌkeɪtrɪks ˈnatʃəraɪ/ *noun phrase* E19 Latin. The healing power of nature.

vista /ˈvɪstə/ *noun* M17 Italian (= view). **1** M17 A view, a prospect, *especially* one seen through an avenue of trees or other long narrow opening. **2** L17 A long narrow opening, especially one created deliberately in a wood etc., through which a view may be obtained, or in itself affording a pleasant prospect. **b** E18 An open corridor or long passage in or through a large building; an interior portion of a building affording a continuous view. **3** L17 *figurative* A broad prospect or vision presented to the imagination; a mental view, in prospect or retrospect, of an extensive period of time or series of events, experiences, etc.

vis viva /ˌvɪs ˈviːvə/ *noun phrase* L18 Latin. *Mechanics* The operative force of a moving or acting body, equal to the mass of the body multiplied by the square of its velocity.

vita /ˈviːtə/ *noun* M20 Latin (= life). **1** M20 A biography, a life history, *especially* a short Latin biography of a saint. **2** M20 A CURRICULUM VITAE.

vita nuova /ˌviːtə ˈnwəʊvə/ *noun phrase* M20 Italian (= new life). A fresh start or new direction in life, especially after some powerful emotional experience.

■ With allusion to the title of a work by Dante describing his love for Beatrice.
1975 P. Organ *House on Cheyne Walk* Not a very good way to begin *la vita nuova*, with more lies.

vitello tonnato /viˈtɛllo tonˈnɑːto/ *noun phrase* M20 Italian (from *vitello* veal + *tonno* tuna). An Italian dish consisting of roast or poached veal served cold in a tuna and anchovy mayonnaise.

viva /ˈviːvə/ *noun* **1** *& interjection* M17 Italian (= live!, 3rd person singular present subjunctive of *vivere* to live, from Latin). (A cry or cheer) wishing long life and prosperity to or expressing approval of an admired person or thing: hurrah! long live! Cf. VIVAT, VIVE (interjection).

viva /ˈvaɪvə/ *noun* **2** *& verb* L19 Latin (abbreviation of VIVA VOCE). **A** *noun* L19 A VIVA VOCE examination. **B** *transitive verb* L19 past tense *vivaed, viva'd* /ˈvaɪvəd/. Subject to a viva voce examination, examine orally.

A 1996 *Spectator* The candidate in search of a doctorate was not alone in being taken aback by the honesty of Richard at their *viva* when he stated that he had not read all of the thesis.

vivandier /vivɑ̃djə/ *noun* (feminine **vivandière** /vivɑ̃djɛr/) plural pronounced same L16 French. *History* In the French and other Continental European armies, a supplier of provisions to troops in the field.

vivarium /vaɪˈvɛːrɪəm/, /vɪˈvɛːrɪəm/ *noun* plural **vivaria** /vaɪˈvɛːrɪə/, **vivariums** E17 Latin (= warren, fish-pond, use as noun of *vivarius* from *vivus* alive, from *vivere* to live). **1** E17 A place for keeping living animals, especially fish, for food; a fish-pond. *obsolete* except *historical*. **2** L17 A structure used for keeping animals under conditions approximating to the natural conditions, for observation or study.

vivat /ˈvaɪvat/, /ˈviːvat/ *interjection & noun* L16 Latin (= may he or she live, 3rd person singular present subjunctive of *vivere* to live). (A cry or cheer) wishing long life and prosperity to or expressing approval of an admired person or thing: hurrah! long live! Cf. VIVA, VIVE.

viva voce /ˌvʌɪvə ˈvəʊtʃɪ/ *adverb, adjective, & noun phrase* M16 Medieval Latin (literally, 'by or with the living voice'). **A** *adverb phrase* M16 Orally rather than in writing. **B** *adjective phrase* **1** E17 Expressed in speech rather than writing, spoken. **2** E19 Of an examination: conducted orally; *specifically* of a supplementary oral examination following a written one. **C** *noun phrase* M19 A viva voce examination.

■ In the nominal sense frequently abbreviated to VIVA (noun 2).

vive /viv/ *interjection* L16 French (= may he, she, or it live, from *vivre* from Latin *vivere* live). Wishing long life and prosperity to or expressing approval of an admired person or thing; long live! Cf. VIVA (interjection), VIVAT.

vive la bagatelle /viv la bagatɛl/ *interjection* M18 French (literally, 'success to frivolity or nonsense'). Expressing a carefree attitude to life.

vive la différence /viv la diferɑ̃s/ *interjection* M20 French. Expressing approval of the difference between the sexes.

■ In jocular use; also transferred (see quotation).
1995 *Times* Three compatriots argued that there was little scope for significant tax cuts . . . But—*vive la différence*—two others argued for higher public spending.

viveur /vivœr/ *noun* plural pronounced same M19 French (= a living person). A person who lives a fashionable and social life. Cf. BON VIVEUR.

vivier /vivje/ *noun* plural pronounced same. LME Old and Modern French. A fish-pond; a tank for storing live fish etc.

viz. abbreviation of VIDELICET.

vlakte /ˈflaktə/ *noun* L18 Afrikaans (from Dutch). In South Africa: an extent of flat open country; a plain. Frequently in *plural*.

vlei /fleɪ/, /vlʌɪ/ *noun* L18 Afrikaans (from Dutch *vallei* valley). **1** L18 In South Africa: a shallow pool of water; a piece of low-lying ground covered with water during the rainy season. **2** L19 A swamp. *United States local.*

vobla /ˈvɒblə/ *noun* (also **wobla**) M20 Russian. Dried and smoked roach eaten in Russia as a delicacy.

voce di gola /ˌvɒtʃe di ˈɡoːla/ *noun phrase* L19 Italian (literally, 'throat voice'). *Music* A throaty or guttural voice.

voce di petto /ˌvɒtʃe di ˈpɛtto/ *noun phrase* M18 Italian (literally, 'chest voice'). *Music* The chest register.

voce di testa /ˌvɒtʃe di ˈtɛsta/ *noun phrase* M18 Italian (literally, 'head voice'). *Music* The head register; formerly also, the falsetto voice.

vodka /ˈvɒdkə/ *noun* E19 Russian (diminutive of *voda* water). A colourless alcoholic spirit made especially in Russia by distillation of grain etc.; a glass or drink of this.

voetganger /ˈfʊtˌxaŋə/ *noun* E19 Afrikaans (from Dutch = pedestrian, from *voet* foot + *ganger* goer). **1** E19 A locust in its immature wingless stage. **2** E20 A pedestrian. Also (*colloquial*), an infantryman. *South African.*

voetsek /ˈfʊtsɛk/ *interjection & verb* (also **voetsak** /ˈfʊtsak/) M19 Afrikaans (*voe(r)tsek*, from Dutch *voort zeg ik* be off I say). **A** *interjection* M19 Especially to a dog: go away!, off you go! **B** *verb* **1** *transitive verb* L19 Chase (a dog) away. **2** *intransitive verb* M20 Leave, go away. *South African.*

voeu /vø/, /və:/ *noun* plural **voeux** (pronounced same) E20 French (= vow, wish). A non-mandatory recommendation made by an international conference.

vogue la galère /vɔɡ la ɡalɛr/ *interjection* M18 French (literally, 'let the galley be rowed'). Let's get on with it! Let's give it a go!

voilà /vwala/, /vwɑːˈlɑː/ *transitive & intransitive verb* (*imperative & impersonal*) (also **voila**) M18 French (from imperative of *voir* see + *là* there). There is, are, etc.; see there.

■ Also as an interjection: 'there it is!', 'there you are!'
1996 *New Scientist* Just as there is nothing north of the North Pole, so there was nothing before the Big Bang. Voilà! We are supposed to be convinced by that . . .

voilà tout /tu/, /tu:/ *interjection* E19 French. That's all! That's it! There is nothing more to do or say.

voile /vɔɪl/, /vwal/ *noun & adjective* L19 French (= veil). **A** *noun* L19 A lightweight open-texture material of cotton, wool, silk, or acetate, used especially for blouses and dresses. **B** *attributive* or as *adjective* L19 Made of voile.

voir dire /ˈvwɑː ˌdɪə/ *noun* (also **voire dire**) L17 Law French (from Old French *voir* true, truth + *dire* to say). *Law* A preliminary examination by a judge or counsel of the competence of a witness or (occasionally) a juror; an oath taken by such a witness. Also, an investigation into the truth or admissibility of evidence, held during a trial.

voix céleste /vwa səlɛst/, /ˌvwɑː sɪˈlɛst/ *noun phrase* plural **voix célestes** (pronounced same) L19 French (= heavenly voice). An organ-stop having an 8-ft pitch, with 2 pipes to each note, tuned slightly apart, producing an undulating tone traditionally regarded as reminiscent of celestial voices. Also called *vox angelica.*

volage /vɔˈlɑːʒ/ *adjective* LME Old and Modern French (from Latin *volaticus* winged, inconstant). Giddy, foolish; fickle, inconstant.

■ Formerly fully naturalized; now in literary use, reintroduced from modern French.

volante /vəˈlanti/ *noun* 1 L18 Spanish (from present participle of *volar* to fly, from Latin *volare* to fly). A horse-drawn carriage or wagon, especially of a two-wheeled covered type, used in Cuba and formerly in other Spanish-speaking countries.

volante /vəˈlanti/ *noun* 2 L19 Italian (= flying). *Music* The rapid execution of a series of notes in singing or playing; *especially* in violin-playing, a bowing technique in which the bow bounces from the string in a slurred staccato.

vol-au-vent /ˈvɒlə(ʊ)ˌvɒ̃/ *noun* E19 French (literally, 'flight in the wind'). A (usually small and round) flat-bottomed case of puff pastry filled with chopped meat, fish, egg, etc., in sauce.

volens /ˈvəʊlɛnz/ *adjective* L19 Latin (present participle of *velle* to be willing). *Law* Consenting to the risk of injury. Cf. NO-LENS VOLENS.

volet /ˈvɒleɪ/, *foreign* /vɔlɛ/ (*plural same*) *noun* M19 Old and Modern French (literally, 'shutter', from *voler* from Latin *volare* to fly). Each of the wings or side-compartments of a triptych. Also called *volant.*

volk /fɒlk/ *noun* (also (German) **Volk**) L19 Afrikaans (from Dutch or German = nation, people). **1** L19 The Afrikaner people. Also (frequently *derogatory*), the Coloured employees of a White (especially Afrikaner) master collectively. *South African.* **2** M20 The German people (especially with reference to Nazi ideology).

1 1996 T. Alexander *Unravelling Global Apartheid* . . . was access to global markets amd finance ultimately more important than self-determination and local supremacy for the Afrikaner *volk*?

Völkerwanderung /ˈføːlkərˌvandərʊŋ/, /ˈfɜːlkəˌvɑːndərʊŋ/ *noun* plural **Völkerwanderungen** /ˈføːlkərˌvandərʊŋən/ M20 German (from *Völker* nations + *Wanderung* migration). A migration of peoples; *specifically* that of Germanic and Slavonic peoples into and across Europe from the second to the eleventh centuries.

völkisch /ˈføːlkɪʃ/ *adjective* M20 German. Populist, nationalist, racialist.

volksgeist /ˈfɒlksɡʌɪst/ *noun* (also **Volksgeist**) M20 German. The spirit or genius that marks the thought or feeling of a nation or people.

1995 *Spectator* I first read Herder in a seminar organised by Nazi students at Freiburg in 1938, and it soon became clear to me that Herder's *volksgeist*—the spirit of a nation—could be stretched to cover a dangerous doctrine of racial supremacy.

volkslied /ˈfɒlksliːd/, /ˈfɒlksliːt/ *noun* plural **volkslieder** /ˈfɒlksliːdə/ (also **Volkslied**) M19 German (or Afrikaans (from Dutch)). **1** M19 A German folk-song; a song or other piece of music in the style of German folk-songs. **2** L19 A national anthem; *specifically* (*historical*) that of the nineteenth-century Transvaal Republic. Also, a South African folk-song.

volta /ˈvɒltə/ *noun* L16 Italian (= turn; cf. VOLTE). The LAVOLTA.

volte /vɒlt/, /vəʊlt/ *noun* L16 French (from Italian *volta* turn, use as noun of feminine past participle of *volgere* to turn, from Latin *volvere* to roll). **1** L16–E17 The LAVOLTA. **2** L17 *Fencing* (now *historical*) A sudden jump or other movement to avoid a thrust. **3** E18 *Horsemanship* A small circle of determined size (proposed with a radius equal to the length of a horse); a movement by a horse sideways around the point of such a circle. **4** E20 (A) complete change. *rare.*

volte-face /vɒltˈfɑːs/, /vɒltˈfas/ *noun* E19 French (from Italian *voltafaccia*, from *voltare* to turn (ultimately from frequentative of Latin *volvere* to roll) + *faccia* (ultimately from Latin *facies*) face). The act or an instance of turning so as to face in the opposite direction. Chiefly *figurative*, a complete change of attitude, opinion, or position in an argument.

1995 *Times* This volte-face confirms the suspicion that the earlier limits were set artificially low by the health education industry . . .

volupté /vɔlypte/ *noun* E18 **French**. Voluptuousness.

volute /və'l(j)uːt/ *noun* (also (earlier) in Latin form **voluta**, plural **volutae**) M16 **French** (Latin *voluta* use as noun of feminine of *volutus* past participle of *volvere* to roll, to wrap). **1** M16 *Architecture* A spiral scroll characteristic of Ionic capitals and also used in Corinthian and composite capitals. **2** M18 A spiral part or object; a convolution. **3** M18 (A shell of) any of numerous gastropod molluscs of the family Volutidae.

vomitorium /vɒmɪ'tɔːrɪəm/ *noun* plural **vomitoria** /vɒmɪ'tɔːrɪə/ M18 **Late Latin** (use as noun of neuter of Latin *vomitorius* vomitory). *Roman Antiquities* **1** M18 A passage or opening in an amphitheatre or theatre, leading to or from the seats. Usually in *plural*. **2** E20 A room allegedly for vomiting deliberately during feasts, to make way for other food.

voorloper /'fʊəlʊəpə/ *noun* M19 **Afrikaans** (from *voor-* before + *loop* to run). In South Africa: the leader of a span of oxen, usually a young African or Coloured boy.

Voortrekker /'fʊətrɛkə/ *noun* L19 **Afrikaans** (from *voor-* before + *trekken* to trek). *South African History* A Boer pioneer, *especially* one who took part in the Great Trek from Cape Colony *c.*1835.

vorlage /'fɔːlɑːgə/ *noun* plural **vorlages**, **vorlagen** /'fɔːlɑːgən/ M20 **German**. **1** M20 *Skiing* A position in which the skier leans forward without lifting the heels from the skis. **b** M20 In *plural* Skiing trousers. **2** M20 An original version of a manuscript from which a copy is produced.

vorlaufer /'fɔːlaʊfə/ *noun* M20 **German** (*Vorläufer*, from *vorlaufen* run on ahead). A skier who travels a course before a race to establish that it is within the capacity of the competitors.

Vorspiel /'fɔːrʃpiːl/ *noun* plural **Vorspiele** /'fɔːrʃpiːlə/ L19 **German** (from *vor* before + *Spiel* play). *Music* A prelude.

Vorstellung /'fɔːrʃtɛlʊŋ/ *noun* (also **vorstellung** plural **Vorstellen** /'fɔːrʃtɛlən/ E19 **German**. *Philosophy* and *Psychology* An idea, a mental picture.

vortex /'vɔːtɛks/ *noun* plural **vortexes** **vortices** /'vɔːtɪsiːz/ M17 **Latin** ((variant of VERTEX) an eddy of water, wind, or flame, from *vortere, vertere* to turn). **1 a** M17 In

Cartesian theory: any of the rapidly revolving collections of fine particles supposed to fill all space. Usually in *plural*. **b** M19 *Physics* A rapid motion of particles round an axis; a whirl of atoms, fluid, or vapour. **2** M17 A violent eddy of the air; a cyclone. Also, an eddying mass of fire. **3** E18 A swirling mass of water; a whirlpool. **4** *figurative* **a** M18 A whirl or constant round of frenetic activity, rapid change, etc. **b** L18 A place or state into which people or things are irresistibly drawn. **5** E20 *The Vortex* A group of modernist British artists (*c.*1914–15).

voulu /vuly/ *adjective* L19 **French** (past participle of *vouloir* to wish). Lacking in spontaneity; contrived.

voussoir /'vuːswɑː/ *noun* ME **Old French** (*vausoir, vaussoir*, etc. (modern *voussoir*) from popular Latin *volsorium* ultimately from Latin *vols-* past participial stem of *volvere* to roll, to turn). Each of the wedge-shaped or tapered stones, bricks, etc., forming an arch or vaulting.

vox angelica /ˌvɒks an'dʒɛlɪkə/ *noun phrase* M19 **Latin** (= angelic voice). A VOIX CÉLESTE.

vox humana /ˌvɒks hjʊ'mɑːnə/ *noun phrase* E18 **Latin** (= human voice). An organ reed-stop, having an 8-ft pitch, producing a tone supposedly resembling the human voice.

vox nihili /ˌvɒks 'nʌɪ(h)ɪlʌɪ/, /ˌvɒks 'nʌɪ(h)ɪliː/ *noun phrase* L19 **Latin** (literally, 'voice of nothing'). A worthless or meaningless word, *especially* one produced by a scribal or printer's error.

vox populi /ˌvɒks 'pɒpjʊlʌɪ/, /ˌvɒks 'pɒpjʊliː/ *noun phrase* M19 **Latin** (= voice of the people). Expressed general opinion; common talk or rumour.

■ In colloquial use abbreviated to *vox pop* (M20), usually (but not always—see quotation) with derogatory connotations of 'uninformed opinion, as expressed in the media by members of the public'. The Latin tag from which the phrase derives, *vox populi, vox Dei* 'the voice of the people is the voice of God' has been cited or alluded to in English from the fifteenth century.

1996 *Times* Vox pop is not, after all, baying for blood; on the contrary, it calls justly for guns to be taken out of our hands.

voyagé /vwajaʒe/ *noun & adjective* plural of noun pronounced same M20 **French** (past participle of *voyager* to travel). *Ballet* (Designating) a movement in which the pose is held during progression.

voyant /vwajɑ̃/ *noun* plural pronounced same M20 French (from as next). A visionary; a seer.

voyant /vwajɑ̃/ *adjective* E20 French (present participial adjective of *voir* to see). Showy, gaudy, flashy.

voyeur /vwɑːˈjəː/ *noun* E20 French (from *voir* to see). A person who obtains sexual satisfaction from covert observation of the sexual organs or actions of others. Also (*transferred*) a powerless or passive spectator.

> **1996** *Spectator* So there I sit like James Stewart in *Rear Window*, a voyeur in spite of myself . . .

voyou /vwaju/ *noun* plural pronounced same E20 French. A street urchin; a lout, a hooligan.

vozhd /vəʊʒd/ *noun* M20 Russian (*vozhd'*). A leader, a person in supreme authority; *specifically* (*historical*) Stalin.

vrai réseau /vrɛ rezo/ *noun phrase* plural **vrais réseaux** (pronounced same) M19 French (= true net). A fine net ground used in making handmade (especially Brussels) lace. Cf. RÉSEAU sense 1.

vraisemblable /vrɛsɑ̃blablˌ/ *adjective* M19 French (from *vrai* true + *semblable* like). Believable, plausible.

vraisemblance /vrɛsɑ̃blɑ̃s/ *noun* plural pronounced same E19 French (from *vrai* true + *semblance* likeness). **1** E19 Verisimilitude. **2** M19 A representation *of* a person or thing.

vrais réseaux plural of VRAI RÉSEAU.

vrouw /vraʊ/ *noun* (also **vrow**) E17 Dutch (= German *Frau*). A woman, a wife; *especially* one of Dutch origin. Chiefly *South African*.

vue d'ensemble /vy dɑ̃sɑ̃bl/ *noun phrase* plural **vues d'ensemble** (pronounced same) M19 French. A general view of matters; an overview.

vulgarisateur /vylgarizatœr/ *noun* plural pronounced same M20 French (from *vulgariser* to popularize, vulgarize). A popularizer, a vulgarizer.

vulgarisation /vylgarizasjɔ̃/ *noun* M20 French. Vulgarization. Cf. HAUTE VULGARISATION.

W

Wabenzi /wɑ'bɛnzi/ *noun plural* (also **Wa-Benzi**) M20 African languages (invented to resemble the name of an African people: from human plural prefix *wa-* + Mercedes-*Benz*). In Africa: Black politicians, civil servants, entrepreneurs, etc., whose status is marked by their ownership or use of a Mercedes-Benz or similar luxury car.

wabi /'wabi/ *noun* M20 Japanese (literally, 'solitude'). In Japanese art, a quality of simple and serene beauty of a slightly austere or melancholy kind expressing a mood of spiritual solitude recognized in Zen Buddhist philosophy. Cf. SABI.

wadi /'wɑ:di/, /'wɒdi/ *noun* (also **wady**) *plural* **wadis**, **wadies** E17 Arabic (*wādī* valley, river-bed). In certain Arabic-speaking countries, a rocky watercourse which is dry except during the rainy season; the stream running through such a watercourse.

■ French *oued*, a later (M19) introduction, represents the same Arabic word. *Oued* now mainly occurs in English with reference to placenames in Francophone North African territories.

wagon-lit /vagɔ̃'li:/ *noun plural* **wagon-lits** /vagɔ̃'li:z/, **wagons-lits** /vagɔ̃'li:/ L19 French (from *wagon* railway coach + *lit* bed). A sleeping-car on a train in Continental Europe.

wagon-restaurant /vagɔ̃ rɛstɔrɑ̃/ *noun plural* **wagons-restaurants** (pronounced same) E20 French (from *wagon* railway coach + *restaurant*). A dining-car on a train in Continental Europe.

wahala /wə'hala/ *noun* L20 Hausa. In Nigeria: trouble, inconvenience; fuss, bother.

wahine /wɑ:'hi:ni/, *foreign* /wa'hine/ *noun* L18 Maori (cf. VAHINE). **1** L18 In New Zealand: a Maori woman or wife. **2** M19 In Polynesia: a VAHINE. **3** M20 A girl surfer. *surfing slang.*

wai see under NAMASKAR.

waka /'waka/ *noun* 1 E19 Maori. In New Zealand: a Maori canoe.

waka /'wakə/ *noun* 2 M20 Japanese. **1** M20 A form of classic Japanese lyrical poetry developed from ancient traditional ballads. **2** M20 A TANKA.

wakame /'wakameɪ/ *noun* L20 Japanese. An edible Japanese seaweed.

wakf /wɑ:kf/ *noun* (also **waqf**) M19 Arabic (*waqf* stoppage, immobilization (sc. of ownership of property), from *waqafa* to stop, come to a standstill). In Islamic countries, endowment or settlement of property under which the proceeds are to be devoted to a religious or charitable purpose; land or property endowed in this way.

waldhorn /'valthɔːn/ *noun* M19 German. A French horn. Also, a natural valveless horn.

Waldsterben /'valt‚ʃtɛrbən/ *noun* L20 German (from *Wald* wood, forest + *Sterben* dying, death). *Ecology* Disease and death in forest trees and vegetation as a result of atmospheric pollution.

■ The term has been current in English since about 1983, originally with reference to dieback through environmental causes affecting Germany's forest trees, but now applied to the same phenomenon elsewhere.

wallah /'wɒlə/ *noun* (also **walla**) L18 Hindi (*-vālā* suffix expressing relation, from Sanskrit *pālaka* keeper). **1** L18 A person, formerly usually a servant, concerned with or in charge of a usually specified thing, task, etc. Chiefly as second element of combination. **2** M19 An Indian Civil servant appointed by competitive examination. More fully *competition-wallah*. **3** M20 Any functionary doing a routine administrative job; a civil servant, a bureaucrat.

■ The Hindi suffix was commonly apprehended by Europeans as a noun with the sense 'man, fellow'; in Anglo-Indian speech it was used chiefly as the second element in combinations such as *box-wallah* ('an itinerant Indian pedlar'). *Wallah* is now only used colloquially with a derogatory suggestion of 'an office-bound functionary' (see quotation 1974) and generally (harking back to the Anglo-Indian usage) with a defining word (see quotation 1996).

3 1974 *Courier-Mail* (Brisbane) Some wallahs in Canberra are sitting in air-conditioned offices telling us what has been flooded and what hasn't.

3 1996 *Times* As the heritage wallahs lord it in

the media during the summer tourist season, they would do well to reflect upon how shallowly rooted and fragile is their present high status.

Walpurgisnacht /valˈpʊrgɪsˌnaxt/ *noun* E19 German (genitive of *Walpurga* (name) + *Nacht* night). The eve of May Day, marked (according to German folklore and especially Goethe's *Faust*) by a witches' sabbath or a feast of the powers of darkness; *transferred* an orgiastic celebration or party.

■ St Walpurga (or Walburga) was an eighth-century Anglo-Saxon nun who became abbess of Heidenheim in Germany. May Day marks the occasion of the translation of her bodily remains to Eichstätt, where her shrine became a pilgrimage centre. The connection with the powers of darkness is nothing to do with the saintly abbess but is a fortuitous association with pagan festivities formerly celebrated on that date.
1996 *Spectator* . . . the new freedom she finds is mirrored by the licentiousness of her lover's half-mad identical twin, who turns up at her house to burn her books and caper in a demonic spirit of *Walpurgisnacht*.

wampum /ˈwɒmpəm/ *noun* M17 Algonquian (*wampumpeag* (from *wap* white + *umpe* string + plural suffix *-ag*) abbreviated on the erroneous analysis of the word as *wampum* + *peag*). **1** M17 Chiefly *History*. Beads made from the ends of shells rubbed down, polished, and threaded on strings, worn by North American Indians as decoration or (formerly) used as money or for mnemonic or symbolic purposes. **2** L19 *generally* Money. *slang*.
■ Chiefly North America.

wamus /ˈwaməs/ *noun* E19 Dutch (probably from Dutch *wammes* contraction of *wambuis* from Old French *wambois* gambeson, tunic). In southern and western United States: a warm knitted jacket resembling a cardigan.

Wanderjahr /ˈvandərjɑːr/ *noun* plural **Wanderjahre** /ˈvandərjɑːrə/ L19 German (*wander* wander + *Jahr* year). A year of wandering or travel, especially one undertaken by a young person.
■ Formerly a period of travel by an apprentice to improve his skill and broaden his experience; cf. LEHRJAHR. Also occurs in English form *wanderyear* (L19).

wanderlust /ˈwɒndəlʌst/ *noun* E20 German. An eagerness or fondness for wandering or travelling.

1996 *Times* But what America really seems to suit is her wanderlust, her sparkle.

Wandervogel /ˈvandərføːgəl/ *noun* plural **Wandervögel** /ˈvandərføːgəl/ E20 German (literally, 'bird of passage'). A member of a German youth organization founded at the end of the nineteenth century for the promotion of outdoor activities (especially hiking) and folk culture; *transferred* a rambler, a hiker.

waqf variant of WAKF.

wasabi /wəˈsɑːbi/ *noun* E20 Japanese. A cruciferous plant, *Eutrema wasabi*, whose thick green root is used in Japanese cookery, usually ground as an accompaniment to raw fish.

washi /ˈwaʃi/ *noun* L20 Japanese. Japanese paper; *specifically* a thin handmade variety used to make lantern shades, kites, etc.

wat /wat/ *noun* M19 Thai (from Sanskrit *vāṭa* enclosure). In Thailand or Cambodia (Kampuchea): a Buddhist monastery or temple.

wayang /ˈwɑːjaŋ/ *noun* E19 Javanese (*wajang, wayang*). In Indonesia and Malaysia: a theatrical performance employing puppets or human dancers; *specifically* a Javanese and Balinese shadow puppet play (also *wayang kulit* /ˈkuːlɪt/ (Javanese = skin, leather)).

wazir /wəˈzɪə/ *noun* E18 Arabic (*wazīr* helper). *History* A high state official, especially in the Ottoman empire; a vizier.

wedeln /ˈveɪd(ə)ln/ *noun* (also **wedel** /ˈveɪd(ə)l/) M20 German (see next). *Skiing* A technique using a swaying movement of the hips to make a series of short parallel turns.

wedeln /ˈveɪd(ə)ln/ *intransitive verb* (also **wedel** /ˈveɪd(ə)l/) M20 German (literally, 'wag (the tail)'). *Skiing* Use the wedeln technique. Also, perform a similar movement on a skateboard.

Wehmut /ˈveːmuːt/ *noun* E20 German. Sadness, melancholy, wistfulness, nostalgia.

Wehrmacht /ˈveːrmaxt/ *noun* M20 German (literally, 'defence force'). *History* The German armed forces, especially the army, between 1921 and 1945.

Wehrwirtschaft /ˈveːrvɪrtʃaft/ *noun* M20 German (from *Wehr* defence + *Wirtschaft* economy). The principle or policy of directing a nation's economic activity towards preparation for or support of a war effort, especially as applied in Germany in the 1930s.

wei ch'i /weɪ 'tʃiː/ *noun* L19 Chinese (*wéiqí* (Wade–Giles *wei-ch'i*), from *wei* to surround + *qí* (*ch'i*) chess). A traditional Chinese board game of territorial possession and capture. Cf. GO.

weiner variant of WIENER.

weinkraut /'vaɪnkraʊt/ *noun* M20 German (from *Wein* wine + *Kraut* cabbage). Pickled cabbage cooked with white wine and apples.

Weinstube /'vamʃtuːbə/, /'vamstuːbə/ *noun* plural **Weinstuben** /'vamʃtuːbən/, **Weinstubes** L19 German (from *Wein*, wine + *Stube* room). A small German wine bar or tavern. Cf. BIERSTUBE.

Wein, Weib, und Gesang /'vaɪn 'vaɪp ʊnt gə'zaŋ/ *noun phrase* L19 German. Wine, woman, and song.

Weisswurst /'vaɪsvə:st/, /'vaɪsvʊəst/ *noun* M20 German (from *weiss* white + *Wurst* sausage). (A) whitish German sausage made chiefly of veal.

Weltanschauung /ˌvɛltan'ʃaʊʊŋ/ *noun* plural **Weltanschauungen** /ˌvɛltan 'ʃaʊʊŋən/, **Weltanschauungs** M19 German (from *Welt* world + *Anschauung* perception). A particular philosophy or view of life; the world-view of an individual or group.

> 1996 *Spectator* In my case, of course, this shattering event would have to be something pleasant, since my *Weltanschauung* is one of nihilistic despair—that is to say, I am a realist.

Weltbild /'vɛltbɪlt/ *noun* M20 German (from *Welt* world + *Bild* picture). WELTAN-SCHAUUNG.

Weltliteratur /'vɛltlɪteraˌtuːr/ *noun* (also **Weltlitteratur**) E20 German (from *Welt* world + *Literatur* literature). A literature of all nations and peoples; universal literature.

Weltpolitik /'vɛltpoliˌtiːk/ *noun* E20 German (from *Welt* world + *Politik* politics). International politics; a particular country's policy towards the world at large.

Weltschmerz /'vɛltʃmɛrts/ *noun* L19 German (from *Welt* world + *Schmerz* pain). A weary or pessimistic feeling about life; an apathetic or vaguely yearning attitude.

> 1996 *Times* The music does not have to drip with emotion, but surely a love-song can be allowed to exude Weltschmerz as well as passion.

Weltstadt /'vɛltʃtat/ *noun* plural **Weltstädte** /'vɛltʃtɛːtə/ L19 German (from *Welt* world + *Stadt* town). A city of international importance or cosmopolitan character; a cosmopolis.

wendigo variant of WINDIGO.

wen jen /'wɛn ʒɛn/ *noun phrase* plural M20 Chinese (*wénrén* man of letters, from *wén* writing + *rén* (Wade–Giles *jên*) man). Chinese men of letters.

wen-yen /'wɛnjɛn/ *noun* (also **wenyen**, **wenyan**) M20 Chinese (*wényán*, from *wén* writing + *yán* speech, words). The traditional literary language or style of China, now superseded by PAI-HUA.

wertfrei /'veːrtfraɪ/ *adjective* E20 German (from *Wert* worth + *frei* free). Free of value judgements; morally neutral.

■ In sociological contexts often in English translation as *value-free*; cf. WERTFREIHEIT.

Wertfreiheit /'veːrtfraɪhaɪt/ *noun* M20 German (from as preceding + -*heit* -hood). The quality of being *wertfrei*.

■ *Wertfreiheit* (also frequently in English 'value-freedom'), was recommended by the German sociologist Max Weber (1864–1920) as an ideal to which sociologists should aspire in that they should not allow their own values to influence their judgements on the people and institutions they study.

Westpolitik /'vɛstpɒlɪˌtiːk/ *noun* L20 German (from *West* west + *Politik* policy: cf. OSTPOLITIK). *History* In European politics, a policy of establishing or developing diplomatic and trading relations with Western nations, especially formerly on the part of Communist States.

whare /'wɒri/ *noun* E19 Maori. In New Zealand: a (Maori) house or hut; *generally* a hut, a shed, *specifically* one on a sheep station, where the hands sleep or eat.

wickiup /'wɪkiʌp/ *noun* (also **wickyup**) M19 Algonquian ((Menominee *wikiop*), perhaps a variant of *wikiwam* wigwam). A rough hut consisting of a frame covered with brushwood, used by nomadic peoples in the west and south-west of the United States; *colloquial* any small hut or shanty.

wiederkom /'viːdəkɒm/ *noun* (also **wiederkomm**, **Wiederkomm**) L19 French (*vidrecome* goblet, ultimately from German *wiederkommen* to return, come again). A tall cylindrical German drinking-vessel made of (usually coloured or painted) glass.

wiener /'vi:nə/ *noun* (in sense 2 also **weiner** /'wi:nə/) L19 German (adjective from *Wien* Vienna). **I** *attributive* **1** L19 Used *attributively* to designate things from or associated with Vienna. **II 2** E20 *Elliptically for* WIENERWURST. *North American.*

weiner schnitzel see under SCHNITZEL.

wienerwurst /'vi:nə‚və:st/, /'wi:nə‚wə:st/ *noun* L19 German. Viennese sausage.

wili /'vɪli/ *noun* (also **willi**) M20 German or French (from Serbo-Croat *víla* nymph, fairy). *Mythology* In Slavonic and eastern German legends, a spirit of a betrothed girl who has died from grief at being jilted by her lover (used especially with reference to the ballet *Giselle*).

wiliwili /'wi:lɪwi:li/ *noun* L19 Hawaiian. A coral tree, *Erythrina tahitensis*, of Hawaii and Tahiti, which bears clusters of orange flowers; the wood of this tree, used to make surfboards.

willi variant of WILI.

willy-willy /'wɪlɪ‚wɪli/ *noun* L19 Aboriginal. In North West Australia: a cyclone or dust-storm.

windigo /'wɪndɪɡəʊ/ *noun* (also **wendigo** /'wɛndɪɡəʊ/) plural **windigo(e)s** E18 Ojibwa (*wintiko*). In the folklore of the northern Algonquian Indians, a cannibalistic giant, the transformation of a person who has eaten human flesh.

Wirtschaft /'vɪrtʃaft/ *noun* M19 German (in sense 2 abbreviation of *Gastwirtschaft* hotel). **1** M19 (Domestic) economy, housekeeping. **2** E20 A hostelry, inn.

Wirtschaftswunder /'vɪrtʃafts‚vʊndər/ *noun* (also **Wirtschaftwunder**) M20 German (*Wirtschaft* economy + *Wunder* miracle). The economic recovery of West Germany after the war of 1939–45. Also *transferred*.

> **1996** *Times* But this ominous comparison makes no impression on the self-confidence of German public and political opinion, still mesmerised by the myth of the *Wirtschaftswunder* of the 1950s.

Wissenschaft /'vɪsənʃaft/ *noun* M19 German. (The systematic pursuit of) knowledge, science; learning, scholarship.

witblits /'vɪtblɪts/ *noun* (also **witblitz**) M20 Afrikaans (from *wit* white + *blits* lightning). In South Africa: home-brewed brandy, a strong and colourless raw spirit.

witdoek /'vɪtdʊk/ *noun* plural **witdoeke** /'vɪtdʊkə/, **witdoeks** L20 Afrikaans (from *wit* white + DOEK). In South Africa: a member of a largely Black conservative vigilante movement operating in the townships around Cape Town, identifiable by the wearing of a white cloth or scarf about the head. Usually in *plural*.

witloof /'wɪtlu:f/ *noun* L19 Dutch (literally, 'white leaf'). A variety of chicory grown for blanching, with broad leaves and midribs.

wobla variant of VOBLA.

wok /wɒk/ *noun* M20 Chinese (Cantonese). A large bowl-shaped frying-pan used in especially Chinese cookery.

> ■ The *wok*, introduced into Western kitchens in the 1970s, rapidly became a standard item of kitchen equipment.
>
> **1988** D. Lodge *Nice Work* 'I thought we could put the electric wok away. We never use it. A microwave would be more useful.'

wongi /'wɒŋɡi/ *noun* E20 Aboriginal. A talk, a chat; a speech. *Australian slang.*

wonton /wɒn'tɒn/ *noun* (also **won ton**) M20 Chinese ((Cantonese) *wān t'ān*). In Chinese cookery, (a dish consisting of) a small round dumpling or roll with a savoury filling (especially of minced pork), usually eaten boiled in soup.

woonerf /'vu:nə:f/ *noun* plural **woonerfs**, **woonerven** /'vu:nə:v(ə)n/ L20 Dutch (from *woon-* residential (from *wonen* to live) + *erf* ground, premises). A road in a residential area, in which a number of devices are employed to create a safer environment by reducing and slowing the flow of traffic.

Wunderkammer /'vʊndərkamər/ *noun* L20 German (from *Wunder* wonder + *Kammer* chamber). A chamber or cabinet of wonders; *historical* a place exhibiting the collection of a connoisseur of curiosities.

wunderkind /'vʊndəkɪnt/ *noun* (also **Wunderkind**) plural **wunderkinds**, **wunderkinder** /'vʊndəkɪndər/ L19 German (from *Wunder* wonder + *Kind* child). **1** L19 A highly talented child; a child prodigy, especially in music. **2** M20 A person who achieves remarkable success at an early age. *colloquial*.

2 1996 *Times* Marion's lyricist, the 20-year-old *wunderkind* Jaime Harding, wails hard and long . . .

wurst /vəːst/, /wəːst/; *foreign* /vʊrst/ *noun* M19 **German**. Sausage, especially of the German or Austrian type; a German or Austrian sausage.

wushu /wuːˈʃuː/ *noun* L20 **Chinese** (*wǔshù*, from *wǔ* military + *shù* technique, art). The Chinese martial arts.

wu ts'ai /wuːˈtsʌɪ/ *noun* E20 **Chinese** (*wǔcǎi* (Wade–Giles *wu ts'ai*), from *wǔ* five + *cǎi* colour). Polychrome; polychrome decoration in enamels applied to porcelain; porcelain with polychrome decoration.

X

xenodochium /zɛnəˈdɒkiəm/ *noun* plural **xenodochia** /zɛnəˈdɒkiə/ (also *xenodochion*) M16 **Late Latin** (from Late Greek from as *xeno-* stranger + *deskhesthai* to receive). *History* A house of reception for strangers and pilgrims, especially in a monastery.

xoanon /ˈzəʊənɒn/ *noun* plural **xoana** /ˈzəʊənə/ E18 **Greek** (related to *xein* to carve). Chiefly *Greek Antiquities* A primitive simply carved image of a deity, originally of wood, and often said to have fallen from heaven.

xystus /ˈzɪstəs/ *noun* plural **xysti** /ˈzɪstʌɪ/ (also Anglicized as **xyst**) M17 **Latin** (from Greek *xustos* smooth, from *xuein* to scrape). *Classical Antiquities* A long covered portico or court used by ancient Greek athletes for exercises. Also, an open colonnade or terrace walk planted with trees and used by the Romans for recreation and conversation.

Y

yabba /ˈjabə/ noun L19 Twi (*ayawá* earthen vessel, dish). In Jamaica: a large wooden or earthenware vessel used for cookery or storage.

yacca, yacker variants of YAKKA.

yad /jɑːd/ noun E20 Hebrew (*yād*, literally, 'hand'). *Judaism* A pointer used by a reader of the Torah in a synagogue to follow the text, usually in the form of a rod terminating in a hand with an outstretched index finger.

yager see under JÄGER.

yagna variant of YAJNA.

yahrzeit /ˈjɑːtsʌɪt/ noun M19 Yiddish (from Middle High German *jarzît* anniversary, from Old High German *jar* (German *Jahr*) year + *zît* (German *Zeit*) time). *Judaism* The anniversary of the death of a person, especially a parent.

yajna /ˈjʌdʒnjə/ noun (also **yagna**) E19 Sanskrit (*yajña* worship, sacrifice). In Hinduism, a sacrificial rite with a specific objective, often involving the burning of substantial offerings.

yakitori /jakɪˈtɔːri/ noun M20 Japanese (from *yaki* toasting, grilling + *tori* bird). A Japanese dish consisting of pieces of chicken grilled on a skewer.

yakka /ˈjakə/ noun (also **yacca, yacker**) L19 Aboriginal. Work, toil.
■ Australian slang, especially in the phrase *hard yakka*.

yaksha /ˈjʌkʃə/ noun L18 Sanskrit (*yakṣa*). *Indian Mythology* (A statue or carving of) any of a class of demigods or nature spirits often serving as tutelary guardians.

yakuza /jəˈkuːzə/ noun plural same M20 Japanese (from *ya* eight + *ku* nine + *za* three, with reference to the worst kind of hand in a gambling game). A Japanese gangster or racketeer. Usually *plural* meaning such gangsters etc. collectively.
attributive **1995** *Spectator* Yakuza gangsters, with extreme right-wing connections, were instantly recognisable by their dress and demeanour . . .

yang /jaŋ/ noun & adjective L17 Chinese (*yáng* sun, positive, male genitals). **A** noun L17 In Chinese philosophy, the male or active principle of the two opposing forces of the universe. Cf. YIN. **B** attributive or as adjective L17 That represents yang; masculine.

yang ch'in /jaŋ ˈtʃɪn/ noun phrase L19 Chinese (*yángqín*, from *yáng* high-sounding, foreign + *qín* (Wade–Giles *ch'in*) musical instrument, zither). A Chinese dulcimer.
1996 *Times* But from the moment Lisa Gerrard appeared on stage, . . . and gracefully glided swan-like over to her *yang-ch'in* (that's Chinese dulcimer to you), I knew this was going to be something special.

yanggona /jaŋˈɡəʊnə/ noun (also **yaqona**) M19 Fijian (*yaqona*). KAVA.

yantra /ˈjantrə/ noun L19 Sanskrit (= device or mechanism for holding or fastening, from *yam* to hold, support). A geometrical diagram used as an aid to meditation in tantric worship; any object used similarly.

yaourt see under YOGHURT.

yaqona variant of YANGGONA.

yarmulke /ˈjɑːmʊlkə/ noun (also **yarmulka**) E20 Yiddish (*yarmolke*, from Polish *jarmułka* cap, probably from Turkish *yağmurluk* raincoat, cape, from *yağmur* rain). A skullcap worn by male Jews.

yashmak /ˈjaʃmak/ noun M19 Arabic (*yašmak* from Turkish *yaşmak* use as noun of *yaşmak* to hide oneself). A veil concealing the face below the eyes, worn by Muslim women in public.

yataghan /ˈjatəgan/ noun (also **ataghan** /ˈatəgan/) E19 Turkish (*yatağan*). Chiefly *History* In Muslim countries, a sword or long dagger having a handle without a guard and often a double-curved blade.

yenta /ˈjɛntə/ noun (also **yente**) E20 Yiddish (originally a personal name; see quotation). A gossip, a busybody; a noisy, vulgar person; a scolding woman, a shrew. *North American colloquial.*
1968 *Encounter* Yenta, I am told, was a perfectly acceptable name for a lady, derived from the Italian *gentile*—until some ungracious *yenta* gave it a bad name.

yentz /jɛnts/ transitive verb M20 Yiddish (from *yentzen* to copulate). Cheat, swindle. *United States slang.*

yerba /ˈjəːbə/ *noun* E19 Spanish (= herb). MATÉ sense 2. More fully *yerba maté*.

yeshiva /jəˈʃiːvə/ *noun* plural **yeshivas**, **yeshivot(h)** /jəˈʃiːvɒt/ M19 Hebrew (*yĕšībāh*, from *yāshab* to sit). An Orthodox Jewish college or seminary; a Talmudic academy.

yeso /ˈjɛsəʊ/ *noun* (also **yesso**) M16 Spanish (from Latin *gypsum*; cf. GESSO). Gypsum, plaster of Paris; *especially* gypsum-rich dust used to control acidity during the making of sherry.

yeti /ˈjɛti/ *noun* M20 Tibetan (*yeh-teh* little manlike animal). A creature said to resemble a large ape, whose tracks have supposedly been found in snow on the Himalayan mountains. Also called *Abominable Snowman*.

yé-yé /jɛˈjɛ/ *adjective & noun* M20 French (representing *yeah-yeah* reduplication of *yeah*, common in popular songs of the 1960s). **A** *adjective* M20 Designating or pertaining to a style of popular music, dress, etc., typical of the 1960s, especially in France; associated with or enthusiastic about this or subsequent forms of popular optimistic youth culture. **B** *noun* M20 A person associated with the yé-yé style. Also, rock or pop music.

yichus /ˈjɪkəs/, /ˈjɪxəs/ *noun* E20 Yiddish (from Hebrew *yiḥūs* pedigree). Social status, prestige. Chiefly *United States colloquial*.

yin /jɪn/ *noun & adjective* L17 Chinese (*yīn* shade, feminine, the moon). **A** *noun* L17 In Chinese philosophy, the female or negative principle of the two opposing forces of the universe. Cf. YANG. **B** *attributive* or as *adjective* M20 That represents yin; feminine.

ying ch'ing /jɪŋ ˈtʃɪŋ/ *adjective & noun phrase* E20 Chinese (*yīngqīng* (Wade–Giles *ying ch'ing*) literally, 'shadowy blue'). (Designating) a type of Chinese porcelain with a bluish-white glaze produced in Jiangxi and other provinces, chiefly during the Song dynasty.

ylang-ylang /iːlaŋˈiːlaŋ/ *noun* (also **ilang-ilang**) L19 Tagalog (*ilang-ílang*). A tree of tropical Asia, *Cananga odorata*, with fragrant greenish-yellow flowers from which a perfume is distilled; the perfume obtained from this tree.

yoga /ˈjəʊɡə/ *noun* L18 Sanskrit (literally, 'union'). In Hindu philosophy, union of the self with the supreme being; a system of ascetic practice, meditation, etc., designed to achieve this.

■ Frequently specifically HATHA YOGA.

yoghurt /ˈjɒɡət/ *noun* (also **yogurt**) E17 Turkish (*yoğurt*). A semi-solid, somewhat sour foodstuff, now often fruit-flavoured, made from milk curdled by the addition of certain bacteria; a carton of this substance.

■ The spelling *yaourt* /ˈjaʊət/ (E19) as a represention of the pronunciation of *yoğurt* is now rare or obsolete.

yogi /ˈjəʊɡi/ *noun* (in sense 1 also **yogin** /ˈjəʊɡɪn/) E17 Sanskrit (*yogin*, nominative singular *yogī*, from YOGA). **1** E17 A person practising, or proficient in, yoga. **2** E20 YOGA.

yogini /ˈjəʊɡiniː/ *noun* L18 Sanskrit (*yoginī* feminine *yogin* yogi). **1** L18 Hindu Mythology A female demon, *especially* one of a group attendant on Durga or Siva. **2** M20 A female yogi.

yokozuna /jəʊkəˈzuːnə/ *noun* M20 Japanese (from *yoko* crosswise + *tsuna* rope (originally a kind of belt presented to the champion)). A grand champion sumo wrestler.

yom tov /jɒm tɒv/ *noun phrase* M19 Yiddish (from Hebrew *yōm* day + *ṭōb* good). A Jewish holiday or holy day.

yoni /ˈjəʊni/ *noun* L18 Sanskrit. Chiefly *Hinduism* A figure or representation of the female genitals as a sacred symbol or object.

yordim /jɔːˈdɪm/ *noun plural* L20 Hebrew (plural of *yored* person who descends). Emigrants from the State of Israel.

yorgan /jɔːˈɡʌn/ *noun* E20 Turkish. A Turkish quilt.

yourt variant of YURT.

yuan /jʊˈɑːn/ *noun* (also **Yuan**) plural same E20 Chinese (*yuàn* courtyard). In China: any of several government departments.

yüeh ch'in /ˈjʊə tʃɪn/, /kɪn/ *noun* M19 Chinese (*yuèqín* (Wade–Giles *yüeh-ch'in*) literally, 'moon guitar'). A Chinese lute with four strings and a flat circular body.

yuga /ˈjʊɡə/ *noun* (also **yug** /jʊɡ/) L18 Sanskrit (*yuga* yoke, an age of the world). In Hindu cosmology, each of four periods, each shorter than and inferior to its predecessor, together totalling 4,320,000 years. Cf. KALPA.

yugen /'juːg(ə)n/ *noun* E20 Japanese (from *jū* faint, distant + *gen* dark, unfathomable). In traditional Japanese court culture and Noh plays, a hidden quality of graceful beauty or mystery; profound aestheticism.

yukata /jʊˈkata/ *noun* E19 Japanese (from *yu* hot water, bath + *kata(bira)* light kimono). A light cotton kimono, frequently with stencil designs, worn after a bath, or as a housecoat.

yurt /jʊət/ *noun* (also **yourt**) L18 Russian (*yurta* (through French *yourte* or German *Jurte*) from Turkic *jurt*). A circular tent of felt, skins, etc., on a collapsible framework, used by nomads in Mongolia and Siberia. Also, a semi-subterranean hut, usually of timber covered with earth or turf.

Z

zabaglione /zaba'ljəʊni/ *noun* L19 Italian (perhaps ultimately from late Latin *sabaia* an Illyrian drink). A dessert consisting of egg-yolks, sugar, and (usually Marsala) wine, whipped to a frothy texture over a gentle heat and served either hot or cold. Cf. SABAYON.

zabuton /za'buːtɒn/ *noun* L19 Japanese (from *za* sitting, seat + *buton* variant of FUTON). A flat floor cushion for sitting or kneeling on.

zaftig /'zaftɪg/ *adjective* (also **zoftig** /'zɒftɪg/) M20 Yiddish (from German *saftig* juicy). Of a woman: plump, having a full rounded figure. North American colloquial.

zaguan /za'gwan/, /sa'gwan/ *noun* M19 Spanish (*zaguán* = vestibule, hall, from Arabic *'ustuwān*, perhaps ultimately from Greek *stoa* porch). In South and Central America and in the south-western United States: a passage running from the front door to the central patio of houses.

zaibatsu /zʌɪ'batsuː/ *noun* plural same M20 Japanese (from *zai* wealth + *batsu* clique). Commerce Originally, a Japanese capitalist organization usually based on a single family having controlling interests in a variety of companies. Now, (the members of) a Japanese business cartel or conglomerate.

zaikai /'zʌɪkʌɪ/ *noun* M20 Japanese (from *zai* wealth + *kai* world). In Japan: (the élite who control) the world of business and high finance.

zaitech /'zʌɪtɛk/ *noun* L20 Japanese (= financial engineering). Playing the money and stock markets as a business practice to enhance a company's profitability.

zakat /zə'kɑːt/ *noun* E19 Persian and Urdu (*zakā(t)*, Turkish *zekât*, from Arabic *zakā(t)* almsgiving). An obligatory payment made annually under Islamic law on certain kinds of property and used for charitable and religious objects.

zakuska /za'kuska/ *noun* (also **zakouska**) plural **zakuskas, zakuski** /za'kuski/ L19 Russian (usually as plural *zakuski*). An hors d'oeuvre.

zamarra /θa'marra/, /sa'marra/ *noun* M19 Spanish. In Spain: a kind of sheepskin jacket.

zampogna /zam'pɒnjə/, *foreign* /tsam'pɒɲɲa/ *noun* M18 Italian (from (late) Latin *symphonia*). Music A traditional mouth-blown bagpipe of southern Italy having two chanters and two drones. Also, any of various other woodwind instruments.

zapateado /za,patɪ'ɑːdəʊ/, *foreign* /θa,pate'ado/, /sa,pate'ado/ *noun* plural **zapateados** /za,patɪ'ɑːdəʊz/, /sa,patɪ'ɑːdos/, /θa,pate'ados/, /sa,pate'ados/ M19 Spanish (from *zapato* shoe). **1** M19 A flamenco dance involving complex syncopated stamping of the heels and toes in imitation of castanets. **2** M20 Dancing or footwork of this kind.

zarape variant of SERAPE.

zarda /'zɑːdə/ *noun* L19 Persian and Urdu (*zardah*, from Persian *zard* yellow). A Persian and Indian sweet dish consisting of rice cooked with saffron and often almonds and raisins or sultanas.

zareba /zə'riːbə/ *noun* (also **zereba, zariba, zeriba**) M19 Arabic (*zarība* pen or enclosure for cattle). **1** M19 In Sudan and neighbouring countries: (a camp fortified by) a fence, usually made of thorn trees, for defence against enemies or wild animals. **2** L19 *transferred* and *figurative* A defensive force or barrier.

zari /zari/ *noun* M20 Persian and Urdu (*zarī*, from Persian *zar* gold). Indian gold and silver brocade; *colloquial* a sari decorated with this.

zariba variant of ZAREBA.

zarzuela /θar'θwela/, /sar'swela/ *noun* L19 Spanish. **1** L19 A traditional form of operetta in Spain, with spoken dialogue, songs, and dances. **2** M20 A Spanish dish consisting of various kinds of seafood cooked in a rich sauce.

zastruga variant of SASTRUGA.

zawiya /'zɑːwɪə/ *noun* (also **zawiyeh**) M19 Arabic (*zāwiya* corner, prayer room). In North Africa: a Sufi religious community's mosque, especially when containing the shrine of a holy person.

zazen /zɑːˈzɛn/ *noun* E18 Japanese (from *za* sitting, a seat + *zen* Zen). Zen meditation.

zearat variant of ZIARAT.

zeitgeber /ˈtsaɪtgeːbər/, /ˈzʌɪtgeɪbə/ *noun* plural same, **zeitgebers** M20 German (from *Zeit* time + *Geber* giver). *Physiology* A rhythmically occurring event, especially in the environment, which acts as a cue in the regulation of certain biological rhythms in an organism.

Zeitgeist /ˈtsaɪtgaɪst/, /ˈzʌɪtgʌɪst/ *noun* M19 German (from *Zeit* time + *Geist* spirit). The spirit of the age; the trend of thought or feeling in a period, especially as reflected in its literature, art, etc.

> 1995 *Times* Like the seasoned politician he [sc. M. Mitterand] is, he has once again identified the *zeitgeist* in France, where dying has become the subject of some debate.

zek /zɛk/ *noun* M20 Russian (representing pronunciation of *z/k*, abbreviation of *zaklyuchënnyĭ* prisoner). In countries of the former USSR: a person held in a prison or forced labour camp.

zemstvo /ˈzɛmstvəʊ/, *foreign* /ˈzemstvo/ *noun* plural **zemstvos**, **zemstva** /ˈzemstva/ M19 Russian (from *zem'* (now *zemlya*) land). *History* Any of the elected district or provincial councils set up in Russia by Alexander II in 1864 as part of his reforms.

Zen /zɛn/ *noun* E18 Japanese (from Chinese *chán* quietude, from Sanskrit *dhyāna* meditation). A school of Mahayana Buddhism emphasizing meditation and personal awareness.

■ Also more fully *Zen Buddhism*. Influential in Japanese life from the thirteenth century onwards, *Zen* became significantly fashionable in the West during the 1960s.

zenana /zɛˈnɑːnə/ *noun* M18 Persian and Urdu (*zanānah*, from *zan* woman). **1** M18 In the Indian subcontinent: the part of a house in which high-caste women are or were secluded. **2** E20 A light quilted thin fabric used for women's dresses.

zendo /ˈzɛndəʊ/ *noun* plural **zendos** M20 Japanese (*zendō*, from ZEN + *dō* hall). A place for Zen Buddhist meditation and study.

zeppole /ˈzɛpʊleɪ/ *noun* plural **zeppoli** /ˈzɛpʊli/ M20 Italian. A kind of doughnut. *United States.*

zereba, zeriba variants of ZAREBA.

zeugma /ˈzjuːgmə/ *noun* LME Latin (from Greek, literally, 'yoking', from *zeugnunai* to yoke, related to *zugon* a yoke). A rhetorical figure by which a single word is made to refer to two or more words in a sentence, especially when applying to them in different senses.

ziarat /ziːˈɑːrət/ *noun* (also **zearat**) L18 Urdu (from Persian *ziyārat* from Arabic *ziyāra(t)* visit, pilgrimage). A Muslim pilgrimage to a shrine.

zibeline /ˈzɪbəlɪn/, /ˈzɪbəliːn/, /ˈzɪbəlʌm/ *noun* L16 French (of Slavonic origin). **1** L16 The sable. Now *rare* or *obsolete*. **b** M19 The fur of this animal. **2** L19 A soft smooth woollen material with a long nap pressed flat, used especially for women's coats. Also *zibeline cloth*.

zibib /ˈzɪbɪb/, /zəˈbiːb/ *noun* M19 Arabic (*zabīb* (Egyptian Arabic *zibīb*) dried grapes, raisins). A strong colourless spirit made in Egypt from raisins.

Zigeuner /tsɪˈgɔmə/ *noun* plural same (feminine **Zigeunerin** /tsɪˈgɔmərɪn/, plural **Zigeunerinnen** /tsɪˈgɔmərnən/) M19 German. A Gypsy.

zingana /ˈzɪŋgənə/, /zɪŋˈgɑːnə/, /ˈtsɪŋgənə/ *noun* E18 Italian. **1** (*Zingana*) A Gypsy girl or woman. *rare*. **2** M20 Striped wood furnished by various African trees; zebrano.

Zingaro /ˈzɪŋgərəʊ/, /ˈtsɪŋgərəʊ/ *noun* & *adjective* (also **zingaro**) E17 Italian. **A** *noun* E17 plural **zingari** /ˈzɪŋgəri/ (feminine **zingara** /ˈzɪŋgərə/, plural **zingare** /ˈzɪŋgəreɪ/). A Gypsy. **B** *attributive* or as *adjective* L18 Of or pertaining to Gypsies.

zita /ˈziːtə/ *noun* plural **zite** /ˈziːteɪ/, **ziti** /ˈziːti/ M19 Italian. Pasta in the form of tubes resembling large macaroni.

zocalo /ˈzɒkələʊ/ *noun* plural **zocalos** L19 Spanish (*zócalo*). In Mexico: a public square, a plaza.

zoco /ˈzɒkəʊ/ *noun* plural **zocos** L19 Spanish (from Arabic *sūḳ* souk). In Spain and North Africa: a souk; a market-place.

zoftig variant of ZAFTIG.

zollverein /ˈtsɔlfəraɪn/ *noun* M19 German (from *Zoll* toll + *Verein* union). *History* A union of States with a uniform rate of customs duties from other countries and free trade within the union; *specifically* that between States of the German Empire in the nineteenth century.

zombie /ˈzɒmbi/ *noun & verb* E19 Bantu (cf. JUMBY). **A** *noun* **1** E19 Originally, a snake-deity in voodoo cults of or deriving from West Africa and Haiti. Now (especially in the West Indies and southern United States), a soulless corpse said to have been revived by witchcraft. **2** M20 A dull, apathetic, unresponsive, or unthinkingly acquiescent person. *colloquial*. **3** M20 In the war of 1939–45, a man conscripted for home defence. *Canadian military slang* (*derogatory*). **4** M20 A long mixed drink consisting of several kinds of rum, liqueur, and fruit juice. **B** *transitive verb* M20 *zombie out.* Exhaust; disorientate.

zoppa /ˈtsɔppa/ *adjective & adverb* M18 Italian (feminine of *zoppo* limping). *Music* In a syncopated rhythm, especially one in which the second quaver of a 2/4 bar is accented.

■ Frequently in the phrase *alla zoppa*.

zori /ˈzɔːri/ *noun plural* **zoris**, same E19 Japanese (*zōri*, from *sō* grass, (rice) straw + *ri* footwear, sole). A Japanese sandal, having a simple thong between the toes and a flat sole originally of straw but now often of rubber, felt, etc.

Zouave /zuːˈɑːv/, /zwɑːv/ *noun* M19 French (from Kabyle *Zouaoua* name of a tribe). **1** M19 A member of a body of light infantry in the French army, originally formed of Algerian Kabyles, and long retaining the original oriental uniform. **b** M19 *History* More fully *Papal* or *Pontifical Zouave*. A member of a corps of French soldiers formed in Rome for the defence of the pope between 1860 and 1871. **c** M19 *History* A member of any of several volunteer regiments of Union troops in the American Civil War which adopted the name and in part the uniform of the French Zouaves. **2** M19 A garment resembling part of the Zouave uniform; *specifically* **a** *History* (in full *Zouave jacket, bodice*) a woman's short embroidered jacket or bodice, with or without sleeves; **b** in *plural*, peg-top trousers, as worn by men in the late nineteenth century and women in the late twentieth century (also *Zouave trousers, pants*); **c** a wide loose skirt with a looped or tucked up hemline (also *Zouave skirt*).

2.b 1981 *Washington Post* First came the ankle-length Zouaves, looking a bit like baggies gone beserk . . . Then came the shorter Zouaves, like knee-length bloomers.

zouk /zuːk/ *noun* L20 French (apparently from Antillean creole *zouk* to party, possibly influenced by United States slang *juke* (or *jook*) to have a good time). An exuberant style of popular music originating in Guadeloupe in the Lesser Antilles.

■ Developed in Paris as a style of Antillean popular music intended to hold its own against Western pop and disco music, *zouk* was popularized in France during the 1980s by the group called Kassav, and began to feature on the British and American music scene at the end of the decade (see quotation).

1987 *Guardian* Tonight, the first ever zouk on British soil kicks off this year's Camden Festival International arts programme . . . Zouk, especially Kassav, is the pulse of Paris streets and the soundtrack for her nightclubs.

zucchetto /tsʊˈkɛtəʊ/ *noun plural* **zucchettos** (also **zucchetta** /tsʊˈkɛtə/) M19 Italian (*zucchetta* diminutive of *zucca* gourd, head). The skullcap worn by Roman Catholic ecclesiastics, black for priests, purple for bishops, red for cardinals, and white for the Pope.

zucchini /zʊˈkiːni/ *noun plural* (also **zucchinis**) E20 Italian (plural of *zucchino* small marrow, courgette, diminutive of *zucca* gourd). Courgettes.

■ Chiefly in North America and Australia; in Britain *courgettes* is the usual word.

zufolo /ˈtsuːfələʊ/, /ˈzuːfələʊ/ *noun* (also **zuffolo**) plural **zufoli** /ˈtsuːfəli/ E18 Italian. *Music* A flageolet, a small flute or whistle.

Zugunruhe /ˈtsuːkˌʊnruːə/ *noun* M20 German. *Ornithology* Migratory restlessness; the migratory drive in birds.

zugzwang /ˈzʌɡzwaŋ/ *noun* E20 German (from *Zug* move + *Zwang* compulsion, obligation). *Chess* A position in which a player must move but cannot do so without disadvantage; the obligation to make a move even when disadvantageous.

■ Frequently in *in zugzwang*.

zuppa di pesce /ˌtsuppa di ˈpeʃe/ *noun phrase* M20 Italian. Fish soup.

zuppa inglese /ˌtsuppa iŋˈɡlese/ *noun phrase* M20 Italian (= English soup). A rich Italian dessert resembling trifle.

zurla /ˈzʊələ/ *noun plural* **zurle** /ˈzʊəleɪ/ M20 Serbo-Croat (*sûrla*, from (as) next). *Music* A kind of shawm introduced to the

Balkans from the Middle East by Gypsies.

zurna /ˈzʊənə/ *noun* L19 Turkish (from Persian *surnā* festival pipe). *Music* A kind of shawm found in Turkey, Arabic-speaking countries, and various neighbouring regions.

zut /zyt/ *interjection* E20 French. Expressing irritation, contempt, impatience, etc.

■ Also *zut alors!*, in which *alors* acts as an intensifier.
1996 *Times: Weekend* So just what is it in the end that brings together the woman with the hair lip, the dirty dancer, a quixotic French cameraman—zut alors!—and a group of troglodyte descendants of lost Vikings with a liking for high technology?

zwieback /ˈtsviːbak/ *noun* L19 German (= twice-bake). A (sweet) rusk or biscuit made by baking a small loaf, and then toasting slices until they are dry and crisp.

zwischenzug /ˈtsvɪʃənˌtsuːk/ *noun* M20 German (from *zwischen* intermediate + *Zug* move). *Chess* A move interposed in a sequence of play in such a way as to alter the outcome.

Appendix

Aboriginal languages

EIGHTEENTH CENTURY
boomerang
cooee
corroboree
gibber
koradji

NINETEENTH CENTURY
alcheringa
billabong
binghi
bunyip
gilgai
goondie
gunyah
mallee
mulga
tjurunga
willy-willy
yakka

TWENTIETH CENTURY
bombora
didgeridoo
wongi

African languages

SEVENTEENTH CENTURY
harmattan
juju

EIGHTEENTH CENTURY
buckra
kierie
marimba

NINETEENTH CENTURY
accra
donga
impi
indaba
induna
inkosi
intombi
inyanga
jumby
lobola
mabele
mbira
nagana
sangoma
tokoloshe
umfaan
umfundisi
yabba
zombie

TWENTIETH CENTURY
alhaji
balafon
dashiki

kalimba
kente
kwashiorkor
kya
lappa
manyatta
mau-mau
patha patha
piri-piri
soukous
tsotsi
Wabenzi
wahala

Afrikaans/Dutch

SEVENTEENTH CENTURY
dagga
jong

EIGHTEENTH CENTURY
doek
hanepoot
kaross
kraal
krans
mebos
naartjie
sjambok
skoff
springbok
stoep
veld
vlakte
vlei

NINETEENTH CENTURY
berg
biltong
bond
dop
hamel
inspan
jukskei
kappie
katel
kêrel
klompie
konfyt
kop
koppie
laager
lammervanger
maas
mealie
meisie
Nagmaal
oblietjie
oom
ou
oubaas
pondok
rand

remskoen
rondavel
rooinek
schlenter
skepsel
sosatie
takhaar
tameletjie
togt
trek
Uitlander
veldskoen
voetganger
voetsek
volk
voorloper
Voortrekker

TWENTIETH CENTURY
apartheid
baasskap
boerewors
braai
braaivleis
dominee
klonkie
koeksister
kragdadig
kwela
lekker
melktert
naat
oudstryder
ouma
oupa
outjie
platteland
swart gevaar
tot siens
vaaljapie
verkrampte
verligte
witblits
witdoek

American Indian languages

SEVENTEENTH CENTURY
moccasin
peag
pocosin
powwow
wampum

EIGHTEENTH CENTURY
coontie
menhaden
pemmican
quipu
shaganappi
tepee
windigo

NINETEENTH CENTURY
cassareep
cheechako
hogan
kachina
kiva
piki
wickiup

TWENTIETH CENTURY
mola

Anglo-Indian

SEVENTEENTH CENTURY
brinjal

EIGHTEENTH CENTURY
chi-chi
serang

NINETEENTH CENTURY
chota
memsahib
topi

Arabic

SIXTEENTH CENTURY
cadi
cafila
faki
hashish
jubba
kebaya
muezzin
mufti
reis
sharif
sheikh

SEVENTEENTH CENTURY
arak
eid
fakir
fatwa
hakim
haram
imam
kebab
khamsin
kiblah
laban
madrasah
mastaba
sakia
salaam
sayyid
sura
ulema
wadi

EIGHTEENTH CENTURY
afreet
bismillah
dhow

fellah
galabiya
ghazi
Hadith
hajj
hanif
id ul-fitr
ihram
khalifa
kohl
naskhi
rebab
simoom
talak
tarboosh
tekbir
wazir

NINETEENTH CENTURY
aba
abaya
agal
alfa
askari
azan
bint
fana
fedai
gandoura
ghibli
gimbri
halal
hammada
hamza
inshallah
izar
jebel
jellaba
jihad
jinnee
kaid
kameez
keffiyeh
khat
khutbah
kief
Kitab
loofah
Mahdi
Majlis
mancala
mashallah
masjid
Maulana
mihrab
mimbar
sabkha
santir
serdab
shadoof
shahada
shahid
sheikha
shott
souk
sudd
tazia
umma
umrah

urs
wakf
yashmak
zareba
zawiya
zibib

TWENTIETH CENTURY
Bedu
burghul
falafel
harka
hijab
hummus
imshi
intifada
ishan
maleesh
mazar
medina
reg
seif
sharifa
shufti
shura
tabbouleh

Aramaic

SEVENTEENTH CENTURY
Kaddish
tefillin

NINETEENTH CENTURY
kiddushin
Kol Nidre

Bantu languages
see under African
languages

Bengali

NINETEENTH CENTURY
surbahar

TWENTIETH CENTURY
esraj

Breton

NINETEENTH CENTURY
korrigan
menhir

Catalan

NINETEENTH CENTURY
paella
talayot
taula

TWENTIETH CENTURY
sardana

Chinese

SEVENTEENTH CENTURY
ginseng
li
sampan
yang
yin

EIGHTEENTH CENTURY
feng-shui
hong

pe-tsai
souchong
T'ai Chi

NINETEENTH CENTURY
chopsuey
chow mein
k'ai shu
kowtow
kung fu
kylin
Lohan
nien hao
pak-choi
pa-kua
san-hsien
taipan
t'ing
te
ti-tzu
tong
wei ch'i
yang ch'in
yüeh ch'in

TWENTIETH CENTURY
an-hua
cheongsam
dazibao
dim sum
erh hu
fu yung
ganbei
ganbu
gung-ho
hoisin
ko
kuei
kwai-lo
lei
li
ling chih
mah-jong
mee
mei ping
pai-hua
pakapoo
p'an
putonghua
qinghaosu
samfu
san ts'ai
subgum
tou ts'ai
tu-mo
ve-tsin
wen jen
wen-yen
wok
wonton
wushu
wu ts'ai
ying ch'ing
yuan

Corsican

TWENTIETH CENTURY
macchia
tafone

Czech

TWENTIETH CENTURY
háček
kolach

Danish

TWENTIETH CENTURY
landnam
landrace
mor
smørrebrød

Dutch

SIXTEENTH CENTURY
kermis
monsoon

SEVENTEENTH CENTURY
maelstrom
polder
soya
vendue
vrouw

EIGHTEENTH CENTURY
baas
kloof
poort
snoek
stoop

NINETEENTH CENTURY
Boer
matje
poffertje
riem
riempie
rijsttafel
roemer
spruit
stelling
taal
wamus
witloof

TWENTIETH CENTURY
kraak porselein
woonerf

Egyptian
(Ancient)

NINETEENTH CENTURY
ankh
shabti
ushabti

TWENTIETH CENTURY
shawabti

Eskimo
languages

EIGHTEENTH CENTURY
angekok
kabloona
kayak
parka
umiak

NINETEENTH CENTURY
igloo
nunatak
tupik

TWENTIETH CENTURY
anorak
pingo
qiviut

Fijian
NINETEENTH CENTURY
sulu
yanggona

Finnish
NINETEENTH CENTURY
sauna
TWENTIETH CENTURY
kantele

French
OLD ENGLISH
philosophe
MIDDLE ENGLISH
accidie
amour
avoirdupois
bourdon
chemise
corvée
douce
flèche
fleur-de-lis
godet
haras
hydria
impayable
jupe
langue
largesse
lieu
Madame
ménage
Messiah
noblesse
orfèvrerie
par
parure
patron
peridot
potage
reverie
richesse
sans
sec
sous-
tablier
tache
trebuchet
venue
voussoir
LATE MIDDLE ENGLISH
absinth
adieu
aigre-doux
antipodes
avant-garde
ballade
Bedouin
beguine
bergerette
blancmange

bourg
bruit
cameo
carte
catechumen
ceinture
cenacle
cham
chaperon
chasse
chaussure
chevalier
chevauchée
chevelure
chevron
cicatrice
cohabitation
commissar
confrère
congé
couchant
couleur de rose
coup
crise
dariole
dauphin
difficile
distrait
douceur
droit
envoi
equivoque
fête
finesse
fleuron
gabelle
gourmand
haut-pas
hélas
hydra
introit
jaune
jour
jujube
jupon
lardon
legerdemain
lèse-majesté
lierne
Mademoiselle
meridional
migraine
muscatel
musette
nadir
noir
nonpareil
obit
or
orgeat
oriflamme
oyer
oyez
pain
pavé
péage
pensée
petit
plage

puissance
rebec
regardant
reinette
reprise
rouge
sanglier
tendresse
tisane
toile
triste
tristesse
tuile
vigneron
vignette
vinaigrette
vivier
volage
FIFTEENTH CENTURY
blond
brochette
chanson
cheval
convenance
entremet
faubourg
jumelle
parole
portail
recueil
regime
réplique
sachet
serviette
sou
tambour
tapis
tranche
tourbillion
valet
vignoble
SIXTEENTH CENTURY
abbé
adage
à la
à la mode
aliquot
antes
armoire
auberge
banderole
bastide
baton
bayadère
bibliothèque
bocage
bon
bonjour
bonne
bonze
bourgeois
bourse
bricole
brocard
brunet
burnous
cabochon
cachou

cafard
caloyer
camaieu
canaille
canton
cap-à-pie
capriole
capuche
cartel
cestui
chamois
champignon
chancre
chaton
clientele
commis
concierge
confiture
cordelle
corps
corps de garde
courante
croissant
démenti
demoiselle
diable
divan
doge
dolman
éloge
emir
escritoire
esplanade
esprit
faille
feme covert
feme sole
feuillemorte
framboise
fricassee
fugue
fusee
gabion
gendarme
gendarmerie
gigot
girasol
gnomon
gonfalonier
goût
guidon
haut-goût
hippodrome
jacquerie
kermes
kumis
lien
limaçon
loup-garou
lunette
luxe
maison
maître d'hôtel
malgré
marron
massif
mignon
monad
mot

moustache
muguet
muscat
mystagogue
nacre
naïf
nebulé
paladin
panache
patisserie
pavane
pensionnaire
perdu
petite
phaeton
piquant
pique
pomade
portmanteau
puisne
qui vive
ravelin
reglement
rendezvous
réseau
rondeau
santon
seigneur
sequin
serin
sorbet
sultan
taille
tarot
tercet
terreplein
tilleul
toque
villanelle
violon
visitant
vivandier
vive
volte
volute
zibeline

SEVENTEENTH CENTURY
aide-de-camp
allemande
allumette
amende honorable
ampoule
andouille
andouillette
à outrance
apropos
arabesque
arrêt
assegai
atelier
attentat
aubade
au reste
au revoir
baccalaureate
badinage
bagatelle
ballet

banquette
baragouin
bascule
beau
beau monde
bel esprit
belle
belles-lettres
berceau
bidet
bienséance
bigarreau
bijou
billet-doux
bisque
bizarre
bon vivant
bon voyage
boucan
bouilli
bouillon
bourgade
bourrée
boutade
brouillon
brusque
bureau
burin
burlesque
cabaret
cachet
cadet
caique
caisson
calotte
calumet
capot
caprice
caracole
carousel
carte blanche
cartouche
casque
cassolette
catafalque
cervelat
chaconne
chagrin
chaise
chandelier
chanterelle
charivari
chassis
chef-d'œuvre
chevaux de frise
chicane
ciboule
cirque
clairvoyant
coiffure
colon
commissionaire
compote
comte
console
contretemps
coquet
coquette
corps de logis

cortège
corvette
couchee
coup d'état
coup de grâce
courbette
court bouillon
couscous
creole
cresson
critique
croisette
croupade
culet
curé
cuvette
dégagé
de haut en bas
délicatesse
démarche
dernier
dernier ressort
déshabillé
dey
domino
douane
double entendre
doyen
dragée
éclaircissement
éclat
embarras
embonpoint
enceinte
en déshabillé
en passant
en prince
entre nous
environs
epode
ergot
espalier
estacade
estrade
étourdi
etui
exergue
faïence
fainéant
fainéantise
fanfaronade
farceur
faux pas
feu d'artifice
feu de joie
flageolet
flambeau
forte
fronton
gala
garçon
gare
gavotte
gazette
genie
gens de la robe
gigue
girandole
glacis

globule
goitre
gondolier
grand monarque
grand seigneur
gratin
grillade
gueux
haricot
hauteur
honnête homme
hôtel-Dieu
impromptu
intendant
intime
jalap
jargonelle
je ne sais quoi
jet d'eau
knout
kremlin
lansquenet
legume
levee
liaison
mâche
maladroit
malapropos
mal-entendu
manège
marabout
marc
Mardi gras
marionette
marquise
mascaron
mélange
mêlée
menus plaisirs
minaret
mistral
moire
mon cher
mouche
mousseline
musée
naive
naïveté
neroli
niche
nom de guerre
nonchalance
nouvelle
odalisque
odeum
opuscule
orangerie
ordonnance
ortolan
par excellence
parterre
partie
passade
passementerie
passe-partout
pastille
patois
paysage
penchant

pension
percale
père
peristyle
picot
pignon
piquet
pirogue
pirouette
pis aller
plafond
point
poivrade
politique
porte-cochère
potager
pot-pourri
pour passer le
    temps
pratique
procès-verbal
ragout
rapport
rasant
ratafia
ratelier
ravissant
rebus
recherché
religieuse
religieux
renversement
reveille
rigadoon
rodomontade
rouleau
routier
sabot
sagamité
sainfoin
salon
sans cérémonie
sans façon
sarabande
saucisson
seigneurie
sobriquet
sottise
sou markee
spirituel
suede
suite
tableau
table d'hôte
tabouret
taille-douce
talus
terre-verte
tête-à-tête
toison d'or
tombac
topinambour
tourniquet
tourte
tracasserie
traineau
treillage
tremblement
trente-et-quarante

tribade
tric-trac
tutoyer
vade-mecum
valet-de-chambre
valise
vedette
vin
voir dire

EIGHTEENTH CENTURY
abatis
accouchement
accoucheur
acharnement
agiotage
agrément
aigrette
aiguille
à la daube
allée
amateur
à merveille
amour propre
ancien régime
aplomb
appliqué
à propos de bottes
assemblé
assemblée
assiette
à tort et à travers
aubergine
au contraire
au courant
au fait
au fond
au pied de la lettre
avalanche
badigeon
baguette
bain-marie
balancé
ballonné
bal masqué
banco
bandeau
barbette
barcarole
bas bleu
batardeau
bateau
batterie
batterie de cuisine
béchamel
bergère
bigarade
bistre
bivouac
blanc
blanquette
bon-bon
bonhomie
bon mot
bonne bouche
bon ton
borné
bosquet
bossage

boudoir
bougie
boulevard
bouleversement
bouquet
bouquetier
bourgeoise
bourgeoisie
boutique
bouts rimés
bravo
brisé
brochure
buffet
cabriole
cabriolet
cache
cadastre
cadeau
café au lait
cannelure
cantaloup
caoutchouc
carafe
carillon
carmagnole
carriole
carte du pays
casserole
cassette
catalogue raisonné
cause célèbre
celadon
centrifuge
chalumeau
chambranle
chanterelle
chapeau-bras
charade
chargé d'affaires
charlotte
chasse
chasseur
château
chatoyant
chenille
chère amie
chez
chiffon
chiffonier
chignon
chou
ci-devant
cipolin
civet
clique
colporteur
comme il faut
compagnon de
    voyage
compère
comptoir
comptoir
connoisseur
conservatoire
contrecoup
cordon bleu
corps diplomatique
coterie

cotillion
coup d'œil
coup de foudre
coup de main
coup de théâtre
coupé
coureur
crèche
crêpe
cretin
critique
cromorne
croquette
croupier
cuisine
cul-de-sac
curette
cyme
dalles
dame de
    compagnie
daube
débouché
debris
début
dehors
déjeuner
demi-caractère
demilune
demi-saison
denouement
de nouveau
depot
derrière
detour
de trop
dévot
diablerie
Directoire
divertissement
dormeuse
douanier
douche
duchesse
duvet
eau-de-vie
ébauche
echelon
écrevisse
égalité
élégante
élite
embarras de
    richesse
embouchure
embrasure
émeute
emigré
empressement
en attendant
enceinte
encore
en face
en famille
enfilade
en gros
en l'air
en masse
ennui

ennuyant
ennuyé
enragé
en route
ensemble
en suite
en train
entrechat
entrée
entrepôt
entresol
en ventre sa mère
epaulette
epigramme
épris
esprit de corps
esprit fort
esquisse
etamine
etiquette
étourderie
exigeant
extrados
farce
farouche
faute de mieux
fauteuil
femme de chambre
fête champêtre
fichu
figurant
fille de joie
fourchette
foyer
fracas
fricandeau
frisson
fronde
frondeur
gage d'amour
gaieté de coeur
galère
galette
galipot
gauche
gaucherie
gîte
grande dame
grand monde
grippe
grisette
gros
guillotine
ha-ha
haute noblesse
homme d'affaires
hors d'oeuvre
hors de combat
hôtel de ville
hôtel garni
houri
illuminé
insouciance
intrados
intriguant
jalousie
jeu
jeu d'esprit
jeu de mots

jeu de paume
jeunesse
jongleur
julienne
kaolin
kasbah
lande
langue d'oc
langue d'oïl
lavage
lettre
lettre de cachet
levee
liqueur
locale
loge
longueur
loup
maisonette
majuscule
malaise
mal de mer
mandolin
maniéré
mannequin
manqué
maréchaussée
marinade
marivaudage
matelote
mauvais
mauvais sujet
mentor
meringue
mésalliance
messagerie
métayer
métier
mézair
mezzanine
mignonette
minaudière
mirabelle
molleton
mon ami
monde
moraine
morale
morceau
mordoré
mousquetaire
nacarat
née
negligée
nonchalant
nouvelle
noyau
nuance
oeil-de-boeuf
ombres chinoises
opéra comique
orné
oubliette
outré
palette
panne
papier mâché
papillote
parloir

paroli
parti
partie carrée
pas
pas de deux
pas de trois
passacaille
passé
pâté
patronne
patte
paupiette
paysanne
perruquier
persiflage
petit-maître
petit pain
piaffe
picotee
pièce de résistance
pierrot
pisé
piste
place d'armes
plat
plateau
politesse
polonaise
pompadour
pompon
port-crayon
port de voix
posé
poste restante
postiche
pot-au-feu
pot de chambre
poudre
poupée
pourparler
praline
précieux
précis
preux chevalier
prie-dieu
protégé
purée
quadrille
quatorze
radeau
raisonné
rapporteur
récolte
redingote
régie
restaurateur
reticule
ricochet
rinceau
riposte
rissole
robe de chambre
rôti
rôtisseur
rouge-et-noir
roulade
roulette
rusé
saccade

salep
salle
salle-à-manger
salmi
salpicon
sang-froid
sans pareil
sansculotte
savant
savante
savoir vivre
savonette
secretaire
séjour
sève
siffleur
silhouette
sissonne
socle
soi-disant
soirée
solitaire
Soubise
soubrette
soupçon
soupe
souterrain
souvenir
tafia
tant bien que mal
tant mieux
tant pis
terre-à-terre
terrine
tiers état
tirailleur
ton
tonneau
tontine
toujours gai
toujours perdrix
toupet
tournee
tournure
tout
tout au contraire
tout compris
tout court
tout de suite
tout ensemble
tout le monde
tout seul
traiteur
trajet
triage
tricorne
tricot
tripotage
trottoir
troubadour
trouvère
tuyère
tzigane
uhlan
usine
valse
vaudeville
velours
vendange

verd-antique
vers de société
veuve
vin blanc
vin du pays
vingt-et-un
vin mousseux
vis-à-vis
vive la bagatelle
vogue la galère
voilà
volupté

NINETEENTH CENTURY
à bas
abattoir
abonné
abonnement
abri
à cheval
à contrecœur
à deux
affaire
affiche
à fond
agent provocateur
aide-mémoire
à la brochette
à la carte
à la fourchette
à la lanterne
à la russe
âme damnée
amour courtois
amourette
anis
anonym
aperçu
aperitif
après nous le
   déluge
après coup
aquarelle
arête
argot
arme blanche
arrière-pensée
arrondissement
artiste
à trois
attaché
au grand sérieux
au gratin
au mieux
aumônière
au naturel
au pair
au sérieux
Av[o]u[é]
baba
baccarat
bagarre
bagasse
bahut
baignoire
bal costumé
ballon
ballon d'essai
barbotine

barège
barré
basse-taille
bassinet
batiste
battement
battue
batture
bavaroise
béarnaise
beau ideal
beau rôle
beau sabreur
beauté du diable
beaux arts
beaux yeux
beignet
berceuse
beret
bertillonage
bête noire
bêtise
beurre noir
bibelot
biberon
bidon
bien entendu
bien-être
bijouterie
blague
blagueur
blancbec
blanc de chine
blanc de perle
blanc fixe
blasé
bleu-du-roi
bois brûlé
boiserie
bombe
bon appétit
bonbonnière
bon enfant
bon gré mal gré
bonheur du jour
bonne femme
bonne fortune
bordereau
bouchée
bouclé
bouffant
bouillabaisse
boulevardier
bouleversé
bouquet garni
bouton
boutonnière
brandade
brasserie
breloque
bretelle
bric-à-brac
brioche
briquette
broché
broderie anglaise
brouhaha
brut
burette

butte
caba
cabane
cabotage
cache-peigne
cache-pot
cadre
café
café chantant
café noir
cafetière
cagnotte
calembour
camaraderie
camisole
canapé
canard
cancan
capable de tout
capitonné
capote
carnet
carte-de-visite
cartonnage
carton-pierre
casse
cassis
causerie
causeuse
celeste
cep
cerise
chacun à son goût
chaise longue
champlevé
changement
chanson de geste
chansonette
chansonnier
chantage
chanteuse
chapelle ardente
charabanc
charcuterie
chargé
charlotte russe
chartreuse
chassé
chassé croisé
Chateaubriand
chatelaine
chaud-froid
chaussée
chechia
chef
chef d'école
chef d'orchestre
chemin de fer
chemisette
cheval de bataille
chevalet
chevet
cheville
chibouk
chic
chiffonnade
chiffonnier
chiné
chinoiserie

chipolata
chocolatier
chose jugée
choucroute
chouette
chronique
   scandaleuse
chypre
cire perdue
clair-de-lune
clairvoyance
claque
claqueur
clavecin
cliché
cloche
cloisonné
clou
cocasse
coco-de-mer
cocotte
cohue
coiffeur
col
colportage
comble
comédie humaine
comédie
   larmoyante
comedienne
communard
communiqué
compte rendu
concessionaire
conférencier
confrérie
consigne
consommé
conte
conteur
contredanse
coque
coquillage
coquille
cor anglais
corbeau
corbeille
cordon sanitaire
corniche
corps à corps
corps d'élite
corps de ballet
corsetière
coryphée
costumier
coteau
couac
coudé
coulée
coulisse
couloir
coup de fors
coupe
courge
couvade
couvre-pied
cracovienne
crémaillère
crème

crème brûlée
crème de la crème
crème de noyau
crêpe de Chine
crêpeline
crépinette
crépon
cretonne
crevasse
criard
criblé
crochet
croquis
croustade
croûton
cru
culotte
cupidon
curettage
cuvée
dame d'honneur
danse du ventre
danse macabre
danseur
danseuse
débâcle
débat
débutant
débutante
déclassé
décolletage
décolleté
décor
degras
dégringolade
délassement
de luxe
déménagement
demi-mondaine
demi-monde
demitasse
démodé
dénigrement
de rigueur
dernier cri
dernier mot
détenu
diable au corps
dinanderie
diorama
diseuse
distingué
divorcee
doctrinaire
dolmen
donnée
dos-à-dos
dot
doublé
double entente
doublure
doyenne
drageoir
dramaturge
droit de seigneur
du reste
du tout
duxelles
eau

eau-de-Cologne
eau de Javel
eau-de-Nil
eau sucrée
éboulement
écarté
éclair
écorché
écossaise
ecru
ecuelle
églomisé
élan
email ombrant
embarras de choix
empiecement
emplacement
employé
empressé
en avant
en beau
en bloc
en cabochon
enchaînement
en clair
enclave
encoignure
en échelon
en évidence
enfant gâté
enfantillage
enfant terrible
en fête
engagé
en garçon
engobe
en grande tenue
en grand seigneur
en noir
en pension
en permanence
en place
en plein
en plein air
en prise
en rapport
en règle
en retraite
en revanche
ensilage
entente
entente cordiale
entourage
en tout cas
entrain
entr'acte
entrecôte
entredeux
entrepreneur
épaulement
épée
erg
escargot
esclandre
espacement
espadrille
espagnole
espagnolette
espieglerie

estaminet
estouffade
etagere
étang
étrenne
étude
exalté
exposé
fabliau
façon de parler
façonné
fait accompli
famille de robe
famille jaune
famille noire
famille rose
famille verte
farandole
faux-bourdon
femme de ménage
femme du monde
femme incomprise
femme savante
fer-de-lance
ferronnière
feu
feu follet
feuilleton
fiancé
ficelle
filé
filet
filet de boeuf
fillette
fils
fin de siècle
fine champagne
fines herbes
flacon
flageolet
flambé
flâneur
fleur-de-coin
flic
flicflac
foie gras
folie
folie de grandeur
folie du doute
fondant
fondue
force majeure
foudroyant
fouetté
foulard
foulé
fourreau
franc tireur
frappé
frisé
frotteur
frou-frou
fusain
fusillade
galop
gamin
gamine
gangue
garde champêtre

gare
garigue
gateau
gêné
gêne
genre
gilet
girouette
glacé
glissade
gloire
gloriette
gouache
goujon
gourmet
grand battement
grand coup
grande horizontale
grande passion
grand mal
Grand Prix
grand siècle
graticule
grecque
grenadine
grès
grimoire
griot
grisaille
gros bleu
grosgrain
gros point
guéridon
guichet
guilloche
guimpe
guipure
habitué
hachure
haute bourgeoisie
haute école
haut monde
haut-relief
haut ton
hollandaise
horizontale
hors concours
houp-la
idée fixe
immortelle
impair
impasse
imprévu
inconnu
ingénue
insouciant
intriguante
introuvable
jabot
jacquard
japonaiserie
jardinière
jaspé
j'adoube
jeté
jeu de société
jeune fille
jeune fille bien
    élevée

jeune premier
jeunesse dorée
joie de vivre
jolie laide
juge d'instruction
juste milieu
kepi
kermesse
La
lacet
laissez-aller
laissez-faire
langouste
langue de chat
larmoyant
lavaliere
layette
lectrice
legionnaire
levée en masse
lever de rideau
lié
lingerie
lisse
littérateur
livraison
lorgnette
louche
luthier
lycée
Lyonnais
macabre
macédoine
madeleine
maillot
maison de santé
maison tolérée
maître
maître d'
maître d'armes
maître de ballet
maîtresse en titre
maîtresse femme
malade imaginaire
maladif
maladresse
mal élevé
mandat
mange-tout
manoir
maquereau
maquillage
maquis
marabou
mariage de
  convenance
mari complaisant
marmite
marron glacé
martelé
massage
massé
massecuite
masseur
matelassé
matériel
matinée
mauvaise langue
mauvais pas

mauvais quart
  d'heure
mayonnaise
mazurka
méchant
méfiance
ménage à trois
mère
métairie
métayage
metif
metis
meunière
milieu
millefeuille
mille-fleurs
mirage
mirepoix
mirliton
mise en scène
misère
modiste
moellon
mofette
moiré
mondain
montagnard
montagne russe
mont de piété
mon vieux
moquette
morgue
mot d'ordre
motif
motte
moue
moule
moulin
mousse
mousseux
moyen-âge
museau
musicale
mystique
nappe
naturelle
navarin
nécessaire
Niçois
noblesse oblige
nocturne
noel
noisette
noix
nom de théâtre
nostalgie de la
  boue
note verbale
nougat
nouille
nous autres
nouveau riche
nouveaux arrivés
noyade
nuit blanche
objet
objet d'art
oeil-de-perdrix
œuvre

ombré
on dit
opéra bouffe
ouvrier
paillette
pair
Palais Royal
paletot
palmette
papeterie
parados
paratonnerre
par éminence
par exemple
parfait
parfumerie
pari-mutuel
parquet
parsemé
parti pris
parvenu
pas d'âne
pas de basque
pas de ciseaux
pas de quatre
passe
pas seul
pastiche
pastourelle
pâte
pâte brisée
pâté de foie gras
pâte dure
pâte-sue-pâte
pâte tendre
patte de velours
pavillon
paysan
peau d'Espagne
peau-de-soie
peignoir
pelure
pendeloque
père de famille
perfide Albion
permis de séjour
persiennes
personnel
pervenche
pétillant
petit bourgeois
petite noblesse
petit four
petit mal
petit point
petits chevaux
petits pois
petits soins
petit verre
pétrissage
pétroleur
physique
picaresque
picayune
pièce d'occasion
pièce de
  circonstance
pied-à-terre
pierrette

pince-nez
piolet
pipette
piqué
piton
placement
planchette
plastique
plein-air
plein-airiste
plein jeu
plié
plique à jour
plissé
plombière
plumeau
pochade
pochette
poêlée
point d'appui
point d'orgue
point de repère
pointe
polisson
pomme de terre
pompier
pontil
porte-bouquet
portée
porte-monnaie
portière
pose plastique
poseur
potiche
poudré
pouf
poule au pot
poulet
poulette
poult-de-soie
pourboire
pour encourager les
  autres
pour rire
pousse-café
premier cru
premier danseur
première
première danseuse
pré salé
primeur
printanier
prix fixe
procédé
profiterole
projet
prononcé
pur et simple
pur sang
puy
quadrille
quai
quand même
quantité
  négligeable
quartier
quel
quenelle
questionnaire

quincaillerie
racloir
raconteur
raconteuse
raffiné
raison d'état
raison d'être
rangé
rappel
rapprochement
rastaquouère
rataplan
ratatouille
ravigote
rayonnant
razzia
réchauffé
récit
réclame
recueillement
reculer pour mieux
    sauter
redowa
reflet
régisseur
reine
relâche
relevé
remanié
remarque
remontoir
rémoulade
remplaçant
Renaissance
renseignement
rente
rentier
rentrée
renvers
repoussé
repoussoir
restaurant
résumé
retable
retraite
retroussé
revanche
réveillon
revenant
revers
revolte
revue
rien ne va plus
rillettes
ris de veau
risqué
ritournelle
riverain
rivière
robe de nuit
rocaille
roche moutonnée
rococo
rognon
roi fainéant
roi soleil
roman-à-clef
roman à thése
roman de geste

ronde
rondelle
rond-point
rongeur
rosé
rotisserie
roué
rouget
routinier
roux
ruche
ruse de guerre
sabreur
salle d'armes
salle d'attente
salle des pas perdus
salon des refusés
sang-de-boeuf
sans-gêne
sans peur
sans phrase
sans recours
sans reproche
sans serif
saphir d'eau
sartage
saut
sauté
sauve qui peut
savarin
savate
savoir
savoir faire
scène à faire
secateur
secretariat
secret de
    Polichinelle
selon les règles
serein
serré
servante
sévigné
shako
sicilienne
sirop
soigné
soirée dansante
soit
soixante-neuf
sommelier
sommité
soubresaut
soubriquet
soufflé
souffrante
souffre-douleur
soufrière
soupirant
souple
sous-entendu
soutache
soutane
spécialité
succès d'estime
succès de scandale
succès fou
sucrier
suprême

surah
surveillant
svelte
sympathique
tableau vivant
tapotement
tartine
tâtonnement
tel quel
tempête
temps
tenue
terrasse
terre cuite
tête-bêche
tête de boeuf
tête montée
thé dansant
tic
tic douloureux
tierceron
timbale
tirade
tirage
titre
tombola
tonnelle
torchon
torque
torsade
tortillon
tour de force
tourmente
tournasin
tournedos
tragédienne
tranchet
travers
trembleuse
très
tricoteuse
tripot
trompe l'oeil
trousseau
trouvaille
trumeau
tulle
veilleuse
velouté
vendangeur
ventre à terre
verglas
vernis martin
versant
vers d'occasion
vicereine
vie d'intérieur
vie de Bohème
vie intime
vieux jeu
vieux rose
ville
vin compris
vin cuit
vin de paille
vin fou
vin gris
vin jaune
vin ordinaire

virgule
visa
viveur
voilà tout
voile
voix céleste
vol-au-vent
volet
volte-face
voulu
vrai réseau
vraisemblable
vraisemblance
vue d'ensemble
wagon-lit
wiederkom
Zouave

TWENTIETH CENTURY
acte gratuit
adage
affairé
a gogo
aileron
aioli
à la broche
à la Florentine
à la page
ambiance
amuse-gueule
anomie
à point
appellation
    contrôlée
après
après-ski
à rebours
arrivisme
arriviste
art brut
art nouveau
à terre
attentisme
attrait
aubusson
auguste
auteur
autoroute
avant la lettre
ballet blanc
bal musette
barre
barrette
bateau-mouche
beau geste
Beaujolais nouveau
béguin
belle époque
belle laide
belote
beur
beurre manié
bidonville
bien pensant
bistro
blanc de blanc
bled
bloc
blouson

bœuf
bœuf bourguignon
boîte
bombé
bondieuserie
boudin
boule
brassière
bricolage
bricoleur
brise-soleil
bustier
cabotin
cache-sexe
café complet
cagoule
calque
calvados
cambré
camouflage
carte d'identité
cassoulet
c'est la guerre
c'est la vie
chaîné
chaise percée
chambré
charmeuse
chef d'équipe
cherchez la femme
cher maître
chétif
chèvre
chichi
chou moellier
cinéaste
cinematheque
cinéma-vérité
ciné-vérité
cinq-à-sept
ciré
clementine
clochard
cloqué
collage
comédie noire
comme ci, comme
   ça
commère
communautaire
comtesse
conche
concours
   d'élégance
contre-jour
coq au vin
coque
couchette
coulis
coupe
courgette
course libre
couture
couverture
craquelure
crème caramel
crème Chantilly
crème de cacao
crème de menthe

crème fraîche
crème renversée
crêpe Suzette
cri de cœur
crime passionnel
crise de conscience
crise de nerfs
croque-monsieur
crotale
croûte
cru classé
crudités
cuir-ciselé
cuivré
danseur noble
debitage
decalage
découpage
déjà entendu
déjà lu
déjà vu
demi-glace
demi-pension
demi-sec
demi-vierge
de nos jours
dépaysé
déraciné
derailleur
désaxé
détente
détraqué
développé
diamanté
digestif
dirigisme
dirigiste
discothèque
dix-huitième
domaine
douçaine
douceur de vivre
dressage
eau de toilette
ébéniste
élan vital
embourgeoisé
embourgeoisement
embusqué
emincé
éminence grise
en brosse
en croûte
en daube
engrenage
en pantoufles
en poste
en primeur
en principe
en regard
entrée en matière
épatant
épater
épater les bourgeois
épicerie
éponge
équipe
escarole
esprit de l'escalier

étalage
etatism
etrier
événement
évolué
explication de texte
extraordinaire
façade d'honneur
façon de Venise
faisandé
faits divers
fantaisiste
farci
fauve
faux
faux amis
faux bonhomme
faux marbre
faux-naïf
femme de trent ans
femme fatale
ferronnerie
fête galante
fiche
filet mignon
film noir
filtre
fin de saison
fine
fléchette
folie à deux
fonctionnaire
force de frappe
fou rire
franc fort
franglais
frisée
froideur
fromage blanc
fromage frais
frottage
fruits de mer
fuselage
gaffe
gaga
galanterie
gaminerie
garconnière
gargouillade
gazon coupé
georgette
gigolo
glissé
grand cru
grand jeté
grande amoureuse
grande sonnerie
Grand Guignol
gratiné
grège
grognard
guêpière
gueule de bois
haute Bohème
haute couture
haute cuisine
haute-luxe
haute vulgarisation

homme moyen
   sensuel
hotelier
hotel particulier
idée reçue
idiot savant
inédit
intimism
intimist
j'accuse
jeté en tournant
jeton
jus
jusqu'au bout
kir
laissez-passer
lamé
langoustine
lapiés
le tout
lettrisme
levade
lissoir
livre de chevet
livre de
   circonstance
longeron
madérisé
madrilene
maison clos
maison de couture
maison de passe
mal du siècle
mal vu
manière criblée
maquette
maquillé
maquisard
marcottage
mariage blanc
marocain
marque
marquisette
Marxisant
matelot
matière
maudit
mauvais coucheur
mauvaise foi
médaillon
melusine
merde
messaline
méthode
   champenoise
metro
metteur en scène
midinette
millegrain
minuterie
mise au point
mise-en-page
mixte
moderne
moeurs
moi
monocoque
monstre sacré
montage

motard
mot de Cambronne
mot juste
mouchette
moulage
mouton enragé
mouvementé
moyen sensuel
musique concrète
mutuel
nacelle
nature morte
navarin printanier
navette
né
négociant
Negritude
ninon
noceur
non
notes inégales
nouveau
nouveau pauvre
nouveau roman
nouvelle cuisine
nouvelle vague
nuancé
nuée ardente
numéro
oeufs en cocotte
œvre de
   vulgarisation
oursin
ouvert
palais
palais de danse
palmier
panier de crabes
paperasserie
papier collé
papier déchiré
papier poudré
parc fermé
parlementaire
partouse
pas d'action
pas de bourrée
pas de chat
pas de cheval
pas devant
passéisme
pasticheur
pastis
pâté de campagne
pâte de verre
pâté en croûte
pâté maison
patissier
patronat
peloton
pelouse
pelure d'oignon
penchée
pétanque
petit battement
petit beurre
petite amie
petite bourgeoisie
petit marmite

petit poussin
petit suisse
petit tranchet
pièce à thèse
pièce noire
pièce rose
pied d'éléphant
pied noir
pilotis
pinard
piperade
piqûre
pissaladière
pissoir
planche
plastiqueur
plat du jour
plein-airisme
plongeur
plus ça change
poché
pochoir
poète maudit
poilu
point de départ
pointillé
pointillisme
policier
pomme
poncif
popote
port de bras
porteur
portrait parlé
pot-et-fleur
poudreuse
poule
poule de luxe
pour le sport
pourriture noble
pour-soi
poussin
praire
pratiquant
prêt-à-porter
princesse lointaine
problematique
profil perdu
protocolaire
provocateur
prunelle
pudeur
quatre-couleur
quête
quiche
rabat
raccourci
raclette
rafale
raisonneur
rapide
rapportage
rasta
raté
ratine
ravalement
ravinement
razet
razeteur

reblochon
Récamier
réchaud
recherche du temps
   perdu
règlement de
   compte
relais
relance
remaniement
remboîtage
remuage
remueur
rendu
repêchage
répétiteur
résistant
retardataire
retiré
retroussage
réussi
reverdie
revirement
rimaye
rite de passage
robe de style
romaine
romancé
roman-fleuve
roman noir
roman policier
rond de cuir
roquette
rouge de fer
rouge flambé
rouille
roulement
sabayon
sabotage
saboteur
salade niçoise
salariat
salaud
salle d'eau
salle de jeux
salle privée
salonnière
salopette
sans blague
saucier
sautoir
semis
sensibilité
sensiblerie
se-tenant
singerie
snobisme
soigneur
soirée musicale
solfège
sondage
sonde
son et lumière
sons bouchés
sorbetière
sottisier
sous vide
souteneur
soutenu

sportif
strapontin
sur place
système D
tabac
tac-au-tac
tailleur
tapénade
tapette
tapis vert
taqueté
tastevin
taupe
taxe de séjour
téléphérique
témoignage
temps perdu
tendu
terrain vague
terre pisée
terroir
tête de cuvée
tête de nègre
thé complet
tiens
tiercé
tiers monde
tole
tomme
torchère
touché
tour d'horizon
tournette
tourtière
tout simple
tragédie lyrique
trahison des clercs
trait d'union
tranche de vie
tranchette
travaux
   préparatoires
tremie
triptyque
tronc
trotteur
truite au bleu
tutu
urinoir
va banque
vacherin
vague
vendeuse
vérité
vernissage
veronique
verre églomisé
vers libre
vespasienne
vice anglais
vichyssoise
vie de château
vie en rose
vie intérieure
vie romancée
vieux marcheur
ville lumière
vin d'honneur
vin de table

vin doux (naturel)
vin rosé
vin rouge
violette de Parme
violon d'Ingres
virage
visagiste
visite de digestion
vive la différence
voeu
voyagé
voyant
voyeur
voyou
vulgarisateur
vulgarisation
wagon-restaurant
yé-yé
zouk
zut

French (American)
EIGHTEENTH CENTURY
bayou
NINETEENTH CENTURY
jambalaya
tignon
travois
TWENTIETH CENTURY
beguine

French (Canadian)
NINETEENTH CENTURY
babiche
frazil
parfleche
tuque
TWENTIETH CENTURY
joual

French (and German)
NINETEENTH CENTURY
galant

French (and Italian)
SEVENTEENTH CENTURY
bis
NINETEENTH CENTURY
cantatrice

French (or Latin)
SEVENTEENTH CENTURY
concordat

French (or Urdu)
SEVENTEENTH CENTURY
tandoor

Gaelic
LATE MIDDLE ENGLISH
loch
sennachie

SIXTEENTH CENTURY
quaich
strath
SEVENTEENTH CENTURY
deoch an doris
machair
EIGHTEENTH CENTURY
pibroch
sporran
taisch
NINETEENTH CENTURY
piob mhor
slainte
toman
urlar
TWENTIETH CENTURY
glaistig
port-a-beul

Gaelic (and Irish)
LATE MIDDLE ENGLISH
clachan

German
MIDDLE ENGLISH
Hanse
SIXTEENTH CENTURY
junker
SEVENTEENTH CENTURY
automat
Fräulein
Graf
krummhorn
sauerkraut
shaman
EIGHTEENTH CENTURY
gneiss
hausfrau
Heimweh
jäger
landau
meerschaum
noumenon
posaune
pumpernickel
schema
sinter
torte
Totentanz
NINETEENTH CENTURY
Abiturient
ablaut
alpenhorn
alpenstock
althorn
anlaut
Anschauung
an sich
Aufklärung
Auslese
backfisch
barouche
bebung
bergschrund
blutwurst
buhl
bund

conservatorium
Dasein
delicatessen
Ding an sich
docent
dom
doppelgänger
Drang
dummkopf
durchkomponiert
erbswurst
ersatz
euchre
Ewigkeit
Fach
fest
firn
flügelhorn
föhn
Fraktur
frankfurter
Frau
gasthaus
gasthof
Gelehrte
gemshorn
gemütlich
Gemütlichkeit
Gesellschaft
giro
glockenspiel
glühwein
graupel
Grenzbegriff
Grübelsucht
gugelhupf
haff
Heft
horst
Identitäts-
   philosophie
idioticon
Kaffeeklatsch
Kaiser
kapellmeister
kaput
Karren
Karrenfeld
karst
katzenjammer
kindergarten
kinder, kirche,
   küche
kirsch
klaberjass
knallgas
Kneipe
knödel
kobold
kohlrabi
Kommers
kraut
kriegspiel
krimmer
krug
kuchen
kulturgeschichte
kulturkampf
kümmel

Kunstforscher
Kunstgeschichte
Kur
Kurhaus
Kurort
kursaal
lager
lammergeyer
ländler
Landsturm
Landwehr
Lebenslust
leberwurst
Lehrjahr
leitmotiv
liebchen
Liebestod
liebling
lied
loess
maar
Märchen
Mettwurst
Minnelied
Minnesinger
mit
Mittelschmerz
mordent
motiviert
Nachlass
Nachschlag
Naturphilosophie
pickelhaube
polka
poltergeist
pralltriller
pretzel
prosit
rackett
rauschpfeife
rinderpest
ritter
Romanze
Sängerfest
sastruga
sauerbraten
Schadenfreude
schappe
schiller
schinken
schlemiel
schloss
schmelz
schnapps
schnitzel
schottische
schrund
Schuhplattler
schwa
schwärmerei
Sehnsucht
singspiel
skat
Spätzle
stadthaus
staffage
stoss
strudel
Sturm und Drang

ephemeron
gnosis
haltere
Logos
mimesis
nemesis
omega
organon
pathos
peripeteia
telos
tmesis

SEVENTEENTH CENTURY
Aceldama
acropolis
acroterion
agape
agon
agonistes
apokatastasis
atlantes
bema
boustrophedon
eidolon
eureka
euthanasia
exegesis
glaucoma
hapax legomenon
Hebe
hexapla
hoi polloi
horme
ichor
kinesis
lambda
miasma
narcosis
nous
octapla
pentathlon
periegesis
pseudepigrapha
stoa
strophe
threnos
trauma
upsilon

EIGHTEENTH CENTURY
amnesia
anabasis
anagnorisis
analgesia
anamorphosis
anti
bathos
demos
epsilon
eupepsia
hamartia
kudos
laura
martyrion
melos
mythos
naos
onomasticon
peplos

pleroma
protome
xoanon

NINETEENTH CENTURY
agapemone
agraphon
anthemion
aphasia
apo koinou
aryballos
ascesis
ataraxia
benthos
boule
calliope
chi-rho
chiton
chroma
daimon
Diaspora
dromos
dysphoria
epyllion
ethos
eunomia
halma
hetaera
hubris
ion
kelebe
kenosis
koine
kylix
larnax
lebes
lekythos
macron
megaron
melisma
metanoia
micro
nabla
noesis
nostos
odeon
oenochoe
olpe
omphalos
ostracon
Phi Beta Kappa
pithos
pneuma
polis
pou sto
psychopompos
rhyton
sepsis
skene
sphendone
stele
temenos

TWENTIETH CENTURY
cathexis
esoterica
eudaimonia
ganosis
hegemon
kafenion

kairos
kernos
koinonia
kore
kouros
kurtosis
labrys
lekane
lexis
macro
mega
migma
moron
mythopoeia
noema
nomos
orthosis
paideia
philia
polloi
semiosis
skandalon
tephra
topos

Greek (ecclesiastical)

EIGHTEENTH CENTURY
Homoousion

NINETEENTH CENTURY
Homoiousion

Greek (Late)

NINETEENTH CENTURY
gammadion

Greek (Modern)

SEVENTEENTH CENTURY
dolmas

NINETEENTH CENTURY
iconostasis
katavothron
ouzo

TWENTIETH CENTURY
bouzouki
enosis
feta
filo
gyro
katharevousa
keftedes
mastika
mavrodaphne
meltemi
pitta
retsina
saganaki
souvlaki
stifado
tahina
taverna
tsipouro
tzatziki

Haitian (creole)

NINETEENTH CENTURY
mamaloi
papaloi

TWENTIETH CENTURY
loa

Hawaiian

NINETEENTH CENTURY
aa
aloha
hula
kahuna
ki
lanai
lei
luau
pahoehoe
pali
ukeke
ukulele
wiliwili

TWENTIETH CENTURY
kapu
laulau
makai
muu-muu

Hebrew

MIDDLE ENGLISH
aleph

LATE MIDDLE ENGLISH
Methuselah

SIXTEENTH CENTURY
dagesh
sephira
shekel
sheva
Thummim
Urim

SEVENTEENTH CENTURY
bethel
haham
hazzan
Masorah
Megillah
mezuzah
mitzvah
mohel
shibboleth
tallith
tohu-bohu
tsitsith

EIGHTEENTH CENTURY
gaon
kiddush
minyan

NINETEENTH CENTURY
bar mitzvah
cherem
chuppah
etrog
genizah
gett
goy
hametz
haroseth
hasid
hebra
heder
ketubah
kosher

lulav
maror
melamed
menorah
Mizpah
nabi
parnas
parochet
pilpul
shalom
shechita
shiva
shochet
shofar
succah
trefa
tsaddik
yeshiva
TWENTIETH CENTURY
bat mitzvah
challah
eruv
halutzim
Kahal
Kashrut
lamdan
lechayim
Magen David
maven
Mitnagged
nahal
olim
rimmon
shomer
simchah
temura
tzedaka
yad
yordim

Hebrew (Modern)
NINETEENTH CENTURY
mazel tov
TWENTIETH CENTURY
kibbutz
kippa
kvutza
moshav
sabra
ulpan

Hindi
SEVENTEENTH CENTURY
pukka
EIGHTEENTH CENTURY
sari
wallah
NINETEENTH CENTURY
apsara
corah
ganja
jheel
mung
TWENTIETH CENTURY
bhaji
darshan
dhania
gherao

goonda
namaskar
namaste

Hindustani
SIXTEENTH CENTURY
achar
SEVENTEENTH CENTURY
dhal
dhoti
ghat
ghee
lakh
pan
puggaree
punkah
ranee
EIGHTEENTH CENTURY
babu
bania
dacoit
dak
veranda
NINETEENTH CENTURY
ankus
bandar-log
basmati
burra
chapatti
chappal
chela
dekko
dhobi
ek dum
haldi
jalebi
jat
kutcha
lassi
lathi
maharani
pachisi
raj
terai
tika
TWENTIETH CENTURY
achkan
choli
dilruba
gharana
hartal
kisan
nimbu-pani
pakora
paratha
puri
raita
roti
thali

Hungarian
NINETEENTH CENTURY
cimbalom
csardas
goulash
paprika

Icelandic
NINETEENTH CENTURY
sandur

Indonesian
TWENTIETH CENTURY
legong
tempeh

Irish
LATE MIDDLE ENGLISH
currach
FIFTEENTH CENTURY
clairschach
SEVENTEENTH CENTURY
crannog
curragh
leprechaun
turlough
EIGHTEENTH CENTURY
caoine
feis
ogham
shebeen
NINETEENTH CENTURY
brogan
ceilidh
immram

Italian
MIDDLE ENGLISH
tramontana
SIXTEENTH CENTURY
alto
amoretto
bagnio
basta
bazaar
biretta
bordello
botargo
bravo
campagna
canto
canto fermo
canzone
cupola
duo
duomo
fresco
gamba
gesso
gondola
illuminato
impresa
inamorato
lavolta
lazaretto
macaroni
Madonna
madrigal
magnifico
majolica
mezzo-relievo
motto
nuncio
pasquinade
per contra

phantasma
piazza
presto
Rialto
saltarello
scagliola
seraglio
signor
signoria
sordino
stanza
stucco
sultana
villanella
viola da gamba
volta
SEVENTEENTH CENTURY
adagio
agio
albergo
allegro
alto-relievo
antipasto
baldachin
basso-relievo
beccafico
campanile
capriccio
chiaroscuro
contadino
Corso
dado
ditto
dogana
felucca
flebile
furioso
generalissimo
ghetto
giro
gusto
inamorata
incognita
incognito
in petto
intaglio
internuncio
largo
lazzaro
lido
lingua franca
manifesto
minestra
monte di pietà
morbidezza
mortadella
orlo
ovolo
padrone
palazzo
palio
passacaglia
pergola
piano
piano piano
Pietà
pietra commessa
portico

prunello
putto
recitativo
regatta
relievo
ritornello
scorzonera
signora
sirocco
sonata
stiletto
tarsia
tempo
vermicelli
vino santo
virtuoso
vista
viva
Zingaro

EIGHTEENTH CENTURY
addio
alfresco
alla breve
alla cappella
allegretto
al segno
andante
appoggiatura
arco
aria
arietta
arioso
arpeggio
a tempo
ballerina
bambino
bassetto
basso
basso continuo
battuta
bravura
breccia
brillante
brio
buffo
cadenza
cantabile
cantata
cantilena
capriccioso
cara sposa
caro sposo
casino
cassino
castrato
cavaliere servente
chitarrone
cicerone
cicisbeo
cinquecento
clavicembalo
coda
cognoscente
coloratura
con amore
concertante
concertino
concerto

concerto grosso
condottiere
conoscente
conservatorio
continuo
contralto
conversazione
cortile
crescendo
da capo
del credere
dilettante
diminuendo
divertimento
divisi
duetto
fagotto
falsetto
falsobordone
fantasia
fantoccini
finale
finocchio
flautino
flauto
forte
forte-piano
fortissimo
furore
giallo antico
imbroglio
impasto
impresario
influenza
intermezzo
larghetto
lazzarone
legato
lentamente
lento
libretto
literato
loggia
maestoso
maestrale
maestro
malaria
maraschino
messa di voce
mezza voce
mezzo
mezzo-soprano
mezzo termine
minuetto
moderato
motivo
moto
mozzetta
obbligato
operetta
oratorio
ottava rima
pasticcio
pastorale
patina
penseroso
pianissimo
piano
pianoforte

più
pococurante
ponticello
portamento
prestissimo
prima
prima donna
primo
pronto
propaganda
rifacimento
ripieno
ripresa
risoluto
riviera
rondo
rosso antico
rubato
scaglia
segue
semplice
senza
sgraffito
siciliana
sinfonia
solfatara
solfeggio
sonatina
soprano
sostenuto
sotto voce
spiccato
staccato
stretto
subito
tarantella
tasto
tempo giusto
tempo rubato
tenore
tenuto
terracotta
terzetto
testo
toccata
toccatina
tondino
torso
tremolo
trio
tufa
tutti quanti
verde antico
villeggiatura
viola bastarda
viola d'amore
violetta
violoncello
virtu
voce di petto
voce di testa
zampogna
zingana
zoppa
zufolo

NINETEENTH CENTURY
a cappella
accelerando

acciaccatura
agitato
albarello
aleatico
alla marcia
allargando
amorino
ancona
andantino
ballabile
basso cantante
basso ostinato
basso profundo
bel canto
ben trovato
bersaglieri
bianco sopra
bianco
brava
calando
Camorra
canzona
capotasto
carabiniere
carissima
cassone
cavatina
cembalo
codetta
commedia dell'arte
commendatore
con brio
confetti
con moto
con sordino
contadina
contessa
contrabasso
contrafagotto
coperta
cotta
credenza
cymbalo
dal segno
decrescendo
disinvoltura
diva
dogaressa
dolce far niente
duettino
espressivo
faenza
far niente
fata morgana
fermata
fianchetto
fiasco
fioritura
fiumara
flautando
flautato
forzando
franco
fresco buono
fresco secco
frottola
fugato
fughetta
fustanella

galleria
giocoso
Giuoco Piano
glissando
gnocchi
graffito
grandioso
granita
grappa
grazioso
grissino
gruppetto
inferno
intarsia
intermedio
intonaco
isolato
karezza
lamentoso
largamente
lasagne
latticinio
leggiero
maestria
Mafia
Mafioso
malebolge
mancando
mandorla
mantelletta
marcato
maremma
martellato
marzacotto
mascara
meno
mesto
mezzani
millefiore
minestrone
molto
Moresca
mosso
moto perpetuo
muta
niello
niente
oboe da caccia
oboe d'amore
ocarina
ombrellino
omertà
opera buffa
opera seria
ossia
ostinato
pallone
panforte
parlando
parmigiana
parroco
partita
pasta
piano
piano nobile
piccolo
pietra dura
pizza
pizzicato

pomposo
precipitato
predella
prima ballerina
prima vista
quattrocento
rallentando
rapido
ravioli
religioso
reticella
reticello
ricotta
rinforzando
Risorgimento
risotto
ritardando
ritenuto
rosalia
rosolio
salami
salto
scampi
scarpetti
scenario
scherzando
scherzo
scordatura
scuola
secco
sempre
sestina
sforzando
sforzato
sfumato
sgraffiato
signorina
sinopia
smorzando
sopra bianco
spaghetti
spianato
stiacciato
stile
    rappresentativo
stracchino
strepitoso
stretta
stringendo
tagliarini
tagliatelle
tanto
tazza
tedesco
tempera
tempietto
tenebroso
tenore di forza
tenore di grazia
tenore robusto
tenorino
terraglia
terra rosa
terra rossa
terribilità
terza rima
tessitura
tombolo
tondo

tragedietta
tranquillo
trascinando
traverso
trecento
tremolando
tutti-frutti
una corda
valuta
vendemmia
vendetta
vernaccia
vibrato
vino cotto
viola da braccio
voce di gola
volante
zabaglione
zita
zucchetto

TWENTIETH CENTURY
aggiornamento
agnolotti
al dente
autostrada
basso buffo
biennale
bimbo
calamari
calzone
cannelloni
capo
cappuccino
cassata
ciabatta
ciao
classico
contrapposto
Cosa Nostra
crostini
diabolo
dolce vita
doppione
duce
espresso
farfalle
fettucine
focaccia
frittata
fritto misto
fusilli
gelato
gonzo
graffiti
gran turismo
grosso modo
imprimatura
irredenta
ladino
lamento
libero
linguine
lupara
manicotti
marinara
mascarpone
modello
mondo

moscato
mozzarella
mysterioso
noia
novella
numero uno
orzo
osso bucco
ottocento
paliotto
pancetta
panettone
panino
panzanella
papabile
paparazzo
pappardelle
partigiano
passeggiata
pastiglia
pecorino
penne
pensiero
pentimento
pepperoni
pesto
pizzeria
prominenti
pro-nuncio
prosciutto
provolone
pulvino
radicchio
ricordo
rigatoni
romanità
rucola
sacro egoismo
saltimbocca
salumeria
scala mobile
scaloppine
scungille
seicento
settecento
sinfonietta
sopranino
sottoportico
spaghettini
spinto
sprezzatura
spumante
spumoni
stagione
stelline
stile antico
stile concitato
stracciatella
studiolo
taleggio
targa
terra irredenta
terrazzo
tiorba
tiramisu
tombarolo
tortellini
trapunto
trasformismo

tre corde
troppo
trullo
uomo universale
vaporetto
veduta
verismo
vino dolce
vino nero
vino rosso
vino secco
vinsanto
vita nuova
vitello tonnato
zeppole
zucchini
zuppa di pesce
zuppa inglese

Italian (and Latin)
SEVENTEENTH CENTURY
villa

Italian (and Spanish)
SIXTEENTH CENTURY
punto
EIGHTEENTH CENTURY
tsarina
NINETEENTH CENTURY
marina
triduo
TWENTIETH CENTURY
ambiente
punto banco

Italian, Spanish, Portuguese
SIXTEENTH CENTURY
padre

Japanese
SEVENTEENTH CENTURY
inro
kami
kimono
mochi
sake
samisen
shogun
tabi
tatami
EIGHTEENTH CENTURY
adzuki
awabi
daimyo
kana
katakana
katsuo
kirin
koi
koto
miso
samurai
satori
shoyu
tofu

torii
zazen
Zen
NINETEENTH CENTURY
banzai
bugaku
bushido
futon
go
gobang
habutai
haiku
hakama
hara-kiri
hibachi
hiragana
hokku
jinricksha
joruri
judo
ju-jitsu
kabuki
kagura
kakemono
kamikaze
ken
kombu
koro
kudzu
kyogen
makimono
netsuke
Noh
nori
obi
ojime
raku
renga
rikka
ronin
ryu
san
sashimi
satsuma
sayonara
sennin
sensei
seppuku
shakudo
shakuhachi
shiitake
shippo
shogi
soba
soshi
sumo
surimono
sushi
taiko
tanka
temmoku
togidashi
tsuba
tsukemono
tsunami
tycoon
uchiwa
ukiyo-e

yukata
zabuton
zori
TWENTIETH CENTURY
aikido
ama
banzuke
basho
bonsai
Bunraku
butoh
dan
dojo
dotaku
emakimono
fugu
gagaku
gaijin
haniwa
harai-goshi
hibakusha
honcho
ikebana
ippon
janken
jigotai
juku
kaizen
kanban
kanji
karaoke
karate
karoshi
kata
katsura
keiretsu
Kempeitai
kendo
koan
kuzushi
kyu
mama-san
manga
mingei
mompei
mondo
narikin
nembutsu
ninja
ninjutsu
nisei
nogaku
nunchaku
onnagata
origami
orihon
oyama
pachinko
ramen
randori
sabi
sanpaku
sansei
seiza
shabu-shabu
shiatsu
shibui
shosagoto

shosha
shunga
shuriken
sogo shosha
sokaiya
suiboku
sukiya
sukiyaki
sumi
sumotori
suzuribako
takamakie
tamagotchi
tamari
tempura
teppan-yaki
teriyaki
tsugi ashi
tsutsumu
udon
ukemi
uki
wabi
waka
wakame
wasabi
washi
yakitori
yakuza
yokozuna
yugen
zaibatsu
zaikai
zaitech
zendo

Javanese
NINETEENTH CENTURY
batik
gamelan
saron
wayang
TWENTIETH CENTURY
lahar

Kiswahili
NINETEENTH CENTURY
baraza
boma
bwana
safari
shamba
TWENTIETH CENTURY
kanzu
khanga
kiboko
kikoi
ngoma
panga
shauri
shenzi
simba
simi
toto
uhuru
ujamaa

Korean

NINETEENTH CENTURY
kimchi

TWENTIETH CENTURY
chaebol
tae kwon do

Kurdish

TWENTIETH CENTURY
peshmerga

Lappish

SIXTEENTH CENTURY
tundra

Latin

OLD ENGLISH
genesis
paternoster
polenta
rhagades
Te Deum
Thule

MIDDLE ENGLISH
alpha
amphora
ave
Ave Maria
benedicite
beta
credo
cursor
delta
et
et cetera
gloria
jubilate
magnificat
magus
miserere
origanum
pallium
pater
placebo
requiem
solidus

LATE MIDDLE ENGLISH
Agnus Dei
alias
amphisbaena
ampulla
aqua vitae
aura
aurora
bubo
cathedra
cave
chimera
cicada
clepsydra
colossus
consul
contra
corpus
cortex
crepusculum
cum
custos

decemvir
de profundis
ecce
echinus
ergo
fenestella
feria
fiat
finis
foetus
forum
fungus
gamma
genitor
genius
gratis
gutta
gypsum
habeas corpora
habeas corpus
halcyon
herpes
hyperbole
idem
index
in excelsis
in pontificalibus
item
lamia
lanx
lapis
lapis lazuli
lector
limbo
macula
magma
manes
matrix
mausoleum
mea culpa
medusa
memento
mittimus
noli me tangere
obelus
palaestra
palladium
papyrus
pax
per
plectrum
Priapus
pro
proconsul
pro tempore
proviso
quietus
quorum
regimen
salve
sanctum sanctorum
sanctus
sarcophagus
scilicet
scoria
sede vacante
sedile
sepia
sigma

sistrum
speculum
sphinx
stadium
summa
susurrus
synecdoche
synthesis
teste
thorax
tiro
toties quoties
triumvir
tumulus
ut supra
venire facias
vertex
vertigo
videlicet
vidimus
virago
zeugma

FIFTEENTH CENTURY
aqua fortis
aureola
exeunt
memorandum
modicum
mutatis mutandis
patella
paterfamilias
prima facie

SIXTEENTH CENTURY
abacus
ab origine
ab ovo
absit omen
acanthus
acumen
ad hominem
ad idem
ad rem
adsum
albumen
alga
alter ego
ambrosia
anaphora
Anno Domini
annulus
anta
ante meridiem
anthropophagi
antonomasia
a priori
arcanum
armiger
atrium
ballista
basilica
boletus
bona fide
cacoethes
caduceus
caesura
callus
cantor
cantus

caries
caveat
caveat emptor
cerebellum
cestus
cloaca
coccyx
codex
colloquium
colostrum
compendium
coram
coryza
cymatium
daemon
decorum
de jure
delirium
Deo gratias
diaeresis
dictum
dilemma
dixit
domine
ecce signum
Elysium
emporium
encomium
ephemeris
epiphora
epithalamium
epitome
errata
erratum
esse
Et tu, Brute
exit
ex nihilo
ex officio
exordium
ex professo
extempore
facetiae
fasces
fascia
fidus Achates
flora
forma pauperis
garum
genus
gymnasium
helix
helot
hiatus
hippocampus
homo
hyperbaton
iambus
icon
id est
ignoramus
in articulo mortis
indecorum
in esse
in extremis
in fine
infinitum
in infinitum
in nubibus

innuendo
in posse
in rerum natura
interim
interregnum
interrex
interstitium
invita Minerva
ipse dixit
ipso facto
ipso jure
janitor
jure divino
jus gentium
ladanum
lar
lemma
lignum vitae
limes
lunula
lustrum
Lyceum
mater
materia prima
medium
menses
metamorphosis
metope
meum
militia
minimus
miscellanea
modulus
modus
molossus
murex
naumachia
nepenthes
nolens volens
non placet
nonplus
non sequitur
novus homo
nunc dimittis
obiter
occupatio
o tempora, o
    mores!
panacea
pari passu
paronomasia
passus
peccavi
penates
periphrasis
per se
petitio principii
piscina
placet
pontifex
pontificalia
postscriptum
primus
principium
pro forma
proprium
pro rata
pubes
punctum

quaere
quantum
quid
quid pro quo
quondam
quot homines, tot
    sententiae
radius
radix
rectum
redivivus
reductio ad
    impossibile
remora
rhombus
rostrum
sanctum
Saturnalia
scarabaeus
scotia
scrutator
sempervivum
simplex
simulacrum
solus
sortes
sphincter
stigma
stria
striges
summum bonum
summum genus
summum jus
sumpsimus
superficies
supra
Sursum corda
symposium
taenia
talaria
tenet
terminus ad quem
terminus a quo
terrae filius
theatrum mundi
thermae
thesaurus
thyrsus
tiara
torus
transire
triquetra
trochilus
tympanum
ultimo
umbra
una voce
vale
veni, vidi, vici
viaticum
vide
vivat

SEVENTEENTH CENTURY
ab initio
ab urbe condita
addendum
ad hoc
ad infinitum

ad libitum
ad nauseam
ad valorem
ad vivum
adytum
aegis
afflatus
a fortiori
agenda
agnomen
album
alibi
alluvium
Alma Mater
alumnus
amanuensis
a mensa et thoro
analemma
angelus
antenna
apex
apodyterium
a posteriori
aqua regia
arbor vitae
argumentum ad
    hominem
armilla
auditorium
automaton
brutum fulmen
calyx
canephora
cantoris
caput mortuum
caret
cavea
cella
census
cento
cerebrum
cestus
choragus
chorea
cognomen
collectanea
coma
compos mentis
consensus
continuum
copula
coran judice
coryphaeus
crux
cui bono
culmen
cultus
cumulus
curia
data
decennium
decretum
de facto
Dei gratia
de minimis
de novo
desideratum
dies non juridicus
differentia

digamma
diploma
discus
dithyramb
doli capax
doli incapax
dolus
dominie
donatio mortis
    causa
duodecimo
duumvir
dyspnoea
Ecce Homo
effluvium
elenchus
embolus
eo ipso
eo nomine
Eros
ex animo
ex cathedra
exempli gratia
exequatur
exit
ex parte
ex pede Herculem
ex post facto
ex relatione
exuviae
facies
facilis descensus
    Averni
farrago
felo de se
ferae naturae
festina lente
focus
frustum
fulcrum
genius loci
germen
hic jacet
homunculus
honorarium
honoris causa
horresco referens
hortus conclusus
hortus siccus
hypogeum
hysterica passio
ibid
idolum
impedimenta
imperium
impetus
imprimatur
in abstracto
in concreto
index librorum
    prohibitorum
indicium
in flagrante
in medio
in nomine
in partibus
in perpetuum
in potentia
in propria persona

in puris
  naturalibus
in re
insignia
insomnia
instanter
in statu quo
inter alia
inter alios
in terrorem
in vacuo
involucrum
jus naturae
juvenilia
lacuna
lamina
lapsus
lapsus linguae
larva
latex
legator
lex talionis
liberum arbitrium
literati
longo intervallo
lues
lumbago
lumen siccum
lusus
mala fide
mala fides
mare clausum
mare liberum
mens sana in
  corpore sano
minerval
momentum
mons Veneris
more
more majorum
motu proprio
mutato nomine
mystes
narthex
nebula
nemine
  contradicente
ne plus ultra
nexus
nil desperandum
nimbus
nolle prosequi
non compos mentis
non est factum
non plus ultra
nostrum
numen
nuntius
obiit
odium
oestrus
olim
onus
opprobrium
ovum
pabulum
pancratium
parergon
patera

pelta
penetralia
peplum
perpetuum mobile
philosophia prima
pinax
plenum
post factum
post meridiem
praecognitum
praenomen
praetorium
prolegomenon
pronaos
proscenium
pruritus
psyche
pudendum
pudor
qua
quadra
quadriga
quantum meruit
quantum sufficit
quia timet
quinquennium
quoad
quod erat
  demonstrandum
quod erat
  faciendum
quotum
rara avis
Regius
reliquiae
res
res gestae
residuum
resurgam
retiarius
rota
salvo
scintilla
sederunt
septum
serum
silenus
sine die
sine qua non
specie
spectrum
sputum
status
stemma
stimulus
sub judice
sub rosa
sub silentio
sudarium
sui juris
sylva
talio
telamon
tenendum
terra firma
terra incognita
tessera
testimonium
tholos

tirocinium
toga
totidem verbis
toto caelo
triclinium
tu quoque
umbilicus
vae victis
vagitus
vallum
varia lectio
vates
venire
vesica
vestigium
veto
via media
vice versa
vi et armis
vinculum
vis
vis major
vivarium
vortex
xystus

EIGHTEENTH CENTURY
ad captandum
  vulgus
ad eundem
ad interim
ad litem
ad usum Delphini
adversaria
aegrotat
angina pectoris
apologia
aurora australis
aurora borealis
bibliotheca
bona fides
caldarium
camera lucida
camera obscura
campus
carcinoma
casus foederis
cervix
cilium
cippus
cirrus
cithara
columbarium
comes
conceptus
contra mundum
conversus
crotalum
curiosa felicitas
cursus
datum
decani
dementia
Deo volente
detritus
detur
discobolus
disjecta membra
dominium

dramatis personae
dux
dyspepsia
emeritus
excelsior
exeat
exedra
ex gratia
ex-voto
frigidarium
gradus
habitat
heroon
humus
ibidem
imago
inertia
in flagrante delicto
ingesta
in medias res
in personam
in rem
in situ
in toto
in utero
lapillus
laquear
laudator temporis
  acti
lavabo
lex loci
literae humaniores
locus
locus poenitentiae
lucus a non
  lucendo
magna mater
magnum
magnum opus
materfamilias
memorabilia
minutia
morituri te
  salutamus
multum in parvo
muscae
musica
musica figurata
nemine
  dissentiente
nil admirari
nota bene
notitia
nucleus
nugae
nugae difficiles
nymphaeum
omnium
optime
opus
opus signinum
ore rotundo
otium
pace
panem et circenses
pars pro toto
pastoralia
pendente lite
periplus

phobia
pileus
podium
pons asinorum
post-mortem
pro bono publico
propugnaculum
propylaeum
prospectus
pullus
quaesitum
quieta non movere
quod vide
re
rectus
reductio ad
  absurdum
remittitur
restitutio in
  integrum
rictus
rus in urbe
sacrum
sequela
signum pantheum
simplex munditiis
situs
sola
stela
stet
stylus
succus
sui generis
tacet
taedium vitae
triduum
triforium
ultima Thule
ultimatum
ultra vires
umbo
variorum
vexillum
via
virgo intacta
vis comica
vis inertiae
vis viva
vox humana

NINETEENTH CENTURY
abortus
absurdum
actio in distans
ad lib
aetatis
alumna
animus
ante
ante-bellum
antefix
ante-mortem
anthrax
arbiter elegantiae
arboretum
Arcades ambo
armamentarium
ave atque vale
candelabrum

castrum
casus belli
celebret
circa
circiter
cogito
cognitum
coitus
collegium
compluvium
consortium
conspectus
corrigendum
crux ansata
culpa
cum laude
cunnilingus
curiosa
curriculum
damnosa hereditas
damnum
defluvium
dies irae
dies non
distinguo
dum casta
ego
ejecta
epos
et al.
et seq.
ex
excreta
excursus
exemplum
ex-libris
exotica
extra dictionem
faciendum
facile princeps
famulus
fecit
fides Punica
filioque
flagellum
flagrante delicto
floreat
flore pleno
floruit
fons et origo
functus officio
furor scribendi
generalia
gens
Homo sapiens
horae
idem sonans
imbrex
impluvium
in absentia
in antis
incipit
incognita
in contumaciam
incunabulum
in dictione
indumentum
in extenso
infra

infra dig
ingenium
injuria
in limine
in loco parentis
in memoriam
in nuce
in ovo
in pari materia
in pectore
in se
in statu pupillari
inter partes
inter se
inter vivos
intra vires
intra vitam
in vitro
ipsissima verba
jus cogens
jus primae noctis
lapsus calami
latifundium
lex domicilii
lex fori
litera scripta
loc. cit.
locus classicus
locus standi
loquitur
ludo
magna cum laude
membrum virile
memento mori
mens rea
mirabile dictu
mons pubis
more meo
mores
more suo
musica ficta
naevus
natura naturans
natura naturata
navicula
nisi
nolo contendere
nominatim
nominis umbra
non est
non nobis
notabilia
nova
noxa
nulla bona
nulli secundus
obiit sine prole
obiter dictum
oculus
officina
op. cit.
optimum
opus sectile
oratio obliqua
oratio recta
passim
pax Romana
perceptum
per impossibile

persona designata
philosophia
perennis
pinetum
post-bellum
post eventum
post festum
post hoc
post-partum
pre-mortem
primus inter pares
proxime accessit
proximo
pteroma
pulpitum
quadrennium
quadrivium
quasi in rem
raptus
rariora
recte
recto
redux
referendum
requiescat
responsum
rubella
saeva indignatio
sancta simplicitas
secundus
senex
sensibile
sensu stricto
separatum
sequitur
sic
signum
situla
solarium
solatium
status quo
status quo ante
studium generale
sub specie
  aeternitatis
sub specie temporis
sub voce
summa cum laude
tabula rasa
tacenda
tegula
tepidarium
tertius
tertius gaudens
textus receptus
tinnitus
triennium
trivium
turba
uberrima fides
ultima ratio
ultra
ultra crepidam
unda maris
unicum
urbi et orbi
vera causa
vera copula
verbum sapienti

verso
vesica piscis
vexata quaestio
Via Crucis
Via Dolorosa
vicus
vim
virtute officii
vis a fronte
vis a tergo
vis medicatrix
    naturae
viva
volens
vox angelica
vox nihili
vox populi

TWENTIETH CENTURY
academia
ad personam
aloe vera
anima
argumentum e
    silentio
biennium
cancellandum
cancellans
circulus vitiosus
colluvium
compactum
consolatio
contra proferentem
curriculum vitae
cursus honorum
damnatio
    memoriae
de mortuis
deus absconditus
diabolus in musica
difficilior lectio
dis aliter visum
dissensus
eheu fugaces
ex silentio
ex vivo
felix culpa
figura
filius nullius
furor academicus
furor poeticus
gravida
gravitas
humanitas
id
in corpore
in parvo
intacta
in vivo
lacrimae rerum
Latino sine flexione
lectio difficilior
lente
libido
locum
locus desperatus
media
memento vivere
miles gloriosus

mirabilia
more hispanico
murus gallicus
musica plana
musica reservata
mysterium
    tremendum
nihil obstat
nomen dubium
nomen nudum
nominatum
numerus clausus
orans
orientalia
patria
persona
personalia
pessimum
pietas
planctus
Pluvius
post coitum
prima materia
proferens
punctum
    indifferens
punctus
puris naturalibus
rarissime
rectius
refugium
res cogitans
res extensa
res non verba
sensu lato
sententia
sic et non
sigillata
spiritus rector
stricto sensu
sub verbo
terminus ante
    quem
terminus post
    quem
terra alba
terra cognita
terra ignota
tertium
    comparationis
titulus
tremendum
ubi sunt
urbs
vagantes
Vanitas
victor ludorum
virga
visibilia
vita

**Latin
(ecclesiastical)**
OLD ENGLISH
exodus
rabbi
LATE MIDDLE ENGLISH
Abba

Apocrypha
SIXTEENTH CENTURY
anathema
apotheosis
hypostasis
SEVENTEENTH CENTURY
charisma
EIGHTEENTH CENTURY
catechesis
NINETEENTH CENTURY
albedo
coenobium

Latin (Late)
OLD ENGLISH
manna
MIDDLE ENGLISH
incubus
LATE MIDDLE ENGLISH
antithesis
arsis
enchiridion
hydrophobia
hyle
ignotum per
    ignotius
oedema
syncope
thesis
SIXTEENTH CENTURY
antepenultima
antistrophe
aporia
bolus
cornucopia
dogma
ens
homoeoteleuton
hypothesis
hysteron proteron
in saecula
    saeculorum
intermedium
latria
litotes
mamzer
metastasis
metathesis
metempsychosis
onomatopoeia
phenomenon
plethora
prosthesis
succuba
trapezium
vanitas vanitatum
SEVENTEENTH CENTURY
ab extra
acedia
anorexia
campana
catheter
colophon
explicit
ex proprio motu
golgotha
gravamen

labarum
melancholia
moloch
phallus
prognosis
psychomachia
sensorium
sigillum
uti possidetis
EIGHTEENTH CENTURY
anacoluthon
herbarium
siglum
tertium quid
vomitorium
NINETEENTH CENTURY
anorexia nervosa
bacillus
exceptis excipiendis
in camera
natatorium
obscurum per
    obscurius
persona grata
septennium
TWENTIETH CENTURY
persona non grata
realia
romanitas
tabula gratulatoria

Latin (Medieval)
MIDDLE ENGLISH
Kyrie eleison
LATE MIDDLE ENGLISH
cranium
dulia
duodenum
hiera picra
lac
non-obstante
nux vomica
oesophagus
quodlibet
retina
succubus
terra sigillata
versus
FIFTEENTH CENTURY
Magna Carta
primum mobile
seriatim
spermaceti
verbatim
SIXTEENTH CENTURY
affidavit
anima mundi
antependium
cabbala
ciborium
confrater
factotum
hegira
hendiadys
hyperdulia
ignoratio elenchi

morbilli
praxis
regalia
viva voce

SEVENTEENTH CENTURY
ambo
anglice
ephemera
incisor
linctus
literatim
malum in se
paraphernalia
quota
suppositum

EIGHTEENTH CENTURY
cancrizans
dulciana
schola cantorum
scriptorium

NINETEENTH CENTURY
ante rem
cantus firmus
Mater Dolorosa
necessarium
novena
opus Alexandrinum
opus anglicanum
opus araneum
opus consutum
opus Dei

TWENTIETH CENTURY
post rem
significacio

Latin (Modern)

SIXTEENTH CENTURY
cyma
guaiacum
ignis fatuus
larynx
lemur
meiosis
per accidens
per diem
pomatum
scholium
stratum
utopia

SEVENTEENTH CENTURY
ab intra
abscissa
amicus curiae
annus mirabilis
bene esse
catalysis
ceteris paribus
chiasmus
coma
deus ex machina
entasis
euphoria
ex hypothesi
experimentum
  crucis
florilegium
lachryma Christi
materia medica

meniscus
millennium
modus operandi
necrosis
per annum
per capita
per centum
per mensem
per stirpes
pharmacopoeia
rebus sic stantibus
risus sardonicus
sal volatile
sarcoma
strabismus
substratum
succedaneum
symbiosis
Valhalla

EIGHTEENTH CENTURY
ad referendum
anaesthesia
condominium
currente calamo
fauna
memoria technica
menologium
neurosis
parens patriae
respondentia
stasis
suppressio veri

NINETEENTH CENTURY
advocatus diaboli
amoeba
anacrusis
apparatus criticus
aquarium
asphyxia
axiomata media
bacterium
catharsis
cyanosis
delirium tremens
editio princeps
horribile dictu
horror vacui
inedita
modus vivendi
moratorium
sanatarium
sanatorium
sebum
suggestio falsi
torticollis
uraeus
via affirmativa
via negativa

TWENTIETH CENTURY
annus horribilis
candida
contrafactum
ex ante
ex post
imponderabilia
minifundium
trivia
unum necessarium

Malagasy

EIGHTEENTH CENTURY
raffia

Malay

SIXTEENTH CENTURY
kris

EIGHTEENTH CENTURY
adat
kain
kramat
rambutan
tuan
tuṇku

NINETEENTH CENTURY
agar-agar
gutta-percha
nasi
parang
sambal
sarong

TWENTIETH CENTURY
ikat
jadam
kathi
merdeka
pahit
satay

Maori

EIGHTEENTH CENTURY
tiki
wahine

NINETEENTH CENTURY
haka
hangi
kai
kapai
korero
kuri
mana
pakeha
pikau
taihoa
waka
whare

TWENTIETH CENTURY
karanga

Maori (and Hawaiian)

NINETEENTH CENTURY
hui

Marathi

TWENTIETH CENTURY
rangoli

Melanesian

TWENTIETH CENTURY
kula

Nepali

NINETEENTH CENTURY
kukri

New Guinea

TWENTIETH CENTURY
kuru

Norwegian

SEVENTEENTH CENTURY
fiord

EIGHTEENTH CENTURY
kraken

NINETEENTH CENTURY
aquavit
fjeld
halling

TWENTIETH CENTURY
gjetost
gravadlax
klister
kril
langeleik
rosemaling
ski-joring
slalom
smørbrød
springar

Old Norse

MIDDLE ENGLISH
kist

EIGHTEENTH CENTURY
Ragnarok
saga
skald

NINETEENTH CENTURY
jotun

Pali

NINETEENTH CENTURY
bhikkhu

TWENTIETH CENTURY
dhamma
nibbana
tathata

Panjabi

TWENTIETH CENTURY
bhangra
gurdwara
jatha
khaddar
kirpan
tikka

Persian

LATE MIDDLE ENGLISH
khan

SIXTEENTH CENTURY
caravanserai
shah

SEVENTEENTH CENTURY
attar
hafiz
hajji
khanum
mullah

EIGHTEENTH CENTURY
baksheesh
durgah

ezan
ghazal
narghile
peri
simurg

NINETEENTH CENTURY
gul
hom
izzat
kanoon
kenaf
qanat

TWENTIETH CENTURY
ayatollah
kulah
takht

Persian (and Urdu)

SIXTEENTH CENTURY
amir
bhang

SEVENTEENTH CENTURY
begum
chadar
charpoy
chokidar
durbar
farrash
havildar
moulvi
sahib
satranji
shikar
syce
tamasha

EIGHTEENTH CENTURY
bundobust
hookah
howdah
khalsa
khidmutgar
masala
mofussil
munshi
nawab
zenana
ziarat

NINETEENTH CENTURY
badmash
bibi
burka
chaprassi
chikan
huma
khaki
kofta
korma
numdah
numnah
purdah
sarod
shalwar
shikari
sitar
tabla

tarkaski
zakat
zarda

TWENTIETH CENTURY
balti
biryani
garam masala
kurta
nan
rogan josh
samosa
shisha
tandoori
zari

Polish

EIGHTEENTH CENTURY
hetman

TWENTIETH CENTURY
kielbasa
oberek

Polynesian

NINETEENTH CENTURY
poi
poipoi

Portuguese

SIXTEENTH CENTURY
amok
banyan
betel
pagoda
typhoon

SEVENTEENTH CENTURY
aldea
copaiba
fidalgo
ipecacuanha
maraca
nabob

EIGHTEENTH CENTURY
auto-da-fé
ayah
commando
cuspidor
elephanta
piranha
senhor

NINETEENTH CENTURY
amah
bucellas
carioca
fazenda
fazendeiro
feijão
garimpeiro
guarana
lingua geral
samba
senhora
senhorita
serra
sertão
vigia
vindaloo
vinho

vinho branco
vinho tinto

TWENTIETH CENTURY
bossa nova
churrasco
fado
favela
favelado
feijoada
lundum
maxixe
pinga
pousada
retornado
saudade
tanga
vinho corrente
vinho da casa
vinho de consumo
vinho verde

Portuguese (Brazilian)

TWENTIETH CENTURY
lambada

Portuguese (and Spanish)

SIXTEENTH CENTURY
copra

SEVENTEENTH CENTURY
peon

TWENTIETH CENTURY
tristeza

Provençal

NINETEENTH CENTURY
alba

TWENTIETH CENTURY
mas
pistou
tian

pseudo-French

EIGHTEENTH CENTURY
bêche-de-mer

NINETEENTH CENTURY
bon viveur
nom de plume

TWENTIETH CENTURY
en travesti

pseudo-German

TWENTIETH CENTURY
sitzkrieg

pseudo-Italian

SIXTEENTH CENTURY
braggadocio

pseudo-Latin

SIXTEENTH CENTURY
mumpsimus
omnium gatherum

NINETEENTH CENTURY
celesta

pseudo-Greek

NINETEENTH CENTURY
agoraphobia

Romanian

TWENTIETH CENTURY
sarmale
tsuica

Romany

NINETEENTH CENTURY
chal
patrin
vardo

Russian

SIXTEENTH CENTURY
boyar
kvass
muzhik
sevruga
tsar

SEVENTEENTH CENTURY
steppe
tsaritsa

EIGHTEENTH CENTURY
balalaika
isba
Raskolnik
tsarevich
ukase
yurt

NINETEENTH CENTURY
artel
ataman
blin
bortsch
chernozem
dacha
droshky
druzhina
duma
feldsher
karakul
kasha
kulak
kurgan
mazut
pirog
polynya
samovar
shchi
starover
taiga
tchin
troika
tsarevna
vodka
zakuska
zemstvo

TWENTIETH CENTURY
agitprop
apparat
apparatchik
babushka
Bolshevik
glasnost
Gulag

intelligentsia
kazachoc
kissel
kolkhoz
kulturny
narod
nekulturny
niet
nilas
nitchevo
nomenklatura
paskha
pelmeny
perestroika
piroshki
podzol
pogrom
Politbureau
Presidium
prisiadka
proletkult
rassolnik
rendzina
residentura
rezident
riza
sambo
samizdat
shashlik
sierozem
skaz
smetana
sobornost
solod
solonchak
solonetz
solyanka
sovkhoz
sputnik
starets
subbotnik
talik
tokamak
tolkach
tovarish
tvorog
ukha
vobla
vozhd
zek

Samoan
NINETEENTH CENTURY
lava-lava

Sanskrit
SIXTEENTH CENTURY
raja
SEVENTEENTH CENTURY
guru
maharaja
puja
sannyasi
vihara
yogi
EIGHTEENTH CENTURY
atman
avatar

brahman
chakra
dharma
gandharva
gopi
kalpa
linga
maharishi
mantra
maya
moksha
mukti
naga
om
om mani padme
   hum
purusha
raga
rasa
samadhi
soma
suttee
swami
tantra
vajra
veena
yaksha
yoga
yogini
yoni
yuga

NINETEENTH CENTURY
acharya
ahimsa
Arhat
bhakta
bhakti
bhikshu
chaitya
deva
devadasi
dharmsala
garuda
gopura
Jina
jiva
Kama Sutra
karma
kundalini
mahatma
mandala
mudra
nirvana
nritya
padma
padmasana
raja yoga
rakshasa
rasa
sadhu
samsara
samskara
samyama
sangha
sarangi
shanti
shikhara
siddha

stupa
sutra
swastika
tilak
torana
vahana
varna
vimana
yajna
yantra
TWENTIETH CENTURY
ashram
ayurveda
bhajan
brahmacharya
gramdan
hatha yoga
hatha yogi
karana
kumkum
lasya
nada
nritta
panchshila
pata
sabha
satyagraha
shrikhand
sunyata

Sardinian
NINETEENTH CENTURY
nuragh

Serbo-Croat
EIGHTEENTH CENTURY
kolo
NINETEENTH CENTURY
slivovitz
TWENTIETH CENTURY
chetnik
hum
uvala
zurla

Sinhalese
NINETEENTH CENTURY
dagoba
pansala

Somali
TWENTIETH CENTURY
shifta

Spanish
SIXTEENTH CENTURY
alcaide
alcalde
alguacil
armada
bacalao
batata
bonito
cacique
cedilla
copal

cordovan
don
frijoles
hidalgo
infanta
machete
mestizo
Morisco
muchacho
olla podrida
panada
peccadillo
salina
sanbenito
sarsaparilla
sassafras
savannah
señora
seron
sierra
sombrero
tercio
tinaja
tinto
yeso
SEVENTEENTH CENTURY
alcazar
alforja
balsa
bandolero
caldera
chilli
chinchilla
conde
condor
contrayerva
dinero
duenna
embargo
estancia
flota
huaca
jornada
llano
manta
matador
mirador
mondongo
montera
mulatta
olla
paco
picaro
pimento
pimiento
plaza
pundonor
rancheria
santo
señor
siesta
toreador
toro
tortilla
tumbaga
vega
vicuña
vino tinto

tienta
tonto
tostada
turron
ultreya
vargueño
veleta
vendimia
vino blanco
vino corriente
vino dulce
vino maestro
vino tierno

Spanish (American)

SEVENTEENTH CENTURY
atole
charqui
chicha
chuño
metate
pulque
puna
teocalli
trapiche

EIGHTEENTH CENTURY
calinda

NINETEENTH CENTURY
bombilla
cafeteria
campo
chicharron
chicle
cholo
enchilada
galpon
gaucho
hornito
jarabe
marijuana
panatela
penuche
peyote
pinole
pulperia
remuda
tango
temblor

TWENTIETH CENTURY
bongo
burrito
cha-cha
chino
clave
conga
cueca
exacta
guacamole
mambo
merengue
montuno
palomino
panga
perfecta
quinella
ruana

rumba
sancocho
sopaipilla

Spanish (Mexican)

SEVENTEENTH CENTURY
tamale

EIGHTEENTH CENTURY
Apache
coyote

NINETEENTH CENTURY
alfilaria
amole
cenote
chaparejos
ejido
huarache
jacal
mecate
milpa
octli
pilón
serape
tequila
tilma

TWENTIETH CENTURY
ayahuasca
charro
chipotle
fajita
huevos rancheros
jalapeño
jojoba
machismo
macho
maquiladora
mariachi
menudo
molcajete
mole
mordida
nacho
pachuco
palapa
pochismo
pocho
taco
taqueria
tepache
tomatillo

Spanish (South American)

SEVENTEENTH CENTURY
guano

EIGHTEENTH CENTURY
poncho

NINETEENTH CENTURY
llanero

TWENTIETH CENTURY
basuco
bombachas
pina colada
seviche

Spanish (West Indian)

NINETEENTH CENTURY
dengue
guajiro

TWENTIETH CENTURY
guajira

Spanish (and Italian)

SEVENTEENTH CENTURY
amoroso
vino

NINETEENTH CENTURY
cantina
municipio

Spanish (and Portuguese)

SIXTEENTH CENTURY
auto
corral
infante
mulatto

SEVENTEENTH CENTURY
junta
recado

EIGHTEENTH CENTURY
albino
curare
quinta

NINETEENTH CENTURY
selva

TWENTIETH CENTURY
norteamericano

Swedish

EIGHTEENTH CENTURY
isblink

NINETEENTH CENTURY
polska
smorgasbord

TWENTIETH CENTURY
fartlek
glögg
ombudsman
palsa
pipkrake
rya
tjaele
varve

Swiss French

EIGHTEENTH CENTURY
chalet
ranz-des-vaches

NINETEENTH CENTURY
luge
névé
seiche
serac

Swiss German

TWENTIETH CENTURY
muesli
putsch
roesti

Tagalog

NINETEENTH CENTURY
ylang-ylang

TWENTIETH CENTURY
boondock

Tahitian

TWENTIETH CENTURY
vahine

Tamil

SEVENTEENTH CENTURY
catamaran
pariah

NINETEENTH CENTURY
patchouli
poppadam

TWENTIETH CENTURY
kavadi
sambar

Thai

NINETEENTH CENTURY
wat

Tibetan

SEVENTEENTH CENTURY
lama

NINETEENTH CENTURY
sherpa

TWENTIETH CENTURY
gompa
yeti

Tongan

EIGHTEENTH CENTURY
kava
taboo

Turkic

NINETEENTH CENTURY
barchan
khatun

Turkish

SIXTEENTH CENTURY
aga
bey
caftan
dervish

SEVENTEENTH CENTURY
baklava
bezesteen
effendi
hammam
harem
khoja
pasha
pashalic
pilau
raki
serai
sherbet
tekke
turbeh
yoghurt

NINETEENTH CENTURY
fez
kilim
kismet
konak
macramé
rahat
rayah
tughra
yataghan
zurna

TWENTIETH CENTURY
bulgur
dolmus
doner kebab
imam bayildi
karaburan
lokum
meze
millet
moussaka
mukhtar
sheshbesh
shish kebab
yorgan

Urdu (see Persian (and Urdu))

Vietnamese
TWENTIETH CENTURY
nuoc mam

Welsh
SEVENTEENTH CENTURY
cromlech

EIGHTEENTH CENTURY
Gorsedd
NINETEENTH CENTURY
bach
crwth
cwm

West Indian creole
EIGHTEENTH CENTURY
goombah
TWENTIETH CENTURY
soucouyant

Yiddish
SEVENTEENTH CENTURY
halva
NINETEENTH CENTURY
chutzpah
farfel
frum
gefilte fish
golem
kehilla
kittel
koppel
kreplach
kugel
lokshen
matzo
meshuga
meshumad
mikva
narrischkeit
nebbish
oy

reb
rebbe
rebbitzin
schmuck
schnorrer
shemozzle
shidduch
shiksa
shul
tzimmes
yahrzeit
yom tov
TWENTIETH CENTURY
bagel
blintze
cholent
dreidel
dybbuk
heimisch
kibbutznik
kibitz
kishke
klezmer
klutz
knaidel
knish
kvell
kvetch
landsman
latke
lekach
luftmensch
macher
mazuma
mensch
meshugaas

meshugener
naches
nosh
nudnik
pastrami
platzel
schalet
schlep
schlepper
schlimazel
schlock
schlong
schmaltz
schmooze
schmutz
schnozz
schwartze
shegetz
shlub
shmatte
shmear
shonda
shtetl
shtibl
shtick
shtoom
teiglach
tokus
trombenik
tsatske
tsores
yarmulke
yenta
yentz
yichus
zaftig